FAITH AND THE PRESIDENCY

Faith and the Presidency

From George Washington to George W. Bush

Gary Scott Smith

UNIVERSITY PRESS

2006

OXFORD
UNIVERSITY PRESS

Oxford University Press, Inc., publishes works that further
Oxford University's objective of excellence
in research, scholarship, and education.

Oxford   New York
Auckland   Cape Town   Dar es Salaam   Hong Kong   Karachi
Kuala Lumpur   Madrid   Melbourne   Mexico City   Nairobi
New Delhi   Shanghai   Taipei   Toronto

With offices in
Argentina   Austria   Brazil   Chile   Czech Republic   France   Greece
Guatemala   Hungary   Italy   Japan   Poland   Portugal   Singapore
South Korea   Switzerland   Thailand   Turkey   Ukraine   Vietnam

Copyright © 2006 by Oxford University Press, Inc.

Published by Oxford University Press, Inc.
198 Madison Avenue, New York, New York 10016

www.oup.com

Oxford is a registered trademark of Oxford University Press

Library of Congress Cataloging-in-Publication Data
Smith, Gary Scott, 1950–
Faith and the presidency : from George Washington to George W. Bush
/ Gary Scott Smith.
    p. cm.
Includes bibliographical references and index.
ISBN-13 978-0-19-530060-4
ISBN 0-19-530060-2
1. Presidents–United States–Biography.   2. Presidents–United
States–Religion.   3. Christianity and politics–United States.
I. Title.
E176.1.S648 2006
973.09'9–dc22   2006004639

9 8 7 6 5 4 3 2 1

Printed in the United States of America
on acid-free paper

Separation of church and state is one thing. Separation of religion and politics is another thing altogether. Religion and politics flow back and forth in American civil society all the time—always have, always will. How could it be otherwise?

Jean Bethke Elshtain

TODAY A DEBATE rages over the place of religion in American public life. What role did Christianity play in the founding of the United States? Should the government aid this religious tradition or refuse to support it in any way? Does the concept of church-state separation mean that religion must be totally divorced from government at the local, state, or federal level? In the past five years, hundreds of editorials, op-ed pieces, newspaper and magazine articles, television talk shows and news programs, dozens of books, and numerous academic conferences have examined these questions. Controversy has erupted over the inscriptions on coins, Bible reading and prayer in public schools, the Pledge of Allegiance, the display of the Ten Commandments in public buildings, and a host of other issues. George W. Bush's faith-based initiatives and foreign policy have raised concerns about the separation of church and state, the use of religious language, and God's relationship with the United States.

Numerous indicators (recent elections, polls, levels of church attendance and charitable giving, and the numbers and impact of parachurch organizations) suggest that religious faith continues to be very important in the United States. Almost all Americans profess belief in God. Sixty-three percent of them belong to a church, synagogue, or mosque, and about 40 percent of them attend religious services on an average weekend. Only 7 percent of Americans consider themselves atheists or agnostics or have no religious preference. Recent polls also indicate that the majority of Americans want religion to have a greater influence in the nation's life.[1] Many protest that the secularization of the media, public education, and the business world has gone too far and call for a rejuvenation of religious values in the public square. Meanwhile, America's religious communities are deeply divided over many political and social issues.

Recent years have witnessed a spirited debate between those who argue that the United States' founding and history until the 1960s was infused with Christian principles and directed by godly leaders and those who see its creation and development as guided by more secular ideologies and statesmen.[2] Many proponents of the first position contend that the United States is obligated to follow biblical norms in its public life. They complain that "today's politicians are more apt to talk about the vague 'faith' aspects of religion rather than about religion as a standard of right public action."[3] Others counter that biblical teachings and denominational doctrines are potentially divisive, are irrelevant to the public arena, and should be confined to private life. Policy making should be based on objective, scientific, pragmatic, prudential, "neutral" factors, not religious presuppositions or values. They insist that the intrusion of religious commitments into policy making "is disturbing, if not downright dangerous."[4]

Wilfred McClay argues that the United States' elite culture, especially its media and universities, "is now almost entirely committed to a standard of antiseptically secular discourse." Supreme Court decisions have significantly reduced the opportunity to publicly display "traditional religious symbols and sentiments" and helped to produce a "naked public square." Religion has been "confined to a sort of cultural red light district." People can believe what they want in private, as long as they do not try to use their beliefs as a basis for public action. Others see "secularism's seeming hold over the moment" as "illusory, unpopular, elitist and doomed to fail." They contend that people of faith have vigorously defended religion's "appropriate role as an essential player in public life."[5] As a result, questions about whether and how government officials can express their religious convictions have become increasingly contentious, as the 2004 presidential election underscored.

The religious views and values of presidents are very important to many Americans today. In a 2004 poll conducted by the Pew Forum on Religion and Public Life, 72 percent of respondents said they want the president to have strong religious beliefs.[6] Although the Constitution prohibits religious tests for holding political office, it cannot prevent Americans from imposing a religious litmus test on candidates. "One day, a truly secular candidate might be able to run for president without suffering at the polls," writes Franklin Foer in the *New Republic*. "But that day won't be soon."[7]

Nevertheless, as former Minnesota Senator Eugene McCarthy once observed, in Washington "only two kinds of religion are tolerated: vague beliefs strongly affirmed and strong beliefs vaguely expressed." "His witticism," argue Kenneth L. Woodward and Martha Brant, "bespoke the genial religiosity of presidents like Eisenhower (vague expression) and Reagan (vague beliefs).... The lesson for candidates seems to be: if you want to be president of all the people, invoke a generic deity everyone can salute." "When you get down to specifics," they conclude, "history offers little evidence of direct interplay between faith and presidential leadership."[8] Similarly, one religious conservative laments that professing Christians "may still hold office, provided they either aren't sincere about their faith or they keep it" locked in the closet.[9] Moreover, it is difficult to delineate precisely how the faith of various presidents affected their actions and policies because many factors play a role.

This study of eleven presidents demonstrates, however, that faith affected how numerous occupants of the Oval Office performed their duties. Their faith influenced their philosophy of governing, relationship with religious constituents, electoral strategies, and approach to public policies. Moreover, it helped shape their convictions and character, as well as their views of the separation of church and state, civil religion, and American chosenness. "Despite our much-vaunted separation of church and state, America has always had a quasi-religious understanding of itself, [as] reflected in the messianism of Puritan founder John Winthrop"; the providentialism of George Washington; the biblically based optimism of Thomas Jefferson; Abraham Lincoln's emphasis on redemptive suffering; the focus on civic righteousness and biblical morality by Theodore Roosevelt, Woodrow Wilson, and Jimmy Carter; and the belief of Franklin Roosevelt, Dwight Eisenhower, John F. Kennedy, Ronald Reagan, and George W. Bush that Nazism, Communism, or terrorism must be opposed on a global scale because these ideologies embodied evil.[10]

Despite the vast evidence that presidents' faith deeply affected their lives and their administrations, many scholars have ignored this fascinating and fertile subject. They have also disregarded the fact that religion matters enormously to many Americans and that "such concepts as Original Sin, the Atonement, and the Resurrection...actually have serious and enduring meanings" to them.[11] Secularism, lack of interest in religion, or overreactions to popular portrayals of Washington and Lincoln as pious, devout, orthodox Christians have all contributed to this neglect.

This book explores the "profound, troubled, and inescapable interaction" between religious faith and politics in the United States.[12] It argues that religion has played a major role in the lives and administrations of numerous presidents. As the federal government has grown larger and more powerful and as its policies have had a greater impact, the influence of a president's faith on his performance of his duties and the role of religion in shaping policies have become even more important. This study analyzes both the personal beliefs and the public policies of presidents. While it examines the specific content of their religious convictions (what they believed about God, Christ, human nature, the Bible, prayer, providence, salvation, life after death, and other topics), it does not try to measure "how religious" they were. It takes their religious beliefs seriously and seeks to assess how these beliefs affected their presidencies. I have investigated and reported what scholars, friends, associates, and critics have said about the religious beliefs of presidents, but I have especially scrutinized presidents' own words in both their public and private statements.

"Because religion is often tightly interwoven with particular cultures and ethnic groups," William Martin maintains, it is very difficult to "disentangle discrete components and label them correctly as secular or religious, sincere or manipulative, beneficial or dangerous." When individuals "profess or appear to be acting from religious motives," it is tempting to ignore them as ignorant, insincere, or insubstantial or to try to discover their " 'real' " motives, which must involve money, power, or fame.[13] Although presidents have used religious rhetoric to justify economic and political policies, bolster social control, and appeal to prospective voters, their religious beliefs have also helped direct their actions and influence their responses to important events. Religious convictions are not simply the product of social, economic, and political forces. They can furnish ideals and inspire actions. While recognizing that numerous factors and varied motives affected presidents' thinking and behavior, I argue that religious beliefs have been a key ingredient in the mix for many of them.

Numerous presidents have chosen, like former Colorado Senator Gary Hart, "not to place my beliefs in the center of my appeal for support because . . . I believe that one's religious beliefs—though they will and should affect one's outlook on public policy and life—are personal."[14] George Washington and Thomas Jefferson best exemplify this approach. Others, by contrast, frequently discussed how important their faith was to them and argued that politicians must bring their faith into the public arena. Woodrow Wilson, Jimmy Carter, Ronald Reagan, and George W. Bush are notable examples of this approach.

Another 2004 poll found that Americans were evenly divided about whether a president's faith should guide him in making political decisions. Some protest that presidents have promoted certain policies that reflect the priorities of particular religious communities and complain that they have favored some religious groups over others. Others object that overly pious presidents (like George W. Bush) have tried to use their office to demolish the wall of separation between church and state, impose their values on other Americans, and use federal funds to finance religious goals and programs. Still others want presidents to emphasize widely shared religious values and advance policies that embody these convictions. By providing in-depth analysis of the faith of eleven presidents and exploring how their religious commitments influenced their work, I hope to further inform public debate about the contentious relationship between religion and politics in the United States.

I have tried to reproduce all quoted material as it is in the cited sources. All italics in the quoted material represent emphasis in the original text.

ACKNOWLEDGMENTS

ONE DOES NOT write a book of this size and scope without significant help from others. The Earhart Foundation of Ann Arbor, Michigan, provided generous grants that enabled me to visit presidential libraries in Abilene, Kansas; Atlanta; Boston; Hyde Park, New York; Simi Valley, California; and West Branch, Iowa, as well as the Houghton Library at Harvard University and the Library of Congress in Washington, D.C. The foundation's aid also gave me release time from teaching four intersessions at my college. Finally, its subvention allowed the length of the book to be increased without increasing its price. I want to thank the trustees and administrators of Grove City College for the sabbatical I received during the fall semester of 2004 and my colleagues for helping cover my courses, counsel my advisees, and take over my departmental chair responsibilities. I am also indebted to colleagues at Grove City College who read chapters of my manuscript and made helpful suggestions for revision: Michael Coulter, Gillis Harp, Paul Kemeny, Paul Kengor, Jeff Patterson, and Earl Tilford. Other scholars also provided excellent advice: Daniel Dreisbach of American University, Garrett Ward Sheldon of the University of Virginia at Wise, Ronald Wells of Calvin College, Thomas J. Carty of Springfield College, and John Woolverton, the editor of *Anglican and Episcopal History.* Four student assistants at Grove City College helped with research and revision: Leah Ayers, Caroline Harp, Amy Martin, Elizabeth Miller, and Mandy Tharpe. I also want to thank my son Joel, a graphic designer, who helped with the jacket design.

Librarians at various institutions provided invaluable assistance. Conni Shaw and Joyce Kebert of Grove City College helped me locate and procure hundreds of books and articles through interlibrary loan. Librarians at Slippery Rock University and the Jimmy Carter, John F. Kennedy, Franklin D. Roosevelt, Dwight D. Eisenhower, Herbert Hoover, and Ronald Reagan presidential libraries also helped me identify, locate, and analyze important primary sources. I would like to especially thank Albert Mason of the Jimmy Carter Presidential Library, James W. Leyerzapf of the Dwight D. Eisenhower Library, and Wallace F. Dailey, the curator of the Theodore Roosevelt Collection at the Houghton Library of Harvard University.

I owe a very large debt to Theo Calderara of Oxford University Press. He helped me reduce a very long manuscript to a long book, painstakingly edited each chapter, and provided excellent suggestions to tighten my arguments and clarify my prose. Joy Matkowski's copy editing was outstanding. Her meticulous checking of facts and stylistic revisions saved me from many errors and made the book read better.

I especially want to thank my wife, Jane. She accompanied me on several trips to presidential libraries and used her skills as a reference librarian to help in the research process. She also helped me find obscure sources, critiqued chapters, and lovingly completed many tasks at home, giving me additional time to write. Without her support and encouragement, this book would not have been completed.

CONTENTS

FAITH AND THE PRESIDENCY

Introduction

The White House is the pulpit of the nation and the president is its chaplain.

James Reston, cited in Thomas Cronin, "The Textbook Presidency and Political Science," *Congressional Record*, Oct. 5, 1970

The president's duties are "essentially pastoral. . . . He is the shepherd of the sheep, nearly 200 million of them."

Frederic Fox quoted in Charles Henderson Jr., *The Nixon Theology*

Americans expect the president "to play a priestly role and even to bring salvation. On the one hand, they want a person of principle, but they are very skeptical about the political process. They are bound to be disappointed because the state is not the agent or place of redemption. Even when a President is devoutly religious a dualism remains between the city of God and the city of man. Religious conviction can strengthen a President's resolve and integrity and help him deal more effectively with inevitable frustrations and defeats."

Charles P. Henderson Jr., "The Politics of Love: Religion or Justice?" *Nation*, May 8, 1976

Whenever a president speaks openly of his religious faith, citizens want to know how that faith affects his political priorities. And we look for clues. But the lines between religious convictions and public policy are seldom clear, even in retrospect.

Kenneth Woodward, "Gospel on the Potomac," *Newsweek*, Mar. 10, 2003

SPEAKING TO 15,000 people at an ecumenical prayer breakfast during the Republican National Convention in Dallas in August 1984, Ronald Reagan declared, "The truth is, politics and morality are inseparable. And as morality's foundation is religion, religion and politics are necessarily related. We need religion as a guide. We need it because we are imperfect, and our government needs the church because only those humble enough to admit they're sinners can bring to democracy the tolerance it requires in order to survive."[1] Reagan's remarks prompted a firestorm of protest. Many accused the Republican of violating the "traditional separation of church and state."[2] Charles Krauthammer contended in *Time* that Reagan had crossed "the line that in a pluralist society divides civil discourse from demagoguery." Claire Randall, the general secretary of the National Council of Churches, insisted that Reagan's position fell "far short of the standard of tolerance for the beliefs of others which must undergird religious freedom in a diverse society."[3] This reaction was due in part to the fact that his words were spoken during a political campaign and that many disagreed with Reagan's support of political policies favored by the religious right (evangelical and fundamentalist Protestants and conservative Catholics), especially a school prayer amendment, tuition tax credits, a strong military defense, and efforts to reduce welfare payments and government regulations on businesses. Some saw Reagan's campaign to decrease abortions, pornography, drug usage, and sex outside marriage (actions also favored by the religious right) as either beyond the role of government or interfering with personal freedoms.

Reagan was not the first president to make this argument. George Washington, Abraham Lincoln, Theodore Roosevelt, Franklin Roosevelt, Dwight Eisenhower, and numerous other presidents also maintained that politics and morality were indivisible and that religion was the principal foundation of morality. Nor was he the first chief executive whose religious rhetoric provoked controversy. Scholars today uniformly praise Lincoln's Second Inaugural Address as one of the greatest American political documents, as a "charter of Christian statesmanship," and the "most far-reaching" reflection on Providence by "a major figure in American public life."[4] However, the Washington *Daily National Intelligencer* predicted the day after Lincoln delivered the address that it was likely to irritate those who advocated strict separation of church and state. And it did. The *New York World*, for example, complained that the president's theology strongly smacked of "the dark ages" and accused him of "abandoning all pretense of statesmanship" and taking "refuge in piety."[5]

The objections of many pundits, politicians, and even some religious leaders to Reagan's and Lincoln's speeches raise a larger issue: What is the proper relationship between religion and politics? Is it appropriate for a president's religious convictions to direct him in performing his duties and devising and implementing his policies? Does the concept of the separation of church and state require presidents to confine their religious values to their private lives and operate from a secular perspective in fulfilling their responsibilities? George W. Bush's frequent testimony to his Christian faith; support for faith-based initiatives; opposition to gay marriage, abortion, and the use of new embryonic stem cells in research; and claims of critics that Bush believes God led him to invade Iraq evoke much debate today. This book examines these questions by exploring the faith of eleven American presidents. It focuses on those chief executives for whom religion was an important issue because of their own beliefs, the issues they confronted, the elections they participated in, and/or the times in which they lived.

Religion and politics have been deeply intertwined throughout American history. Interaction between them, James Wolfe contends, "has been a staple of American life."[6] From the Pilgrims on, many Americans have considered themselves chosen by God for special blessings and responsibilities. Its leaders have repeatedly asserted that the United States has a divine mission to promote freedom, peace, and justice in the world and serve as a haven for the persecuted and oppressed and a land of opportunity for the ambitious and devout.[7] Politicians have continually sought to link their policies to the nation's historic ideals, which are largely religiously based. In the oft-quoted words of G. K. Chesterton, the United States has been a "nation with the soul of a church."[8] All forty-three presidents "have been friendly toward organized religion." Thirty-two have been church members, and all of them attended church at least occasionally and "considered themselves in some sense to be Christians." Every inaugural address, except George Washington's very brief second one, acknowledged God and invoked his blessing on the nation. Presidents have employed religious language and images to express heart-felt convictions, unify and inspire citizens, woo voters, and help legitimate their policies.[9]

There is a long and rich tradition of both scholarly and popular analysis of American presidents. Many of our nation's best and brightest historians, political scientists, and biographers have produced perceptive, provocative assessments of the lives and contributions of our presidents. They have examined their backgrounds, ideological commitments, campaigns, improprieties, and legacies. Few scholars, however, have analyzed the specific nature of presidents' religious convictions or the impact of these beliefs on their thinking and actions. This neglect has persisted despite the fact that during the last twenty-five years other scholars have produced important books assessing the relationship of religion and politics in the United States. These studies have focused primarily on church-state issues; civil religion; the connections between religious beliefs, practice, and affiliation and partisanship and voting behavior; and the rise and impact of the new religious right. Most students of the presidency have paid little attention to the religious convictions of presidents and the relationship of their administrations with religious constituencies. They have also largely ignored the role religion has played in formulating and implementing their policies or in the elections that sent them to the White House (except for those of 1928, 1960, 1976, 1980, 1984, and 2004). Only a handful of the plethora of books written about the presidency as an institution, comparative studies of chief executives, and biographies of individual presidents have focused on these topics. Specialists in religion and theology have not corrected this deficiency.

Although numerous books explore the presidents' personal piety and use of civil religion rhetoric, few books or articles examine, or even suggest, that their religious convictions influenced their policies and performance as our nation's chief executives. From Parson Weems's *Life of George Washington* in the early nineteenth century until the present, authors have discussed the faith of an individual president or all the presidents. Most of these authors have been committed Christians who portrayed their subjects as virtuous, pious, and theologically astute. A few have been enemies of organized religion who sought to prove that the presidents were not very devout or orthodox. Usually simplistic, superficial (especially ones that discuss all the presidents), and unsophisticated, these popular works have either exaggerated or depreciated the faith of the nation's chief executives, either lionizing or demonizing their subjects.[10] There are only three major scholarly treatments of selected occupants of the White House: Robert Alley's *So Help Me God: Religion and the Presidency, Wilson to Nixon* (1972), Richard G. Hutcheson Jr.'s *God in the White House: How Religion Has Changed the Modern Presidency* (1988), and Richard V. Pierard and Robert D. Linder's *Civil Religion and the Presidency* (1988). There are a few solidly researched, insightful monographs on the religious commitments of the founding fathers and the faith of individual presidents, especially Abraham Lincoln, Woodrow Wilson, Jimmy Carter, and George W. Bush.[11] Scholars have also produced valuable articles on various aspects of religion and the presidency.[12]

In the last two decades, the publication of hundreds of informative, instructive analyses of the nation's religious past has contributed to a growing recognition of the importance of religion in American history. Despite this literature and the significant role religion has played in the lives of many presidents, recent biographers have given very little attention to presidents' faith. Perhaps because of their own ideological perspectives, these authors have largely ignored the religious commitments of their subjects. "Religion," argues Garry Wills, "embarrasses the commentators. It is offbounds" for many journalists and scholars.[13] Religious perspectives have been treated with "stereotyping, condescension, dismissal, ignorance, [and] neglect." Religion has been "caricatured in history books, left out of TV documentaries on public issues," portrayed "in stock negative images by columnists and editorialists, treated as a curiosity, or welcomed when it is 'our kind,' i.e., 'progressive.'"[14] Most members of the academy and the media, James Wall, a former editor of

Christian Century, contends, have "either personally rejected a religious worldview, or, if they still" retain "any religious belief," know that it is "not acceptable to admit such a belief in polite society." The rational, logical, modern worldview prevails. It says, "if you do have religious faith, for God's sake keep quiet about it."[15] To many scholars and pundits, the religious views and values of the presidents are either avocations with no more relevance to their public lives than stamp collecting or bird watching or pious cant, spoken to satisfy public expectations, which does not express deep conviction or have major formative influence. Whether or not it was genuine, their faith was a private matter that had little impact on their presidencies.[16] When scholars have analyzed presidents' religious convictions, most have treated them as derivative, as epiphenomenal, as the result of social, political, or economic factors. For a variety of reasons—high levels of public interest, concerns about culture wars, the debate over how George W. Bush's faith affects his presidency, the entrance of more individuals with strong religious commitments into academia—historians and political scientists have recently begun to pay more attention to the relationship between religion and the presidency.

Nonetheless, scholarly treatment of Ronald Reagan illustrates my general point. After his death in June 2004, numerous religious leaders, politicians, associates, and family members accentuated the importance of Reagan's faith.[17] Editorials, television and radio talk shows and news programs, newspaper and magazine articles, and sermons all discussed his faith in God. Speaking for many, his son Ron Jr. declared at Reagan's funeral that his father was "a deeply, unabashedly religious man."[18] His wife, Nancy, praised his "strong, unshakable religious beliefs."[19] As president, Reagan claimed that his relationship to God was vital to him and strongly influenced his perspective on life. He spoke frequently to religious groups, repeatedly discussed spiritual and moral issues in his public addresses, wrote about his personal faith in hundreds of letters, and spent a significant amount of time with Protestant and Catholic religious leaders. Nevertheless, biographers, historians, and political scientists have paid scant attention to Reagan's religious background, convictions, or rhetoric.[20] They have overlooked his considerable knowledge of Scripture, commitment to prayer, and friendships with pastors and priests. While discussing specific issues such as Reagan's lack of church attendance, interest in the biblical battle of Armageddon, superstitious habits, and mystical experiences and his wife's fascination with astrology, other journalists and scholars have also largely ignored the nature and importance of his faith. Moreover, much of the analysis of Reagan's religious commitments has been negative. Wilbur Edel and Haynes Johnson, for example, accuse Reagan of disingenuously constructing his message and rhetoric to appeal to religious conservatives.[21] Like any politician, Reagan wanted to win elections and was sensitive to the potential impact of his proposals and policies. Nonetheless, during his presidency, he remained remarkably true to his core principles and values, which were significantly shaped by his religious commitments. Few scholars, however, have examined the nature of Reagan's faith or how it affected his performance and policies as president.

Americans have long been fascinated with the public and private lives of presidents. Their personalities and performance have been intensely scrutinized. Presidents have been thought to embody, represent, and speak for the American people, and religious elements have helped shape how they played this role.[22] In a sense, the president has been both the nation's pastor and prophet, called on at times to comfort and assure Americans and at others to challenge and inspire them. In the United States, Ronald Isetti points out, the president not only directs the government "but also symbolizes and speaks for the nation in his roles as king, prophet, and priest."[23] Although the Constitution forbids a religious test for the presidency, most Americans have been interested in the religious convictions of their presidents. They have wanted their chief executives to possess and display a substantial religious faith, especially on important public occasions and in times of crisis. Although not required to say the words, every president has ended his oath of office with "So help me God." Most Americans have wanted their presidents to affirm transcendent principles and promote traditional morality while avoiding a sectarian religious agenda and religious fanaticism. Many have also desired presidents to be moral exemplars, to set high standards for ethics and excellence.[24] "The President is expected to personify our betterness in an inspiring way," wrote James David Barber, "to express in what he does and is (not just in what he says) a moral idealism."[25] Franklin Roosevelt maintained that the "president sets the moral tone for our nation. He is a mirror in which we see what kind of people we are."[26] "When there is a moral issue involved," Harry Truman proclaimed, "the President has to be the moral leader of the country."[27] Presidents have affirmed and furthered the American democratic faith. Many have regarded themselves as divinely appointed leaders called to help the United States both to model true religion, individual liberty, and political democracy and to export it to other nations. Fulfilling these diverse expectations has been a great challenge. It has led most presidential candidates to present themselves as "deeply reverent but never sanctimonious," as orthodox Christians who were not narrowly sectarian, and above all as firm believers in religious freedom.[28] At the same time, however, many presidents have also been guided, in some cases in large part, by their personal religious commitments in performing their duties. They have often commingled their public and private faiths.

A New Approach to Religion and the Presidency

Even though thousands of volumes have been written about America's presidents, we do not know much about the precise nature of their faith or how it affected their performance and policies. This book aims to fill this void by providing an in-depth analysis of the religious convictions and practices of eleven presidents who lived in different historical eras and had different denominational backgrounds: George Washington, Thomas Jefferson, Abraham Lincoln, Theodore Roosevelt, Woodrow Wilson, Franklin Roosevelt, Dwight Eisenhower, John Kennedy, Jimmy Carter, Ronald Reagan, and George W. Bush. The religious affiliation (defined by either membership or church attendance) of this group is three Presbyterians, three Episcopalians, one Dutch Reformed, one Roman Catholic, one Baptist, one Christian Church (Disciples of Christ), and one Methodist. These individuals have been selected because either they were the most deeply religious American presidents (Lincoln, Wilson, Carter, Reagan, and Bush), because their perspectives on religion significantly influenced key public policies (Washington, Jefferson, Lincoln, Franklin Roosevelt, Eisenhower, Reagan, and Bush), because their religious faith differed substantially from mainstream Protestantism (Jefferson and Kennedy), and/or because their elections or administrations involved major controversies about religious issues (Jefferson, Lincoln, Theodore Roosevelt, Kennedy, Reagan, and Bush).[29] Each chapter examines the religious beliefs, commitments, affiliation, and practices (church attendance, prayer, Bible reading, and personal morality) of one of these presidents, discusses the influences upon and nature of his faith, and assesses how it contributed to his understanding of political ideology and practice. Each chapter also analyzes how a president's religious views and values helped shape the way he formulated and promoted several specific policies. In addition, chapters examine how presidents dealt with religious constituencies, interest groups, and leaders; evaluated religious issues (such as religious liberty, the relationship between church and the state, government support for religion, the proper place of religion in public life, and the connection between religion, public morality, and civic duty); and appraised key public policy matters (such as combating the Great Depression, ensuring civil rights, promoting peace, and resolving international conflicts). Although chapters explore social and cultural factors that influenced these presidents, they focus primarily on the intellectual and moral presuppositions that helped guide their understanding of political and religious issues and their actions while in office.

Scholars have devised several schemes to classify the theological convictions or religious perspectives of the presidents. In *So Help Me God*, Alley divides the presidents into three categories. The first is goal-oriented presidents, most of whom had Congregationalist or Unitarian backgrounds and leaned toward deism. This group, which includes Jefferson and Lincoln, tended to equate religion with morality. The second group, "legalist" presidents, had fairly close ties to more theologically and/or socially conservative Christian bodies (Presbyterian, Methodist, Baptist, and Quaker): Theodore

Roosevelt, Wilson, and Eisenhower. (Reagan and Bush could be added to this category.) Influenced by Calvinism, they interpreted national endeavors as righteous crusades. A third type, "situational ethics" presidents, grew up in Episcopal churches or elite families, found in tradition a middle ground between rationalism and revealed religion, and were more flexible and pragmatic in their approach to both religion and the presidency (Washington, Franklin Roosevelt, and Kennedy).[30]

More interested in the ideological and theological components of presidential leadership, political scientist Charles Dunn devised a paradigm that compares liberal and conservative tendencies of belief on twenty-four issues, including the ultimate source of knowledge, moral standards, conception of God and human nature, the basis of salvation, the locus of government power, the role of government, how justice is achieved, economic perspective, and preferred rate and type of change. Dunn uses this paradigm to classify American presidents on ideological and theological continuums from conservative to liberal. Although he argues that some presidents are hard to categorize because their theological and ideological convictions conflicted (he lists Jefferson and Carter as examples), he concludes that "ideological and theological components tend to reinforce each other."[31] Those who are conservative in both theology and political ideology have tended to be Republicans (McKinley, Theodore Roosevelt, Hoover, Reagan, and George H. W. Bush), and those who are liberal in both categories have usually been Democrats (Jefferson, Wilson, Franklin Roosevelt, and Kennedy). Dunn labels Lincoln as conservative in theology and liberal in political ideology and Eisenhower as liberal in theology and conservative in political ideology.[32]

Another way to classify American presidents is to describe the nature or focus of their faith, while recognizing that many of them can be placed in more than one category. The faith of some presidents such as Jefferson and Theodore Roosevelt focused primarily on the cognitive and moral aspects of Christianity. A strong devotional component is evident in the faith of other presidents, most notably Carter and George W. Bush. The faith of these presidents and Wilson strongly shaped their views of the world and their policies as president. The faith of Ronald Reagan was deeply personal, but it powerfully influenced his understanding of the world and his actions as chief executive. Kennedy's faith was traditional or formal and appeared to have little impact on his thinking or performance as president. The faith of Franklin D. Roosevelt and Eisenhower is enigmatic. Their religious convictions appear to have deeply affected some aspects of their lives and policies but to have had little influence on other facets.

Although these categorizations are helpful, in some ways these labels confuse more than they clarify. All the presidents confronted the issues of how to best deal with religious constituencies and how to effectively relate their religious beliefs to leading the nation, organizing their administrations, speaking to the public, and devising policies without violating cherished American ideals of religious diversity and the separation of church and state. Despite similarities in how they approached these matters, the presidents' personalities and religious backgrounds, the changing nature of American society, and the particular domestic and foreign problems they faced led to many significant differences. Where appropriate in this book, I discuss common denominational backgrounds and theological commitments and similar styles of making decisions, ways of relating to religious groups, and use of religious rhetoric. Each administration, however, is unique because of the specific political, economic, social, and religious issues it confronted, the political composition of Congress, the nation's economic and social conditions, the relative strength of religious constituencies, the general ideological climate, and different global contexts.

Five Central Themes

In evaluating the faith of these eleven presidents and the role of religion in their administrations, I paid special attention to five themes: the nature of their convictions, the separation of church and state, civil religion, America as a chosen nation, and the issue of character. One major theme this book explores is the ideological convictions or worldview of its subjects. "A worldview is a conceptual scheme" by which individuals "consciously or unconsciously place or fit everything" they believe and by which they "interpret and judge reality."[33] The worldview of many people does not explicitly function as "a systematic conception of life," a philosophy, or a creed. Nevertheless, this "integrative and interpretative framework" provides a blueprint for understanding, explaining, and managing reality and a foundation for everyday thinking and acting.[34] Worldviews determine which ideas individuals consider important and color their perceptions of all aspects of life. Worldviews, argues philosopher Phil Washburn, provide answers to the most "fundamental aspects of human experience": human nature, "moral values and actions," "society and one's place in it," "knowledge and understanding," and transcendence.[35] They determine what people believe about God, humanity, society, and ethics; stipulate how the world should be; offer a vision for the future; and strongly influence people's actions.[36]

Although the perspective and positions of their party and their own political ideologies shaped the thinking and actions of most presidents more than their particular religious traditions, their religious convictions played a significant role in certain decisions and policies of all the chief executives examined in this study. "It is difficult to find an instance in which a President's formal religious attachment," Robert Michaelsen wrote in *Christian Century*, "was of decisive importance in determining the outcome of a major policy decision." For the most part, the influence of a president's faith "has been a subtle . . . part of the total fabric" of his personality and character. The role of religion in the life of any president is best seen in "his total outlook on life" and the way he executed his duties. Did he rely "on a power greater than himself? What issues were of pre-eminent importance to him? What did he value?"[37] Although varied beliefs, ideals, and life experiences helped shape the worldviews of these presidents, their religious socialization, involvement, and study played a substantial part. Because of their training, interests, or lack of access to relevant sources, scholars have rarely recognized any relationship between the religious backgrounds or commitments of presidents and their particular behaviors, actions, or policies. Direct correlations are difficult to establish, but many presidents' religious convictions have significantly influenced their philosophy of governing and some specific programs and policies they promoted.

I explored several factors to explain the worldviews of these eleven pres-idents: their stated beliefs in letters, interviews, and speeches; testimony by those who knew them well; their actions, most notably their participation in religious activities such as church services, prayer, and reading of the Bible and devotional and theological books; and their personal relationships with religious leaders. Cynics argue that neither the church attendance nor the addresses of presidents, especially ones since Hoover who depended on speech-writers, are accurate barometers of their religious convictions. Their atten-dance at religious services, use of pious language, invocation of God, and discussion of religious themes allegedly do not reflect their genuine convic-tions but are usually done to please the public and provide a moral gloss for their positions and policies. Nevertheless, examining presidents' involvement in religious activities and religious beliefs throughout their lives and the amount and nature of their religious rhetoric does provide clues about what they actually believed.

The Separation of Church and State

Since Christianity began, Western societies have struggled with how the church and the state should be related.[38] The American colonies rejected the idea of clerical rule and, following the example of Protestant reformers, sep-arated the offices and responsibilities of ministers and magistrates. Never-theless, some colonies established churches and enforced various religious regulations on all citizens. After the founding of the United States, Americans continued to grapple with the relationship between the church and the state. Neither the Declaration of Independence nor the Constitution affirms specific Christian convictions. Although the First Amendment prohibited Congress from establishing a national church and guaranteed freedom of worship to individuals, it did not resolve the issue of how organized religion and the government should interact. Because this nation has many churches (denominations) and three levels of government—federal, state, and local—the relationship between institutional religion and the state has been complicated.

The perceived ideal relationship between church and state has varied in different periods of American history, depending on the prevailing religious and ideological climate.[39] During the nation's first century, Protestant Christianity was its semiofficial faith, as evident in countless statements by presidents, Supreme Court justices, and Congressmen and in numerous government practices. In the early national years, Americans, including Washington and Jefferson, were strongly influenced by both Enlightenment deism and traditional Protestantism.[40] During the 1820s and 1830s, the Second Great Awakening stamped the values, ethos, and practices of Protestant evangelicalism deeply into American culture and significantly influenced American politics.[41] Religious groups solicited the aid of the federal government, worked to incorporate Christian values into its operation, and strove to shape its policies.[42] This pattern continued after the Civil War. Despite the vehement objections of a few secularists, the vast majority of Americans, whether Protestant or Catholic, saw their nation as essentially Christian. In a unanimous 1892 decision, *Church of the Holy Trinity v. United States,* Supreme Court justices declared: "Our laws and institutions necessarily are based upon and embody the teachings of the Redeemer of mankind.... [I]n this sense and to this extent our civilization and our institutions are emphatically Christian.... [T]his is a Christian nation."[43] During the Progressive era, most Protestants and Catholics accentuated the Bible's teaching on justice and urged Christians to advance the Kingdom of God by promoting social reform at home and missions abroad.[44] Before 1925, few challenged the notion that the United States was a Christian country, protested government aid of religion, or argued that the state and church worked too closely together. Escalating ethnic, religious, and ideological diversity led to the "disestablishment" of Protestantism in the years between 1900 and World War II and the acceptance of three major religious traditions—Protestantism, Catholicism, and Judaism—as furnishing the foundation for national life. While elite culture became increasingly secular after 1925, the Protestant establishment and its Catholic and Jewish allies continued to defend traditional religious standards of morality and the value of religion.[45]

Since 1947, a series of Supreme Court decisions significantly affected the place of organized religion in the public arena, especially schools, public buildings, and government practices, and produced heated debate about the relationship between church and state. Because of these rulings, even greater religious pluralism, the growing secularization of American society, presidents' own education and experiences, and the rise of organizations like the American Civil Liberties Union and Americans United for the Separation of Church and State, which demand rigid separation between religious organizations, rituals, and symbols, and public life, presidents have been more careful in their use of religious rhetoric and more evenhanded in their treatment of religious communities. Although the relationship between church and state has traditionally been one of "friendly separation," Supreme Court decisions in the early 1960s ruled prayer and Bible reading in the public schools unconstitutional, and more recent verdicts have prohibited the display of religious symbols in public places.[46]

Nevertheless, during U.S. history, the concept of church-state separation has not prevented Congress from opening its sessions with prayer, the military from appointing chaplains, or the government from minting coins stating "In God We Trust." Nor has it inhibited presidents from proclaiming days of prayer and thanksgiving. Moreover, some chief executives held prayer breakfasts, worship services, or hymn sings at the White House. Eisenhower and all his successors regularly participated in presidential prayer breakfasts. Many chief executives have insisted that religious faith is crucial to the well-being of the republic. No president has totally segregated religion and politics.[47]

The debate over what role religious bodies should play in the political arena has also been heated. Religious groups have participated extensively in public policy debates over slavery, civil rights, poverty, abortion, and national defense, often striving to pass legislation as well as to transform individual attitudes, mores, and social institutions. Many religious denominations and parachurch organizations have worked diligently to influence governmental policies in ways that accord with their members' understanding of Scripture.[48] Generally speaking, those groups deemed most supportive or most powerful have gained direct access to the nation's chief executive, while those regarded as less loyal or important have dealt only with White House staff. Although presidents usually tried not to favor specific religious organizations, they inevitably had closer relationships with some than with others. Many religious groups insist that the separation of church and state does not mean that religion must (or should) be divorced from the government. Most Americans have agreed with the Founding Fathers that the nation's churches should help maintain order, further the common good, and promote essential religious beliefs such as God's providential direction of the world and reward of virtue and punishment of evil.[49]

American Civil Religion

A third issue that has significantly affected American politics and presidents is the nature, use, and consequences of civil religion. In his seminal

1967 essay, sociologist Robert Bellah argued that the United States had "an elaborate and well-instituted civil religion," which was "alongside of and rather clearly differentiated from the churches."[50] Also known as civic piety, religious nationalism, public religion, the common faith, and theistic humanism, civil religion provides a religious sanction for the political order and a divine justification of and support for civic society and a nation's practices. This generalized form of faith combines "religious metaphors with nationalistic aspirations." It is the "state's use of consensus religious sentiments, concepts, and symbols for its own purposes." Transcending specific denominations, it "mixes piety with patriotism and traditional religion with national life until it is impossible to distinguish between them."[51] "As a system of established rituals, symbols, values, norms, allegiances, all of which function in a practical way in the ongoing life of the community, it serves as the social glue which binds a people together and gives them an overarching sense of spiritual unity."[52]

While this civil religion incorporates many biblical archetypes—"Exodus, Chosen People, Promised Land, New Jerusalem, Sacrificial Death and Rebirth"—it also includes convictions, sacred events and places, prophets and martyrs, and solemn rituals and symbols that are peculiarly American. Supported and perpetuated by mores and folkways rather than by law, it involves beliefs (but no formal creed), revelatory events (most notably the American Revolution and the Civil War), prophets (especially Washington, Jefferson, and Lincoln), sacred places (Washington, D.C., with its shrines to Washington, Lincoln, and Franklin Roosevelt; Bunker Hill; the Alamo; and Gettysburg), sacred texts (the Declaration of Independence, the Constitution, Lincoln's Gettysburg Address, and key inaugural addresses), ceremonies (Memorial Day, Independence Day, and Veterans' Day celebrations and the pageantry of presidential inaugurals, all of which fuse piety and patriotism), hymns ("God Bless America" and "My Country Tis of Thee"), and rituals (prayers at public events such as inaugurals and the beginnings of sessions of Congress, deferential behavior toward the flag, and national days of prayer).[53] From the earliest days of the American republic, this religion, while sharing "much in common with Christianity," Bellah maintains, was not in "any specific sense Christian"; "never anticlerical or militantly secular, on the contrary, it borrowed selectively from the [Judeo-Christian] religious tradition in such a way that the average American saw no conflict between the two."[54] As Conrad Cherry explains, this civil religion asserts that God has chosen America, God is the source of human rights, and sacrifice is required to achieve the nation's destiny.[55]

By presiding over the nation's rituals and reaffirming its creeds, presidents have served as the prophets and priests of this civil religion. They have employed civil religion to unite Americans and to frame and win support for specific policies. These national magistrates, whatever their private religious beliefs, have been guided by America's civil religion in performing their official duties, and their religious commitments have helped shape the civil religion of particular periods.[56] Regularly invoking God in inaugural addresses and on other solemn occasions, the president has functioned as the nation's "principal prophet, high priest, first preacher, and chief pastor."[57] American chief executives, argues Michael Novak, "conduct high public liturgies, constantly reinterpret the nation's fundamental documents and traditions, [and] furnish the central terms of public discourse." They venerate the nation's "holy calendar, its sacred cities and monuments and pilgrimages, its consecrated mounds and fields."[58] From 1776 to the present, increasing religious and cultural pluralism has broadened the basis of civil religion from "evangelical consensus to Protestantism-in-general, to Christianity-in-general, to the Judeo-Christian tradition, and finally to deism-in-general." Throughout American history, however, the nation's religious pluralism has prompted presidents to use generic and sometimes vague religious language and imagery.[59] All of them have struggled to find "in the midst of a startling diversity of faiths, a common ordering faith on which national life can be based."[60] In their inaugural addresses and other speeches and proclamations, especially ones declaring national thanksgiving and days of prayer, presidents have portrayed God as a benevolent father who blesses America much more than as celestial judge who holds the nation accountable to his standards.[61] They have also frequently quoted biblical passages and alluded to scriptural narratives, parables, and stories. The Bible has given them "a rich store of rhetorical devices to illustrate and dramatize the points" in their speeches.[62]

This book examines the ways its eleven subjects conceptualized and used civil religion and, in the case of Washington and Lincoln, became part of the nation's civic faith, in light of scholarly assessment of this concept and its historical effects.

America as God's Chosen Nation

Closely connected with American civil religion has been the widespread conviction that America has a unique calling from God. This theme is evident in the nation's sacred ceremonies, quasi-sacred scriptures, and presidents' inaugural addresses. All nations have seen themselves as chosen people, Russel Nye contends; "the idea of special destiny is as old as nationalism itself." Nevertheless, he argues, "No nation in modern history has been quite so consistently dominated as the United States by the belief that it has a particular mission in the world."[63] Strongly identifying with ancient Israel, many Americans have concluded that God chose them to play a principal role in bringing his kingdom on earth. The Puritans insisted that they had a "divinely appointed errand in the wilderness." John Winthrop, the first governor of Massachusetts Bay Colony; Jonathan Edwards, America's greatest theologian; Timothy Dwight, an early president of Yale; and countless lesser known citizens have trumpeted this theme. As Winthrop put it in his 1630 sermon, "A Model of Christian Charity," "For we must consider that we shall be as a city upon a hill, the eyes of all people are upon us." Edwards expected a "great work of God" to soon begin in America.[64] His grandson Dwight claimed that the new nation was "by Heaven designed, th' example bright to renovate mankind."[65] Americans pushed relentlessly westward "under the banner of Manifest Destiny" and endowed their wars with "apocalyptic meaning."[66]

While ministers, theologians, businessmen, educators, reformers, governors, and senators have all maintained that God assigned America a special mission, presidents have also strongly promoted this conviction. They have repeatedly asserted that America must both embody and export democracy, civility, freedom, and morality. Washington contended in his first inaugural address that "the preservation of the sacred fire of liberty and the destiny of the republican model of government" depended on America's success. Jefferson labeled the American experiment "the last best hope of mankind," and Lincoln called the Union "the last best hope of earth." "Upon the success of our experiment," alleged Theodore Roosevelt, "much depends, not only with regard to our own welfare, but as regards the welfare of mankind."[67] "Our nation is chosen by God and commissioned by history," declared George W. Bush, "to be a model to the world of justice."[68] This conviction has helped motivate and vindicate America's actions at home and abroad.[69] Positively, it has helped inspire the United States to engage in acts of self-sacrifice, generosity, and charity. Negatively, this belief has contributed to imperialism, concepts of racial superiority, cultural insensitivity, and unwarranted interference in the internal affairs of other nations. The idea that God has chosen America to fulfill his purposes has promoted self-righteousness and hubris on the one hand and self-criticism and humility on the other. It has also fueled Americans' sense of identity and purpose.

Presidential Character

Finally, this book examines the character of these eleven presidents. Biblical writers and Greek philosophers stressed that the character of rulers is closely associated with the welfare of their subjects.[70] The Old Testament is replete with examples of how Israel prospered under kings with godly character and foundered under ones with despicable character. In Plato's *Republic*, character is the most important qualification of the ruling class. The Founding Fathers argued that the success of America's democratic experiment depended on the character of both its leaders and its people. "The destiny of the republican model of government," Washington declared in his First In-augural Address, hinged on Americans practicing a high level of both private and public morality.[71] "To suppose that any form of Government will secure liberty or happiness without any form of virtue in the people," asserted James Madison in 1788, "is a chimerical idea."[72] Although all the subjects of this study appealed to the concepts of character, duty, and honor, these concepts were especially important to Theodore Roosevelt. The American republic, he maintained, rested "on the moral character and educated judgment of the individual."[73]

In *The Character Factor: How We Judge America's Presidents* (2004), James P. Pfiffner contends that most students of American politics agree that character is as significant to presidents as intelligence, leadership abilities, or public speaking skills. He maintains that a chief executive's character strongly influences his actions. Moreover, we judge our presidents both by how well they perform their duties and by how effectively they serve as role models. We expect our chief executives to promote the public good and to be moral exemplars. Pfiffner asserts that the traits of trustworthiness, integrity, loyalty, sincerity, candor, self-restraint, compassion, consistency, and prudence are especially valuable in evaluating presidents' performance and character.[74] This study examines the character of these eleven presidents, especially the role that religious training, biblical study, and spiritual piety played in shaping their characters. It also analyzes how their characters influenced their work as president, the importance they attributed to this concept, and their character flaws and alleged moral indiscretions.[75] As William James put it, an individual's philosophy and actions express his "intimate character."[76]

A Final Observation

Several factors make the study of faith and the presidency very challenging. As Martin Fausold notes, scholars who assess American presidents often reach different conclusions "depending on their sources of information, their times, and their values."[77] Presidential biographer Joseph Ellis argues that "the past is a foreign country with its own distinctive mores and language." Therefore, all efforts to evaluate chief executives in light of present knowledge and ideals "invariably compromise the integrity of the historical context" that made them who they were.[78] Moreover, it is difficult to determine whether presidents' speeches, proclamations, and interviews represent their true convictions or simply express what they think the public wants to hear and what will advance their personal popularity and policies. Because Franklin Roosevelt and his successors have all employed speechwriters, it has become even tougher to determine the actual convictions of more recent presidents. Examining presidents' personal correspondence is therefore essential, but most of them wrote with posterity in mind at least part of the time. Finally, many presidents considered their faith to be a private matter and were reticent to discuss it even with intimate friends. Although these issues are significant, scholars have begun to more closely scrutinize the faith of presidents and other politicians.

Although numerous factors influenced the thinking and actions of these eleven presidents, their religious convictions affected the rhetoric they used, the policies they pursued, and the ways they promoted them. These chief executives drew effectively on elements of their own personal faith and the nation's civil religion to gain support for many of their policies. The impact of presidents' religious commitments on their actions is constrained by a variety of other factors, including the goals of their supporters, the federal bureaucracy, Congress, and public expectations. However, the religious beliefs of all of the presidents examined in this book, except Kennedy, played a significant part in shaping key aspects of their administrations. Understanding "the dynamic relationship that exists between a president's religious faith and the public policies he pursues and the political actions he takes," writes Jeff Walz, requires much more work.[79] This book aims to illuminate important dimensions of this understudied subject that is often shrouded in myth and misconception. By carefully examining the religious convictions of eleven key presidents and how these convictions affected these presidents' work, I seek to help both scholars and ordinary Americans better understand and participate more fruitfully in the frequently heated, always interesting, and vitally important dialogue about the relationship between religion, politics, and public policy in contemporary America.

CHAPTER ONE

George Washington
and Providential Agency

The disadvantageous circumstances... under which the war was undertaken can never be forgotten. The singular interpositions of Providence in our feeble condition were such, as could scarcely escape the attention of the most unobserving; while the unparalleled perseverance of the armies of the United States... was little short of a standing miracle....

Farewell Orders to the Armies of the United States, Nov. 2, 1783

When I contemplate the interpositions of Providence, as it was visibly manifested, in guiding us through the Revolution, in preparing us for the reception of a general government, and in conciliating the good will of the People of America toward one another after it's [sic] adoption, I feel myself... almost overwhelmed with a sense of divine munificence.

To the... Common Council of the City of Philadelphia, April 1789

No people can be bound to acknowledge and adore the invisible hand which conducts the affairs of men, more than the people of the United States. Every step by which they have advanced to the character of an independent nation seems to have been distinguished by some token of providential agency.

First Inaugural Address, April 30, 1789

ON JULY 9, 1755, the "most catastrophic" day in Anglo-American history, Colonel George Washington was traveling with General Edward Braddock's army toward Fort Duquesne when they were ambushed by Indians and

French hiding in the woods. In the ensuing massacre, hundreds of British soldiers, including Braddock, were killed or seriously wounded. Perched on their horses, officers were perfect targets. One after another, they were hit. Bullets ripped through Washington's coat, knocked his hat off, and killed two of the horses he rode. Before dying, Braddock ordered Washington to ride forty miles through the pitch-dark night to summon reinforcements. The remainder of the British army eventually staggered back to Philadelphia.[1] Rumors circulated that Washington had been killed. On July 18, he wrote his brother from Fort Cumberland, "As I have heard since my arriv'l at this place, a circumstantial acct. of my death and dying Speech, I take this early oppertunity [sic] of contradicting both, and of assuring you that I now exist and appear in the land of the living by the miraculous care of Providence, that protected me beyond all human expectation."[2] The colonel wrote to Robert Jackson two weeks later, "See the wondrous works of Providence! The uncertainty of Human things!"[3] Preaching to a volunteer company of militia, Presbyterian minister Samuel Davies declared, "As a remarkable instance" of military ardor, "I . . . point . . . to . . . that heroic youth, Colonel Washington, whom I cannot but hope Providence has hitherto preserved in so signal a manner for some important service to his country."[4] And so began the stories about Washington's faith in God and divine selection to lead the American people.

Although the religious convictions and practices of many presidents have been ignored, Washington's have been closely scrutinized and endlessly debated. Some authors have portrayed the Virginian as the epitome of piety, and others have depicted him as the patron saint of skepticism. The fact that Washington said almost nothing publicly or privately about the precise nature of his beliefs has evoked competing claims that he was a devout Christian, a Unitarian, a "warm deist," and a "theistic rationalist." One point, however, is not debatable: Washington strongly believed that Providence played a major role in creating and sustaining the United States. In public pronouncements as commander in chief and president, he repeatedly thanked God for directing and protecting Americans in their struggle to obtain independence and create a successful republic. Arguably, no president has stressed the role of Providence in the nation's history more than Washington.

The Virginian planter was a giant even among the remarkable generation of America's founders. At six feet two inches, he physically towered over almost all of them. His powerful physique, athletic prowess, quick reflexes, stately bearing, personal magnetism, and incredible stamina impressed his contemporaries. More significantly, because of his exceptional character and extraordinary contributions, he has been deemed indispensable to the success of the patriot cause and the new republic. Risking his reputation, wealth, and life, he commanded an undermanned and poorly supplied army to an improbable victory over the world's leading economic and military power. He presided over the convention that produced the United States' venerable Constitution. For nearly a quarter of a century (1775–99), Washington was the most important person in America.[5] Indeed, some call these years the "Age of Washington."[6] As president, he kept the new nation from crashing on the shoals of anarchy, monarchy, or revolution. His impressive appearance, stately demeanor, sterling character, monumental contributions to American independence, and leadership as president combined to produce an aura that gave added weight to his public statements on all subjects, including religion.[7]

To a certain extent during his life and even more after his death, Washington was elevated to sainthood. An American civil religion arose that revered him as God's instrument and a larger-than-life mythological hero.[8] In life and death, he has been seen as "the deliverer of America," the savior of his people, the American Moses, and even a demigod.[9] In the oft-quoted words of future Supreme Court Chief Justice John Marshall, as spoken by Henry Lee, Washington was "First in war, first in peace, and first in the hearts of his countrymen.... Pious, just, humane, temperate, and sincere...his example was as edifying...as were the effects of his lasting example."[10] Both the mythmakers and the debunkers have so distorted the historical Washington that it is very difficult, if not impossible, for his biographers to separate the man from "the myths and images surrounding him."[11]

Because the Virginian wrote little about his religious convictions, analyzing their influence on his presidential policies is more challenging than it is for most other chief executives examined in this book. One place where they are clearly evident is in his pivotal role in helping establish religious liberty and toleration as key principles of the new nation.

The Faith of George Washington

Among American presidents, only Abraham Lincoln's religious convictions and practices have been so painstakingly examined as those of Washington. Of all the varied aspects of the Virginian's life, few have caused as much contention as his religious beliefs and habits. Moreover, no other chief executive has had his religious life so distorted by folklore. As Paul Boller Jr. puts it, Washington's religious outlook has been "thoroughly clouded by myth, legend, misunderstanding, and misrepresentation."[12] Many of the hundreds of books, articles, sermons, and essays published about his faith since 1800 have advanced ideological agendas and told pious fables about Washington that have little basis in historical fact. Other authors have been so preoccupied with refuting these myths that they have paid scant attention to his actual religious beliefs and practices.[13] The fact that Washington, unlike some other founders, never expounded his convictions in a systematic way makes unearthing and analyzing his religious perspective very challenging. Although he frequently used the "language of faith," it was not that "of any particular, readily identifiable faith."[14]

Scores of books and articles have extolled the first president as "a Christian hero and statesman," "the founder of a Christian republic," "Christ's faithful soldier and servant," "the great high priest of the nation," and a "man of abiding faith."[15] Celebrating Washington's piety, they feature stories of the general arranging Communion services before battles and inspiring parishioners in small country churches where he worshiped with religious zeal. Mason Locke "Parson" Weems and other enthusiasts insisted that he regularly attended church services, said grace before all meals, actively participated in church work, filled his public and private statements with religious exhortations, and prayed almost constantly wherever he was—"in his library, in his army tent, at the homes of friends and strangers, and in the woods, thickets, groves and bushes." If Washington were truly as devout as these effusive testimonies portray him, Boller contends, he would have "had time for little else but the ritual of piety." Boller demonstrates that most of these claims, which are based on hearsay and legends, are implausible.[16]

The most famous fable about Washington's piety pictures him kneeling in prayer in the snow at Valley Forge during the winter of 1777–78, when the American cause seemed desperate. According to the story as first told by Weems, Washington had established his headquarters in the home of Isaac Potts, a Quaker pacifist. "One day, when the prospects, morale, and physical state of the Continental Army were at their lowest," Potts saw Washington on his knees in prayer in the woods.[17] Eventually the general arose and returned to his headquarters "with a countenance of angelic serenity."[18] Although this story is "utterly without foundation in fact," it has been memorialized in poetry, inscribed on a plaque at the base of Washington's statue in New York City, commemorated on a postage stamp, and etched in stained glass at both the Washington Memorial Chapel at Valley Forge and a private chapel in Washington, D.C., used by members of Congress.[19]

To these authors, "abundant evidence" demonstrates Washington "was a true Christian in every sense that the word implies."[20] They point to the piety of his parents, who instructed him in the Anglican catechism, faithfully took him to church, and read him Matthew Hale's *Contemplations*. Moreover, Washington received much of his early education in Fredericksburg at a school run by the rector of St. George's Church. Arguing that he served diligently as a vestryman, contributed liberally to churches, attended church consistently, had private devotions regularly, followed biblical moral principles devotedly, and relied repeatedly on God's providence, they conclude that his "every word and act showed clearly" that he was a Christian.[21] Numerous evangelical authors have recently contended that Washington (and many other founders) was an orthodox Christian.[22]

Rejecting these perspectives, many scholars maintain that Washington's faith was not very deep or meaningful. They argue that his "interest in religion" was "perfunctory," that he "lacked a personal religious faith," and that his practice of Christianity "was limited and superficial because he himself was not a Christian." His refusal to take Communion after the Revolutionary War indicated he "was no longer a faithful Episcopalian." The Virginian was ambivalent toward orthodox Christianity and organized religion in general, attended church sporadically, and participated "little in the life of the local church."[23] David Holmes asserts that "with only a few exceptions... Washington's speeches, orders, official letters, and other public communications on religion... seem clearly to display the outlook of a Deist." He regularly substituted deist terms such as "the Supreme Being," "the Grand Architect," and the "Great Ruler of Events" for "God," "Father," "Lord," and "Savior."[24] In his public addresses, Washington seldom referred to Jesus or even to Christianity specifically. In itself, this is not remarkable. As other chapters will demonstrate, in an effort to be as inclusive as possible, presidents frequently alluded to God, often using generic titles, but rarely to Christ. What is more significant is that in his private correspondence Washington mentions Christ or Christianity only a handful of times.

Although Washington stressed that God directed the development of the world, Holmes avers, he considered him "somewhat distant and impersonal."[25] Pierard and Linder argue that Washington's faith centered around a "genuine but generalized faith in God as the Creator and Ruler of the universe." Like other "Unitarian-deists," he regarded God as above the world, "not communicating directly with humanity," but somehow providentially guiding affairs on earth.[26] In the late eighteenth century, some of them "were privately skeptical, others belligerently argumentative, and still others simply philosophically curious about theology... but at least in America, they believed in God and generally in life after death." They revered Jesus as a great moral teacher and role model but did not consider him divine. Although they valued the Bible as a source for virtuous conduct, they denied its miracles and accepted only its teachings that accorded with reason. Peter Henriques labels Washington a "warm deist" because he rejected the belief of most eighteenth-century deists that God was a watchmaker who did not intervene in human affairs and held instead that he regularly shaped and molded history.[27] Others use the term "enlightened deist" to describe Washington and some of the other founders.[28]

Perhaps a better label for what Washington and other like-minded founders believed is theistic rationalism. This "hybrid belief system" mixes "elements of natural religion, Christianity, and rationalism," with rationalism serving "as the predominant element." Although maintaining that these three components were generally in harmony, they used reason to resolve any conflict among them. To theistic rationalists, God was active in human affairs, and prayer therefore was effectual. They contended that religion's primary role was to promote morality, which was indispensable to society. Theistic rationalists asserted that "revelation was designed to complement reason" and had a higher view of the person of Jesus than deists.[29] Because most deists denied God's active involvement in the world, the deity of Christ, and the Bible as God's revelation, the concept of theistic rationalism seems preferable to that of "Unitarian-deist," "warm deist," and "enlightened deist" in describing Washington and other founders such as John Adams, Benjamin Franklin, James Wilson, and Thomas Jefferson.[30]

In 1795, Washington wrote to James Anderson that "in politics, as in religion[,] my tenets are few and simple."[31] A very private individual, the first president seldom confided his deepest thoughts or emotions on any subject in his diary or in letters to friends. Presbyterian pastor Samuel Miller asserted that he displayed an "unusual, but uniform, and apparently deliberate, reticence on the subject of personal religion."[32] Moreover, as Garry Wills explains, "By inclination and principle, he shied away from demonstrations of piety."[33] These factors make it very difficult to determine what Washington actually believed.

Washington's religious views were shaped by parents, his half-brother Lawrence, the teachings and practices of the Episcopal Church, the ideas of the Enlightenment, the tenets of Freemasonry, his wife, Martha, and his military and political experiences. The future president was raised to revere God, respect biblical teaching, and participate in the rituals of the Church of England. Like his role model, Lawrence, Washington "practiced the Anglican faith without bigotry, pious ostentation, or notable fervor." Like many other upper-class Virginians, he was baptized, married, and buried according to Anglican (or Episcopal, as the denomination was called after 1783) rites.[34] In the years before the Revolution, Washington read such prominent Enlightenment authors as Alexander Pope, Voltaire, and Thomas Paine. He became a Freemason in his early twenties and remained one throughout his life. Members of this fraternal order expressed belief in God but disliked traditional Christian forms. In 1759, Washington married Martha Dandridge Custis, a wealthy widow with two young children, with whom he enjoyed a satisfying marriage for the next forty years. Martha was a devout Episcopalian who faithfully adhered to the eighteenth-century concept of duty to God and family. She attended church every Sunday and spent an hour each day reading the Bible and sermons and praying.[35] She regularly received Communion and discussed the consolation her faith had afforded her through her many trials and her hope of a "blessed immortality."[36]

Judged by the standards of the second half of the eighteenth century, Washington was fairly religious. His support for chaplains and religious services, pattern of church attendance, attitude toward worship and the sacraments, and views of the Bible, prayer, God, Christ, salvation, human nature, and life after death all help substantiate this claim. During his military service prior to the Revolution, Washington read services for his troops on Sundays when no chaplains were available. He observed all the fast days the Church of England prescribed for army members.[37] As a commander in chief of the Continental Army, he recruited chaplains for his troops, required his soldiers to attend Sunday worship, and held thanksgiving services after victories.

While residing at Mount Vernon, he periodically attended two churches— Pohick Church in Fairfax County and Christ Church in Alexandria. The lack of rectors to conduct services, the distance he had to travel, and occasionally poor weather limited his attendance.[38] On many occasions, however, Washington skipped church to visit with relatives and friends, go foxhunting, or spend a quiet morning alone at Mount Vernon. Prior to the Revolution, he attended church about once a month, but he worshiped more frequently during times of political crisis.[39] After the war ended, Washington resumed attending either Pohick or Christ Church about once a month.[40] During his presidency, however, perhaps because of the burden of his office or because he wanted to set a positive example, Washington attended church almost every Sunday. Although he usually worshiped in Episcopal churches, he sometimes attended Congregational, Lutheran, Dutch Reformed, German Reformed, and Roman Catholic services (and occasionally contributed to their building funds).[41] While New York was the nation's capital, the president worshiped primarily at St. Paul's Chapel of Trinity Parish. When the capital was moved to Philadelphia, he most often attended Christ Episcopal Church.

Eleanor Parke "Nelly" Custis, Martha Washington's granddaughter, claimed that the general worshiped with "reverent respect," and William White, the bishop of Pennsylvania and senior rector of three Episcopal churches in Philadelphia during the 1790s, insisted he was "always serious and attentive" in church.[42] Nevertheless, Washington did not participate in two vital Episcopal rites. Like many other Episcopalian founders, he was never confirmed. In this rite, individuals publicly professed their faith in Christ. However, only bishops had the power to confirm, and there were no American bishops until the mid-1780s, making confirmation both extremely difficult and very rare.[43] More significantly, he apparently did not take Holy Communion. During the eighteenth century, most Episcopal churches celebrated this sacrament four times a year. Only a small percentage of churchgoers stayed for Communion following the regular service, except at Easter. Although some claimed that Washington did receive the Lord's Supper after the Revolutionary War, Custis and White testified that he did not. Custis reported that she and the general always left after the regular service, while Martha stayed. White admitted in 1835 that "General Washington never received the communion, in the churches of which I am parochial minister."[44] Moreover, James Abercrombie, the rector who oversaw Christ Church, was so upset that the president and others left the service before Communion that he preached a sermon protesting the "unhappy tendency of . . . those in elevated stations who invariably turned their back upon the celebration of the Lord's Supper." Considering this "a very just reproof" aimed especially at him and concluding that he was setting a bad example, Washington never again worshiped at Christ Church when Communion was celebrated.[45] Three factors may have deterred Washington from taking Communion. He may not have felt worthy to do so, he may not have believed in the Episcopal view of what the sacrament symbolized, or he may have been reluctant to publicly declare faith in Jesus Christ. His refusal to take Communion has led some historians to conclude that to him religion was principally a social obligation, not a heartfelt conviction.

Although some claim that Washington avidly read and "supremely prized" the Bible, the evidence suggests that he did not. Unlike most other presidents examined in this study, Washington rarely quoted or alluded to Scripture in his addresses.[46] Moreover, he said very little specifically about the Bible. In his circular letter to state governors in June 1783, Washington asserted that "the pure and benign light of Revelation" had "had a meliorating influence on mankind and increased the blessings of Society." The general applauded a proposal in late May 1783 to give Bibles to his soldiers but noted that most of them had been discharged and it was too late.[47] His name headed a list of subscribers when Scottish Presbyterian John Brown's "Self-Interpreting Bible" was published in New York in 1792, but no Bible is included in the list of books at Mount Vernon compiled in 1783. The 1799 inventory of Washington's estate lists three Bibles, but one is in Latin and the other two appeared to be gifts.[48] The only definitive reference in Washington's voluminous correspondence to his reading the Bible is in a letter to Charles Thomson in 1795. Washington wrote that he had read the "first part" of Thomson's translation of the Septuagint and the New Testament. Although it is unlikely that Washington "diligently searched the Holy Volume,"[49] his fairly frequent citation of biblical passages in his letters to friends and acquaintances indicates that he was familiar with many scriptural themes and verses.[50]

Washington professed belief in the power of prayer. After his first inaugural, he attended a prayer service at St. Paul's. He frequently asked religious bodies to pray for him, especially in his work as president, thanked groups for praying for him, and told individuals he was praying for them.[51] He thanked Methodist bishops in May 1789 for their promise to present prayers "at the Throne of Grace for me" and pledged to pray for them as well.[52] "Let us unite our fervent prayer to the great ruler of the Universe," Washington wrote to the residents of Richmond in August 1793, that Americans might "continue in the uninterrupted enjoyment" of the blessings of peace.[53] "I shall not cease to supplicate the Divine Author of Life and felicity," he told the Philadelphia clergy in 1797, "that your Labours for the good of Mankind may be crowned with success."[54]

Washington firmly believed that God controlled human events. In both his public and private writings, he repeatedly discussed how God providentially helped the United States win its independence against incredible odds, create a unified country out of diverse and competing interests, establish a remarkable constitution, and avoid war with European powers that still had territorial ambitions in North America. Because God created and actively ruled the universe, Washington insisted, people must revere, worship, and obey him. Although members of his staff wrote most of Washington's public statements, including his military orders, he oversaw the process and approved them, and therefore they expressed what he wanted to convey.[55] Furthermore, Washington routinely used similar language in private letters he wrote. On the other hand, Washington's constant use of religious rhetoric in his orders, addresses, and official letters should not be overemphasized because during the late nineteenth century, state legislatures, town councils, and other civic bodies regularly employed similar phrases.

Throughout his life, Washington appealed to "an all-powerful Providence" to protect and guide him and the nation, especially in times of crisis.[56] Throughout the War for Independence, he asked for and acknowledged God's providential guidance and assistance hundreds of times.[57] He told Reverend William Gordon in 1776 that no one had "a more perfect Reliance on the alwise, and powerful dispensations of the Supreme Being than I have nor thinks his aid more necessary."[58] "The hand of Providence has been so conspicuous" in the war, the general asserted in 1778, that anyone who did not thank God and "acknowledge his obligations" to him was "worse than an infidel that lacks faith, and more than wicked."[59] After the war ended, Washington declared, "I attribute all glory to that Supreme Being," who had caused the several forces that contributed to America's triumph to harmonize perfectly together.[60] No people "had more reason to acknowledge a divine interposition in their affairs than those of the United States," he wrote in 1792.[61]

Washington also rejoiced that God was infinitely wise, just, and benevolent. His faith in an "All Wise Creator" who "orders the Affairs of Men" helped him deal with personal and national problems.[62] Washington saw God's gracious hand in General John Burgoyne's surrender at Saratoga in 1778, the United States' alliance with France, the arrival of the French fleet, the rescue of West Point "from Arnold[']s villainous perfidy," and the victory at Yorktown.[63] The decrees of Providence, Washington told a friend, were "always just and wise."[64] Because their cause was just, the general contended, Americans had "every reason to hope the divine Providence" would enable them to win their independence from Britain.[65] The planter asserted that God was "beneficient" [sic] and the "supreme Dispenser of every Good."[66] Using a phrase that utilitarians would later popularize, Washington declared that God's ultimate goal was to provide "the greatest degree of happiness to the greatest number of his people."[67] He repeatedly argued that the course of events justified his belief in "the blessings of a benign Providence."[68]

Although God directed all events, Washington insisted, his plans were ultimately inscrutable. Because God was wise, good, and just, people must trust him, even when their finite minds could not fully understand his purposes.[69] That the United States was able against tremendous odds to defeat Britain, establish a stable government, and frame such a promising constitution convinced Washington that God was working for good in the world. That his poorly trained, clothed, fed, and equipped army could defeat the world's premier military seemed nothing short of miraculous.[70] Reflecting on these developments, he wrote to a friend in August 1788, "I can never trace the concatenation of causes, which led to these events, without acknowledging the mystery and admiring the goodness of Providence." Because God's decrees were always for the best, Americans must accept them without protest.[71] "I will not lament or repine at any act of Providence," he added.[72]

Washington's confidence that God determined the course of events helped inspire his prodigious efforts and keep him humble. He firmly believed that God, not fate or random chance, governed the universe and that God used humans to accomplish his purposes. Washington's conviction that God was perfect helped make him more conscious of his own flaws and failures and prompted him to usually downplay his achievements when showered with effusive tributes. His conviction that he was simply an "instrument of Providence" typically led him to attribute America's successes to God, not himself. "To the Great ruler of events, not to any exertions of mine," the president declared in 1795, "is to be ascribed the favourable terminations of our late contest for liberty."[73] Although God was sovereign, Washington maintained, he worked through people. If they wanted to experience "the smiles of Providence," Americans must put forth "Vigorous Exertions."[74] "Providence has done much for us," the general told a Maryland congressman in 1782, soon after the United States and Britain had agreed to a preliminary peace treaty, "but we must do something for ourselves, if we expect to go triumphantly through with it."[75] Moreover, his confidence in divine Providence helped fuel his courage, resoluteness, and calm in the face of adversity and keep him from discouragement and despair when he suffered defeat.

Although Washington repeatedly stressed God's providence, he said very little about Christianity or Christ in public or private writings. As John G. West Jr. puts it, the "evidence on the subject" of what Washington believed about these matters "is partial, contradictory, and in the end, unsatisfactory."[76] His general orders on July 9, 1776, declared his hope "that every officer and man, will endeavour so to live . . . as becomes a Christian Soldier."[77] Washington's order of May 2, 1778, states, "To the distinguished Character of Patriot, it should be our highest glory to add the more distinguished

Character of Christian."[78] In his 1783 circular letter to the governors, he asked God to give all Americans qualities that characterized "the Divine Author of our blessed Religion," a clear reference to Jesus. Although some have used this phrase to argue that Washington believed Christ was divine, Boller points out that he did not make any similar references to Christ in any of his public addresses or private letters. Moreover, unlike most deists and Unitarians, he never asserted that Jesus was a great ethical teacher.[79]

Washington did refer to Christianity in a few of his private letters. After Major General Israel Putnam's wife died, the Virginian urged him to "bear the misfortune with that fortitude and complacency of mind, that becomes a Man and a Christian."[80] On several occasions, Washington applauded efforts to "civilize and christianize the Savages of the Wilderness."[81] In his many letters to religious bodies, he usually spoke of religion in general terms, mentioning Christianity only three times. Boller argues that given the Christian commitment of some of Washington's speechwriters, such scant use of Christian terminology demonstrates his reserve on the subject.[82]

While convinced that his countrymen were more virtuous than the residents of the Old World, Washington, like most other founders, placed little faith in human goodness. Like other Whig-Republicans, he insisted that all people were "actuated by selfish interests."[83] Without reading John Calvin or Thomas Hobbes, he concluded that individuals and nations "were driven by interest not ideals."[84] "We must take human nature as we find it," he declared. His experiences in the Revolutionary War taught Washington that although patriotism could "push Men to Action . . . , to bear much," and to tolerate difficulties, it would not endure unless it was assisted by self-interest.[85] On other occasions, the planter expressed even greater pessimism about human nature. He complained to John Jay in 1786 that virtue had "in a great degree, taken its departure from us." "We have probably had too good an opinion of human nature in forming our confederation," he wrote about the same time.[86] The word of God proved "that the best Institutions may be abused by human depravity . . . and . . . may even, in some instances be made subservient to the vilest of purposes." For reasons unknown to mortal man, Washington wrote, God had allowed "the restless and malignant passions of man, the ambitious and sordid views of those who direct them, to keep the affairs of this world in a continual state of disquietude." Thus the "prospects of peace" and the "promised millenium" [sic] were "at an awful distance from our day." In his Farewell Address, Washington insisted that people were motivated by a "love of power, and [a] proneness to abuse it."[87]

Whether Washington believed in life after death has also been the subject of considerable debate. As with many other issues, the Virginian never systematically discussed the topic, so his perspective must be gleaned from his correspondence. Washington typically took a stoic attitude toward death and seemed to be skeptical about seeing loved ones after death. While urging the bereaved to seek consolation in religion, he never assured them that they would spend eternity with God or be reunited with their family members in heaven.[88] He viewed death—of others and himself—with resignation, fortitude, and calmness, and as a part of the divine order. People must submit to "the will of the Creator whether it be to prolong, or to shorten the number of our days."[89] His letters contain no "Christian images of judgment, redemption through the sacrifice of Christ, and eternal life for the faithful."[90] On the other hand, Washington rejected the concept of annihilation and did believe in a type of life after death. He referred to going to "the world of Spirits," "the land of Spirits," and "a happier clime."[91] Strikingly, however, these references to immortality are vaguer and more impersonal than those of John Adams, Benjamin Franklin, Thomas Jefferson, and even Thomas Paine.[92]

After his last surviving brother died in 1799, Washington told a friend that when "the giver of life" summoned him to follow, "I shall endeavor to obey it with a good grace."[93] The general strove to deal with the deaths of relatives and friends by following the eighteenth-century ideal: submitting to God's authority and displaying little grief in public. Privately, however, he mourned deeply when those close to him died.[94] Approaching the subject philosophically, he urged the grieving to accept God's decrees "with as little repining, as the sensibilities of our natures" permitted and provided little emotional comfort.[95]

For much of his adult life, Washington was an actor playing various roles: "the classical republican general, the patriot king, [and] the father of his country." He planned to face his own death with "good grace" in order to maintain his sterling reputation.[96] Throughout his long military career, Washington "displayed a stoic's contempt for death . . . that awed his contemporaries," and he often put his life at risk (especially during the French and Indian War) by venturing onto the battlefield.[97] His final struggle with what he once called "the grim King" tested his fortitude and resolve one last time.[98] Making his rounds at Mount Vernon on December 12, 1799, he was stricken with a virulent infection that claimed his life two days later. While on his deathbed, he did not pray, request God's forgiveness, express fear of divine judgment or hope of an afterlife, or call for an Episcopal rector. According to his personal secretary Tobias Lear and attending physicians, Washington, after uttering "Tis well," died peacefully and was buried following Episcopal and Masonic funeral services.[99]

Lear wrote that he hoped to be reunited with Washington in heaven, but he resisted putting such words in the planter's mouth.[100] Others, most notably Parson Weems, did not. In his fabricated account, Washington asked everyone to leave his room so he could pray alone, and his last words were " 'Father of mercies, take me to thyself.' "[101] While rejecting Weems's version, other nineteenth-century biographers portrayed Washington as emulating Socrates: accepting the inevitable, the general fearlessly prepared to die.[102]

Many of his contemporaries emphasized Washington's composure and stoicism as he lay dying.[103] Every major newspaper published his doctors' account of his last moments, and eulogists embellished it. Dying in a rational, self-controlled, dignified manner, the general evinced no pain. Peter Henriques argues that Washington lived and died as if he were more interested in attaining secular than spiritual immortality. In consoling others who lost loved ones and in contemplating his own death, he often stressed the importance of being revered in life, lamented in death, and "remembered with honor in history."[104]

Washington also never clearly expressed his views on the Christian concept of salvation. He apparently thought that conduct, more than belief, made individuals acceptable to God. He told a friend that he constantly strove to walk "a straight line" and endeavored to properly discharge his "duties to his Maker and fellow-men."[105] No person "who is profligate in his morals," Washington maintained, "can possibly be a true Christian."[106]

Although Washington did not publicly profess Christian faith, and his views of life after death and salvation did not accord with traditional doctrines, many clergy and early biographers considered him an orthodox believer. When the president's second term ended in March 1797, twenty-four pastors from the Philadelphia area proclaimed that "we . . . acknowledge the countenance you have uniformly given to his holy religion."[107] Many of his first biographers—such as John Marshall, Jared Sparks, and novelist Washington Irving—argued that Washington was a faithful Christian.[108] In Marshall's words, while Washington made no "ostentatious professions of religion, he was a sincere believer in the Christian faith, and a truly devout man."[109]

On the other hand, several individuals either urged Washington to affirm his faith in Christianity publicly or expressed regret that he had not. Shortly after the Virginian became president, Congregationalist Samuel Langdon sent Washington a sermon praising his character and contributions. They had spent time together during the Revolutionary War when Langdon was president of Harvard and the general was commanding troops in Boston. Langdon rejoiced that in his public addresses Washington had frequently acknowledged "the supreme Lord of heaven & earth for the great things he hath done for us." He challenged the president, however, to openly declare that he was "a disciple of the Lord Jesus Christ" who sought "the honors of that kingdom which he has prepared for his faithful Servants."[110] Characteristically, Washington replied that anyone who could "look on the events of the American Revolution without feeling the warmest gratitude towards the great Author of the Universe whose divine interposition was so frequently manifested in our behalf" "must be bad indeed," but he said nothing about Christ to either Langdon or the American people.[111] Shortly after Washington died, Benjamin Tallmadge, who had served as his chief of intelligence during the Revolutionary War, lamented that the deceased president had never explicitly professed his "faith in, and dependence on the finished Atonement of our glorious Redeemer."[112]

When the subject was being publicly debated in the 1830s, William White admitted that he could not recall "any fact which would prove" that Washington believed "in the Christian revelation" except that he constantly attended church.[113] Another Episcopal bishop, James Madison, asserted that Washington paid little attention to the creeds of various denominations and stressed that he regularly worshiped "according to the received forms of the Episcopal Church in which he was brought up."[114] Boller concludes that if belonging to a Christian church, fairly regularly attending services, believing that God directed human affairs, and emphasizing the social benefits of religion is enough to be a Christian, then Washington was one. If, on the other hand, to be a Christian, one must publicly affirm the divinity and resurrection of Christ and his atonement for humanity's sin and participate in the Lord's Supper, then Washington cannot be considered a Christian.[115]

Washington and Character

What made Washington the most remarkable man of an extraordinary generation? He was not an intellectual giant like Franklin, Adams, Jefferson, or Madison. Compared with most other founders, he was not well educated (he attended school for only about five years), and, unlike many of them, he disliked abstract philosophical discussions.[116] Some of his contemporaries criticized his lack of education. John Adams insisted, for example, "That Washington . . . was too illiterate, unlearned, unread for his station and reputation is . . . past dispute."[117] Despite this negative assessment, Washington was intelligent, well informed, and astute, but he was neither a polished writer nor a spellbinding speaker. Moreover, he was not particularly warm or affectionate, said little in public meetings, and lacked the charisma of many of his successors. Defeating the British with his ragtag army was an impressive feat, but he certainly was not a traditional military hero. He won no spectacular victories during the Revolutionary War. Although he is admired as an outstanding president, few of his policies were stupendous successes.

While praising his military and political record, many scholars contend that Washington's genius lies principally in his character. The only other American president who has been so highly extolled for his exemplary character is Lincoln. Since Washington, all presidents have been ultimately measured "not by the size of their electoral victories," not by the success of their legislative programs, "but by their moral character."[118] His character helped sustain his troops throughout the travails of the Revolutionary War, convince delegates to the Constitutional Convention to assign significant powers to the presidency, secure the ratification of the Constitution, and enable the new republic to survive in a hostile world.[119]

Washington's moral character, especially his refusal to yield to temptation, set him apart from others. He took the standards of his age very seriously and diligently strove to be virtuous. To many, the crowning achievement of Washington's character was his simultaneous resignation in 1783 as the commander in chief of the American army and his retirement from the world of politics. Throughout the Western world, his unprecedented relinquishing of power was widely heralded. Unlike other victorious generals, he did not expect a political or financial reward for his military exploits.[120] Washington's character, Jefferson argued, probably prevented the American Revolution from subverting the liberty it sought to establish.[121] The Virginian had a sterling reputation for integrity and honor, dedication to duty and his country, and remaining above the political fray.[122]

The most important sources in shaping Washington's highly lauded character were *Seneca's Morals*; Joseph Addison's 1713 play, *Cato*; the *Rules of Civility*; various handbooks on civility, courtesy, and politeness he read as an adult; and Christianity. Like many other founders, Washington was fascinated with the Romans. He read *Seneca's Morals* as a teenager and practiced many of its precepts throughout his life. He saw productions of *Cato* many times, frequently quoted lines from it, and sought to emulate its liberal, virtuous classical hero. As a youth, Washington copied all 110 of *The Rules of Civility and Decent Behavior in Company and Conversation*, formulated by French Jesuits in 1595.[123] His Christian nurture, understanding of Scripture, participation in worship, and respect for biblical morality also helped form and sustain his character.

Eulogists and early biographers imputed many virtues to Washington. They praised his wisdom, judgment, astounding courage on the battlefield, and dignified authority. Congress elected him the first chief executive, they insisted, principally because its members trusted his moral character. Portraits and assessments of Washington celebrated his military zeal and political passion on the one hand and his "self-restraint and civil moderation" on the other. Blending Stoic and Christian traditions, eulogists extolled Washington's "rational, calculated, and systematic" perseverance in the midst of setbacks. Many admirers considered Washington's self-control the "keystone of his character."[124] He could master events because he had mastered himself. Despite being surrounded by fear, despair, indecisiveness, treason, and the threat of mutiny, he remained confident and steadfast. Eulogists also heralded his self-sacrifice, devotion to the common good, compassion, generosity, and benevolence.[125] American literary great Washington Irving praised the Virginian's prudence, sagacity, "immovable justice," unfaltering courage, unflagging patience, truthfulness, and magnanimity.[126] No one else in history, argued naval official James Paulding, equaled "the virtues he exhibited."

America's first Catholic bishop, John Carroll, praised Washington's "pure and enlightened" morality.[127]

To many Americans, the most important facet of the planter's character was his piety. During the late eighteenth century, most Americans revered God, highly valued biblical teachings and morality, and wanted their president to be a pious man.[128] Edwin Gaustad points out that even though Washington's religious views were similar to those of Jefferson, the public reaction to their convictions differed sharply. Unlike Jefferson, Washington was never censured as a "howling atheist" or condemned as an enemy of institutional religion. Americans continually pressed Jefferson, as well as Adams and Franklin, for more details about their religious principles, but not Washington. The fact that the first president believed in a God who watched over and protected America seemed to be enough for most citizens.[129]

Often projecting their values onto him, many ministers in their funeral sermons and other public statements transformed the president's somewhat vague beliefs into Christian orthodoxy.[130] They repeatedly affirmed that Washington "was not ashamed" of his faith and acknowledged and adored "a GREATER SAVIOR whom Infidels and deists" slighted and despised.[131] The Virginian strove to follow Christian moral standards and attributed his accomplishments to God's power. An Episcopal rector described Washington's faith as very well balanced, "rational and consistent," and "sincere and ardent."[132] Yale College president Timothy Dwight argued that if the general were not actually a Christian, he acted "more like one than any man of the same description, whose life had been hitherto recorded.[133]

As president, Washington strove to establish public confidence in the new government and to demonstrate that political leaders could act virtuously. He believed his character was much more important to the success of the republic than his policies, and he spent much of his adult life "creating and maintaining a public image of integrity and public virtue."[134] In August 1788, the planter wrote to his trusted confidant Alexander Hamilton, "I hope I shall always possess firmness and virtue enough to maintain (what I consider the most enviable of all titles) the character of *an honest man*."[135] His character helped hold the other founders together in the midst of tremendous trials and reassured them that they could construct a workable republic. His example of "self-sacrifice, discipline, moral rectitude, and virtue" helped elevate the status of the presidency.[136]

Both as commander in chief of the Continental Army and president, Washington worked to form "an independent, national American character." Throughout the War for Independence, he expected both his officers and soldiers to act morally and "display the character of republicans" appropriate to "Christian Soldier[s]" who were defending their country's "dearest Rights and Liberties."[137] Speaking to the nation's governors in 1783, Washington argued that Americans could "establish or ruin their national Character forever." As John Winthrop had done in his 1630 sermon "A Model of Christian Charity," Washington reminded his countrymen that "the eyes of the whole World" were "turned upon them." Guided by the complementary principles of revelation and reason, Americans must fulfill their civic duties because they were "Actors on a most conspicuous Theatre . . . peculiarly designated by Providence for the display of human greatness and felicity."[138]

In 1783, Washington urged Americans to build their new nation on four pillars: a permanent union of the states, lasting peace, public justice, and the proper dispositions of its citizens. In underscoring this fourth prop, the general exhorted his countrymen to "forget their local prejudices and policies," "to make those mutual concessions which are requisite to the general prosperity," and to be willing "to sacrifice their individual advantages to the interest of the Community." "I now make it my earnest prayer," Washington concluded, "that God . . . incline the hearts of Citizens" to obey the government, to practice "brotherly affection and love for one another . . . to do Justice, to love mercy," and to exercise "Charity, humility and pacific temper of mind."[139] In 1789, Washington exchanged his "peaceful abode for an Ocean of difficulties" in large part because he believed that as president he could further delineate and develop the national character.[140] To succeed, the American republic required good laws and moral citizens, both of which the first chief executive aimed to help produce. By defining, personifying, and promoting what he deemed the principal "habits and dispositions of this national character," Washington strove to found "a new order of the ages."[141] He urged the nation's elected officials to provide a positive example and devise laws that promoted private virtue, public justice, social accord, and human happiness.[142] In his first inaugural address, the president asserted that "the foundation of our national policy" must rest upon "the pure and immutable principles of private morality." God had established "eternal rules of order and right" that must be followed to preserve the "sacred fire of liberty." "The destiny of the Republican model of Government" depended on Americans practicing a high level of both private and public morality.[143]

Despite his reputation for exemplary character, Washington's personal ethics, sexual behavior, vanity, and ownership of slaves have been criticized. He engaged in three practices many Christians of his era detested: swearing, drinking, and gambling. When he was frustrated, the Virginian frequently used insulting or vulgar language. He "drank heavily by today's standards" (as his requisitions as both commander in chief and president reveal) but not by the standards of his time.[144] As president, Washington spent 7 percent of his $25,000 salary on wine and liquor to entertain guests.[145] The general enjoyed gambling, especially while playing cards.[146]

More significantly, Washington promoted several governmental policies that enlarged his own wealth. He gave himself the best government western land bounties assigned to soldiers who fought in the French and Indian War.

He urged the federal government to build a canal connecting the Potomac to Ohio, where he owned nearly 60,000 acres, which would have greatly increased the value of his property. Washington received no pay during his eight years as commander in chief of the Continental Army, but he insisted that all his expenses be paid. His supposedly selfless act further enhanced his reputation, but members of Congress considered some of his expenditures exorbitant.[147]

In an era when womanizing was generally not considered a matter of public concern, Washington struggled with sexual passions, but there is no creditable evidence that he was ever unfaithful to his wife.[148] In September 1758, about four months before he married Martha Custis, the colonel wrote a letter to Sally Fairfax, the wife of George William Fairfax, one of Washington's in-laws who owned a plantation near Mount Vernon, which seemed to discreetly express his affection. Washington was very attracted to his witty, bright, and charming neighbor, but Fairfax pretended not to comprehend his fondness for her. Recognizing that his feelings would not be reciprocated, Washington married the affluent and affable Custis in January 1759, and thereafter the two families were amicable neighbors. No evidence indicates that George Fairfax ever had any inkling that Washington was in love with his wife, and the men remained good friends.[149] In 1798, Washington wrote Fairfax, then a widow, in England that the happiest moments of his life had been spent in her company.[150] Although "Fairfax always retained a special place in his heart," almost all scholars conclude that their friendship never involved sexual intimacy.[151] Recognizing that appearances mattered tremendously, Washington carefully constructed "his public persona to deny his very real passions."[152]

There is also some debate over whether Washington fathered a child by a mulatto household slave named Venus Ford, who belonged to his brother John Augustine Washington. The Washington family accorded both her son West, born in either 1784 or 1785, and Venus's parents preferential treatment, suggesting that the future president or someone else in his family was West's father. One Ford family oral tradition has Venus declaring that "the old general" fathered her child. No scientific proof has established Washington's paternity, and if he were indeed sterile, as some scholars conclude, then he could not have been West's father, although this would not prove he never had sexual relations with her.[153]

To a few critics in the 1790s and many today, Washington's biggest character flaw was owning slaves. Prominent English abolitionist Edward Rushton denounced the president in 1796 for holding "hundreds of his fellow beings in a state of abject bondage." "[Y]ou who conquered under the banners of freedom—you who are now the first magistrate of a free people are . . . a slave holder. . . . Shame! Shame! . . . Ages to come will read with Astonishment that the man who was foremost to wrench the rights of America from the tyrannical grasp of Britain was among the last to relinquish his own oppressive hold of poor unoffending negroes."[154] Agreeing with this assessment, many historians have faulted Washington for owning slaves and refusing to publicly condemn the institution. Why, one asks, did he never use "his enormous prestige and public veneration" to openly deplore a system that he expressed distaste for and apprehension about in his private letters and hoped would "either wither naturally or be abolished by legislative action"?[155] Many regard his silence about the most important moral issue of his era as reprehensible.[156]

Before the Revolution, Washington shared the perspective of other Virginia planters and seemed to have no qualms about owning slaves. Like his father, many other relatives, and many other wealthy Southerners, he was not morally troubled by owning slaves.[157] Washington initially resisted efforts to allow free blacks to fight in the Continental Army, but the British offer of freedom to slaves who enlisted in their army, coupled with the continual need for more troops, changed American policy. The general came to admire the courage and skill of black soldiers, which undoubtedly influenced his attitude toward slavery.[158]

His Revolutionary War colleague, the Marquis de Lafayette, urged him twice during the 1780s to join him in emancipation schemes. He suggested that they free some of their slaves and make them tenant farmers on Washington's western lands to inspire other slaveholders to follow their example. The Frenchman also proposed freeing slaves and sending them to a French Guiana farm to show what they could accomplish.[159] Because of Washington's lack of interest, neither plan came to fruition. Privately, he called liberating slaves an exercise of "humanity," but publicly he refused to support either gradual or immediate abolition, arguing the latter would produce "much inconvenience and mischief."[160] Nevertheless, after the war, Washington was deeply troubled by the institution. In 1786, he asserted that no one "wishes more sincerely than I do, to see a plan adopted for the abolition of it."[161]

Scholars concur that Washington, partly because of self-interest, provided adequate food, clothing, and shelter and competent medical care for his slaves at Mount Vernon. Tobias Lear, Washington's personal secretary and an avowed abolitionist, admitted that the planter's slaves were clothed and fed as well as paid laborers.[162] Washington expected his slaves to work hard from daybreak until dusk, and unremitting labor, close supervision, and coercion characterized Mount Vernon.[163] While stereotyping blacks as ignorant, dim-witted, malingering, irresponsible, and deceitful, Washington admitted that they had little incentive to work hard. Unlike many of his contemporaries, he did not separate family members by sale. By his death in 1799, Washington and his wife owned 316 slaves, almost 50 percent more than they did in 1783. Although his hatred of slavery grew, Washington continued to let his economic interests trump his moral principles.[164]

While still privately lamenting the evils of slavery, Washington never condemned slavery publicly during his presidency, even in his farewell address to the nation or his last address to Congress.[165] Doing so, he feared, would discredit him with Southerners and fracture the Union. When Quakers and the Pennsylvania Society for Promoting the Abolition of Slavery petitioned Congress in 1790 to end the foreign slave trade immediately, some Southern states threatened to secede if Congress did. Washington denounced the campaign as "an ill-judged piece of business" and expressed pleasure at its defeat.[166] As president, he signed the Fugitive Slave Act of 1793, which allowed Southerners to cross state lines to retrieve runaway slaves.[167]

Critics fault Washington for not leading a crusade to end slavery during the 1790s. His defenders counter that the United States was very fragile. During the Constitutional Convention, Northerners were not willing to "sink their ship" by confronting the Southern states about slavery. Although some Northern states abolished slavery in the 1780s, none of them introduced an amendment condemning slavery at their conventions to ratify the Constitution. Among Washington's peers, only Franklin publicly deplored slavery in the 1780s. By the 1790s, hostility toward the antislavery activities of Quakers and Methodists had increased in the South. Even in the North, only a small minority opposed slavery. To accomplish the rest of their agenda, Washington and other founders sacrificed the abolition on slavery on the altar of national unity. The first president was not willing to risk his vital role in holding the infant nation together by supporting a controversial and, from his perspective, "quixotic attempt to challenge the South's peculiar institution." Moreover, like many of his peers, he feared the potentially disruptive behaviors of the poor of any color. Regarding social stability and the sanctity of private property as key bulwarks of the new republic, he rejected immediate abolition but, like many other Americans, thought that slavery would die a natural death, especially after the slave trade ended (presumably in 1808).[168]

In his will, Washington freed all 123 of the slaves he personally owned, the only founder who did so. He provided funds to help them buy property and gain an education, and he also attempted, but failed, to raise enough money to free the slaves Martha controlled as a result of her first marriage.[169] Undoubtedly speaking for many abolitionists, Richard Allen, pastor of a black congregation in Philadelphia, applauded Washington's action. He "let the oppressed go free, he undid every burden—he provided lands and comfortable accomodations [sic] for them" so that they could "rejoice in the day of their deliverance."[170] Henry Wiencek lauds Washington for providing for his former slaves' education in his will and insisting on their right to live in America. "Of all the great Virginia patriots, only Washington ultimately had the moral courage and the farsightedness to free his slaves." Nevertheless, it was a "tragedy for the nation" that Washington did not free his slaves while he was president and set a precedent that the chief executive could not hold slaves.[171]

Washington and American Civil Religion

As president, Washington was the first major spokesperson and practitioner of American civil religion, and after his death he became a principal figure in its development. In his first inaugural address, the president thanked God for his past guidance and sought his favor for the nation's future. He offered his "fervent supplication to that Almighty Being who rules over the universe, who presides in the council of nations, and whose providential aids can supply every human defect, that His benediction may consecrate to the liberties and happiness of the people of the United States." "In tendering this homage to the Great Author of every public and private good," he continued, "I assure myself that it expresses your sentiments not less than my own. . . . No people can be bound to acknowledge and adore the Invisible Hand which conducts the affairs of men more than those of the United States." Every step in establishing the republic demonstrated God's "providential agency." The president asked that "his divine blessing" would be "equally conspicuous in the enlarged views, the temperate consultations, and the wise measures on which the success of this Government must depend."[172]

Throughout his presidency, Washington continued to link "piety and patriotism, God and country, and divine benevolence with the well-being of the nation" in his public pronouncements.[173] In his annual message to Congress in 1794, he asserted, "Let us unite . . . in imploring the supreme Ruler of nations" to protect the United States.[174] Moving from priestly to prophetic civil religion, the president urged Americans to confess their corporate sins in order to procure God's aid. Washington began the custom of setting aside special days for national thanksgiving. In proclaiming the last Thursday of November 1789 such a day, he exhorted all citizens to humbly offer "prayers and supplications to the great Lord and Ruler of Nations, and beseech him to pardon our national and other transgressions."[175]

Washington also helped shape America's civic faith by repeatedly emphasizing that religion provided an essential foundation for "public morality, republican institutions, and national happiness."[176] He frequently asserted that religion helped promote virtue, order, and social stability and praised the efforts of churches to make people "sober, honest, and good Citizens, and the obedient subjects of a lawful government."[177] In his farewell address, the nation's civil pastor called religion and morality "indispensable supports" of "political prosperity" and human happiness. Despite the positive influence of "refined education," "reason and experience both forbid us to expect that National morality can prevail in exclusion of religious principle. It is substantially true that, virtue or morality is a necessary spring of popular government." Therefore, he urged all Americans "to respect and to cherish them."[178]

Catherine Albanese explains that the "creed, code and cultus (system of worship)" of American civil religion were already set by the time Washington delivered his first inaugural address.[179] The creed asserted that God had chosen the United States to incarnate and promote republican government throughout the world. The code demanded that all Americans, especially their political leaders, act virtuously to help accomplish this mission. The cultus of this civic faith created national saints and shrines, sacred objects, ritual practices, and patriotic holy days to reinforce belief in the creed and code.

Not only did Washington help mold and popularize the nation's civil religion but also he became a significant part of its cultus. Because of the disagreements and dissension of the Revolutionary era, Americans needed a collective faith and symbols to express their shared commitments and strengthen their unity. Having no established church, the new nation required "a religious ground of being, a transcendent locus," a civic faith that transcended political and religious differences, to direct its public life.[180] Because of his colossal contributions to American independence and his exalted reputation, Washington provided a unifying center and symbol for the new nation. Given the nation's history, it was fitting that its "collective symbol" was "a man—a farmer, a soldier, and, at least metaphorically, a father."[181]

To many Americans, Washington was a titan who embodied the best of classical antiquity.[182] He represented "the ideals of character and consciousness" patriots understood as expressing the most excellent way of life. Almost overnight, Washington became a " 'blessed object," "a sacramental center" who pointed to and personified the spiritual power of the fledgling country and exemplified its moral values.[183] Even before he died, people treasured locks of his hair, named their babies for him, and circulated stories about his miraculous feats. After the British surrendered at Yorktown in 1781, Washington was saluted as a demigod and the nation's savior.[184] Worship services, community bonfires, songs, addresses, and cannon fire commemorated his exploits. Orators lavished effusive praise on him, and his birthday was elaborately celebrated. A typical example of these panegyrics was Ezra Stiles's 1783 election sermon: "O Washington! . . . How have I often adored and blessed thy God for creating and forming thee the great ornament of human kind!"[185]

Contemporaries frequently compared the general to both biblical and Roman heroes. Like Moses, he liberated his people from bondage; like Joshua, he led them into the Promised Land.[186] They hailed the Virginian as "godlike," "our savior and guide," "immortal," and "next unto the trinity."[187] A few even dared to compare Washington with Jesus. Washington "was destined by Heaven," declared a Baptist minister, "to be the instrumental Saviour of his country."[188] A Georgian jurist predicted that future generations would re-member Mount Vernon as fondly as Mount Calvary.[189] Other admirers stressed that like the Roman general Cincinnatus, Washington had left his farm to fight for his country and after achieving victory relinquished power and returned home. Washington's journey to New York in April 1789 to be inaugurated as the nation's first president resembled the victory procession of a Greek emperor. In Philadelphia and New York, large crowds paid him homage by erecting arches and singing lyrics to Handel's "See the Conquering Hero Come."[190] Such deification led physician Benjamin Rush to protest that "we ascribe all the attributes of the Deity to the name of General Washington.... God would cease to be who HE is if he did not" punish Americans for their blasphemy.[191]

After his death on December 14, 1799, Washington continued to help hold the nation together. Pastors and politicians in New York, Boston, and Phi-ladelphia, as well as in London, Paris, and Amsterdam, delivered stirring eulogies. Washington's eulogists were a diverse group: ministers, lawyers, and politicians; Northerners and Southerners; Congregationalists, Presbyterians, Episcopalians, Baptists, Quakers, deists, and Masonic grandmasters; Feder-alists and Republicans. Their encomiums, however, were remarkably simi-lar.[192] James Smylie argues that American clergymen clothed "Washington in republican prestige" and "cast over him a religious, historical, and moral aura" that has been "associated with him and the office ever since."[193] Ap-pealing to the biblical archetypes of Moses and David, they pictured him "as a model republican prophet and king."[194] They made the general an ideal type, "a standard of republican leadership" by which his successors could be judged.[195] Funeral sermons and addresses depicted the Southern planter as both God's instrument and "a servant of the people."[196]

The Moses analogy was especially important in giving Washington an exalted place in the nation's civil religion.[197] Throughout the war, the gen-eral's tactics were sometimes compared with those of Moses. Ministers typ-ically viewed the Continental Army's retreats "not as defeats but as acts of deliverance."[198] After the war, some ministers and editors declared that "God [had] raised up a Washington just as He earlier" had "raised up Moses."[199] Scores of eulogies, especially those by New England clergy, compared the first president with Israel's lawgiver. As a Massachusetts minister put it, God pitied "the abject and servile condition of our American Israel [so] he gave us a second Moses" to free us "from the bondage and tyranny of haughty Britain."[200] Ministers stressed the parallels between the lives and deeds of the two deliverers, noting that both were trained in the wilderness and reluctantly answered God's summons to serve their people.[201] Confronting the major powers of their day, neither hero initially had much hope of victory. Both had to defeat their people's oppressor and quell the protests of their domestic detractors.[202]

Moreover, like Moses, Washington was depicted as a great lawgiver, an outstanding civil leader, and a virtuous man. By leading Americans through the wilderness of the Articles of Confederation, presiding at the Constitutional Convention, and serving as the first president, Washington had shaped thirteen independent states into one unified nation.[203] Like the Jewish prophet, Washington excelled as a civil chief and a military commander.[204] Having served so effectively in both capacities, the two heroes left their people with wise counsel in their farewell addresses.[205] Both deliverers devotedly loved their people and served them zealously and faithfully.[206] Both men had leadership thrust upon them, fought against tremendous odds to achieve a glorious goal, displayed great courage, and trusted God.[207]

New Englanders with Federalist political commitments most fully developed the American Moses concept. To them, Washington's life and death helped verify that Americans were still God's chosen people who must faithfully follow his laws and serve as an example of true religion and liberty for the world.[208] Biographies written before the Civil War uniformly portrayed Washington as "a demigod who descended to earth (his character already fully developed and flawless even in childhood), freed his people from oppression, steered their government for a few years, and then returned to heaven."[209] In nineteenth-century textbooks, Washington more closely resembled Jesus Christ than any other person.[210] Throughout the century, Americans often reasserted these themes to reassure themselves that God reigned over and directed their nation.

Washington's Philosophy of Government

Three ideologies especially influenced Washington's political thought: American political theory, Christianity, and Freemasonry. Washington read many American political essays and treatises, discussed political issues with numerous contemporaries, and received much counsel from James Madison and Alexander Hamilton.[211] He insisted that God ruled the universe and established laws to direct private and public life. The Virginian argued that government should promote justice and virtue and that by inculcating morality, religion played a crucial role in ensuring order and stability. Washington enjoyed the pageantry of the Freemasonry and its symbolic and ceremonial support for the ideas and goals he espoused.[212]

Rejecting relativism, Washington asserted that people were responsible to transcendent standards. Washington contended that the United States would be successful only if its people adhered to biblical principles. "It is to be hoped, that if our cause is just, as I do most religiously believe it to be," he wrote his brother John in May 1776, "the same Providence which has in many Instances appear'd for us, will still go on to afford its aid."[213] America's triumph over

Britain, he wrote in 1782, was "due to the *Grand Architect* of the Universe," who refused to allow "his Superstructures" or "justice to be subjected to the princes of this World, or to the rod of oppression."[214] On several occasions, he warned his fellow countrymen that God would stop showering his blessings upon them if they acted unjustly or selfishly.[215] The United States, he declared in 1783, could achieve happiness only if its citizens imitated Christ and practiced justice, loved mercy, and exuded humility and charity.[216] Any nation that disregarded "the eternal rules of order and right, which Heaven itself has ordained," he proclaimed in his first inaugural address, could not expect God's favor. He maintained that the same transcendent norms should direct both individual conduct and government practices. "The foundations of our national policy," he promised in 1789, "will be laid in the pure and immutable principles of private morality."[217] Only a government that formulated and enforced "wise, just, and constitutional laws," promoted peace, and protected its citizens could be assured of God's approval.[218]

Like many other founders, Washington insisted that religion had a central role to play in producing the virtuous citizens necessary to a republic's success. Providence, he averred, had "connected the permanent felicity of a Nation with its virtue."[219] The Virginian maintained that "general prevalence of piety, philanthropy, honesty, industry and oeconomy [*sic*]" were necessary to advance America's happiness.[220] Religion and morality, he asserted, "are the essential pillars of Civil society."[221] As both commander in chief and president, Washington contended that virtuous conduct was essential to the nation's success.[222] Considering religion to be indispensable to the discipline, morale, and proper behavior of his troops, Washington provided chaplains, required his soldiers to attend Sunday services, and tried to set a good example. He also ordered his men to obey the special days of "Fasting, Humiliation, and Prayer" prescribed by the Continental Congress. "By their unfeigned and pious observance of their religious duties," the troops could "incline the Lord and Giver of Victory, to prosper our arms."[223] When Congress called for days of thanksgiving, Washington directed chaplains to hold services to "express our grateful acknowledgement to God for the manifold blessings he has granted us."[224] Moreover, after the American victory at Saratoga in 1777, the conclusion of an alliance with France in 1778, and the British surrender at Yorktown, Washington ordered chaplains to hold thanksgiving services without any directive from Congress.[225] The general repeatedly reminded his troops that they had little hope of God's blessing if they insulted him by their impiety, profanity, and folly.[226]

Like almost all the founders, Washington contended that both reason and revelation furnished moral precepts that should direct private and public life. Evangelicals like John Witherspoon, Patrick Henry, Samuel Adams, and John Jay and theistic rationalists like John Adams, James Madison, and Thomas Jefferson all concurred that "reason and revelation spoke with one voice" about morality.[227] Similarly, Washington appealed to the authority of "Reason, religion, and Philosophy" and "Prudence, Policy, and a true Christian Spirit."[228] God had so designed the universe, he argued, that there was "an indissoluble union between virtue and happiness; between duty and advantage; between the genuine maxim of an honest and magnanimous policy, and the solid rewards of public prosperity and felicity."[229]

"We now have a National character to establish," Washington declared in 1783, "and it is of the utmost importance to stamp favorable impressions upon it."[230] Contemplating the future expansion of the United States, the Virginian rejoiced that new areas would someday sing "the praises of the Most High." The whole continent would eventually provide "glorious displays of Divine Munificence."[231] As president, he strove to enhance the new nation's reputation by paying its Revolutionary War debts, putting its finances on a sound foundation, protecting American trade, maintaining domestic tranquility, and avoiding foreign entanglements and war. In his foreign policy, Washington pursued both America's interest and international justice. In his farewell address, he urged his countrymen to "observe good faith and justice toward all nations." "Religion and morality enjoin this conduct, and can it be that good policy does not equally enjoin it?" The president sought to promote harmony and positive exchanges with all nations, which "policy, humanity and interest" all recommended.[232]

Washington and Religious Liberty

Washington used his enormous prestige and influence as both commander in chief and president to promote freedom of worship and religious tolerance and to cultivate positive relations among America's various religious bodies. By his words and actions—along with Jefferson and Madison, who led efforts to establish religious liberty in Virginia and frame the First Amendment—he helped ensure that religious freedom and liberty of conscience prevailed in the United States. Washington played a leading role in America's shift from state-established religion to the prohibition of a national church and the guarantee of freedom of worship. Washington spoke out forcibly for religious freedom while many states, including his native Virginia until 1786, continued to have religious restrictions and while many of his compatriots opposed complete religious liberty.[233] Historians argue that the separation of church and state, the absence of religious tests for holding office, and freedom for worship were the most radical aspects of the American Revolution. Some Western nations had no king and had invested political authority in elected bodies, but none had separated church and state and allowed full religious liberty.

Like Jefferson and Madison, Washington supported freedom of conscience and religious practice for both ideological and practical reasons. He wrote that "the mind is so formed in different persons as to contemplate the same objects in different points of view," leading to differences "on questions of the greatest import, human and divine."[234] Writing to Lafayette in 1787, Washington declared that he was inclined to allow Christians to take "that road to heaven which to them shall seem the most direct[,] plainest[,] easiest and least liable to exception."[235] Religion had historically fostered division, discord, and even war. Therefore, he argued, as the most denominationally diverse and ethnically eclectic nation in world history, the United States could flourish only if its citizens enjoyed a religious freedom that helped produce social harmony.

As commander in chief, Washington refused to tolerate religious prejudice among his soldiers. As American troops prepared to attack Canada in September 1775, Washington instructed them to avoid ridiculing their northern neighbor's religious ceremonies and to protect the country's "free Exercise of the Religion" and "the Rights of Conscience in religious matters."[236] "While we are contending for our own Liberty," the general added, "we should be very cautious of violating the Rights of Conscience in others," because "God alone is the Judge of the Hearts of Men."[237] Although Washington was clearly, in this case, trying to gain Canadian Catholic support for the American cause, his statements and actions over a twenty-five-year period testify to his genuine commitment to religious tolerance. Inspired by the same combination of principle and practicality, Washington prohibited his troops from celebrating "Pope's Day"—the "ridiculous and childish custom of burning the Effigy of the pope," as his orders put it.[238] The general also upheld the right of John Murray, the founder of Universalism in America, to serve as a chaplain in the army. Other chaplains petitioned Washington to remove Murray, arguing that his teachings undermined morality and promoted atheism. Eager to avoid religious controversy among his troops, the general instructed each brigade to choose its own chaplain without applying any theological tests.[239]

Quaker pacifism presented Washington with a much more difficult problem during the Revolutionary War. He initially defended draft exemptions for the "conscientiously scrupulous," but in May 1777, when the war shifted to Pennsylvania, like many other patriots he protested that Quaker neutrality was essentially pro-British.[240] Nevertheless, he usually treated Quakers warmly.[241]

Only once during the war did Washington publicly declare religious liberty to be an objective for which Americans fought. In November 1782, he told a group of Dutch Reformed ministers and laymen that because he was convinced "that our Religious Liberties were as essential as our Civil," he had always promoted them both.[242] Nevertheless, the commander in chief clearly assumed that religious and civil liberties were intertwined in the American struggle for independence. Shortly after the peace treaty was signed, he told another religious body that "the establishment of Civil and religious Liberty was the Motive which induced me into the Field."[243]

Washington's denomination had long enjoyed a preferential position in Virginia. When legislators devised plans to disestablish the Episcopal Church, the planter initially supported a proposal to tax residents to provide support for all religious bodies in the state. Although no one was "more opposed to any kind of restraint upon religious principles" than he was, Washington wrote to George Mason, he agreed with "making people pay toward the support of that which they profess," whether they were Christians, Jews, or Muslims. However, after learning that "a respectable minority" rejected the assessment plan and fearing that its adoption would produce conflict, he hoped the bill would "die an easy death."[244] This experience helped convince him that all state aid of religion was potentially divisive and therefore detrimental.[245]

After becoming president, Washington continued to promote religious liberty. He promised Methodists that he would do all he could to preserve "the civil and religious liberties of the American People" and to be "a faithful and impartial Patron of genuine, vital religion."[246] Of all human animosities, Washington wrote to a friend in 1792, those caused by differences in religion were "the most inveterate and distressing." He hoped that the present age's "enlightened and liberal policy" would enable Christians to never carry their religious disputes "to such a pitch as to endanger the peace of Society."[247] Many of the exchanges between Washington and denominational leaders who wrote to congratulate him on becoming president directly discuss religious liberty, especially their hope that he would protect the freedom of religious minorities.[248] In his replies, Washington insisted that freedom of conscience was a right, not a privilege. The chief executive rejoiced "to see Christians of different denominations dwell[ing] together in more charity, and conduct[ing] themselves in respect to each other with a more christian-like spirit than ever they have done . . . in any other nation."[249] When Virginia Baptists complained that the new Constitution did not sufficiently protect liberty of conscience, Washington assured them that if he had "the slightest apprehension" that the document "might possibly endanger the religious rights of any ecclesiastical Society," he would never have signed it.[250] The liberty Americans enjoyed to worship "Almighty God agreeable to their Consciences," Washington wrote to Quakers, "is not only among the choicest of their *Blessings*, but also of their *Rights*."[251]

Given the predominantly Protestant heritage of the new United States, Catholics and Jews were especially concerned about safeguarding their religious liberty. Before the adoption of the Constitution, numerous states restricted office holding to Protestants. When a leading New York newspaper argued in 1789 that the federal government should give Protestants special consideration because of their role in founding the republic, Bishop John

Carroll responded that many Catholics had fought in the Continental Army, strongly supported the work of the Constitutional Convention, and worked to build a republic that promoted "justice and equal liberty."[252] The next year, Washington urged citizens not to "forget the patriotic part" Catholics had played in winning the Revolutionary War and in establishing the new government, or the "important assistance" the United States had received from Catholic France. He rejoiced that American Catholics were "animated alone by the pure spirit of Christianity" and "faithful subjects of our free Government."[253]

As part of a historically beleaguered minority, members of the nation's tiny Jewish community (numbering about 3,000) were eager to protect the civil and religious rights they had gradually won during the colonial years. Jewish leaders sent Washington several letters expressing their gratitude that their rights far surpassed those of their coreligionists in any other country. Savannah Jews praised his role in dispelling the "cloud of bigotry and superstition" that long had plagued them and in giving them "all the privileges and immunities of free citizens." "May the same wonder-working Deity" who had delivered "the Hebrews from their Egyptian Oppressors," the president replied, "make the inhabitants of every denomination participate in the temporal and spiritual blessings of that people whose God is Jehovah."[254] Washington assured the Jews in Newport, Rhode Island, that in the United States all citizens possessed "liberty of conscience" and the same rights.[255]

While Baptists, Quakers, Catholics, and Jews wanted to ensure freedom of worship, other religious groups protested that the Constitution did not acknowledge God's ultimate authority. Presbyterians were thankful that it did not contain a religious test for office, "that grand engine of persecution in every tyrant's hand." They praised the president for not elevating one denomination over others and for guaranteeing that all Americans had the same liberties. Nevertheless, they complained that "the Magna Charta of our country" had no "Explicit acknowledgement of the *only true God and Jesus Christ, whom he hath sent.*"[256] Without directly responding to their objection, Washington insisted that "the path of true piety" was so plain that it required "little political direction." As ministers "instruct[ed] the ignorant" and "reclaim[ed] the devious" and the government promoted morality, Americans could "confidently expect the advancement of true religion, and the completion of our happiness."[257]

Convinced that religious tolerance was essential to national unity and abhorring sectarian quarrels that threatened to disrupt the social order, Washington exulted in 1792 that America's "civil & religious liberty" was "perhaps unrivalled by any civilized nation." The next year he added, "We have abundant reason to rejoice that in this Land the light of truth & reason has triumphed over the power of bigotry and superstion [*sic*], and that every person may here worship God according to the dictates of his own heart." In

America, an individual's religious tenets would "not forfeit the protection of the Laws, nor deprive him of the right of attaining & holding the highest office."[258] Although his contributions were not as significant as those of Jefferson and Madison, Washington played an important role in reducing denominational privileges and firmly establishing religious freedom in the new United States. As one eulogist concluded, "The oppressed corners of every land have felt some alleviation by his priceless labours" for religious liberty.[259]

A Final Assessment

Although Washington faced less criticism than any of his successors, the Republican press subjected the president to a "litany of vitriolic comments," attacking his character, "questioning his statesmanship, [and] mocking his leadership style."[260] A few Republican editors denounced him as a gambler, a cheapskate, a dictator, and "a most horrid swearer and blasphemer."[261] Detractors castigated him as "the American Caesar" who did not deal effectively with revolutionary developments at home or abroad.[262] Claiming that Washington had arrogated the powers of a king, some sneeringly called him George IV. Bitter that Washington had refused to help procure his release from a French jail cell, Thomas Paine denounced the president as "treacherous in private friendship ... and a hypocrite in public life." He predicted that "the world will be puzzled to decide whether you are an apostate or an imposter, whether you have abandoned good principles or ever had any."[263]

Despite Washington's reputation for exemplary character, he was far from flawless. Throughout his life, he battled a quick temper. As a young man, Washington was very concerned about accumulating wealth, frequently harangued his military superiors, and disobeyed orders to engage the French, leading to the surrender of Fort Necessity. As commander in chief, he sometimes hesitated to act, unwisely deferred to subordinates, and utilized poor strategies. Washington abhorred criticism and disloyalty and had trouble accepting responsibility for his mistakes.[264]

None of this seemed, however, to matter to most Americans. John Adams, Benjamin Rush, and others resented Washington's exalted reputation and protested that one person should not be given credit for results that required the sacrifice of thousands. As early as 1777, Adams denounced in Congress the "superstitious veneration sometimes paid to General Washington."[265] "The History of our Revolution will be one continued Lie from one end to the other," he later complained to Benjamin Rush. "The essence of the whole will be that Dr. Franklin's electrical Rod smote the earth and out sprung General Washington." Thereafter, the two of them "conducted all the Policy, Negotiations, Legislatures and War."[266]

Almost all historians rate Washington as one of the nation's greatest presidents. Inspired in part by his faith in God's providential direction of events, he successfully shaped an office unknown in world history, effectively governed a fragile republic that aspired to set an example for other nations, pursued policies that strengthened the nation and ensured its survival in the midst of a hostile environment, and left citizens with an inspiring farewell discourse.[267] Admirers insisted that Washington had helped restore the nation's credit, ensure that justice, peace, and liberty prevailed, and gain the world's respect for the new republic.[268] Without Washington, the United States would not have defeated Britain, ratified the Constitution, functioned successfully as a republic, or prevented Britain, France, or Spain from controlling most of North America. To John Marshall, Washington was "the founder of our federate republic—our bulwark in war, our guide in peace."[269] Because of his leadership, civilians controlled the military, and the United States did not experience a dictatorship, military coup, or political oppression, as did other countries that obtained independence from colonial rulers.[270] Repudiating portrayals of Washington as "a popular figurehead" and a passive political leader, Stuart Leibiger argues that "he was the central politician of his age." Although the Virginian typically acted behind the scenes, his impact was tremendous.[271]

Washington's faith contributed to his pursuit of peace as president. In 1788, he wrote a Frenchman that he hoped agriculture and commerce "would supersede the waste of war ... that the swords might be turned into plough-shares, the spears into pruning hooks, and ... 'the nations learn war no more.'" "Certainly it is more consonant to all the principles of reason and religion (natural and revealed) to replenish the earth with inhabitants, rather than to depopulate it by killing those already in existence," he added. He rejoiced that "the Philosophers, Patriots, and virtuous men in all nations" viewed "our rising Republics" "as a kind of Asylum for mankind. God grant that we may not disappoint their honest expectations, by our folly or per-verseness."[272] Although Washington spent much of his life in the military, as president he avoided war, which required skillful diplomacy during his second term. He kept the United States out of the European war, convinced the British to leave the Northwest Territory, and satisfactorily resolved America's major differences with Spain.[273]

Widely lauded as one of America's greatest documents, Washington's 1796 Farewell Address has had a powerful influence.[274] It warned Americans against the dangers of factions and entangling alliances and helped shape subsequent American political attitudes and practices. Washington urged Americans to develop a strong, self-determined, and independent foreign policy and expressed his hope that America's principles and practices would inspire change around the world.[275] The address reiterated his staunch belief that religion and morality were essential to upright conduct, social tranquility, and national success. "It will be worthy of a free, enlightened and, at no distant period, a great Nation, to give mankind the magnanimous and too novel example of a People always guided by an exalted justice and benevolence."[276]

Although Washington had no biological children, he has rightly been called the father of his country. Without him, the United States may never have been created or survived its infancy. Although many factors helped inspire Washington's monumental contributions, his faith played a major role. Scholars and ordinary Americans will continue to debate the precise nature of his faith, but clearly it became deeper as a result of his trying and sometimes traumatic experiences as commander in chief of the Continental Army and the nation's first president, and it significantly affected his understanding of and his actions in both positions.

CHAPTER TWO

Thomas Jefferson
and the Separation of Church and State

*Can the liberties of a nation be thought secure when we have removed
their only firm basis, a conviction in the minds of people that these
liberties are a gift of God?*

> Notes on the State of Virginia, 1785

*For I have sworn upon the altar of God, eternal hostility against every
form of tyranny over the mind of man.*

> Jefferson to Benjamin Rush, Sept. 23, 1800

*And may that Infinite Power, which rules the destinies of the universe,
lead our councils to what is best.*

> First Inaugural Address, Mar. 4, 1801

ALTHOUGH MANY OF George Washington's contemporaries portrayed him
as a devout Christian and even a saint, Thomas Jefferson's foes depicted him as
an infidel and an atheist.[1] During the 1800 campaign, a Massachusetts Federalist insisted that God would not "permit a howling atheist to sit at the head
of this nation."[2] During Jefferson's first term as president, a Federalist cartoon
pictured him, aided by the devil, pulling down a column on which the names
of Washington and Adams were inscribed.[3] Shortly after her husband's defeat
in the election of 1800, Abigail Adams complained that Jefferson did not
believe in "an all wise and supreme Governour [*sic*] of the World" and
therefore was not a Christian.[4] Her son and the future president, John Quincy
Adams, lamented later the negative impact "free-thinking and irreligion" had
on Jefferson's life. "If not an absolute atheist, he had no belief in a future

existence. All his ideas of obligation or retribution were bounded by the present life."[5] Given how similar their religious views and practices were, these radically different appraisals of Washington and Jefferson are ironic.

Like Washington's, Jefferson's life and legacy have remained of great interest to both the scholarly world and the general public. Academic analysis of Jefferson's life, career, and contributions is growing at a geometric rate.[6] Scholarly studies, popular books, films, and musicals examine his accomplishments. Controversy rages over whether he fathered the children of his slave Sally Hemings. Principal author of the Declaration of Independence; a Southern planter; governor of Virginia; minister to France; the nation's first secretary of state, second vice president, and third president; and founder of the University of Virginia, the sage of Monticello has loomed large in America's history. As a young man, Jefferson could "calculate an eclipse, survey an estate, tie an artery, plan an edifice, try a cause, break a horse, dance a minuet, and play a violin."[7] Often labeled a "Renaissance man," the Virginian's intellectual appetite had few limits. He feasted on archaeology, architecture, classical languages and literature, politics, law, history, rhetoric, music, and science, and he contributed significantly to many of these fields. He mastered Greek and Latin and spoke French and Italian. Although Jefferson wrote only one book, his addresses and more than 20,000 letters testify to his broad erudition and insightful mind. From 1796 to 1815, he served as president of the American Philosophical Society, the nation's first learned association.[8]

Jefferson informed John Adams that he tried to "say nothing of my religion. It is known to my God and myself alone. Its evidence before the world is to be sought in my life; if that has been honest and dutiful to society, the religion which has regulated it cannot be a bad one."[9] He told his former minister that "I not only write nothing on religion, but rarely permit myself to speak on it."[10] Despite such statements, few presidents have displayed as much interest in religious matters. As Edwin Gaustad argues, religion mesmerized, tantalized, alarmed, and sometimes inspired Jefferson, and he discussed religious issues, movements, and leaders often in his conversation and correspondence and occasionally in his addresses and published writings.[11] His personality, political prominence, and life experience made Jefferson very reluctant to reveal his own religious convictions. He did not share his private faith with either his nation or his children, grandchildren, and nephews. He wanted his family members to investigate religious matters and develop their own convictions.[12] Thus his personal faith can be gleaned only from his letters to friends.

Religious issues played a major role in Jefferson's life and presidency. He wrote the Virginia Statute for Religious Freedom (1786) that disestablished the Episcopal Church, enshrined the principle of freedom of conscience, and helped prepare the way for the First Amendment.[13] For almost sixty years, his metaphor of a "wall of separation" between church and state has dominated

Constitutional debate over the proper place of religion in public life and policy. Although he repudiated much of orthodox Christianity and his alleged lack of faith was a major issue in the hotly contested election of 1800, the Virginian was a deeply religious man.[14] He read widely in religious literature and wrote much about biblical, theological, and ethical issues in his private letters.[15] Like other enlightened thinkers, he denounced metaphysical and theological speculation as worthless, relished the Renaissance's rediscovery of classical culture, evaluated religion by whether it accorded with reason and benefited society, and emphasized the moral aspects of Christianity.[16] Rejecting all the "mythic, mysterious, and miraculous" aspects of Christianity, he stressed the worship of one God who created and sustained the universe and revealed himself through nature.[17] In an effort to discover the historical Jesus, he devised two different editions of the Gospels for his own use that eliminated all miraculous elements and focused on Christ's ethical teachings. America's "most self-consciously theological" president criticized the church for corrupting Jesus' pure and sublime teachings and strove to reform Christianity by shifting its focus from theology to ethics. In discussing religious issues, succeeding generations have frequently appealed to Jefferson's views and have paid almost as much attention to his personal beliefs as they have to those of Washington and Lincoln.[18] Although his supporters, his opponents, and academicians have, for the past two centuries, debated the character of his faith and whether he should be labeled an Episcopalian, a deist, or a Unitarian, many scholars do not recognize how important Jefferson's religious convictions were to his political philosophy and career.[19]

Jefferson's Faith

Examining Jefferson's religious socialization, pattern of church attendance, approach toward worship and prayer, the thinkers who shaped his worldview, and his views of God, Jesus, human nature, morality, education, life after death, and the Bible provides insight into his life and his presidency. The future president's father, Peter, served as a vestryman in the Anglican parish in Fredericksville, Virginia. As a youth, Jefferson was immersed in the Bible, the Book of Common Prayer, and the Anglican liturgy. He studied many subjects, including the Bible, under the tutelage of two Anglican rectors, William Douglas and James Maury. From 1760 to 1762, Jefferson attended America's second oldest college, William and Mary, whose seven faculty members included six Anglican clergymen.[20] Nevertheless, during these years Jefferson began to question many aspects of Anglicanism. Although remaining a nominal Episcopalian the rest of his life, he rejected many of the denomination's doctrines.

Jefferson attended church more regularly than Washington and used his own well-worn prayer book. Worshiping as frequently as most other Episcopalians, he earnestly read the congregational prayers and responses, preferred singing psalms to hymns, and appreciated the liturgy.[21] Jefferson contributed generously to Episcopal, Presbyterian, and Baptist congregations and devised the plans for St. Anne's Episcopal Church in Charlottesville.[22] He long enjoyed a close relationship with the congregation's rector, Charles Clay.[23] The parish elected Jefferson a vestryman, but probably more because of his social prominence than for his piety.[24] Although many praised Washington for going to church while serving as the nation's chief executive, Jefferson's enemies denounced as a political ploy his attendance of worship services at the House of Representatives while he was president.[25] After returning to Monticello in 1809, Jefferson often attended services in Charlottesville.[26] His children were undoubtedly baptized and received Episcopal religious instruction. Jefferson explained to a French correspondent in 1788 that he could not be a godparent for any of his friends' children because sponsors had to make a "solemn promise before God and the world, of faith in the articles, which I had never enough sense to comprehend, and it has always appeared to me that comprehension must precede assent."[27] Like Washington, Jefferson participated in Episcopal worship and espoused its central moral teachings, but he did not accept much of its theology.[28] However, an Episcopal clergyman officiated at his funeral, and, in some ways, Jefferson was a lifelong Episcopalian.

Jefferson had a greater interest in devotional activities than Washington did. His mother taught him to pray, and he was sometimes asked to recite the Lord's Prayer for guests as a young child. Charles Sanford argues that Jefferson had "an Anglican reverence for God . . . and a fondness for worship and private devotions." He insists that the Virginian's "habit of private prayer" gave him personal strength and helped shape his political philosophy.[29] Jefferson frequently promised to pray for people's health, happiness, and prosperity and for peace.[30] Jefferson told Meriwether Lewis that he would pray for his safety on his journey to explore the Louisiana Territory.[31] He prayed that other nations would establish republican governments. May "Heaven help their struggles, and lead them, as it has done us, triumphantly thro' them," Jefferson wrote the citizens of Alexandria, Virginia, in 1790.[32] He prayed that France would "speedily obtain liberty, peace & tranquility."[33] He wrote a neighbor that he would "fervently and sincerely pray" for his efforts to abolish slavery.[34] Jefferson often ended his letters with "God bless you."[35] He wrote, for example, to Delaware Republican Caesar A. Rodney, "I offer daily prayers that ye love one another, as I love you. God bless you."[36]

As will be discussed later, Jefferson did not consider the Bible God's inspired Word because he believed that divine inspiration could not be verified empirically and that the Scripture contained "gross effects and palpable falsehoods."[37] Nevertheless, he derived encouragement and comfort from it, and for the last fifty years of his life, Jefferson read the Bible almost every day, often in Greek or Latin. "I never go to bed," he wrote to a friend in 1819, "without an hour or half an hour's previous reading of something moral." More than any other book, Jefferson read the Bible before retiring. When grieving, he found solace in both testaments.

Jefferson's faith involved the head much more than the heart, and he displayed few feelings about religion.[38] "Deep or moving religious experience," Merrill Peterson contends, "seems never to have touched him."[39] Jefferson criticized emotionally oriented worship services. In 1822, for example, he complained about Richmond women who in "night meetings and praying parties" poured "forth the effusions of their love to Jesus, in terms as amatory and carnal, as their modesty would permit them to use to a mere earthly lover."[40]

Jefferson's personal habits were similar to Washington's. Like many other Virginian planters, Jefferson preferred French wine to Irish whiskey and spent lavishly to stock his wine cellar. Visitors to Monticello testified that Jefferson drank large quantities of liquor but held it "like a gentleman."[41] The wine bill during Jefferson's first term as president was almost $10,000, a tenth of his salary.[42] He lamented that "the poison of whiskey" was "desolating" American homes but approved of wine, if consumed moderately.[43] Some scholars claim he never used profanity.[44]

Jefferson's worldview was shaped primarily by his wide reading of classical authors, especially the Epicureans and Stoics, Enlightenment philosophes, rationalistic Christians, and the Bible.[45] "From any country and from any period," Gaustad maintains, Jefferson amassed "ideas as a reaper gathered corn, selecting and retaining the most delectable."[46] He denounced philosophical systems as "prisms of the mind." He viewed thought as a tool for directing everyday life, not for devising an overarching scheme.[47] At William and Mary, Jefferson was introduced to the principal figures and themes of the Enlightenment. He learned about Francis Bacon's emphasis on logic and induction, Isaac Newton's revolution in science and mathematics, and John Locke's new views of education, politics, philosophy, and religion. Jefferson absorbed their ideas and helped advance Enlightenment principles in America. Accepting Locke's empiricism, Jefferson rejected the belief that the Bible was God's infallible Word, as well as the concept of innate ideas, and concluded instead that experimentation, education, and experience paved the path to truth. Newton's writings convinced the future president that God's world was orderly, predictable, and dependable. Bacon, Newton, and Locke all taught him to explore, observe, measure, and collect and to trust the "perceptions of the present rather than the precedents of the distant past."[48] The writings of Henry Saint John Viscount Bolingbroke (1678–1751), Anthony Ashley Cooper (1671–1713), and English deists Lord Herbert of Cherbury (1583–1648), John Toland (1670–1722), and Matthew Tindal (1657–1733) also had a strong impact on Jefferson's worldview. Bolingbroke questioned the historic Christian doctrines of God and the atonement.[49] Cooper argued that nature was be-nevolent and that people could behave properly by following their innate moral sense. Toland strove to prove that Christianity was a rational, natural religion and discarded everything in the Bible that did not accord with reason. Rejecting revelation as unnecessary and miracles as implausible, Tindal reduced religion to morality. While appropriating selectively, Jefferson also was influenced by the works of Frenchmen Montesquieu, Diderot, and Voltaire; English Unitarians such as Richard Price; and Scottish philosophers David Hume and Francis Hutcheson.

The writings of Joseph Priestley, an English chemist who discovered oxygen—and a Unitarian minister—especially affected Jefferson's religious views. "I have read Priestley's books over and over again," Jefferson told Adams in 1813, "and I rest on them...as the basis of my own faith."[50] Gaustad argues that Priestley's *History of the Corruptions of Christianity* (1782) had more impact on Jefferson's religious convictions than any other book. It helped convince the Virginian that he had not rejected Christianity, only degraded forms of it. Priestley contended that neither the Bible nor Jesus taught that God was triune and that reason denied it. Christ's crucifixion demonstrated his selfless devotion and amazing love but did not atone for humanity's sin by satisfying God's wrath. Jefferson found refreshing the scientist's emphasis on the oneness of God and the morality of Jesus.[51]

These varied writers, especially the deists and Unitarians, prompted Jefferson to espouse a religion based on reason rather than revelation or mystical experience, to reject miracles, to relish the historical study of religion, and to argue that theologians had corrupted Christ's original teachings.[52] "Reason and free enquiry," he maintained, "are the only effectual agents against error." Let them loose and they would "support the true religion, by bringing every false one to their tribunal, the test of their investigation."[53] Jefferson urged his nephew Peter Carr in 1787 to question every religious claim, including God's existence, because if he did exist, he would "certainly more approve the homage of reason than of blindfolded fear."[54] People must begin not with presuppositions or speculative systems but with the hard data of experience that could be measured, counted, and evaluated.[55] Reason, rather than revelation, was the final "umpire of truth."[56] Yet Jefferson considered reason to be God's gift to enable people to understand their world and make sense of their lives; "everyone is responsible to the God who planted it [reason] in his breast, as a light for his guidance."[57]

In enlightened thought, nature was even more important than reason because it was so adaptable and useful. The philosophes employed the word *nature* in different contexts as natural law, natural philosophy, natural religion, natural rights, the state of Nature, and Nature's God.[58] Those who shared Jefferson's perspective disagreed over the possibility and extent of revelation, but they concurred that the creation itself was the primary source for knowing about God. The Virginian clearly preferred natural religion to revealed religion. People could learn about moral philosophy simply by observing the physical world.[59] Jefferson cautioned his nephew to carefully examine any biblical facts that contradicted the laws of nature to determine which was more probable: incorrect reporting or "a change in the laws of nature." To Jefferson, the answer was self-evident, because nature was orderly and unchanging. The splendid design of the universe convinced him that God existed. Accepting Thomas Aquinas's cosmological argument, Jefferson insisted that nature's "design, cause and effect" revealed "a fabricator of things from matter and motion."[60] Jefferson relished the poetry of the Psalms and the aesthetics of the Anglican ritual because they testified to God's awe-inspiring creation.[61]

Like Washington, Jefferson repeatedly referred to God in his addresses and letters and called him by a wide variety of terms, including "Almighty," "Supreme Being," "Fabricator," "Intelligent and Powerful Agent," and "Superintending Power."[62] The statesman considered himself both a theist, because he believed a first cause had produced the universe, and a deist, because he believed in one God, not a Trinity, who had created the world and people.[63] He rejected the doctrine of the Trinity as incomprehensible, irrational, and ahistorical. Beginning at an early age, Jefferson wrote, he could not accept the triune nature of God because of the "difficulty of reconciling the ideas of Unity and a Trinity" in the Godhead.[64] Jefferson did not understand how anyone could "believe in the Platonic mysticisms that three are one, and one is three, and yet one is not three, and the three are not one."[65] He insisted further that neither Jesus nor the earliest church fathers "expressly declared" this doctrine. Rather, Jesus clearly stated that God was one. The church never "affirmed or taught" the Trinity before the Council of Nicaea in 325.[66] Christ's religion, Jefferson wrote in 1820, was "founded in the Unity of God," which helped "it triumph over the rabble of heathen gods." He protested that the "metaphysical insanities" of fourth-century theologian Athanasius (who helped establish the Trinitarian Nicene Creed), reformer John Calvin, and Ignatius of Loyola, founder of the Jesuits, were "mere relapses into polytheism."[67]

Although he thought that people could not comprehend God's nature, Jefferson argued that they could discern some of his attributes by studying the physical world, history, and human nature. Rather than providing special revelation to chosen people or miraculously intervening in human affairs, God revealed himself to all individuals "at all times and in all places through the natural wonders of his created universe."[68] Jesus taught that God "is good and perfect," Jefferson stressed, but he never defined God, "and we have neither words nor ideas" to do so either.[69] If all Christians followed Jesus' example, "we should all be of one sect, doers of good and eschewers of evil."[70]

Like Washington, Jefferson believed that God was all-powerful, wise, just, and benevolent and that he providentially directed human affairs. Rejecting the "watchmaker" metaphor, Jefferson averred that "a superintending power" must "maintain the universe in its course and order."[71] Like Jonathan Edwards, he insisted that God's presence in the world was continuous and benevolent.[72] His first inaugural address recognized the role of "an overriding Providence" in American history and invoked the "infinite Power which rules the destinies of the universe" to lead the government to do "what is best" and give Americans "peace and prosperity."[73] In his first annual message to Congress, the president thanked "the beneficent Being" for preserving the nation's peace "through so perilous a season."[74] In his second inaugural address, Jefferson professed that he would need "the favor of that Being . . . who has covered our infancy with his providence, and our riper years with his wisdom and power."[75] Jefferson's confidence in God's direction of history, coupled with his belief in people's essential goodness, assured him that humanity would progress in education, politics, science, commerce, the arts, and morality.[76] His privileged position and wealth prevented him from seeing much of the world's privation or worst problems and contributed to his generally sanguine perspective. God had so designed the world, he insisted, that human liberty would continually expand.[77] He affirmed Bolingbroke's contention: "Since infinite wisdom had established it, the system of the universe must be necessarily the best of all possible systems."[78] Jefferson was confident that sound education and scientific advancement would overcome human defects and someday eradicate all social ills.[79]

His belief that God guided the world sustained Jefferson in his political battles. Because God's power and laws governed the universe, he wrote, "Our efforts are in His hand, and directed by it; and He will give them their effect in his own time."[80] His public addresses, like those of Washington, contain dozens of references to God's "overruling Providence which governs the destinies of men and nations."[81] "When great evils happen," he tried to discover "what good may arise from them." Because Providence had "established the order of things," most evils produced "some good."[82]

Jefferson rejoiced that God was just. God's "even-handed justice" convinced him that Americans would win their independence. As a statesman, he relied on the fact that God had built moral laws of justice into the universe.[83] Jefferson also asserted that God loved and watched over human beings. "The God whom you and I acknolage [sic] and adore," Jefferson wrote Adams, is the "benevolent governor of the world."[84] God delighted "in the happiness of man here, and his greater happiness hereafter."[85] The Virginian thanked God for his love, protection, and guidance.[86] Confident that God cared for people, Jefferson frequently sought his guidance for himself, others, and the United States.[87] The planter's assurance that God was beneficent contributed to his belief that reason and nature could be trusted and helped inspire his optimism and shape his political philosophy.

While espousing an orthodox view of God the Father, Jefferson repudiated the Christian contention that Jesus was God's unique Son. Publicly, he tactfully tried to avoid the question of Jesus' divinity.[88] Privately, however, he argued that Jesus was neither divine, as orthodox Christians proclaimed, nor an imposter, as some skeptics charged.[89] He insisted that "Jesus did not mean to impose Himself on mankind as the Son of God," but his followers made him a "second pre-existing being."[90] He was instead "the first of human sages," whose teachings surpassed those of Socrates and all other philosophers and whose character was more "eloquent and sublime" than any other person's.[91] Jefferson wished that Christians and other theists would stop debating Christ's divinity and focus on his character and moral teachings.[92] The planter rejected the doctrines of Christ's virgin birth, vicarious atonement, and bodily resurrection.[93] The idea that God sacrificed his sinless son to appease his own wrath made no sense to Jefferson.[94] He insisted that the repentance of sinners was sufficient to satisfy God's justice and evoke his mercy.[95] Jesus' crucifixion was deplorable, but his teachings and example inspired people to live more righteously and create a better society.[96] Jesus taught three simple doctrines that promoted human happiness: "there is one God" who is "all-perfect," "there is a future state of rewards and punishments," and "to love God with all thy heart, and thy neighbor as thyself, is the sum of religion."[97] In short, Jefferson portrayed Jesus as an Enlightenment philosophe who urged people to relinquish their inadequate moral systems and instead practice "the most sublime moral code" ever devised.[98] Although he rejected "the corruptions of Christianity," he told Benjamin Rush that he accepted "the genuine precepts of Jesus himself. I am a Christian in the only sense in which I believe Jesus wished any one to be: sincerely attached to his doctrines, in preference to all others; ascribing to himself every human excellence, and believing he never claimed any other."[99]

In addition to rejecting orthodox Christology, Jefferson repudiated the concept of a fall that corrupted human nature, damaged people's moral sense, and prevented them from knowing and doing good.[100] He was convinced that people had an intrinsic disposition to do good rather than evil, to live an upright rather than an immoral life. Denouncing the Calvinist doctrines of predestination and original sin, Jefferson argued that people were free to choose good and avoid evil. He contended that the Creator had made "the moral principle so much a part of our constitution as that no errors of reasoning or speculation might lead us astray from its observance in practice."[101] The moral instinct was as innate as people's ability to see and hear. That some seemed to lack it or had an impaired instinct was no different than the fact that some people had impaired sight or hearing or lacked these senses altogether. Moreover, education, reason, peer pressure, legal punishments, and "the prospects of a future state of retribution" could improve the behavior of those with flawed moral natures.[102] "Happiness is the aim of life," Jefferson asserted, "but virtue is the foundation of happiness."[103] "God has formed us as moral agents," he added, so "that we may promote the happiness" of others "by acting benevolently towards all."[104] Both the moral law and the structure of the physical universe revealed God's wisdom and enhanced his glory.[105] Rejecting the orthodox Christian position, Jefferson argued that conscience rather than divine revelation, properly interpreted, was the best guide to morality.

Although Jefferson repudiated the doctrine of original sin and refused to call human beings sinners, his work as a lawyer and a politician and his knowledge of history made him very aware of human selfishness, treachery, injustice, and cruelty. The events of life—the murder of his friend George Wythe in 1806, the conspiracies of Aaron Burr that same year, the attacks on him by clergy during the election of 1800 and by New Englanders for his Embargo Act of 1807—convinced him that people often acted in wicked ways.[106] He lamented that all people contained elements of depravity and that the seductions of "self-love" prevented them from doing what was right.[107]

Christ's ethical teachings guided Jefferson's personal conduct and work as a statesman. Christian ethics, he argued, provided the best norms for directing human relations. They acknowledged people's divinely bestowed moral sense and taught individuals to serve one another.[108] Christian ethics were superior to classical ethics because they emphasized public goodness and welfare and social development, whereas the latter stressed private goodness and welfare and self-perfection.[109] Christ's moral doctrines "were more pure and perfect than those of the most correct of philosophers and . . . went far beyond [them] in inculcating . . . philanthropy not only to kindred and friends, to neighbors and countrymen, but to all mankind, gathering into one family, under the bond of love, charity, peace, common wants and common aids." Jesus' teaching also surpassed those of other philosophers because he dealt with people's motives.[110] He labeled Christ's teachings on love, repentance, forgiveness, and universal fraternity "the most sublime and benevolent code of morals" for human social relations.[111]

Like Washington, Adams, and virtually all his successors, Jefferson asserted that because religion fostered morality, stability, and social cohesion, it was indispensable to the republic. The new nation would succeed only if it protected civil and religious liberty, promoted virtue, and produced people who were industrious, independent, and willing to make sacrifices for the common good. Jefferson insisted that Christ's teaching could best inspire these traits. In "the original purity and simplicity of its benevolent founder," Christianity was "most friendly to liberty, science, and the freest expression of the human mind."[112] No system of morality could effectively motivate people, he argued, unless it had "the sanction of divine authority stamped upon it."[113] Although Jefferson disliked Christians' focus on doctrine and evangelism, he appreciated their zealous efforts to encourage both private and public morality through their congregations and interdenominational societies.

While contending that religion and morality were closely linked, Jefferson sought to create a state-sponsored and controlled education system in Virginia that greatly restricted the role of revealed religion. He tried to construct an educational system that stretched from the primary grades through professional schools based on "common moral pursuits grounded in an understanding of and commitment to the Author of that morality and of all creation."[114] Moral understanding was critical both to self-governance and to the success of a republic, and young children therefore must be taught how to make moral choices. He advised schools not to assign Bible reading to elementary-age children, however, because "their judgments are not sufficiently matured for religious enquiries." Jefferson wanted public schools to teach those matters on which reason and nature agreed, such as that God was the creator, sustainer, and supreme ruler of the universe and the source of morality. Religious "truths" that were rational and universal were "neutral" and thus should be included in the curriculum. On the other hand, public schools should eliminate all sectarianism and dogmatism.[115]

Realizing he could not eradicate all Episcopal influence from William and Mary, after leaving the presidency Jefferson decided to create a new university near Monticello. He designed the buildings, superintended the grounds, devised the curriculum, arranged the library, and selected the professors and the books. Seeking to make this institution a beacon of enlightened liberalism in the New World, he stressed science and government and depreciated theology. His proposed curriculum excluded biblical and theological studies and instead emphasized the study of ancient and modern history as the primary means of strengthening commitment to republicanism. Although Jefferson refused to appoint a professor of divinity at the University of Virginia, he wanted the professor of ethics to discuss the proofs for God's existence as the "supreme ruler of the universe [and] the author of all the relations of morality."[116] The institution would provide instruction in "religious opinions" and "duties" because people's relationship with their maker and responsibilities to him were extremely "interesting and important."[117] He wanted different denominations to establish divinity schools on the perimeter of the University of Virginia to enable students to participate in the religious exercises of their faith community and divinity students to hear scientific lectures at the university.[118] This arrangement would help students espouse Christ's principal ethical teachings and be virtuous citizens of the new republic.

Jefferson's proposed educational system clashed with the one advocated by most orthodox Christians, and his beliefs about eternal life conflicted with those of historic Christianity. His views of the afterlife changed over time and are somewhat contradictory.[119] His emphasis on empirical verification led him to argue that people could not know for sure whether there was life after death.[120] Moreover, his understanding of the nature of people's existence after death was murky and unclear. Influenced by the laws of science, Jefferson had difficulty believing that people had a soul or spirit that would survive death. His materialistic philosophy, however, conflicted with both his conviction that a righteous God would recompense people according to their earthly deeds in an afterlife and his desire to be reunited with loved ones. As he aged, therefore, Jefferson increasingly discarded his mechanistic perspective in favor of a view that left room for belief in human immortality.[121]

Jefferson affirmed Jesus' teaching about a future state because it was crucial to his understanding of the morality of the universe. Like German philosopher Immanuel Kant, he reasoned that because virtue was not always recompensed on earth and justice did not always prevail, there must be a "future state of rewards and punishments." Jesus' emphasis on an afterlife helped supplement "other motives for moral conduct";[122] "the prospects of a future state" where good conduct was rewarded and evil behavior punished was necessary to stimulate people to live upright lives.[123] Jefferson argued that people should live "with pious resignation to the Divine will" until God rewarded them at their "journey's end," based on their merit.[124]

The loss of many loved ones also affected Jefferson's view of death. His father died when the future president was fourteen. Half of his eight siblings died in their youth. Only two of Jefferson's six children lived to maturity, and one of them died at age twenty-five. After a long illness, his beloved wife, Martha, died in 1782. Their ten years of marriage had been very happy, and Jefferson was grief-stricken. His bereavement undoubtedly contributed to his hope that people continued to live in another place. Jefferson consoled friends who lost loved ones with New Testament assurances of life after death. Quoting St. Paul, he wrote to his college friend John Page, "We sorrow not then as others who have no hope."[125] Comforting John Adams after the death of his wife, Abigail, Jefferson declared that they would soon leave their sorrow and suffering and "ascend in essence to an ecstatic meeting with friends we have loved and lost and whom we shall love and never lose again."[126] In a poem he wrote shortly before his own death, Jefferson envisioned the "welcoming shore" and the "two seraph," his deceased wife and daughter, greeting him as he arrived in heaven.[127] Jefferson and Adams frequently discussed meeting again in the hereafter, where their questions would be answered, their current frustrations ended, and peace and rest provided.[128]

To Jefferson, a person's status in the afterlife depended on virtuous behavior, not correct belief. Those who lived righteously, he wrote, would someday "find themselves united in concert [in heaven] with the reason of the supreme mind."[129] He maintained that if he ever founded a new denomination, its "fundamental principle would be the reverse of Calvin's, that we are saved by our good works which are within our power, and not by our faith which is not within our power."[130] Individuals who steadily observed "those moral precepts in which all religions concur," Jefferson wrote to a Quaker in 1813, "will never be questioned, at the gates of heaven, as to the dogmas in which they differ."[131] The next year Jefferson argued that there were "different roads we may pursue . . . to that our last abode." In heaven, there were no Quakers, Baptists, Presbyterians, Episcopalians, or Catholics. On entering, people left "those badges of schism behind" and were "united in those principles only in which God has united us all."[132]

Like Washington, Jefferson was calm and composed as he approached death. Unlike his fellow Virginian, however, Jefferson's last words invoked Scripture: "Lord, now lettest thou thy servant depart in peace."[133] Nevertheless, although admirers created pietistic legends about Washington's last moments and alleged final words, few mentioned Jefferson's parting sentence.

In an effort to purify Christianity, end futile doctrinal debates, and improve moral practices, Jefferson devised three summaries of biblical teaching. In 1803, he told Joseph Priestley that he planned to provide an analysis "of the life, character, and doctrines of Jesus," who strove to revise Jewish theology and morality to accord with "the standard of reason, justice, and philanthropy."[134] Jefferson wanted to explain why many traditional Christian doctrines were arcane, repulsive, and detrimental and why Christ's "system of morality was the most benevolent and sublime." He also sought to demonstrate that the character of Jesus was "the most innocent" and "most eloquent" anyone had ever exhibited. In the two-page "Syllabus" Jefferson soon prepared and sent to Priestley, Rush, a few other trusted friends, and his daughters, he argued that "unlettered and ignorant" men had so "mutilated" and "misstated" Jesus' teachings that they were "often unintelligible."[135] Rush was "much pleased to find" that the president was "by no means so heterodox" as his enemies depicted him but disagreed with Jefferson's view of Christ's nature and mission.[136]

In March 1804, Jefferson completed a forty-six-page booklet on Christ's character and morality entitled "The Philosophy of Jesus of Nazareth," which he disseminated to a small group of friends and used for his own study. Although Jefferson had an impressive understanding of Greek philosophers, Roman historians, and the early church fathers, he was not a biblical scholar, a skilled exegete, or an expert in ancient manuscripts. Lacking the knowledge of textual transmission, oral traditions, and other tools that higher criticism would later supply, he used his understanding of the Greco-Roman world and of reason and nature to decide what Jesus had actually said.[137] The president cut out verses of the four Gospels that he thought best expressed the "pure and unsophisticated doctrines" of Jesus. Separating Christ's authentic statements from Platonic and clerical additions, he told John Adams, was as easy as distinguishing "diamonds in a dunghill."[138] His presuppositions and interests led Jefferson to retain many of Christ's parables and ethical teachings and excise the miraculous and theological. When Jefferson told Rush he planned to send him his "little volume" on Jesus, the physician replied that unless it affirmed Christ's divinity and argued that "his death as well as his life" were "necessary for the restoration of mankind," he would not "accord with its author."[139] Loathing theological controversy and fearing that his political enemies would use this document to further attack him, Jefferson did not make it public during or after his presidency.

In 1819 or 1820, Jefferson finished a more extensive volume, *The Life and Morals of Jesus of Nazareth*. Based on Greek, Latin, French, and English versions of the New Testament, the so-called Jefferson Bible was not published until 1904. Like later German theologians, Jefferson sought to separate the Jesus of history from the Jesus of faith, which he believed could supply an "anchor for republican virtue," values, and a basis for social harmony as liberal individualism increasingly tore apart the fabric of American society. Four factors motivated Jefferson's quest to find the historical Jesus: Federalist policies that endangered the "virtuous agrarian republic" he envisioned, acrimonious political debates that threatened to shatter civility and social accord, his belief that adherence to Christian moral standards would increase social agreement and cooperation, and his opponents' continued assault on his religious views.[140]

Jefferson had previously considered publishing a book to instruct Indians in Christianity but changed his mind because of an incident that occurred in 1816. He told longtime friend Charles Thomson that he was planning to write a small volume on the philosophy of Jesus that would acknowledge that "I am a *real Christian*, that is to say, a disciple of the doctrines of Jesus, very different from the *Platonists*." This statement prompted Thomson to tell others that the former president had become an orthodox Christian and intended to produce a book on the subject. A disgusted Jefferson sought to quell the rumors that circulated, further convincing him to keep his religious beliefs private.[141] Explaining his views, he wrote to Margaret Bayard Smith that he had always considered religion "a concern purely between our god and our consciences" alone. "I never told my own religion, nor scrutinized that of another," he continued. "I never attempted to make a convert, nor wished to change another man's creed."[142]

About twice the size of "The Philosophy of Jesus of Nazareth," *The Life and Morals of Jesus* examines his ministry and some of his doctrinal teaching, whereas the former focuses on Jesus' moral teachings. Jefferson omitted almost all passages that pertained to the supernatural or prophecy. He cut and pasted among the four Gospels to strip away the layers of distortion he believed Christ's followers had added. Jefferson hoped to purify Christianity by tying it directly to reason and removing all mystery and irrational dogmatism.[143] He selected passages that emphasized Jesus' "sublime code of morals" and omitted ones that made him a miracle worker. The former president consistently excluded verses in which Jesus declared he was divine, as well as passages describing his resurrection, appearance to his disciples as the risen Lord, and ascension into heaven. Labeling Paul the "first corrupter of the doctrines of Jesus," he included nothing from his epistles. Seeking to neither shock nor offend, Jefferson tried to separate the "absurdity," "untruth, charlatanism, and imposture" from the "passages of fine imagination, correct morality," and "most lovely benevolence."[144]

Despite Jefferson's protestations to the contrary, Edwin Gaustad argues that he was a religious reformer who wanted to substitute "morals for mysteries," the unity of God for the Trinity, and "cosmic justice for chaos or parochial self-interest." Like Alexander Campbell, who founded the Disciples of Christ in the early nineteenth century, Jefferson wanted to get "back to the plain and unsophisticated precepts of Christ" and to restore "his genuine doctrines." Their understanding of primitive Christianity differed markedly, however.[145] Jefferson lamented that theologians and clergy had transformed Christ's simple teachings into a complex metaphysical system few could comprehend. The Virginian especially blamed the Neoplatonists, Athanasius, and Calvin for introducing "absurdities" and "sophisms" into Christianity. Scholastic theologians, he protested, had "distorted and deformed the doctrines of Jesus," introducing "mysticisms, fancies, and falsehoods" that shocked "reasonable thinkers."[146] By demonstrating that Jesus was "a great reformer" and moral teacher, Jefferson sought to prevent educated individuals from rashly pronouncing him "an imposter."[147] Moreover, the philosopher-president believed that recapturing the true teachings and inspiring ethics of Jesus would advance the cause of religious liberty, spiritual enlightenment, and social reform.[148]

While seeking to revise Christianity, Jefferson repeatedly criticized the churches. As did many deists, Jefferson faulted Christianity for creating a priestly class that had invented mysterious doctrines to fortify their power by making themselves indispensable mediators between God and individuals. The Virginian castigated clergy as cannibals, mountebanks, charlatans, necromancers, mystery mongers, pseudo-Christians, false shepherds, and pious and whining hypocrites.[149] Many laypeople were no better. While preaching poverty, harmony, charity, and humility, Jefferson protested, they lived lavishly, exuded self-righteous pride, and sowed discord.[150] By distorting Jesus' ethical teachings, which were essential to a virtuous republic, Christians were harming society. Many theologians and ministers had converted Christ's teachings into "an engine for enslaving mankind." They "constitute the real Anti-Christ."[151] He praised the Quakers, who had no ministers and instead judged biblical texts "by the dictates of common sense and common morality."[152] When Connecticut took steps to disestablish the Congregationalist Church in 1817, Jefferson rejoiced that the "den of priesthood" had been broken up and "a Protestant popedom" would no longer "disgrace the American history and character."[153]

Creeds, Jefferson claimed, had "been the bane and ruin of the Christian church." Throughout history, they had "made Christendom a slaughter house, and this day divided it into Casts of inextinguishable hatred to one another."[154] Accentuating dogma caused divisions, whereas emphasizing morality promoted unity and harmony. "My religious reading has long been confined to the moral branch of religion," Jefferson wrote in 1809, "which is the same in all religions; while in that branch which consists of dogmas, all differ." "For one sermon on a moral subject," Jefferson complained, "you hear ten on the dogmas of the sect."[155] If Americans obeyed the teachings of Jesus and reflected on the purity of his life, they could transcend their religious and political parochialisms and create a stronger republic. Jefferson opined that "there would never have been an infidel if there had never been a priest."[156]

Jefferson especially excoriated Calvin and Presbyterians. He accused the Genevan reformer of worshiping a "malignant" "daemon" and blaspheming God by assigning him "atrocious attributes."[157] He denounced the "five demoralizing dogmas of Calvin": belief in the Trinity and election, denial of the importance of "good works and love of neighbor" and of the "use of reason in religion," and creation of an "incomprehensible faith."[158] Presbyterian clergy, he protested, "are the loudest, the most intolerant of all sects, the most tyrannical, and ambitious." Given the opportunity, they would burn at the stake other heretics who denied the Trinity, just as Calvin had torched poor Servetus.[159]

In the final analysis, Jefferson's religious views are difficult to label. He sometimes called himself a deist, and many historians have applied this label to him. Americans deists devoted the January 1802 issue of their magazine, *The Temple of Reason,* to defending Jefferson's religious principles.[160] Gaustad terms him a " 'warm deist' " or a "Newtonian deist," who believed that God was constantly shaping and directing the universe.[161] Joseph Ellis chastises Jefferson for categorizing himself as a quasi-Christian instead of a "deist who admired the ethical teaching of Jesus as a man rather than as the son of God."[162] Walter Isaacson argues that the third president shared a "rather vague Enlightenment-era" deistic belief with Benjamin Franklin. He "did not believe in a God who intervened directly in the daily affairs of mankind."[163] Willard Sterne Randall contends that Jefferson "believed in a supreme being who had set the world on its foundation and stepped aside."[164] These claims contradict Jefferson's expressed convictions that God actively sustained the universe, guided history, and heard and answered prayer. Rejecting the central deist contention that God was aloof, remote, and impersonal, the Virginian insisted that God both created and controlled the universe. This was the foundation on which his life and thought rested, Gaustad argues; "without it, his universe collapsed."[165] Eugene Sheridan's assertion that Jefferson almost perfectly embodied Peter Gay's "compelling portrait of the typical philosophe as a modern pagan whose intellectual development" involved a "dialectical progression" from rejecting Christianity to embracing classicism to pursuing modernity also seems at odds with the facts.[166]

Labeling Jefferson a Unitarian seems more accurate. He shared many affinities with the Unitarians, with whom he frequently corresponded. During his presidency, he often exchanged letters with Joseph Priestley (until his death in 1804) and Englishman Richard Price. In later years, he corresponded with Unitarians such as Harvard physician Benjamin Waterhouse, Baltimore pastor Jared Sparks, and Dutch immigrant Adrian Van der Kemp. He attended a Unitarian church in Philadelphia while serving as secretary of state, but there were no Unitarian congregations in either Washington or near Monticello while he lived in those places. Jefferson hoped that Unitarian graduates of Harvard Divinity School would plant churches in Charlottesville.[167] He praised the sermons of Unitarian Aaron Bancroft for restoring "to us primitive Christianity in all the simplicity in which it came from the lips of Jesus."[168] Their shared commitment to many Unitarian principles provided a congenial context for Jefferson and Adams to discuss philosophical and political issues.[169] Like Unitarians, Jefferson abhorred speculative theology and insisted that the primary purpose of religion is to promote goodness and justice.[170] On the other hand, Jefferson noted that Unitarians disagreed among themselves, insisted that he did not accept all their views, and never publicly stated that he was a Unitarian.[171] He also claimed that he never allowed himself to "meditate a specified creed."[172] Near the end of his life, however, Jefferson confidently predicted that rational religion would soon dominate the United States. He rejoiced in 1821 to see "the advances toward rational Christianity." The next year, he proclaimed that "there is not a young man now living in the United States who will not die a Unitarian."[173] Despite his disagreement with some doctrines of this denomination, classifying Jefferson a Unitarian is better than calling him a deist or rationalist. However, the term *theistic rationalist*, applied to Washington in the previous chapter, describes Jefferson even better than the name Unitarian does.[174]

Avoiding labels, some contemporaries and scholars stress that Jefferson's faith was strong and important to him. Several of Jefferson's closest friends were impressed by his religious devoutness. Robert Brent labels Jefferson a "deeply spiritual man," while Elliott Wicks claims he had "a profound faith in God."[175] Perhaps Jefferson's 1819 confession to a friend best summarizes his faith: "I am of a sect by myself, as far as I know."[176]

The Election of 1800

Pitting Federalist incumbent John Adams against Republican Thomas Jefferson, the election of 1800 was one of the most contentious campaigns in American history, in part because of the Virginian's religious views.[177] Not again until 1928, when Catholic governor of New York Al Smith ran against Quaker Herbert Hoover, would religion play such a major role in a presidential election. Some ministers had questioned Jefferson's orthodoxy as early as the mid-1780s because of his staunch support of disestablishment in Virginia. In defending the right of conscience in his *Notes on Virginia* (1785), Jefferson argued that "it does me no injury for my neighbor to say that there are twenty gods or no gods. It neither picks my pocket nor breaks my leg."[178] Although Jefferson was emphasizing that the state should be concerned about the social consequences rather than the ideological components of religion, some Federalist clergy concluded that he was indifferent toward the essential distinctions among monotheism, polytheism, and atheism. "Let my neighbor once persuade himself that there is no God," William Linn, pastor of a Dutch Reformed church in New York, later warned, "and he will soon pick my pocket and break not only my *leg* but my *neck*.[179] An anonymous writer urged George Washington in January 1792 to replace "the impudent, obscene, unworthy" Jefferson as secretary of state. This atheist's "absurd" opinions endangered the "existence of all Government."[180]

Jefferson's religious beliefs had not been an issue during the 1796 campaign, when he lost to Adams (but by coming in second became vice president), although the public prayer of Jedidiah Champion of Litchfield, Connecticut, shortly after the election expressed the concerns of some Federalists: "O Lord: wilt Thou bestow upon the Vice President a double portion of Thy grace, for Thou knowest he needs it."[181] Moreover, his participation in a public reception in his honor on a Sunday during the summer of 1798 convinced some Federalist editors that Jefferson had contempt for Christianity.[182] In 1800, however, Federalists measured his beliefs and behaviors against those of the recently deceased first president.[183] Dozens of eulogies early that year praised Washington's piety and reminded prospective voters how important it was for the United States to have a Christian president.[184] Meanwhile, Federalists accused the Republican candidate of being a libertine, a pagan, an atheist, and a heretic and urged citizens of the most Christian country on earth not to elect someone who denied key tenets of the gospel. New Haven lawyer David Daggett claimed incorrectly that Jefferson never attended public worship while he lived in New York or Philadelphia.[185] The Federalist *Gazette of the United States* insisted that the "grand question" of the campaign was would citizens "continue in allegiance to GOD—AND A RELIGIOUS PRESIDENT [John Adams]" "or impiously declare for JEFFERSON— AND NO GOD!!!"[186] Alexander Hamilton exhorted New York governor John Jay to take some "legal and constitutional step" "to prevent an atheist in religion, and a fanatic in politics from getting possession of the helm of state."[187]

In widely circulated pamphlets and sermons, many of the North's leading ministers sought to persuade pious voters to support Adams by portraying Jefferson as an infidel. Although Jefferson's attempt to disestablish the church had won him the support of Baptists and some other evangelicals, it aroused the concern of the presidents of the nation's "two most prestigious evangelical colleges"—Yale and Princeton—and key leaders of interdenominational co-operation. In addition, these Federalists disliked Jefferson because of his ad-miration of the French philosophes and the general course of the French Revolution.[188] Because Jefferson had spent several years in France, spoke French fluently, and had many French friends who were considered atheists, his political enemies labeled him a "French infidel." The French Revolution vividly portrayed what happened when nonbelievers controlled government: The Bible was ridiculed, churches were ransacked, and Christ was replaced by a "goddess of Reason." Timothy Dwight warned that if Jefferson were elected, "our churches may become temples of reason and our psalms of praise Marseillois hymns"; "we may see the Bible cast into a bonfire . . . and our children . . . chanting mockeries against God."[189] Electing a "Jacobin" presi-dent, Federalists charged, could produce an alliance with France and war with Great Britain, undermine morality, and create anarchy. Many clergy com-plained that Jefferson viewed religion and politics as separate compartments of life.[190] Federalist ministers derisively labeled him a "philosopher," implying that he was "dangerous, politically unreliable, and an enemy of religion." Like many other philosophers and scientists, they argued, Jefferson investigated nature to discredit the Bible and promoted atheism and materialism.[191]

During the campaign, Jefferson was stigmatized as an atheist or a French infidel in hundreds of pulpits in New England and the Middle Atlantic states.[192] Presbyterian minister John Mitchell Mason warned Christians that making "an open enemy of their religion, their Redeemer, and their hope" chief magistrate would be "a crime never to be forgiven," "mischief to them-selves, and sin against God." Jefferson intended to administer the government "without any religious principle. . . . Pardon me, Christian: this is the morality of devils."[193] Linn denounced Jefferson for disbelieving the Bible, rejecting Christianity, and openly professing deism. Conferring the presidency on a "manifest enemy to the religion of Christ . . . would be an awful symptom of the degeneracy" and "rebellion against God."[194] Echoing these charges, Fed-eralist editors argued that the election of "infidel Jefferson" would mean the "the seal of death" for "our holy religion."[195] Rumors spread that, if elected, Jefferson would use public funds to entice civil servants, teachers, military officers, and even ministers to either ignore religion or teach secularism, to pay lecturers to discuss Thomas Paine's *Age of Reason*, and to endow colleges to propagate deism.[196] Such rhetoric prompted many Federalists in New Eng-land, after hearing that the Virginian had won, to bury their family Bibles in their gardens or hide them in their wells so that his administration could not confiscate and burn them.[197]

Refuting these charges, Republican editors and ministers portrayed Jef-ferson as a tolerant, benevolent, and wise leader who ardently defended constitutional government and religious freedom and sought to maintain the proper relationship between religion and politics.[198] They lauded the Virginian as a patriot and a man of proven character and invaluable experience and rebutted allegations that Jefferson was an infidel or atheist. In the words of one pamphleteer, the Republican was "a sincere professor of Christianity—though not a noisy one."[199] They quoted statements of Jefferson that affirmed his belief in God and insisted that Christian faith could be expressed in a variety of ways.[200] Rather than demonstrating his indifference to Christianity, Jefferson's championing of religious freedom revealed his commitment to defeat bigotry and promote liberty of conscience. His supporters claimed that Jefferson was being attacked because he did not want Quakers, Methodists, or Baptists to have to pay the salaries of the pastors of other denominations or Catholics and Jews to be persecuted for their beliefs.[201] A New Haven lawyer accused Federalists of wanting to impose religious tests for officeholders on the entire nation.[202] A Republican newspaper charged that Federalists had allowed ministers to use the government to achieve their purposes and thus had polluted both "the holy altars of religion" and "the seats of Justice." Republicans, by contrast, stood for "good government without the aid of priestcraft, or religious politics."[203] Some of Jefferson's other supporters, by contrast, felt compelled to counter claims that Jefferson had rejected Christianity because they agreed with Federalists that Christian faith was essential to both morality and government.[204]

Deeply hurt by the assault on his character and convictions during the campaign, Jefferson wrote confidant Joseph Priestley two weeks after his inauguration, "What an effort . . . of bigotry in politics and religion have we gone through."[205] Responding publicly to Federalist salvos would have been fruitless. Because it was impossible "to contradict all their lies," he had decided "to contradict none."[206] Privately, he wrote that he would leave his detractors "to the reproof of their own consciences. If these do not condemn them," these false witnesses would someday "meet a judge who has not slept over his slanders."[207]

Strikingly, although Adams's personal religious convictions were quite similar to Jefferson's, they were not an issue in the campaign. On the other hand, Republicans used his issuing of a national "day of solemn humiliation, fasting, and prayer" in March 1799 to portray him as a tool of conservative Christians, especially Presbyterians, who allegedly wanted to establish a national church. Adams complained later that a "general suspicion prevailed" that Presbyterians sought to make their denomination the national church. He was falsely labeled a Presbyterian (he actually belonged to a Congregationalist church) and accused of directing this project. "The secret whisper ran through all the sects, 'Let us have Jefferson, Madison, Burr, anybody, whether they be philosophers, Deists, or even atheists, rather than a Presbyterian President.'" Adams's contention that this issue cost him the election is dubious, but it undoubtedly cost him votes.[208]

Jefferson's Relationship with Religious Constituencies

Throughout his presidency, Jefferson enjoyed a cordial relationship with many Republican clergy and laypeople, but Federalist Christians continued to criticize him. Speaking for numerous Republican ministers, Baptist John Leland declared shortly after Jefferson's election, "What may we not expect, under the auspices of heaven, while JEFFERSON presides.... Now the greatest orbit in America is occupied by the brightest orb."[209] Less than a year later, on January 1, 1802, Leland presented Jefferson with a "mammoth" cheese, measuring thirteen feet in circumference and weighing 1,235 pounds, made by the staunchly Republican and largely Baptist residents of Cheshire, Massachusetts. When the president personally accepted the cheese on New Year's morning, Cheshire citizens exulted that "the Supreme Ruler of the Universe ... has raised up a JEFFERSON for this critical day, to defend Republicanism."[210] Numerous other Baptist groups thanked Jefferson for the peace, justice, reduced taxes, and civil and religious liberty they enjoyed under his administration.[211]

Although Baptists were Jefferson's strongest supporters, he also had pleasant relationships with some Methodists and Episcopalians. Speaking for many of their coreligionists, Methodists in Pittsburgh, Pennsylvania, wrote to Jefferson in November 1808 to applaud his "valuable services" to the nation. Although his enemies had warned that his administration would open "the floodgates of infidelity," these Methodists rejoiced that Christianity was flourishing in the United States.[212] Despite his earlier opposition to the Anglican establishment in Virginia, Jefferson enjoyed warm friendships with numerous Episcopalians: Bishop James Madison, his former pastor Charles Clay, and several childhood Tidewater friends.[213]

Radical New England clergyman Elias Smith claimed that Jefferson was the sixth angel of the apocalypse described in the Book of Revelation, who set the stage for God to destroy Babylon. The discerning could see the "fierceness of God's wrath in the electoral misfortunes of the Federalists and the progressive collapse of established religion." Jefferson's presidency, Smith argued, was preparing the way for the second coming of Christ.[214] Federalist clergy, by contrast, steadily attacked Jefferson's character and actions during his presidency.[215] Two weeks after his inauguration in 1801, Jefferson offered to transport Thomas Paine from France, where he had barely escaped the guillotine, to the United States on a government ship. To Jefferson, Paine was a hero who had helped Americans win their independence and had tried to help the French do the same. To many Americans, however, Paine was the despised author of *The Age of Reason*, a vicious assault on Christianity. After his arrival in America, Paine aroused further controversy by attacking orthodox religion. Jefferson's public support of Paine (he also invited him to live at the

White House for several weeks) prompted the Federalist press to castigate the president as an "arch infidel" who had befriended a "vile, corrupt, obnoxious sinner."[216] David Osgood, pastor of the Congregationalist church in Medford, Massachusetts, insisted that Americans had to choose between being a "friend of Jesus Christ or of Thomas Paine."[217] Christians, a Federalist editor contended, must either renounce "their savior, or their president."[218]

Federalists also assailed Jefferson on other grounds. While Washington was the nation's King David, Osgood maintained, Jefferson, like David's rebellious son Absalom, had departed from his predecessor's prudent path.[219] Another Massachusetts Congregationalist implied that Jefferson was like Jeroboam, who after succeeding David and Solomon, basely misrepresented "the wise measures" of his previous administrations.[220] Echoing charges made during the campaign of 1800, Clement Clark Moore, the New York minister who achieved lasting fame by penning "A Visit from Saint Nicholas," sharply criticized the impious implications of Jefferson's *Notes on Virginia*.[221]

Whereas Jefferson seemed to Elias Smith to be a harbinger of the Second Coming of Christ, he appeared more like the Antichrist to Congregationalists and Presbyterians. Such attacks prompted the distraught president to compare his treatment by the New England clergy with Christ's crucifixion. He expected "no mercy" from them, Jefferson wrote to Levi Lincoln. "They crucified their Saviour, who preached that their kingdom was not of this world; and all who practise on that precept must expect the extreme of their wrath."[222]

Jefferson, Religious Liberty, and the Separation of Church and State

Jefferson was already the nation's best known advocate of religious liberty many years before he became president. Influenced by the writings of John Locke and others, he devised several laws, most notably, "A Bill for Establishing Religious Freedom in Virginia," to further the cause of religious freedom.[223] In drafting a constitution for Virginia in 1776, he proposed that "all persons shall have full and free liberty of religious opinion; nor shall any be compelled to frequent or maintain any religious institution."[224] Because Virginia did not include this law in its constitution, after Jefferson became governor in 1779, he introduced another bill to provide religious freedom, but it met substantial opposition. Patrick Henry proposed an alternative bill to make Christianity "the established Religion of this Commonwealth." Henry advocated collecting tax monies and distributing them to all approved denominations. Jefferson and Madison argued that this bill betrayed the civil and religious freedoms for which Americans had fought in the Revolutionary War. Madison's *Memorial and Remonstrance* expressed their shared conviction that the denial of equal exercise of religious freedom to all citizens offended God.[225] Moreover, they contended, history showed that the establishment of religion had a malignant, sometimes disastrous, effect. It had produced false piety, hypocrisy, self-righteousness, corruption, and tyranny. Why were citizens who had risked "their lives and fortunes" to gain civil freedom, Jefferson asked in his *Notes on Virginia*, willing to accept "religious slavery"? Rulers could have authority over such natural rights only if citizens acquiesced to them. "The rights of conscience we never submitted, we could not submit. We are answerable for them to our God." Baptists and Presbyterians also opposed this bill. As noted in the previous chapter, this divisive bill never came to a vote and was allowed to "die an easy death" in 1785, as Washington desired. To Jefferson, the religious freedom that residents of Pennsylvania and New York enjoyed was the ideal situation. Numerous religious groups flourished, peace and order prevailed, and if a sect arose "whose tenets would subvert morals," the good sense of the people laughed "it out of doors, without suffering the state to be troubled with it."[226]

In 1786, the Virginia legislature finally passed the bill Jefferson had first proposed seven years earlier. The "Bill for Establishing Religious Freedom" asserted that no citizen "shall be compelled to frequent or support any religious worship, place, or ministry whatsoever" or suffer any penalties because of "his religious opinion or belief." It declared that "all men shall be free to profess, and by argument to maintain, their opinions in matters of religion," and this would in no way "diminish, enlarge, or affect their civil capacities."[227] Jefferson's bill helped changed the course of Western civilization. It prodded democratic governments to recognize that "religious freedom was not a privilege to be condescendingly bestowed but a natural right to be zealously preserved."[228] Moving beyond Locke's policy of toleration, it provided complete religious freedom to all religious groups, including Jews, Muslims, and Hindus.

Jefferson advocated religious freedom for several reasons. First and foremost, he insisted that because God did not force individuals to believe or practice religion, the state must not do so either. "Almighty God hath created the mind free," Jefferson argued in the preamble to the statute Virginia passed in 1786. Therefore, "all attempts to influence it by temporal punishments or burthens, or by civil incapacitations, tend only to beget habits of hypocrisy and meanness, and are a departure from the plan of the Holy Author of our religion." When either civil or ecclesiastical authorities "assumed dominion over the faith of others," he argued, it tended "to corrupt the . . . very religion it is meant to encourage."[229] An all-wise and all-powerful God did not force people to believe and did not want "fallible and uninspired men" to have "dominion over the faith of others."[230] Jefferson argued that differences of opinions, like differences of appearance, "are a law of our own nature, and should be viewed with the same tolerance." Debate about religious opinions, he contended, would allow truth to triumph, as false ideas were shown by investigation to be wrong.[231] Civil rights did not depend on people's religious opinions, any more than on their opinions in physics or geometry. "Truth is great," Jefferson trumpeted, "and will prevail if left to herself."[232] As denominations engaged in dialogue and debate, Christ's central ethical teachings, which were essential to creating a virtuous republic, would be distilled and disseminated.[233]

Disestablishment would also compel ministers and laypeople to be more zealous about spreading their faith, which would strengthen their congregations and improve public morality. Instead of trying to force their religious and moral views on others, Jefferson thought people should ask questions about what others believed and did.[234] Jefferson argued that the freedom of thought during the sixteenth century enabled the Reformation to purge "the corruptions of Christianity." If free inquiry were now restrained, "the present corruptions will be protected and new ones encouraged."[235] Jefferson supported religious freedom not because he was a relativist who believed that all "truths" were equal or because he was a skeptic who doubted the veracity of the major ethical tenets of Christianity, but because he was convinced that an open discussion of competing interpretations of biblical theology and ethics was the best way to discover and disseminate central religious truths. He wanted Americans not to be free from religion but free to pursue whatever religion their reason and conscience led them to adopt. He demonstrated his personal commitment to the voluntary support of churches by giving generously to various ministers and congregations.[236]

Jefferson's views and actions have had a tremendous impact not only on religious liberty but also on the American understanding of the separation of church and state. On January 1, 1802, he wrote a letter to the Danbury Baptist Association, an alliance of twenty-six congregations, most of which were in Connecticut. A religious minority in a state where Congregationalism was legally established, they admired Jefferson's unwavering commitment to religious freedom.[237] In October 1801, association leaders had praised the president's staunch support of religious liberty. They hoped that Jefferson's views would prevail "till Hierarchy and tyranny be destroyed from the Earth."[238]

In responding to citizens' addresses, Jefferson sought to sow "useful truths & principles among the people, which might germinate and become rooted among their political tenets."[239] Recognizing that his address to the Danbury Baptists would be widely published in Baptist and partisan papers throughout the nation, he strove to explain why he did not proclaim days for public prayer, fasting, and thanksgiving.[240] Unlike the first two presidents and almost all state governors, Jefferson refused to declare such days because he believed the First Amendment prohibited the federal chief magistrate from issuing religious proclamations of any kind. He agreed with the Danbury Baptists that religion "lies solely between Man & his God, that he owes account to none other for his faith or his worship, [and] that the legitimate powers of government reach actions only, & not opinions." The First Amendment, Jefferson argued, built "a wall of separation between Church & State." As president, he was bound to respect "this expression of the will of the nation in behalf of the right of conscience."[241] Responding in January 1808 to a request from Presbyterian minister Samuel Miller to recommend "a day of *religious observance*," Jefferson further explained his position. Both the First Amendment and the Tenth Amendment, which reserved to the states the powers not delegated to the United States, he asserted, prevented the federal government from "intermeddling with" "the doctrines, discipline, or exercises" of religious institutions. Because the Constitution did not give the federal government explicit power to prescribe any religious exercises or assume any authority in religious matters, these powers must rest with the states. Jefferson noted that Miller had asked him to only recommend, not designate, a day of fasting and prayer and that his predecessors had stipulated such days. However, he concluded that the president possessed only "civil powers" and had "no authority to direct the religious exercises of his constituents."[242] While insisting that the federal government lacked the authority to designate such days, Jefferson thought it was proper for state and local governments, religious organizations, and private citizens to do so.[243]

Two days after issuing his missive to the Danbury Baptists, the president attended religious services at the Hall of the House of Representatives, where John Leland was preaching. Recognizing that his letter would unleash Federalist attacks on his position, Jefferson sought to reassure Christians of all political persuasions that he valued religion by worshiping in this prominent public forum. His attendance, which was widely reported by newspapers, helped to counter negative impressions created by his refusal to issue thanksgiving and fast proclamations. Throughout the remainder of his tenure, Jefferson often attended similar worship services, which strengthened his "political base in God-fearing areas like New England" and implied that he valued religion.[244]

Many other statesmen disagreed with Jefferson that a president, by proclaiming days of thanksgiving, was establishing religion or directly exercising power over religion. They emphasized that the First Congress, which devised the First Amendment, asked George Washington to designate "a day of public thanksgiving and prayer" and appointed chaplains to the Senate and House who were paid with public funds. Washington and Adams declared other days for religious observances.[245] Thus, by arguing that the federal government must maintain a "wall of separation" on this issue, Jefferson was taking a more radical position, which he acknowledged was not accepted by most Americans.[246] Although the First Amendment prohibits the federal government from establishing religion or denying citizens religious liberty, Jefferson's phrase seems to restrict both government and religious organizations by mandating separation between them.[247]

Scholars have closely scrutinized Jefferson's views on the relationship between church and state, especially because of Justice Hugo L. Black's use of his letter to the Danbury Baptists in a landmark Supreme Court case in 1947.[248] "In the words of Jefferson," wrote Black, the First Amendment "clause against the establishment of religion by law was intended to erect 'a wall of separation between church and State.'... That wall must be kept high and impregnable. We could not approach the slightest breach."[249] Although the First Amendment imposes explicit restrictions only on Congress, Daniel Dreisbach explains, Jefferson's wall of separation metaphor has been interpreted by some to proscribe "all admixtures of religion and politics," deny "all government endorsement of and aid for institutional religion," and promote "a religion that is strictly voluntary and essentially private." For the past half century, Justice Black's perspective has dominated political and legal discourse. Meanwhile, Americans have vigorously debated whether "Jefferson's metaphor merely makes explicit that which is implicit in the constitutional arrangement or whether it exceeds—and, indeed, reconceptualizes— the constitutional mandate."[250] Harold Hammett argues that the "wall of separation" "has become more than a mere symbol or a basis for analysis; it is a rule of law."[251] This metaphor "has become a cherished symbol for a strict separationist policy that champions a secular order in which religious influences are systematically removed from public life."[252]

Defenders of the wall metaphor argue that it "promotes private, voluntary religion and freedom of conscience in the secular polity by preserving the independence of both religious institutions and the civil state from interference or domination by the other, by preventing religious establishments or even dangerous entanglements between governmental and ecclesiastical authorities, and by avoiding destructive sectarian conflict among denominations competing for government favor and aid."[253] Religion is most likely to flourish when it depends on voluntary support from its adherents and avoids assistance from or intertwining with civil government.[254] Critics counter that the metaphor misconstrues the First Amendment, hinders the ability of religious organizations to shape public morality and policy, prevents citizens from using religious convictions to guide their participation in political life, and restricts the opportunity of religious groups to fulfill their civic mission. They complain that Jefferson's trope has been elevated to a Constitutional principle that tends to create an adversarial relationship between religious bodies and the government, silence religious voices in the marketplace of ideas, and "segregate faith communities behind a restrictive barrier." Moreover, the wall metaphor "provides little practical guidance" on how to apply First Amendment principles to church-state controversies, "short of recommending a policy of absolute separation."[255] Finally, they argue that whereas Jefferson's wall explicitly separated the church as an institution from the federal government, Black's "high and impregnable" wall separates religion from all levels of civil government.[256] Robert L. Cord contends that the separation of church and state requires "only that government not pursue sectarian goals, not establish a religion, and not prefer one religion or religious point of view over others."[257]

Several factors indicate that Jefferson used the wall of separation metaphor in a restrictive, not absolute, sense. James H. Hutson maintains that he consistently supported "the principle of government hospitality to religious activity (provided that it be voluntary and offered on an equal opportunity basis)."[258] Although the civil government could not legally establish one church or creed as a national faith and support it financially, Jefferson came to believe that the civil state, as long as it remained "within its well appointed limits," "could provide 'friendly aids'" to religious denominations.[259] Moreover, he used the term "church" rather than "religion" in restating the First Amendment to stress that "the constitutional separation was between ecclesiastical institutions and the civil state."[260] As noted, throughout his presidency, Jefferson attended religious services held on government property. He aided infant congregations in the newly created capital by allowing them to hold services in the Treasury and War office buildings, and he signed a federal law that provided tax exemption for churches in the District of Columbia.[261] Moreover, in colonial and state government settings, Jefferson supported issuing religious proclamations. As a member of the Virginia House of Burgesses, he helped draft a resolution in 1774 designating a "Day of Fasting, Humiliation, and Prayer."[262] In 1779, as governor of Virginia, Jefferson appointed "a day of publick and solemn thanksgiving and prayer to Almighty God." He endorsed and may have helped devise a bill, submitted to the Virginia legislature in 1785, that authorized state officials to stipulate days for thanksgiving and fasting and fined ministers who did not hold services and preach sermons in their churches on these days.[263] As president, Jefferson approved the use of federal funds to support a Catholic missionary who worked with the Kaskaskia Indians in Illinois and to help build a church for them. He also extended three times a federal law, first passed in 1796, that granted federal land to a United Brethren society to assist them in evangelizing Indians in the West.[264] Thus, to use the words, "high," "impregnable," and complete" to describe Jefferson's wall is at odds with what he what he said and contradicts what he did.[265]

Jefferson's Philosophy of Government

It is difficult to delineate Jefferson's philosophy of government because he did not develop a "comprehensive and consistent set of ideas about government."

Nevertheless, he consistently adhered to certain fundamental political tenets for more than half a century.[266] Jefferson's belief that a just, benevolent Creator directed human affairs and that Jesus' moral code was the best guide for private and public life is evident in much of his political theory and practice.[267] The Declaration of Independence and the Virginia Statute for Religious Freedom illustrate this contention, as do his views of God's moral law, human rights, man's moral nature, and the role of government, and his commitment to peace.

Jefferson's political philosophy combined elements of Lockean liberalism, Scottish Common Sense realism, classical republicanism, and Christianity. Garrett Sheldon argues that Lockean liberalism predominated during the Revolutionary and anti-Federalist periods and republicanism after 1800, but both were present at all times.[268] Deeply influenced by the Scottish Enlightenment, especially the moral philosophy of Francis Hutcheson, Jefferson rejected Locke's unbridled individualism and adopted a more communal or collectivist approach.[269] "His emphasis on political participation, an economically independent and educated citizenry, [and] a natural aristocracy of wisdom and virtue ... all reveal" the influence of such theorists as Aristotle, Cicero, and Montesquieu. In the final analysis, Jefferson's political theory was distinctly American and encompassed "psychology, philosophy, economics, ethics, education, and religion within a single worldview."[270]

Jefferson's philosophy of government was based on his belief that God had created the world with a moral structure and man with a moral nature. His conviction that God had endowed people with fundamental rights and that his moral law governed human affairs helped shape his understanding of human rights and assured him that Americans could successfully sustain a republic. Jefferson argued in the Declaration of Independence that Americans had the right to revolt to ensure life, liberty, and the pursuit of happiness because these rights were inalienable or, as he originally put it, "sacred and undeniable."[271] God granted people rights and worth that the government could neither bestow nor withhold. "The God who granted us life, gave us liberty at the same time; the hand of force may destroy, but cannot disjoin them," Jefferson declared.[272] God placed within humans a hunger for freedom and equal rights.[273] In addition, God granted people the right to rule themselves by choosing their form of government.[274] "Can the liberties of a nation be thought secure," he asked in Notes on Virginia, "when we have removed their only firm basis, a conviction in the minds of the people that these liberties are the gift of God? That they are not violated but with his wrath?"[275] Because these rights were decreed, bequeathed, and authenticated by nature's God and built into the very structure of the universe, no government could abolish them. Because upright behavior was essential to social well-being, the Virginian argued, the Creator had impressed moral precepts "so indelibly on our hearts that they shall not be effaced by the subtleties of our brain."[276] Because Christian ethics were the "most advanced...morals governing human relations," they were the best suited to man's social nature and to the best form of government—a republic.[277]

Rejecting Lockean liberalism's conception of human beings as independent and isolated, Jefferson, following Aristotle, saw people as innately social and political. Humans were social by nature because they possessed an innate moral sense consisting of "three distinct but interrelated qualities": a capacity for moral choices, sympathy for others, and a natural sense of justice. This final quality made social life possible and beneficial and individual happiness attainable.[278] A "wise Creator must have seen" an inherent desire for justice as "necessary in an animal destined to live in society."[279] Jefferson argued that the state must foster citizens' inherent desire to live communally by enabling them to participate in community life and governance and by providing the requisite political, educational, and economic resources. An ethical system, best embodied by Christianity, that promoted social cooperation and harmony would help achieve this end.[280] "Our Maker has given" every person a conscience, Jefferson proclaimed, as a "faithful internal Monitor."[281] Teachers, ministers, and politicians must help individuals develop their moral capacity.[282] The government could do so by creating a social environment that encouraged people to act morally and live harmoniously together.[283]

Their differing understanding of human nature helped shape the contrasting political approaches of Federalists and Republicans. Federalists contended that people, "while capable of noble and even altruistic behavior, could never entirely escape" the influence of their "inborn baser passions," especially the love of power and money. Jeffersonian Republicans countered that people had "virtually boundless capacity" to become good or evil, depending on their circumstances. Thus Federalists sought to check and harness people's evil drives to promote the general good, whereas Republicans strove to reduce the power and size of government and to eliminate as many social evils as possible.[284]

Jefferson insisted that nations, like individuals, must fulfill moral duties and maintain a good character.[285] "I have but one system of ethics for men as for nations," he declared.[286] "Moral duties are [as] obligatory on nations as on individuals....It is strangely absurd to suppose that a million human beings, collected together, are not under the same moral laws which bind each of them separately."[287] Jefferson insisted that justice was "the fundamental law of society." Individuals' God-given sense of right and wrong was the foundation for both personal and public morality.[288] "My principle is to do whatever is right," Jefferson declared, "and leave consequences to Him who has the disposal of them."[289]

When war erupted between England and France in 1803, Jefferson strove to keep the United States out of the conflict and preserve its neutrality.

"While we regret the miseries" of this war, "let us bow with gratitude to that kind Providence which...guarded us from hastily entering into the san- guinary contest," he told Congress. In June 1807, a British ship attacked the USS *Chesapeake* off the coast of Virginia. After forcing it to surrender, the British seized four sailors and claimed that they were deserters from their navy. This act, which killed three and wounded eighteen American sailors, impugned American honor, and violated its sovereignty, enraged the nation. Protesting that combat caused millions of deaths, immense human suffering, great physical destruction, and loss of belief in moral principles, Jefferson resisted the clamor for war. He repeatedly thanked God for keeping the United States at peace.[290] The president proposed instead, and Congress passed in December, the Embargo Act, which prohibited ships from leaving American ports to trade with other nations. By withholding its commerce, the United States sought to force belligerent nations into treating it justly and to show that commercial coercion was more effective than war. British im- pressments of American sailors and British and French interference with American trade, Jefferson declared, had "arbitrarily wrested" the ocean from the United States. "Superior force" had trampled on "maxims consecrated by time, by usage, and by an universal sense of right." The United States would not trade with the belligerents, the president proclaimed, until it could be done under a "sense of moral obligations which constitute a law for nations as well as individuals."[291] Jefferson believed that the embargo incarnated the principles of Christian morality and the spirit of the Enlightenment: benev- olence, peace, reason, law, and free trade.[292]

The Embargo Act did not produce the results Jefferson hoped it would, was repealed in March 1809, and caused him more pain than any other event in his long political career. Some scholars claim the embargo devastated the American economy and simply postponed war for five years.[293] Affecting America more than Europe, it put 30,000 seamen out of work, bankrupted many merchants, filled jails with debtors, and crippled countless farmers. Other historians counter that the embargo rested on sound principles, stimulated domestic manufacturing, and kept the United States out of war.[294] Although Jefferson's peaceful alternative was prompted by his principles, practical factors also played a role. His campaign pledges to eliminate internal taxation and reduce the national debt had required him to slash the size of the nation's armed forces. Jefferson viewed the types of compromise that might have eased or even ended conflict with Great Britain as betraying both American interests and international law. Moreover, his belief that the United States' well-being was essential to the spread of liberty made compromise in some situations impossible.[295] The Virginian believed that his empire of liberty would spread throughout the world "by the sheer majesty of ideas and ideals." America's "great republican experiment would be an example and a beacon" to the rest of humanity.[296] Its failure "would decide forever the destinies of mankind" and support "the political heresy that man is incapable of self-government."[297]

Jefferson and Character

As a member of the Virginia gentry, Jefferson adopted its code of conduct, which "synthesized classical Greek and Christian ethics" and emphasized character and courtesy, and he was widely hailed as "the consummate gentleman."[298] Like the Puritans, he praised industry, integrity, temperance, and courage. Although persistently striving to provide an "example of habitual right choice," Jefferson at times was deceitful, duplicitous, and dishonest.[299] His character was assaulted more than any other American's during the early years of the republic.[300] In the early 1800s, his opponents vilified him as "mad Tom," a frenzied radical, an ineffectual philosopher, and an infidel. Jefferson detested the vileness, the personal abuse, and the intrigue that surrounded the presidential office even more than Washington did.[301]

As with his fellow Virginian, the two major attacks on Jefferson's character focused on his alleged romantic and sexual relationships with women and his ownership of slaves. His enemies charged that Jefferson engaged in affairs with two married women, Elizabeth Walker and Maria Cosway, and kept a black mistress, Sally Hemings. At the age of twenty-five, the unmarried Jefferson made unsolicited advances to the wife of a close friend and neighbor, John Walker. By almost all accounts, nothing happened between them. Only after public allegations were made in 1802 did Jefferson confess, without offering any details, that as a young man he had inappropriately "offered love to a handsome lady" and publicly apologized to her husband.[302] In 1786, Jefferson, by then a widower, and Cosway, the beautiful, charming, twenty-seven-year-old Anglo-Italian wife of British painter Richard Cosway, spent six weeks visiting art galleries, exploring classical ruins, and strolling through Paris. Most historians view their relationship as "a mild flirtation" or infatuation that never moved beyond a romantic interlude.[303]

In September 1802, James Callender published an article in the Richmond *Recorder* claiming that "it is well known" that Jefferson had for many years kept his slave Sally Hemings as a concubine. The features of her eldest son Tom bore "a striking . . . resemblance to those of the President himself."[304] Having failed to discredit Jefferson with their allegations of atheism, cowardice during the American Revolution, financial dishonesty, and Jacobinism, Federalist editors welcomed Callender's story. While admitting they did not know if his charges were true, they repeatedly rehashed them, referring to Hemings as "Black Sal," the "African Venus," and the "mahogoney [*sic*] colored charmer."[305]

Callender had previously done much to malign Jefferson's opponents, including John Adams, with the Virginian's approval and financial support, but he became disgruntled when the president refused to appoint him as Richmond's postmaster. When Callender publicized this fact, Jefferson deprecated him as "a lying renegade from Republicanism" and released statements denying he had paid Callender for his attacks on Federalists. Callender, however, had saved Jefferson's incriminating letters, which he distributed to the Federalist press, catching the president in a blatant lie.[306] This, in turn, "enhanced the credibility of Callender's other charges" about Jefferson's more titillating sexual escapades with Hemings.[307]

Three factors gave Callender's charges a measure of plausibility. First, in 1797, he had exposed the adulterous relationship between Alexander Hamilton and Maria Reynolds. Second, Hemings had several children who obviously had a white father, and some of them resembled Jefferson. Third, Callender correctly accused Jefferson of making the unsolicited advances toward Elizabeth Walker discussed earlier.

Those who believe Jefferson fathered Hemings's children point to other facts. The planter was at Monticello nine months before the birth of each of Hemings's children. Unlike the other slaves born at Monticello, Hemings's children all were given names that were closely linked to the Jefferson family. Jefferson freed the four Hemings children who lived to be adults (but only three or four of his other slaves). Although Sally left no written accounts, her son Madison claimed in an 1873 interview that his mother had told him that Jefferson was the father of Eston, two other siblings, and himself.[308] Jefferson never admitted having a sexual relationship with Hemings, but he never publicly denied it.[309]

A 1998 article in *Nature* further fanned the flames of controversy by reporting on DNA evidence revealing that Jefferson or another male relative, such as his younger brother Randolph (1755–1815), could have been Eston's father. A research committee assembled by the Thomas Jefferson Foundation concluded in 2000 that the DNA results, coupled with written and oral historical accounts and statistical data, indicated a high probability that Jefferson was the father of Eston and perhaps of all six of Hemings's children.[310] After analyzing the same data, a committee of thirteen scholars commissioned by the Thomas Jefferson Heritage Foundation contended that it was much more likely that Randolph fathered her children than that the third president did.[311] Moreover, as Willard Randall argues, there were at the time twenty-five Jefferson males living within twenty miles of Monticello who had the same Y chromosome. Twenty-three of them were younger than Jefferson, who was sixty-five when Eston was conceived.[312]

Writing much earlier, Douglass Adair offered a different perspective. He emphasized that Jefferson persistently refused to sue his detractors for libel or issue statements denying their worst charges.[313] In an 1805 letter, Jefferson admitted his youthful indiscretion with Elizabeth Walker but claimed that Callender's other allegations against him were not "founded on truth."[314]

Moreover, Adair argued, Jefferson did not respond to these charges and gave the Hemings children preferential treatment because his father-in-law, John Wayles, was Sally's father.[315] In addition, two witnesses—Jefferson's grandson, Thomas Jefferson Randolph, and Edmund Bacon, Monticello's overseer from 1806 to 1822—reported that Jefferson's nephew Peter Carr had a long-term sexual relationship with Sally and fathered her children. Adair also contended that Hemings's claim that Jefferson was the father of her children is not convincing. She "falsified the date of her first pregnancy to buttress the story she told her children that she became Jefferson's mistress in France." Her story, Adair maintained, contradicts Jefferson's attitude toward and taste in women and his behavior when in love. The Virginian was attracted to women who had artistic, musical, or literary talents and interests and could provide intellectual as well as physical stimulation. It is inconceivable that Jefferson would reject the "delectable" Maria Cosway "to seduce a markedly immature, semieducated, teen-age virgin" who was his slave, a half-sister to his deceased wife, and the companion of his young daughters.[316]

Taking a similar position, Joseph Ellis argues that these "accusations of sexual promiscuity defy most of the established patterns of Jefferson's emotional life"—not because he was too honorable to do so, "but because his deepest urges were more self-protective and sentimental than sexual."[317] The Federalist allegations of sexual impropriety did little political damage to Jefferson's presidency, but more recently, Jefferson's relationship with Hemings has created considerable controversy.

Like Washington, Jefferson has also frequently been criticized for owning slaves. To many, he seems even more culpable. How could the man who declared that "all men are created equal and endowed by their Creator with certain unalienable rights" own about two hundred other human beings for more than sixty years? Throughout his life, Jefferson displayed a deep ambivalence toward slavery. On the one hand, he often denounced the institution and worked to eradicate it. On the other, he refused to take a leading role in the abolitionist cause and freed only a handful of his own slaves.

Jefferson often deplored slavery and urged Americans to end it. In 1784, the Virginian proposed closing the new western territories to slavery in an ordinance he prepared (a proposal Congress defeated). His *Notes on Virginia*, published in 1785, reiterated Jefferson's contention, made before the Virginia Assembly and the federal Congress, that slavery violated the principles of the American Revolution. He condemned slavery as a "political and moral evil" and "a hideous blot" on the United States, caused by "sordid avarice."[318] Ruminating about the blatant contradiction between human bondage and a republic of citizens with inherent freedoms, Jefferson declared that the liberties Americans enjoyed were "the gift of God" and that violating them was likely to provoke his wrath. "Indeed, I tremble for my country when I reflect that God is just; that his justice cannot sleep forever." Because of "supernatural interference," blacks might someday dominate whites.[319] Although his sharp denunciations of slavery aroused the ire of many members of the Virginia gentry, he continued during the second half of the 1780s to censure slavery as immoral. Moreover, he proposed a program of gradual abolition based on ending the slave trade, prohibiting slavery in the western territories, and freeing all children of slaves born after 1800. In 1788, he argued that nobody was "more willing to encounter every sacrifice" to abolish not only the slave trade but also slavery itself.[320]

Although never ceasing to believe that slavery was an abomination, in the 1790s, Jefferson shifted from crusader to cautious diplomat and waited for public opinion to support emancipation.[321] Deeply disliking controversy and unwilling to lead a battle that provoked strong opposition, Jefferson adopted a much more passive approach.[322] "By temperament, experience, and practice," the statesman preferred to achieve reforms by persuasion, not by agitation.[323] Like many other founders, he feared that controversy over slavery would produce such "mortal hatred and eternal discord" that it would destroy the republic they had built.[324] His belief that abolition was politically infeasible ultimately led Jefferson to bequeath the problem to the next generation.[325] While frequently condemning slavery as incompatible with republican values, Jefferson argued that slaves must be liberated in a gradual and orderly fashion; freeing them suddenly before they were adequately prepared would be like "abandoning children."[326] The planter rejoiced that Congress passed legislation outlawing the slave trade (which he signed in 1807). His standard reply to those who urged him to help end slavery, however, was that if he could have a "decisive effect," he would take action. Until then, Jefferson refused to publicly denounce slavery because it might limit his influence in the future.[327] For much of his life, Jefferson hoped that the unprofitability of slavery would lead to its demise, but the invention of the cotton gin made slaves more valuable and spread the institution throughout the lower South. Eventually concluding that slavery was not likely to die because of market forces and technological advances, Jefferson blurted out the dilemma of American slavery in 1820: "We have the wolf by the ears; and we can neither hold him, not safely let him go. Justice is in one scale, and self-preservation in the other."[328] The battle to eliminate slavery, he told a friend in 1814, "is for the young.... It shall have all my prayers, and these are the only weapons of an old man."[329]

Jefferson carefully arranged his life to limit his direct confrontations with slavery. From his design of Monticello to his use of overseers, Jefferson shielded himself from the harsher realities of slavery and usually was able to keep his thoughts about liberty and human bondage in separate compartments.[330] He rarely sold slaves against their will and typically sold slaves who asked to be reunited with their families. Jefferson viewed himself more as a "paternalistic employer and guardian" than as a slave master.[331] "By all accounts," writes Merrill Peterson, "he was a kind and generous master" who cared about his slaves' health and welfare.[332]

Despite repeatedly criticizing slavery as immoral and supporting schemes for gradual emancipation, Jefferson freed only a few of his own slaves. Several factors explain why. First, on the verge of the Revolution, half of the residents of the English colonies were either slaves or indentured servants and legally unfree, a fact that helped Jefferson rationalize his ownership of slaves, focus on being a humane owner, and protest the violent aspects of the institution.[333] Similarly, Jefferson argued that the status of British soldiers, sailors, and wage laborers differed little from that of American slaves.[334]

Second, Jefferson accepted racist arguments that blacks were deficient in reason and reflection. Whether they were created this way or became so as a result of "time and circumstances," they were physically and mentally inferior to whites.[335] Although ancient slavery was much harsher than American slavery, Jefferson argued, some white Greek and Roman slaves had excelled in art, science, and philosophy, whereas African slaves had not. Blacks had not composed music, painted pictures, made important discoveries, or expressed eloquent thoughts.[336] This produced Jefferson's "famous dilemma": He believed that "slaves should be freed and that they could not live with whites as equals."[337] For most of his life, Jefferson insisted that free blacks must be resettled in Africa or somewhere else. If the two groups tried to live together in America, the "deep rooted prejudices" of whites, the injuries blacks had sustained, their bitter memories of slavery, "new provocations," and "the real distinctions of nature" would make whites and blacks bitter rivals and probably lead one race to exterminate the other.[338] Third, Jefferson's financial position prevented him from freeing his slaves. By 1790, he recognized how deeply in debt he was and how much he depended on the work and financial value of his slaves.[339]

Although Jefferson's position on slavery as a younger man was progressive, his tortured approach as a mature man displays "self-serving paralysis and questionable integrity." Liberating his slaves was a lower priority than ensuring the survival of "the ideal republic for which he had risked his life and fortune" or maintaining his personal lifestyle.[340] Shortly after Jefferson died, all of his remaining possessions, including his slaves, were auctioned off to pay his massive debts.[341] Unlike Washington, he failed to free them. Some argue that celebrating Jefferson as the father of freedom is wrong and even sickening, given his blatant racism, halfhearted attempts to abolish slavery, and comfortable lifestyle made possible by slave labor.[342] Other historians are less harsh: Jefferson's position was inconsistent and deplorable, but it is understandable, given his personal financial problems and his fears that debates over slavery would tear the nation apart.

A Final Assessment

The founders of other nations have typically been mythical figures like Romulus and Remus or King Arthur, shrouded in the mist of a distant past. America's, by contrast, were flesh-and-blood men who struggled to embody the traits Jefferson labeled the "natural aristocracy": compassion, conviviality, civility, virtue, and public service.[343] Although he had many faults, the versatile Virginian incarnated these qualities as well as any American. As early as 1782, a French admirer noted that Jefferson, without ever having left America, had become "a musician, draftsman, astronomer, natural philosopher, jurist, and a statesman."[344] To this list could be added a gentleman farmer, an important inventor, an inquisitive scholar, a gifted writer, a skilled diplomat, and a successful politician.

Jefferson's achievements are as monumental as his intellect. His far-reaching political and ideological impact has led historians to term the first two decades of the nineteenth century the age of Jefferson. Many praise the sage of Monticello for powerfully promoting provocative principles, most notably democracy and intellectual and religious freedom. Since his death in 1826, very divergent political movements and many opposing causes have claimed his mantle.[345] One of Jefferson's greatest legacies is his staunch defense of religious freedom. Even Leonard Levy, who has exposed Jefferson's "dark side" on numerous civil liberties matters, praises his record on religious liberty.[346] With the help of Washington and Madison, Jefferson constructed such a solid foundation for religious liberty that political discord, civil war, economic recessions, and "unprecedented religious fecundity" could not topple it.[347]

In directing that the words "author of the Declaration of Independence and of the Virginia Statute for Religious Freedom, and father of the University of Virginia" be placed on his tombstone as the achievements "by which I most wish to be remembered," Jefferson hoped that future generations would view him as a spokesperson for revolutionary ideas.[348] More than any other founder, Jefferson expected the United States to export democracy to the world.[349] However, while desiring to establish an "empire of liberty" at home, Jefferson excluded some groups, most notably blacks, Native Americans, and women, from full participation.[350] Moreover, Jefferson's actions contradicted much of what he wrote. Levy argues that the Virginian's rhetoric about freedom often conflicted with his political policies. As president, he sometimes set aside his idealistic democratic principles to make pragmatic decisions. He championed limited government but expanded the powers of the federal government and doubled the size of country.[351] Jefferson opposed a permanent standing army but used a new fighting force—the U.S. Marines—to battle the Barbary pirates. He wanted to reform American religion, yet he confined his views to private letters.

Biographer Dumas Malone labels Jefferson's faith "the religion of a reasonable man." Unitarian minister Henry Wilder Foote contends that no other president has equaled Jefferson's "knowledge of and admiration for the teachings of Jesus."[352] Charles Sanford argues that "Jefferson's faith in God and the moral purposes" of life made him a courageous leader, gave him enduring meaning, and helped him deal with defeats.[353] The conclusion of his great-grandson rings true: Jefferson did not believe in miracles, the divinity of Christ, or the doctrine of the atonement, "but he was a firm believer in Divine Providence, in the efficacy of prayer, [and] in a future state of rewards and punishments."[354] While rejecting many orthodox Christian doctrines, Jefferson had a strong faith in God as the creator of the universe and the director of human affairs.

Mark Noll argues that the "great religious outcry against Jefferson" in the election of 1800 was ironic because he was "among the most moral and upright of Presidents," set a high ethical standard for his administration, and pursued policies that in some key areas "comported well with basic Christian values." Noll also suggests that Jefferson's policies may have adhered to biblical norms more than did those of the Federalists, whom most evangelical Presbyterians and Congregationalists supported. The Virginian scrupulously monitored federal funds, dispensed patronage with great probity, limited the size and scope of the government, worked to ensure freedom of religious expression for all Americans, and labored vigorously to keep the United States out of war with Britain and France.[355]

The principal author of the Declaration of Independence was invited to speak at a ceremony in Washington, D.C., on July 4, 1826, to commemorate the fiftieth anniversary of its signing. Because his faltering health prevented him from traveling, Jefferson sent a speech in which he rejoiced that the American commitment to freedom, democracy, and knowledge was spreading throughout the world.[356] As a statesman, diplomat, and author, Jefferson played a significant role in this development. While Americans celebrated this jubilee with rallies, picnics, and addresses, the nation's second and third presidents quietly died at Braintree and Monticello, respectively. Noting this remarkable fact, President John Quincy Adams proclaimed that "the time, the manner, [and] the coincidence" of the death of his father and Jefferson were "visible and palpable marks of Divine favor."[357] The "hand that penned the ever-memorable Declaration and the voice that sustained it in debate . . . were by one summons, at the distance of 700 miles from each other, called before the Judge of All to account for their deeds done upon earth. They departed cheered by the benedictions of their country, to whom they left . . . the memory of their bright example."[358] This amazing event, Adams declared, certified that the founding of the republic was "Heaven directed" and demonstrated once again that God watched over America.[359] Thousands of other Americans reached the same conclusion: The God who had chosen the United States to model liberty and self-government for the world, and had so richly blessed its residents, had called Adams and Jefferson home on the golden anniversary of American independence to assure the present generation that they could continue what the founders began. The simultaneous glorious departure of these patriarchs and correspondents helped renew Americans' faith in their providential selection and their republican experiment. To the editor of the Richmond *Constitutional Whig*, Jefferson's death on the nation's fiftieth birthday signified God's approval of his life and work: "It hallows the Declaration of Independence as the Word of God, and is the bow in the Heavens, that promises its principles shall be eternal, and their dissemination universal over the Earth."[360] Much maligned as an infidel during his life, Jefferson ironically became, in death, a symbol of God's benediction.[361]

CHAPTER THREE

Abraham Lincoln:
Saving the Last Best Hope of Earth

I now leave, not knowing when, or whether ever, I may return, with a task before me greater than that which rested upon Washington. Without the assistance of that Divine Being who attended him, I cannot succeed. With that assistance, I cannot fail.

Farewell Address at Springfield, Illinois, Feb. 11, 1861

I shall be most happy indeed if I shall be an humble instrument in the hands of the Almighty, and of this his almost chosen people....

to New Jersey legislators, Feb. 21, 1861

In giving freedom to the slave, we assure freedom to the free.... We shall nobly save, or meanly lose, the last hope of earth.

Annual Message to Congress, Dec. 1, 1862

[A]mid the greatest difficulties of my Administration, when I could not see any other resort, I would place my whole reliance in God, knowing that all would go well, and that He would decide for the right.

To the Baltimore Presbyterian Synod, Oct. 24, 1863

LIKE GEORGE WASHINGTON'S, Lincoln's faith has been closely scrutinized, hotly debated, and often misunderstood. Both men attributed their success in war to divine providence, proclaimed days of public thanksgiving and prayer as president, rarely mentioned Jesus, and were intensely private about their personal beliefs. Lincoln was never baptized, never received Communion, and never joined a church, but he had a thorough knowledge of the Bible, "plumbed depths of spirituality never touched by Washington," and peppered his speeches with biblical references and allusions.[1] Many investigators conclude that in his later years, Lincoln had a profound sense of God's presence, accepted many central scriptural tenets, and valiantly strove to follow Christian ethics.[2] Lincoln cited the Scriptures and discussed theologically significant questions in his addresses more than the avowedly Christian statesmen of the late-nineteenth and early-twentieth centuries, most notably British Prime Minister William Gladstone, Dutch Prime Minister Abraham Kuyper, and President Woodrow Wilson.[3] He has been labeled "a man of more intense religiosity" than any other American president, a "biblical prophet," the "theologian of American anguish," and a "witness to God."[4] Intrigued by "the anomaly of an unbaptized saint in the White House," scholars and religious authors have written more about Lincoln's faith than about that of any other president.[5] He has also undoubtedly been the subject of more sermons than any other chief executive.[6]

Lincoln came from a poor and humble background in the American backwoods. He lacked family pedigree, formal education, and social prominence. Nevertheless, as president, he successfully guided the nation through its most harrowing experience, saved the Union, freed the slaves, and analyzed political issues, historical events, and God's providence in profound addresses that will forever live in the nation's history. Lincoln urged Americans to confess their sins, mend their ways, practice charity, and forsake revenge. Struck down by an assassin's gunshot, he has been revered as a martyr who died so that his people might live in freedom and harmony. Many scholars consider Lincoln the nation's best president, and no person occupies a higher place in the American pantheon than the near-saint from Illinois.[7]

What William Barton wrote in his 1920 book, *The Soul of Abraham Lincoln,* is still true today: No other aspect of Lincoln's life "has evoked more interest than that of his religious faith and experience," and the perspectives investigators have offered are "hopelessly contradictory."[8] Lincoln's mythic stature has made his religious views prone to apocryphal stories, prejudiced pleading, "pious oversimplification and partisan exploitation."[9] Some friends and associates claimed he remained all his life an unbeliever who attended church and employed religious language to win voters, gain support for policies, and convince Americans to trust him. Others, who knew the sixteenth president equally well, contended that he became an orthodox Christian who regularly read the Bible, prayed habitually, and frequently used scriptural passages and illustrations to express his personal convictions.

Unraveling what Lincoln truly believed is challenging for two reasons. First, Lincoln's religious views, like those of Washington, Jefferson, and John Quincy Adams, were complex and intensely personal. To him, religion was a private matter between an individual and God.[10] Lincoln's son Robert and his campaign manager, David Davis, insisted that he rarely discussed his own faith. Unlike many other statesmen, he did not keep a diary or pen an autobiography, and he was reticent to share his deepest beliefs in private letters. Second, as with Washington, much mythology confounds the historical record. To promote themselves, numerous ministers falsely claimed to have met with Lincoln, and others who actually did put improbable words into his mouth. Historical facts must be separated from pious tales and unlikely legends.[11] Thanks to the painstaking work of scholars, this task has become easier, but many perplexing questions remain about Lincoln's religious convictions.[12] Assessments of his faith depend largely on which sources scholars accept as true.

Although Protestant evangelical impulses were "fragmented, indecisive, and inchoate" during the Revolutionary and early national periods, by the 1840s, they dominated the intellectual and cultural landscape and were central to the conception of America as a chosen nation.[13] Jefferson's 1822 prediction that all young men would soon become Unitarians proved false, as Trinitarian Christian denominations flourished. The number of their congregations quadrupled between 1820 and 1860, and they created a vast empire of benevolent organizations to reform American society. Serving as president during a period in American history when Christian values, language, and ethos had arguably their greatest impact, Lincoln successfully appealed to a biblical frame of reference, moral commitments, and a sense of divine mission that many Americans shared. As chief executive, he compellingly articulated "the synthesis of evangelicalism, republicanism, and common sense" that had become the nation's "most powerful value system."[14] More than any other nineteenth-century president, he became known for seeking to base public policies on scriptural principles and as a "Christian" chief executive.[15]

Moreover, Lincoln labored valiantly to discover the meaning of the Civil War and played a pivotal role in the development of American civil religion, especially the prophetic version. After his death, Lincoln became the "second great hero" of the nation's civil faith. Popular prints portrayed Washington receiving Lincoln into heaven with open arms. While Washington was the "saintly father figure and the American Moses," Lincoln was "the Christ figure and the first great martyr." Following his assassination, grieving Victorians elevated the often harshly criticized president to sainthood. Lincoln bore "the moral burdens of a blundering and sinful people," suffered vicariously for them, proclaimed cherished Christian virtues and values, and sacrificed his life for the causes he loved: the Union and freedom.[16] Episcopal Divinity School professor William Wolf hails Lincoln as one of America's greatest theologians because he believed God was intimately involved in the affairs of nations. This "later-day prophet" grasped "the complexity of historical processes" and recognized people's mixed motives and "incurable self-righteousness." Historian Mark Noll insists that "by transcending the moment," Lincoln's faith "preserved both political effect and spiritual power."[17]

Americans continue to debate Lincoln's religious and political convictions today because of his immense value in the nation's culture wars.[18] Because he is the icon "for the pivotal event in American history," "enlisting him on a particular side of the modern political, moral, economic, or religious" argument provides significant advantages.[19] In some circles, the question "What would Lincoln do?" is more important than the query "What would Jesus do?"

The Faith of Abraham Lincoln

While living in Kentucky, Lincoln's parents belonged to the Little Mount Separatist Baptist Church and participated in the revivals that swept the state during the early years of the Second Great Awakening. Like Washington and Jefferson, Lincoln lost a parent as an adolescent; his mother died when he was nine.[20] During his formative years, his mother sang hymns and recited Bible verses as she did her household chores, taught him to read the Bible, and told him many of its principal stories.[21] As a child, Lincoln read the Scriptures and memorized many verses. Testifying to her tremendous impact, Lincoln wrote that "all that I am or ever hope to be, I owe to my angel mother."[22] While living in Spencer County, Indiana, Lincoln's father and second wife, Sarah Bush Lincoln (who married in 1819), joined the Little Pigeon Creek Baptist Church, a "hard-shell" Calvinist congregation in which Lincoln's father played a leadership role.[23] Separatist Calvinist Baptists argued that preaching would benefit only those God had elected to salvation and refused to support social reform movements, mission organizations, Christian colleges, or seminaries.[24] As a teenager, Lincoln sometimes attended church and listened attentively, but, according to his stepmother, he "had no particular religion."[25] He also loved to mimic the hellfire and brimstone preachers he heard.[26] Although Lincoln did not accept many of the specific beliefs that his parents and church espoused, he grew up in an environment where biblical teaching, morality, and predestinarianism predominated.[27]

While living in New Salem, Illinois, in the early 1830s, Lincoln heard numerous sermons at church and campground meetings. However, he also met with a group of freethinkers who denounced many doctrines and practices of the frontier sects, strove to reconcile the Bible with new scientific perspectives, and avidly read skeptics who reduced religion to morality. During these years, Lincoln displayed a fondness for Robert Burns's poem "Holy Willie's Prayer," which satirizes a smug Scottish Presbyterian who excuses his own sins but vehemently attacks those of the nonelect.[28]

After moving to Springfield in 1837, Lincoln became more reluctant to share his religious opinions. He wrote in 1841 that he intended to read the Bible regularly and called it the "best cure for the 'Blues' could one but take it according to the truth."[29] While he was dating Mary Todd, Lincoln sometimes accompanied her to the Episcopal church she regularly attended in Springfield. In 1843, Lincoln lost a Whig nomination for the Illinois legislature in part because of accusations he was an infidel.[30] Opponents contended, he complained, that "no Christian ought to go for me, because I belonged to no church [and] was suspected of being a deist."[31] When he faced the well-known flamboyant Methodist evangelist Peter Cartwright in an 1846 contest for the U.S. Congress, a whispering campaign repeated the charge that Lincoln was "an open scoffer at Christianity." Three days before the election, Lincoln issued a handbill to refute these rumors: "That I am not a member of any Christian Church is true; but I have never denied the truth of Scriptures; and I have never spoken with intentional disrespect for religion in general, or any denominations of Christians in particular." Lincoln added that he would not vote for a candidate who was "an open enemy of, and scoffer at, religion."[32] Although Lincoln denied being hostile to Christianity, he did not affirm any specific doctrines or even profess to be a Christian.[33]

Many of Lincoln's friends during his early years in Springfield, most notably Joshua Speed, James Matheny, and John Stuart, described him as a religious doubter. Speed declared, "When I knew him in early life, he was a skeptic."[34] Matheny, a Springfield court clerk, reported that Lincoln often challenged the veracity of various biblical passages: "Sometimes Lincoln bordered on absolute Atheism." Stuart claimed that Lincoln frequently "denied that Jesus was the Christ of God."[35] As rumors of his infidelity and deism spread in Springfield, "Christian Whigs hated to vote for Lincoln."[36]

Some historians maintain that Lincoln's faith became much more important to him during the 1850s, especially as a result of the death of his son Eddie and his relationship with James Smith, the pastor of the First Presbyterian Church in Springfield from 1849 to 1856. Nevertheless, in 1860, the best spin his friends could put on Lincoln's religion was to describe him as "a regular attendant upon religious worship" and "a pewholder and liberal supporter of the Presbyterian Church."[37] More scholars contend that Lincoln's faith became deeper during his presidency as he dealt with personal tragedy—the loss of close friends and his eleven-year-old son, Willie, and the emotional breakdown of his wife—and the crisis of secession and civil war. These events strengthened his relationship with God, leading him to pray frequently and to analyze God's direction of history.[38] The judgment of these historians rests in part on the claim of numerous of Lincoln's friends and political associates that his faith grew stronger as he dealt with the burdens of the presidency. Fellow Illinois attorney Leonard Swett asserted that during these years his reverence for God's "justice and overruling power" intensified.[39] Newspaper reporter Noah Brooks contended that Lincoln underwent "a process of crystallization" in his faith and prayed daily.[40] Joshua Speed, his closest friend, insisted that as president, Lincoln "sought to make the Bible a preceptor to his faith and a guide for his conduct."[41]

Assessing Lincoln's worldview; church participation; views of the Bible; beliefs about God, Christ, and Providence; and perspective on prayer, sin, salvation, life after death, and morality provides insight into his religious convictions. Lincoln's wide reading and life experience, biographer Allen Guelzo argues, supplied "three large-scale contexts" that shaped his worldview. One was the rigid Baptist Calvinism to which his parents and church attendance in Kentucky and Indiana exposed him. Moreover, after 1850, Lincoln usually worshiped in Old School Presbyterian churches, which emphasized Calvinist theology and opposed revivals and the interdenominational reform societies of the Second Great Awakening, and he had close relationships with his pastors in Springfield and Washington. Because of his love of rationality and Whig politics, Lincoln preferred the more cerebral Old School Presbyterian theology of Charles Hodge's Princeton Seminary to the New School's reformist, revivalist faith.[42] Although Lincoln rejected Calvinism as a doctrinal system because he could not make "ultimate intellectual sense of it," he accepted its tenet that God had predestined events. The book that probably most helped him reaffirm his belief in Christianity was James Smith's *The Christian's Defense*.[43] Smith used evidence from history and the natural sciences to make a logical case for the existence of God, the reliability of the Bible, and the truth of Christianity, an approach that appealed to Lincoln's preference for rational argument over religious affections. Lincoln never wrote anything about this book, but Smith claimed in an 1867 letter that he made "a most patient, impartial and searching investigation" of the arguments of both Christians and non-Christians and concluded that opponents could not answer "the argument in favor of the [Bible's] divine authority and inspiration."[44] Lincoln's brother-in-law Ninian W. Edwards and Thomas Lewis, an elder in the First Presbyterian Church in Springfield, insisted that Lincoln had told them that reading Smith's "evidences of Christianity," listening to his sermons, and discussing disputed issues with the minister had convinced him "of the truth of the Christian religion."[45]

A second intellectual context for Lincoln's worldview was the Lockean Enlightenment, which contributed to his skepticism about religion, especially in the 1830s and 1840s, his suspicion of Rousseauian passions, and his conviction that individual rights were superior to community conventions.[46] The third impact on Lincoln's thinking was classical liberalism and Jeremy Bentham's utilitarianism, which he thought provided a "rational—and thoroughly deterministic—cause for human conduct in self-interest." He came to believe, however, that liberalism could not unshackle individuals and help them improve their lives "without appealing to a set of ethical, even theological principles," outside and above this philosophy.[47]

On one hand, Lincoln was very logical and analytical. He loved the clarity of mathematics and often used propositions to bolster his arguments. In 1838, Lincoln declared, "Reason, cold, calculating, unimpassioned reason, must furnish all the materials for our future support and defense. Let those [materials] be molded into *general intelligence*, [sound] *morality* and ... *a reverence for the constitution and laws....*"[48] Springfield lawyer Charles Zane maintained that his Lincoln "relied upon reason at all times."[49] As Mark Noll argues, Lincoln believed reason could "clarify conundrums, explicate problems, and convince open-minded listeners of the truth."[50] He closed several of his important speeches by insisting that reason could solve the nation's political and social problems.[51] On the other hand, however, Lincoln, like many others who lived on the frontier, was superstitious.[52] His belief that dreams, signs, and portents presaged the future seems to clash with his exaltation of reason, as well as with his criticism of some aspects of the popular religion of his day.[53] Moreover, Lincoln apparently participated in several séances, occasionally consulted mediums, and displayed interest in necromancy.[54] Historians maintain that to please (or protect) his wife, Lincoln attended several séances in Georgetown and one in the White House.[55] Joshua Speed introduced Lincoln to two mediums and "believers in the spirits."[56] Despite his keen interest in dreams, spiritual mediums, and mystical intuitions, David Hein argues, Lincoln did not think they provided any specific otherworldly guidance.[57]

As an adult, Lincoln's church attendance was sporadic until 1850, when his son Eddie died at age three.[58] From then until early 1861, Lincoln apparently worshiped regularly at the First Presbyterian Church in Springfield.[59] During his presidency, the prairie politician rented a pew at New York Avenue Presbyterian Church in Washington and faithfully attended services there. Lincoln may have also periodically gone to the congregation's midweek services, but, if he did, he listened to the Bible readings and prayers while sitting in the pastor's office because he feared his presence in the sanctuary would be disruptive.[60]

Many of his contemporaries faulted Lincoln for never joining a church, and scholars debate his reasons for this decision, especially because doing so would have brought political advantages. Like Jefferson, Lincoln deeply disliked theological disputes and sectarian wrangling.[61] He often complained that Christians focused more on theological hairsplitting and emotional experiences than on upright conduct and good works. Lincoln reputedly told Connecticut Congressman Henry C. Deming:

> I have never united myself to any church because I have found difficulty in giving my assent without mental reservation to the long complicated statements of Christian doctrine which characterize their articles of belief and confessions of faith. When any church will inscribe over its altar as the sole qualification for membership the Savior's condensed statement of the substance of both law and gospel: "Thou shalt love the Lord thy God with all thy heart and with all

thy soul and with all thy mind, and love thy neighbor as thyself," that church I will join with all my heart.[62]

To Lincoln, practicing Christian charity was much more important than affirming specific theological tenets, which often generated conflict and antagonism among Christians. His integrity apparently prevented him from publicly avowing specific doctrines, namely, those of Old School Presbyterianism, whose veracity he questioned.[63] Guelzo argues that Lincoln's feelings of moral inadequacy rather than his intellectual doubts prevented him from joining the church. Lincoln was inhibited by his "sense of being helpless and unworthy in the estimate of the glowering Father who" demanded a perfection he could not attain.[64]

Few American statesmen cited or alluded to the Bible in public addresses as much as Lincoln; among presidents, perhaps only Wilson knew it better than he did. Some scholars argue that the Republican's knowledge of the Bible's content exceeded that of most clergymen of his day.[65] As Carl Sandburg explains, Lincoln "read the Bible closely, knew it from cover to cover," and quoted it in talks to juries, speeches, and letters.[66] As president, Lincoln constantly read the Bible, his private secretary John Nicolay declared, "and had great faith in it."[67] One of his bodyguards claimed that he read one or two chapters from the Bible each morning.[68] His frequent use of biblical texts as rejoinders to political opponents prompted Stephen Douglas to complain in 1858 about Lincoln's "proneness for quoting Scripture." He also cited biblical passages, phrases, and stories to make people laugh, correct others' misquotations or misuses of the Bible, and make political points.[69] Because most of his listeners were familiar with key Bible stories and statements, Lincoln used them to bolster his arguments.[70] Although he was not a Protestant evangelical, his religious rhetoric resonated with many who were.[71]

Lincoln revered the Bible and derived great inspiration and insight from it.[72] In 1864, he declared that the Bible "is the best book God has given to man. All the good from the Savior of the world is communicated in this Book."[73] Lincoln contended that its maxims were "truly applicable to human affairs."[74] David Donald claims that Lincoln sought answers to his questions during the Civil War "in the well-thumbed pages of his Bible."[75] Lincoln's son Robert recalled that "in the later years of his life, he always had a Bible ... very near him," and it comforted him "at all times."[76] In the 1860s, Lincoln used a devotional book entitled *The Believers' Daily Treasure; or, Texts of Scripture Arranged for Every Day in the Year.*[77]

Jefferson was willing to accept only the parts of the Bible that his reason affirmed, and Lincoln long struggled to reconcile scriptural teaching with the dictates of his reason. In 1864, however, Lincoln counseled Joshua Speed to take as much of the Bible "upon reason that you can, and the balance on faith, and you will live and die a better man."[78] His belief that the Bible contained "an immense amount of evidence for its own authenticity" may have led him to provide this advice.[79]

A friend testified that Lincoln believed in "a Creator of all things" who possessed "all power and wisdom."[80] Like Washington and Jefferson, Lincoln used many terms for God, most of which stressed his power and authority rather than his personal presence. His favorite names included Almighty and Merciful Ruler of the Universe, Great Disposer of Events, Divine Providence, God of Right, God of Nations, Great and Merciful Maker, and Omniscient Mind.[81] Lincoln looked to God for moral guidance and wisdom. For him, "God was the final court of appeal" when he was trying to decide moral questions.[82] "I am responsible," Lincoln declared, "to the American people, to the Christian world, to history, and on my final account to God."[83] After being reelected president, he told Noah Brooks, "I should be the veriest shallow and self-conceited blockhead" on earth, "if in the discharge" of presidential duties "I should hope to get along without the wisdom that comes from God."[84]

Like Washington, Lincoln very rarely used Christ's name in his correspondence or addresses, but he frequently quoted his teachings.[85] Lincoln reputedly proclaimed that Christ said more for humanity's benefit in a single parable than the critics of Christianity did in the "heaps of their heartless reasonings." Moreover, his Sermon on the Mount contained more about "justice, righteousness, kindness, and mercy" than all the books of "ignorant doubters from the beginning of human knowledge."[86] Although Lincoln highly valued Jesus' teachings, it is unclear whether he believed in Christ's divinity. William Herndon and a few other Springfield friends claimed that Lincoln never said anything to them that "remotely implied" he had "slightest faith in Jesus as the Son of God and the Saviour of men."[87] Herndon maintained that Lincoln ridiculed the concept of the virgin birth "and did not believe that Jesus was God."[88] Lincoln never explicitly stated that he was a Christian in his speeches, addresses, or letters, but he used the term "Savior" numerous times in his speeches. In his 1858 senatorial campaign, he referred to "the Savior" several times, and in 1864, Lincoln called Jesus "the Saviour of the world."[89] The evidence for Christ's divinity, Lincoln allegedly told Springfield tailor James Keyes, came "in somewhat doubtful Shape." Thus the doctrine that "Christ is God" had to "be taken for granted—for by the test of reason all might become infidels on that subject."[90] According to Illinois superintendent of public education Newton Bateman, Lincoln declared in 1860 that opposition to slavery was right because "Christ teaches it, and Christ is God."[91]

Lincoln was convinced that a higher power controlled human destiny, but for many years, he seemed to be unsure of its actual nature. Repelled by the emotionalism of frontier evangelicalism and by doctrinal disputes among Christian denominations, as a younger man, he accepted what he termed the "Doctrine of Necessity." "No man had a stronger or firmer faith in Providence," explained Herndon, Lincoln's law partner, but this did not prove "that he believed in a personal God." "At its barest," contends Allen Guelzo, "providence was for Lincoln nothing more than the 'necessity' imposed by cause and effect." Nevertheless, even in his thirties, Lincoln sometimes used personal language in discussing Providence. Whatever God "designs he will do for me yet," Lincoln wrote to a friend in 1842. "'Stand still and see the salvation of the Lord' is my text just now."[92]

Although some scholars argue that Lincoln remained his entire life a fatalist who believed that an impersonal force directed history, much evidence indicates that he eventually embraced the Christian doctrine of Providence.[93] Herndon claimed that Lincoln often said, "What is to be will be, and no efforts nor prayers of ours can change, alter, modify, or reverse the decree."[94] Guelzo maintains that during the 1850s, Lincoln accepted a deist view of Providence and thought that natural processes, rather than a personal God, "worked generally to secure harmony and progress in the universe." He used language that accorded with the religious sensibilities of Christians without committing himself to what they believed.[95]

However, if Lincoln's public statements after 1859 expressed his own beliefs rather than simply satisfied the expectations of his listeners, then his belief in God's providential direction of his own life and the United States was strong.[96] He frequently asserted that God directed events to accomplish his purposes.[97] The Republican told well-wishers as he left Springfield, Illinois, to begin his duties as president: "Without the assistance of that Divine Being . . . I cannot succeed. With that assistance I cannot fail. Trusting in Him who can go with me, and remain with you, and be everywhere for good let us confidently hope that all will be well. To His care commending you, as I hope in your prayers you will commend me, I bid you an affectionate farewell."[98] As president, Lincoln frequently took comfort in his belief that God controlled the universe. Having "chosen our course," he told Congress on July 4, 1861, "let us renew our trust in God and go forward without fear."[99] Lincoln told a delegation of Lutherans that he believed God "determines the destinies of nations."[100]

Apparently, personal tragedy and the atrocities and stalemate of civil war helped convince him that God, not simply impersonal forces or laws, directed the universe. His 1862 "Meditation of the Divine Will" shows that these experiences compelled him to confront "the Calvinist God who could not be . . . domesticated into Tom Paine's Almighty Architect," a God who intervened in history and shaped human destinies.[101] Lincoln allegedly told Joseph Gillespie that "he could not avoid believing in predestination," even though it was hard to reconcile "with responsibility for one's acts."[102] Byron Sunderland, pastor of First Presbyterian Church in Washington, claimed that Lincoln stated in 1862 that "I am no fatalist. I believe . . . that men are responsible beings; that God . . . will hold them, to a strict personal account" for their deeds.[103]

More than many professed Christians, Lincoln struggled to determine and follow God's will for his own life and the nation. Believing that God was just and that his plans would prevail, Lincoln strove to discern his will for himself as president and his nation torn by war. Certainly, there is no contending against God's will, Lincoln wrote, "but still there is some difficulty in ascertaining, [and] applying it, to particular cases."[104] Replying to a group of religious leaders from Chicago who urged him in September 1862 to free the nation's slaves, Lincoln explained that clergymen who were "equally certain that they represented the divine will" gave him opposite advice. Was it not more likely that God would reveal his will to him than to others on this issue? Lincoln asserted that "it is my earnest desire to know the will of Providence in this matter. And if I can learn what it is, I will do it." Because these were not "the days of miracles," he did not expect to receive "a direct revelation." Therefore, he "must study the plain physical facts of the case . . . and learn what appears to be wise and right."[105] That same month, Lincoln wrote privately that the "will of God prevails." His purpose in the Civil War might be quite different than that of either the North or the South. God "could have saved or destroyed the Union without a human contest. Yet the contest began." Moreover, "he could give the final victory to either side any day. Yet the contest proceeds."[106] After two more years of death and destruction, Lincoln wrote to a Quaker that the "purposes of the Almighty are perfect and must prevail, though we erring mortals may fail to accurately perceive them in advance. We hoped for a happy termination of this terrible war long before this," he added, "but God knows best and has ruled otherwise. We shall yet acknowledge his wisdom and our own error." Using the best light God provided, Unionists must trust that their labor "still conduces to the great ends he ordains. Surely he intends some great good to follow this mighty convulsion. . . ."[107] "I claim not to have controlled events," Lincoln wrote a Kentucky newspaper editor in 1864, "but confess plainly that events have controlled me. . . . If God now wills the removal of a great wrong, and wills also that we of the North as well as you of the South, shall pay fairly for our complicity in that wrong, impartial history will find therein new cause to attest and revere the justice and goodness of God."[108]

Lincoln believed that in directing history, God used people to accomplish his plans, and he saw himself as God's agent on earth. This motivated him and helped him cope with problems and defeats.[109] Register of the Treasury Lucius E. Chittenden maintained Lincoln told him that God uses "human agencies, and directly intervenes in human affairs, is one of the plainest statements of the Bible. . . . I am satisfied that when the Almighty wants me to do or not do a particular thing, he finds a way of letting me know."[110] While emphasizing that God's actions were often difficult to understand and his purposes frequently clashed with human desires, Lincoln counseled Americans to trust in God's goodness and submit to his will. Calling himself a "humble instrument in the hands of our Heavenly Father," he insisted in 1862 that "we must believe" that

God permitted the war "for some wise purpose of His own, mysterious and unknown to us . . ." and "that He who made the world still governs it."[111]

Unlike the vast majority of statesmen, Lincoln refused to identify God's will with his own cause. Because humans could not fully understand God's purposes, they should not presume that he was on their side. Lincoln was the rare person who could govern during a crisis "without equating his interpretation of the task with the divine wisdom."[112] Repudiating a "God bless America" theology that ignored the nation's sins and culpability, Lincoln urged all Americans to reflect and repent. As Garry Wills emphasizes, "Lincoln mourned for the South, instead of denouncing it" and "mourned for the North, instead of celebrating it." As did many African American Christians, Lincoln emphasized forgiveness and trusted that God was accomplishing his purposes in the midst of people's affliction.[113]

Lincoln strongly valued prayer, primarily as a means of conforming to God's will. Numerous creditable witnesses, including Lincoln's wife, friends, and political associates, all reported that he prayed regularly and devoutly during his years as president. John Nicolay declared, "Mr. Lincoln is a praying man. . . . I have heard him request people to pray for him, which he would never have done had he not believed that prayer is answered."[114] Noah Brooks reported that Lincoln told him, "I have been driven many times upon my knees by the overwhelming conviction that I had nowhere else to go."[115] After the death of his son Willie in early 1862, Lincoln expressed gratitude that Christians across the nation were praying for him. "I need their prayers," he declared.[116] On many other occasions, the president solicited the prayers of visitors or permitted them to pray with him.[117] "I am upheld and sustained by the . . . prayers of God's people," Lincoln wrote to Iowa Quakers in 1863. "Without His favor," he added, "our highest wisdom is but as foolishness and . . . our most strenuous efforts would avail nothing in the shadow of His displeasure."[118] Many friends were impressed with his spirituality, which was deepened by his personal Gethsemane while president. Lincoln, by contrast, confessed, "I have often wished I was a more devout man."[119]

Lincoln did not express a personal need for Christ's atoning sacrifice on the cross, and like John Quincy Adams, he seemed to be unable to accept the Christian concept of salvation. Although he occasionally referred to Jesus as "the Saviour," he never called him "my Savior." Speed maintained that Lincoln "tried hard to be a believer, but his reason could not grasp and solve the great problem of redemption."[120] Some evidence suggests that the prairie politician was a universalist who believed that all individuals would ultimately be saved. Lincoln's tutor in New Salem insisted that he interpreted I Corinthians 15:22—"in Christ shall all be made alive"—to mean that by his atonement Christ saved everyone.[121] According to his longtime friend Isaac Cogdal, "Lincoln did not believe in Hell."[122] In his view, punishment for sin had as "its object, aim, and design . . . the good of the offender; hence it must cease when justice is satisfied."[123] As the supreme Ruler, Lincoln allegedly contended, Christ could not leave any outside the fold.[124] Fellow attorney William Hanna claimed Lincoln told him that he was "a kind of universalist" who never could believe "in Eternal punishment."[125] Because God was good and willed that no one would perish, all would ultimately be saved. Moreover, because God predestined everything and all human actions were foreordained, punishment in the next world would be unfair.[126]

Lincoln also rejected the hard-shell Baptist and Old School Presbyterian belief in human depravity and viewed people as having a mixture of attributes. The Bible taught, and experience confirmed, Lincoln averred, that all people were "desperately selfish."[127] Like most of the Founding Fathers, he contended that people's self-interest strongly shaped their actions. Human beings were sinful and needed to repent and reform their ways.[128] Although individuals were naturally egotistic, they had some sympathy for others and an intrinsic sense of justice.[129] Lincoln insisted that while slavery was "founded in the selfishness of man's nature," opposition to it rested upon "his love of justice."[130] His belief in humans' innate kindness and concern for justice led Lincoln to appeal to the "better angels of our nature" in his First Inaugural Address as a basis for preserving the Union.[131]

Most evangelicals of his day would have been troubled by aspects of Lincoln's theology, especially his views of Christ and the atonement, and by his dabbling in spiritualism, occasional vulgarity, lack of strict Sabbath observance, and frequent attendance at the theater. William Herndon asserted that when speaking to friends, Lincoln was often "indecently vulgar."[132] A journalist maintained that one of Union commander George McClellan's many miscalculations led Lincoln to swear "like a Philistine," but Francis Carpenter, by contrast, reported that he never heard the president use crude language.[133] A political associate claimed that Lincoln sometimes swore "in a moment of vexation" and did not "observe the Sabath [sic] very scrupulously."[134] Although Lincoln did not always use Sundays for worship and rest, as Washington did during the Revolutionary War, Lincoln charged troops to observe the Sabbath in an orderly fashion, which was "the sacred rights of Christian soldiers and sailors." He insisted that this practice deferred to "the best sentiment of a Christian people" and displayed a "due regard for the Divine Will." On Sundays Union forces were to perform only duties that were of "strict necessity" to avoid profaning "the day or the name of the Most High."[135] Although secular Whigs had begun to reform the theater by the 1850s, most evangelicals still complained that its values conflicted with those of biblical religion and that theaters often stimulated raucous, coarse behavior and sometimes even permitted prostitutes to recruit customers in the upper tiers. For these reasons, Christians should not attend the theater.[136]

On the other hand, evangelicals applauded several of Lincoln's other personal habits. Unlike most of his male peers, Lincoln did not smoke, chew tobacco, fistfight, or consume large amounts of alcohol. Close friends testified that Lincoln did not drink, and scholars concur that he was nearly a teetotaler.[137] Although he supported temperance, Lincoln urged advocates to focus on persuading individuals to stop drinking and display compassion for those who struggled with alcohol.[138]

Like evangelicals, Lincoln revered the Scriptures' "perfect moral code." It spoke to people "in all conditions of life" and inculcated "all the duties" they owed their Creator, themselves, and their fellow men.[139] Rejecting moral relativism, Lincoln maintained that without the Bible, people would not "know right from wrong." It contained "all things most desirable for man's welfare, here and hereafter."[140] To Lincoln, the Bible's moral commands were consistent with the dictates of human reason. Indians needed Christian moral training, he told Congress in 1863, to supply them with "elevated and sanctifying influences" and the "hopes and consolation of the Christian faith."[141] Lincoln urged schools to assign "the scriptures and other works... of a religious and moral nature."[142]

Like most of his contemporaries, Lincoln lost many loved ones at young ages. His mother died when he was nine; his older sister died shortly after she married; Ann Rutledge, to whom he was once engaged, died as a young woman; and two of his sons died as children. Although his pastor in Washington, Phineas Gurley, claimed that Lincoln never tired of discussing "the state of the soul after death," his own writings and the reports of friends rarely mention the subject.[143] Richard Carwardine contends that Lincoln's recorded words provide little evidence that "he believed in an afterlife, no matter how often he brooded about death, or how much he wanted" to be reunited "with loved ones beyond the grave."[144] When Joshua Speed's fiancée became very ill in 1842, Lincoln comforted him by writing, "Should she... be destined to an early grave, it is indeed a great consolation to know that she is so well prepared to meet it. Her religion... I will venture you now prize most highly."[145] When his father was near death in 1851, Lincoln urged his stepbrother John D. Johnston to "tell him to remember to call upon, and confide in, our great, and good, and merciful Maker... who will not forget the dying man who puts his trust in Him.... If it be his lot to go now, he will soon have a joyous [meeting] with many loved ones gone before; and where [the rest] of us, through the help of God, hope ere long [to join] them."[146] On the other hand, while president, Lincoln told an elderly woman who said she would meet him in heaven, "I am afraid with all my troubles I shall never get there."[147]

The Battle over Lincoln's Soul

Lincoln's faith has been more vehemently disputed than that of any other president. Contradictory stories abound, many of which are based on hearsay, wishful thinking, and pious imagining. Because those who professed to know what he believed "were scarcely disinterested parties," we must carefully scrutinize their often conflicting judgments.[148] Like Washington, legends about Lincoln's faith are plentiful: He was converted during an 1839 Methodist revival, or after Willie's death, or after the battle of Gettysburg; he was secretly baptized.[149] Shortly after the Union triumphed at Gettysburg, Lincoln reputedly told Willie's nurse, Rebecca Pomeroy: "When I was first inaugurated, I did not love my Saviour." When "God took my son . . . still I did not love him; but when I stood on the battle-field of Gettysburg, I gave my heart to Christ and I can now say I do love the Saviour."[150] Accounts such as these prompted Benjamin Talbot to write to Lincoln in December 1864, "I cannot refrain from expressing to you my joy (& I doubt not the joy of every Christian heart throughout our land), at the statement recently made in the religious press that you have sought and found the Saviour, that you 'do love Jesus.' "[151]

After Lincoln died, the dispute over his faith intensified, and it has continued to the present day. Those closest to Lincoln sharply disagreed about his religious beliefs. To many of his friends, Lincoln was a devout "man of God" whose religious convictions, despite his never joining a church, were largely orthodox. They maintained that his faith became much stronger while he was president and that in later life Lincoln "was a firm believer in the Christian religion."[152] Francis Carpenter argued that "no man had a more abiding sense of his dependence upon God, or faith in the Divine government, and in the power and ultimate triumph of Truth and Right in the world."[153] Noah Brooks contended that Lincoln believed in the "saving knowledge of Christ; he talked always of Christ, his cross, his atonement; he prayed regularly."[154] James Smith declared that Lincoln affirmed "the Divine Authority and Inspiration of the Scriptures."[155]

Other friends and associates countered that the sixteenth president remained a skeptic his whole life and labeled him a "freethinker," an "agnostic," or "an unbeliever."[156] Isaac Cogdal and Jesse Fell insisted he was a deist or a Unitarian. For those who held this position, Lincoln's alleged confession to Newton Bateman in 1860 that "I am not a Christian" remained true all his life.[157]

Lectures, books, and articles in magazines and newspapers moved the debate into the public arena shortly after Lincoln's assassination. In his 1866 biography, newspaper editor Josiah Holland contended that Lincoln was "eminently a Christian President" whose faith grew stronger as the Civil War progressed.[158] The next year, the American Sunday School Union published Z. A. Mudge's *The Forest Boy* to celebrate Lincoln's virtues and devout Christian belief.[159] In an 1873 article in *Scribner's*, James A. Reed, pastor of First Presbyterian Church in Springfield, featured letters from many of Lincoln's friends testifying to his Christian faith. Phineas Gurley wrote that after Lincoln's son Willie died, the president insisted his "heart was changed"; "he loved the Savior," and he intended to "soon make a profession of religion."[160] Similarly, Brooks asserted that Lincoln "believed in the Savior" and was seriously considering joining the church before he died.[161] In subsequent decades, dozens of other ministers, authors, and lecturers depicted Lincoln as "an impeccable Christian gentleman" and a "martyr-saint," and some of them asserted that Lincoln had a conversion experience.[162] Speaking for many, G. Frederick Owen portrayed the sixteenth president as a deeply committed Christian whose heart "yearned for God."[163] Those who view Lincoln as a devout Christian have accentuated his frequent use of Scripture in his addresses and relied on questionable testimonies to validate his theological orthodoxy.

Others claim that Lincoln rejected many fundamental Christian doctrines and sprinkled his speeches with biblical references to achieve political ends. Based on their own experiences, the accounts of some of Lincoln's neighbors and associates, and his failure to publicly profess Christian faith or join a church, several friends, leading agnostic Robert Ingersoll, and numerous freethinkers maintained that he was an unbeliever.[164] In an 1872 biography, Ward Hill Lamon, who practiced law with Lincoln in Illinois, argued that the Republican's lack of faith produced his melancholy.[165] Unitarian minister Jesse Fell claimed that Lincoln's positions on human depravity, Christ's nature, the atonement, biblical infallibility, miracles, future punishments, and many other subjects were "utterly at variance" with orthodox Christianity.[166] In his frequently given public lecture, "The Religion of Abraham Lincoln," and in *Herndon's Lincoln* published in 1889, his former law partner mixed his personal observations with letters from Lincoln's friends and associates to portray the Illinois politician as a religious skeptic.[167] Herndon asserted that Lincoln did not believe that Jesus was God or that the Bible was a divine revelation. If Lincoln truly believed in "the faith of three Gods, Revelation, Inspiration, Miraculous Conception" would he "not have boldly said so?" asked Herndon.[168] The Republican died as he lived: as "a free religionist" and "an infidel."[169] Lincoln used Christian "ideas, language, speech, and forms" because he was the president of a nation of Christians, not because they expressed his personal views.[170] "Let it be written in history and on Mr. Lincoln's tomb," Herndon declared, "'He died an unbeliever.'"[171]

Following the trail blazed by Herndon, others have argued that Lincoln pretended to be orthodox to please a largely Christian populace, but his true convictions were very unconventional. In *Abraham Lincoln: Was He a Christian?* (1893), John E. Remsburg maintained that the clergy conspired to suppress Lincoln's infidelity.[172] Another freethinker claimed that during his presidency, Lincoln wrote to a judge: "My earlier views of the unsoundness of the Christian scheme of salvation and the human origin of the scriptures, have *become clearer* and stronger with advancing years and I see no reason for thinking I *shall ever change them*."[173] Gore Vidal alleges that Lincoln's Christianity was "a superfluous veneer" he "occasionally paraded for political purposes." Hans J. Morgenthau contends that Lincoln's frequent references to biblical persons, events, and texts had little "religious significance." William Lee Miller is not persuaded that Lincoln ever accepted "the central Christian creedal affirmations."[174]

Stewart Winger argues that this debate "has presented a false choice between Lincoln as a conventional nineteenth-century evangelical" and as "a skeptic in the tradition of Thomas Paine." Winger offers a third possibility: "Lincoln's use of religious language reflected a Romantic and poetic understanding of religion." Although usually very skeptical of religious authority, Romantics often "found unorthodox ways to reaffirm surprisingly traditional, Christian descriptions of the human condition." Winger faults historians for generally dismissing the obvious religiosity of Lincoln's speeches and writings "as politically expedient hokum or evidence of a kind of battle fatigue" that "made him more compassionate" "but otherwise mattered very little." The argument that the Republican did not truly believe what he said is not substantiated by the historical record and is counter to his general honesty. Winger contends that "a close contextual reading of Lincoln reveals that his religious words were neither calculated concessions to the supposedly naïve religion of the time nor the personal testimony of an anguished soul." Rather, his religious rhetoric was part of a broad Romantic quest to define America's purpose in a way that was morally and theologically winsome.[175]

Lincoln and Civic Religion

Like Washington, Lincoln has played a major role in American civil religion. Sociologist W. Lloyd Warner insists that Lincoln has loomed over Memorial Day rituals "like some great demigod over the rites of classical antiquity."[176] Most other presidents primarily promoted a "priestly" civil religion, but Lincoln exercised a "prophetic" civil religion, which many scholars have praised.[177] To Sidney Mead, Lincoln was the most insightful "theologian of the religion of the republic"; to Mark Noll, he was "the nation's most profound public theologian"; and to Wolf and Trueblood, he was a prophet of America's destiny.[178] Robert Bellah claims that the sixteenth president embodied "civil religion at its best." Pierard and Linder label Lincoln's public faith "pietistic, pastoral, prophetic, evangelical, and enlightened."[179]

Drawing on his own theological insights and understanding of Scripture, Lincoln concluded, as did Washington, Jefferson, and John Quincy Adams, that the United States had been created to serve God's purposes. He venerated the Bible, the Declaration of Independence, the Constitution, and the nation's laws. Lincoln used masterful prose to express the central convictions of the nation's public religion and devised a civil theology that emphasized America's mission and the importance of religious faith to national unity. He powerfully fused "the dominant evangelical-biblical religion with democratic ideals" and helped create a "civil religion version of the 'city upon a hill.' "[180] In so doing, he continually insisted that Americans were required to obey God's standards and were subject to his judgment. Lincoln persistently refused to identify the aims of the United States with God's will. During the Civil War, a minister expressed his hope that "the Lord was on our side." The president countered that his constant concern and prayer instead was "that I and this Nation should be on the Lord's side."[181] Mark Hatfield, a longtime senator from Oregon, argued that Lincoln never implored "God to give victory to the North." Instead, he urged citizens to confess their sins and seek God's wisdom. He did not try "to sanctify a nation, society, party, system of government, or economics."[182] Lincoln elevated the war to save the Union into a larger struggle to uphold the ideal of freedom for people around the world. The sixteenth president added two great civil religion texts—the Gettysburg Address and his Second Inaugural Address—to the nation's other sacred documents: the Mayflower Compact, John Winthrop's "A Model of Christian Charity," the Declaration of Independence, and the Constitution.[183]

Throughout the Civil War, Lincoln repeatedly called on Northerners to repent and submit to God. Following the Union's disastrous defeat at Bull Run in July 1861, he urged citizens to "confess and deplore their sins," admit their "faults and crimes as a nation and as individuals," ask God for mercy, and humbly accept his reprimands.[184] Because the Bible taught that "nations like individuals are subjected to punishments and chastisements in this world," Lincoln proclaimed in naming April 30, 1863, a National Fast Day, "may we not justly fear that the awful calamity of civil war...may be but a punishment, inflicted on us, for our presumptuous sins" to reform the American people? Americans had received "the choicest bounties of Heaven," but, Lincoln lamented, "we have forgotten God" and "vainly imagined...that all these blessings were produced by some superior wisdom and virtue of our own." If citizens truly repented, then God would pardon their national sins and restore unity and peace to their "divided and suffering Country."[185]

While counseling citizens to repent of their sins, Lincoln overestimated the power of American ideals and "the godly potential of the American people." Although he was convinced that God wanted to use the United States to spread democracy to the world, unlike most other presidents, Lincoln was ambivalent about whether America had a unique relationship with God. He called it a "favored land" and referred to its residents as God's "almost chosen people," but Lincoln frequently condemned its practices and warned that its transgressions were thwarting its ability to accomplish God's purposes.[186] Because Americans fell far short of the noble ideals they professed, he argued, they were suffering God's righteous judgment.[187] To Lincoln, the Civil War was clearly "a divine punishment for the sin of slavery" in which both Northerners and Southerners participated.[188]

Lincoln's Relationship with Religious Constituencies

Several factors enabled Lincoln to enjoy generally positive relationships with Northern religious bodies. His commitment to Protestant values and intense interest in ethics gave him much in common with northern evangelicals. Moreover, the president selected several individuals with strong religious convictions to be part of his administration. Presbyterian minister Edward D. Neil, pastor of a number of prominent congregations and chaplain to a Minnesota regiment during the Civil War, was Lincoln's correspondence secretary. Quaker Isaac Newton served as the first commissioner of the Department of Agriculture. Lincoln's secretary of state, William Seward, an Episcopalian, and his secretary of war, Edwin Stanton, a Presbyterian, were both men of faith. Seward was well known for his argument that a "higher law" than the Constitution, the Bible, condemned slavery.[189] Stanton frequently consulted with religious leaders and asked them to pray that God would guide the Union army.[190]

In addition, Lincoln worked diligently to maintain cordial relationships with religious groups and frequently lauded their work. Lincoln almost daily entertained individual ministers, representatives of Protestant, Catholic, and Jewish bodies, editors of religious journals, leaders of philanthropic organizations, or denominational executives. He listened patiently to their "words of congratulation, counsel, admonition, exhortation, and sometimes reproof."[191] Although Lincoln quickly tired of clergy who sought political appointments or favors or claimed to have a direct pipeline to God, he deeply appreciated visitors who dispensed genuine spiritual advice. Religious groups presented the president with hundreds of resolutions and addresses, usually praising, but sometimes criticizing, his policies. Recognizing that they had substantial power and hoping to develop a "deep reservoir of goodwill," the president dealt "sensitively and respectfully" with religious constituencies. By interacting with ministers, Lincoln sought to discern public opinion and influence those who helped shape it. Through carefully crafted responses to their formal addresses, he strove to gain the clergy's aid.[192] Lincoln declared that he was "profoundly grateful" for the support many religious bodies provided for the war and the Emancipation Proclamation.[193] He thanked them for furnishing chaplains for regiments and hospitals and ministering to the physical and spiritual needs of soldiers and their families. "God bless the Methodist Church—bless all the churches," he proclaimed in 1864, "and blessed be God, Who, in this our great trial, giveth us the churches."[194] That same year, he rejoiced that Christian communities were "zealously giving" "effective and almost unanimous support" to the country.[195]

Prior to Lincoln's issuing the Emancipation Proclamation in September 1862, many Northern ministers criticized his administration for failing to make the freedom of slaves a central aim of the war. They protested that the North was fighting principally to preserve the Union and only secondarily to abolish slavery, whereas God's priorities were precisely the opposite.[196] After the proclamation was issued, hundreds of clergy praised it in their pulpits, and numerous congregations and denominations applauded Lincoln's action.[197] A Wesleyan Methodist conference, for example, congratulated Lincoln on his "noble, humane & Christian proclamation" and hailed the day it took effect "as a glorious Epoch in our Nation's History."[198] A few Southern Christians also extolled the proclamation. Members of the Baptist Church in Beaufort, South Carolina, gave the president "hearty thanks for the Proclamation," declared that they prayed regularly for him, and urged him to continue "to conquer this rebellion."[199]

As the war dragged on, numerous Northern pastors became discouraged and disheartened.[200] Others, like Boston Methodist Gilbert Haven, encouraged their parishioners to persevere. In July 1864, he emphasized the Union's "military and moral victories," especially the issuing of the Emancipation Proclamation, the abolition of the Fugitive Slave Law, and many Northerners' deeper appreciation for their country. If Unionists were "faithful to God," he concluded, "He will give us victory."[201]

Their respect for Lincoln and approval of his policies, coupled with important Union victories shortly before the election, led most Northern pastors to back Lincoln in 1864. Richard Carwardine argues that Lincoln "seized every reasonable opportunity to harness to his chariot of reelection the patriotism of religious bodies." Although some liberal Protestants sharply criticized his administration, the Garrisonian abolitionists and most Northern evangelicals supported Lincoln. Boston pastor and Union chaplain George Hepworth claimed that ministers backed the president because they believed that he was on God's side.[202] Methodist Bishop Matthew Simpson, Congregationalist Henry Ward Beecher, and numerous other clergy actively campaigned for Lincoln.[203] The agents of interdenominational tract societies distributed pro-Lincoln literature. Many religious newspapers endorsed the president, and hundreds of Baptist, Methodist, Presbyterian, and Congregational ministers urged their members to vote the Republican ticket. Lincoln shrewdly proclaimed Sunday, September 10, a day of thanksgiving for Union victories at Mobile and Atlanta and issued a Proclamation of Thanksgiving three weeks before the election to express the Union's hope under "our Heavenly Father" of "an ultimate and happy deliverance" from the war and of the triumph of "the cause of Freedom and Humanity."[204] Carwardine calls the last two months of the campaign "the most complete fusing of religious crusade and political mobilization in America's electoral experience."[205] Although occasional rumors portrayed Lincoln as religiously unorthodox, many Northerners viewed him as an honest, highly principled man whom God had used to bring emancipation. Several clergy, such as William D. Potts, a minister and physician in Newark, New Jersey, denounced the president's policies and urged Americans to elect his Democratic rival, George McClellan.[206] Rejecting such pleas, Protestants voted overwhelmingly for Lincoln.[207]

During the war, Lincoln grappled with several religious issues, most notably how to ensure religious freedom. He struggled to preserve the religious liberty of citizens while preventing disloyalty to the Union and subversion of its purposes. Lincoln exhorted ministers to use their pulpits to proclaim the gospel, not to advance political agendas.[208] In 1862, Union troops barred Samuel B. McPheeters, a Presbyterian minister with Southern sympathies, from preaching in his church in St. Louis. His supporters and opponents both came to see Lincoln. After listening to their conflicting views, Lincoln reportedly responded, "I can't allow my generals to run the churches, and I can't allow . . . ministers to preach rebellion. Go home, preach the gospel, stand by the Union, and don't disturb the Government any more."[209] Lincoln later suspended a military order that expelled McPheeters from the state.[210] When Stanton gave a Northern Methodist bishop the authority to remove disloyal pastors in the Methodist Episcopal Church South in 1864, Lincoln pressured his secretary of war to change his order. "I have never interfered . . . as to who shall or shall not preach in any church," he argued; "nor have I knowingly" allowed "any one else to so interfere by my authority."[211]

During his presidency, Lincoln's closest clergy friends were Phineas D. Gurley, pastor of New York Avenue Presbyterian Church in Washington, and Matthew Simpson. Lincoln began attending Gurley's church soon after taking office. He appreciated his pastor's gifts as a preacher, opposition to slavery and secession, and confidence in the Union. Gurley served as a confidant, friend, and spiritual counselor to Lincoln, and their relationship deepened as a result of Gurley's ministry to Lincoln's family after Lincoln's son Willie contracted typhoid fever and died in February 1862.[212] Gurley claimed they sometimes prayed together, especially before important battles and during various crises. He was at Lincoln's bedside when he died, gave the funeral sermon at the White House service, and traveled with Lincoln's body to Springfield, where the sixteenth president was buried.[213] Lincoln also frequently met with Simpson, asked him for advice, and prized his perspective on political matters. Inspired by Simpson's address at a meeting of the Missionary Society of the Methodist Church in 1863, Lincoln joined the society and agreed to serve on its board of directors.[214] The bishop worked vigorously to help reelect Lincoln and preached the funeral sermon at his burial service at Springfield.[215]

Lincoln also enjoyed cordial relationships with and warm support from other ministers. Henry Ward Beecher, pastor of Plymouth Congregational Church in Brooklyn, campaigned energetically to help elect the Springfield lawyer in 1860.[216] Despite later complaining about Lincoln's leadership, he traveled to England to solicit help for the Union cause, and the president hosted him at the White House.[217] Other leading Congregationalists also praised Lincoln's policies, most notably Theodore Tilton, the editor of the *Independent*; Julian Sturtevant, the president of Illinois College in Jacksonville; and Illinois Congressman Owen Lovejoy.[218] Episcopal Bishop Charles P. McIlvaine met frequently with Lincoln during his presidency and applauded many of his actions.[219]

Methodists and Presbyterians, however, gave Lincoln the most vocal and enthusiastic support. In May 1864, Lincoln declared that the "Methodist Church sends more soldiers to the field, more nurses to the hospital, and more prayers to Heaven, than any" other denomination.[220] Both German Methodists and Primitive Methodists adopted resolutions lauding the work of his administration.[221] Reformed, United, and Old School Presbyterians also sent the president numerous resolutions pledging their sympathy, support, and prayers. The Presbyterian Church USA General Assembly declared in 1863, for example, that "all good citizens" had a "religious duty" "to sustain the government" and to work diligently to suppress "insurrection and rebellion."[222]

Lincoln also enjoyed a friendly relationship with Quakers, especially given their opposition to the Civil War. Lincoln told Rhode Island Quakers in 1862 that although he was directing a great war, he deeply appreciated their "principles of peace."[223] Fearing that the Civil War might produce conflict with other nations, New England Quakers entreated "our much respected President, to use every means which become an enlightened Christian nation, to preserve peace, & prevent the Shedding of blood." If direct negotiation failed, they urged him to submit the issue "to the decision of some disinterested tribunal, instead of resorting to the awful arbitrament of the Sword."[224] Although he did not do this, Quakers believed, Eliza Gurney asserted in 1864, that Lincoln was "conscientiously endeavoring...to discharge the solemn duties of his high and responsible office," not as a "man-pleaser, but 'in simpleness of heart, fearing God.'"[225]

Despite the burdens of the war, Lincoln maintained generally cordial relations with the leaders of the nation's Catholics and Jews. Archbishop John Hughes of the Diocese of New York, a staunch abolitionist, strongly supported Lincoln, and the president asked him to recommend priests to serve as hospital chaplains.[226] The archbishop traveled to Europe in 1862, along with McIlvaine and New York politician Thurlow Weed, to try to gain backing for the Union. Despite Hughes's endorsement of Lincoln, most Catholics voted for McClellan in the 1864 election.[227] Two of Lincoln's most loyal Jewish supporters were rabbis Sabato Morais of Philadelphia and Isaac Wise of Cincinnati.[228] Lincoln named the nation's first Jewish foreign ambassador.[229] Lincoln met several times with groups of rabbis to discuss matters of special concern. After hosting a Jewish delegation who protested against laws limiting army chaplains to ministers of "Christian denominations," Lincoln urged Congress to change the laws, which it did in 1862.[230] The president also countermanded General

Ulysses S. Grant's order that prohibited Jewish merchants from trading with the Army of Tennessee.[231]

Lincoln's Philosophy of Government

Lincoln's religious views helped shape his political thought and actions.[232] He frequently asserted that God created and ruled the world and insisted that political leaders and nations were accountable to him. All people, he declared, should devoutly submit to "the Supreme Authority and just Government of Almighty God," who reigned over "all the affairs of men and of nations." Lincoln urged Americans to "recognize the sublime truth, announced in the Holy Scriptures and proven by all history that those nations only are blessed whose God is the Lord."[233] Because God was Lord of all life, institutions as well as individuals were responsible to him. People must confess their sins "as a nation and as individuals" and obey his norms.[234] Like other Romantic Protestants, Stewart Winger contends, he "accepted much of the evangelical worldview, especially as it related to political morality."[235] "Let us have faith," Lincoln declared, "that right makes might."[236]

Lincoln insisted that the nation's deepest problems did not have political solutions. He argued, for example, that slavery "must be settled on some philosophical basis" that could be sustained by public opinion.[237] Guelzo maintains that for Lincoln this foundation must be "a coherent intellectual scheme of things which transcended mere politics."[238] As a young legislator, Lincoln fought for issues he believed were just, no matter how great the opposition. "The *probability* that we may fall ... *ought not* to deter us from the support of a cause we believe to be just," he announced; "it *shall not* deter me."[239] At the same time, however, Lincoln was a practical politician who valued prudence and realism and differed sharply with the "utopians, perfectionists, moralizers, fanatics and absolutists" of his day.[240] Through moral reasoning, debate, and compromise, Lincoln strove to reconcile "what was morally desirable with what was politically possible."[241] "To an unusual degree," he stated "with great force, clarity, and persistence the moral arguments" that underlay his positions.[242]

Lincoln maintained that God granted human beings rights that could be known through reason, study of the natural world, and his revelation in Scripture. The government must safeguard citizens' liberties, which were "given to mankind directly by the Maker."[243] The Republican argued that the American political system protected civil and religious liberty better than any previous government and labeled ensuring these liberties "the noblest" of causes.[244] "All good people could agree," Lincoln averred, that it was imperative to implore "the gracious favor of the God of Nations" in the struggle to preserve the "precious birthright of civil and religious liberty."[245]

Lincoln repeatedly appealed to the Bible and the Declaration of Independence as the nation's primary sources of moral authority. He especially emphasized the Golden Rule, which to him summarized the Law and the Prophets. To Lincoln, the "ethical core of biblical religion" and "the rational principle of popular government" were identical. Both Christianity and democracy supported the concept of human equality and opposed slavery.[246]

Lincoln sometimes seemed to accord the Declaration the same status as the Scriptures. It expressed the founders' "lofty, wide, and noble understanding of the justice of the Creator to His creatures." These "wise statesmen ... established these great self-evident truths" so that future generations could "renew the battle ... which their fathers began—so that truth, and justice, and mercy, and all the humane and Christian virtues might not be extinguished from the land" and that the "great principles on which the temple of liberty" was built would stand firm.[247] The Declaration's central truth that "all men are created equal," Lincoln insisted, was "the father of all moral principle."[248] Like the Apostles, the Founding Fathers, he maintained, proclaimed God's justice; the humane virtues they espoused mirrored Christian values.[249] Thus Lincoln made the principles of the Declaration, not America itself, "his moral lodestar."[250]

Like Washington, Jefferson, and many other founders, Lincoln believed that God had chosen the United States to model republican government for the rest of the world. America had a divine mandate to extend democracy and "held out a great promise to all people of the world" for "all time to come."[251] Because it was freedom's "last, best hope," it must be preserved.[252] In his address to Congress in December 1862, Lincoln did not encourage "an egotistical national complacency" or a sense of American superiority. Rather, he challenged Americans to "nobly save," not "meanly lose," their God-given opportunity to show the world that democracy could work.[253] At a time when many Europeans predicted that the U.S. experiment in self-government would fail and few other nations had become republics, Lincoln resolved in his Gettysburg Address that "this nation, under God, shall have a new birth of freedom and ... shall not perish from the earth." Like John Quincy Adams, Lincoln believed that the United States must not try to impose its principles on the rest of the world, but rather make them attractive by its example.[254] The Republican repeatedly reminded Americans that their practice fell far short of their ideals. Convinced that God was sovereign, Lincoln sought his will for the nation, insisted that biblical norms should guide public life, stressed corporate responsibility, and promoted democracy.

His belief that God ruled over the nations led Lincoln to trust the integrity and wisdom of the American people. He maintained that "the Maker of the universe" would "through the instrumentality of this great and intelligent people" bring the United States through its difficulties.[255] In his First Inaugural Address, the president exhorted citizens to have "patient confidence in the ultimate justice of the people" because there was no "better or equal Hope" in the world. The "eternal truth and justice" of "the Almighty Ruler of nations" would "surely prevail, by the judgment of this great tribunal, the American people." Urging Southerners not to take up arms, he argued that if their position on slavery was right, God would convince federal officials to make the necessary adjustments. "Intelligence, patriotism, Christianity, and a firm reliance on Him, who has never yet forsaken this favored land," he insisted, could best resolve "our present difficulty."[256] Despite three years of war, Lincoln told a pastor, "I have faith in the people. Let them know the truth, and the country is safe."[257] At the same time, though, Lincoln insisted that "truth and right were not matters of majority vote." Only belief that transcendent standards governed human affairs could safeguard the rights of minorities.[258] The principles of republican government, not America itself, had a sacred character. He exhorted Americans to adopt a polity and practices more consistent with the tenets of the Declaration.[259]

Lincoln and Presidential Policies

Two issues best illustrate how Lincoln's faith helped shape his policies as president: his approach to dealing with slavery and his interpretation of the Civil War. From the 1830s until the Southern attack on Fort Sumter in April 1861, Lincoln consistently opposed the extension of slavery, strove to prevent a confrontation between the North and the South, and worked to gradually abolish slavery where it existed.[260] In deciding what policies to pursue, Lincoln typically relied on biblical teaching, moral principles, and practical reasoning. As Richard Carwardine explains, Lincoln's "hybrid faith, with its rationalist, Universalist, Unitarian, fatalist," and "residually Calvinist elements," helped shape his "approach to slavery as a morally-charged political issue."[261] He concluded that slavery was wrong because it contravened God's laws by robbing individuals of the fruit of their labor and failing to treat them according to the Golden Rule, contradicted democracy because slaves did not consent to their condition, and violated such key principles of the Declaration of Independence as liberty and equality.[262]

Although the prairie politician was neither an abolitionist nor a leader in the antislavery crusade, he insisted for three decades that slavery was a moral evil. Lincoln risked his political future by denouncing slavery as a member of the Illinois legislature in the 1830s and 1840s, when the state passed laws to prevent free blacks from settling there.[263] In 1837, Lincoln signed a petition that declared slavery was both unjust and a "bad policy."[264] "If slavery is not wrong," Lincoln proclaimed, "nothing is wrong."[265] He strongly opposed the Kansas-Nebraska Act of 1854 because it implied that enslaving fellow human beings was right, contravened the principle of liberty, and contradicted the views of the "fathers of the republic."[266] Moreover, permitting the extension of slavery would upset the sectional balance and make compromise more difficult and civil war more likely.[267] His 1855 letter to Joshua Speed reveals his disgust for slavery and other forms of discrimination: "As a nation, we began by declaring that '*all men are created equal.*' We now practically read it 'all men are created equal, *except negroes.*' When the Know-Nothings get control it will read 'all men are created equal except negroes, *and foreigners, and Catholics.*'" If this occurred, he preferred to emigrate to "some country where they make no pretence of loving liberty."[268] In 1858, he called the battle over slavery a crucial part of "the eternal struggle between ... right and wrong ... throughout the world."[269]

Lincoln's approach differed from that of most abolitionists in two major ways. First, his condemnation of slavery did not primarily rest on biblical teaching. As William Lee Miller explains, he made "deft, tangential, illustrative use of the Bible," repeatedly referring to God's justice, the Golden Rule, and the curse requiring Adam to provide for himself by his own labor, not someone's else's. He was careful, however, not to claim he knew how God ultimately judged slavery. Although he made few forthright religious assertions, his argument had "a powerful religious undertone." Nevertheless, in repudiating slavery, Lincoln appealed principally to the Declaration of Independence and people's "natural sense of justice." He highlighted the incongruity between the Declaration's assertion of human equality and the nation's practice of slavery.[270] Christ commanded, Lincoln told a large audience in Chicago in 1858, that "As your Father in Heaven is perfect, be ye also perfect." No one could reach this standard, but people should strive to attain "the highest degree of moral perfection." Thus Americans must seek to implement "the principle that all men are created equal" "as nearly ... as we can."[271] Second, while opposing the expansion of slavery on moral grounds, Lincoln, unlike most abolitionists, refused to excoriate slaveholders and pointed out the moral flaws of both owners and their critics.[272]

In his debates with Stephen Douglas in 1858, as they vied to represent Illinois in the Senate, Lincoln strongly opposed allowing residents of newly created states to choose whether they wanted slavery. Douglas's position, he contended, eradicated "the light of reason and the love of liberty in this American people."[273] Lincoln also attacked a pamphlet of Old School Presbyterian Frederick A. Ross entitled *Slavery as Ordained by God*. If blacks truly were inferior to whites, the Republican asked, then should whites take from them the little they had? "'Give to the needy' is the Christian rule of charity; but 'Take from him that is needy' is the rule of slavery." "The sum of proslavery theology," Lincoln continued, seemed to be: "Slavery is not universally right" or "universally wrong; it is better for some people to be slaves; and in such cases, it is the will of God that they be such." But if slavery was "good for some people," as Ross argued, why did no one ever seek this particular good for himself?[274]

Campaigning for the presidency in 1860, Lincoln declared that both revelation and "natural theology" proved that slavery was "morally wrong and a direct violation" of the "principle of equality."[275] When a nation "dared the Almighty" by enslaving any group, its citizens "had cause to dread His wrath." He reminded Americans of Jefferson's warning: " 'I tremble for my country when I remember that God is just!' "[276] In his speeches, Lincoln repeatedly expositated the biblical text "In the sweat of thy face, thou shalt eat bread." Because God commanded all human beings to labor, "the effort of *some* to shift their share of the burthen to the shoulders of *others*" was despicable. Because work was "originally a curse for transgression upon the whole race," when it was "concentrated on a part only," it became "the double-refined curse of God upon his creatures."[277] When "those professedly holy men of the South . . . in the name of Him who said 'As you would all men should do unto you, do ye even so unto them,' " "appealed to the Christian world to aid them in doing to a whole race of men, as they would have no man do unto themselves," Lincoln protested, "they contemned and insulted God and His Church, far more than did Satan when he tempted the Saviour with the Kingdoms of the earth."[278] At the same time, Lincoln repeatedly reminded Northerners that they shared in the sin of slavery because the Founding Fathers condoned it and their region profited financially from it.

Like many of his contemporaries, Lincoln struggled to solve the problem of slavery. He lamented that "the friends of the Union" had diverse views of slavery: Some wanted to perpetuate it; others wanted to abolish it immediately without reimbursing owners; still others wanted to abolish slavery gradually with compensation; some wanted to colonize free blacks in another country, while others preferred they remain in the United States.[279] Although Lincoln long supported colonization, he eventually decided that sending emancipated slaves to Liberia was impractical. However, if blacks were freed and stayed in the United States, they would be "underlings" whose condition might not be any better than it was as slaves. Lincoln sadly concluded that because of white prejudices and self-interest, "We can not . . . make them equals."[280] In late 1860, Lincoln allegedly told Newton Bateman that he knew God "hates injustice and slavery. I see the storm coming, and I know that His hand is in it." "Christ and reason" both said "that a house divided against itself cannot stand."[281]

As president, Lincoln continued to denounce slavery as immoral, but he insisted that two factors prevented him from trying to abolish it: The Constitution protected it, and attempts to eradicate it might demolish the Union. Lincoln repeatedly emphasized that he had taken an oath to "preserve, protect, and defend the Constitution." This venerable document, he argued, prohibited Americans from abolishing slavery where it already existed without Southern approval.[282] Therefore, he could not act on his personal view that slavery was a moral abomination.[283] Like most Northerners, Lincoln lamented, he had to deny his feelings to maintain his "loyalty to the constitution and the Union."[284] Thus for years he had fought to prevent slavery from spreading into new territories and to gradually emancipate blacks.

Lincoln feared, with good justification, that efforts to eliminate slavery would push the border states into the Confederacy and prompt Northern Democrats to oppose the war. For Lincoln, preserving the Union was a higher goal than ending slavery because he believed the United States, despite its practice of slavery, was the chief vehicle for advancing liberty in the world. Abolishing slavery instantly without compensating owners and giving blacks equality, he warned, would produce even more violence, permanently split the nation, and end its republican experiment. Responding in August 1862 to an open letter from Horace Greeley, the editor of the *New York Tribune*, that demanded immediate emancipation, Lincoln declared, "My paramount object in this struggle *is* to save the Union, and is *not* either to save or to destroy slavery." Functioning as a pragmatic statesman, not a moral prophet, he added, "If I could save the Union without freeing *any* slave I would do it, and if I could save it by freeing *all* the slaves I would do it; and if I could save it by freeing some and leaving others alone, I would also do that."[285] Nevertheless, Lincoln told two ministers from Chicago three weeks later, "Whatever shall appear to be God's will [with regard to slavery] I will do."[286]

Before issuing the Emancipation Proclamation in September 1862, Lincoln took other steps to help slaves. He proposed a plan for gradual, compensated emancipation of slaves residing in the District of Columbia, which Congress passed in April 1862. The president also offered financial aid to any border states that devised a plan to slowly free their slaves.

Prior to September, however, Lincoln felt that he was caught in a vise. If he argued that the Civil War was primarily about slavery, he would alienate residents of the border states, which were crucial to the North's success. On the other hand, if he ignored the importance of slavery to the conflict, he risked losing support from other nations (or, worse yet, having them aid the South). Weighing his alternatives, Lincoln initially chose to de-emphasize slavery, hoping the British and French would appreciate his predicament and understand "that slavery was indeed the great issue dividing North and South."[287] His fear that European governments might recognize the Confederacy led Lincoln to draft a resolution he hoped supporters of the Union cause abroad, especially in England, would adopt. It declared in part: "for the first [time] . . . an attempt has been made to construct a new Nation . . . with the primary, and fundamental object to maintain, enlarge, and perpetuate human slavery." No such state "should ever be recognized by, or admitted into, the family of christian and civilized nations."[288]

Two members of Lincoln's administration testified that he told his cabinet on September 22, 1862, that he had promised God that if the Union Army defeated the Confederates at Antietam, he would free the slaves in the rebellious states. According to Secretary of the Treasury Salmon P. Chase, Lincoln told his cabinet that he had resolved that as soon as the Confederates were driven out of Maryland, he would "issue a Proclamation of Emancipation. . . . I made the promise to myself and . . . to my maker. The rebel army is now driven out, and I am going to fulfill that promise."[289] Secretary of the Navy Gideon Welles testified that Lincoln said "he had made a vow . . . that if God gave us the victory in the approaching battle, he would consider it an indication of Divine will, and . . . move forward in the cause of emancipation."[290] David Hein points out that these two diary accounts differ in a significant way. In Chase's version, it appears that Lincoln had already decided what he would do and his "promise to God was a way of solemnizing" his momentous choice. Welles's account suggests that Lincoln was bargaining with God: If you give us a victory, then I will free the slaves. It implies that Lincoln had not yet determined to liberate them. In fact, Lincoln wrote the Emancipation Proclamation long before the Battle of Antietam. Despite the pleas of the abolitionists, however, he waited for a decisive Union victory before issuing it so his administration did not seem desperate.[291]

"In *giving* freedom to the *slave*," Lincoln asserted in his annual message to Congress in December 1862, "we *assure* freedom to the *free*. . . . The way is plain, peaceful, generous, [and] just—a way which, if followed, the world will forever applaud, and God must forever bless."[292] In issuing the Emancipation Proclamation on January 1, 1863, which freed the slaves only in states in rebellion against the Union, Lincoln declared that "upon this . . . act of justice, warranted by the Constitution . . . I invoke the considerate judgment of mankind and the gracious favor of Almighty God."[293]

Lincoln's faith also influenced his understanding of the Civil War. The scope, length, and fury of the Civil War surprised almost all Americans and strengthened Lincoln's conviction that it had a divine purpose. "War, at its best," he declared, "is terrible, and this war of ours, in its magnitude and in its duration, is one of the most terrible."[294] The Republican came to view the war not only as a means of restoring the Union but also of purging the land of slavery. His changing view of the war's purpose led Lincoln to reflect more deeply on how God directed history.[295] Although political, economic, and social factors contributed to the Civil War, he contended, its ultimate cause was God's judgment upon the United States.

During the Civil War, Scripture, theological reasoning, and religiously charged rhetoric were very important in America. Mark Noll argues that most theologians took predictable positions. During the first half of the war, Northerners saw God's chastisements in the frequent defeats of their armies, while Southerners praised the Almighty for Stonewall Jackson and Robert E. Lee's great victories. After Grant began to command the Army of the Potomac, the situation reversed, as the North experienced God's blessing while the South "endured his cleansing wrath." Although a few ministers and laypeople questioned this interpretation, no one's analysis of God's purposes in the war was as astute as Lincoln's.[296]

Lincoln's most profound appraisal of the war's meaning is in his Second Inaugural Address, delivered about a month before his assassination. Frederick Douglass called it "a sacred effort" that was "more like a sermon than a state paper." Church historian Philip Schaff argued that no "royal, princely, or republican state document of recent times" featured such "genuine Christian wisdom and gentleness."[297] Despite these encomiums, the address was not widely lauded at the time. Recent scholars, however, have profusely praised it. William Wolf calls it "one of the most astute pieces of Christian theology ever written." Deeply rooted in "a biblical understanding of God, humanity, and history," Pierard and Linder argue, Lincoln's "speech is a charter of Christian statesmanship and the most lofty expression of prophetic civil religion in the English language." Noll labels it the "most far-reaching" reflection "on Providence" by "a major figure in American public life."[298]

Lincoln the layman articulated a more complex, nuanced understanding of God's providence than the nation's theologians. The Republican questioned the ironclad certainty of many of his forebears and contemporaries that America was God's chosen nation, but he never completely rejected this concept. He emphasized, however, that the United States was subject to the same transcendent standards of justice as other countries. Although the outcome of the war reinforced the belief of many Northern ministers that the United States had a unique role in bringing the kingdom of God on earth, Lincoln was not so sure.[299]

Moreover, Lincoln disputed the widely held conviction that God's plans were transparent and relatively easy to discern. He asserted instead that God's ends were frequently difficult to fathom and sometimes incomprehensible to mere mortals.[300] "The Almighty has His own purposes," Lincoln proclaimed. He then suggested what to many of his listeners was probably unimaginable: Perhaps American slavery was such a great offense that God gave both the North and the South "this terrible war" as a punishment. Was this conclusion inconsistent with "those divine attributes which the believers in a Living God" had always ascribed to him? "As was said three thousand years ago, so still it must be said, 'the judgments of the Lord, are true and righteous altogether.' "[301]

Finally, in contrast to the cries of his compatriots that Southern "traitors" be punished, Lincoln called for leniency, charity, forgiveness, and reconciliation. While ministers, newspaper editors, civic leaders, and social reformers demanded judgment and condemnation (the incarceration of Confederate leaders, the hanging of Jefferson Davis, and confiscation of Southerners' goods), Lincoln proposed mercy and clemency.[302] The president advocated "malice toward none" and "charity for all." Unlike many other Northerners, he refused to denounce Southerners as evil and to proclaim the war a holy crusade.[303] Instead, he sought to bring healing between the sections and to establish a solid, enduring peace. Lincoln stressed that the residents of both regions were guilty and deserved divine punishment and that their shared suffering could serve as a basis for reunion. He urged Northerners to repudiate revenge and concentrate on binding "up the nation's wounds," caring for widows and orphans, and laboring to "achieve and cherish a just, and a lasting peace." Only reconciliation between regions and a just peace would make the horrific devastation and unparalleled sacrifices of the war worthwhile. Moreover, this alone would enable the United States to model democracy for "all nations."[304]

The Response to Lincoln's Death

A few minutes after Lincoln died on the morning of April 15, 1865, Phineas Gurley, who had spent all night with his mortally wounded parishioner, comforted mourners with a prayer that ended "Thy will be done." Raising his head, Edwin Stanton quietly declared, "Now he belongs to the ages."[305] During the next three weeks, seven million Americans paid their respects to their slain president in the Capitol Rotunda or as his funeral train traveled 1,700 miles from Washington through many major Northern cities to Springfield. The circumstances of Lincoln's death and the condition of the national psyche, deeply battered and bruised by four years of bitterness and bloodshed, combined to unleash a massive, spontaneous torrent of grief that surpassed any the nation had previously experienced. As had Washington, Lincoln quickly became an object of civil religion, as Americans transformed him from a prairie politician to the "Savior of the Union" and Father Abraham. His assassination a week after the end of a conflict that he and many other Americans "saw in millennial terms" magnified its meaning.[306] Moreover, Lincoln's death was a crushing blow to many Americans who were convinced that he could best achieve a "speedy pacification of the country, the restoration of the Union, and the return of harmony and love."[307]

The nation's most renowned pulpiteers and professors and hundreds of less-known pastors preached funeral sermons that helped transform Lincoln "from man to myth."[308] They extolled their murdered leader as a "saint who symbolized the ideals" of American democracy.[309] Many Americans felt that they had lost their father.[310] Sermons on "Black Easter" and in subsequent weeks frequently compared Lincoln with Washington, Moses, and Jesus. While Washington was the nation's founder and father, ministers averred, Lincoln was its restorer and redeemer. Since Washington, the United States had not had "a purer statesman, a wiser, a nobler, a more Christian man" heading its government.[311] Like Moses, the Republican deliverer had led his people through the wilderness and died before entering the promised land.[312] Because they viewed Lincoln as their liberator, many freed blacks were exceptionally grief-stricken by his death.

Struck down on Good Friday, Lincoln, like Jesus, was a martyr who shed his blood and offered a redeeming sacrifice. Orators, editors, ministers, and statesmen across the North exalted Lincoln as the "savior of his country." Hundreds of clergymen evoked Isaiah's image of "the Suffering Servant." Whereas Christ died so that people could enjoy heaven, Lincoln died so they could have a better life on earth. After accomplishing the "painful salvation of the republic," Lincoln, proclaimed a Presbyterian pastor, had "been offered [as] a bloody sacrifice upon the altar of human freedom."[313] A Baptist minister argued that it was fitting that "the second Father of our Republic" was slain on Good Friday. "Jesus Christ died for the world, Abraham Lincoln died for his country." Ohio congressman, Union general, and future president James A. Garfield insisted that Lincoln's death paralleled "that of the Son of God who cried out, 'Father, forgive them for they know not what they do.' "[314]

In making Lincoln the nation's redeemer, ministers had to surmount two major difficulties: that he was fatally shot in a theater, an embarrassingly unsanctified place for a savior, and that he had not explicitly testified to his faith in Christ. The clergy rationalized his attendance at Ford Theater, arguing that he gone reluctantly to please his wife and gratify others.[315] Although some pastors "bitterly regretted that he did not make a public profession of . . . faith in the Lord Jesus Christ," others countered either that his actions demonstrated his faith or that he had accepted Christ as his savior in response to Willie's death in 1862, at Gettysburg in 1863, or at some other unknown time.[316] In their funeral sermons at Washington and Springfield, respectively, Gurley and Simpson, the two ministers who knew Lincoln best, said little about his personal faith. Gurley stressed that he had an "abiding confidence in the overruling providence of God and in the ultimate triumph of truth and righteousness through the power and the blessing of God." Simpson emphasized that the president had "read the Bible frequently, loved . . . its great truth and its profound teachings," and sought to follow its precepts. He claimed that Lincoln "believed in Christ the Saviour of sinners" and had sincerely striven to live by "the principles of revealed religion." No other ruler had shown as much "trust in God."[317] Other ministers agreed that although Lincoln did not publicly profess to be a Christian, he certainly lived as one.[318] Many extolled Lincoln's character, sometimes "elevating him to an almost superhuman status."[319] Gurley insisted that his "integrity was thorough . . . all-controlling, and incorruptible."[320] People had never seen "a more sympathetic, unselfish, large-hearted, forgiving man," proclaimed a Baptist pastor from Philadelphia. Episcopal rector Phillips Brooks called him the world's "gentlest, kindest, most indulgent" ruler.[321]

Jewish rabbis and civil leaders also compared the fallen president with Abraham, Moses, and Washington. God chose Lincoln, like Abraham, a New York City rabbi contended, to "be the protector and father of a great people."[322] Like Moses, the Republican refused to compromise with evil and led his people to the River Jordan but was not allowed to cross over and enjoy the fruit of his labors.[323] Like Washington, Lincoln was a "defender of freedom" and would have a place in American hearts "next to the Father of our Country.[324] In addition, rabbis celebrated Lincoln's faith, character, principles, and accomplishments; argued that his tragic death compelled Americans to confess their sins; and urged listeners to complete his work. They exhorted Jews to emulate Lincoln's trust in God and "implicit faith in the justice of providence."[325] Isaac Mayer Wise, who later funded Reform Judaism, called Lincoln "the highest jewel, the greatest hero, and the noblest son of the nation."[326] Other rabbis acclaimed the slain president as an "illustrious martyr," "our sainted President," and "the Messiah of this country."[327] Henry Vidaver of St. Louis urged his congregation to practice Lincoln's principles: justice, liberty, mercy, forgiveness, and "brotherly love to the misled and defeated."[328] His death demanded that people become "better men, better citizens, [and] true children of the living God."[329] The best way to honor the sixteenth president was to embrace his "sacred principles" and finish his work.[330]

A Final Assessment

Despite his unorthodox views, many laud Lincoln as the nation's most exemplary Christian chief executive. The sixteenth president "stands at the spiritual center of American history," Sidney Mead argued, and many consider him a profound theological thinker. To William Wolf, Lincoln was " 'a biblical prophet' who saw himself as 'an instrument of God' and his country as God's 'almost chosen people' called to world responsibility." No other president, Robert Michaelsen maintained in *Christian Century,* so fully expressed "in word and deed the Christian virtues of charity and compassion under trying conditions." No American, declared Theodore Roosevelt, more fully applied what the churches taught than Lincoln. In Reinhold Niebuhr's judgment, Lincoln's religious convictions were deeper and purer than the political and religious leaders of his era. Few have surpassed the rhetoric of the prairie politician's first post-death biographer, Josiah Holland, who lauded him as a "statesman . . . savior of the republic, emancipator of a race, [and] true Christian."[331]

Although Lincoln has been revered as a paragon of piety, a champion of freedom, a demigod, and the national redeemer in the years since his death, some of his contemporaries harshly criticized him. During the 1860 campaign, the *Charleston* (South Carolina) *Mercury* described the Republican candidate as "a cross between the nutmeg dealer, the horse-swapper, and the nightman."[332] Henry Raymond contended in the *New York Times* in 1865 that the president had experienced more "hate and obloquy" than "any other great leader in modern history."[333] Southern newspapers portrayed Lincoln as an uncouth, ugly man who enjoyed vulgar humor, and cartoons, poems, melodramas, and musical satires poked fun at him.[334] Confederates denounced Lincoln as a "Yankee Attila, a mobocrat, a lunatic, the biggest 'ass' in the United States, the evil chief of the 'Black republican, free love, free Nigger' North that strove to subjugate the white man's South."[335]

Contemporary critics contend that Lincoln's use of total war violated just war standards and helped hasten the appalling assaults on human rights unleashed by twentieth-century warfare. Some scholars fault Lincoln for not transcending his racist culture and more forcefully condemning slavery. His refusal to affirm full civil and social rights for blacks helped fuel the nation's racial crisis in the years after 1875.[336] Critics also castigate the Illinois Republican for using scriptural language to justify enlarging the government and violating people's civil liberties. Allegedly disregarding the Constitution, he expanded presidential powers to an unparalleled degree in his quest to save the Union. Functioning as a "dictator," Lincoln illegally spent public funds, blockaded Southern ports, defied the Supreme Court, created new governmental agencies, seized property, incarcerated political enemies without trials, and closed newspapers that criticized his policies.[337] Others argue that Lincoln needed to have broader presidential powers to achieve his wartime objectives. Moreover, he sought congressional approval for his actions, did not completely censor the Northern press, rarely vetoed measures, and gave his cabinet members considerably freedom.[338] Finally, critics accuse Lincoln of employing biblical rhetoric to identify "God's purposes with the purposes of America as interpreted by the Republican Party." His defenders counter that while Lincoln maintained that America's status as the world's largest and most successful republic gave it a unique role, he challenged the widely held view that the United States was God's chosen nation. Lincoln also rejected the argument of some of his contemporaries that moral progress was inevitable, human depravity had been overcome, and America would bring the "spiritual regeneration of humanity."[339]

Since his assassination, many Americans have extolled Lincoln as a man of exemplary character, a near saint. They have assigned him their "most noble traits—honesty . . . tolerance, hard work, a capacity to forgive . . . a clear-sighted vision of right and wrong, a dedication to God and country, and an abiding concern for all." Joshua Speed insisted that "unlike all other men there was an entire harmony between his public and private life." Another close friend, Joseph Gillespie, maintained Lincoln had an "extremely acute" sense of "right & wrong."[340] Stephen Oates argues that "Lincoln was as honest in real life as in the legend."[341] The Republican was able to take strong moral positions without appearing smug or self-righteous. Numerous close observers praised his self-control, calm demeanor, unending patience, and even temperament.[342] Although Lincoln occasionally lashed out in anger and sometimes ridiculed his adversaries, it is remarkable how rarely his temper erupted, considering how much abuse he suffered.[343] Many have stressed Lincoln's willingness to pardon his political opponents and military enemies.[344] He declared that he was "always willing to forgive on the Christian terms of repentance."[345] Dealing graciously and generously with the South, Lincoln proposed mild terms for Southerners' readmission to the Union. As William Lee Miller puts it, he showed "magnanimity to rivals and critics, mercy to the accused, patience with insolent generals, eloquent sympathy to the bereaved, generosity to associates and subordinates, [and] nonvindictiveness to enemies."[346] Some have even compared Lincoln with Christ. Russian novelist Leo Tolstoy called him a "Christ in miniature" and "a saint of humanity," and John Hay labeled him "the greatest character since Christ."[347] Admirers claim that, like Jesus, he was able to share other people's suffering—especially their feelings of pain, loss, and guilt. He consoled those who failed and did not boast about victories or take credit when he succeeded. He was more ready "to pardon than to punish."[348]

Lincoln confided to Aminda Rankin in 1846 that "probably it is to be my lot to go on in a twilight, feeling and reasoning my way through life, as questioning, doubting Thomas did."[349] Earlier on the day he was shot, Lincoln allegedly told his wife that when his presidency ended, he wanted to "visit the Holy Land and see those places hallowed by the footsteps of the Savior."[350] Guelzo argues that his plan to visit Palestine, as thousands of Christian pilgrims and numerous skeptics, including Herman Melville and Charles Gordon, had done, was consistent with Lincoln's lifelong "search for religious truth." Guelzo calls the transformation of Lincoln into a second Jesus, a "political redeemer," "the most cruel of ironies" because Lincoln did not believe "in the possibility of redemption for himself." He "never found enough acceptance or grace or religious peace to embrace" Christ as his Savior.[351] The Republican could neither believe nor be comfortable with his unbelief.[352] Unable to accept God's love, mercy, and grace, the tormented Lincoln felt helpless "before a distant and implacable Judge who revealed himself only through crisis and death." Guelzo attributes his difficulty in part to the "overweening moral rigorism of Victorian evangelicalism" that made it difficult for people to accept "forgiveness and grace." Mid-nineteenth-century evangelical Protestantism's "ruthless self-honesty" imparted to Lincoln "a crushing sense of worthlessness." "Lincoln was a typical Victorian doubter" who was influenced by the Enlightenment, "shaped by classical liberalism, and nurtured in angst when the Enlightenment's confidence in its own optimistic solutions proved illusory." Guelzo argues that throughout his life Lincoln "remained, by any technical definition, an 'infidel.'" He attended church "but more as a matter of intellectual respect for any religion that painted the same backdrop of necessity, providence, and predestination which colored his own perceptions of the world."[353] John Patrick Diggins contends that the best label for Lincoln is "a 'Christian pragmatist'": "a thinker who sees history as contingent, politics as morally ambiguous, and God as the inscrutable silent presence." Although Lincoln quietly rejected Christianity's doctrinal core, William Lee Miller maintains, "he grasped its moral meaning better than most believers."[354]

Neither Lincoln's discouraging prediction nor these scholarly assessments capture the essence of his faith. Throughout his life, Mark Noll maintains, "strands of determinism, rationalism, scripturalism, and providentialism" are all evident. Like many of his contemporaries, Lincoln turned to reason and duty to help him deal with the sense of anxiety and helplessness he often experienced. Rejecting the skepticism and aimlessness of many Victorian intellectuals, however, he somewhat paradoxically relied on his faith in God's providence to help him make sense of the world and cope with death, destruction, and frustration, especially during the nation's bloody fratricide. As he grew older, his life circumstances and relationships with Christians helped Lincoln move from questioning Christianity to accepting many of its central doctrines. Through years of wrestling with God, Lincoln developed a deep but unconventional faith. Although he did not become a born-again evangelical, he was fascinated with religion and seriously studied the Scriptures. Over time he became "more receptive to Protestant orthodoxy" and his view of God became more Calvinist and conventionally Protestant.[355] His gloomy disposition, profoundly biblical understanding of Providence, and existential awareness of the transitory nature of life enabled him to offer explanations of reality that many American find compelling. Lincoln's personal anguish and despair helped him empathize with grieving citizens engulfed in the tragedy of Civil War, express their pathos and pain, and assuage their sorrow and suffering.[356] Like Job, before his death, Lincoln appeared to trust God without needing to know his reasons for everything.[357] In the final analysis, the assessment of Joseph Gillespie, who observed him for more than thirty years, rings true: "Lincoln cared but little for tenets or sects but had strong & pervading ideas of the infinite power & goodness of Deity and of mans [sic] obligation to his Maker and to his fellow beings."[358] So does the conclusion of John Nicolay: "Benevolence and forgiveness were the very basis of his character. His nature was deeply religious . . . he had faith in the eternal justice and boundless mercy of Providence, and made the Golden Rule of Christ his practical creed."[359]

During the most trying time in American history, Lincoln testified to God's sovereignty, held together a coalition of free and border slave states, kept his fragmented party from falling apart, defeated the rebel states militarily, liberated four million enslaved people, and preserved the Union. His greatest achievement, argues Guelzo, is "that he made the idea of the nation—a single people, unified rationally . . . around certain propositions that transcended ethnicity, religious denominationalism, and gender—into the central political image of the republic."[360]

Quaker Eliza Gurney predicted shortly after Lincoln issued the Emancipation Proclamation that "generations of children yet unborn" would call him "blessed" for his "magnificent deed" of loosing "the bands of wickedness" and letting "the oppressed go free."[361] Henry P. Tappan, the president of the University of Michigan, wrote Lincoln in 1862 that he hoped the history of the country would someday read: "Then the United States redeemed and regenerated commenced a new career of prosperity and glory; and Abraham Lincoln was hailed by his countrymen & by Mankind as the Second father of his country, and the hero of Liberty."[362] Gurney and Tappan's wishes have largely been granted.

CHAPTER FOUR

Theodore Roosevelt and the Bully Pulpit

Most of us enjoy preaching, and I've got such a bully pulpit.

Quoted in George Haven Putnam, "Roosevelt, Historian and Statesman"

I consider it my greatest joy and glory that, occupying a most exalted position in the nation, I am enabled, simply and sincerely, to preach the practical moralities of the Bible to my fellow country-men.

Roosevelt to Ferdinand Iglehart, c. 1906

The Decalogue and the Golden Rule must stand as the foundation of every successful effort to better our social or political life. "Fear God and walk in his ways" and "Love thy neighbor as thyself"—when we practice these two precepts, the reign of social and civic righteousness will be close at hand.

"Christian Citizenship," December 1900

We are the citizens of a mighty republic consecrated to the service of God above, through the service of man on this earth.

"Fear God and Take Your Own Part," *Works*

THEODORE ROOSEVELT WAS one the most colorful, flamboyant, and interesting personalities of his time. Few individuals have played so many diverse roles: historian, naturalist, explorer, rancher, war hero, journalist, and reform-minded civil servant. He branded cattle, led a cavalry charge up San Juan Hill, and challenged America's corporations. Roosevelt was lauded as a demigod and denounced as a demon. To some, he was larger than life, like his monument later carved in stone on Mount Rushmore. The sage of Oyster Bay was an exemplar of manliness and "muscular Christianity" and an exceptional public servant who led a crusade for social justice.[1] To others, Roosevelt was a jingoist, a nativist, a hot-tempered, unpredictable fanatic, and an egomaniac who put his own interests above America's good.

Roosevelt professed faith in Christ at age sixteen and joined the church. As a student at Harvard, he regularly taught Sunday school, and throughout most of his adult life, he faithfully attended church and read the Bible. Sharing many of the views of the Social Gospel movement, which arose in the 1880s in an attempt to alleviate a wide array of social ills, he worked to achieve much of its agenda and frequently wrote for one of its leading publications, *The Outlook*. Roosevelt's political philosophy and policies were guided by Judeo-Christian principles. He highly valued biblical morality and considered it vital to personal and public life, including politics. He downplayed doctrine and theological differences and strongly stressed the importance of good works and character. Contemporaries called him a preacher of righteousness, and he labeled the presidency a bully pulpit, which he used to trumpet the importance of social justice, civility, and virtue. By word and deed, he labored vigorously to convince Americans that the gospel was the "moral foundation upon which all true national greatness must rest" and to promote individual and social righteousness.[2] Building on the work of William McKinley, Roosevelt further enlarged the power of the presidency, boldly attacked many of the nation's ills, and made the United States a major force in international affairs.[3]

Roosevelt's Faith

Roosevelt's father was a devoted Christian who taught poor children at mission Sunday schools, distributed evangelistic tracts, and helped found the New York Children's Aid Society and several other philanthropic organizations. A proponent of muscular Christianity who depicted Jesus as a valiant "soldier of righteousness," he encouraged the efforts of the Young Men's Christian Association (YMCA) to promote both sports and spirituality and supported the revivals of Dwight L. Moody. Theodore Sr. provided extensive religious training for his children and sought to instill in them "Christian piety and social obligation."[4] The family prayed together before breakfast each morning and regularly read the Bible together. Roosevelt required his children to summarize the sermons they heard in church, which he discussed with them.[5] He spent one day each week helping New York City's poor with their physical, material, and spiritual problems and took his children to visit numerous Christian missions that aided the indigent.[6] He was highly respected for his Christian character, philanthropy, and business success.[7]

When Roosevelt was sixteen, he met with James M. Ludlow, the pastor of the Collegiate (Dutch) Reformed Church of St. Nicholas in New York City, where he had been baptized as a child, and declared:

I would like to become a member of the church. You know how strictly I have been raised . . . in Christian faith and denominational doctrine. . . . I feel that one who believes so firmly in the Bible and Christianity as I do, should say so publicly, and enter openly into the active service of the church; to drill with the troops and fight in the battle-front with the soldiers of the Cross. . . . I want to be a witness for Christ; a doer of the word.

Inspired by his father's example, Roosevelt taught a mission class in New York City for three years before going to Harvard. When the future president departed for college, his father advised him, "Take care of your morals first, your health next, and finally your studies."[9] Faithful to this admonition, he prayed each morning, worshiped at Phillips Brooks's Trinity Cathedral, and taught Sunday school at Christ Episcopal Church in Cambridge. After three years of doing so, he taught a Sunday morning class at a Congregationalist mission in East Cambridge.[10] His father's influence and his personal convictions led Roosevelt to avoid profanity, smoking, and gambling, to drink sparingly, and to eschew premarital sex.[11] He later wrote that his fellow students would have looked down on his teaching Sunday school if he had not "also been a corking boxer, a good runner, and a genial member of the Porcellian Club."[12] When his father died in 1878, Roosevelt found consolation in his faith. "It is lovely to think of our meeting in heaven," he wrote in his diary. "Nothing but my faith in the Lord Jesus Christ," he added, "could have carried me through this, my terrible time of trouble and sorrow." "With the help of my God," he vowed, "I will try to lead such a life as Father would have wished me to." After this, however, Roosevelt rarely expressed such deep religious emotions. Even the death of his first wife and his mother on the same day in 1884 did not evoke similar declarations.[13]

As a child, Roosevelt memorized many biblical passages, and as an adult he had a thorough knowledge of and a deep appreciation for the Bible. He also read widely in religious literature (his favorite work was John Bunyan's classic *Pilgrim's Progress*). William Sewall reported that when Roosevelt stayed at his camp in Maine as a teenager, he went off by himself on Sundays to an isolated place to read his Bible, and while ranching in Dakota Territory in his twenties, he regularly read his Bible.[14] Friends reported that his Bible was well worn. His wife, Edith, testified it was the one book he always kept on his reading stand. She claimed that he could recite long portions of Scripture and that his "deep knowledge of the Bible" played a major part in his life.[15] Roosevelt's sister, Corrine Roosevelt Robinson, insisted that he read the Bible "a great deal" for both "inspiration and consolation."[16]

Although he did not quote Scripture as often in his addresses as some other presidents, his speeches and writings are peppered with biblical allusions, and he often testified to the importance of the Bible in his own life and the life of the nation. No other book, Roosevelt insisted, spoke to him so powerfully as did the Bible.[17] Its teachings, he declared, were deeply "interwoven and entwined with our whole civic and social life." Roosevelt urged Americans to pursue "a closer and wider and deeper study of the Bible" in order to "go forth and do the work of the Lord."[18] A 1904 national appeal issued by the American Bible Society included these words from Roosevelt: "The social fabric of modern states has no surer foundation than the Bible, especially in a republic like ours, which rests on the moral character and educated judgment of the individual."[19] Roosevelt urged secular colleges to provide courses in the Scriptures and insisted that those who faithfully studied God's Word would develop high moral standards and find personal inspiration.[20]

Roosevelt faithfully attended church and regularly took Communion. While he was president, whether he was in Washington or traveling, he went to church almost every Sunday. In Washington, Roosevelt attended the Grace Reformed Church, and when at his home in Oyster Bay, he worshiped at Christ Episcopal Church. When traveling, he usually sought out a Dutch or German Reformed Church, although he also attended Lutheran, Episcopal, and Methodist churches.[21] According to observers, Roosevelt participated enthusiastically in worship services. Although not a good singer, he knew many hymns by heart, and his voice often could be heard above other worshipers.[22] During his presidency, a popular tale depicted Roosevelt arriving in heaven and reorganizing the angelic choir. After assigning 10,000 sopranos, 10,000 altos, and 10,000 tenors, he declared, "And I'll sing bass."[23] Roosevelt often outlined the main points of sermons and discussed how they used Scripture. G. E. Talmage, Roosevelt's pastor at Oyster Bay, wrote, "Would that preachers had always so kindly a critic as he—one who could follow what they say, commend utterances that were worth while, and suggest books to read if the views were divergent."[24]

Because there was no Dutch Reformed Church in Washington, Roosevelt attended a small German Reformed Church about a mile from the White House. His participation helped inspire members to build a new church, which opened in 1903. During the services, he often took notes to remind himself to find help for people with special needs.[25] The president participated in both the cornerstone-laying and dedication ceremonies of the new building and hosted church members at the White House.[26] "After a week on perplexing problems and . . . heated contests," Roosevelt allegedly confided to Methodist pastor Ferdinand Iglehart, "it does my soul good to come into the House of the Lord and worship and to sing . . . to commune personally with Christ . . . . I get . . . a superhuman strength in fighting the moral evils I am called to confront."[27]

Not surprisingly, Christian organizations solicited Roosevelt to write articles and pamphlets to encourage other Americans to attend church. In

"Nine Reasons for Going to Church," published by the American Tract Society, Roosevelt insisted that a "churchless community" would go downhill quickly. Participation in the worship and ministry of the church stimulated people to care more about others and to demonstrate their faith by their works. At church services, people could sing inspiring hymns, hear beautiful biblical passages and possibly a helpful sermon, and enjoy fellowship with good neighbors. Roosevelt also strongly urged parents to ensure that their children received moral and spiritual training both at church and at home.[28]

Roosevelt adhered to traditional Christian standards in his personal moral practices. He did not fish, hunt, or play sports on the Sabbath and rarely transacted any business.[29] Friends testified that Roosevelt never used God's name in vain or even said "damn." He refused to tell jokes about any religion or to relate or countenance vulgar stories.[30] Roosevelt did not smoke, though he served cigars and cigarettes to his guests.[31] During his political career, opponents often charged that his "constantly ruddy complexion" and strange outbursts of laughter and anger proved he was a heavy drinker. Roosevelt treated these attacks as part of the price of public life, but increased accusations during the 1912 presidential campaign finally led him to bring a libel suit against the editor of *Iron Ore*, a weekly newspaper in Michigan, who claimed Roosevelt was frequently inebriated. For five days in 1913, family members, former cabinet officials, and journalists testified in court that Roosevelt never drank to excess. The editor could not produce a single witness who ever saw Roosevelt intoxicated. The ex-president told the court he had filed suit to clear his reputation, not to gain money; accordingly, the editor was fined a whopping six cents.[32]

It is difficult to determine how Roosevelt viewed his relationship with God or what he believed about many major Christian doctrines. The words of Christian Reisner, the pastor of Broadway Temple in New York City, ring true: Although Roosevelt had a "workable creed, he seldom talked about or detailed it."[33] After Roosevelt's death, Reisner interviewed many of his closest friends, his sister, and his cousin, who all agreed that he was "very reticent" to discuss "personal religion." They also concurred, however, that his faith "was an indispensable part of his being."[34] His reluctance to explain his specific religious convictions may have stemmed in large part from his staunch belief that actions speak louder than words.[35] Conduct, he repeatedly affirmed, was "infinitely more important than dogma."[36] Many emphasized that his regular reading of the Bible, church attendance, exemplary ethical ideals, everyday conduct, promotion of biblical teachings, and service to others abundantly demonstrated his faith in God and Christian commitment.[37] While admitting that Roosevelt made few public professions of faith, his close friend Jacob Riis maintained that he was "a reverent man" who in private and public consistently lived in "accord with the highest ideal of Christian manliness," a key concept for this generation.[38] Journalist William Allen White judged Roosevelt "fit to stand with Paul and Luther."[39] William Sewall, who accompanied Roosevelt on many of his later wilderness expeditions, insisted that he frequently read the Bible and "prayed without ceasing, for the desire of his heart was always to do right."[40] Another close friend, Arthur Lee, by contrast, never heard Roosevelt speak about religious matters, and the former president told journalist John J. Leary that religion was too private to discuss.[41] Reisner goes to great lengths to try to prove that Roosevelt prayed regularly, but his evidence is inferential, oblique, and circumstantial.[42]

What Roosevelt believed about salvation and the person of Christ is also unclear. Unlike McKinley, he never testified to having had a distinctive conversion experience, although Reformed Christians were much less likely than Methodists or Baptists to do so. After age twenty, he never spoke in all his voluminous writings of having a moving, intimate experience with God. Edward Wagenknecht quotes Roosevelt as saying, "I am mighty weak in the Lutheran and Calvinistic doctrine of salvation by faith . . . [but] I do believe in the gospel of works as put down in the Epistle of James."[43] In 1917, Roosevelt argued that a person should join the church to show "his faith by his works; I leave to the professional theologians the settlement of the question, whether he is to achieve his salvation by his works or by his faith which is genuine only if it expresses itself in works." But Roosevelt also insisted that walking humbly with God was a "necessary corrective to the Gospel of works alone"[44]; "the work of regeneration," he added, "often means such a complete change in a man's nature as is equivalent to the casting out of devils."[45]

Their close working relationship with *The Outlook* and extensive correspondence gave editor and pastor Lyman Abbott a good vantage point for evaluating Roosevelt's doctrinal beliefs. He did not try "to explain the Godward side of Jesus," Abbott explained, "but was attracted to and imitated the manward side of service."[46] Like Jefferson, Roosevelt seemed to be most inspired by Jesus' ethical teaching. "The life of Christ, as set forth in the four Gospels," he argued, "represents an infinitely higher and purer morality than is preached in any other book."[47] Roosevelt's lack of specificity about his religious convictions led his friends to reach very different conclusions. William Howard Taft maintained that Roosevelt accepted the Unitarian view of Christ. On the other hand, Nicholas Murray Butler, president of Columbia University, maintained that Roosevelt did not doubt the divinity of Jesus.[48] And Ferdinand Iglehart claimed that Roosevelt "believed in Jesus Christ as the Son of God as the Saviour of the world, and his own personal Redeemer."[49]

Unlike Washington, John Quincy Adams, Lincoln, and McKinley, Roosevelt rarely referred directly to God's providential direction of history, although he often acknowledged God's influence on human affairs.[50] In 1901, Roosevelt urged Americans to constantly "thank the Giver of all good for the countless blessings of our national life." "Our strength is as nothing," the president added in his 1904 proclamation, "unless we are helped" by "the Author of all blessings." In his 1905 inaugural address, the president proclaimed that "the Giver of Good has blessed us with the conditions which have enabled us to achieve so large a measure of well-being and of happiness."[51]

What Roosevelt believed about life after death is also not clear. As previously discussed, as a young man he found consolation after his father's death in his belief they would be together in heaven. After college, however, in his letters expressing sympathy to those who had lost loved ones, he rarely referred to God or heaven. Wagenknecht concludes that a belief in immortality was not a source of comfort to him.[52] Roosevelt told John J. Leary in 1916: "To love justice, to be merciful, to appreciate that the great mysteries shall not be known to us, and . . . to face the great beyond without fear—that is life."[53] Shortly before he died, Roosevelt wrote a friend, "It is idle to complain or rail at the inevitable; serene and high of heart we must face our fate and go down into the darkness."[54] Sharply disagreeing with most of Roosevelt's contemporaries, Gamaliel Bradford argued that this quotation accurately summarized the New Yorker's views. "I cannot find God insistent or palpable anywhere" in his writings, he declared.[55]

Clearly, Roosevelt placed more value on the morality of Christianity than on its meditative or theological aspects. Like many other presidents, Roosevelt contended that religion strongly encouraged good conduct and service. He agreed with Washington's contention in his Farewell Address that "morality is a necessary spring of popular government," which could not be maintained without religion.[56] He frequently quoted, "By their fruits ye shall know them," to bolster his argument that the ultimate test of religious belief was whether it produced upright behavior. The best way to help others, Roosevelt asserted, was to live by the "great ethical principles" taught by Jesus and the New Testament writers.[57] "In business and in work, if you let Christianity stop as you go out the church door, there is little righteousness in you."[58] The most "useful" person was the one whose religion drove him "to advance decency and clean living and to make the world a better place."[59] In his 1902 thanksgiving proclamation, Roosevelt urged Americans to praise God "not by words only, but by deeds." Roosevelt wrote in his autobiography that "the law of service is the only right law of life."[60] Roosevelt also stressed Romans 12:11—"Not slothful in business, fervent in spirit, serving the Lord"—and in his speeches and articles, often quoted James 1:22: "Be ye doers of the word and not hearers only."[61] He even more frequently quoted Micah 6:8. In 1916, he told John J. Leary that "To do justly, to love mercy, and to walk humbly with thy God" is "to me the essence of religion. . . . It is all the creed I need."[62]

Throughout his life, Roosevelt supported the efforts of Christian missions to both convert souls and improve social conditions. His interest probably began when, as a youth, he read the African adventures of explorer and missionary David Livingstone. To Roosevelt, "Every earnest and zealous believer... is a lifelong missionary in his or her field of labor—a missionary by precept, and, by what counts a thousandfold more... by practice."[63] He served on the foreign missions committee of the Students' Movement at Harvard and addressed numerous missionary groups.[64] Clergy and laypeople were obligated, he contended, to furnish leadership for all social movements that promoted righteousness and strove "to realize the kingdom of God in this world."[65] While hunting in Africa in 1910, Roosevelt frequently visited missionaries, observed their work, and attended their services. He expressed great respect for their labors and challenged critics to investigate firsthand what missionaries were accomplishing.[66] Roosevelt also applauded collaborative efforts of missionaries to spread the gospel. When the World Missionary Conference met in Edinburgh, Scotland, in 1910, he rejoiced that for the first time in four centuries, Christians from all corners of the world were assembling to discuss how best to make "their common Christianity... a vital force" among the two-thirds of the world's people who knew little or nothing about it.[67]

Although Roosevelt valued all forms of Christianity and pled with Christians to work closely together, he insisted that Christianity was superior to other faiths. He objected that Benjamin Kidd in *Social Evolution* (1898) treated all religious beliefs "as if they were all substantially similar and of the same value." The beliefs of Christianity, Islam, Buddhism, ancestor worship, and fetishism were in many ways contradictory and therefore could not all be true. If there were valid reasons to believe a particular religion and its "supernatural authority," Roosevelt maintained, then there could be no justification for accepting "all religions good and bad alike." Kidd's implication that all religions were essentially the same offended "every earnest believer."[68]

"Roosevelt always thought of himself as a preacher," wrote a contemporary, "and he was always looking for a pulpit."[69] When he did use biblical texts in his speeches, they often took the form of moral exhortations or homilies. Although Washington and Lincoln had created the bully pulpit, Roosevelt made greater use of it than they did. He spoke directly to the American people to marshal public support for his policies and overcome Congressional opposition. William Allen White argued that Roosevelt repeatedly exhorted Americans to "be good, be good, be good; live for righteousness, fight for righteousness, and if need be die for it."[70] Roosevelt insisted that many important public issues involved basic questions of right and wrong, and he frequently denounced those who opposed his policies as "evildoers." Using his bully pulpit, he strove to persuade citizens to conserve the nation's resources; treat individuals equally regardless of race, religion, or reputation; make America a moral force in the world; improve home life;

practice honesty in politics and business; support religious institutions; and promote joy in work, well-rounded character, and service.[71] Some of his bitterest enemies, protested Oscar Straus, Roosevelt's secretary of commerce and labor and the first Jew to serve in the cabinet, claimed that Roosevelt spoke and acted as though he had discovered the Ten Commandments.[72] At lectures he gave at Pacific Theological Seminary in 1911, Roosevelt argued that preaching, whether by a minister or a layman, was worthwhile only if it moved people to action. The former president urged people to practice the same morality in business activities and private affairs.[73] He challenged Americans to treat their spouses and children, neighbors, business associates, competitors, customers, and government officials with compassion and justice.[74] In driving home this point, Roosevelt tended to reduce Christianity to ethics, arguing that the forces of right would triumph if people were "decent, God-fearing, law-abiding, honor-loving, justice doing," fearless, and strong.[75]

Roosevelt also placed tremendous value on character. Good character was even more significant than keen minds and robust bodies.[76] "The foundation-stone of national life is, and ever must be, the high individual character of the average citizen."[77] To Roosevelt, "character was tantamount to goodness." Those with good character practiced "a virtuous way of life as defined by traditional Christian morality."[78] "Material well-being," Roosevelt proclaimed, was "a great good" chiefly because it supplied a basis for building "a high and fine type of character, private and public." Upon the foundation of prosperity, Americans must construct "a lofty national life" because "righteousness exalts a nation."[79] Unless Americans lived "in accordance with the laws of the highest morality," he warned in his 1906 thanksgiving proclamation, its unprecedented prosperity in the long run would be a "curse instead of a blessing." An exponent and exemplar of physical fitness and an advocate of the strenuous life, Roosevelt emphasized that Christianity was for the strong. Only those who possessed "strength and courage" could live effectively as Christians.[80] Christianity must combine virtue with vigor and not "leave strength to those who serve the devil."[81]

Like proponents of the Social Gospel, Roosevelt insisted the church must play a major role in reforming society, including improving living conditions and promoting justice for wage earners.[82] The church, he declared, should be a "potent force in social uplifting."[83] He praised the work of institutional churches that were actively ministering to the material needs of their communities.[84] Roosevelt also strongly supported the ministry of the YMCA and the Salvation Army, which strove to meet people's spiritual and physical needs.[85] Nevertheless, he maintained that the spiritual was ten times as important in the nation's civic and social life as the material.[86] Abundant prosperity, he warned, would not save America if its spiritual senses atrophied.[87]

The frequency and fervency of his "preaching" led many to label Roosevelt a "religious force" in America. Admirers lavished superlatives on the

Republican. The *Independent* praised his "homiletic passion."[88] The president's distinctly religious influence, a minister declared, had a "wholesome and stimulating" impact on the nation's political and domestic life. Although Roosevelt did not frequently refer to God or explicitly discuss matters of faith, his continuous emphasis on morality in his speeches and the way he lived, this pastor argued, demonstrated his Christian commitment. By stressing the importance of character, good citizenship, fair play, and honesty and by urging parents to raise morally upright children, he maintained, Roosevelt had greatly improved public life.[89] Others argued that Roosevelt provided a wonderful personal example by his love for his wife and children.[90] Leading Social Gospeler Washington Gladden praised Roosevelt for courageously attacking the nation's economic injustice.[91] His close friend Gifford Pinchot lauded Roosevelt as "the greatest preacher of righteousness in modern times."[92] As a preacher, Edward Cotton asserted, Roosevelt deserved a place alongside Martin Luther, John Wesley, and George Whitefield, none of whom had "raised higher the standard of moral excellence."[93] To Jane Addams, founder of Hull House in Chicago, the New Yorker was "a veritable preacher of social righteousness with the irresistible eloquence of faith sanctified by work."[94]

Roosevelt and Religious Controversies

Three religious issues caused considerable controversy during Roosevelt's tenure in office: his attempt to remove "In God We Trust" from certain coins, the "Dear Maria" affair, and concerns about Taft's Unitarianism during the 1908 presidential campaign. In 1905, Roosevelt asked sculptor Augustus Saint-Gaudens to design a new penny and ten- and twenty-dollar gold pieces. Considering the words "In God We Trust" an "artistic intrusion," the sculptor recommended that they be eliminated, and the president concurred. Although the U.S. Mint had been stamping "In God We Trust" on some coins only since the 1860s, many objected to removing this phrase as unpatriotic and unchristian. Local chapters of social, labor, and religious organizations censured the new coins, first issued in November 1907, and demanded that the motto be restored. Ministers preached sermons entitled "In God We Trust," religious bodies sent resolutions to Congress, and laypeople wrote hundreds of letters to newspapers.[95] Some religious journals supported the president's actions, arguing either that the separation of church and state required it or that religion did not need state aid.[96] Many more church leaders, however, denounced the new coins as part of a secular crusade to remove religious influences from public life.[97]

This unanticipated barrage of criticism led Roosevelt to issue a public letter to explain his action. He labeled the inscription a "sacrilegious association of God and mammon."[98] "In all my life," Roosevelt asserted, "I have never heard anyone speak reverently of this motto on the coins."[99] Instead, the motto was a "constant source of jest and ridicule" that "cheapened and trivialized the trust in God it was intended to promote."[100] Critics countered that the inscription inspired "lofty emotions," not irreverence. Would Roosevelt also favor expunging the Decalogue, the *United Presbyterian* asked, "because some men treat it with lightness and irreverence"?[101] Some detractors accused him of wanting to replace the motto with "In Theodore We Trust," and a Congressman decried the new coins as "godless."[102] Responding to this public outcry, Congress passed a bill to restore the inscription on all coins minted after July 1, 1908. Although he regretted the controversy his actions had caused and resented the negative motives ascribed to him, Roosevelt, while refusing to veto the bill, continued to oppose it to the end. Because most religiously committed Americans either did not understand or disagreed with his position, this episode probably decreased their respect for the president.

In 1906, Roosevelt requested the resignation of America's ambassador to Austria-Hungary, Bellamy Storer, because of the persistent efforts of his wife, Maria Longworth Storer, to have Archbishop John Ireland made a cardinal. An adult convert to Catholicism, Maria Storer bombarded McKinley and then Roosevelt with letters, beseeching them to intervene with the pope on behalf of Ireland. Although both presidents were personal friends of the wealthy Republicans from Cincinnati, they steadfastly refused on the grounds that it would be an unwarranted intrusion into the affairs of the Catholic Church. Roosevelt told Bellamy Storer in 1903 that he would be "delighted" to see Ireland, for whom he had "the heartiest admiration," made a cardinal. He realized, however, that Rome would resent his meddling in its affairs and that Protestant Americans would be incensed. I cannot as president, he wrote to Bellamy in another letter, "help any clergyman" obtain high rank in his denomination.[103]

Despite such direct statements, Maria Storer continued to badger Roosevelt on behalf of Ireland, hinting to her friends at the Vatican that he supported the nomination but that political pressures prevented him from openly acknowledging this. Roosevelt warned Maria in 1905 that letters she was writing to support Ireland were "utterly improper" in her position as the wife of an American ambassador and that, if they continued, he would be forced to remove her husband from the diplomatic service. When others had approached him to ask the Vatican that particular individuals be appointed cardinals, he had "always positively and unequivocally refused." He would no more try to pressure the pope to make Ireland a cardinal than he would try to "get the Archbishop of Canterbury to establish an Archbishopric in America."[104] Because Maria persisted in writing letters and speaking on Ireland's behalf, her husband was recalled in 1906.

Enraged, the Storers told their version of the story to friends on Capitol Hill, who leaked it to the press. For a week, headlines, editorials, and cartoons in newspapers across the nation discussed the "Dear Maria" scandal. Lacking direct information, journalists pieced together the details of the relationship between the president and the Storers and made moral judgments. Roosevelt's opponents accused him of rashness, deception, and even anti-Catholic bias. Near the end of 1906, as the quarrel was fading from the front pages, the Storers published a lengthy pamphlet defending their actions. Containing much of the correspondence between themselves and Roosevelt since the 1890s, it was mailed to numerous prominent government officials. Long excerpts of their letters printed in newspapers caused Roosevelt to provide a rebuttal, reiterating that his office precluded him from participating in ecclesiastical politics. Although some denounced Roosevelt's dismissal of Storer as an inappropriate punishment for the offense, others insisted the president had allowed him to remain in the diplomatic service too long. Many complained that "diplomacy and ecclesiastical affairs" had been, "for a time at least, disastrously entwined" and insisted that the episode vividly illustrated the dangers of not keeping church and state separate.[105]

During the 1908 campaign, many evangelical Protestants objected to Roosevelt's handpicked successor, William Howard Taft, on the grounds that as a Unitarian he did not believe in the divinity of Christ. Others protested that Taft had been too favorable toward Catholics when he was the governor of the Philippines, an allegation Roosevelt used to urge Catholics to work to elect Taft.[106] Convinced that a man's religious creed should not be a political issue, Roosevelt was alarmed by the hundreds of letters he received from "bigoted, narrow-minded, honest evangelical ... Methodists, Lutherans, Baptists, and some Presbyterians," as he referred to them. The editor of one religious journal protested, "Think of the United States with a President who does not believe that Jesus Christ is the Son of God, but looks upon him ... as a common bastard and low, cunning imposter."[107] Although fuming about bigotry in his private letters, Roosevelt decided it was best for Taft and him not to address the issue publicly. After Taft returned to Washington in October from a campaign tour of the South, where many evangelicals had been hostile to him, Roosevelt attended church with him. He did this, he explained to his son Kermit, to encourage the "sincere but rather ignorant Protestants" among his supporters to vote for Taft.[108]

As soon as the election was over, Roosevelt responded publicly to a letter from J. C. Martin, a piano dealer from Dayton, Ohio, which exemplified the hundreds he had received. He had refused to answer these letters earlier because a person's religious convictions should have no bearing on a political election. Taft had wisely refused to explain his religious beliefs because that might have prompted people to vote for or against him. To discriminate against a candidate because he belonged to a particular church or because, like

Lincoln, he did not belong to any church violated an individual's liberty of conscience, which was "one of the foundations of American life." People were not entitled to know matters that were "purely between a man and his Maker." If it were proper to oppose a candidate for being a Unitarian, as were John Quincy Adams and Edward Everett Hale, the current chaplain of the Senate, "then it would be equally proper to support or oppose a man because of his views on justification by faith, or the methods of administering the sacraments." Roosevelt protested further that Martin slandered fellow Protestants when he declared that most of them would not vote for a Catholic for president. (This was not a direct issue with Taft, but Martin, like many others, had claimed incorrectly that Taft's wife and brother were Catholics.) He argued that citizens should vote for the most qualified candidates, regardless of whether they were Protestants or Catholics. He predicted that in the years to come, the United States would have Catholic and Jewish presidents.[109]

Roosevelt's letter evoked a variety of responses. Catholic and Jewish journals called it a "ringing pronouncement of religious liberty and of political equality."[110] Praising Roosevelt for publicizing the Ten Commandments and refurbishing the Beatitudes, *Woman's Home Companion* commended and published the president's letter.[111] To many evangelical Protestants, the issue was not bigotry, religious toleration, or even the divinity of Christ, but fear that a Catholic president would take orders from the pope and disregard the separation of church and state. "A vote for a Roman Catholic," the Baptist *Watchman* of Boston declared, "is a vote for the Roman Church, and is a vote for the subversion of the very principle President Roosevelt was defending, that no one should be discriminated against because of religion." The fear of having a Catholic president, the Presbyterian *Interior* of Chicago explained, was primarily due to "the papacy's failure definitely to renounce its claim of 'temporal sovereignty.'" The Methodist *Christian Advocate* of New York warned that a Catholic president would try to channel public funds to support his church's causes.[112] The doctrine that the pope was supreme in both the political and the ecclesiastical spheres, *The Lutheran* argued, meant that a devoted, consistent Catholic president must use his power to advance his church.[113] The Evangelical Lutheran Church of North America insisted that its members could vote for a Unitarian or a Jew as president but not for a committed Catholic. Quoting numerous papal encyclicals, they contended that Catholic doctrine was antagonistic to the Constitution, liberty of conscience, and the separation of church and state. Their position was not prompted by "narrow bigotry" but by Catholic actions that had frequently "proved disastrous to the peace and prosperity of nations."[114] Others even protested that Roosevelt had furnished clandestine support to the Catholic Church.[115] In some ways, the issues raised by the 1908 campaign were a rehearsal for the much more acrimonious elections of 1928 and 1960.

Roosevelt's Relationship with Religious Constituencies

Despite these controversies, because of his personal convictions, public pronouncements, governmental policies, and personal friendships, Roosevelt managed to maintain a positive relationship with most American Protestants. Roosevelt shared many of the commitments of Social Gospelers and had close connections with key leaders of the movement, most notably Lyman Abbott and Washington Gladden. He consulted Walter Rauschenbusch, a professor of church history at Rochester Theological Seminary, several times on policy matters after his book *Christianity and the Social Crisis* made him a public figure in 1907.[116] During his presidency, Roosevelt spoke to numerous Protestant groups, usually emphasizing civic righteousness and applied Christianity.[117] The Republican appointed several proponents of muscular Christianity to major administrative posts, most notably Gifford Pinchot, James R. Garfield, William Phipps, Henry Stimson, and William Henry Moody.[118]

While having respect for all Protestants, Roosevelt especially valued the convictions and contributions of Reformed Christians and Episcopalians, with whom he usually worshiped, as well as Lutherans and Methodists. Roosevelt confessed he had "special regard for the Lutherans," especially because they supported his policies.[119] While president, Roosevelt wrote, he had gained a great appreciation for Methodists. "Most emphatically," they were doing "the work of the Lord," and they embodied "a peculiarly strong and virile type of American citizenship."[120] During the 1904 campaign, Roosevelt proposed that his vice presidential candidate Charles Fairbanks, a Methodist, appeal to his coreligionists and insisted that the hundreds of Methodist pastors in New York City could do much to help the Republican cause.[121]

As a legislator, New York City's police commissioner, and governor of New York, Roosevelt had established cordial relations with Catholics by means of both his policies and personal friendships, most notably with A. P. Doyle, editor of the *Catholic World*. His frequent attacks on religious bigotry endeared him to Catholic leaders. In an 1894 article in the *Forum*, Roosevelt denounced the efforts of the American Protective Association to discriminate against Catholics "both politically and socially" as "utterly un-American," "base, and contemptible."[122] Each person deserved "a square deal" without regard to "his creed, his ancestry, or his birthplace."[123] Roosevelt strove to persuade YMCA officials to allow Catholic priests and laymen to become directors of local branches.[124] Throughout his lengthy political career, Roosevelt frequently corresponded with Catholic leaders, including Eugene Philbin of New York, Archbishop John Ireland of St. Paul, and James Cardinal Gibbons of Maryland.[125] Roosevelt regularly consulted Catholic priests and laymen on issues affecting their church and maintained close contact with Catholic politicians. The Republican applauded Catholic efforts to help the poor and downtrodden. "I can recall priest after priest," he wrote, "whose disinterested parish work...represented one continuous battle for civilization and humanity."[126] Roosevelt repeatedly emphasized that Protestants, Catholics, and Jews all served in his cabinet.[127] "Some of the men in my administration I most trusted and on whom I most relied were Catholics," Roosevelt told Raymond Robins in 1915.[128]

Roosevelt enjoyed much more cordial relations with Catholics than most other Republican presidents had. He rejoiced that "Catholics and Protestants, Jews and Gentiles, are learning the grandest of all lessons—that they can best serve God by serving their fellowmen, and best serve their fellowmen, not by wrangling among themselves, but by a generous rivalry in working for righteousness and against evil."[129] Roosevelt regarded Catholics as allies, praised their teachings and actions that promoted "social and civic righteousness, and commended their efforts to inculcate Christian values in new immigrants."[130] In his campaigns for both governor and president, Roosevelt worked harder than most Republicans to win Catholic votes and enjoyed greater success.

Nevertheless, several matters caused friction between Roosevelt and Catholics. He disliked the doctrine of papal infallibility and the church's authoritarian structure. Catholics saw his strong endorsement of the public school system as an implicit criticism of parochial schools.[131] Moreover, he inherited from McKinley the problem of the Catholic Church's role in the Philippines. The church owned large amounts of land and had significant wealth, and under Spanish control, the friars had wielded significant political influence. This had fueled discontent against Spain and continued to cause problems after the Spanish-American War ended. Like his predecessor, Roosevelt wanted to diminish the priests' political power, buy the land owned by the Catholic Church, and resell it to the Filipino people, goals some American Catholics vehemently opposed.[132] Whereas McKinley wanted to "Christianize" the islanders (convert them to Protestantism), Roosevelt declared that their "uplifting...must come chiefly through making them better Catholics and better citizens."[133] Roosevelt was very surprised and upset by Catholic criticism of his administration's policies in the Philippines and urged his Catholic friends to defend him. In response, Archbishop John Ireland told the press that no president had been "more fair-minded and impartial in religious matters than Theodore Roosevelt."[134]

Roosevelt stressed treating all people equally regardless of religion, and unlike many other members of his social class, he displayed no anti-Semitism. As New York's police commissioner, Roosevelt hired many Jews and often extolled Jewish officers. He loved to tell the story about a German clergyman who came to the city to hold meetings attacking Jews. Roosevelt could not prevent him from speaking, but "to make him look ridiculous," he assigned forty Jewish policemen to maintain order while he spoke. "So he made his speeches denouncing the Jews, protected exclusively by Jews."[135] Despite appointing Oscar Straus as secretary of commerce and labor, however, Roosevelt, while president, was not particularly sympathetic to Jewish concerns.[136] Illustrative of his approach was a 1903 incident involving Russian Jews. Actions falsely attributed to Jews in Kishinev evoked a pogrom that killed forty-five, injured more than five hundred, and left thousands homeless. These atrocities produced vigorous protests by American Jews, efforts to aid victims, and pleas to the administration to appeal to the Russian government to stop these injustices. Although initially unresponsive, Roosevelt eventually supported sending a protest petition to the czar. The Russians denounced the petition for interfering with their internal affairs. Nevertheless, Roosevelt's largely symbolic actions increased Jewish support for him at home.[137]

As part of their carefully crafted appeal during the 1904 campaign to ethnic, socioeconomic, and religious groups, Republicans worked diligently to "enlist religious bodies in the Roosevelt coalition." Campaign staff created the Independent Roosevelt Committee for Jewish voters and published endorsements, like that of a prominent New York Jew who praised the president's "sympathy for our people in Russia." His appointment of Catholics and record in the Philippines helped Roosevelt run well among Catholics.[138]

Roosevelt's Philosophy of Government

Although imperialist, Darwinian, and racial assumptions influenced Roosevelt's worldview, Christianity, especially the version espoused by turn-of-the-century Social Gospelers, played a significant role in shaping his philosophy.[139] He shared their fervent commitment to the concept of justice and right. Roosevelt maintained that the government must work to provide an "even distribution of justice" and pass legislation that was good "for the Nation as a whole."[140] Achieving these ends required honest, upright public servants.[141] The American republic would flourish only if its people had a "keen sense of righteousness and justice." Because God had given so much to Americans, he expected much in return, as the Parable of the Talents illustrated.[142]

The good society could best be created, Roosevelt argued, by a public-private partnership that based national and individual life on biblical principles and promoted gradual, not radical, change. He strove to steer the American republic safety through perilous straits without crashing on the rocks of either revolution or reaction and by avoiding the dangers of both extreme individualism and collectivism. He identified crusading journalists, scientific socialists, and callous capitalists as the principal threats to the nation.[143] "In social and economic, as in political reforms," he explained, "the violent revolutionary extremist is the worst friend of liberty, just as the arrogant and intense reactionary is the worst friend of order."[144] Taking an image from Bunyan's *Pilgrim's Progress*, Roosevelt denounced journalists who he thought exaggerated society's problems as "muckrakers." Their "sensational, lurid," indiscriminate, and sometimes untruthful attacks on the character of businessmen and public officials did more damage than the crimes they sought to expose.[145]

Roosevelt also thundered against certain types of socialists. He recognized that socialists came in many forms and insisted he could work with those he labeled moral socialists or opportunistic socialists, the ones who rejected the materialism and atheism of Karl Marx. However, he despised doctrinaire socialists who were bitterly opposed to private property, religion, marriage, and conventional morality. The solutions they proposed for industrial and economic problems were "not merely false, but fatal." The true remedies for the nation's maladies were "partly economic and partly spiritual." Efforts by individuals and groups to alleviate social ills and to pass just laws were necessary. So were religious and moral teachings that increased "the spirit of human brotherhood," an educational system that trained people for "every form of useful service," a distribution of industrial profits that enabled "intelligent and thrifty" wage earners to become businessmen, and a "strong, just, wise and democratic" government that forcefully promoted these ends.[146] Thus, Roosevelt sought to undercut support for socialism by building a partnership between government agencies and private organizations that accomplished its most worthy objectives.[147]

"Nine-tenths of my fighting," Roosevelt wrote in 1908, "has been against men of enormous wealth, and their henchmen" in the world of business or politics and the lawyers and newspaper editors "who do their bidding."[148] As long as these men promoted evil, it was necessary "to smite them with the sword of the Lord and of Gideon!"[149] Through legislation and judicial reform, Roosevelt sought to remedy social and economic evils and curb the power of corporations.[150] To achieve these ends and thwart the growth of socialism, anarchism, and other dangerous ideologies, Roosevelt argued, the "sphere of the State's action should be extended very cautiously" and only when it would not crush "healthy individual initiative." By working through voluntary organizations, individuals could avoid the dangers of both state control and excessive individualism.[151] Roosevelt's pursuit of policies he believed furthered the public interest, most notably settling the coal strike in 1902 and prosecuting the Northern Securities Company in 1904, upset many wealthy Republican businessmen, some of whom regarded him as an overly zealous progressive and others as a dangerous radical.[152]

Roosevelt repeatedly urged Americans to apply the Ten Commandments and the teachings of the Old Testament prophets and Jesus, especially the

Golden Rule, more fully to their public lives. In speeches and essays, he emphasized practicing Christian citizenship and civic helpfulness and obeying the eighth and ninth commandments in politics.[153] He exhorted Americans to love, respect, and honor God by loving neighbors, treating people justly and mercifully, and ensuring justice for all. The United States must apply the same standard to all—men and women, rich and poor, employer and employee—and give everyone "a reasonable equality of opportunity." Roosevelt challenged Americans to do their "duty well and manfully," to "uphold righteousness by deed and word," to "be both honest and brave, [and] to serve high ideals, yet use practical methods."[154] Those who did not were "a nuisance . . . a source of weakness, [and] an encouragement to wrongdoers."[155] Raising the nation's moral consciousness, he insisted, was essential to passing progressive economic and social legislation; these laws, in turn, were crucial to achieving a more just, humane, righteous society.[156] Nevertheless, he contended, "Great advances in general social well-being" could rarely be achieved by legislation alone; normally, they were a result of incessant individual effort.[157] Thus, "self-reliance, self-help, and self-mastery" were the keys to constructive social change.[158]

Roosevelt argued in his autobiography that "I did greatly broaden the use of executive power. . . . I acted for the common good . . . whenever and in whatever manner was necessary."[159] Insisting that the president was "the steward of the public welfare," Roosevelt strove to counterbalance the power of large corporations and remedy major societal problems by passing a pure food and drug law, supervising insurance companies, curbing child labor, improving working conditions and wages, enacting workers' compensation laws, and regulating railroad rates.[160] "To an impressive degree," argues Lewis Gould, Roosevelt succeeded in making the federal government "the most effective instrument in advancing the interests of the people as a whole."[161]

Roosevelt's understanding of the U.S. role in the world was shaped by his conviction that nations, like individuals, were bound by moral codes that exalted character and social responsibility.[162] America's "steady aim," he averred, must be to "raise the ethical standard of national action just as we strive to raise the ethical standard of individual action."[163] He insisted that the United States stood for the "ideals of democracy, of liberty under the law, of social progress through peaceful industry, education and commerce and of uncorrupted Christianity," which largely involved fulfilling Micah 6:8.[164] As H. W. Brands argues, "To an even greater degree than in domestic matters, he believed that his arm wielded the sword of righteousness in international affairs."[165] Honesty, justice, and mercy, Roosevelt proclaimed, should govern America's relations with other nations. "We must treat other nations as we would wish to be treated in return, judging each in any given crisis as we ourselves ought to be judged—that is by our conduct in that crisis."[166]

Injecting a "mixture of nationalism and practical idealism into global affairs," Roosevelt insisted that the United States had a "moral obligation to overawe bullies, maintain order, and uplift backward peoples."[167] As America became a world power, it gained "world duties." The United States had become the world's leading economic nation, but it had not developed the diplomatic and military strength to match. It must do so to protect American interests, promote democracy and prosperity, and deter evil.[168]

Roosevelt was an advocate of peace through strength. To him, justice and righteousness were more important than peace. In fact, true peace depended on justice.[169] He preferred to obtain righteous arrangements through peaceful means but was willing to use force to achieve this end. "We infinitely desire peace," he declared in 1903, "and the surest way of obtaining it is to show we are not afraid of war."[170] "The most important service I rendered to peace," Roosevelt argued in his autobiography, was sending the American battle fleet around the world.[171] The United States must deal justly with weaker nations and show the strongest that it could maintain its rights. While speaking courteously and dealing fairly, America must "keep itself armed and ready."[172] If the English Puritans and the American Founding Fathers had valued peace more than righteousness, Roosevelt contended, they would never have resorted to war to overthrow oppression.[173] The colonel declared, however, that he abhorred war and rejoiced that during his seven and a half years as president, not a single soldier fired a bullet against a foreigner.[174]

Roosevelt's most famous aphorism—"Speak softly and carry a big stick"—gave him a reputation for being bellicose and impetuous. Numerous critics claimed that "he rarely spoke softly and wielded his Big Stick all too readily."[175] They objected that he greatly expanded the power of the presidency to conduct foreign affairs without Congressional consent and radically redefined the Monroe Doctrine.[176] In reality, Roosevelt's rhetoric was much more bellicose than his actions. He skillfully negotiated the peaceful settlement of numerous disputes, including the Russo-Japanese War (for which he received the first Nobel Prize awarded to an American), a conflict over Morocco in 1906, and several clashes between Central American countries.[177] Roosevelt boasted that at the end of his presidency, the United States was "at absolute peace, and there was no nation in the world...whom we had wronged, or from whom we had anything to fear."[178] Blessed by not having to deal with a major international crisis, Roosevelt improved relations with Great Britain, dealt adroitly with Germany, began construction of an isthmian canal, made the United States dominant in the Caribbean, and pursued as enlightened a policy in the Philippines as America's imperialist assumptions allowed.[179]

Roosevelt repeatedly declared that he stood for certain principles, most notably justice, righteousness, and fairness, which he refused to compromise. "I am in honor bound," he asserted, "to act up to my beliefs and convictions."[180] Roosevelt wrote to Raymond Robins that "when I have felt that a fundamental issue of morals or of vital national interest or honor was concerned, I have never hesitated to follow my belief, even though I was certain that to do so would hurt me in the estimate of the people as a whole." While not sacrificing their principles, he insisted, public officials must be willing to compromise on programs and policies. To be effective, Roosevelt argued, politicians must combine the ideal with the practical, as had the framers of the Constitution.[181] Ignoring the "fact that a reform must be practicable" to be valuable, many ardent reformers, he protested, proposed unworkable panaceas. He strove instead to use the government's power to take concrete steps to diminish social evils.[182]

Roosevelt's Faith and Public Policies

Roosevelt's religious commitments are clearly evident in many of his policies, including his regulation of trusts, support for marriage, campaign for workmen's compensation laws, attitude toward blacks, settlement of the Russo-Japanese War, and enactment of pure food and drug laws. Concerned about the nation's rampant "moral decadence and materialism," he waged a crusade to defeat the "malefactors of great wealth" and elevate America's moral standards to save "our own national soul."[183] To illustrate his approach, I will focus on three key issues: his role in mediating the 1902 anthracite coal strike, "taking" Panama to build an isthmus canal, and promoting conservation.

Roosevelt endorsed the right of workers to organize to advance their welfare. He recognized the "enormous economic, political and moral possibilities of the trade union," but he did not always "champion the cause" of workers because he thought their strikes were often unwarranted and their methods harmful.[184] Roosevelt argued that low wages, excessive hours, and poor working conditions led to "wholesale moral as well as economic degeneration," whereas decent wages, fewer hours, and an improved working environment brought "intellectual, moral and social uplift."[185] The government must provide a "square deal" for both labor unions and corporations.[186] In the interest of justice and fair play, however, it "must inevitably sympathize" with those "struggling for a decent life" rather than those who were "fighting for larger profits." Roosevelt rejoiced that unions were growing in power and wisdom and were doing much to solve industrial problems; reduce poverty, disease, industrial accidents, and unemployment; further industrial democracy; and attain greater social and industrial justice.[187] Roosevelt sought to make the federal government "a model employer" by giving all employees an eight-hour day and passing a workmen's compensation law. He also took steps to improve working conditions in the

District of Columbia and to end child labor. Roosevelt was convinced that his approach would prevent class warfare and enable the interests of wage earners and employers to be "harmonized, compromised and adjusted."[188] To him, the "great captains of industry" were entitled to "great rewards" as long as they efficiently served the public, but they must not be tolerated when they behaved as "the masters of the public."[189] His strategy was not to prevent the formation of trusts but to control them "in the interest of the public welfare."[190]

In the spring of 1902, about 140,000 miners working in northern central Pennsylvania struck to obtain higher wages, an eight-hour day, a fairer system for weighing coal, and union recognition. The continuing flood of unskilled immigrants, coupled with the "courts' granting of injunctions against organized labor and their interpretation of antitrust laws in an anti-labor fashion," had made the miners' situation very difficult. Their pay was inadequate, "their hours were backbreakingly long," and the mines were "appallingly dangerous." Moreover, the coal companies controlled almost every aspect of their lives, owning their houses, grocery stories, churches, and even the cemeteries "where they were buried, often prematurely."[191] John Mitchell, the president of the United Mine Workers (UMW), offered to submit the miners' grievances to binding arbitration, but the owners refused. They expected a shortage of coal "and violence and sabotage in the minefields" to compel Roosevelt to use the military to end the strike.[192] As winter approached, this shortage threatened to bring calamity. To Roosevelt, the situation confronting the New England and Middle Atlantic states was as "serious as if they had been threatened by the invasion of a hostile army of overwhelming force." Yet initially, he felt there was little he could do because he had no clear jurisdiction for intervening unless the governor of Pennsylvania asked for federal help. Nevertheless, his sense of morality and justice, belief that the strike was a test of his presidential authority, and fear of the dire results of a prolonged strike impelled him to act. By the early fall, violence was escalating in the coalfields. Aggravated assaults, riots, and arson were common. Bridges had been blown up, mines flooded, and trains wrecked. The president blamed the failure to settle the strike primarily on the capitalists who controlled the coal business. "They knew that the suffering among the miners was great; they were confident" that if the government did not intervene, "they would win; and they refused to consider that the public had any rights in the matter." They were guided by an extreme individualism that upheld the "rights of property and the freedom of individual action" and ignored the public good. The owners failed to recognize that both their interests and those of the miners must be subordinated to the interests of the whole community.[193] Their ignoring "the terrible nature of the catastrophe impending over the poor" threatened to generate a "great social disturbance."[194] Roosevelt recognized that the miners had a huge disadvantage in the conflict: The coal companies "could easily dispense with the services of any particular miner," who would have great trouble finding another job.[195]

Roosevelt was reluctant to intervene, but desperate situations (to him, only the Civil War was a more serious crisis) called for radical measures.[196] Admitting he had no "right to intervene...on legal grounds," Roosevelt asked the owners of the coal mines and Mitchell to meet with him in Washington in early October. For the first time in American history, a president sought to mediate between capitalists and laborers. At this meeting, the owners asked Roosevelt to abolish the UMW because it was a trust and to use troops to reopen the mines. Roosevelt was upset with the owners' belligerence and favorably impressed with Mitchell's willingness to arbitrate. Moreover, the owners' provocative pronouncements inflamed public opinion. Their chief spokesman, George Baer, wrote to a resident of Wilkes-Barre: "The rights and interests of the laboring man will be protected," "not by the labor agitators, but by the Christian men to whom God in his infinite wisdom has given the control of the property interests of the country, and upon the successful management of which so much depends.... Pray earnestly that right may triumph, always remembering that the Lord God Omnipotent still reigns, and that his reign is one of law and order, not of violence and crime."[197] The letter soon appeared in print, provoking heated rejoinders. The *New York Times* labeled it very close to "unconscious blasphemy." The doctrine of the divine right of kings, protested the Baptist *Watchman* of Boston, was not as "intolerable as the doctrine of the divine right of plutocrats to administer things in general with the presumption" they were doing the will of God.[198] Despite such criticisms, some religious leaders cautioned Roosevelt not to intervene in the strike; they argued that it was not his role and that he already had too much to do.[199]

His positive appraisal of labor unions prompted the president to treat the UMW as a legitimate participant in the bargaining process. While pursuing a just solution to the strike, Roosevelt "established the precedent that the White House would not remain aloof during a domestic economic crisis."[200] Although it took considerable maneuvering to satisfy both sides, Roosevelt assembled a commission to investigate the strike. The miners returned to work in late October, and in March 1903, the commission issued its report. Both sides won concessions. Miners received a 10 percent pay hike, a nine-hour workday, their own checkers to weigh the coal, and "a system for arbitrating job-related disputes."[201] The commission also refused to recognize the UMW, strongly denounced the union's boycotting tactics and use of violence, and recommended that owners raise the price of coal 10 percent. Although his actions hurt his relationship with some captains of industry, the biggest winner was Roosevelt, who was widely praised at home and abroad. He had used binding arbitration to settle a labor dispute, made the federal government a broker between capital and labor, and underscored his belief that the public interest was more important than that of either party.[202] Rarely one to be modest, Roosevelt later concluded that the resolution of the dispute was a triumph "not only of industrial but of social reform and progress."[203] He rejoiced that justice had prevailed and capitalists and laborers had begun to consider each other's perspectives.[204] Speaking for many, William Allen White proclaimed Roosevelt's settlement of the strike "a victory for sheer righteousness."[205]

Even though Roosevelt repeatedly appealed to a higher law and stressed ethical principles, historians have tended to view him as a warrior more than a moralist. They have often assumed that his "preaching" was "either hypocritical or blindly 'self-righteous.'"[206] Thomas Bailey accuses him of browbeating "other nations into submission." Howard Beale contends that Roosevelt believed the United States "could never act unjustly or wrongly."[207] Nowhere is this accusation made more forcefully than with regard to the U.S. acquisition of the right to build the Panama Canal in 1903. One of the most strongly condemned actions in the history of American foreign relations, it has been described as the "rape of Colombia," "a big black mark," and "cowboy diplomacy." To most historians, it is a blatant example of Roosevelt's use of the "big stick" and American imperialism. Critics contend it displays Roosevelt's insensitivity to Latin American opinion and excessive personal ambition. Few have accepted Roosevelt's contention that his actions were based on moral principles. Disagreeing with these assertions, Frederick Marks concludes that Roosevelt usually approached "issues in terms of right and wrong" and preached "with genuine conviction," and this was the case with Panama in 1903.[208]

Roosevelt's argument for "taking" Panama revolved around several historical, diplomatic, and practical contentions. First was the history of Panama and its relationship with Colombia. After obtaining independence from Spain in 1821, Panama was at times a sovereign nation and at others part of a confederation. In 1886, Colombia stripped Panama of its autonomy and thereafter exploited Panama, taking most of the revenue from the isthmus railway tolls and providing no schools, hospitals, or other public facilities in return. The Panamanians repeatedly tried to gain their independence, displaying both their intense dissatisfaction with their subjugation and Colombia's inability to keep order on the isthmus. If American troops had not stopped several revolts at Colombia's request and to ensure the smooth operation of the isthmus railroad, Panama would have become an independent nation much earlier.[209]

Second, Roosevelt argued that Colombia was willing to accept all the American terms for building the canal except those relating to price. Its ambassador had agreed to American terms for building the canal in January 1903, but Colombia's president, José Marroquin, and a specially called congress had failed to ratify the treaty. The Colombians insisted that an initial payment of $10 million and annual payments of $250,000 were grossly inadequate to compensate their nation for giving up its sovereignty over a six-mile-wide strip of land. Colombia appeared to be biding its time in hopes of improving its negotiating position and securing more money from the United States. Colombian greed, Roosevelt protested, prevented progress and constituted "international blackmail."[210] He argued that the Colombians were "absolutely impossible to deal with" because they were corrupt and "governmentally utterly incompetent."[211] Although the United States had dealt justly and generously with the Colombians, he contended, they had not been reasonable or trustworthy and cared only about their own interests.[212]

Third, Roosevelt accepted the argument of John Bassett Moore, a professor of international law at Columbia University, that an 1846 treaty with Colombia guaranteed the United States the right to build a canal across the isthmus. Fourth, construction of a canal promised great benefits to Panama, the United States, and the world. It would link the oceans, speed communications, increase trade, benefit the United States industrially and militarily, and help Latin American nations commercially. He wrote John Hay that "the Bogotá lot of jack rabbits" should not be "allowed permanently to bar one of the future highways of civilization."[213] The needs of the civilized world took precedence over the interests of "the little wildcat republic of Colombia," Roosevelt told his son Kermit.[214] Since announcing its intention to construct an interoceanic waterway, he emphasized, the United States had received "assurances of approval and encouragement" from around the world.[215]

Fifth, Roosevelt alleged, the United States did not officially endorse or directly aid the two-day Panamanian revolution in November that involved almost no bloodshed. While privately confiding he would be delighted if Panama became an independent state, the president said nothing publicly to encourage revolution.[216] In his January 4, 1904, message to Congress, he claimed that no one in his government had played "any part in preparing, inciting, or encouraging the . . . revolution on the Isthmus of Panama."[217] On the other hand, the United States aided the revolt by expressing extreme hostility toward Colombia, not discouraging the rebels' plans, and sending three battleships to the waters around Panama to prevent Colombian troops from landing. Moreover, it quickly recognized Panama as an independent nation. Justifying his actions, Roosevelt claimed, "I simply ceased to stamp out the different revolutionary fuses that were already burning" and insisted that the United States had helped Panama gain self-government and freedom from "alien oppressors."[218] He was convinced the revolution represented the will of the vast majority of Panamanians.[219] "Every consideration of international morality and expediency, of duty to the Panama people, and of satisfaction of our own national interests and honor," Roosevelt wrote, compelled the United States to recognize Panama.[220]

In December 1903, the Panamanian government accepted the original terms offered to Colombia for the American right to build a canal and exercise sovereignty over the canal zone. Although most Americans were pleased that the canal was going to be built and the Senate voted 66 to 14 to approve the treaty with Panama, many criticized Roosevelt's use of presidential power and military threat to obtain this end and considered his defense of American actions disingenuous. "This mad plunge of ours is simply and solely a vulgar and mercenary venture," protested the *New York Evening Post*, "without a rag to cover its sordidness and shame."[221] Expressing the view of more Americans, the *Detroit News* declared, "Let us not be mealy-mouthed about this. We want Panama."[222]

These considerations led Roosevelt to maintain that American actions accorded "with the highest standards of international morality." Those who criticized them were either misinformed or had a twisted morality. If the United States had acted differently, it would have betrayed its own, Panama's, and the world's interests. Colombia had hoped to "seize the French company's property for nothing," an act of "bandit morality."[223] Roosevelt insisted that during the entire affair, the United States acted with "good faith," "extraordinary patience and large generosity."[224] In 1914, when the Senate was discussing paying Colombia a $25 million indemnity to express its regret for American actions with regard to Panama, Roosevelt protested vehemently: "Either the course we took in 1903 was right," he argued, in which case it was outrageous to pay this "belated blackmail," or "it was wrong, in which case we now have no right to be on the Isthmus. . . ." "Every action we took," he reiterated, was consistent with "the highest principles of public and private morality."[225]

In his autobiography, Roosevelt labeled the construction of the Panama Canal as one of the greatest accomplishments of his presidency, comparable to the Louisiana Purchase.[226] As Nathan Miller argues, "Personal ambition, intense patriotism," and his belief that "superior" nations were responsible for weaker ones all influenced his actions.[227] Yet, given Roosevelt's worldview, these factors were insufficient to justify his conduct. To take the course he did, he had to be convinced—and he was—that he acted to promote justice, righteousness, and the welfare of civilization. The barrage of criticism his actions provoked led Roosevelt to defend the morality of his actions in dozens of letters, conversations, speeches, and his autobiography.[228]

A third issue that was dear to Roosevelt's heart, furnished him with some major victories, and provoked extensive controversy was conservation. As in the cases of the coal strike and Panama, critics claimed Roosevelt exceeded his authority and acted hastily and illegally.[229] As one who loved to hunt, fish, and hike in the woods and who had operated a cattle ranch in the Dakota Territory, explored vast sections of the American wilderness, and written extensively about natural history, Roosevelt deeply desired to preserve

America's scenic treasures and wildlife and conserve its natural resources.[230] When he became president, little had been done to prevent the destruction of its soil, forests, wildlife, or ecosystems.[231]

Roosevelt's efforts focused on three areas: reclamation, preservation, and conservation. In its first seven years, the Reclamation Act of 1902 provided funds for thirty projects, including many large dams. Roosevelt established more than fifty wildlife refuges, created five national parks, tripled the amount of timberland set aside by his predecessors, and designated millions of acres as public land because of its mineral wealth, potential for water-power, or scenic beauty. Reclamation produced no controversy because it took nothing from anyone and interfered with no one's benefits. The con-servation of forests, coal and mineral lands, oil reserves, and potential power sites, however, was strongly opposed by various groups. Logging companies, mine operators, power companies, cattle ranchers, western developers, po-tential settlers, and some officials in western states wanted to use these re-sources for private purposes.[232] Congressmen objected that the president's plan to rely on bureaucrats and experts to oversee conservation policies would prevent them from representing the will of the citizens they most directly affected. Roosevelt countered that the management of natural re-sources was too complex to be directed by "the whims of the democratic process." It must be controlled in a nonpolitical and disinterested way for the common good and not be subject to the pressures of competing interest groups.[233] Prevailing over his opponents, Roosevelt created several govern-ment agencies to further his ends—the U.S. Reclamation Service, the Inland Waterways Commission, and the Country Life Commission (to help farmers)— and enlarged the power of the Bureau of Forestry.

In 1908, Roosevelt convened the nation's governors, members of Con-gress, the Cabinet, Supreme Court justices, prominent conservationists, and noted businessmen to discuss the issue of conservation. The conference in-spired a full-fledged conservation movement and led to the creation of conservation commissions in thirty-six states and the National Conservation Commission, which produced an inventory of America's forest, land, min-eral, and water resources.[234] The United States, Roosevelt asserted, must expand its knowledge of and better use its natural resources so that its population could grow, its industries multiply, and its hidden wealth be de-veloped for the benefit of humanity.[235] As he did in the case of the coal strike and the building of the Panama Canal, he argued that the interests of the few must give way to the larger welfare. The United States must no longer allow individuals "to injure the future of the Republic" for their "own temporary and immediate profit." Americans had "the right and duty" to prevent the destruction of their natural resources.[236] Succinctly put, "the rights of the public to...natural resources outweigh[ed] private rights."[237]

Roosevelt was a committed conservationist not because it was politically popular but because of his life experiences, love of nature, and belief that the president must be a steward of public resources. He strove to modify American behavior toward nature, worked to educate the public about the social and moral virtues of conservation, and tried to persuade citizens to pressure Congress to pass his policies. Roosevelt insisted that people must exercise dominion over nature. This, in turn, would promote economic growth and provide increased opportunity and liberty. In short, Roosevelt sought to make conservation a salient political issue by linking it to "socially valued ideas and beliefs." He implied that conserving natural resources would "re-generate the American spirit."[238] After leaving the presidency, Roosevelt called conservation a "great moral issue" that helped ensure "the health and continuance of the nation."[239] Despite achieving many victories, he failed to create a unified conservation policy because of Congressional opposition, bureaucratic barriers, and rival beliefs, especially in the sanctity of private property.[240] Unlike his actions in Panama, subsequent generations have ap-plauded his contributions to the field of conservation, and many consider them his greatest legacy.

A Final Assessment

"I am not in the least concerned as to whether I will have any place in history," Roosevelt told journalist William Allen White in November 1906.[241] Although Roosevelt's claim seems dubious, countless others strove to eval-uate his place. They could hardly have done otherwise. Roosevelt was argu-ably the world's most dominant personality during the early twentieth century. Larger than life, he was continually the center of attention in America. "Father always wanted to be the bride at every wedding and the corpse at every funeral," one of his sons allegedly quipped. In the judgment of Nathan Miller, "no president was more successful in holding the lime-light."[242] A man of enormous energy, Roosevelt played tennis, hiked in the woods and streams, walked so briskly his Secret Service agents had to hustle to keep up, read a book a day, and entertained an endless flow of intellectuals, politicians, artists, former Rough Riders, and Harvard alumni as guests at the White House.[243] Flamboyant, dramatic, colorful, courageous, and brash, Roosevelt used his power as president to ensure that the world's greatest economic power played a more active role in global affairs. Lewis Gould concludes that Roosevelt "posed some of the right questions about conser-vation, the control of corporations, the welfare of the average American, and what constituted a just society."[244]

While some proclaimed him superior to Washington and Lincoln, others denounced his motives as dishonorable and accused him of instigating dastardly plots.[245] Many canonized him; others detested him; few were neutral. The *Christian Advocate* reported that some revered Roosevelt as a demigod, and others cursed him as a demon. To admirers, he exhibited "the highest statesmanship" and "the most splendid courage" and was "the most exalted" political and social reformer of the age. To enemies, Roosevelt was a half-crazy, bombastic, hypocritical self-seeker who masqueraded as an expert in everything.[246] He was compared with "Julius Caesar, Andrew Jackson, Napoleon, [and] Kaiser Wilhelm II" and called "a combination of Simple Simon and Machiavelli."[247]

Despite disagreeing with him on some issues, many religious leaders lauded Roosevelt's high ideals and valiant fight for righteousness. The *United Presbyterian* rejoiced that his administration had awakened "righteousness throughout the nation." By both preaching righteousness and passing legislation based on moral principles, *The Lutheran* argued, Roosevelt had "made it popular to profess moral purposes and ideals" and act righteously. His ability to achieve his goals without surrendering his principles had been "an illustrated sermon . . . more convincing than the formal preaching of the churches."[248] "His influence as a moral reformer," wrote Lyman Abbott, had strongly shaped American life.[249]

The fictional character Roosevelt most admired was Greatheart, Christian's guide in Bunyan's *Pilgrim's Progress*.[250] The colonel frequently alluded to this literary hero to underscore his arguments. "We gird up our loins as a nation," he thundered, "to play our part manfully in winning the ultimate triumph . . . and with unfaltering steps tread the rough road of endeavor . . . battling for the right, as Greatheart . . . battled in Bunyan's immortal story."[251] After Roosevelt died, others made the comparison as well. Rudyard Kipling penned a poem in his memory, which he titled "Greatheart." Ferdinand Iglehart argued that, like Bunyan's fictional hero, Roosevelt sought to remove the difficulties and dangers in the pathway of life to help others escape harm and discover truth.[252] "Greatheart he was," wrote William Allen White, "passionate, brave, generous, kind, and wise—a great heart that revived to righteousness a nation that was fattening in greed, languishing in iniquity." Roosevelt had entered politics "for the fun of the game and the glory of God." This "flaming prophet of justice" had continually exhorted Americans to live by biblical standards.[253]

Others offer a different perspective. Detractors denounced Roosevelt as "cunning, selfish, vindictive, melodramatic, megalomaniacal, dishonest, shallow, and cynical."[254] Editors and politicians decried him as a destroyer, a demagogue, a revolutionary, and a lunatic. Critics alleged he violated all his own maxims. "Despite Roosevelt's high moral tone," Nathan Miller argues, "he possessed a streak of ruthlessness and at times broke his own rules for fairness and justice." He occasionally condemned people without a hearing and used the tactic of guilt by association. The Republican rarely admitted he was wrong and sometimes accused opponents of being traitors.[255] "Roosevelt always liked to believe that the American people endorsed his actions," H. W. Brands argues, but when the evidence made this hard to do, he often justified his actions in terms of "the fundamental laws of righteousness." In Brands's judgment, Roosevelt, who loved to quote Micah 6:8, was always "strongest on justice, weaker on mercy, and often conspicuously deficient in humility."[256] Critics also charge that he perverted democratic ideals, centralized power in the White House, and laid the foundation for the "imperial presidency."[257]

Brands concludes that because the president held an "idealized image of his father" and strove throughout his life to gain "his father's posthumous blessing," Roosevelt never made the transition from a youthful interpretation of the world as a place of good and evil to a more mature understanding of the world as complicated, confusing, and saturated with shades of gray. Instead, he remained a moral absolutist his entire life, a romantic who believed that most wrongs could be righted. Although recognizing that evil resulted both from the deliberate acts of bad men and "banal and pernicious institutional arrangements," he naively believed that all social ills had solutions. Brands seems to imply that all those who believe in transcendent truth or absolute principles that are not relative to place and time are immature and naive.[258] Roosevelt, however, was part of a long tradition of Judeo-Christian moralists who asserted that ultimate standards should guide both private and public conduct. Like other proponents of this view, he sometimes failed to live by his own ideals. Personal ambition, pride, and practical politics occasionally led him to contravene his principles. Nevertheless, on the whole, he faithfully articulated and sought to realize his conviction that government should incarnate and strive to implement eternal norms of righteousness and justice.

Brands maintains further that prior to Roosevelt's famous declaration in 1912 after receiving the Progressive Party's nomination for president, "We stand at Armageddon, and we battle for the Lord!" "he had left the Lord pretty much out of his politics."[259] The evidence strongly indicates otherwise: As president, much of Roosevelt's philosophy and policies rested on fundamental Judeo-Christian tenets. "Without being able clearly to formulate the reasons for my philosophy," Roosevelt wrote to a friend in 1906, "I am perfectly clear as to the philosophy itself. I want to be a straight and decent man and do good service" and "to realize the ideals of good government."[260] Roosevelt told another friend that "God had raised me up to lead the nation in its desperate fight . . . against the illegal despotism of combined wealth in collusion with corrupt municipal, state and federal officeholders."[261] As president, Roosevelt labored diligently to craft policies consistent with biblical precepts and to elevate the level of personal and public morality in America.

To Brands, Roosevelt was so popular and successful because he was "the last of the romantics" in an era when Americans yearned for heroes and pined for the lost frontier. Had he lived earlier, when heroes were more plentiful, or later, when romanticism had died because of the carnage and seeming futility of World War I, he either would not have stood out or would have appeared "woefully naïve."[262] Although Roosevelt's personality and policies were especially suited to the circumstances of the Progressive era, it is difficult to believe that he would not have left a large imprint on any age.

Roosevelt changed the power, scope, and possibilities of the presidency.[263] When he took office following McKinley's assassination, many feared that the nation's youngest president, whom they considered impetuous and tactless, would not be safe for America. In an article published in Christian periodicals throughout the country, Jacob Riis reassured the public that Roosevelt could be trusted. He was "a man of duty and principle" who typified what it meant to be a "Christian gentleman."[264] As he had done as police commissioner of New York City and as governor of New York, Roosevelt would work closely with church leaders and other reformers to abolish corruption and improve social conditions. Convinced that the essence of religion was morality and not theology, deeds and not doctrines, he pressed Americans to do good works and help one another, especially the poor and afflicted. Whether Roosevelt was safe for America depends on how "safe" is defined. The record indicates, however, that on the whole, he was good for America.

CHAPTER FIVE

Woodrow Wilson: Presbyterian Statesman

There is a mighty task before us and it welds us together. It is to make the United States a mighty Christian nation and to christianize the world.

Nov. 20, 1905

My life would not be worth living if it were not for the driving power of religion, for faith, pure and simple.

Wilson to Mrs. Crawford H. Toy, Jan. 3, 1915

I believe in Divine Providence. If I did not, I would go crazy. . . . I do not believe there is any body of men . . . that can defeat this great enterprise [the establishment of the League of Nations].

Sept. 18, 1919

Our civilization cannot survive materially unless it be redeemed spiritually. It can be saved only by becoming permeated with the spirit of Christ. . . .

"The Road Away from Revolution," *Atlantic Monthly*, Aug. 1923

HIS CONTEMPORARIES, SUBSEQUENT historians and biographers, and Woodrow Wilson himself have all agreed that his religious convictions are crucial to understanding the Democrat's political thought and actions. Wilson's "career can in no wise be understood," wrote his first biographer, Ray Stannard Baker, "without a clear knowledge of [his] profound religious convictions." All who knew Wilson intimately affirmed "the seriousness, the sincerity of his faith."[1] In the words of his foremost biographer, Arthur Link, Wilson was "the prime embodiment, the apogee, of the Calvinist tradition among statesmen of the modern epoch."[2] His "forceful, eloquent speeches fusing political issues with Christian idealism and moral imperatives," insists John M. Mulder, enabled Wilson to win the allegiance and confidence of many Americans.[3]

While concurring that Wilson's faith is pivotal to understanding him, scholars disagree over whether it had a positive or negative impact on his performance as president and his policies. Moreover, many historians and political scientists have misconstrued the nature of Wilson's faith.[4] Contemporary critics denounced him as "a pious phrasemonger and hypocrite" and a "master of bloated blarney" and accused him of spiritual arrogance, hypocrisy, and stupidity.[5] The publication of Wilson's papers and recent studies of American Protestantism and of the "moral and religious influences that decisively shaped" political and cultural life during the years around 1900 have, however, helped scholars "gain a richer and more nuanced" understanding of Wilson and the factors that influenced him.[6]

As a respected scholar, an influential author, a prominent professor and president of an Ivy League university, a successful governor, and a two-term president during some of the most turbulent years in the nation's history, Wilson had a deep impact on American life. Wilson's firmly rooted and fervently cherished faith significantly influenced his thought and actions as president. Clearly America's preeminent Presbyterian statesman, Wilson's faith is evident in his philosophy of government, his view of America's role in the world, and many of his major domestic and foreign policies, especially his attempts to mediate among the combatants in World War I, his decision to involve the United States in the war, and his role in devising the Paris Peace treaties and the League of Nations.

Wilson's Faith

With strong and deep Presbyterian roots on both sides of his family, Wilson's Presbyterian credentials are impeccable. In Scotland, many members of his mother's family were Presbyterian theologians or elders. For six generations, at least one of them was a pastor, including his maternal grandfather, Thomas Woodrow, who immigrated to the United States in the early nineteenth century. His mother's brother, James Woodrow, taught for many years at Columbia Theological Seminary in South Carolina. The future president's father, Joseph Ruggles Wilson, was a graduate of Princeton Theological Seminary who helped found the Southern Presbyterian Church in 1861, pastored congregations in four states, served his denomination as the stated clerk of the General Assembly for almost forty years, and taught at Columbia and Southwestern seminaries.[7] Woodrow grew up in manses where daily devotions, Bible study, hymn singing, the Westminster Catechism, and church history were emphasized. On Sunday mornings, his family attended Sunday school and worship services, and in the evenings, they either attended a second worship service or sang hymns at home. At age sixteen, Wilson accepted Christ as his personal savior at a chapel service at Columbia Seminary, and soon thereafter he joined the First Presbyterian Church of Columbia.[8] He frequently accompanied his father on pastoral calls and helped him edit the *North Carolina Presbyterian* and prepare the minutes of the General Assembly. They shared similar intellectual and religious interests and maintained a very close relationship until the elder Wilson died in 1903.[9] Wilson was educated at Princeton, the bastion of conservative Presbyterianism in late-nineteenth-century America, under the tutelage of its highly respected president, James McCosh.[10]

His religious upbringing, most notably Calvinist covenant theology and the ethos of Southern Presbyterianism, significantly shaped Wilson's views of the church, society, and government.[11] Covenant theology stressed both God's authority and love. God was sovereign over the world's affairs, but he related to "people in love, not arbitrary power."[12] The Covenanter tradition insisted that all of life, including politics, must be based on God's justice and righteousness. As Link puts it, Wilson completely absorbed his denomination's belief in the "omnipotence of God, the morality of the universe, a system of rewards and punishments, and the supreme revelation of Jesus Christ."[13] Like many in his generation, Wilson was socialized to believe in the importance of hard work, success, morality, and service. Herbert Bell insisted that Calvinism helped endow Wilson with dynamism, endurance, and courage.[14] His Covenanter heritage strongly shaped his character and convictions, helping to account for his strengths and accomplishments but also for his political weaknesses.[15] Many of those who did not understand this tradition often found Wilson's attitudes and actions incomprehensible and bizarre.

Link argues that his Christian faith was the primary source of Wilson's strength. In thinking about both private and public matters, Wilson sought to "decide what faith and Christian love commanded." Like other committed Calvinists, he believed that God was sovereign, just, and loving, that moral laws governed nations and individuals, that Jesus Christ was God's supreme revelation and humanity's redeemer, and that the Bible was "the incomparable word of God and the rule of life." Wilson's integrity, sense of justice, devotion to duty, and much of his motivation, Link adds, "stemmed from his spiritual resources."[16] Wilson wrote in 1911 that he strove to put himself under the command of the spirit of God, revealed in his son, Jesus Christ, our savior.[17]

Wilson told his future wife Ellen that he hoped "to construct a perfect Christian home from which pure influences shall go out to those around us."[18] Honoring this pledge and continuing the patterns of his youth, he regularly worshiped at home with his wife and three daughters, studied the Bible, and prayed. The Presbyterian insisted that religion was best communicated by example. "If you wish your children to be Christians," Wilson told a Sunday school convention in 1904, "you must really...be

Christians yourself."[19] Wilson and his wife required their children to memorize the Westminster Shorter Catechism and learn many Bible stories, as they themselves had done.[20]

Wilson was deeply involved in churches he belonged to in Bryn Mawr, Pennsylvania; Middletown, Connecticut; and Princeton. He sang in the choir of all these churches. Two Princeton congregations elected him an elder, and he served on both session and presbytery committees. While he was president, Wilson and his wife worshiped in the Central Presbyterian Church in Washington, D.C.[21] After his wife Ellen died and Wilson married Edith Bolling Galt in December 1915, they alternated between attending Central and her church, St. Margaret's Episcopal.[22] He worshiped almost every Sunday, whether he was in Washington, on official trips in the United States or abroad, while on vacation, and even aboard ship. Wilson worshiped unpretentiously and did not want to call any attention to himself, although his special car, Secret Service agents, and personal fame made that impossible.[23] From 1913 until his death in 1924, Wilson enjoyed a close friendship with Central's pastor, James Taylor.[24] He listened attentively to sermons, sang heartily, prayed passionately, and gave generously to the church.[25] In his letters, Wilson often analyzed the content and quality of the sermons he heard and frequently contended that Presbyterian ministers provided the most biblically sound preaching.[26] Although sometimes upset by the poor musical quality of the churches to which he belonged, Wilson generally enjoyed Presbyterian services and was especially moved by the Lord's Supper and hymns.[27] Although he protested that some churches put too much emphasis on feelings, his own faith was more emotional than intellectual, and church music sometimes caused him to cry.[28] Nevertheless, Wilson, like most other presidents, was reluctant to discuss his religious experiences with others and displayed little interest in theological speculation or debate.[29]

Unlike most other Victorian intellectuals or his wife Ellen, who read Hegel and Kant to try to find answers for her religious questions, Wilson apparently never had any doubts about the veracity of Christianity or his own personal faith. He espoused the long-standing apologetic tradition that held people must believe before they could understand. "I *saw* the intellectual difficulties but I was not *troubled* by them," he wrote in 1889; "they seemed to have no connection with my faith in the essentials of the religion I had been taught. . . . I am capable . . . of being satisfied spiritually without being satisfied intellectually."[30] In 1916, he gave the same testimony: "[N]ever for a moment have I had one doubt about my religious beliefs. There are people who *believe* only so far as they *understand*," he declared, "that seems to me presumptuous and sets their understanding as the standard of the universe."[31] As Link puts it, "in matters of basic Christian faith, Wilson was like a little child, never doubting, always believing, and drawing spiritual sustenance from Bible reading, church attendance, and prayer."[32]

Despite spending a quarter of a century as a college professor and president of one of the nation's leading universities, Wilson seemed undisturbed by the controversies over Darwinism and higher criticism that rocked the academic world. He was convinced that true science and true religion could never conflict and that the Bible was the infallible, authoritative Word of God.[33] Wilson remained largely aloof from the doctrinal debates of the early twentieth century that culminated in the fundamentalist-modernist controversy of the 1920s.[34]

Until about 1908, Wilson was critical of the Social Gospel movement that deeply affected American Protestantism in the forty years following 1880, despite studying at Johns Hopkins under one of its leading proponents, Richard T. Ely. Although Wilson argued that people's faith should drive them to social service, he sometimes protested that sermons had become political manifestos, and until the last fifteen years of his life, he consistently asserted that the primary role of the church was to save souls and only indirectly to purify society.[35] Yet like proponents of the Social Gospel, Wilson repeatedly insisted that service, rather than worship, piety, or theology, was the most essential aspect of religion. He maintained that individuals achieved self-fulfillment by sacrificially serving others.[36]

Although Princeton had long sought to promote evangelical Christianity and serve the national interest by producing cultured and civic-minded graduates, during Wilson's tenure as president, the institution began to focus much more on its public mission than on its religious mission. Preparing well-rounded leaders to shape the nation's political, commercial, and social life required curricular revision. Abandoning the evangelical Protestant commitment to a curriculum centered on biblical studies and a Christian perspective of all subjects, Princeton devised a broader, more liberal set of courses. Wilson strove to substitute an emphasis on character and service for its historically more narrowly sectarian approach. To achieve this end, the university's first lay president abolished the required Sunday evening chapel service, decreased the number of daily chapel services students had to attend, eliminated mandatory Bible courses, and reduced the importance of ethics, apologetics, and philosophy in the curriculum. Seemingly unconcerned about the integration of faith and learning in the classroom, he hired professors based on their scholarship rather than their religious commitments.[37] Wilson wanted the university to "serve the public as a model Christian community," with Christianity defined primarily as "a moral system based on high ideals."[38] Although he believed that education "was essentially spiritual in character" and that religion was "a spirit that infused the curriculum," like most theologically conservative Protestants, he wanted universities to help Christianize America.[39]

Wilson revered the Bible and wore out several of them during his life. In 1917, he signed a membership card of the Pocket Bible League, pledging to "read at least one chapter of the Bible each day," a discipline he followed all his life that supplied him with guidance, comfort, and inspiration.[40] Those who did not read the Bible every day, he declared, deprived themselves of strength and of pleasure.[41] In a letter to American soldiers and sailors during World War I, the president proclaimed, "The Bible is the word of life." By reading long passages rather than "little snatches here and there," they would discover this themselves.[42] Wilson considered the "incomparable and unimpeachable Word of God" the "foundation for all thought." The Bible, he proclaimed, "is the one supreme source of revelation" about "the meaning of life, the nature of God, and the spiritual nature and needs of men." It was the source of both "individual and social regeneration."[43] Wilson's 1911 address, "The Bible and Progress," was read by probably a million Americans and widely distributed in the 1912 presidential campaign. He declared that the Scriptures supplied "the fixed and eternal standard" by which people must judge themselves.[44] "No great nation can ever survive its own temptations and its own follies," Wilson trumpeted, "that does not indoctrinate its children in the Word of God. . . ." The Bible could help the world's people transcend their many divisions and attain harmony and international cooperation. Through spreading the gospel, Wilson proclaimed in 1916, Christians strive to make all the nations "of one mind" and "motive, driven . . . by one devotion and one allegiance."[45]

Prayer was also essential to Wilson. He prayed every day on his knees and said grace before every meal. "I do not see," he wrote, "how any one can sustain himself in any enterprise without prayer. It is the only spring at which he can renew his spirit and purify his motive."[46] A Presbyterian minister remembered that Wilson "prayed like a man who knew God not only as . . . a doctrine in theology or an ideal in ethics, but as an experience in his own soul."[47] Wilson sometimes started his cabinet meetings by asking members to pray about important decisions that needed to be made.[48] Like most other presidents, the Presbyterian periodically proclaimed national days of prayer.

Wilson closely adhered to Presbyterian standards in his personal life. He strictly observed the Sabbath all his life and during election campaigns refused to speak or attend political meetings on Sundays.[49] As president, he urged American troops to reverently keep the Sabbath, arguing that this was "dictated by the best traditions of our people and by the convictions of all who look to Divine Providence for guidance and protection."[50] Upsetting many Washington socialites, the Democrat did not host an inaugural ball, largely because his wife thought that modern dancing was indecent.[51] Wilson did not smoke and rarely drank alcohol.[52]

Many have argued that Wilson's faith was the primary source of his integrity, sense of justice, devotion to duty, and willingness to stand by his convictions.[53] In 1912, he nearly ruined his chances to receive the Democratic nomination for president by rejecting the support of newspaper publisher William Randolph Hearst, whom he despised. As president, he refused to give in to public demands that the U.S. armed forces march through Germany or to accept changes to the Versailles Treaty to get the Senate to approve American participation in the League of Nations. In Link's judgment, few other American statesmen surpassed Wilson's example of morality in politics.[54] Wilson "set a moral tone that permeated his entire administration," enabling it to endure a war and demobilization without a single significant scandal.[55]

Like Theodore Roosevelt, Wilson accentuated the importance of character. The Bible taught, he announced in 1911, that God judged people "according to their characters." Character alone could produce the morality necessary to sustain democracy.[56] Wilson, however, advised Christians to concentrate on service, not character. If they focused on their duties to others, their character would "take care of itself. Character is a by-product, and any man who devotes himself to its cultivation . . . will become a selfish prig. . . . Christ came into the world to save others . . . and no man is a true Christian who does not think constantly of how he can lift his brother . . . [and] how he can enlighten mankind. . . ."[57]

Influenced by his Calvinist heritage, Wilson strongly stressed the sovereignty, majesty, and love of God. As the lord of history, nations, and individuals, God directed all events and accomplished all his purposes. Both individuals and nations were accountable to him and would experience divine condemnation if they violated his moral laws. Wilson believed that God was constantly at work in human affairs, "shaping, directing, and controlling history" in order to advance "justice, righteousness, and human welfare."[58] "The providence of God," he declared in 1911, "is the foundation of affairs." Wilson argued that because people could not thwart the purposes of God, "those little, scheming contemptible creatures" who sought to do so were doomed to fail. "I believe very profoundly in an over-ruling providence," Wilson wrote to a friend in January 1912, "and do not fear that any real plans can be thrown off track."[59] He also emphasized God's redeeming love in Christ.[60] In sharp contrast to stereotypes of Calvinists as fixated on fire and brimstone, Wilson contended that no one "was ever drawn into heaven for fear he would go to hell." Rather, the Scriptures proclaimed a "gospel of love."[61]

Wilson's faith helped sustain him during his trying years as president. Not only did he have to decide whether to push for American participation in the Great War but also he lost his wife, underwent a deep depression, courted, married, and endured a stroke. "Faith in God's providence," he told a friend in 1914, "sustains more than anything else can."[62] In the midst of the difficulties of World War I, he insisted that "the wise heart never questions the dealings of Providence, because the great, long plan, as it unfolds, has a majesty about it and a definiteness of purpose . . . which we are incapable of conceiving." In presenting the Versailles Treaty to the Senate in July 1919, Wilson declared that "the hand of God" had produced it.[63] After the Senate voted a second time not to ratify the treaty, Wilson told his personal physician, "If I were not a

Christian, I think I should go mad, but my faith in God holds me to the belief that He is in some way working out His own plans through human perversities and mistakes."[64] Wilson eventually accepted American failure to participate in the League of Nations as God's will, quipping, "Perhaps God knew better than I did after all."[65]

These convictions, coupled with his belief in a progressive form of post-millennialism (the belief that conditions will gradually improve until Christ's return), led Wilson, like many of his Christian contemporaries, to conclude that the world was getting better and better.[66] He contended that Christ's teachings were "making actual progress in the world." While "older dogmatic forms" of Christianity had less hold, "the real spirit of Christ, translated into terms of service and personal devotion," was "more widespread and dominate than ever before."[67] Like many other presidents, Wilson repeatedly argued that religion was one of the nation's primary pillars of morality and progress.[68] He insisted that progress could not be divorced from religion and that Christ's teachings supplied the only solid platform for societal reform.[69] As did many other Protestants during this era, Wilson maintained that God's kingdom was advancing steadily and systematically on earth, especially in America.[70]

Toward the end of the first decade of the twentieth century, Wilson's view of the role of the church in the world changed significantly. Prior to his entrance into the political arena, he was a committed proponent of individualism. His study of English advocates of laissez-faire and classical economists, coupled with Southern Presbyterianism's almost complete opposition to organized social action by religious or political groups, led him to long reject the use of the state's power to ameliorate social and economic ills. During his years as a college professor, Wilson accepted the individualistic, pietistic perspective of many evangelicals and thought little about the church's relationship to society. He shared the view of Southern Presbyterians and numerous other Protestants that the church should seek to save souls and nurture individual faith rather than mobilize parishioners for political action or societal improvement.[71] Like many other theological conservatives, Wilson feared that focus on social ministries would divert the attention of ministers and congregations "from the effectual preaching of the Word."[72] "Christianity did not come into the world" primarily "to set crooked things straight," or to regenerate social life. Its "end and object . . . is the individual, and the individual is the vehicle of Christianity."[73] Although "Christ was not a reformer," he asserted in 1906, he inspired individuals to "reconstruct and better human life" through their vocations.[74]

As president of Princeton, Wilson delivered the sermons at graduation ceremonies and spoke at many seminaries, Sunday school conventions, YMCA assemblies, and other religious meetings. This forced him to examine his own religious convictions more deeply, and by 1910, he saw the role of the church quite differently. While continuing to affirm that it must work to redeem sinners, he maintained that the church also had a direct responsibility to improve social structures and inspire reform movements.[75] The church was a brotherhood of believers commanded to serve individuals and society. "The spirit of Christianity," he told the Federal Council of Churches in 1915, "is the spirit of assistance, of vitalization, of intense interest in everything that affects the lives of men and women and children."[76] The Christian church, Wilson argued, stood at the center not only of philanthropy but also of education, science, philosophy, and politics. Thus ministers must explicate the spiritual dimensions of all aspects of life.[77]

Wilson's Relationship with Religious Constituencies

Although Wilson's family background, education, and many years as a professor and the president of Princeton made him a devoted Presbyterian, he was very ecumenically minded. As governor of New Jersey and president, he strongly supported the ministry of the American Sunday School Union and the Federal Council of Churches. Soon after Wilson's inauguration in March 1913, the council praised the president's Social Gospel ideals: "your conviction . . . that our social order must be fashioned after the Kingdom of God . . . together with your public faithfulness and your personal faith, lead the churches of the nation to look with confidence to the performance of the serious and solemn duties of the coming years."[78] Undoubtedly speaking for many Protestants, the *Presbyterian Banner* declared that Wilson was a "man of unusual ability, training and fitness" for the presidency. His religious convictions and policies enabled Wilson to maintain a cordial relationship with most Protestants, especially the leaders of the Federal Council, during his tenure in office.[79]

Wilson had a close friendship with several Protestant clergymen. He greatly admired Methodist missions advocate John R. Mott.[80] Wilson lauded him as "the best man in America" and repeatedly implored Mott to serve as the American ambassador to China.[81] Wilson sent Mott to help settle the U.S. conflict with Mexico in 1916 and to Russia in 1917 as part of a special diplomatic mission.[82] Mott and Wilson corresponded regularly, and Mott visited Wilson numerous times at the White House.[83] Wilson also enjoyed close friendships with Azel Washburn Hazen, his pastor in Middletown, Connecticut, and Sylvester Beach, his pastor at Princeton, as well as Bishop James Freeman II of the Episcopal Diocese of Washington.[84]

Throughout his life, Wilson displayed a strong interest in Christian missions, probably in part because his grandfather Thomas Woodrow had served as a missionary and his daughter Margaret aspired for a while to be one.[85] Paul Varg concludes that "no president was more sympathetic to the missionary movement" than Wilson.[86] The Democrat especially monitored missions work in China. The secretary of the American Presbyterian Mission in Tsingtao (now Qingdao in Shandong), China, wrote Wilson regularly about the political and religious conditions in the country. The president contended that the United States must promote democracy and teach Christian morality in China to help it become more peaceful and prosperous. Wilson recognized the government of Yuan Shikai in 1913, hoping it would bring the stability necessary for missions and commerce to flourish.[87]

His stance on prohibition strained Wilson's relationship with some Protestants. As support for a national prohibition amendment became stronger, Wilson argued during the 1916 campaign that the liquor issue was "essentially non-political, moral, and social in its nature" and should be decided by local communities. He termed the Volstead Act "the wrong way of doing the right thing." Placing "unreasonable restrictions" on people's liberty was bound to "end in failure and disappointment." Only public opinion, not laws, could persuade most people to change their behavior.[88] Many religious editors criticized Wilson's opposition to a prohibition amendment and insisted that it was the best way to reduce drunkenness and the evils caused by the liquor industry.[89] Nevertheless, Wilson retained the support of many Protestants who liked his strong personal faith, progressive political positions, and stress on moral principles in foreign policy. Those who sought to reinterpret the "old ideals of a Protestant, agrarian America" in an increasingly industrial, urban, and pluralistic culture applauded the president's emphasis on biblical morality and Christian idealism.[90]

Although Wilson was a staunch Presbyterian, he appreciated other religious groups and perspectives.[91] Like many Protestants, he worried about the massive immigration of Eastern European Catholics during the early twentieth century and disliked the temporal claims of the papacy, but he exhibited few prejudices toward Catholics. During the 1912 campaign, Wilson was paradoxically attacked for being both too friendly with and overly critical of Catholics. In a public letter, Wilson refuted charges that he was a member of the Knights of Columbus (as a non-Catholic, he was not even eligible) and denounced allegations that he was hostile to Catholics as "petty and ridiculous." Wilson insisted that he strove to "treat every creed and class with impartiality and respect." His staff detailed the numerous Catholics he had appointed to prominent posts in New Jersey and highlighted his addresses that praised the political contributions of Catholics.[92]

While serving as the governor of New Jersey, Wilson employed a young Catholic lawyer, Joseph P. Tumulty, as his private secretary. Many Catholic papers praised Wilson for keeping Tumulty as his private secretary when he became president. The Methodist *Christian Advocate* protested that Tumulty might hinder Protestants from communicating with Wilson, especially when they offered criticism of the Catholic Church.[93] Calling such claims "absurdly and utterly false," Wilson insisted in 1914 that all correspondence was open to him.[94]

In the closely contested election of 1916, Wilson's relationship with Catholics caused him considerable difficulty. Some Catholics accused Wilson of treating Catholic prelates discourteously, and others chastised him for allegedly refusing to meet with a representative of the pope. Wilson's relationship with Catholics was further damaged by his policies toward Mexico. Most Catholics strongly disliked his recognition of Venustiano Carranza's Constitutionalist government. Protesting that Mexico's leader was "the avowed enemy of the Catholic Church," a Catholic newspaper in New Orleans urged coreligionists to help defeat Wilson.[95] A few Catholics even blamed Wilson personally for the destruction of Catholic churches and the deaths of priests and nuns that occurred during the Mexican revolution.[96] Rumors circulated that some Catholic leaders were doing all they could to defeat the president and that James Cardinal Gibbons had declared that "any Catholic who votes for Wilson should be damned."[97] A priest in Connecticut was so upset that he threatened to advise every Catholic in the state to vote against Wilson in the fall election.[98]

Wilson and his campaign team sought to rebut these criticisms. The president denied that he had refused to meet with Catholic leaders or had insulted them. Gibbons and William Cardinal O'Connell published statements in the *New York World* declaring that they had no right to tell Catholics how to vote. The Wilson campaign selectively distributed a pamphlet citing complaints from Protestants that Wilson was pro-Catholic and enumerating the benefits Catholics had received during his tenure.[99] Another leaflet contended that reports of atrocities toward Catholics in Mexico had been greatly exaggerated and pointed out that many countries, some of them Catholic, had officially recognized Carranza's regime.[100]

During World War I, Wilson's relationship with Catholics focused primarily on their loyalty to the war effort, Catholic chaplains, Pope Benedict XV's peace proposal, and Catholic concerns about world missions. Soon after the United States declared war, Catholic archbishops publicly pledged their "most sacred and sincere loyalty and patriotism" to "our government."[101] Gibbons strove to guarantee that Catholics gave unswerving fidelity to Wilson's administration.[102] Numerous archbishops argued Catholics had not wanted the United States to enter the war, but now they wholeheartedly endorsed the war effort. The Knights of Columbus promised "unconditional support of the President and the Congress . . . in their determination" to advance the "ideals of humanity and right."[103] Catholics created the National Catholic War Council to coordinate their wartime ministry. Pressure from Catholics prompted the Wilson administration to significantly increase the number of priests serving as chaplains in the armed forces.[104] In August 1917, Pope Benedict XV appealed to all warring nations to immediately stop fighting, substitute arbitration for arms, and settle their differences equitably and justly. Wilson praised the pope's proposal and assured him that the United States wanted peace, if it could be founded on "genuine and impartial justice."[105]

Nevertheless, like other Allied leaders, he insisted that the Allies must continue to fight because German leaders did not represent the views of their constituents and because a German victory would harm the world.[106] At the Paris Peace Conference, Wilson worked with the Catholic Church to ensure that the settlement did not inhibit mission work.[107]

During his presidency, Wilson had limited contact with Jews and dealt with few issues that concerned them.[108] Despite the objections of big business, he nominated Louis D. Brandeis, a favorite of progressives and labor leaders, to be the first Jew on the Supreme Court and strongly supported him during the confirmation process.[109] In addition, Wilson named Henry Morgenthau as the American ambassador to Turkey. Although he praised the work of Jewish philanthropic and relief agencies, Wilson declined to publicly condemn the mistreatment of Jews in Europe before the United States joined the Great War because he believed that doing so would compromise American neutrality.[110] He did, however, designate January 27, 1916, as Jewish War Sufferers Relief Day. In negotiating the Versailles Treaty, Wilson strove to protect the rights of Jews, and in 1919, he publicly endorsed efforts to establish a homeland for Jews in Palestine.[111]

Wilson's Philosophy of Government

At age nineteen, Wilson wrote that all statesmen should trust Christ and follow scriptural standards. A nation could prosper, he insisted, only if the Bible's "eternal principles of right and wrong, of justice and injustice, [and] of civil and religious liberty" undergirded its laws.[112] Throughout his life, Wilson's understanding of Christian social and political duties continued to inform his views on the role of government.[113] Christians, he trumpeted, must carry out God's commands in "a world of good and evil."[114] Because the world was a battleground between these forces, Christians could not compromise their principles. Wilson insisted that people could comprehend these unchanging norms and implement them in society.[115]

Wilson imbibed the Calvinist covenantal tradition's emphasis on "order, structure, and wholeness." In this worldview, God, individuals, and society each had "definite roles and responsibilities." This "gospel of order" helped Wilson define his personal goals, structure his marriage, direct his friendships, and form his conception of society and politics.[116] The Presbyterian saw life in holistic terms and tended to reduce all issues to "clearly defined moral categories." "There are definite comprehensible practices, immutable principles of government and right conduct in the dealings of men with one another," he declared.[117]

As president, Wilson preached a "public faith that stressed obligation, duty, and service." Viewing himself as the nation's president and prophet, he strove to help the United States conform to biblical standards and fulfill its divine mission.[118] Shortly before his inauguration in 1913, he confided to a party leader, "God ordained that I should be the next President of the United States."[119] Scholars have labeled Wilson a "political missionary" and a "secular evangelist" who sought to spread the gospel of American political ideals and institutions and inspire its citizens to reform the world. Because of its unique history and special calling, the Democrat contended, the United States was well equipped to fulfill this mission. Like most other members of his generation, Wilson was a cultural absolutist who believed in the superiority of Anglo-Saxon civilization and constitutionalism.[120]

When Wilson was convinced he understood God's will, a contemporary argued, he stood resolutely, whether friends supported or deserted him, whether he was praised or condemned.[121] Like his Covenanter forebears, Wilson displayed a "striking ambivalence toward power" because he believed God was sovereign over all things but delegated authority to humans who held offices in the family, church, school, and state. The Presbyterian sought to deal with this dilemma by linking humans' exercise of power with God's unchanging moral laws.[122] When Wilson determined that a certain course of action embodied God's principles of justice and righteousness, he was resolute and inflexible because he believed he had no right to compromise.[123] If power was based on moral principles and used to benefit others, he argued, it should not be challenged. In theory and practice, Wilson made the leader himself the supreme judge of how to apply those principles.[124] Although he wrote that "the power that lasts has as its center the just conception to which men's judgments assent, to which their hearts and inclinations respond," he tended to consider his personal principles universally valid and to be intolerant toward his opponents.[125] Robert Ferrell attributes Wilson's difficulty with compromising to his Presbyterian convictions.[126] Because of his moral certitude, Wilson rarely capitulated to political pressures or pursued expedient policies. Even though some of his most impressive achievements resulted from listening to all parties and reaching a consensus, his inflexibility sometimes kept Wilson from resolving disputes.[127] In his later years, Wilson came to understand the ambiguous nature of moral decisions, but throughout his life, he tended to (sometimes simplistically) divide right and wrong, fight for moral ideals, and eschew compromise.

Although Wilson's approach to politics gradually became more flexible and pragmatic, he continually stressed the importance of ideals and insisted that most political conflicts were over principles, not personalities.[128] People's wills must be regenerated and their purposes rectified, Wilson contended, before laws could be passed to embody transcendent moral standards. Laws that reflected the moral values of small minorities would fail because most people either would not understand them or would not obey them. Effective laws expressed the moral consensus a community had already reached.[129]

Wilson sought to motivate individuals and groups to rise above their own selves and instead promote widely shared ideals.[130] John Milton Cooper contends that Wilson was a supreme "realist" because he strove to create political institutions and processes that could constrain people's competing interests and marshal them for progress.[131] Wilson sought to construct a government that "could regulate without stifling," Kendrick Clements explains, and "protect the helpless without suppressing initiative."[132] Unlike social Darwinists who thought the state's only role was to guarantee individual freedom, Wilson maintained it must create the conditions necessary for social progress. "The State," he wrote, "is the eternal, natural embodiment and expression of a higher form of life than the individual.... [I]t makes individual life ... full and complete."[133] In his first inaugural address, Wilson proclaimed that "the firm basis of government is justice.... Justice, and only justice, shall always be our motto." The government must serve humanity, pursue policies that promote morality and its citizens' spiritual and physical welfare, and ensure public justice.[134]

Wilson's Presidential Policies

Arthur Link maintains that Wilson's "every action and policy" as president "was ultimately informed and guided by his Christian faith."[135] His faith is evident in numerous domestic policies, including lowering tariffs, passing an income tax amendment, establishing the Federal Reserve, creating a Federal Trade Commission, and supporting legislation to regulate the labor of women and children and give railway workers an eight-hour day.[136] However, because foreign policies loomed so large in his administration, only they are discussed in this section. Given his lack of experience and interest in international relations, Wilson told a friend shortly before taking office, "It would be an irony of fate if my administration had to deal chiefly with foreign affairs."[137] Irony prevailed, as the Presbyterian faced more significant foreign policy challenges than any other president since Thomas Jefferson. Wilson's belief that the president's control over foreign affairs was "very absolute," coupled with his domineering personality, driving ambition, and conviction that he was intellectually superior and an instrument of God's purposes, led him, despite his previous inexperience, to direct foreign affairs.[138] Especially in areas he regarded as vitally important—dealing with Mexico, European belligerents, and the Allies during World War I and negotiating a peace settlement—Wilson assumed almost total personal control.[139] Guided by the long-standing conviction that America was destined to spread democracy and liberty, Wilson strove to reshape the world.

Link argues that Wilson's foreign policy was based on "a consistent body of principles and assumptions" that were deeply rooted in his "general thinking before 1913 about cosmology, ethics, the nature and ends of government," America's task in the world, and divine providence.[140] Whittle Johnston maintains that Wilson's belief that the United States had a special role to play in spreading Christianity and democracy strongly contributed to his abhorrence of imperialism, firm support for decolonization, and vehement hatred of war.[141] Wilson insisted that immediate aims and material interest must be subordinated to transcendent ethical standards and moral and spiritual purposes. Convinced that democracy was the most benevolent and biblical form of government, the president worked vigorously to promote it worldwide.[142]

Influenced by social Darwinism and late-nineteenth-century Christian optimism, Wilson expressed great confidence in human goodness and the possibility of progress.[143] While never explicitly repudiating the Calvinist doctrine of human depravity, he often ignored it. Wilson assumed that people were inherently good, that progress was inexorable because God willed it, and that all countries would someday become republics. "When properly directed," he asserted, no people were incapable of self-government.[144] Moreover, he reasoned that "a peaceful world community, governed by universal public opinion and united for mutual advancement," could exist only when democracy triumphed everywhere.[145] These convictions led Wilson to internationalize the goals of progressivism and broaden the scope of American foreign policy to include the whole world.[146] The impact of his Christian convictions on foreign policy can most readily been seen in his treatment of Latin American republics, his decision to commit the United States to the Great War, and his role in devising the Treaty of Versailles and the League of Nations.

Because the American people were unique politically (the United States had organized a hundred million individuals of diverse backgrounds into a republic), socially (they affirmed equality and rejected the caste and class systems of Asia and Europe), and morally and spiritually (Christianity had strongly shaped the nation's institutions, laws, mores, and practices), they had a divine mission in the world. As a prosperous, multiethnic republic, Wilson averred, the United States furnished a marvelous example for other countries. Its residents, constitution, and system of government more than that of any other nation, Wilson argued, incarnated Christian love and brotherhood.[147] He insisted that nothing provided a "more profound" basis for "belief in Providence than the history of this country."[148] Would America now use its immense power to exploit other nations or to work for "peace and the salvation of society"?[149] His Presbyterian heritage and temperament helped convince Wilson that God had spared America from the conflicts and corruptions that bedeviled European and Asian societies so it could fulfill its destiny.[150] America's mandate was not to increase its wealth and power but to serve humanity, further morality, and promote peace, cooperation, and brotherhood.[151] "America was born a Christian nation," Wilson trumpeted. It was created to exemplify the societal righteousness God demanded in Scripture. Only America's commitment to biblical ideals made it great.[152] Wilson agreed with Social Gospelers that the United States must "assume the messianic mantle of the suffering servant" and promote righteousness around the world.[153] America, Wilson averred, strove to procure liberty and justice for all people and lead God's crusade for progress and peace.[154] As Christ had done, the United States must minister to others.[155]

Believing that the United States shared some of the responsibilities of the Christian church, Wilson worked with Secretary of State William Jennings Bryan to create a "missionary diplomacy," which exalted eternal truths over expediency and strove to help less-developed countries become more stable and democratic.[156] Wilson repeatedly denounced self-interest as "an insufficient and morally bereft" basis for American policy.[157] In dealing with political issues, Wilson asserted in 1913, "morality and not expediency . . . must guide us."[158] He promised to judge other nations by whether they promoted the common good, and he wanted to mediate conflicts and promote harmony, fraternity, and freedom around the world.[159] Link argues that Wilson was not a moralist who thought that specific scriptural norms could be easily applied to complex international situations, but rather a Christian realist who tried to base his foreign policy decisions upon biblical presuppositions about God's direction of history, human nature, and social relations.[160]

His approach led critics to accuse Wilson of "Messianism" and "missionary constitutionalism," of seeking to force other nations to accept American institutions and of imprudently basing political decisions on moral principles.[161] Wilson and Bryan, Robert Crunden maintains, devised a "Presbyterian foreign policy" that asserted Americans had virtuous motives and superior ideals and insisted they had the right to force politically unstable countries to accept those ideals. Both men were Presbyterian elders who believed that God was all-powerful and that righteousness would ultimately prevail.[162] They wanted to discontinue policies that had enabled American businesses to exploit developing nations. Invoking John Winthrop's image of America as "a city on a hill," Wilson declared in 1913 that the United States must shine "unobstructed the light of the justice of God" throughout Latin America.[163] Wilson and Bryan sought to elevate the political and business practices of poorer countries and improve the spiritual and material lives of their citizens. The president insisted that in the long run, creating democracies in Latin America and developing friendship with its residents would do much more to increase trade between this region and the United States than supporting pro-American dictators, imposing unfair economic terms, or using gunboat diplomacy to gain territory.[164]

Because the United States had a divine mission to liberate oppressed peoples and promote democracy, Wilson insisted, it "had the right and duty to intervene whenever and wherever" its leaders thought it was prudent.[165]

Eager to spread the blessings of Christianity, republicanism, political stability, and social justice, Wilson and Bryan thought they knew what other nations needed better than their own leaders did and thus frequently interfered in their affairs.[166] Their policy produced some positive results: thirty conciliation treaties with other countries in 1913–14, a benevolent approach toward China, pressure on Japan to lessen its demands on China in 1915, significant advances in self-government for Puerto Rico and the Philippines, and an apology to Colombia for the way the United States procured the rights to build the Panama Canal. On the other hand, often ignoring historical precedents, economic realities, and the political situations of poorer nations, Wilson used this policy to justify several military forays into Latin America.[167] Although Roosevelt is remembered for carrying a big stick, Wilson's impact on the region was much greater, as he sent troops to Mexico (1914, 1916), Haiti (1915), the Dominican Republic (1916), and Cuba (1917).[168] Wilson interfered numerous times in Mexico's domestic affairs, betraying his ideals and leaving a "legacy of bitterness."[169] Confident that creating a democratic Mexico was a divinely sanctioned goal, Wilson sought to save it politically.[170] This attempt to "apply constitutional and democratic criteria" to unstable states prompted "military intervention or diplomatic pressures" that seemed to contradict Wilson's emphasis on self-determination.[171] He also sent troops to Europe to defend democracy—first to defeat the Central Powers (1917–18) and then to try to topple the Bolshevik government in Russia (1918–20).

Crunden lambastes Wilson's foreign policy as "provincial, culture-bound, intolerant, and arrogant." Portraying themselves as Sunday school teachers instructing the immature, Wilson and Bryan strove to enforce "American ideas of morality, contract, democracy, legality, and constitutionalism" on reluctant pupils. They denounced economic self-interest and imperialism and professed to be inspired by biblical morality and a deep concern for poor people. Wilson and Bryan assumed that non-Protestants in poorer nations would eventually recognize their inferior ways and adopt American moral principles and political practices.[172] Blinded by his faith in democracy, Wilson resorted to armed intervention to end political turmoil, prevent revolution, and eradicate poverty in developing nations. Wilson's ideology, Frederick Calhoun maintains, kept him from seeing that American help was often unwanted and thwarted people's efforts to choose their own destiny: "The Christian in him cried out for a crusade; the American in him defined its nature"; and the world offered abundant opportunities for reforming expeditions.[173] Wilson desired to knit the two Americas together "by a process of peace, friendship, helpfulness, and good will," but many of his policies unfortunately produced distrust, anger, and conflict instead.[174] Even though the Presbyterian renounced imperialism, his intervention into Latin American affairs and insistence on political conformity, coupled with growing American economic influence there, were just as objectionable to residents of the region as the earlier, cruder form of colonialism or William Howard Taft's "dollar diplomacy." Scholars contend that Wilson's ethnocentrism and inability to see the world from the perspectives of the citizens of other countries caused many of his foreign policy failures. Motivated not by security concerns or economic interests but by patronizing benevolence, Wilson sought to force Haiti and the Dominican Republic to become republics, a goal no military expedition could achieve. Although he often asserted that democracy must evolve gradually, America's strength seduced him into believing that it could sometimes be quickly imposed on nations.[175]

World War I

Many of Wilson's guiding assumptions about foreign policy are evident in his approach toward World War I, which erupted in July 1914. Initially, almost all of the nation's religious groups endorsed his position that Americans should be neutral in thought and action toward the war in Europe. Wilson designated October 4, 1914, as a national day of prayer, asking Americans to pray for an end to hostilities.[176] Speaking for many clergy, a Baptist pastor in South Carolina praised the president, a man whom God had chosen to lead America at "such a time as this," for infusing a strong sense of righteousness into American foreign policy.[177]

The first two decades of the twentieth century were pervaded by a deep religious sensibility, and for many Americans the Great War had profound religious significance.[178] The war raised two thorny questions: Had Christianity failed because it had not been properly applied and, even more troubling, had God failed to accomplish his purposes? Because Protestant progressives, including Wilson, believed that good would invariably triumph and that the world would get continually better, they had to explain how the war benefited humanity. While arguing that war was unavoidable in a sinful world, some maintained that its evils helped build character and taught important lessons about service, sacrifice, and suffering that could not be learned otherwise.[179] Others explained that God's immutable moral law required people to endure the negative consequences of their freely chosen wicked acts.[180]

Prompted in part by Bryan, who argued that it was America's duty "as the leading exponent of Christianity and as the foremost advocate of world-wide peace" to try to mediate between the combatants, Wilson made several attempts to end the war.[181] He sent his aide, Colonel Edward House, to Europe early in 1915 to discuss options for settling differences among the belligerents, but House discovered that both sides hoped to win a decisive victory and impose a harsh settlement on the loser. Less than a year later, House visited London, Paris, and Berlin, but all three governments refused to negotiate meaningfully. Shortly thereafter, Wilson called for a conference to discuss peace, but the belligerents declined to meet. The editors of *The Outlook* refused to support Wilson's reelection because of his continued neutrality. They accused the president of "playing safe" and could not understand why he refused to support the Allies when the European war involved transcendent principles of right and wrong.[182] Defending the president, Democratic Party Chairman Ollie James, a senator from Kentucky, declared, "I can see . . . Christ on the battlefield, with the dead and dying all around him . . . and I can hear the Master say to Woodrow Wilson, 'Blessed are the peace-makers, for they shall be called the children of God.' "[183]

In a 1915 book entitled *The Fight for Peace*, Stanley Gulick identified three different means Americans advocated to restore world peace: military force, judicial arbitration, and Tolstoyan nonresistance. During the first year of the war, Wilson, like the leaders of the Federal Council of Churches and members of the Church Peace Union, stressed arbitration. In 1915, however, Wilson and many progressive clergy began to slowly move toward supporting the Allies, inspired by their belief that America must redeem the world. In late 1915, Wilson asked Congress to increase the size of the American army and navy in case the United States entered the war. To justify his action, he quoted Ezekiel 33:2–6, which includes the injunction, "When he seeth the sword come upon the land, he blow the trumpet, and warn the people."[184] Religious support for preparedness initially came principally from Presbyterians and Episcopalians. Before 1917, many religious leaders, especially numerous evangelicals, fundamentalists, Lutherans, Quakers, Mennonites, Brethren, Catholics, and Jews, argued against preparedness and American entry into World War I. Deploring the atrocities of war, arguing that neither side fought for just reasons, and insisting that God was punishing belligerent nations for their past sins, they urged the United States to remain neutral.[185] Speaking for many of them, Bryan, who had resigned as secretary of state in June 1915 because of the bellicose tone of Wilson's response to the Germans' sinking of the *Lusitania*, protested that Wilson's policy was both "a menace to our peace and safety" and "a challenge to the spirit of Christianity."[186]

Despite increasing the size of the nation's military, Wilson still hoped to avoid American participation in the war. In December 1916, he asked the warring European nations to state their aims. The president blamed both "German militarism" and "British navalism" for causing "this vast, gruesome contest of systematized destruction."[187] Hoping to discover common ground that would pave the way for negotiations, he instead irritated the British, who felt betrayed by the United States' previously sympathetic and friendly attitude. Arguing that ending the war at this point would prevent righteousness from triumphing, the murder of innocent civilians from being avenged, and the violation of God's laws from being punished, more than sixty prominent American churchmen issued a statement denouncing Wilson's diplomatic effort. Peace, they argued, "is the triumph of righteousness and not the mere sheathing of the sword."[188] Addressing the Senate on January 22, 1917, Wilson made a final appeal for ending the fighting in what became known as his "Peace without Victory" speech. "Only a peace between equals can last," he declared. If the victors imposed terms on the vanquished, war would soon erupt again. Thus, he urged warring nations to forsake victory in order to construct a better world. He proposed that the United States join other civilized nations in ensuring a permanent peace based on the consent of the governed, freedom of the seas, a league of nations rather than alliances, and reduced armaments. Such a settlement would "win the approval of mankind" and convince Americans to end 150 years of isolationism and work with other nations to "guarantee peace and justice throughout the world."[189] Accusing Wilson of being too proud to fight, Theodore Roosevelt paraphrased (or perhaps misquoted) Judges 5:23: "Curse ye, Meroz, said the angel of the Lord . . . because they came not to help the Lord against the wrongdoings of the mighty." Wilson had "earned for the nation the curse of Meroz," Roosevelt protested, because he had "not dared to stand on the side of the Lord" against German aggression.[190] Early in 1917, as relations between Germany and the United States deteriorated further, largely because of Germany's renewed use of submarine warfare, many clergy called for America's entry into the war.[191]

For nearly three years, the war in Europe haunted Wilson. In March 1917, he finally faced his Gethsemane.[192] The monumental decision of whether the United States should go to war depended to a large degree on him alone. The president had tried to be genuinely neutral so he could mediate between the combatants. He deplored British interference in American trade with Germany. They had intercepted merchant ships headed to Germany, planted mines in the North Sea, blockaded German ports, and blacklisted almost a hundred American firms. The British had rejected all of Wilson's proposals to arbitrate and ruthlessly crushed a rebellion in Ireland in 1916. Germany, however, had invaded Belgium, France, and Russia, had inhibited Americans from freely sailing the sea by its submarine attacks, and had killed Americans by sinking passenger liners. In March, the British intercepted a telegram from German Foreign Secretary Arthur Zimmermann to his minister in Mexico, promising that if Mexico declared war against the United States, Germany would help it recover its "lost territory in Texas, New Mexico, and Arizona." The economic and cultural ties of the United States with England and France and Wilson's fear that German domination of Europe would have devastating consequences also played a role in his decision. Only by participating in the war could Wilson ensure that the Allies won and that he played a leading role in shaping the peace. On the other hand, Wilson dreaded sending millions of young men into battle, the sacrifices that would be needed at home, and the negative impact the war was likely to have on civil liberties and the national psyche. "If there is any alternative," he cried, echoing Christ's agony in the garden before his crucifixion, "for God's sake, let's take it."[193]

After a week of anguish, Wilson decided the United States must join the battle against the Central Powers. He concluded that American participation in the Great War was necessary to stop German aggression, liberate oppressed peoples, and provide a sounder, more secure basis for fraternity and peace. When men took up arms to "set other men free," warfare could be "sacred and holy." "I will not cry 'peace,'" Wilson added, "so long as there is sin and wrong in the world."[194] As he put it in his speech asking Congress for a declaration of war against Germany on April 2, 1917, "It is a fearful thing to lead this great peaceful people . . . into the most terrible and disastrous of all wars, civilization itself seeming to be in the balance. But right is more precious than peace, and we shall fight for the things which we have always carried nearest to out hearts"—democracy, consent of the governed, the rights of small nations, and justice—in order to bring "peace and safety to all nations." In his mysterious providence, God would use the United States to accomplish his purposes.[195]

In his speech to Congress, Wilson announced that America's objective was "to vindicate the principles of peace and justice" that "selfish and autocratic power" opposed. The president agreed with Social Gospelers that "the same standards of conduct and of responsibility" held for governments as for individual citizens of their states and that Germany therefore must be held accountable for its actions.[196] By fighting a vicarious war on behalf of others, Americans sought to make "the world itself at last free." "The world must be made safe for democracy," Wilson announced. "We have no selfish ends to serve. We desire no conquest, no dominion. We seek . . . no material compensation for the sacrifices we shall freely make. We are but one of the champions of the rights of mankind." Although Wilson thought he was articulating widely respected moral reasons for American participation in the war, many in other nations heard claims of American moral superiority. The president concluded, "America is privileged to spend her blood and her might for the principles that gave her birth and happiness and the peace which she has treasured." Paraphrasing Martin Luther's closing declaration at the Diet of Worms in 1521, he added, "God helping her, she can do no other."[197] The next day, William Gibbs McAdoo, the president's son-in-law and secretary of the treasury, wrote Wilson, "I firmly believe that it is God's will that America should do this transcendent service for humanity . . . and that you are his chosen instrument."[198] He could not have expressed Wilson's own convictions more clearly.

During the Senate's debate over the president's request, numerous senators denounced Germany as the enemy of both civilization and Christianity.[199] Several even compared America's mission in defeating the Central Powers to Christ's sacrificial death on the cross.[200] A senator read a telegram from a Methodist convention supporting a declaration of war: "Even the patient Christ, whose ambassadors we are," they stated, "in times of extremity, when pacific measures had failed, said, 'He that hath no sword, let him sell his garment and buy one.' "[201] On Good Friday, April 6, the Senate voted 82 to 6 to go to war, and the House approved Wilson's declaration of war 373 to 50.

The contention that the United States would fight to "make the world safe for democracy" and "end all wars" helped many Americans, especially Protestant elites, overcome their moral qualms about war. In the ensuing months, many Christian clergy used pulpit and print to strongly support this "war for righteousness." Elevating the war above the sordid realm of "national ambition, rivalry, and interests . . . into the rarified world of ideals, abstractions, and politicized theology," they provided interpretations of the United States, Germany, and "the war's ultimate meaning that were indispensable to waging total war."[202] Wilson fostered this image of the United States as a righteous, redemptive agent, calling the nation "an instrument in the hands of God" to secure liberty for humanity.[203] In a 1917 book, socialist George D. Herron wrote from Switzerland that Wilson believed "that the Sermon on the Mount is the ultimate constitution of mankind." He saw the United States as "a colossal Christian apostle, shepherding the world into the kingdom of God."[204] In 1917, Wilson told the publisher of Herron's book that the theologian understood his "motives and purposes."[205] The Democrat also managed to convince many secular progressives that the Great War would institute a new order of justice and peace.[206]

Agreeing with Wilson, many clergy "portrayed the United States as a righteous nation" fighting a modern crusade to liberate the world's oppressed. They expected its final outcome to remove the scourge of war from the earth and bring worldwide democracy and brotherhood.[207] Some clergy pictured the war as "a new atoning sacrifice" that would accomplish "humanity's final, collective redemption."[208] Moreover, some pastors, like Wilson, identified the United States as a servant nation or as a modern messiah.[209] Unlike neoorthodox theologian Reinhold Niebuhr in the 1930s and 1940s, few clergy chastised Americans for identifying the kingdom of God with their nation.[210] While praising America as a pure, sacrificial agent of worldwide redemption, many clergy condemned Germany as "corrupt, selfish and pagan." They pictured it as a blood-saturated barbarian and "the Antichrist hell bent on world domination."[211] Although God was not on the side of the United States against Germany, argued Congregationalist William Barton, he was "on the side of justice against injustice." Thus America would prevail because it was allied with "the cause of humanity, which is God's own cause."[212] Speaking for many church leaders, Presbyterian Arthur Judson Brown declared that never had a nation "entered a war in such an altruistic spirit." The United States was "absolutely right" to join this war to fight for "righteousness, justice, liberty and brotherhood," a war that was fundamentally "between Pagan and Christian ideas of the organization of the world." Americans were participating in the war to "advance the Kingdom of God on earth."[213] Many religious progressives considered an international order built on Christian principles to be "the capstone of the social structure of the Kingdom of God."[214] Seeing war as a divine mission, some clergy blended patriotism and religion. "Loyalty to the flag swiftly is coming to be recognized as of equal or even greater virtue than fidelity to a church," the *New York Morning Telegraph* editorialized in 1918. "Soldiers of Christ" and "soldiers of Democracy" have united "in the one Grand Army of Liberty."[215]

After the United States declared war, the churches enthusiastically supported mobilization. Protestant denominations and interdenominational organizations created more than forty wartime committees or commissions, many of which focused on supplying chaplains to soldiers and sailors.[216] To promote the war, the Federal Council of Churches, the Church Peace Union, the World Alliance, and the League to Enforce Peace together created the National Committee on the Church and the Moral Aims of the War. Responding to Wilson's request, clergy encouraged parishioners to increase their productivity, reduce their consumption, and buy Liberty Bonds.[217] Leaders of mainline Protestants, Social Gospel organizations, the Federal Council of Churches, and the YMCA rarely criticized any facets of the war effort.[218] Exuding remarkable optimism, some progressive clergy expected the Great War to produce a "socially conscious, activist, and unified church, a renewed social order, and a fraternal new world order."[219]

While displaying similar confidence in the war's salutary effects and recognizing that American military might had played a decisive role in its outcome, Wilson gave God the ultimate credit. In his Thanksgiving Day proclamation in November 1918, he intoned: "God has in His good pleasure given us peace. . . . It has come as a great triumph of right. Complete victory has brought us . . . the confident promise of a new day . . . in which justice shall replace force. . . . In a righteous cause they [our gallant armies] . . . have nobly served their nation in serving mankind. God has indeed been gracious."[220] Investing the war with eschatological significance, Wilson declared that it had accomplished humanity's "final emancipation."[221]

Crunden argues that by entering World War I, Wilson sought to impose his "vision on a world that rarely accepted his goals and never understood his principles." Rejecting Wilson's values, European statesmen saw Christian morals as essentially private and "not applicable to nations or armies."[222] A French newspaper maintained that Wilson's "Peace without Victory" speech was an outstanding sermon on "what human beings might be capable of accomplishing if only they weren't humans."[223] A leading French student of American diplomacy accuses Wilson of presuming that the United States was more moral than other countries and that it alone possessed the "formula for a just and durable peace."[224] Despite the exuberant hopes of Wilson and other religious progressives, World War I did not usher in a new era in international relations, establish a righteous, peaceful world order, or bring the kingdom of God on earth. Few of the moral aims for which Americans fought were realized. Despite the best intentions and zealous efforts of Wilson, other national leaders, and millions of soldiers and civilians, World War I and the treaty that ended it instead sowed the seeds for a second catastrophic conflict. Moreover, Wilson's worst fears were realized at home, as civil liberties became a casualty of the war.[225]

The Treaty of Versailles and the League of Nations

Wilson's Christian convictions also helped shape his work in devising the Treaty of Versailles and the League of Nations. While American troops fought in Europe in 1918, Wilson enunciated American peace aims in three major addresses: Fourteen Points (January 8), Four Principles (February 11), and Five Particulars (September 27). Seeking to win popular support for the cause of freedom, Wilson proposed to substitute collective security for the destructive alliance that characterized Europe's old balance-of-power system. Restating the basic tenets of nineteenth-century liberalism, his Fourteen Points called for freedom of the seas, open markets, and reduced armaments. In these speeches and others, Wilson stressed "all that was high and holy in the Western democracies and Christian traditions."[226] Wilson hoped to incorporate these principles in the treaty the Allies crafted after Germany's surrender in November 1918.

On the way to the Paris Peace Conference the next month, "Wilson the Just," as French premier Georges Clemenceau lampooned him, "became a many-faceted symbol of hope to millions around the world."[227] America's progressive clergy saw Wilson as representative of their principles. To them, a just treaty and a league of nations would incarnate the biblical ideals of service and brotherhood and therefore help bring God's kingdom on earth.[228] Even secular journals described the president's mission in religious terms. "His revolutionary program," declared *Current Opinion*, "is really the application of the principles of Christian missions to statecraft."[229] Upon his arrival in France, Wilson was hailed as a "conquering hero" and "heralded as almost the Second Coming of Christ Himself."[230] "He was transfigured in the eyes of men," wrote English novelist H. G. Wells. "He ceased to be a common statesman; he became a Messiah."[231] Perceiving himself as the apostle of a new political order, Wilson told the plenary session, "Wrong has been defeated" and "the rest of the world is more conscious than ever of the majesty of right."[232] Less optimistically, Clemenceau quipped, "God gave us his Ten Commandments, and we broke them. Wilson gave us his Fourteen Points—we shall see."[233]

At Paris, as he had done at Princeton and Washington, Wilson battled entrenched interest groups. Striving to transcend party concerns and national boundaries, he appealed to universal needs and fundamental moral principles. In joining the war, the United States had fought, he told delegates, for "the cause of justice" and liberty for all people.[234] Rejecting the long-standing commitment to a balance of power in international relations, Wilson called for a new world order based on "a community of power" and an "organized common peace."[235] Following the example of his "very stern ancestors," the Covenanters, he urged delegates to create an international organization to achieve this end. The Solemn League and Covenant they had established in seventeenth-century Scotland was a tripartite agreement between God, the king, and the people. By using the term *covenant* rather than *contract, agreement*, or *constitution*, Wilson implied that God would be one of the contracting parties.[236] Wilson told a British audience in 1918 that he wanted the whole world to enter into "a great league and covenant" to ensure the "triumph of right."[237] In addition, he proposed to locate the League of Nations' headquarters in Geneva, Switzerland, the city where John Calvin had sought to establish a model Christian commonwealth four centuries earlier.

Wilson went to Versailles to lay the groundwork for a lasting peace, not to gain territory for the United States. He insisted that vanquished nations be treated fairly, that Germany not be saddled with more reparations than it could reasonably pay, that all nations have the right of self-determination, and that every country, not just Germany, drastically reduce their armaments. Wilson's time on Mount Olympus was fleeting, as the peace conference soon turned contentious. Delegates strove to advance the interests of their own nations, rather than create a new world order. Determined to receive compensation for their losses, the victors rejected most of Wilson's liberal vision. Inflamed by vengeance, they disarmed Germany, took away its colonies, forced it to take sole blame for the war, and imposed $56 billion in reparation payments. More positively, the treaty recognized the independence of several European nations and established mandates for Germany's former possessions, which prepared the way for their eventual independence. Although the treaty was not totally satisfactory, Wilson insisted, it signaled the demise of autocracy, militarism, and imperialism.[238] It was "severe," he explained, but the treaty liberated new groups of people, abolished the right of conquest, and recognized the principle of self-determination, the rights of minorities, and "the sanctity of religious belief and practice."[239] The treaty contained many compromises and imperfections, but it created a much needed league of nations.

Robert Crunden argues that Wilson failed at Versailles because delegates perceived him to be "rigid, theological, unprepared, vague, and malicious."[240] Upset with the results of the peace conference, British economist John Maynard Keynes protested that Wilson's "Presbyterian temperament" wove the "web of sophistry and Jesuitical exegesis that was finally to clothe with insincerity the language and substance of the whole Treaty."[241] British diplomat Harold Nicolson accused Wilson of viewing the League Covenant as "the solution of all human difficulties" and of sacrificing "his Fourteen Points one by one" before this "Ark of the Covenant."[242]

Speaking to the Senate on July 10, 1919, Wilson invoked God's authority in an attempt to convince members to ratify the treaty. "The stage is set, the destiny is disclosed," he declared. "It has come about by no plan of our conceiving, but by the hand of God who led us into this way. . . . It was of this that we dreamed at our birth. America shall in truth show the way."[243] Because the treaty was divinely inspired and God used the United States to advance his purposes, rejecting it, he implied, would "defy both God and destiny" and lead America to wander for years in the wilderness rather than enter the Promised Land.[244]

Contending that the treaty violated most of Wilson's Fourteen Points, was too harsh toward Germany, and would impede world unity, some progressives condemned it.[245] The editors of Christian Century accused the president of capitulating to the "moral confusion of greedy, cunning and fear-bound diplomacy," of surrendering his idealism, and of compromising "the truth of God at the supreme moment." This "unjust and vicious" treaty betrayed fraternity and democracy. Because its terms were "punitive, vindictive, and terrorizing" to Germany, they were "neither redemptive nor Christian."[246] Three leading secular progressives—Herbert Croly, Walter Lippmann, and John Dewey—also denounced the Treaty of Versailles.[247]

Seventeen senators—fourteen Republicans and three Democrats—known as the "irreconcilables," totally opposed U.S. participation in the league. The majority of Republican senators, however, were willing to support American membership if the treaty were amended to clearly state that nations were not surrendering their sovereignty to a "superstate."[248] With the treaty bottled up in the Foreign Relations Committee, Wilson's sense of mission and faith in the American people prompted him to embark on a public tour to gain popular support to pressure senators to ratify the treaty without what he considered crippling changes.[249] Traveling more than nine thousand miles by train, the president gave thirty-seven speeches in twenty-two days in September 1919 to large and friendly crowds before collapsing in Colorado. A week later, he suffered a devastating stroke that made him a reclusive invalid for the rest of his second term. In these addresses, the president repeatedly argued that if the United States did not ratify the covenant, thousands of American soldiers and sailors would have died in vain.

Many religious leaders supported America's participation in the League of Nations. Shortly before the peace conference began, the Federal Council of Churches collected the signatures of hundreds of pastors who endorsed the league and sent a delegation to Paris to meet with Wilson to express their approval.[250] In May 1919, the council urged churches to give "their fullest support" to the league because it embodied a Christian pattern for international relations.[251] Such prominent Protestant progressives as Baptist Harry Emerson Fosdick, Presbyterian Robert Speer, and Congregationalist Charles Jefferson applauded the league. In Speer's words, it was "an indispensable and unavoidable implication of all our Christian faith and endeavor in the world."[252] The editors of *Christian Century* labeled the league an "extension" of the kingdom of God.[253] To most religious progressives, it was not simply a pragmatic mechanism that could resolve conflicts but "the fulfillment of a spiritual ideal." In response to a plea from the Federal Council in September 1919, 17,000 pastors signed a petition imploring the Senate to support both the treaty and the league.[254]

Women's groups, the American Federation of Labor, and the American Bar Association also endorsed the league, but many other groups opposed it, arguing that the British would use it to advance their empire or that it would limit American independence and perhaps even force the nation into a war against its will. Had Wilson compromised with his opponents, he probably could have gained almost all the treaty's "valuable and workable" provisions, as well as American membership in the League of Nations. The president's illness and unwillingness to negotiate, however, coupled with the reservations of many senators, led to the final defeat of the treaty on March 19, 1920.[255]

A Final Assessment

Although he was much maligned by his political opponents, numerous newspapers, and some ethnic groups, a Methodist argued in 1925, Wilson stood above other statesmen in his support "for justice, mercy, square-dealing, and Christian fellowship in a world groaning under the weight of its own iniquity and pain."[256] Other contemporaries called him the noblest statesman in history, praised him as a peacemaker, and compared him with Abraham Lincoln.[257] No other American, not even Washington or Lincoln, proclaimed the editors of *Christian Century* in 1924, compelled them as much to use spiritual vocabulary to properly assess his significance for the world. No other twentieth-century world leader, not even Lenin or Gandhi, had evoked so much hope and faith or drawn from such great spiritual depths, as had Wilson.[258] To his admirers, Wilson was a powerful prophet, a visionary, and the "champion of the weak and oppressed."[259] He desired the praise of God, one of them argued, rather than the applause of people.[260] After Wilson's death in 1924, the Federal Council declared that the Democrat had forcefully articulated "the ideals of the churches." He had "stirred the soul of America" and challenged its citizens to serve the world.[261] God sent Woodrow Wilson, proclaimed Charles Macfarland, the council's general secretary from 1912 to 1931, "to bear witness" to Christ as the "light of the world."[262] The depth of his convictions, the intensity of his faith, the integrity of his character, and the fervency of his purpose, a historian added, enabled Wilson to foster the "ideal of world peace and brotherhood under the rule of justice and equity."[263] What John Calvin attempted to do in Geneva, Wilson sought to accomplish for the world: to create a social order grounded upon biblical principles. Deeply influenced by both the ideals of political progressivism and the biblical mandate to transform culture, Wilson strove to redeem a corrupt Europe, reform Latin America, and rescue Russia from communism.[264] The Presbyterian exhorted Americans to revere God's laws, serve one another, and help their neighbors around the world. He repeatedly argued that the United States existed to promote freedom, democracy, and justice for the world.[265] Wilson's superior intellect, strong religious conviction, sense of destiny, integrity, boldness, and resolution, Link maintains, made him "at times a superb political leader."[266]

Others, by contrast, showered vicious, venomous invective on Wilson while he was president. They complained that he was cold and austere, held many petty prejudices, and had been bamboozled by other world leaders at Versailles.[267] Theodore Roosevelt accused Wilson of being enthralled by the power of words, of cloaking "weakness or baseness behind insincere oratory on behalf of impractical ideals."[268] Wilson was an "adroit, tricky" "demagogue" who had no "spark of loftiness" "in his cold, selfish and timid soul."[269] The editors of the *Nation* protested in 1919 that the United States had regressed during Wilson's presidency because of his "hypnotic powers" to substitute "empty phrases for real leadership."[270] Even admirers admitted that Wilson had great difficulty accepting constructive criticism or forgiving and forgetting.[271] Link contends that Wilson often gave evasive answers, told half-truths, and even directly lied "when he thought the public interest demanded dissimulation."[272] Despite this president's repeated emphasis on selfless service and the depth of his Christian commitment, John Mulder asserts, Wilson deeply desired to be revered as a great leader who elevated the ideals and improved the practices of the world's nations.[273]

Although Wilson's two terms were free from political scandals, some critics attacked his personal life, especially his relationship with Mary Allen Hulbert Peck. Wilson first met Peck, the wife of a wealthy businessman, in Bermuda in 1907. Wilson turned to Peck for comfort, encouragement, and affirmation in the midst of his battles over the direction of Princeton. Suffering through marital difficulties, Peck found that her relationship with Wilson filled a void in her life. For the next eight years, they exchanged affectionate letters that lavished praise on one another.[274] He called her his "dearest, sweetest Friend" and signed his letters "with infinite tenderness."[275] Peck wrote that she missed Wilson "horribly" when they were apart, called him "adorable," and termed their friendship "the greatest honor and happiness and privilege of her life."[276] In addition to corresponding regularly until 1915, Wilson often visited Peck in New York after she separated from her husband. Whether their relationship ever moved from emotional attachment to physical intimacy is impossible to determine.[277] When rumors began to circulate after Wilson became president that they had an amorous relationship, Wilson assured Colonel Edwin House that their friendship was only "platonic," but he admitted that his letters to Peck had been warmer "than was prudent."[278]

Some of Wilson's bitterest enemies could not believe that he and Peck had had an affair. "Heaven knows I hated Wilson like poison," wrote his Princeton rival dean Andrew F. West, "but there is not one word of truth in this nonsense. It simply is not in character."[279] John Mulder concludes that the strains of Wilson's final years at Princeton may have led him to "uncharacteristic and indiscreet behavior" and that "his tendency to compartmentalize his thinking" may have enabled him to separate "his strict morals" from his personal conduct.[280] Considering Peck a competitor for her husband's affection, Ellen accused him in 1908 of having "emotional love" for Peck. Woodrow responded that her charge was "a cutting and cruel judgment and utterly false."[281] Ellen apparently accepted their friendship and even visited Peck in 1910, but their relationship remained cool and formal.[282]

More recent critics argue that Wilson's presidency contributed to the demise of progressivism, the weakening of the Christian impulse to reform society, and the growing secularization of American politics and society. Ironically, the linking of progressivism with World War I helped make it politically impotent in the 1920s. In 1917, progressives enjoyed a prominent position in both major parties and were poised to dominate American politics. They had taken the legislative initiative in many states and the federal government and had popularized a "new ethos of social responsibility and civic engagement," but during the 1920s, progressivism declined dramatically.[283] Disillusioned by the war, concerned about the threat of communism, distracted by the "perils of prosperity," and affected by increasing secularization, many Americans in the 1920s rejected Wilson's belief in the United States' providential mission to spread the blessings of democracy, capitalism, and Christianity to the world. Many younger intellectuals revolted against the Victorian values of "universal morality, progress, and culture," which they linked with "snobbery, racial pride . . . prudery, and the Wilsonian version of the Allied cause."[284] Progressivism, Robert Crunden contends, "died with his failures." Robert Linder argues that Wilson's crusading Christian idealism was "the last gasp" of political progressivism and the Protestant urge to reform the nation.[285] As Pierard and Linder explain, the "unregenerate world" did not accept Wilson's "moralism and messianic vision," and "the Protestant piety on which it was predicated was steadily losing its hold at home."[286] While denouncing traditional imperialism as antithetical to American values, Wilson strove to use his nation's power to improve the world. During his eight years in office, the United States sought to "uplift and enlighten others," but Wilson's policies antagonized many citizens of developing countries and failed to resolve the conflicts over values and interests among the world's nations.[287] Mulder suggests that "the Wilsonian mix of religion and politics" may have ironically "contributed to the secularization of religion, the sacralizing of politics, and the relativizing of the moral order."[288]

Offering a more positive perspective of his idealism, Link contends that because Wilson rejected "narrow nationalism and materialism as the bases for foreign policy" and articulated the "noblest traditions of Western culture," he spoke with "universal authority" when he pleaded with Germany to stop using submarines, proclaimed that the aim of the Great War was to provide justice for the vanquished as well as the victors, and called for a league of nations "based on the ideals of peace and co-operation." Wilson was an effective war leader and a successful statesman because he extolled what most Westerners, including his opponents, acknowledged were their own highest ideals. Link praises the Presbyterian for exalting "the traditions of humanity and the ideal of justice" at a time when "hatreds and passions threatened to wreck Western civilization."[289]

Yet Link admits that Wilson's "faith in the goodness and rationality of men, in the miraculous potentialities of democracy, and in the inevitable triumph of righteousness sometimes caused him to . . . devise quixotic or unworkable solutions."[290] Others accuse Wilson of ignoring the Calvinist conception of human depravity and expecting too much of people.[291] Deviating from his religious tradition, Wilson stressed "the essential nobility of man" and assumed that human brotherhood and world order could be achieved.[292] Moreover, Link asserts, "his almost romantic faith" in democracy prompted him to naively believe that progressive governments could be established through free elections in Central America, Caribbean states, Mexico, and Russia. Wilson's preoccupation with fundamental principles sometimes prompted him to oversimplify "the vast complexities of international politics." He thought that "civilized gentlemen controlled by enlightened public opinion and common moral standards" could direct foreign relations and that "decency, good will, and free discussion" could settle all international conflicts. This assumption led him to emphasize universal principles, diplomacy, conciliation treaties, and national friendships and usually to avoid threats or violence.[293] Moreover, Wilson believed that his "motives and purposes were purer" than those of his opponents.[294] Influenced by diplomat George Kennan and international relations expert Hans Morgenthau, the "realist" school of historians that emerged in the 1950s similarly criticized Wilson for focusing on abstract ideals and ignoring "strategy, bases and armed power."[295] They argued that his reputedly "universal moral principles" furnished an "inadequate, if not disastrous, foundation for American foreign policy." The United States should pursue its own national interest because it lacked the power to impose its ideals on the world.[296]

Although Wilson sometimes appeared to believe that he was a "messiah divinely appointed to deliver Europe," Link insists, he was "in fact the supreme realist." Arguing that his approach was "more perceptive, more in accord with ultimate reality, and more likely to win the long-run approval of societies professing allegiance to the common western, humane, Christian traditions," Link labels it a "higher realism."[297] Wilson, Link writes, almost always judged "policies on the basis of whether they were right by Christian standards, not whether they brought immediate material or strategic advantage." He assumed that nations, like individuals, were required to obey the law of Christian love. Link argues that Wilson's quest to establish an enduring, peaceful international order was vastly superior to other leaders' attempts at Versailles to destroy their ancient foes, ensure their national security, or gain spoils. Only a settlement based on reconciliation, not vengeance, on disarming all combatants, on preventing annexations and indemnities, and on constructing an international peacekeeping organization could have transcended "the passions and hatreds" that had inflamed Europe and retained the long-term support of most of the world's people. To gain some of his major objectives, Wilson had to compromise. Recognizing that the treaty contained serious flaws, he signed it, nonetheless, as the best one he could negotiate and hoped that the passage of time and the actions of the League of Nations could rectify them.[298] Both on the battlefield and at the conference table, Wilson helped to defeat the autocracy, imperialism, and militarism of the Central Powers and make them anathema throughout the world. Tragically, however, he was unable to devise "a fair and generous peace" that prevented future German aggression.[299]

Individual wickedness and national self-interest kept Wilson's grand designs for world brotherhood, justice, and peace from being attained. Ignoring his own religious tradition's argument that no country was God's special agent, he portrayed the United States as a redeemer nation. His lofty hopes for what America could help the world become were dashed on the hard rocks of European power politics. World War I and its aftermath brought great disillusionment. By conservative estimates, the war killed ten million people and wounded twenty million more. Russia, France, Belgium, and Germany were physically devastated. A new era of peace was not inaugurated. The world's pluralism, diverse ideologies, and lack of political consensus prevented the realization of Wilson's exuberant expectations.[300] Nevertheless, the Presbyterian exalted transcendent ideals that, if followed, could significantly improve international relationships and the quality of people's lives. More than any other political leader of his generation, Wilson challenged his world to exalt fraternity, sacrifice, democracy, and peace above fratricide, selfishness, autocracy, and warfare.

Although Wilson's approach to foreign policy seemed like a failure in the 1920s, it reemerged during the Cold War, usually stripped of its more blatant religious themes, to direct America's approach to global affairs. Lloyd Ambrosius contends that Wilson's liberal internationalism, based on the principles of national self-determination, "Open Door economic globalization," collective security, and a progressive view of history, provided the dominant ideology for American foreign policy in the twentieth century.[301] Wilsonianism asserted that the United States would use its military power, economic resources, and cultural influence to try to advance the interests of the whole world, not just its own.[302] Because most American political leaders espoused Wilsonianism rather than the alternatives of realism or new left revisionism, his legacy has significantly shaped U.S. involvement in international affairs from World War II to the present. Like Wilson, numerous American presidents, including George W. Bush, have "committed the United States to defend and promote a progressive, democratic, capitalist, and peaceful world order against its enemies."[303] The impact of this Presbyterian statesman lives on.

When Wilson was elected a ruling elder in the Presbyterian Church in 1897, his father proudly told a friend, "I would rather that he held that position than be President of the United States."[304] Wilson served as both elder and president, and the connection between his Presbyterian faith and his presidency was direct and strong. As Link puts it, Wilson's work as president "was informed, shaped, and controlled by insights . . . that flowed from Christian faith."[305] Shortly before his death, Wilson wrote to Norman Davis, "I have done the best I know how. . . . I am confident that what I have fought for . . . is for the benefit of this nation and of mankind. If this is so, I believe it will ultimately prevail, and if it is not, I don't want it to prevail."[306] To the end of his life, Wilson believed that God controlled the universe and that he was his instrument.

CHAPTER SIX

Franklin Delano Roosevelt and the Quest to Achieve an Abundant Life

Philosophy? I am a Christian and a Democrat—that's all.

Quoted in Frances Perkins, *The Roosevelt I Knew*

The Great Teacher said "I come that ye may have life and that ye may have it more abundantly." The object of all our striving should be to realize that "abundant life."

A Letter to the Chaplains of the Military and Naval Services, Feb. 13, 1934

Let us pray God to hasten the day when acceptance of His Word will change the hearts and minds of men, and make the kingdoms of this world in truth and fact the Kingdom of God.

Roosevelt to Francis C. Stifler, Editorial Secretary, American Bible Society, Sept. 20, 1941

We must all unite in labor and in prayer in achieve victory and to bring back to the world an international order dominated by true Christian principles.

Roosevelt to William Cardinal Dougherty, Oct. 19, 1942

ON EASTER SUNDAY in 1934, Franklin D. Roosevelt conducted a worship service off the coast of the island of San Salvador aboard the private yacht of a friend. The president led the entire service and preached a short sermon to the assembled American and British soldiers (two U.S. destroyers had accompanied the yacht and a British light cruiser had joined them) about the religious significance of the spot where Columbus had first set foot in the

Americas. Roosevelt argued that Columbus's faith in God had given him "the courage and confidence" to undertake his voyage and to persevere when he was "threatened by disaster and mutiny."[1] Roosevelt's own faith helped him deal with the many challenges he faced during his twelve years in the Oval Office.

Scholars have provided scant analysis of Roosevelt's personal faith, regular use of religious rhetoric, relationship with religious constituencies and leaders, or the impact of his religious convictions on his policies as president. Influenced by his father, James, and his mentor at Groton, Endicott Peabody, Roosevelt repeatedly emphasized the importance of the Bible, prayer, and Christian morality. In numerous speeches and letters, he urged Americans to work for spiritual renewal, promote social justice, and strive to achieve a more abundant material and spiritual life. He frequently asserted that God directed history, considered himself to be God's agent, and insisted that the United States would prosper only if its citizens sought divine guidance and followed biblical principles. His courage, confidence, and calm in dealing with the Great Depression and World War II sprang from his temperament, life experiences, and faith. Interested much more in the moral, character-building, and social justice emphases of Christianity than its theological or devotional aspects, Roosevelt's faith was sincere but not intellectually sophisticated. Like his approach to politics, his faith focused more on action than contemplation, more on results than on principles. More than any other twentieth-century president, Roosevelt managed to maintain cordial relations with Protestants (especially ones concerned about social justice), Catholics, and Jews. During his twelve years in office, Roosevelt greatly expanded the scope of the federal government, substantially increased the power of the president, built a coalition that transformed the Democratic Party into a major political force for the rest of the century, constructed a new American foreign policy based on collective security and international aid, and made the United States the principal player in global politics.[2]

Roosevelt's Faith

Relatively little attention has been devoted to Roosevelt's religious views and practices.[3] Assessing the New Yorker's faith is difficult because he considered his religious beliefs to be very personal and rarely discussed them with his wife or his closest companions. Nevertheless, the testimony of friends, associates, and observers; Roosevelt's expressed convictions; his involvement with the Episcopal Church; his actions as president; and his private and public statements all provide insights into his religious faith.

Roosevelt's father was raised in the Dutch Reformed Church, but when he moved to Hyde Park, he began attending the St. James Episcopal Church. For more than forty years, the elder Roosevelt was a member of the vestry at St. James, and he was known as a kind, helpful, "upright Christian man" who "adorned the doctrine of Christ . . . by a consistent walk and holy life."[4] Four years after the death of his first wife in 1876, James married Sara Delano, and Franklin was their only child. Franklin's mother grew up in a family that had long been Unitarians, but she also became an Episcopalian.

Endicott Peabody, the founder and headmaster at Groton, an elite boarding school Roosevelt attended as a teenager, had even more influence on the future president's faith than his father. Through his daily chapel talks, classroom instruction, and fatherly guidance, the Episcopal rector emphasized morality, character, and service. He challenged students to serve God, their nation, and humanity through numerous avenues, including participation in politics.[5] While at Groton, Roosevelt played the organ for worship services held in mission houses for the destitute.[6] Peabody performed Roosevelt's wedding, supervised the education of his four sons at Groton, and helped lead the president's inaugural day prayer services in Washington. The two men maintained a lifelong friendship and deeply respected each other.[7] In 1935, Peabody wrote to Roosevelt, "It is a great thing" to have a leader "who cares primarily for spiritual things." He rejoiced that Roosevelt was bringing "fresh power to the individual and to the cause of Christ and His Church."[8] In 1941, Roosevelt wrote to Peabody, "I count it among the blessings of my life" that during my "formative years . . . [I had] the privilege of your guiding hand and benefit of your inspiring example."[9]

Several of those who knew Roosevelt best claimed he was "a deeply religious man."[10] Based on their thirty-year relationship, his assistant Stephen Early called the Democrat "one of the finest Christian gentlemen" he knew.[11] Roosevelt's son James testified that "Father never preached much to us—or to anyone—about piety and virtue, but, to him, religion was a real and personal thing from which he drew much strength and comfort."[12] His personal secretary Grace Tully insisted that the New Yorker had "profound respect for religious piety in any form."[13] After his death, Eleanor declared that her husband always considered religion "an anchor and a source of strength and guidance."[14]

Journalists echoed this assessment. Shortly after the 1932 election, the *Presbyterian Banner* declared, "The country is fortunate in having again called to its chief office a man of unspotted character and Christian profession."[15] Although their opinion would later change, the editors of *Christian Century* argued in 1934 that Roosevelt's personality was "spiritually deep and spiritually sound." The American people considered him a "religious leader" who sought to build a "righteous community."[16] Numerous Catholics also lauded his "deep and profound interest" in spiritual matters.[17]

Roosevelt displayed little interest in the intellectual aspects of Christianity. He was uninterested in theology, despised disputes about religious doctrines, and had few doubts about his own faith. When their children were young, Eleanor asked her husband whether he thought they should teach them about religion or allow them to choose their own religious convictions as they grew older. Roosevelt replied that their children should "go to church and learn what he had learned. It could do them no harm." Eleanor retorted, "But are you sure that you believe in everything you learned?" "I really never thought about it," he answered. "I think it is just as well not to think about things like that too much."[18] Disliking doctrinal rigidity and controversy, he applauded the "new scientific" understanding of Christianity developing in the 1920s, which he saw as "opening the way to a simpler faith, a deeper faith, a *happier* faith, than ever our forefathers had."[19]

To the extent that Roosevelt embraced a theological perspective, he largely affirmed the tenets of early-twentieth-century liberal Christianity. He most highly valued the Bible's ethical teachings and stressed God's goodness and love, the Ten Commandments, and Christ's Sermon on the Mount.[20] Like other theological liberals, he rejected the doctrine of human depravity and asserted, instead, that people were essentially good. Those who acted improperly did so because of their evil environments, which could be rectified through social reform.[21] Speaking the language of theological liberalism, the president wrote to Helen Keller in 1942 that the "brotherhood of man" depended on "the fatherhood of God and if we neglect our obligation to the Most High we can hardly fulfill our duty" to society.[22] Roosevelt testified to his belief in the deity of Jesus Christ.[23]

Roosevelt urged Americans to respect "honest differences of religious belief." To him, the primary battle was not between theological systems but "between belief and unbelief," and he welcomed all allies in the war. Around the globe, irreligion was challenging religion. Thus he pleaded with Protestants, Catholics, and Jews to transcend their sectarian creeds and "unite in good works" whenever they could "find common cause."[24] While celebrating religious diversity, he urged religious groups to collaborate to promote morality and spirituality and to reform society.[25]

Like his father before him, Roosevelt served as a vestryman, beginning in 1906, and later as the senior warden of St. James Episcopal Church in Hyde Park, a position he held the entire time he was president. Taking this role seriously, Roosevelt met periodically with other members of the vestry to make administrative and financial decisions on behalf of the congregation.[26] He sometimes interrupted meetings with cabinet members and advisors in the Oval Office to talk on the telephone with the other St. James senior warden about routine church affairs.[27] As president, Roosevelt oversaw a budget of billions, but he sometimes spent time trying to help this relatively small congregation (the church seated 250) save a few hundred dollars.[28] He enjoyed a close relationship with Frank Wilson, who served as the parish's rector from

1929 to 1942.[29] The Democrat also served as a trustee of the Cathedral of St. John the Divine in New York City, where he occasionally worshiped.[30]

"[Y]our going to church," Peabody wrote Roosevelt in 1935, "means more to the people throughout the land than almost anything else that you can do."[31] Despite his mentor's exhortation, Roosevelt did not attend church regularly while he was president. On Sundays, he typically slept late, relaxed, dictated letters, visited with friends, and worked on his stamp collection. Because of his physical condition and celebrity status, he considered church attendance to be more of an ordeal than a benefit.[32] He claimed it was difficult to worship God with so many people staring at him. "I can do almost everything in the 'Goldfish Bowl' of the President's life," he told Frances Perkins, "but I'll be hanged if I can say my prayers in it."[33] Roosevelt apparently attended church about once a month.[34] The president occasionally took visiting dignities to church, including Winston Churchill, King George VI and Queen Elizabeth of England, Canadian Prime Minister MacKenzie King, and Princess Juliana of the Netherlands.[35] Roosevelt described himself as "very Low Church" and admitted he preferred a Presbyterian, Methodist, or Baptist sermon to an Episcopal one.[36] His son James reported that he particularly enjoyed "hearing and singing rousing Methodist and Baptist hymns."[37] Nevertheless, Roosevelt felt most comfortable with the liturgy of the Episcopal service. Some criticized his irregular church attendance. A Methodist pastor in Kansas City urged the president to give up his "political powwows, fishing trips, and sailboat rides" and instead "attend church every Sunday and set a good example for the nation's youth." Norman Vincent Peale, pastor of the Marble Collegiate Church in New York City, accused Roosevelt of being indifferent to the church and "flippant toward religion."[38]

Conservative Christians and traditional moralists were disappointed not only with Roosevelt's infrequent church attendance but also with his smoking in public and his attitude toward liquor and divorce. Unlike Hoover, who enjoyed both cigars and pipes privately, Roosevelt smoked cigarettes openly and was often pictured with a long cigarette holder in his mouth. Although Roosevelt relished alcoholic beverages, especially cocktails, he drank more discreetly. Many complained, however, that liquor was served at the White House.[39] His support for repealing Prohibition hurt him with religious conservatives more than any other issue. Some also protested that Roosevelt seemed to condone the divorces of two of his children.

Although Roosevelt frequently used biblical themes and stories in his public addresses, he rarely discussed religious matters with even his closest associates or privately witnessed to others. One notable exception was a conversation he had with Russian ambassador Maxim Litvinov in 1933. "Your father and mother," Roosevelt reminded the ambassador, "were believers and practiced the Jewish religion. They hoped you might become a Rabbi. . . . Now

Mr. Litvinov...before you die you will think of...the religion that they taught you. Mr. Litvinov, before you die, you will believe in God." Impressed by this incident, Winston Churchill promised to recommend Roosevelt to be the next Archbishop of Canterbury if he were not reelected president.[40]

According to Grace Tully, Roosevelt "believed in the efficacy of prayer and sought God's guidance in all the momentous decisions" he made.[41] He was convinced that God responded to prayer and felt very confident about decisions he made after praying, which gave him great serenity.[42] Eleanor maintained that "he felt guided in great crises by a strength and wisdom higher than his own, for his religious faith was simple and direct." He could not have made such critical decisions "without faith in spiritual guidance."[43] The editor of *Reader's Digest* quoted Roosevelt as saying, "I believe that religion is a seven-day help to human beings.... This country was founded by men who had an acute faith in Almighty God.... Such men have always relied on our Heavenly Father to guide them through life.... They prayed with the sincere belief that if they asked for help they would get it."[44] Before each of his four inaugurals, Roosevelt held a prayer service. Much to the dismay of Republicans, he also offered a short prayer on election eve of each of his three reelection campaigns.[45]

Before each of his four inaugurals and every year on the anniversary of his inauguration, Roosevelt held a special worship service at St. John's Episcopal Church, the church he most often attended in Washington. The services, which featured hymns, collects, and Bible readings, were conducted with "due Episcopal dignity and decorum." Moreover, during World War II, Roosevelt hosted a service on Thanksgiving Day at the White House, attended by his cabinet members, head administrators, military chiefs, and their wives, for which he selected all the hymns and the prayers from the Episcopal Book of Common Prayer.[46] These services, Eleanor claimed, expressed "his religious faith."[47]

Roosevelt frequently urged Americans to pray, thanked others for praying for him, and included prayers in his addresses. Proclaiming September 8, 1940, a day of prayer, he exhorted citizens to beseech "the Ruler of the universe to bless our Republic, to make us grateful for our heritage and firm in its defense, and to grant to this land and to the troubled world a righteous, enduring peace." Roosevelt ended a 1942 address by quoting from a prayer that had been written for the Allies. It declared, " 'God of the free,... Grant us victory over tyrants who would enslave all free men and Nations.... Yet most of all grant us...a common faith that man shall know...justice and righteousness, freedom and security...throughout the world.' "[48] During World War II, the president set aside three special days of prayer to "solemnly express our dependence on Almighty God."[49] Roosevelt's most famous prayer was the one he composed and then read during the D-Day invasion on June 6, 1944. He appealed to people of all faiths to join him as the Allies began the final push to liberate Europe and defeat the ungodly Axis powers. It began: "Almighty God: Our sons...have set upon a mighty endeavor, a struggle to preserve our Republic, our religion, and our civilization, and to set free a suffering humanity." Echoing words used to encourage earlier Christian crusaders, the president added, "Some will never return. Embrace these, Father, and receive them, Thy heroic servants, into Thy kingdom." He continued, "help us, Almighty God, to rededicate ourselves in renewed faith in Thee in this hour of great sacrifice." After exhorting people to pray continuously, Roosevelt concluded, "With Thy blessing, we shall prevail over the unholy forces of our enemy.... Lead us ... with our sister Nations into a world unity that will spell a sure peace.... Thy will be done, Almighty God."[50] Roosevelt rejoiced in March 1945 that more than fifty organizations were calling for special services to pray for the success of the San Francisco conference to organize the United Nations. Permanent peace, he declared, depended on prayer.[51]

Roosevelt expressed a great appreciation for the Bible and reverence for its teachings. At each inaugural, he took the oath of office on a prized family Bible open to I Corinthians 13. The most "stern and searching criticism" had not destroyed the Bible's "prevailing and persistent power." Scripture, he added, had played a major role in "shaping the advances of the Republic." When Americans had most consistently obeyed its precepts, they had "attained the greatest measure of contentment and prosperity." He praised the Bible's unique "system of ethics, of moral and religious principles" and commended "its thoughtful and reverent reading to all our people." He argued that the Scriptures had strongly influenced the Founding Fathers and helped shape the republic they created.[52] According to Frances Perkins, Roosevelt frequently read both the Bible and the Book of Common Prayer.[53]

Few presidents, Ronald Isetti argues, "employed biblical symbols, religious language, and moral injunctions in their public addresses more often than Roosevelt did—and arguably none more effectively and eloquently."[54] "Probably no American politician," James MacGregor Burns contends, gave "so many speeches that were essentially sermons rather than statements of policy."[55] In all four of his inaugural addresses, Roosevelt used biblical images, referred to religious ideals, and invoked God's blessing upon the nation. In 1933, he charged that the "practices of unscrupulous money changers"— dishonest financiers, shady stock traders, and corrupt bankers—had caused the Great Depression. As Jesus had cleansed the temple in Jerusalem by driving out the moneychangers, Americans must expel these modern-day money-changers.[56] "These dark days will be worth all they cost us," Roosevelt added, "if they teach us that our true destiny is not to be ministered unto but to minister...to our fellow men." He ended his address by asking God to "protect each and every one of us. May He guide me in the days to come."[57] Roosevelt's second inaugural address drew on John Bunyan's *Pilgrim's Progress* and employed the imagery of the Exodus: "Shall we pause now and turn our back on the road that lies ahead?" he asked his countrymen. "Shall we call this the promised land? Or shall we continue on our way?" Americans must forge ahead, he argued, presumably with the prophet of Hyde Park as their latter-day Moses. Roosevelt promised to serve the American people while "seeking Divine guidance to . . . give light to them that sit in darkness and to guide our feet into the way of peace."[58] His third and fourth inaugural addresses emphasized the importance of advancing according to "the will of God." In 1945, he concluded by declaring, "The Almighty God has blessed our land in many ways." America's faith had "become the hope of all peoples in an anguished world." He prayed that its people would clearly "see the way that leads to a better life for ourselves and for all our fellow men—and to the achievement of His will to peace on earth."[59]

In campaign speeches, radio addresses, public proclamations, and state of the union addresses, Roosevelt also frequently used scriptural language and stories. In a 1936 campaign speech, Roosevelt denounced Republican leaders who had given the nation "nine mocking years with the golden calf and three long years of the scourge" and insisted that his government was "still on the same side of the street with the Good Samaritan and not those who pass by on the other side."[60] In messages to Congress, the president discussed the parable of the good seed, warned against the flattery of "false prophets," and argued that "by their fruits ye shall know them."[61]

In dozens of addresses and letters to groups and individuals, Roosevelt accentuated the need for national spiritual renewal. In a radio address in 1936, Roosevelt proclaimed, "No greater thing could come to our land today than . . . a revival that would . . . stir the hearts of men and women of all faiths" to reassert their belief in God and rededicate themselves to do his will. Such a spiritual awakening would remedy all social, political, and economic ills.[62] "I doubt there is in the world a single problem," he wrote in 1938, which could not be easily solved if people and nations ruled "their lives according to the plain teaching of the Sermon on the Mount."[63] Not since the Constitution was framed, he argued in 1942, did Americans have "a greater need" to "return to the teachings of the Master."[64]

As president, Roosevelt also repeatedly emphasized the importance of faith and social justice. The spirit of America, he alleged, sprang from "faith in the beloved institutions of our land, and a true and abiding faith in the divine guidance of God."[65] The Democrat maintained that both the Constitution and the practices of the United States presupposed a "belief and trust in God" and urged people to affirm their faith in him.[66] He rejoiced that social justice was "becoming an ever-growing factor and influence in almost every part of the world."[67] To some, Roosevelt was a prophet of social justice. In presenting the president with the Churchman Award in 1942, an editor declared, "When a man echoes the cry of Amos, 'Let justice roll on like waters and righteousness as a perennial stream,' and acts accordingly;" when he stands for the common man, champions the unprivileged, defends victims of racial prejudice, and promotes international brotherhood, and by so doing exposes himself to great ridicule, "then he is religious in the highest traditions of Judaism and Christianity."[68]

Roosevelt's 1935 Letter to the Clergy

In September 1935, Roosevelt sent a letter to more than 120,000 "representative Clergymen" to ask them for "counsel and advice," particularly about the impact of his administration's new social security legislation and public works program. He asked ministers, priests, and rabbis to describe conditions in their communities and suggest ways that the government could better serve citizens. Some clergy considered the letter a political ploy; many doubted that Roosevelt would read the letters; most, however, appreciated being asked to assess the impact of his administration's policies.[69] Thousands replied. Judging by the length, tone, and content of their letters, most thought their advice would be taken very seriously. Their responses focused much more on economic and material issues than spiritual ones and offered much specific advice. Surprisingly few ministers quoted Scripture. The letters reveal how the clergy perceived Roosevelt and his policies during his first term and how they viewed the nation's material and spiritual conditions in the mid-1930s.

Some respondents lauded Roosevelt's personal qualities and religious faith. The editors of the *Lutheran* hoped that his "high ideals and principles" would motivate Americans.[70] The *Presbyterian Messenger* extolled Roosevelt's "personal courage," "brave spirit in spite of handicaps," "unfailing resourcefulness," and sincere concern for the welfare of the " 'forgotten man.' "[71] A Catholic priest thanked God that Roosevelt's "wise, energetic, prudent hands" were piloting the nation through troubled waters.[72] A Baptist pastor in Chicago was confident that Roosevelt would courageously follow God's plan because he believed in God and prayer. A Polish priest in Chicago proclaimed that most Americans looked to Roosevelt for "guidance and salvation," and he expected the president to "lead them to the promised land of plenty and happiness."[73]

Other clergy exhorted Roosevelt to develop a deeper personal faith and more strongly promote spiritual renewal. A Presbyterian minister challenged the president to emulate William Gladstone, Queen Victoria, James Garfield, and William McKinley and "publicly acknowledge Christ as Lord."[74] The pastor of the First Church of Christ in Elmira, New York, insisted that Americans would be greatly encouraged if Roosevelt displayed more personal spirituality.[75] Clarence Macartney, the pastor of First Presbyterian Church in Pittsburgh, accused Roosevelt's administration of being "cold and indifferent to the spiritual and moral interests of the people."[76] A few ministers contended that the Depression was God's chastisement for America's sins.

Others maintained that moral and spiritual reform must precede social and material improvement.[77] A Catholic priest in Chicago insisted that prosperity would not be restored, despite Roosevelt's heroic efforts, until Americans humbled themselves and begged "Almighty God to . . . forgive their sins of Murder-Adultery-Stealing-Birth Control-Divorce . . . sins which cry to heaven for vengeance."[78] Some counseled Roosevelt to call a national day of prayer to encourage Americans to confess their individual and national sins and dedicate themselves to making the United States a Christian nation.[79] An editor from South Carolina urged Roosevelt to follow the example of Theodore Roosevelt, Woodrow Wilson, and Herbert Hoover and pursue "sacred stewardship, brotherhood and humility before God."[80]

Others complained that Roosevelt had waited so long to seek the counsel of the clergy, adopted detrimental policies, and broken his campaign promises. "The President has turned at last," editorialized the *United Presbyterian*, "from the brain trusters, fascists, communists, astrologers, magicians, soothsayers and sorcerers to men of God [so] that the light of divine truth might shine on his dark and dangerous troubled way."[81] Rejecting the advice of ministers, Roosevelt had reestablished the "liquor traffic in all its fury," destroyed large amounts of food even though millions were in dire need, and spent money prodigally, "as if national resources were infinite."[82] Southern Methodist bishop James Cannon Jr. argued that Roosevelt's administration had "an unparalleled record of broken pledges." Campaign pledges had "been tossed aside with such recklessness and callousness" that thoughtful citizens no longer trusted Roosevelt's promises.[83] The editor of the *Religious Telescope* of Dayton, Ohio, protested that the president's policies had consistently flouted Christian principles.[84]

Ministers had many other criticisms of Roosevelt. A few deplored his infrequent church attendance, his involvement in recreational and govern-mental activities on Sundays, and his apparent condoning of his children's divorces.[85] Some disliked his approach to politics. Yale Divinity School pro-fessor Charles Brown complained that Roosevelt appeared to have "no settled policies or convictions"; he was an opportunist who adopted policies he deemed popular and recklessly gave away other people's money.[86] A Baptist clergyman from Hornell, New York, insisted that Roosevelt had surrounded himself with "brainy men who had definitely turned away from God." A Catholic priest in Chicago predicted revolution would soon occur unless the growth of the cancerous Depression was soon stopped.[87] A Baptist pastor in Syracuse, New York, warned that the millions of Americans who blindly trusted Roosevelt to lead them into the Promised Land were bound to be disappointed. J. Oliver Buswell Jr., the president of Wheaton College, de-nounced the "socialistic or communistic tendencies" of Roosevelt's adminis-tration, especially his social security and public works legislation, as "entirely contrary to the spirit and detailed teachings of the Word of God."[88]

Most religious leaders praised Roosevelt's effort to help the poor, jobless, elderly, and handicapped as consistent with Christian principles but insisted that some of the methods his administration employed were harmful.[89] Although a substantial minority thought that conditions in their communities had remained the same or grown worse, most clergy concluded that Roosevelt's policies had improved both morale and material well-being. Many of them applauded the president's public works program for requiring participants to provide services in exchange for the money they received and keeping them from becoming dependent on charity.[90] Some, however, maintained that most projects were useless and that many workers "shirked terribly."[91] Although supporting public works programs, Charles S. Macfarland, a former president of the Federal Council of Churches, wanted to safeguard the "impulses to private philanthropy." Others objected that the public works and relief programs were producing "an almost unbearable burden of taxation" and feared the consequences of deficit spending.[92] Roosevelt's administration had done far more than its predecessors to help working people, a group of prominent clergy and educators argued, but it had not gone far enough. With ten million people still unemployed and twenty million still on relief, the nation remained deeply distressed. Palliative adjustments to the capitalist system, they contended, would not produce permanent recovery. Solving America's economic problems required nationalizing basic industries, furnishing consumer goods through cooperatives, and redistributing wealth.[93]

Most clergy strongly endorsed Roosevelt's social security legislation, which provided assistance to handicapped children, pensions for the elderly, and unemployment insurance.[94] To the clergy of the Episcopal Diocese of Long Island, the federal government's assumption of responsibility for everyone's needs accorded with the Christian principle "that the strong should bear the burdens of the weak."[95] Some, like a rabbi serving in Newark, New Jersey, insisted that the legislation was "a remarkable and courageous step forward" but was "dreadfully inadequate."[96] Several ministers contended that many citizens feared the increasing centralization of the government, disliked bureaucracy, and deeply resented efforts by the executive branch to usurp the Constitutional authority of the legislative and judicial branches.[97]

Although not directly asked about the subject, many clergy complained that the repeal of Prohibition had greatly harmed their communities. This "slap at God and the church" had led to substantial immorality, debauchery, poverty, crime, and injury to women and children.[98] Many were "morally outraged" by the Roosevelt administration's approach to the "liquor question and its attending evils."[99] A pastor in Bakersfield, California, deplored the "wreck and ruin to the bodies and souls of our citizenry" that "the nefarious and iniquitous" act of repeal had caused.[100] Despite Roosevelt's campaign promise that liquor would be sold under strict legal restrictions, that illicit sales would cease, and that the old-time saloon would not be reestablished, James

Cannon Jr. lamented, legal and illicit sales had greatly increased, as evident in the record number of arrests for drunkenness, the death toll caused by drunk drivers, and the presence of saloons everywhere.[101] An Episcopal rector in Penn Yan, New York, argued that repeal violated Christ's parable of the Good Samaritan and was a "disastrous piece of Social Insecurity Legislation."[102] Maintaining that the negative effects of repeal surpassed all the positive impacts of Roosevelt's social programs, some pastors called for reinstituting Prohibition.[103] A few conceded, in the words of a Presbyterian pastor in Burlingame, California, that Roosevelt was not personally responsible for the "orgy of liquor and licentiousness" and torrent of "automobile tragedies and broken homes" repeal had unleashed.[104]

Although Roosevelt's letter asked only about domestic issues, some respondents criticized his administration's military spending and urged him to keep America at peace. A Congregationalist minister in Oak Lawn, Illinois, deeply deplored the nation's vast expenditures on the army and navy and advised Roosevelt to take instead the "road of international co-operation, economic justice and good will."[105] A pastor in Wellsville, New York, told Roosevelt that the churches opposed his program of military expansion because it made war more likely and threatened republican institutions and civil liberties.[106] In a joint letter, several eminent educators and clergymen denounced the nation's excessive spending on armaments, while millions of Americans remained in dire need and public education languished, as "a serious misdirection of our national resources."[107]

Aubrey Mills of the Commerce Department, assigned to assess the results, quantified the number of positive and negative responses to Roosevelt's social security program and the clergy's evaluations of whether local business conditions had improved, remained the same, or become worse. Of the 8,294 replies received by October 17, 1935, Mills calculated that 49 percent were favorable, 33 percent were favorable with criticism, and 18 percent were unfavorable.[108] Most of the letters, however, contained both favorable and unfavorable comments, so they were difficult to divide into these three general categories.[109] Roosevelt's staff discussed how best to use the information they obtained and how to respond most effectively to the flood of letters they received. Their handwritten notes on many of these letters indicate that staff read them carefully.[110] Although positive responses outnumbered negative ones, Roosevelt and his advisors undoubtedly were disappointed with the response. Moreover, numerous newspapers published replies that were highly critical of the president. In the end, the results of the poll were not revealed, and two years later, Stephen Early labeled the survey "a sad mistake."[111] Roosevelt's much greater contact with theologically liberal pastors, who tended to favor public efforts to improve social conditions and aid the poor, than with evangelical and fundamentalist ministers, who often did not, perhaps led him to miscalculate the support his programs enjoyed among clergy and to overestimate the positive response his letter would elicit.[112]

Roosevelt's Relationship with Religious Constituencies

While maintaining generally positive relations with Protestant groups, Roosevelt developed much closer connections with Catholics and Jews than had his predecessors, which significantly increased their political influence. His relationship with the Federal Council of Churches was friendly and mutually supportive, in part because the president and the council's executives shared a commitment to social justice. During his tenure in the White House, Roosevelt met with the council's officers at least once a year. Speaking at the council's twenty-fifth anniversary meeting in 1933, the president promised to initiate programs to help the poor and unemployed that were "wholly in accord with the teachings of Christianity" and exhorted churches to work for social justice.[113] Roosevelt publicly endorsed the council's annual Race Relations Sunday and Week of Universal Prayer.[114] Despite agreeing on the importance of interdenominational cooperation, economic and social reform, and religious revival, the president and council leaders often disagreed about American foreign policy and military spending. Even though its leaders had considerable access to Roosevelt, the council's political influence was limited during his presidency. The council had no permanent office in Washington until 1945 and "lacked the power, the cohesive organization, and the grassroots support" necessary to exert major political pressure. Given its diverse constituency and the low level of commitment to the organization, its leaders could not guarantee that they spoke for a significant portion of the twenty million members of the denominations that belonged to the council.[115] Moreover, in the early 1940s, theological conservatives created two organizations—the American Council of Churches and the National Association of Evangelicals—to advocate their interests and counteract the clout of the Federal Council of Churches. These groups had little relationship with or impact on the Roosevelt administration, but their attacks on the Federal Council of Churches underscored the divided nature of Protestantism, tarnished the council's image, and further reduced its influence.

Roosevelt also had a cordial relationship with the leaders of the National Committee for Religion and Welfare Recovery and strongly praised their work. The more than two hundred bishops, pastors, priests, rabbis, college presidents, and prominent Catholic, Protestant, and Jewish laypeople on the committee promoted spiritual and moral renewal and raised funds to achieve these ends. Roosevelt encouraged Americans to attend church on Loyalty Day, which the committee sponsored each year, and endorsed its stewardship conventions that strove to increase contributions for philanthropic purposes.[116]

Three prominent Protestant clergymen had significant contact with Roosevelt: G. Bromley Oxnam, a Methodist bishop who served the Boston area; Henry St. George Tucker, the presiding bishop of the Episcopal Church; and Daniel Poling, the editor of the evangelical journal *Christian Herald*. Roosevelt lauded Oxnam's emphasis on the ethical foundation for world order, economic justice, and racial harmony and appreciated Methodist support for his efforts to establish world order and law.[117] Tucker corresponded frequently with Roosevelt in the early 1940s on issues ranging from war and peace to the importance of Christian ethics in industry.[118] Through editorials in the *Christian Herald*, service as president of the World's Christian Endeavor Union, membership on the executive committee of the Christian Conference on War and Peace, his articles for other religious journals, his book titled *A Preacher Looks at War* (1943), and travel throughout the world as an ambassador for America's war effort, Poling, a Republican, strongly promoted Roosevelt's foreign policy.[119]

Although many Protestants appreciated Roosevelt's efforts to assist the poor and underprivileged,[120] others vehemently attacked Roosevelt. A Presbyterian minister from Indiana claimed that "a very large majority of the clergy" he knew opposed the president, and some of them regarded his re-election as "a national catastrophe." In 1936, he urged those committed to a Christian approach to recovery and reform, international and domestic peace, social welfare and good will, and integrity in public office to give Roosevelt a "thumping rebuke at the polls." Another Protestant insisted that "a godless President and New Deal" did "not deserve the support of...American Christians." To some Protestants, Prohibition was still the paramount issue in 1936. "Whatever you may say in favor of the president," one of them declared, nothing could "atone for his leadership in the Introduction of the Curse of the Liquor traffic."[121]

Catholics gained unprecedented recognition and political power during Roosevelt's presidency, largely because of his political philosophy and skills and the significant similarities between the ideology underlying the New Deal and the church's social and economic teachings. Roosevelt developed a deep respect for Catholics while working with them as a state senator and governor of New York. He campaigned vigorously for Al Smith when he ran for governor of New York in 1920 and 1924 and president in 1928. Roosevelt attacked religious bigotry and advised Smith on how to refute Protestant charges that a Catholic could not effectively serve as president.[122] His defense of Catholicism in the 1928 election, support while governor of the Hayes Bill that outlawed inquiries about the religious beliefs of candidates for teaching positions in New York public schools, and choice of Catholics James Farley and Edward J. Flynn as political advisors, coupled with the belief that Hoover had profited from the anti-Catholicism of the 1928 election, led most Catholics to vote for the New Yorker in 1932. The Catholic journal *Commonweal* praised Roosevelt's campaign speech in Detroit for bringing religion into politics "in a wholly appropriate and beneficial manner" by quoting statements on social justice by Pope Pius XI, the Labor Day message of the Federal Council of Churches, and the Social Justice Commission of the Central Conference of American Rabbis.[123]

As president, Roosevelt recognized the political clout of Catholics, and many church leaders interpreted the New Deal as "an American version of the papal encyclicals." Ignoring the influence of the Protestant Social Gospel, some of them claimed that papal encyclicals had largely prepared the way for Americans' warm response to New Deal reforms.[124]

Roosevelt's patronage policies, cordial relationship with numerous Catholic clergy, social programs, and frequent quotation of papal encyclicals to justify federal assistance to the needy led many Catholics to strongly support his administration. In 1933, Roosevelt received an honorary degree from Catholic University of America and spoke to the National Conference of Catholic Charities. He appointed significantly more Catholics to administrative posts than did his predecessors. Although only four Catholics had served as cabinet members prior to 1932, Roosevelt's first cabinet included two: Postmaster General James Farley and Attorney General T. J. Walsh. Only one of twenty-five judicial appointments during the Republican regimes of the 1920s had been Catholics, but a quarter were during Roosevelt's tenure.[125]

Numerous archbishops, bishops, priests, the Catholic press, and Catholic organizations praised the president's policies during his first term. George Cardinal Mundelein of Chicago was one of Roosevelt's earliest and most enthusiastic supporters. John Ryan, the director of the Department of Social Action of the National Catholic Welfare Conference, advised and vigorously defended the Roosevelt administration through articles and addresses.[126] Speaking for many Catholics, a priest declared in 1934 that "Almighty God raised up FDR—the Apostle of the New Deal."[127] In 1935, 133 prominent Catholic clergy and laymen signed a statement on "Organized Social Justice" that expressed strong support for many of Roosevelt's programs.[128]

Some Protestants protested that Catholics had too much power in Roosevelt's administration and received special benefits. A group called Protestant Action, A Militant Educational Body for the Preservation of American Rights and Protestant Civilization, claimed that a bloc of voters controlled by Irish Catholic political machines in large Northern cities held the balance of power in Congress, the Electoral College, and the national conventions of both major parties. The boast of some Catholic publications that essential New Deal policies were based on the encyclicals of Popes Leo XII and Pius XI irritated members of Protestant Action.[129] Other Protestants complained that parochial schools were receiving federal funds and that Catholic chaplains in the military far exceeded the percentage of Catholics in the nation. Many Protestants criticized Roosevelt's sending of Episcopal industrialist Myron Taylor as his personal envoy to Pope Pius XII in early 1940.[130] When it appeared that Roosevelt might establish permanent diplomatic relations with the Vatican, the Federal Council of Churches objected that this would "confer upon one Church a special preferential status." This act would also violate the separation of church and state, which had been the "great bulwark of religious freedom in America" and had ensured "a policy of equal treatment of all religious bodies by the national government."[131]

In 1939, Attorney General Frank Murphy, Secretary of the Interior Harold Ickes, and several liberal Catholic bishops pressured Roosevelt to lobby the pope to appoint Bishop Bernard James Sheil as the archbishop of Chicago. Because maintaining good relations with the United States was so important to the Vatican and Roosevelt was the most powerful leader in the world, they argued, the pope would probably grant his request. Insisting that a similar attempt by Theodore Roosevelt to convince the pope to elevate John Ireland had failed, the president refused to intervene to try to get a Catholic (who supported his political policies) appointed as archbishop.[132]

Although Catholic leaders rejoiced that more Catholics were serving in federal government positions, applauded many of Roosevelt's policies, and voted for the New Yorker in droves (one priest estimated that 103 of the 106 American bishops voted for Roosevelt in 1936),[133] some of them deplored the president's refusal to denounce the Mexican government's persecution of Catholics. Catholic leaders and organizations strongly urged the president to intervene to stop anticlericalism and ensure religious freedom in Mexico. Although Roosevelt refused to interfere in Mexican affairs, he did reassert the right of all people to enjoy religious freedom.[134] Other Catholics were troubled by his children's divorces, his wife's support of birth control, his deficit spending, and his alleged lack of respect for the Constitution.[135]

Roosevelt's most vociferous Catholic critic was Father Charles Coughlin, who served the parish of Royal Oak, Michigan. Beginning in the fall of 1930, CBS radio carried his sermons over its national network, and by the end of 1932, Coughlin was supplying simplistic explanations of why the Depression had occurred and how prosperity could be restored to an estimated weekly audience of 30–45 million. He supported Roosevelt in the 1932 election, claiming it was "Roosevelt or Ruin," and proclaimed two years later that "the New Deal is Christ's deal." However, he increasingly criticized specific Roosevelt policies. By 1934, he was receiving more mail than the president and was speaking to the largest regular radio audience in the world.[136] Coughlin's attack on Roosevelt intensified the next year, and in June 1936, he announced the creation of a new Union Party, which endorsed North Dakota's William "Liberty Bell" Lemke for president. To Coughlin, the key issues of the campaign were "the decline of democracy, the increase in centralization of government powers, and the possible emergence of the absolute state."[137] His reckless charges that Roosevelt was a dictator, a liar ("Franklin Double-Crossing Roosevelt"), a "scab President," a communist, and even the anti-Christ embarrassed the president's Catholic supporters and even repelled many of the priest's devoted followers.[138] Although Roosevelt refused to condemn Coughlin publicly and the Catholic hierarchy chose not to openly censure or try to silence him, many bishops, priests, and laypeople found his increasingly strident language repulsive.

Numerous Catholic leaders defended Roosevelt against Coughlin's charges during the campaign.[139] Cardinal Mundelein of Chicago, Maurice Sheehy of Catholic University, the Boston millionaire Joseph P. Kennedy, and many others praised Roosevelt's record and religious faith. Kennedy labeled the president "a God-fearing ruler who has given his people an increased measure of social justice."[140] Catholics had many reasons to support Roosevelt and few to vote for Republican Alf Landon or for Lemke, who had no chance to win, and Roosevelt received 70–80 percent of the Catholic vote in the 1936 election.[141] Feeling personally slighted by Roosevelt, however, Kennedy and Farley soon broke with the president. Like a significant number of other Catholics, they resented the increasing influence of intellectuals, liberals, and internationalists in his administration. Even though *The Catholic World* denounced the Democrat as an inconsistent, unpredictable warmonger, a large majority of Catholics voted for Roosevelt in 1940.[142] Although still high, Roosevelt's percentage of the Catholic vote declined in 1944.

Catholics valued many of the president's programs, the recognition and patronage they received, and their cordial relationship with him. More than his predecessors, Roosevelt understood and respected Catholics and worked hard to maintain close personal contacts with influential churchmen. Although Roosevelt realized that Catholics had substantial political power and was sympathetic to many of their concerns, he rarely allowed their advocacy of a particular policy to significantly influence his final decisions.[143]

Roosevelt also appointed many more Jews to government posts than had his predecessors. In fact, Jews played such an important role in his administration that some bigoted detractors denounced the New Deal as the "Jew Deal," and Nazis alleged that the president himself was Jewish. During Roosevelt's tenure, Jews were approximately 3 percent of the American population but about 15 percent of his top appointments. Samuel Rosenman served Roosevelt as a speechwriter until 1943, when he became special counsel to the president.[144] Ben Cohen wrote important New Deal legislation, and Felix Frankfurter was appointed a Supreme Court justice. Bernard Baruch was an important member of Roosevelt's "brain trust." Detractors devised a Star of David that featured leading Jews or Jewish sympathizers at each apex and listed other prominent Jewish members of Roosevelt's administration beside them. They complained that 18,000 of these "alien-minded New Deal" advisors were "dictating American policies."[145] Roosevelt's appointment of Jews and attention to their interests contrasted sharply with the nation's strong anti-Semitism in the 1930s and 1940s and produced their over-whelming political support for him (90 percent of Jews voted for him in 1940 and 1944).[146]

During the Roosevelt years, American Jews were especially concerned about the discrimination against their coreligionists in Europe. Critics argue that Roosevelt should have devised a more liberal immigration policy to help Europe's persecuted Jews. Instead, they protested, he adhered to the letter of American immigration law, which allowed only a small group of refugees to obtain asylum in the United States. Roosevelt refused to support changing American immigration laws that required applicants to bring records of good conduct, various official documents, and enough cash to ensure that they and their dependents would not require relief, which was impossible to do for those fleeing Nazi Germany. Despite an appeal by the American Civil Liberties Union in September 1933, signed by thirty-six prominent Americans, including Reinhold Niebuhr, Felix Frankfurter, John Haynes Holmes, Charles Beard, and Jane Addams, that called for revising immigration laws to "admit religious and political refugees, particularly from Germany," Roosevelt refused to budge. Even after the 1938 Kristallnacht (Night of Broken Glass) pogrom, when the Nazis torched every synagogue in Germany, smashed the windows of Jewish businesses, shipped 25,000 Jews to concentration camps, and fined Jews a billion marks for the damage, Roosevelt did not support increasing the nation's quota for European immigrants. By taking this position and by never officially protesting the actions of Hitler's government, critics contend, Roosevelt contributed to the death of hundreds of thousands of European Jews.[147]

Others counter that Roosevelt did all he could to help Jewish victims of Nazi persecution, given the opposition of an isolationist Congress, a powerful anti-immigration constituency, and strong nativist and anti-Semitic sentiment at home. They maintain that during the 1930s the United States accepted twice as many Jewish refugees as the rest of the world combined and that Roosevelt worked diligently to help them find safety in other lands. After the German invasion of Austria in 1938, Roosevelt called an international conference to deal with the refugee crisis. Delegates from twenty-nine nations established the Inter-Governmental Committee to pressure the German government to permit Jews to migrate with enough resources to start over again in other countries. Plans to resettle Jews from Germany and Austria were thwarted by the demands of Poland and Romania that they have the same right to expel their Jewish residents. (There were fewer than 500,000 Jews in Germany and Austria but 3.5 million in Eastern Europe.) Responding more forcefully to Kristallnacht than other national leaders, Roosevelt recalled the American ambassador, an unprecedented move, and extended the visas of all Germans and Austrians in the United States who felt their lives would be jeopardized by going home. A sluggish bureaucracy, strict immigration laws, and religious and ethnic prejudice all hampered Roosevelt's efforts. Congressional leaders warned the president that some might try to use efforts to increase quotas as an opportunity to reduce them. No one at this time, of course, foresaw the horror of the Holocaust. During the war, Roosevelt strongly condemned the "wholesale systematic murder" of European Jews, promised retribution to the perpetrators, and urged the "free peoples of Europe and Asia temporarily to open their frontiers to all victims of oppression."[148] Based on these considerations, some scholars argue that Roosevelt did more to help European Jews than any other nation's chief executive and insist that it is very ironic that the man Nazi Propaganda Minister Joseph Goebbels vilified as "that Jew Rosenfeld" "should be faulted for being indifferent" to their genocide.[149]

Still other scholars take a middle position. They emphasize that before 1937 American diplomacy with the Third Reich focused primarily on limiting armaments and preventing Germany from defaulting on loans owed to American investors and stress that "few people anywhere . . . understood the depth of Nazi anti-Semitism."[150] They contend that Roosevelt's desires to help Jewish refugees was hindered by several factors: his need for the support of congressmen who favored restrictive immigration policies "to keep alive his weakened New Deal coalition"; his sensitivity to criticisms of the New Deal as the "Jew Deal"; the fact that American Jews were small in number, already were committed to the Democratic Party, and therefore had limited political clout; and American fears that a large influx of refugees would exacerbate the nation's economic problems and (after 1939) enable Nazi agents to infiltrate the country. The United States did accept almost 250,000 refugees in the years from 1933 to 1941, more than any other nation including Palestine, but substantially below the number the quota system allowed. These scholars fault Roosevelt for permitting the State Department to erect administrative barriers after 1940 that reduced the number of refugees to minimal levels, giving in to "a wave of hysteria over national security," and refusing to use the presidency as a pulpit to attack racism or assert the nation's long tradition of providing asylum for victims of religious and political persecution. On the other hand, they praise Roosevelt's efforts to resettle large numbers of refugees in Africa and his establishment of a War Refugee Board in January 1944 that helped save the lives of many Hungarian, Romanian, and Bulgarian Jews. Given the political opposition Roosevelt faced and the determination of the Nazis to destroy the Jews, even much more vigorous efforts would probably not have prevented the Holocaust.[151]

Although some American Jewish leaders urged Roosevelt to provide more help for their beleaguered comrades, many expressed their profound gratitude for what he had done. The American Jewish Congress, for example, implored the president to "once again warn the Nazis that they will be held to strict accountability for their crimes" and to appoint an American commission to examine "all evidence of Nazi barbarities against civilian populations."[152] On the other hand, the director of the American Committee for Hebron Yeshivah wrote Roosevelt: "The Jewish people know well the spiritual quality of our President . . . who has truly been sent by Heaven to rescue the world from utter annihilation."[153] The *Jewish Day* insisted that Roosevelt had "stood like a rock against the tyranny of Hitler." Someday everyone would "recognize Roosevelt's achievements as . . . a savior of Democracy and the Jewish people," as a second Lincoln who "had freed the entire world."[154]

Roosevelt's Faith and Public Policies

Roosevelt concluded his 1936 State of the Union Address by quoting the "words of a wise philosopher at whose feet I sat many, many years ago" (presumably Endicott Peabody): " 'Fear not, view all the tasks of life as sacred, have faith in the triumph of the ideal. . . . [C]arry on the work of righteousness, of charity, of courage, of patience, and of loyalty. . . . This world in its crisis called for volunteers, for men of faith in life. . . . I volunteered to give myself to my Master—the cause of humane and brave living.' "[155] Roosevelt's secretary Stephen Early claimed that his "very life, his labors as President, his approaches to the problems of his office" were all "a practical application of his religious beliefs."[156] Biographer Kenneth Davis argues that Roosevelt's religious faith provides "the most potent of clues to the innermost working of his psyche."[157]

Roosevelt was convinced that God directed the universe and that he was God's agent. This made him very sanguine about human potential and progress.[158] Nothing—not his own physical handicap, the woes of the Great Depression, the horror of World War II, or the perils involved in building a peaceful postwar world—destroyed his optimism. At his first inaugural, he told his countrymen that "the only thing we have to fear is fear itself." His final speech proclaimed: "The only limit to our realization of tomorrow will be our doubts of today. Let us move forward with strong and active faith."[159] These beliefs prompted him "to sermonize and moralize," as he fought the financial interests, an allegedly reactionary Supreme Court, or the putative foes of freedom and democracy. They also persuaded him that his cause was right and would succeed, no matter how difficult the circumstances or strong the opposition.[160] Rex Tugwell explained, "The secret of his unassailable serenity" and positive attitude lay in his "sense of oneness with the ongoing processes of the universe and his feeling of being. . . in tune with the infinite."[161]

Like Hoover, Roosevelt argued that moral and spiritual problems lay beneath the nation's material ones. His New Deal programs sought to give Americans a reasonable level of physical comfort so that they could focus on spiritual values.[162] "The great objective which church and state" were both demanding, he explained, in 1933 was " 'a more abundant life.' "[163] The "object of all our striving," he added the next year, should be to help citizens realize the abundant life Christ said he came to bring.[164] Roosevelt wanted to ensure that "all elements of the community" had an equitable share of the nation's resources. The federal government's social planning, he contended, was "wholly in accord with the social teachings of Christianity." He called for the government and the churches to work hand in hand to devise "a new definition of prosperity" "built on spiritual and social values rather than on special privilege." The government should exhort the churches to teach the ideals of social justice, while religious bodies should prod the government to promote a richer, more fruitful life.[165] He saw the laws he devised, the agencies he created, the policies he pursued, and the political strategies he employed as the means of enabling all Americans to achieve this more abundant life. It included the right of individuals to have a useful, remunerative job, of farmers to have just compensation for their products, of businessmen to be protected from unfair competition, of every family to have a decent home, and of every person to have adequate medical care, a high-quality education, and material comfort in old age.

To accomplish this, his New Deal strove to stimulate economic production, create jobs, ensure equality of opportunity, provide good schools, and redistribute wealth through taxation. Rejecting Thomas Jefferson's maxim that the government is best that governs the least, Roosevelt claimed to follow a utilitarian adage: "Seek only the greater good of the greater number of Americans."[166] Only through cooperation, commitment to the common good, and dedication to serving others could the abundant life be achieved. "No man lives to himself," Roosevelt trumpeted, "and no man dies to himself; but living or dying, we are the Lord's and each other's."[167] To Roosevelt, this concept of social responsibility expressed biblical teachings more fully than any other arrangement. Efforts to achieve social justice through governmental action were vastly superior to the laissez-faire approach that allowed the "fittest" to triumph. "The thing we are seeking," he proclaimed, "is justice" guided by the concept of "Do unto your neighbor as you would be done by."[168]

Ronald Isetti challenges the contention of Richard Hofstadter, William Leuchtenburg, and other historians that the temper of the New Deal was secular and had little in common with the more religiously oriented progressive movement of the early twentieth century. Isetti argues convincingly that for all its secular spirit, the New Deal "was firmly anchored in the moral-religious tradition of earlier reform movements in American history." It was "highly moralistic, prophetic, and even biblical in its inspiration and tone." He maintains that Roosevelt strove to defend, maintain, and advance a "regulatory Progressive state based in political liberalism and Christian humanitarianism, which for Roosevelt were pretty much the same."[169] Although social Christianity was not as strong in the 1930s as it had been between 1900 and 1925, many pastors and seminary professors continued to attack the injustices in American social and economic life and to call for increased efforts to help the poor and oppressed. Roosevelt agreed philosophically and practically with many of their prophetic pleas, and much of his approach was consistent with their aims. In many ways, these politically liberal, Social Gospel proclamations and policies resonated with Roosevelt's personal preferences and convictions.

While championing social justice, Roosevelt did not make combating widespread segregation or discrimination against blacks a priority of the New Deal. The failure of his administration to enact any Civil Rights legislation, especially a federal antilynching bill, irritated blacks. Roosevelt denounced lynching as a "vile form of collective murder" and as "deliberate and definite disobedience" to the commandment "Thou shalt not kill," and he rebuked those who condoned it.[170] He was unwilling, however, to make a federal antilynching measure a priority because of his fear that Southern Congressional committee chairmen would retaliate by refusing to support his economic proposals. On the other hand, during Roosevelt's tenure in office, the "federal government aided blacks to an unprecedented extent, both substantively and symbolically."[171] Black federal employees tripled in the 1930s, and the administration began to desegregate federal restrooms, secretarial pools, and cafeterias. Blacks received substantial relief monies, and several New Deal agencies treated blacks and whites equally.[172] Secretary of the Interior Harold Ickes hired many African Americans and gave black families much of the new housing built in urban areas. Meanwhile, Eleanor Roosevelt forcefully promoted black Civil Rights. Seven of the eight justices Roosevelt appointed to the Supreme Court became strong advocates of Civil Rights and later contributed to major decisions that ended discriminatory practices. Considering the economic woes of the 1930s, the political obstacles he confronted, and that when Roosevelt took office, the vast majority of whites had no desire to end racial segregation or discrimination, considerable Civil Rights progress was made during his presidency. By the time Roosevelt died, black expectations had risen, their sense of powerlessness had diminished, articulate African American leaders were proclaiming a gospel of racial equality, white hostility had decreased, and the groundwork had been laid for the Civil Rights movement of the 1950s and 1960s.[173] Always the consummate politician, Roosevelt's policies in this area seemed to be inspired more by pragmatic considerations than by religious or moral principles.

Roosevelt's religious convictions also helped shape his approach toward international relations. He continually stressed the importance of spiritual values and the need to protect Judeo-Christian religion from those who sought to obliterate it, and he used religious rhetoric to inspire the Allies to fight the Axis powers and to assure them of ultimate victory. Most religious groups' support of or opposition to Roosevelt before December 1941 was closely correlated with their assessment of his ability to keep the United States out of World War II. Although most church leaders backed Roosevelt after the United States entered the war, before Pearl Harbor, many of them denounced Roosevelt's diplomatic strategy, economic aid to the Allies, and military buildup as belligerent and challenged his contention that Fascists aimed to destroy religion.[174] The president argued that he wanted to make the United States prosperous, free, and strong so that it would be "a light of the world and a comfort to all people." The Bible, moral law, and the "promise of a great era of peace," he insisted, all taught that the "forces of evil shall not prevail" against such a nation. Roosevelt challenged people to "work and pray for the establishment of an international order in which the spirit of Christ" ruled.[175]

Prior to the U.S. entrance into World War II, Roosevelt strove to build a strong military defense, but he also called for "spiritual and ethical preparedness." He urged religious groups to work together to raise "the moral tone of the nation," strengthen national unity, and promote economic justice.[176] Shortly after the Germans invaded Poland, Roosevelt pledged that the United States would remain neutral and insisted that "every effort" of the government would be directed toward keeping his country out of the war. He added that most Americans believed in "the spirit of the New Testament—a great teaching which opposes itself to the use of . . . armed force, of marching armies, and falling bombs."[177]

Nevertheless, before the United States entered World War II, the leaders of the Federal Council of Churches and many prominent clergymen and editors criticized Roosevelt's military and diplomatic policies, especially in the Far East.[178] In 1935, 200 leading churchmen signed a letter to Roosevelt to protest that projected naval maneuvers in the Pacific would "seriously complicate the task of preserving peace" in the region.[179] The next year, more than 450 college presidents, professors, clergy, and businessmen signed an "Appeal to the President and Congress of the United States" that expressed their deep dismay at the nation's tremendous increase in military spending.[180] In 1938, the Federal Council of Churches labeled Roosevelt's effort to "build a navy of overwhelming proportions" "a council of despair." The United States was called to lead the world along the road of "sacrificial peace," not of threat, coercion, and bluster.[181]

The *Christian Century* persistently objected to Roosevelt's diplomatic strategy and level of military spending. The proposed Ludlow Amendment mandating that a national referendum be required before the United States could declare war, its editors insisted in 1937, indicated the "growing lack of confidence in President Roosevelt as a protector of the nation's peace." This lack of confidence sprang largely from his decision to "sabotage the neutrality law," which prevented the United States from participating in foreign wars. If Roosevelt believed that Americans' sympathy for the Chinese or indignation toward the Japanese or the dictatorial states of Europe could be "used to commit them to fighting another overseas war," he was very mistaken.[182] The next year, the editors denounced Roosevelt's "new and disquieting belligerence" sparked by his fear of "a Japanese-controlled eastern Asia," which prompted him "to take some gigantic risks."[183] "Liberals and labor," they insisted, had "no stomach for adventures overseas while the social problems of America remain so far from solution."[184] The editors also protested that Roosevelt had "embarked on a gigantic armament program, designed to shift the national economy to a military basis" and had acquired new bases in the Atlantic and Pacific. By helping defend Great Britain, they argued, the United States was supporting its imperialism in Africa, the Middle East, and Asia and could easily be drawn into the European war.[185]

In his State of the Union Address in January 1939, Roosevelt warned Americans that the "dictator nations" of Europe threatened their safety and sought to destroy religion, which was the source of both democracy and international good will. Religion provided people with a sense of dignity and taught them to respect their neighbors. The ideals of the Prince of Peace demanded that societies be based on religion, democracy, and good will toward other nations. Wherever religion and democracy had vanished, "good faith and reason in international affairs" had given way "to strident ambition and brute force." Roosevelt urged Americans to "prepare to defend not only their homes but the tenets of their faith and humanity on which their churches, their governments and their very civilization are founded."[186] The *Christian Century* lambasted Roosevelt's speech as "the most misleading and dangerous appeal made to the American people by a chief executive in the history of the republic." It was misleading because the prospect of an attack on the United States by the world's totalitarian nations was "fantastic." It was "diabolically dangerous" because it attempted to "rouse religious passion." The president had issued an "invitation to a holy war" in order to destroy "the calm, sober judgment of the American people" and to reduce opposition to his gigantic armament program. The editors urged the nation's churches to repudiate this insult to their ideals and intelligence and disavow the idea that armed force was necessary to defend religion.[187] Arguing that the American frontier was "on the Potomac, not on the Rhine," the editors in February 1939 sharply criticized Roosevelt's apparent strategy of putting the nation's enormous resources on the Allied side to prevent the impending European war and his assumption that the current crisis pitted "good against evil," "the true faith (democracy) against the unbeliever (dictatorships)."[188] They protested further that Roosevelt's partisanship robbed him of moral authority and kept him from being an impartial intermediary who could resolve the hostilities between European nations.[189]

Shortly after war erupted in Europe, the Federal Council of Churches praised Roosevelt's resolve to keep the United States out of the conflict and endorsed his appeal to Americans to refrain from profiting financially from the crisis.[190] Other Protestants, however, criticized his policies. In June 1940, the *Christian Century* called the president "an indignant, resentful, roused man in a fighting mood, determined to take his country just as close to the verge of fighting" as he could, and deplored his pledge to use the nation's material resources to support the Allies.[191] In October, as the 1940 election approached, its editors censured Roosevelt for abandoning "all pretense of neutrality," emasculating laws designed to keep the United States out of war, making America the arsenal of democracy, and conscripting men for the army.[192] In January 1941, they complained that the United States had pledged to loan Great Britain $3 billion in war goods, even though Britain was bankrupt and had not explicitly stated its war aims, and thus it was not clear whether arbitration, compromise, or accommodation was possible.[193] Congress' passage of the lend-lease bill, they objected in March, gave Roosevelt "powers unparalleled in American history" and greater than those of "any other leader of a modern democratic state." They distrusted Roosevelt's pledges to keep America out of the war.[194] In June, the journal noted that the *Saturday Evening Post* had changed from opposing to supporting American entrance into the war because Roosevelt's current policy was "indistinguishable from war." Because of the commitments the United States had made, the only course of action left, the *Post* insisted, was "to support the government as it plunges into an unjustified, unnecessary war."[195] Later that month, the *Christian Century* rejoiced that the activities of the Churchmen's Campaign for Peace through Mediation, the Committee for America First, and numerous other organizations had slowed down the president's drive for war and hoped that he had abandoned "the idea of belligerent participation."[196]

In October 1941, Roosevelt accused Hitler's government of plotting to abolish all religion. The United States had obtained a secret Nazi document that contained a detailed plan to seize all church property, outlaw all religious symbols, and place all clergy in the Western hemisphere in German concentration camps (where many were already being tortured because they had "placed God above Hitler"). The Reich intended to replace churches with an International Nazi Church, the Bible with *Mein Kampf,* and the cross of Christ with the swastika and the sword. If this effort were successful, Roosevelt warned, a "God of Blood and Iron" would "take the place of the God of Love and Mercy."[197] The *Christian Century* denounced this "tale of a secret map and a secret plan for the extermination of religion" as "childish" and "moronic" propaganda. "What evidence is there," the editors asked, "that it represents any acknowledged or official German policy?" The main outlines of the plan had been circulating since May 1938, and the present version of the plan was without a doubt "entirely unofficial and irresponsible." Roosevelt sought to use this alleged threat to religion as means of overcoming the reluctance of the religious groups to support American entrance into the war.[198] In retrospect, although the map was a British forgery, Roosevelt recognized the evil intentions of the Axis powers much more fully than these Christian critics.[199]

After the United States entered the war, religious groups provided varying amounts of assistance. Rarely did they conclude that Roosevelt's support of the Allies or quest to prepare the United States to participate in the war had been wise. Nevertheless, most of them backed the war effort. Shortly after the Japanese bombed Pearl Harbor, the Catholic bishops of the United States promised to do their part to transform the nation's "impressive material and spiritual resources" into weapons that could defeat the forces of "wanton aggression," provide international security, and guarantee individual rights.[200] The next year, they issued "The Bishops' Statement on Victory and Peace." "From the moment our Country declared war," they asserted, "we have called upon our people to make the sacrifices which, in Catholic doctrine, the virtues of patriotism, justice, and charity impose." Only this would prevent the establishment of a "slave world" that "would deprive man of his divinely conferred dignity, reject human freedom and permit no religious liberty." They urged Allied leaders to study the peace proposals of Pius XII, who insisted that only the love of God and human beings provides a secure basis for international justice.[201] About two hundred Protestant clergy signed a statement in July 1942 arguing that Christians must assume their share of the "effort, sacrifice and suffering" necessary to prevent the "enslavement of nations," "the destruction of civil liberties," "the regimentation of conscience," and "the suppression of the free Christian witness" that an Axis victory would bring.[202]

Throughout World War II, Roosevelt repeatedly resorted to religious rhetoric to inspire his fellow citizens and assure them of eventual triumph. Responding to the Japanese bombing of Pearl Harbor, Roosevelt proclaimed that the American people "will gain the inevitable triumph—so help us God."[203] He averred, "In victory we shall not seek vengeance but the establishment of an international order in which the spirit of Christ shall rule the hearts of men and nations."[204] In his State of the Union Address in 1942, Roosevelt claimed that German, Italian, and Japanese warmongers sought to destroy the "material and spiritual centers of civilization. . . . The world is too small to provide adequate 'living room' for both Hitler and God."[205] The Axis powers, Roosevelt declared in 1943, were "implacable foes of every principle by which Christian nations live." "Strangers alike to the love of God and of man," they knew "no Christian impulse—neither mercy, justice, nor compassion."[206] "Without spiritual armor," he avowed in 1943, "we cannot hope to win this war."[207] He proclaimed the next year that "without supreme devotion to our religious beliefs, we could not have borne these burdens. . . . Under God, there can be no other outcome save victory."[208] As great as America's resources and resolve were, the president argued, the nation could not win the war without God's assistance. "A real revival of religion, a quickening of the spiritual life of the nation[,] would strengthen our morale for the war effort and would be our sure guide to a just and lasting peace."[209]

A Final Assessment

Franklin Roosevelt was buried on the eightieth anniversary of Lincoln's death, and many have compared these two titans who guided America during some of its most turbulent years. Historians have ranked both among the greatest presidents, and both have been venerated and derided. Supporters lauded Roosevelt as the savior of Western civilization, while critics lampooned him as its "most persistent, malevolent enemy," who was "the embodiment of Satan."[210] Admirers portrayed Roosevelt as superhuman, an exceptional humanitarian who prevented social revolution, modernized the government, and protected the American way of life. Many extolled Roosevelt's "dauntless spirit" and his triumph over his physical disability.[211] Roosevelt's opponents denounced him as "an impulsive, uninformed opportunist, lacking policy or stability, wasteful, reckless, unreliable in act and contract."[212] Both liberals and conservatives sometimes charged that Roosevelt, if not a dictator, had arrogated too much power.[213]

Many Americans felt the same kind of trust for the president they felt for "a warm and understanding father who comforted them in their grief or safeguarded them from harm."[214] Using "his reassuring radio voice and his religious rhetoric," Roosevelt convinced millions of Americans to hope and persevere during the Great Depression and World War II.[215] His hopefulness, cheerfulness, confidence, idealism, and use of biblical language inspired the nation. The thousands of letters Roosevelt received each week from ordinary Americans indicates that his frequent use of biblical stories, themes, and images resonated with many.[216]

Many historians have overlooked or downplayed the "moral and religious flavor and content" of the New Deal and have missed its continuity with the more liberal phase of social Christianity, "especially as it expressed itself in the New Nationalism of Theodore Roosevelt, but . . . with a more sustained defense of and rationale for the welfare state, often made in terms of biblical archetypes and Judeo-Christian morality."[217] Leuchtenburg labels Roosevelt "a moralist who wanted to achieve certain humane reforms."[218] He sought to make the industrial system more caring, ensure a livable wage, protect workers from exploitation, and provide assistance to the handicapped, aged, and defenseless. His administration strove to develop a society that was more just, prosperous, and tolerant of differences and that divided resources more fairly. "His genuine concern for the welfare of the common man," *Christian Century* declared in 1941, was impressive.[219] During his tenure, the United States adopted a social security system and a minimum wage, guaranteed collective bargaining for union members, prohibited child labor, prevented farmers from losing their property through foreclosures, modernized and expanded public welfare, and regulated public utility companies that previously had exploited both consumers and stockholders. The New Deal created a broker state that tried to balance the interests of various groups—businessmen, farmers, industrial workers, and consumers—in American society. Although this arrangement was better than when business was the nation's only major interest group, the Roosevelt administration tended to grant privileges to constituencies in proportion to their political strength. The New Yorker maintained that the public interest was superior to that of any pressure group, but his policies often ignored the common good and accorded few benefits to groups that were unable to organize effectively—women, blacks, the poor, Native Americans, and other ethnic groups.[220]

The three principal criticisms of Roosevelt's character are his alleged lack of principle, his tendency to distort the truth, and his marital infidelity. Many argue that pragmatism triumphed over principle in his administration and that results were more important than ideology or coherent policies. His lack of concern about consistency implied he cared little about truthfulness and was sly, slippery, and excessively clever, "an opportunistic confidence man."[221] H. L. Mencken charged that the president "had exhibited precisely the same sense" of morality and honor as "a snake-oil vender at a village carnival." Roosevelt's success rested upon his chameleon adaptability. If he became convinced that supporting cannibalism would win him votes, "he would begin fattening a missionary in the White House backyard."[222] The test of whether a particular function should be performed by the private or public sector, the Democrat declared, was simply "which can do it better."[223] Throughout his life, Roosevelt focused much more on the art of politics than on the philosophical underpinnings for political action. Frances Perkins argued that "his emotions, his intuitive understanding, his imagination, his moral and traditional bias, his sense of right and wrong" all helped shape Roosevelt's thinking.[224] Unlike Hoover, who was typically very certain about both ends and means, the Democrat was "usually quite clear about the ends he wished to achieve, but vague about the means."[225]

Roosevelt sometimes took credit for things he did not do, altered the past to suit the present, invented or embellished stories, and even lied. He told newspapermen made-up stories about ordinary citizens who came to see him about their everyday problems and copied in his own handwriting Raymond Moley's typed draft of his first inaugural address with the "deliberate *intent* to deceive posterity."[226] "The shiftiness . . . of his political stratagems," the *Christian Century* alleged, was "evidence of a tragic lack of integrity at the core of his nature."[227] Roosevelt's "predeliction [*sic*] for craft and dissimulation," declared Oswald Garrison Villard in 1944, was "so well established" that he no longer commanded the moral confidence of thoughtful Americans.[228] Revisionist historians have even charged that Roosevelt maneuvered the Japanese into attacking Pearl Harbor as a way of getting the United States into World War II to stop Hitler.[229]

From 1913 to 1918, Roosevelt carried on an extramarital affair with Lucy Mercer, who served as his wife's social secretary. Their affair ended only after Eleanor learned about it and threatened to leave Franklin if he did not terminate the relationship. Recognizing that a divorce would severely damage his political aspirations, Roosevelt agreed, but after becoming president, he began seeing Mercer again. Family members and aides helped hide their relationship from Eleanor. Roosevelt apparently even disclosed classified diplomatic and military information to Mercer. Neither the press nor the public knew about their clandestine relationship, and therefore it had no effect on Roosevelt's reputation during his lifetime. Nevertheless, his unfaithfulness to his wife (who did so much to advance his political career) was a blatant violation of the Christian moral code he claimed governed his life.[230]

Roosevelt exhibited a tendency to doctor the historical record and a deep concern about his reputation. Thus, can we ever know what Roosevelt truly believed? How can we know the essential character and commitments of this "multifaceted, mercurial, enigmatic man"? How can we "penetrate his thick and evidently swiftly changing disguises to reach any understanding of his essential being—of his basic attitudes and motives"?[231] There are ample grounds for suspecting that Roosevelt was always playing a role. Every letter, conversation, and act seemed to reflect his concern about how posterity would perceive him, and thus there were few (or no) unguarded, backstage moments that allow us to see the real man and know his heart. Like other presidents, he clearly employed religious rhetoric to suit his purposes and promote his aims, whether it was winning elections, passing reform legislation, or defeating the Nazis. He skillfully raised the use of civil religion to new heights. Nevertheless, some of the evidence does not fit well with this appraisal. Why did his concern about public opinion not lead him to attend church regularly, especially since he was frequently criticized for not doing so? Why did he do almost nothing as president to publicize his work as the senior warden of the St. James Episcopal Church?

In the final analysis, Roosevelt's faith seems to have been simple but sincere. It was heartfelt, but it did not consistently guide his actions. While he was not very concerned about the intellectual or devotional aspects of Christianity, he appeared to be genuinely moved by biblical stories, episodes in church history, moral ideals, and occasionally by worship experiences, ranging from singing Methodist hymns to participating in the Episcopal liturgy. Although he used biblical teachings and church history to motivate Americans to pursue courses of actions he deemed best, he seemed to be personally inspired as well. Kenneth Davis concludes that Roosevelt's "plain, simple, matter-of-fact Christianity" is the best clue for understanding how his mind worked.[232] He experienced a brief crisis of faith after contracting polio, but thereafter he seemed to maintain a steady belief in God's power, goodness, and love. He frequently spoke about God's providence, saw himself as carrying out God's purposes, and insisted that America would be successful only if its people sought God's guidance and strove to do his will. Despite his polio and other physical afflictions, he constantly maintained a cheerful demeanor. In the midst of a terrible economic depression and the world's most devastating, horrific war, he radiated confidence and courage. Although his mendacity and marital infidelity violated Judeo-Christian teaching, many of his words and deeds expressed its compassion, social justice, and kindness. His personal traits, inspiring rhetoric, use of religious themes, and concern for the destitute and dispirited enabled him to develop positive relationships with many of the nation's religious communities. Perhaps his most fitting epitaph is that offered by the Episcopal bishop of Washington at Roosevelt's funeral: He had "sympathy with the hunger and fears of common men" and "unyielding faith in the possibility of a more just and ordered world."[233]

CHAPTER SEVEN

Dwight David Eisenhower,
Dynamic Conservatism,
and the Religious Revival of the 1950s

I am the most intensely religious man I know.
　　New York Times, May 4, 1948

Religion nurtures men of faith, men of hope, men of love; such men are
needed in the building of a new world reflecting the glory of God.
　　Message to the Opening Session of the Sixteenth Annual Convention,
　　Chaplains' Association of Army and Navy, Oct. 23, 1946

Faith is the mightiest force that man has at his command. It impels
human beings to greatness in thought and word and deed.
　　Address at the Second Assembly of the World Council of Churches,
　　Aug. 19, 1954

Application of Christianity to everyday affairs is the only practical hope
of the world.
　　Life Magazine, Dec. 26, 1955

DWIGHT D. EISENHOWER'S PERSONAL behavior, the mood of the 1950s, and
shrewd publicity combined to make his administration seem more religious
than those of most other presidents.[1] Although the general did not join a
church until the second Sunday after his inauguration, he is considered one of
the most religious presidents in American history. A number of factors contribute to this assessment. Eisenhower attended church regularly, proclaimed

national days of prayer, invited Billy Graham and other influential clergymen to the White House, and helped create an organization called the Foundation for Religious Action. He structured his staff very effectively to handle religious matters and deal with religious organizations. Eisenhower maintained very cordial relations with most of the nation's religious communities. The president met frequently with religious delegations, sent hundreds of messages to religious gatherings and groups, and spoke to numerous religious assemblies. His speeches contained more religious rhetoric than almost any other president, and he repeatedly called for a spiritual revival and a moral crusade to remedy the nation's ills. While he was president, the highly publicized national prayer breakfasts began, the words "under God" were added to the Pledge of Allegiance, and Congress made the phrase "In God We Trust" the national motto. Articles in religious and secular magazines extolled his faith, and his closest friends and admirers—Billy Graham, his pastor Edward Elson, Senator Frank Carlson of Kansas, and many others—praised his commitment to God, prayer, and Christian morality.[2] Rather than creating controversy about breaches of church-state separation, the Eisenhower administration's significant interest in religion seemed to increase the public's esteem and admiration for the man from Abilene.[3] Inspired in part by his faith, Eisenhower promoted a "dynamic conservatism" that prodded voluntary organizations to combat economic and social problems and used the power of the federal government to remedy ills when their resources were insufficient.

The Faith of Dwight Eisenhower

The future president's grandfather Jacob Eisenhower led several Mennonite congregations from eastern Pennsylvania to Kansas in the 1878. There he became a minister of the River Brethren (later called the Brethren in Christ).[4] Like Mennonites and other Anabaptist groups around 1900, the River Brethren, by their conduct and dress, strove to be separate from the world. They practiced foot washing, exchanged "holy kisses," tithed, and did not use tobacco or join secret societies. Like other Anabaptists, they were pacifists. Dwight's father, David Eisenhower, and mother, Ida Stover, married in 1885 and settled near Abilene. Named for his father and the great American evangelist Dwight L. Moody, David Dwight Eisenhower (his first and middle names were later reversed) was the third of six sons. His mother, who had grown up as a Lutheran, displayed a deep interest in religion early in life and easily adjusted to the Bible-centered River Brethren community to which her husband introduced her. Sometime between 1895 and 1900, Ida became a Jehovah's Witness (known as Bible Students until 1931), and her husband eventually did too.

Religion was very important in Eisenhower's family while he grew up. Twice each day, family members gathered to pray and read the Bible. The Scriptures served as an authoritative guide for all aspects of his parents' lives. The Bible, the general later recalled, was a "live and lusty influence in their lives. . . . They tried their best to instill the Bible, its doctrines, its beliefs, [and] its convictions, in their sons."[5] Their six sons were required to attend family devotions and Sunday school, do their chores, get good grades, and, like their parents, refrain from smoking, drinking, swearing, card playing, and gambling.[6] Dwight did not fully embrace his parents' practices and pietism and loved to play poker.

Dwight's parents were committed pacifists, but when he was offered a nomination to the U.S. Military Academy, they did not try to dissuade him from accepting it.[7] As a cadet, Eisenhower did not participate regularly in religious activities—church, Sunday school, Bible studies, or the YMCA—and his conduct record was below average.

Despite claiming to be the "most intensely religious man" he knew, prior to his election as president, Eisenhower's involvement in organized religion as an adult was limited. During his long military career, Eisenhower moved frequently from place to place and occasionally attended chapel services on bases, but his interest in religion seemed to be minimal. Nevertheless, he insisted that soldiers and clergymen had an identical purpose—to advance "the glory of God."[8] As the supreme Allied commander in Europe during World War II, Eisenhower had to make extraordinarily difficult strategic decisions and order hundreds of thousands of soldiers to risk and often sacrifice their lives, which prompted him to reexamine his purpose in life and deepen his relationship with God.

Nevertheless, when the general sought the Republican presidential nomination in 1952, his staff worried that his lack of church affiliation would lose him votes among the religiously devout and urged him to join a church. Despite frequent criticism that he was "a man without a church and without a faith," Eisenhower initially refused to discuss this issue with his campaign team and argued that religion was "an absolutely private matter." While living in Paris, he explained to journalist Clare Boothe Luce that he had grown up in a religious tradition in which one did not have "to join a church in order to be a believing Christian." Joining a church to be elected president "would be an unbearable piece of hypocrisy." If he did, he would have "nothing but contempt" for himself. Although his staff had argued that Eisenhower needed to join the church for political reasons, Luce insisted he needed to join and attend regularly to provide a good example for children. "I can see," she said, "little boys and girls being pried out of bed" on Sunday mornings by their parents and complaining, " 'Why should I have to go to church? The President of the United States . . . refuses to go to church.' " Instead of regarding going to church a "hypocritical gesture," Luce continued, he should consider it "a constructive and necessary" example for both his contemporaries and the next generation. Apparently convinced by her argument, Eisenhower began attending a Presbyterian church in Paris, and the press stopped its criticism.[9] During the summer of 1952, Eisenhower wrote to a friend that although he and his brothers had not joined churches, they were "all very earnestly and seriously religious." Given their upbringing, they "could not help being so."[10]

In February 1953, on the second Sunday after his inauguration, the president was baptized in a private ceremony, and he and his wife joined the National Presbyterian Church in Washington, D.C, a congregation where Andrew Jackson, James Polk, Franklin Pierce, James Buchanan, Grover Cleveland, and Benjamin Harrison had all worshiped. Eisenhower had several reasons for joining this church. Its pastor, Edward Elson, had served as a chaplain under his command in Europe, and when war ended, the general had sent him to discuss the Allied plan for reconstituting the church with German clergy. Elson worked hard to persuade the Republican and his wife, Mamie, to join his congregation, and Billy Graham encouraged them to do so.[11] Mamie had grown up as a Presbyterian, the Eisenhowers had been married in a Presbyterian church, and they had sometimes attended Mamie's home church in Denver. In addition, numerous high-ranking federal officials attended this congregation, including Secretary of State John Foster Dulles, FBI director J. Edgar Hoover, eleven senators, several representatives, three Supreme Court Justices, and numerous military and business leaders and federal judges.[12] Milton Eisenhower explained his brother's decision to join a church this way: The president must provide "spiritual stimulation" "to protect American democracy and freedom in the world." Thus it was "good and right" for their president, like many other Americans, "to go to church regularly."[13] Thousands of congregations and individual clergy and laypeople congratulated and commended the president for joining a church.[14]

After becoming a member, Eisenhower attended faithfully, gave money regularly, occasionally sent copies of Elson's sermons to staff members, and helped lead a campaign to fund the congregation's new $20 million building.[15] In addition to Elson, some of America's most renowned ministers—including Billy Graham, Eugene Carson Blake, John Mackay, Elton Trueblood, Norman Vincent Peale, and Louis Evans—preached at the National Presbyterian Church during his tenure in office. Except when he was ill or conducting important governmental business, the president almost always attended Sunday services.[16] When he did not go to the National Presbyterian Church, he attended Methodist, Episcopal, and Catholic churches in the Washington area, a Presbyterian church near his farm in Gettysburg, Pennsylvania, or services on military bases or in various congregations in towns across the nation. Although he occasionally complained about going to church when he was tired, he sometimes returned from a trip on Sunday mornings and jumped out of his helicopter to rush to National Presbyterian Church. In 1959, Eisenhower invited his houseguest at Camp David, Nikita Khrushchev, the premier of the Soviet Union, to go to church with him. Khrushchev declined his invitation, but Eisenhower traveled twenty-five miles to attend services, much to the delight of the religious press.[17] In addition to going to church himself, the president also verbally encouraged Americans to attend church.[18]

Eisenhower abhorred people trying to capitalize on his religious practices. He complained bitterly to his brother Milton that Elson tried to "extract the maximum publicity from the fact" that he and his wife had joined his church. Elson had promised that there would be a "minimum of publicity," but he told the congregation they had joined without previously informing the Eisenhowers and sent out a press release without asking the president's press secretary.[19] His liaison to religious groups, Frederic Fox, explained that Eisenhower did not "like to parade his faith."[20] He preferred to attend worship services without any fanfare but recognized that this was not possible.[21] In fact, many Americans wrote the president to praise him for worshiping regularly.[22]

Despite this problem, Eisenhower and Elson enjoyed a warm, friendly relationship. They frequently discussed books, sermons, upcoming church events, places where Eisenhower could attend church when traveling at home or abroad, political strategy, administrative policies, and world events.[23] Elson suggested campaign tactics, recommended candidates for administrative positions, and reported his assessment of conditions in the Middle East after traveling throughout the region.[24] Elson occasionally made pastoral calls on the president, and he and his wife were frequent guests at White House dinners.[25] In November 1955, Elson held a special service to bless Eisenhower's farm near Gettysburg.[26] Elson claimed that he never preached particular sermons because the president was attending, but in October 1957, with Eisenhower and Queen Elizabeth II of England in attendance, his sermon was entitled "The Way of the Peacemaker," and the title of at least one of his sermons, "The Tools of Peace," was taken from a phrase Eisenhower had used in a speech.[27] In this latter sermon, Elson praised the president for his spiritual analysis "of false ideologies," appointing Harold Stassen as "virtually a Secretary for Peace," and going to church to pray for peace after arriving in Geneva for an international summit.[28]

Observers reported that Eisenhower actively participated in worship. They claimed that the president sang hymns heartily, joined in unison prayers, and followed sermons closely.[29] He preferred lively, enthusiastic services over dignified, formal ones. Eisenhower admired the same qualities in a preacher as in a soldier or a cabinet member: forthrightness, enthusiasm, integrity, optimism, and devotion. He preferred sermons that applied the message of the Bible to everyday life.[30]

Whereas Franklin Roosevelt was sometimes criticized for his infrequent church attendance, Eisenhower was widely applauded for worshiping faithfully.

Democratic Senator Matthew Neely of West Virginia provoked extensive controversy in 1955 when he complained about Eisenhower being constantly photographed leaving church services and accused him of being a "publican" who prayed to be seen by people. Eisenhower's attempt "to parade his religious associations or connections for political purposes" violated "the teachings of the Scripture." A deluge of letters to the White House and numerous public statements from ministers, Republican congressmen, and ordinary citizens condemned the senator and defended Eisenhower. Irate citizens lambasted Neely as a "stinking swine" and "white trash from the hills" and denounced his assault on Eisenhower as "out of bounds," "a new political low," and a "vicious smear."[31] The president of the National Council of Churches insisted that all people of faith should rejoice when the nation's chief executive provided a positive example by attending church. Robert S. Lutz, pastor of the Corona Presbyterian Church in Denver, which the Eisenhowers attended during summer vacations, maintained that the president had never publicized his worship there. Republican Senator Joseph McCarthy of Wisconsin expressed amazement that a public servant could be condemned "for worshipping God as his conscience directs." Another senator demanded that Neely publicly apologize to the president and "all God-fearing Americans." Neely responded that he had not criticized Eisenhower for going to church but, rather, had deplored the fact that "every time he went to church we had a half-page picture in the Monday papers."[32] The Catholic journal *Commonweal* denounced Neely's attack as unreasonable and unfair. It was unreasonable because everything the president did was newsworthy. It was unfair because it implied that Eisenhower went to church not because of devout belief but to gain "political favor and popularity."[33] Hundreds of ordinary citizens wrote to the president to express their confidence that his faith was genuine and commend his church attendance.[34] Billy Graham wrote to Eisenhower that his faithful participation in spiritual exercises gave "hope and encouragement to millions."[35]

Eisenhower's religiosity was evident in other ways as well. Like Roosevelt, he held a worship service the morning of his inauguration. About 180 members of the incoming administration and their families gathered for prayer and Bible reading at the National Presbyterian Church.[36] Eisenhower and his administrative team took Communion before the opening of each new session of Congress. He chose a Mormon apostle, Ezra Taft Benson, as his secretary of agriculture; active Methodists Arthur Fleming and Robert B. Anderson as his secretary of health, education, and welfare and secretary of the treasury, respectively; Douglas McKay, who belonged to the National Presbyterian Church, as his first secretary of the interior and Episcopalian Fred Seaton as his second; and one of the nation's leading Protestant laymen, John Foster Dulles, as his secretary of state.[37] Dulles consistently sought to apply moral law to international relations and bring "the force of Christianity" to bear on global problems.

In the *Christian Science Monitor*, William Stringer described Eisenhower's faith as simple but vigorous, based more on good works than theology.[38] Biographer Stephen Ambrose maintains that Eisenhower knew and cared nothing about theology, "never discussed his idea of God with anyone," and was not concerned about the specific form or religious content of the spiritual revival he championed.[39] Although his family background and life experiences helped shape Eisenhower's faith more than intellectual arguments or philosophical reasoning did, the design of the universe, the reality of the conscience, the respect people felt for moral law, and the human craving for affection all persuaded him that God existed.[40] One of his favorite sayings was "It takes no brains to be an atheist."

A number of factors provide insights into Eisenhower's religious convictions: his commitment to prayer, view of the Bible, attitude toward death, belief in God's providential direction of history, conviction that the United States rested on a firm religious foundation, argument that religion and democracy were closely related, persistent promotion of religious revival, and depreciation of theological differences. Considerable evidence indicates that Eisenhower believed deeply in the power of prayer. His brother Milton claimed that since childhood he had prayed as naturally as he ate food.[41] When Eisenhower was sixteen, he nearly lost his left leg because of blood poisoning. Fearing he might die if they did not, physicians recommended amputating his leg. Three weeks later, after extensive prayer by Eisenhower's family, his leg miraculously healed, which reinforced the future president's belief in the efficacy of prayer.[42] He told Clare Boothe Luce in 1952: "Do you think I could have fought my way through this war, ordered thousands of fellows to their deaths, if I couldn't have got down on my knees and talked to God and begged him to support me and make me feel that what I was doing was right for myself and the world. . . . I couldn't live a day of my life without God."[43] Indeed, stories about the general praying during World War II took on a legendary quality. On July 9, 1943, as commander of the Allied Expeditionary Forces, he knelt in prayer to ask for God's help on a mountaintop overlooking Malta as the Allies began their all-out assault on Sicily. As the weather rapidly deteriorated, the general had to decide whether to go ahead with the carefully planned invasion. After praying fervently, he ordered the attack to go forward, and it succeeded beyond all expectations.[44] In June 1944, Eisenhower had to make an even more momentous decision—whether to proceed with the D-Day invasion of France. Weather conditions again caused problems, and Eisenhower seized a small window of opportunity to send the Allied troops on shore. "If there were nothing else in my life to prove the existence of an almighty and merciful God," he later reflected, those events did it. He claimed that religious faith "gives you the courage to make the decisions you must make in a crisis and then the confidence to leave the result to a higher Power."[45]

During the early years of the cold war, the president continued to maintain that prayer was vital. Eisenhower admired Lincoln for frequently praying to God for wisdom and discernment. In a campaign speech in 1952, he declared, "I shall live . . . with a fervent prayer for God's direction and compassion, that I may humbly help our people to live in honor, in freedom, and in peace."[46] He wrote to a close friend that he prayed daily for guidance and assistance.[47] Eisenhower began his first inaugural address with prayer. He beseeched God to help his administration serve all Americans "regardless of race, station, or calling" and to "discern clearly right from wrong." "May we all work," he closed, "for the good of our beloved country, and for thy glory."[48] Eisenhower later called his inaugural prayer "a perfectly natural" way to remind Americans that their nation was founded on religious faith. Thousands of letters poured into the White House from Republicans and Democrats alike applauding his act.[49] In the opinion of Frederick Brown Harris, the chaplain of the Senate, Eisenhower's "supplication turned the inaugural platform into a high and holy altar" and thrilled the nation.[50] The Freethinkers of America, on the other hand, denounced his inaugural prayer as a "wholly uncalled for" "vulgar display."[51]

Eisenhower promoted prayer in numerous other ways. In one of his first speeches as president, he told Americans "your prayers for divine guidance on my behalf are the greatest gift you could possibly bring to me."[52] It was widely noted that all his cabinet meetings opened with prayer, usually silent, but occasionally led by cabinet members.[53] Each year of his presidency, Eisenhower proclaimed a national day of penance and prayer. He spoke at several national prayer breakfasts. In 1956, he asserted that by coming together to pray, the country's political and religious leaders were publicly acknowledging that the United States "is still a nation under God" with "great concern for . . . compassion and mercy."[54] He praised the power of prayer to increase mutual understanding and solve problems.[55] Proclaiming prayer "an indispensable part" of religious faith, he reminded Americans that in the "bitter and critical winter at Valley Forge, when the cause of liberty was so near defeat," George Washington engaged in "sincere and earnest prayer."[56] At news conferences, Eisenhower mentioned that he and other members of his administration prayed about policy matters.[57] He frequently expressed his deep appreciation for those who prayed for him.[58] Eisenhower maintained that he asked God for the wisdom to make good choices and for strength and courage to implement his decisions. One morning in 1955, Fred Seaton slipped unannounced into the Oval Office and found the president on his knees praying. Eisenhower explained that he was asking God for guidance in making a crucial decision about the Far East.[59] Before leaving for the Geneva Conference in July 1955, he urged people throughout the world to pray for peace because prayer was "a mighty force," and immediately after arriving in Geneva, he went to a church to pray.[60] That same year, Eisenhower was deeply touched by the millions of prayers offered for him by people across the nation after he suffered a heart attack.[61] Initially, the White House responses to inquiries about Eisenhower's favorite prayer declared that the president believed "most sincerely in the power of prayer" but did not have a favorite one.[62] Eventually, however, replies included copies of either his prayer at the first inaugural or his "The Prayer of Our People" from his second inaugural, which the National Council of Churches also distributed as a pamphlet.[63]

Eisenhower shared Franklin Roosevelt's profound respect for the Bible, but he was more knowledgeable about its teachings. As a child, he memorized the Ten Commandments, the Beatitudes, and other portions of Scripture, and he read the entire Bible twice before the age of eighteen.[64] The president "keeps a red leather Bible at his bedside," *Time* magazine noted, "and, judging from the content of his speeches, he reads it."[65] Eisenhower insisted that the "Bible is the rock on which this republic rests."[66] "Our civilization," he added, "is built upon its words." No other book provided such wisdom and hope.[67] "The message of Scripture," he declared, was "a constant source of light and strength."[68] He often quoted the Bible at staff meetings to illustrate points, and if someone misquoted a verse, Eisenhower usually corrected him.[69] Eisenhower strongly supported the work of the American Bible Society, especially its worldwide Bible-reading program, and the National Bible Week sponsored by the Laymen's National Committee.[70]

Eisenhower's faith and understanding of Christianity were similar to Franklin Roosevelt's in a number of other ways. They shared a strong belief that God directed the world's affairs. Like Roosevelt, Eisenhower saw World War II as a God-inspired crusade to protect democracy and religion against the Axis tyranny.[71] During the war, when soldiers asked the general why they were fighting, "the simplest and best answer" he could give was that "they were defending a free way of life"—a free education, freedom of speech and worship, free enterprise, free homes—"which rested on a religious foundation."[72] "We have seen the hand of Providence in the daily affairs" of America, Eisenhower declared, since its earliest days.[73] He told a group of clergy that "there is nothing America cannot do when her purpose is in conformity with the will of the Almighty."[74]

Eisenhower insisted that the Founding Fathers "wrote their religious faith into our founding documents, stamped their trust in God upon our coins and currency, [and] put it squarely at the base of our institutions."[75] They strove to obey God's commandments, live in freedom, and create a prosperous country.[76] "The knowledge that God is the source of all power" had given birth to and sustained the nation.[77] The concept of free government depended on the conviction that God had endowed all people created in his image "with certain rights."[78] Human dignity sprang from these rights, as so "eloquently stated" in the Declaration of Independence.[79] Those who settled America, Eisenhower asserted, had "faith in a Provident God whose hand supported and guided them; faith in themselves as the children of God, endowed with purposes beyond mere struggle for survival"; and faith in the principles of freedom and justice that were of "divine origin."[80] In adding the words "under God" to the Pledge of Allegiance, Eisenhower declared in 1954, Americans were reaffirming the importance of religious faith in their "heritage and future" and strengthening "those spiritual weapons" that would forever be the "country's most powerful resource, in peace or in war."[81] Speaking on the American Legion's "Back-to-God" program, Eisenhower averred that "recognition of the Supreme Being is the first—the most basic—expression of Americanism."[82] Near the end of his presidency, he warned that a "materialistic America—bereft of spiritual purpose—" would be "a rudderless ship of state" that would eventually crash in "the fury of international storms and internal decay."[83]

Like Roosevelt, Eisenhower argued that religion and democracy were closely linked. All types of free government, Eisenhower proclaimed, had a spiritual basis.[84] Freedom, the president contended, "is rooted in the certainty that the brotherhood of all men springs from the fatherhood of God. And thus, even as each man is his brother's keeper, no man is another's master."[85]

Given these convictions, it is not surprising that Eisenhower, like Roosevelt, continually called for spiritual renewal and challenged citizens to rededicate themselves to religious ideals and moral conduct. The Republican rarely made a speech without referring to the nation's need for greater spiritual strength. Throughout its history, Eisenhower alleged, America's greatness had depended on its acknowledgment of God.[86] Speechwriter Emmett Hughes explained that Eisenhower "exhort[ed] on few subjects so promptly and passionately as 'spiritual' strength or 'spiritual' precepts as the real source of American power and greatness."[87] Like Washington, Eisenhower contended that "national morality could not be maintained without a firm foundation of religious principle."[88] Moreover, religion had always been the most effective agent in "developing human character strong enough" to overcome people's selfishness and inspire them to perform their duty to God, humanity, and country.[89] "Confronted by a militant atheism and brazen materialism," he wrote to a retired general, "our religious institutions" have never been "more important to our way of life."[90]

Eisenhower maintained that the United States had a pivotal role to play in God's plan for civilization. "The world's destiny depended upon America's moral values, sense of order and decency, and cooperative spirit."[91] The United States, he argued, was "the mightiest spiritual force on earth."[92] The president repeatedly insisted that religion and atheism were locked in a global struggle. The world would have peace and prosperity, he predicted, only when its citizens rejected a materialistic philosophy and strove to serve God.[93] Although he continually complained about the "fatal materialism that plagues our age," Eisenhower exulted that most Americans gave "their first allegiance to the kingdom of the spirit."[94]

While asserting that America's leadership was crucial to preserving and expanding the free world, Eisenhower also tried to promote spiritual vitality among its allies. "For a long time," he wrote to Hughes in November 1958, "I have been pondering ... an attempt to center greater attention in ... the free world, on the predominant influence of spiritual values." "We have" considered "bombs and machines and gadgets," he lamented, "the arsenal of our national and cultural strength." However, because of the "spiritual values" they espoused, all nations that were "either philosophically or politically related" to the United States had "a combined potential strength" that was "indestructible."[95] Eisenhower told Hughes that he planned to informally discuss this issue with the leaders of other nations.[96]

Eisenhower's passionate desire for spiritual and moral renewal, coupled with his own religious background, led him, like Roosevelt, to minimize theological differences and stress the importance of religious toleration. "Whatever our individual church, whatever our personal creed, our common faith in God is a common bond among us," he declared.[97] Disliking divisions between denominations, Eisenhower, when talking with church leaders, frequently emphasized their "essential unity of purpose" and the "desirability of toning down their differences."[98] The president lauded the efforts of the National Council of Churches in 1953 to "devise ways and means to cooperate in the great religious life of America, so that differences in dogma, or ritual ... will be minimized and cooperation" would center about the essential truth that people were spiritual beings who derived their dignity from God.[99] Although Eisenhower vigorously promoted religion and spirituality, few complained his policies violated the separation of church and state, perhaps because he accentuated broad religious themes but shied away from supporting more specific programs such as Charles E. Wilson's Prayer for Peace plan and Moral Re-Armament.

His personal secretary Ann Whitman insisted that Eisenhower rarely dwelt on death, even the impending or actual death of close friends. He was greatly affected, however, by Dulles's slow, painful death in 1959.[100] During and after his presidency, he asked Billy Graham if he truly believed people would spend eternity with their loved ones in heaven. The evangelist told him that he strongly believed in Christ's promise of an afterlife with God and fellow believers, which undoubtedly eased Eisenhower's fear of death and increased his hope of being reunited with his mother and other relatives.[101] Based on a 1965 interview, journalist Sherwood Wirt claimed that the general firmly believed in life after death.[102] Shortly before Eisenhower died in March 1969, he and Graham discussed spiritual matters and prayed together at Walter Reed Hospital. His last words were "I want to go; God take me."[103]

During the Eisenhower years, religious activity flourished on Capitol Hill, which prompted many to rejoice and some to refer derisively to "piety along the Potomac." Many prayer breakfast groups, including ones for members of the House, the Senate, and the judiciary, met regularly. Eisenhower regularly attended one organized by the International Council for Christian Leadership that became known as the Presidential Prayer Breakfast. At the first breakfast held in February 1953, more than five hundred congressmen, cabinet members, Supreme Court justices, diplomats, and religious leaders gathered to pray and listen to the president. Eisenhower trumpeted two of his perennial themes: all free governments rested upon "deeply felt religious faith," and prayer was essential because it enabled people to "get in touch with the Infinite."[104] Although noting that morality in Washington seemed to be improving, critics complained that these religious gatherings equated "piety with personal prosperity."[105]

Two areas where Eisenhower's efforts bore little fruit were his endeavors to make an annual day of prayer a new national tradition and to help establish the Foundation for Religious Action (FRA). The American public largely ignored Eisenhower's annual proclamations for a day of prayer, and the accomplishments of the FRA were meager.[106] Cosponsored by such luminaries as Herbert Hoover, Billy Graham, Norman Vincent Peale, George Meany, Henry Ford II, and Henry Luce, the organization sought to "unite all people who believed in a Supreme Being" in a spiritual and ideological crusade against communism.[107]

Eisenhower's two most vocal critics, Carl McIntire and William Lee Miller, came from opposite ends of the theological spectrum. Inspired in part by the sting of rejection, the American Council of Churches, which McIntire served as president, complained that Eisenhower's administration was favoring some religious groups "to the harm and discredit of other religious and minority groups." Delegates to the 1958 annual convention of this ultraconservative body "objected strenuously" to the president addressing the World Council of Churches, attending a special mass for Pope Pius XII in Washington, and participating in the dedication of the Interchurch Center of the National Council of Churches in New York. These activities, done in the name of the American people, undermined the separation of church and state, gave free publicity to these organizations, and violated the canons of fairness.[108]

Miller, a journalist and professor, who embraced Reinhold Niebuhr's neoorthodoxy, protested that Eisenhower promoted religion in general rather than any specific faith or theological perspective. In a series of essays written in the 1950s, Miller insisted that Eisenhower did not use "the God stuff" "simply as a political device," but his constant moral rhetoric was "partly a substitute for a developed social philosophy." Like many Americans, he concluded, Eisenhower was "a very fervent believer in a very vague religion." The float in the parade at his first inaugural representing religion illustrated the president's eclectic convictions. It stood for all religions, had symbols of none, and featured such generic captions as "In God We Trust." To Miller, the float, like Eisenhower himself, emphasized faith not in God but in faith and religion. Devoid of content, the president's religion was designed to appeal to the "widest possible public."[109] Moreover, Miller complained, Eisenhower used religion to endorse America's aims and purposes. The president tended to confuse "the absolute and emotional loyalties of religion with the relative and shifting loyalties of politics." Like some of the decade's other political leaders, he reduced religion to "a national 'resource,' 'advantage,' 'strength,' and 'weapon,' especially useful for anti-Communist purposes." Summarizing this view, FBI Director J. Edgar Hoover declared, "Since Communists are anti-God, encourage your child to be active in the church."[110]

Like Jewish sociologist Will Herberg, Miller labeled the decade's religious "revival" shallow. By many indices—church attendance, giving to religious organizations, construction of new places of worship, and interest in religion as represented by movie themes, book sales, and religious programming on television—religion was flourishing. This revival, however, did not seem to be improving the nation's religious life or elevating its moral practices.[111] Many Americans used religion as a tool to achieve their purposes—to enhance their reputations, solve their personal problems, or protect the nation against ungodly communism.[112] This belief in "religion-in-general" or "spiritual values," Miller argued, failed to recognize the "possibility of idolatry, of false and bad religion, of the need to discriminate among the claims" made by various religious groups.[113]

Other Christians, especially theological liberals, agreed that Eisenhower's "deeply felt faith" was rather vague and vacuous. They contended that he avoided serious theological reflection and ignored the social implications of the gospel. Some of them and numerous secular critics complained that Eisenhower's religiosity was more a public relations ploy than a genuine heartfelt conviction.[114] They insisted that his public piety, as evident in his decision to join a church, faithful participation in worship services and prayer breakfasts, opening of cabinet meetings with prayer, frequent use of religious rhetoric in speeches, and numerous meetings with religious delegations, was designed to enhance his popularity and win votes rather than a reflection of a deep, devout faith.[115]

Many pietistic and theologically conservative Christians, on the other hand, applauded Eisenhower's emphasis on prayer and spirituality. An article in *Decision Magazine*, a publication of the Billy Graham Association, made the president sound like an evangelical. After studying the "astonishing influence of Jesus of Nazareth on human nature, history, forms of government, codes of jurisprudence and civilization in general," Eisenhower had concluded that Jesus was the "essence of Christian faith."[116] The Republican actually said little about Jesus. Given America's religious pluralism and the demands of civil religion, it is not surprising that his public addresses rarely mention Jesus, but neither do his books, diary, or letters.

Various individuals and groups extolled the importance and impact of Eisenhower's faith. Catholic John J. O'Brien argued that Eisenhower had brought "spiritual values to the forefront of government more than any other time since the early years of the republic."[117] In 1955, thirty-one of Eisenhower's top officials expressed "tremendous confidence" "in the sincerity" of his Christian convictions.[118] The Baptist General Conference of America declared that "by both precept and example" Eisenhower stimulated citizens to depend on God.[119] The president of the Washington Ministerial Association asserted that he had "popularized prayer and righteousness" and encouraged business and professional men to join breakfast prayer meetings and attend church with their families.[120] Elson claimed that through his personal example and speeches, Eisenhower had become the "focal point of a moral resurgence and spiritual awakening of national proportions."[121] The Republican National Committee called him "the spiritual leader of our times."[122] In recognition of his religious achievements, Eisenhower received the Lay Churchman Award in 1955 and the Gold Medal Brotherhood Award from the National Conference of Christians and Jews in 1956. "Eisenhower's personal faith in God," declared the editors of Christianity Today, "was the indestructible bastion of his life."[123] Shortly after the president died, Billy Graham assured Americans that "General Eisenhower is in heaven" and "because of our mutual faith in Christ I look forward to seeing him again."[124]

Eisenhower's Two Presidential Elections

While serving as the head of NATO forces in Europe during 1950–51, Eisenhower was increasingly touted as a presidential candidate, even though it was not clear whether he was a Republican or a Democrat. After many meetings with political advisors and considerable soul searching, he returned home in April 1952 to seek the Republican nomination. Although supporters of Robert A. Taft denounced the general as a superficial candidate who stood only for "mother, home, and heaven" and accused him of having a wartime affair with his aide Kay Summersby, he defeated the Ohio senator in the battle for the nomination.[125] Immensely popular because of his exuberant personality and wartime heroics, Eisenhower campaigned primarily against godless communism and political corruption. His speeches were so filled with spiritual content and religious phrases that some advisors urged him to limit these references.[126] Refusing to do so, he argued (as Herbert Hoover had been doing for nearly two decades) that Americans must lead a crusade to defeat the enemies of Christianity, most notably Communist Russia. Eisenhower insisted that the Soviet Union and the United States were irreconcilable enemies, fighting "a war of light against darkness, freedom against slavery, [and] Godliness against atheism."[127] The general pledged to provide peace and prosperity, reduce the size of the federal government, restore dignity to the presidency, and remove all the "communists and crooks in Washington."[128] Because God gave the United States victory in World War II, Eisenhower argued, it must increase its "spiritual, creative, and material strength," "win a just and lasting peace," "build a prosperity not based on war," make its promise of equality a reality for every citizen, improve the welfare of all Americans, and restore honesty to government.[129] In his campaign speeches, Eisenhower repeatedly extolled Americans' "deeply felt religious faith" and called for a revival of "moral and spiritual values," especially "honesty, decency, fairness, and service."[130]

Religion was a very important issue in the 1952 campaign. Before the Republican convention, anti-Semitic groups who wanted to stop the party from nominating Eisenhower conducted a vicious whispering campaign against the general. They implied that he was a Jew by circulating the jest beside his name in his graduating class's yearbook at the U.S. Military Academy: "This is Dwight David Eisenhower, the terrible Swedish Jew." When Gerald L. K. Smith, Joseph Kamp, and others flooded the mails with anti-Semitic materials, some of which attacked Eisenhower, he compared their tactics with those used by Nazis, Fascists, and Communists and declared: "Appeals to prejudice and bigotry have no place in America." He urged all Americans to promise that in political affairs "no taint of religious or racial animosity shall trouble our national unity."[131]

The editors of *Christian Century* complained that politicians were professing piety and that scriptural references and God's holy name were frequently popping up in political speeches. Although some might rejoice that things of the spirit were receiving so much attention, they deplored "the exploitation of religion for political ends." It was "wrong to treat true faith in God as if it were something to be worn once in four years, like a campaign button." At the Republican convention, bands repeatedly played "Onward Christian Soldiers" and clergy portrayed God as "a mythical Uncle Sam." God, they protested, was not a Republican or a Democrat or even an American.[132] Many privately denounced Democratic nominee Adlai Stevenson as an atheist because he was a Unitarian. Others complained that he was divorced or did not mention God enough in his speeches.[133] The editors of the *Episcopal Church News* asked both candidates how their religious convictions would affect their work as the nation's chief executive. "A man's personal religious beliefs," Stevenson declared, "had no proper place in our political life, except as they may influence his public acts and thus affect the public welfare." Eisenhower, by contrast, insisted that only by trusting in God could he effectively carry out the responsibilities of the office and help the United States solve its problems.[134]

America's religious leaders viewed the two candidates very differently. Speaking for many theological and political liberals, John Swomley indicted Eisenhower as a militarist and an ardent nationalist.[135] A professor at the Pacific School of Religion in Berkeley, California, by contrast, lauded the Republican as a "genuine democrat, the man of the people," who embodied the "old-fashioned" "virtues of devotion to duty, personal integrity, courage, fair play, and resolute idealism."[136] Bradshaw Mintener insisted that because of his exemplary character and "great moral strength," Eisenhower would return "honesty, fairness and integrity" to government. He would administer domestic affairs "for the good and benefit" of all Americans and lead the nation to "attain and maintain world peace."[137] Expressing views held by many evangelicals, Donald Grey Barnhouse, pastor of Tenth Presbyterian Church in Philadelphia, maintained that both candidates were men of "very high caliber," of outstanding character and intelligence, who were "exceptionally well fitted to lead the nation." Nevertheless, he was going to vote for Eisenhower because the general had demonstrated that he was a great organizer who had a superb understanding of international affairs and could help people with diverse interests work together. As a Unitarian, Stevenson denied the Trinity, while Eisenhower had a simple, although not "very well informed faith," which was "in line with Christian principles."[138] Most Catholic editors supported Stevenson. *Commonweal* called his election a "matter of vital importance to the nation."[139] While admiring Eisenhower's character, they preferred the Democrat's policies and candor.[140] A group of professors at the University of Notre Dame extolled Stevenson as a man who rose "among us as an act of Providence."[141] Both Catholics and Protestants hoped the campaign would focus on issues and the moral and religious basis for policies rather than personalities.[142]

The election of 1956 featured the same two candidates. Ernest LeFever noted that the response to Eisenhower's religious rhetoric and support of religious causes had generally been enthusiastic and labeled the president's faith "simple, vague, fervent and crusading." Because Stevenson had been reticent to discuss his religious views and was not president, his religious beliefs had been little analyzed. In December 1955, Stevenson had joined a Presbyterian congregation while maintaining his membership in a Unitarian church. The "almost complete lack of comment" about his dual membership indicated that "a nondenominational politics and a bipartisan religion" prevailed in the United States.[143] Both candidates strongly advocated religious tolerance. Although Eisenhower's tolerance tended to "reduce real religious differences to vague belief in man as a 'spiritual being,'" Stevenson's tolerance encouraged "diversity in belief and thought." LeFever accentuated the similarities between Eisenhower and America's leading evangelist, Billy Graham, and between Stevenson and the nation's foremost theologian, Reinhold Niebuhr. While Eisenhower emphasized God's nearness and helpfulness to humanity, Stevenson stressed God's transcendence and sovereignty and human dependence on him. The president wanted to lead the world in a great moral crusade to achieve peace, justice, harmony, happiness, and unparalleled prosperity, but evil men stood in the way. Eisenhower, LeFever contended, thought God was on the side of the free world, America, and the Republican Party. While agreeing that God called people to work through politics to achieve a just and peaceful world, his Democratic challenger insisted that God was not "primarily a source of strength for 'our side,' but a source of wisdom and righteousness," who inspired and judged all men and nations. LeFever complained that Eisenhower did not distinguish between "true religion and American democracy" and obliterated the long-standing "distinction between absolute religious affirmations and relative political loyalties." Stevenson, by contrast, warned against the American passion for crusades and desire for absolutes. LeFever concluded, however, that when they dealt with "grave and complex public issues[,] Eisenhower and Stevenson" were "probably not as far apart" as their religious views suggested.[144]

The responses to LeFever's article provide a barometer of public opinion. A history professor at Mercer University in Georgia argued that his effort to "make a neo-orthodox unitarian out" of Stevenson, who was an advocate of "rationalistic humanism," was not convincing. LeFever's "sneering tone" about Eisenhower's religion, a man from Seattle insisted, was "contemptible in a religious publication." A woman from Elkhart, Indiana, feared that Americans preferred Eisenhower's "vague spiritual religiosity" to Stevenson's "searching biblical faith" and a God who smiled "benignly upon his chosen people" to a righteous God who sat in "judgment over all nations."[145]

Also writing in *Christian Century*, Robert Fitch praised the Eisenhower administration's "essential liberalism" on humanitarian issues. This had forced many liberal journals, Christian and secular, which had opposed his election in 1952, to issue recantations during the past four years. Those who had derided him as a militarist had also been proven wrong. Eisenhower had proved his "inordinate passion for peace." His commitment to world peace, more than anything else, had prompted him to seek a second term. Nevertheless, Fitch complained that Republicans stressed peace, prosperity, and progress and paid too little attention to the social justice the prophets demanded, the love Christ incarnated, and the civil, political, and religious liberties the Bible affirmed. Fitch challenged Christians to use these biblical ideals to evaluate the campaign's most important issues: disarmament, farm problems, the rights of workers and blacks, social welfare, and a "just and creative economy."[146]

Christianity and Crisis, a leading voice of liberal theological opinion, featured articles presenting the case for and against Eisenhower. Paul G. Hoffman, former administrator of the Marshall Plan, praised the president for expanding the opportunities of all Americans, substantially improving the nation's moral and political climate, ending the Korean War, and working diligently to achieve a lasting peace. Former governor of Connecticut Chester Bowles countered that Eisenhower had allowed big business to dominate his administration and had not solved the nation's major domestic and foreign problems. The tension and bloodshed in many parts of the world, the division of Korea, Vietnam, and Germany, the necessity of maintaining an American military of three million men, and the growth of nuclear weapons indicated that the president's quest for world peace had failed.[147]

Writing in *Christian Century*, Kermit Eby protested that the election of 1956 offered an "unsatisfying choice" between "Stevenson's eloquence and Eisenhower's winsomeness." The campaign was based on "personalities rather than issues." Many saw Eisenhower as a "protective, reassuring" father who taught Americans that if they lived right, they would receive "tangible and immediate" rewards because they were "God's special charge." Predicting that this election would deal with fewer issues than any other in the nation's history, Eby urged prospective voters to evaluate the parties' stances on the economy, integration, agriculture, the military, and foreign relations.[148] Trying to help shape the campaign's debate over policy, the National Council of Churches presented recommendations on sixteen major domestic and foreign issues to the Democratic and Republican platform committees. They called for increased funding of education and housing, integration of public schools, protection of the rights of Indians and migrant workers, continued support of the United Nations, greater economic and technical aid to developing countries, arms reduction, and the use of negotiation instead of threat in international relations.[149] Many others complained that the candidates did not discuss the religious and moral aspects of the campaign's chief political issues.[150]

During the campaign, the evangelical periodical *Christianity Today* surveyed "representative clergymen from all sections of the United States" about the Republican and Democratic candidates. Respondents favored Eisenhower eight to one over Stevenson. They praised the president's religious convictions and emphasis on morality and spirituality and applauded his foreign and domestic policies, especially his efforts to combat communism and promote racial desegregation.[151] Billy Graham predicted in June that because of his "complete sincerity, honesty, fairness and religious conviction," Eisenhower would win a greater percentage of the vote than in 1952.[152] In August, he promised the president he would do all he could "to gain friends and supporters" for his cause.[153]

Two leading Catholics, Senator John F. Kennedy of Massachusetts and Mayor Robert Wagner of New York City, were serious contenders for the Democratic Party's vice presidential nomination. A "secret memorandum" argued that if a Catholic were on the ticket, millions of Catholics who had deserted the party to vote for Eisenhower in 1952 would return to the fold.

Detailed analysis showed that a small shift in a dozen states with large Catholic populations could bring victory to the Democratic ticket.[154] Learning about this potential strategy, the editors of *Christian Century* protested that the Catholic Church refused to abide by the First Amendment principle that all denominations must be "on equal footing in their relation to the state." Neither Wagner nor Kennedy had demonstrated that he could be trusted to resist the church's "never ceasing drive...for access to public funds...and for preferential treatment by public figures and bodies."[155] This strategy was not tested, as Tennessee Senator Estes Kefauver narrowly defeated Kennedy for the vice presidential position.

Eisenhower was elected in a landslide, piling up 457 electoral votes to Stevenson's 74, even though Democrats maintained control of both houses of Congress. Strikingly, he won the highest percentage of the Catholic vote by a Republican candidate to that point in history (49–53 percent in various polls). In the opinion of the Catholic journal *America*, the president was reelected because Americans liked, admired, and trusted him.[156] Eisenhower won so decisively, *Christian Century* contended, because of his "distaste for the use of political power" and the credit he received for the nation's peace and prosperity.[157]

Eisenhower's Relationship with Religious Constituencies

The close and cordial relationship Eisenhower enjoyed with religious groups was due to three principal factors: his religious commitments, personality, and appointment of Congregational minister Frederic Fox as special assistant on religious matters in July 1956. Prior to this time, Eisenhower, like his predecessors, had no "clearly defined method for handling religious matters," "general theory for church-state relations," or plan for coordinating the relationship between the White House and various religious groups. Before Fox's appointment, Sherman Adams, Eisenhower's chief of staff, and James Hagerty, his press secretary, made many of the decisions about religious issues. Kevin McCann, an Evangelical and Reformed leader, wrote many of the president's religious proclamations and speeches. Catholics Emmett Hughes and Bernard Shanley oversaw communications with Catholic organizations, and Maxwell Robb, a Jew, did the same with Jewish groups.[158]

With Fox's appointment, all this changed, as the administration's religious activities became centralized. Fox, the first clergyman to serve on the White House staff since the Lincoln administration, coordinated religious activities, responded to citizens who wrote to the president about religious matters, drafted speeches for Eisenhower on religious subjects, and served as a liaison with religious groups. On behalf of the administration, Fox sent thousands of letters of greeting and congratulation to Protestant, Catholic, and Jewish national and regional gatherings, congregations, charitable organizations, and colleges, as well as individual clergy who celebrated significant anniversaries in the ministry. Fox insisted that he did not serve as staff chaplain or as a spiritual counselor to the president. He did research and wrote drafts of some of Eisenhower's speeches, but the president himself supplied the numerous religious references in his speeches. Fox represented Eisenhower at national meetings of educational, charitable, and religious organizations and helped answer the ten thousand letters he received each week from these groups and from individuals about religious matters.[159] During his presidency, citizens sent Eisenhower dozens of sermons, articles on religious subjects, and pamphlets. Individuals asked him countless questions about religion, especially about his favorite biblical passages, prayers, and hymns. Fox often told religious gatherings that the president wanted religious groups to "speak up clear and strong" to help improve the nation.[160] Eisenhower maintained generally friendly relations with liberal and moderate Protestants, evangelicals, Catholics, and Jews. Only with Protestant fundamentalists was his relationship strained.

Eisenhower met personally with National Council of Churches executives several times a year, more frequently than with the leaders of any other religious body. The president's closest advisors typically knew the National Council's position on important matters of domestic and foreign policy, and the president sometimes read their statements on social and economic issues and even distributed them to his cabinet and staff. The National Council and the Presbyterian Church (USA), the president's denomination, received the most attention, in part because their leaders frequently petitioned the White House and represented many Americans. Nevertheless, the National Council tended to support politically liberal policies the president opposed, and its policy statements usually did not reflect the views of most of their constituents.[161] Both factors limited its influence on Eisenhower's administration.

National Council of Churches executives wrote to Eisenhower in 1955 to protest his decision to limit his personal appearances to religious gatherings held in Washington. They complained that this policy would prevent the president from personally encouraging religious communities in the same way he did other important groups. The nation's religious picture, they added, was "not as confusing as the existence of 250 religious sects" suggested. Three major organizations—the National Council, the Synagogue Council of America, and the National Catholic Welfare Conference—spoke for the vast majority of religiously affiliated Americans. National Council leaders offered to help the president decide which invitations to accept from religious bodies, resist the pressures placed upon him by religious groups, and prepare speeches, proclamations, and messages dealing with religious matters.[162]

Although theologically conservative Protestants strongly backed most of Eisenhower's policies, they had less access to the president. Many of them shared the president's conservative political philosophy and admired his character and speeches. Led by the National Association of Evangelicals (NAE, founded in 1942) and International Christian Leadership (ICL, formed in 1943), evangelicals had become involved in political affairs. The NAE established a Washington office and appointed a director of public affairs who advanced the political interests of missionary agencies affiliated with the NAE and closely monitored church-state issues. The ICL established "Fellowship House" as a center for ministering to the nation's political leaders and sponsored prayer breakfasts in Washington and throughout the country.[163] Most evangelicals were very enthusiastic about Eisenhower's election and applauded his administration's efforts to raise the nation's level of morality and spiritual vitality. The NAE's Office of Public Affairs worked to preserve religious liberty and pass legislation to restrict the advertising, manufacture, and sale of liquor and to prohibit the sale of pornographic literature.[164]

Next to his pastor, Edward Elson, Eisenhower's closest spiritual mentor and confidant was Billy Graham. Graham's very successful revival services in Los Angeles in 1949 propelled him onto the public stage. The evangelist's close relationship with Eisenhower (and most of his successors) evoked much criticism. Impressed by Eisenhower's "sincerity, humility, and tremendous grasp of affairs," Graham encouraged him to run for the presidency in 1952 and declared that the "destiny of the Western World" might rest upon his decision.[165] Although Graham did not formally endorse Eisenhower, he met with the general three times before the 1952 election, applauded his "crusade for honesty in government," and frequently echoed the Republican campaign theme that America desperately needed a "strong spiritual leader" who would clean up the capital. He also told Christian audiences that the Republican candidate depended on God, wanted to see a spiritual revival, and would accept "advice from some genuine, born-again Christians."[166] Eisenhower invited Graham to the Commodore Hotel in New York five days before his first inauguration to discuss biblical passages he might use in his address.[167]

While Eisenhower was president, the evangelist wrote dozens of letters, kept him informed about the results of his crusades, sent him copies of his books, visited him occasionally at the White House and Gettysburg, lauded his faith, character, and policies in speeches, interviews, and letters, and advised him on racial issues.[168] "Your constant references to spiritual needs and your faithful attendance at church," Graham declared in September 1953, "have done much" to aid the nation's spiritual awakening. "Millions of Americans," he added in 1954, "thank God for your spiritual leadership." Graham praised Eisenhower for bringing a spiritual emphasis to the White House, promoting good causes, and manifesting "sincerity, integrity, and dedication." He promised the president: "Whatever your ultimate decision" about the U.S. role in Indochina, "I shall do my best through radio and television" to help sell it to the American people.[169] In 1955, he told Eisenhower that both "the overwhelming confidence of the American people" and "divine providence" had placed him in the Oval Office. Graham urged Eisenhower to seek reelection, arguing that his "splendid and courageous leadership" had united the American people and continued to be "absolutely essential." "I shall do all in my power during the coming campaign," the evangelist wrote to the president in August 1956, "to gain friends and supporters for your cause. As always, you have my complete devotion and personal affection."[170] Eisenhower, Graham predicted, "would go down in history alongside of Lincoln." Shortly after the Republican left the presidency, Graham called him "an old friend whom I admire more than any man in the world."[171]

Graham is "remarkably gifted and has accomplished much good," Eisenhower wrote to a friend in March 1956. "Today . . . we discussed . . . how he might" help to solve some of the country's "more serious human problems."[172] Eisenhower especially sought the evangelist's assistance in dealing with the nation's racial problems. Battling the widespread perception that all evangelists were as deceitful and greedy as Elmer Gantry, Graham greatly benefited from the president's public endorsement of his ministry.[173] One of the president's advisors claimed he was happy to see the evangelist anytime.[174] At a 1956 press conference, Eisenhower lauded Graham for going "to the far corners of the earth" to promote peace, mediation instead of conflict, [and] tolerance instead of prejudice."[175] After leaving the presidency, Eisenhower praised Graham's ability to "relate his basic spiritual beliefs to the tough problems of the day."[176]

Several factors help explain their cordial relationship. Each benefited from the other's popularity. Both men sought to promote spiritual and moral revival in America, despite their different perceptions of what that entailed. Both of them insisted that religion was the best antidote to communism.[177] Eisenhower and Graham frequently depicted the conflict between the United States and the Soviet Union as a struggle between God and Satan or good and evil.[178]

The Eisenhower administration was less friendly toward fundamentalist groups, especially Carl McIntire's American Council of Christian Churches, than toward any other religious bodies. During his tenure in office, Eisenhower's staff struggled with how to relate to this organization. In 1954, they debated whether they should send a greeting to the organization's annual meeting. The State Department recommended not doing so because this group had criticized some of Eisenhower's religious statements and the World Council of Churches leaders regarded it as "a reactionary and fanatical organization."[179] Other staff countered that the administration sent greetings to meetings of labor unions and the NAACP, groups that were even more disparaging of the current administration, and that they must not take sides in the rivalry between religious bodies.[180] Throughout Eisenhower's presidency, the American Council persistently sought to obtain an audience with him.

Although he met numerous other religious delegations, their requests were repeatedly rebuffed.[181]

Eisenhower also maintained a generally positive relationship with American Catholics despite appointing few of them to prominent posts in his administration.[182] He regularly corresponded with Catholic leaders and invited some of them to the White House.[183] The Republican addressed several Catholic assemblies and met with Pope John XXIII at the Vatican. Fox worked diligently to develop cordial relationships with the Catholic hierarchy. Unlike most of his predecessors, Eisenhower did not make any major policy decisions that offended Catholics.[184] In 1954, Catholic bishops adopted a resolution urging the president to appoint a Catholic to the Supreme Court. Prompted in part by their arguments, Eisenhower named William Brennan Jr., a Catholic Democrat from New Jersey, to the bench in 1956.[185] Although sometimes critical of the president's specific policies, *Commonweal* praised his commitment to "honesty, decency and fair play at home and conciliation and negotiation abroad."[186] Eisenhower won about half of the votes Catholics cast in both 1952 and 1956.[187]

Pressure from Catholic bishops also influenced Eisenhower's declaration in 1959 that the federal government had no responsibility to dispense birth control information to foreign governments. The editors of *Christian Century* chastised Eisenhower for his unwillingness to take active steps to curb world population growth. They protested that the president was either unaware of the magnitude of the problem and potential solutions for it, used different multiplication tables than demographers, did not realize that most Protestants disagreed sharply with Catholic bishops, or was responsive only to the views of one religious community.[188]

Eisenhower believed that the Jews were God's chosen people who supplied the West with its "high ethical and moral principles." Moreover, the general's "treatment of the Jewish displaced persons whom his armies liberated from the Nazi concentration camps," argued Rabbi Judah Nadich, his advisor on Jewish affairs during World War II, displayed great "understanding and sympathy."[189] As president, however, he did not develop a close relationship with the Jewish community.[190] During the 1952 campaign, the general pledged to work to preserve Israel as a national homeland for the Jews, develop a permanent peace between Israel and its Arab neighbors, relocate Arab refugees who could not be reabsorbed by Israel, and provide political and economic aid to Israel and Arab states that were willing to cooperate with the free world against totalitarian aggression. Nevertheless, the vast majority of Jews voted for Stevenson in both 1952 and 1956, apparently preferring his liberal domestic policies over Eisenhower's conservative ones. Although he sent greetings to Jewish organizations, acknowledged Jewish holy days, and occasionally spoke to Jewish groups, the Republican had no close Jewish friends and rarely met personally with Jewish leaders. The president usually invited spokesmen for the groups most concerned about particular issues to the White House, listened to their perspective, and then explained his position and urged them to support it. However, in formulating American policy on Israel, he did not follow this pattern. Eisenhower was acquainted with some Jewish leaders, most notably Bernard Baruch, Lewis Strauss, and Louis Marx, but he seldom sought their opinion or that of the broader Jewish community. His desire to maintain cordial relationships with Arab states to provide a buffer against the Soviet Union may have prompted this approach.[191]

Eisenhower's Presidential Policies

In his first State of the Union Address, Eisenhower asserted that his administration sought to realize "four ruling purposes": "deter aggression and eventually secure peace"; create an honest, efficient federal government; encourage economic initiatives that boosted productivity and fortified freedom; and ensure equal opportunity for all.[192] During the Eisenhower years, production increased significantly, and general prosperity prevailed. His administration earned generally high marks for its efficiency and honesty.

The president often characterized his approach to politics as "dynamic conservatism": "liberal on human issues, conservative on economic ones."[193] Claiming that Harry Truman's Fair Deal had pandered to various interest groups that put their selfish desires above the public good, he sought instead to take the United States "down the middle of the road between the unfettered power of concentrated wealth . . . and the unbridled power of statism or partisan interests."[194] He believed with Lincoln that "government should do for the people what they could not do well for themselves or at all, but it should keep out of those things that people can do for themselves."[195] Like Hoover, Eisenhower called for sacrifice, cooperation, and commitment to the common good. "By promoting the interrelated forces of "capitalism, free enterprise, democracy, [and] religion," the president maintained, America could get "on the right track again."[196] In foreign affairs, Eisenhower was an internationalist who insisted that the United States must play an active role in the world.

"I have constantly tried to make clear," the president wrote in 1955, "my own belief in the superiority of moral principles as guideposts for the actions and policies of our nation."[197] "To keep our bearings firm in the conduct of international relations," he proclaimed, the government must be guided by ethical precepts.[198] Eisenhower told delegates to the World Council of Churches that many members of Congress periodically met to "consider how religious principles" could be "applied to the practical affairs of our Government." He invited them to "show us additional and better ways" the Christian ethic "can be applied to all sorts of problems."[199]

Eisenhower constantly asserted that belief in God was the surest and strongest foundation for justice and freedom.[200] He insisted that God gave all people the same dignity and rights. Universal recognition of "the fundamental truth that all men are created equal" would set people free.[201] Only by focusing on moral and spiritual values could the world improve race relations and increase international good will and cooperation. Without a commitment to liberty and equality, people could not achieve human brotherhood.[202]

To illustrate how Eisenhower's religious convictions influenced his presidency, his quest to achieve peace and his effort to ensure equality of opportunity will be examined. "Of the various tasks to which I early determined to devote my energies," he explained in *Waging Peace,* "none transcended in importance that of trying to devise practical and acceptable means to lighten the burdens of armaments and lessen the likelihood of war" and "establishing a universal peace with justice and freedom."[203] Eisenhower initially sought "total conventional and nuclear disarmament," but eventually he and his advisors "adopted the far more modest and realistic objective of arms control."[204] He repeatedly argued that his crusade to achieve peace was grounded in his religious convictions. "Human peace and advancement," Eisenhower asserted, "cannot be accomplished by human ingenuity alone." People could attain these ends only if their efforts accorded "with the law and the will of a Power greater than themselves."[205]

Achieving "enduring peace, while living in freedom," Eisenhower proclaimed, "must ever be the overriding goal of our American foreign policy." The only way to counter "a regime that wages total cold war," he insisted, "is to wage total peace."[206] "I doubt whether any of these people, with their academic or dogmatic hatred of war," he wrote to his brother Arthur, "detest it as much as I do."[207] The pursuit of peace, the president added, was both "our religious obligation and our national policy."[208] "Divinely inspired faith" that gave people the "desire to be free," to further justice, and to make sacrifices for their children was crucial to the quest for peace.[209] Eisenhower hoped that people realized "the United States was truly trying to follow in the footsteps of the Prince of Peace, and to establish a just peace for the world."[210]

To attain peace, the United States must understand and advance "the legitimate aspirations and hopes of all peoples."[211] "Bullets and guns and planes and ships" could "produce no real or lasting peace."[212] Neither could "edicts and treaties, no matter how solemnly signed," nor could economic arrangements, no matter how favorable they were.[213] "Only a great moral crusade" carrying out God's will would be successful.[214] Because the United States was "the greatest force that God" had "ever allowed to exist on His footstool," it must help the world attain a secure and lasting peace.[215] The Christmas message of "Peace on Earth, Good Will Toward Men," he proclaimed, was a basic aspiration of "Christian, Jew, Moslem, Hindu, [and]

Buddhist alike—of every person in the world who has faith in an Almighty God."[216]

In 1954, Secretary of Defense Charles E. Wilson urged the president to make a spectacular appeal for peace to all the world's people based on the "Universal Fatherhood of God and the Brotherhood of all men." After months of intensive preparation by people throughout the world, Eisenhower could speak simultaneously to citizens of many nations gathered in their mosques, synagogues, and churches in what would be the "greatest peace effort since Christ came to earth."[217] Eisenhower replied that he and his staff had given "considerable thought to the matter," especially about the "circumstances and timing" that would enable such a plan to have the most appeal and possibility of success. He had appointed Harold Stassen as an unofficial "Secretary for peace" to ensure that one government official worked on this issue full-time.[218] Although Eisenhower never implemented Wilson's proposal, he did frequently appeal to people to pray for peace, most notably at the World Council of Churches in 1954. He urged delegates to invite "every single person, in every single country in the world," who believed "in the power of a Supreme Being, to join in a mighty, simultaneous, intense act of faith." If hundreds of millions prayed fervently and worked "unceasingly for a just and lasting peace...wondrous results would ensue."[219] Inspired by the president's plea, the Executive Committee of the World Council of Churches promised to explore how to organize "an effective world-wide concert of prayer for peace."[220] "To be successful," the deputy director of the United States Information Agency argued, "the world-wide moment of prayer" must involve people of all major religions, each praying in his own tongue and his own way. Such a dramatic event would counter the Soviet claim that the United States was a warmonger and would give the free world the initiative in promoting peace because the Soviet Union could not call for prayers for peace.[221] Although Eisenhower never organized a specific program or event, he did support an American Pray for Peace movement, proclaimed Memorial Day 1960 as "a day of prayer for permanent peace," and rejoiced that many citizens had joined together to pray for a just peace.[222] "The price of peace, our ultimate objective," he declared, "is unceasing sacrifice and prayer."[223]

While urging people to pray for peace, Eisenhower used "many and varied" methods to achieve it. His staff constantly emphasized peace in speeches, day-to-day diplomacy, and discussions with the leaders of friendly governments, and they tirelessly worked to amicably resolve "the clashes of interests" that arose "even among friends." In addition, his administration negotiated treaties, supported the activities of the United Nations, worked to reduce armaments, arranged cultural and educational exchanges, promoted mutually profitable trade, and developed programs for mutual security.[224] In his second inaugural address, "The Price of Peace," the president proclaimed: "The building of a peace with justice in a world where moral law prevails" is "our firm and fixed purpose."[225] To reduce the world's weapons, Eisenhower devised his Atoms for Peace proposal and his Open Skies plan.

In what the media quickly dubbed his "Atoms for Peace" speech, delivered at the United Nations in 1953, the president warned that the appalling growth of nuclear weapons threatened to destroy civilization. He proposed that the three atomic powers—the United States, Great Britain, and the Soviet Union—place most of their fissionable material under the authority of an international atomic energy agency. This would slow the spread of nuclear weapons and calm people's anxieties. "The United States pledges," Eisenhower declared, "to help solve the fearful atomic dilemma"—to ensure that "the miraculous inventiveness of man shall not be dedicated to his death, but consecrated to his life."[226] Eisenhower's much celebrated speech produced few concrete results. The Soviets protested that his proposal would encourage nuclear proliferation, some Congressmen worried that the plan would divulge American atomic secrets, and critics called it a propaganda ploy. Finally established in 1957, the International Atomic Energy Agency had little impact because its staff and budget were small and it was given little power to control atomic research and development.[227]

In July 1955, Eisenhower traveled to Geneva, Switzerland, to implore the Soviets, British, and French to develop more positive, peaceful relations and reduce their weapons. Because the citizens of the free world believed in a supreme being and the Golden Rule, he argued, they strove to promote justice, respect for others, and peace. Before leaving, he exhorted all Americans to pray for peace to demonstrate "the sincerity and depth of our aspirations for peace."[228] Eisenhower proposed that the United States and the Soviet Union give each other a complete blueprint of their military establishments and provide facilities for aerial reconnaissance of the other nation.[229] Speaking for many theologically moderate and liberal Christians, Kenneth W. Thompson praised the president's willingness to go anywhere to advance the cause of peace. He lamented, however, that summit participants had not seriously discussed the issues that "so painfully divided" the "unhappy postwar world."[230] Eisenhower resorted to "resounding moralisms and glittering generalities," Thompson protested, instead of discussing the "hard facts of the cold war."[231] Arguing that Eisenhower's actions did not match his rhetoric, the editors of Christian Century appealed to the president to "end our national schizophrenia and to commit all our energies to peace."[232] Although the Atoms for Peace and Open Skies initiatives did not produce any major arms reductions, they expressed Eisenhower's belief that the superpowers could identify "limited aspects of arms control" on which they agreed and then gradually "extend their cooperation to larger and more complex aspects."[233]

World War II taught Eisenhower two lessons that governed his approach to foreign affairs: America was morally superior to other nations, and dictatorships respected force more than ideals. Like most of the nation's leaders of his generation, he was convinced of U.S. moral preeminence.[234] America would triumph over its godless, immoral foe, the Soviet Union, Eisenhower contended, because it rested on spiritual and moral principles and defended democracy, a system of government that recognized human dignity and protected individual rights.[235] In waging ideological warfare with communism, Eisenhower sometimes contrasted the Soviet Union's material achievements with U.S. spiritual accomplishments. America's moral vitality was more impressive than Soviet missiles that hit the moon and orbited the sun. While communists put their faith in their triumphs in space, Americans put their faith in the "service of God and man." "Our Protestant beliefs and convictions," Eisenhower trumpeted, provided a sound basis for "our civilization and government."[236] Eisenhower castigated "Russia's hostility to free government—and to the religious faith" on which it "is built."[237] The free world, Eisenhower repeatedly insisted, must use spiritual, intellectual, and material weapons to defeat communism.[238] Caroline Pruden argues that Eisenhower's "basic distrust of the Soviet Union" hampered his efforts to "pursue genuine, sustained negotiations." Because he perceived the USSR as an aggressive, imperialist, atheistic power, he demanded "terms of inspection that the Soviets, equally fearful of espionage, would not accept."[239] The editors of the *Nation* bemoaned "the evangelical certainty" with which the president "described the 'forces of good and evil' now locked in mortal combat in the world." This characterization thwarted efforts to resolve disputes between the United States and the USSR. Unlike George Kennan, who devised the "containment" thesis, Eisenhower failed to realize that there had been "fault on both sides."[240]

Although working tirelessly to curb the growth of armaments, Eisenhower argued that peace would be assured only if the United States maintained enough military strength to deter Soviet aggression. Guided by the biblical principle that "When a strong man armed keepeth his palace, his goods are in peace," the president announced, the United States would remain strong and seek allies that observed the moral values embedded in the Judeo-Christian faith.[241] Some religious leaders, especially those holding more liberal theological perspectives, criticized his administration for spending too much on defense and continuing to test nuclear devices. During the 1956 campaign, the editors of *Christian Century* supported Stevenson's call for a ban on nuclear testing as a way to break the arms control deadlock, decrease the threat of radioactive fallout, prevent the spread of nuclear weapons, and enhance American prestige in Europe.[242] Eisenhower admired the World Council of Churches' resolutions calling for "universal enforcement of disarmament through the United Nations" and the elimination of atom and hydrogen bombs. However, this could not be achieved in a world where many people were "selfish and greedy and ignoble." While working for peace, America must be strong to ensure its safety and security.[243] The United States, joined by

Canada, France, and Britain, proposed in August 1957 that all nations suspend nuclear testing for a period of up to two years, but the Soviets rejected the offer. Although Eisenhower initially protested that unilaterally ending testing could cause America to fall behind the Soviets, the United States suspended testing in 1959 and 1960 and presented other limited test ban proposals to the Soviets, which they also refused to accept.

If spending on armaments could be reduced, Eisenhower argued, it would increase the world's security and could free money to feed, clothe, house, and educate the world's hungry, poor, illiterate people. He suggested that a "substantial percentage of the savings achieved by disarmament" be devoted to a "fund for world aid and reconstruction" to finance a war against "the brute forces of poverty and need."[244] The world's nations, he lamented, spent billions for weapons and "not one cent for peace."[245] Substantially lowering this amount would enable "every nation, great and small, developed and less developed, to advance the standards of living of its people."[246] In a world of finite resources, "every gun that is made, every warship launched, every rocket fired signifies, in the final sense, a theft from those who hunger and are not fed, those who are cold and are not clothed." By building more arms, he argued, the world was not simply squandering money. It was "spending the sweat of its laborers, the genius of its scientists, [and] the hopes of its children. The cost of one modern heavy bomber," Eisenhower calculated, was equivalent to the price of a "modern brick school in more than thirty cities" or "two fine, fully equipped hospitals."[247]

Convinced that world peace could not be achieved by the efforts of governments alone, Eisenhower applauded the activities of private citizens "working singly and together in organizations" to promote the understanding that was "so essential to the building of peace."[248] "To work with all our hearts for peace in the world," he told a Jewish audience in 1954, "is a task not alone for the solder, the diplomat, the scholar, the statesman—peace is a job for every one of us": businessman, clerk, farmer, doctor, engineer, minister, teacher, parent, and child.[249] Eisenhower urged Americans in 1959 to work as "individuals,... corporations, labor unions, professional societies, [and] communities to help peace and good will to prevail on earth."[250]

Despite his administration's eight years of unremitting efforts to achieve peace, Eisenhower admitted that its accomplishments were "almost negligible." Besides founding the International Atomic Energy Agency, his only other achievement had been to educate "all civilized peoples" about "the growing need for disarmament and the reasons for our failure to achieve tangible results."[251] Despite his pessimistic assessment, Eisenhower strengthened the NATO alliance and by visits to Africa, Asia, and Latin America showed that the United States "cared as much for those regions as the communists did."[252] By the end of his presidency, the United States was in a strong position economically and militarily, cold war tensions had been reduced, and despite all the turmoil in the world, American armies were not fighting any-where.[253] Yet by emphasizing the containment of communism and collective security, Eisenhower's administration passed to its successors "commitments that would outstrip American capabilities."[254]

The Republican powerfully and poignantly proclaimed his fears about the escalation of armaments and the cold war in his farewell address to the nation, delivered on January 17, 1961. "We face," he declared, "a hostile ideol-ogy, global in scope, atheistic in character, ruthless in purpose, and insidious in method." He warned Americans that this conflict would pressure the nation to spend increasingly larger sums to develop new and better weapons. To maintain peace and protect its freedom, the United States had built a huge military establishment, which ironically now threatened to create a garrison state that destroyed liberty. In words that would be the most quoted and remembered of his entire presidency, he asserted: "This conjunction of an immense military establishment and a large arms industry is new in the Amer-ican experience. The total influence—economic, political, even spiritual—is felt in every city, every statehouse, every office of the federal government. In the councils of government," he exhorted, "we must guard against the ac-quisition of unwarranted influence, whether sought or unsought, by the military-industrial complex." Two new dangers threatened liberty: "the conjunction of an immense military establishment and a large arms industry" and the federal government's domination of research.[255] Eisenhower urged Americans to avoid "plundering, for our own ease and convenience, the precious resources of tomorrow. We cannot mortgage the material assets of our grandchildren without risking the loss of their political and spiritual heritage." Eisenhower concluded his presidency the same way he began it—with a prayer. "We pray," he said, "that all peoples of all faiths, all races, [and] all nations may have their great human needs satisfied . . . ; that all who yearn for freedom may experience its spiritual blessings . . . ; that the scourges of poverty, disease and ignorance will be made to disappear from the earth; and that . . . all peoples will come to live together in a peace guaranteed by the binding force of mutual respect and love."[256]

Widely heralded as one of the most prophetic statements by an American leader in the nation's history and as comparable with Washington's Farewell Address, the speech expressed Eisenhower's frustration with his "inability to stop the waste, duplication and parochialism of the military."[257] His experi-ence as a general and the nation's commander in chief, coupled with his acclaim as a war hero and revered president, increased the speech's impact. Ironically, however, his administration did little to thwart America's growing tendency to consolidate military, corporate, scientific, and technological power.

Eisenhower's religious convictions are also evident in his Civil Rights policy. Although he declared in his first message to Congress in February 1953 that "we expect to make true and rapid progress in civil rights," he adopted a gradualist approach.[258] The Republican insisted in his memoirs that because of conviction, not political expediency, he had sought to steer a "difficult course between extremist firebrands and extremist diehards."[259] Moving faster, he maintained, would have caused the South to erupt into riots and bloodshed. Inflamed by *Brown v. Board of Education* (1954), Southerners began organizing White Citizens Councils, which by 1956, had 250,000 members committed to preventing integration. The president asked Billy Graham to help convince Southern ministers to support a "moderate," "sensible course of action" that steered a path between "the foolish extremists on both sides of the question."[260] He hoped the clergy would promote and publicize black progress and prevent quarrels rather than simply help pick up the pieces after "an unfortunate fight." Following their conversation in March 1956, Eisenhower wrote Graham that conciliation could produce "more lasting and stronger" results than could "force and conflict." He asked the evangelist to consider ways to increase the number of qualified blacks elected as city and county commissioners and school board members, to prod universities to base entrance to their graduate schools strictly on merit, and to develop plans to seat blacks and whites more efficiently on public transportation. He wanted ministers to discuss these matters in their pulpits, affirm the Catholic archbishop of Louisiana who had courageously desegregated the New Orleans parochial schools, and stress the racial progress the border states were making. This would pressure federal judges to make decisions that promoted greater racial justice.[261] Graham agreed that churches must exercise spiritual leadership on this crucial issue.[262] In June, Graham reported to Eisenhower that he had met with numerous prominent black and white pastors to persuade them to "take a stronger stand" for desegregation while still "demonstrating charity and, above all, patience." He had asked Southern religious leaders to tell the president how they planned to promote racial reform. If the Supreme Court went slowly and "the extremists on both sides" quieted down, Graham concluded, the nation could achieve a "peaceful social readjustment" within ten years.[263]

Eisenhower repeatedly exhorted religious, Civil Rights, and business leaders to encourage Americans to strive to better understand blacks and work to end discrimination. National Prohibition demonstrated that coercive laws could not produce racial progress; only education, persuasion, and personal example could do so.[264] Nevertheless, he rarely used his personal popularity or the prestige of his office to directly challenge citizens to work for racial justice. Instead, he urged blacks to be patient in their crusade for equal rights. Eisenhower hosted black leaders only once during his presidency. In their brief meeting with him in June 1958, Martin Luther King Jr., Roy Wilkins, and others failed to convince Eisenhower to use his "moral authority to persuade his fellow Americans that integration was right and just."[265] Because their long-standing patterns and the entrenched prejudices of their residents made most states and communities reluctant to end discriminatory practices, Eisenhower's emphasis on local activism rather than national initiatives did little to further Civil Rights progress.

More positively, the Republican completed the desegregation of the armed forces and barred discrimination on all federal property, including military bases, Veterans Administration hospitals, and facilities in the District of Columbia. Hoping to make Washington a model for the country, he worked to persuade owners of the city's hotels and movie theaters to serve blacks. He sponsored and signed the first Civil Rights act since 1870. Passed in 1957, this bill created a national nonpartisan Civil Rights commission, established a Civil Rights division in the Department of Justice, and struck down the laws and practices of Southern states that long had disenfranchised blacks. To enforce the Supreme Court decision integrating the schools, he sent federal troops to Little Rock, Arkansas, the first time a president had dispatched troops to the South since Reconstruction. A second Civil Rights act, passed in 1960, further strengthened black voting rights. As Pach and Richardson argue, however, his "actions were more symbolic than substantive, since they did little to ensure black access to the ballot box or to integrated schools."[266] When Eisenhower left office, only a small percentage of Southern blacks were registered to vote, few Southern schools were integrated, and most Southern restaurants, hotels, theaters, and buses remained segregated.

A Final Assessment

During his presidency, critics accused Eisenhower of reading Westerns and playing golf and bridge with wealthy capitalists while his associates ran the country in his name. Shortly before he left office, a story made the rounds about a Japanese toy called the Eisenhower doll: "You wind it and wind it and it doesn't do a blessed thing."[267] This "aging hero" allegedly "lacked the energy, motivation, and political skill" to significantly affect events and left important decisions to his subordinates.[268] This perspective of Eisenhower dominated the 1960s. A poll of American historians rated him an average president, and critics charged that he did not control his administration. Many argued that because of his political inexperience and dislike of politics, he had not understood complex national issues or functioned effectively as chief executive. Numerous scholars judged the Eisenhower administration to be "standpattist in domestic affairs, unimaginative in . . . foreign policy, and neglectful of the nation's defenses."[269] Eisenhower sought to improve public perceptions of his administration through his memoirs, *Mandate for Change, 1953–1956* (1963) and *Waging Peace, 1956–1961* (1965), but many reviewers criticized these books as "impersonal, officious, and less than candid."[270]

During the 1970s, revisionists began to offer more positive assessments of Eisenhower's presidency. The work of political scientist Fred Greenstein, published in the early 1980s and based on painstaking research, revolutionized scholarly perceptions of Eisenhower. He and others concluded that Eisenhower was very politically astute and made all of his administration's important decisions. Labeling his approach to governing "hidden-hand leadership," Greenstein argued that Eisenhower disguised the fact that he made the critical policy choices to avoid antagonizing either the conservative or moderate factions of the Republican Party and to remain above partisan controversy in order to preserve his personal popularity.[271] Accepting this interpretation, many recent analyses of Eisenhower's presidency contend that he "shrewdly used his power, often behind the scenes, to accomplish his purposes." Although not an intellectual or even well read, Eisenhower quickly digested information from his staff and penetrated to the core of issues. His extraordinary experience in world affairs, coupled with his exceptional analytical skills, enabled him to craftily "dissect the arguments of his associates" and direct his administration's policies.[272]

Scholars and journalists have criticized Eisenhower on other grounds. H. W. Brands argues that Eisenhower was "a prisoner of his popularity. On a number of occasions, when national interest demanded strong leadership and a willingness to risk contention," such as denouncing McCarthyism or pushing harder for arms control, Eisenhower failed to provide it. Robert Divine accuses the Kansan of "placing a greater premium on his adulation by the American people than on any particular achievement."[273] Eisenhower refused to "mount the bully pulpit," Brands maintains, "because it would have threatened his popularity" and led many to view him "as a soldier who had forsaken the true and noble call of duty for the base allure of political ambition."[274]

Why was Eisenhower so admired during the 1950s? Some point to the general's personal traits as the primary reason for his phenomenal popularity. He was a sincere, warm, unpretentious, dependable, confident, likable father figure who calmed Americans' anxieties about the cold war and the nuclear threat. Hundreds of ordinary citizens wrote the president each week to ask him to help them solve their personal problems or to answer their religious questions.[275] Others attribute Eisenhower's high public esteem to his impressive achievements. More than any other individual (except perhaps Franklin Roosevelt), he had defended America against autocracy and helped save Europe during some of its darkest days. In addition, during his presidential years, the United States enjoyed a baby boom, full employment, low inflation, a surfeit of consumer goods, countless technological innovations, the highest standard of living ever achieved by such a large number of people, and generally positive international relations.[276] Still others insist Eisenhower was so popular because he embodied the "authentic American center." He stood at the center of American politics and culture, and he incarnated its core habits and values. Because of his character and commitment to "Americanism, spiritual values, and moral crusades," he seemed to transcend politics.[277] Throughout his tenure in office, Eisenhower promoted this image by his style of leadership and dignified demeanor. He inspired a trust among ordinary Americans "that was as broad and deep as that of any president since George Washington."[278] He frequently compared himself with that other general-president, who transcended parties and factions and represented all the people.

Like many other Americans, Eisenhower preferred individualistic to collectivistic solutions to the nation's social problems, and he expressed the widespread belief that social progress depended more on changing human hearts than on altering social structures. He insisted that people's welfare was best advanced "not by government paternalism but by helping people help themselves."[279] Led by "those with strong moral motivation and spiritual resources," Americans could work together through families and voluntary associations to remedy all their social ills.[280]

Finally, most Americans found Eisenhower's personal faith attractive. He "was close to the moderate center of American theological thinking." His personal theology was orthodox, but he valued other religious perspectives. Like many other Americans, his faith was sincere and more experientially than intellectually grounded; it was meaningful but not very sophisticated or theologically astute. If Eisenhower's political philosophy and faith were more at home in turn-of-the-century Abilene than in "modern metropolitan America," so were those of millions of other Americans.[281]

Although few doubted the sincerity of Eisenhower's faith, some questioned its quality and political effect. They accused him of being unconcerned about the content of faith. To support this contention, these critics frequently quoted his statement made shortly after the 1952 election: "Our form of government has no sense unless it is founded in a deeply felt religious faith and I don't care what it is."[282] Others countered that Eisenhower was arguing that a public religion or widely held faith made free government possible. The latter perspective seems more plausible: Eisenhower did not maintain that the nature of religious belief made no difference but rather that all three major American faiths—Protestantism, Catholicism, and Judaism—supported the moral values and spiritual ideals on which the nation rested.

Some protested that Eisenhower personified America's shallow piety and embodied the worst aspects of its civil religion. Critics claimed that Eisenhower accentuated God's blessing and approval of America but rarely discussed God's disappointment or disapproval of its actions.[283] "His easy blend of individualistic pietism, secular optimism and strong patriotism," argued Ernest LeFever in 1956, "is perhaps the most popular and merchandisable product on the American market today." Some objected that

Eisenhower used religion to validate America's objectives. The president claimed that God was on the United States' side; he was "a source of strength, a weapon, a resource and a moral sanction for our purposes." Eisenhower seldom asked if we were "instruments of His purpose."[284] The president reduced religion, William Lee Miller complained, to an advantage and strength; it furnished a "wholesale endorsement of the aims and purposes of America."[285] Pierard and Linder conclude that Eisenhower's civil theology "emphasized God as the wellspring of individual and national strength, government as resting on a spiritual foundation, faith as a public virtue, and the utilitarian nature of religion in the apocalyptic struggles against communism."[286] Although Eisenhower, like Roosevelt, masterfully used the language of civil religion, he frequently went well beyond the conventions of this discourse and stressed God's control of the world and the importance of prayer, spiritual renewal, and obeying God's commandments.

Writing in the *New Republic* in 1954, R. W. B. Lewis charged that the "thin religiosity" that permeated many of the activities and ceremonies of the Eisenhower administration was one of its most effective defenses. This new religiosity was "a formidable weapon" that caused "serious strategic difficulties" for the administration's critics. Those who questioned the president were made to sound as though they "favored the instant abolition of Sunday Schools."[287]

Perhaps more than any other president, Eisenhower was closely connected with the religious climate and conditions of his era. Through his personal practices and religious rhetoric, much more than his administrative policies, Eisenhower prodded Americans to rededicate themselves to traditional moral values and the religious convictions of their forefathers. By repeatedly referring to God, religion, and spirituality in public addresses, arguing that spiritual revival was essential to national renewal, worshiping regularly, and supporting religious groups and activities, Eisenhower encouraged Americans to deepen their spiritual lives and improve their moral practices. As evidence of religious resurgence, people pointed to significant increases in church membership and attendance, evangelistic crusades, huge sales of religious books, religious programming on television, the immense popularity of religious films and songs, and prayer chains.[288] Those who wanted the nation to move in new, more "progressive" or radical theological directions or to reemphasize the social implications of the gospel were disappointed with both Eisenhower's faith and the nature of the decade's religious revival. To them, the revival was superficial, inspired by fear of nuclear holocaust, and overly concerned with external appearances and social acceptability, and it ignored America's pressing social problems.

To some historians, Eisenhower was more of a "hawk than a prince of peace." He devised a "military posture that made it almost impossible for the United States to fight anything short of nuclear war" and threatened to use nuclear weapons more often than Truman or any of his successors.[289]

Eisenhower admitted on numerous occasions that his greatest failure in foreign policy was that he had not improved relations with the Soviets or reduced the arms race. Nor had Communism been contained. It spread into Vietnam and more menacingly, Cuba, ninety miles from American shores. Moreover, Eisenhower's fervent "anti-Communism coupled with his penchant for seeing Communists wherever a social reform movement or a struggle for national liberation was under way" contributed to "his overthrow of popularly elected governments in Iran and Guatemala," to "over-commitment in Indochina, and to millions of residents of the Third World profoundly mistrusting the United States."[290] Others defend Eisenhower's record in foreign affairs. "For eight years," Robert Divine contends, "he kept the United States at peace, adroitly avoiding military involvement in the crises of the 1950s." Ambrose contends that he almost single-handedly slowed the pace of the arms race; refused to escalate defense spending; strengthened the NATO alliance; maintained generally positive relations with Arab states, Latin American republics, Japan, South Korea, and Formosa; and managed international crises effectively. Pach and Richardson praise Eisenhower for "framing defense issues in not just economic, but in moral terms."[291]

In his final State of the Union Address, the Republican declared that his administration had achieved its goal of increasing "the spiritual, moral and material strength of the nation." He pointed to ending the war in Korea, resolving crises in the Suez and Lebanon, deposing communist regimes in Guatemala and Iran, preserving the freedom of West Berlin, strengthening America's military defenses and space program, significantly improving its economy, developing the federal highway system, quadrupling the outlays for medical research, advancing black Civil Rights, greatly increasing funding for education, and broadening Social Security coverage.[292]

Pach and Richardson conclude that Eisenhower "used his power resourcefully—and often successfully—in domestic and foreign affairs" to accomplish his basic goals of peace and prosperity.[293] Despite his personal political conservatism and desire to limit the scope of the federal government and decrease the regimentation and bureaucracy of American society, Eisenhower's humanitarian concerns prodded him to extend the benefits of Social Security, ensure that all American children were vaccinated against polio, create the Department of Health, Education, and Welfare, expand health coverage through the concept of "vocational rehabilitation," increase federal aid to education and public housing, launch urban renewal, and take an interest in the plight of ordinary people.

To what extent was Eisenhower's presidential and personal behavior consistent with his professed religious faith? The United States, declared a Congregationalist pastor in 1955, was "exceedingly fortunate to have as President...a man of such moral integrity, courageous independence, and earnest purpose" as Eisenhower.[294] The editor of the Catholic journal

Commonweal insisted that the Republican had healed "old political wounds" and restored "a shattered unity of purpose" because he was "fair, judicious, honest, tolerant, reasonable, cautious, loyal, and reverent."[295] The editor of *U.S. News and World Report* claimed that Eisenhower had earned the tribute of Scripture, "Well done, thou good and faithful servant."[296] Many of Eisenhower's closest associates praised him as a man of principle who asked what was right for America rather than what was politically expedient.[297]

On the other hand, some accused Eisenhower of significant character flaws, most notably having a bad temper and being dishonest. Many testified that he could be moody and had a terrible temper that he rarely displayed in public. In his rage, Eisenhower often used profanity, including taking God's name in vain. Despite being highly esteemed for his integrity, Eisenhower, anxious to achieve an arms control agreement with Khrushchev, approved a series of "patently false cover stories" about American U-2 espionage flights over the Soviet Union.[298] Moreover, his desire not to divulge too much information, reveal administrative plans, or appear too much in control of the government led Eisenhower in press conferences to feign ignorance, try to confuse reporters, and even flatly deny knowing things he clearly did know. Arthur Schlesinger Jr. contends that the Eisenhower papers reveal a man who pretended to be above politics and politically innocent but in reality was "wily ... calculating, crafty, and unerringly self-protective" and who spoke incoherently to conceal his purposes. His belief that America's aims were righteous, Pach and Richardson conclude, led him to sanction "unsavory methods—covert intervention, assassination attempts—to frustrate Communist designs."[299] Brands argues that by using "covert and admittedly repugnant means" to wage the cold war, Eisenhower and his advisors engaged in actions that haunted America's conscience and eventually damaged its interests.[300] Writing in *Esquire* in 1967, Murray Kempton called the Kansan "the sneakiest, most cunning, most devious, most Machiavellian, and in some respects most treacherous, meanest President we've ever had."[301]

The most significant moral questions raised about Eisenhower's personal life concern his relationship with Kay Summersby of Ireland, who served on his staff during World War II. During the 1950s, detractors occasionally insinuated that they had had an affair during the war and that the general and his wife "stayed together only for appearances."[302] In a 1976 autobiography, *Past Forgetting: My Love Affair with Dwight David Eisenhower*, Summersby claimed that they had spent countless hours together, expressing their mutual passion by holding hands and kissing. On two occasions, they tried to have intercourse but failed because the general was impotent. All the evidence suggests that Summersby's story is fabricated. None of the people closest to Eisenhower in England believed at the time or later that they were romantically involved. Summersby offered no material evidence to substantiate her claim, and her story is filled with holes.[303]

In the final analysis, how genuine was Eisenhower's faith and how much did it influence his actions as president? Did he faithfully engage in public worship and use extensive religious rhetoric primarily to express his heartfelt convictions or mainly to gain political advantages during a decade of piety and religious renewal? The many individuals who testified that his faith was sincere and that his knowledge of the Bible was substantial typically had ulterior reasons for doing so: to promote their own organizations or causes or to make a president they liked look good. To what extent did the Republican understand Christian political philosophy? Clearly, Eisenhower did not have a well-developed biblical worldview grounded in extensive study of the Scriptures and Christian literature. No evidence indicates that he read works on how to apply Christian principles to political practice or policies or that he directly discussed this subject with experts or friends except on rare occasions. Was Eisenhower truly a deeply religious man as he claimed? Or was he a hypocrite who used the façade of religious piety to further his political purposes? Did he simply float on the religious tide of the decade and cultivate a reputation for religiosity to increase his personal popularity? Some claimed that he attended church primarily for public relations purposes (which many others strongly rebutted), a few protested the way he used civil religion, and William Lee Miller censured "piety along the Potomac." On the whole, though, Eisenhower's religious convictions or practices were little criticized during the 1950s. What did he truly believe about the nature of God, the deity of Christ, the atonement, the existence of heaven, and other fundamental Christian doctrines? Despite his many addresses, voluminous correspondence, and memoirs and the extensive analysis of his life and ideology by scholars of all sorts, we simply do not know. Was a scriptural worldview integral to his policy analysis, or was his frequent use of biblical principles and quotations window dressing designed to appeal to the prevailing mind-set and mood of the 1950s? In his memoirs of his presidential years, Eisenhower rarely explains how his faith had an impact on his work as the nation's chief executive. On the other hand, his commitment to prayer and church attendance (which continued to the end of his life), support of religious organizations and endeavors, and recurrent discussion of religious themes suggest that his faith was genuine and meaningful and that it helped shape his thinking and actions as president. Although his faith was authentic, not hypocritical or pretentious, it appears not to have been as central to Eisenhower's philosophy and persona as he apparently believed or wanted others to think.

CHAPTER EIGHT

John F. Kennedy:
The First Catholic President

I am not the Catholic candidate for president. I am the Democratic candidate for president who happens to be a Catholic.

Kennedy to the Greater Houston Ministerial Association, Sept. 12, 1960

The White House is not only the center of political leadership, it must be the center of moral leadership—a "bully pulpit" as Theodore Roosevelt described it.

Campaign speech, June 1960

I personally believe, as did the Founding Fathers, that religion is a vital aspect of the life of any people and conducive to the right ordering of civil affairs.

Kennedy to B. F. Skinner, Jan. 24, 1958

[L]et us go forth to lead the land we love, asking His blessing and His help, but knowing that here on earth God's work must truly be our own.

Inaugural Address, Jan. 20, 1961

THE CONTRAST BETWEEN the Republican who left office and the Democrat who succeeded him on January 20, 1961, could hardly have been greater. The nation's youngest elected president replaced the country's oldest one. Although Dwight D. Eisenhower and John F. Kennedy both fought in World War II, their temperaments, religious convictions, political philosophies, and approaches to the presidency differed markedly. They both attended church regularly while president and used religious rhetoric extensively in their speeches, especially in discussing their quest for world peace. Eisenhower, however, provided strong governmental support for the Judeo-Christian tradition, whereas Kennedy maintained a much stricter separation between church and state.

Both were very popular presidents. Serving two full terms, Eisenhower retired after a lengthy and impressive career of public service. Kennedy was struck down by an assassin's bullet in the prime of life, prompting national anguish and projections of what he might have accomplished. His vitality, idealism, powerful rhetoric, and charisma inspired many younger Americans to social activism and evoked comparisons with the legend of Camelot. Many insisted Kennedy would have led Americans to new heights had he lived.

Of all the presidents in this book, Kennedy is the most difficult to analyze. As the nation's only Catholic president, whose religious affiliation was a major issue in the 1960 election, he is central to any examination of religion and the presidency. Moreover, his assassination and funeral evoked a torrent of religious rhetoric, analysis, and emotion and reinforced the importance of civil religion in American society. On the other hand, his faith had much less influence on his thinking and policies than that of the other presidents examined. In addition, beneath his exuberant, commanding public persona were private vices that contradicted his Catholic faith.

Kennedy's Faith

Kennedy's mother, Rose, was a devout Catholic who attended mass every morning and maintained close relationships with many church leaders. She wanted her children to become committed Catholics and took them to mass every Sunday and all holy days, regularly discussed sermons with them, made them say grace at meals, listened to their nightly prayers, and required them to recite their catechism lessons each week.[1] Thomas Reeves argues that Rose implanted in her children a ritualistic form of Christianity "in which form mattered more than substance, public performance more than private conviction."[2] John had only one year of Catholic education at Canterbury, a prep school in Connecticut. At both Choate, an elite Episcopal preparatory school in Connecticut, and Harvard, he frequently attended mass, and in college he belonged to St. Paul's Catholic Club. Nevertheless, as a youth he did not appear to be interested in Catholic piety or devotional life.[3] Like many adolescents, Kennedy underwent a period of religious doubt. His sister Eunice explained that "he was always a little less convinced about some [religious] things than the rest of us." Nevertheless, his roommate at Choate reported, "Never can I remember Jack not saying his prayers on his knees every night before going to bed."[4] His roommate at the Navy PT training school in Melville, Rhode Island, contended that this uncertainty persisted during

Kennedy's young adult years.[5] Albert Menendez concludes that the future president made an intellectual accommodation with Catholicism before running for Congress, perhaps as a result of his combat experiences in World War II, his search for meaning in life, or his belief that an ex-Catholic could not be elected in Massachusetts.[6]

Lawrence Fuchs argues that Kennedy never showed "any special interest in Catholicism." Privately, he "displayed a remarkably candid irreverence toward ecclesiastical authorities."[7] Although appearing to have few deep religious convictions, Kennedy attended mass every Sunday. He told a friend that it was "one of the things I do for my father."[8] Biographer Hugh Brogan alleges that Kennedy "enjoyed good sermons."[9] Menendez argues that he had little intellectual interest in religion.[10] Theodore Sorensen, his long-time policy advisor and speechwriter, contends that he did not care "a whit for theology." "It is hard for a Harvard man to answer questions in theology," Kennedy wrote to a Catholic editor.[11] On the other hand, Father Albert Pereira of St. Stephen's Church in Middleburg, Virginia, claimed, based on conversations with Kennedy, that the president "displayed a remarkable awareness of the finer points of Catholic dogma."[12] Kennedy apparently believed in God as a supernatural force and accepted most traditional Catholic dogmas, but he rarely discussed these matters. Sorensen reports that Kennedy never talked about his views of God during the eleven years they worked closely together. Nor did Sorensen ever hear him pray aloud or see him "alter his religious practices for political convenience." Kennedy did not know or care about the religious beliefs of his staff. Yet Sorensen also insisted that the president never "downgraded his Catholic faith" or concealed his church attendance.[13]

Moreover, Sorensen reported that Kennedy resented the characterization of an early biographer that he was "not deeply religious," and some devout Christians insisted that the Democrat's faith was genuine and meaningful.[14] Kennedy was "a man of deep faith who knew how to pray," maintained Richard Cardinal Cushing, the archbishop of Boston, who married John and Jacqueline Bouvier in 1953, baptized their children, prayed at his inaugural, and performed the funeral for their infant son. Cushing insisted that Kennedy "felt his religion profoundly" and "never failed to put his confidence in the hands of the Unchanging God." He was as good a Catholic as he was an American. His "grace of style, his boundless courage, his patient suffering, his self-assurance and the warmth of his affection—all these were firmly rooted in a faith that was anchored ... truly in God Himself."[15] Brooks Hays, an eight-term Congressman from Arkansas and a dedicated Southern Baptist who served as Kennedy's liaison with Protestants, wrote to a citizen that the president was "a devout Christian whose dedication to the work of [o]ur Lord is beyond challenge."[16] In another letter, Hays declared that "his consciousness of Christian principles is evident in his every word and action."[17]

As a senator, Kennedy and his family attended the Holy Trinity Church in Georgetown, a parish of about eight hundred families. After he was elected president, people wondered where the Kennedys would worship. The White House was within the limits of another parish, St. Matthew's Cathedral, and Catholics were usually expected to worship at the church in the parish where they resided. Kennedy spokesmen suggested that this may not be prudent, however, because St. Matthew's was very near Washington's hotels and shopping district and therefore more likely to attract large numbers of tourists who wanted to see the president. This issue proved to be moot: Kennedy spent few weekends at the White House and thus rarely worshiped at either church.[18] The Kennedys bought a country home near Middleburg, Virginia, and while there on the weekends, attended St. Stephen's Church.[19] They also worshiped quietly at local parishes in Hyannis Port, Massachusetts, and Palm Beach, Florida. Although Eisenhower's church attendance often attracted major media attention, Kennedy's usually did not, largely because he considered it a private act and strongly discouraged publicity.

Shortly after his election, a close friend told *U.S. News* that as a senator, Kennedy went to church every week, prayed regularly at night, went to confession, and fasted during Lent. "He has a solid religious commitment, but it is not the ostentatious kind." Kennedy spokespersons said that the president would continue to faithfully attend mass, go to confession, and observe the Catholic practice of not eating meat on Fridays. Trying to alleviate the fears of some Protestants, they emphasized that in the confessional booth Catholics were required to divulge only actions that violated the Ten Commandments or Christ's teachings, and thus Kennedy would not have to disclose any information pertaining to his work as president.[20]

In responding to letters from ordinary Americans, Kennedy frequently testified to his faith. "I rely upon God's guidance," he wrote in October 1961, "and I believe that one of America's greatest strengths is its spiritual faith."[21] Kennedy told the audience at the presidential prayer breakfast in 1963 that "all of us believe in and need prayer." He professed to be very moved by people's assurances that they were praying for him.[22] Kennedy often thanked citizens for their prayers, which he declared were a "source of help and inspiration" in discharging his duties.[23] Authors Hugh Brogan and Jim Bishop claim that Kennedy prayed frequently.[24] Cushing asserted that Kennedy prayed every night before he went to bed.[25] In an effort to emphasize his faith, some Catholics circulated the story that Kennedy, who often had his right hand in his pocket, kept a rosary there, which he turned to in times of crisis.[26] Kennedy often stressed his need of God's aid. At the Springfield, Illinois, Armory in October 1960, he quoted Lincoln's farewell speech to his friends in that town: "Without the assistance of the Divine Being . . . I cannot succeed. With that assistance, I cannot fail." In February 1961, Kennedy asserted that every president had "placed special reliance upon his faith in God" and had "taken comfort and courage when told . . . that the Lord 'will be with thee. He will not fail thee or forsake thee.' "[27]

The morning of his inauguration, Kennedy went alone to mass at Holy Trinity Church. His mother later wrote that "he wanted to start his presidency by offering his mind and heart . . . to Almighty God, and asking His blessing as he began his great duties."[28] Kennedy invited four religious leaders to pray at his inauguration: a Catholic priest, a rabbi, a Greek Orthodox priest, and a Disciples of Christ minister.[29] Yet when he placed his left hand on the family Bible and swore to uphold the Constitution, he was thinking, he confided to Tip O'Neill that evening, "how the hell" did George Kara, a powerful Boston businessman, manage to procure a seat right behind the Kennedy family.[30] For his inaugural address, Kennedy and Sorensen obtained lists of potential biblical quotations from Billy Graham and Isaac Franck, the director of Washington's Jewish Community Center.[31] In his address, he urged both the free and communist worlds to heed the command of Isaiah to " 'undo the heavy burden . . . [and] let the oppressed go free.' " He challenged Americans to rejoice in hope and be "patient in tribulation" while fighting "tyranny, poverty, disease and war." He concluded by declaring, "[L]et us go forth to lead the land we love, asking His blessing and His help, but knowing that here on earth God's work must truly be our own."[32]

Richard Hutcheson argues that Kennedy played the "role of 'high priest of the public religion' with consummate grace." He quoted the Bible frequently and appropriately and did nothing to offend Protestants or Jews.[33] Kennedy spoke at all three presidential prayer breakfasts during his years in office. He called the Bible "the foundation upon which the great democratic traditions and institutions of our country stand." The president hoped all Americans would "turn to the Bible and refresh mind and soul with the truth which undergirds personal integrity and fortifies the life of the nation." In a letter commending National Bible Week, he proclaimed that by following the Bible's "invaluable guideposts," the United States could be a "shining example and symbol of human liberty and social justice."[34]

Writing in the *Nation* in 1964, Thomas J. Fleming claimed that trying to identify what was uniquely Catholic about Kennedy's philosophy and style was "a sterile and futile pursuit because . . . there was nothing uniquely Catholic" about his public life. Kennedy had smashed "the illusion that there is a 'Catholic' way of thinking about everything—not merely religion. The complex apparatus of scholastic philosophy . . . was totally foreign to Kennedy's mind."[35] James Wolfe concurred: "Kennedy's fidelity to his church seemed to be one of identification, affiliation, and ritual observance rather than one of thought or worldly action." Considering church teaching irrelevant to politics and having little personal faith, Kennedy sought to achieve a "technically based consensus" to direct politics, similar to the one that guided the scientific community.[36] John Cogley, editor of *Commonweal*, took a different position.

When Kennedy ran for the presidency, some were disappointed that such an atypical Catholic spoke for their community. They were "as uncomfortable with Kennedy's pragmatism as he was with the scholastic-flavored thought of the Catholic universities." Kennedy, Cogley maintained, would never be mistaken for a saint, "but he was a man of faith and of steady, unspectacular loyalty to his Church." Like leading Protestant theologian Reinhold Niebuhr, Kennedy "instructed the nation on the responsible use of power." His approach recognized "the two foundations of Catholic political thought: an appreciation of power . . . and . . . the pre-eminence of reason."[37]

Kennedy's private behavior, especially his vulgarity, sexual infidelity, and deceit, differed sharply from his public persona and violated Christian moral teachings. "Kennedy uses profanity with the unconcern of a sailor," wrote a *Look* magazine reporter.[38] Sorensen admitted that Kennedy's language and humor were often "coarse in private conversation."[39] In a 1975 book, Benjamin Bradlee defended the president's vulgarity as common among those whose "vocabularies were formed in the crucible of life in the World War II Navy."[40] Besides using crude sexual language, Kennedy repeatedly took God's name in vain.[41] Bradlee insisted that Kennedy was also "exceedingly vain . . . penurious, insensitive, spiteful . . . and extremely manipulative. He slipped secret government documents to reporters in return for favors, got drunk . . . and denigrated liberals."[42]

Kennedy's many sexual partners while living in the White House are well documented. He had affairs with film stars Marilyn Monroe and Jayne Mansfield, aspiring actresses such as Judith Campbell, White House employees, burlesque queens, and socialites such as Florence Pritchett. He also frequently had sexual relations with casual acquaintances or total strangers.[43] Strong evidence indicates that Kennedy discussed sensitive national security issues with some sexual partners and that his affairs made him vulnerable to manipulation by J. Edgar Hoover, Teamster Union leader James Hoffa, and mobsters who had relationships with Kennedy's paramours or knowledge of his activities.[44]

Throughout his life, Kennedy carefully covered up not only his sexual indiscretions but also his serious health problems. Throughout his presidency, Kennedy was portrayed to the public as a paragon of good health, whereas in fact he suffered from Addison's disease, major back problems, gastric disorders, and partial deafness in his right ear. To ease his pain, Max Jacobson, a New York physician known as "Dr. Feel Good," regularly injected the president with amphetamines. Although legal at the time, they involved numerous risks—hyperactivity, impaired judgment, hypertension, addiction, and even psychosis.[45]

Although he violated several basic biblical teachings in his private life, Kennedy frequently quoted the Bible and used scriptural allusions in his addresses, especially to illuminate such themes as courage, integrity, righteousness, God's guidance of history, and human dependence on God. Some contend either that his speechwriters supplied these materials or that Kennedy used them because they had rhetorical value and civil religion demanded them.[46] Cushing, by contrast, insisted that Kennedy was "a great reader of the Bible." His many scriptural references in his public addresses, Cushing added, were a "vital and integral" "part of the man himself."[47]

Like other presidents, Kennedy publicly professed "belief in a benevolent God" who looked "favorably on the new Zion of the United States."[48] The sovereign God used America to fulfill his purposes. Shortly before he assumed office, he declared, "I have been guided by the standard of John Winthrop, set before his shipmates on the flagship Arabella 331 years ago, as they, too, faced the task of building a new government in a new and perilous frontier. 'We must always consider,' he said, 'that we shall be as a city upon a hill—the eyes of all people are on us.' "[49] "The guiding principle and prayer of this Nation," he declared, "has been, is now, and shall ever be 'In God We Trust.' "[50]

Like many of his predecessors, Kennedy emphasized America's religious heritage and insisted that God had commissioned the United States to promote freedom around the world. Faith in Almighty God, he contended, "was a dominant power in the lives of our Founding Fathers."[51] Kennedy urged Americans to "dwell upon the deep religious convictions of those who formed our nation" and remember that many of the nation's leaders had "relied upon Almighty God for vision and strength of purpose."[52] Almost every public document in American history, he claimed, had recognized "our obligation to God."[53] He asserted in his inaugural address that "the rights of man come not from the generosity of the state but from the hand of God."[54] "We cannot have liberty ourselves, much less insure its success in the world," he wrote to a Jewish organization, "unless we also partake of the spirit of the Lord, which proclaims truth, justice, and charity of all men toward all men."[55] In his 1963 State of the Union Address, Kennedy trumpeted, "With thanks to Almighty God for seeing us through a perilous passage, we ask His help anew in guiding the 'Good Ship Union.' "[56] In his second State of the Union message, he asked God to "watch over the United States" as it strove to fulfill its mission to defend freedom. Religious freedom, Kennedy added, meant little unless it was accompanied by religious conviction.[57] In calling for a national day of prayer in 1961, Kennedy emphasized that members of the Constitutional Convention understood "that without the concurring aid of Providence they would succeed in political building 'no better than the builders of Babel.' " Americans, he added, must be "conscious of our continuing need to bring our actions under the searching light of Divine Judgment."[58] Kennedy frequently urged Americans to be grateful for the blessings God had showered on them.[59] He saw value in all religious traditions and lauded religious toleration.[60] "I firmly believe," Kennedy wrote, "that our religious and cultural pluralism has been . . . one of our principal sources of strength."[61]

Kennedy sometimes used religious language to describe his personal sense of mission. In accepting the Democratic nomination for the presidency, he proclaimed, "Recall with me the words of Isaiah: 'They that wait upon the Lord...shall mount up with wings like eagles; they shall run, and not be weary....' "[62] Speaking in Frankfurt, Germany, in June 1963 about the importance of maintaining peace and spreading freedom, Kennedy quoted Lincoln's remarks before the Civil War broke out, " 'I know there is a God. I see a storm coming. If he has a part and place for me, then I am ready.' "[63] He especially liked the counsel of nineteenth-century Boston pulpiteer Phillips Brooks: "Do not pray for tasks equal to your powers. Pray for powers equal to your task."[64]

The Election of 1960

Like the election of 1928, the one in 1960 pitted a Catholic Democrat against a Republican Quaker who had been a key part of the previous administration and had substantial ties to the West Coast. The issue of religion was as controversial and acrimonious in 1960 as it had been in 1928. In the late 1940s and 1950s, most Catholics and Protestants disagreed over federal funding for parochial schools, Sunday blue laws, birth control statutes, divorce laws, and the propriety of sending an ambassador to the Vatican. In 1948, the National Catholic Welfare Conference declared, "If tomorrow Catholics constituted a majority of our country, they would not seek a union of church and state. They would then, as now, uphold the Constitution...." Despite this statement, many Protestants remained unconvinced that Catholic leaders viewed the separation of church and state the same way they did. Because Catholics were a quarter of the American population and seemed loyal not to a subculture within the United States (like the Amish or Jehovah's Witnesses) but to a foreign-based church, many Protestants considered them much more threatening than other religious minorities. In 1949, Unitarian Paul Blanchard published the first of his five books on the subject, *American Freedom and Catholic Power*, alleging that Catholics threatened to destroy "the American way of life." According to Blanchard, the church's views on medicine, education, marriage, divorce, and censorship were adverse to American liberty. He claimed that individuals could not be good Catholics and believe in the primacy of individual conscience, which was a crucial element in the success of democratic societies.[65] During the 1950s, three Jesuits—John Courtney Murray, Gustave Weigel, and Robert Drinan—took the lead in rebutting these charges and revising Catholic positions on church-state issues and interreligious dialogue.[66]

Kennedy's quest to gain the Democratic vice presidential nomination in 1956 provoked new fears among Protestants about how Catholics viewed civic power. Several factors prevented him from garnering the nomination—his youth and unimpressive record in the Senate, the opposition of Lyndon Johnson and Hubert Humphrey, and the relatively small number of electoral votes in Massachusetts—but none was as important as his faith.[67] Some Democratic leaders feared that placing a Catholic on the ticket would contribute to its defeat. Discussion of the issue became more intense after Kennedy announced he was a candidate for the presidency in 1959. In an interview in *Look* magazine in March, Kennedy declared that no matter what religion they professed, officeholders were bound "to uphold the Constitution... including the First Amendment and the strict separation of church and state." He insisted that he firmly opposed appointing an ambassador to the Vatican and giving federal aid to parochial schools (both of which he had supported as a congressman), prompting the Jesuit weekly *America*, the Paulist *Catholic World*, the liberal lay Catholic journal *Commonweal*, and many other Catholic periodicals to accuse him of being a poor Catholic, a poor politician, and a poor moralist.[68] Kennedy told James MacGregor Burns, "My faith is a personal matter and... it is impossible that my obligation as one sworn to uphold and defend the constitution could be changed in any manner by anything the Pope could say or do."[69] In dozens of letters to concerned individuals, Kennedy stated, "As a public official, sworn to uphold the Constitution, I have no obligation to any private institution, religious or otherwise. My obligation is to my conscience and the public good."[70]

Most Jews and many Protestants applauded Kennedy's views on the separation of church and state, but some Protestant spokesmen protested that his views were too secular. To James Pike, the Episcopal bishop of California, Kennedy seemed to "represent the point of view of a thoroughgoing secularist, who really believes that a man's religion and his decision-making can be kept in two watertight compartments." Charles Hayes wrote that while two other Democratic candidates, Protestants Hubert Humphrey and Stuart Symington, affirmed the connection between their beliefs and political positions, Kennedy offered a "defensive, almost apologetic assurance" that he would be "a good public official in spite of his Christian commitment."[71] To Lutheran Martin Marty, an editor of *Christian Century*, the Democrat was "spiritually rootless and politically almost disturbingly secular."[72]

In April 1960, Kennedy tackled the religious issue in a speech to the American Society of Newspaper Editors. Every contender for the 1960 Republican and Democratic nominations, he alleged, was "dedicated to the separation of church and state, to the preservation of religious liberty, to the end of religious bigotry, and to the total independence of the officeholder from any form of ecclesiastical dictation." "I want no votes solely on the account of my religion," he insisted. "Any voter, Catholic or otherwise, who feels another candidate would be a superior President should support that candidate." "I have made it clear," he added, "that I would neither veto nor sign... a bill on any basis except what I considered to be the public interest without regard to my private religious views." "Are we going to admit to the world," he concluded, "that a Jew can be elected mayor of Dublin, a Protestant can be chosen Foreign Minister of France, a Moslem can serve in the Israeli Parliament—but a Catholic cannot be President of the United States?"[73]

The pivotal event in Kennedy's capturing the Democratic nomination was his decisive defeat of Hubert Humphrey in May in West Virginia, a state where only 4 percent of the population was Catholic. Kennedy effectively dealt with the religious issue, inflamed by his competitor's use of "Give Me That Old-Time Religion" as his theme song. "Nobody asked me," he declared, "if I was a Catholic when I joined the United States Navy." In the oath of office, he explained, the president swore to "support the separation of church and state." If he broke that pledge, he committed a "crime against the Constitution" and a "sin against God."[74]

Before Kennedy's nomination, both evangelical and mainline Protestant leaders cautioned citizens about electing a Catholic chief executive. They frequently emphasized that the pope had never renounced his authority over civil rulers.[75] Could a Roman Catholic layman freely carry out his duties as president, asked John Mackay, the former president of Princeton Theological Seminary, and remain "in good . . . standing in his communion?" The decisive question a Catholic candidate must answer was: What would he do if he had to choose between a mandate of his church on a specific issue and what he as a public servant believed to be right?[76] A Baptist minister claimed that a Catholic president would "be obliged to put the Pope ahead of his country."[77] Kennedy also faced significant opposition from Catholic politicians and religious leaders. Many Democratic governors and Congressmen feared that by accentuating the religious issue and inflaming Protestant prejudices, Kennedy's candidacy would make it harder for other Catholic candidates to win. Some Catholic leaders, most notably Francis Cardinal Spellman of New York and James Cardinal McIntyre of Los Angeles, disliked Kennedy's political liberalism. Other members of the hierarchy thought that a Protestant president would do more to advance their interests than Kennedy, who would be inhibited by his desire to prove his fairness.[78] Their opposition prompted Kennedy's colorful complaint, "Now I understand why Henry VIII set up his own church."[79]

During the campaign, most mainline Protestant denominations and journals did not take any position on the election and left the matter up to individual members. *Christian Century*, for example, argued that it was far more important to examine a candidate's record in public office and personal sensibilities and sympathies than it was "to scrutinize his religious affiliation."[80] In October, it evenhandedly featured pro and con articles on Kennedy's candidacy. Charles Andrews argued that a liberal Catholic president would be better able to deal with the pressures from the hierarchy of his church than would a Protestant.[81] Harold Bosley countered that until Rome gave "her official blessing to religious freedom," Protestants had "genuine cause for concern" about electing a Catholic president.[82]

Many evangelical and fundamentalist Protestant leaders, however, strongly opposed Kennedy's candidacy. Some asserted that a Catholic president could not be independent from the pope, others disliked Kennedy's stands on religious issues, and still others denounced his political liberalism.[83] Despite Kennedy's many assurances, they questioned whether he truly could resist pressures from church leaders, often emphasizing that he reneged on a promise to speak at an interfaith event in Philadelphia in 1947 after the Archbishop of Philadelphia told him not to do so.[84] Bob Jones, Carl McIntire, and Harvey Springer, the cowboy evangelist of the Rockies, issued "vocal and often vicious anti-Catholic propaganda."[85] Other Protestants distributed millions of pamphlets that proclaimed "Is Catholic Control Possible in America?" "How the Roman Catholic Church Would Change the Constitution," "Catholic Political Power vs. Religious Liberty," and "Can Roman Catholics Be Loyal Both to America and the Vatican?"[86] Hundreds of ministers, including prominent evangelical pastors Harold John Ockenga of Park Street Congregational Church in Boston and W. A. Criswell of First Baptist Church in Dallas, preached sermons questioning whether Kennedy could avoid "church domination" and urging congregants to vote for Nixon.[87] A "converted Catholic priest" insisted that Kennedy's claim that he was free of Rome was "either ignorance, wishful thinking, or a bold-face lie."[88] Although Kennedy had pledged to honor the separation of church and state, the Catholic Church would not allow him to carry out his own desires, warned the editor of *Eternity* magazine. Its leaders had made it "unmistakably clear" that he must be a Catholic first and president second in matters involving the church.[89] In an article in *Christianity Today*, distributed as a pamphlet by Protestants and Other Americans United for Separation of Church and State (POAU), C. Stanley Lowell predicted that if Catholics became a numerical majority and gained political control, they would make Catholicism the nation's official religion, restrict Protestant worship, prohibit evangelistic services, and forbid criticism of the Catholic Church in print or on the air.[90] At their annual meetings, the National Association of Evangelicals, the Church of God, and the Southern Baptist Convention expressed similar fears.[91] Even Charles Clayton Morrison, the long-time editor of *Christian Century* and usually a voice of moderation, insisted in *Christianity Today* that contemporary democratic societies faced "two powerful monarchical" competitors—"the Communist Dictatorship and the Infallible Papacy"—and argued that Kennedy's allegiance to the Constitution "would be qualified by his prior and equally sacred allegiance to another State."[92] In a confidential letter to Eisenhower, Billy Graham urged the president to "stump the country" on behalf of Nixon.[93] Graham resisted strong pressures to explicitly endorse Nixon, but five days before the election, he gave an invocation at a Nixon rally in Columbia, South Carolina, and the next day he appeared with Nixon and Eisenhower at a campaign stop in Pittsburgh.[94] A group of 150 Protestant ministers, including Norman Vincent Peale, well-known author of *The Power of Positive Thinking*, and Daniel Poling, editor of *Christian Herald*, issued a public statement on September 7 questioning whether a Catholic president could successfully resist pressures from the Catholic hierarchy.[95]

Although this statement drew intense criticism from other Protestants, it prompted Kennedy to gamble: He decided to directly discuss the religious issue at a speech on September 12 before the Greater Houston Ministerial Association.[96] Hoping he could satisfy the qualms of Protestants while not antagonizing Catholics, Kennedy sought to counter religious objections to his candidacy and convince Americans that he would respect the separation of church and state. He insisted that no Catholic prelate should tell a Catholic president how to act and that no Protestant minister should tell his parishioners for whom to vote. The United States, he argued, was not officially Catholic, Protestant, or Jewish. No public official should request or accept "instructions on public policy from the Pope, the National Council of Churches or any other ecclesiastical source." Religious bodies must not try to impose their "will directly or indirectly upon the general populace or the public acts of its officials." He asked prospective voters to "judge me on the basis of my 14 years in the Congress—on my declared stands against an ambassador to the Vatican [and] against unconstitutional aid to parochial schools." Kennedy protested the widespread dissemination of printed materials that used quotations, often out of context, from Catholic leaders, usually from other countries and centuries, to argue that the Catholic Church opposed the separation of church and state. These publications also ignored the 1948 statement by the American bishops endorsing the concept, which reflected the views of almost all American Catholics. "I do not speak for my church on public matters," he assured the audience, and "the church does not speak for me." If elected, he would decide issues "in accordance with what my conscience tells me to be the national interest and without regard to outside religious pressures or dictates."[97]

Despite such guarantees, many Protestants remained unconvinced, and the religious issue did not disappear. Many pastors made a last-ditch effort on Reformation Sunday, October 30, to persuade parishioners not to vote for Kennedy, but others used the occasion to argue that religious bigotry, not Catholicism, was the problem.[98] Throughout the campaign, the National Conference of Christians and Jews spearheaded efforts to eliminate religious prejudice, especially through its "Standards for Decent Political Campaigning."[99] Meanwhile, Kennedy's staff tried to use the issue of Kennedy's religion to attract Catholic, Jewish, and African American voters, while the Nixon campaign persistently refused to discuss the Democratic senator's faith to avoid being labeled religious bigots.[100]

Others offered a very different perspective of Kennedy and Nixon. Church historian Winthrop Hudson complained that their religious convictions did not differ significantly. Their faith had "been shaped more by the contemporary cultural climate than by any church." Both candidates reflected "the general cultural conviction" that although religion was a good thing, it was "a purely private affair which had few implications for the political order." Nixon frankly admitted he was not an orthodox Quaker, and Catholic theologians freely acknowledged that Kennedy was not a conventional Catholic and insisted that if he had been educated in Catholic schools, his policies would be more in accord with church doctrine. Both men insisted that the major religious division was between those who believed in God and those who did not. "Presumably it makes little difference what God one believes in," Hudson complained. They both reduced God to "an empty symbol" and made religion "irrelevant to the issues of our common life."[101] Echoing this judgment, James Wall, the editor of *Christian Century*, called Kennedy's speech in Houston the "paradigmatic modern moment" for the nation's academic, media, and political elites who considered religion to be a negative influence on government. The Democrat assured the nation's cultural arbiters, "the protectors of society's secular faith," that he would not base his public policies on his personal faith.[102] Reinhold Niebuhr added that both Kennedy and Nixon were "too ambitious politically" to candidly discuss the world's major problems.[103]

Kennedy won the electoral vote 303 to 219, but he received only about 120,000 more popular votes than Nixon, out of 68 million cast. Although many factors determined the outcome, analysts conclude that the religious issue played a major role. In 1960, there were fourteen Northern states, with a combined 261 electoral votes (only seven less than needed for victory), in which Catholic voters were numerous enough to decide the outcome. Many Catholic Republicans voted for Kennedy, helping him capture most of these key states. On the other hand, Kennedy's religion significantly reduced his vote in the South and the Midwest, as Protestants who normally voted Democratic defected. In the final analysis, Kennedy's religious affiliation decreased his popular tally but helped him win the decisive electoral vote.[104] As Thomas Carty puts it, "many Catholics voted to overturn the unwritten law that no Catholic could occupy the White House."[105] After the election, Billy Graham predicted that Kennedy's election would help improve Protestant-Catholic relations and declared it "proved that there was not as much religious prejudice in the United States as many people feared."[106] Other Protestant, Catholic, and Jewish leaders echoed this judgment.[107] The result of the election underscored the point that religious pluralism was a political and social reality in the United States.

Kennedy's Relations with Religious Constituencies

Throughout his presidency, Kennedy's staff worked hard to maintain positive relations with Catholics, Protestants, and Jews and in some ways were more successful with the latter two groups. During the early 1960s, American Catholicism was undergoing cataclysmic changes, as reflected by Vatican II. During his tenure in office, Kennedy met with numerous Catholic groups and leaders, spoke to several Catholic groups, and often praised papal encyclicals and church teaching.[108] When Pope John XXIII died in June 1963, Kennedy praised "his wisdom, compassion, and kindly strength" in fulfilling "the highest work of any man": protecting and carrying on "the deepest spiritual heritage of the race."[109] Kennedy argued that the pope's encyclical *Pacem in Terris* provided a "penetrating analysis" of the "great problems" of social welfare, human rights, disarmament, international order, and peace that demonstrated that Christianity could provide "counsel on public affairs" that was "of value to all people of good will." He pointed out, however, that statements by Protestant denominations and the World Council of Churches had expressed similar convictions and aspirations.[110] Kennedy met briefly with Paul VI shortly after the new pontiff was elected.

Despite these actions, the Catholic hierarchy did not enjoy as close a relationship with Kennedy as either he or they had hoped. Controversy began early, prompted by Fletcher Knebel's article, "The Bishops versus Kennedy," published in *Look Magazine* in May 1961. Catholic leaders repudiated Knebel's claim that the American bishops had opposed Kennedy's election and continued to embarrass him after his election. The Bureau of Information of the Archdiocese of New York declared that although the bishops disagreed with Kennedy's position on federal aid to education, they were pleased by the president's general conduct in office.[111]

Kennedy's stance on federal aid to parochial education produced the most problems in his relationship with Catholics. The bill the president sent to Congress in 1961, requesting $2.3 billion over the next three years to construct, operate, and maintain public schools and pay teachers' salaries, excluded sectarian schools. The U.S. Catholic Conference and most Catholics, both liberal and conservative, opposed the bill. Although almost half of Catholic children were currently attending parochial schools without public support, Cardinal Spellman protested that passing this bill would destroy Catholic education in America. "Of what value is the right of parental freedom in education," the editors of *America* asked, "if exercise of that right has been priced out of existence by massive Federal grants to one school system to the detriment of others?"[112] Calling Kennedy's understanding of the Constitution "dubiously narrow," the editors of *Commonweal* insisted that "a good Constitutional case can be made ... for certain kinds of aid to private education" and charged that "denial of such aid amounts to an injustice." Many other Catholics, however, approved of Kennedy's position, insisting that the needs of public schools took precedence over parochial ones.[113] Cardinal Cushing, Kennedy's most loyal Catholic supporter, supported the bill, arguing that federal aid to parochial schools would bring government control and secularization. Kennedy's aides strove to persuade Catholic opponents that his "proposals were sound, constitutional, and in no way anti-Catholic."[114] Federal funds, they insisted, could be used to pay for school lunches, health services, and transportation, but not for direct educational expenses. Most Protestant denominations and the National Education Association opposed providing federal aid to parochial schools. Speaking for most Protestants, *Christian Century* alleged that the bill did not discriminate against Catholics and accused them of "demanding not equality but preference and patronage."[115] A Southern Baptist Convention resolution praised the president for following the Constitution and "not giving federal aid to church schools."[116] *Christianity Today, Christian Herald,* and a numerous other Protestant journals all commended Kennedy for resisting strong pressure from the Catholic hierarchy.[117]

The editors of the Jesuit journal *America* concluded that Kennedy's conduct toward his church was "more or less" what might have been expected from any Catholic president "in a land largely dominated, in a cultural sense, by a strong residual Protestant tradition." Nevertheless, they complained that unlike Franklin Roosevelt, Kennedy had not sought "the advice, assistance, companionship, and friendship of highly placed Catholic dignitaries." They protested that Kennedy's relationship with his own church had been rather negative and that his approach to Protestants was politically motivated.[118] They could have added that Kennedy had relatively few Catholics on his staff (far fewer than Nixon) and had not appointed a significant number of core-ligionists to major administrative posts. Moreover, quietly but significantly, the federal government increased its support of birth control and population control by expanding research grants, cooperating with United Nations efforts, and furnishing information to nations requesting it. Others agreed that Kennedy was less supportive of the Catholic political agenda than any Protestant president would have been. Many Catholics were upset, but not surprised, that Kennedy did not send an ambassador to the Vatican.

Because of shrewd public relations, his staunch commitment to the separation of church and state, and his staff's attention to their concerns, Kennedy enjoyed generally good relations with most Protestants, despite the opposition of many of them to his election. Brooks Hays, president of the Southern Baptist Convention from 1957 to 1959, served as a special assistant to the president for intergovernmental affairs.[119] In this capacity, he responded to articles and editorials about the Kennedy administration in Protestant journals, answered correspondence on religious matters, met with Protestant leaders, and gave dozens of speeches to religious groups, often stressing the moral aspects of various Kennedy programs.[120] He met with the pope and made a guest appearance on the *Jack Paar Show*. Hays regularly apprised the president about how various Protestant groups viewed his administration.[121] He corresponded with many Protestant leaders and pointed out that "the overwhelming majority" of Kennedy's appointments to federal courts were Protestants.[122] Hays also regularly met with religious groups in Washington to discuss their concerns.[123] Kennedy sometimes personally hosted Protestant delegations and spoke to a number of Protestant groups.[124] Billy Graham promised Kennedy privately that if he won the election, he would give the Democrat his "wholehearted support." A few days before the inauguration, they played golf, had lunch together, and discussed spiritual matters in Palm Beach, Florida. They met a few other times and even discussed going to Latin America together, but their correspondence was meager, and Graham provided no substantive counsel to the president. The evangelist's "public critique of the inaugural festivities—too much liquor, fine clothes and night life"—instead of "soberness, repentance, prayer, and faith in God" undoubtedly dampened his relationship with the new president.[125]

Numerous Protestants, including Glenn Archer, executive director of POAU, who opposed Kennedy's election because of fears he would not uphold the separation of church and state, professed delight at how he had handled this issue.[126] E. S. James, editor of the *Baptist Standard*, declared that Kennedy had "disillusioned many of us who felt that a Roman Catholic could not make a good President" and praised his political appointments and rigid adherence to the separation of church and state.[127] Kennedy had "compiled a better record" on this issue, editorialized *Christian Century*, than any other president in the past thirty years.[128] A few Protestants, however, continued to express concern. The Bible Presbyterian Church protested Kennedy's sending official representatives to attend the opening sessions of Vatican II, a letter to the pope commending this council, and Lyndon Johnson to visit the pontiff.[129] The National Association of Evangelicals urged the president in January 1963 to assess major proposals such as federal aid to education, the Peace Corps, and the Alliance for Progress in light of "our cherished American tradition of church-state separation in order to eliminate and avoid compromises of our national policy."[130]

Despite the fact that his father had been accused of being both anti-Semitic and pro-Nazi, Kennedy enjoyed generally cordial, if not close, relations with the Jewish community. This was undoubtedly a result of the fact that most Jews supported the Democratic Party. Moreover, Deputy Special Counsel to the President Myer Feldman played a similar role with Jews as Brooks Hays did with Protestants. He spoke to many Jewish groups and handled much of the correspondence with Jewish leaders, organizations, and individuals.[131] Kennedy appointed Arthur Goldberg secretary of labor and

Abraham Ribicoff secretary of health, education, and welfare, the first time the United States had two Jewish cabinet members. The administration's stance on Zionism and assistance to persecuted Jews in the Soviet Union provoked minor controversy. The American Council for Judaism denounced the Kennedy administration in 1962 for supporting the Zionist perspective that Israel was the homeland of all Jews and could speak for all Jewish people.[132] Many Jews wrote the White House to ask the president to assist their compatriots in the Soviet Union who were undergoing intense persecution. The administration took the position that formal American protests were likely to be counterproductive, given past unfavorable reactions by the Soviet government. Wherever possible, the government supported efforts to improve the situation of Soviet Jews and reduce discrimination against them.[133] Kennedy met periodically with Jewish groups and sent greetings to various Jewish groups and to all Jews on their high holy days.[134]

School Prayer

The most intense religious controversy during Kennedy's tenure was provoked by the June 1962 Supreme Court case (*Engel v. Vitale*) that ruled that school-sponsored prayers as part of a regularly scheduled devotional exercise violated the Constitution. The plaintiffs objected specifically to the nonsectarian New York Regents' Prayer, which stated: "Almighty God, we acknowledge our dependence upon Thee, and we beg Thy blessing upon us, our parents, our teachers, and our country." In many public school classrooms across the nation, similar prayers or the Lord's Prayer was recited every day, and the Bible was read without comment. The court's ruling evoked a massive nationwide protest, primarily from evangelical Protestants and Catholics. Cardinal Spellman called the decision "a tragic misreading of our Founding Fathers" and protested that it struck at "the very heart of the Godly tradition."[135] Cardinal Cushing termed the verdict "asinine, ridiculous, and absurd" and warned that it was "fuel for Communist propaganda."[136] Cardinal McIntyre of Los Angeles labeled it "positively shocking and scandalizing." The editors of *America* protested that it spit in the face of the nation's history, tradition, and heritage as a religious people.[137] Billy Graham denounced the decision as "another step toward secularism" and called for a national referendum to determine whether the United States should allow prayer and Bible reading in its public schools.[138] Democrats and Republicans from all sections of the country sponsored Constitutional amendments to overturn the court's verdict. Billboards demanded the impeachment of Chief Justice Earl Warren, and many lamented that the court had "kicked God out of the schools."[139]

Thousands of concerned citizens, churches, and civic and religious organizations wrote to the president to protest the ruling. They argued that the decision was contrary to the intent of the First Amendment and to the wishes of the great majority of the American people. The Regents' Prayer did not establish a religion; it only reaffirmed the nation's faith in God.[140] Prayers in public schools, argued the president of the University of Tennessee, helped youth to depend on "God in all matters and situations of life."[141] Because hundreds of thousands of children had no other religious teachings, asserted the Santa Monica Bay Woman's Club, banning prayer in the schools robbed them of the knowledge of God and faith.[142] An attorney from Media, Pennsylvania, chastised the president for refusing to use the prestige of his office to defend "our dearest and most fundamental tradition."[143] Groups of citizens from New Jersey and New York protested that the ruling was likely to frustrate the aspiration of suppressed peoples living in atheistic countries and was a "cause of joy" for Khrushchev.[144] Many feared that this decision would contribute to eliminating recognition of God from other aspects of American life, including the currency, the Pledge of Allegiance, oaths of public officials, and chaplains in the military and the Senate.[145]

Asked at a news conference about prayer in public schools, Kennedy replied, "I think that it is important ... that we support the Supreme Court decisions even when we may not agree with them." In this case, he added, we have "a very easy remedy": "to pray ourselves. ... We can pray a good deal more at home, we can attend our churches with a good deal more fidelity, and we can make the true meaning of prayer much more important in the lives of all our children."[146] Albert Menendez argues that Kennedy's response revealed both his "admiration of genuine voluntary religious experience" and "his fundamental respect for the legal process."[147] It also demonstrated his political astuteness and desire to offend neither side on this volatile, emotionally charged issue. His shrewd, middle-of-the-road position prompted little public criticism.

Those who supported the ruling argued that it was just, prudent, and beneficial. Many agreed with the president that prayer must begin at home. "Any religion that can be deprived of power, usefulness and vitality by not being honored or promoted" in the schools, a citizen wrote to Kennedy, did not have these qualities in the first place.[148] The *Baptist Standard* termed the decision "proper, fair, and correct."[149] Supporters denied the claim that the verdict exalted "minority rights at the expense of the rights of the majority" and imposed "secularism as a way of life" on people who were "by and large religious." The court's fundamental premise was that government sponsorship of religion was inappropriate. Moreover, although the nation must respect the right of majorities, it could not allow them to impose their will on minorities.[150] A United Church of Christ agency argued that even though it was nondenominational and its recitation was voluntary, the prayer violated the Establishment Clause of the First Amendment because it was sponsored by the government. In a public statement, thirty-one prominent Protestants representing twelve denominations agreed with the court that the government "should stay out of the business of writing and sanctioning official prayers." The ruling protected "the integrity of the religious conscience and the proper functioning of religious and governmental institutions."[151] Everyone remained free to pray as they wished, declared the *New York Times*, expressing the perspective of most of the nation's major newspapers, but they could not use "official power to make others pray that way."[152] Others added that the decision prevented children who did not participate in the prayer from being labeled as nonconformists or antireligious by their classmates.[153] In the years since 1962, this issue has repeatedly resurfaced, as both houses of Congress have held committee hearings and introduced amendments on the floor, but the verdict, reinforced by other Supreme Court rulings, has stood.[154]

Kennedy's Philosophy of Governing

Shortly after World War II ended, Kennedy wrote in a loose-leaf notebook that to be a "positive force for public good," a politician needed to have "a solid moral code governing his public actions."[155] He told the National Conference of Christians and Jews in 1961 that "we all draw our guidance, inspiration, and sense of moral direction from . . . the Bible."[156] Yet his approach to the presidency often did not explicitly demonstrate a commitment to either biblical teaching or a "solid moral code." In the judgment of Richard Hutcheson, no American president "adhered more rigorously . . . to the gentlemen's agreement to keep personal faith separate from public life."[157]

Presidential advisor Arthur Schlesinger Jr. argued that although Kennedy was devoted to the Catholic Church and sometimes found solace in mass, there was "little organic intellectual connection between his faith and his politics." His social thought was not based on a desire to apply the principles of Catholic encyclicals, most notably *Rerum Novarum*, to American life. The strong connection he felt with Pope John XXIII was based on the pontiff's character and policies, not on theology or morality. Kennedy's religion, Schlesinger concludes, "was humane rather than doctrinal. He was a Catholic as Franklin Roosevelt was an Episcopalian—because he was born into the faith, lived in it, and expected to die in it. . . . He had little knowledge of or interest in the Catholic dogmatic tradition." Kennedy rejected the approach of both Senators Thomas Dodd of Connecticut and Eugene McCarthy of Minnesota, who embodied the divergent forms of intellectual Catholicism at the time. Unlike Dodd, he did not participate in the Catholic subculture and expressed little reverence for the Catholic hierarchy. He rejected the "black-and-white moralism, the pietistic rhetoric, the clericalism, the anti-intellectualism, the prudery, [and] the fear of Protestant society" that had long characterized parts of the American Irish Catholic community. But, unlike McCarthy, he also had no desire to "rescue Catholic doctrine from fundamentalism and demonstrate its relevance to the modern world." His indifference to the scholastic tradition caused some Catholic scholars to sharply criticize him. His philosophy of life, however, was quite "compatible with the sophisticated theology of Jesuits like Father John Courtney Murray, whom he admired greatly." Kennedy's example, Schlesinger contended, helped inspire the progressive Catholicism that emerged in the 1960s and showed that Catholics could participate fully in American society.[158]

Numerous scholars argue, however, that Kennedy's Catholicism was totally irrelevant to his political worldview. "He was not a Catholic President. He was a secular President who was affiliated with the Catholic Church," argues Robert Alley. Had conservative Protestants truly understood Kennedy's ideology, Alley contends, they would have opposed him as being a secular humanist. Catholic sociologist Andrew Greeley maintains that Kennedy "did not seem to perceive any connection between the teachings of his religion and his social and political commitment, nor much relationship between the morality of his Church and the problems he faced in the world's most important office." Tom Wicker concludes that Kennedy's "religious belief and discipline had no effect whatever on his Presidential conduct and judgment."[159]

Kennedy insisted that presidents must make "informed, prudent, and resolute" choices among men, measures, and methods. These choices would determine what issues had priority in national life and "the mode and success of their execution."[160] Nowhere, however, does Kennedy clearly identify what principles guided him in making these choices. Menendez concludes correctly that "Kennedy's secular education, his appreciation of history, and his disinterest in Catholic social teaching played far more significant roles in the development of his character [and, I would add, his worldview] than his residual Catholicism."[161] His lack of theological education, belief that Catholic hierarchy had little political insight, and sensitivity to concerns about Catholic political power led Kennedy to avoid the guidance of explicitly Catholic positions in forming his policies.

According to Sorensen, Kennedy freely admitted that he entered Congress "with little or no political philosophy." Reeves maintains that Kennedy "had little ideology beyond anti-Communism and faith in active, pragmatic government. . . . What convictions he did have, on nuclear proliferation or civil rights or the use of military power, he was often willing to suspend," particularly to avoid confrontation with Congress or being labeled soft, or to win votes.[162] Kennedy's pragmatism is evident in his lack of metaphysical assumptions and his testing the meaning of propositions by their consequences. Bored by abstractions, he "never took ideology very seriously."[163] Taught by his father that "substantive political and moral issues were secondary" to winning at the ballot box, Reeves argues, he was "pragmatic to the point of amorality; his sole standard seemed to be political expediency." He "lacked a moral center" and an ideological standard that "went beyond self-aggrandizement."[164]

More positively, Kennedy strove to be a strong, active president in the tradition of Wilson and Franklin Roosevelt in order to "advance social justice at home and American interests abroad."[165] His New Frontier appealed to the same messianic impulses as had Wilson's New Freedom and Roosevelt's New Deal. Kennedy was "a sort of centrist Democrat," who sought to use the federal government to "right a number of wrongs" and advance the common welfare.[166] Urging Americans to pursue the common good rather than their individual interests, Kennedy quoted Matthew 6:24: "No man can serve two masters: for either he will hate the one and love the other, or else he will hold to the one, and despise the other. Ye cannot serve God and mammon." He exhorted people to "serve only the public and love that master well."[167]

Kennedy and Public Policy Issues

Given Kennedy's pragmatic style of governing, perspective toward Catholicism, and lack of a coherent philosophy, there does not seem to be much relationship between his policies and his faith. Nevertheless, he did present moral rationales for his stances on numerous issues, including education, juvenile delinquency, women's rights, world hunger, poverty, and the Alliance for Progress. To assess Kennedy's approach, three issues will be examined: the Peace Corps, Civil Rights, and the Limited Test Ban Treaty. Considered by some to be Kennedy's "most affirmative and enduring legacy," the Peace Corps enabled thousands of Americans to serve overseas as ambassadors of good will and agents of change.[168]

The mythology surrounding the Peace Corps suggests that Kennedy initiated and strongly promoted the organization. The organization adopted as its slogan a phrase from his inaugural address, "help people help themselves," and emphasized key words of Kennedy's New Frontier: challenges, sacrifice, and pioneers. Moreover, its mission resonates with many of Kennedy's pronouncements.[169] The president contended that America's relief efforts, especially its Food-for-Peace Program, helped fulfill the biblical injunction to feed the hungry and care for the sick.[170] "The supreme reality of our time is our indivisibility as children of God and our common vulnerability on this planet."[171] Americans "must lead the way" in relieving "oppression, hunger and despair so that all may share the age-old vision of a good and righteous life."[172] Despite such rhetoric, the origins of the Peace Corps lie in the ideas of others, and after his election Kennedy initially resisted its implementation.

Several programs provided the inspiration for the Peace Corps: the National Youth Administration of the New Deal and Truman's Point Four Program and Operation Crossroads Africa, which both functioned during the 1950s. In the late 1950s, Congressman Henry Reuss of Wisconsin and Hubert Humphrey called for a service organization to spread knowledge and skills in developing countries and improve America's image abroad. Students at the University of Michigan responded very enthusiastically at a campus rally to Kennedy's query: "How many of you are willing to spend ten years in Africa or Latin America or Asia working...for freedom?" Only through such selfless service, he argued, could free societies compete successfully with communist ones. While campaigning in San Francisco three weeks later, Kennedy argued similarly that communist influence could be countered only by "a peace corps of talented young men and women," who understood the language, circumstances, and customs of the host countries and were "willing to spend their lives serving the cause of freedom."[173]

Several factors converged after Kennedy's election to transform the Peace Corps from a concept to a reality. The idea had phenomenal popular support, it concretely embodied Kennedy's promise to improve international relations, and key members of his administration strongly supported it. Most important, Kennedy named his brother-in-law Sargent Shriver, an idealist with extensive experience in business, education, and international relations, its director.[174] Although the organization was not his brainchild and he did little to ensure its success, Kennedy's charisma and inspiring rhetoric did help attract volunteers. By promoting political and spiritual freedom, Kennedy repeatedly claimed, the Peace Corps was thwarting the spread of communism.[175] By his death, almost seven thousand volunteers were serving in forty-four countries, providing numerous services (surveying roads, building schools, drilling wells, starting industries, and mainly providing instruction in English), teaching important skills, and helping develop better relations with poor nations.[176]

The reaction of America's religious community to the Peace Corps was mixed. A Methodist minister in Milwaukee lauded the idea as a partial fulfillment of Christ's Great Commission.[177] In 1963, the Religious Heritage Foundation selected Shriver as its "Church Man of the Year," the first Catholic layman ever chosen, because of his leadership of the Peace Corps.[178] However, at his Los Angeles crusade that year, Billy Graham attacked the corps, claiming it was "almost completely materialistic in its aims" and did not place "God at its center." Shriver countered that the evangelist's denomination, the Southern Baptist Convention, had endorsed the Peace Corps.[179] Lawrence Fuchs, who served as the director of the Peace Corps in the Philippines from 1961 to 1963, estimated that about 40 percent of the six hundred staff who served there were Catholics, many of them ex-seminarians.[180] In 1965, Samuel Proctor, a former associate director of the organization, wrote that although church leaders had initially feared that the "Peace Corps would eclipse the Christian mission abroad," they now realized that its success had opened new doors for missionaries.[181]

Civil Rights

Although Kennedy hoped to expand black Civil Rights "gradually, smoothly, and with a minimum of conflict," this quest was the most contentious and time-consuming domestic issue of his administration.[182] The confrontational tactics of Civil Rights activists combined with staunch and often violent resistance from Southerners to prod Kennedy to take action to abate racial discrimination more forcefully and quickly than he desired. Although the president's response to the challenges of the Freedom Rides of 1961, efforts to desegregate the University of Mississippi in 1962 and the University of Alabama in 1963, and the demonstrations at Birmingham, Alabama, in 1963 disappointed black leaders and their white supporters, he went beyond Truman and Eisenhower in promoting black rights and played a leading role in passing the Civil Rights Act of 1964. Kennedy had promised during the 1960 campaign to combat racial injustice, but his small margin of victory, the lack of public support, and Congressional opposition, especially from Southern Democrats, limited his options and led him to move slowly. As Schlesinger explains, Kennedy was initially ambivalent about Civil Rights because he believed Congress would not pass a Civil Rights bill and feared that pushing too hard for Civil Rights would alienate the Southern support he needed for other important legislation.[183] Kennedy appointed more blacks to federal positions than any previous president, and the Justice Department brought more than nine times as many suits against violations of black voting rights in the South during his three years in office than in Eisenhower's eight. Despite the extensive obstruction, violence, and intimidation employed by Southern officials, during his presidency the percentage of Southern blacks registered to vote increased substantially. On the other hand, the Civil Rights Commission Congress created in 1957 protested that his administration was moving too slowly on Civil Rights, and many Americans complained that he had not ended discrimination in housing, something he boasted in his campaign could be accomplished with a "stroke of the presidential pen."[184] Moreover, Kennedy did not censure segregationist judges in the South and did little to combat school segregation, which was extensive in the South and increasing in the North.

In February 1963, Kennedy sent a message to Congress detailing how the nation's social practices violated the principles of the Constitution. Racial discrimination hampered economic growth, harmed America's image abroad, increased the costs of public welfare, and contributed to crime, delinquency, and disorder. "Above all," the president declared, "it is wrong."[185] While appreciating Kennedy's eloquent prose, Civil Rights leaders were disappointed by the piecemeal measures he recommended to Congress to improve black voting rights, extend the Civil Rights Commission, and provide technical aid to school districts that voluntarily tried to desegregate.

In April 1963, Martin Luther King Jr. organized a protest in Birmingham, where only the interstate bus terminals had been integrated, that included pray-ins, street marches, and sit-ins in downtown stores. King's moving "Letter from the Birmingham Jail," coupled with the arrests of many other demonstrators and the brutality of Police Commissioner Eugene "Bull" Connor, whose officers used dogs, high-pressure fire hoses, and nightsticks against protesters, increased support for the black cause and pressured the federal government to act.

These events and Governor George Wallace's attempt to prevent two blacks from enrolling at the University of Alabama in June 1963 led Kennedy to give a televised speech that month to stress that Civil Rights was a moral issue. The government must act, he told Americans, not simply to preserve order, protect lives and property, and enforce court orders, but because justice required it. He reminded viewers that their nation was "founded on the principle that all men are created equal" and that blacks were serving in the armed forces around the world to "promote and protect the rights of all who wish to be free." The nation's segregation and blatant discrimination confronted Americans with a "moral issue" that was "as old as the Scriptures" and "as clear as the . . . Constitution." The key question was: Were all Americans "to be afforded equal rights and opportunities"? Given the situation, would whites would be willing to trade places with blacks or "be content with counsels of patience and delay?" The nation's unjust treatment of blacks made its defense of freedom around the world appear hypocritical. He urged Americans to reexamine their consciences and pled with business and municipal leaders to work to end discrimination. Insisting that this moral crisis could not be resolved by token measures and must not be settled by demonstrations in the streets, he announced that he was submitting a comprehensive Civil Rights bill to Congress.[186] Kennedy, *Newsweek* announced, had thrown "the full weight of his prestige and power behind the Negro's struggle for equality of opportunity."[187]

Several factors prompted Kennedy to focus on the moral dimensions of Civil Rights: his experience with bigotry in the 1960 election, compassion for blacks, sense of fairness, recognition that the nation's discrimination was hurting its image, blacks' public relations successes in Birmingham, and Northern whites' increased sympathy for the black struggle.[188] Achieving equality for blacks, Kennedy wrote to Benjamin Mays in January 1963, required "a humanitarian and moral consensus which, expressed publicly in the actions of our people, will indicate their firm desire" to accord human dignity to all.[189] Reeves argues that Kennedy believed prejudice was "a waste of emotion and time." It harmed America's economy and damaged its international relations. For Kennedy, black demands ultimately "were just politics, a volatile issue to be defused."[190] Yet he realized that fighting for equal rights for blacks involved more political liabilities than advantages, and he did so anyway.[191] The conclusion of Theodore Hesburgh, who served on the Civil Rights Commission, seems accurate: Although the Civil Rights issue was imposed on the Kennedy administration by the march of events, the president supported black Civil Rights not just because he thought it was expedient but because he thought it was right.[192]

Six days after his televised speech, Kennedy met with about two hundred of the nation's religious leaders, Protestant, Catholic, and Jewish, white and black, to solicit their help in battling discrimination. His staff encouraged him to seek their help in doing what was "both morally right and essential for civil order." They insisted that his administration must promote justice, love, and peace, the "themes so eloquently expressed in the peace encyclical of the late and beloved Pope John." His staff urged Kennedy to praise the statements of religious bodies affirming human equality and to stress that black ministers had a key role to play in the Civil Rights movement. Finally, Kennedy should exhort the clergy to proclaim in their pulpits that "all men are equal under God and that segregation and discrimination offend the consciences of all truly religious people."[193]

In supporting equality for blacks, Kennedy appealed to pragmatic considerations—fears about public safety, concerns about the loss of national prestige, and desires for economic growth—but he increasingly emphasized moral issues and social responsibility. "As we approach the 100th anniversary ... of the Emancipation Proclamation," Kennedy declared, "let the acts of every branch of the Government—and every citizen—portray that 'righteousness does exalt a nation.' "[194] In July 1963, he announced, "[W]e are trying to erase for all time the injustices and inequalities of race and color in order to assure all Americans a fair chance ... as equal children of God."[195] Black leaders believed Kennedy was on their side but were frustrated until the summer of 1963 by his unwillingness to make Civil Rights a priority. Kennedy was annoyed by their expectation that he could persuade millions of unwilling whites to grant equal rights to blacks.[196] Although recognizing that the president could not eradicate personal prejudice, blacks argued he could do much more to end state-sponsored discrimination.

For the remainder of Kennedy's life, a Civil Rights bill, which eventually included guaranteeing all citizens equal access to all public facilities, removing barriers that prevented blacks from voting, and desegregating schools, was hotly debated. Although this landmark act was not passed until 1964, Kennedy deserves much of the credit for its enactment. He promoted it in press conferences, public addresses, messages to Congress, private conversations with congressmen, and dozens of meetings with governors, businessmen, labor leaders, ministers, editors, Civil Rights activists, and educators.[197] Reinhold Niebuhr praised Kennedy for giving blacks "the full support" of the federal government and summoning the nation to solve a "great moral crisis."[198]

The Limited Test Ban Treaty

Daniel Callahan argued in *Commonweal* that before 1961, Catholics had been "conspicuously absent among those pressing for disarmament [or] cessation of nuclear tests." Convinced that communism was the main source of evil and danger in the world, Catholics had primarily been concerned with the proper use, rather than the limiting, of nuclear weapons. They had put their trust in military strength and urged the United States to develop as much deterrent power as possible.[199] Although most Catholics, especially Polish and Irish ones, supported the "moralistic and ideological" approach of John Foster Dulles, Kennedy rejected Dulles's "rhetoric of liberation."[200] In sharp contrast to Eisenhower, who had strongly emphasized America's religiosity as an antidote to communism's godlessness, Kennedy declared, "I do not regard religion as a weapon in the Cold War."[201]

During the 1960 campaign and throughout his presidency, Kennedy trumpeted the theme of peace, often using biblical rhetoric to underscore his arguments. "[P]eace is our deepest aspiration," Kennedy declared, "and when it comes we will gladly convert not our swords into plowshares, but our bombs into peaceful reactors, and our planes into space vessels. 'Pursue peace,' the Bible tells us, and we shall pursue it with every effort and every energy that we possess."[202] "[T]he making of peace," he told ministers in Houston, was "the noblest work of a God-fearing man. It is the righteous way. And righteousness exalteth a nation."[203] Kennedy insisted in a Christmas message that peacemakers were "truly blessed."[204] Speaking at the United Nations in September 1961, Kennedy declared, "Together we shall save our planet, or together we shall perish in its flames. Save it we can—and save it we must—and then we shall earn the eternal thanks of mankind and, as peacemakers, the eternal blessings of God."[205] That year, he told Congress that "we seek only the day when 'nation shall not lift up sword against nation, neither shall they learn war any more.' "[206] In 1963, he urged Americans to fervently ask "God for guidance in our efforts to achieve a peaceful world."[207] A speech Kennedy had planned to give on November 22, 1963, at the Trade Mart in Dallas declared his hope of achieving "in our time and for all time the ancient vision of 'peace on earth, good will toward men.' That must always be our goal, and the righteousness of our cause must always underlie our strength."[208]

These convictions played a major role in Kennedy's efforts to negotiate with the Soviets to reduce the tensions of the cold war and limit nuclear weapons. Building on Eisenhower's work, Kennedy strove to negotiate a test ban treaty with the Soviets.[209] In his inaugural address, he urged both nations to "formulate serious and precise proposals for the inspection and control of arms."[210] Early in 1961, he proposed banning nuclear testing in the atmosphere, halting the production of nuclear weapons, ending the Soviet and American policies of giving nuclear weapons to their allies, and destroying many of each nation's weapons. Talks in Geneva during 1961 accomplished little because of disagreement about on-site inspections. That September, Kennedy told United Nations delegates that war could no longer settle disputes or produce unconditional victory. All people lived "under a nuclear sword of Damocles, hanging by the slenderest of threads, capable of being cut at any moment" by accident, miscalculation, or madness. "The mere existence of modern weapons—ten million times more powerful than the world has ever seen, and only minutes away from any target on earth," he continued, "is a source of horror, and discord and distrust."[211] Kennedy faced the daunting challenge of finding a formula for bargaining with the Soviets that the disparate elements of his administration could accept and of building and sustaining public and congressional support for negotiations, despite Soviet obstructionism and poor East-West relations.[212] The Cuban Missile Crisis helped convince him that a world of nuclear weapons was not only irrational but also intolerable. Meanwhile, a rift between China and the Soviet Union both tarnished the image of Marxism as a universal ideology that overrode all national interests and dissolved all historic conflicts and prompted the Soviets to reevaluate their relationship with the United States.[213] The resumption of nuclear testing in the atmosphere (breaking an unofficial moratorium) by Soviets in September 1961 and Americans in April 1962, which prompted protests by many around the world, provided an additional incentive.

The pace of disarmament talks accelerated quickly, following the resolution of the Cuban Missile Crisis of October 1962. Early in 1963, several leading American politicians denounced a test ban, claiming it made too many concessions to the Soviets, would be unenforceable, and would prevent the development of a neutron bomb and antiballistic missiles.[214] The Joint Chiefs of Staff also opposed the ban, arguing that the proposed six annual inspections of the Soviet Union were not enough to monitor compliance. Despite this opposition, Kennedy pressed on, haunted by the fear that unless the negotiations were successful, by 1975 there would be as many as twenty nuclear powers instead of the present four.[215] Discussion foundered on the issue of how many on-site inspections were necessary. Meanwhile, public pressure for a treaty was growing. Scientists around the world argued that the "radioactive fallout from nuclear tests was poisoning the planet." Thirty-four senators introduced a resolution calling for "banning all tests that contaminate the atmosphere or the ocean." The country's best-selling book was *Fail-Safe*. This novel's frightening plot involved the United States dropping nuclear bombs on Moscow as the result of an electronic glitch and then destroying New York City to prevent Soviet retaliation.[216]

On June 10, 1963, Kennedy dropped a bomb of his own in the form of a commencement address at American University in Washington that redefined the American attitude toward the cold war.[217] It repudiated "the self-righteous cold war rhetoric" of several recent secretaries of state and "attempted to force Americans to face new international realities."[218] The threat of total war, Kennedy declared, required the United States to make achieving peace its highest priority. Such a peace could not be "enforced on the world by American weapons of war." It must be a "genuine peace," the kind that made life worth living and enabled people "to build a better life for their children." He challenged Americans to reexamine their attitudes toward peace, the Soviet Union, and the cold war. They must reject the dangerous and defeatist conclusion that "war is inevitable, that mankind is doomed, that we are gripped by forces we cannot control." Although human nature could not be transformed, social institutions could be gradually improved, and concrete agreements could be reached that benefited the entire world. World peace did not "require that each man love his neighbor," only that people "live together in mutual tolerance, submitting their disputes to a just and peaceful settlement." Taking a cue, some argued, from Pope John XXIII's *Pacem in Terris*, Kennedy insisted that "no government or social system is so evil that its people" were without virtue.[219] Citizens of both countries abhorred war and had never fought each other. Because war would have devastating effects on the Soviet Union and the United States and both were spending "massive sums of money" to build weapons that "could be better devoted to combating ignorance, poverty and disease," he reasoned, both countries and their respective allies had an immense incentive to attain "a just and genuine peace" and to halt the arms race. Finally, Kennedy urged Americans to reassess their attitude toward the cold war. Rather than "distributing blame or pointing fingers of judgment," the United States must help communists see it was in their best "interests to agree on a genuine peace."[220] The international community, the Soviets, and most Americans responded very favorably to the address. Khrushchev allowed the Voice of America to broadcast it freely and the Soviet press to reprint the entire address.[221] Leaders of the National Council of Churches wrote to Kennedy to express their "heartfelt gratitude and strong support" for his speech. They applauded his commitment to justice, freedom, and human rights for all people, his search for ways to relax East-West tensions, and his efforts to achieve disarmament with adequate safeguards.[222]

Signed in Moscow by the United States, the United Kingdom, and the Soviet Union on August 5, 1963 (and within the next six weeks by almost a hundred nations), the Limited Test Ban Treaty prohibited nuclear tests in the atmosphere, in outer space, and under water. Although he admitted that the treaty would not reduce nuclear stockpiles, halt the production of nuclear weapons, or prevent their use in the case of war, Kennedy labeled it "an important first step—a step toward peace—a step toward reason—a step away from war."[223] In September, Kennedy told the United Nations that the treaty would neither eliminate basic conflicts nor secure freedom for all. Kennedy urged his listeners to use it as a lever to move the planet "to a just and lasting peace" and to pursue peaceful cooperation.[224]

On September 24, the Senate ratified the treaty by a vote of 80 to 19. It neither ended the cold war nor guaranteed world peace. It was, however, the first major thaw since the war began and had several benefits: It indicated that the Soviets had accepted American nuclear superiority, had confidence in American restraint, and had developed a new view of nuclear deterrence. It slowed the bilateral arms race and had the potential to prevent nuclear proliferation and bring about agreements on more general disarmament issues.[225] Accordingly, the *Bulletin of Atomic Scientists* moved its "death watch"—an imaginary clock symbolizing the threat of nuclear disaster—from 11:52 to 11:48. Niebuhr hoped that the test ban treaty would "go down in history as the beginning of a new era in the Cold War."[226]

Although the accord stopped the radioactive fallout produced by atmospheric testing, it did little to reduce either the amount or magnitude of the superpowers' weapons.[227] The hope that the treaty would improve political relations between the United States and the Soviet Union dissipated in the jungles of Vietnam, and the arms race soon accelerated again. Despite establishing a hotline between Moscow and Washington in June 1963, concluding this treaty in August, and arranging a wheat deal in October, the two nations did not develop a more positive relationship. Yet the treaty did signal the desire of American leaders to balance halting the spread of communism and avoiding nuclear holocaust.[228] It also helped pave the way for arms agreements during the 1970s and 1980s.

Kennedy's Death and Funeral

Many Americans had feared Kennedy would not respect the separation of church and state, but he scrupulously maintained this distinction. Ironically, his assassination evoked a fusion of church and state, as these institutions combined their resources to help Americans deal with their anguish and dismay. James Wolfe contends that Kennedy's death caused Americans to question such basic assumptions as the sovereignty of God, the rationality of the universe, and America's status as an innocent and invincible chosen nation.[229] Few events in the nation's history prompted such an outpouring of grief and confusion. The intensity of Americans' reactions, British journalist Henry Fairlie wrote, was similar to those of Egyptians who thought when a pharaoh died that "the sun would be darkened forever."[230] In pulpits across the nation, Catholic, Protestant, and Jewish clergy expressed Americans' passionate grief and showered effusive praise on the slain president. Theological differences were ignored and "the separation of church and state forgotten," as "Americans knelt at the national altar, proclaiming their common devotion to God, country, and Kennedy."[231] Although Kennedy was not canonized, he was certainly idolized as a hero and a martyr.[232]

Many ministers, priests, and rabbis lauded Kennedy's faith. A Lutheran called him "a just man, a devout Christian, a man of moral character, intellectual stature, and social understanding to which few men in politics attain."[233] "He was a devout adherent of his faith," a Baptist pastor proclaimed.[234] Kennedy, asserted a Methodist minister, "was a sincere and practicing Christian" whose "faith was a vital part of the fabric of his life."[235] "Kennedy revered God," asserted a Jewish rabbi. "He was a man of faith."[236] Few American presidents, opined an Episcopal rector in Dallas, were as devoted Christians as Kennedy.[237] A priest argued that he "was a Catholic in the mind and heart and spirit of Pope John XXIII," committed to charity, justice, and peace.[238]

As had happened following Lincoln's and McKinley's assassinations, many judged Kennedy's death to be vicarious. In his benediction at Kennedy's funeral, Cardinal Cushing asserted that Kennedy had made "the supreme sacrifice of dying for others."[239] To Norman Vincent Peale, Kennedy "literally died for his country."[240] Several clergymen quoted Jesus' words in John's Gospel: "Greater love has no man that this, that a man lay down his life for his friends."[241] He was "a martyr to the cause of human freedom," asserted a Lutheran pastor.[242] Because Kennedy gave his life for the cause of justice, peace, and good will, a Methodist maintained, he had not died in vain.[243] Some admirers even compared Kennedy with Christ and the Apostle Paul: "like Christ he did not shirk from his cross, but welcomed it"; like Paul, he had fought the good fight.[244]

Many praised Kennedy for his political policies, his family life, and his personal attributes. Eulogists celebrated his stand on the separation of church and state, dedication to the cause of peace, negotiation of the nuclear test ban treaty, and commitment to Civil Rights.[245] Kennedy, insisted Niebuhr, worked harder to avoid "nuclear catastrophe than any other contemporary leader."[246] Hundreds applauded his efforts to ensure equal justice for black Americans. Speaking for many, a minister extolled Kennedy's "almost unmatched devotion to the poor, the outcast, and the depressed."[247] They lauded the Democrat's "exemplary devotion to his family."[248] Pastors, college presidents, and politicians also commended many of Kennedy's personal traits, especially his courage and compassion.[249]

In sharp contrast to the assassination of McKinley, which most Americans blamed solely on the irrational act of an anarchist, Kennedy's death was widely attributed to the national climate of hate, malice, intolerance, injustice, and fanaticism, to which many had contributed.[250] Kennedy's civil rights legislation, argued a Methodist pastor, had made him "a traitor and an enemy to millions of Americans." "By vilification, innuendo, scathing criticism, scurrilous remarks, and profane abuse," he had been "murdered a thousand times in the hearts of his enemies."[251] Many ordinary Americans emphasized national shame and corporate guilt.[252] "We must confess," declared a Unitarian minister, "that everyone who has not played a full part . . . [in] working for an enduring peace between the nations, and working for justice between the races—and this includes most of us—is also responsible" for Kennedy's death.[253] A Presbyterian pastor insisted that all Americans shared a complicity in the neglect of law, decline of morality, glorification of violence, and atmosphere of hate that had produced the assassination.[254] Lee Harvey Oswald was "simply the executioner," argued a Methodist minister, who had "millions of accomplices."[255] A Presbyterian attributed the packed churches the Sunday following Kennedy's death not simply to people's need to express their grief but to their need for cleansing.[256] Many ministers challenged parishioners to search their souls, repent, and mend their ways.[257] They urged listeners to move beyond "superficial and sentimental grief coupled with self-righteous condemnation of Oswald" as an oddball, a Marxist, or an insane man and to recognize that all Americans had contributed to the president's death.[258]

Ministers used the tragedy to discuss other spiritual and civil themes. They accentuated the fleetingness of life, the importance of being prepared to meet God, the resurrection of Christ, and the promise of eternal life.[259] Numerous sermons assured Americans, as a Presbyterian pastor put it, that Kennedy "walks with God."[260] His death was a blunt reminder of the power of sin and evil in the world.[261] Pastors rejoiced that the orderly transition of power demonstrated the soundness and stability of the American government.[262] Clergy proclaimed that God was still sovereign, grappled with the problem of evil, and urged Americans to take up the causes Kennedy championed. Numerous ministers argued that God would bring good out of this evil event.[263] A rabbi insisted that their misery and pain could inspire people to be more compassionate and fight against evil.[264] God's answer to evil, declared the Archbishop of Canterbury, was the "Cross of Christ on Calvary and the Resurrection on Easter morning," which demonstrated how God could "turn suffering into a triumph of love and sacrifice."[265] Struggling to find meaning in the midst of sorrow, numerous pastors hoped that Kennedy's death would stimulate Americans to fight to extend freedom, justice, and righteousness and to end discrimination and hunger.[266] "His martyred blood," announced a black pastor in Mobile, Alabama, would "produce new champions of our cause."[267] Others urged people to rededicate themselves to obeying the law, acting responsibly, exercising courage, and eradicating the forces of hate, bigotry, and violence.[268] Arthur Schlesinger Jr. argued that Kennedy's death involved even "greater pathos" than Lincoln's or Franklin Roosevelt's because he had so much more "to give to his family, his nation, his world. . . . The best way to serve his memory" was to promote the values of decency, rationality, civility, and honor for which he gave his life.[269]

A Final Assessment

Despite Kennedy's deceit and sexual exploits, his presidency was not marred by any major scandals. To the end of his life, as the funeral eulogies reveal, he was considered a superior role model, a near-saint, and a superman, who would have done many other good things if he had not been murdered.[270] He was extolled as "the pride of western civilization," and his administration was praised for its virtue, style, and wisdom.[271] To his admirers, Kennedy's accomplishments were legion. He brought new hope for peace on earth, abolished "nuclear diplomacy," strengthened America's defense, aided the developing world, and helped make the republic "brave, civilized, rational, . . . tough, [and] questing," as the founders intended.[272] Under Kennedy's leadership, Sorensen contended, the federal government assumed a larger role in directing higher education, combating mental illness, ensuring Civil Rights, and conserving natural resources. He inspired hope "for a life of decency and equality" and "for a world of reason and peace."[273] Through the Peace Corps, Food for Peace, and AID programs and the Alliance for Progress, Kennedy helped improve America's image in Latin America, Asia, and Africa.[274] Kennedy was hailed for making "world peace a more feasible ideal" and negotiating "honorably with the Soviets" to achieve it.[275] Albert Menendez argues that Kennedy "exemplified the best in Catholic and American traditions" and was a "Catholic humanist statesman . . . in the tradition of Thomas More, Lord Baltimore, Charles Carroll, and Lord Acton."[276]

Critics, by contrast, fault Kennedy for his "faint-hearted response" to Civil Rights until near the end of his presidency, his failure to pass most of his New Frontier programs, and his willingness to "risk national security for sexual pleasure."[277] Reeves labels him "a reluctant spokesman for social justice."[278] Although Kennedy worked to lessen the intensity of the cold war and reduce nuclear weapons, his administration significantly increased America's supply of missiles, which prompted the Soviet Union to enlarge their forces, fueled the arms race, and produced parity in the 1970s.[279] Kennedy clearly "abused his high position for personal gratification. His reckless liaisons with women and mobsters" posed "enormous potential for scandal and blackmail." Kennedy had ample courage, but he lacked essential ingredients of good character: a core set of convictions, commitment, compassion, and integrity. Like Lyndon Johnson and Richard Nixon, he was "pragmatic, bellicose, secretive, and deceptive."[280] "Kennedy's private life and personal obsessions," Seymour Hersh argues, negatively affected both domestic and foreign policy "more than has ever been known."[281]

During the early 1960s, Catholics began to engage more fully and fruitfully with the larger American culture. By issuing two very influential encyclicals—*Mater et Magistra* and *Pacem in Terris*—and convening Vatican II, Pope John XXIII played an important role. So did American Catholic periodicals, universities, church leaders, governors, and congressmen. The 1960 campaign and Kennedy's presidency, however, were arguably the most significant. His approach to the office and policies helped convince Protestants and Jews that Catholics would not seek to impose their views of faith and morality on others when they held political power and helped increase dialogue between Catholics and other Americans.[282] Kennedy demonstrated that Catholics could "enter wholly and without apology into the mainstream of American society."[283] No longer were Catholics excluded from the highest office in the land.[284] Kennedy's promotion of "relatively liberal goals and values" made them more acceptable to Catholics.[285] Thanks to Kennedy, a priest contended, the Catholic Church had become better known and more respected throughout the United States, and prejudice toward Catholics had declined greatly. The whole world witnessed a Catholic funeral after the president was slain.[286] Kennedy's presidency, especially his scrupulous adherence to the separation of church and state, had helped improve relations between Catholics and Protestants.[287] Millions of young Americans considered him "an authentic hero," enhancing Catholicism's image.[288]

Kennedy's life demonstrates the irreducible complexity of human beings: Many people's beliefs and behaviors seem to others to be inconsistent, if not contradictory. How Kennedy could regularly attend church, profess to be a good Catholic, and convince some of his closest associates that his faith was genuine while violating his church's most fundamental teachings about marital fidelity, sexual purity, and honesty is difficult to understand. Why was Kennedy willing to risk his reputation and the success of his presidency to gratify his sexual desires? Incredibly sensitive about his public image in almost every other area, Kennedy displayed a reckless abandon about his philandering. Some argue that Kennedy's poor relationship with his wife, the unusual circumstances of his career, and his temperament—which supposedly pushed him toward illicit sexual encounters—excuse his behavior.[289] It is unclear how Kennedy justified his sexual practices to himself. Perhaps he rationalized that his psychic and physical needs (he claimed he got a migraine headache if he did not have sex every day) and his incredible political pressures justified his actions. He may have reasoned he was simply following the example of his father, who had numerous paramours, most notably Gloria

Swanson.[290] Perhaps his mind was so compartmentalized that he simply did not consider the contradiction between Christian morality and his sexual practices.[291]

Had Kennedy lived in another place and time when rulers were not held to the same standards as others, his sexual appetites could have been sated in socially acceptable ways. He lived, however, in a society that affirmed the Judeo-Christian norm of marital sexual fidelity, and he publicly supported Christianity's moral teachings. Nor could Kennedy use the common justification for affairs—that he was in love with the women with whom he had them.[292] Menendez asserts that Kennedy's philandering does not automatically prove he is a poor Catholic.[293] However, most Catholic, Protestant, Jewish, Muslim, and secular humanist Americans would condemn his hundreds of sexual trysts with women, many of whom were total strangers, as well as his persistent lying and endangering of national security. Although the difference between people's public image and private behavior is often striking, in Kennedy's case the disparity was especially stark and significant.

James MacGregor Burns extensively analyzed Kennedy's relationship with the Catholic Church but never discussed how Catholicism shaped his views, aims, or policies.[294] Menendez describes Kennedy's faith as "tolerant, pragmatic, flexible, vague, and—most important of all—tidily compartmentalized and rarely expressed in public," which, he maintains, is "the way most American seem to prefer."[295] This conclusion is questionable. While wanting their presidents to be open-minded and not rigidly dogmatic, most Americans also appear to prefer that their presidents have a substantial personal faith, practice upright private behavior, and exhibit public religiosity, especially by attending church and using religious rhetoric to both challenge and comfort the nation. Although the evaluations of Kennedy's faith disagree sharply, it is tempting to regard testimonies of his devoutness as either expressions of loyalty, projection of the observers' own convictions onto the president, or attempts to strengthen his public image. Kennedy seemed to believe that people could control their own destiny and that the traditional moral standards did not apply to him.[296] Belief in God as the creator, director of history, and ultimate judge did not seem to guide Kennedy's thinking or actions. His frequent use of religious language appears primarily to be window dressing rather than the expression of heartfelt convictions or the ideological foundation for his public policies.

CHAPTER NINE

Jimmy Carter: First Servant of the Nation

The most important thing in my life is Jesus Christ.

Kenosha, Wisconsin, April 2, 1976

We have a responsibility to try to shape government so that it does exemplify the teaching of God.

Plains, Georgia, June 27, 1976

I recognize that I ought to be not "First Boss" but "First Servant."

To the employees of the Department of Health, Education, and Welfare, Feb. 16, 1977

There is no way to understand me and my political philosophy without understanding my faith.

Dec. 28, 1983

JIMMY CARTER'S DECISION in March 1976 to answer reporters' questions about his religious faith openly and honestly created a commotion that reverberated from coast to coast. Americans allow, even expect, politicians to talk about morality or spirituality and its importance in government and public life. But Carter went much further. He confessed that he was a born-again, evangelical Southern Baptist whose faith influenced every area of his life, including his political positions and style of governing. Journalists, most of whom had little understanding of conservative Protestantism, scrambled to figure out what it meant to be born again and how a politician's faith could guide his work. Carter's disclosures of his religious convictions, practices, and experiences and his claim to have an intimate relationship with God evoked amazement, interest, and fear. Many evangelicals rejoiced that one of their own was running for the presidency and that the media were discussing the nature and importance of the Christian conversion experience. Many liberal Protestants, Catholics, Jews, and agnostics openly worried that, if elected, Carter would use the power of his office to try to impose his particular brand of religion on the nation or would make political decisions based on alleged personal revelations from God. Countless Americans insisted that religion and politics simply did not mix. Soon, however, their relationship was being discussed at offices, factories, sporting events, and parties across the nation, and *Newsweek* declared 1976 to be "the Year of the Evangelical." In July, the spiritual patriarch of the African American community, Martin Luther King Sr., endorsed Carter's candidacy in his fervent benediction at the Democratic National Convention: "Surely the Lord sent Jimmy Carter to . . . bring America back to where she belongs."

Carter's faith played a major role in both the 1976 presidential campaign and his presidency. This is evident in his speeches, relationship with religious constituencies, approach to politics, stance on several controversial religious issues, and many of his domestic and foreign policies.

The Faith of Jimmy Carter

Carter grew up in the Southern Baptist Church that had dominated many parts of the South since the Civil War. As a child, he regularly attended Sunday school, worship services, and the Royal Ambassadors, an organization for young boys that focused on missions, at the Baptist church in Plains, Georgia. At age eleven, Carter publicly professed his faith in Jesus Christ as his personal Savior and Lord, was baptized, and joined the church. Thereafter, he participated faithfully in the Baptist Young People's Union. Carter's religious convictions and social attitudes were strongly shaped by his mother, Lillian. In 1958, Carter was ordained as a deacon, the governing office in Southern Baptist congregations, and he ushered, led public prayers, and preached lay sermons at his home church. His failure to win the Democratic nomination for governor in 1966 prompted Carter to reassess his faith. Challenged by a sermon entitled "If You Were Arrested for Being a Christian, Would There Be Enough Evidence to Convict You?" and conversations with his sister, evangelist Ruth Carter Stapleton, he vowed to make serving Christ and others his primary aim. During the 1966 governor's race, he had spent sixteen to eighteen hours a day trying to convince Georgians to vote for him. "The comparison struck me," Carter wrote, "300,000 visits for myself in three months, and 140 visits for God [to witness to others] in fourteen years!" Carter soon experienced a more intimate relationship with Christ and inner peace. He read the Bible "with new interest" and concluded that he had been a Pharisee. He went on witnessing missions, attended several religious conferences, and oversaw the showing of a Billy Graham film in Americus, Georgia.[1]

Historian E. Brooks Holifield identifies three major influences on Carter's ideology: Southern evangelicalism, Baptists' views of the separation of church and state, and the Christian realism of Reinhold Niebuhr. Like other Southern evangelicals, Carter emphasized an intimate relationship with Christ and personal holiness. He embodied "a Calvinist piety filtered through Puritan introspection and revivalist exhortation."[2] Their understanding of the Bible and experience as cultural outsiders in early American history led Baptists to advocate a firm division between church and state, a position that had a powerful impact on Carter's approach to politics. Carter's reading of numerous books by and about Niebuhr helped shape his perspective on "Christian political involvement, . . . the notion that love should be translated into justice, and the tension between idealism and realism."[3] Niebuhr helped convince him, Carter explained, that "the highest possible goal of a government . . . is justice: to treat people fairly, to guarantee their individual rights, to guard against discrimination, to try to resolve arguments peacefully."[4]

Leo Ribuffo contends that Carter was the nation's "most introspective president since Abraham Lincoln." He thought deeply about many matters and tried to become an expert in numerous fields. Surprisingly, however, he paid little attention to the intellectual aspects of religion. Prior to becoming president, Carter never took a course in religion or theology at any level. He displayed minimal knowledge of biblical criticism, biblical history, or systematic theology. Ribuffo surmises that "perhaps unconsciously he chose to keep religious faith—a realm of release, reassurance, and warmth—relatively unscathed by the technical complexities that affected other parts of his life."[5] Carter drew inspiration from a variety of neoorthodox, liberal Protestant, existentialist, Jewish, and Catholic authors, especially Niebuhr, Dietrich Bonhoeffer, Karl Barth, Paul Tillich, Soren Kierkegaard, Martin Buber, and Hans Kung.[6] However, he rarely read or conversed with any of the leading evangelical political analysts and practitioners of the 1970s, most notably Mark Hatfield, Carl F. H. Henry, John Anderson, Steven V. Monsma, or Harold Hughes.[7]

"The most important thing in my life," Carter declared during the 1976 campaign, "is Jesus Christ."[8] He considered Christ's admonition to "love God with all your heart and soul and mind, and love your neighbor as yourself" a foundation for life.[9] By words and actions, he accentuated the importance of spirituality and church involvement. Carter repeatedly asserted that he was a born-again Christian who attended church regularly, prayed constantly, and read the Bible faithfully.[10] He worshiped every Sunday either at First Baptist Church in Washington, D.C., at various churches across the United States or abroad, or at special services at Camp David.[11] Before, during, and after his presidency, he taught a Sunday school class. He relied on prayer to guide him in his political responsibilities.[12] During the 1976 presidential primaries, he asserted, "I spent more time on my knees the four years I was governor . . . than I did all the rest of my life put together."[13] In 1980, Carter insisted that he had depended even more on God's help while he was president.[14] The Georgian later explained that when he prayed, he asked three key questions: Are my goals appropriate? "Am I doing the right thing, based on my personal moral code, my Christian faith, and the duties of my current position?" "Have I done my best, based on the alternatives open to me?" When he followed this approach, he concluded, things usually worked out well.[15] Carter declared, "I've been steeped in the Bible since early childhood" and insisted that the study of the Bible "is a very important part of my life."[16] He read at least one chapter of the Bible each night before bed, often in Spanish, and frequently with his wife, Rosalynn.[17] He explained that they "read the Bible together . . . not as some sort of mystical guidebook, as some might think, to give us quick and simple solutions to every problem of a nation or personal life, but because we find new insights and new inspirations" in its pages.[18]

In most ways, Carter's personal faith was typical of Southern Baptists and most other evangelicals. He believed in the deity of Christ, the need to accept Christ as Savior and Lord (being born again, saved, or spiritually regenerated), the importance of evangelism, the sinfulness of human beings, and the authority of the Bible.[19] Carter claimed that he deeply loved his wife, that he was sexually and emotionally faithful to her, and that their common faith in Christ helped sustain and strengthen their marriage.[20] However, he rejected traditional evangelical taboos against drinking alcohol, attending movies, dancing, and working on Sundays.[21]

One of the most devout Christians to serve as the nation's chief executive, Carter often discussed his personal faith while in office. During the 1976 campaign, he assured voters that his effort to pattern his life after Christ's would help him remain calm in the midst of crises and the challenges of the presidency.[22] Toward the end of his term, Carter said, "my own personal faith . . . is stronger now than it's ever been before."[23] While it resonated with many religiously committed Americans, his use of scriptural language, principles, and themes seemed to be more of a natural expression of his convictions than rhetoric employed to win votes. Nevertheless, he made fewer explicit references to either biblical passages or to his own faith in speeches and public statements than many other presidents, including Lincoln, Franklin Roosevelt, Eisenhower, and Reagan.[24] Three factors explain why. First, as previously noted, Carter strongly endorsed the separation of church and state. "Baptists," he contended, "are among the most fervent advocates of all legal separation between the church and the state."[25] The Constitution prohibited "an unwarranted intrusion of the state . . . into religion or vice versa."[26] He claimed that he would never let his religious beliefs "interfere" with his presidential duties and that he strove to "separate his Christian convictions from his role as

President."[27] As had Kennedy, Carter assured Americans that no church leaders would determine his decisions.[28] Second, Carter respected America's religious diversity and realized that to govern effectively, he needed the support of liberal, mainline, evangelical, charismatic, and fundamentalist Protestants, as well as of Catholics, Jews, Muslims, and the unchurched. Carter frequently appealed to beliefs people shared in common. "We can be fervent believers in our own religion," he averred, "and still work for peace and harmony, good will, love, and a sense of brotherhood throughout the world."[29] Third, Carter wanted to assure critics and skeptics that he was not a religious extremist committed to converting the United States into a theocracy. In an effort to dispel what his White House chief of staff, Hamilton Jordan, called the "weirdo factor," Carter stressed that many other Americans shared his religious commitments. His faith was "not a mysterious or mystical or magical thing."[30] He did not have a direct pipeline to God or think that he was incapable of making mistakes. "The fact that a person has deep religious convictions," Carter explained, "does not mean that that person thinks he's always right" or that God placed him in a prominent position.[31] He repudiated Catholic social theorist Michael Novak's contention that individuals who saw themselves as highly moral could easily convince themselves that they were incapable of doing wrong. This belief, Carter argued, violated Christ's teaching that all people were sinful. He insisted that his constant search "for better answers to questions" was "a matter of public record."[32]

Carter's worldview rested upon an amalgam of factors: his family, educational, and religious background, as well as his varied life experiences in the military, business, and politics. He was a Southerner, a populist, a Democrat, an engineer, a Washington outsider, and a Baptist evangelical, so his evangelical Christian convictions should not be overemphasized in explaining his political perspective.[33] At times, in fact, Carter minimized the impact that his Christian view of life had on how he carried out his political responsibilities. When reporters asserted during the 1976 campaign that some Americans felt uneasy about having in the White House "a Southern Baptist, a 'born again' Christian, a man who is not hesitant to talk about his religious views in public," Carter reminded them that the United States had already had a Southern Baptist president—Harry Truman—who had demonstrated that "deep religious beliefs" and public service were compatible.[34] In a 1978 press conference, he declared, "I have never found" that being a devout Christian "interfered with my performance of duties as governor or as a candidate or as president of our country."[35] Carter told the National Religious Broadcasters in January 1980, "I serve Christ. I also serve America. And I have never found any incompatibility between these two responsibilities for service."[36] Like other people, Carter's worldview and actions were often inconsistent, in part because he spent little time "formulating a coherent political philosophy."[37] Despite his use of such terms as *interference* and *incompatibility*, Carter frequently argued paradoxically that his faith affected all his thoughts and actions and was integral to his work as president. He repudiated the idea that Christians should restrict their faith to their private lives instead of applying it to the public areas of economics, education, social relationships, and politics. Carter's Christian values affected the goals he set, the policies he developed, the legislation he proposed, and the way he related with leaders of other nations, his cabinet, his staff, and the public. "I can be a better President," Carter insisted, "because of my faith."[38] During the campaign, he promised that if elected president, "I would try to exemplify in every moment of my life those attitudes and actions of Christianity that I believe in. I would ask God for guidance on decisions affecting our country and make those decisions after evaluating the alternatives as best as I could."[39] As president, he insisted that his faith provided a "very sound basis" for his political actions and that his religious convictions strongly influenced his political decisions.[40] All Christians, Carter contended, had an obligation to "try to elevate" their nation's standards and practices to meet those "set for us by Jesus Christ."[41] Isaiah and Jeremiah had "pronounced God's judgment in the very center of political power," demonstrating that individuals were required to bring their own "personal religious life" into the political arena.[42] Carter told the audience at the National Prayer Breakfast in January 1979 that people must not separate their governmental duties from their responsibilities to God.[43]

Carter often seemed reluctant, however, to discuss how his faith affected specific political decisions. When a Polish journalist invited him in December 1977 to describe how his "evangelical principles" helped him solve "any complicated problem," he did not give any concrete examples.[44] In March 1979, Carter was asked on what scriptural basis he supported the Equal Rights Amendment (ERA). Instead of discussing the Bible's emphasis on treating people equally regardless of their race, ethnicity, or sex, Carter replied that his position was not based on Scripture, which could be used both to support and oppose the ERA. He did add, however, that he looked "to the Bible as a source of guidance" and believed "that Christ meant for all of us to be treated equally," which he demonstrated "in many ways."[45] His refusal to cite specific biblical passages to support his positions disappointed many conservative Christians.

Carter argued that the 1980 election should focus on issues and his record as president, not the religious convictions of the candidates. In late October, he was asked why so many evangelical leaders were endorsing Reagan. The president blamed the Moral Majority's establishment of a "religious test for political acceptability." He added that he had never found anything in Scripture that specified whether the federal government "should create a Department of Education or build B-1 bombers or air-launched cruise missiles, or share the operation of the Panama Canal with Panama." Carter repudiated the Moral Majority's use of candidates' stances on these issues to evaluate whether they were obeying God.[46] Nor did Carter mention any general biblical principles pertaining to the nature of education, the responsibility of government, or the importance of justice that helped shape the positions he took on these issues. Moral Majority founder Jerry Falwell and other conservative Christians, by contrast, discussed scriptural norms they believed justified their stances.[47] Responding to a similar question two days later, Carter replied, "I'm not in favor of a religious definition of an acceptable politician."[48] James Wall, the editor of the *Christian Century*, who ran Carter's 1976 campaign in Illinois, agreed with the president's position. "It would be unconstitutional, impolitic and just plain bad theology," he argued, "for Mr. Carter to insist that his Christian perspective provide[s] him with specific answers to policy questions." He had to translate his personal perspective that Jesus Christ is Lord into an approach to guide national policies. Wall affirmed T. S. Eliot's argument in *The Idea of a Christian Society* that "the Christian and the unbeliever do not, and cannot behave very differently in the conduct of office; for it is the general ethos of the people they have to govern, not their own piety, that determines the behaviour of politicians." This was why, Wall reasoned, Carter did not mention God or Christ in his inaugural address and why he "consistently appealed to a national sense of higher ideals, not to a specific religious faith." He sought to lead the nation by appealing to Americans' "agreed-on values and commitments, based on common experience, history and goals." Wall maintained that Carter's Christian perspective guided all the decisions he made, "but it would be inappropriate to say that any single decision" he made was more "'Christian'" than any other. The president never claimed that his decisions were spiritually superior to those who disagreed with him.[49] On other occasions, however, as discussed later, Carter did argue that the Bible provided a basis for his policies.

Carter believed he could function as a Christian president because the United States was based "on an awareness of the will of God" and a willingness to do it.[50] Since its beginning, he maintained, the American political framework had depended in part on religious faith, as evident in the Declaration of Independence, the Constitution, laws, coins, and the Pledge of Allegiance. Although the Constitution did not explicitly mention God, he declared, in it, "we recognize God as the guiding leader of us all."[51] "Our founding fathers," he insisted, made "Judeo-Christian ethics and a belief in God . . . a foundation for the Constitution and the laws of our nation. There is no basic incompatibility between them, although in practice there is a sharp delineation."[52] The Georgian insisted that there was a higher authority than man's law for both interpersonal and international relations. This was "biblical moral standards," which, he averred, were "compatible with the laws of our country."[53] Thus Carter thought it was proper to try to elevate the principles of government "to meet the standards set for us by Jesus Christ."[54]

These convictions led Carter to conclude that his faith could properly play an important role in the political decisions he made.[55] He maintained that God had created the United States for a purpose: "to set an example for the rest of the world" by protecting human rights and providing equality of opportunity.[56] Although Americans had been "given great natural resources and great wealth," Carter insisted, they had "no special claim to be God's chosen people."[57] He was convinced that God directed history and was in charge of all events, but Carter never claimed that God had specifically chosen him to be president to accomplish his purposes.[58] His firm belief that God worked for good in the lives of those who loved him helped him deal with defeats and criticism.[59]

Carter did not see himself as the nation's spiritual leader: "I don't look on the presidency as a pastorate."[60] He was a political leader, "not a priest nor a bishop, nor someone who fills a religious pulpit." If the nation engaged in a sinful act, it was his responsibility as president to "stop that act and to atone through action for [the] inequities or suffering" the act had caused, but it was not his personal "responsibility to repent before God for what our nation has done in the past or may even do while I am in the White House."[61] Nevertheless, Carter argued that the president was the only one who could "set a standard for morals, decency and openness" and "call on the American people for sacrifices" and explain their purpose and consequences.[62] Although he routinely made proclamations on special religious subjects such as National Prayer Day and Bible Reading Week, Carter seemed less interested in them than other presidents. Perhaps because he was so personally pious and well known for his Christian faith, he felt less compelled to display his religious commitment in visible, official ways.[63]

Carter's faith also influenced how he related to the leaders of other nations. He witnessed to Park Chung Lee of South Korea; the first secretary of the Communist Party in Poland; Deng Xiaoping, the head of the People's Republic of China; and other heads of state. The president urged Deng to allow the use and printing of Bibles in China and to permit Christian worship. Carter regularly attended religious services when traveling abroad, sometimes contributing a Bible reading or prayer. Carter concluded that "in a quiet way, I was able to let the world know about my Christian beliefs without being too ostentatious."[64]

The Election of 1976

The 1976 election featured the most religiously devout pair of major party nominees since William McKinley defeated William Jennings Bryan in 1896. Incumbent President Gerald Ford regularly attended Congressional prayer breakfasts, continually prayed for guidance, read the Bible daily, and occasionally quoted Scripture in interviews and speeches. During the campaign, he addressed the Southern Baptist Convention, courted influential Catholic priests, and received covert assistance from Billy Graham.[65] Nevertheless, it was Carter's faith that became a controversial issue in the campaign. Journalists largely ignored his religious convictions early in the campaign, but his sister Ruth's interview in the *Washington Post* in mid-March and Carter's victories in several primaries prompted them to ask the Georgian about his faith.[66] After that, Carter frequently talked candidly about his religious convictions and how they affected his political positions, something few presidential candidates have done.[67] Reporters and political commentators who had limited knowledge of religious groups, issues, and theology found it difficult to understand Carter's religious commitments, which they often misrepresented.[68]

Although Carter never explicitly asked Americans to support him because of his faith, others did. Stapleton urged people to vote for her brother because of the spiritual leadership he would provide.[69] When speaking to black congregations, his wife, Rosalynn, strongly stressed her husband's religious commitments.[70] Detroit mayor Coleman Young implored blacks to vote for Carter because of his Christian beliefs.[71] A group calling themselves Citizens for Carter placed a full-page ad in *Christianity Today* that answered its question "Does a Dedicated Evangelical Belong in the White House?" with a resounding yes.[72] Other supporters produced a poster portraying Carter with long flowing hair and dressed in biblical grab with the caption, "J. C. Can Save America."[73] Evangelicals published two laudatory books—Howard Norton and Bob Slosser's *The Miracle of Jimmy Carter* and David Kucharsky's *The Man from Plains*—to promote his candidacy.

The nature and sincerity of Carter's religious convictions—and how they might affect his performance as president—quickly became major issues. Many political pundits criticized Carter's campaign strategy and religious commitments. Fellow Southern Baptist Bill Moyers called the Democratic convention that nominated Carter "a combination of religion, politics, and manipulative techniques."[74] Historian Arthur Schlesinger Jr., who had served as a political advisor for the Kennedy administration, chided Carter for implying that evangelical principles could solve "social, economic, and international perplexities."[75] Political scientist James Burnham maintained that the Carterian virtues of goodness, decency, compassion, idealism, and trust were a "manifest absurdity" in foreign policy that would thwart America's ability to achieve its prudential interests.[76] Richard Reeves labeled Carter a "phony," "an actor, [and] a salesman."[77]

Before the party conventions, Mark Hatfield, a Republican senator from Oregon and the nation's most outspoken evangelical politician, exhorted Carter, Ford, and Ronald Reagan, who all professed to be Christians, to openly declare their commitment to protect the poor and oppressed against institutional exploitation, reject "all forms of violence and militancy," repudiate America's materialism, and view "political leadership as servanthood."

Although Carter agreed with Hatfield on most of these points, he did not respond publicly to the senator's challenge. Neither did his opponents.[78]

As in the elections of 1928 and 1960, the separation of church and state was a contested issue. During these earlier campaigns, Protestants protested that church officials would unduly influence the political decisions of Catholic candidates Al Smith and John F. Kennedy. In 1976, some Catholics, Jews, liberal Protestants, and secularists warned that a theologically conservative Southern Baptist might transgress the often difficult to discern line between church and state. Catholic priest, sociologist, and novelist Andrew Greeley wrote an article "Catholics Should Be Fearful of Carter," and the editors of *America* reminded readers that Southern Baptists had historically been anti-Catholic.[79] Carter worked hard to reassure prospective voters that he shared Baptists' historical commitment to the need for a rigid separation between the church and the state.

In late September, Carter's now infamous interview with *Playboy* magazine hit the newsstands. His startling admission that he had lusted after women in his heart amazed many, amused some, and confused others.[80] His willingness to do an interview for a pornographic magazine upset some religious conservatives, as did his use of the terms "shack up" and "screw."[81] Although some commentators praised Carter's candid discussion of social and political issues, numerous editorial columns and cartoons lampooned the Georgian. One showed him looking lustfully at a sensuous nude Statue of Liberty. Some even questioned whether his emphasis on morality, religion, and decency was merely a political ploy. Carter's once-large lead over Ford evaporated, his remarks were dissected and debated in many American pulpits, and he was forced to defend his actions both in interviews and in the third presidential debate.[82] Carter pointed out that such luminaries as Albert Schweitzer, Arnold Toynbee, and Walter Cronkite had been interviewed in *Playboy* and insisted that this forum enabled him to present the gospel to many people who did not attend church or read religious literature.[83] The interview, however, undoubtedly lost him some evangelical votes.

Although "armed with the advantages of outsider status and broad centralist appeal, and competing against the uninspiring and unelected Gerald Ford against a backdrop of Watergate, defeat in Vietnam, and rising economic distress," Carter beat Ford by only 2 percent of the popular vote.[84] Many factors contributed to his narrow victory. The social and political climate—a divisive war, three assassinations, demonstrations, riots, the resignation of a Republican vice president and president in disgrace, Ford's pardon of Nixon, political fraud, a sputtering economy, and increases in crime and drug usage—combined to produce a desire for change. Untainted by Washington's corruption, Carter understood America's mood and "offered absolution to a country plagued with guilt for its sins."[85] Although Ford received about

60 percent of evangelical votes, the Georgian won 20 percent more of their votes than any of his recent Democratic predecessors.[86] Like Carter, Ford professed to be born again, and more evangelicals (an estimated 30 percent of the population) were registered as Republicans than Democrats. In addition, Carter opposed and Ford supported several issues that were important to evangelicals: tuition tax credits, federal aid to parochial schools, school prayer, a repeal of the Supreme Court's position on abortion, and preservation of the tax-exempt status of all church-owned property. Nevertheless, many evangelicals voted for Carter because he was "one of them," a Christian brother they could count on, who spoke their language and stressed the importance of family values and morality in public life. Most of them applauded his emphasis on integrity, compassion, brotherhood, and sacrifice for the common good.[87] His religious rhetoric reaffirmed Americans' faith in themselves and their nation, helped voters trust him, enabled many who had strong religious commitments to identify with him, and generated considerable media attention.[88] To countless evangelicals, Carter's election proved not only that mainstream society had accepted some of their convictions but also that they had become the most important force in American religion.

Carter's Philosophy of Government

Carter strongly stressed the themes of morality, virtue, justice, forgiveness, humility, servanthood, peace, human rights, concern for the poor, and stewardship. He claimed that the Bible provided a solid foundation for the modern state and delineated its major responsibilities. The Old Testament, he wrote, taught that government is based on "a voluntary covenant rather than force—the idea of equality before the law and the supremacy of the law over the whims of any ruler."[89] "We should try to assure that secular law is compatible with God's laws...[and] obey the government" when it does not "conflict with God's command to us."[90] The Bible instructed Christians to alleviate hunger, suffering, and discrimination, promote peace, and foster human rights.[91]

Because God's law was the ultimate authority for all life, Carter argued, national policies should be based on what was morally right rather than politically expedient. During the 1976 campaign, he accused the Ford administration of ignoring human rights and putting "self-interest above principle."[92] He insisted that Nixon and Ford had tarnished America's image by their "Machiavellian tactics—secret diplomacy, back channels, 'Lone Ranger' diplomacy, excessive concern with power politics"—and their "neglect of principles and morality."[93] Carter promised that his administration would not intervene in the domestic affairs of other countries, would ensure that economic aid benefited the citizens of recipient nations, and would vigorously protest human rights violations.[94] "In dealing with other nations, the United States" should abide by the standards of "morality, justice, and freedom . . . in its own Constitution."[95] When America had adhered to Christian norms in its relationship with other nations, Carter averred, it had been stronger, not weaker.[96] Moreover, he argued, the United States must do what was best for the citizens of other nations.[97] He declared in August 1980 that he had sought to "do what is right and proper in the interest of our country and . . . of justice" and had "let the political consequences take care of themselves."[98]

His Christian commitment also prompted Carter to strongly emphasize the importance of virtue and insist that public officials should set an "absolutely exemplary" standard.[99] Carter sought to maintain high standards of integrity for himself and his administration. In May 1977, he submitted the Ethics in Government Act, which required all policy-making officials to publicly disclose their financial interests, increased restrictions on the revolving door between government and private industry, and established a new Office of Government Ethics.[100] He urged Americans to follow the same standards of morality in business and politics as they did in their personal and family lives.[101] Carter contended that the Judeo-Christian tradition provided a moral vision and a transcendent basis for ethics.[102] Its "honesty, integrity, compassion, love, hope, charity, [and] humility" should guide people's lives.[103] He rejoiced that the United States was dedicated to advancing "basic moral and philosophical principles," and he strove to ensure that the nation fulfilled its "deepest moral and religious commitments."[104]

In his inaugural address, Carter quoted Micah 6:8, which commands human beings to act justly, love mercy, and walk humbly with God. The president tried to promote justice in international affairs, racial relations, tax programs, and the courts.[105] Carter pledged to use his office "to translate love into simple justice." Influenced by Niebuhr's book *Moral Man and Immoral Society,* Carter insisted that God's mandates for individuals were much higher than those for society. Individuals were required to practice "complete agape love," whereas nations must "institute simple justice." Although accepting this distinction, Carter was much more optimistic than the neoorthodox theologian that Christian love could be expressed in public affairs. Unlike Niebuhr, he seemed to believe that societies could further Christian causes and virtues. Carter concluded that the aims of individuals, religious bodies, and nations were similar: to advance ideals, promote peace, alleviate suffering, and express love by providing justice.[106] Biographer Betty Glad faults Carter for failing to recognize that justice, rather than love, is "the relevant virtue for the political realm" or to understand that "justice requires power be confronted and somehow constrained. While individuals may sacrifice themselves for a higher good, statesmen could not sacrifice their nation's security for a higher goal."[107] When Carter spoke of a government "which was as loving as its people," Calvin College professor Paul Henry protested, he forgot that a "government acts not as an agent of love, but as a final resort to force when love, compassion, and volunteerism have failed."[108]

Carter's concern for mercy was evident in his first presidential act: unconditionally pardoning all those who had evaded the draft during the Vietnam War and had not engaged in a violent act. Moreover, he urged Americans to care for "the family of all humankind" and to forgive one another.[109] Echoing Niebuhr, who called pride the root of sin, Carter frequently denounced hubris and praised humility. "Christ admonishes us against self-pride, against the condemnation of others," he declared, "since we too are sinful."[110] "Like all human beings," he admitted, "I am sinful and certainly have made mistakes."[111] On the one hand, Carter claimed that nations as well as individuals were fallible, sinful, and afflicted with pride, and he urged them to repent and receive God's forgiveness. Both America's embarrassments—most notably the Watergate scandal, the Vietnam War, and CIA and FBI excesses—and Niebuhr's emphasis on the immorality of nations prompted Carter to insist that the United States must acknowledge its failures.[112] On the other hand, though, Carter repeatedly called for a government as compassionate and competent as the American people; he often praised American achievements and citizens and even entitled a 1977 compilation of his speeches *A Government as Good as Its People.*[113]

Motivated by Christ's example, Carter strove to adopt the attitude and approach of a servant. Power, Carter maintained, should be used to serve others. As president, he could "greatly magnify" his opportunities to serve and love others and to help the poor and afflicted.[114] Those who served Christ and others were truly great. He admitted, however, that it was hard for the president to be "a genuine servant."[115] The privileges, prerogatives, and protections of the office made it very difficult to take on the attitude and role of a servant. The president's time is extremely precious, access to him is very limited, everyone defers to him, he is always the center of attention, and he alone can speak for the American people. All of these factors prompt him to consider himself more important than others. Moreover, no one becomes president without selling himself, as well as his policies. Peter Bourne claims that Carter regularly asked himself: "How do you reconcile a lifelong belief that deep humility is an essential part of achieving God's kingdom on earth with the egotistical self-promotion of politics?"[116]

Carter's faith also helped to inspire his efforts to promote peace throughout the world. The president reminded Americans that the Bible commanded them to "Seek peace, pursue it—pursue it actively, search for peace."[117] The Old Testament offered a vision of what "peace might mean in its deepest sense."[118] Carter insisted that peace was more than the "mere absence of war." It involved stamping out international terrorism and "unceasing effort to preserve human rights."[119] Despite all their difficulties and conflicts, Carter believed that nations would someday "obey the Biblical injunction to 'follow after the things which make for peace.'"[120]

The Laws and the Prophets of the Judeo-Christian tradition deeply influenced Carter's commitment to human rights. God's law was superior to the laws of individual nations. The Bible instructed nations to respect human dignity, help the indigent, and live peacefully together despite their differences in religion and ideology.[121] National Security Advisor Zbigniew Brzezinski argued that Carter's advocacy of human rights was based on both "his religious beliefs" and "his political acumen."[122] Carter's focus on human rights was the cornerstone of his foreign policy and differed sharply with the position of his predecessors. He declared in his inaugural address, "Our commitment to human rights must be absolute." The Baptist maintained that the United States had a moral obligation to defend the human rights set forth in the Helsinki Accords of 1975.[123] His administration sought to promote "freedom from arbitrary arrest and imprisonment, torture [and] unfair trial . . . rights to food, shelter, health care, and education . . . [and] freedom of thought, speech, assembly, religion, press, movement, and participation in government."[124] As Gladdis Smith contends, foreign policy traditionally required that "every move must be justified in terms of national advantage. In a sinful world, no leader could endanger the survival of the nation by blind adherence to an absolute moral standard."[125] As a result, Carter applied his human rights agenda selectively.[126] Unlike Woodrow Wilson, he "refused to intervene militarily to advance political reform." Like John F. Kennedy, he often judged American security as "sufficiently compelling to warrant overlooking flagrant violations of human rights by friendly or potentially friendly regimes."[127] Some critics complained that Carter's human rights policy was naive; others protested that it was inconsistent: He berated some regimes but ignored the violations of others when the United States had important security or economic interests at stake.

Carter often expressed his concern for those who suffered because of poverty, discrimination, imprisonment, or injustice. He claimed that both as governor of Georgia and as president, he spent considerable time exploring how to feed the hungry, provide shelter for the homeless, educate the illiterate, eliminate the "stigma of poverty or racial discrimination," prevent crime, rehabilitate prisoners, and ensure justice.[128]

More than any other president, Carter urged Americans to be good stewards of God's creation and warned them about the perils of materialism. God had given people dominion over the earth to improve the quality of life for the poor among them and the next generation.[129] Carter complained that too many Americans worshiped "self-indulgence and consumption" and stressed that owning and using things did not satisfy the human longing for meaning.[130] He lamented that the world was spending more on the military than ever before.[131] Carter wanted the world's natural and financial resources to provide "a better quality of life, not measured by material possessions," but by people's use of "the talents and ability that God gives us."[132]

Carter and Controversial Religious Issues

As previously mentioned, Carter's positions on several issues, most notably abortion, school prayer, and tuition tax credits, were at odds with those of many evangelicals and Catholics. Carter repeatedly asserted that he strongly believed abortion was wrong (but he avoided calling it murder or offering an opinion of when life began).[133] However, he promised to abide by the 1973 *Roe v. Wade* decision that made abortion legal during the first trimester of a woman's pregnancy. He maintained that the president could not change a Supreme Court ruling.[134] Moreover, he pointed out that while he was governor, Georgia passed the strictest abortion law permissible.[135] Although Carter was legally required to enforce this decision, he could have denounced it and supported a Constitutional amendment to reverse the Court's position, but the Democratic Party's many pro-choice constituents prevented him from taking this approach.

Carter did promise to try to reduce abortions, especially by encouraging sex education, providing more access to contraceptives, improving adoption procedures, and reforming the welfare system.[136] He called for "a permanent, nationwide system of family planning...to ensure that every child is a wanted child."[137] Carter largely ignored the pro-life argument that fetuses are created in God's image and have a right to life and therefore that abortion is murder.[138] He also scrupulously avoided directly attacking the belief that women had the right to control their own bodies. Theologically conservative Christians frequently criticized Carter's position, and he refused to meet with their leaders to discuss abortion.[139]

On the other hand, Carter's refusal to use federal funds to pay for abortions except in cases where a woman's life was threatened or where pregnancy resulted from rape or incest irritated pro-choice advocates.[140] In July 1977, a reporter asked him whether a woman's ability to have an abortion should depend on her financial resources. Carter declared that "there are many things in life that are not fair, that wealthy people can afford and poor people can't." He added that neither the states nor the federal government "should be required to finance abortions."[141] The next day, aide Midge Costanza wrote to the president that she had received many phone calls from public interest groups, individuals, and White House staff members "expressing concern and even anger" over his remarks. By presenting his personal view on this subject, callers claimed, Carter had "provided negative guidance to legislators and governors and interfered...in an unfair way." She added, callers "hope you will...support the use of Federal funds for abortion when 'medically necessary.'" Beside this statement, Carter wrote in pen, "no." At the bottom of the communiqué, Carter replied: "My opinion was well defined...during [the] campaign. My [campaign] statement is actually more liberal than I feel personally."[142] When asked a few days later how he reconciled his denial of federal funds for abortions with his concern for the poor, the president responded that federal funds could be better used to provide preventive health care and immunization programs, care for the elderly, and adequate housing and food.[143]

Carter also consistently opposed efforts to permit public schools to set aside a specific time for voluntary prayer. Although deeply committed to prayer, Carter contended that this proposal interfered with the right of Americans to worship as they saw fit. Moreover, America's religious pluralism made it difficult to implement, and it would cause embarrassment to students who could not in conscience participate. Although affirming the importance of prayer in the home, the school, and the Oval Office, he declared that the government should not tell people "they have to worship at a certain time and in a certain way."[144] Because prayer was "a private matter between a person and God," the government "should stay out of the prayer business."[145]

During the 1976 campaign, Carter insisted that it was important to give all children "a healthy diversity of educational opportunity."[146] Nevertheless, he promised to do everything he could to prevent Congress from passing legislation to provide tuition tax credits. The Georgian insisted that these credits were unconstitutional, too costly, and unjust, because they would furnish more aid to the wealthy than to the middle class or the poor. If enacted, they would weaken public schools by making it easier for parents to send their children to private schools.[147] Unlike many evangelicals, Carter did not complain about the public schools' secular curriculum and limited instruction about moral values. He believed they had a vital role to play in preparing children for the future, inculcating traditional American values, and teaching basic subjects.

Carter's Relationship with Religious Constituencies

Despite his strong personal faith, Carter did not meet regularly with the leaders of any religious groups, solicit their advice or opinions frequently, or respond very favorably or effectively to their wishes. He spoke to few religious gatherings and did not name a liaison to religious groups until the spring of 1979.[148] Carter promised during the 1976 campaign that he would not hold special worship services at the White House or give special access to evangelicals.[149] Nevertheless, numerous religious leaders expected to have Carter's ear. Many of them soon, however, became frustrated (and some disillusioned) by the president's lack of availability and sensitivity to their concerns.[150] Despite his solid evangelical credentials and success with evangelical voters in 1976, Carter did not enjoy a close or cordial relationship with this group. The Democrat had pledged that if elected he would appoint some evangelicals to administrative posts, but he did not do so.[151] Carter took this approach because he did not want to be perceived as overly favorable toward religious communities, especially evangelicals. His limited attention to their interests and many of his political policies antagonized evangelicals and other religious constituencies. This, in turn, hindered his efforts to implement aspects of his political agenda and contributed to his defeat in the 1980 election.

Southern Baptist minister Robert Maddox served as Carter's liaison to religious groups during the last year and a half of his presidency.[152] During this time, he focused on trying to "put out fires with conservatives who were deeply set against" Carter.[153] Maddox tried to rebuild rapport with disgruntled religious communities by visiting ministers, denominational executives, and lay leaders throughout the country. He attended conferences; spoke at numerous churches, colleges, and theological seminaries; and met with key leaders to solicit support for administrative policies. Although many of these leaders shared much in common with Carter, his failure to involve them more directly in the political process limited their support for him. As Claire Randall, the general secretary of the National Council of Churches, put it in 1979, "More than any other President in memory, Jimmy Carter speaks the language similar to our own, shares many of our assumptions, [and] looks at the world through our lenses."[154] They wanted, however, to participate in drafting legislation, not simply help sell it after it was written.[155]

Maddox lamented that the Carter administration had especially overlooked fundamentalists and other theologically conservative groups that comprised a constituency of 40 million people.[156] Theological conservatives, most notably Jerry Falwell, Pat Robertson, and Jim Bakker, head of the popular television ministry PTL, agreed with most of Carter's religious convictions but disagreed strongly with many of his political positions. Although Carter reached out to this constituency as the 1980 election approached, he did not adopt a specific strategy for appealing to religious groups.[157] In January 1980, Carter held a breakfast meeting with fourteen influential conservative leaders, many of whom were critics of his administration, to answer their questions about his policies. The president discussed his views on prayer in public schools, abortion, national defense, ERA, the White House Conference on Families, and other issues.[158] The next month, Carter spoke to the National Religious Broadcasters, and in August he hosted important moderate evangelical leaders to listen to their concerns and encourage them to work for his reelection. His staff also met with prominent ecumenical leaders to discuss similar issues.[159]

Carter's relationship with Southern Baptists during his presidency was closer and more cordial than with other groups. He met and corresponded regularly with key denominational leaders, spoke at several Southern Baptist gatherings, and hosted a dinner and reception to raise funds for a Southern Baptist missions organization. At their annual conventions, Southern Baptists adopted resolutions supporting many of Carter's priorities and policies, including multilateral arms control, national security, peace, world hunger, relief for refugees, and lobby disclosure legislation.[160] On the other hand, most Southern Baptists disagreed with Carter's position on ERA, abortion, and homosexual civil rights. Although many Southern Baptists craved greater attention, some complained that Carter had established "a Baptist Vatican on the Potomac."[161]

As it was with evangelicals, Carter's relationship with Catholics was generally troubled. He claimed that his positions on abortion and school vouchers created more problems with the Catholic hierarchy than with Catholic laypeople.[162] Upset by his stances on these issues, most Catholic clergy and editors favored Ford in 1976.[163] Carter won 55 percent of the Catholic vote, but this percentage was significantly lower than most of his recent Democratic predecessors had received.[164] As had Franklin Roosevelt, Nixon, and Ford, Carter appointed a personal representative to the Vatican, which Catholics heartily approved. Both evangelical Protestants and militant secularists protested that this violated the separation of church and state.[165] Catholics also appreciated Carter's hosting of Pope John Paul II at the White House in October 1979 during his historic six-day visit to the United States.[166] In a public address welcoming the pontiff, the president stressed their mutual efforts to promote human dignity and rights and to achieve arms limitations and peace.[167] American Catholics were also pleased when Carter visited the pope at the Vatican in June 1980. The president praised the pope for focusing the world's attention upon those suffering from hunger, poverty, disease, and political repression. John Paul II voiced their shared conviction that "justice could be obtained only if human dignity was recognized."[168] Despite these actions and Carter's periodic meetings with Catholic leaders, they often felt slighted and ignored.

During the 1976 Democratic primaries, Jews supported rival candidates and expressed concerns about Carter's religious conservatism. Even though the Baptist believed that the state of Israel had been established to fulfill biblical prophecy and strongly supported Israel, most Jews felt more comfortable with theologically liberal Christians.[169] Carter strategists sought to woo Jewish voters by distributing a letter from several prominent Jews living in Atlanta that affirmed his commitment to Israel's independence and asserted that Jews did not need to worry about his religious convictions.[170] Jews had several reasons to view Carter's presidency very favorably. He appointed many Jews to key positions in his administration, including two to his cabinet. He championed the rights of Jews around the world, and the policies and pressure of his administration enabled hundreds of thousands of Jews to emigrate from the Soviet Union and other nations to the United States and Israel. He negotiated the Camp David Accords that brought peace between Israel and Egypt, helping to ensure Israel's survival. In addition, Carter spoke to, met with, and corresponded fairly frequently with Jewish leaders and groups. Nevertheless, despite these actions and most Jews' close affinity with the Democratic Party, his relationship with them was problematic. Many

Jews feared that Carter's Southern Baptist beliefs would intrude into his presidency. Two incidents caused trouble: when Carter was accused of blaming Jews for the crucifixion of Christ and when the president of the Southern Baptist Convention declared that "God Almighty does not hear the prayers of a Jew."[171]

Jewish leaders generally appreciated Carter's deeply held religious convictions, many of which were rooted in the Old Testament, as well as his commitment to the security and permanent peace of Israel and his extraordinary accomplishment in facilitating the Camp David Accords. Many of them, however, resented his pressure on Israel to accept an agreement that diminished "the quality, nature, and scope of the peace" it could expect after withdrawing from the Sinai.[172] Many Jewish leaders also disagreed with Carter's position that the Palestinians living in Israel should be granted a permanent homeland.[173]

Carter's Faith and Presidential Policies

Carter explains in his autobiography, *Keeping Faith*, that his inaugural address focused on his "most important values—human rights, environmental quality, nuclear arms control, and the search for justice and peace."[174] His Christian commitment is evident in these and other of his priorities as president, most notably his work to strengthen families, reduce poverty, reform welfare, curb energy usage, and slow world population growth.

During the 1976 campaign, Carter asserted, "I intend . . . to make sure that . . . our government . . . helps our families rather than hurts them." He promised to convene a conference on the American family to enable leaders of government and the private sector, as well as ordinary citizens, "to discuss specific ways we can better support and strengthen our families."[175] In 1979, he insisted that his administration had significantly helped families by creating eight million new jobs; reforming the nation's "ineffective, inefficient welfare programs"; greatly increasing funding for social services, health, housing, and education; and working to pass comprehensive health insurance and legislation to prevent child abuse and sexual exploitation of children. His administration had also revamped the food stamp program, strengthened Social Security, enacted new laws to promote part-time employment and flexible hours, and asked Congress to help poor families pay their higher energy bills.[176] After preliminary meetings in forty-eight states, three national meetings were held in 1980 in connection with the White House Conference on Families. The president pledged to reduce the "marriage penalty tax," to meet with major corporations to discuss how to develop more family-friendly policies, to work with public and private organizations to better serve families, and to adopt other measures "to enhance family strengths."[177]

Carter's understanding of biblical stewardship significantly affected his strong commitment to protecting the environment. The president protested that human beings had "despoiled God's Earth." They had not properly preserved the "carefully balanced, very delicate" environment God had created.[178] Despite tremendous opposition from timber, mineral, oil, and gas interests, he signed a bill in December 1980 to keep a third of Alaska from commercial development. One of the most important pieces of environmental legislation in American history, this bill doubled the size of national parks and wildlife refuges. Carter also signed separate laws that prevented strip mining and promoted reclamation and established a "Superfund" to eliminate dangerous chemicals that had been dumped or spilled into the environment.[179]

His Christian convictions also helped inspire Carter's effort to reform welfare and reduce poverty. During the 1976 campaign, he asserted that helping "those who are poor, deprived, despised, unfortunate, illiterate, [and] afflicted," would be his "prime responsibility."[180] The Democrat failed to achieve his specific goals in this area. The number of Americans living under the poverty line increased significantly during his presidency, and a coherent welfare system was not created. The welfare "system" Carter sought to revamp, however, was a "mess" and "a monument to the power of special interests and to the prevalence of hostile stereotypes of poor people."[181] Moreover, the nation's economic woes during the late 1970s pushed more people onto welfare rolls, making reform much more difficult. This, coupled with Congressional opposition and his commitment to balancing the budget, led Carter to eventually abandon his attempts to reconstruct the welfare system and to reduce poverty.[182]

Carter's willingness to tackle tough problems, ask Americans to make sacrifices, and address long-term issues are especially evident in his quest to develop a national energy policy. As John C. Barrow puts it, this issue reveals "the strength of Carter's leadership—his willingness to confront inherently difficult national problems without regard to political costs and his conception of the presidency as leadership for the public good." Throughout his tenure in office, the Baptist stressed that the serious challenges and choices confronting Americans required them to make sacrifices. Carter sought to devise public policies that provided "comprehensive, long-range solutions," not "politically safe, short-term fixes."[183]

In a nationally televised speech in April 1977, Carter termed the energy problem the "greatest challenge," with the exception of preventing war, the United States would face in the next generation.[184] He recognized that many of his proposals would be unpopular because they required Americans to reduce their energy consumption and endure inconveniences, but he believed that, as the national trustee, he had a moral responsibility to deal with the problem. Accepting the pessimistic projections of the Club of Rome, Carter asserted that the oil and natural gas Americans depended on so heavily were quickly running out and warned that all the world's proven oil reserves could be exhausted by 1990 unless "profound changes" in consumption patterns occurred. Labeling the United States "the most wasteful nation on Earth," he argued that Americans must drastically change their ways. He proposed a national energy plan to maintain the American standard of living, protect jobs and the environment, lessen America's vulnerability to energy embargoes, guarantee equal sacrifices from all regions, classes, and interest groups, reduce demand through conservation, and develop alternative sources of energy.[185] Addressing a joint session of Congress two days later, Carter warned that unless the federal government adopted a comprehensive national energy policy, catastrophe would result.[186]

Carter created a new Department of Energy, but Congress stymied his national energy policy. In November 1977, he reemphasized that if Americans did not act today, they would "face a greater series of crises tomorrow—energy shortages, environment damages, ever more massive Government bureaucracy and regulations, and ill-considered, last-minute crash programs."[187] Nevertheless, despite considerable lobbying by the president, Congress did not pass his national energy plan until October 1978, and it did not include many of Carter's initial proposals.[188]

New energy initiatives Carter proposed in April 1979 evoked extensive opposition, and energy prices and inflation continued to rise in May and June.[189] By the end of June, the nation was in the throes of an energy crisis, prompting Carter to plan another major public address on the subject. Thirty hours before he was scheduled to appear on television, the White House mysteriously canceled the speech. During the next eleven days, the president met with nearly 130 leaders from government, business, labor, religion, and academia to discuss the nation's energy policy.[190] Advisors sharply disagreed over whether the tone of his address should be optimist, realistic, or pessimistic, and whether it should focus primarily on energy or on broader themes.[191] After much deliberation, Carter decided to discuss the crisis of the American spirit. In his speech, Carter called the energy emergency a symptom of America's deeper "moral and spiritual crisis." America's "crisis of confidence"—evident in surveys, declining productivity, and failure to save for the future—threatened to destroy the nation's "social and political fabric." Carter lamented that many had abandoned "hard work, strong families, close-knit communities, and . . . faith in God" for self-gratification and consumerism.[192] "All the legislation in the world," the president contended, could not "fix what's wrong with America." The nation's problems could be solved only by a revival of faith: "faith in each other, faith in our ability to govern ourselves, and faith in the future of the nation." Carter insisted that solving energy problems could also help "conquer the crisis of spirit in our country" by "rekindling America's sense of unity, inspiring confidence in the future, and providing a new sense of purpose." The president again called for setting import quotas, developing alternative sources of fuel, and conserving energy. He concluded that there were no short-term solutions to the nation's long-range problems. Sacrifice was unavoidable.[193]

Although the immediate reaction of journalists, politicians, and ordinary citizens to Carter's address was largely favorable, it was soon widely and derisively referred to as his "malaise" speech, although he never used this word.[194] Many religious groups and leaders, however, applauded Carter's address and endorsed his energy policy. Major Jewish organizations praised his plan.[195] Southern Baptists produced a series of television and radio advertisements to help win support for the administration's energy policies.[196] Dozens of prominent religious spokespersons signed a statement lauding the president's plan. They agreed with Carter that America's energy predicament pointed to "a greater moral crisis . . . lack of commitment to a common good." Like him, they lamented that Americans were experiencing an "erosion of confidence and trust in one another and in the institutions of public life," that "the great majority of Americans" were "far too dependent on the ethics of materialism," and that Americans consumed "an inordinate share of the earth's resources." They promised to intensify their efforts to reduce energy consumption, provide emergency assistance to the poor, elderly, and disabled, and discuss the moral issues underlying the present crisis.[197]

Barrow argues that Carter sought to devise a rational, comprehensive solution to the nation's energy usage. Disliking political horse trading, he appointed a task force to "evaluate policy options on the basis of merit rather than political considerations." Seeking to promote the national interest, Carter worked to mobilize public support for his proposals to counter the influence of lobbyists on Capitol Hill. The president, however, "alienated members of Congress and interest groups by failing to consult extensively with them," while pursuing a public policy "that had no highly organized constituency." Moreover, he failed to "convince Americans that the costs of his programs would be offset by future benefits."[198] Inspired by his Christian convictions, Carter courageously attacked materialism and exhorted Americans to adopt a simpler lifestyle and make sacrifices for the common good. History demonstrates that it is extremely difficult to persuade large numbers of people to forgo comforts in the present to provide projected benefits to their heirs. Carter accepted pessimistic appraisals of global resources that turned out to be unduly gloomy but seemed very reasonable to many experts in the 1970s. However, his willingness to forsake short-term political advantage to supply long-term solutions to America's energy crisis is laudable.

Spurred by a spate of alarmist books, the population explosion became a major international concern during the 1970s. The world's rapidly accelerating population (between 1960 to 1975, it increased from 3 billion to 4 billion) caused great anxiety and prompted substantial efforts to limit population growth. Closely connected with this dramatically increasing population was extensive hunger and malnutrition, largely concentrated in the Indian subcontinent, Southeast Asia, and sub-Saharan Africa. About a quarter of the world's people were hungry or undernourished, 500 million suffered from malnutrition, and thousands died of starvation every day. In 1978, Carter established the Presidential Commission on World Hunger, which embodied his commitment to reducing world hunger for both humanitarian and national security reasons. He promised that his administration would work to increase world food production and improve food distribution, reduce population growth, and help people lift themselves out of poverty.[199] Reflecting Carter's priorities, the commission stressed that the right to food was the most basic human right. All other rights became a mockery for those who had to "spend all their energy merely to maintain life itself." The United States should make eliminating hunger "the primary focus of its relations with the developing world." Because of its agricultural productivity, advanced food technology, and market power, the United States had "a special responsibility to lead the campaign against world hunger."[200] Prodded by Carter, the Vienna Economic Summit Conference held in June 1980 urged both the United Nations and the world's most industrialized nations to work to slow population growth and help the world's poorest nations increase "their ability to feed themselves."[201]

The philosophical commitments of a president can be seen most clearly in his foreign policy because it involves fewer constraints and greater latitude than domestic matters. Carter played a decisive role in the Panama Canal treaties, the Camp David Accords, and other important negotiations.[202] In 1977, the president argued that America's foreign policy should reflect the nation's character, rest on unchanging moral values, and use "power and influence" to achieve humane purposes. The rise of nearly a hundred new nations since 1945 had made the policy of containing the Soviet Union and promoting "global stability" through alliances with non-Communist, industrial nations no longer viable. The United States must instead help to shape a new world where peoples had higher aspirations for "justice, equity, and human rights." Carter announced "five cardinal principles" that would direct America's new approach: fostering "commitment to human rights," strengthening the bonds among democratic allies, halting the East-West arms race, working to achieve peace in the Middle East, and preventing the spread of both nuclear and conventional weapons.[203]

Carter was convinced that turning control of the Panama Canal over to the Panamanians would improve America's relations with other Latin American countries, increase its influence in the Western hemisphere, discourage the spread of hostile ideologies in Latin America, ease tensions in Panama, and enhance the United States' strength, security, and trade.[204] Nevertheless, his actions were motivated first and foremost by his belief that the original treaty with Panama was blatantly unjust.[205] The president called the new treaties "a gracious apology" for "past wrongdoing."[206] They demonstrated that the United States was willing to "deal fairly and honorably" with smaller nations.[207] Moreover, this issue would reveal to the world how a superpower planned to treat smaller and relatively defenseless nations.[208] Latin America provided a "special opportunity to apply the philosophy of repentance and reform—admitting past mistakes." Carter also wanted to make "the region a showcase" for his human rights policy and replace paternalism with "mutual respect and partnership."[209]

Despite its bipartisan support (Kennedy, Johnson, Nixon, and Ford had all endorsed it), passage of the proposal initially seemed hopeless, as more than three quarters of Americans and most senators opposed giving Panama sovereignty over the canal. During the 1976 Republican primaries, Reagan repeatedly argued that "we built it, we paid for it, it's ours, and . . . we are going to keep it." He and other political conservatives protested that Carter's proposals "were illegal, unpatriotic, a cowardly yielding to blackmail, a boon to communism, and a threat to our nation's security." Many fundamentalist Christians agreed. Carter worked tirelessly in the fall of 1977 and the winter of 1978 to convince senators to ratify the treaties by meeting privately with almost all of them.[210] The president and his staff also labored to gain the support of key religious leaders for the treaties. In a January 1978 briefing with them, Carter emphasized that his foreign policy demonstrated respect for human dignity and the rights of others.[211] In April 1978, the Senate ratified the agreement to transfer control of the waterway to Panama in 2000, giving Carter one of his most important victories.

Carter's other major diplomatic triumph—the Camp David Accords—also rested in large part on his Christian commitment to justice and peace. He considered Israel to be a homeland for the Jews "ordained by God." His "moral and religious beliefs," the Baptist explained, made his "commitment to the security of Israel unshakable."[212] Carter insisted that preserving Israel was "a basic cornerstone" of American foreign policy.[213] His goals in the Middle East were the same as all the other administrations from Truman to Ford: "independence and security for Israel, access to oil, and containment of Soviet influence."[214] Carter was able to negotiate a formal peace agreement between Israel and Egypt because of his understanding of the Middle East, his ability to form friendships with the leaders of both nations, and the power of his core convictions. He devoted more time to the Middle East than to any other issue during his time in the White House.[215] Carter deeply respected the faith of both Israel's Prime Minister Menachem Begin and Egypt's President Anwar Sadat, and both leaders visited him in Washington during the early months of his presidency.[216] In welcoming Begin in July 1977, Carter praised his "deep and unswerving religious commitments" and quoted Isaiah's words: " 'the work of righteousness shall be peace.' "[217] In his memoirs, Carter wrote that he admired Sadat more than any other leader.[218] In the judgment of Gladdis Smith, the only relationship between an American president and a foreign leader that was closer than their relationship was Franklin Roosevelt's bond with Winston Churchill.[219]

On November 20, 1977, Carter attended a special prayer service for peace in the Middle East at First Baptist Church in Washington. "My prayer," he explained to reporters, "recognized that this whole world wants peace; that Christ, our Savior, is the Prince of Peace." He rejoiced that Begin and Sadat, both of whom were "deeply religious" men, had that day prayed to God in a Jewish temple and a Muslim mosque, respectively. Because Muslims, Jews, and Christians "all worship the same God," they had "an avenue of communication and a common purpose."[220] The three leaders had prayed for the success of Sadat's historic visit to Israel, which began that day. Sadat's address, broadcast live in the United States, echoed Carter's convictions. It inspired hope in millions, changed the way many Americans viewed Egypt, and led most Arab leaders to condemn Sadat as a traitor and eventually break diplomatic relations with his country.[221] As 1978 began, Carter traveled to the Middle East and convinced King Hussein of Jordan and the Shah of Iran to support Sadat's initiative. Soon thereafter, Carter met with Sadat and Begin separately to try to ease the suspicion that was growing between them.[222]

Convinced that the United States should take the lead in devising a settlement in the Middle East, Carter invited Sadat and Begin to meet at Camp David on September 5, 1978. No American president had been so deeply and personally involved in diplomatic negotiations since Wilson had helped formulate the Versailles Treaty in 1919. The next day, the three leaders issued an unprecedented "Call for Prayer." It stated: "despite vast human efforts, the Holy Land does not yet enjoy the blessings of peace. . . . [W]e place our trust in the God of our fathers, from whom we seek wisdom and guidance. . . . [W]e request people of all faiths to pray with us that peace and justice will result from these deliberations."[223] During thirteen days, Carter, Sadat, and Begin hammered out an agreement few thought possible. Their "Framework for Peace in the Middle East" provided guidelines for a bilateral Egyptian-Israeli peace treaty and for a comprehensive settlement involving the other occupied territories and the Palestinians. When Begin and Sadat were unable to finalize the bilateral peace treaty, Carter made a dramatic visit to Jerusalem and Cairo in March 1979 and persuaded the two nations to complete the accord. Peter Bourne argues that for six months Carter kept the peace process together "by sheer force of personality," by his sympathetic understanding of the two principals, and by his "determination never to give up."[224]

The Election of 1980

Many conservative Protestants who had been drawn to Carter in 1976 soon discovered that he was more liberal both politically and theologically than they had thought. Moreover, many of them disagreed with him about how Christian convictions should be translated into public policies. Carter's focus on social justice resonated more with religious liberals than conservatives, who disliked the president's positions on abortion, school prayer, tuition tax credits, and many other issues. In 1979, the religious right created four organizations—the National Christian Action Coalition, the Moral Majority, Religious Roundtable, and Christian Voice—to promote its agenda. Entering directly into politics for the first time, religious conservatives took many specific political positions, issued report cards on Congressmen, targeted liberal Democratic senators for defeat, and worked to elect Reagan. The Republican standard-bearer's rhetoric and policies strongly appealed to many evangelicals and fundamentalists. Other Christians who were political moderates supported independent candidate John Anderson, a long-time Congressman from Illinois. Some influential Protestant conservatives, most notably Jimmy Allen, Jim Bakker, and Oral Roberts, endorsed Carter. But the Democrat stressed his religious convictions and personal piety much less than in 1976 and did not implement Maddox's schemes for soliciting the support of specific religious groups.[225] Carter's troubles were exacerbated by the nation's high rates of inflation and unemployment—termed *stagflation*—which combined with rising energy prices to throttle the economy. Moreover, there was no unifying "consensus, no program, no set of principles on which a majority of Democrats agreed."[226] Meanwhile, the Soviet Union invaded Afghanistan, the Iranians seized fifty-two American hostages, and Carter seemed powerless to bring them home.

Unlike Carter and Anderson, Reagan accepted an invitation to address 10,000 conservative Christians, including 2,500 pastors, at a "National Affairs Briefing" in Dallas in August. His address to this gathering, closely allied with the National Religious Broadcasters, was very enthusiastically received. "I know you can't endorse me," Reagan concluded, "but I want you to know that I endorse you and what you are doing."[227] Buoyed by his support for their political agenda, Bailey Smith, president of the Southern Baptist Convention, Jerry Falwell, Pat Robertson, and other leaders of the religious right privately promised Reagan they would work for his election.[228] Doug and Bill Wead's *Reagan in Pursuit of the Presidency* lauded his religious commitments, and Bakker interviewed him on his *PTL Club* show.[229] In a direct-mail campaign and nationwide newspaper ads, Christian Voice argued that Reagan was the best alternative for Christian voters.[230] Believing that Reagan represented "all the political positions" they held dear, and that his moral and spiritual commitments were "genuine and relevant to his campaign," the Moral Majority worked to elect him by registering new voters, mobilizing precinct workers, and producing campaign literature.[231] Reagan talked frequently about moral issues and the importance of moral absolutes. Whereas his campaign produced many "slick, sophisticated" pieces specifically targeting the conservative religious community, Carter's sent only one brochure late in the campaign to about 250,000 ministers.[232]

Reagan scored a decisive victory, receiving 51 percent of the popular vote (compared with Carter's 41 percent) and 489 electoral votes to Carter's 49. He won about two thirds of the votes of conservative Protestants and 51 percent of the Catholic vote. Carter's percentage of Catholic votes was almost 20 points lower than in 1976 and less than that of any Democratic nominee since 1924. Moreover, for the first time in fifty years, a Democratic candidate did not win a majority of Jewish votes (Carter captured only 45 percent).[233] "Carter's publicly expressed doubts about American virtue left him vulnerable to a rival who never questioned that God was on our side."[234] Undoubtedly speaking for many evangelicals, Tim LaHaye declared that Reagan won because "our Heavenly Father . . . saw thousands of us working diligently to awaken his sleeping church to its political responsibilities."[235]

A Final Assessment

During the 1976 campaign, Carter asserted that if he could increase freedom, justice, and equality, restore foundational American principles, and enhance citizens' trust in government, "that would be a notable achievement."[236] In his inaugural address, the president expressed his hope that during his tenure the United States would remember the words of Micah and renew its "search for humility, mercy, and justice."[237] To what extent were these goals achieved during his four years in office? How did his faith contribute to his accomplishments and failures as president?

Several factors inhibited Carter's ability to attain his objectives. One was of his own making, but it is perhaps inevitable in the electoral process. Sociologists identify a revolution of rising expectations: Politicians often promise far more than they can deliver, causing people to become disillusioned. "Tantalizing the public by announcing a series of immediate and usually 'comprehensive' legislative initiatives in such intractable areas as welfare reform, tax code revisions, national health care, and energy policy, the new president promised prompt and decisive action on each." By the count of his own staff, Carter made over two hundred campaign promises, more than any other president in the twentieth century.[238] He sometimes admitted his own expectations for his administration were too high. Many of his advisors warned that he was trying to do too much too fast.[239]

External events over which Carter had no control also thwarted his efforts. The 1970s was one of America's most dismal decades. Journalist Tom Wolfe labeled it the "me decade"; others called it the "Bangladesh of the decades" and the time of the "nowhere generation."[240] Hal Lindsey's extremely popular *Late Great Planet Earth* (1970) predicted social and economic collapse and the imminent demise of the world. Disaster films such as *Airport* (1970, sequels in 1975 and 1977), the *Poseidon Adventure* (1972), *Jaws* (1975, sequel in 1978), and

The China Syndrome (1979) were a popular genre. The two most watched situation comedies, *All in the Family* and *M*A*S*H*, "reveled in the cultural conflict of the decade" and depicted social authority as simply absurd, respectively. *Winning through Intimidation* and *Looking Out for #1* topped the bestseller charts, suggesting that many Americans were more concerned about their personal goals than the public good. Median family income declined in real dollars, the divorce rate rose, whites complained about "reverse discrimination," and public confidence plummeted.[241] While the national confusion and shame connected with the Vietnam War and Watergate still lingered, Carter was also forced to grapple with the energy crisis, high rates of inflation, an economic recession, and the Iran hostage crisis. In his inaugural address, Carter proclaimed, "We have learned . . . that we can neither answer all questions nor solve all problems." He later explained that this concept was "to prove painfully prescient and politically unpopular. . . . We simply could not afford everything" Americans wanted.[242]

Evaluations of the impact of Carter's religious faith on his performance as president vary greatly. As he began his presidency, his approach to government reminded many of Wilson's, evoking the image of a " 'preacher-professor' " who made political decisions after receiving "direct communiqués from God."[243] Michael Novak warned, "There is a grave danger that President Carter will do damage to the role of organized religion. . . . [H]e wears religion on his sleeve more than any other president in history." If he is seen as "inept, incompetent, and amateurish, he is likely to bring piety into disrepute."[244] Although few pundits concluded that Carter had either based his policies on divine revelations or discredited Christianity, many agreed with Erling Jorstad's contention that his presidency demonstrated that " 'moral man' does not necessarily have superior resources to reform 'immoral society.' "[245] Others, however, such as Republican Senator William Armstrong of Colorado, a leading evangelical, praised Carter for fostering spiritual values in his work.[246]

Historian Kenneth Morris insists that Carter had no "ascendant political 'idea.' " The Baptist's evolving Christian "individualistic and apolitical philosophy" did not induce him "to develop a social vision." Although Carter was guided "by a consistent set of values and beliefs," Peter Bourne argues, he did not translate it into a coherent Christian political philosophy.[247] To this day, Carter has never systematically discussed in a speech, article, or his numerous books how biblical principles inform his approach to politics. He often stresses that his faith is very important and powerfully influenced his performance of his presidential duties and policies. But Carter nowhere provides a sustained, reasoned, scriptural analysis of politics. Despite his reading of many influential theologians, daily study of Scripture, and regular teaching of Sunday school, Carter's political philosophy was not explicitly based on a biblical foundation. He applied his Christian values to political issues more in a pietistic, piecemeal fashion than in a principled, methodical manner. Although the Georgian was "a supreme public moralist" and had many good ideas, Morris concludes, he "flitted erratically from proposal to proposal" and was never able to translate his personal faith into a moral vision to inspire the nation.[248]

Rather than offering a vision for the nation or discussing issues, Carter's campaign primarily emphasized his character. He promised and delivered competence and integrity, but Americans needed more than a moral exemplar; they needed a leader who could stimulate them to greater achievements and restore their faith in American values. In his inaugural address, Carter admitted, "I have no new dream to set forth today."[249] Morris faults Carter for failing "to rally his party and the nation around a positive vision of government." Had he possessed "a governing philosophy that extended beyond . . . [his] personalistic Christian faith" and been able to articulate his agenda "in a more positive and compelling way," his presidency may have produced more substantial results.[250]

A major reason Carter did not develop a coherent Christian political philosophy may have been his lack of a network of supportive Christian politicians to provide counsel, guidance, or criticism. This was due in part to the nature of the evangelical community. Prior to the mid-1970s, evangelicals had largely avoided politics and had failed to "devise a genuinely positive and constructive social ethic."[251] However, by this time, numerous evangelicals were serving in Congress, and some professors and politicians had begun to examine political issues from a distinctively evangelical perspective. They insisted that Christian political task must be communal, not a "one man show."[252] Some evangelical politicians met regularly for fellowship, prayer, and discussion. Carter, however, did not appoint committed Christian advisors, develop close relationships with religious leaders, or interact with nonpartisan evangelical political organizations, which deprived him of potentially helpful biblical and theological analysis of his positions.

Overall assessments of Carter's domestic and foreign policy vary greatly. Some have labeled his presidency "spectacularly inept"—a colossal failure, if not a tragedy.[253] Others contend that Carter was a mediocre president. Burton Kaufman argues that he never gained the support of the institutions and interests in Washington that he needed to govern effectively; he was "smart, caring, honest, and well-informed," but he "self-righteously believed that what he thought was right should prevail."[254] Fink and Graham maintain that Carter "lacked the political skills, experience, and temperament to do the job."[255] Any president who began in 1977 would have faced a Herculean task because of the impact of the Vietnam War and Watergate, double-digit inflation, an energy crisis, tension in the Middle East, the nuclear arms race, the Iranian hostage crisis, and the Soviet invasion of Afghanistan. Nevertheless, Kaufman concludes that many Americans viewed Carter's presidency as "ineffective in dealing with Congress, incapable of defending American honor abroad, and uncertain about its purposes, priorities, and sense of direction."[256]

Charles O. Jones counters that Carter downplayed "short-term electoral considerations" and viewed himself as a "trustee"—an official who represented "the public or national interest." This administrative style favors "doing what's right, not what's political," an approach Carter often adopted. The president, who represents all the people, must craft a political agenda, propose policies, counterbalance special interests, and make decisions for the public welfare even if they are unpopular and politically damaging.[257] Shortly after the 1980 election, Carter claimed he had resolved "a number of difficult and sometimes unpopular issues" "for the good of our country and the peace of the world."[258]

Several factors prompted Carter to see himself as the national trustee. His engineering background led him to believe "that if he knew enough details about a subject, he could make a decision that was in the public interest rather than in the interests of particular groups."[259] It also convinced him that there was a "right," scientific way to govern.[260] Moreover, Carter was not part of the Washington establishment. He was a Southerner, a governor with no experience inside the Beltway, more conservative than many Democratic Congressmen, and a deeply committed Christian functioning in a political world where many believed that religious convictions were either irrelevant or a hindrance. Carter recognized that the Bible spoke only indirectly to many political and social issues and that the United States was a pluralistic nation whose people held a smorgasbord of ideological convictions that must be respected in the political arena. Yet his commitment to such biblical ideals as justice, peace, righteousness, and concern for the poor clearly helped guide his political thinking and shape his policy making. He pursued policies he considered broadly beneficial and did not pander to special interests. If Carter had been more willing to compromise not on principles but on programs, he could have attained more of his domestic goals.[261]

Carter worked hard to gain support for his policies and programs but "failed to establish the base of public support and political legitimacy" necessary to succeed "in his role as a trustee president."[262] Some commentators conclude that Carter antagonized many Congressmen by continually trying to go over their heads to the people.[263] Moreover, the mood and moralism that helped elect Carter was directed against Nixon's corrupt actions, not toward a new style of politics. Thus, Jones argues, Carter "encountered serious opposition, criticism, even ridicule, when he sought" "to change Washington politics and policy making."[264] In addition, Carter's religious sensibilities clashed with the secularity of the cultural leaders "who set the tone" for society. These academic, media, and political elites, James Wall argues, tended to resent and resist "any combination of religion and power."[265] By his cast of mind, region, religion, and previous occupations and experience, Carter was not part of the community that had governed America in the twentieth century.[266]

Carter adopted a more prophetic stance than almost all his predecessors. Most presidents provided a priestly type of civil religious leadership, celebrating and supporting the nation's common faith. Because of Carter's influence, Mark Hatfield concluded, the approach, common among his predecessors, that mixed piety with patriotism and failed to distinguish between civil religion and biblical faith, seemed to be diminishing.[267] He and others applauded Carter for challenging a wayward public, confronting the nation with its shortcomings, and calling for collective repentance.[268] However, the Democrat's willingness to tell the American people what they did not want to hear—that they must tighten their belts, reduce their wastefulness, and live simpler lifestyles—contributed to his political difficulties.[269] Few other major political leaders have asked Americans to "sacrifice current benefits to better the lives of future generations."[270]

Although Carter insisted during the 1976 campaign that the United States "must have a coherent foreign policy," scholars debate whether his administration ever developed one, and if it did, whether it remained consistent during his four years in office.[271] Kaufman and William Stueck argue that Carter's approach to foreign policy shifted during his four years in office. Kaufman identifies his primary foreign policy goals as replacing global confrontation with global interdependence, promoting human rights, and creating a "new world order based on mutual cooperation, stability, justice, and peace." Nevertheless, by the end of his tenure he had adopted a cold war posture similar to that of presidents from Truman to Johnson.[272] Stueck agrees that Carter abandoned much of the framework he articulated in his campaign and followed early in his presidency. Although Carter expanded the nation's military machine, he avoided new quagmires abroad, improved America's relationship with China, and pointed out the human rights violations in the Soviet bloc. These actions put Reagan in a position to end the cold war and helped create a world where one adversary did not dominate American foreign policy, nuclear weapons could be reduced, and conflicts between nations could be more readily resolved—goals Carter initially sought to achieve.[273]

At the level of principle, however, Carter's foreign policy was quite consistent. Although recognizing the sinfulness of humanity and the problem of self-interest, Carter insisted that moral principles should guide America's interaction with other nations.[274] Because of its wealth, power, and resources, the United States was obligated to play a positive role in world affairs. The Baptist agreed with Niebuhr that "nations must use their power" as "an instrument of justice and a servant of interests broader than their own."[275] Carter repeatedly asserted that America should actively promote peace and human rights, work to reduce arms, and use its foreign aid to alleviate hunger, slow population growth, and stop environmental devastation. He argued that in the long run pursuing morality and justice in international affairs would benefit the United States more than seeking immediate, narrowly defined interests.[276] Gladdis Smith praises Carter for articulating a "morally responsible and farsighted" vision and challenging Americans to "think as citizens of the world with an obligation to future generations." Tragically, however, "the clamor of political critics, the behavior of the Soviet Union, the discordant voices of his advisors . . . all combined to make his vision appear naïve."[277]

Carter initially underestimated the extent to which moral values clash, advisors disagree, facts are unclear, and events occur that even a powerful nation has little ability to control. He increasingly realized that in international relations "coercive power counts more than good intentions and virtue."[278] Recognizing the world's complexity and America's security needs, Carter did not try to apply moral principles to foreign policy in a simplistic or dogmatic manner.[279] The Democrat acknowledged that the world was "imperfect," "complex," and "confused." "I understand fully the limits of moral suasion."[280] Wall argues that Carter sought to apply general biblical principles to particular situations rather than make decisions based on "a rigid set of rules." His faith encouraged him to seek "not the absolute perfect answer, but the best possible answer" available at that particular moment.[281] The Baptist also insisted that America was not the world's policeman or judge. He refused to intervene in some situations where it appeared Communists were gaining an upper hand or governments were being established that were not favorable toward the United States.

In summary, Carter's religious faith is quite evident in his character, convictions, and contributions. Both critics and supporters agree he was honest, trustworthy, hardworking, intelligent, and exceptionally well prepared. Many admired his considerate, compassionate, generous nature, which has been further demonstrated by his public service since leaving office. Inspired by Scripture, he emphasized the public good, human rights, justice, peace-making, and the stewardship of resources. His policies helped reduce world hunger, fortify families, advance peace, and protect the environment. Carter strongly supported the civil rights of blacks and women, strengthened relations with black Africa, sought to slow the arms race, and powerfully promoted human rights around the world.[282] His administration challenged traditional American approaches to international affairs, worked hard to control nuclear arms, based its foreign policy on "an effective combination of morality, reason, and power," and strove to make decisions on the basis of "a lasting world order beneficial to all people" rather than on "short-term calculation of American advantage over the Soviet Union."[283] Carter engineered the passage of the Panama Canal treaties, negotiated the Camp David Accords, and normalized relations with China. His "emphasis on human rights inspired dissidents in the Soviet Union and Eastern Europe" and "scored some notable success in Africa, Latin American and Third World countries."[284] It also made it impossible for Reagan and his successors to ignore this issue, and the Georgian initiated many of the policies the Republican pursued in the 1980s in his quest to end the cold war.[285] Considering the obstacles he faced, Carter's efforts to achieve justice in a fallen world were impressive.

CHAPTER TEN

Ronald Reagan: Making America
God's Shining City on a Hill

My daily prayer is that God will help me to use this position so as to serve him.

Letter to Greg Brezina, Oct. 25, 1982

Religion is a guide for me. To think that anyone could carry out the awesome responsibilities of this office without asking for God's help through prayer strikes me as absurd.

"Written Responses to Questions Submitted by France *Soir* Magazine," Nov. 3, 1984

We can work to reach our dreams and to make America a shining city on a hill.

Address to National Religious Broadcasters, Jan. 31, 1983

RONALD REAGAN'S RELIGIOUS convictions were crucial to his under-standing of the world and performance as president, but few scholars have provided substantive analysis of his faith and its impact on his policies during his tenure in the White House.[1] Although the circumstances of Reagan's life and the seeming inconsistencies between his beliefs and his practices make his faith difficult to explain, it appears to have been genuine, very meaningful to him, and essential to his political philosophy. Reagan firmly believed and often declared that God intended America to be a beacon of hope, faith, freedom, and democracy, "a city on the hill."[2] Although the nation was in moral decline, its citizens still retained the power, as Thomas Paine put it in *Common Sense*, "to begin the world over again."[3] Reagan's presidency was devoted to helping the United States fulfill this divine destiny. Like other presidents, Reagan's tenure is filled with ironies. His bellicose rhetoric and fierce anticommunism scared many, but his use of force was limited and he helped end the cold war. Reagan oversaw a huge military buildup but negotiated the first treaty that reduced nuclear weapons. He promised to reduce the size and scope of government, but the federal debt, the number of government employees, and federal spending increased. His admirers considered him to be a forceful and effective leader, but his critics lampooned him as an "empty suit," "a disengaged manager" whose staff deserved credit for the accomplishments of his administration.[4] Although critics offer radically different assessments of his administration, he helped the United States and the world realize more fully the values of this shining city.

Reagan's Faith

Like several other presidents, Reagan had a godly mother (Nelle) who was his primary religious influence. She was baptized into the Christian Church (Disciples of Christ) on Easter in 1910, after a deeply moving conversion experience.[5] For the rest of her life, she was active in the church. She taught Sunday school and Bible school classes, wrote columns for the church newspaper, served as president of the missionary society, led a women's Bible study, passed out tracts and food to prisoners, cared for the destitute, and wrote plays for the congregation she joined in Dixon, Illinois.[6] Nelle imparted her optimistic outlook to her son.[7] Maureen Reagan claimed that her grandmother "had the gift of making you believe you could change the world."[8] Nelle taught her son to "believe that God has a plan for everyone," "that everything in life happened for a purpose." She maintained that "even the most disheartening setbacks" "were part of God's Plan."[9] Reagan insisted that his mother planted her faith in God's goodness "very deeply in me."[10]

Reagan was baptized on June 21, 1922, symbolizing his commitment to Christ and the Disciples' church, and as a youth he attended church several times a week.[11] He gave dramatic recitations and acted in church plays and skits written by his mother. While in high school, Reagan taught Sunday school classes, led Bible studies and prayer meetings, participated in a Christian Endeavor group, and entertained patients at Dixon State Hospital in his church's monthly programs there.[12] Interested in both religious matters and the minister's daughter, Margaret, whom he dated for several years, Reagan spent a lot of time at the home of his pastor, Ben Cleaver. Garry Wills argues that Cleaver served as a father figure to Reagan, advising him on many issues and helping him get into college.[13] One of Reagan's favorite books as a youth was Harold Bell Wright's *That Printer of Udell* (1903). The book, Reagan explained, "made a lasting impression on me...because of the goodness of the principal character."[14] Like other Social Gospel novels, Wright's hero applies the principles of Christianity to remedying social ills. By the end of the book, upright businesses have replaced burlesque shows, and the indigent and disreputable have found wholesome jobs.[15] When Reagan finished reading the book, he told his mother, "I want to be like that man," and a few days later he requested to be baptized.[16]

After graduating from high school, Reagan attended Eureka College in Illinois, a small school affiliated with the Disciples. Biographer Anne Edwards claims that the Bible "was a daily and vital part" of Reagan's life during his four years at Eureka.[17] Stephen Vaughn argues that his church and college training during these years strongly influenced many of Reagan's later beliefs as president, instilling in him "faith in Providence and prayer,... [the] presumption that poverty is an individual problem" best dealt with by private charity rather than the state, belief in the work ethic, admiration of the wealthy, hatred of communism, commitment to family values, and the conviction that God had chosen America to serve his purposes.[18]

During his years as a radio broadcaster and a Hollywood film star, Reagan's involvement in organized religion was minimal. In an article entitled "My Faith," which he wrote for *Modern Screen* in 1950, Reagan admitted that his participation in the church was limited and his religious convictions were not very specific. He occasionally attended Hollywood Beverly Christian Church. The Christian Church, he claimed, "has little hard and fast dogma but is based on a literal interpretation of the New Testament." "I wouldn't attempt to describe what God is like, although I place my greatest faith in Him." The Bible declared that God is love, Reagan asserted, which described God as closely as words could. Reagan argued that "an all wise and loving father" would not "condemn any of his children to eternal damnation." "I believe in prayer," he testified. "There hasn't been a serious crisis in my life when I haven't prayed and when prayer hasn't helped me."[19]

During the 1960s, Reagan became acquainted with several influential charismatic evangelicals, and in 1964 he started attending Bel Air Presbyterian Church and formed a friendship with its evangelical minister, Donn Moomaw.[20] Only after being elected governor of California in 1966, as he wrestled with the immense challenges of the job, however, did his faith again become more significant in his life. The week before he was inaugurated, Reagan declared his intention to follow the teachings of Jesus in his work as governor and to rely on God's help in discharging his duties. After a few months in this position, Reagan declared, "I have spent more time in prayer these past months than in any previous period I can recall." He thanked God for the "wisdom and strength" he received "from these times of prayer."[21] While governor, he twice invited Billy Graham to speak to the state assembly, often stressed the importance of the Bible and prayer in letters and addresses, attended prayer breakfasts, and occasionally prayed in his office with evangelical friends.[22]

In October 1970, Reagan and his wife, Nancy, hosted George Otis of High Adventure Ministries, entertainer Pat Boone, and others at their home in Sacramento. As these guests prayed with the Reagans, Otis prophesied that if Reagan remained faithful to God, someday he "would reside at 1600 Pennsylvania Avenue." Years later, Otis was "struck by the fact that his prayer-turned-prophecy had been so precise about Reagan's future." To many charismatic supporters, Reagan's election as president in 1980 demonstrated God's approval of his actions.[23]

Reagan firmly believed that God had a plan for his life, although sometimes he was not sure what it was.[24] "I've always believed there is a certain divine scheme of things," he told an interviewer in 1968.[25] Reagan declared in 1976, "Whatever I do has meaning, only if I ask that it serves His purpose."[26] Reagan "felt 'called' to lead the nation," biographer Frank van der Linden argued in 1981, "as ministers are 'called' to their congregations." The president had "a remarkable serenity that comes directly from his belief that God has a plan for his life."[27] Patti Davis reports her father as declaring, "I pray that whatever God's will is, I'll be able to accept it with grace and have faith in His wisdom."[28] "Is there any truth that gives more strength," Reagan asked the National Religious Broadcasters in 1988, "than knowing that God has a special plan for each of us?"[29]

Nine weeks after taking office, Reagan gave a speech at the Washington Hilton. As he exited the hotel, John Hinckley Jr. fired six shots at the president. One of them bounced off his limousine, struck Reagan under his left arm, and stopped in his lung, only an inch from his heart. Bleeding profusely and gasping for breath, Reagan was rushed to George Washington University Hospital, where surgeons operated to remove the bullet. Lying on a stretcher in the hospital, Reagan "silently asked God to help him [Hinckley] deal with whatever demons had led him to shoot us."[30]

The attack fortified Reagan's faith. As he recuperated, he concluded that God had intervened to preserve his life. Terence Cardinal Cooke of the Archdiocese of New York visited the president in the hospital to discuss why his life had been spared, provide spiritual counsel, and pray with him. "I have decided that whatever time I have left," Reagan confided to Cooke, "is for Him."[31] Reagan also shared this testimony with Moomaw, Graham, Mother Teresa, and other religious leaders.[32] Reagan wrote in his diary, "Whatever happens now I owe my life to God and will try to serve him in every way I can."[33] The president emerged from this experience, declared aide William Norton Smith, "more convinced than ever that he was doing God's work."[34]

Reagan's faith is demonstrated by several factors. He maintained relatively close relationships with a number of Christian leaders, including Moomaw, Boone, Graham, Cardinal Cooke, Mother Teresa, Jerry Falwell, Louis Evans Jr., Pat Robertson, and Richard Halverson.[35] Reagan was very interested in biblical prophecy, the Shroud of Turin, creationism, and other religious topics.[36] In many addresses, proclamations, letters, and private conversations, Reagan stressed his faith in God and prayer, the inspiration of the Bible, and the divinity of Jesus. "Faith," Reagan declared, "is integral to my public and personal life. Having had a brush with death, I realized that my time on earth belongs to someone else."[37] He assured many who wrote to him that the Lord could live in people's hearts.[38] By talking openly and freely about spiritual matters, Patti Davis testified, her father passed on to her a "deep, resilient faith that God's love . . . is constant, unconditional, and eternal."[39]

Reagan repeatedly asserted his belief in the power of prayer and thanked Americans for praying for him in hundreds of public statements and personal letters. In closing his speech accepting the Republican nomination in 1980, he asked, "Can we begin our crusade joined together in a moment of silent prayer?"[40] In his first inaugural address, Reagan declared that he was "deeply grateful" for the "tens of thousands of prayer meetings being held this day."[41] He repeatedly emphasized the role prayer had played in American history, lauded the benefits of prayer, and called on Congress to pass an amendment to restore prayer in the schools. He reminded citizens that William Bradford, George Washington, Abraham Lincoln, and many other Americans leaders had relied on God's power to lead them in trying times; that the Mayflower Compact and the Declaration of Independence asserted America's recognition of God's power and authority; that Benjamin Franklin, John Jay, Thomas Jefferson, and James Madison all accentuated God's providential guidance and the importance of prayer;[42] and that the Founding Fathers ensured that Congress began each day with prayer because they valued it so highly.[43] "At every crucial turning point in our history," Reagan insisted, Americans' faith had enabled them to "overcome great odds." "Prayer has sustained our people in crisis, strengthened us in times of challenge, and guided . . . our daily lives since the first settlers came to this continent."[44] It had helped make America free, secure, and a force for good.[45] Reagan lamented that secularizing trends were "removing religion from its honored place" and especially deplored the banning of prayer and Bible reading in public schools.[46]

Reagan rejoiced that God answered prayers, and he claimed to derive great benefits from praying.[47] "My mother gave me a great deal," he said, "but nothing she gave me was more important than . . . the knowledge of the happiness and solace to be gained by talking to the Lord."[48] "I grew up in a home," he explained, "where I was taught to believe in intercessory prayer."[49] "My father taught me to talk with God," wrote Patti Davis. Although God answered all prayers, he told her, people did not always get the answers they desired.[50] Reagan often echoed Lincoln's assertion that as president "he had been driven to his knees because he had nowhere else to go."[51] When individuals told him that they were praying for him, he often joked that if they ever got a busy signal, it was because he was there ahead of them.[52] "Nothing means more to us," Reagan told Mother Teresa, "than the many prayers that are offered on our behalf."[53] Considering prayer to be deeply personal, not for public display, Reagan never permitted the press to photograph him praying. Aides reported that Reagan sometimes knelt in the Oval Office and prayed with visitors and that when pastors occasionally laid their hands on his head and prayed for him, he was visibly moved.[54] Unlike Eisenhower, he did not open cabinet meetings with prayer. When someone suggested that he do so, he replied, "I do," implying that he prayed privately about the meetings before they began.[55] His friend Pat Boone and some of Reagan's aides hoped that Reagan would someday be bold enough to lead the nation in prayer, but unlike Franklin Roosevelt, he never did.[56] He regularly prayed for his family and friends, world peace, and God's will to be done on earth.[57] Reagan also prayed for specific world leaders and for divine assistance at his summits with Mikhail Gorbachev.[58]

Reagan professed deep respect for the Bible and cited it frequently in public addresses. He insisted that he had never had any doubts about the Bible's divine origin, especially because Old Testament prophecies had "predicted every single facet" of Christ's life and death hundreds of years before he was born.[59] Moomaw labeled Reagan's knowledge of the Scriptures impressive.[60] From 1981 to 1985, he and Nancy served as the honorary chairpersons for Laymen's National Bible Week. Proclaiming 1983 to be the Year of the Bible, Reagan urged Americans to read and study God's Word. He agreed with Lincoln that the Bible was " 'the best gift God has given to man.' "[61] Like many other presidents, he asserted that no other factor was "more fundamental and enduring than the Bible" in shaping the United States."[62] Within its covers are answers "to all the problems that face us today."[63] Around the world, millions had been "imprisoned, tortured, [or] harassed for even possessing a Bible or trying to read one," a privilege too many Americans took for granted.[64] Reagan identified II Chronicles 7:14 and John 3:16 as his favorite verses. At both of his inaugurations, the Bible he used—his mother's—to affirm his oath was open to the former verse: "If my people . . . shall humble themselves, and pray, and seek my face, and turn from their wicked ways, then will I hear from heaven . . . and will heal their land."[65] The New Testament verse, a favorite of evangelicals, declares, "For God so loved the world that he gave his only son, that whoever believes in Him should not perish but have everlasting life."[66]

Reagan told David Frost in a 1968 interview that the person he most admired was Jesus, an assertion he repeated on other occasions.[67] Reagan complained in a 1978 radio address that many seminaries were minimizing Christ's divinity and regarding him as "merely human"; by so doing, they were explaining away the world's greatest miracle—the incarnation.[68] That same year, he used a well-known argument of Christian apologist C. S. Lewis in responding to a Methodist pastor who had written Reagan that he esteemed Christ's teachings but did not believe he was the son of God. Jesus' own statements, Reagan replied, "foreclose . . . any questions as to his divinity. It doesn't seem to me that he gave us any choice: either he was what he said he was, or he is the world's greatest liar. It is impossible to believe that a liar or charlatan could have had the effect on mankind he has had for 2000 years."[69] Reagan also testified to his belief in Christ's bodily resurrection, "the triumph of life over death."[70] Like other presidents, Reagan rarely mentioned Jesus in public addresses, except as the Man from Galilee, unless he was speaking to Christian audiences. However, in a national radio address in 1983, Reagan declared, "Some celebrate Christmas as the birthday of a great teacher and philosopher. But to other millions of us, Jesus is much more. He is divine, living assurance that God so loved the world He gave to us his only begotten Son so that believing in Him and learning to love each other we could one day be together in paradise."[71]

Although Reagan was reluctant to parade his faith and often reticent about sharing his personal testimony with others, he sometimes discussed his faith with friends and strangers, expressed concern about others' spiritual state, witnessed to individuals, and praised evangelism. People sometimes wrote Reagan to ask him theological questions. A sixteen-year-old Argentine inquired, "Is it possible that the present world is just a big chaos and not a perfect and marvelous creation of God?" In a lengthy letter, Reagan responded that the world "could become perfect if we would all pray to God for help in learning our roles in His plan to save a fallen world."[72] Learning that his agnostic father-in-law was dying, he wrote in his diary, "I want so much to speak to him about faith. . . . I want so much to help him" turn to God. Reagan wrote him a letter to explain how faith in Jesus Christ was essential to salvation and eternal life.[73] On several occasions, Reagan confessed he had had "an unholy desire" to serve "the most fabulous gourmet dinner that has ever been concocted" to some atheists and then "ask them if they believe there was a cook."[74] Congratulating Billy Graham on his sixty-fifth birthday, Reagan declared that as a result of his ministry "countless thousands" had "made decisions that changed their lives forever. God has surely blessed your work and you have kept the commandment of the Lord Jesus" to proclaim the gospel to all nations.[75]

While many conservative Christians strongly supported Reagan because of his personal faith and political policies, they (and others) were troubled during his presidency by his infrequent church attendance and his wife's interest in astrology. His absence from church seemed to contradict his professed beliefs and disappointed the widespread expectation that presidents display public piety. Reagan claimed that he yearned to attend church but did not want to endanger and inconvenience other worshipers. He feared that his entourage of Secret Service agents, police, SWAT teams, and reporters would distract others from worshiping. Because of the assassination attempt and subsequent threats on his life, the Secret Service required certain crowds, including worshipers, to be electronically screened when the president appeared in public.[76] Moreover, like Franklin Roosevelt, Reagan often felt ill at ease in church, fearing that his mere presence would distract others from worshiping.[77] In his debate with Walter Mondale in 1984, Reagan was asked why he did not go to church. "I have gone to church regularly all my life," he replied with considerable exaggeration, "and I started to here in Washington." However, it did not seem right to attend church if it threatened the lives of several hundred others. He noted that his minister (Moomaw) supported him in this decision and added, "I miss going to church, but I think the Lord understands."[78] Billy Graham also defended Reagan's decision.[79] His biggest disappointment about the weekends he spent at Camp David, Reagan noted in his autobiography, was that he could not go to church. Offering a rationalization that neither Theodore Roosevelt nor many other Christians accepted, he continued, "But I prayed that God would realize that when I was out in the beautiful forest I felt as if I was in His temple."[80] Although still accompanied by Secret Service agents, the Reagans resumed attending church after he left office, took membership classes, and joined the Bel Air Presbyterian Church, where they had worshiped periodically before 1980.[81]

During his presidency, those concerned about the president's spiritual nurture or public image proposed remedies. In February 1982, Jack Reitz encouraged the president to attend religious services of different denominations to promote the theme "America Prays Together." Church members at services the president chose to attend would gladly submit to the necessary screenings. By attending church and holding services in the East Room, he argued, Reagan could publicly affirm his belief that God had saved his life and could worship with minorities and the poor.[82] Others also urged Reagan to hold private services on Sundays at the White House as Nixon had done, but the president rejected this alternative.[83] Concerns about the safety of others, critics stressed, did not prevent him from spending time with groups of Hollywood celebrities or businessmen. (Nor did they later stop George H. W. Bush, Bill Clinton, or George W. Bush from attending church, although none of them almost died from an assassin's bullet.) Had Reagan been more concerned with appearances, he would probably have attended church, as almost all his predecessors did, despite the risks (or at least held private services at the White House) because of public expectations.

Even more damaging to Reagan was his wife's fascination with astrology, which became a public issue in 1988. Nancy had long been interested in astrology, and before Reagan became president, they both had regularly read their horoscopes.[84] Her interest in the stars increased after her husband was shot, and she turned to astrology, especially the services of Joan Quigley, in an effort to determine the most propitious times for him to schedule trips, major addresses, and other events.[85] Although advisors such as Michael Deaver and Donald Regan considered her "zodiacal inclinations inconvenient, sometimes irritating, and potentially embarrassing," they tolerated them.[86] After resigning, however, a disgruntled Regan revealed Nancy's practices in his 1988 memoirs, provoking an uproar. "Virtually every major move and decision the Reagans made during my time as White House Chief of Staff," he claimed, "was cleared in advance with a woman in San Francisco who drew up horoscopes to make certain the planets were in a favorable alignment for the enterprise."[87] Others asserted that Reagan scheduled INF Treaty negotiations with the Soviets after astrological consultation and that he chose press conferences according to the fullness of the moon. The president insisted that astrology played no role in his daily schedule and that he had never made any policy decisions based on astrological predictions.[88] Several of Reagan's closest aides testified that he never discussed astrology with them.[89]

Despite Reagan's denials, concerned Christian friends, including Pat Boone and George Otis, exhorted him to renounce any involvement with astrology. Unlike many other Americans who faithfully attended church and regularly consulted their horoscopes, they and most other evangelicals saw the practices as contradictory. While publicly declaring that the daily astrology forecast was "no more interesting or meaningful" to Reagan than a comic strip, Boone privately reminded the president that "God decisively" condemned "astrology as a counterfeit religion" and warned that anyone who placed confidence in it would be led astray and suffer. Because the concerns of the Christian community were "deep and valid" and the practice was so spiritually dangerous, he counseled Reagan to definitively denounce it.[90] Otis warned Reagan that if he did not repudiate the practice of astrology, it would legitimize "the occult and set our nation on a collision course with God."[91] Other leading evangelicals protested that consulting the stars was incompatible with Reagan's frequent profession that the Bible was God's inspired Word.[92] Religious Roundtable founder Ed McAteer lamented that the president's actions showed he did not have "a good grasp of biblical truth." Conservative columnist Cal Thomas called the Reagans' alleged use of astrology "the last straw for a lot of religious people. The president used to say, 'The answer to all of life's problems can be found in the Bible.' I guess he put God on hold and consulted Jeane Dixon."[93] The president of the Moral Majority, on the other hand, insisted his constituency would be worried only if it was conclusively shown that Reagan "had consulted the stars in making political decisions."[94] Hundreds of thousands of Americans signed petitions urging Reagan to "Say No to Astrology in the White House."[95] Despite this pressure, Reagan never publicly condemned the practice of astrology.[96]

Had they known, conservative Christians would have also been upset by Reagan's apparent belief in mystical experiences and spiritual visitations, his conviction that he had inherited some of his mother's psychic powers, his superstitious practices, and his entertaining the possibility that ghosts might be real. He asserted that at his father's funeral in 1941, he heard Jack say, "I'm okay and where I am it's very nice. Please don't be unhappy." Convinced that his father had spoken to him, Reagan's desolation disappeared.[97] He insisted that some of his mother's belief in hunches had rubbed off on him and that sometimes he knew, or at least had a strong feeling, that particular things would happen.[98] His press secretary, Marlin Fitzwater, claimed that Reagan considered some numbers to be lucky. Aides revealed that he knocked on wood and kept a good-luck penny in his pocket.[99] The frightened reaction of his dog Rex to the Lincoln Bedroom, Reagan wrote in *An American Life*, nearly convinced him that Lincoln's ghost haunted parts of the second floor of the White House.[100]

Another issue that might have caused trouble for Reagan was his belief in the Battle of Armageddon, described in the Book of Revelation as the climatic confrontation of good and evil. While governor of California, Reagan frequently discussed with evangelical friends how the founding of Israel in 1948 fulfilled biblical prophecy and suggested that the end of the world was near. Reagan invited Graham to speak to a joint session of the state legislature about the Second Coming of Christ. The future president read Hal Lindsey's 1970 best-seller, *The Late Great Planet Earth*, which depicted this final ferocious battle. In an interview in 1980 on Jim Bakker's PTL Network, Reagan declared, "We may be the generation that sees Armageddon." As president, he discussed Armageddon so often with so many people that one of his campaign strategists feared that the media might publicize his fascination with the topic.[101] It did surface briefly in the 1984 campaign, when Reagan was asked during his second debate with Mondale if the U.S. plans for nuclear war were related to his belief in Armageddon. No one knows, Reagan responded, if "Armageddon is a thousand years away or the day after tomorrow. So I have never seriously warned that we must plan according to Armageddon." Some liberal Protestant and Jewish leaders feared that "a theology of nuclear Armageddon" might unduly influence Reagan's foreign policy, but the subject did not become a significant campaign issue.[102]

The next year, Reagan's use of a biblical text to support a stronger national defense provoked considerable controversy. Speaking to business and trade representatives at the White House and the National Religious Broadcasters at their annual convention on the same day in February 1985, Reagan invoked Scripture to justify his policy. He reminded the audiences of Jesus' words in Luke 14:31–32: "What king, when he sets out to meet another king in battle will not first sit down and take counsel whether he is strong enough with 10,000 men to encounter the one coming against him with 20,000. Or else, while the other is still far way, [he] sends a delegation and asks the terms of peace." Applying the passage to America's situation, the president concluded, "I don't think the Lord that has blessed this country, as no other country has ever been blessed, intends for us to have to someday negotiate because of our weakness."[103] Asked at a news conference a couple weeks later whether it was appropriate to use the Bible to defend political positions, Reagan replied that he had consulted several clergymen and theologians who assured him that he had interpreted the passage correctly and therefore its use was "perfectly fitting." He had never exploited the "Bible to further political ends," he added, but it contained "an answer to just about everything and every problem that confronts us."[104] Critics accused the president of ignoring hundreds of other verses that promoted peace and nonresistance. They urged him to avoid the "business of Bible interpretation" and to refrain from using the Scriptures to defend specific policies.[105]

Unlike many of his predecessors, there was little about Reagan's personal morality that religious conservatives would have considered objectionable. As will be discussed later, they tended to ignore the fact that he was divorced. He occasionally drank a glass of wine, normally at public events.[106] He told some stories that many of them would have deemed somewhat irreverent, and he occasionally used profanity in male company.[107] No evidence indicates that Reagan was ever sexually unfaithful to his wife.

Considering Reagan's assertions and actions, it is not surprising that friends, associates, and journalists did not fully agree about the nature of his faith. Like many other presidents, he was quite private about his relationship with God, as close friends and observers noted. Nevada Senator Paul Laxalt insisted that Reagan was a "loner" in his relationship with God. Charles Wick and his wife were one of the couples closest to the Reagans, but he was unable to tell an interviewer much about Reagan's religious beliefs.[108] Dinesh D'Souza, who worked as a policy analyst in the Reagan administration, argues that the Republican was "reserved and understated about his personal beliefs because he didn't want to sound self-righteous or exhibitionistic."[109] On the other hand, evangelical friends and colleagues such as Pat and Shirley Boone and Senator Roger Jepsen and his wife, Dee, reported that Reagan talked openly about his faith in private conversations.[110] Others claimed that Reagan interjected biblical ideas into cabinet meetings, sessions with senior advisors, and at dinners.[111] "The president," Attorney General Edwin Meese insisted, "was able to talk about religion in a comfortable way."[112] "God is real to him," declared Peggy Noonan, who wrote speeches for Reagan for five years.[113]

Catholic Patrick Buchanan, who served as the White House communications director, and Moomaw called Reagan "a self-taught Christian." He was "a very simple Christian," Buchanan added, who focused on his "personal relationship with God." Later in his life, he had "become more and more an outspoken believer in God. He talks about it often." From 1963 on, Reagan maintained a close relation with Moomaw, whom he called "my pastor" even while he was living in Washington. Moomaw helped lead a special worship service at St. John's Episcopal Church prior to Reagan's first inauguration.[114] The Presbyterian gave the invocation at both inaugurals, and they communicated fairly frequently. Moomaw insisted that they were "friends and Christian brothers" who shared a "deep loyalty."[115] Reagan has a "deep private faith," Moomaw insisted, "that has not been instructed too much by Bible classes, prayer meetings, or worship services." He did read the Bible, pray, and worship, but the last had not been a regular experience for him throughout his life. His faith, Moomaw judged, was "more experiential than intellectual."[116] Like many other Americans, Reagan's faith was "highly individualistic." It rested on a personal relationship with God and had little theological specificity.[117]

Others who observed Reagan closely offered a different view of his spirituality. Some described his faith as earnest but superficial.[118] To historian Martin Marty, Reagan's religion was "sincere but inauthentic."[119] Others denounced it as bland, shallow, politically motivated, and self-serving. One critic labeled it "Revised Standard Country Club Piety."[120] Another censured him as a "stay-in-bed faker who used the alibi, 'Oh, I don't go to church because the Secret Service men would disturb the congregation.'"[121] Some accused Reagan of hypocrisy. His infrequent church attendance, meager donations to charities, and estrangement from his son Michael, maintained Robert Kaiser, indicated that it was "extremely unlikely that religion means much in Reagan's life."[122] Calvin College professor Richard Mouw lamented that Reagan did not "show the marks of an evangelical Christian"—personal spirituality, a solid grasp of Christian doctrine, or desire to help the poor.[123]

The issue of whether Reagan was born again in the way most evangelicals use the term is also difficult to determine definitively. In 1976, he announced, "I certainly know what the meaning" of born again "is today.... [I]n my own experience there came a time when there developed a new relationship with God.... So yes, I have had an experience that could be described as 'born again.'"[124] During the 1980 campaign, Reagan told a reporter that his joining the Christian Church at age twelve "represented a conscious decision to accept Christ. 'If that's what you mean by born-again, you could call me born-again.'"[125] The term, he told another questioner, was not used in the Christian Church in which he was raised. "But there you were baptized when you yourself decided that you were, as the Bible says ... born again."[126] That same year, Adrian Rogers, a prominent Southern Baptist pastor, directly asked Reagan, "Do you *know* the Lord Jesus or do you only know *about* Him?" To which he replied, "I *know* Him," testifying that he had a personal relationship with Christ as his redeemer.[127] Similarly, Reagan told Moomaw that had he died after he was shot in 1981, he would have been all right with God because he had accepted Jesus as his savior.[128] In a statement in the files of his presidential library, entitled "Ronald Reagan's Religious Beliefs," he wrote, "Jesus Christ has been a part of my life almost from the time I was born.... There was no great dramatic moment when I accepted Christ."[129] The Web site of the Reagan Library states under the heading "Religion" that Reagan "considers himself a 'born-again Christian.'"[130] Although disappointed that Reagan did not consistently state unequivocally during his presidency, as did Carter, that he was a born-again Christian, most evangelicals considered Reagan one of them. Ignoring Carter, Pat Robertson declared, "He is probably the most evangelical president we have had since the founding fathers." Herb Ellingwood insisted that he was "a born again Christian."[131] Pierard and Linder argue, on the other hand, that Reagan's somewhat vague explanations put him "squarely in the mainstream of general Protestantism" and assured Americans he was not a religious fanatic.[132]

Although historians debate the nature of Reagan's spirituality, they concur that he used religious rhetoric, discussed religious themes, and spoke to religious groups more than any other twentieth-century president. Arguably, of all American presidents, only Lincoln talked about spiritual and moral issues as often as Reagan. Critics protested that Reagan's religiosity was evident in every pronouncement "from his State of the Union Address to the quickest offhand comments."[133] Whereas Carter was better known for his personal religiosity, he spoke much less frequently to religious groups and discussed religious topics in substantive ways much less often than Reagan. His use of religious metaphors, biblical quotations, and evangelical theology, Paul Boase argues, "pales by comparison with Reagan's direct, blunt use of religious terminology."[134] No president spoke to more religious gatherings during his tenure in office than Reagan.[135] Moreover, evidence indicates that Reagan played a major role in writing his speeches in which he emphasized the nation's religious heritage, the importance of public and private morality, and the necessity of national dependence on God.[136] He argued that public policies must rest on moral values, insisted that America's problems stemmed in large part from its citizens' disobedience to God's commandments, and called for spiritual renewal.

Like many other presidents, Reagan stressed (critics said he exaggerated) the religious commitments of the Founding Fathers and maintained that the United States would flourish only if its people acted morally. The founders "believed faith in God was the key to our being a good people and America's becoming a great nation."[137] The Western ideas of freedom and democracy, he insisted, sprang "directly from the Judeo-Christian religious experience."[138] Reagan regularly recounted how great Americans, especially Washington, Lincoln, and Eisenhower, had relied on God in leading the nation.[139]

Reagan often asserted that America's success depended on its relationship with God. The nation had overcome many challenges by relying on God's power and protection.[140] "If we ever forget that we're one nation under God," he proclaimed in 1984, "then we will be a nation gone under."[141] He also repeatedly maintained that God had chosen America for a special mission. "Can we doubt," he told the Republican National Convention in 1980, "that only a Divine Providence placed this land . . . here as a refuge for all those people in the world who yearn to breathe free?"[142] "I've always believed," he declared in 1983, "that this blessed land was set apart in a special way."[143] Because God had given America such freedom and abundance, it must aid "less fortunate brothers and sisters around the world."[144] The mission of America was to model liberty, democracy, free enterprise, and Christianity and to export them to other nations. "Democracy," Reagan argued, "is just a political reading of the Bible."[145] The nation's "intellectual and spiritual values," Reagan proclaimed, "are rooted in...a belief in a Supreme Being, and a law higher than our own."[146]

Reagan repeatedly contended that the First Amendment was not meant to "keep traditional moral values away from policymaking." It was "not written to protect people and their laws from religious values" but rather "to protect religion from the interference of the government and to guarantee...'the free exercise of religion.'"[147] As a pluralistic society, the United States must protect all religions, but it must not twist the concept of freedom of religion "to mean freedom against religion."[148] Recent court rulings, Reagan protested in 1984, displayed instead "government hostility to religion," which must be changed.[149] "We establish no religion in this country, nor will we ever," Reagan declared. "We command no worship. We mandate no belief. But we poison our society when we remove its theological underpinnings." Those with faith "must be free to speak of and act on their belief, to apply moral teaching to public questions."[150]

To Reagan, America's many problems stemmed from its failure to live by God's teachings and to fulfill the mission he had assigned it. The breakdown of the family; lack of community; spread of secularism; rampant pornography and sexual promiscuity; large numbers of abortions, teenage pregnancies, and children born out of wedlock; and eroding patriotism all plagued America. Throughout history, great empires had fallen, he warned, after their people had forsaken their gods. "I don't want us to be another great civilization that began its decline by forsaking its God."[151] Reagan denounced efforts to end the tax-exempt status of churches, eliminate the words "under God" from the Pledge of Allegiance, and remove "In God We Trust" from the currency.[152] He argued that if the United States curbed the size and power of the federal government, unleashed the entrepreneurial spirit of its citizens, and reformed its moral practices, it could be a shining city on a hill, arrest the spread of atheism and communism, and promote liberty, democracy, and capitalism around the world.[153] Like Franklin Roosevelt and Eisenhower, Reagan repeatedly called for a national spiritual revival or rejoiced that one was occurring.[154] In 1983, for example, to buttress his claim that the nation was in the midst of a "spiritual awakening and a moral renewal,"[155] he pointed to surveys that revealed an overwhelming majority of Americans disapproved of adultery, teenage sex, pornography, abortion, and hard drugs and expressed a deep reverence for family ties and religious beliefs.

Reagan's Relations with Religious Constituencies

As president, Reagan sought to maintain close bonds with the religious right, improve his relationship with mainline Protestants, and gain the support of both groups for his policies. His administration assigned several staff members in the Office of Public Liaison to work with Protestants.[156] They arranged meetings between Reagan and key Protestant groups and leaders, met with selected religious constituents, conferred with influential leaders, and spoke to Protestant gatherings. These liaisons also circulated drafts of legislation to Protestant ministers, editors, and parachurch leaders and conveyed their concerns to the president.[157]

Believing they had played a major role in Reagan's victory and that the president shared many of their values, conservative Christians expected to be richly rewarded with political appointments, attention, and the implementation of their social agenda. Although they had greater access to Reagan's administration than to any other in the twentieth century, many of them were still disappointed by his actions. A few evangelicals received high-level posts. Donald Hodel, James Watt, and Elizabeth Dole served, respectively, as secretary of the interior, secretary of the interior, and secretary of transportation.[158] C. Everett Koop was named surgeon-general and Bob Billings assistant secretary of education for nonpublic schools.[159] Other evangelicals served in the Justice Department, Health and Human Services, as liaisons with religious conservatives or women, and as speechwriters. Reagan appointed relatively few religious conservatives to his administrative team because few of them had the proper credentials, because he wanted to distance himself somewhat from the Christian right, and because of the opposition of his inner circle.[160] On the other hand, there were enough committed Christians in the Reagan White House for Bible study and prayer groups to flourish.[161]

During his first two years, Reagan also upset many evangelicals by not pressing their issues as strongly as they desired. This stemmed in part from the argument of his pollsters that abortion, school prayer, and busing were "no-win issues." As the 1984 election approached, Reagan improved his relationship with evangelicals by speaking to several of their conventions, holding briefings for their leaders, meeting privately with their spokespersons, and emphasizing the importance of faith, prayer, and God's designs for America in major speeches. He repeatedly called for spiritual renewal and reasserted his promises to work for tuition tax credits, a school prayer amendment, and more restrictive abortion laws.[162] Administration officials also hosted the Evangelical Press Association in May 1984 to discuss Reagan's policies on family issues and civil liberties.[163] Despite their disappointments, conservative Protestants remained firmly in Reagan's camp, providing support not only for the administration's moral and social agenda but also for its economic and defense policies.[164] During his second term, Reagan and his staff met regularly with evangelicals to solicit their help to push his agenda on the family, education, tax reform, Central America, South Africa, and other matters.[165]

While providing considerable access to religious conservatives, Hadden and Shupe argue, no twentieth-century president "so completely snubbed" the nation's "established religious leadership" as did Reagan.[166] The protests of mainline Protestant leaders that Reagan was ignoring them prompted his staff to schedule twelve briefings with several hundred of them in 1984 and 1985.[167] Each briefing dealt with the moral dimensions of a particular policy, such as tax reform, Central America, South Africa, family, civil rights, arms control, refugees, or social and economic justice.[168] Persuaded by the arguments they heard, some participants supported Reagan's policies in sermons, articles, and radio programs. Others, however, accused administrative spokespersons of presenting only carefully selected facts that backed Reagan's positions.[169] Reagan's aides refuted the criticism that Reagan was "absolutely in concert with the far Right Religious community." They emphasized that many religious conservatives had opposed Sandra Day O'Connor's nomination to the Supreme Court and protested Reagan's establishing of formal diplomatic relations with the Vatican. They also claimed that the White House was eager to hear the views of mainline Protestants, Catholics, Mormons, and Jews.

During Reagan's tenure, some Protestants were troubled by other matters. Various groups protested that the government was interfering in religious affairs, especially through its Internal Revenue Service policies that appeared to try to enforce certain social policies on religious organizations and its alleged use of missionaries in Central Intelligence Agency operations.[170] Numerous Protestants censured the Reagan administration's support of the contras in Nicaragua.[171]

The Reagan administration also took many steps to try to establish good rapport with Catholics, who had become a major force in American politics. They accounted for more than a quarter of the members of Congress, and church leaders were issuing strong statements on a host of political issues. Robert Reilly, a former staff member of the U.S. Information Agency, served the longest as Reagan's liaison to Catholics.[172] Reagan spoke to many Catholic groups, typically discussing abortion, school prayer, tuition tax credits, and volunteerism and often quoting Pope John Paul II and Catholic theologians and authors.[173] Catholics played many important roles in the Reagan White House: His three national security advisors—Richard Allen, William Clark, and Robert C. McFarland—were all Catholics. Clark, who was one of Reagan's most trusted advisors, regularly read the Bible and prayed with him.[174] Reagan's two secretaries of state (Alexander Haig and George Shultz), CIA director William Casey, Attorney General William French, Communications Director Patrick Buchanan, and Health and Human Services Secretary Margaret Heckler were all Catholics. So were speechwriters Tony Dolan and Peggy

Noonan and Ambassador Vernon Walters. The president met with John Paul II three times and worked closely with him to aid Catholic churches in Poland and undermine communism.[175] Reagan met with Mother Teresa several times, corresponded with her, and awarded her the Presidential Medal of Freedom.[176]

Reagan's opposition to abortion and campaign for tuition tax credits endeared him to many Catholics. So did his support for traditional family values, efforts to restore prayer in the schools, condemnation of human rights violations in Communist countries, and fight against drugs and pornography. Three Catholic lay organizations, most of whose members were blue-collar Reagan Democrats, especially supported his social policies: the Knights of Columbus, the Catholic Daughters of America, and the Catholic Golden Age.[177] Many Catholics were pleased with his decision in January 1984 to appoint an ambassador to the Vatican. Speaking for the majority of Catholics, James Malone, the president of the U.S. Catholic Conference, insisted that this act affirmed the role played so effectively by John Paul II and his predecessors "on behalf of peace and justice in the world." The president of the Southern Baptist Convention declared that he was "'deeply disappointed'" by Reagan's decision and warned that it might hurt his reelection campaign. Upgrading relations with the Vatican, Jerry Falwell contended, set "a bad precedent." Would Mecca request an ambassador next? he asked. Many mainline Protestant and Jews, most notably Americans United for the Separation of Church and State, also denounced Reagan's act.[178]

Meanwhile, many leading Catholics, especially the American Catholic bishops, strongly disagreed with Reagan's policies on the economy, defense, and Central America, despite diligent efforts by administration officials to shape Catholic perspectives on these matters. His staff especially concentrated on trying to influence the National Conference of Catholic Bishops' letters on war and peace and social and economic issues and on working with conservative Catholics who supported their positions on these issues.

In December 1982, twenty-four Catholic Congressmen defended Reagan's peace-through-strength position. Quoting frequently from statements by popes, Catholic theologians, bishops, and John F. Kennedy, they challenged many of the positions espoused in the recent draft of the bishops' pastoral letter. The policies of the Soviet Union, these Catholic legislators argued, had made the arms race necessary. America's nuclear deterrent was not "a threat to peace, but... a guarantor of peace." In condemning nuclear weapons, they protested, the bishops ignored the fact that conventional weapons could be just as destructive. The bishops also ignored the United States' extensive efforts to limit nuclear weapons. These Catholic politicians urged the bishops to remember, foreshadowing Reagan's "evil empire" speech, that the crisis they confronted did "not involve two morally equally forces, but... human freedom against totalitarianism." Peace without justice, they contended was "moral violence."[179]

In January 1983, State Department officials met with a delegation of Catholic bishops to discuss the bishops' stance on defense spending and nuclear weapons. They emphasized Reagan's commitment to achieving world peace and negotiating arms control agreements. They discussed the moral dilemmas inherent in political action and in dealing with an adversary whose "behavior required our . . . insistence on strong defense." Officials emphasized that the pope had recently reaffirmed the morality of nuclear deterrence as long as it was coupled with efforts to stop the buildup of arms.[180] Despite these efforts, the bishops' *Pastoral Letter on War and Peace* issued in May 1983 supported a nuclear freeze and declared that "the deliberate initiation of nuclear warfare, on however a restricted scale," could not "be morally justified."[181] Disagreeing with this position, four Catholic organizations created the American Catholic Conference to support Reagan's defense policies.[182]

In 1983, Catholic bishops also began a study of the relationship between Christianity and capitalism, focusing on employment, poverty, trade, and economic policy.[183] Fearing that their letter would attack free enterprise, political conservatives strove to counteract its "potentially negative impact." They urged Catholic businessmen, community leaders, professors, and students to discuss with their bishops and priests "why the letter should recognize the positive moral role played by the free market economy," and they created a commission of prominent Catholic professionals to study Catholic social thought and the economy.[184] The first draft of the bishops' *Pastoral on Catholic Social Teaching and the U.S. Economy,* issued in November 1984, pronounced "the level of inequality in income and wealth in our society" "morally unacceptable."[185] Contesting this perspective, the commission's report argued that the American economic system was "concerned for the welfare of all," including the unemployed and needy.[186]

Other Catholics also criticized the bishops' letter. Business executive Gerald Lynch argued that the economic and political programs the bishops supported had "been implemented and found wanting in every country of the Western World." Moreover, they ignored factors that had always "propelled the American economy, such as capital formation, incentive, . . . risk, reward, productivity, [and] discipline." Capitalism was "infinitely superior in terms of economic results" to all other economic systems, including modern-day versions of socialism.[187] As with the earlier pastoral letter, the efforts of the Reagan administration and its supporters had little impact on the final draft of the bishops' letter issued in late 1986.[188] In sum, conservative Catholics who agreed with Reagan's stance on abortion, school prayer, tuition tax credits, pornography, drugs, and family values provided strong support for his administration. More liberal Catholics, especially the National Conference of Catholic Bishops, who disliked his policies on defense, Central America, and the economy, were some of his most vocal critics.

Reagan and his staff, led by Orthodox Jew Marshall Breger, also worked diligently, with limited success, to maintain positive relations with Jews. Reagan praised Jewish contributions to Western civilization, denounced anti-Semitism, worked to stop the persecution of Jews in the Soviet Union and to facilitate their emigration, and celebrated the Jewish religious heritage.[189] He spoke to numerous Jewish organizations and met personally with dozens of Jewish leaders.[190] Other administration officials met with many Jewish groups and spoke at Jewish gatherings.[191] Reagan appointed Morris Abrams to the Civil Rights Commission, Elliot Abrams as an assistant secretary of state, and Alan Greenspan and Murray Weidenbaum as economic advisors.

During his first term, Reagan enjoyed generally good relations with Jews, in large part because he strongly supported Israel, which he did for both strategic and moral reasons.[192] The president backed a Jewish homeland as a compensation for their long-standing persecution, as a fulfillment of biblical prophecy, and as a strategic bulwark to help stop Soviet intervention into the Middle East.[193] The American Jewish community was also pleased by Reagan's promise in 1983 that if Israel were ever forced out of the United Nations, "the United States and Israel would leave together."[194] On the other hand, some Jewish leaders and organizations objected to Reagan's close relationship with conservative Christians and argued that he ignored the separation between church and state.[195] Administration officials countered that the president strongly endorsed "religious tolerance and forbearance" but objected to recent court decisions that limited religious freedom.[196] During the 1984 campaign, a few Jews urged their coreligionists to vote for Reagan because of his economic policies and "liberal softness toward Israel."[197] Although many Jews were repulsed by the religious right's alleged efforts to abolish the wall of separation between church and state and Christianize America, Reagan won about 35 percent of the Jewish vote in 1984, a high percentage for a Republican candidate.[198]

Controversy erupted in April 1985 over Reagan's scheduled trip to West Germany. He had accepted an invitation from Chancellor Helmut Kohl to lay a wreath at a cemetery in Bitburg to commemorate the fortieth anniversary of the end of World War II and to demonstrate that their two nations were now allies. Bitburg was the staging area for the Battle of the Bulge, the final German assault on the western front. When Reagan agreed to go, he did not know that forty-nine members of the Waffen SS had been buried at this cemetery in 1945. Veterans' groups, prominent Republicans, and Jewish leaders all pointed out the negative implications of visiting Bitburg and begged him not to go.[199] Clergymen exhorted Reagan to cancel his visit to underscore the point that the Holocaust was "the greatest moral crime of the century."[200] In remarks to reporters before leaving for Germany, Reagan accepted the distinction the Germans made between the regular SS forces, the Nazi regime's most fanatical agents, and the Waffen SS, who were young teenagers "forced into military service in the closing days of the Third Reich." Thus, he argued, "they were victims," just as were those who died in the concentration camps. Moreover, he insisted, Americans should not "ask new generations of Germans to live with this guilt forever without any hope of redemption. This should be a time of healing."[201] Reagan's efforts to equate the slain SS soldiers with the Jewish victims of the Holocaust convinced few and outraged many. The *New York Times* labeled the episode the "biggest fiasco" of Reagan's presidency.[202] Lou Cannon contends that "Reagan abandoned the moral high ground of his intense convictions about the Holocaust" to help Kohl politically.[203] Dinesh D'Souza counters that Reagan wanted to underscore the point that the West could better "resist the contemporary evil of totalitarianism by permitting postwar Germany to outlive its Nazi past, recover its national pride, and join the fraternity of free nations on an equal basis."[204] In private letters, Reagan defended his decision as "the morally right thing to do."[205] The president paid a high price for going to Bitburg: He was severely criticized and never regained the trust of the Jewish community.[206]

The Election of 1984

Pierard and Linder argue that "probably in no election campaign in American history, not even 1928 or 1960, did religion receive a larger billing than in 1984," a campaign that pitted Reagan and George H. W. Bush against Carter's vice president, Walter Mondale, and New York Congresswoman Geraldine Ferraro, a Catholic.[207] The Christian right, Catholic bishops, and black Protestants all spoke loud and often about political matters, and religion touched on numerous issues, most notably abortion, school prayer, tuition tax credits, the threat of nuclear war, and how to best help the poor. While two large black denominations—the National Baptist Convention and the African Methodist Episcopal Church—supported Mondale and the Catholic bishops attacked Reagan's economic policies and refusal to support a nuclear freeze, the Christian right engaged in Herculean efforts to reelect the president.[208] Moreover, Reagan's repeated use of religious rhetoric during the campaign provoked considerable controversy. *Newsweek* contended that the religious differences between Reagan and Bush and their Democratic opponents involved "a whole range of assumptions and beliefs about the nature of society and a Christian's role in it."[209] At stake in the election, added *Time*, were several "specific policy matters with a clear religious dimension" and more abstract questions, such as "How should faith inform public policymaking?" and "Should clergy involve themselves and their congregations directly in politics?"[210]

In the late 1970s, many conservative Christians became convinced that they could arrest negative social trends by political activism. They were disappointed that Reagan had not done more to advance other items of their agenda: promotion of family values and opposition to abortion, the Equal Rights Amendment, affirmative action, environmentalism, school busing, and gun control.[211] Nevertheless, they generally admired Reagan's economic policies and anticommunism, efforts to provide a strong defense, support for a school prayer amendment, and willingness to combat abortion, pornography, and moral decline. They applauded his seemingly strong personal faith and his frequent discussion of spiritual and religious themes. Although disappointed that he had not appointed more evangelicals to positions in his administration, they appreciated their increased access to the president and his sensitivity to some of their concerns. Now that the economy was improving, religious conservatives hoped Reagan would concentrate on fighting the social evils they despised. Certainly, Mondale would not advance their agenda. Moreover, Reagan worked vigorously in 1984 to "rally religious conservatives of all stripes to his cause."[212] He stressed the importance of a spiritual revival in his State of the Union Address and proclaimed January 22 "National Sanctity of Human Life Day." At major evangelical conclaves and in speeches to other groups, Reagan called for tuition tax credits, protection for unborn children, and "voluntary" school prayer.

All these factors prompted many leaders of the religious right to labor strenuously to help Reagan win. During the campaign, three evangelical publishers issued books accentuating Reagan's religious commitments.[213] Christian Voice distributed almost a million copies of a "Presidential Biblical Scoreboard" that rated the candidates on fifteen "biblical-family-moral issues." Especially important was the creation of the American Coalition for Traditional Values (ACTV) in June 1984. Led by Tim LaHaye, its thirty-three board members included many of the nation's most influential televangelists and evangelical pastors, who promised to encourage their followers to vote for "pro-moral candidates." In July, the ACTV invited three hundred evangelical and fundamentalist ministers to Washington to hear Reagan speak and meet with Bush, Meese, and Clark. That same month, Senator Paul Laxalt, the Republican campaign chair, sent letters to 45,000 carefully chosen ministers and priests to exhort them to persuade their parishioners to register to vote and to work for Reagan's reelection.

Leaders of the religious right also played a prominent role at the Republican National Convention by endorsing Reagan's policies and assuring Americans that he represented moral righteousness. Evangelist James Robison opened the convention with a prayer, thanking God for Reagan's leadership. W. A. Criswell, pastor of the First Baptist Church of Dallas, gave the closing benediction. In platform appearances, Falwell called Reagan and Bush "God's instruments in rebuilding America" and E. V. Hill, a prominent black pastor in Los Angeles, labeled Republicans the "Prayer Party."[214] During the convention, Reagan addressed a huge ecumenical prayer breakfast at Reunion Arena, declaring religion and politics "inseparable."[215]

Reagan's religious rhetoric during the campaign prompted a barrage of criticism. William Safire charged that he wanted to "impose a religious government," and others protested that he did not respect the separation of church and state.[216] *Washington Post* writer Sidney Blumenthal castigated Reagan for considering the evangelical right "a division of Christian soldiers in the conservative army" who believed the GOP was on the "path of political salvation."[217] The *Atlanta Constitution* indicted the president for trying to base public policy on "religious dogma" and granting "governmental favor to some religious groups."[218] Other critics denounced Reagan as a "self-appointed national preacher-in-chief" who sought to "enshrine the social-policy particulars" of the religious right into national law.[219] Some detractors even claimed Reagan identified himself with God, sought to Christianize America, and made himself the judge of what was good and bad religion. They accused him of maintaining that "good Christians" supported "school prayer, a ban on abortion, and unlimited military spending and opposed a nuclear freeze and social programs for the poor."[220]

Reagan's staff countered that the president sought not to make the government religious but rather to make it "tolerant and accommodating toward religious belief, expression, and conduct." Rather than promoting religion, his administration respected "religious convictions that individuals adopt[ed] entirely apart from government." Republican advisors counseled Reagan to avoid general statements about the role of religion in politics, which the "establishment media" could turn against him, and focus instead on the "specific application of moral principles and values to the task of governing."[221] During the last days of the campaign, Reagan sought to strike a delicate balance, as he solicited the support of the Christian right while trying not to drive away other voters by appearing to be a religious zealot.

Rebuffing Reagan, Mondale echoed the argument of New York Governor Mario Cuomo that "religion and faith were private matters, not symbols to be exploited by partisan politicians."[222] Nevertheless, the former vice president felt compelled to defend his religious pedigree and convictions. In the first presidential debate, he emphasized that his father was a Methodist minister. "I don't know if I've been born again, but I know I was born into a Christian family. . . . I have a deep religious faith. . . . It's probably the reason I'm in politics. I think our faith . . . instructs us about the moral life we should lead." He denounced the "growing tendency to try to use one's own personal interpretation of faith politically . . . and to try to use the instrumentalities of government to impose those views on others." The United States was the most religious nation on Earth because it had prevented politicians and the state from interfering with the personal exercise of faith.[223] Ignoring such statements, Tim LaHaye, in attempting to discredit the Democrat with conservative Christians, contended that "Mondale admits he's a humanist."[224]

While Reagan's staff worked hard to retain the support of the religious right, they also developed a comprehensive strategy to win Catholic votes and convince Catholics to make the GOP "their new permanent political home." A public effort to achieve this aim might cost Republicans votes in the Bible Belt or the Deep South. Therefore, the "best way to disguise this maneuver" was to emphasize moral issues rather than appeal directly to Catholics. Strategists recommended cultivating close relations with the Vatican, consulting frequently with Catholic prelates, developing cordial associations with various Catholic groups, appointing Catholics to major administrative posts, speaking at Catholic gatherings, increasing the number of Catholic leaders in the Republican Party, and focusing on issues that were important to Catholics: abortion, tuition tax credits, family values, sex and violence on television, anticommunism, and the concept of volunteerism.[225] Strategists also insisted that the president's positions on these issues must be widely publicized in Catholic and ethnic communities. The values he shared with most Catholics and ethnic Americans must be constantly accentuated through the media. Because of the liberal bent of the U.S. Catholic Conference, advisors suggested, the Reagan administration must work closely with other Catholic organizations that were "neutral and objective."[226] During the campaign, his team put ads in many Catholic newspapers showing him meeting with Pope John Paul II and proclaiming his support for "basic family values," "the rights of the unborn," voluntary prayer in schools, and tuition tax credits. Catholics for a Moral America and the Catholic Center for Private Enterprise, Strong Defense, and Traditional Values labored vigorously for Reagan's re-election.[227] Although many Catholic prelates disliked Reagan's positions, the bishops' pastoral letter strongly criticized his defense policies, and Ferraro was a Catholic (although pro-choice on abortion), Reagan captured 55 percent of the Catholic vote, the highest percentage ever won by a Republican candidate.[228]

The efforts of conservative Christians to register voters and mobilize support for Reagan were very successful, as about 80 percent of white evangelicals cast ballots for the president, contributing to his landslide victory (Reagan won 59 percent of the vote and forty-nine states).[229] Many commentators conclude, however, that Reagan could have won handily without the enthusiastic support of religious conservatives because his personal popularity was so great and Mondale's campaigning so lackluster. Richard Pierard's assessment rings true: "the election was essentially a referendum on his performance as president, not an affirmation of his social policy."[230] Nevertheless, Mondale and Ferraro's argument that religious values did not "belong in the political arena" and their assault on Reagan's religious convictions and policies as unchristian backfired, because millions of Americans felt their own beliefs were under attack.[231]

Reagan's Faith and Public Policies

Reagan proclaimed in 1984 that "politics and morality are inseparable." "And as morality's foundation is religion, religion and politics are necessarily related. We need religion as a guide."[232] Although Reagan's faith affected many of his policies, his endeavors to curb abortion, pass a school prayer amendment, secure tuition tax credits, and oppose communism shed the most light on the relationship between his religious convictions and his policies.

Many who shared his religious presuppositions applauded his approach to these issues, but others who disagreed sharply with his guiding assumptions denounced it as misguided, improper, unfair, dangerous, and detrimental. The editors of the *New Republic* rejected the president's claim in 1983 that "policy decisions must have religious reasons." "By what authority does this man claim to administer the Judeo-Christian tradition? We elected a President, not a priest." Reagan "is not in the White House to save our souls, but to protect our bodies; not to do God's will, but the people's." Reagan did not understand, they argued, that the positions he repudiated—communism without and secularism within—were based not in sin but on different points of view. He misrepresented the views of the Founding Fathers on the separation of church and state, oversimplified issues, and offered a religious analysis of abortion and school prayer that contradicted "the American political tradition." Reagan's rhetoric, they protested, was "deeply divisive."[233] No president had "presumed to associate God with his political philosophy," complained Wilbur Edel in 1987, "as persistently" as Reagan.[234]

Reagan's opposition to abortion is well known. He campaigned in 1980 and 1984 as an opponent of abortion, and he strove to reduce the number of abortions in the country by writing a short book on the subject and sponsoring pro-life bills in 1987 and 1988. He repeatedly denounced abortion as a slaughter of innocents and "a wound of our national conscience."[235] In the final analysis, however, he was unable to stem the tide, and many pro-life proponents expressed disappointment that he had not devoted more time, energy, and political resources to the cause. While governor of California, Reagan, urged on by his physician father-in-law, had signed a therapeutic abortion bill, even though pro-life groups strongly opposed it. Although he later professed regret that he had signed the law, and he privately deplored the state's huge increase in abortions, he never tried to tighten the law during his tenure as governor.[236]

As president, however, Reagan's approach was different. He met with the leaders of the pro-life movement at least once each year.[237] Reagan appointed C. Everett Koop, a staunch antiabortion advocate, as surgeon general, frequently denounced abortion in major speeches, and wrote *Abortion and the Conscience of the Nation* (1984) to promote the pro-life position. The president protested that abortion diminished the value of all human life. He endorsed the Respect Human Life Bill, which prohibited the federal government from paying for abortions except to save the lives of pregnant women. The president denounced late-term abortions and urged Americans to work to overturn *Roe v. Wade*. In numerous speeches, Reagan called the protection of human life "the first duty of government."[238] "This nation," he declared in 1984, "cannot continue turning a blind eye and deaf ear to the taking of 4,000 unborn children's lives every day." Since 1973, fifteen million "helpless innocents" had been slaughtered. "Doesn't the constitutional protection of life, liberty, and the pursuit of happiness extend to the unborn"? The medical evidence indicated that the unborn were living human beings, he said, [239] and abortion was rampant because many Americans, ignoring Judeo-Christian teaching, viewed sex as a purely physical act that had no "potential for emotional and psychological harm."[240] The president commended efforts to improve foster care, increase adoptions, and provide crisis counseling centers and other services for pregnant women.[241]

Although Reagan spoke out often and forcefully against abortion, he did not invest as many political resources in obtaining an antiabortion amendment to the Constitution as evangelicals wanted. The president refused to address in person the March to Life rally that assembled each year on the anniversary of *Roe v. Wade*. Reagan provided little support for the 1981 Human Life Statute, which contributed to its defeat and baffled and annoyed most opponents of abortion. This bill declared that "human life shall be deemed to exist from conception." If passed, it would have enabled the states to define abortion as murder. Conservatives were further frustrated when Reagan failed to endorse the Family Protection Act in 1981, which included, among its thirty-one provisions, a measure to prohibit abortion. They also fought unsuccessfully against the nomination of Sandra Day O'Connor for the Supreme Court because of her position on abortion. In 1982, Reagan did endorse an antiabortion bill and lobbied for its passage, but the bill was defeated in the Senate.[242]

Given the views of the Supreme Court justices and the Congress, Reagan realized that *Roe v. Wade* could not be overturned. He therefore focused his efforts on trying to pass a bill to further restrict public funding for abortion. In 1987, Reagan sent to Congress the President's Pro-Life Bill, also called the Hyde Amendment, the first antiabortion legislation initiated by a president. It argued that abortion took the life of an unborn human being and criticized *Roe v. Wade* for not recognizing the humanity of the fetus. It mandated that no federal funds be used to perform abortions except when a woman's life was endangered and that private organizations that provided or referred clients for abortions (such as Planned Parenthood) would not be eligible for government monies.[243] Stripped of this second provision, the Hyde Amendment passed in 1988, and Reagan signed it into law.

Several considerations prompted Reagan to drag his feet on abortion: Nancy pressured him to not push the issue, Republicans were divided over abortion, and many of his aides urged him to avoid the subject for political reasons.[244] Many conservative Christians complained that Reagan did not make the fight against abortion a high enough priority.[245] Others pronounced Reagan's abortion crusade harmful because his policies were not consistently pro-life (he did not oppose the death penalty or support gun control or a nuclear freeze). By linking abortion to a larger conservative political agenda that was "decidedly not pro-life," Jim Wallis, editor of *Sojourners*, protested, Reagan had "cut the moral heart out of his concern for the sacredness of life."[246] Another evangelical castigated him for funding the "slaughter of children in Central America," escalating the risk of nuclear war, and severely reducing "social service programs necessary for the survival and health of low-income children."[247] Supporters of abortion rights complained that his proposals, if implemented, would rob women of the right to choose, place immense psychological and financial burdens on them, limit the ability of poor women to have abortions, and bring into the world unwanted children who were likely to be neglected and mistreated. Shortly before leaving office, Reagan declared that his greatest disappointment as president was that he had not been able to do more to protect the unborn. As long as abortion on demand was legal, he added, the United States would never be "completely civilized.[248] In another interview the same week, he urged Americans to continue to pray for "the end of the abortion holocaust."[249]

Reagan made passing a school prayer amendment a higher priority but had no success. In May 1982, he submitted an amendment stating, "Nothing in this Constitution shall be construed to prohibit individual or group prayer in public schools or other public institutions. No person shall be required by the United States or any State to participate in prayer." In dozens of addresses, Reagan urged Congress to pass this amendment and offered reasons they should do so. School prayer should be reinstated, he argued, because it was consistent with the Constitution and a long-standing American practice. It acknowledged God's authority, would benefit children, and could help restore morality ("if we could get God and discipline back in our schools, maybe we could get drugs and violence out").[250] Moreover, he insisted that schoolchildren should have the same right as members of Congress to begin each day with prayer and emphasized that the vast majority of Americans favored school prayer.[251] The argument that voluntary prayers violated the rights of others, Reagan alleged, was "twisted logic."[252] "The Constitution was never meant to prevent people from praying," he argued; "its declared purpose was to protect their freedom to pray."[253] In a radio address in February 1984, Reagan contended that if religious exercises were not allowed in schools, religion was "placed at an artificial and state-created disadvantage." The refusal to permit such exercises was not state neutrality but "the establishment of the religion of secularism."[254] "No one will ever convince me," he added, "that a moment of voluntary prayer will harm a child or threaten a school or State."[255] "God, source of all knowledge," Reagan repeatedly objected, "should never have been expelled from our children's classrooms." He continually denounced court decisions that prohibited schoolchildren from saying grace before meals, voluntarily meeting for prayer or Bible study, reciting poems with religious motifs, or simply getting together to talk about their faith.[256]

Behind the scenes, Reagan's staff worked to garner support for a school prayer amendment. They assembled lists of Christian organizations and celebrities who supported it, sent letters to hundreds of Christian leaders to urge them to work for its passage, mailed materials to newspaper and magazine editors across the country, called senators to try to persuade them to vote for the bill, and wrote op-ed pieces for leading newspapers.[257] Reagan met several times with Congressmen and groups of supporters to promote the amendment.[258]

Many Protestants and Catholics and some Jews lobbied for the bill. The Leadership Foundation distributed more than 42 million pamphlets and letters supporting school prayer and produced a television special, "Let Our Children Pray," which aired on more than a hundred stations. Christian Voice created Project Prayer Coalition to push for the amendment, and Pat Robertson of CBN spearheaded "a massive grassroots letter-writing campaign" to persuade senators to support the amendment.[259] While admitting that school prayer would not save souls, supporters argued it recognized God's supremacy and could help reverse the trend toward secularism and promote revival. Despite Reagan's passionate exhortations in dozens of speeches, the Senate vote on the amendment in the spring of 1984 fell eleven short of the two-thirds majority required. In 1985, his administration began a second push for an amendment, but the Senate eventually defeated it as well.[260] Some analysts argue that the White House did not strongly pressure Senators to pass the amendment because a number of prominent Republicans disliked it.[261]

Opponents contended that school prayer was a state-imposed religious practice, divisive, and a meaningless exercise. This vacuous faith in faith did little to help theists and offended unbelievers or made them uncomfortable. "The inherently religious ritual of public prayer," argued a rabbi from New York City, "must be reserved for synagogue, church, or home."[262] House Speaker Tip O'Neill charged that Reagan's advocacy of the amendment was "politically inspired" and opined that a man who did not go to church should not talk about prayer.[263] Although some saw no Constitutional objections to school prayer, they instead urged the government to focus on supplying vouchers or tuition tax credits to enable parents who wanted the option to send their children to religious schools, where each day could begin with genuine prayer.

Reagan also failed to obtain tuition tax credits. He regularly promised religious groups he was working to secure these credits for deserving families.

Attracted by their strong religious values and high educational standards, five million American children, Reagan emphasized, attended private schools. Their families, most of whom earned less than $25,000 a year, paid tuition for their children to attend these schools while also paying taxes to support public schools. They were entitled to relief.[264] Responding to critics, Reagan argued that tuition tax credits "would only threaten public schools if you believe that more competition, greater parental choice, and stronger local control will make our schools worse, not better."[265] These credits would help the nation by promoting educational diversity and excellence, allowing the working class and poor to send their children to private schools, and jolting "public education out of its lethargy."[266] "I have not forgotten my promise regarding tuition tax credits," Reagan wrote to a Catholic bishop in April 1982, "but have been constrained by our economic situation and the unwillingness of leaders on the Hill to move on this matter."[267] In June, Reagan submitted a bill to Congress entitled "The Educational Opportunity and Equity Act," to furnish tuition tax credits to parents whose children attended private elementary and secondary schools, but it was defeated by the Senate in 1983. He blamed its failure principally on the opposition of the National Education Association, which strongly lobbied against the bill.[268]

Unlike abortion, school prayer, and tuition tax credits, the battle against communism did not intrinsically involve religion. For Reagan, however, the war against communism was at heart religious, and he made its defeat a central goal of his administration.[269] Reagan departed radically from Carter's course. The Democrat had initially portrayed the Soviet behemoth as having a limited capacity to affect the world.[270] Although events, especially the Soviet Union's invasion of Afghanistan in late 1979, changed Carter's mind, he never, like his successor, denounced the USSR as a belligerent, godless regime. To Reagan, by contrast, communism was an inherently evil and expansionist system that was destined to fail because it was contrary to human nature, biblical principles, and God's plan for history. Because God directed the course of events, "free men and women, inspired by their deeply held religious beliefs and values," could turn the historical tides and set "them running again in the cause of freedom."[271] Communism's central flaw was that it denied people freedom, which was essential to human happiness and economic prosperity.[272] "The cause of freedom," he trumpeted, "is the cause of God."[273] Because Communist governments rejected God, they denied people religious, political, and economic freedom. They ignored "the rights God bestows" and suppressed freedom of speech, restricted emigration, jailed dissidents, and put intellectuals in mental hospitals.[274] Reagan complained that the Communist Party had "substituted Karl Marx for God" and insisted that the "Marxist vision of man without God" would "eventually be seen as an empty and false faith."[275] He claimed that the United States and the Soviet Union offered competing worldviews. "Two visions of the world remain locked in dispute," he declared in 1983. "The first believes all men are created equal by a loving God who had blessed us with freedom. . . . The second vision believes that religion is the opium of the masses. It believes that eternal principles like truth, liberty, and democracy have no meaning beyond the whim of the state."[276] "The struggle between freedom and totalitarianism," Reagan insisted, was not ultimately a battle of arms or missiles, but a "spiritual struggle."[277] Because it was the enemy of God and freedom, communism could not last.[278]

In March 1983, Reagan delivered the most controversial speech of his presidency to the National Association of Evangelicals in Orlando, Florida. "There is sin and evil in the world," Reagan averred, "and we're enjoined by Scripture and the Lord Jesus to oppose it with all our might." "If history teaches anything," he proclaimed, "it teaches that simple-minded appeasement or wishful thinking about our adversaries is folly." The president then turned his guns on the atheistic philosophy and sins of the Soviet Union. Following Lenin, the Soviets repudiated all religion and contended that morality was "entirely subordinate to the interests of class warfare." Because the Soviets "preach[ed] the supremacy of the State" and sought to dominate the planet, he argued, "they are the focus of evil in the modern world." He urged Americans to pray that "all who live in that totalitarian darkness" would "discover the joy of knowing God." Attacking those who supported a nuclear freeze, Reagan warned against the temptation to believe that both sides were equally to blame for the arms race. Doing so ignored "the facts of history and the aggressive impulses of an evil empire." Those who took this approach retreated "from the struggle between right and wrong and good and evil." The United States, he maintained, must "never stop searching for a genuine peace," but it must be a "peace through strength." He urged his listeners to support his administration's efforts to "keep America strong and free, while we negotiate real and verifiable reductions in the world's nuclear arsenal and one day, with God's help, their total elimination." "I've always maintained," he concluded, that this struggle "will never be decided by bombs or rockets, by armies or military might. The real crisis we face today is a spiritual one; at root, it's a test of moral will and faith."[279]

Many evangelicals (and other Reagan supporters) enthusiastically applauded his message.[280] Since the 1920s, many conservative Christians had made defeating communism a focal point of their politics. It served to "funnel more diffuse fears of atheism, evolution, and modernism into a single embodied enemy."[281] Despite the fact that Wilson had accused the Bolsheviks of "mass terrorism," "barbarism," and "wanton acts," and Eisenhower decried communism as a "hostile," "atheistic," "ruthless" ideology, numerous commentators deplored Reagan's "stunning breach of international protocol."[282] Judging by how frequently they quoted him, many agreed with Henry Steele Commager that it was "the worst presidential speech in American history" because of its "gross appeal to religious prejudice."[283] Hugh Sidey protested in *Time* that Reagan's "fiery sermon mixed statecraft and religion." "How we deal with the Soviets," he argued, "is not something that can be decided by self-appointed soldiers of God armed with unbending judgments about who and what are good and moral."[284] In the *New York Times*, Anthony Lewis condemned the speech as "simplistic," "terribly dangerous," "outrageous," and "primitive." By attempting to "apply religious concepts to the contentious technical particulars of arms programs," he argued, Reagan ignored the facts that the United States had led the way in almost every new weapon development in the last thirty years, that millions of Americans did not agree with conservative Protestant or Catholic theology, and that many religious groups had endorsed a nuclear freeze.[285] Jim Wallis complained in *Sojourners* that it was "not only bad theology, but dangerous heresy to suggest that evil in the world" was "mostly located to the north of the Caspian Sea."[286] A *Washington Post* editorial accused Reagan of enlisting "God on our side in the Cold War."[287] Many Western Europeans, fearful that they would be caught in the cross fire of a nuclear war between the superpowers, deprecated Reagan as a "binary-minded simpleton" who thought complex issues "could be reduced to checked boxes marked YES or NO."[288] Not surprisingly, the Soviet press and leadership vehemently objected to Reagan's characterization of them as international pariahs.[289]

Although many disagreed at the time, Reagan saw himself as a peacemaker and often declared that his ultimate goal was to halt the production of nuclear weapons and then reduce their number.[290] He insisted, however, that the United States must first achieve military superiority over the USSR and be able to negotiate from a position of strength. To a Catholic priest, Reagan wrote, "I'm sure the Bishops supporting the 'freeze' and unilateral disarmament are sincere and believe they are furthering the cause of peace. I am equally sure that they are tragically mistaken. What they urge would bring us closer to a choice of surrender or die."[291] Although nuclear freeze "had a nice-sounding emotional appeal," Reagan argued in 1990, the agenda of its supporters "could have been written in Moscow." Like his religious critics, Reagan saw nuclear war as both immoral and unwinnable. It would cause hundreds of millions of casualties, poison the planet, and end civilization.[292] Reagan proposed his Strategic Defense Initiative (SDI), a shield to stop incoming missiles, because the United States had a "moral obligation to pursue technological breakthroughs that could permit us to move away from exclusive reliance on the threat of retaliation and mutual nuclear terror."[293] SDI would eliminate the necessity of mutually assured destruction (MAD), which he despised on moral grounds, and move the world closer to his dream of "a world free of nuclear weapons." Reagan denounced MAD as "madness," the "craziest thing I ever heard of." It was like "two westerners standing in a saloon aiming their guns at each other's head—permanently."[294]

Moderating his militant rhetoric during his second term, Reagan developed a good working relationship with Mikhail Gorbachev, who became the Soviet premier in 1985. Holding four summits in two and a half years (Geneva in 1985, Reykjavik in 1986, Washington in 1987, and Moscow in 1988), they negotiated the Intermediate-Range Nuclear Forces (INF) Treaty, which eliminated all intermediate-range missiles and, for the first time in history, reduced the nuclear arsenal of each nation. After the historic Washington summit, which included the signing of the INF Treaty, Reagan told a nationwide television audience, "Let us then thank God for all His blessings to this nation, and ask Him for His help so that we might continue the work of peace and foster the hope of a world where human freedom is enshrined."[295]

Reagan also sought to provide greater spiritual opportunities for the residents of Communist nations. He was convinced that many living behind the Iron Curtain had a deep desire for spiritual things and that, despite Communist antagonism, a religious revival was occurring there. Although overthrowing this repressive system was his ultimate goal, Reagan also tried to further this revival by working to increase the freedom of citizens of Communist countries to worship God, discussing religious themes in his speeches to them, and exhorting Americans to pray for them. In a 1983 address, Reagan quoted British writer Malcolm Muggeridge: " 'The most important happening in the world today is the resurgence of Christianity in the Soviet Union....' " Reagan claimed that "the most awesome military machine in history" was "no match for that . . . single man, hero, strong yet tender, Prince of Peace. His name alone, Jesus, can lift our hearts, soothe our sorrows, heal our wounds, and drive away our fears."[296] In 1987, Reagan maintained that Billy Graham's recent crusades in the Soviet Union confirmed the "hunger for religion there."[297] In numerous addresses, Reagan expressed his hope that people behind the Iron Curtain would come to know "the liberating nature of faith in God."[298]

Reagan repeatedly denounced the lack of religious freedom in Communist nations, met with several Soviet dissidents, and urged the Soviet Union to allow more Jews to emigrate.[299] Both Marx and Lenin, he asserted, recognized that religious belief would subvert communism.[300] In 1983, Reagan warned that those who sought to "crush religious freedom," jailed believers, closed churches, confiscated Bibles, and harassed priests and rabbis would "never destroy the love of God and freedom that burns in their hearts."[301] Later that year, he protested that people in many countries were not "even allowed to read the Bible. It is up to us to make sure that the message of hope and salvation gets through."[302] Reagan continually applauded and secretly supported the struggle of the Polish people to throw off the yoke of Soviet oppression. "Nowhere in the world is there a more splendid affirmation of this connection between religious values and political freedom," Reagan avowed, "than in the ideals, the faith, and heroism of the Polish people and the leaders of Solidarity."[303] Reagan also asserted in 1983 that the communist-inspired revolution in Central America was "no match for the much greater force of faith that runs so deep among the people," as demonstrated by Pope John Paul II's recent visit to the region.[304]

Reagan frequently used his opportunities to speak to communist audiences to stress religious themes. He argued in 1988 that "the most fitting way to mark the millennium of Christianity in Kiev Rus" would be to grant all Soviets the right to "worship their God, in their own way."[305] During his trip to Moscow in May of that year to meet with Gorbachev, Reagan told religious leaders that he hoped the Soviet Union was ready to reopen churches. He argued that faith was as elemental to the nation as its dark and fertile soil and hoped that perestroika would "be accompanied by a deeper restructuring, a deeper conversion" and that glasnost would "let loose a new chorus of belief, singing praises to the God who gave us life."[306]

Historians have extensively debated the factors that led to the demise of the Soviet Union and the end of the cold war. Many give Gorbachev the lion's share of the credit for transforming East-West relations.[307] Some insist that communism was doomed to fail and emphasize factors beyond the control of leaders: The USSR's bloated bureaucracy and economic inefficiency, low birth rate, problems with alcoholism, and lagging technology combined to make its rate of economic growth far below that of the United States. Meanwhile, the cost of supporting Communist nations in Eastern Europe, Africa, Asia, and the Caribbean, fighting a war in Afghanistan, and trying to compete militarily with the United States drained its resources. Suffering from chronic economic problems, diminished productivity, low morale, political mismanagement, and overextension, the Soviet Union collapsed under its own weight. Both Reagan and Gorbachev hastily improvised to keep up with these forces and events. To these scholars, Reagan simply happened to be president when the Soviet Union changed, for reasons he neither understood nor influenced. This lucky bumbler was too ill informed and inept to have engineered the toppling of the empire he denounced as evil.[308] Others maintain that all the presidents from Truman to Reagan deserve equal credit for the victory over communism.[309] Many of those who attribute the end of the cold war to the Reagan administration credit his staff, not Reagan himself, whom they judge to have been too aloof and passive to have managed the effort.[310]

Rejecting these interpretations, other scholars insist that Reagan resolutely directed some major aspects of his administration's foreign policy, including its relationship with the world's other superpower. Lou Cannon maintains that Reagan, not his staff, set the priorities for his administration, including the nation's military buildup and the decision to negotiate with Gorbachev.[311] Some of those who argue that Reagan played the decisive role in bringing down the Soviet Union and ending the cold war maintain that he devised and coordinated a comprehensive strategy for doing so.[312] According to this view, his carefully conceived plan for toppling the Soviet Union centered on improving the American economy, overseeing the largest peacetime military buildup in the nation's history, changing the foreign policy from détente to confrontation, deploying Pershing and cruise missiles, and trying to develop a missile shield to protect the nation from a Soviet nuclear attack. Recognizing that the Soviet Union's resources were stretched dangerously thin, the Reagan administration worked to further weaken its economy by denying it favored-nation trade status, increasing the global production of oil to undercut Soviet revenue, using diplomacy to prevent the construction of a Soviet oil pipeline, and supporting anticommunist insurgency around the world, especially by aiding Solidarity in Poland, the contras in Nicaragua, and the mujahedin in Afghanistan.[313] Reagan insisted the Soviet Union's economic woes and seething discontent made it very vulnerable. It was "ultimately too weak to withstand a challenge from the morally and technologically superior West."[314] Despite widespread disapproval of his defense policies, "criticism from elder statesmen, ridicule from the media, and withering attacks from his political opponents," Reagan relentlessly pursued his grand design.[315] Although many American scientists and military experts dismissed SDI as unfeasible, Gorbachev and other Soviet leaders took it seriously. They feared that trying to compete militarily would wreck their economy and prevent perestroika from succeeding.[316]

By acting tough toward Moscow during his first term (upsetting the doves) and conciliating Gorbachev during his second term (antagonizing the hawks), Reagan accomplished what Henry Kissinger termed "the greatest diplomatic feat of the modern era."[317] To save itself from imploding, the Soviet Union had to change. Communism had failed to deliver what it promised, economically or politically. The Soviet Union collapsed, Reagan concluded in his autobiography, because communism had bankrupted the nation "economically and spiritually," sapping people's incentive to "produce and excel," and inhibiting their opportunity to worship their Creator.[318] When congratulated for ending the cold war, Reagan countered that it was "not my success, but a team effort [directed] by divine providence."[319] Although he had substantial help from Gorbachev, John Paul II, Great Britain's Prime Minister Margaret Thatcher, Czech President Vaclav Havel, and Solidarity leader Lech Walesa, D'Souza argues, Reagan played the decisive role in ending the cold war. He possessed what Edmund Burke called moral imagination, the belief that there was right and wrong in the world.[320] Thatcher put it simply: "Ronald Reagan won the cold war without firing a shot."[321]

A Final Assessment

A chorus of critics demeaned Reagan's intelligence, deprecated his leadership, denounced his policies, and deplored their consequences.[322] In religion, as in every other facet of life, Reagan was a "virtuoso politician," a journalist averred, a man who played "the emotions the way Artur Rubinstein played a Steinway."[323] Unfortunately, Reagan did not use "his considerable communication skills to rally people to noble causes or to remind them of their obligations to others."[324] Critics attributed Reagan's accomplishments to "'incredible luck'" (he was the "beneficiary of vast social and political trends he had little or nothing to do with") and argued that "his short-term gains" would be "greatly outweighed by the long-term liabilities" with which he had "burdened the country."[325] They complained that his huge tax cuts, trade policies, and mammoth defense budget produced unprecedented budget deficits. By slashing government social programs, his administration brought greater hardships to minorities and the poor.[326] Many Catholics and mainline Protestants argued that Reagan's policies toward the destitute and unemployed violated the "norms of Christian compassion and justice."[327] While opposing abortion, Reagan pursued a "broader ideological agenda" that degraded "human life in favor of private profit and military dominance."[328] Reagan preached the importance of morality and, like Carter, "was widely viewed as incorruptible," Lou Cannon argued, but he never established an ethics code for his administration, tolerated dishonesty, and practiced cronyism. As a result, ethical practices tended to depend on the personal standards of officeholders, and his administration was riddled with improprieties and scandals, most notably the Iran-contra affair.[329] The Reagan years, predicted a journalist, would be remembered "for hustling, hypocrisy, lying, sleaze, and stasis."[330] Protesting that Reagan had done little to combat racism, global environmental problems, nuclear mismanagement, homelessness, the financial IOUs we are leaving our children, corruption in government, or income disparity, the Catholic journal *Commonweal* insisted that what the nation needed after eight years of his presidency was "a fierce and cleansing wind."[331]

Some castigated Reagan for presiding over a decade of decline, decay, debt, despair, and unfulfilled dreams. To Haynes Johnson, the 1980s produced neither the spiritual revival nor the widespread prosperity Reagan prophesied. Rather, it brought an orgy of materialism and self-gratification and an even larger gap between the rich and the poor. Top-rated television shows like *Dallas* and *Dynasty* and songs like Madonna's "Material Girl" portrayed Americans' self-absorption and preoccupation with acquisition. Tycoons on Wall Street, politicians in Washington, and televangelists across the country all proclaimed the virtues of selfishness and bellowed that "greed is good."[332]

Others refuted many of these charges. To Alonzo Hamby, many of liberals' criticisms of Reagan reflect their acceptance of a postmodern mentality that rejects the idea of ultimate truth and clear-cut moral distinctions. Unlike many of his detractors, Reagan believed there were objective standards for truth and virtue. The Republican's conviction that God had a special plan for his life,

Hamby adds, drove "his critics to a fury."[333] Even his generally sympathetic biographer Edmund Morris criticized "the fundamentally childlike, bipolar quality" of Reagan's mind, "its tendency to see all moral questions in terms of opposites."[334] Meanwhile, many conservatives complained privately that "Reagan was a kindly old bumbler," a "malleable figurehead" who was "easily controlled by his wife and pragmatic advisors." Both camps, D'Souza maintains, greatly underestimated Reagan. They failed to understand how he conceived and realized his grand objectives.[335]

Supporters laud Reagan's domestic and foreign policies. He halted inflation, cut taxes, and presided over the greatest economic expansion in American history. Admirers claim that his supply-side economics were rooted in compassion and justice, which focused on creating wealth, not simply redistributing it. Writing in the *Washington Post*, T. R. Reid labeled the 1980s a decade of creed, not greed, when the number of Americans who gave their time to religious, civic, and educational causes increased much faster than the population.[336] *Christianity Today* rejoiced that Reagan had "heightened the visibility of Christianity in America by taking virtually every opportunity to convey a God-centered philosophy of life." Thus he had also helped to counter the nation's unbridled secularism that strove to marginalize religion.[337] His defenders also argued that Reagan rebuilt America's defenses, restored its prestige, dealt with the Soviets from a position of strength, negotiated arms limitations and reductions, and helped overthrow communism in Eastern Europe and the Soviet Union. When he left office, peace, democracy, and capitalism were flourishing in many parts of the world, they said, and Americans' morale was high once again.[338] Only Washington, Lincoln, and Franklin Roosevelt could "claim a legacy of comparable distinction."[339]

Others object to the way Reagan used religious rhetoric, the type of religion he promoted, and the impact his approach and actions had on religion in America. Pierard and Linder fault Reagan for elevating civil religion to new heights and basing national moral and spiritual renewal on "a highly generalized, albeit theistic, public faith." To them, his repeated calls for restoring prayer in the public schools illustrate this point. Had his amendment passed, schoolchildren would have invoked the name of the deity of American civil religion, not the God worshiped by Christians, Jews, Muslims, or any other religious group. Though possessing a meaningful personal faith, Reagan sacrificed it on the altar of public theology to promote the nation's purposes as he understood them and his own political agenda.[340] Like many of his predecessors, Jim Wallis contends, "Reagan promulgated an American civil religion, which was an amalgam of the Judeo-Christian heritage and the national experience." It "mixes piety with patriotism, invokes God's name when speaking of the national destiny, and generally blurs the distinction between biblical faith and cultural religion." Reagan was the "new high priest of American civil religion," who comforted citizens, assured them of "their basic goodness and the soundness of their institutions," and proclaimed "the righteousness of the national purpose and destiny." In his theology, the United States was the "first, best, richest, most righteous, and always, most powerful [nation] in the world." It favored "the rich over the poor [and] the strong over the weak." Instead of subjecting himself to the Word of God, Reagan claimed to be on God's side. He reduced God to "a narrow American tribal deity" and used him to bless American ambitions and aspirations.[341]

Other critics were equally caustic. As a result of Reagan's alliance with the televangelists, Johnson maintained, the combination of religion and politics became "a new and disturbing phenomenon in American life."[342] Wilbur Edel protested that Reagan transformed the presidency into an amalgamation of "Theodore Roosevelt's 'bully pulpit,' a fundamentalist chapel, a Hollywood stage, and a Madison Avenue public relations office." He accused Reagan of trying to "alter the basic framework of the Constitution to accommodate his fundamentalist religious principles." "Reagan's frequent plea for a return to the religious precepts of the Founding Fathers" reflected a "child's view of American history—sincere, reverent, and patriotic, but with little understanding of the forces and ideas that have shaped U.S. society."[343]

Still others castigated Reagan for using conservative Christians to serve his own purposes.[344] He "kept his Religious Right followers happy through rhetoric and symbolic gestures," argues William Pemberton, "rather than through effective action on their agenda."[345] The rates of abortion, out-of-wedlock births, divorce, and drug usage continued at high levels; sex and violence increased on television and in the movies; and prayer was still not allowed in public schools. Although most religious conservatives never wavered in their support of Reagan, many disliked some aspects of his administration, his party, and his lifestyle. Although frustrated that their votes were courted but their views were often ignored, they had nowhere else to turn. By the end of Reagan's tenure, many evangelicals feared that they had become pawns in the political power game. Some lamented that they had succumbed to the allure of power, the attraction of being invited to the political table for the first time.[346] Speaking for this group, Ed Dobson argued that during the Reagan years, the Christian right had access and influence but made little progress in promoting its social agenda, except for the publicity it received in the three presidential elections of the 1980s.[347] Others countered that Reagan's legitimation of their causes and their organizations had a very positive impact. Moreover, they argued, his relationship with religious conservatives, as well as their political activism, dominance of the airwaves, and increasing numerical and financial strength, coupled with the decline of mainline Protestantism, shifted the balance of religious power in America.[348]

Most religious conservatives strongly supported Reagan, even though they disliked his divorce and earlier participation in a Hollywood culture they viewed as a den of modernism, hedonism, and sexual immorality. Like them, the president strongly stressed the importance of families, and he was portrayed by his supporters as an exemplar of family values, even though he did not have a close relationship with his four children.[349] While they emphasized active participation in the life of the local church through Sunday morning worship, Sunday school classes, Bible studies, and discipleship groups, he rarely even attended worship services during his presidency. Linder and Pierard term the transformation of a veteran movie actor into "'a great man of faith'" "one of the most remarkable public relations stories of the twentieth century."[350]

Why, then, did most religious conservatives support Reagan over Carter—who was perceived to be more devout, thought to know the Bible better, participated much more in church activities, and was much more willing to publicly discuss his personal relationship with God? Garry Wills contends that they found Reagan more appealing because Carter lacked his exuberant confidence in people and their achievements and in America. Carter believed in original sin and people's aggressive tendencies, argued there were limits to growth, and called for sacrifice and self-denial. Reagan, by contrast, painted a more glowing, optimistic picture of human potential and America's future. Carter's religion was more in line with historic Calvinism or what William James called the "sick soul." It stressed man's fall, need for repentance, and humility. Reagan's religion, Wills maintains, is what James labeled "healthy-mindedness." For it, sadness, rather than sin, was the enemy of human nature. Evangelicals were moving up in the world. They preferred Reagan's upbeat emphasis on national pride and assertiveness, economic growth, and success over Carter's pessimistic jeremiad of national peril and stagnation and the need to accept limits.[351] Many evangelicals rejected Carter, a sincere believer in the gospel, and embraced Reagan, who held a "hodgepodge of make-believe beliefs," Wills maintained, because he offered "a more marketable God." While Carter's God was a "downer," Reagan's God cheered people up, enabled them to stand tall, filled their pockets, liked Americans more than other people, and did not demand individual or national humility or repentance. Reagan's "God" was an idol that he carried around "in his pocket with his other amulets and rabbit's feet."[352]

Another critic accused Reagan's religious supporters of idolatry. Captivated by his charisma and character, they portrayed him as chosen and anointed by God, as a man "of great faith and Christ-like forbearance and rectitude." Religious conservatives saw Reagan as God's agent, who would bring spiritual renewal and political redemption. If the United States recaptured its Christian identity, it could help redeem the rest of the world. "Reagan's power over the faithful, then, stemmed from his ability to summon up a world of memory and illusion and to equate divine and national purpose in an overarching world mission."[353]

Although a number of these assertions cannot be substantiated, others contain elements of truth. They overlook, however, the simpler explanation for why many religious conservatives were so enthusiastic toward and sup- portive of Reagan. Despite their differences with him, which they largely ignored, most members of the religious right (including conservative Cath- olics and Mormons) considered him a brother in Christ, a kindred spirit. Reagan spoke their language often, beautifully, not just to individuals or congregations, but to the nation and the world. He shared their opposition to secularization, moral decay, and the spread of iniquity, and perhaps most important, he shared their political conservatism. Reagan invited them to the White House, gave them private briefings and opportunities for photo-ops, listened to their concerns, spoke at their gatherings, and provided them with enough political appointments and social legislation to assure them that he was on their side. Moreover, he strove valiantly to remedy the nation's vices and heal its sin. Reagan called for a spiritual revival, insisted God had chosen America to fulfill his purposes in the world, and advanced many of their causes. For many of them, this was what ultimately counted.[354]

Moreover, these critics often overstate their case, provide little or no evidence to support their claims, or base their analysis on debatable as- sumptions about goodness and truth. Although Reagan's personal life was not a paragon of evangelical piety, his worldview was strongly shaped by his understanding of biblical teaching.[355] To religious conservatives, Reagan's quest to inject spiritual and moral values into the nation's government and life was commendable. Pierard and Linder argue that Reagan performed the role of "the high priest of American civil religion" "more unabashedly, forcefully, compellingly, and with greater national acceptance than any pre- vious president."[356] However, he not only emphasized the priestly, com- forting aspects of civil religion but also stressed its prophetic dimension. While in the priestly version the president makes the nation itself, rather than God, the ultimate standard for judging the country's actions, Pierard and Linder explain, in the prophetic version he evaluates the nation's actions in relationship to God's will.[357] Although frequently accused of asserting that God supported his positions, Reagan declared that "we must be cautious in claiming God is on our side. I think the real question we must answer is, are we on His side."[358] Reagan argued that Americans were accountable to transcendent standards, lamented that in many ways they fell short of them, and urged them to repent. Only then would God heal their land and use them as his instrument. While very proud of America's achievements and ex- tremely optimistic about its potential, Reagan did not make the United States the ultimate reference point or suggest that its behavior was blameless. Reagan never claimed that God had chosen the United States in the same way that he had selected Israel to be his unique agent in the world. Rather, God could use the United States (and other nations) to carry out his mission in the world. But Americans must put their own house in order before they could be a beacon of freedom, hope, and democracy.

Like the Puritans and numerous other presidents, Reagan believed that the United States had a larger role to play in God's plans than other nations. His inveterate optimism led him to conclude that revival was occurring, morality was improving, and God's kingdom was growing on Earth. Near the end of his presidency, he rejoiced that Americans had "done great things" in the last eight years, inspired by the "brilliant vision of America as a Shining City on a Hill."[359] "I've spoken of the shining city all my political life," Reagan proclaimed in his Farewell Address. "[I]t was a tall, proud city built on rocks, . . . God-blessed, and teeming with people of all kinds living in harmony and peace." "We made the city stronger," Reagan concluded, and "we made the city freer." "We meant to change a nation," he trumpeted, "and instead we changed the world."[360] "Reagan may not have been a great president," Cannon maintains, "but he was a great American" with "a compelling vision of his country."[361] By his powers of persuasion, argued the *Albuquerque Journal,* he made Americans feel good about themselves and "brought us measurably closer to the ideal of a 'shining city upon a hill.'"[362] Although the United States did not embody all the aspects of this city during Reagan's watch, it did take significant steps toward realizing some of its principal values.

CHAPTER ELEVEN

George W. Bush: A Faith-Based Presidency

Christ, because he changed my heart.

Bush's response when asked to name the philosopher who had most
influenced him during a debate in De Moines, Iowa, among Republican
presidential candidates on Dec. 13, 1999

*My administration will put the federal government squarely on the side
of America's armies of compassion.*

National Prayer Breakfast, Feb. 1, 2001

*There is only one reason that I am in the Oval Office and not in a bar. I
found faith. I found God. I am here because of the power of prayer.*

Bush to religious leaders, Sept. 2002

*I don't see how you can separate your faith as a person from the job of
being president.*

Aug. 12, 2004, interview on *Larry King Live*

ALTHOUGH GEORGE W. BUSH is not more personally devout than William
McKinley, Woodrow Wilson, or Jimmy Carter, religious issues have played an
even more important role in his presidency than for any of his predecessors.
Writing in *Newsweek*, Howard Fineman labeled his presidency "the most
resolutely 'faith-based' in modern times."[1] The impact of Bush's faith is evident in his personality, rhetoric, campaigns, appointments, and policies. It has
helped shape his electoral strategy, his political agenda, and his relationship
with domestic constituencies and leaders of other nations. The nature of his
personal faith, the many religious factors involved in his campaigns, and the
influence of his religious convictions on his policies have provoked an

immense amount of discussion, debate, and disagreement. Bush has delivered national radio addresses that both admirers and detractors label sermons, regularly "injects religious ideas into his domestic policy," and frequently argues that faith can help solve America's social ills.[2] More than that of any other president, his White House is filled with individuals who have strong faith commitments. All these factors are forcing Americans to reevaluate the role of religion in public life.

Few presidents, a trio of *Newsweek* staff contend, "have invoked faith more openly than, or as often as, Bush."[3] Soon after rising, most other recent presidents examined news summaries or overnight intelligence dispatches. By contrast, Bush, like Carter (and Woodrow Wilson and John Quincy Adams in earlier eras), instead reads the Bible or devotional literature. His first day in office, Bush proclaimed the following Sunday a national day of prayer and thanksgiving: "I cannot succeed in this task without the favor of God and the prayers of the people."[4] Like several of his predecessors, Bush has sought to bring religious principles and organizations into the battle against the nation's social problems. His faith has encouraged millions of Americans and alarmed many others. "Revered or ridiculed, followed or feared, perhaps no American president has brandished religion so potently as George W. Bush," writes a French foreign correspondent.[5] Three religious biographies, hundreds of magazines and newspapers, as well as documentaries on PBS and A&E, have explored his religious beliefs and practices.

Bush has been frequently accused of being a Christian zealot who wants to remake America in accordance with his own religious views, as evident in his domestic agenda, political appointments, and approach to international relations. Bush has awarded substantial amounts of federal money to religious organizations that provide social services, banned human cloning and partial birth abortions, limited stem-cell research, supported government vouchers for students who attend religious schools, increased funding to teach sexual abstinence, devised pro-life foreign aid policies, and dispensed federal money to prison programs that use Christian principles to transform convicts.[6] He has nominated pro-life judges and given many positions in the White House and federal agencies to conservative Christians. He has supplied federal funds to strengthen marriages and worked to reduce the persecution of Christians abroad. By repeatedly referring to the war on terrorism as a "conflict between good and evil," critics contend, Bush has turned a political conflict into a religious crusade.[7]

Detractors also protest that many of Bush's policies and his belief that he is God's instrument violate First Amendment guarantees of church-state separation and are extremely dangerous. The Texan's conviction that he has a divine mandate to be president, they object, gives him an "unabashed certainty about his policies."[8] After launching the war against Iraq, Bush confided that he sought to "be as good a messenger" of God's "will as possible." Some maintain that the term "messianic militarist" more accurately describes him. During the 2004 campaign, Ralph Nader complained that church and state were "not at all separated in Bush's brain," which "is extremely disturbing."[9]

Bush's approach to the presidency, notes the British *Economist*, has produced "a flood of partisan books and films" and "a storm of Bush-hatred, both at home and abroad." Millions paid to see Michael Moore's documentary *Fahrenheit 9/11* and many anti-Bush polemics grace the *New York Times* best-seller list. Bush "has rewritten the rules of American foreign policy," "recast much [of the nation's] domestic policy," and "become a transformational president."[10]

The Faith of George W. Bush

Raised by devout parents, Bush's father, George H. W., received additional Christian nurture through the Episcopal Church and chapel services at prep school. Barbara, who was grew up Presbyterian in a wealthy family in New York, has a deep faith, has maintained a close relationship with Billy Graham, and has been "the vital spiritual influence in her family."[11] Throughout their marriage, the senior Bushes have regularly prayed together before going to bed.[12]

As a child, George W. attended First Presbyterian Church in Midland, and as a youth, he served as an altar boy at St. Martin's Episcopal Church in Houston.[13] While at Yale, Bush rarely attended church.[14] Following his marriage to librarian Laura Welch in 1977, Bush usually worshiped at First Presbyterian Church in Midland, where he also taught Sunday school. After their twin daughters were baptized in 1982, however, he joined the First Methodist Church, to which Laura belonged. An active member, he served on the church's finance and administrative committees.

Like his parents, Bush cannot point to a single spiritual experience that transformed his life. Three midlife incidents helped rekindle the faith his parents and involvement in the church planted in Bush. In April 1984, eccentric evangelist Arthur Blessitt came to Midland to hold revival services. One of Bush's oilmen friends, Jim Sale, an organizer of the crusade, arranged a meeting between Bush and Blessitt. Blessitt's Web site says the following exchange took place:

> "If you died this moment, do you have the assurance you would go to heaven?" [Blessitt asked].
>
> "No," he replied.
>
> "Then let me explain to you how you can have that assurance and know for sure that you are saved."
>
> He replied, "I like that."

Blessitt claims he then explained the biblical basis of personal salvation through trust in Christ to Bush, and they held hands and prayed for him to receive Jesus as his Savior.[15] Although Bush has never denied this conversation happened, he does not mention it in his autobiography, and two of his closest spiritual confidants, Don Evans and Karen Hughes, have never heard Bush discuss it.[16]

Whatever happened at his meeting with Blessitt, Bush remained spiritually unsatisfied. The Texan points to an experience he had the next year as beginning the renewal of his faith. The words Billy Graham shared with several members of Bush's family one summer weekend in 1985, Bush declared, "sparked a change in my heart." A personal conversation with Graham "planted a mustard seed" in Bush's soul that germinated the next year.[17] Graham asked Bush, "Are you right with God?" "No," Bush retorted, "but I want to be."[18] Although he had "always been a religious person," that weekend started Bush on a journey that soon led to him to recommit his heart to Jesus Christ.[19] Bush realized that "God sent His Son to die for a sinner like me" and came to know "God's amazing grace" through Christ. Bush's closest friends agree that this encounter was decisive in moving him from simply assenting to basic Christian doctrines to being a disciple of Christ.[20] He began reading the Bible regularly and, encouraged by Evans, a childhood friend, joined a men's group, Community Bible Study (CBS), in Midland. Begun in 1975, CBS involved an intensive study of a New Testament book for a year.[21] Bush's interest in the Scriptures became much stronger, and "the words became clearer and more meaningful."[22] Meanwhile, he and Laura actively participated in the First Methodist Church in Midland.

By 1986, Bush was under immense pressure. His oil company, Spectrum 7, was deeply in debt, and he was not drawing a salary.[23] That July, Bush and his wife went to Colorado Springs to celebrate his own and two other friends' fortieth birthdays. Bush, who for many years had consumed significant amounts of alcohol, drank too much at their party. While jogging the next morning, he felt miserable and decided to stop drinking. Neither a DUI arrest, Laura's pleas, nor social embarrassment had previously caused him to stop.[24] Although this was "not specifically a 'spiritual' decision, it had profound spiritual consequences."[25] It helped confirm Bush's experiences with Blessitt, Graham, and CBS and make him a more devoted Christian. The Texan does not use the terms "born again" or "saved" to describe his relationship with Christ but rather speaks of "renewing" his faith, rededicating his life to Christ, or being a disciple of Jesus.[26]

Bush's favorite hymn, "A Charge to Keep I Have," encapsulates his faith. It proclaims: "A charge to keep I have, a God to glorify.... To serve the present age, my calling to fulfill; o may it all my powers engage to do my Master's will." His 1999 autobiography takes its title from this hymn, and a painting it inspired hangs in the Oval Office. As Bush began his first term as president, he echoed words Harry Truman spoke in 1945: "I ask only to be a good and faithful servant of my Lord and my people."[27]

While frequently professing that his faith is strong and very important to him, what Bush believes about a variety of specific issues is not clear. David Aikman had considerable access to Bush's senior officials and friends when he wrote *A Man of Faith* (2004), but no one gave him "a sort of credo" of what Bush believes. Forced to "intuit" many facets of the president's faith, he concluded that he is "a mainstream evangelical with a higher-than-normal tolerance of dissent." Stephen Mansfield contends in *The Faith of George W. Bush* (2003) that he is "a conservative Christian" but adds that on many issues Bush is not very doctrinaire. Tim Goeglein, Bush's liaison with Christian groups, argues that the president is "an evangelical" who "also fits theologian C. S. Lewis's definition of a 'mere Christian'—someone who" focuses on central, Christian teachings.[28] Despite Bush's lack of specificity on many issues, examining his understanding of faith, the Bible, God, Providence, Christ, salvation, human nature, and prayer; his pattern of church attendance; his personal habits; and his views of witnessing and religious tolerance can shed significant light on his religious convictions.

Bush repeatedly emphasizes that his faith is central to his life and work.[29] "My relationship with God through Christ has given me meaning and direction," he declares. "My faith has made a big difference in my personal life and my public life as well."[30] The Texan argues that faith provides individuals "a framework for living."[31] "My faith frees me," Bush asserts, "to put the problem of the moment in proper perspective," "to make decisions that others might not like," "to try to do the right thing, even though it may not poll well," and "to enjoy life and not worry about what comes next." "Faith changes lives," he adds. "I know, because it has changed mine."[32] "Without it," he told a National Prayer Breakfast audience in 2001, "I doubt I'd be here today."[33]

Since he became involved with CBS in 1985, Bush has faithfully read the Scriptures. Even during his two grueling campaigns for the presidency and as the nation's chief executive, Bush has closely studied the Bible each day. Employing the skills he developed in CBS, Bush examines key words in the passages he reads, evaluates their context, and meditates on their meaning.[34] While president, Bush also has typically read a selection from Scottish pastor Oswald Chambers's devotional work, *My Utmost for His Highest*.[35] Bush has engaged almost exclusively in private study of the Bible and has not participated in any of the numerous weekly study groups in the White House.[36] Although Bush has not specified whether he accepts the belief of many evangelicals that the Bible is God's infallible Word, he argues that "the church is built on the absolute principles of the Word of God."[37]

Bush stresses the love, grace, forgiveness, power, and sovereignty of God. "I believe in a God who calls us, not to judge our neighbors, but to love them. I believe in grace, because I have seen it; in peace, because I have felt it; in forgiveness, because I have needed it."[38] Like all the other presidents examined in this book, Bush believes strongly that God providentially directs history and that his plans are inscrutable. "He speaks of being called to the presidency, of a God who rules in the affairs of men, and of the United States owing her origin to Providence," writes Mansfield. "I . . . believe in a divine plan that supersedes all human plans," Bush declared.[39] In a 2001 radio address, Bush affirmed his trust in "a Creator who . . . loves us, and has a plan for our lives." Speaking at a memorial service for the victims of 9/11 at the National Cathedral in Washington, D.C., Bush emphasized that God's direction of history did not always produce the results people expected and urged listeners to yield "to a will greater than our own."[40] In his 2003 State of the Union Address, the president declared, "We do not claim to know all the ways of Providence, yet we can trust in them. . . . Behind all of life and all of history, there's a . . . purpose, set by the hand of a just and faithful God."[41] History "has a visible direction," Bush averred in his second inaugural address, set by "the Author of Liberty."[42]

Bush seems to affirm the traditional Christian doctrines of Jesus' divinity and atonement and of human nature. He asserts that "Christ bore the sins of man when he was crucified on the cross."[43] Bush calls Christ's death "the perfect example of unconditional love."[44] The Texan often argues that all people are sinners and refers to himself as a "lowly sinner" who needs Christ's redemption.[45] Although people are created in God's image, they are "flawed and fallible."[46] Bush has "adopted a nuanced position" on the issue of salvation. In a 1994 interview, he suggested that only those who accept Christ as their personal savior would go to heaven. In 1998, Bush apologized to the Anti-Defamation League for this remark and stressed that he respected all faiths, and during the 2000 campaign, he denied he had ever made an "exclusivist claim about salvation." He told NBC's Tim Russert, "What I said was, my religion teaches . . . that you accept Christ and you go to heaven. . . . Governors don't decide who gets to go to heaven. . . . God decides."[47]

Bush considers prayer indispensable. In a 2003 interview, he said, "I pray daily . . . in all kinds of places. . . . I pray a lot . . . as the Spirit moves me."[48] As president, he begins every day in prayer. Aides have reported seeing him on several occasions praying while facedown on the floor in the Oval Office. Bush sometimes prays with visitors to the White House who tell him about their concerns.[49] Cabinet meetings often begin with prayer, usually led by one of the secretaries.[50] "I firmly believe in the power of intercessory prayer," he declares, "and know I could not do my job without it."[51] "I pray for strength, . . . for forgiveness, and . . . to offer my thanks" to "a kind and generous Almighty God."[52] He agrees with Lincoln that the burdens of the presidency are "too great for any man" and thus must be carried "to God in prayer."[53] "I pray for guidance . . . wisdom and patience and understanding."[54] As he began his first term, Bush urged Americans "to pray that everyone in my administration...always remembers the common good."[55] The president rejoices that the United States "is a nation of prayer" and frequently calls prayer the "greatest gift" people can give him.[56] Bush was pleased that during Operation Iraqi Freedom many Americans adopted soldiers to pray for and wore prayer bracelets to remind themselves to intercede for the troops.[57] The president argues that prayer helps unify Americans, comforts them in their grief, and gives them strength, resolve, wisdom, a sense of compassion, and a concern for justice.[58] Because of its people's continual prayers, the United States "had been delivered from many serious evils and wrongs."[59] Bush's personal commitment to prayer, pleas for intercessory prayer for his administration, and the terrorist attacks of 9/11 prompted Christians to create the Presidential Prayer Team in mid-September 2001 to pray daily for Bush, his cabinet members, and other political leaders.[60] By May 2003, organizers reached their goal of enlisting 2.8 million members, 1 percent of the nation's population, to pray for these groups and for military personnel. Like most of his predecessors, Bush has declared several national days of prayer, humility, and fasting.

Bush worshiped faithfully from 1977 to 2001, first in Midland, then at the Highland Park United Methodist Church in Dallas from 1989 until 1995, and finally at the Tarrytown United Methodist Church in Austin, Texas, while serving as governor.[61] At Highland Park, Bush participated in a ministry that provides a variety of programs for low-income, primarily Hispanic families.[62] Amy Sullivan insists that even "many of the president's fiercest supporters" do not know that he attends church infrequently when he is in Washington. According to Sullivan, Bush's defenders maintain either that the leader of the free world does not "have time to go to church" or (like Reagan's supporters) that "the security precautions necessary for a presidential visit would drive congregants away." They add that "Bush doesn't feel the need to prove his religiosity." Privately, however, some Bush partisans confess they are baffled by Bush's failure to attend church habitually.[63] Others sharply disagree and insist that Bush worships regularly at St. John's Episcopal Church in Washington or the chapel at Camp David when he is there on weekends.[64]

For many years, Bush engaged in a number of personal habits that most religious conservatives detest: swearing, smoking, chewing tobacco, and drinking. The Texan has struggled with swearing most of his life. As a young man, he "cursed harder than a grease-stained roustabout."[65] As Bush neared forty, his secretary complained that he still cursed "like a sailor." After smoking for many years, Bush finally quit in the early 1990s. His problems with alcohol are well known. By the time he became governor of Texas in 1994, Bush had stopped smoking, chewing tobacco, and drinking, but he still struggled with swearing.[66] Bush continues to occasionally use foul language, although he apparently never uses God's name in vain.[67]

Bush frequently shares his personal spiritual journey with groups and individuals. After his speech to the National Religious Broadcasters in 2003, for example, Bush met privately with religious social workers and discussed his faith in Jesus Christ. "I would not be president today," he told them, "if I hadn't stopped drinking 17 years ago. And I could only do that with the grace of God."[68] As president, Bush has talked about the significance of the cross with Russian Prime Minister Vladimir Putin, discussed his faith with Chinese president Jiang Zemin, and prayed with Macedonia's president Boris Trajkovski.[69]

While espousing strong Christian beliefs, Bush has celebrated the value of all the nation's major religious faiths. In accepting the Republican nomination for president in 2000, Bush declared, "I believe in tolerance, not in spite of my faith, but because of it."[70] Speaking to a Jewish group the same month, he said, "Our nation is chosen by God and commissioned by history to be a model to the world of justice and inclusion and diversity without division." Jews, Christians, and Muslims are all committed "to a kind, just, tolerant society."[71] Bush has regularly issued statements celebrating Christian, Jewish, and Muslim holidays. "I believe the Lord can work through many faiths"—Christian, Jewish, Muslim, and Hindu—because they all emphasize the "universal call . . . to love your neighbor."[72] "An American President serves people of every faith, and serves some of no faith at all." While Americans should treat each other graciously, the president avers, they are not required "to abandon deeply-held beliefs."[73]

The Election of 2000

When Bush decided to run for the presidency in 2000, his strategy, as devised by Karl Rove, focused on two primary goals: acquiring funding from businessmen and winning the votes of evangelicals, conservative mainline Protestants, and Catholic traditionalists.[74] His personal faith and emphasis on values helped him achieve his second objective. In his battle for the Republican nomination, Bush faced a formidable challenge in gaining the support of the religious right. Gary Bauer, Alan Keyes, and Orrin Hatch also had credentials that made them attractive to religious conservatives.[75] Nevertheless, several factors gave Bush advantages over these other contenders. Bush had gained the respect of many and the friendship of some religious conservatives while working as his father's liaison to them during the 1988 presidential campaign and while serving as governor of Texas, a state with a huge evangelical population.[76] His "compassionate conservatism," which emphasized mentoring, tough love on crime, and faith-based welfare, was attractive to many evangelicals. Moreover, Bush shrewdly courted the religious right. In 1998 and 1999, he held several meetings in Texas with ministers of large congregations from across the country. As he prepared to announce his candidacy in 1999, Bush invited prominent pastors to the governor's mansion to "lay hands" on him and told them he felt "called" to run for the presidency.[77] That year, Texas evangelist James Robison hosted the governor twice on his television program and prayed for him on the air.[78] He talked naturally about his faith. Early in his campaign, Bush wrote a testimonial about his faith that was widely circulated on the Internet and also appeared in numerous publications.[79] Many members of the Christian right found his religious experiences, convictions, and sensibilities, as well as his personality, appealing. In addition, many of them liked the policies Bush implemented in Texas and his stand on national issues. They also recognized that as the son of a former president and a successful governor of one of the nation's largest states, Bush could raise large amounts of money and was likely to win the Republican nomination.[80] At the same time, Bush's Presbyterian, Episcopal, and Methodist roots and connections helped him relate to and gain the support of many mainline Protestants, a traditional GOP constituency.

Bush's December 1999 comment during a debate among Republican candidates in Iowa helped propel religion to the forefront of the campaign. Asked to name the philosopher or thinker he identified with most, the Texan replied, "Christ." "When you turn your heart and your life over to Christ, when you accept Christ as the Savior," he elaborated, "it changes your life." Whether Bush's statement was politically calculated or a spontaneous testimony to his convictions, it "packed a powerful punch among conservative Christians." Speaking for many of them, leading Southern Baptist Richard Land simply responded, "Wow."[81]

Others took a different view. *New York Times* columnist Maureen Dowd lambasted Bush for "playing the Jesus card." Bush had taken something deeply personal and paraded it for political gain, making him "guilty of either cynicism or exhibitionism." Did the governor want Jesus as his "personal savior or political savior," she asked.[82] "The scorn on this side of the Atlantic," wrote a journalist in the *London Times*, "could not have been greater if he'd said Homer Simpson."[83] The director of the Anti-Defamation League of B'nai B'rith called Bush's remark "a disconcerting inclusion of religion into politics," while the head of Americans United for the Separation of Church and State denounced "the politicizing of religion."[84]

Undeterred by such criticism, Bush primarily sought to woo religious voters throughout the campaign, as Jimmy Carter did in 1976, by telling them his life story and openly discussing how his faith sustained him. While some other candidates tried to court evangelicals by stressing their positions on issues such as abortion and gay rights, "Bush talked about his faith," Bauer explained, "and people just believed him—and believed in him."[85] Speaking for many evangelicals, Houston pastor Ed Young declared, "He talks to God. That's all I need to know."[86]

Religious factors and concerns about morality also played a large role in the general election. After securing the Republican nomination, Bush faced

Vice President Al Gore, a Southern Baptist. Both candidates emphasized their spiritual pilgrimages and the religious foundations for their policies. Franklin Foer argued that these two baby boomers had led "parallel spiritual lives." They grew up in the 1960s, when old religious orthodoxies were not popular, and in the 1970s, both experienced "midlife anxiety" and "spiritual hunger."[87] Like Bush, Gore frequently quoted Scripture, discussed his religious background and piety, and talked about the biblical and moral aspects of policies. His running mate, Senator Joseph Lieberman of Connecticut, an Orthodox Jew, repeatedly called religion the basis of morality, claimed secularism produced a "vacuum of values," gave "Silver Sewer" awards to "Hollywood's worst moral offenders," and urged Americans to dedicate themselves and their nation to "God's purpose."[88] Tired of claims that GOP stood for "God's Only Party," one of Gore's policy advisors told the *Boston Globe*, "The Democratic Party is going to take back God this time."[89] Throughout his campaign, the vice president accentuated his faith and sought to discuss issues in spiritual terms. Gore stressed that he had attended religious revivals as a child, been born again while attending Harvard in 1968, and been baptized in his midthirties.[90] The Democrat explained that he often asked, "What would Jesus do?" when confronted with choices.[91] He repeatedly declared that faith was central to his belief system, insisted that the United States had "a divine destiny to fulfill," and, like Bush, argued that the federal government should provide funds to help faith-based organizations do their work.[92] While identifying himself as a Protestant and a Baptist, he maintained that all those labels were less significant to him than his "own personal religious faith."[93]

During the campaign, numerous polls indicated that many Americans thought their nation had "lost its moral compass," and voters pondered which party could "best point the country toward true north."[94] Numerous potential voters identified moral decay and family decline as the most significant issue facing the country. Meanwhile, 70 percent of respondents in a 2000 Pew Research Center poll declared that they wanted presidential candidates to be religious. Appealing to these concerns, Bush stressed traditional values, spiritual renewal, and compassionate conservatism. Billy Graham, who usually refrained from explicitly endorsing presidential candidates, declared shortly before the election while standing next to Bush in North Carolina, "We believe there's going to be a tremendous victory and change . . . in the direction of the country—putting it in good hands. I believe in the integrity of this man."[95] Exit polls indicated that Gore's faith did not resonate with most religious conservatives. Although the Democrat had been a Southern Baptist all his life, few evangelicals saw his faith as orthodox. Fellow Southern Baptist Richard Land called his views "profoundly out of step" with the denomination. Moreover, Gore's pro-choice position on abortion alienated many religious conservatives.[96]

While striving to capture the votes of the religious right and mainline Protestants, Bush also worked diligently to win Catholic votes. In February 1999, the Republican National Committee, chaired by Catholic Jim Nicholson, formed a task force to reach out to Catholics. During his campaign, Bush met with various influential Catholics, such as Deal Hudson, editor of *Crisis*, a conservative Catholic magazine, and Father Frank Pavone, head of Priests for Life.[97] Bush's decision to speak at fundamentalist Bob Jones University in early 2000 to shore up conservative Christian support in South Carolina hurt his relationship with Catholics. After John McCain accused him of endorsing the institution's historic anti-Catholicism, Bush publicly apologized to John Cardinal O'Connor of New York for failing to denounce the university's views. During the rest of the campaign, Bush frequently consulted conservative Catholic leaders, often discussed issues traditional Catholics considered important, and regularly quoted Pope John Paul II. At the Republican Convention, priests played a very visible role, and a special skybox showcased prominent Catholics. After Labor Day, Bush appealed to conservative Catholics by emphasizing broad ethical themes, spiritual renewal, and faith-based social programs and met with more than a dozen bishops.[98] Soon after their meeting, Archbishop Roger Mahoney of Los Angeles issued a pastoral letter urging Catholics to vote for those "who share our commitment to the fundamental rights of the unborn." Campaign workers made phone calls and sent two direct mail pieces to a group of three million Catholics who attended mass weekly to accentuate the Republican position on issues such as same-sex marriage and abortion.[99] Staff also placed pro-Bush articles in the newspapers of most Catholic dioceses.

Although Bush won the presidency by a razor-thin electoral margin (271–266) in a contested result decided by the Supreme Court, his efforts to court religious voters helped him defeat a relatively popular vice president who had presided over the eight most prosperous years in American history.[100] Bush's overt religiosity, extensive use of biblical language, and "careful cultivation of the 'parachurch' network" during his years as governor of Texas and in the campaign helped him capture 84 percent of the votes of highly committed evangelicals (exceeding the 75 percent Reagan won in 1984 and 70 percent his father garnered in 1988).[101] The positive relationship Bush crafted with religious groups as governor enabled him to assemble a similar coalition on the national level and attract many religiously conservative voters.[102] He managed to integrate many leaders of the Christian right into his winning coalition "without provoking negative attention."[103] During the campaign, Bush rarely emphasized "hardcore Religious Right issues" and did not take a hard line on abortion or homosexuality.[104] Moreover, his "compassionate conservatism" appealed to many religious and political conservatives who believed that government social welfare programs tended to undercut personal responsibility, create a culture of dependency, and increase poverty in the long run.[105]

Bush did very well among "traditionalist" evangelicals, mainline Protestants, and white Catholics (winning, respectively, 80, 82, and 70 percent of their votes), reasonably well among "centrists" (garnering 49, 71, and 56 percent of their votes), and poorly among "modernists" (carrying only 46, 29, and 35 percent of their votes). He also lost by landslide margins among secular, Jewish, Hispanic Catholic, and African American voters (winning only 35, 29, 26, and 4 percent of their votes, respectively). Evangelical traditionalists provided a third of Bush's total votes, and the evangelical community (about 25 percent of Americans) furnished almost 40 percent of his votes. Combined with mainline and Catholic traditionalists and Mormons (who gave Bush 91 percent of their votes), Bush received 60 percent of his votes from theological conservatives.[106] According to CNN exit polling, Bush defeated Gore 57 to 40 percent among those who attended religious services weekly and 63 to 36 percent among those who attended more often than weekly. Bush bested Gore 80 to 18 percent among white voters who identified with the religious right. He defeated Gore 63 to 34 percent among white Protestants and 52 to 45 percent among white Catholics.[107]

Polls indicated that voters' concerns about morality contributed significantly to the Republican victory. Asked to identify the "most important issue" confronting the American government, almost half of evangelical traditionalists, a third of mainline traditionalists, and a quarter of Catholic traditionalists named a moral concern.[108] Bush won two thirds of the votes of the 57 percent of those who described the "moral climate of the country" as "seriously off on the wrong track."[109]

The Election of 2004

In late 2003, Jim Wallis chastised Democrats for assuring Americans that they would not let "their religious beliefs . . . affect their political views" and challenged them instead to discuss the moral and religious foundations of their policies.[110] They should stress biblical imperatives for social justice and peacemaking; argue on religious grounds for providing all Americans with economic security, health care, and quality education; and assert that spiritual values supplied the best basis for a just foreign policy. Finally, he urged Democrats to label as religious issues and moral failures the Bush administration's neglect of the environment and working families and its waging a preemptive and unilateral war based on false claims. This would enable Democrats to appeal to many religiously committed Americans who cared about how faith affected public policies.[111] At the same time, leading Democrats expressed fears that an increasingly religious public saw "their party as opposing God and moral values." "I think we've made a mistake by not putting our values up front," asserted Congressman Richard Gephardt of Missouri. To correct these problems, veteran political activist Amy Sherman launched a campaign to help Democrats talk more openly about faith. Sherman and others crafted a blueprint to enable their party to appeal to swing evangelicals that stressed Democrats' support for environmental stewardship and faith-based social service initiatives and criticized Bush for failing to "live up to his evangelical language."[112] Democrats, however, rarely made the kinds of explicit connections Wallis and Sherman called for.[113] In the minds of many Americans, the election was, as Newt Gingrich put it, "Michael Moore versus Mel Gibson."[114] In many ways, Bush's electoral strategy and victory replicated that of his first campaign.

As it had been in 2000, Bush's faith was an important issue in 2004. In the campaign, *Newsweek* quipped, Jesus was "practically a GOP consultant."[115] Almost two thirds of Americans thought Bush struck the proper balance in discussing his personal faith, and a majority of Americans judged his "reliance on religion in policymaking appropriate."[116] A documentary entitled *George W. Bush: Faith in the White House* was released in August to counter Michael Moore's *Fahrenheit 9/11*. Its producer credited Bush with creating "the most faith-based presidency since Abraham Lincoln." Using "candid testimony from both critics and presidential contacts," he argued, it depicted "Bush's extraordinary faith and prayer life." Although the Bush campaign did not make the documentary, it distributed 300,000 copies to churches.[117] Frank Rich complained in the *New York Times* that the video depicted the president as "God's essential and irreplaceable warrior on earth."[118]

Throughout the campaign, both Bush and his supporters discussed how his faith influenced his work as president. Pat Robertson told CNN, "I just think God's blessing is on him." Some Americans protested, in the words of a thirty-year-old interior designer from Denver, that Bush brought "too much of his own religion into play."[119] Barry Lynn complained that the "God-supports-Bush" theme was popular among the president's supporters because he did nothing to discourage it.[120] Kevin Phillips complained in *Christian Century* that "Kerry's divergences from Vatican doctrine" were "front-page news," while the impact Bush's religious beliefs had on his decision to invade Iraq was "studiously ignore[d]."[121]

As he did in 2000, Bush appealed strongly to evangelicals, and a high percentage of them backed him. Rove estimated that four million evangelicals had stayed home on election day 2000, causing Bush to lose the popular vote, and strove to make sure they went to the polls in 2004.[122] Bush's campaign staff provoked controversy when they sought to identify 1,600 congregations "where voters who were friendly to the president might gather on a regular basis" in the swing state of Pennsylvania and urged churches to send the campaign their membership directories.[123] Critics protested that this action violated campaign finance and tax laws, which require congregations to remain neutral to retain their tax-exempt status. The Republican convention featured

Joni Eareckson Tada, a quadriplegic who opposes stem-cell research; Max Lucado, a best-selling religious writer; and the Christian rock band Third Day. Bush made highly publicized visits to several evangelical organizations that received grants from his faith-based initiatives. The Republican National Committee devised a Web site entitled www.kerrywrongforevangelicals.com. Bush strategists talked regularly with prominent evangelical Christians, such as Richard Land and James Dobson, head of Focus on the Family. Ralph Reed, the former executive director of the Christian Coalition, served as the campaign's coordinator for the Southeast. Many evangelicals campaigned for Bush, dispensed forms to use to register to vote, and secured the signatures need to place anti–gay marriage initiatives on the ballots of eleven states.[124] Most evangelicals applauded Bush's efforts to keep America's military strong, fight global terrorism, eliminate weapons of mass destruction, protect Israel, and promote religious freedom abroad.[125] Christian radio talk show host Kevin McCullough asserted in October: "The church community is more strongly supportive of this President than any other I can remember in my lifetime."[126]

Steven Waldman, the editor of Beliefnet.com, argues that large numbers of evangelicals supported Bush not so much because of his policies but for broader reasons. Many of them believed "God put him in office for a reason" (a point made in materials distributed in churches during the campaign) and that his presidency validated their importance in American society because Bush was one of them. They were confident he would continue to repudiate moral relativism and promote Christian values in public life.[127] Evangelicals' connection with Bush "is deep and personal" because it is grounded in their understanding of "how God transforms men and chooses leaders."[128]

Not all evangelicals supported Bush in 2004. Some, like Jim Wallis, preferred Kerry. Others could not support either candidate. After analyzing seven key issues—race, the value of life, taxes, trade, medicine, religious freedom, and the international rule of law—leading evangelical historian Mark Noll reported in September that he disagreed substantially with the policies of both Bush and Kerry and therefore would almost certainly cast his vote for "none of the above."[129]

As in 2000, religious and moral themes were prominent in 2004. Bush appealed to "voters angry at the permissiveness of popular culture" and the policies of liberal Democrats. Lambasting the "If it feels good, just go ahead and do it" mentality, he called for "a culture of responsibility."[130] The Bush campaign used moral issues to woo the large group of Hispanic voters. It aired "Vote Your Values" radio and television spots on Spanish-language media, emphasizing Bush's positions on abortion, same-sex marriage, and stem-cell research.[131] Like Carter in 1976 and Clinton in 1992 and 1996, Democrats also sought to craft a message that appealed to the millions of Americans for whom personal faith and moral values were very important, but they were much less successful.

Several factors hindered Democrats' efforts to win the votes of religious Americans.[132] They nominated Massachusetts Senator John Kerry, the first Catholic to head a major party ticket since 1960. A political liberal who attended a nontraditional Catholic church, the Paulist Center on Boston's Beacon Hill, his views of abortion, homosexuality, and stem-cell research clashed with those of his church. Democrats tried to create specific religiously based organizations and a party structure to counter those of Republicans, but it was a case of too little, too late. In November 2003, liberal Protestants, Catholics, and Jews organized to mobilize voters who opposed Bush's policies, especially on the economy, health care, civil liberties, and the war in Iraq. Its members wanted to resurrect the "biblical mandates" to pursue justice and peace.[133] Both the Kerry campaign and the Democratic National Committee hired directors of religious outreach and recruited religious leaders to speak on behalf of the senator.[134] Because their party included a large wing of secularly minded individuals, it was much harder for Democrats than Republicans to emphasize religious grounds for their positions.[135] Many secular liberals and Jews, who are a significant part of the Democrats' base, abhor blending religion and politics and strongly supported gay marriage and abortion rights, which religious conservatives opposed.[136] Finally, Kerry's discomfort with discussing personal faith and the religious basis for his policies enabled Bush to dominate the field.[137]

Nevertheless, Democrats did try to inject religious values into the campaign, especially at their convention. Kerry announced in his acceptance speech that "we welcome people of faith." Although "I don't wear my own faith on my sleeve," he added, "faith has given me values and hope to live by."[138] Keynote speaker, Barack Obama of Illinois, argued that Kerry understood "the ideals of community, faith and service." Repudiating the idea that only Republicans turned to religion for inspiration, he declared, "We worship an awesome God in the blue states."[139] Kerry emphasized that he regularly attended Sunday mass and took Communion and agreed with Catholic positions on many social justice issues. While rarely citing Scripture, Kerry sometimes argued that his policies were grounded in moral imperatives informed by his faith. Catholic teaching, he asserted, emphasized protecting the environment, helping the indigent, and promoting fairness, peace, and brotherhood, which the Bush administration was failing to do.[140] After examining the voting records of his colleagues on moral issues of concern to the U.S. Conference of Catholic Bishops, Senator Dick Durbin of Illinois concluded that Kerry had the highest ranking.[141] Kerry's staff stressed that he wore a crucifix and carried a rosary, a prayer book, and a St. Christopher medal with him on the campaign trial.[142] During the last month of the campaign, Kerry proclaimed, "Faith is central to my life. . . . [M]y . . . faith is strong and sure."[143]

While declaring that his faith was vital to him, the Massachusetts senator frequently insisted it did not affect his policies. Like Kennedy, Kerry insisted,

"I'm not running to be a Catholic president. I'm running to be a president who happens to be Catholic."[144] Kerry told reporters that "I fully intend to continue to practice my religion as separately from what I do with respect to my public life."[145] The Democrat explained, "I don't make decisions in public life based on religious belief" because of the "separation of church and state."[146] Kerry accused Bush of overemphasizing religion, failing to respect the separation of church and state, and not practicing the principles he professed. He indicted Bush for using religious language inappropriately, ignoring the nation's ideological diversity, and making many Americans uncomfortable.[147] Kerry also chided the president for not implementing the compassionate conservatism he preached, citing James 2:14: "What good is it, my brothers, if a man claims to have faith but has no deeds?"[148] Unlike the Good Samaritan, when Bush saw people in need, Kerry protested, he "crossed over to the other side of the street."[149]

Despite his efforts to either ignore religion or use it to his advantage, it caused Kerry considerable difficulty and discomfort during the campaign. While Kennedy was criticized as being too Catholic, Kerry was chastised for not being Catholic enough. Numerous non-Catholics had complained that Kennedy would do the bidding of the pope; many Catholics protested that Kerry did not follow the teachings of the pope closely enough.[150] The Democrat's position on abortion caused him significant problems with the American Catholic hierarchy. "I don't like abortion," Kerry stated. "I believe life does begin at conception." But, he added, "I can't take my Catholic belief, my article of faith, and legislate it on a Protestant or a Jew or an atheist" because of the nation's separation of church and state. Kerry repeatedly declared that he wanted to keep abortion "safe, legal, and rare," but his long-standing support for abortion measures led several Catholic archbishops to state that they would not serve Communion to him in their dioceses.[151] In June 2004, the nation's Roman Catholic bishops issued a statement entitled "Catholics in Political Life" that contended politicians who supported abortion rights were "cooperating with evil."[152] Although Kerry insisted that he was "personally opposed" to abortion, Deal Hudson maintained, few senators had worked so diligently to promote it.[153] Another Catholic, George Neumayr, warned that because of his stances on abortion, stem-cell research, euthanasia, and several other core issues, a Kerry presidency would be the "most anti-Catholic" one in American history.[154]

During the campaign, some conservative Catholic bishops and like-minded Catholic groups blanketed churches with voters' guides identifying abortion, gay marriage, and the stem-cell debate as among a small number of "non-negotiable issues." "[N]ever before have so many bishops so explicitly warned Catholics so close to an election," wrote two New York Times reporters, that voting a certain way would be committing a sin. Meanwhile, some parishes disseminated "Catholic Answers," which asserted it was a sin to vote for a candidate who supported any one of five "non-negotiable issues": abortion, euthanasia, embryonic stem-cell research, human cloning, or homosexual marriage. Possessing far fewer resources, more liberal Catholics urged their coreligionists to take a more global approach and consider a much broader range of issues when voting, including war, poverty, the environment, and immigration.[155]

Polls suggested that Kerry's reluctance to discuss his religious views cost him many votes because nearly three quarters of Americans wanted a president who had a "strong religious faith."[156] Kerry rarely met with evangelical groups to discuss his positions or listen to their concerns, and he condoned late-term abortions. Despite his repeated declarations that he was a practicing Catholic, to many religious conservatives, "he seemed a secular extremist."[157] Critics accused Kerry of ignoring Catholic teachings when they contradicted his views (such as abortion) and emphasizing them when they coincided with his views (such as the minimum wage).[158]

Although Bush won more decisively in 2004 than in 2000, his margin of victory in the electoral college was the second smallest for any incumbent president. The most common explanation is that moral issues and the nation's religious divide were the keys to his reelection. Exit polls revealed that more than 20 percent of voters cared most about moral values, and four fifths of them cast ballots for Bush.[159] This was substantially less than the almost 50 percent of American voters who rated moral issues most important in 1996 and 2000. In those previous elections, however, America was not fighting a war on terrorism or trying to recover from a recession. Under these circumstances, the *Economist* claimed, it was remarkable that a fifth of voters were most "concerned about moral matters."[160] However, various polls showed that for many voters "moral values" included straight talk, the "personal qualities" of the candidates, and a traditional lifestyle, not simply moral issues. For many white Protestant and Catholic voters, Kerry's emphasis on economic issues was not as compelling as Bush's stress on religious and moral values defined in this way.[161]

"The split between Democrats and Republicans," a journalist wrote in *USA Today*, "is now defined by the ideological moat that separates faithful and secular Americans."[162] People who attend church once a week or more voted for Bush by nearly two to one (64 to 35 percent). By contrast, Kerry won 62 percent of voters who "never" go to church compared with Bush's 36 percent. Two thirds of all white Protestants voted for the president. In 2000, 71 percent of evangelicals voted for Bush; in 2004, 78 percent of them did. Catholics gave Bush 52 percent of their votes and Kerry 47 percent. Catholics who attend mass weekly preferred Bush 56 to 43 percent.[163] Thus both evangelicals and Catholics were very important to his victory.

A trio of op-ed pieces in the *New York Times* attributed Kerry's defeat to a national outburst of religious fervor. Maureen Dowd accused Bush of "dividing the country along fault lines of fear, intolerance, ignorance, and religious rule" to secure his reelection. The election demonstrated, Thomas Friedman argued, that "we disagree on what America is." Bush's reelection, lamented Garry Wills, signaled the end of the Enlightenment. Only the Muslim world matched America's "fundamentalist zeal," "rage at secularity, religious intolerance, fear of and hatred for modernity."[164] Many Europeans were even more negative. "The conservative rural red-neck Calvinist vote," asserted the *Economist*, "has captured America." The cover of Germany's most popular newsweekly, *Der Spiegel*, pictured the Statue of Liberty "blindfolded by an American flag." "How can 59,054,087 people be so DUMB?" asked Britain's *Daily Mirror*.[165]

Challenging the conventional wisdom that "Red America values voters surged to the polls" to reelect Bush, David Brooks pointed out that evangelicals made up the same percentage of the electorate in 2000 and 2004 (although the turnout was much higher in 2004). He argues that all voters take moral values into consideration and that Bush won primarily because 53 percent of them approved his performance as president and 58 percent of them trusted him to fight terrorism. The alleged values divide between "the metro force of enlightenment and reason" and the "retro forces of dogma and reaction" fell apart under scrutiny, as Americans had "a complex layering of conflicting views about faith leadership, individualism, American exceptionalism,... economic opportunity...and a zillion other issues."[166] Similarly, after reviewing nearly all the published data, Morris Fiorina and his colleagues found that "on a variety of supposedly hot-button issues (school vouchers, the death penalty, immigration, equal rights for women)," attitudes among residents of red and blue states differed little.[167] Leon Wieseltier of the *New Republic* maintained that Bush's reelection was not due to concerns about values but to Kerry's failure to persuade 3.6 million additional voters that he would keep America secure.[168] Other researchers concluded that the religion gap between Republicans and Democrats was minimal among people who attend church less frequently than every week when such measures of religiosity as belief, prayer, and Bible reading are examined.[169]

Bush and Religious Constituencies

Based on interviews with Christian political activists, in December 2001 the *Washington Post* proclaimed Bush the religious right's new leader.[170] Author Kevin Phillips contends that Bush's close relationship with fundamentalists, evangelicals, and Pentecostals rests on three principal pillars: his conspicuous personal religiosity, his belief in the power of prayer, and his biblically centered rhetoric.[171] Speaking for many, religious broadcaster Janet Parshall exulted, Bush is "so unhesitatingly unembarrassed by his faith. He works it into his verbiage, his public policy, [and] his comportment."[172] The private joke inside the Beltway, declared a National Association of Evangelicals official in 2004, is that conservative Christians do not need a staff person in the White House to converse with the president because "We've got one in the Oval Office."[173] Numerous religious leaders insist that the Bush White House is much more attentive to their concerns than Reagan's or George H. W. Bush's was. Although the staffs of his Republican predecessors took their calls, Richard Land explains, the Bush administration calls us to ask what we think.[174] Catholic bishops and Jewish groups also have significant access to the Oval Office, but liberal mainline Protestant leaders, especially the executives of the National Council of Churches, have lost the close connection they enjoyed with several of Bush's predecessors, including Clinton.[175]

Like every president since Eisenhower, Bush employs staff to relate to religious constituencies. Tim Goeglein, an Evangelical Lutheran, who directs the White House Office of Public Liaison, serves as Bush's principal contact with Christians, answers thousands of e-mail messages and phone calls, speaks to hundreds of groups, and meets with scores of leaders.[176] "The wonderful thing about serving George W. Bush," Goeglein declares, "is that we serve another King and Kingdom."[177]

Bush has surrounded himself with conservative Christians and emphasized personal morality among White House staff. An estimated 40 percent of the five hundred White House staff participate in the various Bible studies or prayer fellowship meetings held weekly in the White House–Old Executive Office Building complex.[178] "The Bush administration hums to the sound of prayer," reported a BBC correspondent.[179] On his first day in office, Bush mandated that all staff "maintain the highest standards of integrity."[180] Former speechwriter David Frum, a Jew, insists that Bush is determined to keep his administration morally clean. His staff want "very badly to do the right thing." Evangelicals set the tone and are the White House's "gentlest souls, the most patient, [and] the least argumentative."[181] "We understand that the political vision we serve," one staffer declared, "is fueled by faith."[182] In Frum's judgment, Bible study in the White House is, "if not compulsory, not quite *uncompulsory* either."[183] Other officials claim that the White House "is suffused with an aura of prayerfulness."[184] Critics object that Bush's staff have not consistently followed these high moral standards.

During Bush's first term, many pivotal members of his team were people of strong faith. Especially important were speechwriter Michael Gerson, White House Communications Director Karen Hughes, Secretary of Commerce Don Evans, National Security Advisor Condoleezza Rice, and Attorney General John Ashcroft. Gerson, a graduate of evangelical Wheaton College in Illinois, wrote the president's major speeches. Hughes, a Presbyterian elder, helped compose important addresses.[185] Both Evans and Rice are committed Christians. Ashcroft, a devout Assembly of God layman, selected numerous

Christian conservatives to run important aspects of the Justice Department.[186] Many other Christians held key positions in the White House, including Education Secretary Rod Paige, a Baptist deacon, and Bush's chief of staff, Andrew Card, who is married to a Methodist minister.[187]

As president, Bush has enjoyed a close relationship with a trio of Texas ministers: Tony Evans, Kirbyjon Caldwell, and Mark Craig. Evans is the senior pastor of the six-thousand-member Oak Cliff Bible Fellowship Church in Dallas. He influenced Bush's views on faith-based initiatives and has prayed with the Texan on several occasions. Caldwell pastors the nation's largest Methodist congregation, Windsor Village in Houston. Although Caldwell is a Democrat, many insiders believe that he is Bush's closest spiritual confidant.[188] Craig, pastor of the Highland Park United Methodist Church in Dallas, spoke at the 2000 Republican National Convention and preached a sermon at special services before Bush's first inaugural.

During his first term, evangelicals had significant influence on Bush's policies on abortion and human rights issues abroad, including reducing religious persecution, fighting AIDS, stopping human sex trafficking, and trying to end the genocide in the Sudan.[189] In a 2003 resolution, the National Religious Broadcasters praised Bush's "godly" leadership, support for "the sanctity of life in all its forms," and tax cuts and proclaimed that God had appointed him "to leadership at this critical period."[190] On the other hand, many evangelical Democrats questioned the implicit connections Bush makes between his faith and his conservative political agenda.[191]

After Bush's reelection in 2004, commentators debated whether he would reward evangelical supporters by pursing policies and laws they favored—conservative judicial appointments, an amendment to the Constitution prohibiting gay marriage, stricter obscenity laws, school vouchers, a ban on human cloning, and abortion restrictions—or take a more centrist approach, recognizing that he would not need their votes again. Some suggested that because Bush had won a narrow victory, thanks in large part to the massive support of Christian conservatives, he would feel immense pressure to translate their religious convictions into public policy. "We're going to put God back into the public square," declared Tom DeLay, the GOP's House majority leader, the day after the election.[192] Evangelicals disagreed among themselves about whether Bush owed them. "Now that values voters have delivered for George Bush," argued D. James Kennedy, "he must deliver for their values."[193] The president of Bob Jones University urged Bush to use his electoral mandate to appoint conservative judges and pass legislation "defined by biblical norm[s]."[194] Charles Colson, on the other hand, counseled evangelicals not to seek or expect any payback from Bush.[195] Given the various groups that supported him, Bush may continue to employ "the three 'S's—symbolism, sympathy, and selective concessions" to satisfy his diverse constituencies.[196] Some pundits maintain that "Bush's skillful handling of the Christian right—giving them just enough to keep them in line—is probably his most impressive political credential."[197] Rather than being captured by the religious right, Bush has worked to make it "a captive of the Republican Party."[198]

Bush also has ideological affinities with traditional Catholics, and they played a major role in both of his victories. He has maintained close relationship with many of their leaders, appointed many Catholics to significant positions, and frequently lauded Catholic teaching. A *New Republic* correspondent argues that "Bush has courted the Catholic vote more doggedly than any modern president...placing 'compassionate conservatism' within the context of the Catholic tradition of aiding the underprivileged and protecting the sanctity of life."[199] White House aides regularly discuss strategy and issues with leading Catholic conservatives, including pollster Steve Wagner, the Acton Institute's Reverend Robert Sirico, and Princeton political scientist Robert George. Editor Deal Hudson served as the principal liaison between Bush and the conservative Catholic community from 1998 until the summer of 2004. On his trips around the country, the president often meets privately with senior members of the Catholic clergy.[200]

Bush has appointed many Catholics to important posts. Both directors of the White House Office of Faith-Based Services have been Catholics, professor John DiIulio and attorney James Towey. Three Catholics served in Bush's cabinet during his first term: Wisconsin Governor Tommy Thompson headed the Department of Health and Human Services, Mel Martinez oversaw the Department of Housing and Urban Development, and Tom Ridge was the nation's first secretary of homeland security. Bush has also met with many Catholic groups, spoken to important Catholic gatherings, and repeatedly cited Catholic social teaching. Bush frequently praised Pope John Paul II, calling him "a great world leader" and "a hero of history" and underscoring his defense of the "culture of life."[201] Traditionalist Catholics applaud the president's opposition to abortion, emphasis on the sanctity of marriage and the family, and support of faith-based initiatives and vouchers for education.[202] A few pundits protest that the Republican Party is "pursuing the Roman Catholic Church's agenda."[203] Some Catholics accuse Bush of trying to "sanctify his political positions by associating them" with Catholic teaching while conveniently sidestepping "the many positions on which he diverges sharply from the church," most notably the death penalty, tax cuts for the wealthy, and his alliance with big business.[204]

David Frum contends that Bush fuses the three personality types most calculated to frighten and annoy Jews: the redneck, the Bible thumper, and the upper-class frat boy. Because most Jews dislike his social conservatism, apparent anti-intellectualism, and life of privilege, he began his tenure as president with fewer Jewish supporters than any chief executive since Eisenhower. Although he appointed no Jews to his cabinet, Bush named Ari Fleischer his press secretary and appointed Richard Perle and Paul Wolfowitz as foreign policy advisors and Elliott Abrams to the National Security Council. Moreover, during his first term, Bush became one the staunchest supporters of Israel "ever to occupy the Oval Office."[205] Many evangelicals believe that the United States has a biblical and moral duty to defend Israel, and some of them insist that Israel has a pivotal role to play in God's plans for the end of history, leading many op-ed writers to hint that Bush shares their apocalyptic vision.[206] Bush, however, has never publicly justified Israel's existence on biblical grounds. His support for Israel rests primarily on his belief that it is "a loyal friend," a strategic ally, "an island of democracy in the Middle East, and a nation with a historic right to exist."[207] The director of the Jewish Institute for National Security Affairs labels Bush's administration the best one for Israel since Truman's.[208]

During the 2000 election, the nation's million Muslim voters apparently voted heavily for Bush.[209] After the 9/11 attacks, Bush visited the Islamic Center in Washington to reassure frightened American Muslims, an act many Muslim clerics applauded. Hoping to undercut bin Laden's support, maintain cordial relations with American Muslims, and prevent attacks against them by vengeful Americans, Bush proclaimed his high regard for Islamic faith, called Islam a religion of peace, and insisted that bin Laden's rhetoric and actions contradicted the teachings of the Koran.[210] The president invited an imam to speak at the memorial service at the National Cathedral because he wanted to emphasize that terrorists, not Muslims, were the enemy.[211] Most American Muslims, he argued, "love this country as much as I do."[212] In his speech on September 20, Bush insisted that he respected Islam. "Its teachings are good and peaceful, and those who commit evil in the name of Allah blaspheme" his name. He argued that Osama bin Laden and his followers practiced a fringe form of Islamic extremism that Muslim scholars and "the vast majority of Muslim clerics" rejected. Sharply disagreeing with the president, some political conservatives insisted that terrorists were natural products of radical modern Islam.[213] Others noted that few American Muslim leaders had unequivocally condemned bin Laden or the culture of extremism espoused in some American mosques.[214] Leaders of the religious right were especially incensed by Bush's characterization of Islam. On 60 Minutes, Jerry Falwell deprecated Mohammad as "a terrorist . . . a man of war."[215] Franklin Graham called Islam "wicked" and "violent" and disagreed with Bush that Christians and Muslims worshiped the same God.[216] Bush insisted that such comments did not reflect the views of his administration or most Americans.[217] In November 2001, Bush hosted the first-ever White House dinner to recognize the beginning of Ramadan, and he has met frequently with Muslim leaders.[218] Visiting the Islamic Center in Washington, D.C., in December 2002, Bush declared that "we respect the vibrant faith of Islam which inspires countless individuals to lead lives of honesty, integrity, and morality."[219] New York Times columnist Nicholas Kristof lauded Bush for displaying "real moral leadership after 9/11 when he praised Islam as a 'religion of peace' and made it clear that his administration would not demonize it."[220] Although Bush's antiterrorist measures soon strained his relations with many American Muslims, his actions helped to protect their safety and rights. The frequency and intensity of Bush's praise for Islam in the face of criticism from the religious right suggests that he firmly believes what he says.[221] Nevertheless, upset by the war in Iraq and civil liberties issues at home, 93 percent of Muslims voted for Kerry in 2004.[222]

Bush, Compassionate Conservatism, and Faith-Based and Community Initiatives

Bush's aides claim that the president's "quiet but fervent Christian faith gives him strength but does not dictate policy."[223] Bush identifies his two major goals as "expanding peace and freedom throughout the world and helping our country become a more compassionate and prosperous nation."[224] In his first inaugural address, Bush promised to "speak for greater justice and compassion."[225] Speechwriter Michael Gerson labels Bush an "incrementalist" who believes that "social consensus must precede change."[226] Influenced by Marvin Olasky, a journalism professor at the University of Texas and the editor of *World* magazine, and Myron Magnet, a neoconservative with the Manhattan Institute, Bush, while governor of Texas, adopted a philosophy called "compassionate conservatism."[227] It stresses the worth, dignity, and power of each individual, the importance of limited, efficient government, and the value of free markets and free trade. Bush claims that basis of American society has shifted from sacrifice to selfishness. Refusing to accept personal responsibility, many expect the government to solve their problems, which encourages a culture of dependency. Americans must instead reduce the "scope of the federal government" and put more responsibility on local government, neighborhoods, voluntary organizations, and individuals. In most instances, Bush argues, community programs, charities, and religious institutions are the best vehicles to help Americans rebuild broken lives. American society can be changed only one heart at a time.[228] Bush's presidential Web site explains that "compassionate conservatism means providing vigorous and thorough support for those in need, while preserving the dignity of the individual and fostering personal responsibility." Rather than giving the poor handouts, Americans must help them take personal responsibility and better their lives.[229]

As president, Bush has heralded this philosophy in addresses and sought to implement it through various policies, especially his faith-based initiatives and developmental assistance programs. In his first inaugural address, Bush pledged, citing the Parable of the Good Samaritan, that "when we see that wounded traveler on the road to Jericho, we will not pass on the other side." Compassionate conservatism, Bush asserted in April 2002, involves aggressively fighting poverty and encouraging work, community spirit, responsibility, and "the values that often come from faith." "God has a special concern for the poor," Bush told Southern Baptists in 2002, "and faith proves itself through . . . acts of kindness and caring for those in need." The president has repeatedly argued that "the measure of true compassion is results."[230] On dozens of occasions, he has declared his desire to "rally the armies of compassion so that we can change America one heart, one soul at a time."[231]

John DiIulio, the first director of the White House Office of Faith-Based and Community Initiatives, delineated Bush's promises that reflect his compassionate conservatism: to provide health insurance for all children, help the working poor get tax credits, strengthen federal welfare reform laws, increase funding for the "armies of compassion," give more aid to the large cities where many poor people live, assist the families of prisoners, and implement "No Child Left Behind."[232] Although they applaud many of Bush's aims, critics argue that his policies have generally made matters worse for the poor. Compassionate conservatism was supposed to supply the central organizing concept for domestic policy, but it was soon reduced in practice to an "agglomeration of little ideas."[233] Critics insist that Bush has not pushed Congress to fund his compassionate conservative programs the same way he fought for tax cuts and the Iraq war.[234] Judged by Bush's pledges, his record is poor, concludes Robin Weinstein. His administration has systematically dismantled the social welfare net, especially by restructuring and reducing funding for Temporary Assistance for Needy Families, Head Start, and housing voucher programs.[235] Others protest that Bush proposed to eliminate after-school programs for half a million children and to cut juvenile delinquency programs and children's health programs. Kristof accuses Bush of contradicting Jesus' teaching in the Sermon on the Mount by financing tax breaks for the wealthy and by reducing services for the indigent.[236] Ron Sider, who heads Evangelicals for Social Action, urges Bush to expand the earned-income tax credit, provide more food stamps, ensure a living wage, and end "the scandal of 42 million Americans without healthcare."[237] Bush supporters counter that while throwing billions of dollars at problems, government programs have changed few lives, absolved individuals of personal responsibility, and created dependency. They advocate providing tax cuts to increase economic growth, reducing government regulations, improving education, accentuating values, and enabling private organizations to play a greater role in alleviating poverty through faith-based initiatives and charity tax credits.

At the heart of Bush's efforts to help the poor is his faith-based social service initiative. While Bush was governor, Texas became a national leader in using faith-based organizations to fight social problems. After the passage of the Charitable Choice Act in 1996, he encouraged state agencies to partner with faith-based groups to provide social services. In 1997, Texas passed legislation that encouraged prison ministries, deregulated religious drug-treatment programs, and permitted child care centers, most of which were church based, to seek private accreditation.[238] Explaining his motives, Bush argued, "Faith is a powerful tool for change." "[G]overnment can't make people love one another. I wish we could. I'd sign that law."[239]

Because it raises important issues of "religious autonomy, government intervention, and public accountability," Bush's faith-based initiative has been one of the president's most controversial policies.[240] Considering this proposal central to his compassionate conservatism, Bush devoted substantial time and energy during his first term (especially the first eight months) to promoting it. His initiative builds on the Charitable Choice legislation, which made it easier for faith-based groups that provide social services to receive government funds while respecting their integrity, protecting their clients from discrimination, and maintaining church-state separation.[241] Bush's initiative raises policy questions about the best ways to aid the nation's poor; constitutional questions about the meaning of First Amendment religion clauses; political questions about his relationship with the religious right, Catholics, and minorities; and pragmatic questions about whether it can deliver the kinds of services and produce the kinds of results he envisions.[242]

During his first term, Bush gave more than forty speeches touting his faith-based initiative, and he devoted parts of each of his state of the union addresses to this theme. He also met with numerous groups of ministers and heads of faith-based organizations to solicit support for his proposal. In his speeches, the president commended the social ministry of faith-based groups and exhorted Americans to promote justice and practice compassion.[243] In May 2001, Bush declared that he supported faith-based initiatives for both the moral reason that God gave people social obligations and the practical reason that religious groups achieved good results.[244] His experience in Texas led the president to argue that religious organizations can "outperform their secular equivalents and so should be allowed to compete for the same government funds."[245] "I understand that government must not...endorse a religious creed or directly fund religious worship," he stated. However, faith-based programs should be allowed to compete for taxpayers' money if they pro-vided necessary services, produced positive results, and helped all those in need regardless of their faith.[246] Bush insisted that the nation's founders had approved using federal money to fund the activities of religious groups that promoted morality and improved social conditions but not those that spread their beliefs.[247] He also stressed the importance of providing a "level playing field" for religious organizations.[248] Because of his own struggle with alcohol and his religious renewal in midlife, Bush saw immense value in programs that worked from the bottom up instead of the top down.

In January 2001, Bush created the White House Office of Faith-Based and Community Initiatives and satellite offices in five cabinet departments to en-sure that religiously affiliated organizations could compete for federal money to carry out secular parts of their mission. He issued an executive order to remove obstacles to their participation and proposed legislation to reduce other legal barriers.[249] In addition, Bush proposed giving tax breaks to motivate individuals, especially the 70 percent of taxpayers who did not itemize their deductions, to donate more money to charities. Embodying classic conservative principles, these actions recognized the great potential of private organizations to help the needy and empowered "individuals in the civil sector instead of government."[250] Bush's faith-based initiative passed the House but died in the Senate over the issue of whether religious groups furnishing social services could hire only applicants who shared their faith. By the end of Bush's first term, ten cabinet agencies had established offices on faith-based services that funded pilot projects with religious organizations and encouraged greater participation by these groups.[251] Jim Towey argues there is "a great deal of interest in the faith-based initiative when you get out of Washington." In the capital, however, "faith-based forces have bogged down in incremental trench warfare." Four key stumbling blocks have forced the Bush administration to drastically lower its goals: the battle over whether religious organizations could receive money if they discriminated in hiring, the local nature of most faith-based groups, the complexity of the federal bureaucracy, and the inability of the White House to mobilize citizens "to pressure Congress to pass significant legislation."[252]

Most white, black, and Hispanic evangelicals, Orthodox Jews, and the U.S. Catholic Bishops Conference back the initiative, although some of them are concerned about certain aspects of it.[253] Supporters note that poverty has been increasing even though the federal government has spent hundreds of billions to fight it. Dave Donaldson and Stanley Carlson-Thies argue that "the decline in personal responsibility" and the failure of "churches to serve their needy neighbors" is the heart of the problem. They contend that the faith-based initiative can induce churches to reenlist in the battle against poverty and provide needy Americans with "not only help, but also hope."[254] Supporters argue that it encourages individuals to exercise compassion, recognizes the positive role religious groups play in society while respecting their "mission, integrity, and autonomy," emphasizes the plight of the poor, and stops discrimination against religious groups by government agencies. Moreover, they stress that the White House's example has inspired more than a hundred state agencies and liaison organizations to create similar programs on the state and local level.[255]

Most mainline Protestants and Reform and Conservative Jews oppose the concept. They maintain that federal funds will be used to proselytize, that groups with harmful ideologies might be awarded grants, that government funds always come with strings attached, that the concept violates the separation of church and state, and that no reliable evidence shows that religious organizations deliver social services more effectively than secular ones.

Moreover, the initiative ignores the structural causes of poverty and indirectly subsidizes the religious mission of faith-based organizations. Others claim that Bush's program will favor religious organizations over secular ones and is politically motivated. Opponents acknowledge that the government has funded faith-based groups that provide social services, most notably the Salvation Army, Catholic Charities, and Jewish Family Services, but emphasize that these organizations have incorporated separately, refrained from evangelizing, and followed federal nondiscrimination policies in hiring. They argue that it is impossible to totally separate the proselytizing goals of religious groups from the social services they provide because they consider personal transformation essential to behavioral change. In the churches of Bush's "beloved South" and "in the thousands that sponsored *Left Behind*," wrote Michelle Cottle in the *New Republic,* "the idea of not spreading the good word runs absolutely counter to God's directive. The underlying goal, no matter how gentle and indirect, will remain . . . to help lost souls see the light."[256] The editors of *Commonweal* feared that funds might go to the Nation of Islam, whose leaders have expressed anti-Semitic views.[257] Conservative Christians complained that groups like the International Society for Krishna Consciousness (ISKCON) and the Church of Scientology might receive government aid to spread their ideas.

Many insist that government grants will force religious organizations to change aspects of their approach or their goals and compel them to devote their already meager resources to complying with bureaucratic regulations. Even some of Bush's staunchest supporters, such as Marvin Olasky and Pat Robertson, worry that the government might meddle with the mission and message of religious groups that accept funds. Robertson warns that the faith-based initiative is "a Trojan horse that would bring government mandates inside the church."[258] Jerry Falwell also fears that government strings would accompany government subsidies.[259] According to James Dunn, head of the Baptist Joint Committee: "The notion that public funds will not alter the religious character of faith-based programs requires a leap of faith that even Kierkegaard could not negotiate."[260] The *New York Times* complains that the president's executive orders "punched a dangerous hole in the wall between church and state," wrongly cut Congress "out of the loop," and allowed "faith-based organizations to use tax dollars to win converts and to discriminate in hiring."[261] Others attack Bush's argument that faith-based groups produce better results than secular providers. They insist that because little empirical research has been completed, the Bush administration has largely relied on "anecdotal evidence to support the view that faith-based approaches produce better long-term results."[262] Some protest that Bush's approach focuses on the need to change individual attitudes and behaviors and ignores the structural causes of joblessness. Although defenders of Bush's plan contend that the government will not directly subsidize religious worship, sectarian instruction, or evangelism, critics respond that the government would be indirectly funding such activities because the money these groups receive would allow them to shift resources to accomplish these purposes.[263] Others maintain that under the new guidelines, faith-based groups have received preferential treatment.[264] Some even suggest that Bush's primary motives for his faith-based initiative are political, especially to reward conservative Christian groups that support him.[265]

Amy Sullivan argues that Bush's policies have been "neither compassionate nor conservative." Unless additional money is appropriated to help the poor, the faith-based initiative simply transfers funds from some groups to others. Worse yet, his administration has slashed social service budgets and given "token grants" to religious constituencies with "almost no effort to monitor their effectiveness." Meanwhile, Bush's plan to increase tax credits for charitable giving has floundered. Because the overall amount of money for social services has decreased, "well-established organizations that have provided services for decades are now competing with—and, in some cases, being displaced by—unproven, often less successful groups," hurting those who most need help.[266] David Kuo, who served as a special assistant to the president and as deputy director of the faith-based initiative, concludes similarly that the program has not been given the resources it needs to change lives. Bush submitted three huge budgets with billions of dollars for other domestic "priorities" but no new requests for his "compassion agenda." Kuo blames the limited success of Bush's faith-based agenda on the indifference of Republican senators, the hostility of Democratic senators, the minimal commitment of senior White House staff to the cause, the lack of an effective lobby to push for it, and the attack of "secular liberal advocacy and interest groups" on "every little thing the faith-based initiative did."[267] Other analysts maintain that the Bush administration could achieve much better results by concentrating on passing legislation either to provide charitable tax credits or to give vouchers to needy individuals. Tax credits for tuition payments to private schools, commentator Kate O'Beirne contends, would furnish much larger resources "with no corrupting strings attached.""[268] Others insist that instead of funding organizations, the government should give vouchers to individuals, who could spend them on the social services they want, giving them more control over their lives.[269]

Bush and Foreign Policy

In his 1999 autobiography, Bush argued that as the world's only superpower, the United States must use its power "in a strong but compassionate way to help keep the peace and encourage the spread of freedom."[270] As president, Bush has often stressed these three themes of compassion, peace, and freedom.

In his 2003 State of the Union Address, Bush proclaimed: "The qualities of...compassion that we strive for in America also determine our conduct abroad." In his second inaugural address, he claimed that justice and peace were possible only if people enjoyed basic rights and freedoms, and he maintained that the advance of freedom depended on private character, service, mercy, and "a heart for the weak."[271] Bush argues that "protecting human dignity and promoting human rights should be at the center of America's foreign policy."[272] American assistance to other nations must display compassion and promote responsibility. By aiding developing nations, the United States can diminish resentment, conflict, and terror. Simply giving them vast amounts of money without holding them accountable for its use, however, has often produced misery, poverty, and corruption. In 2002, Bush proposed to increase American development assistance by 50 percent during the next three budget years. He announced that through his Millennium Challenge Account, the United States would give "greater development assistance to nations that govern justly, invest in their people and encourage economic freedom."[273] In exchange for these funds, recipient nations would have to eliminate corruption, open their markets, and respect human rights.[274] The United States, Bush insisted, must "help the afflicted," "defend the peace," seek to resolve the "regional conflicts that enflame violence," and promote free trade.[275]

Supporters insist that Bush's desire to alleviate human suffering is especially evident in his policies toward Africa.[276] In his 2003 State of the Union Address, Bush pointed out that nearly fifty million Africans had the AIDS virus (as many as a third of the population in several African nations), but only fifty thousand were receiving the medicine they needed.[277] He asked Congress to provide $15 billion over the next five years to fight AIDS in Africa, a bill its members passed four months later.[278] Calling the AIDS "tragedy" "the responsibility of every nation," he also tried to persuade other countries to fight the disease.[279] Bush insisted that the Bible's emphasis on compassion inspired his AIDS policy.[280] Critics complain that Bush has not done nearly enough to combat Africa's AIDS epidemic.[281]

Bush claims that promoting peace and extending freedom are also major aims of his foreign policy. Although circumstances sometimes required using arms, the United States must "lead the world to peace." "Our greatest export is freedom," the Texan trumpeted, "and we have a moral obligation to champion it throughout the world." The United States must "create a balance of power that favors human freedom," "where great powers cooperate in peace instead of continually prepare for war."[282] Freedom is not "America's gift to the world," Bush declared; "it is God's gift to humanity."[283] Developments since 1945 demonstrated, Bush asserted in a 2003 speech, that "in every region of the world, the advance of freedom leads to peace." Skeptics alleged that "the traditions of Islam" were "inhospitable to representative government," but after World War II, many had argued that democracy was very unlikely to work in

Japan, India, or Germany. Moreover, the number of democracies in the world had skyrocketed from 40 in 1970 to 120 in 2000. Establishing a free Iraq in the center of the Middle East would "be a watershed event in the global democratic revolution." Advancing freedom, he concluded, is "the calling of our country."[284] Throughout the 2004 campaign, Bush heralded "the transformational power of liberty." It was, a *New York Times* reporter argued, his way of describing his mission. He wanted to turn the Middle East "into what Japan had become": prosperous and peaceful with "its own distinctive form of democracy."[285] "I believe that God wants everybody to be free," Bush asserted in the final presidential debate in 2004. "And that's been part of my foreign policy."[286]

Religious freedom is especially important to Bush. "Religious freedom," he declared, "is a cornerstone of our Republic, a core principle of our Constitution, and a fundamental human right."[287] The president promised that his national security strategy would include "special efforts to promote freedom of religion and conscience and defend it from encroachment by repressive regimes."[288] On trips to Russia and China in 2002, Bush trumpeted the importance of religious liberty. After visiting a church and a synagogue in St. Petersburg and talking with religious leaders, Bush declared he was impressed with the amount of religious liberty in Russia.[289] Speaking in China, by contrast, Bush urged Chinese leaders to reaffirm their nation's long-standing "tradition of religious tolerance" and allow people to "worship as they wish." Faith benefited nations, he added, by pointing to a higher moral law and teaching people to love and serve others. Therefore, the tens of millions of Chinese who were "relearning Buddhist, Taoist and local religious traditions or practicing Christianity, Islam and other faiths" were not a "threat to public order" but rather likely to be "good citizens."[290]

Numerous observers argue that Bush's religious commitments guide his approach to foreign policy. After 9/11, Tony Carnes contends, Bush's perspective "became coherent and deeply linked to his Christian convictions." Jay Lefkowitz, deputy assistant to the president, reports that Bush begins every policy discussion by asking, "What is the morally correct thing to do?"[291] The *Weekly Standard* describes Bush's foreign policy as "morality-based," and *Newsweek*'s Howard Fineman calls it "faith-based."[292] Don Evans declares: "It's love your neighbor like yourself. The neighbors happen to be everyone on the planet." Some leading conservative Catholics, Jews, and evangelicals applaud Bush for promoting international human rights, religious freedom, democracy, free trade, and public health.[293] The president believes that "America has a special role to play in spreading freedom and human dignity around the world," Richard Land maintains.[294] Carol Hamrin, a former State Department expert on China, argues that Bush's actions have been prompted by his belief that God uses his people "to do justice" in foreign affairs.[295] Bush's "vision clearly includes an ambitious reordering of the world through preemptive and, if necessary, unilateral action," Bob Woodward avers, "to reduce suffering and bring peace."[296]

Many others, by contrast, are alarmed by the influence Bush's religious principles have on his foreign policy. Some protest that Bush has abandoned the spirit of humility that as a candidate in 2000 he promised would characterize his foreign policy. Greg Smith of Great Britain asserts that Bush's religion "is not true Christianity" but rather "a nationalistic heresy, a mirror image of some of the extreme forms of politicized Islam." Bush, contends University of Washington Professor David Domke, has blended his "religious fundamentalist worldview" with his political agenda and used "strategic language choices and communication approaches" to sell it to the American people. Many worry that Bush's campaign to bring freedom and peace to the world will instead produce widespread conflict.[297]

Two members of Clinton's National Security Council, Ivo Daalder and James Lindsey, argue in *America Unbound* (2003) that Bush has engineered "a Copernican revolution in foreign policy." Since 9/11, Bush has used a doctrine of preemption to justify action against deceitful nations that construct weapons of mass destruction or aid terrorists. Proclaiming that America is the world's only superpower and eschewing multilateral cooperation, he has acted virtually alone. They reject the conventional view that "Bush was duped into adopting his ambitious grand strategy by a stealthy cabal of neoconservative thinkers" and assert that the president is the architect of the revolution. They contend that the Republican has repudiated the internationalist approach of Harry Truman and Franklin D. Roosevelt, as well as "the nation's oldest foreign-policy traditions by arguing that 'the United States should aggressively go abroad searching for monsters to destroy.' "[298]

Leading diplomatic historian John Lewis Gaddis reaches a very different conclusion in *Surprise, Security, and the American Experience* (2003). He avows that Bush is working to complete the task Woodrow Wilson began almost a century earlier: to make the entire world "safe for democracy."[299] Gaddis alleges that Bush has developed America's third "grand strategy" to envision its mission, define its interests, and set its priorities. The first strategy, developed by James Monroe and John Quincy Adams, focused on making the United States secure through territorial expansion. The second, formulated by Franklin Roosevelt, emphasized establishing free markets, promoting self-determination in Europe, and creating the United Nations. Bush's strategy centers on preventing terrorists and rogue states from obtaining nuclear weapons and on bringing democracy to the Middle East.[300]

Bush's approach is not revolutionary, Gaddis maintains. Rather, it reasserts "the guiding principles of pre-emption, unilateralism, and hegemony" originally devised by Adams himself. Adams justified American expansion into Texas and other parts of the West and helped frame the Monroe Doctrine, which proclaimed American hegemony in the western hemisphere.

During World War II, Roosevelt overcame "America's go-it-alone isolationism" and forged "a multilateral system" that combined "U.S. power and leadership with cooperative alliances and new international institutions." The terrorist attacks, Gaddis contends, forced the United States, "strategically adrift since the end of the Cold War, to return to older principles." Although contemporary conditions may require preemption and some unilateral actions, he concludes, they will be successful only if America uses supreme diplomatic tact and caution.[301]

Numerous Catholics, including parish priests, the U.S. bishops, and the pope, strongly oppose this doctrine of "preponderance"—that the United States should exercise "its superior power, for its own good and that of the world." Its underlying principles, maintains Philip Berryman, "are very much at odds with the Catholic understanding of world politics." The neoconservative internationalists who have argued for this policy for a decade "challenge the assumptions not only of internationalists, who advocate working cooperatively with other nations, but also of Kissinger-style realists, who see international affairs in terms of a balance of power." Bush and his advisors divide the world into enemies (terrorists and rogue states) and friends (nations that support the United States). This dichotomy, Berryman argues, contradicts Catholic belief that humanity is a family. Advocates of preponderance simplistically picture recent history as the triumph of the forces of freedom, led by the United States, over totalitarianism. Such claims should make Catholics suspicious because "no ruler, no regime, no political system is free of sin. Greater power tends to lead to greater abuses."[302]

Bush and the War on Terrorism

The nature and impact of Bush's approach to foreign policy can be seen most vividly in the war on terrorism and the American-led invasion of Iraq. September 11, 2001, dramatically changed Bush's presidency. The horrific terrorist attacks on the World Trade Center and the Pentagon confronted him with a unique challenge: How could a nation of 285 million people with thousands of miles of open borders and a long tradition of extensive personal freedoms be protected from further attacks, and how should the United States respond to this appalling assault? Many argue that Bush provided exemplary leadership as he visited the site of the tragedy, consoled mourners, and galvanized the nation. The day of the attacks, he told Americans, I pray that those who grieve "will be comforted by a power greater than any of us, spoken through the ages in Psalm 23: 'Even though I walk through the valley of the shadow of death, I fear no evil for You are with me.' "[303] The president declared September 14 a national day of prayer and remembrance and scheduled a special service at the National Cathedral in Washington, D.C. Bush confided to a journalist that he prayed a lot before the speech he gave there because he wanted "the good Lord to shine through."[304] Echoing Lincoln's second inaugural, Bush proclaimed: "God's signs are not always the ones we look for. We learn in tragedy that His purposes are not always our own." He assured Americans that God heard and understood the prayers of the sufferers and asserted: "This world He created is of moral design." "[W]e ask almighty God to watch over our nation, and grant us patience and resolve in all that is to come," he declared. "We pray that He will comfort and console those who now walk in sorrow. We thank Him for . . . the promise of a life to come."[305]

Shortly before addressing Congress on September 20, Bush met with a diverse group of twenty-seven religious leaders at the White House. Attendees included evangelists Luis Palau and Franklin Graham; Protestant pastors Max Lucado, Bill Hybels, and T. D. Jakes; Bernard Cardinal Law of Boston and Edward Cardinal Egan of New York; and Mormon, Buddhist, Hindu, and Sikh clerics. Only religious leaders, Bush told them, could comfort Americans and answer their spiritual questions. The president of the Lutheran Church–Missouri Synod told Bush that "you are a servant of God called for such a time like this." "I accept the responsibility," he responded.[306] In his address that evening, the president urged all those around the world who believed "in progress and pluralism, tolerance and freedom" to join the battle against terrorism. "No one should be singled out for unfair treatment or unkind words because of their ethnic background or religious faith." "Prayer has comforted us in sorrow," Bush reminded Americans, "and will help strengthen us for the journey ahead." "Freedom and fear, justice and cruelty, have always been at war, and we know that God is not neutral between them." Bush assured his listeners that the United States would "meet violence with patient justice—assured of the rightness of our cause, and confident of the victories to come. In all that lies before us, may God grant us wisdom, and may He watch over the United States."[307]

Bush's rhetoric after 9/11 sought to balance the dispassionate "realism of the warrior" with "the compassion and care" of the humanitarian.[308] When the president spoke extemporaneously, he often paraphrased Romans 12:21, "Be not overcome by evil, but overcome evil with good."[309] "We don't seek revenge," he proclaimed; "we seek justice."[310] When the Taliban in Afghanistan did not comply with Bush's demands to surrender al Qaeda leaders and close terrorist training camps, the United States and other nations began a military campaign to achieve these ends. Wanting his country to be viewed as a "liberator" rather than a "conqueror," the president directed U.S. transport planes to drop humanitarian aid while other planes bombed military targets in Afghanistan.[311] Bush announced the creation of "America's Fund for Afghan Children" and asked every American child to give a dollar to provide food and medical supplies. In the ensuing months, the United States provided large amounts of food and medicine and rebuilt many schools.[312]

Many praised Bush's leadership after 9/11. Since the attacks on the World Trade Center, declared Tony Carnes in *Christianity Today*, Bush "has led the nation with a deft spiritual presence that radiates solidarity with people of all faiths" and has skillfully expressed spiritual and moral convictions. Many viewed the catastrophe as "a spiritually defining moment for the country and its leader."[313] Stephen Mansfield insisted that 9/11 prompted Bush to speak more boldly about his faith and gave him greater confidence. "Bush's greatest gift to the country after September 11," asserted David Frum, "was his calm and self-restraint."[314]

Although they did not enthusiastically endorse the attack on Afghanistan, as did many evangelicals, or laud Bush as a courageous Christian example, the leaders of most mainline denominations offered few criticisms. Like Clifton Kirkpatrick, the Stated Clerk of the Presbyterian Church (USA), most of them offered guarded support for the American war effort. Kirkpatrick also urged the president to work to establish political institutions that were broadly supported and that respected Afghan cultural traditions and to increase American efforts to help the Afghan people and achieve lasting peace in the Middle East.[315]

Some leading cultural analysts praised the way the president responded to 9/11. Journalist Anthony Lewis insisted that the attack on Afghanistan was justified because most Afghans were victims of terrible cruelty, Taliban leaders were closely allied with Osama bin Laden and were "preaching his hatred and following his orders," and bin Laden had sought weapons of mass destruction. By arguing that America was waging war against terrorists, not Islam, Bush refused to let bin Laden "define the terms of the conflict," political scientist Alan Wolfe maintained, and deprived him of the "religious battle he so intensely desires." Sociologist Peter Berger declared that Bush's promotion of pluralism at home was "remarkable," especially compared with the way Japanese Americans were treated after Pearl Harbor.[316]

Bush and the Iraq War

When Saddam Hussein refused to abdicate and leave Iraq, an American-led coalition attacked the country on March 20, 2003. In the decision to go to war against Iraq, several religious issues were prominent: Did Bush use religion to sell the war? Did Bush claim God directed him to attack Iraq? Was this a just war? Which religious groups supported and opposed the war, and why did they do so?

David Domke complained that Bush used religious rhetoric to persuade Americans to support the war on terrorism and the invasion of Iraq. In *God Willing? Political Fundamentalism in the White House, the "War on Terror" and the Echoing Press*, he argues that Bush systematically referred to religion in speeches on these subjects. Moreover, in several of them, the president "explicitly linked his administration's goals and policies to divine intention."[317]

A few claimed Bush believed that God directed him to attack Iraq. Kevin Phillips asserted that Bush's sense of religious intention in planning the war against Iraq was "unprecedented." The Israeli newspaper *Haaretz* reported in June 2003 that the president informed the Palestinian prime minister that "God told me to strike at al-Qaeda and I struck them, and then he instructed me to strike at Saddam, which I did, and now I am determined to solve the problem in the Middle East."[318] Bush's most trusted supporters, argues Esther Kaplan, "believe the United States is engaged in a holy war."[319] Norman Podhoretz, editor of the conservative Jewish journal *Commentary*, voiced the opinion of many that Bush felt called by God to "eradicate the evil of terrorism from the world," just as Reagan had "rid the world of the 'evil empire.'"[320]

Except for this statement quoted in *Haaretz*, which the White House denies the president made, Bush has never publicly claimed that God led him to attack Iraq.[321] Moderator Bob Schieffer asked the Texan during the third presidential debate what he meant when he said that he had not consulted with his father about the Iraq invasion but with a "higher authority." Bush replied that he meant he had prayed a lot about the decision.[322] The president told Bob Woodward that he prayed "for the strength to do the Lord's will" in Iraq. "I'm surely not going to justify war based on God. . . . Nevertheless, . . . I pray I will be as good a messenger of His will as possible."[323]

As Bush contemplated attacking Iraq during late 2002 and early 2003, the pope, the U.S. Catholic Bishops, the Methodist Council of Bishops, the National Council of Churches, numerous Jewish groups, most Muslim clerics, and many other religious leaders and organizations urged him not to use military force to oust Hussein. *Sojourners* editor Jim Wallis argued that a wide spectrum of religious bodies—Catholic, mainline Protestant, evangelical, Pentecostal, and Orthodox—all took "the threat posed by Saddam Hussein seriously," but they did not see "war as the best response."[324] Instead, he asserted, "international law, political wisdom, and moral principle" should direct the United States in its efforts to persuade Iraq to stop violating its citizens' human rights, developing weapons of mass destruction (WMD), and threatening the peace of the region.[325] Bishop Thomas Gumbleton of Detroit led Catholic opposition to invading Iraq, declaring that it would violate "every value we hold as people of faith and conscience."[326] Gary Kohls accused the president in the *New Catholic Times* of "unapologetically planning the un-Christ-like mass slaughter of innocent Iraqi children."[327] During the past two decades, mainline Protestant leaders responded to few events as forcefully as they did to Bush's threat of war against Iraq. In mid-September 2002, a group of primarily liberal mainline church officials sent Bush a letter denouncing war against Iraq on moral grounds.[328] Most major denominations except the Southern Baptists and the Assemblies of God expressed strong opposition to war.

In November 2002, the National Council of Churches adopted a resolution against war and complained that Bush's "demonizing of adversaries" contradicted "Christians' beliefs in the dignity and worth of each individual as a child of God."[329] An ad in the *New York Times* the next month, spearheaded by the NCC's general secretary Bob Edgar and signed by 125 religious leaders and laypeople, insisted that an invasion of Iraq "would violate the teachings of Jesus Christ. It is inconceivable that Jesus Christ, our Lord and Savior, the Price of Peace, would support this proposed attack."[330]

Scores of executives, bishops, and pastors in Bush's denomination, the United Methodist Church, also opposed an American invasion of Iraq. The president of its Council of Bishops sent a pastoral letter to the denomination's 8.4 million members to argue that a preemptive assault on Iraq would violate "our understanding of the gospel."[331] Jim Winkler, the head of the denomination's General Board of Church and Society, insisted that Christians could not condone war and violence. "I cannot profess Christ as my savior," he added, "and simultaneously support preemptive war."[332]

Numerous critics, including Pope John Paul II and the American Catholic bishops, contended that Bush's reasons for proposing to attack Iraq did not satisfy the criteria of just war theory.[333] Methodist bishop Melvin Talbert insisted that Bush's plan to invade Iraq contradicted "the teachings of his own church" and of other denominations that espoused a just-war doctrine.[334] Jimmy Carter asserted that "a substantially unilateral attack on Iraq" would damage America's foreign alliances and contradict international law. Preemptively striking Iraq, averred Susan Thistlethwaite, president of Chicago Theological Seminary, would show that Americans had "learned nothing from 1,500 years of moral reasoning." The United States had a "just cause," others added, only if Bush was correct that Hussein had the "ability and desire to do terrible things to us." The editors of *Christian Century* labeled arguments for war as "extreme and unfounded," and Winkler complained of "an astonishing lack of evidence" to justify military intervention.[335] Some ethicists doubted whether an invasion of Iraq would pass the test of proportionality—that its good results would outweigh its evils and unintended consequences.[336] Many feared that invading Iraq would produce substantial civilian casualties, further destabilize the Middle East, and hurt America's reputation and interests. Church World Service, an association of faith-based relief agencies, predicted "horrendous humanitarian consequences."[337]

Some politicians and journalists, including Henry Kissinger and Dick Armey, the Republican majority leader in the House, also raised both principled and prudential objections against a preemptive attack: It would violate American political principles and the long-standing conventions of international law, be difficult to accomplish, and divert attention from the war against terrorism.[338] Moreover, others argued, Hussein's fear of losing his power, nation, and life would deter him from using biological, chemical, or nuclear weapons against Israel or the United States.[339] Still others objected that a preemptive assault against Iraq contravened the American tradition of not striking first and "could destabilize other countries in the Middle East, trigger more terrorism from Saddam or others, [and] leave Israel more vulnerable to attack."[340] "An America war against Iraq," warned Israeli Amos Oz in February 2003, "is liable to heighten the sense of affront, humiliation, hatred and desire for vengeance that much of the world feels toward the United States."[341] The *New York Times* urged the president to help the world "unite it around a shared vision of progress, human rights and mutual responsibility," not further split it into "squabbling camps."[342] Bush's grounds for war with Iraq were so weak, Maureen Dowd argued, that he could justify it only "by believing God wants it."[343]

During the last three months before the assault on Iraq began, many religious groups and leaders intensified their opposition to war and took steps to try to resolve the crisis. In December 2002, Chicago religious leaders exhorted Bush to continue working to achieve greater security in the Middle East and Persian Gulf and to avoid "if at all possible, a costly, dangerous and destructive war."[344] In February 2003, 150 faculty at John Carroll University, a Catholic school in Cleveland, sent Bush a petition arguing that attacking Iraq would spread violence throughout the Middle East, dramatically escalate human suffering, and "breed new hatreds."[345] Denominational executives, pastors, and seminary professors helped organize protests in the United States and abroad. A group of American church leaders, led by Jim Wallis and Clifton Kirkpatrick, met with Tony Blair in late February to discuss alternatives to invading Iraq.[346] Four days before the invasion, Wallis and Bishop John Chase of the Episcopal Diocese of Washington, D.C., backed by key Presbyterian, Methodist, and American Baptist leaders, presented a six-point plan to avoid war. They urged the United Nations Security Council to establish an international tribunal to indict Hussein for "war crimes and crimes against humanity," provide more aggressive weapons inspections, organize a massive humanitarian effort to help the Iraqi people, and work to settle the Israeli-Palestinian conflict.[347]

Although opponents outnumbered supporters among religious leaders, many evangelicals, especially Southern Baptist and Assemblies of God spokespersons, as well as some conservative Catholics, backed Bush's decision to invade Iraq. They insisted that Bush had ample moral grounds for removing Hussein. James Nicholson, the U.S. Ambassador to the Vatican, asserted that the threat the Iraqi dictator posed to the world required a new interpretation of the Christian concept of a "just war."[348] Disagreeing with the pope, Catholic lay theologian Michael Novak contended while lecturing in Rome in February 2003 that invading Iraq would be "the lawful conclusion to the just war fought and swiftly won" in 1991.[349] University of Chicago ethicist Jean Bethke Elshtain maintained that Hussein's refusal to grant basic human rights to the Iraqi people gave foreign governments a moral right to intervene.[350] Other Bush supporters added that just war theory allowed using military force against regimes that aided terrorists.[351] Richard Land; D. James Kennedy, president of Coral Ridge Ministry; Bill Bright of Campus Crusade; Prison Fellowship's Charles Colson; and other evangelical luminaries published a letter arguing that Hussein's actions justified using military force to depose him. An attack on Iraq, they averred, would meet all five just war theory criteria: "just intent" (to restore justice), "last resort" (Hussein had not responded to numerous United Nations resolutions), "legitimate authority" (the authorization of Congress), "limited goals," and "reasonable expectation of success."[352] A few days before the invasion, a number of leading evangelicals, including Land, Colson, Kennedy, Franklin Graham, Jerry Falwell, and Pat Robertson, issued a statement urging Americans to pray and fast for peace, and they insisted that a war against Iraq was morally justified.[353]

Defenders of the invasion emphasize that Hussein fought a long, bloody war with Iran in the 1980s, invaded Kuwait in 1991, brutally oppressed his own people, used poison gas against the Kurds in northern Iraq, fired Scud missiles at Israel during the Gulf War, built biological and chemical weapons, tried to produce nuclear weapons, and persistently declined to allow U.N. weapons inspectors into Iraq, hampered their work, or failed to comply with their mandates. "After 12 years of economic sanctions, two different arms-inspection forces, several Security Council resolutions and, now, with more than 200,000 American and British troops at his doorstep," wrote John McCain several days before the war began, "Hussein still refuses to give up his weapons of mass destruction." Removing Hussein and disarming Iraq, he argued, would liberate the Iraqi people from ruthless oppression, make the region and the world safer, and diminish "antipathy toward the United States in the Islamic world."[354]

Despite the vocal opposition of many moderate and liberal religious leaders, the rank and file of Christians supported war. Gallup found in February 2003 that two thirds of Americans who attended church at least once a week backed an attack on Iraq. A Pew Research Center survey in mid-March reported that 77 percent of evangelicals and 62 percent of both Catholics and mainline Protestants supported a preemptive attack.[355]

During the six-week war and the subsequent occupation of Iraq, critics continued to condemn American actions on both moral and strategic grounds. Catholic Bishop Thomas Gumbleton denounced the war as "sinful," and the General Assembly of the Presbyterian Church (USA) condemned it as "unwise, immoral and illegal."[356] Moderate Muslims accused Bush of a "pro-Christian, pro-Israel bias" and lambasted the United States for denigrating "their societies and cultures."[357] A chorus of critics protested that the United

States did not have the authority or resources to police the world.[358] Sociologist Robert Bellah claimed that the war was part of the president's plan for "American world domination."[359] Others contended that America was striving to build an empire or maintain its status as the world's financial center while deflecting attention from its industrial weakness, financial problems, and predatory character.[360] Detractors denounced Bush's plan to transform Iraq into a "prosperous, capitalistic, and democratic state under U.S. tutelage" as "far-fetched if not preposterous."[361]

Is Bush's theology, Jim Wallis asks, "really Christian, or merely American? Does it take a global view . . . or just assert American nationalism?" The terrorist attacks of 9/11 demonstrate that real evil exists, Wallis asserts. However, to say that "they" are evil and "we" are good and to claim that in this war "others are either with us or against us" is "bad theology." Bush's "simplistic 'we are right and they are wrong' theology," Wallis maintains, "rules out self-reflection and correction." It also ignores America's sins, which have produced "widespread global resentment against us." Because humans are all sinners, Wallis declares, "every nation, political system, and politician falls short of God's justice." God has not given the United States the responsibility to overcome evil. Instead of demonizing our enemies and claiming we are on God's side and completely upright, Wallis concludes, Americans should repent and pursue justice. Bush "invokes God's blessing on our activities, agendas, and purposes," Wallis complains, rather than entreating God to hold us accountable to his aims—to pursue "justice, compassion, humility, repentance, and reconciliation." American Christians must decide if they will stand with the worldwide church, which does not generally support Bush's foreign policy goals, or with their own government. Bush's "nationalist religious" theology confuses "the identity of the nation with the church and God's purposes with the mission of American empire." "America's foreign policy is more than pre-emptive, it is theologically presumptuous; not only unilateral, but dangerously messianic; not just arrogant, but bordering on the idolatrous and blasphemous."[362]

Robert Jay Lifton contends that we are experiencing "an apocalyptic face-off" between Islamist and American forces. Both sides see themselves as engaged in a mission to combat evil in order "to redeem and renew the world." "More than mere domination," Lifton avers, the American colossus "now seeks to control history." "Our excessive response to Islamist attacks creates more terrorists and more terrorist attacks, which in turn leads to an escalation of the war on terrorism."[363] James Carroll argues that the U.S. war against terrorism is "essentially religious." Bush's Jesus, like that of the medieval crusaders, Carroll contends, is the savior "whose cross is wielded as a sword." After 9/11, "divinely sanctioned violence" has expressed Bush's "deepest urge." The Republican sees this war as "a cosmic battle between . . . the transcendent forces of good and evil."[364]

Before invading Iraq, Bush and his staff primarily stressed four major reasons for invading Iraq: suspicion of WMD, Hussein's past and potential use of these weapons, his support of terrorism, and the liberation of Iraqis from decades of oppression.[365] In the months after the invasion, enormous controversy arose when inspectors were unable to find any WMD and the link between Hussein and Al Qaeda proved tenuous. Bush supporters emphasized that everyone, including the Clinton administration, other leading Democrats, the French and Russians, and the United Nations Security Council, believed that Hussein had stockpiles of WMD.[366] Moreover, the Bush administration continued to assert that Hussein aided and abetted terrorists. Refuting the argument that the attack on Iraq has distracted the United States from the war on terror, the president's defenders insist that they are closely related and emphasize that the United States has not been attacked since 9/11. After the war began, Bush increasingly stressed the importance of spreading democracy in the Middle East. He and others also claim that the ousting of Hussein has freed the Iraqi people from one of the most hellish regimes in history. Lawrence F. Kaplan and William Kristol contend that Hussein's brutal human-rights abuses against his own people justified deposing him. Others insist that ousting the dictator prevented him from adding to the 300,000 Iraqis he had already executed.[367] Critics object that the Bush administrations emphasized these humanitarian arguments only after the allegations about WMD and Iraqi links to al Qaeda proved to be false.

Time will tell whether Bush's decision to invade Iraq has more good than bad results.[368] It could lead to increased support for terrorist groups and a repressive theocratic regime like that of Iran. On the other hand, it could produce a much more stable, prosperous, just society and help spread democracy in the Middle East. To date, things have not gone as planned in Iraq, as religious and political factions have not worked together and insurgents have killed thousands of Iraqi citizens and American troops, causing support for the war to plummet at home. Despite the claims of critics, Bush has never asserted that God willed Hussein's removal or told him to invade Iraq. While asking God for help to do his job wisely, Bush told NBC's Tom Brokaw, he based his decision to invade Iraq on what he considered "the best interests of the American people."[369]

Critiques of Bush's Faith-Based Presidency

The number and vehemence of the attacks on how Bush's faith affects his work as president are unprecedented in American history. Many contend that the Texan allows his "private" religious faith to guide his public policies, uses religious rhetoric inappropriately, and ignores the separation of church and state. Bush believes, others allege, that God has selected him to be president, that God directly reveals his will to him, and that America is God's chosen nation. This, along with his Manichaean philosophy, messiah complex, and faulty eschatology, put the United States at great risk. Some protest that Bush has made the Christian right the nation's "most favored constituency" and has tried to force its values on America.[370] Numerous theologically and socially liberal Christians argue that many of Bush's policies contradict the teachings of Christ and the Scriptures.

Many criticize Bush's use of religious rhetoric. The Republican referred to the "Almighty so frequently," complained Frank Rich, that God became "his de facto running mate" in 2004.[371] C. Welton Gaddy, executive director of the Interfaith Alliance, and Elaine Pagels, a religion professor at Princeton University, argue that the way Bush uses religious language "discourages political discourse, disenfranchises members of other faiths and puts the country at greater risk of attack by non-Christian militants."[372] Another scholar contends that Bush often employs double coding in his speeches, enabling him to communicate different messages to secular and religious audiences. Buried beneath his overt rhetoric are veiled references to biblical texts and themes.[373] Wallis accuses Bush of frequently quoting the Bible and hymns either out of context or "in ways quite different from their original meaning."[374] "The media's God police go crazy every time President Bush mentions Jesus," U.S. News declared. In reality, like other presidents, Bush "rarely invokes Jesus's name."[375] "The historical record shows," a journalist adds, that "Bush's language in God and faith is like that of most presidents—and perhaps more temperate."[376]

Although Bush has repeatedly called the separation of church and state "a really important principle" and promised to honor it, many accuse him of seeking to demolish the long-standing "wall" between them.[377] Barry Lynn argues that Bush has "enormous difficulty separating his personal religious commitment from his public policy positions."[378] Illinois Senator Richard Durbin claims that through his faith-based initiative, Bush is trying to change the "balance between government and religion that our founding fathers struck over 200 years ago." "Again and again, this President has demonstrated that he doesn't understand the Constitution, or just doesn't care about it," contends New York Congressman Jerry Nadler.[379] Others protest that Bush is trying to create a theocracy or to make the federal government a subsidiary of the Christian right. "Bush laces his speeches with biblical language, allows faith-based groups to compete for federal funding regardless of whether they proselytize, and enlists churches to register voters and actively assist his campaign," a journalist complained in The Nation.[380]

Some critics claim that Bush believes God chose him to be the nation's chief executive and that God discloses his will to him. Bush felt that God spoke through Mark Craig's sermon in 1999 to encourage him to seek the presidency. Soon thereafter, Bush told James Robison, "I've heard the call."

"I believe God wants me to run for president."[381] Numerous columnists have quoted Richard Land as saying that Bush told him, " 'God wants me to be president.' " Land explained in a letter to the *New York Times* that this was a misleading truncation. The Texan actually said, "I believe that God wants me to be president. But if that doesn't happen, that's O.K. I'm loved at home, and that's more important. I have seen the presidency up close and personal. I know it's a sacrifice, and I don't need it for personal validation." The entire quotation, Land argued, conveyed a very different message. "Does anyone really think George Washington, John Adams, Abraham Lincoln, Woodrow Wilson, Franklin Roosevelt, John Kennedy, Jimmy Carter and Ronald Reagan did not believe that God wanted them to be president?"[382] Bush has been careful never to say anything publicly that even hints God has specifically selected him to be president.[383] Nevertheless, others insist that 9/11 confirmed for Bush that God specifically chose him to be president.[384] In *Bush at War*, Bob Woodward observed that the Texan cast "his vision and that of the country in the grand vision of God's master plan."[385] Gaddy argues that Bush regards himself as "a divinely chosen leader for this moment in history."[386] After September 11, Michael Duffy alleges, the president spoke of "being chosen by the grace of God to lead." Bush does not have to say that he is ordained by God, Ron Suskind contends; his followers say it for him.[387] Steve Waldman agrees: Bush's supporters, most notably Robison, Land, and Janet Parshall, have insisted that God put him in the White House. Republican Congressman Tom DeLay told a group of Texas Baptists that God was using Bush "to promote a biblical world-view."[388] When a retired jeweler told the president during a 2004 Florida campaign rally that "this is the very first time that I have felt that God was in the White House," Bush simply said, "Thank you," as his supporters roared their approval.[389]

Many contend that Bush's belief that he knows God's will for the United States strongly influences his key policy decisions and makes him rigid, arrogant, and condescending. Maureen Dowd accuses Bush of believing he has "detailed and perfect knowledge of everything that God wants." John Kennedy had to combat allegations that "his Oval Office would take orders from heaven. For W., it's a selling point." Bush, as Pat Robertson puts it, gets "his direction from the Lord."[390] After discussing the president's ironclad confidence in his book on former Bush Treasury Secretary Paul O'Neill, Suskind says that numerous politicians called him to relate anecdotes about Bush's "preternatural certainty." Bruce Bartlett, a treasury official in George H. W. Bush's administration, alleges that the Methodist has a "Messianic idea of what he thinks God has told him to do," which leads him to disregard "inconvenient facts." "He truly believes he's on a mission from God." His "absolute faith...overwhelms a need for analysis."[391]

Critics also argue that Bush promotes "the appealing delusion" that America is a nation with a special calling to redeem the world.[392] His use of "the language of righteous empire, of God being on our side," Jim Wallis complains, frightens the Arab world. Like many other presidents, Bush seems to encourage Americans' pervasive "God loves us more than you" mentality.[393] The idea that America is a redeemer nation called to regenerate the world, insists George Will, has perhaps never before had such impact on U.S. policy as it does under Bush. The president, contends Wilfred McClay, puts forward this "vision of America with the greatest energy of any president since Woodrow Wilson."[394] Land counters that Bush believes that the United States is a unique nation but not that it is "God's chosen people."[395] "We cannot," the president declared in May 2001, "assert a special claim on his [God's] favor."[396] Americans do not consider themselves a "chosen nation," Bush proclaimed in his second inaugural address. "God moves and chooses as he wills."[397] Nevertheless, like most of his predecessors, Bush implies that God's concern for the United States exceeds his concern for other countries and comes close to asserting that God is on our side. As have many other chief executives, Bush insists that God has chosen America to serve as a model of justice and liberty and to export democracy to other nations.[398]

Bush's belief that he is God's messenger, some warn, entails great dangers for the United States. The Texan's "calm assurance that most of the world and much of his nation is wrong," Garry Wills contends, rests more on his conviction that God is on his side than on geopolitical calculations. Thus his opponents are not simply "mistaken, miscalculating, misguided, or even . . . malevolent. They are evil."[399] Bush's belief "that he is doing God's will" as president, maintains Rutgers professor Jackson Lears, encourages "dangerous simplifications" and produces self-righteousness.[400] Labeling Bush's "evident conviction that he's doing God's will" problematic, historian Martin Marty urges him to heed Lincoln's reminder that "The Almighty has His own purposes."[401]

Bush's staff and supporters counter these allegations. Michael Gerson, who crafted nearly all of the president's major speeches during his first term, argues that although Bush believes God is working in his life, he has not claimed "that God is behind his presidency or U.S. foreign policy." Gerson insists that he and Bush have done their best to avoid identifying the president's or American purposes "with the purposes of God." Bush's "references to the role of providence in human affairs," Gerson contends, "have been carefully calibrated and [are] fully within the tradition of American civic religion."[402] Bush does not claim to hear an audible voice or to see handwriting on the wall, explains Stephen Mansfield. Like many other Christians, he simply feels "promptings" to choose certain courses of action.[403] Richard John Neuhaus, editor of the journal *First Things*, asserts that Bush's effort to discern God's purposes for his life and country is conventional Christian piety and faith that should not "raise any alarms." All devout Jews and Muslims also try to determine God's plans. "There is nothing that Bush has said about divine purpose, destiny and accountability that Abraham Lincoln did not say." Former Bush speechwriter David Frum explains, Bush "told us that he does not ask God to tell him what to do, but asks God for wisdom and judgment and calm. If you said to him, 'Does God want you to invade Iraq?' he'd say, 'I don't know.' He'd say, 'I asked for the best wisdom I could have to make that decision.' "[404] Supporters insist that Bush's faith has more impact on how he makes decisions than on their outcome. They do agree with critics that Bush's faith gives him astonishing self-confidence after he has chosen a course of action.[405]

Critics also complain that Bush simplistically divides the world into good and evil. As did Winston Churchill and Franklin Roosevelt in their battle against Nazism during World War II, Bush cast the war against terrorism in moral terms.[406] The day after the attack on the World Trade Center and the Pentagon, Bush asserted, "This will be a monumental struggle of good versus evil, but good will prevail."[407] Bush's contention in his 2002 State of the Union address, that Iraq, Iran, and North Korea constituted an "axis of evil," has evoked great controversy. In May 2002, Bush told the members of the German Bundestag that the convictions that free nations espouse "are universally true and right." "Moral truth is the same in every culture, in every time, and in every place," Bush declared at West Point's 2002 commencement. "America will call evil by its name."[408] As Tony Carnes contends, after 9/11, "Bush no longer sounded like a balance-of-power realist, but like an abolitionist intent on ridding the world of vice."[409]

Many Americans, especially ones with strong religious commitments, find Bush's assessment accurate and his rhetoric reassuring. *Newsweek* declared that "his Manichaean descriptions of good versus evil, with us or against us," "rooted in his reading of the Bible," struck many Americans "as strong, righteous and decisive." The *Washington Post* declared that Bush's appraisal of Iraq, Iran, and North Korea as an axis of evil had "the advantage of being true."[410] Many others, however, denounce Bush's language as inappropriate and inflammatory. Some accuse the president of improperly invoking "a higher authority" who led "him to battle 'the evildoers' " and intruding his religious beliefs into foreign policy.[411] Bush's language implies "a sort of insight and ultimate judgment" that makes most Christians uncomfortable, claims James Dunn, a professor at Wake Forest University. His type of "ultimate certainty" has produced the Crusades, the Inquisition, and the Puritan witch trials. Others insist that Bush's rhetoric prevents Americans from examining the problems that prompted the terrorist attacks and seeking to solve them. "We have not seen the face of evil; we have seen the face of an enemy who comes at us with a full roster of grievances, goals, and strategies," argues Stanley Fish, an English professor at the University of Illinois. "If we reduce that enemy to 'evil,' " he protests, "we conjure up a shape-shifting demon . . . beyond our comprehension and therefore beyond the reach of any counterstrategies."[412] Similarly, popular evangelical speaker Tony Campolo urges Christians to concentrate on addressing the issues of hunger, poverty, and injustice that produced the rage and destructive acts of terrorists.[413]

Juan Stam, a Costa Rican pastor and theologian, charged in the *Nation* that Bush espouses the ancient heresy of Manichaeism that divides all reality into absolute good and total evil. He alleges that Bush often proclaims that the United States has a "divine calling" and identifies God with his own projects.[414] In his 2003 State of the Union Address, the president declared that the nation must "confound the designs of evil men" because "our calling, as a blessed country, is to make the world better."[415] The editors of the *Progressive* insist that Bush's public statements, Woodward's *Bush at War*, and Frum's *The Right Man* portray a president who is "on a divine mission." They are frightened by a president who "feels divinely inspired to reshape the world through violent means," whose "religious fundamentalist beliefs spill over into his job," and who "uses religious rhetoric in inflammatory ways." Chip Berlet, senior analyst for Political Research Associates, contends that "Bush is very much into the apocalyptic and messianic thinking of militant Christian evangelicals." Bush's belief that he is "carrying out God's will" makes him likely to take "inappropriate and scary" risks. In *Blowback: The Costs and Consequences of American Empire*, Chalmers Johnson indicts Bush for using theological language to justify his actions.[416] Such critics usually ignore Bush's predecessors who have argued that God chose America to advance democracy, freedom, and justice throughout the world.

Others claim that Bush has been strongly influenced by "Kingdom Now" or Dominionist theology that calls for Christians to seize earthly power to rescue the world, which may lead him to view himself as God's agent to achieve this end.[417] Some scholars point out that Bush's rhetoric has moved from a Wesleyan theology of personal transformation to a more Calvinist focus on a sovereign God who directs world history.[418] Others worry that Bush subscribes to the view of millions of Americans "that the Bible foretells regime change in Iraq, that God established Israel's boundaries millennia ago, and that the United Nations is a forerunner of a satanic world order." A few even suggest he attacked Iraq because he saw it as "the new Babylon" and because his fundamentalist followers viewed this "as a prelude to Christ's return."[419] Bush has not publicly stated that he believes this apocalyptic scenario, and his aides insist he does not. His conversations with the president lead Richard John Neuhaus to conclude that "the whole realm of biblical prophecy . . . with respect to the Middle East" is "quite alien" to Bush's thinking.[420]

Finally, some theologically and socially liberal Christians contend that many of Bush's policies are at odds with biblical teaching. In *May God Bless America: George W. Bush and Biblical Morality* (2004), Joseph J. Martos argues that Bush's policies on tax reform, the federal debt, health care, education, the environment, human rights, and war clash with New Testament precepts. Neither Bush nor his advisors appear to "consult the Bible when formulating policy, or ask, 'What would Jesus do?'" The Bush administration violates "virtually everything the Gospels teach about compassion, loving one's enemy, caring for the needy and non-violence."[421] Similarly, Jim Wallis faults Bush for failing to embrace "the social activism of John Wesley who said poverty was not only a matter of personal choices but also of social oppression and injustice." He does not serve the God who requires social justice and challenges "the wealthy and powerful."[422]

A Final Assessment

Although all presidents have endured virulent criticism from their opponents, the bashing of Bush has reached new rhetorical heights. Countless articles in major newspapers and magazines and books with provocative titles like *I Hate George W. Bush: Why He's Wrong about Absolutely Everything*, *How George W. Bush (Mis)leads America*, *Big Bush Lies: The 50 Most Telling Lies of President George W. Bush*, *The Bush Betrayal*, *Losing America: Confronting a Reckless and Arrogant Presidency*, *Bushworld: Enter at Your Own Risk*, *Global Village Idiot*, *The Bush-Hater's Handbook: A Guide to the Most Appalling Presidency of the Past 100 Years*, and *Losing America: Confronting a Reckless and Arrogant Presidency* excoriate the Texan. The view from abroad is equally negative. The European press frequently depicts Bush as "a shallow, gun-loving, abortion-hating, Christian fundamentalist Texan buffoon."[423] Speaking for many, Jonathan Chait declares in the *New Republic*, "I hate President George W. Bush. . . . I think his policies rank him among the worst presidents in U.S. history." Columnist Robert Novak declares, "I have never seen [such hatred] in 44 years of campaign watching."[424]

Hatred of Bush rests principally on the following grounds: He does not deserve to be president because of his intellectual, moral, and character flaws; he lacks principles, ignores facts, prohibits disagreement, disregards the public good, tries to prevent oversight of his administration, besmirches his opponents, refuses to admit errors, and lies incessantly. "Bush's personal life," Chait argues, "is just as deep an affront to the values of the liberal meritocracy [as Clinton's]." "Bush is a dullard lacking any moral constraints in his pursuit of partisan gain." He is "loyal to no principle save the comfort of the very rich."[425] To many, Bush is a moralist who lacks intellectual firepower. His foes claim that he is "ruthless, dishonest and corrupt."[426] *New York Times Magazine* writer James Traub charges that many liberals see Bush as "a craven, lazy, hypocritical nitwit."[427] "In the 21st century reign of King George II," argues Maureen Dowd, "flattery is mandatory, dissent is forbidden," faith is more important than facts, and "loyalty trumps competence."[428] Even some political conservatives protest that the Bush administration "seems to act first and then create ex post facto rationalizations" for decisions instead of engaging in serious deliberation.[429] Numerous critics aver that the White House practices "groupthink."[430] Paul Krugman maintains that no administration since Nixon's has insisted so strongly that "it has the right to operate without oversight or accountability."[431] Some allege that the Bush White House has utilized more smear tactics than Nixon's.[432] Detractors accuse the Republican of hubris and emphasize his unwillingness to admit in presidential debates that he had made any mistakes.[433]

Many claim that Bush frequently lies to accomplish his political purposes. Some "distrust Bush so much," the editor of the *New Republic* explains, "that they automatically assume everything he says must be false."[434] Michael Moore's scathing documentary depicts Bush as "fundamentally dishonest, perhaps even evil," a view shared by many liberals.[435] Bushwatch.com has a special "Bush Lies" section.[436] Columnists Paul Krugman of the *New York Times*, E. J. Dionne and Dana Milbank of the *Washington Post*, and editor at large Harold Meyerson of *The American Prospect* all suggest that Bush has a serious problem with the truth, and others, including *The Nation*'s Eric Alterman, call Bush "a liar."[437] Many indict the Bush administration for misleading the nation into war in Iraq.[438] Nicholas Kristof contends that to Bush, reality "is not about facts, but about higher meta-truths."[439] For Bush, writes Milbank, "facts are malleable."[440] Al Gore accuses Bush and his staff of using "Orwellian language to disguise their true purposes."[441] Bush's defenders counter that such charges spring from his opponents' "unquenchable hatred for" him.[442] They maintain that Bush has told the truth as he understood it and that there is a difference between "repeating unreliable information and willfully lying."[443] In *Plan of Attack*, Woodward points out that Bush believed Hussein had WMD and told CIA director George Tenet several times, "Make sure no one stretches to make our case."[444]

Analysts disagree sharply about the impact of the Republican's policies. "Bush promised us a foreign policy of humility and a domestic policy of compassion," Joe Klein writes in *Time* magazine. "He has given us a foreign policy of arrogance and a domestic policy that is cynical, myopic, and cruel." "History will show," opines Bob Herbert, "that the Bush crowd of incompetents brought tremendous amounts of suffering to enormous numbers of people."[445] Bush's decision to invade Iraq "without reliable intelligence, real international backing, legitimate United Nations authority or serious postwar planning has exacted a high price," editorializes the *New York Times*. His "policies have badly damaged America's alliances with its most important economic and military allies in Europe" and estranged Latin America governments.[446] While Bush has pursued his "megalomaniacal vision of changing the world," declares West Virginia Senator Robert Byrd, "the Middle East peace process is in shambles," "terrorism proliferates . . . the American economy struggles . . . the deficit balloons, and we have lost friends around the world."[447] Detractors maintain that Bush has seriously eroded "the economic security, the access to health care, the civil rights and civil liberties, and the environmental protections of the American people." Bush has "been profligate" with Americans' money, created "a mountain range of deficits," and led the nation into a war with tragic results.[448] Ignoring the public interest, he has served "his political base—extremist elements of the Republican Party—the religious right, Fortune 500 CEOs," and "neoconservative ideologues."[449]

Many conservatives also criticize some of Bush's policies. William Safire, George Will, Rush Limbaugh, and others complain that Bush rapidly increased federal discretionary spending, refused to veto pork-barrel spending or push for nationwide vouchers or tax credits to provide greater parental choice in education, and has done little to develop a compassionate conservative agenda.[450] Doug Bandow of the libertarian Cato Institute argues that except for tax cuts, none of Bush's policies has advanced conservatives' goals. He complains that Bush has increased "the size and power of the U.S. government both at home and abroad."[451]

Others praise Bush's intellect, character, leadership, and accomplishments. Kristof claims the president is very bright and has "an awesome memory, great management skill and a tremendous emotional IQ."[452] While admitting that Bush "is impatient and quick to anger" and "often uncurious and as a result ill informed," David Frum maintains that his virtues—"decency, honesty, rectitude, courage, and tenacity"—outweigh his faults.[453] Frum argues that Bush has been "nothing short of superb as a wartime leader" because of his "moderation, persistence, and boldness." He praises his emphasis on tolerance of Muslim Americans, swift and massive aid for the people of Afghanistan, and "generous reconstruction program for New York." Bush acted with "remarkable caution, circumspection, and deliberation" and steadfastly adhered to his war aims.[454] "No one could have been better suited" to confront the peril that America faced after 9/11, biographer Ronald Kessler contends. Bush had the necessary "vision, courage, patience, integrity, focus, discipline, determination, decisiveness and dedication" to his country to successfully face the immense challenges.[455] The president's admirers credit his actions with prompting Libyan dictator Muammar Kaddafi to announce in December 2003 that he would stop producing weapons of mass destruction and submit to inspections of all "nuclear activities" and with contributing to promising developments in the Middle East: Egypt's signing of a free trade agreement with Israel and Israel's decision to withdraw Jews from Gaza.[456]

As previously noted, critics and supporters reach dramatically different conclusions about Bush's faith and its impact on his presidency. Many secular members of the mainstream media depict Bush as a "fire-breathing . . . Puritan whose rigid faith is an enemy to reason—even reality—and to the nation itself." They paint the president as a "Christian bigot whose worldview blinds him to facts, reason, and reality."[457] Numerous detractors argue that Bush's "faith is insincere at best," hypocritical at worst, "and mostly a political cover for his right-wing agenda."[458] Others grant that his faith may be sincere but insist it is shallow.[459] Some protest that Bush considers himself the nation's "preacher-in-chief."[460] Woodrow Wilson, Jimmy Carter, and Ronald Reagan were also men of ardent faith, argues Arthur Schlesinger Jr., but none of them "applied religious tests to secular issues" or exploited his religion for political benefit, as has Bush. The Texan is "the most aggressively religious president in American history."[461] Critics accuse him of using religious arguments to justify his policies, including the invasion of Iraq. Bush's "faith-based presidency" "is genuinely troubling" because he validates public policies "by invoking God's name."[462] His foes protest that a man "claiming to hear voices from God should not be military commander of a superpower."[463]

Others see Bush's faith very differently. Although Wallis disagrees with many of Bush's policies, he insists that president's faith "is sincere and deeply held." "After talking with Mr. Bush's longtime acquaintances," writes Kristof, "I'm convinced that his religious convictions are deeply felt and fairly typical in the U.S."[464] Bush's supporters argue that his faith gives him "a calm self-assurance" and helps make "him a sound man in a crisis."[465] In the aftermath of 9/11, Derek Davis contends, Bush admirably performed his role as the "national pastor" as he articulated Americans' grief, soothed their hearts, and offered spiritual comfort.[466] Marvin Olasky calls Bush "our first modern president who is born again not only in his heart and mind but in his actions."[467] Aikman concludes that "to a remarkable degree," Bush has made his Christian faith "the lodestar of his course as national leader." "What distinguishes the presidency of George W. Bush" from most of his predecessors, argues Stephen Mansfield, is "that he seems to genuinely believe privately what he says publicly about religion" and "that he seeks to integrate faith with public policy at the most practical level."[468] Although Bush talks more openly about his personal faith than most presidents, his faith is not qualitatively different from that of many of his predecessors. Many presidents have used religious rhetoric as extensively as Bush to achieve the same purposes—to provide comfort in tragedy and assurance in calamity, to help justify policies, and to give thanks for America's blessings. Considered in the larger context of all the occupants of the Oval Office, Bush's faith is neither unusual nor threatening to the republic. Instead, it has sustained him during crises, strengthened his resolve, increased his courage, confidence, and compassion, and shaped his policies in many positive ways.

Conclusion

Things have come to a pretty pass when religion is allowed to invade public life.

Lord Melbourne opposing efforts to end the slave trade in the House of Lords

Every president invokes God and asks his blessing. Every president promises, though not always in so many words, to lead according to moral principles rooted in Biblical tradition.

Howard Fineman, "Bush and God," *Newsweek,* March 10, 2003

THIS EXAMINATION OF the lives of eleven presidents demonstrates that their faith has been vitally important to a substantial number of the occupants of the Oval Office.[1] Of these eleven, only Wilson was the son of an ordained minister, but many of them had religiously devout fathers and mothers (especially Lincoln, Theodore Roosevelt, Eisenhower, Kennedy, and Reagan). Although some of them attended colleges with strong religious traditions (Jefferson, Theodore Roosevelt, Wilson, and Reagan), none of them majored in religion or philosophy. Moreover, none of them attended seminary, did graduate work in religion or theology, took a course in Christianity and politics, or read extensively about this subject. Their personal correspondence and autobiographies suggest that none of them thought deeply or communicated regularly with others about religion and government. Nevertheless, their faith helped shape their character, political philosophy, and style of governing. It also affected their relationships with religious groups and many of their policies. Inspired in part by their faith, these presidents sought to promote liberty, tolerance, righteousness, and charity and to attain peace and justice. The policies they pursued to achieve these ends differed substantially, however, because of the religious traditions to which they belonged; their personalities and interests; their political parties, platforms, and perspectives; and the way they interpreted the Bible and conceived their political duties. This is hardly surprising, because religious groups take different positions on many public policy issues. Some presidents (Franklin Roosevelt, Kennedy, Carter) were much more willing than others (Jefferson, Eisenhower, Reagan) to use the power and resources of the federal government to promote prosperity, attack injustice, and ameliorate social ills.

Despite their differences, all eleven presidents emphasized the nation's religious heritage, trumpeted the value of religion, called for spiritual renewal, and underscored the relationship between religious faith and morality. They all stressed the importance of civic righteousness, most notably Theodore Roosevelt, Wilson, and Carter, three of the nation's most biblically literate presidents.[2] From George Washington to George W. Bush, they argued that God rules the universe, that the dictates of reason and revelation reinforce one another and supply a basis for both individual morality and public policy, and that religious faith best sustains the nation's constitutional democracy and provides the strongest safeguard and support for republican virtue and liberty.[3] They all accepted Washington's exhortation in his general order of July 2, 1776: "Let us therefore rely upon the goodness of the Cause, and the aid of the supreme Being, in whose hands Victory is, to animate and encourage us to great and noble Actions."[4] With John Adams, they believed: "Our Constitution is made for a moral and religious people. It is wholly inadequate to the government of any other."[5] All eleven used religious motifs to define and defend the nation's goals and purposes. Most of them argued that faith in God was essential to sustaining America's traditional values, strengthening its resolve, and solving its problems. Both Roosevelts, Wilson, Eisenhower, Kennedy, Reagan, and Bush emphasized patriotic piety, conventional morality, and the evils of autocracy, fascism, communism, or terrorism.[6] Wilson and Franklin Roosevelt saw German leaders during World Wars I and II as enemies of true religion. Eisenhower viewed the U.S. struggle with the Soviet Union as "a war of light against darkness, freedom against slavery, [and] Godliness against atheism."[7] Reagan denounced the Soviet Union as an "evil empire." Bush declared Iraq, Iran, and North Korea to be an "axis of evil." All seven viewed the United States as carrying out a godly mission by striving to defeat these wicked forces and create a more righteous international order.

Although the subjects of this study all affirmed many central Christian tenets, they disagreed about some major doctrines, most significantly the deity of Jesus Christ, the basis for salvation, and human nature. Some presidents openly declared Jesus to be their savior (Wilson, Carter, and Bush), whereas Jefferson expressed doubts about his divinity. Some asserted that salvation was by grace through faith (Wilson, Carter, Reagan, and Bush), while others insisted that it depended primarily on good works (Washington, Jefferson, and Theodore Roosevelt). Some contended that people were naturally inclined toward evil (Carter and Bush), others saw individuals as essentially good (Jefferson, Wilson, Franklin Roosevelt, and Reagan), and still others maintained humans were a mixture of good and bad (Washington, Lincoln, and Eisenhower).

Many of these presidents had deeply held religious beliefs, but they expressed their faith in different ways. Except for Wilson, Carter, and Bush, they were intensely private about their religious convictions.[8] These three presidents and Lincoln were the most personally devout. Of these eleven chief executives, only Jefferson and Wilson extensively studied Christian theology. Although all of them highly regarded and read the Bible, Jefferson, Lincoln, Wilson, Carter, and Bush read it most faithfully and knew it the best. Only Franklin Roosevelt and Reagan did not attend church regularly while president. To gain public approval, set a good example, obtain personal strength and inspiration, glorify God, fulfill a religious duty, or continue a lifelong pattern, the others worshiped almost every Sunday. All eleven testified that they valued prayer and frequently sought divine guidance in making decisions and leading the nation. They all declared that they needed God's counsel to carry out their momentous responsibilities. Their faith helped these presidents (Kennedy to a much lesser extent) gain perspective, establish priorities, be confident about their decisions, endure trials, and accept defeats.[9] These presidents also regularly employed religious rhetoric in their speeches to comfort the grieving; challenge citizens to promote justice, righteousness, and compassion; appeal to commonly held spiritual values; win support for their campaigns or policies; and invoke God's blessing on America and thank him for his guidance.[10]

These presidents have been both lauded and lambasted for their faith. Although many have praised their personal piety and the influence of their religious convictions on various actions and policies, others have complained that some chief executives have mistakenly (and dangerously) claimed to know God's will on vital issues or that their faith influenced them to adopt policies that have harmed the nation. The faith of some presidents has been widely acclaimed (Washington, Lincoln, Theodore Roosevelt, Eisenhower), whereas the faith of others has frequently been assailed (Jefferson, Kennedy, Carter, and Bush). Opponents protested that the religious commitments of these four presidents (deism, Catholicism, evangelicalism) threatened the nation. No president's religious convictions were more condemned than Jefferson's, who ironically spent many evenings in the White House studying the teachings of Jesus, although those of Kennedy, Carter, and Bush made many Americans uneasy. As the scholarly community and the culture became more secular and skeptical, substantial concerns were raised about the religiosity of some twentieth-century presidents. "A lot of people are worried about Presidents' taking their cues from on high," journalist Hugh Sidey wrote in 1984. "Woodrow Wilson's fervor sank his marvelous ideas about peace. Jimmy Carter's conviction that he had a special relationship with God and could get answers through prayer instead of the National Security Council may have been the biggest cause of his ineptitude. Reagan is at his worst when he is thumping his Bible and counting God among his Cabinet."[11] Many accuse Bush of believing that God directs his policy making. Critics also complain that presidents have often used the Bible selectively and inappropriately to advance their own political interests, ignored many of its central teachings, and frequently quoted it out of context. Instead of using the Bible to scrutinize and criticize American actions, detractors protest, they have generally employed it to justify them. They wanted "God on their side" to help them legitimate their ideas and give them "moral satisfaction" and used "only enough of the Bible or their Christian convictions [to] accomplish their political objectives."[12] Moreover, critics allege, they have portrayed God as sanctifying and expediting America's agenda.

Presidential Convictions

This final chapter evaluates how the five themes discussed in the introduction—the nature of their convictions, the separation of church and state, civil religion, America as a chosen nation, and their character—affected the work of these eleven presidents. This study has demonstrated that the worldviews of its eleven subjects (in many ways, Kennedy is an exception), as informed in part by their faith, helped shape their philosophy of governing and selected policies. All of them saw God as the world's creator, sustainer, protector, and judge. They believed that he directed human affairs and acknowledged him as the ultimate source of authority. These presidents asserted that nations were required to obey God's transcendent standards and faced his condemnation when they did not. They concurred that God created the world with a moral structure and gave human beings a moral nature. These chief executives insisted that God instituted government to provide order and ensure justice. Human rights, all eleven asserted, were a gift of God that government must protect. Although they were elected by the American people, they believed that their authority ultimately came from God. Therefore, in carrying out their duties, they strove to be responsible to both. These presidents tended to depreciate denominational and doctrinal differences and stress the importance of morality, character, good works, and social justice. Some were more sanguine than others, but they all displayed an unshakable confidence in God and the nation's people, institutions, and values. Speaking for all of them, Franklin Roosevelt declared in his final speech, "Let us move forward with strong and active faith."[13]

Some maintain that presidents should confine their religious convictions to their private lives and prevent them from intruding on their work. Voicing this concern, Abraham Foxman, national director of the Anti-Defamation League, argues that when Bush prays "as a private person practicing his own faith, God bless, but when it becomes part of the official function of the president," it is "inappropriate." Others counter that committed Christians, Jews, and Muslims, like other citizens, should be able to support or oppose political policies based on their personal perspective of what is morally right, prudent, feasible, and good for society. The president, they avow, has the same right as any other American to take his private faith into the public arena. The Constitution, argues Martin Marty, does not mandate that faith in Jesus "or action based on faith in him, or faith in other prophets or messiahs" has to "be boxed in, shelved and forgotten in the zone called private."[14] Those with deeply held religious convictions should not be disqualified from public office or from expressing and acting on their commitments.[15] Is it "really so preposterous," others add, for a "person who represents the will of the public...to discuss his personal convictions?" Is it inappropriate for a country where 90 percent of the citizens believe in God to "elect a leader who shares this fundamental belief?"[16]

Like other Americans, presidents should be able to express and act on their religious convictions. They bring to their public service the totality of who they are as people, which is shaped in part by their faith. Although none of them tried to "impose" his personal religious views on the citizenry, the subjects of this study believed that their ideological commitments should direct their actions and policies. Several factors make it difficult for presidents and other elected officials to bring Christian values to bear directly on political life: the pressures of political life, their desire for public approval, the complex, demanding nature of diplomacy, and the necessity of appealing to and satisfying conflicting interest groups.[17] Nevertheless, the influence of their faith is evident in many ways, including Washington's quest to guarantee religious liberty, Jefferson's to ensure peace, Lincoln's to end slavery, Theodore Roosevelt's to settle the 1902 coal strike, Wilson's to devise the Treaty of Versailles, Franklin Roosevelt's to remedy the ills of the Great Depression, Eisenhower's to reduce armaments, Kennedy's to procure black Civil Rights, Carter's to promote human rights around the globe, Reagan's to combat communism, and Bush's to encourage faith-based initiatives.

The Separation of Church and State

Political science professor and former Congressman Stephen Monsma argues that throughout its history, the United States has struggled with four distinct church-state issues: "whether or not government should directly subsidize" the core rituals and practices of religion; whether or not government should "sponsor or endorse public acts of worship or public displays of religious devotion" (Bible reading and prayers in public schools, civic exhibits of the Ten Commandments, religious symbols such as nativity scenes, religious mottos on coins, and prayers at the beginning of legislative sessions); how to best insure the right of citizens to freely exercise their religious beliefs without government interference; and if the government provides and/or financially supports education, health, and social services," may it help fund faith-based services in these areas.[18]

Presidents, because of their duties, visibility, and influence, have played an important role in this debate over the intent of the First Amendment. Through their personal religious practices, rhetoric, and policies, they have a significant impact on American attitudes about church-state relations.[19] All the presidents in this study supported Madison and Jefferson's basic position on the first issue: The government cannot directly fund religious worship or proselytizing. They sometimes inflamed the debate over the second issue by leading the nation in prayer or including scriptural passages in issuing proc-lamations or giving addresses. Many of the presidents in this study, most significantly Washington and Jefferson, strongly promoted religious liberty. Carter, Reagan, and Bush criticized communist nations for restricting the religious freedom of their citizens. Only Lincoln dealt with this issue at length at home, as he wrestled with how to maintain citizens' religious liberty while thwarting disloyalty to the Union and efforts to undermine its purposes. Nu-merous chief executives, especially since Franklin Roosevelt, have been deeply involved in disputes involving the fourth question.

Identifying three possible responses to these church-state issues helps clarify these debates. The first, the strict separation position, advocates very limited aid to "educational and social programs of faith-based groups" and strong safeguards to protect the free exercise rights of religious citizens. Its proponents believe that religion is important, but because it is private and personal, government should neither aid nor impede it. The second approach— formal neutrality—contends that the "government should not use religion as a category either to confer special benefits or to withhold benefits generally available." The government must not single out religious groups for distinctive benefits or liabilities. Some fear that this position will weaken free exercise provisions. Labeled both "positive neutrality" and "substantive neutrality," the third stance calls for examining not only whether a law or governmental action "is neutral in a technical legal sense" but also "whether its *effects* are neutral." Monsma contends that the "strict, no-aid position" often unjustly places faith groups at a disadvantage when the government provides its own secularized education, health, and social services and funds those of private, nonprofit groups that supply these services in a secularized manner but refuses to sub-sidize their similar services.[20]

Advocates of strict separation insist that the government must not take sides in a religiously pluralistic society like the United States; it must remain neutral. Supporters of the "positive neutrality" position counter that the nation's various religious systems of belief and its various nonreligious or secular systems of beliefs are competing worldviews. Whereas proponents of the first view see secular as being neutral, those espousing positive neutrality maintain that public institutions that ignore religion promote secularism, a rival perspective of life. The fundamental point of contention between these camps is: Do nonreligious education, health, and social services "occupy a neutral ground between religious 'belief or disbelief, practice or nonpractice, observance or nonobservance,'" or do they "by default favor religious non-belief, nonpractice, and nonobservance."[21] As the government has grown in size and budget and has funded more enterprises, including many that deal with issues of human sexuality, human origins, racial diversity, abortion, parental consent, the rights of minors, euthanasia, protection of the environment, and numerous other value-laden topics, this debate has grown in importance and fervor.

Considering religion essential to the nation's well-being, all eleven presidents advocated some federal support of religious groups and for religious symbols and practices in public life. Washington profusely praised the contributions and values of the nation's religious communities in a series of letters, connected God's blessing with the welfare of the nation, and in his farewell address, proclaimed religion to be essential to the nation's morality and republican institutions; the other ten followed his example. Eschewing neutrality, they claimed that God ruled the universe and provided norms to direct governmental policies and practices. Although these presidents (most notably Washington and Lincoln) resisted pressures to amend the Constitution to declare the United States to be a distinctively Christian nation, they contended that government officials and the American people were responsible to transcendent standards. They often sought the advice of religious leaders on crucial issues, as did Lincoln during the Civil War, Franklin Roosevelt during the Great Depression, and Bush after the terrorist attacks of September 11, 2001.

These eleven presidents provided governmental support for religion in numerous ways. All of them except Jefferson proclaimed days of public prayer and thanksgiving to God, deeming them constitutionally permissible and beneficial.[22] They officially recognized Christian, Jewish, and, more recently, Muslim holidays. Many of them prayed in the White House with religious groups. Eisenhower and all his successors spoke at the national prayer breakfasts in Washington that began in the 1950s. These eleven presidents typically endorsed such practices as chaplains in the military and Congress, the inclusion of the phrase "under God" in the Pledge of Allegiance, prayers by chaplains at inaugurals, prayer in the public schools, and government funding of private religious schools. Several of them held their own worship services before their inauguration ceremonies. Theodore Roosevelt ordered that the motto "In God We Trust" be removed from various coins. He did so, however, because he thought the phrase trivialized religion, making it a source of jest and ridicule, rather than enhancing it. Kennedy supported Supreme Court rulings prohibiting prayer in public schools and aid to parochial schools, but Reagan strongly supported an amendment to the Constitution to permit school prayer, and both he and Bush pushed for government aid to private schools through either vouchers or tuition tax credits.

While strongly promoting scriptural values of righteousness, peace, justice, and compassion, all eleven presidents respected the separation of church and state. Although they celebrated the nation's Judeo-Christian heritage and emphasized the importance of religion to the well-being of the nation, they did not use the power of their office to push any distinctively sectarian beliefs, practices, or aims or to give special privileges to their own denominations. They all asserted that religious faith helped promote virtue, civility, and social order and wanted the federal government and religious groups to work together to elevate the nation's morality and remedy its social ills.

All of these presidents insisted that the government could supply "friendly aid" to religious groups as long as it did not favor some over others. Although Jefferson, Kennedy, and Carter, because of philosophical commitments and political pressures, adopted the strict separationist position of no government aid most fully, they still promoted religion through various means. Their life experiences, ideological convictions, and religious supporters, as well as the prevailing political climate, prompted other presidents, most notably Wilson, Franklin Roosevelt, Eisenhower, Reagan, and Bush, to prefer the positive neutrality position. To them, the nation's traditional religious values provided a bulwark for combating evil opponents—German autocrats, Nazis, communists, and terrorists—and for rallying the support of the American people. Some of these eleven presidents led the nation in prayer (Roosevelt on D-Day and Eisenhower at his first inaugural), and many of them repeatedly exhorted Americans to pray about domestic and foreign issues. Most of them gave more government support to religion than members of Americans United for the Separation of Church and State argue is permitted by the Constitution or prudent, and Kennedy and Carter maintained a more rigid separation than scores of scholars and religious leaders think is constitutionally required.[23]

Civil Religion

From Washington to Bush, "presidents have symbolized, and in some cases defined, the civil religion or public faith that has held this diverse society together."[24] The myths of civil religion "represent a fusion of biblical and nationalistic imagery; its rites and rituals are associated with the national holidays; its saints and martyrs are" the heroes of American history; and "its priests and prophets are American presidents."[25] Its chief executives have served as the nation's central symbol and as its interpreter in chief who tell Americans what sort of people they should be and help shape the national self-identity.[26] Since its founding, the United States has struggled to find a common faith to undergird its life. The nation's religious and ideological pluralism has steadily increased, and the differences among religious communities over public policies have intensified, making this task even more difficult.[27] Presidents have usually employed broad religious language and eschewed specific Christian or Protestant terms. They have typically referred to God by generic titles and avoided mentioning Jesus or Christian doctrines. Most of them strongly applauded the nation's religious diversity and called for religious toleration. Presidents have minimized theological differences, urged religious communities to work together, and tried to strengthen citizens' commitment to America's core values.[28] They have used civil religion to sanctify the political order, reinforce cherished ideals, appeal to principles shared by the country's many religious communities, and assure citizens that God uses the United States to accomplish his purposes (especially to defeat evil and spread democracy) and endorses its policies. Often linking piety with patriotism and love of God with love of country, the subjects of this study stated or intimated that God's hand was evident in the creation and preservation of the United States.

Washington and Lincoln played a crucial role in developing the nation's civil religion and became its patron saints. Setting a pattern for his successors, Washington declared in his inaugural address in 1789:

> It would be improper to omit in this first official act my fervent supplications to that Almighty Being who rules over the universe... and whose providential aids can supply every human defect.... In tendering this homage to the Great Author of every public and private good, I assure myself that it expresses your sentiments not less than my own, nor those of my fellow citizens at large less than either.[29]

Washington saved the infant nation four times—by defeating the British, presiding over the Constitutional Convention, serving effectively as president, and relinquishing power as both commander in chief and chief executive. Lincoln preserved the Union and died for America's sins. They, along with Franklin Roosevelt, who "saved" the country from the Great Depression and the world from the Nazi onslaught, all credited their successes to God's power and goodness, not their own acts.[30]

Scholars distinguish between priestly civil religion, which offers God's comfort and solace to people in the midst of tragedy and affliction, and prophetic civil religion, which uses biblical themes to challenge citizens' attitudes and actions. All eleven presidents functioned more as priests than as prophets. They asserted that God had chosen and blessed the United States, provided spiritual inspiration, and consoled their countrymen after tragedies.[31] However, they all sometimes used the rhetoric of civil religion to exhort citizens to reevaluate the nation's goals and actions and to accentuate and seek to implement its best values. When employing the prophetic role, presidents challenged Americans to evaluate "the country's actions in relation" to God's will and standards, condemned the "idolatry of religious nationalism," and urged them to repent of their "corporate political sins."[32] Eisenhower, Reagan, and Bush primarily played the priestly role, reassuring citizens that God rules and loves them as they dealt with disasters in space, communist threats and the cold war, terrorist attacks at home, and military action in Korea, Afghanistan, and Iraq. Lincoln, Franklin Roosevelt, and Carter most often practiced the prophetic version. They emphasized God's transcendence and judgment and urged Americans to repent of their sins, selfishness, and shortcomings, forgive others, make sacrifices, assume personal responsibility, and improve their conduct. Although they used religious rhetoric "to comfort and console," they also frequently employed it to "challenge and to criticize."[33] Even Lincoln, however, best remembered and highly revered for his prophetic role, normally functioned as a priest.[34]

Deeply desiring to hold the nation's disparate elements together, the presidents examined in this study often employed the rhetoric and symbols of civil religion in their efforts to promote unity or provide comfort in times of national trial and tragedy. In the absence of a national church or sanctioned religious credo, and given Americans' substantial religious diversity, their use of this form of discourse is quite understandable. Despite its strong Judeo-Christian heritage, the United States has no official religion. Therefore, when speaking to or for the American people, presidents have tended, no matter what their own personal faith, to use broad, generalized language. More than many critics admit, these presidents employed civil religious rhetoric to criticize the nation's shortcomings and failure to incarnate or implement transcendent standards. Unfortunately, however, they too often used this vocabulary to justify U.S. policies, actions, and principles and to exaggerate its righteousness.

America as God's Chosen Nation

The idea that America is a chosen nation has had a powerful impact on its history. From the Puritan attempt to build a city upon a hill, to Thomas

Paine's vision of America as an "asylum for Mankind," to current arguments that the United States is a refuge for the world's politically oppressed, this concept has inspired millions. Since 1776, most Americans have believed that their nation has a mission and "moral significance in the world."[35] The venerable principles enshrined in the Declaration of Independence, the United States' highly improbable victory over the British, and the country's rapid growth in size, wealth, and power all contributed to this conviction. The messianic myth reached a zenith in the 1860s, when Lincoln, the American Christ, died for the sin of slavery after claiming the United States was the "last hope of earth." Lincoln, Wilson, and other presidents "hallowed" the Civil War as "an awful travail necessary for a new birth of freedom."[36] Throughout the nineteenth century, belief in America's divine mission motivated manifest destiny, and in the 1890s, it inspired overseas expansion. During crusades to defeat German autocracy during World War I, to conquer fascism during World War II, to stem the spread of communism during the cold war, and to combat terrorism, America perceived itself as the defender of the free world and its superior ethical standards.[37]

By their words and actions, presidents have done much to promote this idea. Although none of the subjects of this study claimed that America was the new Israel, all of them asserted that God selected the United States to perform a special mission: to spread democracy, liberty, and biblical morality to the world. They argued that its seemingly miraculous birth; rapid spread across the continent; remarkable increase in population, industry, affluence, and might; successful assimilation of millions of people of diverse ethnic and religious backgrounds; modeling of republican government; and pivotal role in deciding the outcome of international wars all testified to God's choice, use, and blessing of America. Its success and support encouraged people in countries around the globe to throw off the shackles of despotism and embrace democracy. As Eisenhower put it, "The American experiment has, for generations, fired the passion and the courage of millions elsewhere seeking freedom, equality, [and] opportunity."[38] While assigning America an exalted role and responsibility, none of these eleven presidents contended that God approved of all of its actions. They insisted that God wanted to use the United States to benefit the world and exhorted citizens to obey biblical standards. Undoubtedly speaking for all of them, Franklin Roosevelt declared in his final State of the Union Address: "We pray that we may be worthy of the unlimited opportunities God has given us."[39]

The belief that God has especially blessed the United States and selected it for a special mission in the world is biblically suspect. It has inspired Americans to fight injustice at home and abroad, but it has also contributed to simplistic moralizing, overlooking national flaws, a lack of awareness of moral ambiguity, and an understandable hatred abroad of American hubris. William Weeks argues that many American presidents have employed a "rhetoric of empire" to gain public and congressional support for their foreign policies. It consists of three main components: the assumption that the United States is morally superior to other nations, the assertion it must redeem the world by spreading republican government, and "faith in the nation's divinely ordained destiny" to fulfill this mission. This triad of virtue, mission, and destiny has led presidents to reduce many foreign policy issues to a choice between right and wrong or good and evil, rather than subjecting them to reasoned debate. Appealing to this exalted image and crucial calling, they have used stirring rhetoric about "long-aggrieved Americans, evil enemies, and righteous retaliation" to convince citizens to support their foreign policy initiatives. Morality, Weeks argues, has played a paradoxical role in American foreign policy. On the one hand, foreign policy goals have normally required a moral rationale to be acceptable. On the other, presidents have usually believed that tangible national interests are more important than abstract moral principles. They have typically defined "morality as that which serves the American nation and more generally, the global republican revolution."[40] Although the United States has often aided nations striving to create a democratic polity and free institutions, it has frequently supported repressive regimes to further its own interests and try to stop the spread of communism or terrorism.

Lincoln was much less willing than the other presidents examined in this study—most notably Washington, Wilson, both Roosevelts, Reagan, and Bush—to say that God supported his side. He was also much more ambivalent than the rest of them about whether God had selected the United States to accomplish his purposes, calling it God's "almost chosen nation." While repeatedly asserting, as they did, that God directed history, Lincoln rejected the belief that God is on our side that inspired the campaigns and foreign policies of numerous other occupants of the Oval Office.[41] This was much easier to do because he fought against his former countrymen with whom he shared many commonalities and with whom he sought reconciliation, not a foreign power whose people differed in race, culture, and creed and who thwarted America's interests or sought world domination. Yet to his credit, Lincoln persistently refused what must have been a strong temptation to identify his side with God's righteousness and justice.

Given their conviction that America is a chosen nation, not surprisingly, almost all of them believed that God selected them to be president and saw themselves as his instrument. In the words of Woodrow Wilson, "God ordained that I should be the next President of the United States," and no mortal "could have prevented that." Although most of them did not state this claim so boldly, they were inspired by their belief that God had "called" them. This conviction prompted them to pray for God's guidance in leading the nation and to seek to discern his will. Although some of them have been accused of believing that God specifically revealed his will to them, none of them made this claim. Lincoln was the most explicit in declaring that "the Almighty has his own purposes" that people often did not comprehend, but all the subjects of this study strove to discover God's plans for the United States. Although many of them spoke of feeling more confident about important decisions after praying, none of them asserted that God directly told him to take a particular course of action.[42] Theologians argue that the Bible does not teach that national leaders can precisely know God's will for their countries. Rather, it "speaks of an inscrutable God" who often brings "down powerful nations in their prime due to their pride."[43] On the other hand, many Americans would echo the conclusion of historian Paul Johnson: The "most powerful man on earth should feel he is answerable not merely to American opinion and world opinion but to a higher, all-seeing and all-judging power."[44]

Presidential Character

Throughout the nation's history, most Americans have expected their presidents to have sterling character. Although some complain that focusing on the personal morality of statesmen diverts attention from the more important matters of political philosophy and programs, the issue of character has played a significant role in selecting and evaluating presidents. *Character* is an elusive, complex term that is difficult to define. Thomas Reeves argues that for many centuries people have wanted their leaders to have integrity and a desire to serve others and to be "just, wise, courageous, prudent, and temperate in their rule." Good character historically has also included compassion, generosity, prudence, loyalty, responsibility, temperance, humility, and perseverance.[45] After 1945, "as the demands on the chief executive for political savvy, managerial expertise, and communication skills loomed ever larger, the traditional virtues, though still acknowledged, were often slighted."[46] For example, James David Barber emphasizes interpersonal skills, optimism, personal self-esteem, and flexibility more than Judeo-Christian ideas of morality as important to presidential character.[47] Because character has no agreed-on definition, political partisans have defined it differently to make their candidate look preferable to his or her competitors.

Although character includes wisdom, tenacity, courage, and loyalty, at its heart, it is moral character that Americans most value.[48] As Richard Hutcheson argues, for many Americans, character is closely connected to "religiously grounded morality." Most of the presidents examined in this study have been men of exemplary character, but they have not led flawless lives. Critics accuse all eleven of lying to advance their agendas, safeguard their reputations, or supposedly promote the national interest. They claim that Washington, Jefferson, Wilson, Franklin Roosevelt, Eisenhower, and

Kennedy had sexual relations outside marriage, violating biblical moral standards and their commitments to their wives.[49]

Good character, Reeves maintains, is an essential ingredient in "the complex mix of qualities that make an outstanding president and a model leader for a democratic people."[50] Many of the chief executives who are considered great were men of exceptional character. Many Americans agree that "office and the country [are] better served by having Presidents who exemplify the best qualities of integrity, honesty, morality, and strength of character." Nevertheless, scholars generally rate several men widely considered to have had the most integrity (including John Quincy Adams, Hoover, and Carter) as among the least effective presidents. Their admirable character helped them endure extensive criticism as they dealt with ideological divisions, social unrest, and economic difficulties and urged Americans to eschew selfishness and pursue the common good.[51] On the other hand, some who were less upright (including Franklin Roosevelt and Kennedy) were very successful presidents.[52] In the final analysis, their exemplary character, often sustained by their faith, helped numerous presidents, including Washington, Lincoln, Theodore Roosevelt, Eisenhower, and Reagan, lead effectively.

A Final Assessment

Billy Graham exaggerates when he argues that every president has left the office "with a very deep religious faith," but the tremendous responsibilities and pressures and the trials and tribulations of the presidency have inspired many of these eleven chief executives to develop a stronger faith.[53] Crises often drive people to a deeper appreciation of their religious heritage and a closer relationship with God. Many of these presidents testified that the burdens of the office prompted them to seek God's guidance and assistance more than ever before. As we have seen, their faith was important to many presidents and helped inform the way they viewed the world, fulfilled their responsibilities, made decisions, and chose and implemented policies. Although George W. Bush is more outspoken about his faith than most of his predecessors, religious convictions have helped shape and guide the attitudes and actions of many occupants of the Oval Office. Arthur Schlesinger Jr.'s complaint that a "tide of religiosity" is "engulfing a once secular republic" as a result of Bush's presidency displays a misunderstanding of both the presidency and American history.[54]

In the final analysis, we must be careful not to make too much or too little of the influence of presidents' faith on how they performed their duties. Scholars have tended to take it into account too little; some critics and admirers have given it too much attention. The faith of presidents has been viewed and valued differently in various eras in American history, depending on how positively religion was perceived at the time and how the faith of particular presidents fit with the general religious climate and was judged to have affected their work. Because of the nation's religious pluralism, separation of church and state, and demands of civil religion, presidents have struggled to be true to their own religious convictions while trying to satisfy the frequently competing expectations of various constituencies. While not wanting to push their views on others or antagonize those who espoused other perspectives, many of them were guided in their work in part by their faith. Because of their personal temperament, religious background, and sense of propriety, some presidents said very little about their own faith. Others openly shared what they believed. On the whole, the faith of these eleven presidents increased their courage and confidence, helped them persevere during monumental trials, made them better leaders, and encouraged them to pursue policies that promoted justice, righteousness, and compassion. Speaking for many Americans, Pierard and Linder urge presidents to eschew a sectarian religious agenda but to base their administrations on transcendent ethics, promote morality and the common good, and ensure justice.[55]

Applying biblical and moral principles to political life is immensely challenging. Politics, Thomas Reeves contends, "are rough, often dirty, and at best require numerous compromises of principle."[56] George Kennan, Dean Acheson, and many others argue that religious principles are irrelevant to foreign policy. To them, "the times are too perilous ... to allow the luxury of conscience." Moral judgments handicap political leaders dealing with an amoral world.[57] While recognizing that the world's many religions and ideologies and countries' clashing interests made it very difficult to base international relations on biblical principles, these presidents nonetheless often tried to do so. At times, they demonized their enemies or cloaked America's self-serving goals in moral rhetoric, but they frequently pursued policies they believed were based on biblical norms and would benefit other nations. Some claim it is morally obligatory to assess the ethical implications of political, military, and strategic factors and to seek to do God's will on earth.[58] "Great presidents not only encourage the public to strive for the noblest ideals and the highest principles," Reeves maintains, "but pursue the goals in practice."[59] The presidents examined in this study tried to achieve many of humanity's most admirable ideals through their domestic and foreign policies.

Today's often contentious debate over religion, politics, and public policy will be much more productive if Americans accept certain guidelines and better understand their history. Wilfred McClay distinguishes between two types of secularism. Negative secularism involves "an openness to diverse perspectives ... a commitment to free inquiry and free association" and the absence of any " 'official' perspective, including that of militant secularism."

Positive secularism, by contrast, affirms "the secular ideal as an ultimate and alternative comprehensive faith." Americans, he contends, "have by and large accepted the concept of negative secularism, and the fundamental respect for the human person that undergirds it, as an essential basis for peaceful co-existence in a religiously pluralistic society." To participate effectively in contemporary politics, faith communities must adopt negative secularism and accept basic rules for the political game, such as not resorting to appeals to divine revelation to justify their positions. Before doing so, however, they must ask whether such an adaptation compromises their faith or deepens and clarifies it.[60]

Many of the contestants in this animated debate pay insufficient attention to American history. Blatantly partisan and driven by ideological agendas, they often ignore the past. When they do use history, they typically employ it selectively to bolster their side of the argument. Either they exaggerate or minimize the faith of the founders and presidents, or they highlight statements or actions that are unrepresentative or apocryphal. I hope that my investigation of the religious convictions of eleven presidents and analysis of how their faith influenced their work will provide a historical context that sheds more light and reduces the heat of this debate. I have sought to describe the faith of these presidents in the context of their times; to discuss their own statements as well as those of their admirers and critics and more dispassionate scholars; and to reach balanced, judicious, and accurate conclusions. I have aimed to steer a course between those who depict the founders and many presidents as devout, conventional Christians and those who portray them as deists, skeptics, and secularly minded men. Faith—although not always orthodox, Christian faith—had a powerful influence on the thoughts and actions of many presidents. Their understanding of the separation of church and state did not lead these chief executives to confine their religious convictions to their private lives. Instead, their faith affected their work in important ways. Comprehending this can help readers, whether they are politicians, religious leaders, journalists, lobbyists, or simply concerned citizens, better evaluate the approach of George W. Bush and his successors and participate more thoughtfully and effectively in this fascinating debate. This, in turn, can help our nation pursue the ends we all care about: advancing justice, peace, equality, compassion, and virtue.

NOTES

ABBREVIATIONS

AM	Atlantic Monthly	LD	Literary Digest
AQ	American Quarterly	MJPS	Midwest Journal of Political Science
CA	Christian Advocate		
CAC	Christianity and Crisis	MQR	Methodist Quarterly Review
CC	Christian Century	NR	New Republic
CH	Church History	NW	Newsweek
CS	Church and State	NYT	New York Times
CSM	Christian Science Monitor	PB	Presbyterian Banner
CT	Christianity Today	PL	Presbyterian Layman
CMW	Commonweal	PSQ	Presidential Studies Quarterly
FH	Fides et Historia	RRR	Review of Religious Research
JAH	Journal of American History	UP	United Presbyterian
JALA	Journal of the Abraham Lincoln Association	USN	U.S. News and World Report
		VMBH	Virginia Magazine of Biography and History
JCR	Journal of Communication and Religion	WMQ	William and Mary Quarterly
JCS	Journal of Church and State	WP	Washington Post
JPH	Journal of Presbyterian History	WSJ	Wall Street Journal
JSH	Journal of Southern History	WT	Washington Times
LAT	Los Angeles Times		

PREFACE

1. See Steve Farkas et al., *For Goodness Sake: Why So Many Want Religion to Play a Greater Role in American Life* (New York: Public Agenda Foundation, 2001); Pew Forum on Religion and Public Life, *American Views on Religion, Politics, and Public Policy* (Washington, DC: Pew Research Center, 2001); and George Barna and Mark Hatch, *Boiling Point* (Ventura, CA: Regal, 2001).

2. See Peter Marshall Jr. and David Manuel, *The Light and the Glory* (Old Tappan, NJ: Revell, 1977); Marshall and Manuel, *From Sea to Shining Sea* (Old Tappan, NJ: Revell, 1986); Tim LaHaye, *The Battle for the Mind* (Old Tappan, NJ: Revell, 1980); Francis Schaeffer, *A Christian Manifesto* (Westchester, IL: Crossway, 1981); John Whitehead, *The Second American Revolution* (Elgin, IL: David C. Cook, 1982); and

431

David Barton, *Spirit of the American Revolution* (Aldeo, TX: Wallbuilders, 1994). Taking the opposite position is R. Laurence Moore and Isaac Kramnick, *The Godless Constitution: The Case against Religious Correctness* (New York: Norton, 1996). See also Jon Butler, "Why Revolutionary America Wasn't a Christian Nation," in James Hutson, ed., *Religion and the New Republic: Faith in the Founding of America* (Lanham, MD: Rowman and Littlefield, 2000), 187–202; Mark A. Noll, Nathan Hatch, and George Marsden, *The Search for a Christian America* (Westchester, IL: Crossway, 1983); Mark A. Noll, *One Nation under God? Christian Faith and Political Action in America* (San Francisco: Harper and Row, 1988); James H. Hutson, *Religion and the Founding of the American Republic* (Washington, DC: Library of Congress, 1998); Daniel L. Dreisbach, Mark D. Hall, and Jeffry H. Morrison, eds., *The Founders on God and Government* (Lanham, MD: Rowman and Littlefield, 2004); and David D. Kirkpatrick, "Putting God Back into American History," *NYT*, Feb. 27, 2005.

3. Hugo Heclo, "An Introduction to Religion and Public Policy," in Heclo and Wilfred M. McClay, eds., *Religion Returns to the Public Square: Faith and Policy in America* (Washington, DC: Woodrow Wilson Center Press, 2003), 15. See also Wilson Carey McWilliams, "American Democracy and the Politics of Faith," in ibid., 143–62.

4. Ibid., 24.

5. Wilfred M. McClay, "Two Concepts of Secularism," in Heclo and McClay, eds., *Religion Returns*, 33–34; first three quotations from 33, last two from 34.

6. Another Pew poll conducted in 2000 reported that 70 percent of Americans, about the same for Democrats and Republicans, want the president to be a person of faith. Both polls cited in Cathy Young, "Beyond Belief," *Reason* 36 (Oct. 2004).

7. Franklin Foer, "Beyond Belief," *New Republic* 229 (Dec. 29, 2003–Jan. 12, 2004), 22.

8. Kenneth L. Woodward and Martha Brant, "Finding God," *NW* 135 (Feb. 7, 2000), 32.

9. David Limbaugh, "The 'Dangerous' Faith of President Bush," Oct. 19, 2004, http://www.townhall.com.

10. James Carroll, "The Bush Crusade," *Nation* 279 (Sept. 20, 2004), 18.

11. Robert McColley, "Review Essay: *The Inner World of Abraham Lincoln*, by Michael Burlingame, and *Abraham Lincoln: From Skeptic to Prophet*, by Wayne C. Temple," *JALA* 17, no. 2 (1996), 60.

12. Heclo, "Religion and Public Policy," 3.

13. William Martin, "With God on Their Side: Religion and U.S. Foreign Policy," in Heclo and McClay, eds., *Religion Returns*, 347, 346, quotations in that order.

14. Gary Hart, "When the Personal Shouldn't Be Political," *NYT*, Nov. 8, 2004.

INTRODUCTION

1. Ronald Reagan, "Remarks at an Ecumenical Prayer Breakfast in Dallas, TX," Aug. 23, 1984, *Public Papers of the Presidents of the United States, Ronald Reagan, 1981–1989*, 8 vols. (Lanham, MD: Bernan Press, 1995), 4:1167.

2. Haynes Johnson, *Sleepwalking through History: America in the Reagan Years* (New York: Doubleday, 1992), 209.

3. Charles Krauthammer, "Rectifying the Border," *Time* 124 (Sept. 24, 1984), 80; Randall is quoted in *WP*, Sept. 5, 1984, A4. My attention was called to these two sources by Richard V. Pierard, "Religion and the 1984 Election Campaign," *RRR* 27 (Dec. 1985), 104.

4. Richard V. Pierard and Robert D. Linder, *Civil Religion and the Presidency* (Grand Rapids, MI: Zondervan, 1988), 106; Mark A. Noll, "Lincoln's God," *JPH* 82 (Summer 2004), 86; quotations in that order.

5. *Daily National Intelligencer*, Mar. 6, 1865, 2; *New York World*, Mar. 6, 1865, as cited by Ronald C. White Jr., *Lincoln's Greatest Speech: The Second Inaugural* (New York: Simon and Schuster, 2002), 194.

6. Discussant James S. Wolfe in Herbert D. Rosenbaum and Alexei Ugrinsky, eds., *The Presidency and Domestic Policies of Jimmy Carter* (Westport, CT: Greenwood, 1994), 123.

7. See Russel B. Nye, *The Almost Chosen People* (East Lansing: Michigan State University Press, 1966).

8. G. K. Chesterton, *What I Saw in America* in *The Collected Works of G. K. Chesterton* (San Francisco: Ignatius, 1990), Vol. 21, 41–45. See also Sidney Mead, *The Nation with the Soul of a Church* (New York: Harper and Row, 1975). The nature of U.S. religious and ideological roots has been extensively debated. Although some exaggerate the Christian commitment of the Founding Fathers and the religious basis of the American republic, others underestimate them. A balanced assessment of the issue is Mark A. Noll, Nathan O. Hatch, and George M. Marsden, *The Search for Christian America* (Westchester, IL: Crossway, 1983). They argue that the United States is based on the confluence of three streams: the Judeo-Christian tradition, the several varieties of the Enlightenment in Europe, and the ideas of the radical Whigs or Commonwealth men of early-eighteenth-century England. Also helpful are Alan Heimert, *Religion and the American Mind: From the Great Awakening to the Revolution* (Cambridge, MA: Harvard University Press, 1966); Robert Handy, *A Christian America: Protestant Hopes and Historical Realities* (New York: Oxford University Press, 1971); and William Lee Miller, *The First Liberty: Religion and the American Republic* (New York: Alfred A. Knopf, 1986).

9. Pierard and Linder, *Civil Religion*, 17.

10. Books in the former category, which tend to depict the presidents as devoutly religious men, include Louis Banks, *The Religious Life of Famous Americans* (New York: American Tract Society, 1904); Charles E. Kistler, *This Nation under God: A Religious Supplement to American History* (Boston: Gorham, 1924); Vernon Hampton, *Religious Background of the White House* (Boston: Christopher, 1932); Archer Wallace, *The Religious Faith of Great Men* (New York: Round Table, 1935); Bliss Isely, *The Presidents, Men of Faith* (Boston: W. A. Wilde, 1953); Olga Jones, *Churches of the Presidents in Washington* (New York: Exposition, 1961); John S. Bonnell, *Presidential Profiles: Religion in the Life of American Presidents* (Philadelphia: Westminster, 1971); J. W. Storer, *The Presidents and the Bible* (Nashville, TN: Broadman, 1976); John McCollister, *So Help Me God: The Faith of America's Presidents* (Louisville, KY: Westminster/John Knox, 1991); Daniel Ernest White, *So Help Me, God: The U.S. Presidents in Perspective* (New York: Nova Science, 1996); and John McCollister, *God and the Oval Office: The Religious Faith of Our 43 Presidents* (Nashville, TN: W Pub. Group, 2005). Franklin Steiner's *Religious Beliefs of Our Presidents* (Girard, KS: Haldeman-Julius, 1936), on the other hand, argued that most American presidents rejected the morality and supernaturalism of Christianity. More balanced, but still rather superficial, is Edward Fuller and David Green, *God in the White House: The Faith of American Presidents* (New York: Crown, 1968). See also Berton Dulce and Edward J. Richter, *Religion and the Presidency* (New York: Macmillan, 1962).

11. The most noteworthy on the founding fathers are Michael Malbin, *Religion and Politics: The Intentions of the Authors of the First Amendment* (Washington, DC: American Enterprise Institute, 1978), John Eidsmoe, *Christianity and the Constitution: The Faith of the Founding Fathers* (Grand Rapids, MI: Baker, 1987), Edwin Gaustad, *Faith of Our Fathers: Religion and the New Nation* (San Francisco: Harper and Row, 1987); John West Jr., *The Politics of Revelation and Reason: Religion and Civic Life in the New Nation* (Lawrence: University Press of Kansas, 1996); Michael Novak, *On Two Wings: Humble Faith and Common Sense at the American Founding* (San Francisco: Encounter, 2002); Frank Lambert, *The Founding Fathers and the Place of Religion in America* (Princeton, NJ: Princeton University Press, 2003); Alf J. Mapp Jr., *The Faiths of Our Fathers: What America's Founders Really Believed* (Lanham, MD: Rowman and Littlefield, 2003); David L. Holmes, *The Religion of the Founding Fathers* (Charlottesville, VA: Ash Lawn-Highland, 2003); and Daniel Dreisbach, Mark Hall, and Jeffry Morrison, eds., *The Founders on God and Government* (Lanham, MD: Rowman and Littlefield, 2004). On individual presidents, the best works are William E. Barton, *The Soul of Abraham Lincoln* (New York: Doran, 1920); David Hinshaw, *Herbert Hoover: American Quaker* (New York: Farrar, Straus, 1950); Paul Boller Jr., *George Washington and Religion* (Dallas, TX: Southern Methodist University Press, 1963); William Lee Miller, *Piety along the Potomac* (Boston: Houghton Mifflin, 1964); Lawrence H. Fuchs, *John F. Kennedy and American Catholicism* (New York: Meredith, 1967); William J. Wolf, *Lincoln's Religion* (Philadelphia: Pilgrim, 1970); Arthur Link, *The Higher Realism of Woodrow Wilson and Other Essays* (Nashville, TN: Vanderbilt University Press, 1971); Glen E. Thurow, *Abraham Lincoln and American Political Religion* (Albany: State University of New York Press, 1976); David Kucharsky, *The Man from Plains: The Mind and Spirit of Jimmy Carter* (New York: Harper and Row, 1976); Neils C. Nielsen Jr., *The Religion of President Carter* (Nashville, TN: Thomas Nelson, 1977); James T. Baker, *A Southern Baptist in the White House* (Philadelphia: Westminster, 1977); William Lee Miller, *Yankee from Georgia: The Emergence of Jimmy Carter* (New York: New York Times Books, 1978); John M. Mulder, *Woodrow Wilson: The Years of Preparation* (Princeton, NJ: Princeton University Press, 1978); Bob Slosser, *Reagan Inside Out* (Waco, TX: Word, 1984); Charles Sanford, *The Religious Life of Thomas Jefferson* (Charlottesville: University Press of Virginia, 1985); Edwin Gaustad, *Sworn on the Altar of God: A Religious Biography of Thomas Jefferson* (Grand Rapids, MI: Eerdmans, 1996); Dan Ariail and Cheryl Heckler-Feltz, *The Carpenter's Apprentice: The Spiritual Autobiography of Jimmy Carter* (Grand Rapids, MI: Zondervan, 1996); Allen Guelzo, *Abraham Lincoln: Redeemer President* (Grand Rapids, MI: Eerdmans, 1999); William Lee Miller, *Lincoln's Virtues: An Ethical Biography* (New York: Random House, 2002); Stephen Mansfield, *The Faith of George W. Bush* (New York: Penguin, 2003); David Aikman, *A Man of Faith: The Spiritual Journey of George W. Bush* (Nashville, TN: W. Publishing Group, 2004); Paul Kengor, *God and Ronald Reagan: A Spiritual Life* (New York: HarperCollins, 2004); and Paul Kengor, *God and George W. Bush: A Spiritual Life* (New York: HarperCollins, 2004). Also helpful are Albert Menendez, *Religion and the U.S. Presidency: A Bibliography* (New York: Garland, 1986), Cheryl Heckler-Feltz, *Heart and Soul of the Nation: How the Spirituality of Our First Ladies Changed America* (New York: Doubleday, 1997); and Harold I. Gullan, *Faith of Our Mothers: The Stories of Presidential Mothers from Mary Washington to Barbara Bush* (Grand Rapids, MI: Eerdmans, 2001).

12. Especially significant are Paul Boller Jr., "George Washington and Religious Liberty," *WMQ* Series 3, 17 (1960), 486–506; James E. Wood Jr., "The Church-State

Legacy of John F. Kennedy," *JCS* 6 (Winter 1964), 5–11; Robert P. Hay, "George Washington: American Moses," *AQ* 21 (Winter 1969), 780–91; Merlin Gustafson, "The Religious Role of the President," *MJPS* 14 (November 1970), 708–22; Paul Boller Jr., "Religion and the U. S. Presidency," *JCS* 21 (Winter 1979), 5–21; Richard Pierard, "Billy Graham and the U.S. Presidency," *JCS* 22 (Winter 1980), 107–27; Ronald B. Flowers, "President Jimmy Carter, Evangelicalism, Church-State Relations and Civil Religion," *JCS* 25 (Winter 1983), 113–32; Lawrence Jones, "Reagan's Religion," *Journal of American Culture* 8 (Winter 1985), 59–70; and Gregory S. Butler, "Vision of a Nation Transformed: Modernity and Ideology in Wilson's Political Thought," *JCS* 39 (Winter 1997), 37–51. Also valuable is Leo P. Ribuffo, "God and Jimmy Carter," in M. L. Bradbury and James B. Gilbert, eds., *Transforming Faith: The Sacred and Secular in Modern American History* (Westport, CT: Greenwood, 1989), 141–59.

13. Garry Wills, *Under God: Religion and American Politics* (New York: Simon and Schuster, 1990), 18. In covering six presidential campaigns, he never saw a religious writer on a campaign plane (18).

14. "Mr. Reagan's Civil Religion," *CMW*, Sept. 21, 1984, 483. Cf. "Politics and Pulpits," *NR*, Oct. 11, 1980, 5.

15. Discussant: James M. Wall in Rosenbaum and Ugrinsky, *Jimmy Carter*, 120. Wall concludes, "[t]hese leaders encouraged the incorrect impression that a President Carter just might function in the White House with an open line not to Rome, as they feared with John Kennedy, but to Heaven itself."

16. E.g., Lewis L. Gould, *The Presidency of William McKinley* (Lawrence: University Press of Kansas, 1980); H. Wayne Morgan, *William McKinley and His America* (Syracuse, NY: Syracuse University Press, 1963); Nathan Miller, *Theodore Roosevelt: A Life* (New York: William Morrow, 1992); H. W. Brands, *T. R.: The Last Romantic* (New York: Basic Books, 1997); George McJimsey, *The Presidency of Franklin Delano Roosevelt* (Lawrence: University Press of Kansas, 2000); Stephen E. Ambrose, *Eisenhower* (New York: Simon and Schuster, 1984); Chester J. Pach Jr. and Elmo Richardson, *The Presidency of Dwight D. Eisenhower* (Lawrence: University Press of Kansas, 1991); Geoffrey Perret, *Eisenhower* (New York: Random House, 1999); Lou Cannon, *President Reagan: The Role of a Lifetime* (New York: Simon and Schuster, 1991); and William Pemberton, *Exit with Honor: The Life and Presidency of Ronald Reagan* (Armonk, NY: M. E. Sharpe, 1998).

17. E.g., "Foundation Built on Faith: Religious Leaders Note Reagan's Core," AP, June 12, 2004.

18. Ron Reagan Jr., Eulogy for Ronald Reagan, June 14, 2004, http://www.ameri canrhetoric.com/speeches. His other son, Michael, testified, "I believe that his determination and perseverance came from his relationship with the Lord. He played an important role in pointing me to God. I am secure in the knowledge that he is with his Lord and Savior Jesus Christ in heaven" (http://reaganranch.yaf.org/leadership/press/ YAF06_05_04_MR.pdf).

19. Nancy Reagan, "The Eternal Optimist," *Time* 163 (June 14, 2004), 48.

20. The only in-depth analyses of Reagan's faith are Slosser, *Reagan Inside Out*; Kengor, *God and Ronald Reagan*; and Mary Beth Brown, *Hand of Providence: The Strong and Quiet Faith of Ronald Reagan* (Nashville, TN: WND Books, 2004). In *Reagan's God and Country* (Ann Arbor, MI: Servant, 2000), Tom Freiling provides a compilation of Reagan's speeches on a wide variety of religious and moral issues. Garry Wills examines the faith and influence of his mother, Nelle, on the future

president in *Reagan's America: Innocents at Home* (Garden City, NY: Doubleday, 1987), 16–26. See also Stephen Vaughn, "The Moral Inheritance of a President: Reagan and the Dixon Disciples of Christ," *PSQ* 25 (Winter 1995), 109–23.

21. See Johnson, *Sleepwalking*, 193–214 and Wilbur Edel, *Defenders of the Faith: Religion and Politics from the Pilgrim Fathers to Ronald Reagan* (New York: Praeger, 1987), 140–56.

22. Pierard and Linder, *Civil Religion*, 15.

23. Ronald Isetti, "The Moneychangers of the Temple: FDR, American Civil Religion, and the New Deal," *PSQ* 26 (Summer 1996), 684. Cf. Michael Novak, *Choosing Our King: Powerful Symbols in Presidential Politics* (New York: Macmillan, 1974), 3. "The president," he argues, "affects our internal images of authority, legitimacy, [and] leadership... the election of a president is an almost religious task." (4). See also James Smylie, "The President as Republican Prophet and King: Clerical Reflections on the Death of Washington," *JCS* 18 (Spring 1976), 233–52; and Charles Lippy, "The President as Priest: Civil Religion and the American Presidency," *Journal of Religious Studies* 8 (Fall 1980), 29–41.

24. Thomas C. Reeves, *A Question of Character: A Life of John F. Kennedy* (New York: Free Press, 1991), 414; Ronald A. Wells, "American Presidents as Political and Moral Leaders: A Report on Four Surveys," *FH* 11 (Fall 1978), 39–53.

25. James David Barber, *The Presidential Character: Predicting Performance in the White House* (Englewood Cliffs, NJ: Prentice-Hall [1972]), 9.

26. Quoted in Walter Mondale, "Religion Is a Private Matter," *CS*, Oct. 1984, 15.

27. Quoted in Merle Miller, *Plain Speaking: An Oral History of Harry S. Truman* (New York: Greenwich House, 1985), 415.

28. William Burlie Brown, *The People's Choice* (Baton Rouge: Louisiana State University Press, 1960), 130–31, based on a study of campaign biographies from 1824 to 1960.

29. Space does not permit an examination of several other presidents for whom religion was significant, most notably John Adams, John Quincy Adams, James Garfield, Grover Cleveland, Benjamin Harrison, William McKinley, Herbert Hoover, Richard Nixon, Gerald Ford, and George H. W. Bush. Adams was a diligent student of theology, regarded himself as a Christian, and tried to walk a middle road between deism and orthodox Calvinism. See Page Smith, *John Adams*, 2 vols. (Garden City, NY: Doubleday, 1962), 1:24, 29–30; 2:896, 1078–79. Garfield claimed to be a born-again Christian and was a lay preacher for the Disciples of Christ and a very faithful Christian. Because he was shot five months after taking office and died two months later, both his policies and his relationship with religious constituencies were limited. See Theodore Clark Smith, *The Life and Letters of James Abram Garfield*, 2 vols. (New Haven, CT: Yale University Press, 1925), esp. 1:33–38, 54, 83–84; 2:1063; E. V. Smalley, "Characteristics of Garfield," *Century Magazine*, 1882, 168–76; Edward J. Giddings, *American Christian Rulers or Religion and Men of Government* (New York: Bromfield, 1889), 233–40; Banks, *Religious Life*, 53–62; Hampton, *Religious Background*, 58–71; Woodrow Wasson, *James A. Garfield: His Religion and Education. A Study in the Religious and Educational Thought of an American Statesman* (Nashville: Tennessee Book Co., 1952); Allan Peskin, *Garfield: A Biography* (Kent, OH: Kent State University, 1978); and Margaret Leech and Harry J. Brown, *The Garfield Orbit* (New York: Harper and Row, 1978). The son of a Presbyterian minister, Cleveland insisted that his religious socialization affected his perspective on life. See Isely, *Presidents*, 171–76; Allan

Nevins, *Grover Cleveland: A Study in Courage* (Norwalk, CT: Easton, 1989 [1932]); Alyn Brodsky, *Grover Cleveland: A Study in Character* (New York: St. Martin's Press, 2000); and Richard E. Welch, *The Presidency of Grover Cleveland* (Lawrence: University Press of Kansas, 1988). A devout evangelical Presbyterian, Harrison also claimed to be a born-again Christian. See Isely, *Presidents*, 179–84; Banks, *Religious Life*, 237–45; Hampton, *Religious Background*, 341–43; Harry Sievers, *Benjamin Harrison: Hoosier Warrior, 1833–1865* (Chicago: Henry Regnery, 1952), esp. 27–29, 59–63, 111–14; and Harry Sievers, *Benjamin Harrison: Hoosier President* (Indianapolis, IN: Bobbs-Merrill, 1968). Truman, a Southern Baptist, regularly composed short prayers while president, knew the Scriptures well, and called the Bible "the fundamental basis of all government" (Harry S. Truman, *Mr. Citizen* [New York: Bernard Geis, 1960], 135). See also Merlin Gustafson, "Religion of a President," *JCS* 10 (Autumn 1968), 379–87; Merlin Gustafson, "Harry Truman as a Man of Faith," *CC* 90 (Jan. 17, 1973), 75–78; and Alonzo Hamby, *Beyond the New Deal: Harry S. Truman and American Liberalism* (New York: Columbia University Press, 1973). Nixon, a Quaker, enjoyed a close relationship with Billy Graham and held worship services at the White House. See Marshall Frady, *Billy Graham: A Parable of American Righteousness* (Boston: Little, Brown, 1979); William Martin, *Prophet with Honor: The Billy Graham Story* (New York: Quill, 1991), 269–83, 330–71, 420–35; Richard Pierard, "Billy Graham and the U.S. Presidency," *JCS* 22 (Spring 1980), 119–25; Charles P. Henderson Jr., *The Nixon Theology* (New York: Harper and Row, 1972); Ben Hibbs, ed., *White House Sermons* (New York: Harper and Row, 1972); Stephen Ambrose, *Nixon: The Triumph of a Politician, 1962–1972* (New York: 1989), 183–84, 555; Wills, *Under God*, 62, 83; and Fawn M. Brodie, *Richard M. Nixon: The Shaping of His Character* (New York: Norton, 1981). Ford, a churchgoer and faithful Christian all his life, demonstrated a deep and genuine faith in many ways. See Billy Zeoli, *God's Got a Better Idea* (Old Tappan, NJ: Fleming H. Revell, 1978); and James C. Hefley and Edward Plowman, *Washington: Christians in the Corridors of Power* (Wheaton, IL: Tyndale, 1975), 13–36. George Bush, an Episcopalian, presented himself as a born-again Christian and actively sought the support of the religious right in 1988. See George Bush, *All the Best, George Bush: My Life and Letters and Other Writings* (New York: Scribner, 1999), 147, 319–20, 323–25, 409, 501, 504, 509, 513–14; Herbert S. Parmet, *George Bush: The Life of a Lone Star Yankee* (New York: Scribner, 1997), 22–24, 248–49, 302–3, and passim; "Bush on Faith: A Personal Issue," *CT* 32 (Sept. 16, 1988), 40; Richard G. Hutcheson Jr., "Religion in the Bush White House," *CC* 106 (Jan. 18, 1989), 37–38; Kim Lawton, "White House Religion," *CT* 33 (Feb. 17, 1989), 36–37; and "Bush Affirms the Role of Religion in Public Life," *CT* 35 (Apr. 29, 1991), 38–39. These individuals are omitted either because they made a sharp distinction between their private faith and public duties or because they served in close proximity to other presidents whose faith was more significant because of their personal commitments, historical circumstances, or policies. On J. Q. Adams, McKinley, and Hoover, see my essays at www.visandvals.org

30. Robert S. Alley, *So Help Me God* (Richmond, VA: John Knox, 1972), 24–28. I have listed only the presidents in Alley's schematization that I analyze in this book. Michael Novak identifies five versions of Protestant civil religion that have political relevance. His classification scheme includes chief executives and other politicians. The first is "classic mainline Protestantism of New England" promoted by Episcopalians, northern Presbyterians, and the United Church of Christ. For these individuals, "wealth, family background and political and social awareness" derived

through an Ivy League education produced a liberal approach to public policy that emphasizes compromise and tolerance (Charles W. Dunn, "The Theological Dimensions of Presidential Leadership: A Classification Model," *PSQ* 14[1] [1984], 65). Second is the "populist tradition of the lower classes," which is strongest in the South, the Bible Belt, and small towns and rural areas. Suspicious of formal authority, this low-church tradition emphasizes decency and order, tends to be absolutist in its understanding of right and wrong, and therefore usually dislikes compromise. Third is the "denominational moralism of the middle-class heartland churches." "Reformist yet practical," it is more Midwestern than Southern and more Methodist than Baptist. Unlike the low-church tradition, it accepts professionalism, bureaucracies, and expertise. The fourth category is reform Protestantism, a cyclical type that arises in response to a controversial moral issue such as abolition, Prohibition, Civil Rights, or antiwar protest. Novak's final category is based on the black Protestant experience, which is more communal, emotional, interpersonal, and vibrant than that of white Protestants. See Novak, *Choosing Presidents: Symbols of Presidential Leadership* (New Brunswick, NJ: Transaction, 1992), 131–34.

31. Dunn, "The Theological Dimensions of Presidential Leadership," 67–69, quotation from 69.

32. Ibid., 69–71. I have listed only the presidents in Dunn's schematization who I discuss in this book. Dunn concludes that few presidents have had strong theological convictions, in large part because the office seems to moderate staunchly held convictions. Presidents usually have joined or attended mainline Protestant congregations.

33. Ronald Nash, *Faith and Reason: Searching for a Rational Faith* (Grand Rapids, MI: Zondervan, 1988), 24.

34. James Olthius, "On Worldviews," in Paul A. Marshall, Sander Griffioen, and Richard J. Mouw, eds., *Stained Glass: Worldviews and Social Science* (Lanham, MD: University Press of America, 1989), 29. Most people rarely analyze their basic presuppositions, but everyone is guided by fundamental assumptions. See David K. Naugle, *Worldview: The History of a Concept* (Grand Rapids, MI: Eerdmans, 2002), xv. Postmodernists argue that there are no true large-scale interpretations of reality, simply "a plethora of socially and linguistically constructed meaning systems," none of which is better than others, and all of which should be tolerated (174). For postmodernists, worldviews are simply personal stories, not coherent views of life or compelling interpretations of the universe (257).

35. Phil Washburn, *Philosophical Dilemmas: Building a Worldview* (New York: Oxford University Press, 1997), 6–11, quotation from 7. Cf. Michael Kearney, *World View* (Novato, CA: Chandler and Sharp, 1984), esp. 41–42; and James Sire, *Naming the Elephant: Worldview as a Concept* (Downers Grove, IL: InterVarsity, 2004), esp. 23–50.

36. Brian J. Walsh and J. Richard Middleton, *The Transforming Vision: Shaping a Christian World View* (Downers Grove, IL: InterVarsity, 1984), 32. In recent decades, theologians, philosophers, sociologists, anthropologists, psychologists, and historians of science have also analyzed the powerful impact of worldviews in their respective fields. E.g., Peter Berger and Thomas Luckmann, *The Social Construction of Reality* (New York: Anchor, 1967); Thomas Kuhn, *The Structure of Scientific Revolutions* (Chicago: University of Chicago Press, 1970); Michel Foucault, *The Archaeology of*

Knowledge, trans. A. M. Sheridan Smith (New York: Random House, 1972); Lewis Feuer, *Ideology and the Ideologists* (New York: Harper and Row, 1975); J. Richard Middleton and Brian J. Walsh, *Truth Is Stranger Than It Used to Be: Biblical Faith in a Postmodern Age* (Downers Grove, IL: Inter Varsity, 1995); and Edwin Hung, *The Nature of Science: Problems and Perspectives* (Belmont, CA: Wadsworth, 1997).

37. Robert Michaelsen, "Religion and the Presidency—II," *CC* 77 (Feb. 10, 1960), 159.

38. E.g., James S. Wolfe, "Exclusion, Fusion, or Dialogue: How Should Religion and Politics Relate?" *JCS* 22 (1980), 89.

39. John F. Wilson, "Introduction" in Wilson and Donald F. Drakeman, eds., *Church and State in American History: The Burden of Religious Pluralism* (Boston: Beacon, 1987), xv–xx. They identify five different periods of church-state relations in the history of the United States: the struggle for independence and the terms of settlement (1760–1820), the era of republican Protestantism (1820–1860), the recognition of American pluralism (1860–1920), mainstream pluralism (1920–1960), and inclusive pluralism (1960–).

40. Mark A. Noll, "Evangelicals in the Founding and Today," in James H. Hutson, ed., *Religion and the New Republic: Faith in the Founding of America* (Lanham, MD: Rowman and Littlefield, 2000) 146–47, quotation from 147; John M. Murrin, "Religion and Politics in America from the First Settlements to the Civil War," in Mark A. Noll, ed., *Religion and American Politics: From the Colonial Period to the 1980s* (New York: Oxford University Press, 1990), 31. The fifty-five framers of the Constitution included only two Methodists and no Baptists, and only one delegate, Richard Bassett of Delaware, can be definitively labeled a born-again Christian.

41. See Nathan Hatch, *The Democratization of American Christianity* (New Haven, CT: Yale University Press, 1989); Richard J. Cawardine, *Evangelicals and Politics in Antebellum America* (New Haven, CT: Yale University Press, 1993); Curtis D. Johnson, *Redeeming America: Evangelicals and the Road to Civil War* (Chicago: Ivan R. Dee, 1993); and Jon Butler, *Awash in a Sea of Faith: Christianizing the American People* (Cambridge, MA: Harvard University Press, 1990).

42. More than 140 bills on Sunday observance were proposed in Congress between 1888 and 1945; 200 bills were introduced in Congress to overturn the Supreme Court decisions outlawing Bible reading and the Lord's prayer from 1962 to 1983.

43. See Norman De Jong, "The First Amendment: A Comparison of Nineteenth and Twentieth Century Supreme Court Interpretations," *Journal of Political Science* 16 (Spring 1988), 69.

44. Mark A. Noll, "The Scandal of Evangelical Political Reflection," in Richard John Neuhaus and George Weigel, eds., *Being Christian Today: An American Conversation* (Washington, DC: Ethics and Public Policy Center, 1992), 73.

45. E.g., David A. Hollinger, *Science, Jews, and Secular Culture: Studies in Mid-Twentieth-Century American Intellectual History* (Princeton, NJ: Princeton University Press, 1996).

46. Anson Phelps Stokes, *Church and State in the United States*, 3 vols. (New York: Harper, 1950), 1:65. See Terry Eastland, ed., *Religious Liberty in the Supreme Court: The Cases That Define the Debate over Church and State* (Grand Rapids, MI: Eerdmans, 1993); Marvin E. Frankel and Eric Foner, *Faith and Freedom: Religious Liberty in America* (New York: Hill and Wang, 1995); John T. Noonan Jr., *The Lustre of Our Country: The American Experience of Religious Freedom* (Berkeley: University of

California Press, 1998); and Noah Feldman, *Divided by God: America's Church-State Problem—and What We Should Do about It* (New York: Farrar, Straus and Giroux, 2005).

47. See Merlin Gustafson, "Franklin Roosevelt and His Protestant Constituency," *JCS* 35 (Spring 1993), 285–97; and Merlin Gustafson, "The President's Mail," *PSQ* 3 (Winter 1978), 30–44.

48. Some urge religious groups to promote the common good over their special interests and to participate in political battles not as combatants but as facilitators. E.g., James M. Wall, "Who Speaks for the Common Good?" *CC*, Feb. 15, 1984, 155–56; and James Skillen, *Recharging the American Experiment: Principled Pluralism for Genuine Civic Community* (Grand Rapids, MI: Baker, 1994).

49. Conrad Cherry, "Introduction," in Cherry, ed., *God's New Israel: Religious Interpretations of America's Destiny* (Englewood Cliffs, NJ; Prentice Hall, 1972), 13. See also Ernest Lee Tuveson, *Redeemer Nation: The Idea of America's Millennial Role* (Chicago: University of Chicago Press, 1980).

50. Robert Bellah, "Civil Religion in America," in Russell Ritchey and Donald Jones, eds., *American Civil Religion* (New York: Harper, 1974), 21.

51. Robert D. Linder, "Reagan at Kansas State: Civil Religion in the Service of the New Right," *Reformed Journal*, Dec. 1982, 13–14.

52. Robert D. Linder and Richard V. Pierard, "Ronald Reagan, Civil Religion and the New Religious Right in America," *FH*, 23 (Fall 1991), 66.

53. Bellah, "Civil Religion," quotation from 40.

54. Ibid., 29, 34–35, quotations in that order.

55. Cherry, "Introduction," 10. Pierard and Linder argue in *Civil Religion and the Presidency* that five components have contributed to American civil religion: belief that America is a chosen nation; civil millennialism, a secularizing of the themes derived from the First Great Awakening of the 1730s and 1740s; nineteenth-century evangelicalism, which helped establish ethical norms "that stood above parties, denominations, sects, and creeds" (57); the rationalist perspective of the nation's intellectual and political elite that was "compatible with the general evangelical tone of the civil faith" (59); and historical events that appeared to demonstrate that God had selected the United States to spread civil and religious liberty to the world. On civil religion, see also Conrad Cherry, "Two American Sacred Ceremonies: Their Implications for the Study of Religion in America," *AQ* 21 (Winter 1969), 739–54; Louis J. Voskuil, "Jean-Jacques Rousseau: Secular Salvation and Civil Religion," *FH* 7 (Spring 1975), 11–26; Robert D. Linder, "Civil Religion in Historical Perspective: The Reality That Underlies the Concept," *JCS* 17 (Autumn 1975), 399–421; John Wilson, *Public Religion in American Culture* (Philadelphia: Temple University Press, 1979); and Robert Bellah and Phillip E. Hammond, *Varieties of Civil Religion* (San Francisco: Harper and Row, 1980).

56. Bellah, "Civil Religion," 22, 30; Robert Booth Fowler, Allen D. Hertzke, and Laura R. Olson, *Religion and Politics in America: Faith, Culture, and Strategic Choices* (Boulder, CO: Westview, 1999), 116; Alley, *So Help Me*, 24; Charles P. Henderson Jr., "Civil Religion and the American Presidency," *Religious Education* 70 (Sept.–Oct. 1975), 477.

57. Pierard and Linder, *Civil Religion*, 25.

58. Novak, *Choosing Our King*, 309, 127.

59. Linder and Pierard, *Civil Religion*, 63.

60. Richard G. Hutcheson Jr., *God in the White House: How Religion Has Changed the Modern Presidency* (New York: Macmillan, 1988), 238. See also Sydney Ahlstrom, *A Religious History of the American People* (New Haven, CT: Yale University Press, 1972), 842–56; and Don S. Ross, "The 'Civil Religion' in America," *Religion in Life* 44 (Spring 1975), 24–35.

61. See Paul H. Boase, "Moving the Mercy Seat into the White House: An Exegesis of the Carter/Reagan Religious Rhetoric," *JCR*, Sept. 1989, 1. See also Charles V. LaFontaine, "God and Nation in Selected U.S. Presidential Inaugural Addresses, 1789–1945," *JCS* 18 (Winter 1976), 39–60; (Autumn 1976), 503–21; and Cynthia Toolin, "American Civil Religion from 1789–1981: A Content Analysis of Presidential Inaugural Addresses," *RRR* 25 (Sept. 1983), 39–48.

62. Isetti, "Moneychangers," 685.

63. Nye, *Almost Chosen*, 164. See also See William R. Hutchison and Hartmut Lehmann, eds., *Many Are Chosen: Divine Election and Western Nationalism* (Cambridge, MA: Harvard University Press, 1994).

64. Jonathan Edwards, *Some Thoughts concerning the Present Revival of Religion in New England*, in *The Works of President Edwards* (New York: S. Converse, 1830), 128.

65. Quoted by Nye, *Almost Chosen*, 169.

66. James H. Moorhead, "The American Israel: Protestantism Tribalism and Universal Mission," in Hutchison and Lehmann, eds., *Many Are Chosen*, 145–66. See also Winthrop Hudson, ed., *Nationalism and Religion in America: Concepts of American Identity and Mission* (New York: Harper and Row, 1970) and Sacvan Bercovitch, *The American Jeremiah* (Madison: University of Wisconsin Press, 1978).

67. Quoted in Nye, *Almost Chosen*, 170.

68. George W. Bush, speech to B'nai B'rith, Aug. 28, 2000, http://www.beliefnet.com/story/40/story_4049_1.html.

69. Cherry, "Introduction," 19.

70. James Davidson Hunter, *The Death of Character* (New York: Basic Books, 2000), 4.

71. George Washington, "First Inaugural Address," in James D. Richardson, comp., *A Compilation of the Messages and Papers of the Presidents, 1789–1897*, 10 vols. (Washington, DC: Government Printing Office, 1896), 1:52–53.

72. James Madison, "The Virginia Convention Debates, Friday, 20 June 1788," in John P. Kaminski and Gaspare J. Saladino, eds., *The Documentary History of the Ratification of the Constitution: Virginia* (Madison: State Historical Society of Wisconsin, 1993), 10:1417.

73. Theodore Roosevelt, American Bible Society, N.Y., Centennial pamphlets, No. 5, 1916.

74. James P. Pfiffner, *The Character Factor: How We Judge America's Presidents* (College Station, TX: Texas A&M Press, 2004), 3–17. See also David W. Gill, *Becoming Good: Building Moral Character* (Downers Grove, IL: InterVarsity, 2000); James Davison Hunter and Carl Bowman, *The Politics of Character* (Charlottesville: University of Virginia Institute for Advanced Studies in Culture, 2000), 13–19; Deborah Rhode, "Moral Character in the Personal and the Political," *Loyola University of Chicago Law Journal* (Fall 1988), 1–19; and Richard A. Posner, *An Affair of State* (Cambridge, MA: Harvard University Press, 1999), 132–69.

75. Shelley Ross, *Fall from Grace: Sex, Scandal, and Corruption in American Politics from 1702 to the Present* (New York: Ballantine, 1988); Wesley O. Hagood, *Presidential*

Sex: From the Founding Fathers to Bill Clinton (Secaucus, NJ: Carol, 1998); Jeffery D. Schultz, *Presidential Scandals* (Washington, DC: CQ, 2000); Charles W. Dunn, *The Scarlet Thread of Scandal: Morality and the American Presidency* (Lanham, MD: Rowman and Littlefield, 2000).

76. William James, *A Pluralistic Universe*, quoted in Naugle, *Worldview*, xi.

77. Martin Fausold, *The Presidency of Herbert C. Hoover* (Lawrence: University Press of Kansas, 1985), 245.

78. Joseph J. Ellis, oliminate the ponod *American Sphinx: The Character of Thomas Jefferson* (New York: Alfred A. Knopf, 1997), 292.

79. Jeff Walz, "Religion and the American Presidency," in Corwin E. Smidt, ed., *In God We Trust: Religion and American Political Life* (Grand Rapids, MI: Baker, 2001), 209.

CHAPTER 1

1. James T. Flexner, *Washington: The Indispensable Man* (Boston: Little, Brown, 1974), 24–26, quotation from 26; John R. Alden, *George Washington: A Biography* (Baton Rouge: Louisiana State University Press, 1984), 39–44.

2. GW to John Augustine Washington, July 18, 1755, in W. W. Abbot, ed., *Papers of George Washington* (hereafter *PGW*), *Colonial Series*, 9 vols. (Charlottesville: University Press of Virginia, 1983–84) 1:343.

3. GW to Robert Jackson, Aug. 2, 1755, *PGW, Col. Ser.* 1:350.

4. Samuel Davies, *Religion and Patriotism the Constituents of a Good Soldier...* (Philadelphia: J. Buckland, J. Wars, and T. Field, 1756).

5. Richard Brookhiser, *Founding Father: Rediscovering George Washington* (New York: Free Press, 1996), 162.

6. E.g., Fisher Ames, "Eulogy of Washington," Feb. 8, 1800, in William B. Allen, ed., *Works of Fisher Ames* (Indianapolis, IN: Liberty Classics, 1983), 1:519–38.

7. Richard V. Pierard and Robert D. Linder, *Civil Religion and the Presidency* (Grand Rapids, MI: Zondervan, 1988), 74–75.

8. See Catherine Albanese, *Sons of the Fathers: The Civil Religion of the American Revolution* (Philadelphia: Temple University Press, 1976), 143–81.

9. See *Maryland Journal* and *Baltimore Advertiser*, July 8, 1777, 1; and *Pennsylvania Mercury* and *Universal Advertiser*, July 8, 1785, 1, as cited in Robert P. Hay, "George Washington: American Moses," *AQ* (Winter 1969), 781.

10. John Marshall, "Eulogy on Washington: 'First in the Hearts of His Countrymen,'" in Greg L. Gregg II and Matthew Spalding, eds., *Patriot Sage: George Washington and the American Political Tradition* (Wilmington, DE: ISI, 1999), 296.

11. Marcus Cunliffe, *George Washington: Man and Monument* (Boston: Little, Brown, 1958), 213.

12. Paul F. Boller Jr., *George Washington and Religion* (Dallas, TX: Southern Methodist University Press, 1963), vii. Boller's book is the most thorough examination of Washington's religion. Also very important is Michael Novak and Jana Novak, *Washington's God: Religion, Liberty, and the Father of Our Country* (New York: Basic Books, 2006), which was published too close to my book going to press to be incorporated.

13. E.g., W. R. Whittekin, "George Never So Prayed," *Truth Seeker* 56 (July 27, 1929), 474; Franklin Steiner, *The Religious Beliefs of Our Presidents* (Girard, KS:

Haldeman-Julius, 1936), 14–41, 160–72; and John E. Remsburg, *Six Historic Americans: Paine, Jefferson, Washington, Franklin, Lincoln, Grant, the Fathers and Saviors of Our Republic, Freethinkers* (New York: Truth Seeker, 1906).

14. Edwin Gaustad, *Faith of Our Fathers: Religion and the New Nation* (San Francisco: Harper and Row, 1987), 76.

15. B. F. Morris, *Christian Life and Character of the Civil Institutions of the United States* (Philadelphia: G. W. Childs, 1864), 166, 11; Philip Slaughter, *Christianity the Key to the Character and Career of Washington* . . . (Washington, DC: Judd and Detweiler, 1886), 2; William Meade, *Old Churches, Ministers and Families of Virginia*, 2 vols. (Philadelphia: J. B Lippincott, 1878), 2:243; Norman Vincent Peale, *One Nation under God* (Pawling, NY: Foundation for Christian Living, 1972), 14; quotations in that order.

16. Boller, *Religion*, 3–23, quotations from 5.

17. Pierard and Linder, *Civil Religion*, 71.

18. Mason L. Weems, *The Life of George Washington*, Marcus Cunliffe, ed. (Cambridge, MA: Harvard University Press, 1962), 181.

19. Boller, *Religion*, 10. Potts was not anywhere near the army encampment during the winter of 1777. See John C. Fitzpatrick, *The Spirit of the Revolution* (Boston: Houghton Mifflin, 1924), 88–89; Rupert Hughes, *George Washington, the Savior of the States, 1777–1781* (New York: W. Morrow, 1930), 270–77; and Samuel Eliot Morison, *The Young Man Washington* (Cambridge, MA: Harvard University Press, 1932), 38. See also W. Herbert Burk, *The Washington Window in the Washington Memorial Chapel, Valley Forge* (Norristown, PA: Norristown Press, 1926); J. Leroy Miller, "Where Washington Prayed: Thousands Now Will Pray," *American Magazine* 108 (Aug. 1929), 73–74; and Martin E. Marty, "Legends in Stained Glass," *CC* 93 (May 5, 1976), 447.

20. Albert R. Beatty, "Was Washington Religious?" *National Republic* 20 (Feb. 1933), 3.

21. In 1762, the Truro Parish of the Church of England elected Washington a vestryman, and twice during the next twelve years he also served as one of its churchwardens. In this role, he helped supervise the parish's finances, building projects, and daily operations and also oversaw civic matters such as constructing roads and caring for orphans. See Beatty, "Was Washington Religious?" 4–5, 28, and Part II, Mar. 1933, 18–19, 29, quotation from 29; Arthur B. Kinsolving, "The Religion of George Washington," *Historical Magazine of the Protestant Episcopal Church* 18 (Sept. 1949), 326–32. See also Frederick Conrad, "Washington: Christianity and the Moulding Power of His Character," *Lutheran Quarterly* 26 (1896), 89–115; John C. Fitzpatrick, *Washington as a Religious Man*, Pamphlet No. 5 of the series, "Honor to George Washington," Albert Bushnell Hart, ed. (Washington, DC: George Washington Bicentennial Commission, 1931); Francis Landon Humphreys, *George Washington, the Churchman* (Palm Beach, FL, 1932); John S. Littell, *Washington, Christian* (Keene, NH: Hampshire Art Press, 1913); "Washington as a Christian," *Presbyterian* 102 (Sept. 15, 1932), 4; and Vernon B. Hampton, *Religious Background of the White House* (Boston: Christopher, 1932), 330–37.

22. E.g., Peter Marshall and David Manuel, *The Light and the Glory* (Old Tappan, NJ: Revell, 1977); Tim LaHaye, *Faith of Our Founding Fathers* (Brentwood, TN: Wolgemunt and Hyatt, 1987); Verna Hall, *George Washington: The Character and Influence of One Man, A Compilation*, Dorothy Dimmick, ed. (San Francisco: Foundation for American Christian Education, 2000); and Benjamin Hart, *Faith and Freedom: The Christian Roots of American Liberty* (San Bernardino, CA: Here's Life, 1988).

23. Dorothy Twohig, "The Making of George Washington," in Warren R. Hofstra, ed., *George Washington and the Virginia Backcountry* (Madison, WI: Madison House, 1998), 19; Robert F. Jones, *George Washington: Ordinary Man, Extraordinary Leader* (New York: Fordham University Press, 2002), 27; Barry Schwartz, *George Washington: The Making of an American Symbol* (New York: Free Press, 1987), 175; James T. Flexner, *George Washington*, 4 vols. (Boston: Little, Brown, 1965–1972), 2:543; Alden, *Washington*, 217; Paul K. Longmore, *The Invention of George Washington* (Charlottesville: University Press of Virginia, 1999), 169; Pierard and Linder, *Civil Religion*, 74; quotations in that order. Cf. Flexner, *Indispensable Man*, 216; and Willard Sterne Randall, *George Washington: A Life* (New York: Henry Holt, 1997), 256. Joseph J. Ellis labels Washington "a lukewarm Episcopalian" and contends that he thought of God as "a distant, impersonal force" (*His Excellency George Washington* [New York: Alfred A. Knopf, 2004], 45, 151, quotations in that order).

24. David L. Holmes, *The Religion of the Founding Fathers* (Charlottesville, VA: Ash Lawn-Highland, 2003), 84. Paul Boller contends that to Washington, God "was an impersonal force" and insists that he never experienced "personal intimacy or communion" with God (*Religion*, 108–9, quotation from 108). These and other titles he employed all had "a vaguely impersonal, broadly benign, calmly rational flavor" (Gaustad, *Faith*, 77).

25. Holmes, *Founding Fathers*, 85.

26. Pierard and Linder, *Civil Religion*, 73.

27. Peter R. Henriques, "The Final Struggle between George Washington and the Grim King: Washington's Attitude toward Death and an After Life," in Don Higginbotham, ed., *George Washington Reconsidered* (Charlottesville: University Press of Virginia, 2001), 258.

28. E.g., Jones, *Washington*, 95.

29. Gregg Frazer, "The Political Theology of the American Founding" (paper presented at a Symposium on Religion and Politics, Calvin College, May 1, 2004), 1–2; first quotation from 1, second from 2.

30. See Kerry S. Walters, *The American Deists* (Lawrence: University Press of Kansas, 1992), 26–33, 41; Walters, *Elihu Palmer's "Principles of Nature"* (Wolfeboro, NH: Longwood Academic, 1990), 35, 114–15, 231–32; E. Graham Waring, ed., *Deism and Natural Religion: A Source Book* (New York: Frederick Ungar, 1967), x; and Peter Gay, comp., *Deism: An Anthology* (Princeton, NJ: D. Van Nostrand, 1968), 11, 42, 167–68, 176.

31. GW to James Anderson, Dec. 24, 1795, in John C. Fitzpatrick, ed., *The Writings of George Washington* (hereafter *WGW*), 37 vols. (Washington, DC: Government Printing Office, 1931–42), 34:407.

32. Samuel Miller, *Life of Samuel Miller*, 2 vols. (Philadelphia: Claxton, Remsen and Haffelfinger, 1869), 1:123. Many ministers sent Washington sermons dedicated to him that complimented his public service. He thanked them but very rarely commented on the substance of their sermons (Boller, *Religion*, 77). E.g., GW to Nathaniel Whitaker, Dec. 20, 1777, *WGW* 10:175; GW to Uzal Ogden, Aug. 5, 1779, *WGW* 16:51; GW to Israel Evans, Mar. 13, 1778, *WGW* 11:78; and GW to Jedidiah Morse, Feb. 28, 1799, *WGW* 37:140. Boller found only two letters where Washington actually commented on the substance of sermons, and in both cases he simply affirmed their doctrine as sound.

33. Garry Wills, *Cincinnatus: George Washington and the Enlightenment* (Garden City, NY: Doubleday, 1984), 23.

34. The name "Protestant Episcopal Church" was officially adopted in August 1783 and soon became widely accepted. See James Thayer Addison, *The Episcopal Church in the United States, 1789–1931* (New York: Charles Scribers' Sons, 1951), 57.

35. Helen Bryan, *Martha Washington: First Lady of Liberty* (New York: John Wiley, 2002), 35, 72–73, 133, 280.

36. George Washington Parke Custis, *Recollections and Private Memoirs of Washington...*, Benson J. Lossing, ed. (New York: Derby & Jackson, 1860), as quoted by Bryan, *Martha Washington*, 379. See also Margaret Conkling, *Memoirs of the Mother and Wife of Washington* (Auburn, NY: Derby, Miller, 1850).

37. Holmes, *Founding Fathers*, 79.

38. Before 1775, he usually attended the Pohick Church; after 1785, he normally worshiped at the Alexandria Church. See Philip Slaughter, *The History of Truro Parish* (Philadelphia: G. W. Jacobs, 1908), 97.

39. Boller, *Religion*, 29. Holmes, *Founding Fathers*, 79–80; Longmore, *Invention*, 130–31, 138; and John C. Fitzpatrick, *George Washington Himself* (Indianapolis, IN: Bobbs-Merrill, 1933), 130.

40. Holmes, *Founding Fathers*, 80–81. This is what his diary indicates. By contrast, several Continental Army officers testified long after the war that Washington regularly attended religious services and strictly observed the Sabbath.

41. See Dorothy Twohig, ed., *Papers of George Washington, Presidential Series*, 11 vols. (Charlottesville: University Press of Virginia, 1987–2000), 11:579–80.

42. Eleanor Parke Custis to Jared Sparks, Feb. 26, 1833, in Sparks, ed., *The Writings of George Washington*, 12 vols. (Boston: F. Andrews, 1837), 12:406; William White to B. C. C. Parker, Nov. 28, 1832, in Bird Wilson, *Memoir of Life of the Right Reverend William White* (Philadelphia: J. Kay, Jun. & Brother, 1839), 189. On Nelly's faith, see David Riblett, *Nelly Custis, Child of Mount Vernon* (Mount Vernon, VA; Mount Vernon Ladies' Association, 1993), 23 and passim.

43. See Arthur Lyon Cross, *The Anglican Episcopate and the American Colonies* (Hamden, CT: Archon, 1964), 36, 45, 88–112, 154–55, 219–20, 230–31, 248–58, 270–71; and Carl Bridenbaugh, *Mitre and Sceptre: Transatlantic Faiths, Ideas, Personalities, and Politics, 1689–1775* (New York: Oxford University Press, 1962), passim.

44. William White to Hugh Mercer, Aug. 15, 1835, in Wilson, *White*, 197.

45. James Abercrombie to Origen Bacheler, Nov. 29, 1831, *Magazine of American History* 13 (June 1885), 597. Washington allegedly feared that if he started taking Communion, the public would deem it "an ostentatious display of religious zeal arising altogether from his elevated station." See Boller, *Religion*, 33; and Holmes, *Founding Fathers*, 83.

46. Boller, *Religion*, 40. The quotation is from Eliphalet Nott Potter, *Washington a Model in His Library and Life* (New York: E. & J. B. Young, 1895), 181. Cf. Edward McGuire, *The Religious Opinions and Character of Washington* (New York: Harper & Brothers, 1836), 404.

47. George Washington, "Circular to the States," June 8, 1783, *WGW* 26:485; GW to John Rodgers, June 11, 1783, *WGW* 27:1. See also Rodgers to GW, May 30, 1783, George Washington Papers, Library of Congress (hereafter GWP), 1741–1799: Series 4, General Correspondence. 1697–1799.

48. Boller, *Religion*, 40. In addition, his library contained few popular religious works. See Longmore, *Invention*, 217; and Appleton P. C. Griffin, comp., *A Catalogue*

of the Washington Collection in the Boston Athenaeum (Boston: Boston Athenaeum, 1897), 497–503.

49. GW to Charles Thomson, Mar. 5, 1795, *WGW* 30:286.

50. McGuire, *Religious Opinions*, 404. See Daniel L. Dreisbach, "The 'Vine and Fig Tree' in George Washington's Letters: Reflections on a Biblical Motif in the Literature of the American Founding Era," unpublished essay. Dreisbach found nearly fifty references in Washington's letters and addresses to the phrase "vine and fig tree" as used in Micah 4:4. Washington cites the biblical language of converting "swords into plowshares" in at least four letters. He also refers several times to "war and rumors of war." He refers to Mt. 13:25ff in a May 31, 1776, letter to John Augustine Washington (*WGW* 5:93) and to Ps. 121:4 in a March 31, 1779 letter to James Warren (*WGW* 14:313). Washington's 1785 letter to the Marquis de Lafayette contains numerous biblical references, including the argument that Americans must settle the West to fulfill "the first and great commandment, *Increase and Multiply*" (July 25, 1785, *WGW* 28:206–7).

51. E.g., GW, "To the United Brethren of Wachovia, North Carolina," June 1, 1791, *PGW, Pres. Ser.* 8:226; GW to William Gordon, July 19, 1791, *PGW, Pres. Ser.* 8:356–57; GW to Hannah Washington, May 20, 1792, *PGW, Pres. Ser.* 10:403; and GW to Marquis de Lafayette, June 13, 1793, *WGW* 32:501.

52. GW, "To the Bishops of the Methodist Episcopal Church . . ." *PGW, Pres. Ser.* 2:411. See also GW, "To the General Assembly of the Presbyterian Church in the United States of America," May 1789, *PGW, Pres. Ser.* 2:420–21; GW, "To . . . the German Reformed Congregations in the United States," June 1789, ibid., 3:92–93; GW, "To the . . . Protestant Episcopal Church," Aug. 19, 1789, ibid., 3:497; and GW, "To the Congregational Ministers of the City of New Haven," Oct. 17, 1789, ibid., 4:198.

53. GW, "To the Inhabitants of Richmond . . . ," Aug. 1793, *Letter Books*, 30:135, in *Religious References in the Writings, Addresses, and Military Orders of George Washington* (Washington, DC: U.S. Bicentennial Commisison, 1932), 14. Cf. GW to Louis XVI, Mar. 14, 1792, *PGW, Pres. Ser.* 10:108; and GW to Louis XVI, Oct. 9, 1789, *PGW, Pres. Ser.* 4:152–53.

54. GW, "To the Clergy . . . residing in and near the City of Philadelphia," Mar. 1797, *Letter Books*, 31:282, in *Religious References*, 16. Cf. GW, "To the General Assembly of the PCUSA," 2:420; and GW, "To the Bishops of the Methodist Episcopal Church," *PGW*, 2:411.

55. The most significant were Joseph Reed, Tench Tilghman, David Cobb, Jonathan Trumbull Jr., and David Humphreys. Douglas Freeman argued that several of these writers were devout Christians who often added religious phrases to the public statements they drafted for him while he was commander in chief. See Freeman, *George Washington: A Biography*, 7 vols. (New York: Scribner, 1952), 2:387–88, 397; 5:443, 493–94, chap. 3, note 49. John C. Fitzpatrick, on the other hand, contended that Washington "dominated his correspondence" and thus was completely responsible for any statements issued in his name (*WGW* 1:xlv). Moreover, as other footnotes indicate, Washington's private letters are peppered with references to God's providence.

56. GW, "To the Massachusetts Legislature," Mar. 28, 1776, *WGW* 4:441–2; GW to Martha Custis, July 20, 1758, *WGW* 2:242; GW to Israel Putnam, Mar. 26, 1776, *WGW* 4:444; GW to Thomas Ruston, Aug. 31, 1788, *WGW* 30:79. See also Robert P. Hay, "Providence and the American Past," *Indiana Magazine of History* 65 (1969), 79–101. Writing to his wife after being appointed to lead the Continental Army, Washington confessed, "I shall rely . . . confidently on that Providence, which has heretofore

preserved and been bountiful to me...." (June 18, 1775, *WGW* 3:294). Cf. GW to Landon Carter, May 30, 1778, *WGW* 11:492; and GW to Joseph Reed, Jan. 14, 1776, *WGW* 4:243.

57. E.g., GW to Landon Carter, Mar. 25, 1776, *WGW* 4:433–34; and GW to John Augustine Washington, Mar. 31, 1776, *WGW* 4:447–48.

58. GW to William Gordon, May 13, 1776, in Philander D. Chase, ed., *Papers of George Washington, Revolutionary War Series*, 13 vols. (Charlottesville: University Press of Virginia, 1985–) 4:286.

59. GW to Gen. Thomas Nelson, Aug 20, 1778, *WGW* 12:343.

60. GW, "To the Inhabitants of Princeton and... the President and Faculty of the College," Aug. 25, 1783, *WGW* 27:116. Cf. GW, "To the Synod of the Dutch Reformed Church in North America," Oct. 1789, *PGW, Pres. Ser.* 4:263–64: "the glory should be ascribed to the manifest interposition of an over-ruling Providence."

61. GW to John Armstrong, Mar. 11, 1792, *PGW, Pres. Ser.* 10:86.

62. GW to James Anderson, July 25, 1798, *WGW* 36:365; GW to Jonathan Trumbull, July 18, 1775, *WGW* 3:344; quotations in that order. See also GW to Thomas Nelson, Aug. 3, 1788, *WGW* 30:34; GW to Bryan Fairfax, Mar. 1, 1778, *WGW* 11:3; and GW to William Pearce, Mar. 25, 1794, *WGW* 33:375.

63. General Orders, Oct. 18, 1777, *WGW* 9:391; General Orders, May 5, 1778, *WGW* 11:354; GW to Nelson, *WGW* 12:343; GW to John Laurens, Oct. 13, 1780, *WGW* 20:173 (quotation); General Orders, Oct. 20, 1781, *WGW* 23:247.

64. GW to Rev. Bryan Fairfax, Mar. 6, 1793, *WGW* 32:376.

65. GW, "To the Magistrates and Military Officers of Schenectady," June 30, 1782, *WGW* 24:390.

66. GW, "To the Mayor, Corporation, and Citizens of Alexandria," Apr. 16, 1789, *WGW* 30:287; GW to General Philip Schuyler, Jan. 27, 1776, *WGW* 4:281, quotations in that order. Cf. General Orders, May 2, 1778, *WGW* 11:343.

67. GW to Jonathan Trumbull, Sept. 6, 1778, *WGW* 12:406. Washington assured Lafayette that "the great Ruler of events will not permit the happiness of many millions to be destroyed" (Sept. 10, 1791, *PGW, Pres. Ser.* 8:516).

68. GW to John Smith et al., Nov. 28, 1796, *WGW* 35:294.

69. Because people were "ignorant of the comprehensive schemes [God] Intended" (GW to John Robinson, Sept. 1, 1758, *PGW, Col. Ser.* 5:432–43), they should simply trust Providence without perplexing themselves to "seek for that, which is beyond human ken" (GW to David Humphreys, Mar. 23, 1793, *WGW* 32:398). See also GW to Jonathan Trumbull, May 15, 1784, *WGW* 27:399; GW to William Pearce, Dec. 28, 1793, *WGW* 33:218; GW to William Pearce, Sept. 14, 1794, *WGW* 33:499; GW to Henry Knox, Mar. 2, 1797, *WGW* 35:409; GW to Thaddeus Kosciuszko, Aug. 31, 1797, *WGW* 36:22; and GW to Bryan Fairfax, Jan. 20, 1799, *WGW* 37:94.

70. GW to Samuel H. Parsons, Apr. 23, 1777, *WGW* 7:456; Washington, "Farewell Orders to the Armies of the United States," Nov. 2, 1783, *WGW* 27:223.

71. GW to Jonathan Boucher, Aug. 15, 1798, *WGW* 36:414; GW to James McHenry, July 31, 1778, *WGW* 30:30.

72. GW to Joseph Reed, Mar. 7, 1776, *WGW* 4:380.

73. GW to Jonathan Williams, Mar. 2, 1795, *WGW* 34:130. Cf. GW to Tench Tilghman, Apr. 24, 1783, *WGW* 26:358 and GW to Henry Knox, Feb. 20, 1784, *PGW, Conf. Ser.*, 1:136–39.

74. GW to Jonathan Trumbull, Aug. 18, 1776, *WGW* 5:453. Cf. GW, "To the Officers and Soldiers of the Pennsylvania Associators," Aug. 8, 1776, *WGW* 5:398; GW to

Parsons, *WGW* 7:456; GW to Thomas Nelson, Nov. 8, 1777, *WGW* 10:28; and GW, "To the Trustees of the Public School of Germantown," Nov. 6, 1793, *WGW* 33:149.

75. GW to James McHenry, July 18, 1782, *WGW* 24:432.

76. John G. West Jr., "George Washington and the Religious Impulse," in Gregg and Spalding, eds., *Patriot Sage*, 271.

77. General Orders, July 9, 1776, *WGW* 5:245.

78. *WGW* 11:343.

79. Boller, *Religion*, 74–75, quotation from 74. Speaking to the Delaware chiefs in 1779, Washington declared, "You do well to wish to learn our arts and ways of life, and above, all the religion of Jesus Christ" (May 12, 1779, *WGW* 15:55).

80. GW to Israel Putnam, Oct. 19, 1777, *WGW* 9:401.

81. GW, "To the Directors of the Society of the United Brethren for Propagating the Gospel among the Heathen," July 1789, *Letter Books* 29:34 in *Religious References*, 9. See also GW to James Jay, Jan. 25, 1785, *PGW, Conf. Ser.* 2:291–93; GW to the Countess of Huntingdon, June 30, 1785, *PGW, Conf. Ser.* 3:92–93; and GW to John Ettwein, May 2, 1788, *WGW* 29:489. A close associate of John and Charles Wesley, the English countess named Washington an executor for creating an American foundation to finance a college to train missionaries to Indians. Ettwein participated in the Moravian Society for Propagating the Gospel among the Heathen. Washington hoped southern Indians would allow missionaries to live among them to teach them the "great duties of religion, and morality" ("To Commissioners to the Southern Indians," Aug. 29, 1789, *PGW, Pres. Ser.* 3:558). In his 1791 address to Congress, Washington commended teaching Indians the "principles of religion and philanthropy" (GW to the U.S. Senate and House of Representatives, Oct. 25, 1791, *PGW, Pres. Ser.* 9:112.

82. Boller, *Religion*, 70.

83. John E. Ferling, *The First of Men: A Life of George Washington* (Knoxville: University of Tennessee Press, 1988), 359. Cf. Richard Norton Smith, *Patriarch: George Washington and the New American Nation* (New York: Houghton Mifflin, 1993), 279.

84. Ellis, *His Excellency*, 271. He was "fully attuned to the specter of evil in the world," Ellis adds (272).

85. GW to the Secretary for Foreign Affairs, Aug. 1, 1786, *WGW* 28:502–3; GW to John Banister, April 21, 1778, *WGW* 11:286, quotations in that order. "We must take the passions of Men as Nature has given them," he added.

86. GW to John Jay, May 18, 1786, *PGW, Conf. Ser.* 4:55–56 (first quotation); GW to the Secretary for Foreign Affairs, *WGW* 28:502 (second quotation).

87. George Washington, "Undelivered First Inaugural Address: Fragments," section 34, April 1789, *PGW, Pres. Ser.* 2:166 (first quotation); GW to the Earl of Buchan, May 26, 1794, *WGW* 33:383 (second and third quotations); Washington, "Farewell Address," in *George Washington: Writings* (New York: Library of America, 1997), 971 (fourth quotation). Henry Wiencek argues: "Washington's view of human nature was pragmatic—and pessimistic" (*An Imperfect God: George Washington, His Slaves, and the Creation of America* [New York: Farrar, Straus and Giroux, 2003], 231).

88. E.g., GW to David Humphreys, Oct. 10, 1787, *PGW, Conf. Ser.* 5:365–66 and GW to Mary Butler, Jan. 6, 1792, *PGW, Pres. Ser.* 9:386.

89. GW to George Augustine Washington, Jan. 27, 1793, *WGW* 32:315–16.

90. Henriques, "Final Struggle," 259–62, quotation from 262.

91. GW to Robert Morris, May 5, 1787, *WGW* 29:211; GW to Henry Knox, Jan. 10, 1788, *WGW* 29:378; GW to Henry Knox, Feb. 25, 1787, *WGW* 29:170. He declared that he was searching for Elysium, the blissful dwelling place of virtuous people after death. He believed his stepdaughter Patsy Custis had gone "into a more happy & peaceful abode" and that his mother had departed to a "happier place." See GW to Lafayette, Mar. 25, 1787, *WGW* 29:184; GW to James McHenry, Mar. 25, 1799, *WGW* 37:158; GW to Jonathan Trumbull, Jan. 5, 1784, *WGW* 27:294; GW to Burrell Bassett, June 20, 1773; *PGW, Col. Ser.* 9:243–44; and GW to Betty Washington Lewis, Sept. 13, 1789, *PGW, Pres. Ser.* 4:32. He hoped that God would compensate people for their good works (To the Presbyterian Ministers of Massachusetts and New Hampshire, Nov. 2, 1789, *PGW, Pres. Ser.* 4:274).

92. See Lester Cappon, ed., *The Adams-Jefferson Letters*, 2 vols. (Chapel Hill: University of North Carolina Press, 1959), 2:486; Albert Henry Smyth, ed., *The Writings of Benjamin Franklin*, 10 vols. (New York: Macmillan, 1907), 10:84; Albert Ellery Bergh, ed., *The Writings of Thomas Jefferson*, 20 vols. (Washington, DC: Thomas Jefferson Memorial Association, 1904–5), 17:v; and Daniel Edwin Wheeler, ed., *Life and Writings of Thomas Paine*, 10 vols. (New York: V. Parke, 1908), 6:2. Martha Washington expected to be reunited with her husband in heaven. See MW to Jonathan Trumbull, Jan. 15, 1800, in Joseph E. Fields, ed., *Worthy Partner: The Papers of Martha Washington* (Westport, CT: Greenwood, 1994), 339.

93. GW to Burgess Ball, Sept. 22, 1799, W*GW* 37:372.

94. Henriques, "Final Struggle," 257, 259. See Daniel Blake Smith, *Inside the Great House: Planter Family Life in Eighteenth-Century Chesapeake Society* (Ithaca, NY: Cornell University Press, 1980), 265.

95. GW to Tobias Lear, March 30, 1796, *WGW* 35:5. Cf. GW to Burwell Bassett, Apr. 24, 1796, *WGW* 35:27; and GW to William A. Washington, Feb. 27, 1798, *WGW* 35:174.

96. Henriques, "Final Struggle," 252. See also Henriques, *He Died as He Lived: The Death of George Washington* (Mount Vernon, VA: Ladies of Mount Vernon, 2000).

97. Flexner, *Indispensable Man*, 26, 36.

98. GW to Richard Washington, Oct 20, 1761, *PGW, Col. Ser.* 7:80.

99. See David L. Holmes, ed., *A Nation Mourns: Bishop James Madison's Memorial Eulogy on the Death of George Washington* (Mount Vernon, VA: Mount Vernon Ladies' Association, 1999).

100. Tobias Lear, "Journal account," Mount Vernon Ladies' Association. Lear's original journal and "diary" account are available at http://gwpapers.virginia.edu/ project/exhibit/mourning/lear.html. For a discussion of the accuracy of his account, see Henriques, "Final Struggle," 266.

101. Weems, *Life of Washington*, 168. Cf. John Marshall, *The Life of George Washington . . .*, 5 vols. (New York: C. P. Wayne, 1804–7), 319; David Ramsay, *The Life of George Washington . . .* (London: Longman, Hurst, Rees, & Orme, 1807), 319; and Sparks, ed., *Writings*, 12:525.

102. Albanese, *Sons*, 180. E.g., Thomas Condie, *Biographical Memoirs of Gen. George Washington . . .* (Lexington, KY: Downing and Phillips, 1815), 265–66; and Caroline M. Kirkland, *Memoirs of Washington* (New York: D. Appleton, 1857), 457.

103. Marshall, "Eulogy," 297.

104. Henriques, "Final Struggle," 263 (quotation). See also Schwartz, *Washington*, 184–85; Ellis, *His Excellency*, 151; Douglass Adair, *Fame and the Founding Fathers: Essays*, Trevor Colbourn, ed. (Indianapolis, IN: Liberty Fund, 1998); GW to James

Tilghman, June 5, 1786, *PGW, Conf. Ser.* 4:96; and GW to Sarah Cary Fairfax, Sept. 25, 1758, *PGW, Col. Ser.* 6:42.

105. GW to Fairfax, *WGW* 37:94–5.

106. GW, "General Assembly of the PCUSA," 2:420.

107. Philadelphia Protestant Clergy to George Washington, Mar. 3, 1797, *WGW* 35:416–17. One of these clergymen, Ashbel Green, a chaplain in the House of Representatives during Washington's tenure in office and later president of the College of New Jersey, declared that he had no doubt about Washington's orthodoxy. See Ashbel Green, "Jefferson's Papers," *Christian Advocate* 8 (1830), 308.

108. Sparks, ed., *Writings*, 12:399–411. Sparks concluded, "If a man, who spoke, wrote, and acted as a Christian through a long life . . . is not to be ranked among the believers of Christianity, it would be impossible to establish the point by any train of reasoning" (411). See also Washington Irving, *Life of George Washington*, 8 vols. (New York: G. P. Putnam, 1857), 1:162, 397; 2:362–63; 8:123.

109. Marshall, *Washington*, 5:375.

110. Samuel Langdon to GW, July 8, 1789, *PGW, Pres. Ser.* 3:149–51. Few, if any, dared to lament publicly what some did privately: Washington was never "explicit in his profession of *faith in, and dependence on* the finished Atonement of our glorious Redeemer" (Benjamin Tallmadge to Manasseh Cutler, as quoted in Charles Swain Hall, *Benjamin Tallmadge, Revolutionary Soldier and American Businessman* [New York: Columbia University Press, 1943], 167). On February 1, 1800, Jefferson wrote in his journal: "Dr. [Benjamin] Rush told me that he had it from Ash[bel] Green that when the clergy addressed Genl. Washington, on his departure from the govmt, it was observed in their consultation that he had never, on any occasion, said a word to the public which shewed a belief in the Xn. religion, and they thot they should so pen their address as to force him at length to disclose publicly whether he was a Christian or not. . . . However, he observed, the old fox was too cunning for them. He answered every article of their address particularly, except that, which he passed over without notice. . . . Gouverneur Morris . . . has often told me that Genl. Washington believed no more of that system [Christianity] than he himself did" (Jefferson, *PTJ* 31:352–53).

111. GW to Samuel Langdon, Sept. 28, 1789, *PGW, Pres. Ser.* 4:104.

112. Quoted in Hall, *Benjamin Tallmadge*, 161. Cf. Miller, *Life*, 1:123.

113. White to B. C. C. Parker, Dec. 21, 1832, in Wilson, *White*, 193.

114. "Excerpts from Jared Sparks' Journal for 1829–31," *VMHB* 60 (Apr. 1952), 263.

115. Boller, *Religion*, 89–91.

116. Gordon S. Wood, "The Greatness of George Washington," in Higginbotham, ed., *Washington Reconsidered*, 312.

117. Quoted in Cunliffe, *Man and Monument*, 31.

118. Wood, "Greatness," 324.

119. Wills, *Cincinnatus*, 23.

120. Wills, *Cincinnatus*; Wood, "Greatness," 311–16.

121. Wood, "Greatness," 324.

122. Jefferson insisted that his fellow Virginian's "integrity was most pure, his justice the most inflexible I have ever known." He truly was "in every sense of the words, a wise, a good and a great man" (to Dr. Walter Jones, Jan. 2, 1814, in Paul Leicester Ford, ed., *The Writings of Thomas Jefferson* [New York: G. P. Putnam's Sons, 1892–99], 10 vols. 9:448–49).

123. See Letitia Baldridge, ed., *George Washington's Rules of Civility & Decent Behavior in Company and Conversation* (Mount Vernon, VA: Mount Vernon Ladies' Association, 1989).

124. Schwartz, *Washington*, 163–65, 167; quotation from 167.

125. E.g., David Tappan, *A Discourse Delivered...* (Charlestown, MA: Samuel Etheridge, 1800), 28; Jeremiah Smith, *An Oration upon the Death of General George Washington* (Exeter, NH: Henry Raulet, 1800), 70; John Fitch, *A Sermon Delivered... as a Tribute... for... General George Washington* (Peachah, VT: Farley and Goss, 1800); Elisha Pick, "Oration," in *The Washingtonian* (Baltimore: Samuel Sawyer, 1800), 198, 203. See also Barry Schwartz, "Vengeance and Forgiveness," *School Review* 86 (1978), 65–68.

126. Irving, *Washington*, 5:301.

127. Phillips Paxton, "A Sermon Delivered at Chelsea," quoted by William A. Bryan, *George Washington in American Literature, 1775–1865* (New York: Columbia University Press, 1952), 59; James K. Paulding, *A Life of Washington*, 2 vols. (New York: Harper and Brothers, 1835), 2:230–31; John Carroll, *A Discourse on George Washington* (Baltimore: Warner and Hanna, 1800), 14.

128. Schwartz, *Washington*, 171.

129. Gaustad, *Faith*, 77–78.

130. James Smylie, "The President as Republican Prophet and King: Clerical Reflections on the Death of Washington," *JCS* 18 (Spring 1976), 247.

131. Jonathan Sewall, *An Eulogy on the Late General Washington...* (Portsmouth, NH: William Treadwell, 1799), 17–18. Cf. Moses Cleaveland, *An Oration... [on] General George Washington* (Windham, CT: John Byrne, 1800), 14; and Abraham Clarke, *A Discourse Occasioned by the Death of General George Washington* (Providence, RI, n. p., 1800), 8.

132. John Croes, *A Discourse... to the Memory of General George Washington* (Philadelphia: John Ormrod, 1800), 25. Cf. Smith, *An Oration*, 76.

133. Timothy Dwight, *A Discourse... on the Character of George Washington...* (New Haven, CT: Thomas Green and Son, 1800), 28. See also Jonathan Huse, *A Discourse Occasioned by the Death of... Washington* (Wiscasset, ME: n.p., 1800), 11; and Thaddeus Mason Harris, *A Discourse... after... the Death of Washington* (Charlestown, MA: Samuel Etheridge, 1800), 13. "At all times" Washington "acknowledged the providence of God, and never was he ashamed of his redeemer," America's first Methodist bishop Francis Asbury confidently declared. John Carroll praised Washington's "Christian piety" and his affirmation that a "superintending providence" governed all human events (Asbury, *The Journal* of Charleston, SC, Jan. 4, 1800; Carroll, *Discourse*, 5).

134. Glenn A. Phelps, "The President as Moral Leader: George Washington in Contemporary Perspective," in Ethan Fishamen, William D. Pederson, and Mark J. Rozell, eds., *George Washington: Foundation of Presidential Leadership and Character* (Westport, CT: Praeger, 2001), 4. See also Schwartz, *Washington*.

135. GW to Alexander Hamilton, Aug. 28, 1788, in *WGW* 30:67.

136. Phelps, "Moral Leader," 16.

137. Matthew Spalding and Patrick J. Garrity, *A Sacred Union of Citizens: George Washington's Farewell Address and the American Character* (Lanham, MD: Rowman and Littlefield, 1996), 13; General Orders, July 9, 1776, *WGW* 5:245, quotations in that order.

138. Washington, "Circular to the States," *WGW* 26:485–86.

139. Ibid., 26:496.

140. GW to Henry Knox, Apr. 1, 1789, *PGW*, *Pres. Ser.* 2:2–3.

141. Spalding and Garrity, *Sacred Union*, 31, 10, 12, quotations from 10.

142. E.g., GW to John Armstrong, Apr. 25, 1788, *WGW* 29:465.

143. George Washington, "First Inaugural Address," *WGW* 30:294–95.

144. Phelps, "Moral Leader," 9; Flexner, *Indispensable Man*, 30, 157.

145. Wood, "Greatness," 321.

146. Flexner labels Washington a "passionate gambler" (*Indispensable Man*, 30, 51, 248).

147. Phelps, "Moral Leader," 9–10.

148. Flexner, *Indispensable Man*, 367.

149. Bernard Knollenberg, *George Washington: The Virginia Period, 1732–1775* (Durham, NC: Duke University Press, 1964), 78.

150. GW to Sarah Cary Fairfax, May 16, 1798, *WGW* 36:263.

151. Alden, *Washington*, 73–79, quotation from 79. See also Phelps, "Moral Leader," 8; Randall, *Washington*, 168–71.

152. We will never know if he loved Fairfax while president, Glenn Phelps argues, because he did not want to jeopardize the reputation he had crafted or "the health of the nascent republic" he had spent the previous fifteen years "winning, building, and nurturing" ("Moral Leader," 8).

153. Bryan, *Martha Washington*, 272–73. Washington frequently took Ford hunting and fishing and to Christ Church. Ford was set free around 1806 and in 1829 inherited 160 acres from John Augustine Washington's son. See also Linda Allen Bryant, *I Cannot Tell a Lie: The True Story of George Washington's African Descendants* (Writer's Showcase Press, 2001); http://www.westfordlegacy.com; and Wiencek, *Imperfect God*, 292–310. On whether Washington was sterile, see Flexner, *Indispensable Man*, 367; Wiencek, *Imperfect God*, 309; and Ellis, *His Excellency*, 42.

154. Edward Rushton to GW, July 1796, as quoted in Dorothy Twohig, "'That Species of Property': Washington's Role in the Controversy over Slavery," in Higginbotham, ed., *Washington Reconsidered*, 115. Cf. Warner Mifflin to GW, Dec. 12, 1792, *PGW*, *Pres. Ser.* 11:502–8.

155. Twohig, "'Species of Property,'" 116.

156. For the larger context, see also Fritz Hirschfeld, *George Washington and Slavery: A Documentary Portrayal* (Columbia: University of Missouri Press, 1997); and Joseph J. Ellis, *Founding Brothers: The Revolutionary Generation* (New York: Alfred A. Knopf, 2001), 81–119.

157. Ferling, *First of Men*, 475.

158. GW to Daniel Parker, April 28, 1783, *WGW* 26:364; GW to Benjamin Harrison, May 6, 1783, *WGW* 26:401–2; GW to Guy Carleton, May 6, 1783, *WGW* 26: 405–8.

159. Ferling, *First of Men*, 475.

160. GW to Lafayette, Apr 5, 1783 and May 10, 1786, *WGW* 26:300; 28:424, quotations in that order. See Ferling, *First of Men*, 475; Flexner, *Washington*, 4:112–25; Paul Leicester Ford, *The True George Washington* (Philadelphia, J. B. Lippincott Co., 1903), 153–54; and Wiencek, *Imperfect God*, 260–64.

161. GW to Robert Morris, Apr. 12, 1786, *WGW* 28:408.

162. Smith, *Patriarch*, 149.

163. E.g., GW to Anthony Whiting, Nov. 4, Dec. 9, 1792 and Jan. 6, 1793, *WGW* 32:205, 256–57, 292–96; Ferling, *First of Men*, 477–78.

164. Twohig, " 'Species of Property,' " 117, 122.

165. Ferling, *First of Men*, 474.

166. GW to David Stuart, June 15, 1790, *WGW* 31:52. See also GW to Stuart, Mar. 28, 1790, *WGW* 31:30; and Thomas E. Drake, *Quakers and Slavery in America* (New Haven, CT: Yale University Press, 1950), 100–13.

167. Ferling, *First of Men*, 479.

168. Twohig, " 'Species of Property,' " 124–31; first quotation from 124, second from 127. See also Wiencek, *Imperfect God*, 264–72.

169. Dennis J. Pogue, "George Washington and the Politics of Slavery," *Historic Alexandria Quarterly*, Spring/Summer 2003, 1, 6–8; and John P. Riley, " 'Written with My Own Hand': George Washington's Last Will and Testament," *Virginia Cavalcade* 48 (1999), 168–77. Washington's will directed that all his slaves be set free only when Martha died.

170. Richard Allen, "Address," *Philadelphia Gazette*, 1799, in Charles H. Wesley, *Richard Allen, Apostle of Freedom* (Washington, DC: Association Publishers, 1935), 12–3.

171. Wiencek, *Imperfect God*, 356–58, 135, 359; first quotation from 135, second from 359.

172. Washington, "First Inaugural Address," 30:293, 296; first three quotations from 293, last one from 296.

173. Pierard and Linder, *Civil Religion*, 77.

174. Saxe Commins, ed., *The Basic Writings of George Washington* (New York: Random House, 1948), 616.

175. George Washington, Thanksgiving Proclamation, Oct. 3, 1789, *WGW* 30:428.

176. Pierard and Linder, *Civil Religion*, 78.

177. GW, "General Assembly of the PCUSA," 2:420–21.

178. Washington, "Farewell Address," 971.

179. Catherine Albanese, *America, Religion and Religions* (Belmont, CA: Wadsworth, 1999), 295–97, 308–9.

180. Gaustad, *Faith*, 7. See also Pierard and Linder, *Civil Religion*, 78.

181. Albanese, *Sons*, 143.

182. See Bernard Mayo, *Myths and Men: Patrick Henry, George Washington, Thomas Jefferson* (Athens: University of Georgia Press, 1959), 337–56; Albanese, *Sons*, 143–81; Dixon Wecter, *The Hero in America* (Ann Arbor, MI: University of Michigan Press, 1963), 99–147; and Gaustad, *Faith*, 71–84.

183. Albanese, *Sons*, 144, 145, quotations in that order; Schwartz, *Washington*, 9.

184. Gaustad, *Faith*, 78.

185. Ezra Stiles, "The United States Elevated to Glory and Honor (May 8, 1783)," in John W. Thornton, *The Pulpit of the American Revolution* (New York: Da Capo, 1970 [1860]), 448.

186. E.g., George Duffield, "A Sermon Preached in the Third Presbyterian Church...," in Frank Moore, ed., *The Patriot Preachers of the American Revolution* (New York: Charles T. Evans, 1862), 361–62.

187. "The Godlike Washington," *Massachusetts Centinel*, Nov. 7, 1789, in John P. Kaminski and Jill Adair McCaughan, eds., *A Great and Good Man: George Washington in the Eyes of His Contemporaries* (Madison, WI: Madison House, 1989), 160–61; Daniel George, "An Ode for Independence," *Gazette of the United States*, July 1, 1789, in ibid., 131; "Our Saviour and Our Guide," Philadelphia *Federal Gazette*, Aug. 20, 1789, in

ibid., 137; "Next unto the Trinity," Keane *New Hampshire Recorder*, Sept. 9, 1790, in ibid., 143–44.

188. Thomas Baldwin, *A Sermon...Occasioned by the Death of General George Washington* (Boston: Manning and Loring, 1800), 26.

189. Augustin Smith Clayton in *Register of Debates in Congress...*, 14 vols. (Washington, DC: Gales & Seaton, 1825–37), 2nd Congress, Vol. 8, Pt. 2, Feb. 13, 1832, 1797.

190. Albanese, *Sons*, 151. Harvard and Yale bestowed honorary doctorates upon him, actors extolled him on stage, and eight biographies of Washington appeared by 1799.

191. Benjamin Rush to William Marshall, Sept. 15, 1798, in Lyman Butterfield, ed., *Letters of Benjamin Rush*, 2 vols. (Princeton, NJ: Princeton University Press, 1951), 2:807.

192. Schwartz, *Washington*, 98, 223–24, notes 16–17.

193. Smylie, "Republican Prophet," 234. Smylie called my attention to many of the eulogies in this section.

194. E.g., James Madison, *A Discourse on the Death of George Washington...* (Richmond, VA: T. Nicolson, 1800), passim; Patrick Allison, *A Discourse...Dedicated to...General George Washington* (Baltimore: W. Pechin, 1800), 24; and Smith, *An Oration*, 41.

195. Smylie, "Republican Prophet," 251.

196. Ibid., 251. They compared Washington with Moses, Joshua, and three of Israel's greatest kings—David, Hezekiah, and Josiah. See Jonathan Elmer, *An Eulogy on the Character of General George Washington* (Trenton, NJ: G. Craft, 1800), 4; William Linn, *A Funeral Eulogy Occasioned by the Death of George Washington...* (New York: Isaac Collins, 1800), 12, 35; Samuel Macclintock, *An Oration...[on] George Washington* (Portsmouth, NH: Charles Peirce, 1800), 6, 10–11; Samuel Miller, *A Sermon... Occasioned by the Death of General George Washington* (New York: T & J Swords, 1800), 6; Samuel Spring, *God the Author of Human Greatness...* (Newburyport, MA: Edmund M. Blunt, 1800), 11–16; Isaac S. Keith, *National Affliction and National Consolation...* (Charleston, SC: W. P. Young, 1800). See Mark A. Noll, "The Image of the United States as a Biblical Nation, 1776–1865," in Nathan O. Hatch and Mark A. Noll, eds., *The Bible in America: Essays in Cultural History* (New York: Oxford University Press, 1982), 41, 45. Margaret B. Stillwell, "Checklist of Eulogies and Funeral Orations on the Death of George Washington, December 1799–February 1800," *Bulletin of the New York Public Library* 20 (May 1916), 403–41, lists 440 eulogies. See also Clifford K. Shipton, *The American Bibliography of Charles Evans*, vol. 13: *1799–1800* (Worcester, MA: American Antiquarian Society, 1955), 347–79.

197. See Hay, "American Moses," 780–91, who called my attention to many of the sources in this section.

198. Quotation from Schwartz, *Washington*, 29. E.g., Hay, "American Moses" and Harry P. Kerr, "The Character of Political Sermons Preached at the Time of the American Revolution," Ph.D. dissertation, Cornell University, 1962.

199. Samuel Miller, *A Sermon Delivered in the New Presbyterian Church...* (New York: F. Childs, 1795), 6; Cyprian Strong, *A Discourse Delivered at Hebron...* (Hartford, CT: Hudson and Goodwin, 1799), 6.

200. Isaac Braman, *An Eulogy on the Late General George Washington...* (Haverhill, MA: Seth H. Moore, 1800), 5. Cf. Thaddeus Fiske, *A Sermon Delivered...at the Second Parish in Cambridge...* (Boston: James Cutler, 1800), 10.

201. Dwight, *Discourse*, 28; Alexander MacWhorter, *A Funeral Sermon...for the Universally Lamented General Washington...* (Newark, NJ: Jacob Hasley, 1800), 9.

202. E.g., Peter Folsom, IV, *An Eulogy on Geo. Washington...* (Gilmanton, NH, 1800), 6.

203. Madison, *Discourse*, 5; Uzal Ogden, *Two Discourses, Occasioned by the Death of General George Washington...* (Newark, NJ: Mattias Day, 1800), 22; Richard Furman, *Humble Submission to Divine Sovereignty...* (Charleston, SC: W. P. Young, 1800), 11.

204. John J. Carle, *A Funeral Sermon...* (Morristown, NJ, 1800), 10.

205. E.g., Huse, *Discourse*, 11.

206. *Proceedings of the Town of Charlestown...in Respectful Testimony...of the Late George Washington* (Charlestown, 1800), a sermon delivered by Jedidiah Morse, 35. See also Huse, *Discourse*, 7–9.

207. Carle, *Funeral Sermon*, 13, 10–11; Frederick W. Hotchkiss, *An Oration Delivered at Saybrook...* (New London, CT: S. Green, 1800), 13; Joseph Buckminster, *Religion and Righteousness the Basis of National Honor and Prosperity...* (Portsmouth, NH: Charles Peirce, 1800), 8–10; Fiske, *Sermon*, 10–11.

208. Hay, "American Moses," 789.

209. Bryan, *George Washington*, 118.

210. Ruth Miller Elson, *Guardians of Tradition: American Schoolbooks of the Nineteenth Century* (Lincoln: University of Nebraska Press, 1964), 194.

211. See Stuart Leibiger, *Founding Friendship: George Washington, James Madison, and the Creation of the American Republic* (Charlottesville: University Press of Virginia, 1999).

212. Brookhiser, *Founding Father*, 139–51. Critics of these orders, like New England Congregationalists, denounced them as irreligious and generally ignored Washington's participation or claimed he did not truly understand Masonic beliefs and practices.

213. GW to J. A. Washington, *WGW* 5:93.

214. GW to Watson and Cassoul, State of New York, Aug 10, 1782, *WGW* 24:497.

215. E.g., GW to Trumbull, *WGW* 27:399; Washington, "Proposed Address to Congress," Apr. 1789, *WGW* 30:301.

216. Washington, "Circular to the States," 26:496.

217. Washington, "First Inaugural Address," 30:294.

218. Washington, Thanksgiving Proclamation, 30:428 (quotation); GW, "To...the United Episcopal Churches of Christ Church and St. Peters," Mar. 2, 1797, *WGW* 35:410–11.

219. Washington, "Farewell Address," 972.

220. GW, "General Assembly of the PCUSA," 2:420.

221. Washington, "To the Clergy...of Philadelphia," 31:282.

222. Washington, Thanksgiving Proclamation, *WGW* 30:427–28.

223. General Orders, May 15, 1776, *WGW* 5:43.

224. General Orders, Dec. 17, 1777, *WGW* 10:168.

225. E.g., General Orders, May 5, 1778, *WGW* 11:354.

226. E.g., General Orders, Aug. 3, 1776, *WGW* 5:367.

227. West, "Religious Impulse," 279.

228. GW to Knox, *WGW* 35:409; GW to Benedict Arnold, Sept. 14, 1775, *WGW* 3:492, quotations in that order.

229. Washington, "First Inaugural Address," 30:294.

230. GW to Theodorick Bland, Apr. 4, 1783, *WGW* 26:294.

231. Washington, "Undelivered First Inaugural Address," section 23, 2:163.

232. Washington, "Farewell Address," first two quotations from 972, third from 975. See also Matthew Spalding, "The Command of Its Own Fortunes: Reconsidering Washington's Farewell Address," in Fishamen, Pederson, and Rozell, eds., *George Washington*, 26.

233. The best discussions of Washington's views of this subject and pivotal role in promoting religious freedom are Boller, *Religion*, 116–62, and Boller, "George Washington and Religious Liberty," *WMQ*, 3rd ser., 17 (1960), 486–506.

234. Washington, "Proposed Address to Congress," 30:299.

235. GW to Lafayette, Aug. 15, 1787, *PGW, Conf. Ser.*, 5:295.

236. Instructions to Colonel Benedict Arnold, Sept. 14, 1775, *WGW* 3:495–96.

237. GW to Benedict Arnold, Sept. 14, 1775, *WGW* 3:492.

238. General Orders, Nov. 5, 1775, *WGW* 4:65.

239. See John Murray, *The Life of Rev. John Murray, Preacher of Universal Salvation*...(Boston: Universalist Publishing House, 1869), 316–17; General Orders, Sept. 17, 1775, *WGW* 3:497; GW to the President of Congress, June 8, 1777, *WGW* 8:203–4; Boller, *Religion*, 126–28.

240. GW, "To the Pennsylvania Council of Safety," Jan. 19, 1777 and Jan. 29, 1777, *WGW* 7:35, 79.

241. Boller, *Religion*, 131–37; James Sharpless, *A History of Quaker Government in Pennsylvania, 1682–1783*, 2 vols. (Philadelphia: T. S. Leach, 1900), 2:168; Richard Bauman, *For the Reputation of Truth*...(Baltimore: Johns Hopkins University Press, 1971), 190–206. As president, Washington admired the relationship Quakers had with Indians and appreciated the support of Philadelphia Quakers for most of the policies of his administration. See also Paul F. Boller Jr., "George Washington and the Quakers," *The Bulletin of Friends Historical Association* 49 (Autumn 1960), 79–80.

242. GW, "To the...Dutch Church at Kingston, New York," Nov. 16, 1782, *WGW* 25:346–47.

243. GW, "To...the Reformed German Congregation of New York," Nov. 27, 1783, *WGW* 26:249. Cf. GW, "To Hackensack, New Jersey Dutch Reform Church, Nov. 10, 1783," GWP, 1741–1799: Series 4, General Correspondence. 1697–1799.

244. GW to George Mason, Oct. 3, 1785, *WGW* 28:285.

245. Boller, *Religion*, 122. On the factors that contributed to Washington's views of liberty of conscience, see Lemuel Call Barnes, "George Washington and Freedom of Conscience," *Journal of Religion* 12 (Oct. 1932), 493–525.

246. GW, "Methodist Episcopal Church," 2:411–12.

247. GW to Sir Edward Newenham, Oct. 20, 1792, *PGW, Pres. Ser.* 11:246. Cf. GW to Newenham, June 22, 1792, *PGW, Pres. Ser.*, 10:493.

248. Boller, *Religion*, 139. These addresses praised Washington's service to the nation, pledged support for his government, asked God to bless him, and expressed hope that religion and morality would flourish. See also Boller, "George Washington and Religious Liberty," 486–506; and Schwartz, *Washington*, 85.

249. GW, "To the Protestant Episcopal Church," Aug. 19, 1789, *PGW, Pres. Ser.* 3:497.

250. GW, "To the United Baptist Churches of Virginia," May 1789, *PGW, Pres. Ser.* 2:423–24, quotations from 424. See also Isaac Backus to GW, Nov. 15, 1790, *PGW, Pres. Ser.* 6:658–60.

251. GW, "To the Society of Quakers," Oct. 1789, *PGW, Pres. Ser.* 4:266. While citizens must obey the laws of the land and fulfill their social obligations, he added,

they were "responsible only to their Maker for the religion, or modes of faith, which they may prefer or profess." Cf. GW, "To the Society of Quakers," Mar. 1790, *PGW, Pres. Ser.* 5:296–97.

252. *Gazette of the United States*, May 6 to May 9, 1789, 1; June 10, 1789.

253. GW, "To Roman Catholics in America," *PGW, Pres. Ser.* 5:299–301.

254. Savannah Jews to GW, May 1790, *PGW, Pres. Ser.* 5:449n; GW, "To the Hebrew-Congregation of the City of Savannah," May 1790, *PGW, Pres. Ser.* 5: 448–49.

255. Newport Jews to GW, Aug. 17, 1790, *PGW, Pres. Ser.* 6:286; GW, "To the Hebrew Congregation in Newport, Rhode Island," *PGW, Pres. Ser.* 6:285.

256. Ministers and Ruling Elders . . . in Massachusetts and New Hampshire to GW, Oct. 28, 1789, *PGW, Pres. Ser.* 4:275–76. They rejoiced that this constitutional defect had been partially remedied by Washington's piety and devotion in observing the Sabbath and worshiping God and through his thanksgiving proclamation.

257. GW, "To the Presbyterian Ministers of Massachusetts and New Hampshire," Nov. 2, 1789, *PGW, Pres. Ser.* 4:274. Similarly, in January 1789, John Armstrong protested in a letter to the president that the Constitution contained no "Solemn acknowledgement of the One living & true God" (Jan. 27, 1789, *PGW, Pres. Ser.*, 1:254–55, quotations from 254).

258. GW to Robert Sinclair, May 6, 1792, *PGW, Pres. Ser.* 10:359; GW, "To the Members of the New [Swedenborgian] Church at Baltimore," Jan. 1793, *Letter Books*, 30:110 in *Religious References*, 14; General Orders, Apr. 18, 1783, *WGW* 26:336, quotations in that order. Cf. GW, "To the Members of the Volunteer Association and Other Inhabitants of the Kingdom of Ireland . . . ," Dec. 2, 1783, *WGW* 27:254; GW to Rev. Francis Adrian Van der Kemp, May 28, 1788, *WGW* 29:504.

259. Samuel Knox, *A Funeral Oration* . . . (Fredericktown, MD: Matthias Bartgis, 1800), 10–12.

260. Ferling, *First of Men*, 461. See also Freeman, *Washington*, 7:319.

261. *New York Journal*, as quoted in Smith, *Patriarch*, 288. See also George A. Billias, *George Washington's Opponents* (New York: William Morrow, 1969).

262. Smith, *Patriarch*, 132.

263. *Aurora*, Oct. 17, 1796.

264. Leibiger, *Founding Friendship*, 222; Schwartz, *Washington*, 187; Ellis, *His Excellency*, 38.

265. John Adams to the Continental Congress, Feb. 18, 1777, in Morton Borden, ed., *George Washington* (Englewood Cliffs, NJ: Prentice Hall, 1969), 75.

266. Adams to Rush, Apr. 4, 1790 in *Old Family Letters*, series A (Philadelphia: M. B. Lippincott, 1892), 1:55.

267. Ferling, *First of Men*, 480.

268. E.g., Carroll, *Discourse*, 20.

269. Marshall, "Eulogy," 288, 290, 295; quotation from 288.

270. E.g., Martin Lipset, "George Washington and the Founding of Democracy," *Journal of Democracy* 9 (October 1998), 24–38; David Abshire, *The Character of George Washington* (Washington: Center for the Study of the American Presidency, 1999); and Flexner, *Indispensable Man*.

271. Leibiger, *Founding Friendship*, 224.

272. GW to Francois Jean, Comte de Chastellux, April 25, 1788, GWP, 1741–1799: Series 2 *Letterbooks*.

273. Ferling, *First of Men*, 483. See also Frank T. Reuter, *Trials and Triumphs: George Washington's Foreign Policy* (Fort Worth: Texas Christian University Press, 1983).

274. See Spalding, "Command," 20–31.

275. See Samuel Flagg Bemis, "Washington's Farewell Address: A Foreign Policy of Independence," in *American Historical Review*, 39 (Jan. 1934), 250–68.

276. Washington, "Farewell Address," 971–72, quotation from 972.

CHAPTER 2

1. This assault continued long after Jefferson's death. See Merrill D. Peterson, *The Jefferson Image in the American Mind* (New York: Oxford University Press, 1960), 127–29, 165, 219, 243, 301, 447. See, for example, John C. Kilgo, *A Study of Thomas Jefferson's Religious Belief* (Charlotte, NC, n.p., 1900).

2. Thomas Robins, *Courier of New Hampshire* (Concord), Dec. 19, 1800, as quoted in Nobel E. Cunningham Jr., *In Pursuit of Reason: The Life of Thomas Jefferson* (Baton Rouge: Louisiana State University Press, 1987), 230.

3. Roger Butterfield, *The American Past: A History of the United States from Concord to Hiroshima, 1775–1945* (New York: Simon and Schuster, 1947), 32.

4. Abigail Adams to Mary Cranch, Feb. 7, 1801, in Stewart Mitchell, ed., *New Letters of Abigail Adams, 1788–1801* (Boston: Houghton Mifflin, 1947), 266. Adams argued that Jefferson believed religion was useful only when it served political purposes.

5. John Quincy Adams, *Memoirs of John Quincy Adams: Comprising Portions of his Diary from 1795 to 1848*, 12 vols., Charles Francis Adams, ed. (Freeport, NY: Books for Libraries Press, 1969), Jan. 11, 1831, 8:270–71; quotations from 270. Adams also accused Jefferson of having "loose morals" (271). See also *Memoirs*, July 26, 1845, 12:206.

6. See Frank Shuffelton, *Thomas Jefferson: A Comprehensive Annotated Bibliography of Writings about Him, 1826–1980* (New York: Garland, 1983) and Shuffelton, *Thomas Jefferson, 1981–1990: An Annotated Bibliography* (New York: Garland, 1992).

7. James Parton, *Life of Thomas Jefferson, Third President of the United States* (Boston: J. R. Osgood, 1874), as quoted by Merrill D. Peterson, *Thomas Jefferson and the New Nation* (New York: Oxford University Press, 1970), 31.

8. Helpful analyses of Jefferson's life, thought, and legacy include Peterson, *Jefferson*; Merrill Peterson, ed., *Thomas Jefferson: A Reference Biography* (New York: Scriber's, 1986); Cunningham, *In Pursuit of Reason*; Peter S. Onuf, ed., *Jeffersonian Legacies* (Charlottesville: University Press of Virginia, 1993); Joseph J. Ellis, *American Sphinx: The Character of Thomas Jefferson* (New York: Alfred A. Knopf, 1997); and R. B. Bernstein, *Thomas Jefferson* (New York: Oxford University Press, 2003).

9. TJ to Adams, in Lester Cappon, ed., *The Adams-Jefferson Letters*, 2 vols. (Chapel Hill: University of North Carolina Press, 1959), 2:506. Cf. TJ to Miles King, Sept. 26, 1814, in Andrew A. Lipscomb and Albert Ellery Bergh, eds., *The Writings of Thomas Jefferson*, 20 vols. (Washington, DC: Thomas Jefferson Memorial Association, 1905) (hereafter *WTJ*), 14:196: "Our particular principles of religion are a subject of accountability to our God alone."

10. TJ to Charles Clay, Jan. 29, 1815, *WTJ* 6:412. Cf. TJ to Benjamin Rush, May 31, 1813, The Thomas Jefferson Papers, Library of Congress (hereafter TJP): Religion was a subject on which he had been "most scrupulously reserved."

11. Edwin S. Gaustad, *Sworn on the Altar of God: A Religious Biography of Thomas Jefferson* (Grand Rapids, MI: Eerdmans, 1996), xiii–xiv.

12. According to his grandson, Thomas Jefferson Randolph, if family members asked Jefferson's opinions on religious subjects, he typically refused to give it and told them they must "study assiduously" the matter themselves and devise their own views (quoted in Henry S. Randall, *The Life of Thomas Jefferson*, 3 vols. [New York, 1857], 3:672).

13. See Thomas E. Buckley, *Church and State in Revolutionary Virginia, 1776–1787* (Charlottesville: University Press of Virginia, 1977); Buckley, "After Disestablishment: Thomas Jefferson's Wall of Separation in Antebellum Virginia," *JSH* 61 (Aug. 1995), 445–80; Merrill D. Peterson and Robert C. Vaughan, eds., *The Virginia Statute for Religious Freedom: Its Evolution and Consequences in American History* (New York: Cambridge University Press, 1988); and Ronald Hoffman and Peter J. Albert, eds., *Religion in a Revolutionary Age* (Charlottesville: University Press of Virginia, 1994).

14. E.g., TJ to Margaret Bayard Smith, Aug. 6, 1816, *WTJ* 15:60; TJ to John Page, June 25, 1804, *WTJ* 11:32.

15. Jefferson's personal library contained 650 books on religion, ethics, philosophy, biblical study, and church history. See Charles B. Sanford, *Thomas Jefferson and His Library: A Study of His Literary Interests and of the Religious Attitudes Revealed by Relevant Titles in His Library* (Hamden, CT. Archon, 1977).

16. Eugene R. Sheridan, "Liberty and Virtue: Religion and Republicanism in Jeffersonian Thought," in James Gilbreath, ed., *Thomas Jefferson and the Education of a Citizen* (Washington, DC: Library of Congress, 1999), 242–43.

17. Ibid., 257.

18. Gaustad, *Sworn*, xiii. Important works include Edward M. Calish, "Jefferson's Religion," in *WTJ* 17:i–xi; J. Leslie Hall, "The Religious Opinions of Thomas Jefferson," *Sewanee Review* 21 (Apr. 1913), 164–76; William D. Gould, "The Religious Opinions of Thomas Jefferson," *Mississippi Valley Historical Review* 20 (Sept. 1933), 191–208; Royden J. Mott, "Sources of Jefferson's Ecclesiastical Views," *CH* 3 (1934), 267–84; George Harmon Knoles, "The Religious Ideas of Thomas Jefferson," *Mississippi Valley Historical Review* 30 (Sept. 1943), 187–204; Wilder Foote, *Thomas Jefferson: Champion of Religious Freedom, Advocate of Christian Morals* (Boston: Beacon, 1947); Daniel Boorstin, *The Lost World of Thomas Jefferson* (Boston: Beacon, 1948), 151–66; Robert M. Healey, *Jefferson on Religion in Public Education* (New Haven, CT: Yale University Press, 1962); Robert A. Brent, "The Jeffersonian Outlook on Religion," *Southern Quarterly* 5 (1967), 417–32; Elliott K. Wicks, "Thomas Jefferson—A Religious Man with a Passion for Religious Freedom," *Historical Magazine of the Protestant Episcopal Church* 36 (1967), 271–83; Constance Bartlett Schulz, "The Radical Religious Ideas of Thomas Jefferson and John Adams: A Comparison," Ph.D. dissertation, University of Cincinnati, 1973; William B. Huntley, "Jefferson's Public and Private Religion," *South Atlantic Quarterly* 79 (1980), 286–301; Charles B. Sanford, *The Religious Life of Thomas Jefferson* (Charlottesville: University Press of Virginia, 1984); David L. Holmes, *The Religion of the Founding Fathers* (Charlottesville, VA: Ash-Lawn Highland, 2003), 96–106; and Thomas E. Buckley, "The Religious Rhetoric of Thomas Jefferson," in Daniel L. Dreisbach, Mark D. Hall, and Jeffry H. Morrison, eds., *The Founders on God and Government* (Lanham, MD: Rowman and Littlefield, 2004), 53–82.

19. Sanford, *Religious Life*, preface. Jefferson did not systematically develop his theological convictions. They must be culled from his Syllabus, "Bible," addresses, letters, *Autobiography*, and published works.

20. On Anglicanism in Virginia, see George M. Brydon, *Virginia's Mother Church*, 2 vols. (Richmond, VA: Richmond Historical Society, 1947, 1952).

21. Charles B. Sanford, "The Religious Beliefs of Thomas Jefferson," in Garrett Ward Sheldon and Daniel L. Dreisbach, eds., *Religion and Political Culture in Jefferson's Virginia* (Lanham, MD: Rowman and Littlefield, 2000), 61; Sanford, *Religious Life*, 93; Gould, "Religious Opinions," 198. Jefferson especially liked the Psalms. See TJ to John Adams, Oct. 13, 1813, *WTJ* 13:392 and TJ to Thomas Jefferson Smith, Feb. 21, 1825, *WTJ* 16:110–11. For Anglican faith and practice in Virginia during Jefferson's formative years, see John K. Nelson, *A Blessed Company: Parishes, Parsons, and Parishioners in Anglican Virginia, 1690–1776* (Chapel Hill: University of North Carolina Press, 2002), 205–7, 211–17.

22. Gould, "Religious Opinions," 197. His account books record many donations to congregations, chapels, ministers, and missionaries. See Jefferson's *Memorandum Books: Accounts, with Legal Records and Miscellany, 1767–1826*, James A. Bear Jr. and Lucia C. Stanton, eds., 2 vols. (Princeton, NJ: Princeton University Press, 1997). See also Jefferson, "Manuscript in Subscription to Support a Clergyman in Charlottesville," Feb. 1777, in Julian Boyd et al., eds., *The Papers of Thomas Jefferson*, 31 vols. to date (Princeton, NJ: Princeton University Press, 1950–) (hereafter *PTJ*), 2:6.

23. On Clay, see William Meade, *Old Churches, Ministers and Families of Virginia*, 2 vols. (Baltimore: Genealogical Pub., 1966), 2:48–51, 61.

24. Gaustad, *Sworn*, 13.

25. Dumas Malone, *Jefferson and His Time*, 6 vols. (Boston: Little, Brown, 1948–61), 4:199; James T. Hutson, *Religion and the Founding of the American Republic* (Washington, DC: Library of Congress, 1998), 84–93.

26. See Foote, *Champion*, 7–8.

27. TJ to Justin Pierre Plumard Derieux, July 25, 1788, *PTJ* 13:418.

28. Gaustad, *Sworn*, 14.

29. Sanford, *Religious Life*, 100–1, quotations in that order.

30. E.g., TJ to George Washington, Dec. 31, 1793, *WTJ* 9:279; TJ to John Page, Aug. 30, 1795, TJP; TJ to Thomas Paine, Mar. 18, 1801, *WTJ* 10:224–25; TJ to Charles Thomson, Dec. 25, 1808, *WTJ* 12:218; TJ to John Garland Jefferson, Jan. 25, 1810, *WTJ* 12:355; and TJ to James Maury, Apr. 25, 1812, *WTJ* 13:149. Dozens of other examples could be provided.

31. TJ to Meriwether Lewis, June 20, 1803, Instructions, TJP.

32. TJ to William Hunter, Mar. 11, 1790, *WTJ* 8:7. Cf. TJ to John Adams, June 12, 1812, *WTJ* 13:156.

33. TJ to Gouverneur Morris, Oct. 15, 1792, *WTJ* 8:420.

34. TJ to Edward Coles, Aug. 25, 1814, in TJP.

35. E.g., TJ to Archibald Stuart, Aug. 8, 1811, *WTJ* 13:72; and TJ to James Madison, June 6, 1812, *WTJ* 13:155.

36. TJ to Caesar A. Rodney, Feb. 10, 1810, *WTJ* 12:359.

37. Douglas Wilson, ed., *Jefferson's Literary Commonplace Book* (Princeton, NJ: Princeton University Press, 1989), 24–25.

38. Randall, *Jefferson*, 3:553–61; Stuart Gerry Brown, *Thomas Jefferson* (New York: Washington Square Press, 1966), 199–200; Sanford, *Religious Life*, 8. Huntley argues that Jefferson penned no prayers, poetry, or psalms that expressed an intense religious feeling ("Jefferson's Public and Private Religion," 288).

39. Peterson, *Jefferson*, 961.

40. TJ to Thomas Cooper, Nov. 2, 1822, *WTJ* 15:404.

41. Garrett Ward Sheldon, *The Political Philosophy of Thomas Jefferson* (Baltimore: Johns Hopkins University Press, 1991), 126. See also TJ to William Crawford, Jan. 5, 181, *WTJ* 19:252.

42. Herbert E. Sloan, *Principle and Interest: Thomas Jefferson and the Problem of Debt* (New York: Oxford University Press, 1995), 197–201.

43. TJ to M. John de Neufville, Dec. 13, 1818, *WTJ* 15:178. Cf. TJ to Benjamin Waterhouse, June 26, 1822, *WTJ* 15:383; and TJ to Charles Yancey, Jan. 6, 1816, TJP.

44. Gould, "Religious Opinions," 196; Randall, *Jefferson*, 3:555.

45. See Adrienne Koch, *The Philosophy of Thomas Jefferson* (Chicago: Quadrangle, 1964), 15, 17–18, 20, 52; Karl Lehman, *Thomas Jefferson, American Humanist* (Chicago: University of Chicago Press, 1965), 122, 478.

46. Gaustad, *Sworn*, 25.

47. Peterson, *Jefferson*, 45–46 (quotations); Randall, *Jefferson*, 203.

48. Gaustad, *Sworn*, 21. On the Enlightenment, see Peter Gay, *The Enlightenment: The Rise of Modern Paganism* and *The Enlightenment: The Science of Freedom* (New York: Alfred A. Knopf, 1966, 1969); Henry F. May, *The Enlightenment in America* (New York: Oxford University Press, 1976); and Henry Steele Commager, *The Empire of Reason: How Europe Imagined and America Realized the Enlightenment* (Garden City, NY: Doubleday, 1977). Jefferson called Locke, Newton, and Bacon "the three greatest men the world had ever produced." See TJ to Benjamin Rush, Jan 16, 1811, in Paul Leicester Ford, ed., *The Writings of Thomas Jefferson* (New York: G. P. Putnam's Sons, 1892–99), 10 vols. (hereafter, Ford, *WTJ*) 9:295–96.

49. See Douglas L. Wilson, "Jefferson and Bolingbroke: Some Notes on the Question of Influence," in Sheldon and Dreisbach, eds. *Religion and Political Culture*, 107–18; Koch, *Philosophy*, 9–14. Jefferson largely adopted Bolingbroke's rejection of metaphysics, belief in reason as the final arbiter of knowledge, argument that the clergy had corrupted Christianity, and skepticism about the Bible's historical accuracy. See Willard Sterne Randall, *Thomas Jefferson: A Life* (New York: Henry Holt, 1993), 85–86.

50. TJ to John Adams, Aug. 22, 1813, *WTJ* 13:352.

51. Gaustad, *Sworn*, 112–13. Jefferson had a lower opinion of biblical miracles than Priestley and repudiated his belief in Christ's resurrection. Jefferson wrote Priestley of "the pleasure I had in the perusal" of his *Socrates and Jesus Compared* (Apr. 9, 1803, *WTJ* 10:376). See also Ira V. Brown, "The Religion of Joseph Priestley," *Pennsylvania History* 24 (Apr. 1957), 85–100.

52. Sanford, *Religious Life*, 85.

53. Thomas Jefferson, *Notes on the State of Virginia*, William Peden, ed. (Chapel Hill: University of North Carolina Press, 1955), 159.

54. TJ to Peter Carr, Aug. 10, 1787, *WTJ* 6:258.

55. Gaustad, *Sworn*, 28.

56. TJ to King, *WTJ* 14:196. Cf. TJ to John F. Watson, May 17, 1814, *WTJ* 14:136.

57. TJ to William Carver, Dec. 4, 1823, Ford, *WTJ* 10:285. Cf. TJ to John Adams, Aug. 15, 1820, *WTJ* 15:275–76; TJ to Carr, *WTJ* 6:258–60.

58. Gaustad, *Sworn*, 32–33.

59. TJ to Carr, Aug. 10, 1787, Ford, *WTJ* 6:257.

60. TJ to John Adams, Apr. 11, 1823, *WTJ* 15:426–27. See Charles A. Miller, *Jefferson and Nature: An Interpretation* (Baltimore: Johns Hopkins University Press, 1988).

61. Gaustad, *Sworn*, 38.

62. Healey identified twenty-six different terms Jefferson used for God (*Public Education*, 27–28).

63. TJ to John Adams, Apr. 8, 1816, *WTJ* 14:469; TJ to Priestley, *WTJ* 10:375.

64. TJ to Derieux, *PTJ* 13:418.

65. TJ to Adams, Aug. 22, 1813, *A-J Letters*, 2:368. "Had you and I been forty days with Moses on Mount Sinai," Adams responded, and were told that "one was three and three, one, we might not have had the courage to deny it, but we could never have believed it" (Adams to TJ, Sept. 14, 1813, ibid., 2:373).

66. Thomas Jefferson, "Notes on Religion," Ford, *WTJ* 2:96.

67. TJ to Jared Sparks, Nov. 4, 1820, *WTJ* 15:288.

68. Sheridan, "Liberty and Virtue," 245.

69. TJ to Ezra Stiles Ely, June 25, 1819, *WTJ* 15:203 (first quotation); TJ to King, *WTJ* 14:197 (second quotation).

70. TJ to Ely, *WTJ* 15:203–4.

71. TJ to Adams, *WTJ* 15:427.

72. Gaustad, *Sworn*, 37.

73. Thomas Jefferson, "First Inaugural Address," Mar. 4, 1801, *WTJ* 3:320, 323.

74. Thomas Jefferson, "First Annual Message," Dec. 8, 1801, *WTJ* 3:327.

75. Thomas Jefferson, "Second Inaugural Address," Mar. 4, 1805, *WTJ* 3:383. He then invited citizens to join in him in prayer that God would "enlighten the minds of your servants, guide their councils, and prosper their measures, that whatever they do, shall result in your good, and shall secure to you the peace, friendship, and approbation of all nations."

76. Sanford, *Religious Life*, 57.

77. Jefferson, "First Inaugural Address," *WTJ* 3:318–23.

78. Gilbert Chinard, *The Literary Bible of Thomas Jefferson* (Baltimore: Johns Hopkins University Press, 1928), 59–60.

79. E.g., TJ to Samuel Kercheval, July 12, 1816, *WTJ* 15:42.

80. TJ to David Barrow, May 1, 1815, *WTJ* 14:297. Cf. TJ to Samuel Adams, Feb. 26, 1800, *WTJ* 10:154.

81. TJ to Stephen Cross, Mar. 28, 1809, *WTJ* 16:352. Cf. TJ to Society of Tammany . . . , Feb. 29, 1808, *WTJ* 16:303.

82. TJ to Benjamin Rush, Sept. 23, 1800, TJP.

83. E.g., TJ to Governor Dunsmore, June 12, 1775, Ford, *WTJ* 1:459; TJ to George Thacher, Jan. 26, 1824, Ford, *WTJ* 10:289; and TJ to de Marbois, *WTJ* 15:130.

84. TJ to Adams, *WTJ* 15:426–27.

85. Jefferson, "First Inaugural Address," *WTJ* 3:320.

86. E.g., TJ to John Adams, Aug. 10, 1815, *A-J Letters*, 2:454; TJ to Walter Jones, Mar. 5, 1810, *WTJ* 12:373; and TJ to John Langdon, Mar. 5, 1810, *WTJ* 12:379.

87. Sanford, *Religious Life*, cites as examples (218): TJ to the Earl of Buchan, July 10, 1803, *WTJ* 10:400; Jefferson, Reply to Republican Young Men of New London, Feb. 24, 1809, *WTJ* 16:339–40; Jefferson, Reply to Delegates of Massachusetts, Mar. 28, 1809, *WTJ* 16:352; and Jefferson, "Second Inaugural Address," *WTJ* 3:383.

88. Sanford, *Religious Life*, 144.

89. TJ to Derieux, *PTJ* 13:418.

90. TJ to William Short, Aug 4, 1820, *WTJ* 15:261; TJ to Adams, *A-J Letters*, 2:594.

91. TJ to George Logan, Nov. 12, 1816, *WTJ* 12:42.

92. TJ to Priestley, *WTJ* 10:334; TJ to Short, *WTJ* 15:259; TJ to Sparks, *WTJ* 15:288; TJ to Thacher, Ford, *WTJ* 10:288. In his letter to Priestley, Jefferson identified four possible views of Christ's person: "a member of the God-head," "a being of eternal pre-existence," a "man divinely inspired," and "the Herald of truths reformatory of the religions of mankind." He argued that all views of Jesus should be tolerated but clearly preferred the latter.

93. TJ to William Short, Oct. 31, 1819, *WTJ* 15:219–20; TJ to Waterhouse, *WTJ* 15:383–84. In the letter to Short, Jefferson repudiated all aspects of Christ's divinity: his immaculate conception, role in creating the world, miraculous powers, resurrection and visible ascension, and "corporeal presence in the Eucharist." He also rejected "the Trinity, original sin, atonement, regeneration, [and] election" (220–21).

94. TJ to William Short, Apr. 13, 1820, *WTJ* 15:244; TJ to Short, *WTJ* 15:257. Cf. Wilson, ed., *Jefferson's Commonplace Book*, 42–43.

95. Chinard, *Literary Bible*, 57.

96. TJ to George Thacher, Ford, *WTJ* 10:288–89; TJ to Logan, *WTJ* 12:42. On Jesus as a great reformer, see TJ to Priestley, *WTJ* 10:374; TJ to Samuel Kercheval, Jan. 19, 1810, *WTJ* 12:345; TJ to Short, *WTJ* 15:220; and TJ to Adams, *WTJ* 15:430.

97. TJ to Waterhouse, *WTJ* 15:383.

98. Sanford, *Religious Life*, 127; the quotation is from TJ to Priestley, *WTJ* 10:374–75. Benjamin Rush argued that Jefferson affirmed "the divine mission of the Savior of the world" but "did not believe that He was the Son of God the way most Christians believed it" (*Autobiography* [Princeton, 1948], 151–52).

99. TJ to Benjamin Rush, Apr. 21, 1803, *WTJ* 10:379–80.

100. Gaustad, *Sworn*, 37.

101. Peterson, *Jefferson*, 55.

102. TJ to Thomas Law, June 13, 1814, *WTJ* 14:142–43. While Jefferson exalted human reason as a divine gift, he differentiated it from moral sense and seemed to place even more confidence in virtue than in reasoning. See TJ to Maria Cosway, Oct. 12, 1786, *WTJ* 5:430ff.; TJ to Rush, Apr. 21, 1803, *WTJ* 10:386; and Huntley, "Jefferson's Faith," 295–96. On Jefferson's view of human nature, see Koch, *Philosophy*, 113–23.

103. TJ to Short, *WTJ* 15:223–24.

104. TJ to King, *WTJ* 14:197–98.

105. Cf. TJ to de Nemours, *WTJ* 14:491; TJ to Rodney, *WTJ* 12:359 and TJ to John Adams, Oct. 14, 1816, *WTJ* 15:76.

106. Gaustad, *Sworn*, 188.

107. TJ to Law, *WTJ* 14:142; TJ to de Nemours, *WTJ* 14:489.

108. TJ to John Adams, May 5, 1817, *A-J Letters*, 2:512. See also Eugene R. Sheridan, "Introduction," in Dickinson W. Adams, ed., *Jefferson's Extracts from the Gospels* (Princeton, NJ: Princeton University Press, 1983); and Hall, "Religious Opinions," 164–76.

109. Sheldon, *Political Philosophy*, 104. See TJ to Rush, *WTJ* 10:379–80; TJ to John Adams, Oct. 12, 1813, *A-J Letters* 2:384–85; TJ to William Short, Oct. 31, 1816, *WTJ* 15:220.

110. TJ to Edward Dowse, Apr. 19, 1803, *WTJ* 10:377; TJ to Ely, *WTJ* 15:203; TJ to Rush, *WTJ* 10:379–80.

111. TJ to Adams, *A-J Letters* 2:384.

112. TJ to Moses Robinson, Mar. 23, 1801, *WTJ* 10:237.

113. TJ to Charles Clay in 1814, as cited by Gaustad, *Sworn*, 211.

114. Gaustad, *Sworn*, 180.

115. Ibid., 163–64, 169, quotations from 163.

116. Thomas Jefferson, report of the Commissioners for the University of Virginia, Aug. 1–4, 1818, in Saul K. Padover, *The Complete Jefferson* (hereafter *CJ*) (Freeport, NY: Books for Libraries Press, 1969), 1104. See Jennings L. Wagoner Jr., "That Knowledge Most Useful to Us: Thomas Jefferson's Concept of Utility in the Education of Republican Citizens" in James Gilreath, ed., *Thomas Jefferson and the Education of a Citizen* (Washington, DC: Library of Congress, 1999), 130.

117. Thomas Jefferson, "Freedom of Religion at the University of Virginia," Oct. 7, 1822, *CJ*, 957.

118. TJ to Cooper, *WTJ* 15:404–5.

119. See Randall, *Jefferson*, 3:540–47; Foote, *Champion*, 67–68; Koch, *Philosophy*, 33, 38; Sanford, *Religious Life*, 141–71.

120. He told John Adams in 1820 that ignorance about the subject was "the softest pillow upon which I can lay my head" (Mar. 14, 1820, *WTJ* 15:240–1). Cf. TJ to Isaac Story, Dec. 5, 1801, *WTJ* 10:299.

121. While affirming the concept of immortality, Jefferson rejected the concept of a bodily resurrection.

122. Adams, ed., *Jefferson's Extracts*, 334; Jefferson, "Syllabus," in TJ to Rush, *WTJ* 10:385.

123. TJ to Law, *WTJ* 14:142–43. Jefferson insisted that after death, people would be judged by the "scales of eternal justice" (TJ to Charles Thomson, Jan. 29, 1817, Ford, *WTJ* 10:76).

124. TJ to John Page, July 15, 1763, *WTJ* 4:10. Jefferson regularly advised young people to live in such a way as to reap a heavenly reward (e.g., TJ to Martha Jefferson, Dec. 11, 1783, *PTJ* 6:380–81; and TJ to Smith, *WTJ* 16:110).

125. TJ to Page, *WTJ* 11:31.

126. TJ to Adams Nov 13, 1818, *A-J Letters*, 2:529.

127. Sanford, *Religious Life*, 172.

128. E.g., TJ to John Adams, June 1, 1822, *A-J Letters*, 2:577–78; TJ to Adams, June 27, 1822, ibid., 2:580–81; Adams to TJ, May 12, 1820, ibid., 2:565; Adams to TJ, June 11, 1822, ibid., 2:579; TJ to Adams, Jan. 8, 1825, ibid., 2:606. He also told Maria Cosway and Lafayette that he looked forward to being reunited with them in the afterlife (Dec. 27, 1820, *WTJ* 18:309–10; Feb. 14, 1815, Ford, *WTJ* 9:510).

129. TJ to William Canby, Sept. 18, 1813, *WTJ* 13:377.

130. TJ to Thomas B. Parker, May 15, 1819, *TJP*.

131. TJ to Canby, *WTJ* 13:377.

132. TJ to King, *WTJ* 14:197–98. Cf. Jefferson, "Notes on Religion," Ford, *WTJ* 2:100.

133. Randall, *Jefferson*, 3:101–2, 543–47.

134. TJ to Priestley, *WTJ* 10:375.

135. Ibid. Ellis (*American Sphinx*, 215) claims that Jefferson made sure that his essay was leaked to Republican friends to rebut "the anti-Christian system . . . imputed to me by those who know nothing of my opinions" (TJ to Rush, Ford, *WTJ* 8:223).

136. Rush to TJ, May 5, 1803 in L. H. Butterfield, ed., *Letters of Benjamin Rush*, 2 vols. (Princeton, NJ: Princeton University Press, 1951), 2:864.

137. Some German scholars had already begun this work, but Jefferson could not read German.

138. TJ to Adams, *A-J Letters*, 381–83.

139. Rush to TJ, Aug. 29, 1804, *TJP*.

140. Sheridan, "Liberty and Virtue," 253–57; quotations from 253.

141. TJ to Charles Thomson, Jan. 9, 1816, *WTJ* 14:385; Peterson, *Jefferson*, 960.

142. TJ to Smith, *WTJ* 15:60.

143. Edwin S. Gaustad, *Faith of Our Fathers: Religion and the New Nation* (San Francisco: Harper and Row, 1987), 8.

144. TJ to Short, *WTJ* 15:219–20.

145. Gaustad, *Sworn*, 132, 145, quotations in that order.

146. TJ to Timothy Pickering, Feb. 27, 1821, *WTJ* 15:323. See also TJ to Rush, *WTJ* 10:383–84; TJ to Short, *WTJ* 15:244–45; and TJ to Short, *WTJ* 15:257–59.

147. TJ to Kercheval, *WTJ* 12:345; TJ to Pickering, *WTJ* 15:323. Cf. TJ to Peter Carr, Aug. 10, 1787, *WTJ* 6:260–61; TJ to Short, *WTJ* 15:259–60.

148. Sanford, *Religious Life*, 132.

149. Fred C. Luebke, "The Origins of Thomas Jefferson's Anti-Clericalism," *Church History* 32 (1963), 344, 353. E.g., TJ to Waterhouse, *WTJ* 15:384; and TJ to Smith, *WTJ* 15:60.

150. Sheldon, *Political Philosophy*, 106. E.g., TJ to Adams, May 5, 1817, *A-J Letters*, 1:52; TJ to P. H. Wendover, Mar. 13, 1815, *WTJ* 14:279; and TJ to Waterhouse, *WTJ* 15:384.

151. TJ to Kercheval, *WTJ* 12:345–46. Cf. TJ to Canby, *WTJ* 13:377–78; TJ to John Cartwright, June 5, 1824, *WTJ* 16:48–51.

152. TJ to Elbridge Gerry, Mar. 29, 1801, *WTJ* 10:254.

153. TJ to Adams, *A-J Letters* 2:512.

154. TJ to Thomas Whittemore, June 5, 1822, *WTJ* 15:374.

155. TJ to Thomas Leiper, Jan. 21, 1809, *WTJ* 12:237.

156. TJ to Smith, *WTJ* 15:60.

157. TJ to Adams, *WTJ* 15:425.

158. TJ to Waterhouse, *WTJ* 15:384.

159. TJ to Short, *WTJ* 15:246. For other attacks on Calvinism, see TJ to Richard Price, Jan. 8, 1789; *WTJ* 7:252; TJ to Ely, *WTJ* 15:203; TJ to Sparks, *WTJ* 15:288; and TJ to Adams, *WTJ* 15:425.

160. Gould, "Religious Opinions," 199.

161. Gaustad, *Sworn*, 143. Cf. David N. Mayer, *The Constitutional Thought of Thomas Jefferson* (Charlottesville: University Press of Virginia, 1994), 161. See also Kerry S. Walters, *The American Deists: Voices of Reason and Dissent in the Early Republic* (Lawrence: University Press of Kansas, 1992).

162. Ellis, *American Sphinx*, 259. Ellis adds that "in modern-day parlance, he was a secular humanist." This term is not appropriate for Jefferson. Secular humanists are agnostics, do not believe in prayer, see no value in Christian worship, assert that the supreme being is humanity and that ethics is situational and autonomous, and criticize numerous aspects of Christian ethics. See Humanist Manifestos I and II; Paul Kurtz, "A Secular Humanist Declaration," *Free Inquiry* 1 (1980); and Corliss Lamont, *The Philosophy of Humanism* (New York: F. Ungar, 1982). John M. Murrin makes the same argument in "Religion and Politics in America from the First Settlements to the Civil War," in Mark A. Noll, ed., *Religion and American Politics: From the Colonial Period to the 1980s* (New York: Oxford University Press, 1990), 32–33, which Frank Lambert endorses in *The Founding Fathers and the Place of Religion in America* (Princeton, NJ: Princeton University Press, 2003), 279. Murrin contends that Jefferson was a secular humanist because he elevated human reason over divine authority,

believed human problems had human solutions, and embraced ethical relativism. Jefferson exalted reason above revelation, but he valued biblical teaching, asked God to help him deal with varied problems, and considered biblical ethics far superior to other systems.

163. Walter Isaacson, "God of Our Fathers," *Time* 164 (July 5, 2004), 62–63, quotations in that order. Cf. Bernstein, *Jefferson*, 42.

164. Randall, *Jefferson*, 291.

165. Gaustad, *Sworn*, 215.

166. Sheridan, "Liberty and Virtue," 243. See Gay, *Enlightenment*, 1:207–419.

167. TJ to Benjamin Waterhouse, July 19, 1822, *WTJ* 15:392.

168. TJ to John Davis, Jan. 18, 1824, TJP.

169. Gaustad, *Sworn*, 206.

170. Gould, "Religious Opinions," 200.

171. In private letters, Jefferson called himself "an Unitarian by myself." E.g., TJ to Waterhouse, July 19, 1822, Jan. 8, 1825, *WTJ* 15:392; Ford, *WTJ*, 10:336.

172. TJ to Whittemore, *WTJ* 15:373.

173. TJ to Pickering, *WTJ* 15:323; TJ to Whittemore, *WTJ* 15:373; quotations in that order.

174. In *Religion of the Founding Fathers*, Holmes summarizes Jefferson's religion as "monotheistic, restorationist, centered on reason and Jesus, opposed to mystery, medieval theology, and Calvinism, and anti-clerical" (106).

175. Brent, "Jeffersonian Outlook," 431; Wicks, "Thomas Jefferson," 273.

176. TJ to Ely, *WTJ* 15:203. Earlier, Jefferson wrote, "I never submitted my opinions to any party of men in religion or in politics.... If I could not go to heaven but with a party, I would not go there at all!" (to Francis Hopkinson, Mar. 13, 1789, Ford, *WTJ* 5:76).

177. See Charles O. Lerche Jr., "Jefferson and the Election of 1800: A Case Study in Political Smear," *WMQ*, 3rd ser., 5 (1948), 467–91; Foote, *Champion*, 35–43; Luebke, "Jefferson's Anti-Clericalism," 344–56; Noble E. Cunningham Jr., "Election of 1800," in Arthur M. Schlesinger Jr., ed., *History of American Presidential Elections: 1789–1968* (New York: Chelsea, 1985), 101–56; Constance B. Schultz, " 'Of Bigotry in Politics and Religion': Jefferson's Religion, the Federalist Press, and the Syllabus," *VMBH* 91 (Jan. 1983), 73–91; Norman De Jong with Jack Van Der Slik, "The Presidential Election of 1800: Thomas Jefferson's Second Revolution?" in *Separation of Church and State: The Myth Revisited* (Jordon Station, Ontario: Paideia, 1985), 147–68; Mark A. Noll, *One Nation under God: Christian Faith and Political Action in America* (San Francisco: Harper and Row, 1988), 74–89; Philip Hamburger, *Separation of Church and State* (Cambridge, MA: Harvard University Press, 2002), 111–24; Frank Lambert, *The Founding Fathers*, 265–87; and John Ferling, *The Tumultuous Election of 1800* (New York: Oxford University Press, 2004).

178. Jefferson, *Notes*, 159. Detractors also criticized Jefferson's views on the Genesis flood and Adam's universal parenthood, as well as his refusal to teach the Bible to young children in schools, and denounced him for fraternizing with French atheists. See G. Adolf Koch, *Republican Religion: The American Revolution and the Cult of Reason* (Gloucester, MA: Peter Smith, 1964), 265–74; Sheridan, "Liberty and Virtue," 256–57; and Hamburger, *Separation*, 111–29.

179. William Linn, *Serious Considerations on the Election of a President* (New York: John Furman, 1800), 19.

180. Anonymous to GW, c. Jan 20, 1792, in Dorothy Twohig, ed., *Papers of George Washington, Presidential Series*, 11 vols. (Charlottesville: University Press of Virginia, 1987–2000), 9:484. Cf. Anonymous to GW, c. Jan. 3, 1792, ibid., 9:369–70.

181. Quoted in M. Louise Greene, *The Development of Religious Liberty in Connecticut* (Boston: Houghton Mifflin, 1905), 415–16, footnote. One exception is [William Loughton Smith], *The Pretensions of Thomas Jefferson to the Presidency Examined...* (Philadelphia 1796).

182. Peterson, *Jefferson*, 608.

183. In 1796, opponents argued that Jefferson was not fit to be president because he was an impractical philosopher. See Frank Lambert, "God—and a Religious President...[or] Jefferson and No Campaigning for a Voter-Imposed Religious Test in 1800," *JCS* 39 (Aug. 1997), Academic Search Elite, 4; [John Gardiner], *A Brief Consideration of...Mr. Adams for the Presidency...* (Boston, 1796), 27. A few falsely accused Jefferson of not attending worship (e.g., Smith, *The Pretensions of Thomas Jefferson to the Presidency Examined*, 39). Religion was not nearly as important an issue in the 1804 campaign, probably because the dire predictions of Federalists had not come true.

184. E.g., Abiel Abbot, *An Eulogy on the Illustrious Life and Character of George Washington* (Haverhill, MA, 1800), 9, 17–18, 26. See also chapter 1.

185. Connecticutensis, *Three Letters to Abraham Bishop* (Hartford, CT: Hudson and Goodwin, 1800), 28–29.

186. *Gazette of the United States*, Sept. 11, 1800, 2. The *Gazette* repeatedly posed this question during the campaign.

187. Alexander Hamilton to John Jay, May 7, 1800, in Henry C. Lodge, ed. *The Works of Alexander Hamilton* (New York, 1904), 10:372–73. Hamilton helped make religion a central issue in the election of 1800 through articles he published in the New York *Commercial Advertiser*.

188. These included Congregationalists Timothy Dwight, president of Yale College, and Jedidiah Morse, a prominent proponent of foreign missions and theological education, Presbyterians John Mitchell Mason, a pastor in New York City, Samuel Stanhope Smith, president of Princeton, and highly respected lay leader Elias Boudinot. See Mark Noll, "When 'Infidels' Run for Office," *CT* 28 (Oct. 5, 1984), 22.

189. Timothy Dwight, *The Duty of Americans, at the Present Crisis* (New Haven, CT: Thomas and Samuel Green, 1798), in Ellis Sandoz, ed., *Political Sermons of the American Founding Era, 1730–1805*, 2 vols. (Indianapolis, IN: Liberty, 1991), 2:1382. This sermon was widely distributed during the campaign. Also see Gary B. Nash, "American Clergy and the French Revolution," *WMQ*, 3rd ser, 22 (1965), 392–412.

190. A Layman, *The Claims of Thomas Jefferson to the Presidency* (Philadelphia, 1800), 35–36, 46, as cited by Hamburger, *Separation*, 115.

191. See Edwin Martin, *Thomas Jefferson, Scientist* (New York: H. Schuman, 1952), 236–40.

192. Randall, *Jefferson*, 2:567.

193. John Mitchell Mason, *The Voice of Warning to Christians, on the Ensuing Election of a President of the United States*, in Sandoz, ed., *Political Sermons*, 2:1463, 1452, 1462, quotations in that order. Mason accused Jefferson of wanting to take the Bible away from children, disregarding divine worship, showing contempt for the Sabbath, and possessing a "notoriously unchristian character" (1463).

194. Linn, *Serious Considerations*, 20, 24–26, 28.

195. *Hudson Bee*, Sept. 7, 1800, reprinted from the *New-England Palladium*, quoted in Nathan Schachner, *Thomas Jefferson: A Biography* (New York: Thomas Yoseloff, 1951), 641.

196. Martin, *Scientist*, 237.

197. David Saville Muzzey, *Thomas Jefferson* (New York: Charles Scribner's Sons, 1918), 207–8; Albert Jay Nock, *Jefferson* (New York: Harcourt, Brace, 1926), 238; Randall, *Jefferson*, 1:493–96, 2:567–68, 3:620–22.

198. Cunningham, *In Pursuit of Reason*, 225–26.

199. [Tunis Wortman], *A Solemn Address... Upon the Approaching Election of a President of the United States...* (New York: David Denniston, 1800), in Sandoz, ed., *Political Sermons*, 2:1499. Wortman refuted the arguments of Jefferson's enemies, based on Jefferson's published statements and alleged actions (1501–27). Cf. Americanus [John James Beckley], *An Epitome and Vindication of the Public Life and Character of Thomas Jefferson* (Philadelphia: James Carey, 1800), 7. See also Joseph Bloomfield, *To the People of New Jersey*, Sept. 30, 1800, Historical Society of Pennsylvania, Philadelphia; "Marcus Brutus," *Serious Facts Opposed to "Serious Considerations"* (n.p., 1800); and Stanley Griswold, *Truth Its Own Test, and God Its Only Judge* (1800).

200. E.g., "Grotius" [DeWitt Clinton], *A Vindication of Thomas Jefferson* (New York, 1800), 6–7; Abraham Bishop, *Oration... for the Election of Thomas Jefferson* (New Haven, 1801), 94.

201. Bloomfield, *To the People of New Jersey*.

202. Abraham Bishop, *Connecticut Republicanism: An Oration on the Extent and Power of Political Delusion* (New Haven, 1800), 45. On religious tests for officeholders, see Lambert, "God—and a Religious President," 769–89; James H. Smylie, "Protestant Clergy, The First Amendment, and Beginnings of a Constitutional Debate, 1781–1791," in Elwyn A. Smith, ed., *The Religion of the Republic* (Philadelphia: Fortress, 1971), 116–53; and Edwin Gaustad, "Religious Tests, Constitutions, and a 'Christian Nation,'" in Hoffman and Albert, *Religion*, 218–35.

203. *General Aurora Advertiser*, Oct. 14, 1800.

204. Hamburger, *Separation*, 117–120. See William G. McLoughlin, *Soul Liberty: The Baptists' Struggle in New England, 1630–1833* (Providence, RI: Brown University Press, 1991), 194–95, 267–68.

205. TJ to Joseph Priestley, Mar. 21, 1801, *WTJ* 10:228.

206. TJ to James Monroe, Ford, *WTJ* 9:136. '[W]hile I should be engaged with one [lie]," he added, "they would publish twenty new ones."

207. TJ to Uriah McGregory, Aug. 13, 1800, *WTJ* 10:171.

208. Adams to Benjamin Rush, June 12, 1812, in John A. Schutz and Douglas Adair, eds., *The Spur of Fame: Dialogues of John Adams and Benjamin Rush, 1805–1813* (San Marion, CA: Huntington Library, 1966), 224.

209. John Leland, "A Blow at the Root: Being a Fashionable Fast-Day Sermon (Cheshire, MA, Apr. 9, 1801)," in L. F. Greene, ed., *The Writings of the Late Elder John Leland* (New York: G. W. Wood, 1845), 255.

210. Address of the inhabitants of the town of Cheshire, Berkshire County, MA, to TJ, Jan. 1, 1802, reprinted in dozens of newspapers. On Baptist opposition to the Congregationalist establishment and the Federalist Party, see William G. McLoughlin, *New England Dissent, 1630–1833: The Baptists and the Separation of Church and State*, 2 vols. (Cambridge, MA: Harvard University Press, 1971).

211. Appomattox Baptist Association to TJ, Oct. 21, 1807, TJP; Baltimore Baptist Association to TJ, Oct. 15, 1808, ibid.; Ketocton Baptist Association to TJ, Aug. 18, 1808, ibid.; Address of New Hope Baptists, Woodford County, KY, to TJ, Aug. 31, 1807, ibid.; TJ to John Thomas, Nov. 18, 1807, ibid.; Albemarle County, Virginia, Baptist Church to TJ, Mar. 17, 1809, ibid.

212. Pittsburgh Methodist Church to TJ, Nov. 20, 1808, TJP. See also TJ to Pittsburgh Methodist Episcopal Church, Dec. 9, 1808, *WTJ* 16:325–26. Cf. New London, CT, Society of the Methodist Episcopal Church to TJ, *WTJ*, Nov. 21, 1808; 16:320–21, 331–32. See also Jefferson's response: Feb. 4, 1809, *WTJ* 16:331.

213. See especially TJ to Clay, Jan., 29, 1815, *WTJ* 14:233.

214. Elias Smith, *The Whole World Governed by a Jew* . . . (Exeter, NH: Henry Ranlet, 1805), 77; quotes from Michael Kenny, *The Perfect Law of Liberty: Elias Smith and the Providential History of America* (Washington: Smithsonian Institution Press, 1994), 25.

215. See Schultz, "Of Bigotry," 73–91; and Edwin S. Gaustad, "Thomas Jefferson, Danbury Baptists, and 'Eternal Hostility,'" *WMQ*, 3rd ser., 56 (1999), 802–3.

216. Thomas G. Fessenden, *Democracy Unveiled* (New York, 1806), 2:36–37.

217. David Osgood, *A Discourse Delivered at Cambridge* . . . (Cambridge, MA: William Hilliard, 1810), 9.

218. Quoted in Ellis, *American Sphinx*, 216. See also Dumas Malone, *Jefferson the President, First Term, 1801–1805* (Boston: Little, Brown, 1970), 192–200; and Jerry W. Knudson, "The Rage around Tom Paine," *New York Historical Society Quarterly*, Jan. 1969, 34–61.

219. Osgood, *Discourse*, 20.

220. Quoted in Gaustad, *Sworn*, 108.

221. Clement Clark Moore, *Observations upon* . . . *Mr. Jefferson's Notes on Virginia, Which Appear to Have a Tendency to Subvert Religion, and Establish a False Philosophy* (New York, 1804), esp. 18, 30–31.

222. TJ to Levi Lincoln, Aug. 26, 1801, TJP.

223. See Jefferson, "Notes on Religion," Ford, *WTJ* 2:92–103; Jefferson, *Notes*, 223–25; Clinard, *Commonplace Book*, 377–93.

224. Jefferson, Second Draft of Virginia Constitution of 1776, *PTJ* 1:353.

225. On Madison's contribution to religious liberty, see Robert S. Alley, *James Madison on Religious Liberty* (Buffalo: Prometheus, 1985); and Garrett Ward Sheldon, *The Political Philosophy of James Madison* (Baltimore: Johns Hopkins University Press, 2001).

226. Jefferson, *Notes*, 160–61, quotations from 161.

227. Bill for Establishing Religious Freedom, in Jefferson, *Notes*, 224.

228. Gaustad, *Sworn*, 69.

229. Bill for Establishing Religious Freedom, *Notes*, 233–34.

230. Jefferson, *Notes*, 223, 160, three quotations from 223. See also TJ to Matthew Carey, Nov. 11, 1816, *WTJ* 12:42 and TJ to Logan, *WTJ* 12:43.

231. TJ to William Duane, July 25, 1811, *WTJ* 13:67; TJ to Wendover, *WTJ* 14:279.

232. Jefferson, *Notes*, 223–24, quotation from 224. Cf. TJ to Samuel Knox, Feb. 12, 1810, *WTJ* 12:360–61.

233. E.g., TJ to Waterhouse, *WTJ* 15:385.

234. TJ to Thomas Jefferson Randolph, Nov. 24, 1808, *WTJ* 12:199.

235. Jefferson, *Notes*, 159.

236. Peterson, *Jefferson*, 143.

237. See Forrest McDonald, *The Presidency of Thomas Jefferson* (Lawrence: University Press of Kansas, 1976), 17; Greene, *Religious Liberty*, 394, 407.

238. Letter from the Danbury Baptist Association to TJ, Oct. 7, 1801, The Papers of Thomas Jefferson (Manuscript Division, Library of Congress), Series 1, Box 87, Aug. 30, 1801–Oct. 15, 1801, as quoted in Daniel L. Dreisbach, *Thomas Jefferson and the Wall of Separation between Church and State* (New York: New York University Press, 2002), 20.

239. TJ to Levi Lincoln, Jan. 1, 1802, PTJ, Series 1, Box 89, Dec. 2, 1801–Jan. 1, 1802, as cited in Dreisbach, *Jefferson*, 25.

240. On his predecessors' practices, see Anson Phelps Stokes, *Church and State in the United States*, 3 vols. (New York: Harper, 1950), 1:486–91.

241. TJ to the Danbury Baptist Association, Jan. 1, 1802, WTJ 16:282. On the First Amendment, see William Lee Miller, *The First Liberty: Religion and the American Republic* (New York: Alfred A. Knopf, 1986); Thomas Curry, *The First Freedoms: Church and State in America to the Passage of the First Amendment* (New York: Oxford University Press, 1986); Leonard W. Levy, *The Establishment Clause: Religion and the First Amendment* (New York: Macmillan, 1986); and James E. Wood Jr., ed., *The First Freedom: Religion and the Bill of Rights* (Waco, TX: Institute of Church-State Studies, 1990).

242. TJ to Samuel Miller, Jan 23, 1808, WTJ 11:428–30. Cf. Jefferson, "Second Inaugural Address," WTJ, 3:378.

243. James H. Hutson, "Thomas Jefferson's Letter to the Danbury Baptists: A Controversy Rejoined," *WMQ*, 3rd ser., 56 (1999), 780–81; Dreisbach, *Jefferson*, 27; Thomas E. Buckley, "Reflections on a Wall," *WMQ*, 3rd ser, 56 (1999), 800.

244. James H. Hutson, " 'A Wall of Separation': FBI Helps Restore Jefferson's Obliterated Draft," *Library of Congress Information Bulletin* 57 (1998), 163.

245. See Dreisbach, *Jefferson*, 67; Stokes, *Church and State*, 1:486–91.

246. See Rodney K. Smith, *Public Prayer and the Constitution: A Case Study in Constitutional Interpretation* (Wilmington, DE: Scholarly Resources, 1987), 62; Daniel L. Dreisbach, " 'Sowing Useful Truths and Principles': The Danbury Baptists, Thomas Jefferson, and the 'Wall of Separation,' " *JCS* 39 (1997), 465–66. In *Thomas Jefferson*, Dreisbach discusses alternative metaphors for defending religious liberty including George Washington's "effectual barriers," Jefferson's "fences," and James Madison's "great barriers" and "line of separation."

247. Hamburger, *Separation*, 11–14.

248. Dreisbach, *Jefferson*, 7.

249. *Everson v. Board of Education*, 330 U.S. 1, 16, 18 (1947).

250. Dreisbach, *Jefferson*, 2, 4, quotations from 2.

251. Harold Hammett, "The Homogenized Wall," *American Bar Association Journal* (Oct. 1967), 929. Cf. Levy, *Establishment Clause*, 250; and Derek Davis, "What Jefferson's Metaphor Really Means," *Liberty*, Jan.–Feb. 1997, 12.

252. Dreisbach, *Jefferson*, 7.

253. Ibid., 120.

254. See Harold E. Fey, "Problems of Church and State in the United States: A Protestant View," in Dallin H. Oaks, ed., *The Wall between Church and State* (Chicago: University of Chicago Press, 1963), 37; Marvin E. Frankel, "Religion in Public Life— Reasons for Minimal Access," *George Washington University Law Review* 60 (1992), 633–34; and Levy, *Establishment Clause*, 246.

255. Dreisbach, *Jefferson*, 121, 124, quotations in that order. See Paul G. Kauper, "Everson v. Board of Education: A Product of Judicial Will," *Arizona Law Review* 15

(1973), 321; Richard P. O'Brien, *Caesar's Coin: Religion and Politics in America* (New York: Macmillan, 1987), 66; James Davison Hunter and Os Guinness, eds., "The Williamsburg Charter," in *Articles of Faith, Articles of Peace: The Religious Liberty Clause and American Public Policy* (Washington, DC: Brookings Institution, 1990), 136; and Kathleen M. Sullivan, "God as Lobby," *University of Chicago Law Review* 61 (1994), 1665.

256. Dreisbach, *Jefferson*, 125. See also Daniel L. Dreisbach and John D. Whaley, "What the Wall Separates: A Debate on Thomas Jefferson's 'Wall of Separation' Metaphor," *Constitutional Commentary* 16 (1999), 672; Robert L. Cord, "Mr. Jefferson's 'Nonabsolute' Wall of Separation between Church and State," in Sheldon and Dreisbach, eds., *Religion and Political Culture*, 167–88; Dreisbach, *Real Threat and Mere Shadow: Religious Liberty and the First Amendment* (Westchester, IL: Crossway, 1987), 113–34; and Dreisbach, "New Light on the Jeffersonian Model of Church-State Relations," *North Carolina Law Review* 69 (1990), 159–211.

257. Cord, " 'Nonabsolute' Wall," 167.

258. Hutson, "Jefferson's Letter," 789.

259. Hutson, " 'Wall of Separation,' " 163.

260. Dreisbach, *Jefferson*, 51.

261. Hutson, "Jefferson's Letter," 787.

262. "Resolution of the House of Burgesses Designating a Day of Fasting and Prayer," May 24, 1774, *PTJ* 1:105–6. See also Jefferson's explanation in his *Autobiography*, *WTJ* 1:9–10.

263. Report of the Committee of Revisors Appointed by the General Assembly of Virginia in 1776 (Richmond, VA: Dixon and Holt), 60. Dreisbach points out that several scholars believe that Jefferson wrote the bill: Robert L. Cord, *Separation of Church and State: Historical Fact and Current Fiction* (New York: Lambert, 1982), 220–21; Healey, *Jefferson on Religion*, 135; and Donald L. Drakeman, "Religion and the Republic: James Madison and the First Amendment," *JCS* 25 (1983), 441. The bill never passed.

264. Cord, " 'Nonabsolute' Wall," 176–77.

265. Dreisbach, *Jefferson*, 58; Buckley, "Reflections on a Wall," 797–800; and Thomas E. Buckley, "The Political Theology of Thomas Jefferson," in Merrill D. Peterson and Robert C. Vaughan, eds., *The Virginia Statute for Religious Freedom: Its Evolution and Consequences in American History* (New York: Cambridge University Press, 1988), 94–96.

266. Mayer, *Constitutional Thought*, 324–25, quotation from 324; Merrill Peterson, *Adams and Jefferson: A Revolutionary Dialogue* (New York: Oxford University Press, 1978), 41.

267. Sanford, *Religious Life*, 133.

268. Garrett Ward Sheldon, "Liberalism, Classicism, and Christianity in Jefferson's Political Thought," in Sheldon and Dreisbach, eds., *Religion and Political Culture*, 93–105. See also Donald S. Lutz, *A Preface to American Political Theory* (Lawrence: University Press of Kansas, 1992); and Michael P. Zuckert, *The Natural Rights Republic: Studies in the Foundation of the American Political Tradition* (Notre Dame, IN: Notre Dame University Press, 1996).

269. See Garry Wills, *Inventing America: Jefferson's Declaration of Independence* (New York: Vintage, 1979); and Ronald Hanowy, "Jefferson and the Scottish Enlightenment: A Critique of Garry Wills' *Inventing America . . . ,*" *WMQ* 36 (1979), 503–23.

270. Sheldon, *Political Philosophy*, 61, 147, quotations in that order. See also Gordon Wood, *The Creation of the American Republic* (Chapel Hill: University of North

Carolina Press, 1969), 53–58; and Lance Banning, *The Jefferson Persuasion* (Ithaca, NY: Cornell University Press, 1978), 29–46.

271. On Jefferson's work in crafting the Declaration and changing views of the document, see Pauline Maier, *American Scripture: Making the Declaration of Independence* (New York: Knopf, 1997); and Robert M. S. McDonald, "Thomas Jefferson's Changing Reputation as the Author of the Declaration of Independence: The First Fifty Years," *Journal of the Early Republic* 19 (Summer 1999), 169–95.

272. Thomas Jefferson, *A Summary View of the Rights of British America*, Ford, *WTJ* 1:447.

273. Bill for Establishing Religious Freedom, *Notes*, 223–25; TJ to James Fishback, Sept. 27, 1809, *WTJ* 12:315.

274. Koch, *Philosophy*, 136.

275. Jefferson, *Notes*, 163.

276. TJ to Fishback, *WTJ* 12:315.

277. Sheldon, "Liberalism, Classicism, and Christianity," 97

278. Sheldon, *Political Philosophy*, 56. See TJ to Law, *WTJ* 14:141–43; TJ to J Adams, *A-J Letters* 2:492; TJ to John Adams, Feb. 25, 1823, ibid., 2:589.

279. TJ to Adams, *A-J Letters*, 2:492. Cf. TJ to Carr, *WTJ* 6:257–8 and TJ to Francis W. Gilmer, June 7, 1816, *WTJ* 15:25.

280. Sheldon, *Political Philosophy*, 54–55.

281. TJ to Martha Jefferson, *PTJ* 6:380.

282. Jefferson, *Notes*, 146–49; Jefferson, "Bill for the More General Diffusion of Knowledge," *CJ*, 1048–49.

283. Mayer, *Constitutional Thought*, 323–24.

284. Forrest McDonald, *The Presidency of George Washington* (Lawrence: University Press of Kansas, 1974), 18.

285. Jefferson, "The Anas," Ford, *WTJ* 1:332.

286. TJ to Madame D'Enville, Apr. 2, 1790, *PTJ* 16:291.

287. Quoted by Foote, *Champion*, 42. Cf. Jefferson, "Opinion on French Treaties," Apr. 28, 1793, *WTJ* 3:229, 241–43.

288. TJ to Dupont de Memours, Apr. 25, 1816, *WTJ* 14:490–91.

289. TJ to George Logan, Oct. 3, 1813, *WTJ* 13:387. Cf. TJ to the General Assembly of North Carolina, Jan. 10, 1808, *WTJ* 16:300.

290. E.g., TJ, Reply to Ketocton Baptist Association, *WTJ* 16:320; Jefferson, "First Annual Message," *WTJ* 3:327; Jefferson, "Third Annual Message," *WTJ* 3:358.

291. TJ to the Society of Tammany, *WTJ* 16:302.

292. Peterson, *Jefferson*, 883–85, 916–18.

293. E.g., Eric McKitrick, "The View from Jefferson's Camp," *New York Review of Books*, Dec. 17, 1970, 35–38.

294. E.g., Louis Martin Sears, *Jefferson and the Embargo* (New York: Octagon, 1966).

295. Robert W. Tucker and David C. Hendrickson, *Empire of Liberty: The Statecraft of Thomas Jefferson* (New York: Oxford University Press, 1990), 250–51.

296. Julian P. Boyd, "Thomas Jefferson's Empire of Liberty," *Virginia Quarterly Review* 24 (1948), 548.

297. TJ to John Hollins, May 5, 1811, *WTJ* 13:58. Cf. TJ to Priestley, *WTJ* 10:324–25.

298. Sheldon, *Political Philosophy*, 17, 117, 120–21, first quotation from 17, second from 121. See also Rhys Isaac, *The Transformation of Virginia, 1740–1790* (Chapel

Hill: University of North Carolina Press, 1982), 260, 294–95; Melvin Yazawa, *From Colonies to Commonwealth: Familial Ideology and the Beginning of the American Republic* (Baltimore: Johns Hopkins University Press, 1985), 35–36, 131–32, 141, 168; and Louis B. Wright, *The First Gentlemen of Virginia* (Charlottesville: University Press of Virginia, 1940), 3, 8.

299. Gordon S. Wood, "Where Are the Jeffersons of Today?" *Time* 164 (July 5, 2004), 62; Bernstein, *Jefferson*, xv; quotation from Gaustad, *Sworn*, 162.

300. See Linda Kerber, *Federalists in Dissent: Imagery and Ideology in Jeffersonian America* (Ithaca, NY: Cornell University Press, 1970), 11–12, 14, 19, 51–56, 69, 131–33.

301. McDonald, *Presidency*, 180.

302. TJ to Robert Smith, July 1, 1805 in W. C. Ford, ed., *Thomas Jefferson's Correspondence* (Boston, 1916), 114–15. See Malone, *Jefferson*, 1:447–51; 4:216–23; Peterson, *Jefferson*, 708–9; Randall, *Jefferson*, 557–59; and Fawn Brodie, *Thomas Jefferson: An Intimate History* (New York: Norton, 1975), 57, 74–79, 374–75.

303. E.g., Sanford, *Religious Life*, 45 (quotation); Peterson, *Jefferson*, 348–49. Ellis, *American Sphinx*, maintains they were lovers (93–97).

304. *Recorder*, Sept. 22, 1802.

305. See Douglass Adair, "The Jefferson Scandals," in Trevor Colbourn, ed., *Fame and the Founding Fathers: Essays* (Indianapolis: Liberty Fund, 1998 [1974]), 227–73; Virginius Dabney, *The Jefferson Scandals: A Rebuttal* (New York: Dodd, Mead, 1981); and Brodie, *Intimate History*, 339–75.

306. See Michael Durey, *With the Hammer of Truth: James Thomas Callender and America's Early National Heroes* (Charlottesville: University of Virginia Press, 1990). For Jefferson's efforts to deny his past relationships with Callender, see TJ to James Monroe, May 26, 1801, and July 15, 1802, Ford, *WTJ* 8:57–58, 164–68.

307. Ellis, *American Sphinx*, 219.

308. Madison Hemings's reminiscences, *Pike County Republican* 13 (Mar. 13, 1873), in Annette Gordon-Reed, *Thomas Jefferson and Sally Hemings: An American Controversy* (Charlottesville: University of Virginia Press, 1997), 245–48. See also Dumas Malone and Steven Hochman, "A Note on the Evidence: The Personal History of Madison Hemings," *JSH* 41 (Nov. 1975), 523–28.

309. In *Thomas Jefferson and Sally Hemings*, Gordon-Reed argues that the Hemings's oral tradition and the documentary evidence confirm each other. See also James A. Bear Jr., "The Hemings Family at Monticello," *Virginia Cavalcade* 29 (Autumn 1979), 78–87; Douglas L. Wilson, "Thomas Jefferson and the Character Issue," *AM* 270 (Nov. 1992), 57–74; Bryon W. Woodson, *A President in the Family: Thomas Jefferson, Sally Hemings and Thomas Woodson* (Westport, CT: Praeger, 2001); Jan Ellen Lewis and Peter S. Onuf, eds., *Sally Hemings and Thomas Jefferson* (Charlottesville: University Press of Virginia, 1999); Joshua D. Rothman, *Notorious in the Neighborhood: Sex and Families across the Color Line in Virginia, 1787–1861* (Chapel Hill: University of North Carolina Press, 2003), 12–56; and Frasier D. Neiman, "Coincidence or Causal Connection? The Relationship between Thomas Jefferson's Visits to Monticello and Sally Hemings's Conceptions," *WMQ*, 3rd ser., 57 (Jan. 2000), 198–210. See the other articles in this symposium entitled "Forum: Thomas Jefferson and Sally Hemings Redux," ibid., 121–197.

310. See *Report of the Research Committee on Thomas Jefferson and Sally Hemings* (Thomas Jefferson Foundation, 2000).

311. See VI. "Conclusions," in Robert F. Turner, ed., *Jefferson-Hemings Scholars Commission Report on the Jefferson-Hemings Matter* (Thomas Jefferson Heritage Society, 2001).

312. "Debate Stalls on Hemings Street," http://www.cavalierdaily.com/CVArticle. asp?ID=431&pid=459.

313. Adair, "Jefferson Scandals," 234. As Jefferson explained to a friend in 1816, "I should have fancied myself half guilty had I condescended to put pen to paper in refutation of their falsehoods, or drawn to them respect by any notice from myself" (TJ to George Logan, June 20, 1816, Ford, *WTJ*, 11:527n).

314. In 1805, Jefferson confessed to a friend "that when young and single, I offered love to a handsome lady. I acknowledge its incorrectness" (TJ to Smith, July 1, 1805, 114–15). Walker's version of the events is in Malone, *Jefferson*, 1:449–50.

315. Both Isaac Jefferson, a Monticello slave, and Madison Hemings claimed that Wayles fathered six children by his concubine Betty Hemings, who upon his death in 1774, were given to Jefferson and his wife, Martha. See Isaac Jefferson, *Memoirs of a Monticello Slave . . .* (Charlottesville: University of Virginia Press, 1951) and Adair, "Jefferson Scandals," 243–47.

316. Adair, "Jefferson Scandals," 250–73; first quotation from 257–58, second from 259. For Randolph's account, see Henry S. Randall to James Parton, June 1, 1868, in Milton E. Flower, *James Parton, the Father of Modern Biography* (Durham, NC: Duke University Press, 1951), 236–37. For Bacon's account, see Hamilton W. Pierson, *Jefferson at Monticello* (New York: Charles Scribner, 1862), 110–11. For a similar perspective, see White McKenzie Wallenborn, *Thomas Jefferson Foundation DNA Study Committee Minority Report* (1999).

317. Ellis, *American Sphinx*, 219. For an alternative perspective, see Bernstein, *Jefferson*, 195–97.

318. Jefferson, *Notes*, 143, 87 (first and third quotations); TJ to Jean Nicholas Demeunier, January 24, 1786, *TJP* (second quotation). See also TJ to William Short, Sept. 8, 1823, *WTJ* 7:310; TJ to Richard Price, Aug. 7, 1785, *WTJ* 1:377.

319. Jefferson, *Notes*, 162–63, quotations from 163.

320. TJ to J. P. Brissot De Warville, Feb. 10, 1788, *WTJ* 5:66. Cf. TJ to John Holmes, Apr. 22, 1820, Ford, *WTJ* 10:157–58.

321. C. Vann Woodward, "The Old and the New Worlds: Summary and Comment," in Gilreath, ed., *Thomas Jefferson*, 213; Ellis, *American Sphinx*, 88.

322. Ellis, *American Sphinx*, 146, 329. Cf. Peterson, *Jefferson*, 999–1000.

323. Sanford, *Religious Life*, 81.

324. TJ to Short, *WTJ* 15:247–8.

325. Ellis, *American Sphinx*, 88.

326. TJ to Edward Bancroft, 1789, Ford, *WTJ* 5:66. On Jefferson's condemnation of slavery, see TJ to Coles, TJP. See also Edward Coles to TJ, Sept. 26, 1814, TJP.

327. TJ to George Logan, May 11, 1805, *WTJ* 11:71–72. Cf. TJ to Thomas Humphreys, Feb. 8, 1817, *WTJ* 15:103; TJ to Fanny Wright, Aug. 7, 1825; and TJ to William Short, Jan. 18, 1826, Ford, *WTJ* 10:343–45, 361–62.

328. TJ to Holmes, Ford, *WTJ* 10:157–58.

329. TJ to Coles, TJP. Cf. TJ to Frances Wright, Aug. 7, 1825, *WTJ* 16:119.

330. Bernstein, *Jefferson*, 110.

331. Ellis, *American Sphinx*, 152. On the slaves at Monticello, see Lucia Stanton, "'Those Who Labor for My Happiness': Thomas Jefferson and His Slaves," in Onuf,

ed., *Jeffersonian Legacies*, 147–80. Scholars sharply disagree about his record. Wilson, "Thomas Jefferson and the Character Issue," 61–78, defends him. Paul Finkelman, "Jefferson and Slavery: Treason against the Hopes of the World," in Onuf, ed., *Jeffersonian Legacies*, 181–221, strongly attacks his record. The best survey is John Chester Miller, *The Wolf by the Ears: Thomas Jefferson and Slavery* (New York: Free Press, 1977).

332. Peterson, *Jefferson*, 534–35, quotation from 534.

333. See Gordon Wood, *The Radicalism of the American Revolution* (New York: Knopf, 1992), 50–51.

334. TJ to Thomas Cooper, Sept. 10, 1814, *WTJ* 14:183–84.

335. Jefferson, *Notes*, 138–43, quotation from 143. See Winthrop Jordan, *White over Black: American Attitudes toward the Negro, 1550–1812* (Chapel Hill: University of North Carolina Press, 1968), 429–81, on the racist values of the era.

336. Jefferson, *Notes*, 140.

337. James Oakes, "Why Slaves Can't Read," in Gilreath, ed., *Thomas Jefferson*, 191.

338. Jefferson, *Notes*, 138. Cf. TJ to Humphries, *WTJ* 15:102–3.

339. Ellis, *American Sphinx*, 148.

340. Sheldon, *Political Philosophy*, 139.

341. See Stanton, "Those Who Labor," 147–48.

342. Finkelman, "Jefferson and Slavery," 181–221.

343. Wood, "Where Are the Jeffersons?" 82.

344. Quoted in ibid.

345. McDonald, *Presidency*, 168, note 2. See also Ellis, *American Sphinx*, 7; Garrett Ward Sheldon, *What Would Jefferson Say?* (New York: Berkley, 1998); Peterson, *Jefferson Image*, 395–420; and Peter S. Onuf, "The Scholars' Jefferson," *WMQ* 50 (Oct. 1993), 673–75.

346. Leonard Levy, *Jefferson and Civil Liberties: The Darker Side* (Cambridge, MA: Harvard University Press, 1963), 15, 21.

347. Gaustad, *Sworn*, 227.

348. "Epitaph [1826]" in Merrill Peterson, ed., *Thomas Jefferson Writings* (New York: Library of America, 1984), 706; Bernstein, *Jefferson*, ix–x.

349. Bernstein, *Jefferson*, xii.

350. Sheridan, "Liberty and Virtue," 249; Tucker and Hendrickson, *Empire of Liberty*, 161. See also Anthony F. C. Wallace, *Jefferson and the Indians: The Tragic Fate of the First Americans* (Cambridge, MA: Harvard University Press, 1999); Bernard W. Sheehan, *Seeds of Extinction: Jeffersonian Philosophy and the American Indians* (Chapel Hill: University of North Carolina Press, 1973); and Peter S. Onuf, *Jefferson's Empire: The Language of American Nationhood* (Charlottesville: University Press of Virginia, 2000).

351. Levy, *Civil Liberties*, 124–25, 358–66.

352. Malone, *Jefferson* 5:190; Henry Wilder Foote, ed., *The Life and Morals of Jesus of Nazareth* (Boston: Beacon, 1951), 13.

353. Sanford, "Religious Beliefs," 71.

354. Thomas Jefferson Coolidge, "Jefferson in the Family," *WTJ* 15:iv.

355. Noll, " 'Infidels,' " 23–4, quotation from 23; Noll, *One Nation*, 87.

356. TJ to Roger C. Weightman, June 24, 1826, Ford, *WTJ* 10:391.

357. Adams, *Memoirs*, July 9, 1826, 7:125.

358. John Quincy Adams, "Second Annual Address," Dec. 5, 1826, in *A Compilation of the Messages and Papers of the Presidents, 1789–1897*, comp. James D. Richardson, 10 vols. (New York: Bureau of National Literature and Art, 1901–6 [1896–99]), 2:364.

359. Quoted in Peterson, *Jefferson Image*, 5.

360. As reprinted in the Huntsville (AL) *Southern Advocate*, July 21, 1826, quoted by Robert P. Hays, "The Glorious Departure of the American Patriarchs: Contemporary Reactions to the Deaths of Jefferson and Adams," *JSH* 35 (Nov. 1969), 546. See also Peterson, *Jefferson Image*, 3–12.

361. Hays, "Glorious Departure," 552–55.

CHAPTER 3

1. Merrill D. Peterson, *Lincoln in American Memory* (New York: Oxford University Press, 1994), 218.

2. William J. Wolf, *Lincoln's Religion* (Philadelphia: Pilgrim, 1970), 173–94; William E. Barton, *The Soul of Abraham Lincoln* (New York: George H. Doran, 1920), 260–90; Mark A. Noll, *One Nation under God? Christian Faith and Political Action in America* (New York: Harper and Row, 1988), 90–104; Mark Noll, "The Perplexing Faith of Abraham Lincoln," *CT* 29 (Feb. 15, 1985), 12–14; Richard V. Pierard and Robert D. Linder, *Civil Religion and the Presidency* (Grand Rapids, MI: Zondervan, 1988), 96–97, 103–8.

3. Mark A. Noll, *America's God: From Jonathan Edwards to Abraham Lincoln* (New York: Oxford University Press, 2002), 7.

4. James Randall and Richard Current, *Lincoln the President*, 4 vols. (New York: Dodd, Mead, 1945–1955), 4:375; Wolf, *Lincoln's Religion*, 194; D. Elton Trueblood, *Abraham Lincoln: Theologian of American Anguish* (New York: Harper and Row, 1973); and David Hein, "Lincoln's Theology and Political Ethics," in Kenneth W. Thompson, ed., *Essays on Lincoln's Faith and Politics* (Lanham, MD: University Press of America, 1983), 108–56; quotations in that order.

5. Albert Menedez, *Religion and the U.S. Presidency: A Bibliography* (New York: Garland, 1986), 67. In addition to others listed in previous and subsequent notes, on Lincoln's faith and religious views, see Wayne C. Temple, *Abraham Lincoln: From Skeptic to Prophet* (Mahomet, IL: Mayhaven, 1995).

6. Edgar DeWitt Jones, *Lincoln and the Preachers* (Freeport, NY: Books for Libraries Press, 1970 [1948]), 122. See the Lincoln Collection of Harold K. Sage, Milner Library, Illinois State University.

7. William Lee Miller, *Lincoln's Virtues: An Ethical Biography* (New York: Alfred A. Knopf, 2002), xii–xiii.

8. Barton, *Soul*, 19; Stewart Winger, *Lincoln, Religion, and Romantic Cultural Politics* (DeKalb: Northern Illinois University Press, 2003), 3.

9. Noll, *One Nation under God*, 90.

10. E.g., Francis B. Carpenter, *Six Months at the White House* (New York: Hurd and Houghton, 1866), 186: Lincoln only rarely expressed "his most inmost convictions" and only "to his most intimate friends."

11. Wolf, *Lincoln's Religion*, 26–28. See also Noll, "The Perplexing Faith of Abraham Lincoln," 12–14; Trueblood, *Abraham Lincoln*, 95–117; and David Hein, "The Calvinistic Tenor of Abraham Lincoln's Religious Thought," *Lincoln Herald* 85 (Winter

1983), 21–30. Scholars must carefully consider the provenance and substance of quotations ascribed to Lincoln, but they must not totally ignore them. See Don E. Fehrenbacher, *Lincoln in Text and Context: Collected Essays* (Stanford, CA: Stanford University Press, 1987), 277–78, 281.

12. Besides Roy P. Basler, ed., *Collected Works*, 9 vols. (New Brunswick, NJ: Rutgers University Press, 1953–55) (hereafter *CW*, see Peterson, *American Memory*; Michael Burlingame, ed., *An Oral History of Abraham Lincoln: John G. Nicolay's Interviews and Essays* (Carbondale: Southern Illinois University Press, 1996); Don E. Fehrenbacher and Virginia Fehrenbacher, eds., *Recollected Words of Abraham Lincoln* (Stanford, CA: Stanford University Press, 1996) (hereafter *RW*) (which evaluates the reliability of thousands of alleged statements by Lincoln); and Douglas Wilson and Rodney O. Davis, *Herndon's Informants* (Urbana: University of Illinois Press, 1997) (hereafter *HI*).

13. Noll, *America's God*, 15. The evangelicalism promoted by the Second Great Awakening (1800–1840) was the United States' dominant religion until at least the Civil War, and perhaps 1900. It emphasized the Bible as the ultimate authority for religion, the centrality of the Christ's atonement and bodily resurrection, the necessity of a "new birth" experience, and the requirement of personal evangelism. See Mark A. Noll, *Between Faith and Criticism: Evangelicals, Scholarship and the Bible* (Grand Rapids, MI: Baker, 1991), 2; and Bruce L. Shelley, "Evangelicalism," in Daniel G. Reid et al., eds., *Dictionary of Christianity in America* (Downers Grove, IL: InterVarsity Press, 1990), 413–16.

14. Noll, *America's God*, 14. See also Robert Handy, *A Christian America; Protestant Hopes and Historical Realities* (New York: Oxford University Press, 1984); and Mark Y. Hanley, *Beyond a Christian Commonwealth: The Protestant Quarrel with the American Republic, 1830–1860* (Chapel Hill: University of North Carolina Press, 1994). On the relationship of evangelicalism and the Republican Party, see Richard Carwardine, "Lincoln, Evangelical Religion, and the American Political Culture in the Era of the Civil War," *JALA* 18, no. 1 (Winter 1997), 34–55; and Carwardine, *Evangelicals and Politics in Antebellum America* (New Haven, CT: Yale University Press, 1993).

15. Allen C. Guelzo, *Abraham Lincoln: Redeemer President* (Grand Rapids, MI: Eerdmans, 1999), 18.

16. Pierard and Linder, *Civil Religion*, 88, 112; first and fourth quotations from 88, second and third from 112; Harold Holzer, " 'Columbia's Noblest Sons': Washington and Lincoln in Popular Prints," *JALA* 15, no. 1 (1994), 40.

17. Wolf, *Lincoln's Religion*, 24; Noll, *One Nation*, 90.

18. Miller, *Lincoln's Virtues*, 85.

19. Mark A. Noll, "Lincoln's God," *JPH* 82 (Summer 2004), 79, 86. The best overviews of Lincoln's life and presidency include Benjamin P. Thomas, *Abraham Lincoln: A Biography* (New York: Alfred A. Knopf, 1952); Michael Burlingame, *The Inner World of Abraham Lincoln* (Urbana: University of Illinois Press, 1994); Phillip Shaw Paludan, *The Presidency of Abraham Lincoln* (Lawrence: University Press of Kansas, 1994); Douglas Wilson, *Honor's Voice: The Transformation of Abraham Lincoln* (New York: Knopf, 1998); and Richard J. Carwardine, *Lincoln* (Harlow, England: Pearson, 2003).

20. David H. Donald, *"We Are Lincoln's Men": Abraham Lincoln and His Friends* (New York: Simon and Schuster, 2003), 8–9.

21. Carl Sandburg, *Abraham Lincoln: The Prairie Years*, 2 vols. (New York: Harcourt, Brace, 1926), 1:26, 416; Aminda Rankin as quoted in Henry B. Rankin, *Personal Recollections of Abraham Lincoln* (New York: G. P. Putnam's Sons, 1916), 320–21.

22. Quoted in Josiah Holland, *Life of Abraham Lincoln* (Springfield, MA: Gurdon Bill, 1866), 436. See also Clarence E. Macartney, *Lincoln and the Bible* (New York: Abingdon-Cokesbury, 1949), 11; Charles T. White, comp., *Lincoln the Comforter* (Hancock, NY: Herald, 1916), 11–16.

23. William J. Wolf, "Abraham Lincoln and Calvinism," in George L. Hunt, ed., *Calvinism and the Political Order* (Philadelphia: Westminster, 1965), 141.

24. See Ida Tarbell, *In the Footsteps of the Lincolns* (Harper and Brothers, 1924), 108–9; Louis A. Warren, *Lincoln's Youth: Indiana Years, Seven to Twenty-One, 1816–1830* (New York: Appleton, Century, Crofts, 1959), 13, 112–16; Guelzo, *Lincoln*, 36–38; and James L. Peacock and Ruel W. Tyson Jr., *Pilgrims of Paradox: Calvinism and Experience among the Primitive Baptists of the Blue Ridge* (Washington, DC: Smithsonian Institution Press, 1989).

25. Quoted in Guelzo, *Lincoln*, 38. For a while as a youth, Lincoln served as the church sexton, which required him to be there whenever the church was open (Warren, *Lincoln's Youth*, 121–22).

26. Ward H. Lamon, *The Life of Abraham Lincoln: From His Birth to his Inauguration as President* (Boston: James R. Osgood, 1872), 39. Dennis Hanks remembered that Lincoln amused his siblings by parodying sermons, repeating them almost verbatim and mimicking their "Style & tone" (quoted in Guelzo, *Lincoln*, 38). Cf. William H. Herndon (hereafter WHH) interview with Matilda Johnston Moore, Sept. 8, 1865, *RW*, 109–10.

27. Warren, *Lincoln's Youth*, 115–16; Benjamin Thomas, *Portrait for Posterity: Lincoln and His Biographers* (New Brunswick, NJ: Rutgers University Press, 1947), 47–48, Winger, *Lincoln*, 172–73.

28. Wolf, *Lincoln's Religion*, 43–45; Wilson, *Honor's Voice*, 7; Albert Beveridge, *Abraham Lincoln, 1801–1858*, 2 vols. (Boston: Houghton, 1928), 1:138–39. Lincoln read the works of Voltaire, Thomas Paine, and Gibbons's *Decline and Fall of the Roman Empire* (David H. Donald, *Lincoln* [New York: Simon and Schuster, 1995], 48–49).

29. AL to Mary Speed, Sept. 27, 1841, *CW* 1:261.

30. Donald, *Lincoln*, 74.

31. AL to Martin Morris, Mar. 26, 1843, *CW* 1:320.

32. Lincoln, "Handbill Replying to Charges of Infidelity," July 31, 1846, *CW* 1:382. See also AL to Allen N. Ford, Aug. 11, 1846, *CW* 1:384.

33. Wolf argues that because Lincoln was repudiating false charges, his statement did not necessarily express all he believed (*Lincoln's Religion*, 73).

34. Joshua Speed, *Reminiscences of Abraham Lincoln . . .* (Louisville, KY: John P. Morton, 1884), 32. Cf. Speed to WHH, Jan. 12, 1866, in *HI*, 156.

35. James H. Matheny interview, Mar. 2, 1870, in *HI*, 576: Lincoln sometimes commented on biblical passages to show their falsity and "follies on the grounds of *Reason*"; John Stuart as quoted in *Herndon's Life of Lincoln* (Cleveland: Fine Editions, 1949), 355.

36. James H. Matheny interview, Nov. 1866, in *HI*, 432.

37. Guelzo, *Lincoln*, 151.

38. E.g., Donald, *Lincoln*, 337. Mary Lincoln said that her husband first thought about religion "when Willie died—never before." He "felt religious More than Ever

about the time he went to Gettysburg," she added, and he "read the bible a great deal about 1864" (interview with WHH, Sept. 1866, in *HI*, 360). Donald concluded that her assessment testified to their lack of intimacy much more than to the president's state of mind. Others point to Lincoln's trip to Gettysburg as the turning point in his relationship with God. See Carpenter, *Six Months*, 119, 187–88, 192–93; Ida Tarbell, *The Life of Abraham Lincoln*, 2 vols. (New York: Lincoln Memorial Association, 1900), 2:89–90. See also *CW* 6:196–97, 8:550.

39. Leonard Swett to WHH, Jan. 17, 1866, in *HI*, 167–68. He added that Lincoln "believed in God as much as the most approved Church member," but "he had . . . very little faith in ceremonials and forms."

40. Michael Burlingame, ed., *Lincoln Observed: The Civil War Dispatches of Noah Brooks* (Baltimore: Johns Hopkins University Press, 1998), 13, 211; Brooks to James A. Reed, Dec. 31, 1872, in *RW*, 47.

41. Speed to WHH, Jan. 12, 1866, in *HI*, 156. John Nicolay, by contrast, contended that Lincoln did not "in anyway change his religious ideas, opinions, or beliefs from the time he left Springfield to the day of his death" (Nicolay to Herndon, May 27, 1865, in *HI*, 6).

42. Guelzo, *Lincoln*, 154. Lincoln especially liked its view of human dependence and God's providential direction of the world (Winger, *Lincoln*, 195).

43. This book was based on debates between Smith and freethinker Charles G. Olmstead. Ninian Edwards verified that Lincoln read Smith's book, and Thomas Lewis asserted that it helped changed Lincoln's views about Christianity (Guelzo, *Lincoln*, 156).

44. Smith to WHH, Jan. 24, 1867, in *HI*, 549.

45. Edwards to James A. Reed, Dec. 27, 1872, and Lewis to Reed, Jan. 6, 1873, both in James A. Reed, "The Later Life and Religious Sentiments of Abraham Lincoln," *Scribner's Monthly* 6 (July 1873), 338–39; the quotation is from Edwards. According to James Keyes, Lincoln thought "it would have been More miraculous" for "the Order and harmony of nature" "to have Come about by chance, than to have been created and arranged by some great thinking power" (Keyes to WHH, 1865–66, *HI*, 464).

46. Guelzo, *Lincoln*, 455.

47. Ibid., 20–21, quotations in that order.

48. Abraham Lincoln, "The Perpetuation of Our Political Institutions," Jan. 27, 1838, *CW* 1:115. Cf. Lincoln, "Temperance Address," Feb. 22, 1842, *CW* 1:279: "Happy day, when, all appetites controlled [*sic*], all passions subdued, . . . all-conquering *mind*, shall live and move the monarch of the world. . . . Reign of Reason, all hail!"

49. Charles Zane to WHH, 1865–66, in *HI*, 489.

50. Noll, "Lincoln's God," 85.

51. Lucas Morel, *Lincoln's Sacred Effort: Defining Religion's Role in American Self-Government* (Lanham, MD: Lexington, 2000), 164. He points especially to Lincoln's "Perpetuation of Our Political Institutions" and "Temperance Address."

52. He told Joshua Speed, "I always was superstitious" (July 4, 1842, *CW* 1:289), and Barton argued he continued to be (*Soul*, 236). See also AL to James W. Grimes, July 12, 1856, *CW* 2:348; *Herndon's Life of Lincoln*, 352; and Winger, *Lincoln*, 160–65.

53. Stephen B. Oates, *Abraham Lincoln: The Man Behind the Myths* (New York: Harper and Row, 1984), 40. See also Carpenter, *Six Months*, 163–65; Brooks, *Lincoln Observed*, 205–6; Ward Hill Lamon, *Recollections of Abraham Lincoln, 1847–1865*

(Chicago: A.C. McClurg, 1895), 12–13; and Gideon Welles, *Diary of Gideon Welles,* 3 vols. (Boston: Houghton-Mifflin, 1911), 2:282–83.

54. See Jean H. Baker, *Mary Todd Lincoln* (New York: W. W. Norton, 1987), 218–22; and Garry Wills, *Under God: Religion and American Politics* (New York: Simon and Schuster, 1990), 208.

55. Peterson, *American Memory,* 228; Mark Neely Jr., "Religion," in *The Abraham Lincoln Encyclopedia* (New York: McGraw-Hill, 1982), 261. Current claims that Lincoln probably read a book entitled *Further Communications from the World of Spirits . . .* (1861). A critic denounced Lincoln in a tract entitled *Interior Causes of the War: The Nation Demonised, and Its President a Spirit-Rapper* (New York: M. Doolady, 1863) (see Richard N. Current, *The Lincoln Nobody Knows* [New York: Hill and Wang, 1963], 56, 67–68). Others disagree with this perspective. Lincoln's private secretary John Nicolay declared, "I never knew of his attending a séance of Spiritualists at the White House or elsewhere. . . ." Nicolay to Jesse Weik, Nov. 24, 1894, as quoted in Wolf, *Lincoln's Religion,* 202. Wolf maintains there is no creditable evidence that Lincoln attended a séance or met with a medium (202).

56. Speed to AL, Oct. 26, 1863, Abraham Lincoln Papers, Library of Congress (hereafter ALP).

57. Hein, "Lincoln's Theology," 170.

58. According to the testimony of friends and his own admission, Lincoln did not attend church very often during this period. E.g., AL to Mary S. Owens, May 7, 1837, *CW* 1:78.

59. Ida Tarbell claimed that Lincoln's former neighbors in Springfield testified that he attended church weekly and gave "serious attention" to the sermons he heard (*Abraham Lincoln,* 1:238). James Smith reported that Lincoln "was a regular attendant upon my ministry" (Smith to WHH, Jan. 24, 1867, in *HI,* 550).

60. Barton, *Soul,* 244; William J. Johnstone, *How Lincoln Prayed* (New York: Abingdon, 1931), 74–75.

61. See Benjamin Thomas, *Lincoln's New Salem* (Springfield, IL: Abraham Lincoln Association, 1934), 89; Wolf, *Lincoln's Religion,* 41–42.

62. Henry Deming, *Eulogy upon Abraham Lincoln: Before the General Assembly of Connecticut* (Hartford: A. N. Clark, 1865), 42. See also Rankin, *Personal Recollections,* 325–26. James Matheny explained that as Lincoln "grew older he grew more discrete— didn't talk much before Strangers about his religion" (*HI,* 576). David Davis, Lincoln's campaign manager in 1860, asserted in 1866 that he did not "know anything about Lincoln's Religion—don't think anybody Knew . . ." (interview, Sept. 20, 1866, in *HI,* 348).

63. Lincoln allegedly told Gurley that he could not accept all the doctrines of the Westminster Confession of Faith (Barton, *Soul,* 245; cf. 258).

64. Guelzo, *Lincoln,* 155.

65. Wolf, *Lincoln's Religion,* 39.

66. Sandburg, *Abraham Lincoln,* 1:415. See also White, *Lincoln the Comforter,* 11–16.

67. Quoted in William Henry Crook, *Memories of the White House . . .* (Boston: Little, Brown, 1911), 15. Hay reportedly told Elihu Root that sometimes Lincoln awakened him at night to read the Bible to him for twenty or thirty minutes, which helped calm the president. See Michael Burlingame and John R. Turner Ettlinger, eds., *Inside Lincoln's White House: The Complete Civil War Dairy of John Hay* (Carbondale: Southern Illinois University Press, 1997), 345–46.

68. David V. Derickson, "Recollections of Lincoln," *Meadville* (PA) *Tribune Republican*, May 12, 1888.

69. Lincoln quoted Douglas's remark in a speech on July 17, 1858, *CW* 2:252. In his debates with Douglas, Lincoln often corrected his use of the Bible.

70. Guelzo contends that Lincoln quoted Scripture "more by way of proverb and illustration than authority" (*Lincoln*, 318), but sometimes his quotations were integral to his argument. See also Noll, "Lincoln's God," 84.

71. Winger, *Lincoln*, 165.

72. See Macartney, *Lincoln and the Bible*; and S. Trevena Jackson, *Lincoln's Use of the Bible* (New York: Eaton and Maine, 1909).

73. Abraham Lincoln, "Reply to the Loyal Colored People of Baltimore upon Presentation of a Bible," Sept. 7, 1864, *CW* 7:542.

74. Abraham Lincoln, Speech at Cincinnati, Sept. 17, 1859, *CW* 3:462.

75. Donald, *Lincoln*, 514. Carwardine argues that John Bunyan's *Pilgrim's Progress*, the hymns of Isaac Watts, and the King James Bible all had a powerful influence on Lincoln (*Lincoln*, 31).

76. Quoted in Neely, "Books," *The Abraham Lincoln Encyclopedia*, 34.

77. The book was first issued in 1852 and was republished as *Lincoln's Devotional* in 1957. It is not known how much Lincoln read it. See Wolf, *Lincoln's Religion*, 108–9.

78. Speed, *Reminiscences*, 32–33. Cf. Byron Sunderland to James A. Reed, Nov. 15, 1872, in Reed, "Religious Sentiments," 342.

79. Quoted in L. E. Chittenden, *Recollections of President Lincoln and His Administration* (New York: Harper and Brothers, 1891), 449.

80. Keyes to WHH, 1865–66, in *HI*, 464.

81. Wolf identifies thirty-three titles Lincoln used for God (*Lincoln's Religion*, 179–80).

82. Ibid., 20.

83. Abraham Lincoln, "Address at the Baltimore Sanitary Fair," Apr. 18, 1864, *CW* 7:302.

84. Dispatch of Nov. 11 in Sacramento *Union*, Dec. 10, 1864, in *RW*, 52.

85. Two examples are AL to James R. Doolittle, George B. Ide, and A. Hubbell, May 30, 1864, *CW* 7:368; and Lincoln, "Fragment: Niagara Falls," Sept. 25–30, 1848, *CW* 2:10.

86. Quoted in Robert Browne, *Abraham Lincoln and the Men of His Time*, 2 vols. (Chicago: Blakely-Oswald, 1907), 2:426.

87. Quoted in Guelzo, *Lincoln*, 151.

88. Emanuel Hertz, *The Hidden Lincoln: From the Letters and Papers of William H. Herndon* (New York: Blue Ribbon, 1940), 408; WHH to Croyer, Dec. 3, 1866, in ibid., 43.

89. See *CW* 2:442; 501, 511, 3:17. The 1864 reference is Lincoln, "Reply to the Loyal Colored People," *CW* 7:542. He made two other references in his "Speech on the Sub-Treasury," Dec. [26], 1839, *CW* 1:167.

90. Keyes to WHH, 1865–66, in *HI*, 464.

91. Bateman to Josiah Holland, June 19, 1865, in *RW*, 25. It seems unlikely that Bateman correctly remembered Lincoln's words. On Bateman's creditability, see Allen Guelzo, "Introduction" in *Holland's Life of Abraham Lincoln* (Lincoln: University of Nebraska Press, 1998), xx–xxii.

92. Guelzo, *Lincoln*, 153; AL to Joshua F. Speed, July 1842 in *CW* 1:217.

93. See Melvin B. Endy, "Abraham Lincoln and American Civil Religion: A Reinterpretation," *CH* 44 (June 1975), 229–41; Allen C. Guelzo, "Abraham Lincoln and

the Doctrine of Necessity," *JALA* (Winter 1997), 57–81; Guelzo, *Lincoln*, 117–18, 152–55; and Noll, *America's God*, 435. Noll adds that Lincoln's belief that "God communicated with him intuitively also seems more a product of folk religion than of traditional Christianity."

94. WHH to Fowler, Feb. 18, 1886, in Hertz, *Hidden Lincoln*, 142; quotation from WHH to Weik, Feb. 6, 1887, ibid., 167. Herndon claimed Lincoln's wife verified this point, ibid., 406.

95. Guelzo, *Lincoln*, 318, 319, 328, quotation from 318.

96. For the larger context, see John F. Berens, *Providence and Patriotism in Early America, 1640–1815* (Charlottesville: University Press of Virginia, 1978).

97. Abraham Lincoln, "Mediation on the Divine Will," Sept. 2, 1862, *CW* 5: 403–4.

98. Abraham Lincoln, "Farewell Address at Springfield, IL," Feb. 11, 1861, *CW* 6:110. Cf. Lincoln's speech at Buffalo, Feb. 16, 1861, *CW* 4:221.

99. Abraham Lincoln, "Message to Congress in Special Session," July 4, 1861, *CW* 4:441. Cf. Lincoln, "Annual Message to Congress," Dec. 3, 1861, *CW* 5:53 and AL to Rev. I. A. Gere, A. A. Reese, and G. D. Chenoweth, [May 15?] 1862, *CW* 5:215.

100. Abraham Lincoln, "Response to Evangelical Lutherans," May 13, 1862, *CW* 5:213. Cf. *CW*, Oct. 3, 1863, 6:497; and *CW*, May 9, 1864, 7:333.

101. Guelzo, *Lincoln*, 327.

102. Gillespie to WHH, Dec. 8, 1866, *RW*, 168.

103. Sunderland to Reed, Nov. 15, 1872, in Reed, "Religious Sentiments," 343.

104. Abraham Lincoln, "Fragment on Pro-slavery Theology" [Oct. 1, 1858?] *CW* 3:204. Cf. Lincoln, "Reply to Members of the Presbyterian General Assembly," May 30, 1863, *CW* 6:244.

105. Abraham Lincoln, "Reply to Emancipation Memorial Presented by Chicago Christians of All Denominations," Sept. 1862, *CW* 8:28–29.

106. Lincoln, "Mediation on the Divine Will," *CW* 5:403–4.

107. AL to Eliza P. Gurney, Sept. 4, 1864, *CW* 7:535.

108. AL to Albert G. Hodges, Apr. 4, 1864, *CW* 7:282. Cf. Lincoln, "Address at Sanitary Fair," *CW* 7:361.

109. Donald, *Lincoln*, 15.

110. Quoted in Chittenden, *Recollections of President Lincoln*, 448.

111. Abraham Lincoln, "Reply to Eliza P. Gurney," Oct. 26, 1862, *CW* 5:478. Cf. AL to James C. Conkling, Aug. 26, 1863, *CW* 6:410; *CW*, Oct. 20, 1864, 8:56.

112. Reinhold Niebuhr, "The Religion of Abraham Lincoln," in Allan Nevins, ed., *Lincoln and the Gettysburg Address: Commemorative Papers* (Urbana: University of Illinois Press, 1964), 75, 87, quotation from 87. See also Reinhold Niebuhr, *The Irony of American History* (New York: Charles Scribner's Sons, 1952), 171–74, quotation from 172.

113. Wills, *Under God*, 214, 218, quotation from 214.

114. Quoted in William E. Curtis, *The True Abraham Lincoln* (Philadelphia: J. B. Lippincott, 1903), 385–86. See also Noah Brooks to J. A. Reed, Dec. 31, 1878, as cited by Wolf, *Lincoln's Religion*, 124. Mary Todd Lincoln's testimony is in Reed, "Religious Sentiments," 343. Newton Bateman claimed that Lincoln told him he believed in the "duty, privilege, and efficacy of prayer" (Bateman to Josiah Holland, June 19, 1865, in *RW*, 25).

115. Noah Brooks, "Personal Recollections of President Lincoln," *Harper's New Monthly* 31 (July 1865), 226.

116. Pomeroy in *Lincoln Scrapbook,* 54. Cf. Rebecca R. Pomeroy, "What His Nurse Knew," *Magazine of History* 32 (1926), 47–48. Ida Tarbell argues that after this experience, Lincoln "was seen often with the Bible in his hand, and he is known to have prayed frequently" (*Abraham Lincoln,* 2:91–92). Julia Taft Bayne, by contrast, claimed she "never heard him pray" and noted that the Lincolns did not hold family worship (*Tad Lincoln's Father* [Boston: Little, Brown, 1933], 183). Illinois Senator Orville Browning said that "during their long and intimate acquaintance and intercourse," he saw Lincoln reading his Bible on several occasions but never observed him engage in "any other act of devotion" (Browning to Isaac N. Arnold, Nov. 25, 1872, Arnold Papers, Chicago Historical Society, quoted in Burlingame, ed., *Oral History,* 130–31, quotations from 130).

117. E.g., Lincoln, "Reply to Eliza P. Gurney," *CW* 5:478.

118. AL to Caleb Russell and Sallie A. Fenton, Jan. 5, 1863, *CW* 6:39. Cf. AL to Gurney, *CW* 7:535: "I am much indebted to the good Christian people of the country for their constant prayers and consolations." Lincoln frequently invoked God when providing comfort to the bereaved. E.g., AL to Lydia Bixby, Nov. 21, 1864, *CW* 8:117; AL to the parents of Colonel Elmer Ellsworth, May 25, 1861, *CW* 4:386.

119. Abraham Lincoln, "Remarks to the Baltimore Presbyterian Synod," Oct. 24, 1863, *CW* 6:535.

120. Guelzo, *Lincoln,* 160, 155 (Speed quotation). See Lincoln, Speech at Chicago, July 10, 1858, *CW* 2:501. In *How Lincoln Prayed,* Johnstone cites the testimony of many who knew Lincoln, including Nicolay, Brooks, Pomeroy, Bateman, James Jacquess, Judge Joseph Gillespie, James Smith, Presbyterian executive William Henry Roberts, N. W. Miner, Methodist Bishop Edmund Janes, and cabinet member L. E. Chittenden.

121. Menter Graham to B. F. Irwin, Mar. 17, 1874, quoted in Wolf, *Lincoln's Religion,* 48. See also Wolf, "Abraham Lincoln," 145; Rankin, *Personal Recollections,* 306; and Barton, *Soul,* 271–72.

122. Cogdal interview by WHH, 1865–66, in *HI,* 441. Cogdal added that Lincoln "was a Universalist taproot & all in faith and sentiment."

123. Isaac Cogdal to Benjamin F. Irwin, Apr. 10, 1874, *Illinois State Journal,* May 16, 1874, in *RW,* 110.

124. Dictated and signed by Jonathan Harnett to Benjamin F. Irwin, in *Illinois State Journal,* Apr. 20, 1874.

125. William Hanna interview by WHH, 1865–66, in *HI,* 458.

126. Guelzo, *Lincoln,* 50, 154.

127. Abraham Lincoln, "Seventh ... Debate with Stephen A. Douglas," Oct. 15, 1858, *CW* 3:310.

128. E.g., AL to Thurlow Weed, Mar. 15, 1865, *CW* 8:356.

129. Miller, *Lincoln's Virtues,* 264.

130. Abraham Lincoln, "Speech at Peoria, IL," Oct. 16, 1854, *CW* 2:271.

131. Abraham Lincoln, "First Inaugural Address," Mar. 4, 1861, *CW* 4:271.

132. W. H. Herndon, "Lincoln's Religion," in Douglas C. McMurtrie, ed., *Lincoln's Religion* (Chicago: Black Cat, 1936), 17. See also Abner Ellis, statement for WHH, Jan. 1866, *HI,* 171, 173; and H. E. Dummer, interview by WHH, 1865–66, in *HI,* 443.

133. Horace White to Joseph Medill, Mar. 3, 1862, Charles H. Ray MSS, Henry E. Huntington Library, as cited by Burlingame, *Inner World,* 183; Carpenter, *Six Months,* 84.

134. Leonard Swett to WHH, Jan. 17, 1866, in *HI*, 167. Cf. Cyrus Elder to John G. Nicolay, May 5, 1863, ALP.

135. "Order for Sabbath Observance," Nov. 15, 1862, *CW* 5:497–98. See Morel, *Lincoln's Sacred Effort*, 92–95.

136. Guelzo, *Lincoln*, 315–16.

137. E.g., "Conversation with Hon. S. T. Logan at Springfield, July 6, 1875," in Burlingame, ed., *Oral History*, 38. See Beveridge, *Abraham Lincoln*, 1:82–83, 534.

138. Lincoln, "Temperance Address," *CW* 1:279; Morel, *Lincoln's Sacred Effort*, 125–62; and Miller, *Lincoln's Virtues*, 43.

139. Quoted in James Smith to WHH, Jan. 24, 1867 in Springfield *Daily*, *Illinois State Journal*, Mar. 12, 1867. The Fehrenbachers question this quotation because Smith attributes it to an address Lincoln gave to the Bible Society of Springfield, and there is no other evidence of this speech (*RW*, 411).

140. Lincoln, "Reply to the Loyal Colored People," *CW* 7:542.

141. Abraham Lincoln, "Third Annual Message to Congress," Dec. 8, 1863, *CW* 7:48.

142. Abraham Lincoln, "Communication to the People of Sangamo County," Mar. 9, 1832, *CW* 1:8.

143. Quoted in Jones, *Preachers*, 37. David Donald argues that Lincoln did not believe in an afterlife. See *Lincoln's Men*, 5. On the other hand, Lincoln was pre-occupied with death. See Douglas L. Wilson, "Abraham Lincoln's Indiana and the Spirit of Mortal," *Indiana Magazine of History* 87 (June 1991), 155–70; Robert V. Bruce, *Lincoln and the Riddle of Death* (Fort Wayne, IN: A. Warren Lincoln Library and Museum, 1981); and Burlingame, *Inner World*, 92–122.

144. Carwardine, *Lincoln*, 231.

145. AL to Speed, Feb. 3, 1842, *CW* 1:267–68.

146. AL to John D. Johnston, Jan. 12, 1851, *CW* 2:97. According to Herndon, many of Lincoln's Springfield friends contended that he did not believe in immortality but was simply providing consolation as a "dutiful son to his dying father" (Herndon to an unknown correspondent, Nov. 24, 1882, in Hertz, *Hidden Lincoln*, 87).

147. Joshua Speed to WHH, Jan. 12, 1866, in *HI*, 157. Cf. Joshua Speed interview, June 1865, in *HI*, 31.

148. Carwardine, *Lincoln*, 29.

149. Fowler, *Patriotic Orations*, 102; Edward L. Watson, "The Conversion of Abraham Lincoln," Appendix II, in Barton, *Soul*, 309–13, originally published in *CA*, Nov. 11, 1909; Johnstone, *How Lincoln Prayed*, 15–16, 36–41; Tarbell, *Abraham Lincoln*, 2:91; Raymond W. Settle, "Abraham Lincoln's Faith," *CT* 2 (Feb. 3, 1958), 7. G. Frederick Owen, *Abraham Lincoln: The Man and His Faith* (Wheaton, IL: Tyndale, 1981), 163–64, quotes Lincoln as saying that when he saw the thousands of graves at Gettysburg, "I then and there consecrated myself to Christ. Yes, I do love Jesus." There is little reason to believe that this undocumented quotation is authentic. Guelzo discusses the sources for these statements and their lack of plausibility (*Lincoln*, 444–45).

150. Quoted in William H. Bates, "The Religious Opinions and Life of Abraham Lincoln," *Bibliotheca Sacra*, Jan. 1914, 38–63, quotation from 60–61.

151. Talbot to AL, Dec. 21, 1864, ALP. Two months later, a woman from Troy, New York, wrote to Lincoln, "Ever since you have been our President . . . I have thought very many times—'I wonder if he is not a christian'. . . ." But after reading an article in the *American Messenger* discussing Lincoln's faith, her "heart overflowed with gratitude to God, and with increased love and respect for our God-given President—for

I had very often prayed for you, as all christian people have" (Sarah T. Barnes to AL, Feb. 7, 1865, ALP).

152. Carpenter, *Six Months*, 187–88, 192; Carpenter to WHH, in *HI*, 521; James H. Matheny interview by WHH, Dec. 9, 1873, in *HI*, 582; Chittenden, *Recollections of President Lincoln*, 446–51. See also Burlingame, ed., *Oral History*, 14–15. The quotation is from Matheny in Reed, "Religious Sentiments," 335.

153. Carpenter, *Six Months*, 186.

154. See Hugh McLellan, ed., *The Character and Religion of President Lincoln: A Letter of Noah Brooks, May 10, 1865* (Champlain, NY: Privately printed, 1919). Brooks provided no transcript of Lincoln's prayers, and he "had a well-known weakness for exaggerating his intimacy with Lincoln" (Guelzo, *Abraham Lincoln*, 442).

155. Smith to WHH, Jan. 24, 1867, in *HI*, 547.

156. E.g., Abner Y. Ellis to WHH, Dec. 6, 1866, in *HI*, 501; John T. Stuart interview, 1866, *HI*, 519; and David Davis interview, 1866, in *HI*, 529.

157. Bateman to J. G. Holland, June 19, 1865, in Holland, *Abraham Lincoln*, 236–37.

158. Holland, *Abraham Lincoln*, 236–42, 455, 542–44, quotation from 542.

159. Z. A. Mudge, *The Forest Boy: A Sketch of the Life of Abraham Lincoln...* (New York: Carlton & Porter, 1867). Mudge faulted Lincoln for never publicly avowing his Christian faith. Cf. William C. Gray, *Life of Abraham Lincoln. For the Home Circle and Sabbath School* (Cincinnati: Western Tract Society, 1867).

160. Reed, "Religious Sentiments," 339. The Fehrenbachers argue that this "secondhand testimony...probably reflects some wishful thinking by both clergymen" (*RW*, 191).

161. Brooks to J. A. Reed, Dec. 31, 1872, in Reed, "Religious Sentiments," 340.

162. Oates, *Abraham Lincoln*, 5. E.g., Isaac N. Arnold, *The Life of Abraham Lincoln* (Chicago: Jansen, McClurg, 1885); Bates, "Religious Opinions and Life," 38–63; William J. Johnstone, *Abraham Lincoln: The Christian* (New York: Abingdon, 1928 [1911]); John Wesley Hill, *Abraham Lincoln, Man of God* (New York: G. P. Putnam's Sons, 1920); Harlan H. Horner, *The Growth of Lincoln's Faith* (New York: Abingdon, 1939); Ralph Lindstrom, *Lincoln Finds God* (New York: Longmans, Green, 1958); and Robert Flood, *America, God Shed His Grace on Thee* (Chicago: Moody Bible Institute, 1975), 113–29. See the account of Methodist pastor James F. Jacquess, who alleges that Lincoln was converted at Springfield in 1839, and the claim of James Smith in Barton, *Soul*, 125–26, 258, 241–42, 309–13.

163. Owen, *Abraham Lincoln*, esp. 1, 166–78.

164. See Robert Ingersoll, "The Religious Beliefs of Abraham Lincoln," in *The Works of Robert G. Ingersoll*, 12 vols. (New York: Ingersoll League, 1929), 12:248–55; and Eva Ingersoll Wakefield, ed., *Letters of Robert G. Ingersoll* (New York, 1951), 341–46.

165. Lamon, *Abraham Lincoln*, 144, 157–58, 237, 504, and passim.

166. Jesse W. Fell to Ward Hill Lamon, Sept. 22, 1870, in *HI*, 579. See also William Herndon and Jesse Weik, *Herndon's Lincoln: The True Story of a Great Life*, 3 vols. (Chicago: Belford Clarke, 1889), 3:445–46; and Edgar L. Masters, *Lincoln the Man* (New York: Dodd, Mead, 1931), 470–98.

167. Oates argues in *Abraham Lincoln* (6) that Herndon's sources were a combination of "gossip, hearsay, and legend," but three articles have helped rehabilitate the reliability of Herndon and his informants: Douglas L. Wilson, "Editing Herndon's Informants," *Lincoln Herald* 95 (Winter 1993), 115–23; Wilson, "William H. Herndon and His Lincoln Informants," *JALA* 14 (Winter 1993), 15–34; and Rodney O. Davis,

"William Herndon, Memory, and Lincoln Biography," *Journal of Illinois History* 1 (Winter 1998), 99–112.

168. WHH to Croyer, Dec. 3, 1866, in Hertz, *Hidden Lincoln*, 45.

169. Hertz, *Hidden Lincoln*, 409. Cf. C. F. B., "Mr. Lincoln's Religious Beliefs," in McMurtrie, ed., *Lincoln's Religion*, 89; Herndon, "Lincoln's Religion," 23. In this lecture Herndon attacked the accuracy and credibility of all Reed's witnesses.

170. Herndon, "Lincoln's Religion," 17.

171. Ibid., 44.

172. John E. Remsburg, *Abraham Lincoln: Was He a Christian?* (New York: Truth Seeker, 1893). Cf. Joseph Lewis, *Lincoln the Freethinker* (New York: Freethought Press Association, 1934).

173. Quoted by Joseph Lewis, as cited by Peterson, *American Memory*, 227.

174. The Vidal quotation is from Noll, *One Nation*, 92 (see also Gore Vidal, *Lincoln: A Novel* [New York: Random House, 1984], 620–21); Hans Morgenthau, "The Mind of Abraham Lincoln: A Study in Detachment and Practicality," in Thompson, ed., *Essays on Lincoln's Faith and Politics*, 6–16, quotation from 15; Miller, *Lincoln's Virtues*, 85.

175. Winger, *Lincoln*, 4–8, 11; first quotation from 4, second from 6.

176. W. Lloyd Warner, *The Living and the Dead: A Study of the Symbolic Life of Americans* (New Haven, CT: Yale University Press, 1959), 270.

177. E.g., Martin E. Marty, "Two Kinds of Civil Religion," in Russell E. Richey and Donald G. Jones, eds., *American Civil Religion* (New York: Harper and Row, 1974), 47–49.

178. Sidney Mead, *The Nation with the Soul of a Church* (New York: Harper and Row, 1975), 68; Noll, "Lincoln's God," 86; Wolf, *Lincoln's Religion*, 24; Trueblood, *Abraham Lincoln*, 118–19.

179. Robert Bellah, "Civil Religion in America," *Daedalus* 96 (Winter 1967), 9–10; Pierard and Linder, *Civil Religion*, 107; Endy Jr., "Abraham Lincoln and American Civil Religion," 229–41; and Michael P. Zuckert, "Lincoln and the Problem of Civil Religion," in John A. Murley, Robert L. Stone, and William T. Braithwaite, eds., *Law and Philosophy* (Athens: Ohio University Press, 1992), 720–43.

180. Pierard and Linder, *Civil Religion*, 97–99, quotation from 99; Wolf, *Lincoln's Religion*, 58.

181. Quoted in Carpenter, *Six Months*, 282.

182. Quoted in James Hefley and Edward E. Plowman, *Washington: Christians in the Corridors of Power* (Wheaton, IL: Tyndale, 1975), 115.

183. Pierard and Linder, *Civil Religion*, 108, 112.

184. Abraham Lincoln, Proclamation of a National Fast Day, Aug. 12, 1861, *CW* 4:482.

185. Cf. Abraham Lincoln, Proclamation Appointing a National Fast Day, Mar. 30, 1863, *CW* 6:156; and Lincoln, Thanksgiving Proclamation, Oct. 20, 1864, *CW* 8:56. Numerous religious groups and leaders echoed Lincoln's exhortations. United Presbyterians labeled the war "a dire calamity, which the righteous Ruler of the Universe has inflicted upon us because of our sin as a nation" (United Presbyterian Synod to AL, Oct. 28, 1861, ALP). Cf. James Priestley to AL, June 5, 1861 (Resolutions of the General Assembly of the UPCNA), ALP. Alonzo Potter, the Episcopal Bishop of Pennsylvania, wrote to Lincoln that religious leaders in his state unanimously agreed that nation needed to formally acknowledge its dependence on God and repent of its "grievous sins" (Potter to AL, Sept. 27, 1862, ALP). The Triennial Congregational

Convention declared that the crisis demanded that Americans repent of their individual and national sins (Julian M. Sturtevant et al. to AL, Apr. 28, 1864, ALP). Cf. James Delany to AL, Oct. 1863 (Resolutions from the Wisconsin Baptist State Convention), ALP.

186. The first quotation is from Lincoln, "First Inaugural Address," *CW* 4:271; the second is from Lincoln, "Address to the New Jersey Senate at Trenton, NJ," Feb. 21, 1861, *CW* 4:236.

187. Noll, *One Nation*, 103 (quotation); Noll, "Lincoln's God," 87.

188. Stephen Oates, *With Malice toward None: The Life of Abraham Lincoln* (New York: Mentor-New American Library, 1977), 446. Cf. Randall and Current, *Lincoln*, 371.

189. See Glyndon G. Van Deusen, *William Henry Seward* (New York: Oxford University Press, 1967), 37–38, 123–28.

190. See Robert D. Clark, *Life of Matthew Simpson* (New York: Macmillan, 1956), 226; *An Address on the Life and Public Services of Hon. Edwin M. Stanton* (Cincinnati: R. W. Carroll, 1870); and Benjamin P. Thomas and Harold M. Hyman, *Stanton: The Life and Times of Lincoln's Secretary of War* (New York: Knopf, 1962).

191. Lamon, *Recollections*, 91–92.

192. Richard Carwardine, "Abraham Lincoln, the Presidency, and the Mobilization of Union Sentiment," in Susan-Mary Grant and Brian H. Reid, eds., *The American Civil War: Explorations and Reconsiderations* (New York: Longman, 2000), 87–88.

192. Lincoln, "Remarks to the Baltimore Presbyterian Synod," *CW* 6:535.

194. Abraham Lincoln, "Response to Methodists," May 18, 1864, *CW* 7:351.

195. AL to Ide, Doolittle, and Hubbell, *CW* 7:368.

196. David Chesebrough, *"No Sorrow Like Our Sorrow": Northern Protestant Ministers and the Assassination of Lincoln* (Kent, OH: Kent State University Press, 1994), 9–10. Northern clergy strongly influenced Lincoln's decision to issue the proclamation. See John R. McKivigan, *The War against Proslavery Religion: Abolitionists and the Northern Churches, 1830–1865* (Ithaca, NY: Cornell University Press, 1984), 160.

197. E.g., Israel Dwinell, *Hope for Our Country* (Salem, MA: Charles W. Swasey, 1862); and J. E. Rankin, *The Battle Not Man's, But God's* (Lowell, MA: Stone and Huse, 1863).

198. A. C. Hand and W. W. Satterlee to AL, Oct. 11, 1862, ALP. Cf. Pittsburgh Presbyterian Church to Abraham Lincoln, October 1, 1862, ALP.

199. Beaufort, SC, Baptist Church to AL, Jan. 1, 1863, ALP.

200. Chesebrough, *"No Sorrow,"* 10–11. E.g., Byron Sutherland, *The Crisis of Our Times* (Washington, DC: National Banner, 1863).

201. Gilbert Haven, "Three Summers of War," in *National Sermons* (Boston: Lee and Shepard, 1869), 407–20.

202. Carwardine, *Lincoln*, 287. Hepworth to AL, Oct. 24, 1864, ALP. Cf. J. Russell Johnson to AL, June 20, 1864, ALP.

203. E.g., O. T. Lanphear, *Peace by Power* (New Haven, CT: J. H. Benham, 1864). See Chesebrough, *"No Sorrow,"* 12–14.

204. Abraham Lincoln, "Proclamation of Thanksgiving and Prayer," Sept. 3, 1864, *CW* 7:533–34; Lincoln, "Proclamation of Thanksgiving," Oct. 20, 1864, *CW* 8:55–56.

205. Carwardine, *Lincoln*, 288. This section closely follows ibid., 287–92. See also Victor Howard, *Religion and the Radical Republican Movement, 1860–1870* (Lexington: University Press of Kentucky, 1990), 68–89.

206. William D. Potts, *Freeman's Guide to the Polls and a Solemn Appeal to American Patriots* (New York, 1864), esp. 3, 13, 46–47, 100–101.

207. Donald, *Lincoln*, 542, 544. Victor Howard contends that Lincoln won "almost all the evangelical votes" in 1864 (*Religion and the Radical Republican Movement*, 89).

208. Wolf, *Lincoln's Religion*, 92.

209. Quoted in Jones, *Preachers*, 148. Commenting on this case, Lincoln wrote in 1863 that "the U. S. government must not . . . undertake to run the churches" (AL to Samuel R. Curtis, Jan. 2, 1863). See also see Franklin A. Dick to Montgomery Blair, Dec. 19, 1862; Samuel R. Curtis to AL, Dec. 28, 1862 and Dec. 29, 1862; Curtis to AL, Dec. 30, 1862; St. Louis Citizens to AL, Dec. 30, 1862; and St. Louis Presbyterian Church, 1862 (pamphlet), all in ALP.

210. AL to Samuel Curtis, Dec. 27, 1862, *CW* 6:20. A few days later, Lincoln told Curtis he could expel McPheeters if he thought the "public good requires his removal" (AL to Curtis, Jan. 2, 1863, *CW* 6:34).

211. AL to Stanton, Feb. 11, 1864, *CW* 7:179. See also Mordecai J. W. Ambrose to AL, Feb. 2, 1864, ALP.

212. Gurley sometimes wrote Lincoln about political and religious matters. E.g., Gurley to AL, Mar. 30, 1864 and Oct. 12, 1864, ALP.

213. On Gurley, see Jones, *Preachers*, 34–41; D. R. Barbee, "President Lincoln and Doctor Gurley," *Abraham Lincoln Quarterly* 5 (Mar. 1948), 3–24; and David Hein, "A Sermon Lincoln Heard: P. D. Gurley's Man's Projects and God's Results," in *Lincoln Herald* 89 (Winter 1987), 161–66.

214. Jones, *Preachers*, 139.

215. See George R. Crooks, *The Life of Bishop Matthew Simpson* . . . (New York: Harper and Brothers, 1890), 370–76, 389; and Clarence True Wilson, *Matthew Simpson: Patriot, Preacher, Prophet* (New York: Methodist Book Concern, 1929), 69–74.

216. Jones, *Preachers*, 90.

217. See Beecher to AL, Feb. 4, 1865, and Feb. 21, 1865, ALP and Henry Ward Beecher in Allen Thorndike Rice, ed., *Reminiscences of Abraham Lincoln* (New York: North American, 1886), 247–53.

218. See Tilton to AL, Nov. 12, 1864, ALP; and Julian M. Sturtevant to AL, Dec. 2, 1860, ALP.

219. Seward appreciated the "efficient service" McIlvaine rendered in Europe (Seward to AL, June 23, 1862, ALP) and called him "our excellent friend" (Seward to AL, Oct. 25, 1862, ALP).

220. Lincoln, "Response to Methodists," *CW* 7:351.

221. See George Parker and Charles Dawson to AL, May 24, 1864, ALP; AL to William Nast, Oct. 31, 1864, *CW* 8:83.

222. Presbyterian General Assembly to AL, May 27, 1863, ALP. Cf. Edwin F. Hatfield to AL, May 21, 1861 (minutes of Presbyterian General Assembly); Timothy Stillaman to AL, Sept. 18, 1862 (resolutions from Genesee, New York Presbyterian Synod); United Presbyterian General Assembly to AL, May 30, 1862; George D. Henderson to AL, June 3, 1864 (United Presbyterian Church position); and William Brown et al. to AL, Feb. 11, 1864 (Reformed Presbyterian Synod letter), all in ALP.

223. AL to Samuel B. Tobey, Mar. 19, 1862, ALP. See also Society of Friends for New England to AL, Feb. 5, 1862, and Society of Friends for New England to AL, Feb. 5, 1861, in ALP.

224. Society of Friends for New England to AL, Feb. 5, 1862.

225. Eliza P. Gurney to AL, Sept. 8, 1864, ALP. Cf. Caleb Russell and Sallie A. Fenton to AL, Dec. 27, 1862, ALP.

226. AL to John Hughes, Oct. 21, 1861, ALP.

227. See Harold M. Hyman, "Election of 1864," in Arthur Schlesinger Jr. et al., eds., *History of American Presidential Elections, 1789–1968* (New York: Chelsea, 1971), 1155–78.

228. For an overview of Jewish opinion about Lincoln, which was divided during the 1864 presidential campaign, see Myer S. Isaacs to AL, Oct. 26, 1864, ALP.

229. On Jonas, see Isaac Markens, *Lincoln and the Jews* (New York, n. p., 1909), 17–22. The appointee, Sigismund Kaufmann of New York, refused the position.

230. See AL to Arnold Fischel, Dec. 14, 1861, *CW* 5:69; and Henry I. Hart and Myer J. Isaacs to AL, Oct. 6, 1862, ALP. Congress revised the law to allow Jewish chaplains, and the first one was appointed in September 1862.

231. See Markens, *Lincoln and the Jews*, 8–17; and Bertram W. Korn, *American Jewry and the Civil War* (New York: World, 1961). On the issue of army chaplains, see Lee M. Friedman, *Jewish Pioneers and Patriots* (Plainview, NY: Books for Libraries Press, 1974), chap. 4; on Grant's order, see Korn, *American Jewry*, chap. 6; and St. Louis B'nai B'rith to AL, Jan. 5, 1863 ALP.

232. Ronald C. White Jr., "Lincoln's Sermon on the Mount: The Second Inaugural," in Randall M. Miller, Harry S. Stout, and Charles Reagan Wilson, eds., *Religion and the American Civil War* (New York: Oxford University Press, 1998), 208; Glen E. Thurow, *Abraham Lincoln and American Political Religion* (Albany: State University of New York Press, 1976), xii.

233. Abraham Lincoln, Proclamation Appointing a National Fast Day, Mar. 30, 1863, *CW* 6:155.

234. Lincoln, Proclamation of a National Fast Day, *CW* 4:482.

235. Winger, *Lincoln*, 84. Cf. T. Harry Williams, ed., *Selected Writings and Speeches of Abraham Lincoln* (New York: Hendricks House, 1980), xviii.

236. Abraham Lincoln, "Address at Cooper Institute," Feb. 27, 1860, *CW* 549–50. Cf. Lincoln, "Speech on the Dred Scott Decision," June 26, 1857, *CW* 2:409.

237. Abraham Lincoln, "Speech at New Haven, CT," Mar. 6, 1860, *CW* 4:17.

238. Guelzo, *Lincoln*, 19.

239. Lincoln, "Speech on the Sub-Treasury," *CW* 1:179. Lincoln was discussing the 1840 presidential election.

240. Miller, *Lincoln's Virtues*, 228.

241. Quotation from Hein, "Lincoln's Theology," 167.

242. Miller, *Lincoln's Virtues*, 400–1.

243. Roy P. Basler, ed., *The Collected Works of Abraham Lincoln Supplement, 1832–1865* (Westport, CT: Greenwood, 1974), 45.

244. Lincoln, "Address before the Young Men's Lyceum of Springfield, IL," Jan. 27, 1838, *CW* 1:108, 114.

245. AL to Russell and Fenton, Jan. 5, 1863, *CW* 6:40.

246. Harry V. Jaffa, *A New Birth of Freedom: Abraham Lincoln and the Coming of the Civil War* (Lanham: Rowman and Littlefield, 2000), 155; Chittenden, *Recollections of President Lincoln*, 450.

247. Abraham Lincoln, "Speech at Lewistown, IL," Aug. 17, 1858, in *CW* 2:546–47. Cf. AL to George Robertson, Aug. 15, 1855, *CW* 2:318.

248. Abraham Lincoln, "Speech at Chicago," July 10, 1858, *CW* 2:499.

249. Jaffa, *New Birth of Freedom*, 353.

250. Winger, *Lincoln*, 143.

251. Lincoln, "First Inaugural Address," *CW* 4:271; quotation from Lincoln, "Address to the New Jersey Senate," *CW* 4:236.

252. Lincoln, "Second Annual Message to Congress," Dec. 1, 1862, *CW* 5:537. Cf. "Speech to the 189th New York Volunteers," Oct. 24, 1864, *CW* 8:75.

253. Miller, *Lincoln's Virtues*, 464.

254. Hans J. Morgenthau, "Human Rights and Foreign Policy," in Kenneth W. Thompson, ed., *Herbert Butterfield: The Ethics of History and Politics* (Washington, DC: University Press of America, 1980), 103; Hein, "Lincoln's Theology," 165.

255. Abraham Lincoln, "Address to the Legislature at Albany, NY," Feb. 18, 1861, *CW* 4:226.

256. Lincoln, "First Inaugural Address," *CW* 4:270–71; first and second quotations from 270, third from 271.

257. Edward Kirk, July 1864, *RW*, 278.

258. Pierard and Linder, *Civil Religion*, 101. See Lincoln, "First Inaugural Address," *CW* 4:267–71.

259. Lincoln, "Speech at Peoria," *CW* 2:276. See also J. David Greenstone, *The Lincoln Persuasion: Remaking American Liberalism* (Princeton, NJ: Princeton University Press, 1993), 220, 236.

260. Howard Jones, *Abraham Lincoln and a New Birth of Freedom* (Lincoln: University of Nebraska Press, 1999), 23.

261. Carwardine, *Lincoln*, 37.

262. Hein, "Lincoln's Theology," 153; Geoffrey C. Ward, *Lincoln, Slavery, and Civil Rights* (Springfield, IL: Sangamon State University Press, 1978), 21; *CW* 7:368, 542; *Supplement*, 43–45.

263. In 1831, the legislature passed a law requiring free blacks to post a $1,000 bond guaranteeing their good behavior in order to reside in the state. The new state constitution of 1848 prohibited blacks from settling in the state (Neely, *Last Best Hope*, 42).

264. Protest in Illinois Legislature, Mar. 3, 1837, *CW* 1:75.

265. AL to Hodges, *CW* 7:281. Cf. AL to George Robertson, Aug. 15, 1855, *CW* 2:318.

266. Lincoln, "Speech at Peoria," *CW* 2:274.

267. AL to John M. Palmer, Sept. 7, 1854, *CW* 2:228. See also Lincoln, "Speech at Winchester, IL," Aug. 26, 1854, *CW* 2:227; and Lincoln, editorial on the Kansas-Nebraska Act, *Illinois State Journal*, Sept. 12, 1854, in *CW* 2:229–31.

268. AL to Joshua Speed, Aug: 24, 1855, *CW* 2:323.

269. Lincoln, "Seventh . . . Debate with Stephen A. Douglas," *CW* 3:315. Cf. Abraham Lincoln, "Speech at Edwardsville, IL," Sept. 11, 1858, *CW* 3:92.

270. Miller, *Lincoln's Virtues*, 366. E.g., Lincoln, "Speech at Lewiston, IL," Aug. 17, 1858, *CW* 2:546.

271. Lincoln, "Speech at Chicago," July 10, 1858, *CW* 2:501. See also Lincoln, "Speech at Springfield," June 26, 1857, *CW* 2:406; and Lincoln, "Speech at Peoria," *CW* 2:266.

272. Miller, *Lincoln's Virtues*, 150.

273. Abraham Lincoln, "First Debate with Stephen A. Douglas at Ottawa, IL," Aug. 21, 1858, *CW* 3:29.

274. Lincoln, "Fragment on Pro-Slavery Theology," *CW* 3:204–5.

275. Abraham Lincoln, "Speech at Hartford, CT," Mar. 5, 1860, *CW* 4:9.

276. Abraham Lincoln, "Speech at Columbus, OH," Sept. 16, 1859, *CW* 3:410.

277. Abraham Lincoln, "Speech at Cincinnati," Sept. 17, 1859, *CW* 3:462.

278. AL to Doolittle, Ide, and A. Hubbell, *CW* 7:368. Cf. "The President's Last, Shortest, and Best Speech," Dec. 6, 1864, *CW* 8:155.

279. Lincoln, "Second Annual Message to Congress," *CW* 5:530–31. Lincoln told Reformed Presbyterians that he agreed with them that slavery was immoral but disagreed with them about the best way to abolish it ("Remarks to Committee of Reformed Presbyterian Synod," July 17, 1862, *CW* 5:327).

280. Lincoln, "Speech at Peoria, IL," *CW* 2:255–56, quotations from 256.

281. Bateman to Josiah Holland, June 19, 1865 in *RW*, 25.

282. Lincoln, "Speech at Hartford," *CW* 5:5.

283. AL to Hodges, *CW* 7:281–82.

284. AL to Joshua Speed, Aug. 24, 1855, *CW* 2:320.

285. AL to Horace Greeley, August 22, 1862 (clipping from Aug. 23, 1862 *New York Tribune*) in ALP.

286. Abraham Lincoln, "Reply to Emancipation Memorial Presented by Chicago Christians of All Denominations," Sept. 13, 1862, *CW* 5:419–25, quotation from 425.

287. Jones, *Abraham Lincoln*, 39–40, quotation from 40.

288. Abraham Lincoln, "Resolution on Slavery," Apr. 15, 1863, *CW* 6:176.

289. *Diary and Correspondence of Salmon P. Chase* (New York: Da Capo, 1971), 88.

290. Welles, *Diary*, 1:143.

291. Hein, "Lincoln's Theology," 149–50, quotation from 150. For Lincoln's account of these events, see Carpenter, *Six Months*, 77–78.

292. Lincoln, "Second Annual Message to Congress," *CW* 5:537.

293. http://www.archives.gov/exhibits/featured_documents/emancipation_proclamation/. See Allen Guelzo, *Lincoln's Emancipation Proclamation: The End of Slavery in America* (New York: Simon & Schuster, 2004).

294. Abraham Lincoln, "Speech at Great Central Sanitary Fair, Philadelphia," June 16, 1864, *CW* 7:394.

295. Kenneth M. Stampp, "Lincoln's History," in James M. McPherson, ed., *We Cannot Escape History* (Urbana: University of Illinois Press, 1995), 28–29.

296. Noll, *America's God*, 424–26; quotation from 425.

297. Frederick Douglass, *Life and Times of Frederick Douglass* (Hartford, CT: Park, 1882), 407, 403, quotations in that order; Philip Schaff, *Der Burgerkrieg und das christliche Leben in Nord-Amerika* (Berlin, 1866), 68, as quoted by Noll, *America's God*, 6–7.

298. Wolf, *Lincoln's Religion*, 186; Pierard and Linder, *Civil Religion*, 106; Noll, "Lincoln's God," 86. The address mentions God fourteen times, alludes to Scripture several times, and quotes four biblical verses. See also Thurow, *Abraham Lincoln*; Morel, *Lincoln's Sacred Effort*, 163–221; Mark Noll, "'Both . . . Pray to the Same God': The Singularity of Lincoln's Faith in the Era of the Civil War," *JALA* 18 (Winter 1997), 1–26; and Ronald C. White, *Lincoln's Greatest Speech: The Second Inaugural* (New York: Simon and Schuster, 2002). Unlike Lincoln, many Northerners wanted revenge on the South. For examples, see David B. Chesebrough, ed., *"God Ordained This War": Sermons on the Sectional Crisis, 1830–1865* (Columbia: University of South Carolina Press, 1992).

299. See Chesebrough, *"No Sorrow,"* 105–6, for examples.

300. Noll, *America's God*, 430, offers the addresses of Bushnell, German Reformed seminary professors John Williamson Nevin and Philip Schaff, the eulogy of Charles Hodge of Princeton Seminary, and the commentary of Southerner John Adger as

examples of those who thought God's purposes in the Civil War were easily discerned. See Horace Bushnell, "Our Obligations to the Dead," in *Building Eras in Religion* (New York: Charles Scribner's Sons, 1881), 328–29, 341, 352; John Nevin, "The Nation's Second Birth," *German Reformed Messenger*, July 26, 1865, 1; Philip Schaff, *Der Burgerkrieg*, 16–17; Charles Hodge, "President Lincoln," *Biblical Repository and Princeton Review* 37 (July 1865), 439–40; and John Adger, "Northern and Southern Views of the Province of the Church," *Southern Presbyterian Review* 16 (Mar. 1866), 398–99, 410.

301. Abraham Lincoln, "Second Inaugural Address," Mar. 4, 1865, *CW* 8:333.

302. Lincoln's death increased the rage and hatred of Northerners and their demand for revenge and retribution rather than a willingness to forgive, understand, and conciliate. See Chesebrough, *"No Sorrow,"* xx, 54–56, 97–101; and Charles Stewart "The Pulpit and the Assassination of Lincoln," *Quarterly Journal of Speech* 50 (Oct. 1964), 300.

303. Hein, "Lincoln's Theology," 142.

304. All the quotations in this paragraph are from Lincoln, "Second Inaugural Address," *CW* 8:333, except the last one, which is from Lincoln, "Second Annual Message to Congress," *CW* 5:537.

305. See Dorothy Kunhardt and Philip Kunhardt, *Twenty Days: A Narrative in Text and Pictures of the Assassination of Abraham Lincoln . . .* (San Bernardino, CA: Borgo, 1977), 79–80; and Welles, *Diary* 2:286–8.

306. Pierard and Linder, *Civil Religion*, 108.

307. Phineas Gurley, *Faith in God: Dr. Gurley's Sermon at the Funeral of Abraham Lincoln* (Philadelphia: General Assembly of the PCUSA, 1940), 12.

308. Chesebrough, *"No Sorrow,"* 109. Chesebrough identifies and discusses many of the sermons cited in this section. See also Charles Stewart, "Lincoln's Assassination and the Protestant Clergy of the North," *Journal of the Illinois State Historical Society* 54 (Autumn 1961), 268–93; and the fifty-seven full-text sermons at "Our Martyred President: Sermons Given on the Occasion of Abraham Lincoln's Assassination," http://chaucer.library.emory.edu/lincoln/html/.

309. Pierard and Linder, *Civil Religion*, 109. See also Ray P. Basler, *The Lincoln Legend: A Study in Changing Conceptions* (New York: Octagon, 1969), 125–26.

310. E.g., J. B. Wentworth, *A Discourse on the Death of President Lincoln* (Buffalo: Matthews and Warren, 1865), 11; James Reed, "Address," in *Sermons Preached in Boston on the Death of Abraham Lincoln* (Boston, J. E. Tilton, 1865), 302; and Charles C. Everett, *A Sermon* (Bangor, ME: Benj. A. Burr, 1865), 5.

311. Quotation from Denis Wortman, *A Discourse on the Death of Abraham Lincoln* (Albany: Weed, Rider, and Brother, 1865), 9. Others who compared the two presidents include Joshua Tucker, *A Discourse* (Holliston, MA: Plimpton and Clark, 1865), 15; Hiram Sears, *The People's Keepsake* (Cincinnati, Poe & Hitchcock, 1865), 15; Sidney Dean, *Eulogy* (Providence, RI: H. H. Thomas, 1865), 7; William R. Williams, "Sermon I," in *Our Martyr President, Abraham Lincoln: Voices from the Pulpit of New York and Brooklyn* (New York: Tibbals and Whiting, 1865), 18; and Henry B. Smith, "Sermon XXI," in ibid., 366.

312. E.g., Charles Lowe, *Death of President Lincoln* (Boston: Unitarian Association, 1865), 18–19; Clement M. Butler, *Funeral Address* (Philadelphia: Henry B. Ashmead, 1865), 12; and Alonzo H. Quint, "What President Lincoln Did for His Country," in *Three Sermons* (New Bedford, MA: Mercury Job, 1865), 18.

313. Joel Bingham, *National Disappointment, A Discourse Occasioned by the Assassination of President Lincoln* (Buffalo, NY: Breed, Butler, 1865), 35–36.

314. These quotations are from Lloyd Lewis, *Myths after Lincoln* (New York: Reader's Club, 1957), 95–98.

315. Chesebrough, *"No Sorrow,"* 32–33. E.g., Thomas Laurie, *The Discourses* (Dedham, MA: John Cox, Jr., 1865), 33; George Duffield, *The Nation's Wail* (Detroit: Advertiser and Tribune Print, 1865), 17; and Robert Lowry, "Sermon XVII," in *Our Martyr President*, 310–11.

316. Guelzo, *Lincoln*, 441–42. The quotation is from Samuel C. Baldridge, *The Martyr Prince* (Cincinnati: Joseph Boyd, 1865), 12. Cf. Theodore Cuyler, "Sermon IX," in *Our Martyr President*, 169; Joseph P. Thompson, "Sermon X," in ibid., 202; and Henry A. Nelson, "The Divinely Prepared Ruler," in *Two Discourses* (Springfield, IL: Baker and Phillips, 1865), 21. Baptist, Methodist, Presbyterian, Congregational, Episcopal, and Dutch Reformed pastors all told stories about Lincoln's conversion. See Chesebrough, *"No Sorrow,"* 30–31, for examples.

317. Gurley, *Faith in God*, 16, 18, quotations in that order; Simpson, "Oration," 404–5. Cf. Gordon Hall, *President Lincoln's Death: Its Voice to the People* (Northampton, MA: Trumball and Gere, 1865).

318. E.g., Joseph A. Seiss, *The Assassinated President* (Philadelphia, n. p., 1865), 20; Sears, *The People's Keepsake*, 13.

319. Chesebrough, *"No Sorrow,"* 16.

320. Gurley, *Faith in God*, 14–15, quotations from 15.

321. Quoted in Chesebrough, *"No Sorrow,"* 16–17.

322. Samuel Adler, "Excerpt from Address," in Emanuel Hertz, ed., *Abraham Lincoln: The Tribute of the Synagogue* (New York: Bloch, 1927), 179. Cf. Samuel Myer Isaacs, "The President's Death," in ibid., 75.

323. Henry Vidaver, "Discourse," in *Tribute of the Synagogue*, 53; M. R. Deleeuw, "Abraham Lincoln," in ibid., 174.

324. Adler, "Excerpt from Address," 179; Deleeuw, "Abraham Lincoln," 175, quotations in that order.

325. Vidaver, "Discourse," 54; Rabbi Isaac Wise, "Funeral Address," in *Tribute of the Synagogue*, 92 (quotation); Rabbi Isaac Leeser, "Lincoln's Death," in ibid., 137.

326. Wise is quoted in James G. Heller, *Isaac M. Wise: His Life, Work, and Thought* (New York: Union of American Hebrew Congregations, 1965), 371. Cf. Sabato Morais, "An Address on the Death of Abraham Lincoln," in *Tribute of the Synagogue*, 3.

327. Max Lilienthal, "Assassination of Lincoln," in *Tribute of the Synagogue*, 120; Vidaver, "Discourse," 53; Wise, "Funeral Address," 95; quotations in that order.

328. Vidaver, "Discourse," 54–55.

329. Wise, "Funeral Address," 94–95, quotation from 95. Cf. Leeser, "Lincoln's Death," 136.

330. Max Lilienthal, "Lincoln—An Appreciation," in *Tribute of the Synagogue*, 130–31.

331. Sidney E. Mead, *The Lively Experiment: The Shaping of Christianity in America* (New York: Harper and Row, 1976), 73; Wolf, *Lincoln's Religion*, 194; Robert Michaelsen, "Religion and the Presidency—II," *CC* 77 (Feb. 10, 1960), 160; Roosevelt as cited by John McCollister, *So Help Me, God: The Faith of America's Presidents* (Louisville, KY: Westminster/John Knox), 81; Niebuhr, "The Religion of Abraham Lincoln," 72; Holland, *Abraham Lincoln*, 544.

332. Quoted in Guelzo, *Lincoln*, 247.

333. Henry Raymond, "The Last Address of the President to the Country," *NYT*, Apr. 17, 1865, in Herbert Mitgang, ed., *Abraham Lincoln: A Press Portrait: His Life and Times* . . . (Chicago: Quadrangle, 1971), 472.

334. Carolyn L. Harrell, *When the Bells Tolled for Lincoln: Southern Reaction to the Assassination* (Macon, GA: Mercer University Press, 1997), 20. See Michael Davis, *The Image of Lincoln in the South* (Knoxville: University of Tennessee Press, 1971), 62–75; and Thomas Red Turner, *Beware the People Weeping: Public Opinion and the Assassination of Abraham Lincoln* (Baton Rouge: Louisiana State University Press, 1982), 90–99.

335. Oates, *Abraham Lincoln*, 18. See also Don E. Fehrenbacher, "The Anti-Lincoln Tradition," *Papers of the Abraham Lincoln Association* 4 (1982), 7–28; and Davis, *The Image of Lincoln*, 41–104.

336. Noll, "Lincoln's God," 86. See Eugene D. Genovese, "Religion in the Collapse of the American Union," in Miller, Stout, and Wilson, eds., *Religion and the American Civil War*, 74–88; Harry S. Stout, " 'Baptism in Blood': The Civil War and the Creation of an American Civil Religion," *Books & Culture*, July–Aug. 2003, 16–17, 33–35; Michael Vorenberg, *Final Freedom: The Civil War, the Abolition of Slavery and the Thirteenth Amendment* (New York: Cambridge University Press, 2001); and Lerone Bennett Jr., *Forced into Glory: Abraham Lincoln's White Dream* (Chicago: Johnson, 2000). Miller counters that only Charles Sumner, Salmon Chase, Joshua Giddings, and a few other mid-nineteenth-century politicians had a superior record on racial issues, and none of them represented a constituency that was as close to the South as lower Illinois (*Lincoln's Virtues*, 362, 364).

337. Mark Neely, *The Fate of Liberty: Abraham Lincoln and Civil Liberties* (New York: Oxford University Press, 1991); M. E. Bradford, "The Lincoln Legacy: A Long View," *Modern Age* 24 (1980), 358–62. Lincoln's actions, some complain, transformed a decentralized federalist system into a nation-state with much greater powers and responsibilities. See Garry Wills, *Lincoln at Gettysburg: The Words That Remade America* (New York: Simon and Schuster, 1992), 32–40; George P. Fletcher, *Our Secret Constitution: How Lincoln Redefined American Democracy* (New York: Oxford University Press, 2001); and Thomas DiLorenzo, *The Real Lincoln: A New Look at Abraham Lincoln, His Agenda, and an Unnecessary War* (Roseville, CA: Prima, 2002).

338. Hein, "Lincoln's Theology," 159–62.

339. Winger, *Lincoln*, 75–78; first quotation from 75, second from 78.

340. Speed to WHH, Dec. 6, 1866, in *HI* 499; Gillespie to WHH, Dec. 8, 1866, in *HI*, 507.

341. Oates, *Abraham Lincoln*, 16, 52, quotations in that order.

342. E.g., John G. Nicolay, "The Campaign of 1860," unpublished essay, Nicolay MSS; William Crook, *Through Five Administrations: Reminiscences of Colonel William H. Crook, Body-Guard to President Lincoln*, Margarita Spalding Gerry, ed. (New York: Harper and Brothers, 1910), 11; and Charles Dana, *Lincoln and His Cabinet* (New York, n. p., 1896), 31, 41.

343. On Lincoln's temper, see Paul M. Angle, "Abe Lincoln Had a Temper," *Midwest: Magazine of the Chicago Sunday Times*, Feb. 12, 1956, 6; Sandburg, *Abraham Lincoln: The Prairie Years*, 1:392; Thomas, *Abraham Lincoln*, 84; and Burlingame, *Inner World*, 147–48, 208–9, who called my attention to all the sources in this paragraph.

344. E.g., Douglas Good, "Abraham Lincoln: Paradigm of Forgiveness," *FH* 15 (Spring–Summer 1983), 28–43.

345. AL to Reverdy Johnson, July 26, 1862, *CW* 5:343. Cf. his Second Inaugural Address.

346. Miller, *Lincoln's Virtues*, 90.

347. John Hay to WHH, Sept. 5, 1866, Herndon-Weik Papers, Library of Congress.

348. Wills, *Under God*, 216–17, quotation from 216.

349. AL to Rankin, in Rankin, *Personal Recollections*, 324. Although this statement seems to accurately capture Lincoln's views and life experience, Mrs. Rankin did not dictate this conversation to her son until 1889.

350. Noyes W. Miner, pastor of the First Baptist Church of Springfield, claimed that Mary Lincoln told him this. See Miner, "Personal Reminiscences of Abraham Lincoln," manuscript dated 1882, Illinois State Historical Library, in *RW*, 297.

351. Guelzo, *Lincoln*, 435, 446, 419, quotations in that order. Guelzo notes that Lincoln did not suggest in his Second Inaugural Address that the tragic slaughter of the Civil War might serve a redemptive purpose.

352. Alfred Kazin, *God and the American Writer* (New York: Alfred A. Knopf, 1997), 131, 139–41.

353. Guelzo, *Lincoln*, 446, 461–62, 318; first quotation from 446, second from 461, third and fourth from 462, fifth and sixth from 318.

354. John Patrick Diggins, *On Hallowed Ground: Abraham Lincoln and the Foundations of American History* (New Haven, CT: Yale University Press, 2000), 39; Miller, *Lincoln's Virtues*, 365.

355. Carwardine, *Lincoln*, 30, 242, quotation from 30.

356. Noll, "Lincoln's God," 79, 84, 87; quotation from 79. Many sermons emphasized Lincoln's empathy and love for citizens. E.g., Gilbert Haven, "The Uniter and the Liberator of America," in *National Sermons*, 561; Wentworth, *A Discourse*, 19; Simpson, "Oration," 399; and George Hepworth, "Sermon," in *Sermons Preached in Boston*, 114.

357. Hein, "Lincoln's Theology," 198.

358. Joseph Gillespie to WHH, Dec. 8, 1866, in *HI*, 508. Cf. Isaac N. Arnold to WHH, Dec. 18, 1882.

359. John Nicolay, "Abraham Lincoln," *Encyclopedia Britannica*, 9th ed., 14:662.

360. Guelzo, *Lincoln*, 458.

361. Eliza P. Gurney, Interview with AL, Oct. 26, 1862, ALP. Cf. Eliza P. Gurney to AL, Aug. 18, 1863, ALP.

362. Henry P. Tappan to AL, Nov. 22, 1862.

CHAPTER 4

1. See Clifford Putney, *Muscular Christianity: Manhood and Sports in Protestant America, 1880–1920* (Cambridge, MA: Harvard University Press, 2001).

2. Theodore Roosevelt, "At the Centennial Meeting of the Board of Missions of the Presbyterian Church," May 20, 1902, in *Presidential Addresses and State Papers* (hereafter *PA*), Part One (P. F. Collier, 1905?), 46.

3. Kathleen Dalton, *Theodore Roosevelt: A Strenuous Life* (New York: Alfred Knopf, 2002), 7.

4. Dalton, *Roosevelt*, 18–21, 43, 49–50; first quotation from 18, second from 21. Also see David McCullough, *Mornings on Horseback* (New York: Simon & Schuster, 2001), 24, 32, 42, 68, 91, 105, 125, 144.

5. Christian Reisner, *Roosevelt's Religion* (New York: Abingdon, 1922), 28–29, 207–8. On family prayers before breakfast, see Corinne Roosevelt Robinson, *My Brother Theodore Roosevelt* (New York: Charles Scribner's Sons, 1921), 93.

6. Reisner, *Roosevelt's Religion*, 33; Roosevelt, "Centennial Meeting," 45.

7. On the life of Theodore Sr., see Edmund Morris, *The Rise of Theodore Roosevelt* (New York: Coward, McCann, and Geoghegan, 1979); Carleton Putnam, *Theodore Roosevelt: The Formative Years, 1858–1886* (New York: Charles Scribner's Sons, 1958); Dalton, *Roosevelt*; and McCullough, *Mornings*.

8. Interview with James M. Ludlow in Ferdinand C. Iglehart, *Theodore Roosevelt: The Man As I Knew Him* (New York: Christian Herald, 1919), 292.

9. Quoted by Roosevelt in a letter to Martha Bulloch Roosevelt, Mar. 24, 1878, in Elting Morison, ed., *The Letters of Theodore Roosevelt* (hereafter *Letters*), Vol. 1: *The Years of Preparation, 1868–1898* (Cambridge, MA: Harvard University Press, 1951), 33.

10. Roosevelt was dismissed by Christ Episcopal Church because he refused to become an Episcopalian. See TR to Martha Roosevelt, Jan. 11, 1880, *Letters* 1:43; Jacob Riis, *Theodore Roosevelt, the Citizen* (New York: Outlook, 1904), 37–38; Roosevelt, Personal Diary, Jan. 11, 1880, Theodore Roosevelt Papers, Library of Congress (hereafter TRP); Typescript of the Theodore Roosevelt Association, 1968, Theodore Roosevelt Collection (hereafter TRC), Houghton Library, Harvard University.

11. Nathan Miller, *Theodore Roosevelt: A Life* (New York: William Morrow, 1992), 58, 89–90; H. W. Brands, *T. R.: The Last Romantic* (New York: Basic Books, 1997), 73; Roosevelt, Personal Diary, Apr. 18, 1878, Dec. 11, 1879.

12. TR to Edward S. Martin, Nov. 26, 1900, *Letters*, Vol. 2: *The Years of Preparation, 1898–1900*, Elting Morison, ed. (Cambridge, MA: Harvard University Press, 1951), 1443.

13. Roosevelt, Personal Diary, Mar. 16, 17, Apr. 25, 1878. In his March 17 entry, he added, "As my mottos I take: 'Trust in the Lord, and do good.'" See also Putnam, *Theodore Roosevelt*, 148–52; and Dalton, *Roosevelt*, 68–69.

14. Reisner, *Roosevelt's Religion*, 318.

15. "Mrs. Theodore Roosevelt Entertains the Annual Meeting," *Bible Society Record* 68 (July 1923), 101–3, quotation from 103. See also Edward Cotton, *Ideals of Theodore Roosevelt* (New York: Appleton, 1923), 47. Edith, a devout Episcopalian, strongly encouraged her husband to apply his Christian faith to political and civic life. See Dalton, *Roosevelt*, 119.

16. Quoted in Reisner, *Roosevelt's Religion*, 306, 315–17, quotation from 306. See also Corrine Roosevelt Robinson, "Foreword," in Cotton, *Ideals*, xi. On the religious training Roosevelt provided for his children, see Theodore Roosevelt Jr., *All in the Family* (New York: G. P. Putnam's Sons, 1929), 156–65.

17. Edward Wagenknecht, *The Seven Worlds of Theodore Roosevelt* (New York: Longmans, Green, 1958), 47.

18. All these quotations are in "President Roosevelt's Letter on the Bible," *CA* 77 (May 22, 1902), 810.

19. See the American Bible Society, N.Y. Centennial pamphlets, No. 5, 1916. See also *Outlook*, May 27, 1911, 223.

20. See "The Bible and the Life of the People" in Theodore Roosevelt, *Realizable Ideals* (Freeport, NY: Books for Libraries Press, 1969 [1911]), 69. This chapter was also

distributed as a pamphlet by the American Bible Society. The American Bible Society published a booklet entitled *President Roosevelt on the Bible.*

21. E.g., TR to John Hay, Aug. 9, 1903, *Letters,* Vol. 3: *The Square Deal, 1901–1903,* Elting Morison, ed. (Cambridge, MA: Harvard University Press, 1951), 550. Roosevelt even occasionally arranged sermons for troops on ships or in a field. E.g., "The President's First Sunday After Escape," *CA* 77 (Sept. 11, 1902), 1446; and "President Roosevelt at Chickamauga," ibid. (Oct. 16, 1902), 1660.

22. His favorite hymns included "How Firm a Foundation," "A Mighty Fortress Is Our God," "Christ Is Made the Sure Foundation," and "The Son of God Goes Forth to War." Roosevelt often discussed the sermons he heard on his Sunday walks with Nicholas Murray Butler (Reisner, *Roosevelt's Religion,* 344).

23. Cited in John McCollister, *So Help Me God: The Faith of America's Presidents* (Louisville, KY: Westminster/John Knox, 1991), 126.

24. *The Churchman,* as quoted in Reisner, *Roosevelt's Religion,* 332.

25. *Historical Sketch of the Reformed Church and of the Grace Reformed Congregation* (Washington, DC, 1923), 21–25; Cotton, *Ideals,* 40; "President Roosevelt at Church," *CA* 94 (Jan. 16, 1919).

26. See Harold Bolce, "When the President Goes to Church," *Saturday Evening Post,* n. d., TRC; Gabrielle Marie Jacobs, "Where the President Goes to Church," *Woman's Home Companion,* Nov. 1902; "Where the President Will Worship," *Christian Herald,* Dec. 10, 1902, 1042; Ferdinand C. Iglehart, "An After-Church Chat with President Roosevelt," *CA* 94 (Jan. 30, 1919), 134; and S. H. McKinney, Mar. 11, 1906, letter to the editor of the Oil City (PA) *Derrick,* in "Cranberry Folks at Washington" in *The S. H. McKinney History and Family Tree,* John and Emma McKinney, compilers (privately printed, 1992), 166–67.

27. Iglehart, "After-Church Chat," 134.

28. Roosevelt, *Realizable Ideals,* 74, 77–79. Cf. Theodore Roosevelt, "The Word of Micah; The Religion of Service," *Works of Theodore Roosevelt,* 20 vols., National Edition (New York: Charles Scribner's Sons, 1926–27) (hereafter *Works,* nat. ed.), 19:134.

29. Archibald W. Butt, *The Letters of Archie Butt: Personal Aide to President Roosevelt* (New York, 1924), 77. See also Reisner, *Roosevelt's Religion,* 361; and Edmund Morris, *Theodore Rex* (New York: Random House, 2001), 533.

30. Reisner, *Roosevelt's Religion,* 17, 248; Mark Sullivan, "Was Roosevelt Profane?" in Frederick S. Wood, ed., *Roosevelt as We Knew Him: The Personal Recollections of One Hundred and Fifty of His Friends and Associates* (Philadelphia: John C. Winston, 1927), 20–25; John A. Loring, "The Colonel's Abhorrence of Vulgarity," in ibid., 338–39; Brands, *T.R.,* 421.

31. Oscar Straus, "Mr. Roosevelt's Temperate Habits," in Wood, ed., *Roosevelt,* 332.

32. Miller, *Roosevelt,* 534–35; Stefan Lorant, *The Life and Times of Theodore Roosevelt* (Garden City, NY: Doubleday, 1959), 585–86, 588–89; Wagenknecht, *Seven Worlds,* 92–96; "Mr. Roosevelt's Victory," *Lutheran,* June 12, 1913, 600; Straus, "Temperate Habits," 333–38.

33. Reisner, *Roosevelt's Religion,* 15. William Harbaugh argues that Roosevelt's "innermost convictions are unclear." As an adult, he rarely spoke openly about his faith (*Power and Responsibility: The Life and Times of Theodore Roosevelt* [New York: Farrar, Straus and Cudahy, 1961], 221).

34. Reisner, *Roosevelt's Religion,* 228.

35. Corrine Roosevelt Robinson asserted that "he had a profound faith which he believed would show itself in action" (quoted in Reisner, *Roosevelt's Religion*, 229).

36. Roosevelt, *Works*, nat. ed., 5:48.

37. Reisner, *Roosevelt's Religion*, 230–46.

38. Riis, *Theodore Roosevelt*, 305–6. On the subject of manliness, see Putney, *Muscular Christianity*, passim.

39. Quoted in Reisner, *Roosevelt's Religion*, 232.

40. Letter to Reisner, Jan. 7, 1921, in Reisner, *Roosevelt's Religion*, 231. As a youth, Roosevelt often discussed his faith as being very important. His cousin Emlen Roosevelt claimed that he frequently talked about God in a very natural way on their hunting trips when they were young men.

41. Wagenknecht, *Seven Worlds*, 182.

42. Reisner, *Roosevelt's Religion*, 270–73.

43. TR to Taft, Aug. 28, 1908, *Letters*, Vol. 5: *The Big Stick, 1905–1907*, Elting Morison, ed. (Cambridge, MA: Harvard University Press, 1952), 1200. Cf. Roosevelt, "Christian Citizenship," 271.

44. Theodore Roosevelt, "Address to the Franklin Street Methodist Episcopal Church," Sept. 30, 1917, 6, TRC. Cf. TR to Raymond Robins, June 3, 1915, *Letters*, Vol. 8: *The Days of Armageddon, 1914–1919*, Elting Morison, ed. (Cambridge, MA: Harvard University Press, 1954), 928: walking humbly with God was "the necessary antidote . . . to the hard spiritual arrogance . . . brought about by *mere* reliance on the Gospel of Works."

45. Theodore Roosevelt, "Rider Haggard and the Salvation Army," *Outlook*, July 1, 1911, 476–77, quotation from 476. Moreover, the president called evangelist Billy Sunday the "most wide-awake, militant preacher of Christianity I know" (quoted in William McLoughlin, *Billy Sunday Was His Real Name* [Chicago: University of Chicago Press, 1955], 224).

46. Quoted in Wagenknecht, *Seven Worlds*, 183.

47. Roosevelt, *Realizable Ideals*, 72.

48. Reisner, *Roosevelt's Religion*, 238. Lyman Abbott's son Lawrence, declared, "I think that he believed the spirit of Jesus is the finest and divinest spirit . . . but I do not think he was interested in metaphysical or dogmatic arguments" about Christ's nature (quoted in Reisner, *Roosevelt's Religion*, 241). Reisner alleged that Riis told him that Roosevelt believed in "the unique divinity of Jesus" (259).

49. Iglehart, *Theodore Roosevelt*, 296.

50. E.g., Theodore Roosevelt, "At the Mechanics' Pavilion, San Francisco," May 13, 1903, *PA*, Part One, 394; and Roosevelt, "National Duties," *Works*, Executive Edition (hereafter *Works*, ex. ed.), Vol. 12: *The Strenuous Life* (New York: P. F. Collier, 1900), 235.

51. Theodore Roosevelt, "Thanksgiving Proclamation," Nov. 2, 1901, in James Richardson, ed., *A Compilation of the Messages and Papers of the Presidents*, 20 vols. (New York: Bureau of National Literature, 1917), 14:6640; Roosevelt, "Thanksgiving Proclamation," Nov. 1, 1904, ibid., 14: 6890; Roosevelt, "Inaugural Address," Mar. 4, 1905, ibid., 14:6930.

52. Wagenknecht, *Seven Worlds*, 194.

53. Quoted in Cotton, *Ideals*, 307.

54. Quoted in Joseph Bishop, *Theodore Roosevelt and His Time Shown in His Letters*, 2 vols. (London: Hodder and Stoughton, 1920), 2:476.

55. Gamaliel Bradford, *The Quick and the Dead* (Boston: Houghton Mifflin, 1931), 30.

56. Roosevelt, "Word of Micah," 133.

57. Roosevelt, *Realizable Ideals*, 84, 90, and passim; quotations in that order.

58. Theodore Roosevelt, "At Trinity Reformed Church," Sept. 1901, in C. E. Banks and L. Armstrong, *Theodore Roosevelt, Twenty-Sixth President of the United States* (Chicago: E. R. Du Mont, 1901), 163. Church attendance "is not enough. We must study the Bible, but we must not let it end there," Roosevelt added.

59. Theodore Roosevelt, "Athletics, Scholarships and Public Service," *Works*, nat. ed., 15:490. Cf. Roosevelt, "Before the Young Men's Christian Association," Dec. 30, 1900, *Works*, nat. ed., 13:499).

60. Theodore Roosevelt, *An Autobiography* (New York: Macmillan, 1913), 177. Roosevelt's other favorite Scriptures included Romans 12:11 and the end of James 1 and the beginning of James 2 (Wagenknecht, *Seven Worlds*, 48).

61. E.g., Theodore Roosevelt, "Address at Northfield, MA," Sept. 1, 1902, *PA*, Part One, 134–36.

62. Quoted by Cotton, *Ideals*, 306–7. A message he wrote for the flyleaf of Bibles sent to American soldiers in the summer of 1917 featured this passage.

63. Roosevelt, "Centennial Meeting," 45.

64. "News and Comment," *Lutheran*, Aug. 20, 1908, 797.

65. TR to John R. Mott, Oct. 12, 1908, *Letters*, Vol. 6: *The Big Stick, 1907–1909*, Elting Morison, ed. (Cambridge, MA: Harvard University Press, 1952), 1282. See also Roosevelt, "The Awakening of China," *Outlook* 90 (Nov. 28, 1908), 665–67.

66. Cotton, *Ideals*, 45; "Roosevelt's Testimony," *CA* 78 (Jan. 22, 1903), 140; "The President on Home Missions," *Lutheran*, May 28, 1908, 595; "Roosevelt and the Missionary," *Lutheran*, Sept. 9, 1909, 857.

67. TR to Silas McBee, May 16, 1910, *Letters*, Vol. 7: *The Days of Armageddon, 1909–1914*, Elting Morison, ed. (Cambridge, MA: Harvard University Press, 1954), 84–85. If Christians worked "together with earnest sincerity for the common good," they would find "that doctrinal differences in no way interfere[d]."

68. Theodore Roosevelt, "Social Evolution," *Works*, ex. ed., 1:333–43; first quotation from 333, second and third from 341.

69. George Haven Putnam, address to the Century Association in New York City, quoted in Edwin Carty Ranck, "Roosevelt, an Ethical Force," *The* (Episcopal) *Chronicle* 20 (Oct. 1919), 105.

70. William Allen White, "Saith the Preacher" in *Works*, nat. ed., 13:xi.

71. Cotton, *Ideals*, 206–7.

72. Oscar Straus, "The Religion of Roosevelt," *Forum*, Feb. 1923, 1193. See also Straus, *The American Spirit* (New York: Century, 1913), 311–20.

73. Cf. Roosevelt, "Address . . . upon the . . . Bi-centennial Celebration of the Birth of John Wesley," *PA*, Part One, 247; Roosevelt, *Realizable Ideals*, 2–4; Roosevelt, "Addresses at . . . Presbyterian Home Missions," May 20, 1902, ibid., 53.

74. Theodore Roosevelt, "Peace and Justice in the Sudan," in Roosevelt, *European and African Addresses*, Lawrence Abbott, ed. (New York: G. P. Putnam's Sons, 1910), 7.

75. Theodore Roosevelt, "Address at the Banquet of the YMCA," Jan. 19, 1903, *PA*, Part One, 231. Quoting passages from Micah, Isaiah, Amos, Matthew, and James, Roosevelt contended that the Bible defined religion "as service to one's fellow men

rendered by following the great rule of justice and mercy, of wisdom and right-eousness" ("Word of Micah," 139).

76. Theodore Roosevelt, "Character and Success" in *Works*, ex. ed., 12:98–106; Roosevelt, Thanksgiving Proclamation, Nov. 1907; Roosevelt, "At the Banquet . . . in Honor of Dr. Nicholas Murray Butler," *PA*, Part One, 30; Roosevelt, "At Claremont, CA," May 8, 1903 in Roosevelt, *California Addresses* (San Francisco: California Pro-motion Committee, 1903), 22–23. See also Robert V. Friedenberg, *Theodore Roosevelt and the Rhetoric of Militant Decency* (New York: Greenwood, 1990), 28–30.

77. Theodore Roosevelt, "At Washington, D.C.," Apr. 14, 1906, *Works*, nat. ed., 16:424. Cf. Roosevelt, "National Life and Character," *Works*, ex. ed., 1:289–320.

78. David H. Burton, *Theodore Roosevelt: Confident Imperialist* (Philadelphia: University of Pennsylvania Press, 1968), 72.

79. Theodore Roosevelt, "The New Nationalism and the Old Moralities," in Wil-liam Leuchtenburg, ed., *The New Nationalism* (Englewood Cliffs, NJ: Prentice-Hall, 1961), 173. Cf. Roosevelt, "At Bangor, ME," Aug. 27, 1902, *PA*, Part One, 132–33; Roosevelt, "In the Chapel at the University of Minnesota," Apr. 4, 1903, ibid., 294.

80. Roosevelt, "Address to the Holy Name Society," 460–61, quotation from 461.

81. Roosevelt, "Address at the Banquet of the YMCA," 228.

82. Roosevelt, "Address to the Franklin Street Methodist Episcopal Church," 9; Roosevelt, "Word of Micah," 135–37.

83. Theodore Roosevelt, "Reform through Social Work," *McClure's* 16 (Mar. 1901), 448–54.

84. See Roosevelt's introduction to a history of St. George's Episcopal Church, in George Hodges and John Reichert, *The Administration of an Institutional Church* (New York: Harper and Brothers, 1906).

85. See Theodore Roosevelt, "Civic Helpfulness," *Works*, ex. ed., 12:89–91; Roose-velt, "Address at the Banquet of the YMCA," 226–31; TR to John F. Stevens, May 21, 1906, *Letters* 5:281; and Roosevelt, "The Good Citizen," in Leuchtenburg, ed., *New Nationalism*, 143.

86. Roosevelt, "Addresses at . . . Presbyterian Home Missions," 50.

87. Roosevelt, "Word of Micah," 132.

88. "Our Preacher President," *Independent* 61 (Dec. 13, 1906), 1431. Cf. Lynn Meekins, "The Gospel of Preacher and President," *Saturday Evening Post*, Oct. 5, 1901, 12.

89. W. C. Chisholm, "President Roosevelt as a Religious Force," 102, 104–5, quotation from 102, TRC. Cf. William Boyce Thompson, "The Man—Theodore Roosevelt," *Life Boat*, Oct. 1919, 291–93; William Allen White, "Roosevelt: A Force for Righteousness," *McClure's* 28 (Feb. 1907), 386–94; and Philip Loring Allen, *America's Awakening: The Triumph of Righteousness in High Places* (New York: Fleming H. Revell, 1906), 44–58. Allen argued that Roosevelt was the main inspiration for the "civic renaissance" of the early twentieth century (7): "I never knew a man who exemplified more fully in word and deed . . . in private life and public office, the injunction of the prophet, 'To do justly, love mercy and walk humbly before God.'"

90. E.g., Ranck, "Roosevelt," 103–7; Straus, "The Religion of Roosevelt," 1196; A. L. Cheney, *Personal Memoirs of the Home Life of the Late Theodore Roosevelt . . .* (Washington, DC: Cheney, 1919), esp. 153–57; William Crook, "The Home Life of

Roosevelt," *Saturday Evening Post*, Mar. 11, 1911; and Arthur Hewitt, "The President's Rules for the Conduct of Life," *Ladies Home Journal*, Feb. 1907, 21.

91. Washington Gladden, *Recollections* (Boston: Houghton Mifflin, 1909), 391.

92. "Address of Gifford Pinchot" in Iglehart, *Theodore Roosevelt*, 403.

93. Cotton, *Ideals*, 204.

94. Quoted in Reisner, *Roosevelt's Religion*, 205.

95. See " 'In God We Trust,' " *LD* 35 (Nov. 23, 1907), 788; "Religious Press on the Coinage Motto," *LD*, Dec. 7, 1907, 869–70; and "The President and the Motto on the Coins," *Current Literature* 44 (Jan. 1908), 69–70.

96. "The Motto on the Coins," *Churchman*, Nov. 23, 1907, 3; "What Makes a State Christian?" *Independent* 63 (1907), 1263–64; "Religious Press on the Coinage Motto," 869–70; Reisner, *Roosevelt's Religion*, 248–49.

97. The Roman Catholic *New World*, as cited in "The President and the Motto on Our Coins," 68. See Willard Gatewood Jr., *Theodore Roosevelt and the Art of Controversy: Episodes in the White House Years* (Baton Rouge: Louisiana State University Press, 1970), 226, who directed me to most of the sources in this section, and "In God We Trust," *Harper's Weekly* 51 (1907), 1714.

98. Gatewood, *Theodore Roosevelt*, 228.

99. TR to Roland C. Dryer, Nov. 11, 1907, *Letters*, Vol. 4, *The Square Deal, 1903–1905*, Elting E. Morrison, ed. (Cambridge, MA: Harvard University Press, 1951), 842.

100. Arthur Schlesinger Jr., "When Patriotism Wasn't Religious," *NYT*, July 7, 2002; TR to Dryer, *Letters* 4:842; quotations in that order.

101. Quoted in "Religious Press on the Coinage Motto," 870.

102. See *Congressional Record*, 60th Congress, 1st Session, 511–16; Gatewood, *Theodore Roosevelt*, 229–31.

103. TR to Bellamy Storer, Dec. 27, 1903, *Letters* 3:683; quotation from TR to Storer, Dec. 19, 1903, *Letters* 3:672.

104. TR to Maria Storer, Dec. 11, 1905, *Letters* 5:108.

105. The quotation is from "Story of the Storers," *Current Literature* 42 (Jan. 1907), 21–25, quotation from 22. The best account of this episode is Gatewood, *Theodore Roosevelt*, 175–212. See also Mark Sullivan, *Our Times: The United States, 1900–1925*, 6 vols. (New York: Charles Scribner's Sons, 1926–35), 3:99–128; "The Storers," *Collier's* 38 (Dec. 22, 1906), 15; "The Case of Mrs. Bellamy Storer," *Outlook* 84 (Dec. 15, 1906), 901–2; and "Roosevelt vs. Storer," *Nation* 83 (Dec. 13, 1906), 500.

106. TR to Richard Oulahan, Oct. 12, 1908, *Letters* 6:1285.

107. Both quotations are from Harbaugh, *Power and Responsibility*, 360.

108. Quoted in Butt, *Letters of Archie Butt*, 143–44.

109. TR to J. C. Martin, Nov. 6, 1908, *Letters* 6:1333–35. In August, he counseled Taft in rebutting the charges against him to emphasize that Hale was a Unitarian who was revered by clergymen of all denominations; that Thomas Jefferson, John Quincy Adams, and Abraham Lincoln were fiercely attacked as "nonorthodox Christians"; and that the gospel of works in the Epistle of James was the essence of Christianity. See TR to Taft, Aug. 28, 1908, *Letters* 6:1200. See also TR to Starr Beatty, Oct. 16, 1908, *Letters* 6:1290; Hermann Hagedorn, *Roosevelt: Prophet of Unity* (New York: Charles Scribner's Sons, 1924), 54–62; and Roosevelt, "Before the Knights of Columbus," Oct. 12, 1915, *Works*, nat. ed., 18:389.

110. *The American Israelite*, quoted in "Objections to the President's Letter on Religious Tolerance," *Current Literature* 46 (Jan. 1909), 68.

111. "Is the President Right?" *Woman's Home Companion* 36 (Jan. 1909), 6.

112. All of these quotations are in "Objections to the President's Letter on Religious Tolerance," 69–70.

113. "Did Our President Forget?" *Lutheran*, Nov. 19, 1908, 124.

114. "Another Letter to President Roosevelt," *Lutheran*, Nov. 26, 1908, 184. See also A. Spaeth, "A Defense of the Letter to President Roosevelt," ibid., Jan. 21, 1909, 317–18.

115. Robert J. Long, *Is Roosevelt a Safe Leader for Loyal Americans?* (East Orange, NJ, n.d.); *Political Romanism* (New York, 1914), 279–81; 309–11.

116. Dores Sharpe, *Walter Rauschenbusch* (New York: Macmillan, 1942), 413–14.

117. E.g., Theodore Roosevelt, "Address to the Pan-American Missionary Service," Oct. 23, 1903, *PA*, Part Two, 495–500; Roosevelt, "Address at . . . the N. Y. Avenue Presbyterian Church," Nov. 16, 1903, ibid., 501–5.

118. Moody, Garfield, and Pinchot were especially important confidants and advisors to Roosevelt. See Dalton, *Roosevelt*, 208, 296.

119. TR to Theodore Brentano, Sept. 1, 1903, *Letters* 3:583.

120. "Mr. Roosevelt's Letter," *CA* 84 (Mar. 11, 1909), 367. See also "The Address of the President of the United States," ibid. *78* (Mar. 5, 1903), 376–78; and Clarence True Wilson, "Methodist Rights in Politics," *Forum* 76 (Nov. 1926), 669–70.

121. TR to George B. Cortelyou, Aug. 13, 1904, *Letters* 4:892.

122. Quoted in A. B. Hart and H. R. Ferleger, eds., *Theodore Roosevelt Cyclopedia* (New York: Roosevelt Memorial Association, 1941), 518.

123. TR to James F. Smith, July 11, 1904, *Letters* 4:855. Cf. TR to John Crane, July 31, 1902, *Letters* 3:307; Roosevelt, "At St. Louis University," Apr. 29, 1903, *PA*, Part One, 341; Roosevelt, "At the Jamestown Exposition," Apr. 26, 1907, *Works*, nat. ed., 11:313; and TR to John Drain, June 27, 1911, *Letters* 7:299.

124. TR to Cleveland Dodge, Feb. 17, 1911, *Letters* 7:232.

125. See Frank T. Reuter, *Catholic Influence on American Colonial Policies, 1898–1904* (Austin: University of Texas, 1967), 109. Roosevelt corresponded regularly with both Gibbons and Ireland. See *Letters* and TRP.

126. Roosevelt, *Works of Theodore Roosevelt*, Memorial Edition, 24 vols (New York: Charles Scribner's Sons, 1923–26), 21:135–36.

127. His two Catholic appointees were Postmaster Robert Wynne and Charles Bonaparte, who served as secretary of the navy and then attorney general.

128. TR to Robins, June 3, 1915, *Letters* 8:932.

129. Theodore Roosevelt, *Oliver Cromwell* (New York: Charles Scribner's Sons, 1900), 49–50.

130. TR to Storer, June 22, 1901, *Letters* 3:100.

131. E.g., Theodore Roosevelt, "True Americanism" in *American Ideals*, in *Works*, ex. ed., 1:43; "The Most Characteristic Work of the Republic," *CA* 80 (Aug. 17, 1905), 1295.

132. Lewis Gould, *The Presidency of Theodore Roosevelt* (Lawrence: University Press of Kansas, 1991), 58–60.

133. Quoted in Wagenknecht, *Seven Worlds*, 188.

134. Quoted in Reuter, *Catholic Influence*, 152. See TR to Ireland, July 31, 1903, *Letters* 3:536 and TR to Rollo Ogden, Nov. 26, 1902, *Letters* 3:381. On Roosevelt's relationship with Catholics, see also David H. Burton, "Robinson, Roosevelt, and Romanism: An Historical Reflection on the Catholic Church and the American

Ideal," *Records of the American Catholic Historical Society of Philadelphia* 80 (Mar. 1969), 3–16.

135. Roosevelt, *Autobiography*, 205–6. See also TR to George B. Aiton, May 15, 1901, *Letters* 3:78–79; Morris *Theodore Rex*, 244; and Miller, *Roosevelt*, 232.

136. On Straus's relationship with Roosevelt, see his *Under Four Administrations: From Cleveland to Taft* . . . (Boston: Houghton Mifflin, 1922), 163–92.

137. Gould, *Presidency*, 89–90; Morris, *Theodore Rex*, 255–56.

138. The quotations are from Gould, *Presidency*, 140.

139. David Burton explains that the influence of Darwinism led Roosevelt to believe that struggle usually produced progress, "that there were superior and inferior peoples with differing rights and responsibilities," and "that force was frequently appropriate to accomplish good among men and among nations" (*Theodore Roosevelt*, 132–39, quotation from 137). Harbaugh argues that "Roosevelt was too sophisticated a Reform Darwinist to believe blatantly in racial superiority," though a mild undercurrent of racism was evident in his thought (*Power and Responsibility*, 220).

140. Theodore Roosevelt, "At the State Fair," Sept. 7, 1903, *PA*, Part Two, 476.

141. Roosevelt, *Realizable Ideals*, 120–21, quotation from 120.

142. Roosevelt, Thanksgiving Proclamation, 1907. Cf. Roosevelt, "Pan-American Missionary Service," 501; and Roosevelt, *Oliver Cromwell*, 239.

143. TR to Mott, Oct. 12, 1908, *Letters* 6:1282.

144. TR to Ray Stannard Baker, Nov. 28, 1905, *Letters* 5:101.

145. Theodore Roosevelt, "The Man with the Muck-rake," *Works*, nat. ed., 16:415–18. See also "The Man with the Muck Rake," *CA* 81 (Apr. 19, 1906), 549.

146. Theodore Roosevelt, "Socialism Versus Social Reform" in *Works*, nat. ed., 19:96–112, first quotation from 103, the rest from 112. See also Roosevelt, "Reform through Social Work," 448–54; Roosevelt, "Where We Cannot Work with Socialists," *Outlook* 91 (Mar. 20, 1909), 619–23; and Roosevelt, "Where We Can Work with Socialists," *Outlook* 91 (Mar. 27, 1909), 662–64.

147. Sharpe, *Walter Rauschenbusch*, 413–14. When Rauschenbusch told Roosevelt that the United States would soon become a socialist nation, he responded, "Not as long as I am President, for I will sail the ship of state alongside the ship of socialism and I will take over everything that is good in socialism and leave the bad." Rauschenbusch asked, "Do you propose to write into the laws of the nation the social theories of socialism?" "Precisely that," declared Roosevelt, "at least in so far as those theories are wise and practicable for the nation's well-being."

148. TR to Lyman Abbott, June 17, 1908, *Letters* 6:1081. Cf. TR to Charles Bonaparte, Jan. 2, 1908, *Works*, nat. ed., 20:443.

149. Roosevelt, *Autobiography*, 168.

150. TR to Lyman Abbott, Apr. 23, 1906, *Letters* 5:219.

151. Theodore Roosevelt, "Christian Citizenship" in *Works*, ex. ed., 12:265; Roosevelt, "Social Justice: The Brotherly Court of Philadelphia" *Works*, nat. ed., 19:85–89.

152. Brands, *T.R.*, 490. Roosevelt argued that capitalists who did not pay a living wage were enemies of morality, religion, and the state ("The Cause of Decency," *Outlook*, July 15, 1911, 569–70).

153. E.g., Roosevelt, "Christian Citizenship," 262–72; Roosevelt, "The Eighth and Ninth Commandments in Politics," *Works*, ex. ed., 12:107–12; Roosevelt, "The Best and the Good," ibid., 12:113–18; Roosevelt, "Civic Helpfulness," 80–97; and Roosevelt, "The Purpose of the Progressive Party," *Works*, nat. ed., 17:334–40.

154. Theodore Roosevelt, "The Strenuous Life" in *Works*, ex. ed., 12:21.

155. Theodore Roosevelt, "Fear God and Take Your Own Part," *Works*, nat. ed., 18:199.

156. Roosevelt, "New Nationalism," 38.

157. Theodore Roosevelt, "Our Poorer Brother" in *American Ideals*, 239.

158. Ibid., 243. Cf. Theodore Roosevelt, "The Labor Question" in *Works*, ex. ed., 12:256; and Roosevelt, "First Annual Message," Dec. 3, 1901, *Works*, nat. ed., 13:481.

159. Roosevelt, *Autobiography*, 389.

160. Roosevelt, "New Nationalism," 36. Cf. Roosevelt, *Autobiography*, 504.

161. Gould, *Presidency*, 223. See Roosevelt, *Autobiography*, passim.

162. Friedenberg, *Theodore Roosevelt*, 38–39; and Frederick Marks, III, *Velvet on Iron: The Diplomacy of Theodore Roosevelt* (Lincoln: University of Nebraska Press, 1982), 89–128.

163. Theodore Roosevelt, "Sixth Annual Message to Congress" in Richardson, ed., *Messages and Papers of the Presidents* 14:7053.

164. TR to Robins, June 3, 1915, *Letters* 8:928.

165. Brands, *T.R.*, 463.

166. Roosevelt, "Fear God," 200. Cf. TR to Mott, Oct. 12, 1908, *Letters* 6:1282 and Roosevelt, "National Character and the Characters of National Statesmen," *Outlook* 91 (Jan. 23, 1909), 190–93.

167. Miller, *Roosevelt*, 385.

168. Roosevelt, "National Duties," 234 (quotation); Roosevelt, *Autobiography*, 417–19.

169. TR to Charles H. Mohr, Nov. 20, 1911, *Letters* 7:438. Cf. Roosevelt, "Inaugural Address," Mar. 4, 1905, *Works*, nat. ed., 15:268; TR to Carl Schurz, Sept. 8, 1905, ibid., 20:533: "Peace is chiefly valuable as a means to righteousness"; and Roosevelt, "Sixth Annual Message," ibid., 15:402.

170. Roosevelt, "At the Mechanics' Pavilion," 394. Cf. TR to Andrew Carnegie, Aug. 6, 1906, *Letters* 5:346; Roosevelt, "The Peace of Righteousness," *Outlook* 99 (Sept. 9, 1911); and TR to Lyman Abbott, Jan. 3, 1907, *Letters* 5:536.

171. Roosevelt, *Autobiography*, 592.

172. Roosevelt, "Address at the Mechanics' Pavilion," 394.

173. Roosevelt, "Address to the Franklin Street Methodist Episcopal Church," 13.

174. Roosevelt, *Autobiography*, 602.

175. Miller, *Roosevelt*, 385; Thomas Bailey, *A Diplomatic History of the American People* (New York: Appleton-Century-Croft, 1964), 52; Richard Hofstadter, *The American Political Tradition* (New York: Vintage, 1948), 209; I. E. Cadenhead, *Theodore Roosevelt: The Paradox of Progressivism* (Woodbury, NY: Baron's Educational Series, 1974), 89.

176. See Walter Lafeber, "'The Lion in the Path': The U.S. Emergence as a World Power," *Political Science Quarterly* 101 (1986), 705–18.

177. See Marks, *Velvet on Iron*, 89–96, 129–58. Roosevelt believed firmly in the power of arbitration and supported the work of the Permanent Court of International Justice at The Hague, to which he submitted a dispute involving the United States. E.g., TR to Lyman Abbott, June 8, 1905, *Letters* 4:1208.

178. Roosevelt, *Autobiography*, 602.

179. Gould, *Presidency*, 269.

180. TR to Albion Tourgee, Nov. 8, 1901, *Letters* 3:190–91.

181. TR to Lyman Abbott, Jan. 13, 1900, *Letters* 2:1132. Cf. TR to Philip Goepp, Mar. 18, 1901, *Letters* 3:17–8.

182. Roosevelt, *Works*, nat. ed., 10:307 (the quotation is from this source); TR to Abbott, Apr. 23, 1906, *Letters* 5:217. See also Roosevelt, "Reform through Social Work," 448–54; and Roosevelt, *Works*, nat ed. 13:343–44.

183. TR to Bishop William C. Doane, Jan. 26, 1905, The Newspaper Scrapbook Collection, as cited by Dalton, *Roosevelt*, 299; the first quotation is from Dalton; the last two from TR.

184. Roosevelt, *Autobiography*, 518. Cf. Roosevelt, "To the Brotherhood of Locomotive Firemen," Sept. 8, 1902, *PA*, Part One, 159: "I believe emphatically in organized labor."

185. Roosevelt, *Autobiography*, 519.

186. TR to James S. Clarkson, July 16, 1903, *Letters* 3:518.

187. Roosevelt, *Autobiography*, 519–20, quotation from 520. See also Roosevelt, "Law, Order, and Justice," in Leuchtenburg, ed., *New Nationalism,* 160–61; Roosevelt, "Labor and Capital," ibid., 99–107; and "The President and the Leaders of Organized Labor," *CA* 81 (Mar. 29, 1906), 432.

188. See Roosevelt, *Autobiography*, 501–2, 524, quotation from 524.

189. Roosevelt, "New Nationalism and the Old Moralities," 171.

190. Roosevelt, "New Nationalism," 29. See also Irving Greenberg, *Theodore Roosevelt and Labor: 1900–1918* (New York: Garland, 1988).

191. Brands, *T.R.*, 450–51; first quotation from 450, second and third from 451.

192. Miller, *Roosevelt*, 371.

193. Roosevelt, *Autobiography*, 505, 513; all quotations from 513.

194. TR to Winthrop M. Crane, Oct. 22, 1902, *Letters* 3:362.

195. Roosevelt, *Autobiography*, 511.

196. Ibid., 514.

197. Baer to W. F. Clark, July 17, 1902, in Sullivan, *Our Times*, 2:425.

198. These quotations are from ibid., 2:426–27.

199. See "Too Low a View of the President's Office," *CA* 77 (Oct. 2, 1902), 1566; "The President's Second Repulse," *CA*, Oct. 16, 1902, 1648–49. A church in Massachusetts urged Roosevelt to heed Joshua 1:7. He responded, "I shall try to live up to it . . . and turn neither to the right hand nor the left, though I think two-thirds of the people who write to me about this strike seem to desire that I shall turn either to the right hand or to the left." See "The Scriptures Affecting the Settlement of the Coal Strike," *CA*, Oct. 23, 1902, 1684.

200. Gould, *Presidency*, 69.

201. Ibid., 71.

202. Miller, *Roosevelt*, 377.

203. TR to Sydney Brooks, Dec. 28, 1908, 6:1444. On the coal strike, see also Riis, *Theodore Roosevelt*, 370–80.

204. Theodore Roosevelt, "At Omaha, NB," April 27, 1903, *PA*, Part One, 333–34.

205. White, "Force for Righteousness," 389.

206. Marks, *Velvet on Iron*, 89.

207. Bailey, *Diplomatic History*, 230; Howard Beale, *Theodore Roosevelt and the Rise of America to World Power* (Baltimore: Johns Hopkins University Press, 1956), 25.

208. Marks, *Velvet on Iron*, 90.

209. Roosevelt, "Message to Congress," Jan. 4, 1904, *PA*, Part Two, 700–3; Roosevelt, *Autobiography*, 555–57.

210. Gould, *Presidency*, 92. See also TR to George Harvey, Dec. 19, 1903, *Letters* 3:673.

211. TR to Cecil-Spring Rice, Nov. 9, 1903, *Letters* 3:651.

212. Roosevelt, "Message to Congress," Jan. 4, 1904, 697, 713, 716; Roosevelt, *Autobiography*, 569.

213. TR to Hay, Aug. 19, 1903, *Letters* 3:567. Cf. TR to Cecil Spring-Rice, Jan. 18, 1904, *Letters* 3:699.

214. TR to Kermit Roosevelt, Nov. 4, 1903, *Letters* 3:644.

215. Roosevelt, "Message to Congress," Jan. 4, 1904, 751.

216. TR to Albert Shaw, Oct. 10, 1903, *Letters* 3:628. Roosevelt told John Bigelow that Bunau-Varilla "had no assurances in any way either from Hay or myself" that the United States would support revolution. But he should have been able "to make a very accurate guess, and to advise his people accordingly" about America's favorable perspective toward Panamanian independence (Jan. 6, 1904, *Letters* 3:689).

217. Gould, *Presidency*, 98. See also Roosevelt, *Autobiography*, 564.

218. Roosevelt, *Autobiography*, 567.

219. TR to William R. Thayer, July 2, 1915, *Letters* 8:945.

220. Roosevelt, *Autobiography*, 565.

221. Quoted in Gould, *Presidency*, 98.

222. Quoted in Miller, *Roosevelt*, 408.

223. Roosevelt, *Autobiography*, 566.

224. TR to Joseph Cannon, Sept. 12, 1904, *Letters* 4:922.

225. TR to William Joel Stone, July 11, 1914, *Letters* 7:778–79. See also Lyman Abbott, *Silhouettes of My Contemporaries* (Garden City, NY: Doubleday, Page, 1921), 138–39.

226. Roosevelt, *Autobiography*, 553.

227. Miller, *Roosevelt*, 399.

228. On the building of the Panama Canal, see David McCullough, *The Path between the Seas: The Creation of the Panama Canal, 1870–1914* (New York: Simon and Schuster, 1977); and Walter LaFeber, *The Panama Canal: The Crisis in Historical Perspective* (New York: Oxford University Press, 1978).

229. Roosevelt, *Autobiography*, 431–32.

230. See Paul R, Cutright, *Theodore Roosevelt: The Making of a Conservationist* (Urbana: University of Illinois Press, 1985).

231. Roosevelt, *Autobiography*, 430.

232. See Harold Howland, "Roosevelt Introduced Conservation into American Politics," Tom Lansford and Robert Watson, eds., *Theodore Roosevelt: Presidents and Their Decisions* (Farmington Hills, MI: Greenhaven, 2003), 45, 49, 51–52; and Daniel O. Buechler, "Roosevelt Built Support for Conservation by Linking It to American Values," ibid., 61.

233. Gould, *Presidency*, 206. See also Gifford Pinchot, *Breaking New Ground* (New York: Harcourt, Brace, 1947); and Samuel P. Hays, *Conservation and the Gospel of Efficiency* (Cambridge, MA: Harvard University Press, 1959).

234. Sandy Marvinney, "Roosevelt Helped Establish American Environmentalism," Lansford and Watson, eds., *Theodore Roosevelt*, 42.

235. Theodore Roosevelt, "Conservation as a National Duty," *Proceedings of a Conference of Governors* (Washington, DC: Government Printing Office, 1909), 5.

236. Ibid., 10.

237. Roosevelt, *Autobiography*, 437–38.

238. Leroy Dorsey, "Roosevelt Redefined the Frontier Myth to Build Support for Conservation," Lansford and Watson, eds., *Theodore Roosevelt*, 76. See also Stephen

Ponder, " 'Publicity in the Interest of the People': Theodore Roosevelt's Conservation Crusade," *PSQ* 20 (1990), 547–55.

239. Roosevelt, "New Nationalism," 33.

240. Buechler, "Roosevelt Built Support," 59–66.

241. TR to White, Nov. 28, 1906, *Letters* 5:517.

242. Miller, *Roosevelt*, 411.

243. TR to George Trevelyan, Mar. 9, 1905, *Letters* 4:1132.

244. Gould, *Presidency*, 300.

245. Cotton, *Ideals*, 312.

246. "Unexaggerated Account of Prevailing Exaggerations," *CA* 84 (Apr. 15, 1909), 563. Cf. "Exit Roosevelt, Enter Taft," *CA* 84 (Mar. 4, 1909); and "The Inauguration of President Roosevelt," *CA* 80 (Mar. 9, 1905), 365.

247. Miller, *Roosevelt*, 412. Cf. "Theodore Roosevelt," *PB*, Mar. 4, 1909, 1262.

248. "President Roosevelt," *UP*, Nov. 5, 1908, 7; "The Incoming President," *Lutheran*, Mar. 11, 1909, 425. Cf. "Roosevelt, Preacher of Ethics," ibid., Mar. 11, 1909, 426; T. W. Kretchmann, "Our New President," ibid., Mar. 18, 1909, 445; and "Roosevelt and the Outlook," ibid., Apr. 15, 1909, 517.

249. Lyman Abbott, "A Review of President Roosevelt's Administration," *Outlook* 91 (Feb. 27, 1909), 434.

250. Bolce, "When the President Goes to Church."

251. Roosevelt, "National Duties," 244.

252. Iglehart, *Theodore Roosevelt*, 329ff.

253. William Allen White, "Theodore Roosevelt," in Morton Keller, ed., *Theodore Roosevelt: A Profile* (New York: Hill and Wang, 1967), 32, 22, 28, quotations in that order.

254. Miller, *Roosevelt*, 412. Cf. "Theodore Roosevelt," Mar. 4, 1909, 1262.

255. Ibid.

256. Brands, *T.R.*, 487, 716, first quotation from 487; second from TR to O. Gresham, Nov. 30, 1903, *Letters* 3:663; third from 716. Cf. Morris, *Theodore Rex*, 82.

257. Miller, *Roosevelt*, 411.

258. Brands, *T.R.*, 84, 420; quotations in that order.

259. Ibid., 716.

260. TR to White, Nov. 28, 1906, *Letters* 5:517.

261. Iglehart, "An After-Church Chat," 135.

261. Brands, *T.R.*, 812.

263. Miller, *Roosevelt*, 411.

264. Riis, "The Christian Manliness of Roosevelt," 10.

CHAPTER 5

1. Ray Stannard Baker, *Woodrow Wilson: Life and Letters* (hereafter Baker, *WW:LL*), 8 vols. (Garden City, NY: Doubleday, 1927–39) 1:68, 5:171; quotations in that order. David F. Houston, who served as Wilson's secretary of agriculture, wrote that he was "a dyed-in-the wool Scotch Presbyterian . . . with all that implies—in philosophy, ethics, morals, standards of conduct, and practices" (*Eight Years with Wilson's Cabinet, 1913–1920*, 2 vols. [Garden City, NY: Doubleday, Page, 1926], 2:158). Cf. Samuel F. Wells Jr., "New Perspectives on Wilsonian Diplomacy: The Secular

Evangelism of American Political Economy," *Perspectives in American History* 6 (1972), 407, 419.

2. Arthur Link, "Woodrow Wilson: Presbyterian in Government," in George L. Hunt, ed., *Calvinism and the Political Order* (Philadelphia: Westminster, 1965), 157.

3. John M. Mulder, "Wilson the Preacher: The 1905 Baccalaureate Sermon," *JPH* 51 (Fall 1973), 267. Washington Gladden called Wilson "the greatest preacher of the century" (*The Interpreter* [Boston: Pilgrim, 1918], vii).

4. Jan Schulte Nordholt, *Woodrow Wilson: A Life for World Peace*, Herbert H. Rowen, trans. (Berkeley: University of California, Press, 1991), 40–41.

5. Edwin Anderson Alderman, *In Memoriam: Woodrow Wilson* (Washington, DC: Government Printing Office, 1925), 34. E.g., John Maynard Keynes, *The Economic Consequences of the Peace* (New York: Harcourt, Brace and Howe, 1920), 38; and Harold Nicolson, *Peacemaking 1919* (New York: Grosset and Dunlap, 1965 [1934]), 195–200.

6. John M. Mulder, "'A Gospel of Order': Woodrow Wilson's Religion and Politics" in John Milton Cooper Jr. and Charles E. Neu, eds., *The Wilson Era: Essays in Honor of Arthur S. Link* (Arlington Heights, IL: Harlan Davidson, 1991), 224. See David B. Danbom, *"The World of Hope": Progressives and the Struggle for an Ethical Public Life* (Philadelphia: Temple University Press, 1987); Robert M. Crunden, *Ministers of Reform: The Progressives' Achievement in American Civilization, 1889–1920* (New York: Basic Books, 1982); and Peter J. Frederick, *Knights of the Golden Rule: The Intellectual as Christian Social Reformer in the 1890s* (Lexington: University of Kentucky Press, 1976).

7. On the senior Wilson, see John M. Mulder, "Joseph Ruggles Wilson: Southern Presbyterian Patriarch," *JPH* 52 (Fall 1974), 245–71. On Wilson's Scotch-Irish background, see Arthur S. Link, "Woodrow Wilson and His Presbyterian Inheritance" in Link, *The Higher Realism of Woodrow Wilson and Other Essays* (Nashville, TN: Vanderbilt University Press, 1971), 3–20.

8. Baker, *WW:LL* 1:67. There is no doubt, Baker argues, that Wilson regarded this experience as an intellectual and emotional turning point. See also Minutes of the Session, First Presbyterian Church of Columbia, SC, July 5, 1873, in Arthur S. Link et al., eds, *The Papers of Woodrow Wilson* (hereafter *PWW*) 69 vols. (Princeton, NJ: Princeton University Press, 1966–94) 1:22–23.

9. William Bullitt accused Wilson over being overly dependent on his father because he always consulted him about major decisions. See Sigmund Freud and William Bullitt, *Thomas Woodrow Wilson: A Psychological Study* (Boston: Houghton Mifflin, 1967). Other psychohistorical examinations of Wilson include Alexander L. and Juliette L. George, *Woodrow Wilson and Colonel House: A Personality Study* (New York: John Day, 1956); and Edwin A. Weinstein, *Woodrow Wilson: A Medical and Psychological Biography* (Princeton, NJ: Princeton University Press, 1981). Wilson told the Presbytery of the Potomac in April 1915 that his father "was the best instructor" and "the most inspiring companion" a young person ever had. See "The Address of President Wilson to the Presbytery," in James H. Taylor, *Woodrow Wilson in Church: His Membership in the Congregation of the Central Presbyterian Church, Washington, D.C., 1913–1924* (Charleston, SC: Privately printed, 1952), 18–19. See also George Osborn, "The Influence of Joseph Ruggles Wilson on His Son, Woodrow Wilson," *North Carolina Historical Review*, Oct. 1955; John M. Mulder, *Woodrow Wilson: The Years of Preparation* (Princeton, NJ: Princeton

University Press, 1978), 1–51. On his religious experience as a teenager, see Arthur Walworth, *Woodrow Wilson*, 2 vols. (New York: Longmans, Green, 1958), vol. 1: *American Prophet*, 12–16.

10. Mulder points out that Princeton was a strongly Christian institution when Wilson attended. He regularly participated in the prayer meetings his class held twice a week. Wilson's diary for his Princeton years documents his close relationship with God and spiritual growth (*Preparation*, 44, 47). On McCosh, see J. D. Hoeveler Jr., *James McCosh and the Scottish Intellectual Tradition* (Princeton, NJ: Princeton University Press, 1981).

11. Mulder, "'Gospel of Order,'" 223–47. Mulder disputes John M. Cooper's contention that "specifically Calvinist doctrines and viewpoints had comparatively little impact on Wilson." Mulder counters that the influence of Wilson's father on him was tremendous and notes that Cooper concedes that "for Wilson, Presbyterianism was . . . a way of life." Others maintain that Wilson's thought was more a product of late-nineteenth-century evangelicalism than of a distinctively Calvinist perspective. Mulder responds that Wilson was steeped in a "religious tradition that was self-conscious about its Presbyterian and Calvinist identity." See Mulder, "'Gospel of Order,'" 237; John Milton Cooper Jr., *The Warrior and the Priest* (Cambridge, MA: Harvard University Press, 1983), 17–19, quotation from 18.

12. Mulder, *Preparation*, 34.

13. Arthur S. Link, "Wilson the President" in *Lectures and Seminar at the University of Chicago in Celebration of the Centennial of Woodrow Wilson* (Chicago: University of Chicago Press, 1956), 119.

14. Herbert C. F. Bell, "The Genesis of Wilson's Foreign Policy," *Thought* 38 (Dec. 1948), 658. Cf. John M. Blum, *Woodrow Wilson and the Politics of Morality* (Boston: Little Brown, 1956), 7; Mulder, "'Gospel of Order,'" 227.

15. Frank Bell Lewis, "The Man of Faith," in Em Bowles Alsop, ed., *The Greatness of Woodrow Wilson, 1856–1956* (New York: Rinehart, 1956), 37.

16. Arthur S. Link, "Wilson the Diplomatist," in Earl Latham, ed., *The Philosophy and Policies of Woodrow Wilson* (Chicago: University of Chicago Press, 1958), 152 (first two quotations); Link, "A Portrait of Wilson," *Virginia Quarterly Review* 32 (Autumn 1956), 529 (third quotation).

17. Woodrow Wilson, "A Religious Address in Trenton, NJ," Oct. 1, 1911, *PWW* 23:377.

18. Quoted in Arthur S. Link, "Woodrow Wilson and the Life of Faith," *Presbyterian Life*, Mar. 1, 1963, 9, 11.

19. Woodrow Wilson, "The Young People and the Church," in *Selected Literary and Political Papers and Addresses of Woodrow Wilson* (hereafter *SLPP*), 3 vols. (New York: Grosset and Dunlap), 1:177.

20. Mulder, *Preparation*, 112.

21. See WW to Ellen Axson Wilson (hereafter EAW), Aug. 10, 1913, *PWW* 28:132; WW to Mary A. Hulbert, Aug. 10, 1913, in Baker, *WW:LL* 4:271–72. See also *WW:LL* 1:48.

22. On Galt, see Edith Bolling Wilson, *My Memoir* (Indianapolis, IN: Bobbs-Merrill, 1939); Ishbel Ross, *Power with Grace: The Life of Mrs. Woodrow Wilson* (New York: G. P. Putnam Sons, 1975); and Phyllis Lee Levin, *Edith and Wilson: The Wilson White House* (New York: Scribner, 2001).

23. Taylor, *Woodrow Wilson in Church*, 39, 41.

24. Arthur Walworth, *Woodrow Wilson*, vol. 2: *World Prophet*, 122. Taylor visited Wilson frequently at the White House, and they exchanged many letters.

25. Link, "Life of Faith," 12. Cary T. Grayson, Wilson's personal physician and close companion, contends that Wilson loved thoughtful sermons, especially those of Taylor (*Woodrow Wilson: An Intimate Memoir* [New York: Holt, Rinehart and Winston, 1960], 14). See also Taylor, *Woodrow Wilson in Church*, 5, 23.

26. Baker, *WW:LL* 1:208. As examples of Wilson's letters discussing sermons, see WW to Edith Gittings Reid, Feb. 27, 1898, *PWW* 10:462; WW to EAW, Feb. 27, 1898, *PWW* 10:461; and WW to EAW, June 19, 1898, *PWW* 10:565. See also WW to Anson Phelps Stokes, Apr. 30 and May 3, 1907, *PWW* 17:125–26, 129–30; and Diary, Jan. 17, 1904, *PWW* 15:134. Azel Hazen, pastor of the Congregational church the Wilsons attended in Middletown, wrote Wilson, "I can never forget your reverent, worshipful bearing in our services, nor your patient attention . . ." (Hazen to WW, Apr. 1, 1897, *PWW* 10:211).

27. Wilson cherished some of the old hymns of the church, but he complained that others were "silly and meaningless" ("A Religious Address in Trenton," 378). His favorite hymns included "The Son of God Goes Forth to War," "How Firm a Foundation," and "The Strife of Life is O'er" (Grayson, *Woodrow Wilson*, 12).

28. Mulder, *Preparation*, 34; WW to Ellen Axson, Oct. 9, 1887, *PWW* 5:614–15; June 11, 1876, *PWW* 1:138.

29. Josephus Daniels, *The Life of Woodrow Wilson, 1856–1924* (Philadelphia: John C. Winston, 1925), 359; Lewis, "Man of Faith," 41.

30. Journal, Dec. 28, 1889, *PWW* 6:462.

31. Mrs. Crawford H. Toy, "Second Visit to the White House," diary entry, Jan. 3, 1915, Manuscript in the Ray Stannard Baker Collection of Wilsonia, Library of Congress, quoted in Baker, *WW:LL* 5:144.

32. Link, "Wilson the Diplomatist," 152.

33. Link, "Life of Faith," 12.

34. Baker, *WW:LL* 1:209; Mulder, " 'Gospel of Order,' " 239. Wilson's "faith was so incorporated in the sum and substance of his innermost self and such an integral part of his moral constitution," Presbyterian minister Theodore Whitefield Hunt maintained, "that doctrine and duty, thought and life, creed and character were consolidated and fused into the everyday expression of his experience." See Hunt, "Woodrow Wilson's Attitude toward Religion," [1924] n. p., Archives, Princeton Seminary Library, as quoted by P. C. Kemeny, *Princeton in the Nation's Service: Religious Ideals and Educational Practice, 1868–1928* (New York: Oxford University Press, 1998), 146.

35. Woodrow Wilson, notes for a religious address, Jan. 17, 1900, *PWW* 11:376; Wilson, "The Present Task of the Ministry," May 26, 1909, *PWW* 19:221. In 1908, Wilson complained that ministers had become "involved in all sorts of social activities" and thus had "diverted their attention from the effectual preaching of the Word." He feared that congregations would "become great philanthropic societies" instead of providing "spiritual stimulation" to "guide all philanthropic effort" (WW to Mott, May 1, 1908, *PWW* 18:279–80).

36. Woodrow Wilson, *Memorial Book* of the 150th anniversary of the founding of Princeton (New York: Scribner's, 1898), 5; Mulder, *Preparation*, 150.

37. Mulder, *Preparation*, 177. Wilson did insist, however, that "scholarship had been most fruitful when associated with religion." See "The President on Religious Education," *LD*, June 13, 1914, 1438.

38. George M. Marsden, *The Soul of the American University: From Protestant Establishment to Established Nonbelief* (New York: Oxford University Press, 1994), 232. Wilson wrote, "That religion lies at the heart of Princeton's life is shown, not in the teachings of the class room and of the chapel pulpit, but in the widespread, spontaneous, unflagging religious activity of the undergraduates themselves" (Introduction to *The Handbook of Princeton*, c. Aug 1, 1904, *PWW* 15:428–29). Although Wilson in many ways was a theological conservative, his approach to education at Princeton had much more in common with liberal Protestantism. Stressing the immanence of God, this tradition stove to overcome the threat of science to Christianity by sacralizing the curriculum. Convinced that scientific naturalism, historicism, and new philosophical perspectives had undermined the plausibility of the nineteenth-century evangelical worldview, liberal Protestants focused more on broader ethical issues. In an effort to resolve the tensions between universities' civic and religious missions and to try to nurture the faith of their students, they made Bible courses electives and chapel services voluntary and emphasized the value of student religious organizations. See Kemeny, *Princeton in the Nation's Service*, 127–72, esp. 150, 171–72.

39. Kemeny, *Princeton in the Nation's Service*, 128, 129, quotations in that order. Princeton's mission was to provide an education steeped in moral ideals and imperatives, and thus its instruction must be informed "with the spirit of . . . the religion of Christ" (Wilson, "Princeton in the Nation's Service," *PWW* 14:184).

40. Baker, *WW:LL* 7:274.

41. Woodrow Wilson, statement in *The Daily Bible*, Mar. 1913, quoted in Stanley A. Hunter, comp., *The Religious Ideals of a President* . . . (1914), 1–2, first quotation from 1; second and third from 2.

42. Woodrow Wilson, "The Bible," *SLPP*, 2: 251.

43. First two quotations from Wilson, statement in *The Daily Bible* in *Religious Ideals*, 2; third from *Religious Ideals*, 6.

44. Wilson, "The Bible and Progress," *SLPP*, 1:341–55, first quotation from 343, second from 346.

45. "Religious Utterances of the President-Elect," *LD*, Dec. 7, 1912, 1068; Wilson, "Remarks Celebrating the Centennial of the American Bible Society," Mar. 7, 1916, *PWW* 36:630, quotations in that order. Cf. Wilson, "The Young People and the Church," 178.

46. Quoted by Baker, *WW:LL* 1:68. See also William Allen White, *Woodrow Wilson: The Man, His Times, and His Task* (Boston: Houghton Mifflin, 1929), 188–89; and Morris B. Crawford, Wesleyan University *Alumnus*, Mar. 1924.

47. John McDowell to R. S. Baker, quoted in Baker, *WW:LL*, 1:71.

48. Houston, *Eight Years*, 159.

49. Baker, *WW:LL* 3:217. See also "Diary of Ray Stannard Baker," June 21, 1919, *PWW* 61:65.

50. Ray Stannard Baker and William E. Dodd, eds., *The Public Papers of Woodrow Wilson*, 6 vols. (New York: Harper and Brothers, 1925–27) (hereafter *PPWW*), 5:166.

51. White, *Woodrow Wilson*, 278; Baker, *WW:LL*, 4:5.

52. See "Diary of Ray Stannard Baker," Mar. 8, 1919, *PWW*, 55:466; "Editorial Note," July 8, 1910, *PWW* 20:565; and Wilson, "A Campaign Address in Sioux City, Iowa," Sept. 17, 1912, *PWW* 25:151.

53. E.g., Link, "Wilson the President," 121; Arthur S. Link, ""Portrait of the President," in Latham, ed., *Philosophy and Policies of Woodrow Wilson*, 9; Mulder, *Preparation*, 270–72.

54. Link, "Presbyterian in Government," 161.

55. Link, "Wilson the President," 121.

56. Wilson, "Bible and Progress," 1:348 (quotation); Wilson, "The Modern Democratic State," c. Dec. 1–20, 1885, 63; Wilson, "Remarks to the Clerical Conference of the New York Federation of Churches," Jan. 27, 1916, *PWW* 36:5.

57. Woodrow Wilson, "Militant Christianity," *SLPP*, 2:75. Cf. Wilson, "An Address on Francis Asbury," Mar. 31, 1916, *PWW* 36:392.

58. Link, "Presbyterian in Government," 164. In 1883, Wilson wrote his future wife: "Do you think...that I was trying to persuade you that all things do *not* work together for good? I would as soon try to persuade you that there is no God" (WW to Ellen Axson, Dec. 28, 1883, quoted in Baker, *WW:LL* 1:207, emphasis in the original).

59. *Trenton True American*, Oct. 2, 1911, *PWW* 23:378; Wilson, "Bible and Progress," 1:354; WW to Mary A. Hulbert Peck, Jan. 7, 1912, *PWW* 24:6; quotations in that order. See also WW to Hulbert, Mar. 22, 1914, *PWW* 29:372: "There is certainly a Providence overruling all. I can explain nothing, if there is not." Cf. WW to Edward M. House, Aug. 3, 1914, *PWW* 30:336.

60. Link, "Presbyterian in Government," 164, 162.

61. Wilson, "Young People and the Church," 183.

62. WW to Mary A. Hulbert Peck, Sept. 6, 1914, *PWW* 31:3.

63. Wilson, "Remarks to Confederate Veterans," June 5, 1917, *PWW* 42:452; *PPWW* 1:551–52, quotations in that order.

64. Grayson, *Woodrow Wilson*, 106.

65. The first quotation is from H. C. F. Bell, *Woodrow Wilson and the People* (New York: Doubleday, 1945), 379.

66. See James H. Moorhead, "The Erosion of Postmillennialism in American Religious Thought, 1865–1925," *CH* 53 (Mar. 1984), 61–77.

67. Woodrow Wilson, letter to the *Christian Work and Evangelist, Religious Ideals*, 8–9. Cf. Wilson, "The 1905 Baccalaureate Sermon," in Mulder, "Wilson the Preacher," 283.

68. E.g., Woodrow Wilson, "The Clergyman and the State," Apr. 6, 1910, *PWW* 20:329.

69. Wilson, "Bible and Progress," 1:354.

70. E.g., Robert Handy, *A Christian America: Protestant Hopes and Historical Realities* (New York: Oxford University Press, 1971).

71. Mulder, " 'Gospel of Order,' " 240.

72. WW to John R. Mott, May 1, 1908, *PWW* 18:279–80.

73. Woodrow Wilson, "The Ministry and the Individual," Nov. 2, 1909, *PWW* 19:472.

74. Woodrow Wilson, "The Minister and the Community," Mar. 30, 1906, *PWW* 16:349.

75. E.g., Woodrow Wilson, "An Address to the Clergymen and the State at the General Theological Seminary in New York," Apr. 6, 1910, *PWW* 20:330–31. Wilson's baccalaureate sermons at Princeton from 1904 to 1910 reveal his shift from a "religious and political conservative to a political progressive, fired by evangelical zeal" (Mulder, "Wilson the Preacher," 271).

76. Woodrow Wilson, "A New Kind of Church Life," *SLPP*, 2:147.

77. Wilson, "Present Task," 218, 221. Wilson labeled "Christian Socialism" a contradiction in terms because while its aims were Christian, its use of social compulsion violated Scripture ("Address...at the General Theological Seminary," 333). See also

Wilson, "The Banker and the Nation," Sept. 30, 1908, *PWW* 18:426–27; and Gregory S. Butler, "Visions of a Nation Transformed: Modernity and Ideology in Wilson's Political Thought," *JCS* 39 (Winter 1997), 37–51.

78. The Federal Council of the Churches of Christ to WW, Mar. 5, 1913, *PWW* 27:154. Founded in 1908, by 1916 the Federal Council's constituents included two thirds of all Protestant ministers and members. See Henry K. Carroll, ed., *Federal Council Year Book* (New York: Missionary Movement of the United States and Canada, 1917), 109, 214. Charles S. Macfarland, a long-time council executive, stated that Wilson usually responded favorably to its suggestions (*Across the Years* [New York: Macmillan, 1936], 260).

79. "The Election," *PB*, Nov. 14, 1912, 730. While generally supportive of Wilson, Lutherans were sometimes critical of his specific statements or actions. E.g., "The Political Virtues President Wilson Will Need," *Lutheran* 17 (Mar. 6, 1913), 367; "The New Freedom of President Wilson," ibid., 17 (Apr. 3, 1913), 443; and "Two Views of Wilson's First Year, ibid., 18 (Mar. 12, 1914), 382.

80. Link, "Presbyterian in Government," 171.

81. *WW:LL* 4:31.

82. Mott to WW, Nov. 10, 1916, *PWW* 38:631.

83. Mott and Wilson knew each other through their mutual interest in the ministry of the YMCA and Mott's frequent visits to Princeton while Wilson was a professor or the president there. Over the years, they met scores of times. See C. Howard Hopkins, *John R. Mott, 1865–1955, a Biography* (Grand Rapids, MI: Eerdmans, 1979), 446, 449, 459–60, 474–75, 518–19, 524–26, 536, 538–39, 547–48, 552, 579, 596–97, 665–66.

84. Mulder credits Hazen with helping Wilson integrate his religious and political thought more fully (*Preparation*, 107).

85. Walworth, *Woodrow Wilson*, 1:346.

86. Paul Varg, *Missionaries, Chinese, and Diplomats: The American Protestant Missionary Movement in China, 1890–1952* (Princeton, NJ: Princeton University Press, 1958), 146.

87. WW to Bryan, Feb. 11 [or 5], 1913, *WW:LL* 4:31. The best source for Wilson's relationship with missionaries in China is Eugene P. Trani, "Woodrow Wilson, China, and the Missionaries, 1913–1921," *JPH* 49 (Winter 1971), 328–51.

88. Quoted in Joseph P. Tumulty, *Woodrow Wilson as I Know Him* (Garden City, NY: Doubleday, Page, 1921), 411, 410, quotations in that order. For the larger context, see Gaines M. Foster, *Moral Reconstruction: Christian Lobbyists and the Federal Legislation of Morality, 1865–1920* (Chapel Hill: University of North Carolina Press, 2002), 204–13. Doubting the feasibility of prohibition, Wilson vetoed the Volstead Act in 1919, but Congress passed it over his veto.

89. S. D. Lovell, *The Presidential Election of 1916* (Carbondale: Southern Illinois University Press, 1980), 71.

90. Mulder, "Wilson the Preacher," 274.

91. Arthur S. Link, "Woodrow Wilson: Christian in Government,"*CT* 8 (July 3, 1964), 6; August Heckscher, *Woodrow Wilson; A Biography* (New York: Charles Scriber's Sons, 1991), 396.

92. Baker, *WW:LL* 3:386–87, quotations from 386.

93. As cited in "Joe Tumulty Pulls the Strings," *Current Opinion* 54 (Apr. 1913), 285–86. Other Protestants warned that Tumulty would "let the Vatican into the secrets of the White House," a charge Wilson vehemently repudiated (Baker, *WW:LL* 3:458).

94. WW to W. W. Prescott, Jan. 19. 1914, in the John Sharp Williams Papers, as cited by George C. Osborn, "Religious Cross Currents in the Wilson Administration," *Journal of Mississippi History* 2 (July 1940), 139. See also Dragan R. Zivojinovic, *The United States and the Vatican Policies, 1914–1918* (Boulder, CO: Associated University Press, 1978); Tumulty, *Woodrow Wilson*, 64; and Michael Williams, *American Catholics and the War* (New York: Macmillan, 1921).

95. New Orleans *Morning Star*, as quoted in "Catholic Feeling over Carranza," *LD* 51 (Nov. 6, 1915), 1016.

96. E.g., J. A. Thayer to Joseph Tumulty, Aug. 10, 1916, Woodrow Wilson Papers, Library of Congress. These factors led socialist George Herron to argue in 1917 that "the Roman Catholic hierarchy" had labored "tirelessly and malignly" to prevent Wilson's reelection (*Woodrow Wilson and the World's Peace* [New York: Mitchell Kennerley, 1917], 51).

97. Arthur S. Link, *Wilson: Campaigns for Progressivism and Peace: 1916–1917* (Princeton, NJ: Princeton University Press, 1965), 133.

98. Lovell, *Presidential Election of 1916*, 120. See also *PWW* 38:79, 83.

99. See Link, *Wilson: Campaigns*, 134.

100. See William E. Leary, "Woodrow Wilson, Irish Americans and the Election of 1916," *JAH* 54 (June 1967), 57–72.

101. Gibbons to WW, Apr. 18, 1917, National Catholic War Council archives, Catholic University of America, as quoted in John F. Piper Jr., *American Churches in World War I* (Athens: Ohio University Press, 1985), 21. See also "The Hierarchy's Call to Patriotism," *Catholic Mind* 15 (May 1917), 233–34.

102. Baker, *WW:LL* 7:298. Other Catholics felt compelled to defend their fidelity and patriotism. E.g., Joseph McKee, "A Paradox of History," *Catholic World* 106 (Oct. 1917), 82–90.

103. The quotation is from Maurice Francis Egan and John B. Kennedy, *The Knights of Columbus in Peace and War* (New Haven, CT: Knights of Columbus, 1920), as cited in Piper, *American Churches*, 21–24.

104. Baker, *WW:LL* 7:261; Piper, *American Churches*, 121–22.

105. Baker, *WW:LL* 8:484–85, quotation from 485.

106. "The President's Answer to the Pope," *Lutheran* 21 (Sept. 6, 1917), 806. Wilson argued that it would be folly to take the course the pope advocated because unless the Allies defeated the Central Powers there could be no "stable and enduring peace." See Robert Lansing to Pope Benedict XV, Aug. 27, 1917, in Tumulty, *Woodrow Wilson*, 281–84.

107. Tumulty, *Woodrow Wilson*, 482–83.

108. See Abraham J. Karp, *From Haven to Home: A History of Jews in America* (New York: Schocken, 1985), 224–27.

109. Paul A. Freund, "The Liberalism of Justice Brandeis," in *Critical Studies in American Jewish History*, vol. 3 (New York: Ktav, 1971), 98. See also Philippa Strum, *Louis D. Brandeis: Justice for the People* (New York: Schocken, 1989).

110. See Herman Bernstein to WW, Mar. 22, 1916; WW to Tumulty, Mar. 23, 1916, *PWW* 36:356; Simon Wolf to WW, May 25, 1916, *PWW* 37:109–10.

111. Heckscher, *Woodrow Wilson*, 569. Wilson praised the Zionist movement in the United States and Europe. See news report, Mar. 2, 1919, *PWW* 55:386; and WW to Wise, Aug. 31, 1918, Baker, *WW:LL* 8:372–73.

112. Woodrow Wilson, "The Christian Statesman," Sept. 1, 1876, *PWW* 1:188; Wilson, "The Bible," Aug. 25, 1877, *PWW* 1:185. Cf. Wilson, "Christian Progress," Dec. 20, 1876, *PWW* 1:234–35.

113. Link, "Christian in Government," 8.

114. Woodrow Wilson "Baccalaureate Address," June 7, 1908, *PWW* 18:332.

115. Mulder, "'Gospel of Order,'" 221. E.g., Wilson, "An Address to the Pittsburgh Y.M.C.A," Oct. 24, 1914, *PWW* 31:223, 226.

116. Mulder, "'Gospel of Order,'" 228–30. Mulder argues that Wilson's understanding of the modern democratic state was informed by the basic assumptions of covenant theology (*Preparation*, 99, 104). See also Wilson, "Baccalaureate Address," June 12, 1904, *PWW* 15:369.

117. Mulder, "Wilson the Preacher," 273; Woodrow Wilson, "Baccalaureate Address," June 12, 1910, *PWW* 20:523.

118. Richard Pierard and Robert Linder, *Civil Religion and the Presidency* (Grand Rapids, MI: Zondervan, 1988), 153.

119. William F. McCombs, *Making Woodrow Wilson President* (New York: Fairview, 1921), 208. McCombs was the chairman of the Democratic National Committee.

120. Pierard and Linder, *Civil Religion*, 154; Wells Jr., "New Perspectives," 419; Ross Gregory, "To Do Good in the World: Woodrow Wilson and America's Mission," in Frank Merli and Theodore A. Wilson, eds., *Makers of American Diplomacy: From Benjamin Franklin to Henry Kissinger* (New York: Scribners, 1974), 364–67; Arthur S. Link, *Wilson the Diplomatist: A Look at His Major Foreign Policies* (Baltimore: Johns Hopkins University Press, 1957), 14–16.

121. Alderman, *In Memoriam*, 32. Cf. Houston, *Eight Years*, 159: If Wilson could discover what God wanted, "he gave no heed to what anybody else or everybody else wanted or thought."

122. Mulder, *Preparation*, 274–75.

123. Lewis, "Man of Faith," 47; Gerald W. Johnson, "Wilson: Character as Statecraft," in *Woodrow Wilson Centennial Addresses* (Oxford, OH: Miami University, 1957), 27.

124. Mulder, *Preparation*, 276.

125. Woodrow Wilson, "The Statesmanship of Letters," Nov. 5, 1903, *PWW* 15:36.

126. Robert H. Ferrell, *Woodrow Wilson and World War I, 1917–1921* (New York: Harper and Row, 1985), 158–60.

127. Mulder, "Wilson the Preacher," 274.

128. Mulder, *Preparation*, 50–51.

129. Wilson, "New Kind of Church Life," 148. Cf. Wilson, "Remarks to the American Bar Association," Oct. 20, 1914, *PWW* 31:186.

130. Mulder, "'Gospel of Order," 236.

131. Cooper, *The Warrior and the Priest*, 217–21. See also Niels Aage Thorsen, *The Political Thought of Woodrow Wilson, 1875–1910* (Princeton, NJ: Princeton University Press, 1988), 214–34.

132. Kendrick A. Clements, *Woodrow Wilson: World Statesman* (Boston: Twayne, 1987), 116.

133. Woodrow Wilson, "The Study of Administration," c. Nov. 1, 1886, *PWW* 5:370, 373.

134. Woodrow Wilson, "An Inaugural Address," Mar. 4, 1913, *PWW* 27:150–51. See also Wilson, address to voters, Nov. 1912, quoted in Baker, *WW:LL* 6:98.

135. Link, "Presbyterian Inheritance," 4. Cf. Link, "Christian in Government," 10; and August Heckscher, "Woodrow Wilson in Perspective," in *Centennial Addresses*, 36.

136. Through these measures, Wilson strove to promote the interests of the whole nation and to push the government to take the initiative in social reform. See Kendrick

A. Clements, *The Presidency of Woodrow Wilson* (Lawrence: University Press of Kansas, 1992), 44.

137. Quoted in Baker, *WW:LL* 4:55. Link maintains that before 1913 Wilson did not think systematically about "the nature, complexity, and difficulties of foreign policy" ("Wilson the Diplomatist," 151).

138. Woodrow Wilson, *Constitutional Government in the United States* (New York: Columbia University Press, 1908), 77–78.

139. Link, "Wilson the Diplomatist," 160; Arthur S. Link, *Woodrow Wilson: Revolution, War, and Peace* (Arlington Heights, IL: Harlan Davidson, 1979), 14.

140. Link, "Wilson the Diplomatist," 152; Link, "Presbyterian in Government," 171. Cf. Bell, "Genesis," 657; and Loren Baritz, *Backfire: A History of How American Culture Led Us into Vietnam and Made Us Fight the Way We Did* (New York: William Morrow, 1985), 34–37, 41–43, 72, 75, 78, 142, 144, 167.

141. Whittle Johnston, "Reflections on Wilson and the Problems of World Peace," in Arthur S. Link, ed., *Woodrow Wilson and the Revolutionary World, 1913–1921* (Chapel Hill: University of North Carolina Press, 1982), 201–2.

142. Cf. William Merrill, *Christian Internationalism* (New York: Macmillan, 1918), 73.

143. Link, "Wilson the Diplomatist," 152–54.

144. Samuel G. Blythe, "Mexico: The Record of a Conversation with President Wilson," *Saturday Evening Post* 186 (May 23, 1914), 4.

145. Link, "Wilson the Diplomatist," 154. See Woodrow Wilson, *The State: Elements of Historical and Practical Politics* (Boston: D. C. Heath, 1889), 603; and Frederick Lynch, *President Wilson and the Moral Aims of the War* (New York: Fleming H. Revell, 1918), 10.

146. Frederick S. Calhoun, *Power and Principle: Armed Intervention in Wilsonian Foreign Policy* (Kent, OH: Kent State University Press, 1986), 8, 17. See also Thomas Knock, *To End All Wars: Woodrow Wilson and the Quest for a New World Order* (Princeton, NJ: Princeton University Press, 1995); Robert Johnson, *The Peace Progressives and American Foreign Relations* (Cambridge, MA: Harvard University Press, 1995); and Alan Dawley, *Changing the World: American Progressives in War and Revolution* (Princeton, NJ: Princeton University Press, 2003).

147. Calhoun, *Power and Principle*, 18.

148. Woodrow Wilson, "Speech on Patriotism to the Washington Association of New Jersey," Feb. 23, 1903, *PWW* 14:371.

149. Woodrow Wilson, "An Address in Charlotte, North Carolina," May 20, 1916, *PWW* 37:80–82.

150. See WW to W. J. Bryan, Nov. 12, 1912, *PWW* 25:240; Heckscher, *Woodrow Wilson*, 294.

151. Link, "Wilson the Diplomatist," 154–55.

152. Wilson, "Bible and Progress," 1:354–55, 350.

153. Richard M. Gamble, *The War for Righteousness: Progressive Christianity, the Great War, and the Rise of the Messianic Nation* (Wilmington, DE: ISI, 2003), 86–87, quotation from 86. See Wilson, "A Flag Day Address," June 15, 1914, *PWW* 30:186; and Wilson, "A Fourth of July Address," July 4, 1914, *PWW* 30:254–55.

154. Woodrow Wilson, "A Nonpartisan Address in Cincinnati," Oct. 26, 1916, *PWW* 38:542; Wilson, "Address at the Seventh Annual Dinner of the Railway Business Association," Jan. 27, 1916, in *PPWW* 4:28–29; Wilson, "Address at Overflow Meeting

at Soldiers Memorial Hall, Pittsburgh," Jan. 29, 1916, in ibid, 4:26; Wilson, "Address before Manhattan Club," Nov. 4, 1915, in ibid., 3:385–86; Wilson, "Address at Overflow Meeting at Soldiers Memorial Hall, Pittsburgh," Jan. 29, 1916, in ibid, 4:29; Wilson, "Speech at Omaha," Oct. 5, 1916, in ibid., 4:346–47; Woodrow Wilson, "Remarks at a Luncheon in New York," May 17, 1915, *PWW* 33:211; and Wilson, "A Commencement Address," June 5, 1914, *PWW* 30:146.

155. Harley Notter, *Origins of the Foreign Policy of Woodrow Wilson* (Baltimore: Johns Hopkins University Press, 1937), 653; Link, *Wilson the Diplomatist*, 15–16; Lloyd E. Ambrosius, *Woodrow Wilson and the American Diplomatic Tradition: The Treaty Fight in Perspective* (Cambridge: Cambridge University Press, 1987), 12. See Wilson, "Religion and Patriotism," *PWW* 12:474–78.

156. Arthur S. Link, *Woodrow Wilson and the Progressive Era* (New York: Harper and Brothers, 1954), 81–106. See also Emily Rosenberg, *Spreading the American Dream: American Economic and Cultural Expansion, 1890–1945* (New York: Hill and Wang, 1982). Wilson appointed Bryan secretary of state in part because of their shared belief that foreign policy should be based on moral principles (Mulder, "Gospel of Order," 239). On Bryan, see Michael Kazin, *A Godly Hero: The Life of William Jennings Bryan* (New York: Knopf, 2006).

157. Anne R. Pierce, *Woodrow Wilson and Harry Truman: Mission and Power in American Foreign Policy* (Westport, CT: Praeger, 2003), 18.

158. Woodrow Wilson, "A New Latin American Policy," Oct. 27, 1913, in *PPWW* 3:67–69.

159. Woodrow Wilson, "A Statement on Relations with Latin America," March 12, 1913, *PWW* 27:172–73.

160. See Arthur S. Link, "The Higher Realism of Woodrow Wilson," in Link, *The Higher Realism*, 127–39.

161. E.g., Blum, *Woodrow Wilson*, 85; and Lou Hartz, *The Liberal Tradition in America: An Interpretation of American Political Thought since the Revolution* (New York: Harcourt, Brace and World, 1955), 290, 293, 295–97, 300, 304.

162. Crunden, *Ministers of Reform*, 226, 228. After Bryan resigned in 1915, Wilson appointed another Presbyterian elder, Robert Lansing, as secretary of state. Crunden argues that Lansing "completely shared the religious biases already strong" in American foreign policy (231).

163. Woodrow Wilson, "An Address on Latin American Policy," Oct. 27, 1913, *PWW* 28:448–51.

164. *PPWW* 3:130. See also Edward J. Wheeler, "Can President Wilson Inaugurate a Moral Pan-American Empire?" *Current Opinion*, June 1914, 450ff. Although the "dollar diplomacy" of William Howard Taft and his Secretary of State Philander Knox, which Wilson and Bryan repudiated, had first and foremost served American economic self-interest, Crunden contends, it recognized the realities of the marketplace, created jobs in poorer nations, and helped these countries develop their resources (*Ministers of Reform*, 234–35). On Wilson's objections to dollar diplomacy, see Baker, *WW:LL* 4:61–69.

165. Crunden, *Ministers of Reform*, 240.

166. See Link, *Progressive Era*, 81–82; Pierard and Linder, *Civil Religion*, 142; and David Healy, *Drive to Hegemony: The United States in the Caribbean, 1898–1917* (Madison: University of Wisconsin Press, 1988), 199.

167. Crunden, *Ministers of Reform*, 243.

168. Dawley, *Changing the World*, 79.

169. Pierard and Linder, *Civil Religion*, 142, 154, quotation from 154. See also Pierce, *Woodrow Wilson and Harry Truman*, 12.

170. Wells, "New Perspectives," 407.

171. Pierard and Linder, *Civil Religion*, 155. See also Julius Pratt, *Challenge and Rejection: The United States and World Leadership, 1900–1921* (New York: Macmillan, 1967), 84–101.

172. Crunden, *Ministers of Reform*, 235, 237, quotations in that order.

173. Calhoun, *Power and Principle*, 23–44, quotation from 24.

174. "Mexican Question," *Ladies Home Journal*, 33 (Oct. 1916), 9.

175. Clements, *Presidency*, 96, 106, 113; Healy, *Drive to Hegemony*, 181–82.

176. Woodrow Wilson, "A Proclamation," Sept. 8, 1914, *PWW* 31:11.

177. *The* (Newberry, SC) *Herald and News*, Oct. 6, 1914, as quoted by Gamble, *War for Righteousness*, 99. Gamble called my attention to many of the sources cited in this section.

178. Gamble, *War for Righteousness*, 100–2.

179. E.g., William Adams Brown, *Christianity and War* (New York: Association, 1919); Harry Emerson Fosdick, *The Challenge of the Present Crisis* (New York: Association, 1917), 4–5, 14–20; Henry Churchill King, *Fundamental Questions* (New York: Macmillan, 1917), esp. 2, 4–6, 17; Horatio Dresser, *The Victorious Faith: Moral Ideals in War Time* (New York: Harper, 1917), esp. 124, 129–30, 138–43, 219–21; Eugene William Lyman, *The Experience of God in Modern Life* (New York: Charles Scribner's Sons, 1918), esp. 50, 103–4, 145, 149; Robert Latham Owen, *Where Is God in the European War?* (New York: Century, 1918); Edward S. Drown, *God's Responsibility for the War* (New York: Macmillan, 1919); and Charles E. Jefferson, *What the War Has Taught Us* (New York: Fleming H. Revell, 1919).

180. E.g., "The Purpose of the War," *Outlook* 107 (Aug. 29, 1914), 1044; "God Is Not on Trial," ibid., 108 (Sept. 30, 1914), 249–50; "Have We Lost Faith?" ibid., 108 (Nov. 25, 1914), 667; "God in His World," ibid., 111 (Sept. 1915), 17–18; and Charles E. Jefferson, *What the War Is Teaching* (New York: Fleming H. Revell, 1916), 123–24.

181. Bryan to WW, Dec. 1, 1914, *WW:LL* 5:296.

182. "Religion in the Coming Political Campaign," *CC* 32 (Nov. 25, 1915), 3; "Shall We Vote for Wilson?" *Outlook* 113 (Aug. 23, 1916), 941–42.

183. Quoted in Mark Sullivan, *Our Times*, 6 vols. (New York: Charles Scribner's Sons 1935), vol. 5: *Over Here, 1914–1918*, 235.

184. WW to Seth Low, Nov. 8, 1915, *PWW* 25:180–81.

185. See Robert Bolt, "American Involvement in World War I," in Ronald Wells, ed., *The Wars of America: Christian Views* (Grand Rapids, MI: Eerdmans, 1981), 141. Pacifist denominations opposed all wars. They refused to support American involvement, even though they experienced ostracism and in some cases civil penalties. Sizable numbers of conservative Protestants initially did not want to participate in what they deemed to be a secular crusade. Most fundamentalists opposed the war until they began to see it as a fulfillment of biblical prophecy. See Paul Boyer, *When Time Shall Be No More: Prophecy Belief in Modern American Culture* (Cambridge, MA: Harvard University Pres, 1992), 101–3. Many Lutherans argued that because the United States had supplied the Allies with munitions, it had not been truly neutral and thus could not enter the war with clean hands. E.g., "To President Wilson," *Lutheran* 21 (Feb. 22, 1917), 1. Irish American and German American Catholics were hesitant to join

Protestant Anglophiles in a battle with the British against Germany. Before the Russian Revolution in March 1917, Jewish Americans did not want to fight on the side of the czar who had treated their coreligionists so poorly (Dawley, *Changing the World*, 131).

186. Quoted in William Allen White, *Autobiography* (New York: Macmillan, 1946), 514. See also William Jennings Bryan, "Present Peace Problems and the Preparedness Program," May 18, 1916, in *Mohonk Reports, 1916*, 144–46, 149; Clements, *Woodrow Wilson*, 160; and Walter Millis, *Road to War, 1914–1917* (New York: H. Fertig, 1970 [1935]), 187–91, 237–38.

187. Woodrow Wilson, "An Unpublished Prolegomenon to a Peace Note," c. Nov 25, 1916, *PWW* 40:67–68.

188. "No False Peace: A Warning by American Religious Leaders," *Outlook* 115 (Jan. 10, 1917), 63. See Gamble, *War for Righteousness*, 142–43. These leaders included Lyman Abbott; Henry Churchill King, president of Oberlin; Wilson's successor at Princeton, John Grier Hibben; Social Gospel novelist Winston Churchill; New York City pulpiteer Harry Emerson Fosdick; Boston pastor George A. Gordon; Brooklyn minister Newell Dwight Hillis; and evangelist Billy Sunday.

189. Woodrow Wilson, "An Address to the Senate," Jan. 22, 1917, *PWW* 40:533–39.

190. *NYT*, Jan. 29, 1917.

191. E.g., E. W. Diarmid, "On the Eve of Armageddon," *CC* 34 (Feb. 15, 1917), 13; Ernest M. Stires, *The High Call* (New York: E. P. Dutton, 1917), 1–63; *NYT*, Mar. 26, 30, and Apr. 2, 1917; *PWW* 41:353–4; *LD* 54 (Apr. 14, 1917), 1064; and Gamble, *War for Righteousness*, 144–48. Protesting American subservience to British policy and the "collusion of big business, the newspapers, and the elite pulpits," some professors, such as J. Gresham Machen, and congressmen, most notably Claude Kitchin of North Carolina, opposed American entry into the conflict. See Ned Stonehouse, *J. Gresham Machen*, 245–47 and Alex M. Arnett, *Claude Kitchin and the Wilson War Policies* (Boston: Little, Brown, 1937). The quotation is from Gamble, *War for Righteousness*, 147.

192. Walworth, *Woodrow Wilson*, vol. 2: *World Prophet*, 1; Link, *Progressive Era*, 275. For an account of Wilson's actions during this period, see Link, *Revolution, War and Peace*, 64–71.

193. Link, *Progressive Era*, 277. Link argues that Wilson believed that Christians sometimes "had to accept war as the less evil option" ("Presbyterian in Government," 173).

194. Wilson, "Bible and Progress," 1:345.

195. Woodrow Wilson, "An Address to a Joint Session of Congress," Apr. 2, 1917, *PWW* 41:526.

196. Like both Gladstone and Roosevelt, Wilson insisted that nations should be "governed by the same high code of honor that we demand of individuals." Like Roosevelt, Frederick Marks maintains, "Wilson tried to hold other nations to a personal conception of righteousness" (*Velvet on Iron: The Diplomacy of Theodore Roosevelt* [Lincoln: University of Nebraska Press, 1982], 117). Unwilling to separate private moral standards from public policy, Crunden contends, Wilson refused to settle for results that were tolerable rather than ideal (*Ministers of Reform*, 237).

197. Wilson, "An Address to a Joint Session of Congress," 41:519–27; first quotation from 527, second from 525, third and fourth from 527. America could "make the world freer, more just, and more peaceful" only by participating in World War I, so Wilson

decided to "sin boldly" and go to war (Cooper, *Warrior and the Priest*, 322–23). See also Link, *Revolution*, 69–71.

198. McAdoo to WW, Apr. 3, 1917, *PWW* 41:541.

199. See *Congressional Record*, Apr. 4, 1917, vol. 55, 223, 335; ibid., Apr. 5, 1917, vol. 55, 404; and ibid., Apr. 9, 1917, vol. 55, 423.

200. E.g., Frank W. Gunsaulus, "The War and the America of Tomorrow," *CC* 34 (Oct. 25, 1917), 10–11; and Charles S. Macfarland, "Spiritual Unity through Sacrificial Suffering," *Survey* 39 (Dec. 29, 1917), 358–59.

201. See *Congressional Record*, Apr. 4, 1917, vol. 55, 256.

202. Gamble, *War for Righteousness*, 157. See Ray H. Abrams, *Preachers Present Arms* (New York, Round Table, 1933), 55–71. E.g., Lyman Abbott, *The Twentieth Century Crusade* (New York: Macmillan, 1918); Shailer Mathews, "Why We Fight Germany," *New York Times Magazine*, Aug. 1917; and Randolph McKim, *For God and Country or the Christian Pulpit in War Time* (New York: Dutton, 1918).

203. Woodrow Wilson, "Remarks to Confederate Veterans," June 5, 1917, *PWW* 42:451–53, quotation from 452. Two weeks later, a delegation from the PCUSA, the president's own denomination, visited him at the White House and promised to work to persuade their parishioners to support the goals Wilson had delineated (Remarks by Wallace Radcliffe to WW, June 19, 1917, *PWW* 42:535). The Democrat replied that "this is a war which any great spiritual body can support, because I believe if ever a nation purged its heart of improper motives in a war, this nation has purged its heart, and that, if there ever was a war which was meant to supply new foundations for what is righteous and true and of good report, it is this war" (WW to a delegation from the PCUSA, June 19, 1917, *PWW* 42:537).

204. Herron, *Woodrow Wilson*, 77. Herron argued that Wilson, like Lincoln, was "a redeemer of democracy" (73).

205. WW to Mitchell Kennerley, Oct. 1, 1917, *WWLL* 7:288–89.

206. Nordholt, *Woodrow Wilson*, 239. See also Lloyd Gardner, *Safe for Democracy: The Anglo-American Response to Revolution, 1913–1923* (New York: Oxford University Press, 1987). Progressives tended to view the world through the lens of Christian ethics and "to deal with nations as if they were individuals subject to sin, forgiveness, and redemption" (Crunden, *Ministers of Reform*, 248).

207. E.g., J. Lovell Murray, *The Call of a World Task in War Time* (New York: Association, 1918), 2, 20–46; Robert E. Speer, *The Christian Man, the Church and the War* (New York: Macmillan, 1918), esp. 8, 10, 25–26, 31, 68–76; William H. P. Faunce, *Religion and War* (New York: Abingdon, 1918); Herbert L. Willett, "The War and the Kingdom of God," *CC* 35 (Dec. 12, 1918), 6; Arthur Cushman McGiffert, "Democracy and Religion," *Religious Education* 14 (June 1919) 158–61; and Merrill, *Christian Internationalism*, 68–69.

208. See Gamble, *War for Righteousness*, 159; Gunsaulus, "The War," 10–11; and Macfarland, "Spiritual Unity," 358–59.

209. E.g., Charles Reynolds Brown, "Moral and Spiritual Forces in the War," in E. Hershey Sneath, ed., *Religion and the War* (New Haven, CT: Yale University Press, 1918), 17–19, 20; and Charles E. Jefferson, "What Are We Fighting For?" *Independent* 95 (Aug 24, 1918), 266.

210. See Reinhold Niebuhr, *The Children of Light and the Children of Darkness: A Vindication of Democracy and a Critique of Its Traditional Defense* (New York: Charles Scribner's Sons, 1944); Niebuhr, *The Irony of American History* (New York: Charles

Scribner's Sons, 1952); and Hans J. Morgenthau, "The Influence of Reinhold Niebuhr on American Political Life and Thought," in Harold R. Landon, ed., *Reinhold Niebuhr: A Prophetic Voice in Our Time* (Greenwich, CT: Seabury, 1962), 97–116.

211. Gamble, *War for Righteousness*, 161. E.g., Merrill, *Christian Internationalism*, 132–33; Newell Dwight Hills, "What Are We Fighting Against?" *CC* 34 (Oct. 18, 1917), 10–11; *NYT* May 22, July 7, and Sept. 17, 1917; and Hillis, *German Atrocities* (New York: Fleming H. Revell, 1918). For other examples, see Abrams, *Preachers*, 96–116.

212. William Barton, "The Moral Meanings of the World War," *Homiletic Review*, 1918, 242.

213. Arthur Judson Brown, "The Moral Conflict," in Lynch, *President Wilson*, 50–58; first quotation from 51, second from 52, third from 53, fourth and fifth from 55. Cf. William I. Hull, "The President's International Ideal," in ibid., 59–66; Henry Churchill King, "Grounds of Hope in the Present Crisis," in ibid., 67–81.

214. Merrill, *Christian Internationalism*, 12.

215. Quoted in the *LD* 47 (Apr. 13, 1918), 33. Cf. George Pentecost, *Fighting for the Faith* (New York: Doran, 1918), 103. For other examples, see Abrams, *Preachers*, 50, 82.

216. Piper, *American Churches*, 10.

217. See Woodrow Wilson, "An Appeal to the American People," Apr. 15, 1917, *PWW* 42:71–75; "From the President to the People," *Outlook* 115 (Apr. 25, 1917), 729. For clergy support of the war, see Abrams, *Preachers*, 85–86.

218. E.g., Donald Gorrell, *The Age of the Social Responsibility: The Social Gospel in the Progressive Era* (Macon, GA: Mercer University Press, 1988), 279–89.

219. Gamble, *War for Righteousness*, 181–231, quotation from 208. E.g., Merrill, *Christian Internationalism*; Lyman Abbott, "Our God Is Marching On," *Outlook* 119 (Aug. 7, 1918), 547–49; and Harry F. Ward, *The New Social Order: Principles and Programs* (New York: Macmillan, 1919).

220. Woodrow Wilson, "A Thanksgiving Proclamation," Nov. 16, 1918, *PWW* 53:75–76.

221. Richard J. Bishirjian, "Croly, Wilson, and the American Civil Religion," *Modern Age* 23 (Winter 1979), 37.

222. Crunden, *Ministers of Reform*, 247.

223. *L'Homme Enchaine*, as quoted by Crunden, *Ministers of Reform*, 249.

224. Jean-Baptiste Duroselle, in J. Joseph Huthmacher and Warren Susman, eds., *Wilson's Diplomacy: An International Symposium* (Cambridge, MA: Harvard University Press, 1973), 21, 33, 109–11.

225. His administration bears some of the blame for this. Led by George Creel, the Committee on Public Information fanned the flames of hatred for the enemy. Congress passed the Alien Act and Espionage Act in 1917 and the Sedition Act in 1918. Authorities harassed conscientious objectors, silenced opposing perspectives, and countenanced irrational hatred of German Americans (Clements, *Presidency*, 152–56). Wilson warned Navy Secretary Josephus Daniels that "every reform we have won will be lost if we go into this war" (Baker, *WW:LL* 6:506).

226. Pierard and Linder, *Civil Religion*, 157.

227. Dawley, *Changing the World*, 243.

228. Gamble, *War for Righteousness*, 224–25; Ferrell, *Woodrow Wilson*, 139–40.

229. "Religion's Opportunity Now That the War Is Over," *Current Opinion* 66 (Jan. 1919), 45.

230. Gamble, *War for Righteousness*, 224.

231. Quoted in Knock, *To End All Wars*, 1.

232. Woodrow Wilson, "An Address to the Third Plenary Session of the Peace Conference," Feb. 14, 1919, *PWW* 55:117.

233. Quoted in Ferrell, *Woodrow Wilson*, 152. Clemenceau also complained that Wilson thought he was Jesus Christ.

234. Baker and Dodd, *PPWW* 5:355–400.

235. Ibid., 4:410. The quotations are from Wilson's "peace without victory" speech of Jan. 22, 1917.

236. Gerald W. Johnson, "Wilson the Man," *Virginia Quarterly Review* 32 (Autumn 1956), 501.

237. Woodrow Wilson, "An Address in Free Trade Hall," *PWW* 53:552. See also Mulder, *Preparation*, 273–74.

238. *PPWW* 5:378.

239. *PPWW* 5:523.

240. Crunden, *Ministers of Reform*, 253.

241. Keynes, *Economic Consequences*, 38.

242. Nicolson, *Peacemaking*, 7, 15, 28, 36–37, 42, 52–53, 69–79, 146, 164, 170–71, 184, 196–99; quotations from 199, 198, 53.

243. Woodrow Wilson, "An Address to the Senate," July 10, 1919, *PWW* 61:436.

244. Gamble, *War for Righteousness*, 229.

245. See Robert Moats Miller, *Harry Emerson Fosdick: Preacher, Pastor, Prophet* (New York: Oxford University Press 1985), 90.

246. The first quotation is from "The Idealism of Woodrow Wilson," *CC* 41 (Feb. 21, 1924), 231; second and third from "The Common Guilt," *CC* 36 (Sept. 18, 1919), 6–7.

247. Ambrosius, *Woodrow Wilson*, 5. Also see Charles Forcey, *The Crossroads of Liberalism: Croly, Weyl, Lippmann, and the Progressive Era, 1900–1925* (New York: Oxford University Press, 1961), 221–315; and Charles DeBenedetti, *Origins of the Modern American Peace Movement, 1915–1929* (Millwood, NY: KTO, 1978), 3–43.

248. For religious concerns about the league, especially that the pope might be able to dictate the policies of the Catholic nations that belonged, see Ralph Stone, *The Irreconcilables: The Fight against the League of Nations* (Lexington: University of Kentucky Press, 1970), 103–5.

249. Pratt, *Challenge and Rejection*, 196, 201, quotation from 201. Pratt criticizes Wilson for failing to realize that the Senate would not approve the treaty without significant changes and that the league would have benefited far more from American participation than it would have lost because of these modifications (211). Pratt attributes Wilson's inability to see these truths to his illness, stubbornness, and "religious faith in his mission" that sometimes seemed like "a messianic complex" (212).

250. See *Federal Council of Churches Reports, 1918*, 72–73. Wilson did not meet with the delegation, but he promised to give their resolution of support "careful attention." See WW to Frank Mason North, Jan. 14, 1919, *PWW* 54:56.

251. The Federal Council of Churches, *Report of Special Meeting, Cleveland, Ohio, May 6, 7, 8, 1919* (New York: National Office, 1919), 72–74. See also W. G. McAdoo, *A League to Prevent War* (New York: League to Enforce Peace, 1919), 3–4.

252. Robert E. Speer, "The Witness Bearing of the Church to the Nations," *Federal Council Bulletin* 2 (June 1919), 92. See also Miller, *Fosdick*, 91; Jefferson, *War Has Taught Us*, 70; Jefferson, "The Great Peace," *Independent* 96 (Nov. 23, 1918), 243; and Jefferson, "The League of Nations and Religion," *CC* 36 (Mar. 13, 1919), 7–8.

253. "The Dilemma of the Covenanter," *CC* 36 (Sept. 25, 1919), 7–8; "The President's Will," ibid., (Oct. 2, 1919), 6–8.

254. Charles S. Macfarland, *Pioneers for Peace through Religion* (New York: Fleming Revell, 1946), 73.

255. See Stone, *The Irreconcilables*; and Ambrosius, *Woodrow Wilson*.

256. Frederick F. Shannon, "Woodrow Wilson: Martyr," *MQR* 74 (Apr. 1925) 295–308, quotation from 301.

257. David Hunter Miller, *Woodrow Wilson* (New York: Appeal, 1924), 1; Earl G. Hamlett, "The Immortality of Woodrow Wilson," *MQR* 74 (July 1925), 576.

258. "Idealism of Woodrow Wilson," 230.

259. James H. Taylor, "A Great Man Has Fallen," in Taylor, *Woodrow Wilson in Church*, 32–34, quotation from 34.

260. Alderman, *In Memoriam*, 33.

261. *NYT*, Feb. 4, 1924, 1–3.

262. Macfarland, *Across the Years*, 265–66. On Macfarland's relationship with Wilson, see 101, 116–19, 125, 259–63.

263. Lewis, "Man of Faith," 48.

264. See Dawley, *Changing the World*, 335.

265. Pierce, *Woodrow Wilson and Harry Truman*, 18–19. See Wilson, *Presidential Messages*, 3:3–4; ibid., 3:11; Jan. 8, 1915 at Indianapolis; Oct. 25, 1913, *PWW* 32:38–41; at Swarthmore College, *PWW* 28:441; and Wilson, "The Rights of Jews," *SLPP*, 1:369.

266. Link, ""Portrait of the President," 9.

267. "Wilson and Lenin," *CC* 41 (Feb. 21, 1924), 199.

268. Theodore Roosevelt, *Works of Theodore Roosevelt*, national edition, 20 vols. (New York: Charles Scribner's Sons, 1926), 18:204.

269. TR to Owen Wister, Feb. 5, 1916, quoted in Wister, *Roosevelt: The Story of a Friendship* (New York: Macmillan, 1930), 355.

270. "The Failure of Moral Leadership," *Nation* 109 (July 1919), 4.

271. Alderman, *In Memoriam*, 35.

272. Link, "Portrait of the President," 22–23, quotation from 23.

273. Mulder, *Preparation*, 269–70. Cf. Link, "Wilson the Diplomatist," 160.

274. Mulder, *Preparation*, 263, whose account I closely follow in discussing this matter.

275. E.g., WW to Peck, Feb, 25, 1910, *PWW* 20:178.

276. Peck to WW, Feb. 15 and 18, 1910, *PWW* 20:127, 142.

277. Clements, *Presidency*, 2. Francis Saunders concludes that "no unambiguous evidence" proves "how intimate the relationship" became between Wilson and Peck. Wilson called their relationship "a contemptible error," a "madness of a few months," an episode that had left him "stained and unworthy" (Saunders, *Ellen Axson Wilson*, 201; WW to Edith Galt, Sept. 19 and 21, 1915, *PWW* 34:491, 497). In September 1915, Wilson wrote a statement that remained private until after his death. He claimed that "neither in the act nor even in thought was" Peck's "purity or honor "touched or sullied.... Neither was my utter allegiance to my incomparable wife in the least jot abated" (An Admission, c. Sept. 20, 1915, *PWW* 34:496–97). Peck also denied they had had an affair. Levin concludes that her summary probably accurately described their relationship: "Tender yes; but hardly erotic, nor by any means measured of passion." See Mary Allen Hulbert, "The Woodrow Wilson I Knew," *Liberty Magazine*, Jan. 3, 1925. Jeffrey Schultz, by contrast, contends that they had an affair. See *Presidential*

Scandals (Washington, DC: Congressional Quarterly Press, 2000), 232–33). The fullest account of their relationship is Levin, *Edith and Wilson*, 113–38.

278. House Diary, Sept. 22, 1915, quoted in Arthur Link, *Wilson: Confusions and Crises, 1915–1916* (Princeton, NJ: Princeton University Press, 1964), 6.

279. Quoted in Margaret Axson Elliott, *My Aunt Louisa and Woodrow Wilson* (Chapel Hill: University of North Carolina Press, 1944), 202.

280. Mulder, *Preparation*, 262, 263.

281. WW to EAW, July 20, 1908, *PWW* 18:372.

282. See EAW to WW, Feb. 24, 1910, *PWW* 20:172. While courting Edith Galt in the fall of 1915, Wilson feared that his correspondence with Peck might become public and destroy his relationship with Galt. He told Galt about his friendship with Peck, and apparently it did not harm their relationship, because soon thereafter they married (Robert Saunders, *In Search of Woodrow Wilson: Beliefs and Behavior* [Westport, CT: Greenwood, 1998], 71). Their wedding, sixteen months after Wilson's wife Ellen died, surprised many and shocked some. A few detractors even suggested that they had an affair before his first wife's death (Baker, *WW:LL* 6:49–50). There is no evidence they did; Woodrow and Ellen had a loving, affectionate relationship their entire married life, and the president grieved deeply after her death.

283. Dawley, *Changing the World*, 122.

284. Lloyd E. Ambrosius, *Wilsonianism: Woodrow Wilson and His Legacy in American Foreign Relations* (New York: Palgrave Macmillan, 2002), 6. See also Henry May, *The End of American Innocence: A Study of the First Years of Our Time, 1912–1917* (New York: Alfred A. Knopf, 1959).

285. Crunden, *Ministers of Reform*, 273; Robert Linder, "Thomas Woodrow Wilson," *Dictionary of Christianity in America* (Downers Grove, IL: InterVarsity, 1990), 1262.

286. Pierard and Linder, *Civil Religion*, 160.

287. Pierce, *Woodrow Wilson and Harry Truman*, 5, 8, quotation from 8.

288. Mulder, " 'Gospel of Order,' " 242. See also Robert Booth Fowler, *Unconventional Partners: Religion and Liberal Culture in the United States* (Grand Rapids, MI: Eerdmans, 1989).

289. Link, "Wilson the Diplomatist," 156.

290. Ibid.

291. Arthur Link in Huthmacher and Susman, eds., *Wilson's Diplomacy*, 10; H. G. Nicholas in ibid., 80–81; Nordholt, *Woodrow Wilson*, 41–42.

292. Walworth, *Woodrow Wilson*, 2:421.

293. Link, "Wilson the Diplomatist," 156–58; first quotation from 158, second from 157, third from 156. See also Lynch, *President Wilson*, 8, 10, 16–29; Merrill, *Christian Internationalism*, 136.

294. Link, "Wilson the Diplomatist," 158–59; first quotation from 158, second and third from 159.

295. Link, "Higher Realism," 128.

296. Ambrosius, *Wilsonianism*, 146: "For them such a policy was neither immoral nor amoral, but simply realistic." E.g., George Kennan, *American Diplomacy, 1900–1950* (Chicago: University of Chicago Press, 1951); Norman A. Graebner, ed., *Ideas and Diplomacy: Readings in the Intellectual Tradition of American Foreign Policy* (New York: Oxford University Press, 1964); and Hans J. Morgenthau, *A New Foreign Policy for the United States* (New York: Frederick A. Praeger, 1969). The pluralist school

urged American leaders to distinguish between areas where the nation had critical interests and only tangential interests. They urged statesmen to pursue America's own "interests without engaging in liberal crusades" (Ambrosius, *Wilsonianism*, 155).

297. Link, "Higher Realism," 129–30; first quotation from 129, others from 130. Others who share this perspective include Edward H. Buehrig, *Woodrow Wilson and the Balance of Power* (Bloomington: Indiana University Press, 1955); Ernest R. May, *The World War and the American Isolation, 1914–1917* (Cambridge, MA: Harvard University Press, 1959); and Tony Smith, *America's Mission: The United States and the Worldwide Struggle for Democracy in the Twentieth Century* (Princeton, NJ: Princeton University Press, 1994), 30–32.

298. Link, "Higher Realism," 137–39, quotation from 137.

299. Pierce, *Woodrow Wilson and Harry Truman*, 117.

300. While Wilson emphasized global independence, Ambrosius argues, he paid insufficient attention to the world's pluralism. "If foreign leaders disagreed, as they frequently did, he attributed this disagreement to their failure to represent the true interests" of their citizens (*Wilsonianism*, 5, 33, quotation from 33).

301. Ibid., 2. Ambrosius contends that these four principles "were not only difficult to implement but often inherently contradictory" (14).

302. Akira Iriye, *The Cambridge History of American Foreign Relations*, vol. 3: *The Globalizing of America, 1913–1945* (Cambridge, England: Cambridge University Press, 1993), 45, 71–72.

303. Ambroius, *Wilsonianism*, 8. See also Henry Kissinger, *Diplomacy* (New York: Simon and Schuster, 1994); Amos Perlmutter, *Making the World Safe for Democracy: A Century of Wilsonianism and Its Critics* (Chapel Hill: University of North Carolina Press, 1997); and Frank Ninkovich, *The Wilsonian Century: U. S. Foreign Policy since 1900* (Chicago: University of Chicago Press, 1999). On Bush, see Lawrence Kaplan, "Bush, Closet Liberal: Regime Change," *New Republic*, Mar. 3, 2003; and David Kennedy, "What W Owes to WW," *AM* 295 (Mar. 2005), 36–40.

304. Quoted in Daniels, *Woodrow Wilson*, 359.

305. Link, "Life of Faith," 14.

306. Quoted in Walworth, *Woodrow Wilson*, 2:412.

CHAPTER 6

1. James Roosevelt and Sidney Shalett, *Affectionately, F. D. R.: A Son's Story of a Lonely Man* (New York: Harcourt Brace, 1959), 99–101, quotations from 101.

2. See Morton J. Frisch, "Franklin D. Roosevelt and the Modern American Presidency," in Herbert D. Rosenbaum and Elizabeth Bartelme, *Franklin D. Roosevelt: The Man, the Myth, the Era, 1882–1945* (New York: Greenwood, 1987), 230–38; James MacGregor Burns, *Roosevelt: The Soldier of Freedom* (New York: Harcourt Brace Jovanovich, 1970), vii, 339–43.

3. The best sources on this subject are Merlin Gustafson and Jerry Rosenberg, "The Faith of Franklin Roosevelt," *PSQ* 19 (Summer 1989), 559–66; Merlin Gustafson, "Franklin Roosevelt and His Protestant Constituency," *JCS* 35 (Spring 1993), 285–97; Ronald Isetti, "The Moneychangers of the Temple: FDR, American Civil Religion, and the New Deal," *PSQ* 26 (Summer 1996), 678–93; Halford R. Ryan, *Franklin D. Roosevelt's Rhetorical Presidency* (New York: Greenwood, 1988); and Richard V. Pierard

and Robert D. Linder, *Civil Religion and the Presidency* (Grand Rapids, MI: Zondervan, 1988), 161–83.

4. Franklin A. Mahlau, "March 20, 1882—The Baptism of a Future President," manuscript, Vertical File (hereafter VF), Roosevelt, F. D., Religion, Franklin Roosevelt Presidential Library (hereafter FRPL).

5. See Frank D. Ashburn, *Peabody of Groton* (New York: Coward McCann, 1944), esp. 177–79.

6. Chris Farlekas, "FDR: He Took His God Seriously," 4, VF, Roosevelt, F. D., Religion.

7. Peabody's admiration for Roosevelt and his policies grew over the years, and he voted for Roosevelt in 1936, 1940, and 1944 (Ashburn, *Peabody*, 345–51).

8. Quoted in Ashburn, *Peabody*, 343.

9. FDR to Peabody, Jan. 11, 1941, quoted in Ashburn, *Peabody*, 349. On Peabody's impact on Roosevelt's religious views, see Richard Thayer Goldberg, *The Making of Franklin D. Roosevelt: Triumph over Disability* (Cambridge, MA: Abt, 1981), 9–10.

10. Grace Tully, *F. D. R., My Boss* (Chicago: Peoples Book Club, 1949), 6; Samuel Rosenman, *Working with Roosevelt* (New York: Harpers, 1952), 397.

11. Early to Fulton Oursler, Jan. 17, 1945, President's Personal Files 3024, *Reader's Digest*, FRPL.

12. Roosevelt and Shalett, *Affectionately, F. D. R.*, 99. Roosevelt added that his father was eager for all the children "to be active in church affairs," but he encouraged rather than demanded them to do so (103).

13. Tully, *F. D. R.*, 181.

14. Eleanor Roosevelt, *This I Remember* (New York: Harper, 1949), 347. Eleanor developed an international reputation as a writer, lecturer, humanitarian, and social crusader. A rector at St. James described her as a saint, "a single-minded . . . puritan," who relentlessly did good works. In the 1980s, local people still talked about her piety and Christian witness. See Mahlau, "The Baptism of a Future President," 5–6, quotation from 5.

15. "The Election," *PB* 119 (Nov. 17, 1932), 3. Cf. "Faith in God," ibid. (Oct. 6, 1932), 3; Walter L. Lingle, "A Cheerful Heart," *The Christian Observer*, Mar. 29, 1933; "Campaign Slander," *Presbyterian* 102 (Sept. 22, 1932), 5.

16. "A Year of Roosevelt," *CC* 51 (Mar. 7, 1934), 311.

17. See Stephen Early to Father Terence A. Seery, Aug. 21, 1942, Official File (hereafter OF) 76B-76C, Church Matters, Box 4, OF76b, Catholic 1942, FRPL; Harold Ickes, *The Secret Diary of Harold L. Ickes*, vol. 3: *The Lowering Clouds, 1939–1941* (New York: Simon and Schuster, 1954), 383; "The Cardinal and Our President," *New World* 46 (Nov. 18, 1938), 2; and "Prayers for President Requested by Bishops," *Echo*, Mar. 9, 1939.

18. Eleanor Roosevelt, *This Is My Story* (New York: Harper, 1937), 149–50. His response effectively shut her up, but in the ensuing years, when he played golf and she took the children to church, she felt a kind of "virtuous grievance" until finally "her sense of humor came to the rescue" (150). Cf. Roosevelt and Shalett, *Affectionately, F. D. R.*, 106–7.

19. Franklin D. Roosevelt, *Whither Bound* (Boston: Houghton Mifflin, 1926), 14, emphasis in the original.

20. Thomas H. Greer, *What Roosevelt Thought: The Social and Political Ideas of Franklin D. Roosevelt* (East Lansing: Michigan State University Press, 1958), 4. See FDR to Francis Stifler, Oct. 29, 1940, PPF 90, The Bible, 1941–1945, FRPL.

21. Greer, *What Roosevelt Thought*, 9.

22. FDR to Keller, Jan. 12, 1942, PPF 2169, Keller, Helen.

23. Roosevelt affirmed his belief in Christ's bodily resurrection in a statement Daniel Poling asked him to write for the *Christian Herald's* Easter edition in 1945. Roosevelt called the resurrection "the story of man's greatest victory—his triumph over death; it is a source of consolation for those whose loved ones have given their lives" (Jan. 5, 1945, statement in PPF 6680, Religion, FRPL).

24. FDR to Henry St. George Tucker, Sept. 15, 1942, PPF 21 Cont. I, Church Matters, 1934–1943 (quotation); Roosevelt, "Radio Address on Brotherhood Day," Feb. 23, 1936, in B. D. Zevin, ed., *Nothing to Fear: Selected Addresses of Franklin Delano Roosevelt, 1932–45* (Boston: Houghton Mifflin, 1946), 58–59.

25. Franklin D. Roosevelt, "Campaign Address at Cleveland, Ohio," *The Public Papers and Addresses of Franklin D. Roosevelt*, ed. Samuel I. Rosenman, 13 vols. (New York: Random House, Harper, 1938–50), 10:514–15 (hereafter *PPAFDR*), 552.

26. See "President Roosevelt Meets Local Vestry," *Churchman* 145 (Oct. 1, 1935), 19: Roosevelt "regards the affairs of the local church as one of his serious responsibilities"; William Hassett, *Off the Record with FDR* (New Brunswick, NJ: Rutgers University Press, 1958), 238; and Mahlau, "The Baptism of a Future President," 5–6. For other matters pertaining to the vestry, see Bowie, Rev. W. Russell, Jan. 9, 1943; Gerald Morgan to FDR, Jan. 31, 1943; and FDR to Gerald Morgan, Feb. 3, 1943, all in PPF 8292, Wilson, Rev. Frank R. All of these are in President's Secretary's File, Subject File: Hyde Park: St. James Church, 1940–44, Box 139, FRPL. See also FDR to Wilson, Apr. 11, 1941; Oct., 29, 1941; Sept. 26, 1942; Feb. 5, 1943; and FDR to James Roosevelt, Feb. 8, 1944, all in this same file.

27. Stephen Ford, "The Spiritual Side of FDR," VF, Roosevelt, F. D., Religion.

28. Roosevelt and Shalett, *Affectionately, F. D. R.*, 104. While working to ameliorate the nation's massive economic problems, Roosevelt ostensibly did not encourage the congregation to help its local community. Vestry minutes indicate that members did not discuss the church's mission in the community and that in 1938 the church invested its entire surplus funds of $25,000 (a hefty sum at the time) in U.S. government bonds rather than using any part of it for charitable purposes. See Gustafson and Rosenberg, "Franklin Roosevelt," 563.

29. The Roosevelts frequently entertained Wilson and his wife at their homes at both Hyde Park and Campobello, and the Wilsons spent several nights in the White House during Roosevelt's presidency (Roosevelt and Shalett, *Affectionately, F.D.R.*, 105). See also "FDR Brings the Rev. Wilson Joy and Trouble," *PM's Weekly*, Feb. 23, 1941, 37.

30. See Rachel K. McDowell, "Franklin Roosevelt as I Knew Him," *Presbyterian*, Apr. 26, 1945, 9.

31. Quoted in Ashburn, *Peabody*, 343. Peabody added that his church attendance would positively influence his own family, Groton, and the nation.

32. Gustafson and Rosenberg, "Franklin Roosevelt," 561.

33. Quoted in Tully, *F. D. R.*, 6. James Roosevelt reports that all of the president's children had heard him make similar remarks (*Affectionately, F. D. R.*, 102).

34. See "... Religion, Says Former Washington Rector," PPF 1170, Wilkinson, Rev. Howard S. 1940–1945, FRPL. Pastor Allan J. Miller insisted in "A Spiritual Impression of the President" that FDR received his "physical strength, mental vigor and human understanding through constant communion with God." He also explained that few people except the clergymen the president invited to the White House appreciated

Roosevelt's "deep religious sense." See also "Social Traits of Roosevelt Are Analyzed," PPF 1170, Wilkinson, Howard S., 1934–1939, FRPL.

35. In 1939, FDR took King George, Queen Elizabeth, and MacKenzie King to services at St. James. In November 1941, he attended the Dutch Reformed church in Poughkeepsie, New York, with Princess Juliana. See Roosevelt and Shalett, *Affectionately, F. D. R.*, 105; Farlekas, "FDR: He Took His God Seriously," 4. On Christmas morning 1941, Churchill and Roosevelt worshiped at a service at the Foundry Methodist Church in Washington. See "Foundry Facts for Foundry Folks," Jan. 1, 1942, VF, Roosevelt, F. D., Church Services, 1941–1945. Better known is the service that Roosevelt and Churchill attended on the H.M.S. *Prince of Wales* before signing the Atlantic Charter in 1941.

36. Harold Ickes, *The Secret Diary of Harold L. Ickes*, vol. 2: *The Inside Struggle, 1936–39* (New York: Simon and Schuster, 1953), 290–91.

37. Roosevelt and Shalett, *Affectionately, F. D. R.*, 69. Roosevelt's favorite hymns included "All Hail the Power of Jesus' Name," "O Master, Let Me Walk with Thee," and "Be Strong." See Bliss Isely, *The Presidents, Men of Faith* (Boston: Wilde, 1953), 244.

38. *NYT*, July 15, 1936, 2; ibid., Aug. 19, 1936, 2. My attention was called to these articles by Pierard and Linder, *Civil Religion*, 325. Roosevelt regularly gave money to numerous congregations and charitable organizations, especially to Episcopal churches, the Federal Council of Churches, and the Infantile Paralysis Foundation. See Gustafson and Rosenberg, "Franklin Roosevelt," 562. Roosevelt regularly gave money to St. James Episcopal Church. See President's Secretary's File, Subject File, Hyde Park: St. James Church, 1933–39, and 1940–44, Box 139.

39. For Roosevelt's drinking habits, see Roosevelt and Shalett, *Affectionately, F. D. R.*, 93–95.

40. See James Farley, *Jim Farley's Story* (New York: McGraw Hill, 1948), 43–44; Perkins, *Roosevelt*, 142–43.

41. Tully, *F. D. R.*, 6. Cf. Edwin M. Watson to A. J. McCartney, July 1, 1940, PPF 2227, Committee on Religious Life in the Nation's Capital: The President is "a firm believer in the efficacy of prayer."

42. Greer, *What Roosevelt Thought*, 6–7. Roosevelt told a woman whose husband was ill that "spiritual faith and a steadfast belief in prayer" could help them overcome their problems (FDR to Mrs. Frakes, Apr. 22, 1943, PPF 6680, Religion).

43. Roosevelt, *This I Remember*, 67–68.

44. Oursler to FDR, Jan. 31, 1945, PPF 3024, *Reader's Digest*.

45. See *NYT*, Nov. 2, 1936, 2; Nov. 5, 1940, 16; Nov. 7, 1944, 18. My attention was called to this point and these sources by Paul H. Boase, "Moving the Mercy Seat into the White House: An Exegesis of the Carter/Reagan Religious Rhetoric," *JCR*, Sept. 1989, 1.

46. Hassett, *Off the Record with FDR*, 155–56 (quotation) 142; Ickes, *Secret Diary*, 3:143.

47. Roosevelt, *This I Remember*, 69. Cf. Rosenman, *Working with Roosevelt*, 397.

48. Franklin D. Roosevelt, "Radio Address on United Flag Day," *PPAFDR* 11: 288–89.

49. *PPAFDR* 10:514–15; 11:288–89; *NYT*, Nov. 13, 1942, 25.

50. *PPAFDR* 13:152–53. See also F. D. R. Speech File #1519, Container 78, 1507–20, F.D.R. Prayer Read on the Radio, June 6, 1944, FRPL, for Roosevelt's handwritten

revisions to the typed draft. The prayer was published as a pamphlet. See VF, D-Day Prayer.

51. FDR to Clark Eichelberger, Mar. 24, 1945, OF 5557, Dumbarton Oaks Conference on International Security.

52. See "The President's Noble Appreciation of the Bible," *UP*, Oct. 17, 1935, 7 (all quotations); FDR to Roy G. Ross, July 29, 1942, PPF 8129, Religious Education Week; and FDR to Howard Christy, Mar. 6, 1942, PPF 8160, Layman's National Committee Inc.

53. Perkins, *The Roosevelt I Knew*, 139–40, 144.

54. Isetti, "Moneychangers," 678. Isetti challenges the contention of Gustafson and Rosenberg that "many, if not most, of the religious references in his speeches were provided for him by his more knowledgeable speech writers" (563). He provides substantial evidence that Roosevelt was often "an active collaborator" in crafting major speeches. See also Rosenman, *Working with Roosevelt*, 142; Early to Fulton Oursler, Jan. 17, 1945; Tully, *F. D. R.*, 6. Roosevelt's proclamations are also peppered with biblical quotations.

55. James MacGregor Burns, *The Lion and the Fox* (New York: Harcourt, Brace, and World, 1956), 476.

56. Franklin D. Roosevelt, "First Inaugural Address," *PPAFDR* 2:12.

57. Roosevelt, "First Inaugural Address," 16. Some labeled Roosevelt's address as a sermon. E.g., "The Inaugural Address," *CC* 50 (Mar. 15, 1933), 351–52; and "The Faith of Roosevelt," *Nation* 136 (Mar. 15, 1933), 278.

58. Franklin D. Roosevelt, "Second Inaugural Address," in Zevin, ed., *Nothing to Fear*, 90–92, quotations in this order. For a positive appraisal of his address, see "The Second Inaugural," *CC* 54 (Feb. 3, 1937), 134–36, quotation from 135.

59. Franklin D. Roosevelt, "Third Inaugural Address," in Zevin, ed., *Nothing to Fear*, 271; Roosevelt, "Fourth Inaugural Address," *PPAFDR* 13:524–55.

60. Roosevelt, "We Have Only Just Begun to Fight," Oct. 31, 1936, *PPAFDR* 2:382. Cf. Roosevelt, "Your Life and Mine, Though We Work in the Mill, the Office or the Store, Can Still Be a Life in Green Pastures and Beside Still Waters," Sept. 10, 1936, *PPAFDR* 5: 341–48. Isetti explains that during the 1930s, the White House was inundated with "telegrams, notes, cards, poems, and letters" in response to Roosevelt's addresses. Thousands of citizens praised his use of biblical quotations and "commended him for the distinctly religious rhetoric of his major speeches" ("Moneychangers," 687).

61. Roosevelt, "First Annual Message to Congress," Jan. 1934; quotations from Roosevelt, "Third Message to Congress," Jan. 1936.

62. Roosevelt, "Radio Address on Brotherhood Day," 59. Cf. FDR to Raphael Miller, Jan. 23, 1942, PPF 7302, National Christian Mission; FDR to Samuel Thorne, Oct. 27, 1941, PPF 7796; FDR to H. R. Gonner, Apr. 14, 1940, PPF 2300, Catholic *Daily Tribune*; FDR to David McLean, Oct. 31, 1939, PPF 6292, Brooklyn, New York *Citizen*; FDR to A. C. Holland, Mar. 31, 1938, PPF 5280, St. John's Church (Chicago); and FDR to the Bishops of the General Conference of the Methodist Episcopal Church, South, Apr. 20, 1934, PPF 21 Cont. I, Church Matters, 1934–1943. See also James Farley, *Behind the Ballots: The Personal History of a Politician* (New York: Harcourt, Brace, 1938), 208.

63. FDR to Daniel Poling, June 15, 1938, PPF 630, Christian Endeavor Union. Cf. FDR to United Council of American Methodism, Jan. 17, 1938; "President Extols

Methodist Council," *NYT*, Feb. 4, 1938, 18; and FDR to Archbishop Rummel, Oct. 1, 1938, PPF 2773, National Eucharistic Congress, FRPL.

64. FDR to A. Shullenberger, July 6, 1942, PPF 6269, International Convention of the Disciples of Christ.

65. Franklin D. Roosevelt, "The Need for Patriotic and Religious Faith," Oct. 4, 1933, *PPAFDR* 2:382.

66. Franklin D. Roosevelt, "Address before the Inter-American Conference for the Maintenance of Peace," Dec. 1, 1936, *PPAFDR* 5:609–10.

67. Roosevelt, "Patriotic and Religious Faith," 379.

68. Guy Emery Shipler, "Franklin Roosevelt and Religion: Some Revealing Episodes," *Churchman* (1942), 8.

69. Some individuals who worked in other professions also replied to Roosevelt's letter. A manufacturer argued that the letter was a political move designed to stimulate pastors to lead "their congregations to the brook, at the next election," and tell "them where to drink" (A. R. Patten to FDR, Oct. 3, 1935, PPF 21A, Non-Clergy Letters, Container 36, Clergy Letters, Non-Clergy Correspondence). See also "Does Roosevelt Flatter the Clergy?" *Churchman* 149 (Oct 15, 1935), 32; and "The President Consults the Ministry," *UP*, Oct. 3, 1935, 7. Others labeled Roosevelt's letter "political plagiarism" because it was very similar to a letter Governor Philip LaFollette sent to the clergy of Wisconsin. See "Mr. Roosevelt Has Been Poorly Advised," *CC* 52 (Oct. 9, 1935), 1269–70. A Methodist doubted whether the clergy responses would get within "six rods of the President's office." See Harry Earl Woolever, "Washington Observations," *CA* 110 (Oct. 17, 1935), 925.

70. "To the President of the United States," *Lutheran* 18 (Oct. 10, 1935), 13.

71. E. J. Boell to FDR, Oct. 7, 1935, PPF 21A Container 35, Clergy Letters, Authors and Editors. Cf. W. O. Carver to FDR, Oct. 15, 1935, PPF 21A, Container 36, Clergy Letters, Educator; B. L. Jennings to Roosevelt, Oct. 9, 1935, PPF 21A, Container 4, Clergy Letters, CA; Justin Wroe Nixon to FDR, n.d., PPF 21A, Container 21, Clergy Letters, NY.

72. Joseph Ciarrocchi, "A Letter to the President," *Italo-American Detroit Weekly*, Oct. 4, 1935, PPF 21A, Container 35, Clergy Letters, Catholic Officials.

73. Roland J. Brown to FDR, Nov. 19, 1935, PPF 21A, Container 9, Clergy Letters, IL; Edward A. Przybylski to FDR, Nov. 11, 1935, PPF 21A, Container 9, Clergy Letters, IL.

74. E. D. Viser to FDR, Sept. 26, 1935, PPF 21A, TN-TX, Container 30, Clergy Letters, TN.

75. Allan M. Laird to FDR, Sept. 26, 1935, PPF 21A, Container 9, Clergy Letters, NY.

76. "Dr. Macartney's Answer to President Roosevelt," *PB*, Oct. 3, 1935, 10.

77. L. Niermnann to FDR, Oct. 2, 1934, PPF 21A, Container 9, Clergy Letters, IL; C. R. Yost to FDR, Oct. 9, 1935, PPF 21A, Container 36, Clergy Letters, Educators; H. R. Smith to FDR, Oct. 10, 1935, PPF 21A, Container 4, Clergy Letters, CA; F. Vance to FDR, Oct. 11, 1935, PPF 21A, TN-TX, Container 30, Clergy Letters, TN.

78. T. F. Quinn to FDR, Sept. 27, 1935, PPF 21A, Container 35, Clergy Letters, Catholic Officials; F. James Craik Morris to FDR, Oct. 2, 1935, PPF 21A Container 35 Church Officials (Misc.), Clergy Letters, Bishops.

79. Leslie Cook to FDR, Sept. 30, 1935, PPF 21A Container 35, Clergy Letters, Outside the United States. Cf. I. S. Caldwell to FDR, Sept. 28, 1935, PPF 21A, Container 9, Clergy Letters, IL; "An Open Letter to President Roosevelt," *Presbyterian Guardian*,

Oct. 21, 1935, 23; and LaVerne Taylor to FDR, Oct. 2, 1935, PPF 21A, Container 9, Clergy Letters, IL.

80. Edwin R. Errett to FDR, n.d., PPF 21A Container 35, Clergy Letters, Authors and Editors. Cf. J. H. Hamblem to FDR, Sept. 26, 1935, PPF 21A, TN-TX, Container 30, Clergy Letters, TX.

81. "President Roosevelt Seeks Light from Clergymen," *UP*, Oct. 10, 1935, 7. Cf. "Clergymen," *Christian Union Herald*, 56 (Oct. 12, 1935), 5; Daniel Brownlee to FDR, PPF 21A Container 35, Clergy Letters, Church Officials; and L. P. Buroker to FDR, Oct. 18, 1935, PPF 21A, Container 35, Clergy Letter, Church Officials.

82. "The President and the Preachers," *UP*, Oct. 10, 1935, 5.

83. James Cannon Jr. to FDR, Oct 12, 1935, PPF 21A, Container 4, Clergy Letters, CA. Cf. S. L. Hale to FDR, Oct. 2, 1935, PPF 21A, Container 4, Clergy Letters, CA; "The President's Letter to Ministers," *PB*, Oct. 3, 1935, 4; J. Franklin Young to FDR, Sept. 28, 1935, PPF 21A, Container 9, Clergy Letters, IL.

84. W. E. Snyder to FDR, Oct. 8, 1935, PPF 21A Container 35, Clergy Letters, Authors and Editors.

85. E.g., John H. Engle to FDR, Nov. 15, 1935, PPF 21A, Container 4, Clergy Letters, CA; Errol B. Sloan to FDR, n.d., PPF 21A, Container 4, Clergy Letters, CA; and John Evan Stuchell to FDR, Oct. 9, 1935, PPF 21A, Container 4, Clergy Letters, CA.

86. Brown to FDR, Sept. 26, 1935, PPF 21A, Container 36, Clergy Letters, Educators. Cf. Albert W. Beaver to FDR, Dec. 12, 1935, PPF 21A, Container 36, Clergy Letters, Educators.

87. Howard M. Green to FDR, Sept. 27, 1935, PPF 21A, Container 9, Clergy Letters, NY; Father O'Flanagen to FDR, Oct. 2, 1935, PPF 21A, Container 9, Clergy Letters, IL.

88. C. M. Thompson to FDR, Nov. 5, 1935, PPF 21A, Container 9, Clergy Letters, NY; Buswell to FDR, Sept. 26, 1935, PPF 21A, Container 36, Clergy Letters, Educators. Buswell cited twenty-seven biblical passages to support his contentions.

89. E.g., Walter H. Gray to FDR, Sept. 26, 1935, PPF 21A, Container 35, Clergy Letters, Catholic Officials; T. V. Neal to FDR, Sept. 30, 1935, PPF 21A, Container 36, Clergy Letters, Educators; and Henry H. Sweets to FDR, Oct. 4, 1935, PPF 21A, Container 36, Clergy Letters, Educators.

90. E.g., Richard L. McCready to FDR, Oct. 3, 1935, PPF 21A Container 35 Church officials (Misc.) Clergy Letters, Bishops; Frederick A. Doane to FDR, Oct. 5, 1935, PPF 21A, Container 4, Clergy Letters, CA; and F. M. McConnell to Roosevelt, Sept. 30, 1935, PPF 21A, Container 36, Clergy Letters, Educators.

91. M. P. Elder to FDR, Oct. 4, 1935, PPF 21A, TN-TX, Container 30, Clergy Letters, TX, FRPL. Cf. Barr Gifford Lee to FDR, Oct. 7, 1935, PPF 21A, Container 4, Clergy Letters, CA; W. R. Kruszas to FDR, Sept. 30, 1935, PPF 21A, Container 9, Clergy Letters, IL; and Charles J. Deane to FDR, Oct. 28, 1935, PPF 21A, Container 36, Clergy Letters, Educators.

92. Charles S. Macfarland to FDR, Sept. 30, 1935, PPF 21A Container 35, Clergy Letters, Church Officials; Baxter to FDR, Oct. 3, 1935, PPF 21A, Container 36, Clergy Letters, Educators.

93. This group included Jerome Davis of Yale Divinity School, Reinhold Niebuhr of Union Theological Seminary, John Haynes Holmes, pastor of the Unitarian Community Church of New York City, and Rabbi Sidney Goldstein of the Free Synagogue of New York City. See Davis et al. to FDR, Nov. 29, 1935, PPF 21A, Container 36, Clergy Letters, Educators. They claimed that their response reflected the views of 4,700 clergy surveyed by the National Religion and Labor Foundation.

94. See Samuel J. Abrams to FDR, Sept. 26, 1935, PPF 21A Container 35 (Church Officials: Misc.), Clergy Letters, Rabbis, FRPL. The Commission on Social Justice of the Central Conference of American Rabbis published a pamphlet entitled "Judaism and Social Security," expressing its approval of the social security legislation.

95. Cranston Brenton to FDR, Oct. 1, 1935, PPF 21A Container 35, Clergy Letters, Church Officials. Cf. John F. Mormon to FDR, Nov. 12, 1935, PPF 21A, Container 9, Clergy Letters, IL.

96. Leon S. Lang to FDR, Oct. 9, 1935, PPF 21A Container 35 (Church Officials: Misc.), Clergy Letters, Rabbis. Cf. Alva Tompkins to FDR, Nov. 6, 1935, PPF 21A, Container 9, Clergy Letters, IL.

97. E.g., Gray to FDR; G. W. Chessman to Roosevelt, Sept. 27, 1935, PPF 21A, Container 9, Clergy Letters, IL.

98. C. W. Ivie to FDR, Sept. 28, 1935, PPF 21A, Container 9, Clergy Letters, IL. Cf. Otis V. Wheeler to FDR, Sept. 27, 1935, PPF 21A, Container 9, Clergy Letters, NY; and Walter H. McKenzie to FDR, Sept. 27, 1935, PPF 21A, TN-TX, Container 30, Clergy Letters, TX.

99. F. C. Stelzriede to FDR, n.d., PPF 21A, Container 9, Clergy Letters, IL. Cf. William J. Hawley to FDR, Oct. 25, 1935, PPF 21A, Container 9, Clergy Letters, NY.

100. Albert Douglass to FDR, Oct. 7, 1935, PPF 21A, Container 4, Clergy Letters, CA.

101. Cannon to FDR. Cf. Francis C. Ellis to FDR, Nov. 11, 1935, PPF 21A, Container 4, Clergy Letters, CA.

102. William W. Lane to FDR, Sept. 25, 1935, PPF 21A, Container 9, Clergy Letters, NY. Cf. F. D. W. Beggs to FDR, Sept. 28, 1935, PPF 21A, Container 9, Clergy Letters, IL.

103. E.g., Harold E. Carlson to FDR, Oct. 10, 1935, PPF 21A, Container 4, Clergy Letters, CA; R. T. Hodgson to FDR, Oct. 30, 1935, PPF 21A, Container 9, Clergy Letters, NY.

104. Stuchell to FDR. Hundreds of letters protested the adverse effects of drunkenness, especially its contribution to automobile accidents. E.g., Josiah S. Watson to FDR, Sept. 26, 1935, PPF 21A, Container 9, Clergy Letters, IL; and A. D. Creasman to FDR, Oct. 2, 1935, PPF 21A, TN-TX, Container 30, Clergy Letters, TN.

105. Kirk M. Dewey to FDR, Nov. 12, 1935, PPF 21A, Container 9, Clergy Letters, IL. Cf. Theodore Dautenhahn to FDR, n. d., PPF 21A, Container 9, Clergy Letters, IL; Selden Carlyle Adams to FDR, Oct. 5, 1935, PPF 21A, Container 9, Clergy Letters, NY; and George W. Kincheloe to FDR, Oct. 14, 1935, PPF 21A, Container 9, Clergy Letters, NY.

106. M. Huyett Sangree to FDR, Oct. 1, 1935, PPF 21A, Container 9, Clergy Letters, NY.

107. Davis et al. to FDR. They also urged the president to pass a permanent neutrality law that included an embargo on shipments "to belligerents of raw materials needed in the manufacture of weapons and munitions, and on loans and credits for war purposes," and to work with Japan to eliminate the economic causes of conflict in the Pacific region.

108. See PPF 21A, Container 35 (Church Officials Misc.) Clergy Letters, Report of Aubrey Mills, Summary.

109. Mills further divided positive responses into favorable, favorable with suggestions, and favorable with criticism. Mills assigned many replies to the three favorable categories that included substantial criticisms and negative assessments of Roosevelt's personal qualities, policies, and approach to the presidency. Adding the

favorable with criticism and unfavorable categories together, Gustafson concludes that 51 percent of the responses were critical of Roosevelt's policies. See "Franklin D. Roosevelt," page 2. By November 15, 1935, the White House had received 12,096 replies, and thousands more came in after this date. The final response may have been as high as 15 percent of those surveyed. See PPF 21A, Container 35 (Church Officials Misc.) Clergy Letters, Report of Aubrey Mills, Summary.

110. Near the end of October, Mills suggested to Roosevelt's secretary Stephen Early that acknowledgments not be sent until November 6 or 7 to support the supposition that the president had had enough "time to digest some of the replies." See Mills to Early, Oct. 26, 1935, PPF 21A Container 35 (Church Officials: Misc.), Report of Aubrey Mills, (Summary). In a 1936 poll conducted by Literary Digest, 70 percent of 21,606 ministers who replied approved of the New Deal. See "Specific Poll of Clergymen on New Deal," LD 121 (Feb. 22, 1936), 8.

111. See Early to Samuel Rosenberg, July 28 and Aug. 3, 1937, PPF 64.

112. Gustafson, "Franklin D. Roosevelt," p. 2.

113. Franklin D. Roosevelt, "The Right to a More Abundant Life," Dec. 6, 1933, PPAFDR 2:519. The council president declared that Roosevelt's goals for social betterment were consistent with the principles of the organization (Albert W. Beaver to FDR, Dec. 9, 1933, OF 213, Federal Council of Churches, 1933–38). See also Samuel McCrea Cavert to FDR, Dec. 11, 1933, same file.

114. E.g., FDR to F. Ernest Johnson, Nov. 13, 1940, PPF 7073, Johnson, Dr. F. Ernest.

115. Gustafson, "Franklin D. Roosevelt," 5.

116. E.g., FDR to E. Graham Wilson, Aug. 30, 1939, PPF 1685, National Committee for Religion and Welfare Recovery, 1938–45, FRPL; Walter Head to FDR, Sept. 11, 1934; FDR to James W. Gerard; Press Release, Aug. 21, 1937; FDR to Judge McGoorty, Sept. 3, 1938; FDR to Hill Montague, Oct 2, 1940, all in the same file; and "President Praises Loyalty Day Ideal," NYT, Sept. 21, 1936, 12.

117. FDR to Oxnam, Mar. 9, 1943, OF 76A-76B, Church Matters, Box 2, OF 76A Protestant; FDR to Oxnam, May 22, 1944, PPF 21, Container 1, Church Matters, 1944–45. On Oxnam, see Robert Moats Miller, Bishop G. Bromley Oxnam, Paladin of Liberal Protestantism (Nashville, TN: Abingdon, 1990).

118. E.g., Tucker to FDR, May 1, 1941, PPF 7211, Tucker, Bishop Henry St. George; Tucker to FDR, May 20, 1941, and Memorandum, Apr. 6, 1943, both in the same file.

119. Poling strongly endorsed Roosevelt's leadership in his book (Poling to FDR, June 28, 1943, PPF 7800, Poling, Dr. Daniel A.) and called him "a true prophet," "a wise and courageous leader," and "a symbol of freedom" (Poling to FDR, May 18, 1943). Roosevelt called Poling America's "spiritual ambassador of good will" (FDR to Poling, May 15, 1944, same file). See also William Hassett to FDR (May 4, 1944) who called Poling "the most influential Protestant Clergyman on our side."

120. E.g., "The Nation Decides," CC 53 (Nov. 11, 1936), 1486–88.

121. "Correspondence," CC 53 (Nov. 25, 1936), 1578–91; quotations from 1581, 1582, 1583, 1588, 1591.

122. Edmund A. Moore, A Catholic Runs for President: The Campaign of 1928 (New York: Ronald Press, 1956), 72–73; Roosevelt, This I Remember, 40.

123. CMW, Oct. 12, 1932. Roosevelt called Pius's encyclical Quadragesimo "just as radical as I am" and "one of the greatest documents of modern times" (Franklin D. Roosevelt, "The Philosophy of Social Justice through Social Action," Oct. 2, 1936, PPAFDR 1:778). See also "Mr. Roosevelt's Sermon in Detroit," CC 49 (Oct. 12, 1932), 1229.

124. George Q. Flynn, *American Catholics and the Roosevelt Presidency, 1932–1936* (Lexington: University of Kentucky Press, 1968), ix–xi, 44–49, quotation from xi.

125. In addition, Frank Murphy served successively as governor-general of the Philippines, attorney general, and Supreme Court justice. Roosevelt also appointed Robert H. Gore as governor of Puerto Rico, Joseph P. Kennedy as chairman of the Security and Exchange Commission and ambassador to Great Britain, and John F. O'Hara as a delegate to a Pan-American Congress. William Hassett served as a presidential aide and Grace Tully as Roosevelt's personal secretary.

126. See Gerald P. Fogarty, "Roosevelt and the America Catholic Hierarchy," in David B. Woolner and Richard G. Kurial, eds., *FDR, The Vatican, and the Roman Catholic Church in America, 1933–1945* (New York: Palgrave, 2003), 11–43; Edward Kantowicz, "Cardinal Mundelein of Chicago and the Shaping of Twentieth Century American Catholicism," *JAH* 68 (June 1981), 52–68; Flynn, *American Catholics*, 38–42; Francis L. Broderick, *Right Reverend New Dealer: John A. Ryan, the Biography of Priest and Social Reformer Extraordinary* (New York: Macmillan, 1963), 208–22, 229–31, 245. See also John Ryan, "The New Deal and Social Justice," *CMW*, Apr. 13, 1934, 657–59; and Ryan, "An Open Letter to the Editor," *CMW*, Apr. 1936, 22–26.

127. W. D. O'Brien, "The New Deal in Religion," *Extension*, May 1934, 7. Cf. Brooklyn *Tablet*, May 13, 1933, 9.

128. See John Ryan et al., *Organized Social Justice* (Washington, DC, 1935).

129. William H. Anderson to FDR, Dec. 21, 1934, OF 76B, Church Matters, Box 2, Catholic, 1933–34.

130. G. D. Batdorf, president of the Pennsylvania Council of Churches, to FDR, Nov. 25, 1938, OF 76A-76B, Box 2, Church Matters, Protestant, 1933–42, FRPL; "Is There a Quasi-Alliance between the Roosevelt Administration and the Romanist Church?" *Herald of the Epiphany*, July 15, 1940, 1; H. W. Van Delinder to FDR, n. d., same file; Allan G. Frisbie to FDR, Feb. 6, 1935, OF 76B, Church Matters, Box 3, OF 76b, Catholic, 1935–39. See also "The President Explains the Status of Myron Taylor, as His Personal Representative to the Pope," Mar. 14, 1940, *PPAFDR* 9:101–2. Roosevelt believed he could best gain information about the views of the Catholic hierarchy and conditions in Italy through this means. See Tully, *F.D.R.*, 296.

131. "Maintaining the Separation of Church and State," OF 213, Federal Council of Churches, 1944–45. The statement added that while some argued that the Vatican was a state, not a religious institution, that in practice it was "impossible to separate the two." See also Samuel McCrea Cavert to FDR, Dec. 2, 1944, same file. The *Christian Century* took the same position. E.g., A. W. Palmer, "Prophet on the Tiber" 61 (Jan. 12, 1944), 42–43. See also Michael Carter, "Diplomacy's Detractors: American Protestant Reactions to FDR's 'Personal Representative' at the Vatican," in Woolner and Kurial, eds., *FDR*, 179–208.

132. See Ickes, *Secret Diary*, 3:45, 55–56, 64–65, 114–15, 382–83, 403–4.

133. Maurice Sheehy to Marguerite Le Hand, Apr. 10, 1937, OF 76B, Church Matters, Box 3, OF 76b, Catholic, 1935–39.

134. Flynn, *American Catholics*, 160–75; "Washington Notes," *NR*, July 8, 1936, 266. See Roosevelt, "Address at Notre Dame," in Rosenman, *PPAFDR* 4:493–96. See also George Q. Flynn, *Roosevelt and Romanism: Catholics and American Diplomacy* (Westport, CT: Greenwood, 1976) and Philip Chen, "Religious Liberty in American Foreign Policy, 1933–1941: Aspects of the Public Argument between FDR and American Roman Catholics," in Woolner and Kurial, eds., *FDR*, 121–39.

135. James M. Gillis, editor of the *Catholic World*, criticized Roosevelt for enlarging the national debt and disregarding the Constitution. E.g., Gillis, "Our Unconventional President," *CMW*, Feb. 1936, 513–23.

136. William Leuchtenburg, *Franklin D. Roosevelt and the New Deal, 1932–1940* (New York: Harper and Row, 1963), 100–1, quotation from 100.

137. *CMW* 144 (Nov. 1936), 129, 132, quoted in Flynn, *American Catholics*, 206. Coughlin's radio broadcasts generated thousands of letters to Roosevelt, which after 1934 were increasingly critical of the president.

138. Thousands of Catholics wrote to the president to protest Coughlin's "disloyal and disgraceful conduct," to pledge their "sincere respect, confidence and support" (Joseph Lavin to FDR, July 17, 1936, OF 306, Charles E. Coughlin, July 1936) and to denounce the priest's "intolerance, vulgarity, and venomous display of demagoguery" (James C. McCabe to FDR, July 18, 1936, same file).

139. On Coughlin's relationship with Roosevelt, see Charles J. Tull, *Father Coughlin and the New Deal* (Syracuse, NY: Syracuse University Press, 1965).

140. "Kennedy Attacks 'Communist Cry'," *NYT*, Oct. 25, 1936, 33.

141. See Flynn, *American Catholics*, 208–33; and Edgar E. Roosevelt, *They Voted for Roosevelt: The Presidential Vote, 1932–1944* (Stanford, CA: Stanford University Press, 1947), 82, 103, 110, 120, 130, 149, 180.

142. See the November 1940 issue; the editorial was reprinted in the *NYT*, Oct. 23, 1940. See also James O'Hara to James M. Gillis, Oct. 24, 1940, OF 76B, Church Matters, Box 3, OF 76b, Catholic, 1940–41.

143. Lawrence Fuchs, *John F. Kennedy and American Catholicism* (New York: Meredith, 1967), 124; Flynn, *American Catholics*, 239.

144. Stephen Wise, president of the American Jewish Congress, appears to have been Roosevelt's most important supporter and confidant among American rabbis. See Stephen Wise, "President Roosevelt's Leadership of America: Is It Good or Bad?" PPF 1820, Speech Material, Container 14, Speech Material, Religion; FDR to Wise, July 17, 1942, PPF 19, Jewish Matters, 1942–45; Wise to FDR, Dec. 2, 1942, OF 76C, Church Matters, Box 8, Jewish 1942, Oct.–Dec.; Wise to FDR, Jan. 12, 1945, OF 76C, Church Matters, Box 9, Jewish 1944 Aug.–Dec. 1945.

145. "Roosevelt's Supreme Council," OF 76C, Church Matters, Box 8, Jewish 1936.

146. See Geoffrey Ward, *A First-Class Temperament: The Emergence of Franklin Roosevelt* (New York: Harper and Row, 1989), 252–54.

147. Arthur D. Morse, *While Six Million Died: A Chronicle of American Apathy* (Woodstock, NY: Overlook, 1967), 146–49.

148. Franklin D. Roosevelt, "The President Asks That Frontiers Be Opened to Victims of Nazi Oppression . . .," Mar. 24, 1944, *PPAFDR* 13:104–5.

149. William J. vanden Heuvel, "Roosevelt Did All He Could for Europe's Jews," in Brian Grapes, ed., *Franklin D. Roosevelt* (San Diego: Greenhaven, 2000), 215. This paragraph is based on vanden Heuvel's essay. See also Henry L. Feingold, *The Politics of Rescue: The Roosevelt Administration and the Holocaust, 1938–1945* (New Brunswick, NJ: Rutgers University Press, 1970); Robert Divine, *American Immigration Policy, 1924–1952* (New Haven, CT: Yale University Press, 1957); and Patrick J. Hearden, *Roosevelt Confronts Hitler: America's Entry into World War II* (Dekalb: Northern Illinois University Press, 1987).

150. Sheldon Neuringer, "Franklin D. Roosevelt and the Refuge for the Victims of Nazism, 1933–1941," in Rosenbaum and Bartelme, eds., *Franklin D. Roosevelt*, 87. This

paragraph is based on Neuringer's essay, which represents that middle position. See also Neuringer, *American Jewry and United States Immigration Policy, 1881–1953* (New York: Arno, 1980), 205–19; and Lucy S. Dawidowicz, *The War against the Jews, 1933–1945* (New York: Holt, Rinehart and Winston, 1975), esp. 3–28, 77–92, 112–16.

151. Neuringer, "Franklin D. Roosevelt," 85–100, first quotation from 89, second from 98.

152. Letter to FDR signed by various Jewish leaders, Dec. 8, 1942, OF 76C, Church Matters, Box 8, Jewish 1942, Oct.–Dec.

153. Rabbi P. Frank to FDR, Oct. 23, 1940, OF 76C, Church Matters, Box 7, Jewish 1940, Oct.–Dec.

154. "Vote for Roosevelt," *Jewish Day*, Oct. 25, 1940, 3. Cf. Resolution of the Jewish National Fund Regional Conference, Oct. 25, 1942, OF 76C, Church Matters, Box 8, Jewish 1942, Oct.–Dec.

155. Franklin D. Roosevelt, "Annual Message to the Congress," Jan. 3, 1936, *PPAFDR* 5:18.

156. Early to Fulton Oursler, Jan. 17, 1945.

157. Kenneth Davis, "FDR as a Biographer's Problem," *American Scholar* 52–53 (Winter 1983/84), 107.

158. E.g., Roosevelt, "Radio Address on United Flag Day," 288.

159. Roosevelt, "First Inaugural Address," 11; Undelivered address for Jefferson Day, Apr. 13, 1945, *PPAFDR* 13:616.

160. Pierard and Linder, *Civil Religion*, 169–70, quotation from 169.

161. Rexford G. Tugwell, *The Democratic Roosevelt* (Garden City, NY: Doubleday, 1957), 32.

162. E.g., Franklin D. Roosevelt, Campaign address, Sioux City, Iowa, Sept. 20, 1932; Roosevelt, Address dedicating the birthplace of Woodrow Wilson, May 4, 1941; Roosevelt, Address at the White House Conference on Children in a Democracy, Apr. 23, 1939. My attention was called to these sources by Greer, *What Roosevelt Thought*, 10.

163. Roosevelt, "More Abundant Life," 519.

164. Franklin D. Roosevelt, "A Letter to the Chaplains of the Military and Naval Services," Feb. 13, 1934, *PPAFDR* 3:96. Cf. Roosevelt, "Inter-American Conference," 609.

165. Roosevelt, "More Abundant Life," 518–19.

166. Franklin D. Roosevelt, "Campaign Address at Chicago, Illinois," Oct. 14, 1936. *PPAFDR* 5:483.

167. Franklin D. Roosevelt, "Campaign Address at Madison Square Garden," Nov. 5, 1932, *PPAFDR* 1:865.

168. Franklin D. Roosevelt, "Address on Occasion of Receiving the Award for Distinguished Service to Agriculture, Chicago," Dec. 9, 1935, *PPAFDR* 4:489–90. See also Roosevelt, "Social Justice though Social Action," 771–80.

169. Isetti, "Moneychangers," 678, 679, 686, quotations in that order. Isetti points out that in his address "A Wider Opportunity for the Average American Man" (Aug. 9, 1934) Roosevelt quoted a Congressman who declared that "the new deal is . . . as old as Christian ethics, for basically its ethics are the same." See *PPAFDR* 3:375.

170. Roosevelt, "More Abundant Life," 519.

171. Harvard Sitkoff, *A New Deal for Blacks: The Emergence of Civil Rights as a National Issue*, vol. 1: *The Depression Decade* (New York: Oxford University Press, 1978), 331.

172. E.g., Robert C. Weaver, "The Negro and the New Deal: A Look at the Facts," *Opportunity, Journal of Negro Life*, July 1935.

173. Sitkoff, *New Deal for Blacks*, 330–31.

174. Roosevelt insisted that the Good Neighbor Policy that guided his administration in dealing with Latin America and other nations promoted understanding and fellowship and was the "road to spiritual awakening." Stephen Early called this policy "nothing less than an outcropping" of Roosevelt's "religious consciousness," and most church leaders enthusiastically applauded it (Roosevelt, "Radio Address on Brotherhood Day," 59; Early to Oursler, Jan. 17, 1945; Van Kirk to FDR, Mar. 13, 1935).

175. Roosevelt, "Campaign Address at Cleveland, Ohio," 550 (first two quotations); FDR to Daniel A. Poling, July 4, 1941, PPF 630, Christian Endeavor Union, (third quotation).

176. FDR to Everett R. Clinchy, July 30, 1940, PPF 1426, National Conference of Jews and Christians, 1940–1945, FRPL. Cf. FDR to Theodore C. Speers, Sept. 13, 1940, PPF 6862, Greater New York Federation of Churches; FDR to Elmer C. Pedrick, Sept. 25, 1940, PPF 6883, Pedrick, Rev. Elmer, FRPL; and FDR to Buttrick, Dec. 23, 1939, OF 213, Federal Council of Churches, 1939–42.

177. Franklin D. Roosevelt, "Fireside Chat on the European War," Sept. 3, 1939, in Zevin, ed., *Nothing to Fear*, 182.

178. E.g., Walter W. Van Kirk to FDR, Mar. 13, 1935, OF 213, Federal Council of Churches, 1933–38, FRPL.

179. "American-Japanese Relations," a statement adopted by the Executive Committee of the Federal Council of Churches, Mar. 1, 1936, OF 213, Federal Council of Churches, 1933–38. See also Walter W. Van Kirk to FDR, Mar. 8, 1935, same file; "Not Too Late to Mend," *CA* 110 (Mar. 21, 1935), 260.

180. See Memorandum, Van Kirk, Walter, Mar. 3, 1936, OF 213, Federal Council of Churches, 1933–38.

181. Letter to FDR, Feb. 15, 1938, OF 213, Federal Council of Churches, 1933–38.

182. "Peace and the President," *CC* 54 (Dec. 1, 1937), 1479–81, first and second quotation from 1480, third from 1481.

183. "Where Is Mr. Roosevelt Heading?" *CC* 55 (Jan. 12, 1938), 38–40, quotation from 38.

184. "Mr. Roosevelt's Lost Following," *CC* 55 (Apr. 6, 1938), 425.

185. "Foreign Policy in the Campaign," *CC* 57 (Oct. 23, 1940), 1302–4, first two quotations 1303, third and fourth ones from 1304.

186. Franklin D. Roosevelt, "Annual Message to Congress—A Warning to Dictator Nations," Jan. 4, 1939 in Zevin, ed., *Nothing to Fear*, 163. Roosevelt often stressed the close relationship between religion and democracy. See his campaign speeches on November 1, 1940, in Brooklyn (*PPAFDR* 9:532) and the next day in Cleveland (*PPAFDR* 9:550–35), and his 1941 State of the Union message, in which he enunciated the four freedoms (*PPFADR* 10:672).

187. "Invitation to a Holy War," *CC* 56 (Jan. 18, 1939), 78–80, all quotations from 78. See also "The President's Armament Program," *CC* 56 (Feb. 8, 1939), 188–89.

188. "Our Frontier Is on the Potomac," *CC* 56 (Feb. 15, 1939), 206–7, all quotations from 207.

189. "Mr. Roosevelt Intervenes," *CC* 56 (Apr. 26, 1939), 536.

190. Samuel McCrea Cavert to FDR, Oct. 9, 1939, OF 213, Federal Council of Churches, 1939–42.

191. "What Comes Next?" *CC* 57 (June 19, 1940), 790. The editors also denounced the high-pressure propaganda campaigns that portrayed the war as a "struggle by a demonic paganism to destroy the Christian and democratic way of life."

192. "Foreign Policy in the Campaign," 1302.

193. "Mr. Roosevelt's Lost Opportunity," *CC* 58 (Jan. 1, 1941), 6–7.

194. "The New Battleground," *CC* 58 (Mar. 19, 1941), 385–86; first two quotations from 385, third from 386.

195. "Let the President Ponder," *CC* 58 (June 4, 1941), 742–43, first quotation 742, second 743.

196. "The President Listens," *CC* 58 (June 25, 1941), 823–25, quotation from 824.

197. Franklin D. Roosevelt, "We Have Cleared Our Decks and Taken Our Battle Stations," Oct. 27, 1941, *PPAFDR* 10:440.

198. "To Your Battle Stations!" *CC* 58 (Nov. 1941), 1360–62, first two quotations from 1361, second two from 1362. The editors claimed that according to a recent poll, 91.5 percent of Catholic clergy opposed a "shooting war outside the Western hemisphere."

199. Nicholas John Cull, *Selling War: The British Propaganda Campaign against American "Neutrality" in World War II* (New York: Oxford University Press, 1995).

200. Edward Mooney to FDR, Dec. 22, 1941, PPF 18, Catholic Matters.

201. See PPF 18, Catholic Matters.

202. See OF 76A-76B, Box 2, Church Matters, Protestant, 1933–42. The next year, the Federal Council's Commission on a Just and Durable Peace issued a statement entitled "Six Pillars of Peace." Formulated by seventy-five leading Christians, lay and clergy, black and white, it discussed six major areas where international cooperation was necessary to preserve peace in the future.

203. Franklin D. Roosevelt, "December 7, 1941—A Date Which Will Live in Infamy," Dec. 8, 1941, *PPAFDR* 10:525.

204. FDR to Archbishop Edward Mooney, Dec. 24, 1941, PPF 18, Catholic Matters.

205. Roosevelt, "Address on the State of the Union," 35, 41–42. Cf. FDR to Joseph R. Sizoo, PPF 8424, General Synod of the Reformed Church in America.

206. FDR to Henry St. George Tucker, Apr. 6, 1943, PPF 7211, Tucker, Bishop Henry St. George.

207. FDR to Dr. Samuel McCrea Cavert, PPF 1628, Federal Council of the Churches of Christ in America.

208. FDR to Roy C. Ross, July 6, 1944, PPF 8129, Religious Education Week.

209. FDR to Douglas Horton, Apr. 7, 1942, PPF 8004, Congregationalist and Christian Churches of America.

210. Frank Freidel, "Introduction: The Legacy of FDR," Rosenbaum and Bartelme, eds., *Franklin D. Roosevelt*, 1, 7, quotations in that order.

211. E.g., "Editorial," *CA* 110 (Feb. 7, 1935), 1; Goldberg, *Franklin D. Roosevelt*.

212. Arthur Krock, *NYT*, fall 1936, quoted in Freidel, "Introduction," 7.

213. "F.D.R.: President of the World," *NR* 104 (Mar. 31, 1941), 434; Oswald Garrison Villard, "President of the World?" *CC* 58 (Apr. 9, 1941), 492–94; Gerald W. Johnson, *Roosevelt: Dictator or Democrat?* (New York: Harper, 1941).

214. Leuchtenburg, *Roosevelt*, 331.

215. Isetti, "Moneychangers," 689.

216. Leuchtenburg, *Roosevelt*, 346, 331; Isetti, "Moneychangers," 687–88.

217. Isetti, "Moneychangers," 686.

218. Leuchtenburg, *Roosevelt,* 346.

219. "Mr. Roosevelt's Place in History," *CC* 58 (July 9, 1941), 877.

220. See Leuchtenburg, *Roosevelt,* 87–89; Daniel R. Fusfeld, "The New Deal and the Corporate State" in Rosenbaum and Bartelme, *Franklin D. Roosevelt,* 141–42.

221. Davis, "Biographer's Problem," 101.

222. Quoted by Wolfskil and Hudson, *All but the People,* 182.

223. Franklin D. Roosevelt, Address, Syracuse University, July 9, 1930.

224. As quoted by Greer, *What Roosevelt Thought,* 11.

225. Frank Freidel, "Hoover and Roosevelt in Historical Continuity," in *Herbert Hoover Reassessed: Essays Commemorating the Fiftieth Anniversary of the Inauguration of Our Thirty-First President* (Washington, DC: Government Printing Office, 1981), 276.

226. Rosenman, *Working with Roosevelt,* 399; Davis, "Biographer's Problem," 102, emphasis in the original. Davis points out that Samuel Rosenman, Raymond Moley, Rex Tugwell, and James Farley all "record instances of Rooseveltian mendacity, often employed merely to embellish a good story but sometimes with regard to major issues, and of his preference for the devious over the frankly straightforward" (102).

227. "Mr. Dewey's Patriotism," *CC* 61 (Oct. 11, 1944), 1159.

228. Villard, "The Great Deception," *CC* 61 (June 21, 1944), 745–46, quotation from 746. Cf. "As the Campaign Closes," 1249.

229. Most historians dispute this charge.

230. See Ward, *A First-Class Temperament,* 362–67, 412–17, 740, 747.

231. Davis, "Biographer's Problem," 103–4. Cf. Conrad Black, *Franklin Delano Roosvelt: Champion of Freedom* (New York: PublicAffairs, 2003), 39.

232. Ibid., 107.

233. "A Prayer," *Churchman* 159 (May 1, 1945), 9.

CHAPTER 7

1. See Merlin Gustafson, "The Religious Role of the President," *MJPS* 14 (Nov. 1970), 709–10.

2. For discussions of Eisenhower's religious background and convictions, see Paul Hutchinson, "The President's Religious Faith," *CC* 71 (Mar. 24, 1954), 362–69; Bela Kornitzer, *The Great American Heritage: The Story of the Five Eisenhower Brothers* (New York: Farrar, Straus and Cudahy, 1955), 14–17, 133–44; William Lee Miller, *Piety along the Potomac: Notes on Politics and Morals in the Fifties* (Boston: Houghton Mifflin, 1964); Edmund Fuller and David E. Green, *God in the White House: The Faith of American Presidents* (New York: Crown, 1968), 212–18; Merlin Gustafson, "The Religion of a President," *CC* 86 (Apr. 30, 1969), 610–13; Richard V. Pierard and Robert D. Linder, *Civil Religion and the Presidency* (Grand Rapids, MI: Zondervan, 1988), 184–205; and Richard Hutcheson, *God in the White House: How Religion Has Changed the Modern Presidency* (New York: Macmillan, 1988), 50–55, 62, 124.

3. Gustafson, "Religious Role," 710. Helpful analyses of Eisenhower's life and presidency include Charles C. Alexander, *Holding the Line: The Eisenhower Era* (Bloomington: Indiana University Press, 1975); R. Alton Lee, *Dwight D. Eisenhower: Soldier and Statesman* (Chicago: Nelson-Hall, 1981); Robert A. Divine, *Eisenhower and the Cold War* (New York: Oxford University Press, 1981); William B. Ewald Jr.,

Eisenhower the President: Crucial Days, 1951–60 (Englewood Cliffs, NJ: Prentice Hall, 1981); Fred I. Greenstein, *The Hidden-Hand Presidency: Eisenhower as Leader* (New York: Basic Books, 1982); Robert F. Burk, *Dwight D. Eisenhower: Hero and Politician* (Boston: Twayne, 1986); Stephen E. Ambrose, *Eisenhower: Soldier, General of the Army, President Elect, 1890–1952*, and *Eisenhower*, 2 vols. (New York: Simon and Schuster, 1983, 1984); Jo Ann P. Krieg, ed., *Dwight D. Eisenhower: Soldier, President, Statesman* (Westport, CT: Greenwood, 1987); Michael Beschloss, *Eisenhower: A Centennial Life* (New York: HarperCollins, 1990); Chester Pach Jr. and Elmo Richardson, *The Presidency of Dwight D. Eisenhower* (Lawrence: University Press of Kansas, 1991); and Steven Wagner, *Eisenhower Republicanism: Pursuing the Middle Way* (Dekalb: Northern Illinois University, 2006).

4. See Carlton O. Wittlinger, *Quest for Piety and Obedience: The Story of the Brethren in Christ* (Nappanee, IN: Evangel, 1978).

5. "Text of Eisenhower's Speech at Abilene," *NYT*, June 5, 1952, 16.

6. Pierard and Linder, *Civil Religion*, 186. See also Lelia G. Picking, Oral History Transcript, Eisenhower Library (hereafter EL), 4–5; and Rev. Ray I. Witter, ibid., 22.

7. Ida became alarmed by her son's fascination with the Greek and Roman wars of antiquity and substituted such works as *Ben Hur* and *The Pilgrim's Progress*. The latter story seemed to have influenced his spiritual and moral development. See Sherwood Wirt, "The Faith of Dwight D. Eisenhower," Part Two, *Decision*, August 1965, 7. Scholars disagree when Ida became a Jehovah's Witness, with most of them claiming she did so in 1900. Others maintain that she did so in 1895 and was baptized by this group in 1898. Understandably, the Eisenhower brothers minimized their parents' and their own involvement with this group. In various interviews about his faith after becoming president, Dwight did not mention his family's involvement with the Witnesses. He and his siblings continued to sometimes attend the River Brethren Sunday school, and none of them apparently accepted the sect's key distinctives. See Jerry Bergman, "Why President Eisenhower Hid His Jehovah's Witness Upbringing," *JW Research Journal* 6 (July–Dec. 1999).

8. Dwight Eisenhower, "Remarks at a Luncheon Meeting of the General Board of the National Council of Churches," Nov. 18, 1953, *Public Papers of the Presidents of the United States: Dwight D. Eisenhower*, 8 vols. (Washington, DC: Government Printing Office, 1960–61) (hereafter *PP*), 792.

9. Claire Booth Luce, Oral History Transcript, EL, 9–13, quotations from 9, 11, 12.

10. DDE to Cliff Roberts, July 29, 1952, *Papers of Dwight David Eisenhower*, 21 vols., Louis Galambos and Daun Van Ee, eds. (Baltimore: Johns Hopkins University Press, 1989, 1996) (hereafter *Papers*), 13:1284.

11. E.g., Anne Wheaton to Mamie Eisenhower, Dec. 2, 1952, President's Personal File (hereafter PPF) 53-B-1, Box 913, National Presbyterian Church (hereafter NPC) (1), EL. Elson both wrote and called the president, urging him to select his church. Wheaton recommended the National Presbyterian Church because it was designated as the national church by the general assembly, was well designed for security, and had an excellent program. On Elson, see Paul Wooton, "Meet the President's Pastor," *Guideposts*, June 1958, 7.

12. See Edward L. R. Elson, *Wide Was His Parish* (Wheaton, IL: Tyndale, 1986), 110–12, 114–18, 133.

13. Quoted in Kornitzer, *Great American Heritage*, 137.

14. See PPF 1-A-9, Box 17, Church Affiliation of the President (1).

15. The president had fifty copies of Elson's sermon "The Mastery of Moods," preached on January 24, 1954, sent to government officials (PPF, Box 913, 53-B-1, NPC [1]). See DDE to Elson, Nov. 25, 1956, Ann Whitman Series, Box 14, Elson, Dr. Edward L. R. (2) and Dwight D. Eisenhower, Post-Presidential Papers (hereafter PPP), 1961–69, Secretary's Series, A 67–37, Box 10, MacAskill, Robert, EL.

16. William Stringer claims that Eisenhower missed only four Sundays the first year of his presidency. See "The President and the 'Still Small Voice,'" *CSM*, Feb. 26, 1954. In 1956, he attended church 31 Sundays, 23 of which were at the National Presbyterian Church. See "The President's Church Attendance—1956," Ann Whitman File (hereafter AWF), Name Series, Box 9, EL.

17. E.g., "Thanks Mr. President," *Capital Baptist* 5 (Oct. 8, 1959).

18. E.g., "Statement by the President . . . for the . . . the Committee on Religion in American Life," Oct. 31, 1953, *PP*, 736. After his retirement, he faithfully attended the Gettysburg Presbyterian Church until he died.

19. DDE to Milton Eisenhower, Feb. 2, 1953, *Papers*, 14:20. See also *The Eisenhower Diaries*, Robert H. Ferrell, ed. (New York: Norton, 1981), 226. Elson told reporters that Eisenhower's decision to become a member was "the climax of long consideration by the President and instruction by the pastor." Eisenhower, he added, took "religious doctrine very seriously" (*NYT*, Feb. 3, 1953).

20. O. B. Fanning, "Clergyman in the White House," *Christian Advocate for Pastors and Church Leaders* 4 (Jan. 7, 1960), 7.

21. Stringer, "The President."

22. See PPF 1-A-9, Boxes 17 and 18, Church Affiliation of the President (1) and (2).

23. They talked about both reading and then discussing *The Bible as History*. Elson sent Eisenhower a pamphlet entitled "The Manual of Prayer and Victorious Life Lessons." Eisenhower told Elson that his sermon "Men and the Stars" was "helpful in understanding man's relationship to this new era" (PPF, Box 913, NPC [3]). See DDE to Elson, May 13, 1954, PPF 53-B-1, Box 913, NPC (2); Elson to DDE, AWF, Name Series, Box 14, Elson, Dr. Edward L. R.; and Elson to DDE, Oct. 25, 1955, PPF 53-B-1, Box 913, NPC (1). On Elson, see Caspar Nannes, "The President and His Pastor," *Colliers*, Nov. 11, 1955, 29–31; Russell Hitt, "What Ike's Pastor Believes," *Eternity* 5 (Feb. 1954), 10–11, 44.

24. See Elson to DDE, Oct. 6, 1956, and Elson to DDE, Dec. 28, 1956. During the summer of 1957, Elson visited nine nations in his capacity as chairman of the American Friends of the Middle East. Upon his return to Washington, he reported his findings at length to Eisenhower (Memorandum for the Files, Aug. 9, 1957, PPF 53-B-1, NPC [3]).

25. The appointment index cards at the Eisenhower Library show that Elson met with Eisenhower twenty-six times at the White House while he was president.

26. Elson proposed this idea. See the Nov. 26, 1955, memorandum in PPF, Box 913, NPC (2). See also Elson, "The President's Dedicated Home," *Christian Herald*, May 1959, 29–30, 62.

27. See "The Way of the Peacemaker," PPF 53-B-1, NPC (3). On "The Tools of Peace," see DDE to Elson, June 9, 1955; Elson to DDE, Nov. 14, 1955, PPF, Box 913, NPC (2).

28. See Elson, "The Tools of Peace," National Presbyterian Church Pulpit Series 2, No. 8, Dec. 1955 PPF 53-B-1, Box 913, NPC (2), quotations from 4.

29. Hutchinson, "President's Faith," 368.

30. Wirt, "Faith," Part Two, 7.

31. Miller, *Piety*, 47.

32. "The President and His Church: What Senator Neely Says...Some Replies," *USN* 38 (Apr. 8, 1955), 50–52. On Lutz, see Robert Lutz, "The Savior of the Throne," *Eternity* 7 (Jan. 1956), 20–21, 37.

33. John Cogley, "Who's a Hypocrite?" *CMW* 62 (Apr. 15, 1955), 47. Cf. "Senator Neely's Speech," ibid., 33.

34. The standard White House reply to positive letters included: "it is indeed heartening and reassuring to him to know that the overwhelming majority of his fellow citizens have unreserved confidence in his sincerity of purpose." E.g., Sherman Adams to Mrs. Oscar Ahlzres, Apr. 7, 1955. This letter and hundreds of more are in PPF Box 19, 1–4-10.

35. Billy Graham (hereafter BG) to DDE, Mar. 26, 1955, PPF, Box 966, 1052 Graham, Billy (hereafter GB).

36. "Eisenhower Aides Join Him at Church," *NYT*, Jan. 21, 1953, 18; Edward L. R. Elson, *America's Spiritual Recovery* (Westwood, NJ: Fleming H. Revell, 1959), 53–55.

37. On Benson, see *Ezra Taft Benson, Crossfire: The Eight Years with Eisenhower* (Garden City, NY: Doubleday, 1962); and Edward L. and Frederick H. Schapsmeier, *Ezra Taft Benson and the Politics of Agriculture: The Eisenhower Years, 1953–1961* (Danville, IL: Interstate, 1975). On Dulles, see Stanley High to DDE, Nov. 16, 1952, *Papers*, 13:1433–34.

38. Stringer, "The President."

39. Ambrose, *Eisenhower*, 2:38. Eisenhower's personal secretary Ann Whitman claimed that Eisenhower did not conceive of God as a personal being, but much other evidence contradicts this. See Whitman to E. S. Whitman, n. d. (possibly Dec. 1957). Whitman and Eisenhower apparently had an ongoing disagreement about religion. In the same letter, for example, Whitman complained that Eisenhower "preached religion at me all the day long," quizzed her about the differences between translations of the Bible, lectured her on the relationship between democracy and religion, and explained his reasons for believing in God.

40. Wirt, "Faith," Part Two, 13; Ann Whitman to E. S. Whitman, n. d., Personal Papers of Ann C. Whitman, Correspondence—E. S. Whitman, Box 1, EL.

41. Doron K. Antrim, "Why the President Believes in Prayer," *Parade*, Dec. 8, 1957.

42. See "Radio and TV Broadcast: The Women Ask the President," Oct. 24, 1956, *PP*, 267–68. Eisenhower stated that his parents "were very deeply religious people" who prayed continuously during this crisis. He insisted that prayer had unquestionably played a part in his recovery (268).

43. Luce, 10–11.

44. Sherwood Wirt, "Faith of Dwight D. Eisenhower," *Decision*, July 1965, 8. See also Dwight D. Eisenhower, *Crusade in Europe* (Garden City, NY: Garden City Books, 1948); Harry C. Butcher, *My Three Years with Eisenhower: The Personal Diary of Captain Harry C. Butcher* (New York: Simon and Schuster, 1946); and David Eisenhower, *Eisenhower at War, 1943–1945* (New York: Random House, 1986).

45. Statement prepared for the *Episcopal Church News*, Sept. 21, 1952, in *NYT*, Sept. 15, 1952, 1, 16. See also Eisenhower, *Crusade in Europe*, 249–50.

46. "Text of Eisenhower's Speech Ending Campaign with Appeal for National Unity," *NYT*, Nov. 4, 1952, 23.

47. DDE to Mrs. Fred Byington, Feb. 3, 1953, Minnich Series, Cabinet and Legislative Meeting Index, Box 27, EL.

48. Dwight D. Eisenhower, "Inaugural Address," Jan. 20, 1953, *PP*, 1.

49. Dwight D. Eisenhower, "Remarks at the Annual Breakfast of the International Council for Christian Leadership," Feb. 2, 1956, *PP*, 221–22, quotation from 221. In his memoirs, Eisenhower noted that he wanted to point out that Americans "were getting too secular" and express his "deep faith in the beneficence of the Almighty." See Dwight D. Eisenhower, *The White House Years: Mandate for Change, 1953–1956* (Garden City, NY: Doubleday, 1963), 100–1. See also Emmet J. Hughes, *The Ordeal of Power: A Political Memoir of the Eisenhower Years* (New York: Atheneum, 1963), 53, 55–56.

50. Harris, *Washington Star*, quoted in Norman Grubb, *Modern Viking: The Story of Abraham Vereide, Pioneer in Christian Leadership* (Grand Rapids, MI: Zondervan, 1961), 131; "Changes on Inauguration Day," *CA* 131 (Jan. 22, 1953), 107.

51. "Inauguration Spectacle," *CA* 131 (Feb. 12, 1953), 207.

52. Dwight D. Eisenhower, "Remarks Recorded for the American Legion 'Back to God' Program," Feb. 1, 1953, *PP*, 11.

53. Robert J. Donovan, *Eisenhower: The Inside Story* (New York: Harper, 1956), 32–33. See also "President Prays," *America* 92 (Oct. 9, 1954), 29–30; and "Prayer at Cabinet Meetings," ibid. 88 (Mar. 7, 1953), 612. The journal praised him and the Cabinet for "their forthrightness in . . . testifying to their . . . dependence on God's providence." Other important governmental meetings also began with prayer (see Elson, *America's Spiritual Recovery*, 59).

54. Eisenhower, "Remarks . . . [to] the International Council for Christian Leadership," 222.

55. Dwight D. Eisenhower, "Message Recorded for the Observance of World Day of Prayer," Mar. 2, 1954, *PP*, 288; Eisenhower, "Remarks at the Dedicatory Prayer Breakfast of the International Christian Leadership," Feb. 5, 1953, *PP*, 38.

56. Dwight D. Eisenhower, "Remarks upon Lighting the National Christmas Tree," Dec. 24, 1953, *PP*, 858. He had a very high view of Washington's piety and personal faith. E.g., DDE to Lewis Webster Jones, President, National Conference of Christians and Jews, Oct. 22, 1960, Frederic Fox Records (hereafter FFR), Protestant (1), Box 10, EL.

57. E.g., "The President's News Conference of Nov. 23, 1954," *PP*, 1065.

58. E.g., DDE to Elson, May 13, 1954, PPF 53-B-1, Box 913, NPC (2).

59. Antrim, "President Believes in Prayer."

60. Dwight D. Eisenhower, "Radio and Television Address . . . Prior to Departure for . . . Geneva," July 15, 1955, *PP*, 704–5.

61. Antrim, "President Believes in Prayer."

62. See Ann Whitman to Chow Monk, Dec. 9, 1954, PPF 1-A-3, Box 8, Favorite Bible Passages.

63. His favorite hymns were consistently specified as including "O God, Our Help in Ages Past," "God of Our Fathers," "Mine Eyes Have Seen the Glory," "A Mighty Fortress Is Our God," and "Faith of Our Fathers." See ibid.

64. Wirt, "Faith," Part Two, 7.

65. "Ike's Faith," *Time* 61 (Apr. 13, 1953), 91. Cf. "Dwight D. Eisenhower's Bible-Based Legacy," *Bible Society Record*, July–Aug. 1969.

66. Quoted in Wirt, "Faith," 8.

67. Quoted in "Eisenhower's Bible-Based Legacy."

68. DDE to James Nettinga, Oct. 9, 1959, FFR, Box 10, Religious (1), Worldwide Bible Reading message.

69. Stringer, "The President." Those who inquired about Eisenhower's favorite biblical passages were told that he especially liked the book of Genesis, II Chronicles 7:14, Psalms 23, 33:12, 127:1, and John 8:31–32. E.g., "A Thought for Today," *WP*, Mar. 7, 1955; Kevin McCann to Elliott Kraemer, Apr. 4, 1959, PPF 1-A-3, Box 8, Favorite Books and Authors. He also loved the Old Testament prophets ("Eisenhower's Bible-Based Legacy").

70. In 1954, for example, Eisenhower signed an ABS-sponsored "World Good Will Book," declaring that he loved the Bible, respected its teachings, and wanted "to see it more widely disseminated" ("Eisenhower's Bible-Based Legacy").

71. Eisenhower stated, "Because only by the utter destruction of the Axis was a decent world possible, the war became for me a crusade in the traditional sense of that often misused word" (*Crusade in Europe*, 157).

72. Dwight D. Eisenhower, "Remarks at the 22nd Annual Convention of the Military Chaplains Association," May 6, 1954, *PP*, 462.

73. DDE to Frederic Fox, FFR, Religious (2), Box 10. Cf. Eisenhower, "Address...on Accepting the Nomination...," Aug. 23, 1956, *PP*, 715.

74. DDE to Patrick A. O'Boyle, Angus Dun, and Norman Gerstenfeld, Jan. 10, 1953, *Papers*, 13:1495–96.

75. Quoted in Stringer, "The President." Cf. DDE to Eugene Carson Blake, Dec. 2, 1957, FFR, Protestant (4), Box 10; and DDE to Captain John V. Noel, Sept. 12, 1957, same file. See also Eisenhower, "Remarks to...the Military Chaplains National Association," May 9, 1956, *PP*, 483.

76. DDE to James Z. Nettinga, Sept. 28, 1960, FFR, Protestant (1), Box 10.

77. Dwight D. Eisenhower, "Remarks at the Dedication of the Washington Hebrew Congregation Temple," May 8, 1955, *PP*, 477–78, quotations in that order.

78. DDE to Anton Frederick Lorenzen, Sept. 9, 1953, *Papers*, 14:509. Cf. DDE to Rene Pleven, Aug. 13, 1952, ibid. 13:1317; Eisenhower, "'Back to God' Program," 11; Eisenhower, "Address at the American Legion Convention," Aug. 30, 1954, *PP*, 780.

79. Dwight D. Eisenhower, "Address at the Second Assembly of the World Council of Churches," Aug. 19, 1954, *PP*, 737–38. See also "President's News Conference of Nov. 23, 1954," 1067; Eisenhower, "Radio and Television Address...on the State of the Nation," Apr. 5, 1954, *PP*, 373; and Eisenhower, "Address at...Mount St. Mary's College," June 2, 1958, *PP*, 447.

80. "Eisenhower's Speech at Abilene," 16. Cf. Eisenhower, "Remarks Broadcast as Part of the American Legion 'Back to God' Program," Feb. 7, 1954, *PP*, 243–44.

81. "Statement...upon Signing Bill to Include the Words 'Under God' in the Pledge to the Flag," June 14, 1954, *PP*, 563. See also Gerard Kaye and Ferenc M. Szasz, "Adding 'under God' to the Pledge of Allegiance," *Encounter* 34 (1973), 52–56.

82. Dwight D. Eisenhower, "Remarks Recorded for the "Back-to-God" Program of the American Legion," Feb. 20, 1955, *PP*, 274.

83. Dwight D. Eisenhower, "Address at...the National Conference of Catholic Charities," Sept. 26, 1960, *PP*, 731. Cf. Eisenhower, "Remarks at the...Washington Conference for the Advertising Council," *PP*, Apr. 2, 1957, 233.

84. Dwight D. Eisenhower, "True Brotherhood," Dec. 1960, Frederic Fox Papers (hereafter FFP), Box 31. Cf. Eisenhower, "National Council of Churches," 792; and Eisenhower, "Military Chaplains Association," 461.

85. Dwight D. Eisenhower, "'The Greater Purposes,'" *Time* 68 (Nov. 12, 1956), 29. Cf. Eisenhower, "Remarks to a Delegation from the National Council of Churches,"

Sept. 9, 1959, *PP*, 645; and "President's News Conference of Oct. 3, 1957," *PP*, 713. John Tracy Ellis, a professor at Catholic University, warned that Eisenhower's connection of the two threatened to make "a religion of our democracy" (quoted in Hutchinson, "President's Faith," 366). Cf. Ernest LeFever, "The Candidates' Religious Views," *CC* 73 (Sept. 19, 1956), 1074.

86. Dwight D. Eisenhower, "Remarks at . . . the Issuance of the First Stamp bearing the Motto 'In God We Trust,'" Apr. 8, 1954, *PP*, 392.

87. Quoted in Gustafson, "Religion," 611.

88. Dwight D. Eisenhower, "Remarks at the Cornerstone-Laying Ceremony for the Interchurch Center, New York City," Oct. 12, 1958, *PP*, 732.

89. Dwight D. Eisenhower, "Message to the . . . Chaplains' Association of Army and Navy," in Rudolph L. Trevenfels, ed., *Eisenhower Speaks: Dwight D. Eisenhower in His Messages and Speeches* (New York: Farrar, Straus, 1948), 144.

90. DDE to Willard Stewart Paul, Mar. 27, 1954, *Papers*, 15:985.

91. Dwight D. Eisenhower, "Address . . . [to] the United Church Women, Atlantic City, NJ," Oct. 6, 1953, *PP*, 637.

92. Dwight D. Eisenhower, "Speech Accepting the Republican Nomination," *NYT*, July 12, 1952, 4; Eisenhower, "Washington Hebrew Congregation Temple," 477, quotations in that order.

93. Dwight D. Eisenhower, "Remarks at the World Christian Endeavor Convention," July 25, 1954, *PP*, 654–55.

94. Dwight D. Eisenhower, "Annual Message to the Congress on the State of the Union," Jan. 7, 1954, *PP*, 1954, 22–23, quotations in that order. Cf. Eisenhower, "International Council," *PP*, 222.

95. DDE to Hughes, Nov. 20, 1958, AWF, DDE Diary Series A75–22, Box 37, DDE Dictation, Nov. 1958. See also Eisenhower, "Remarks to . . . NATO Naval Chaplains," Oct. 11, 1957, *PP*, 737.

96. He soon did this while meeting with Queen Frederika of Greece. See Conversation with Queen Frederika of Greece, Dec. 9, 1958, AWF, DDE Diary Series A75–22, Box 38, Staff Notes, Dec. 1958 (2).

97. "The Testimony of a Devout President," *Life* 40 (Dec. 26, 1955), 13. Cf. Eisenhower, "Remarks at the Pageant of Peace Ceremonies," Dec. 23, 1957, *PP*, 846.

98. Hutchinson, "President's Faith," 367.

99. Eisenhower, "National Council of Churches," 793.

100. Ann Whitman Diary, Feb. 14, 1959, Feb. 1959 (1), EL. See also "Life and Death—Question and Answer," *NW* 48 (Aug. 13, 1956), 34.

101. Billy Graham, *Just as I Am: The Autobiography of Billy Graham* (San Francisco: Harper, 1997), 204.

102. Wirt, "Faith," Part Two, 13.

103. Ambrose, *Eisenhower*, 2: 674–75, quotation from 675.

104. Eisenhower, "Remarks at the Dedicatory Prayer Breakfast," 38. See also "The March of the News," *USN* 34 (Feb. 13, 1953), 4.

105. Hutchinson, "President's Faith," 368.

106. The year before Eisenhower took office, Congress had mandated the president to "set aside and proclaim" a national day of prayer each year. See Frederic E. Fox, "The National Day of Prayer," *Theology Today* 30 (July 1973), 258–80.

107. The organization held national conferences in Washington in November 1954 and October 1955. The letter inviting conferees in 1954 featured a statement from

Eisenhower, which declared, "Our government has logically been described as a translation into the political field of a deeply held religious faith. This faith holds that man is created in the image of God, and from this fundamental concept springs our dedication to the principle of and our belief in equality under the law, justice, mercy, and the brotherhood of man" (See Official File [hereafter OF] 144-G-1, Box 738, Conference on Moral and Spiritual Recovery [1]), EL. The first conference focused on the spiritual foundations of American democracy and featured an address by Eisenhower that was published as a pamphlet and widely circulated. See National Conference on the Spiritual Foundations of American Democracy and Highlights, First National Conference on the Spiritual Foundations of American Democracy, both in OF, 144-G-1, Box 738, Conference on Moral and Spiritual Recovery (2).

108. Convention News, American Council of Christian Churches, Oct. 30, 1958, OF 144-B, Box 736. See also Carl McIntire, "President Eisenhower's Religion," *Christian Beacon* 19 (Mar. 24, 1954), 1, 5, 8; and McIntire to DDE, Mar. 24, 1954, PPF 1-A-9, Box 17, Church Affiliation of the President (1).

109. Miller, *Piety*, 33, 34, 43–45; first quotation from 33, second from 34, third from 45. See also *NYT*, Jan. 19, 1953.

110. Ibid., 34, 37, 43, 45, quotations in that order, last two from 45.

111. Ibid., 127.

112. Will Herberg, *Protestant-Catholic-Jew: An Essay in American Religious Sociology* (Garden City, NY: Doubleday, 1956), 49–57, 85–113, 276–77.

113. Miller, *Piety*, 128–31, 155; quotation from 128–29.

114. See Gustafson, "Religion," 610.

115. E.g., Hutchinson, "President's Faith," 362.

116. Wirt, "Faith," 8, Part Two, 13 (quotation). In a 1954 article, Russell Hitt maintained that Elson unquestionably believed that Eisenhower had "made a personal commitment to the Lord Jesus Christ" ("What Ike's Pastor Believes," 11). Carl McIntire, by contrast, protested that Eisenhower's beliefs about God, Christ, and salvation were unclear ("President Eisenhower's Religion," 8).

117. John J. O'Brien, "Prayerful President," *The Sign* 33 (Aug. 1953), 19–21.

118. Marvin Boyd to DDE, Apr. 7, 1955, PPF, Box 904, 53-B, Church Matters (1). Boyd interviewed these officials.

119. Resolution of Appreciation to Our President, July 26, 1955, PPF, Box 903, 53 Religion (2). See also Presbytery of Washington City to Eisenhower, Mar. 11, 1953; and the Statement of Faith signed by almost 2,000 residents of Rochester, New Hampshire, both in PPF, Box 903, 53 Religion (1).

120. Quoted in Elson, *America's Spiritual Recovery*, 187.

121. Ibid., 53.

122. "Text of Resolution," *NYT*, Feb. 18, 1955, 28.

123. "Greatness in a Time of Tempest," *CT* 13 (Apr. 11, 1969), 640.

124. Quoted in Edward Plowman, "Ike's Faith," *CT* 13 (Apr. 25, 1969), 705.

125. James T. Patterson, *Mr. Republican: A Biography of Robert A. Taft* (Boston: Houghton Mifflin, 1972), 519, 535–36; Pach and Richardson, *Presidency*, 21.

126. Stanley High, "What the President Wants," *Reader's Digest* 62 (Apr. 1953), 1–4; Stringer, "The President."

127. *NYT*, Jan. 17, 1953.

128. Pierard and Linder, *Civil Religion*, 189.

129. Quoted in "Ike's Faith," 13. See also John R. Greene, *The Crusade: The Presidential Election of 1952* (Lanham, MD: University Press of America, 1985).

130. Hutchinson, "President's Faith," 367. Cf. Miller, *Piety*, 33–34.

131. Judah Nadich, *Eisenhower and the Jews* (New York: Twayne, 1953), 13–14. Cf. "Appeal for Politics without Bigotry," *CC* 73 (Aug. 15, 1956), 939–40.

132. "On God's Coattails?" *CC* 69 (July 30, 1952), 870–71, all quotations from 870. See also "Litany for Political Parties," ibid., May 21, 1952, 608; "Correspondence," ibid. (Aug 20, 1952), 950–51; and "God's Coattails," *NW*, Aug. 11, 1952, 58.

133. "The Stevenson Divorce," *CA* 127 (Sept. 18, 1952), 1152. On Stevenson's sparse references to God, see David L. Cohn, "Politics in a God-Fearin' Key," *Saturday Review* 37 (Apr. 3, 1954), 12.

134. *Episcopal Church News*, Sept. 21, 1952, quoted in "Religion and the Presidency," *CA* 127 (Oct. 9, 1952), 1248.

135. John M. Swomley Jr., "The Eisenhower Portent," *CC* 69 (Jan. 30, 1952), 124–26. See also Robert E. Fitch, "Politics in Christian Perspective," *CC* 73 (Oct. 31, 1956), 1257–58.

136. Robert E. Fitch, letter to the editor in a section titled "Swomley's Eisenhower," *CC* 69 (Feb. 20, 1952), 223.

137. Bradshaw Mintener, "Why I Shall Vote for Eisenhower," *CC* 69 (Oct. 15, 1952), 1188.

138. Donald Grey Barnhouse, "For Whom to Vote," *Eternity* 3 (Nov. 1952), 13–14, 40–42. First two quotations from 13, last two from 42.

139. See E. S. Skillin et al., "Our Choice for President," *CMW* 57 (Sept. 26, 1952), 595–98; "The Eisenhower Victory," *CMW* 57 (Nov. 14, 1952), 131. See also "The Catholic Press on Party Candidates," *America* 88 (Oct. 4, 1952), 5–6; and John Sheerin, "Korea, Communist, Corruption," *CMW* 176 (Nov. 1952), 81–82.

140. See John Cogley, "We Like Ike," *CMW* 54 (Sept. 14, 1951), 542; "The Eisenhower Candidacy," *CMW* 56 (May 9, 1952), 109; "The Trouble with Crusades," *CMW* 56 (Aug. 29, 1952); and "Eisenhower as Eisenhower," *CMW* 57 (Sept. 5, 1952), 525.

141. Quoted in John Sheerin, "President Eisenhower's Task," *CMW* 176 (Dec. 1952), 163.

142. See Sheerin, "Eisenhower's Task," 163; Charles Lucey, "Washington Front," *America* 88 (Oct. 18, 1952), 61; "Moral Issues in the Campaign," *CA* 127 (July 31, 1952), 976; and Kenneth Underwood, "Protestants and Politics," ibid. (Oct. 16, 1952), 1279, 1282.

143. LeFever, "Religious Views," 1072. The evangelical journal *Eternity*, by contrast, argued that "those of us who feel answerable to Jesus Christ could never vote for Mr. Stevenson for any office whatsoever" ("Adlai's Religion," 7 [Aug. 1956], 10).

144. LeFever, "Religious Views," 1072–75, first and second quotation from 1073, third from 1074, fourth from 1075.

145. "Correspondence," *CC* 73 (Oct. 10, 1956), 1166.

146. Robert Fitch, "Politics in Christian Perspective," *CC* 73 (Oct. 31, 1956), 1257–59. Cf. Fitch, "The American President as Philosopher-King," *NR* 135 (Aug. 13, 1956), 11–13.

147. Paul G. Hoffman, "Why I Will Vote Republican," *CAC* 16 (Oct. 15, 1956), 129, 134–36; Chester Bowles, "Why I Will Vote Democrat," CAC, 129, 136–39.

148. Kermit Eby, "Unsatisfying Choice," *CC* 73 (Oct. 31, 1956), 1259–60.

149. "Platform Committees Hear from the Churches," *CC* 73 (Aug. 22, 1956), 963–64.

150. E.g., "Religion in the Campaign," *CA* 131 (June 21, 1956), 788. The editors pointed to the status of Africa, the future of Germany, and the problems of the Middle East, as well as such domestic problems as housing, conservation, immigration, public assistance, and social security for children as campaign issues that had "much to do with religious ideas and ideals." A. Dudley Ward argued that religious bodies should take a keen interest in four main areas during the 1956 campaign: civil rights; health, education, and welfare; international relations and military preparedness; and economic policies. See Ward, "Our Vital Stake in the Fall Election," *CA* 131 (Aug. 23, 1956), 1006–7, 1021, 1030–31. See also T. Otto Nall, "On the Record," *CA* 131 (Aug. 30, 1956), 1045; "The Election Results," *CC* 73 (Nov. 14, 1956), 1315.

151. "Ministers Favor Eisenhower 8 to 1," *CT* 1 (Oct. 29, 1956), 28. Respondents preferred Eisenhower over Stevenson by huge margins on such matters as their "personal stature," party platforms, and attitudes toward corruption in government. These ministers were "selected at random among all denominations," but it seems probable that either the survey was sent primarily to theologically conservative clergy or that this group responded in much larger numbers. See also Don Rosenberger, "The Christian Vote," *Moody Monthly* 57 (Sept. 1956), 74–75.

152. BG to DDE, June 4, 1956, PPF 1052, Box 966, GB.

153. BG to DDE, Aug. 24, 1956, AWF, name series A75–22, GB, Box 16.

154. See Albert J. Menendez, *Religion at the Polls* (Philadelphia: Westminster, 1977), 61–62; James Robert Brown, "Do Catholics Vote Their Religion?" *America* 95 (Aug. 25, 1956), 480–81.

155. "Politics without Bigotry," 939.

156. "Ike in a Landslide," *America* 96 (Nov. 17, 1956), 186.

157. "Election Results," 1315.

158. Gustafson, "Religious Role," 710–11, quotation from 710.

159. Prior to taking this position, Fox graduated from Union Theological Seminary and pastored churches in four states. See "White House Parson," *NW*, Jan. 6, 1958; Warren Unna, "Pastor on the White House Payroll," *Christian Herald*, Feb. 1959, 25, 71–72; Fanning, "Clergyman in the White House," 7–8; "White House Pastor Helps Ike Write Talks and Answer Mail," FFP, Box 28, May 1958; Frederic Fox, "Christian Ideals and Political Realities," *CC* 69 (Oct. 29, 1952), 1249–52; Fox to the Members and Friends of the First Congregational Church, Williamstown, MA, FFP, Box 24, Aug. 1956.

160. "Churches of America Asked to 'Speak Up Clear and Strong,'" Fort Wayne *News-Sentinel*, Dec. 7, 1957.

161. Gustafson, "Religious Role," 718–19.

162. E. F. Adams to DDE, Apr. 1, 1955, General File 118, 1955, Box 679, EL.

163. Grubb, *Modern Viking*, 128–35.

164. James D. Murch, *Cooperation without Compromise: A History of the National Association of Evangelicals* (Grand Rapids, MI: Eerdmans, 1956), 151–52.

165. The first quotation is from Richard Pierard, "Billy Graham and the U. S. Presidency," *JCS* 22 (Winter 1980), 116. The second is from BG to DDE, Dec. 3, 1951, Pre-Presidential Papers (hereafter Pre-PP), Principal File, Grah-Gras (Misc.), EL. Eisenhower thanked the Almighty for Graham's "fight for the old-fashioned virtues of integrity, decency, and straightforwardness in public life" (DDE to BG, Nov. 8, 1951, PPF, Box 966, 1052, GB). During the 1952 campaign, evangelical Arthur Langlie, governor of Washington, suggested that Eisenhower form an organization of religious leaders to work for his election. The general responded that pastors "must necessarily

take a non-partisan approach," but he suggested that some of them might informally support his campaign (DDE to Langlie, Aug. 11, 1952, same file).

166. Graham visited Eisenhower in Paris in March, in Chicago shortly after the Republican convention, and in Denver several weeks later. In Paris, they discussed reasons Eisenhower should run; in Chicago, Graham suggested that Eisenhower make the nation's need of spiritual renewal one of his campaign themes; in Denver, they discussed the importance of Eisenhower joining the church and which congregations he might join. See John Pollock, *Billy Graham: Evangelist to the World: An Authorized Biography of the Decisive Years* (San Francisco: Harper and Row, 1979), 165–66; and Marshall Frady, *Billy Graham: A Parable of American Righteousness* (Boston: Little, Brown, 1979), 255–56.

167. Billy Graham, "God is My Witness," *McCall's*, June 1964, 64. Eisenhower used one of three verses that Graham suggested, but they did not discuss the inaugural prayer, which Eisenhower composed by himself the morning of the inaugural (Pollock, *Billy Graham*, 166).

168. Eisenhower received dozens of letters about Graham, mostly commending his work. See Alphabetical File: Graham, Rev. Billy, EL. Graham sent the president his book *Peace with God*, which Eisenhower said he looked forward to reading (DDE to BG, Nov. 3, 1953, PPF, Box 966, 1052, GB). Graham often reported on his crusades to Eisenhower, and the president occasionally wished him "complete success" (see the same file).

169. BG to DDE, Sept. 28, 1953; Feb. 8, 1954; Nov. 18, 1959; May 10, 1954, PPF 1052, Box 966, GB, quotations in that order. "My private opinion," Graham added, is that Indo-China must be held at all costs" (May 10, 1954).

170. BG to DDE, Aug. 19, 1955, PPF 1052, Box 966, GB; BG to DDE, Aug. 24, 1956, AWF, Name Series, Box 16, GB [race relations, politics], quotations in that order. Graham praised Eisenhower's acceptance speech as "absolutely terrific" and labeled the prayer of dedication at the end of the Republican convention "magnificent" (Aug. 24, 1956).

171. BG to DDE, June 4, 1956, PPF 1052, Box 966, GB; BG to DDE, Aug. 28, 1961, PPP, Principal File 1961, Box 9, GR, quotations in that order.

172. DDE to Frank W. Boykin, Mar. 20, 1956, PPF 1052, Box 966, GB. Boykin, a congressman from Alabama, urged Ann Whitman to recommend that the president solicit Graham's help on the "race question." "No one except the Good Lord," he added, "will ever know of the good that Billy Graham has done for President Eisenhower and our great country" (Boykin to Whitman, Mar. 19, 1956, ibid). See also Boykin to DDE, Mar. 19, 1956, ibid.

173. Pollock, *Billy Graham*, 166.

174. Robert Keith Gray, Oral History Transcript, EL Apr. 10, 1970, 33–35.

175. "President's News Conference of March 21, 1956," *PP*, 338.

176. DDE to J. C. Pollock, Feb. 8, 1865, PPP, Secretary's Series, Messages (ME-2)–Individuals, Box 2, A 67–37. Eisenhower added that he appreciated Graham's "deep faith in the Bible and its teachings" and enjoyed their stimulating conversions.

177. E.g., William Stoneman, "Billy Emerging as No. 1 Enemy of Reds in Europe," *Chicago Daily News*, June 11, 1955.

178. In 1961, for example, Graham wrote that communism had "all the earmarks of the Anti-Christ that is spoken of in Scripture" (BG to DDE, May 16, 1961, PPP, Principal File, Box 9, 1961, GR).

179. Walter K. Scott to Bryce Harlow, Aug. 2, 1954, PPF 47, International Council of Christian Churches, Box 819.

180. Bryce Harlow to DDE, Aug. 5, 1954, PPF 47, International Council of Christian Churches, Box 819. The administration did send a message. See Eisenhower to McIntire, Aug. 6, 1954, same file.

181. Ronn Spargur to Frederic Fox, Sept. 15, 1959; Spargur to Wilton Persons, Apr. 8, 1959; Spargur to Fox, May 7, 1959, all in OF 14-B, Box 736. A March 13, 1959, memorandum declared that "extreme caution should be exercised" in dealing with this group "because of our past experience and information."

182. Eisenhower's most notable Catholic appointee was Labor Secretary James P. Mitchell.

183. His closest Catholic confidant and advisor was Cardinal Francis Spellman of New York. The president called him an "old, old," "good friend" (Eisenhower, "National Council of Churches," 646). Cf. DDE to William E. Robinson, Sept. 12, 1953, *Papers*, 14:518). In addition, Eisenhower was close friends with two priests—John P. Markoe and Edward Conway—whose letters were routinely forwarded to him (Gustafson, "Religious Role," 716–17).

184. Merlin Gustafson, "How a President Uses Religion and How It Uses Him," 6, unpublished paper, EL.

185. Eisenhower preferred a Republican Catholic but apparently could not find one he liked. See Eisenhower, *Diary*, Nov. 16, 1954, *Papers*, 15:1397. See also DDE to Brownell, Mar. 8, 1955, *Papers*, 16:1606–7. The editor of the *Catholic World* applauded Brennan's nomination but noted that Eisenhower's desire to win the "Catholic vote" in the next month's presidential election may have influenced his choice. See John B. Sheerin, "A Catholic Comes to the Court," *CMW* 184 (Nov. 1956), 81–82.

186. "Our Debt to President Eisenhower," *CMW* 63 (Oct. 7, 1955), 3. See also "The President and Politics," ibid. 59 (Nov. 6, 1953), 108–9; "The Ambiguous Blessing," ibid. 60 (Sept. 10, 1954), 549–50; and "Time of Decision," ibid. 64 (Sept. 28, 1956), 623–24.

187. See Samuel Lubell, *The Future of American Politics* (New York: Doubleday, 1956), 236, 238.

188. "President of All the People?" *CC* 76 (Dec. 16, 1959), 1459.

189. Ibid.

190. Maxwell Abbell, president of the United Synagogue of America, quoted in Nadich, *Eisenhower*, 11.

191. Ambrose, *Eisenhower*, 2:387.

192. Dwight D. Eisenhower, "Annual Message to the Congress on the State of the Union," Feb. 2, 1953, *PP*, 12.

193. E.g., "Eisenhower as President," *CC* 71 (Feb. 10, 1954), 167–68.

194. Robert Griffith, ed., *Ike's Letters to a Friend* (Lawrence: University Press of Kansas, 1984), 104.

195. Eisenhower, "Remarks at . . . the Advertising Council," 233. See also "Ike Outlines His Political Creed," *USN* 39 (Sept. 23, 1955), 114–15.

196. Gustafson, "Religion," 611.

197. DDE to Blossom Gray Jaffray, Apr. 8, 1955, OF 136, Box 687, 137 Peace (2).

198. DDE to Ernest A. Gross, Nov. 17, 1958, FFR, Religious (1), Box 10.

199. Eisenhower, "Address at the . . . World Council of Churches," 736. Frederic Fox insisted that religious principles helped guide Eisenhower's administration. Its foreign policy, which emphasized "Peace with Justice in Freedom," rested in part on a religious foundation. Only by seeing all people as children of God could the problem of

Civil Rights be properly handled (Fox to Robert J. Weir, Mar. 10, 1960, General File 118, 1959–60).

200. E.g., DDE to Rabbi Joachim Prinz, Mar. 26, 1953, FFR, Jewish (2), Box 10.

201. DDE to Marion B. Folsom, Feb. 19, 1957, FFR, Religious–Other (2), Box 10.

202. DDE to the National Conference of Christians and Jews, Feb. 18, 1953, FFR, Religious–Other (2), Box 10.

203. Dwight D. Eisenhower, *Waging Peace, 1956–61* (Garden City, NY: Doubleday, 1965), 467.

204. Caroline Pruden, *Conditional Partners: Eisenhower and the United Nations and the Search for a Permanent Peace* (Baton Rouge: Louisiana State University Press, 1998), 168.

205. DDE to members of the American Legion, Feb. 3, 1956, EL. Cf. Eisenhower, "Address at the American Legion Convention," 786: "In the earnest belief that these basic purposes [of his administration] conform to the will of the Highest of All Rulers, the United States will continue to pursue them."

206. Dwight D. Eisenhower, "Annual Message to the Congress on the State of the Union," Jan. 9, 1958, *PP*, 3.

207. DDE to Arthur Eisenhower, May 18, 1943, Pre-PP, Principal File, Arthur Eisenhower (2).

208. Dwight D. Eisenhower, "Address at the American Jewish Tercentenary Dinner," Oct. 20, 1954, *PP*, 921. "I recall that wonderful prophecy of Isaiah," Eisenhower added, "'and the work of righteousness shall be peace....'"

209. Dwight D. Eisenhower, "Address to the National Council of Catholic Women," Nov. 8, 1954, *PP*, 1026, 1028, quotations in that order.

210. Eisenhower, "International Council," 223.

211. Eisenhower, "United Church Women," 636.

212. "President's News Conference of Nov. 23, 1954," 1068.

213. Dwight D. Eisenhower, "Remarks upon Receiving an Honorary Degree from Catholic University," Nov. 19, 1953, *PP*, 794–95, quotation from 794.

214. Eisenhower, "World Christian Endeavor Convention," 655.

215. Eisenhower, "State of the Nation," 381.

216. Dwight D. Eisenhower, "Remarks at the Pageant of Peace Ceremonies," Dec. 23, 1958, *PP*, 867. Eisenhower misunderstood Eastern religions: Hindus are polytheists and Buddhists believe in sacred principles but not a personal God.

217. The quotations are from Wilson to Sherman Adams, May 28, 1954. See also Alphabetical File, Box 2948, Spellman, Francis Cardinal, Cross Reference Sheet. Wilson first asked Eisenhower to adopt a "Peace Plan" in February 1953.

218. Wilson to DDE, Mar. 17, 1955; DDE to Wilson, Mar. 22, 1955, *Papers*, 16:1630. Charles Willis Jr. suggested Wilson's appeal be sent to a group of distinguished Americans for further study (Willis to Sherman Adams, Apr. 27, 1955). Bryce Harlow contended it would turn the president into "a global Billy Sunday," which some people might consider "wacky." Moreover, the president must not overemphasize the role of religion in human affairs (Harlow to Adams, June 8, 1954). See also Wilson to Adams, May 28, 1954; Adams to Wilson, Aug. 23, 1954; and Wilson to DDE, Mar. 17, 1955. All these documents are in OF 136, Box 687, 137, Peace (1).

219. Eisenhower, "Address at...the World Council of Churches," 739. See also *NYT*, Aug. 20, 1954; "Under God," *Time* 64 (Aug. 30, 1954), 7; "Eisenhower at the Assembly," *CC* 71 (Sept. 1, 1954), 1048–49.

220. Samuel McCrea Cavert to DDE, Oct. 27, 1954, OF 144-H, Prayers for Peace, Box 738.

221. Abbott Washburn to L. Arthur Minnich Jr., Nov. 2, 1954, OF 144-H, Prayers for Peace, Box 738.

222. Eisenhower stressed the difficulty of organizing a specific event that would have a greater effect than the "efforts constantly made by the churches throughout the world" (DDE to Samuel McCrea Cavert, Nov. 3, 1954, OF 144-H, Prayers for Peace, Box 738).

223. DDE to Edward Elson, Apr. 16, 1957, FFR, Religious–Other (2), Box 10.

224. Dwight D. Eisenhower, "Remarks and Address at . . . the National Conference on the Foreign Aspects of National Security," Feb. 25, 1958, PP, 178.

225. Dwight D. Eisenhower, "Second Inaugural Address," Jan. 21, 1957, PP, 62.

226. Dwight D. Eisenhower, "Address before . . . the United Nations on Peaceful Uses of Atomic Energy," Dec. 8, 1953, PP, 813–22, quotation from 822. See also Eisenhower, "Remarks at the Ceremony Marking the Issuance of the Atoms for Peace Stamp," July 28, 1955, PP, 744–45.

227. Geoffrey Perret, Eisenhower (New York: Random House, 1999), 523–24.

228. Dwight D. Eisenhower, "Radio and Television Address . . . prior to Departure for the Big Four Conference at Geneva," 701–5; quotation from 705.

229. Dwight D. Eisenhower, "Statement on Disarmament Presented at the Geneva Conference, July 21, 1955," PP, 714–16; first two quotation from 714, second from 716.

230. Kenneth W. Thompson, "Geneva: Triumph and Tragedy," CAC 15 (Oct. 3, 1955), 123–24, quotations from 124.

231. Ibid., 125–26, all quotations in that order.

232. "Sermon and Parade," CC 74 (Feb. 6, 1957), 158–59.

233. H. W. Brands Jr., Cold Warriors: Eisenhower's Generation and American Foreign Policy (New York: Columbia University Press, 1988), 195.

234. Ibid.

235. E.g., DDE to Hazlett, July 19, 1947, Pre-PP, Box 56. Cf. Eisenhower, "United Church Women," 637.

236. "Remarks by the President," National Presbyterian Church, Jan. 6, 1960, OF 144-B-1-A, National Presbyterian Church and Center, Box 736. Our faith, Eisenhower continued, "includes our loyalty to all those qualities of life which are uppermost in the Christian tradition: justice, charity, peace, and the truth that sets men free. . . . In the exercise of them each person finds his highest fulfillment as a grateful and responsible child of God."

237. Eisenhower, "United Church Women," 635.

238. E.g., Dwight D. Eisenhower, "Remarks at the Republican Women's National Conference," May 10, 1955, PP, 481–82.

239. Pruden, Conditional Partners, 169–71, quotations from 171.

240. "The President's Prayer," The Nation, 176 (Jan. 31, 1953), 91.

241. Eisenhower, "International Council," 223.

242. "Bombs and Ballots," CC 73 (Oct. 31, 1956), 1253–54.

243. "President's News Conference of Nov. 23, 1954," 1067.

244. Dwight D. Eisenhower, "The Chance for Peace," Apr. 16, 1953, PP 186.

245. Eisenhower, "Foreign Aspects of National Security," 178.

246. Eisenhower, "Statement of Disarmament," 714.

247. Eisenhower, "Chance for Peace," 182.

248. DDE to Everett Clinchy, May 29, 1958, FFR, Box 10, Religious (1).

249. Eisenhower, "American Jewish Tercentenary Dinner," 928.

250. Dwight D. Eisenhower, "Radio and Television Remarks...Delivered at the Pageant of Peace Ceremonies," Dec. 23, 1959, *PP*, 882.

251. Eisenhower, *Waging Peace*, 468.

252. Brands, *Cold Warriors*, 199–200, quotation from 200.

253. Richard A. Melanson and David Mayers, "Preface," in Melanson and Mayers, eds., *Reevaluating Eisenhower: American Foreign Policy in the Fifties* (Chicago: University of Illinois Press, 1987), 4. See also Thomas F. Soapes, "A Cold Warrior Seeks Peace: Eisenhower's Strategy for Nuclear Disarmament," *Diplomatic History* 4 (Winter 1980), 57–72; Walt W. Rostow, *Open Skies: Eisenhower's Proposal of July 21, 1955* (Austin: University of Texas Press, 1983); Burton I. Kaufman, *Trade and Aid: Eisenhower's Foreign Economic Policy, 1953–61* (Baltimore: Johns Hopkins University Press, 1982); and William B. Ewald Jr., *Eisenhower as President: Crucial Days, 1951–60* (Englewood Cliffs, NJ: Prentice Hall, 1981).

254. Brands, *Cold Warriors*, 211.

255. Dwight D. Eisenhower, "Farewell...Address to the American People," *PP*, Jan. 17, 1961, 1037–38; first quotation from 1037, the rest from 1038.

256. Ibid., 1039–40; first three quotations from 1039; last two from 1040.

257. Perret, *Eisenhower*, 599.

258. Eisenhower, "State of the Union," Feb. 2, 1953, 31.

259. Eisenhower, *Waging Peace*, 154.

260. DDE to BG, Mar. 30, 1956, AWF, Name Series, A75–22, Box 16, GB [race relations, politics]. See also Ann Whitman Diary, Mar. 1956 (1), Mar. 21, 1956; and "The President's News Conference of March 14, 1956," *PP*, 304–5.

261. DDE to BG, Mar. 22, 1956, AWF, Name Series, A75–22, Box 16, GB [race relations, politics]. Cf. "President's News Conference of March 21, 1956," 339.

262. BG to DDE, Mar. 27, 1956, AWF, Name Series, A75–22, Box 16, GB [race relations, politics]. "I will do all in my power," Graham added, "to urge Southern ministers to call upon the people for moderation, charity, compassion and progress toward compliance with the Supreme Court decision [*Brown v. the Board of Education,* 1954]."

263. BG to DDE, June 4, 1956. Eisenhower replied, "I appreciate very much all you are doing toward our mutual goal of improving race relations" (DDE to BG, June 21, 1956, PPF 1052, Box 966, GB). For a similar perspective, see "The Church and the Race Problem," *CT* 1 (Mar. 18, 1957), 20–22; and Harold Lindsell, "The Bible and Race Relations," *Eternity* 7 (Aug. 1956), 12–13, 44.

264. Ambrose, *Eisenhower*, 2:309, 327, 337, 410, 528–29. Eisenhower argued in 1957 that "the sentiment, the goodwill, the good sense of a whole citizenry" was what enforced the law ("The President's News Conference of Oct. 3, 1957," *PP*, 707). He saw the work of Omer Carmichael, the superintendent of schools in Louisville, Kentucky, as a model for his approach. For two years, Carmichael had met with civic leaders and white and black parent groups and had integrated the city's schools without violence. See "Louisville's Integrator," *NYT*, Sept. 10, 1956; DDE to Carmichael, Sept. 14, 1956, FFP, Box 24, Sept. 1956 (2).

265. Pach and Richardson, *Presidency*, 155–56, quotation from 156. Similarly, *Commonweal* called on Eisenhower to "exert a moral force which is unlimited by particularities of creed, nationality, party or geography" to promote black Civil Rights

("Plea to the White House," 65 [Feb. 8, 1957], 477–78, quotation from 478). Cf. "Little Rock and the Future," *CMW* 67 (Oct. 18, 1957), 59–60.

266. Pach and Richardson, *Presidency*, 137.

267. John Cogley, "Dwight Eisenhower, a Good Man," *CMW* 73 (Jan. 20, 1961), 436.

268. Fred I. Greenstein, "Eisenhower Revisited: The Activist President," in Thomas G. Paterson, ed., *Major Problems in American Foreign Policy*, vol. 2: *Since 1914* (Lexington, MA: D. C. Heath, 1989), 456. Cf. Milton Eisenhower, "Portrait of a Brother," in Kenneth W. Thompson, ed., *The Eisenhower Presidency: Eleven Intimate Portraits* (Lanham, MD: University Press of America, 1984), 8.

269. Alexander, *Holding the Line*, xv.

270. Pach and Richardson, *Presidency*, 237.

271. Fred Greenstein, *The Hidden-Hand Presidency: Eisenhower as Leader* (New York: Basic Books, 1982), 58–65. Greenstein based his reassessment of Eisenhower's presidential leadership on three factors: "the transcripts of Eisenhower's conversations and conferences; his markups and insertions in the numerous drafts through which all his major speeches went; and his personal correspondence" (Greenstein, "Eisenhower Revisited," 464).

272. Pach and Richardson, *Presidency*, 237, 40, quotations in that order.

273. Brands, *Cold Warriors*, 191; Divine, *Cold War*, 9.

274. Brands, *Cold Warriors*, 192.

275. See Frederic Fox, Feb. 23, 1968, personal communication, cited in Gustafson, "Religious Role," 712.

276. Ambrose, *Eisenhower*, 2:624.

277. Miller, *Piety*, 7–10, quotations from 7 and 10. See also Arthur Larson, *Eisenhower: The Man and the Symbol* (New York: Harpers, 1951); "The President and Politics," 111.

278. Ambrose, *Eisenhower*, 2:425.

279. Hoffman, "Why I Will Vote Republican," 134. Cf. Dwight D. Eisenhower, "Remarks at the Annual Breakfast of Masonic Leaders," Feb. 24, 1955, *PP*, 297.

280. DDE to Everett Clinchy, President, National Conference of Christians and Jews, May 30, 1956, FFR, Religious–Other (2), Box 10. Cf. Eisenhower, "Address to the National Council of Catholic Women," 1025; and Eisenhower, "Address at . . . the National Conference of Catholic Charities," 730.

281. Gustafson, "Religion," 612–13; first quotations from 612, second from 613.

282. *NYT*, Dec. 23, 1952, 16. For an analysis of how this statement has been quoted and misquoted, see Patrick Henry, "'And I Don't Care What It Is': The Tradition-History of a Civil Religion Proof-Text," *Journal of the American Academy of Religion* 49 (Mar. 1981), 35–49.

283. James Juhnke, "'One Nation under God': Religion and the American Dream," *Mennonite Life*, Dec. 1983, 23, 26.

284. LeFever, "Religious Views," 1073–74; first quotation from 1073, second and third from 1074.

285. Miller, *Piety*, 45, 34, quotation from 34.

286. Pierard and Linder, *Civil Religion*, 199.

287. Lewis, "A Formidable Weapon," *NR* 130 (Jan. 11, 1954), 23.

288. On the religiosity of the decade, see Richard Pierard, "One Nation under God," in Perry Cotham, ed., *Christian Social Ethics* (Grand Rapids, MI: Baker, 1979), 85–98; J. Ronald Oakley, *God's Country: America in the Fifties* (New York: Dembner,

1986), 319–27; and Billy Graham's sermon at the Third Annual Prayer Breakfast, Washington, DC, Feb. 2, 1955, WHCF, Box 819, International Christian Leadership, Inc., 16.

289. Arthur Schlesinger Jr., *The Cycles of American History* (Boston: Houghton Mifflin, 1986), 404, 394, 399; first quotation from 404, second from 394.

290. Ambrose, *Eisenhower*, 2:622. See also Kenneth W. Thompson, "The Strengths and Weaknesses of Eisenhower's Leadership," in Melanson and Mayers, eds., *Reevaluating Eisenhower*, 26–28.

291. Divine, *Cold War*, 154; Ambrose, *Eisenhower*, 2:626; Pach and Richardson, *Presidency*, 238. Cf. Robert J. McMahon, "Eisenhower and Third World Nationalism: A Critique of the Revisionists," *Political Science Quarterly* 101 (1986), 454.

292. Dwight D. Eisenhower, "Annual Message to the Congress on the State of the Union," Jan. 12, 1961, *PP*, 913–30, quotation from 930. All these programs, Eisenhower argued, had enabled the nation to "fully" advance its "spiritual goals" (915).

293. Pach and Richardson, *Presidency*, 238–39, quotation from 239.

294. Howard Conn, "Events of Religious Significance in 1954," 16, PPF 53 (Religion (1), Box 903. See also Bradshaw Mintener to DDE, Jan. 25, 1955; and DDE to Conn, Jan. 31, 1955, same file.

295. Cogley, "Dwight Eisenhower," 436.

296. David Lawrence, "Farewell to the 'Faithful Servant,'" *USN* 50 (Jan. 23, 1961), 112.

297. E.g., Arthur Larson, "Eisenhower's Worldview," in Thompson, ed., *Eisenhower Presidency*, 42–44; Andrew Goodpastor, "Organizing the White House," in ibid, 74; and Eisenhower, "Portrait of a Brother," in ibid., 9.

298. Pach and Richardson, *Presidency*, 231. On May 1, 1960, the Soviets shot down his plane, and pilot Gary Powers ejected. Trying to protect America's reputation and prevent the cancellation of a scheduled summit meeting with the Soviets, the State Department announced that the Soviets had shot down an "unarmed weather plane that had flown off course 'and accidentally violated Soviet airspace'" (Perret, *Eisenhower*, 583). See also Michael R. Beschloss, *Mayday: Eisenhower, Khrushchev and the U-2 Affair* (New York: Harper and Row, 1986). For Eisenhower's defense of his actions, see *Waging Peace*, 544–51.

299. Schlesinger, *Cycles*, 388; Pach and Richardson, *Presidency*, 239.

300. Brands, *Cold Warriors*, 211.

301. Murray Kempton, "The Underestimation of Dwight D. Eisenhower," *Esquire*, Sept. 1967, 108–9, 156.

302. Pach and Richardson, *Presidency*, 43.

303. Perret, *Eisenhower*, 270, 216–17.

CHAPTER 8

1. Rose Kennedy, *Times to Remember* (Garden City, NY: Doubleday, 1974), 161. Kennedy told her children that faith "is a great gift from God . . . to sustain us in our lives on earth, to guide us in our activities, to be a source of solace and comfort, so we should do everything we can to strengthen its roots, to nourish it, and it help it grow and flourish" (161). Her daughter Eunice argued, "She was successful in instilling firm faith in all her children" (165).

2. Thomas Reeves, *A Question of Character: A Life of John F. Kennedy* (New York: Free Press, 1991), 413. This is not the impression one gains from reading her autobiography.

3. Lawrence Fuchs, *John F. Kennedy and American Catholicism* (New York: Meredith, 1967), 205.

4. Quoted in Kennedy, *Times to Remember*, 165.

5. See Clay Blair Jr. and Joan Blair, *The Search for JFK* (New York: Berkley, 1976), 11, 184. See also Robert Dallek, *An Unfinished Life: John F. Kennedy, 1917–1963* (Boston: Little, Brown, 2003), 59.

6. Albert J. Menendez, *John F. Kennedy: Catholic and Humanist* (Buffalo, NY: Prometheus, 1978), 66.

7. Fuchs, *Kennedy*, 164.

8. Kaye Halle Oral History, John F. Kennedy Presidential Library (hereafter KL), as quoted by Reeves, *Character*, 57.

9. Hugh Brogan, *Kennedy* (London: Longman, 1996), 46.

10. Menendez, *Kennedy*, 66. The only religious books Kennedy had in his Bowdoin Street library were a New Testament and a summary of Catholic doctrine.

11. Quoted in John Cogley, "Kennedy the Catholic," *CMW* 79 (Jan. 10, 1964), 42.

12. Quoted in John McCollister, *So Help Me God: The Faith of America's Presidents* (Louisville, KY: Westminster/John Knox, 1991), 170. Pereira's claim seems dubious.

13. Theodore C. Sorensen, *Kennedy* (New York: Harper and Row, 1965), 19, 365, quotations in that order.

14. Quoted in Cogley, "Kennedy," 42.

15. Richard Cardinal Cushing, "Introduction," T. S. Settel, ed., *The Faith of JFK* (New York: E. P. Dutton, 1965), 5–6; quotations in that order. In an interview, Cushing asserted that Kennedy was "just as good a Catholic as I am" and that they held similar ideas (Oral Interview, KL).

16. Hays to William Moffett, Jan. 12, 1962, Brooks Hays Papers (hereafter BHP), Files 1962, Jan., Box 3, KL. See also Hays's Nov. 26, 1963, statement in his files: "Kennedy was a sincere and practicing Christian. . . . My judgments about this . . . are largely based upon his actions and his public declarations, for we seldom discussed the subject" (BHP, Carton 14, Personal Correspondence (hereafter PC), 1963, P-Z, Kennedy Condolences).

17. Hays, BHP, Carton 3, 1962, Correspondence and Chronological Files (hereafter CCF) April 1962.

18. J. B. West with Mary Lynn Kotz, *Upstairs at the White House: My Life with the First Ladies* (New York: Coward, McCann and Geoghegan, 1973), 236.

19. James N. Giglio says that there was no Catholic church in the vicinity and the Kennedys attended mass at the Middleburg Community Center. See Giglio, *The Presidency of John F. Kennedy* (Lawrence: University Press of Kansas, 1991), 105.

20. "With a Catholic as President," *USN* 49 (Nov. 21, 1960), 54–55, quotation from 55.

21. JFK to Mrs. J. Warren Fields, Oct. 3, 1961, White House Central Files (Subject) (hereafter WHCF), Box 885, Religious Matters (hereafter RM) 1–20–61—5–15–62, KL. Most of those who inquired about Kennedy's faith received a form letter emphasizing that the president was a practicing Catholic who regularly attended mass, although some were told that "he has expressed his deep faith in God on many occasions." See WHCF, RM. While a senator, Kennedy told a girl who asked what prayer meant to

him: "I believe that man is created by God with an immortal soul.... [I]t is quite natural that we should turn to Him, our Master, for guidance and relief.... When my crew and I were lost for several days ... I believe that prayers were directly responsible for our finally being rescued" (quoted in G. Darrell Russell Jr., *Lincoln and Kennedy: Looked at Kindly Together* [New York: Carlton, 1973], 39).

22. John F. Kennedy, "Remarks at the 11th Annual Presidential Prayer Breakfast," *Public Papers of the Presidents of the United States, John F. Kennedy, Containing the Public Messages, Speeches, and Statements of the President, 1961–1963,* 3 vols. (Washington, DC: Government Printing Office, 1962–64) (hereafter *PP*), Feb. 7, 1963, 138.

23. JFK to Mrs. J. T. Maynard, Sept. 11, 1961, WHCF, Box 885, RM 1–20–61—5–15–62; JFK to James W. Clark, Apr. 20, 1961, ibid; JFK to Raymond Boyd, Aug. 2, 1961, Box 886, RM 2, Prayers-Prayer Periods, 1–20–61—3–31–62. Several governors promised that they and others would pray daily for Kennedy. E.g., Mark Hatfield to JFK, Feb. 20, 1962; and Norman Erbe to JFK, Feb. 21, 1962, in ibid. During the crisis in Berlin in 1961, Kennedy asked the American people to pray for its successful resolution.

24. Brogan, *Kennedy,* 46; Jim Bishop, *A Day in the Life of President Kennedy* (New York: Random House, 1964).

25. Cushing, "Introduction," 4–5.

26. Russell W. Gibbons, "Catholics and Kennedy," *Nation* 199 (July 13, 1964), inside cover. There is no conclusive evidence that this story is true. Kennedy gave all his salary as president to Catholic, Protestant, Jewish, and interdenominational charities and insisted that these gifts not be publicized. See Kenneth O'Donnell and David F. Powers, Johnny, *We Hardly Knew Ye* (New York: Pocket, 1976), 478.

27. John F. Kennedy, "Remarks at the Dedication Breakfast of International Leadership," *PP*, Feb. 9, 1961, 76.

28. Kennedy, *Times to Remember,* 384.

29. See "J.F.K. as a Theologian," *CC* 80 (May 8, 1963), 631.

30. Tip O'Neill, *Man of the House: The Life and Political Memoirs of Speaker Tip O'Neill* (New York: Random House, 1987), 102.

31. Sorensen, *Kennedy,* 240.

32. John F. Kennedy, "Inaugural Address," *PP*, Jan. 20, 1961, 2–3, first three quotations, 2; last quotation 3.

33. Richard Hutcheson, *God in the White House: How Religion Has Changed the Modern Presidency* (New York: Macmillan, 1988), 54–55, quotation from 54. Two books of Kennedy's biblical quotations were compiled shortly after his death.

34. JFK to Alfred Kunz, Nov. 20, 1961, WHCF, Box 885, RM1, Bibles; JFK to Everett Smith, Oct. 10, 1963, ibid.; JFK to Frank M. Folsom, Oct. 9, 1963, ibid.; quotations in that order.

35. Thomas J. Fleming, "Kennedy the Catholic," *Nation* 198 (June 8, 1964), 571–72, quotations from 572.

36. James Wolfe, "Exclusion, Fusion, or Dialogue: How Should Religion and Politics Relate?" *JCS* 22 (1980), 92–94, first quotation from 92, second from 94.

37. Cogley, "Kennedy," 422–24, first quotation from 422, second from 423, third and fourth from 424.

38. Fletcher Knebel, "What You Don't Know about Kennedy," *Look,* Jan. 7, 1961, 82.

39. Sorensen, *Kennedy,* 28.

40. Benjamin C. Bradlee, *Conversations with Kennedy* (New York: W. W. Norton, 1975), 11.

41. Menendez, *Kennedy*, 94.

42. Reeves, *Character*, 6.

43. Traphes Bryant, *Dog Days at the White House: The Outrageous Memoirs of the Presidential Kennel Keeper* (New York: Macmillan, 1975), esp. 4, 12, 17, 22–25, 35, 40, 62, 66. Cf. West and Kotz, *Upstairs at the White House*, 214–15, 279–82.

44. See Giglio, *Presidency*, 267–69. The literature on this subject is voluminous. See Seymour Hersh, *The Dark Side of Camelot* (Boston: Little, Brown, 1997), 1–12, 294–325, 387–411; Herbert S. Parmet, *JFK: The Presidency of John F. Kennedy* (Norwalk, CT: Easton, 1983), 111–20, 304–7; Reeves, *Character*, 173–74, 322–25; and Richard Reeves, *President Kennedy: Profile of Power* (New York: Simon and Schuster, 1993), 288–93, 315–16. Kennedy also had numerous affairs before becoming president. Additional sources include Judith (Campbell) Exner, *My Story* (New York: Grove, 1977); Anthony Summers, *Goddess: The Secret Lives of Marilyn Monroe* (New York: New American Library, 1986), 239–463; Kitty Kelley, "The Dark Side of Camelot," *People*, Feb. 29, 1988; and Anthony Summers, "Kennedy, the Mafia and Me," London *Sunday Times* magazine, Oct. 6, 1991.

45. Giglio, *Presidency*, 263. The Kennedy family managed to prevent the full story from becoming known until recently. See Dallek, *Unfinished Life*, 33–34, 73–81, 99–105, 117–18, 152–53, 195–97, 281–82, 704–5, and passim.

46. Menendez, *Kennedy*, 73. Hays suggested many of the themes Kennedy used at the three presidential prayer breakfasts he addressed (Hays, Oral Interview).

47. Cardinal Cushing, Oral Interview; Cushing, "Introduction," 5; quotations in that order.

48. Fuchs, *Kennedy*, 189.

49. John F. Kennedy, "History Will Be Our Judge," Jan. 9, 1961, in Jay David, ed., *The Kennedy Reader* (Indianapolis: Bobbs Merrill, 1967), 100.

50. Kennedy, "Dedication Breakfast," 76. Cf. Kennedy, "Message Greeting President Quadros of Brazil . . . ," *PP*, Jan. 31, 1961, 28.

51. John F. Kennedy, "Proclamation of a National Day of Prayer, 1962." Cf. Kennedy, "Proclamation of a National Day of Prayer, 1963."

52. JFK to L. F. Austin, Oct. 2, 1961, WHCF, Box 885, RM 1–20–61—5–15–62.

53. John F. Kennedy, "Remarks at the 11th Annual Prayer Breakfast," *PP*, Feb. 7, 1963, 139.

54. Kennedy, "Inaugural Address," 1. Cf. Kennedy, "Address at Independence Hall, Philadelphia," *PP*, July 4, 1962, 538.

55. JFK to Rabbi Maurice Eisendrath, Nov. 14, 1961, WHCF, Box 887, RM 3–2, Jewish, 1–20–61—9–30–62.

56. John F. Kennedy, "Annual Message to the Congress on the State of the Union," *PP*, Jan. 14, 1963, 19.

57. Kennedy, "Dedication Breakfast," 76.

58. John F. Kennedy, "Proclamation of a National Day of Prayer, 1961," *PP*, 686–87. Cf. Kennedy, "Message . . . [at] the Dedication of the Inter-Faith Chapel, Kings Point, NY," *PP*, May 1, 1961, 342.

59. See his three Thanksgiving Day Proclamations: Oct. 28, 1961, *PP*, 686–87; *PP*, Nov. 7, 1962, 822–23; and *PP*, Nov. 5, 1963, 835–36; and Kennedy, "Proclamation of a National Day of Prayer, 1962," Oct. 11, 1962, *Federal Register*, 27:10147.

60. Sorensen, *Kennedy*, 19.

61. Quoted in James MacGregor Burns, *John Kennedy: A Political Profile* (New York: Harcourt Brace Jovanovich, 1960), 249.

62. John F. Kennedy, "Address... Accepting the Democratic Party Nomination...," July 15, 1960, http://www.jfklibrary.org/j071560.htm.

63. John F. Kennedy, "Remarks at the Romerberg in Frankfurt," *PP*, June 25, 1963, 515–16.

64. Kennedy, "11th Annual Prayer Breakfast," 139.

65. Fuchs, *Kennedy*, 136–41.

66. Ibid., 147. See John Courtney Murray, *We Hold These Truths: Catholic Reflections on the American Proposition* (New York: Shedd and Ward, 1960); Leon Hooper, ed., *Bridging the Sacred and the Secular: Selected Writings of Gustave Weigel* (Washington, DC: Georgetown University Press, 1994); and Robert Drinan et al., *The Wall between Church and State* (Chicago: University of Chicago Press, 1963). For the larger context, see Patrick W. Carey, *The Roman Catholics in America* (Westport, CT: Praeger, 1996), 93–114; and Jay Dolan, *In Search of an American Catholicism: A History of Religion and Culture in Tension* (New York: Oxford University Press, 2002), 157–64, 180–216.

67. Theodore Sorensen's essay, known as the "Bailey Memorandum," argued that because of the distribution of Catholic votes, a Catholic vice president could help the Democrats win. Most Catholic politicians, however, insisted that having a Catholic on the ticket would be a liability in their states. See Sorensen, *Kennedy*, 80–84; "Drive on for a Catholic Vice-President," *CC* 73 (Aug. 15, 1956), 941; and Fletcher Knebel, "Can a Catholic Become Vice President?" *Look* 20 (June 12, 1956), 33–35. A typical Protestant assessment of Kennedy's candidacy is Roy Pearson, "Catholics in Public Office," *CC* 73 (Dec. 12, 1956), 1450–51. See also John C. Bennett, "A Reply to Dean Pearson," ibid., 74 (Jan. 2, 1957), 14; Helen Hill Miller, "A Catholic for President? I—1960 Is Not 1928," *NR* 137 (Nov. 18, 1957), 10–13; "II—Catholic Doctrine and the First Amendment," ibid., Nov. 25, 1957, 10–13; and "III—Public Office and Religious Affiliation," ibid., Dec. 2, 1957, 10–12.

68. See Fletcher Knebel, "Democratic Forecast: A Catholic in 1960," *Look*, Mar. 3, 1959, 14–17. Kennedy issued a public statement explaining that in his remarks "I was simply stating candidly my firmly held belief that a Catholic can serve as President... and fulfill his oath of office with complete fidelity and without reservation." See Pre-Pres., Box 1000, '60 Campaign, Religious Issues Files, Pro-Catholic, Memo on *Look* article. See also Sorensen, *Kennedy*, 109; "A Catholic for President," *CMW* 69 (Mar. 6, 1959), 587–88; and "Aftermath of the Kennedy Statement," ibid., Mar. 20, 1959, 635–36.

69. Quoted in Fuchs, *Kennedy*, 167.

70. E.g., JFK to Rev. Bernard Henninger, July 17, 1959, Pre-Pres., Box 998, '60 Campaign, Religious Issues Files, Religion, General Correspondence. 6–1–59—7–31–59. Cf. JFK to John Stevenson, Jan. 17, 1958, ibid.; and JFK to Rev. Mickey Johnston, Feb. 5, 1958, ibid.

71. Charles Hayes, "Conscience and Public Office," *CC* 77 (May 4, 1960), 545.

72. Quoted in Fuchs, *Kennedy*, 168.

73. John F. Kennedy, "'I Am Not the Catholic Candidate for President," *USN* 48 (May 2, 1960), 90–92.

74. See Sorensen, *Kennedy*, 138–47; Parmet, *JFK*, 38–40; Theodore White, *The Making of a President, 1960* (New York: Atheneum, 1961), 128–29; Peter Collier and David Horowitz, *The Kennedys: An American Drama* (New York: Warner, 1984), 237–38.

75. James A. Pike, "Can a Catholic Be President?" *Life* 47 (Dec. 21, 1959), 79.

76. John A. Mackay, "The Other Side of the 'Catholic Issue,'" *USN* 49 (July 4, 1960), 51. Mackay was responding to an article by Francis J. Lally, "If a Catholic is President," ibid., May 30, 1960, 64–68.

77. "Protestants and a President's Faith," *NW* 55 (Mar. 14, 1960), 33, 36, 38, 40, quotation from 36. See also "A President's Faith," ibid., Mar. 7, 1960, 62; and "Protestants on the Presidency," *CMW* 72 (Apr. 8, 1960), 29.

78. "Catholics and the Presidency," *CMW* 71 (Jan. 1, 1960), 383. Nevertheless, the Catholic press published many articles that presented Kennedy's candidacy favorably. E.g., Raymond Cour, "Catholics in Public Office," *CMW* 72 (Sept. 16, 1960), 491–92; "Who Is the Bigot?" ibid., May 13, 1960, 164.

79. See Parmet, *JFK*, 37–38.

80. Robert Michaelsen, "Religion and the Presidency—II," *CC* 77 (Feb. 10, 1960), 159–61, quotation from 161. See also Michaelsen, "Religion and the Presidency—I," ibid. (Feb. 3, 1960), 133–35.

81. Charles Andrews, "A Catholic President: Pro," *CC* 77 (Oct. 26, 1960), 1241–43. See also *CAC* 20 (Oct. 17, 1960), which featured competing perspectives: Eugene McCarthy, "Why I Will Vote Democrat," 145–48, and Kenneth Keating, "Why I Will Vote Republican," 148–51.

82. Harold Bosley, "A Catholic President: Con," *CC* 77 (Oct. 26, 1960), 1244–47, quotation from 1244.

83. See "Protestant Positions on a Catholic in the White House," *CMW* 72 (Sept. 30, 1960), 11–13. See also Eugene Carson Blake and G. Bromley Oxnam, "Protestant View of a Catholic for President," *Look* 24 (May 10, 1960), 31–34; and "Religious Debate Must Continue," *CC* 77 (May 4, 1960), 533.

84. E.g., "Kennedy and the Catholic Hierarchy," *Christian Heritage*, Mar. 1960; "Campaign: Religion Becomes an Open Issue," *USN* 49 (Sept. 12, 1960), 94.

85. See the issues of *Western Voice* and *Christian Beacon*, summer and fall 1960.

86. See Pre-Pres., '60 Campaign, Religious Issues, Boxes 1018 and 1019, Anti-Catholic Material.

87. Ockenga, "Religion, Politics, and the Presidency," June 5, 1960, Pre-Pres., Box 1021, '60 Campaign, Religious Issues; Criswell, "Religious Freedom, the Church, the State, and Senator Kennedy," July 3, 1960, ibid., Box 1019.

88. Emmett McLoughlin, "Senator Kennedy's Oath," *Baptist Message*, Aug. 11, 1960. Cf. "Kennedy for President? A Catholic Priest Says 'No,'" *Human Events*, July 28, 1960, 1–2.

89. Donald Grey Barnhouse, "The Perils over the Presidency," *Eternity*, Oct. 1960, 8.

90. C. Stanley Lowell, "If the United States Becomes 51% Catholic!" Pre-Pres., Box 1001, '60 Campaign, Religious Issues File. See also "Nixon? Kennedy?" *CC* 77 (Nov. 2, 1960), 1281. For the activities of the POAU during the campaign, see Thomas J. Carty, *A Catholic in the White House: Religion, Politics, and John F. Kennedy's Presidential Campaign* (New York: Palgrave Macmillan, 2004), 69–81.

91. The NAE urged churches to set aside the first prayer meeting of every month to pray for the nation and emphasize the dangers of a Catholic president. They produced special materials for churches to use on either October 23 or 30 to help defeat Kennedy. Protestant pastors were admonished: "We dare not sit idly by—voiceless and voteless—and lose the heritage for which others have died." See "In Times Like These," Pre-Pres., Box 1021, '60 Campaign, Religious Issues, NAE. See also John Pollock, *Billy Graham: Evangelist to the World* (San Francisco: Harper and Row, 1979),

219; and Billy Swift, "Church of God Delegates Vote to Oppose Kennedy," *Commercial Appeal*, Aug. 19, 1960.

92. Charles Clayton Morrison, "Open Letter to Sen. Kennedy," *CT* 4 (Sept. 12, 1960), 32–33, quotations in that order.

93. Graham to Eisenhower, Aug. 4, 1960; Eisenhower Library, PPF 1052. On Graham's role in the election, see Carty, *White House*, 49–58, 64–65.

94. Graham wrote an article for *Life* magazine touting Nixon's strengths, but because of objections from Kennedy's campaign staff, it was not published. Some insist that had the article been published, Nixon would have won. See Billy Graham, *Just as I Am: An Autobiography of Billy Graham* (San Francisco: Harper, 1997), 392–93; Pollock, *Billy Graham*, 219–20; and David Poling, *Why Billy Graham* (Grand Rapids, MI: Zondervan, 1977), 77–78.

95. See *NYT*, Sept. 8, 1960, 25. See also "Catholicism and the Campaign," *CMW* 72 (Sept. 23, 1960), 507–8; Berton Dulce and Edward J. Richter, *Religion and the Presidency: A Recurring Problem* (New York: Macmillan, 1962), 165–71; and Carty, *Catholic in the White House*, 54, 58–63.

96. E.g., on September 11, one hundred religious leaders released a statement asserting that candidates' faith should not be the basis for voting. See "Clergy and Scholars Fight Religious Pleas to Voters," *NYT*, Sept. 12, 1960, 42. James Wine, a judge, Presbyterian elder, and former National Council of Churches executive who advised the Kennedy campaign on religious matters, later declared, "There was no doubt in my mind" that the Houston speech "would make or break us" (James Wine, Oral History, KL). See also Parmet, *JFK*, 42–44; "Kennedy Clarifies Stand to Houston Ministers," *CC* 77 (Sept. 28, 1960), 1109; and "James W. Wine Becomes Kennedy's Aide," ibid., Sept. 7, 1960, 1013.

97. Kennedy's speech is printed in "Both Sides of the 'Catholic Issue,'" *USN* 49 (Sept. 26, 1960), 74–75. Much of the material in this speech was provided by John Cogley, editor of *Commonweal*. See Cogley to JFK, n. d., Pre-Pres., Box 1018, '60 Campaign, Religious Issues, John Cogley.

98. See Patricia Barrett, *Religious Liberty and the American Presidency: A Study in Church-State Relations* (New York: Herder and Herder, 1963), 24–25; "Before the Election," *CMW* 72 (Nov. 11, 1960), 163; "Reformation Sunday," *America*, Nov. 12, 1960, 198; and "The Reformation and the Election," *CC* 77 (Oct. 26, 1960), 1235–36.

99. See also Statement by Rabbi Maurice Eisendrath, President of the Union of American Hebrew Congregations, Sept. 13, 1960, Pre-Pres., Box 1019, '60 Campaign, Religious Issues.

100. Carty, *White House*, 84–97.

101. Winthrop Hudson, "The Religious Issue in the Campaign," *CC* 77 (Oct. 26, 1960), 1239–40. Cf. A. Roy Eckrardt, "When Faith Is Not Faith," CC (Sept. 14, 1960), 1050–52.

102. Discussant: James M. Wall in Herbert D. Rosenbaum and Alexei Ugrinsky, eds., *The Presidency and Domestic Policies of Jimmy Carter* (Westport, CT: Greenwood, 1994), 118. Cf. Garry Wills, *Under God: Religion and American Politics* (New York: Simon and Schuster, 1990), 92.

103. Reinhold Niebuhr, "The Problem of a Protestant Political Ethic," *CC* 77 (Sept. 21, 1960), 1087.

104. See Giglio, *Presidency*, 18; and Louis Bean, "Why Kennedy Won," *Nation* 191 (Nov. 16, 1960), 408–10. Bean argued that many more Republican Catholics voted for Kennedy out of pride than Protestant Democrats voted for Nixon out of prejudice

(410). By contrast, the Survey Research Center of the University of Michigan concluded that Kennedy's Catholicism cost him a net loss of one and a half million votes. See "Religion Was Campaign's Central Phenomenon," *CC* 78 (May 17, 1961), 613–14. More than 70 percent of Catholics and 80 percent of Jews voted for Kennedy. See V. O. Key Jr., *The Responsible Electorate: Rationality in Presidential Voting, 1936–1960* (Cambridge, MA: Belknap, 1966), 118.

105. Carty, *White House*, 127.

106. "Dr. Graham Hails Kennedy Victory," *NYT*, Jan. 17, 1961, 24. Also see Graham, *Just as I Am*, 394–96 and Lowell D. Streiker and Gerald S. Strober, *Religion and the New Majority: Billy Graham, Middle America, and the Politics of the 70s* (New York: Association, 1972), 62.

107. See "End of an Issue?" *NW* 56 (Nov. 28, 1960), 82. The fullest accounts of the religious dimensions of the election of 1960 are Dulce and Richter, *Religion and the Presidency*, 122–221; Carty, *White House*, 49–157; and Barrett, *Religious Liberty*, which contains a sixty-five-page description of campaign materials and an extensive bibliography of contemporary periodical articles. Also helpful are Patricia Barrett, "Religion and the 1960 Presidential Election," *Social Order*, June 1962, 267–85; Sorensen, *Kennedy*, 168–69, 174–77, 186–94; John H. Fenton, *The Catholic Vote* (New Orleans: Hauser, 1960); and James A. Pike and Richard Byfield, *A Roman Catholic in the White House* (Garden City, NY: Doubleday, 1960).

108. E.g., in *Pacem in Terris*, "Pope John XXIII presented to the world a penetrating analysis of today's great problems of social welfare and human rights, of disarmament" and international relations (JFK to William F. Johnson, Apr. 25, 1963, WHCF, Box 886, RM 3–1, Catholic, 1963). Cf. JFK to National Newman Club Federation, July 11, 1963; JFK to Joseph P. Burke Jr., Apr. 25, 1963; JFK to Floyd Anderson, Apr. 23, 1963, both in ibid; and Kennedy, "Remarks . . . at the National Convention of the Catholic Youth Organization," *PP*, Nov. 15, 1963, 859–60.

109. John F. Kennedy, "Statement . . . on the Death of Pope John XXIII," *PP*, June 3, 1963, 433.

110. John F. Kennedy, "Address at the Boston College Centennial Ceremonies," *PP*, Apr. 20, 1963, 336.

111. See Timothy J. Flynn to editor, *Look*, May 17, 1961, WHCF, Box 887, RM 3–1, Catholic, 1961. See also Paul Tanner to Theodore Sorensen, May 12, 1961, ibid.

112. "Church and President," *America*, Jan. 13, 1962, 461.

113. "The Church and Mr. Kennedy," *CMW* 75 (Feb. 9, 1962), 503–4, quotations from 503. A Gallup poll in April found that Catholics favored aid to both public and parochial schools 66 to 28 percent, while Protestants supported aid to public schools only by 63 to 29 percent.

114. Menendez, *Kennedy*, 49.

115. "Catholics Demand Patronage," *CC* 78 (Mar. 22, 1961), 381–82.

116. Menendez, *Kennedy*, 53.

117. E.g., "The President and Rising Pressures for Special Favors to Catholics," *CT* 6 (Feb. 16, 1962), 30; Philip Burton, "Public Funds for Public Schools Only," *CC* 78 (Apr. 5, 1961), 415–17; John C. Bennett, "The Debate on Education and Religion," *CAC* 22 (May 28, 1962), 79; and Maurice Rosenblatt, "Federal Aid to Education," ibid., 81–84. The votes of conservative Democrats and Republicans defeated the bill. Some scholars argue that had Kennedy been willing to compromise with Catholic critics, the bill might have passed, but most contend, given its opposition, the measure could not

have succeeded. See Lawrence J. McAndrews, "Beyond Appearances: Kennedy, Congress, Religion, and Federal Aid to Education," *PSQ* 21 (Summer 1991), 545–57; and Donald C. Lord, *John F. Kennedy: The Politics of Confrontation and Conciliation* (Woodbury, NJ: Barron's, 1977), 113.

118. "Church and President," 461–62. The editorial accused Kennedy of going "out of his way *not* to ingratiate himself with a specifically Catholic constituency" (462). See also "Kennedy and the Clergy," *NW* 59 (Jan. 22, 1962), 48; "Catholic View of J.F.K.," *Time* 79 (Jan. 19, 1962), 58; and "A Catholic Size-Up of Kennedy's First Year," *USN* 52 (Jan. 22, 1962), 53.

119. Hays wrote *This World: A Christian Workshop* (1958) and *A Southern Moderate Speaks* (1959). He was convinced that "a pure religious faith" should direct politics. See Hays to Carlos Camargo, Dec. 3, 1962, BHP, Carton 5, PC, 1962, A-C, Church-State Relations.

120. See Hays to JFK, Jan. 4, 1962, BHP, Files 1962, Box 3, CCF, Jan. 1962.

121. Hays to JFK, June 13, 1962, BHP, Carton 3, 1962 CCF, June 1962. See also Hays to JFK, Sept. 28, 1961, POF, General Correspondence, 1961, HA.

122. E.g., JFK to Caradine Hooton, General Secretary, General Board of Christian Social Concerns of the Methodist Church, Dec. 2, 1961, WHCF, Box 887, RM 3–3, Protestant; Hays to Herman Weinberger, June 26, 1962, BHP, Carton 3, 1962, CCF, June 1962. A study that examined 1,000 appointments to top federal offices and judicial nominations during Kennedy's first year found that 80 percent of appointees were Protestant, 15 percent Catholic, and 5 percent Jewish. See "POAU: No Sectarian Bias in Appointments of President Kennedy," WHCF, Box 885, RM 5–16–62—1–25–63.

123. See Brooks Hays, *Politics Is My Parish: An Autobiography* (Baton Rouge: Louisiana State University, 1981), 224–26.

124. See John F. Kennedy, "Remarks on Greeting the Representatives of the Baptist World Alliance," *PP*, Feb. 2, 1961, 53; M. Chandler Stith to JFK, Feb. 6, 1961, WHCF, Box 887, RM 3–3, Protestant; Kennedy, "Remarks at . . . the Protestant Council of the City of New York," *PP*, Nov. 8, 1963, 838–42.

125. See Billy Graham, "It's Later Than You Think, Sermon," 1961, 2; the quotation is from Richard Pierard, "Billy Graham and the U.S. Presidency," *JCS* 22 (Winter 1980), 121. See also Pollock, *Billy Graham*, 167; and Marshall Frady, *Billy Graham, A Parable for American Righteousness* (Boston: Little, Brown, 1979), 258–59.

126. "Kennedy and the Clergy," 48. Ramsay Pollard, a former president of the Southern Baptist Convention, judged his performance in the area of church-state relations as "excellent." John Bennett of Union Theological Seminary in New York declared that Kennedy had "shown that a Catholic layman" could be "quite independent." Eugene Carson Blake, stated clerk of the Presbyterian Church, argued that he had demonstrated that a Catholic could "govern constitutionally."

127. "Changing Times," *NW* 61 (Mar. 4, 1963), 77.

128. "A Notable Record," *CC* 79 (Jan. 24, 1962), 99. See also "The President's Performance," *CC* 79 (Apr. 11, 1962), 462–63; and "President Allays Protestant Fears," ibid. 78 (Oct. 11, 1961), 1196.

129. General Synod of the Bible Presbyterian Church, Resolution No. 6, Oct. 19, 1962, WHCF, Box 887, RM 3–2, 1963. See also Carl McIntire to Ralph A. Dungan, July 30, 1963, ibid., Box 886, RM3: "we do not believe the President adheres either to the principles . . . [or] the practices" of the separation of church and state." See Kennedy, "Message . . . on . . . the Opening of the Second Vatican Council," *PP*, Oct. 5, 1962, 733–34.

130. See WHCF, Box 885, RM2–1–63—2–20–63. Dungan responded that Kennedy had directed agencies concerned with these issues to make "every effort to conform their activities to the constitutional principles" (Dungan to Donald Gill, Feb. 12, 1963, ibid.).

131. E.g., Feldman to Irwin Herrman, Sept. 27, 1962, WHCF, Box 887, RM 3–2, 1962.

132. See "Rabbi Blasts Israel['s] Claims on Jews in the U.S.," *Chicago Daily Tribune*, Aug. 20, 1962.

133. Letter to Peter Has, Nov. 1, 1963, WHCF, Box 887, RM 3–2, 1963.

134. See John F. Kennedy, "Remarks to . . . the National Conference of Christians and Jews," *PP*, Nov. 21, 1961, 736–37; Kennedy, "Remarks to . . . the Union of American Hebrew Congregations," *PP*, Nov. 13, 1961, 715–16; JFK to Rabbi Maurice Eisendrath, Nov. 14, 1961, WHCF, Box 887, RM 3–2, Jewish, 1–20–61—9–30–62; JFK to Max Bressler, June 28, 1962, ibid.; and JFK to Eisendrath, Nov. 20, 1963, ibid., 1963.

135. Quoted in Russell W. Gibbons, "Conflicts in Catholicism," *Nation* 195 (Dec. 8, 1962), 393.

136. *NYT*, June 27, 1962.

137. "Black Monday Decision," *America* 107 (July 7, 1962), 456. Cf. Knights of Columbus of Rockville Centre, NY, to Kennedy, July 17, 1962, WHCF, Box 886, RM2/ED 7–25–62—8–31–62.

138. The McIntyre and Graham quotations are in the *NYT*, June 26, 1962. See also Streiker and Strober, *New Majority*, 62.

139. Quoted in *Washington Newsletter* of the American Jewish Committee, Sept. 20, 1962, 1.

140. Resolution of the Kiwanis Club of Costa Mesa, CA, to JFK, July 25, 1962, WHCF, Box 886, RM 2/ED, 7/25/62–8/31/62.

141. A. D. Holt to JFK, Aug. 6, 1962, WHCF, Box 886, RM 2/ED, 7/25/62–8/31/62.

142. Resolution on Religious Freedom, WHCF Box 885, RM 9–11–62—1–31–63. Cf. Resolution of the Fort Lauderdale Junior Chamber of Commerce, WHCF Box 886, RM2/ED 1–20–61—7–13–62.

143. Donald Collins to JFK, June 28, 1962, WHCF Box 886, RM2/ED 1–20–61—7–13–62.

144. Letters to JFK, June 26 and June 29, 1962, WHCF, Box 886, RM2/ED 1–20–61—7–13–62.

145. E.g., William D. James to JFK, July 4, 1962,WHCF, Box 886, RM2/ED 1–20–61—7–13–62 and Wade H. Hutto Jr. to JFK, July 2, 1962, ibid.

146. "The President's News Conference," *PP*, June 27, 1962, 510–11. See Harold Siegel to JFK, June 28, 1962, WHCF, Box 886, RM 2/ED, 1–20–61—7–13–62; Ted Baer to JFK, June 28, 1962, ibid; "Religion in Our Public Schools," *Alabama Baptist*, July 12, 1962, 1; John Pemberton Jr., Executive Director, ACLU, to JFK, June 29, 1962, WHCF, Box 886, RM 2/ED, 7/25/62–8/31/62; and National Council Community Relations Advisory Council *News*, June 28, 1962, 1–2.

147. Menendez, *Kennedy*, 57.

148. Floyd Quigg to JFK, June 30, 1962, WHCF, Box 886, RM 2/ED, 7/25/62–8/31/62.

149. "Prayer in the Public School," *Baptist Standard*, July 6, 1962.

150. Robert Hoyt, *The Catholic Reporter*, Appendix to "Statement of the American Jewish Committee . . . on the proposed amendment . . . to permit prayers in the public schools," WHCF, Box 886, RM2/ED 9–1–62—, v.

151. Appendix to ibid., vii, viii; quotations in that order.

152. "Prayer Is Personal," *NYT*, June 27, 1962. See "Editorial Opinion Supporting the U.S. Supreme Court Decision on Prayer in the Public Schools," WHCF, Box 886, RM2/ED 9–1-62.

153. E.g., Statement by Rabbi Alvin I. Fine, June 29, 1962, WHCF, Box 886, RM 2/ ED, 7/25/62–8/31/62.

154. See Robert S. Alley, *School Prayer: The Court, the Congress, and the First Amendment* (Buffalo, NY: Prometheus, 1994), 107–26; and Albert Menendez, *School Prayer and Other Religious Issues in American Public Education: A Bibliography* (New York: Garland, 1985).

155. Quoted in Arthur Schlesinger Jr., *A Thousand Days: John F. Kennedy in the White House* (Boston: Houghton Mifflin, 1965), 106.

156. Kennedy, "Christians and Jews," 736–37.

157. Hutcheson, *White House*, 52.

158. Schlesinger, *Thousand Days*, 107–8. John F. Quinn argues that Kennedy and Murray "inhabited different worlds and differed sharply on certain political questions." Kennedy was a strict separationist who opposed federal aid to parochial schools, while Murray advocated cooperation between civil and religious institutions and supported aid. See Quinn, "John Courtney Murray, SJ: The Man JFK Didn't Understand," *Crisis* 17 (Oct. 1999), 32–37.

159. Robert Alley, *So Help Me God: Religion and the Presidency, Wilson to Nixon* (Richmond, VA: John Knox, 1972), 96, 98, quotation from 96; Andrew M. Greeley, *The Catholic Experience* (Garden City, NY: Doubleday, 1967), 289; Tom Wicker, *JFK and LBJ: The Influence of Personality upon Politics* (New York: William Morrow, 1968), 124.

160. John F. Kennedy, "Foreword," in Theodore C. Sorensen, *Decision-Making in the White House: The Olive Branch or the Arrows* (New York: Columbia University Press, 1963), xii.

161. Menendez, *Kennedy*, 77.

162. Sorensen, *Kennedy*, 21–22; Reeves, *Profile*, 19.

163. Schlesinger, *Thousand Days*, 111.

164. Reeves, *Character*, 414–15, first quotation from 414, the rest from 415.

165. Giglio, *Presidency*, 29.

166. Reeves, *Character*, 414.

167. John F. Kennedy, "Speech at Wittenberg College Stadium," Oct. 17, 1960, quoted in Settel, ed., *Faith of JFK*, 18.

168. Gerald T. Rice, *The Bold Experiment: JFK's Peace Corps* (Notre Dame, IN: University of Notre Dame Press, 1985), ix.

169. E.g., John F. Kennedy, "Remarks on the Forthcoming Presidential Election," Sept. 3, 1960; and Kennedy, "Speech at the Civil Auditorium, Oakland, CA," Sept. 8, 1960, in Settel, ed., *Faith of JFK*, 10, 12.

170. Kennedy, Thanksgiving Proclamation, Oct. 28, 1961, 686–87; Kennedy, "Remarks Connected with the United Nations Freedom from Hunger Campaign," *PP*, Nov. 22, 1961, 740–41; Kennedy, "Remarks upon Proclaiming Voluntary Overseas Aid Week," *PP*, Apr. 9, 1962, 311.

171. John F. Kennedy, "Speech before the Irish Parliament," *PP*, June 28, 1963, 537.

172. John F. Kennedy, "Statement [on] the Jewish High Holy Days," *PP*, Sept. 14, 1962, 682.

173. Quoted in Coates Redmon, *Come as You Are: The Peace Corps Story* (New York: Harcourt Brace Jovanovich, 1986), 19–20.

174. See John F. Kennedy, "Statement...upon...Establishing the Peace Corps," *PP*, Mar. 1, 1961, 134–35; and Kennedy, "Special Message to the Congress on the Peace Corps," ibid., 143–46. On the origins of the Peace Corps, see Rice, *The Bold Experiment*, 32–90; and Sargent Shriver, "The Vision" in Milton Viorst, *Making a Difference: The Peace Corps at Twenty-Five* (New York: Weidenfeld and Nicolson, 1986), 15–24.

175. E.g., "President Recommends Expansion of the Peace Corps," *Department of State Bulletin* 49 (July 29, 1963), 171.

176. Giglio, *Presidency*, 156–58; David Hapgood and Meridan Bennett, *Agents of Change: A Close Look at the Peace Corps* (Boston: Little, Brown, 1968); Kevin Lowther and C. Payne Lucas, *Keeping Kennedy's Promise: The Peace Corps, Unmet Hope of the New Frontier* (Boulder, CO: Westview, 1978).

177. Ensworth Reisner, "Peace Corps," Mar. 19, 1961, WHCF, #670, PCS, 3-8-61–4-19-61. Numerous ministers wrote Kennedy supporting the program. E.g., Dean Kindy to JFK, Feb. 2, 1961, WHCF, #670, PCS, 1-24-61–3-7-61.

178. See Glenn Everett to Brooks Hays, BHP, Carton 14, PC, 1963, p-2, File: Religious News Service.

179. Religious News Service, Aug. 30, 1963; Streiker and Strober, *New Majority*, 62. In their funeral sermons, numerous ministers praised the Peace Corps as one of Kennedy's greatest accomplishments. E.g., C. L. Seasholes, Funeral Sermon, Charles Stewart Papers (hereafter CSP), KL, Box 1, Baptist, Folder 1; David S. Evans, "John Kennedy Memorial Sermon," 2, CSP, Box 3, Methodist, Folder 4.

180. Fuchs, *Kennedy*, 231. See also Fuchs, *"Those Peculiar Americans": The Peace Corps and National Character* (New York: Meredith, 1967), passim.

181. Samuel Proctor, "Foreword," in Roger D. Armstrong, *Peace Corps and Christian Mission* (New York: Friendship, 1965), 7–10, quotation from 7.

182. Giglio, *Presidency*, 159.

183. Schlesinger, *Thousand Days*, 930.

184. Frustrated Americans reminded Kennedy of this promise by flooding the White House with pens in 1961 (Giglio, *Presidency*, 171–72).

185. John F. Kennedy, "Special Message to the Congress on Civil Rights," *PP*, Feb. 28, 1963, 221–30, quotation from 222.

186. John F. Kennedy, "Television Address to the People," June 11, 1963, in Kennedy, *The Burden and the Glory*, Allan Nevins, ed. (New York: Harper and Row, 1964), 181–85; first two quotations from 181, remainder from 182.

187. "JFK in the Bully Pulpit," *NW* 61 (June 24, 1963), 27.

188. E.g., John F. Kennedy, "Statement...on the March on Washington for Jobs and Freedom," *PP*, Aug. 28, 1963, 645.

189. JFK to Mays, Jan. 10, 1963, WHCF, Box 360, HU 2, 12–26–62—6–20–63.

190. Reeves, *Profile*, 62.

191. Schlesinger, *Thousand Days*, 806. Polls in 1963 showed he lost six or seven white votes for every black vote he gained (Reeves, *Profile*, 626).

192. Theodore Hesburgh, Oral History, KL 9, 16, 23–24.

193. "Thoughts for the Proposed Presidential Meeting with Religious Leaders," undated, Personal Papers of Robert Kennedy, Attorney General's Correspondence, Box 11, Folder: Civil Rights: Meeting with Religious Leaders, 6–17–63. See also Louis Oberdorfer, Memorandum to Robert Kennedy, June 17, 1963; and Ralph A. Dungan, Memorandum for the President, June 14, 1963, both in ibid.

194. John F. Kennedy, "Annual Message to the Congress on the State of the Union," *PP*, Jan. 11, 1962, 8.

195. John F. Kennedy, "Remarks at a Dinner Given in His Honor by President Segni," *PP*, July 1, 1963, 549.

196. Reeves, *Power*, 356.

197. See Lord, *Kennedy*, 162–64.

198. Reinhold Niebuhr, "Tribute," in William M. Fine, ed., *That Day with God* (New York: McGraw Hill, 1965), 89.

199. Daniel J. Callahan, "Sin, Power and Politics," *CMW* 73 (Feb. 17, 1961), 529.

200. The first phrase is that of Eugene McCarthy, *The Limits of Power* (New York: Dell, 1968), 29; the second is that of Fuchs, *Kennedy*, 213.

201. Kennedy, "Dedication Breakfast," 77. Cf. Kennedy, "Remarks at the 10th Annual Presidential Prayer Breakfast," *PP*, Mar. 1, 1962, 175: "religion is not an instrument of the cold war."

202. John F. Kennedy, "Speech at the Civic Auditorium, Seattle," Sept. 6, 1960, in *Quotations from the Scriptures by John Fitzgerald Kennedy* (New York: Catholic Family Library, 1965), 1.

203. John F. Kennedy, "Address...to the Greater Houston Ministerial Association," Sept. 12, 1960, http://www.jfklibrary.org/j091260.htm.

204. John F. Kennedy, "Remarks at the Pageant of Peace Ceremonies," *PP*, Dec. 17, 1962, 888. Cf. Kennedy, "Speech at a Bonds for Israel Dinner," Oct. 31, 1960, in Settel, ed., *Faith*, 24.

205. John F. Kennedy, "Address...before the General Assembly of the United Nations," *PP*, Sept. 25, 1961, 626.

206. John F. Kennedy, "Special Message to the Congress on Urgent National Needs," *PP*, May 25, 1961, 406.

207. John F. Kennedy, "Proclamation of a Prayer for Peace, Memorial Day, 1963," Apr. 26, 1963, *Federal Register*, 4279.

208. John F. Kennedy, "Remarks Prepared for Delivery at the Trade Mart in Dallas," *PP*, Nov. 22, 1963, 894. Cf. Kennedy, "Address at the University of Washington's 100th Anniversary Program," *PP*, Nov. 16, 1961, 725.

209. Glenn Seaborg, *Kennedy, Khrushchev and the Test Ban* (Berkeley: University of California Press, 1981), 32–33. On the limited test ban treaty, also see Norman Cousins, *The Improbable Triumvirate: John F. Kennedy, Pope John, Nikita Khrushchev* (New York: W. W. Norton, 1972); Robert Divine, *Blowing on the Wind: The Nuclear Test Ban Debate, 1954–1960* (New York: Oxford University Press, 1978); Michael Beschloss, *The Crisis Years: Kennedy and Khrushchev, 1960–1963* (New York: Edward Burlingame, 1991); and Carl Kaysen, "The Limited Test-Ban Treaty of 1963," in Douglas Brinkley and Richard T. Griffiths, eds., *John F. Kennedy and Europe* (Baton Rouge: Louisiana State University Press, 1999), 95–113.

210. Kennedy, "Inaugural Address," 2.

211. Kennedy, "United Nations," 618, 620, quotations from 620.

212. Bernard J. Firestone, "Kennedy and the Test Ban: Presidential Leadership and Arms Control," in Brinkley and Griffiths, eds., *John F. Kennedy*, 72.

213. Schlesinger, *Thousand Days*, 892–93.

214. See U.S. Congress, Senate Committee on Armed Forces, Preparedness Investigating Subcommittee, *Hearings: Military Aspects and Implications of Nuclear Test Ban Proposals and Related Matters*, 88th Congress, 1st sess. 1963, 21–44.

215. "The President's News Conference" *PP*, Mar. 21, 1963, 280; Schlesinger, *Thousand Days*, 897.

216. Reeves, *Power*, 512.

217. Schlesinger, *Thousand Days*, 900.

218. The first quotation is from Schlesinger, *Thousand Days*, 909; the second is from Lord, *Kennedy*, 211.

219. "JFK in the Bully Pulpit," 27.

220. John F. Kennedy, "Commencement Address at American University," *PP*, June 10, 1963, 459–65.

221. Giglio, *Presidency*, 217.

222. J. Irwin Miller and Ernest A. Gross to JFK, July 11, 1963, BHP, Carton 14, PC, 1962, P-2, RM.

223. John F. Kennedy, "Radio and Television Address...on the Nuclear Test Ban Treaty," *PP*, July 26, 1963, 602. Kennedy insisted that the treaty would help reduce world tension and provide "broader areas of agreement," help free the world "from the fears and dangers of radioactive fallout," help prevent nuclear proliferation, and increase America's security (602–5). In "Special Message to the Senate on the Nuclear Test Ban Treaty," *PP*, Aug. 8, 1963, 622–24, Kennedy explains ten benefits of the treaty.

224. John F. Kennedy, "Address Before the 18th General Assembly of the United Nations," *PP*, Sept. 20, 1963, 695, 698, quotation from 698.

225. Schlesinger, *Thousand Days*, 910–11.

226. Niebuhr, "Tribute," 89.

227. Pierre Salinger, *With Kennedy* (Garden City, NY: Doubleday, 1966), 364.

228. Firestone, "Test Ban," 66–67.

229. Wolfe, "Exclusion," 96.

230. Henry Fairlie, *The Kennedy Promise* (Garden City, NY: Doubleday, 1973), 254.

231. Wolfe, "Exclusion," 98.

232. See William Manchester, *The Death of a President* (New York: Harper and Row, 1967), 562. See also Bradley S. Greenberg and Edwin Parker, eds., *The Kennedy Assassination and the American Public* (Stanford, CA: Stanford University Press, 1965).

233. Theodore A. Daniel, "In Memoriam: John Fitzgerald Kennedy," *Trinity Lutheran* 12 (Dec. 1963), 7. "[W]e know that he believed in God,...confessed Christ as Lord and Savior, knew the power of prayer,...trusted in God's gracious providence, and looked to eternal life."

234. Harvey T. Whaley, Funeral Sermon, CSP, Box 1, Baptist, 4. Cf. Ward B. Hurlburt, Funeral Sermon, ibid.

235. Evans, "Kennedy Memorial Sermon," 2.

236. Alvin I. Fine, "A Thanksgiving Day Sermon," in Charles Stewart and Bruce Kendall, eds., *A Man Named John F. Kennedy: Sermons on His Assassination* (Glen Rock, NJ: Paulist, 1964), 144. The 25 sermons in this book were chosen from the 850 submitted from all fifty states, representing nineteen denominations (10–11).

237. John Mark Kinney, "Hate," in Stewart and Kendall, eds., *Kennedy*, 43.

238. Charles J. Dollen, Eulogy, 3, CSP, Box 1, Catholic, Folder 4.

239. See also Richard Cardinal Cushing, " 'Foretaste of Eternity,' " *Boston Pilot*, Jan. 25, 1964; and Cushing, "Eulogy," Stewart and Kendall, eds., *Kennedy*, 18.

240. Norman Vincent Peale, Funeral sermon, in Fine, ed., *That Day*, 74. This collection of 64 sermons and tributes was pared down from more than 300 selections. It overlaps little with Stewart and Kendall's book.

241. E.g., Joseph Champlin, "President John F. Kennedy," 1, CSP, Box 1, Catholic, Folder 4.

242. Louis Valbracht, "One Martyr in the March," 1, CSP, Box 3, Lutheran, Folder 1.

243. Leroy C. Hodapp, "Reflections on the Death of John F. Kennedy," Stewart and Kendall, eds., *Kennedy*, 126. See also Barry M. Carter, "Where Is Your Brother?" ibid., 84; Colman Colloty, Funeral sermon, CSP, Box 1, Catholic, Folder 5; and William H. Dickson, "Living Out Our Faith," Fine, ed., *That Day*, 8.

244. Quotation from Pius Liu, Funeral sermon, 3, CSP, Box 1, Catholic, Folder 3. See also John J. Flynn, "President Kennedy," ibid.; and Cushing, "Eulogy," 18.

245. James Harris, Funeral sermon, CSP, Box 1, Baptist; Charles Trentham, "Who Caused Our President's Death?" ibid.; and John M. Riley, "Our President," CSP, Box 1, Christian.

246. Niebuhr, "Tribute," 89.

247. Gilbert E. Hoffman, "Eulogy on . . . President John F. Kennedy," 1, CSP, Box 3, Methodist, Folder 4.

248. Harris, Funeral sermon, 2. Cf. Joseph B. Courtney, "Oh God, No!" in Stewart and Kendall, eds., *Kennedy*, 49; Wallace E. Fisher, "John F. Kennedy: Man and Leader," ibid., 185–86; and Dollen, Eulogy, 2.

249. E.g., Grayson Kirk, Memorial Address, in Fine, ed., *That Day*, 83–84; and George M. Docherty, Funeral sermon, ibid., 200–1.

250. Arthur L. Slaikeu, "A Profile of Courage," CSP, Box 1, Baptist, 2; Erwin Knitt, Funeral sermon, CSP, Box 3, Lutheran, Folder 1.

251. Thomas Parry Jones, "An American Tragedy," in Stewart and Kendall, eds., *Kennedy*, 91.

252. Hodapp, "Reflections on . . . Kennedy," 122.

253. Harry B. Scholefield, Funeral sermon, CSP, Box 5, Unitarian.

254. Hubert L. Black, "Sow the Wind," 1–2, CSP, Box 4, Presbyterian, Folder 1.

255. Carter, "Where Is Your Brother?" 80. Cf. William F. O'Brien, Funeral sermon, in Fine, ed., *That Day*, 16.

256. Eugene Ensley, "Why Our President Died," 2, CSP, Box 4, Presbyterian, Folder 1.

257. E.g., Fisher, "Kennedy," 188.

258. Francis Robert Otto, "A Call to Repentance," in Stewart and Kendall, eds., *Kennedy*, 202–5, quotation from 202.

259. Courtney, "Oh God, No!" 48. See also Daniel, "In Memoriam," 7; Hoffman, "Eulogy," 2; Peale, Funeral sermon, 76; and John S. Kennedy, Funeral sermon, in Fine, ed., *That Day with God*, 103.

260. William S. Findley, "Why God, Why?" in Stewart and Kendall, eds., *Kennedy*, 95.

261. Knitt, Funeral sermon, 1; Findley, "Why God, Why?" 101.

262. Daniel, "In Memoriam," 7; Stanley Rabinowitz, "Out of Evil a Blessing," in Stewart and Kendall, eds., *Kennedy*, 25; Peale, Funeral sermon, 77.

263. E.g., Black, "Sow the Wind," 1; Thomas A. Fry Jr., Funeral sermon, 1, CSP, Box 4, Presbyterian, Folder 1; Harold Joppido, Funeral sermon, CSP, Box 1, Catholic, Folder 4; and Dickinson, "Living Out Our Faith," 13.

264. Rabinowitz, "A Blessing," 28, 32.

265. Michael Ramsey, Funeral sermon, in Fine, ed., *That Day*, 55.

266. William J. Rupp, Memorial Address, 2, CSP, Box 4, UCC, Congregational; William D. Goble, "Ask . . . What You Can Do for Your Country," CSP, Box 1, Baptist,

Folder 1; Hodapp, "Reflections on . . . Kennedy," 127; Fine, "A Thanksgiving Day Sermon," 140.

267. Marshall H. Strickland, Funeral sermon, in Fine, ed., *That Day*, 181. Cf. Charles S. Hartman, "Blessed Are They That Mourn," Stewart and Kendall, eds., *Kennedy*, 66.

268. Dickinson, "Living Out Our Faith," 10–13; Kirk, Memorial Address, 85–87; Arthur Goldberg, Eulogy, in Fine, ed., *That Day*, 208.

269. Arthur Schlesinger Jr., "A Eulogy: John Fitzgerald Kennedy," *Saturday Evening Post* 236 (Dec. 14, 1963), 32a.

270. Giglio, *Presidency*, 1.

271. Laura Bergquist and Stanley Tretick, *A Very Special President* (New York: McGraw-Hill, 1965), 2. Cf. Reeves, *Character*, 4.

272. Schlesinger, *Thousand Days*, 1030–31, quotation from 1031. See also "Beyond the Generations," *USN*, Oct. 24, 1988, 33; and "John F. Kennedy: In Memoriam," *Nation* 197 (Dec. 14, 1963), 404.

273. Sorensen, *Kennedy*, 756–57, quotations from 757.

274. Parmet, *JFK*, 352. See also "An Intelligent, Courageous Presidency," *Life*, Nov. 29, 1963; and "A Tragedy for the World," *Manchester Guardian*, Nov. 23, 1963, in David, *Kennedy Reader*, 417–19. For more recent positive assessments, see Ralph G. Martin, *A Hero for Our Time: An Intimate Story of the Kennedy Years* (New York: Macmillan, 1983); Kenneth Thompson, ed., *The Kennedy Years: Seventeen Intimate Perspectives of John F. Kennedy* (Lanham, MD: University Press of America, 1985); and Irving Bernstein, *Promises Kept: John F. Kennedy's New Frontier* (New York: Oxford University Press, 1991).

275. Cogley, "Kennedy," 424.

276. Menendez, *Kennedy*, 106, 85, 108; first and last quotations from 106, second from 85, third from 108.

277. Giglio, *Presidency*, 1. See also Donald W. Jackson and James W. Riddlesperger, *Presidential Leadership and Civil Rights Policy* (Westport, CT: Greenwood, 1995).

278. Reeves, *Character*, 417.

279. Parmet, *JFK*, 352.

280. Reeves, *Character*, 418–20, quotations in that order.

281. Hersh, *Dark Side*, ix.

282. Fuchs, *Kennedy*, 227–35. See also Francis J. Lally, *The Catholic Church in a Changing America* (Boston: Little, Brown, 1962).

283. Fleming, "Kennedy the Catholic," 572. Cf. James O'Gara, "A Catholic in the White House," *CMW* 73 (Feb. 10, 1961), 498.

284. Cogley, "Kennedy," 423.

285. Menendez, *Kennedy*, 108.

286. Champlin, "Kennedy," 2–3.

287. "Love, Hatred and Politics," *CC* 80 (Nov. 20, 1963), 1423.

288. Cogley, "Kennedy," 423.

289. Menendez, *Kennedy*, 80–81.

290. Ted Schwarz, *Joseph P. Kennedy: The Mogel, the Mob, the Statesman, and the Making of an American Myth* (New York: Wiley, 2003), 133–61, 163–68, and passim.

291. Dallek, *Unfinished Life*, 706, argues that Kennedy "probably rationalized his behavior as a diversion comparable with what British aristocrats did, or with the golf, sailing, and fishing presidents traditionally used to ease tensions."

292. Giglio, *Presidency*, 270.

293. Menendez, *Kennedy*, 80.

294. Burns, *Kennedy*, 237–58. See also Hayes, "Conscience and Public Office," 545.

295. Menendez, *Kennedy*, 102. On Kennedy's compartmentalization, see also Reeves, *Profile*, 19.

296. Fuchs, *Kennedy*, 205.

CHAPTER 9

1. Jimmy Carter, *Why Not the Best?* (Nashville, TN: Broadman, 1975), 171–73. On Carter's religious background and views, see Carter, *Living Faith* (New York: Random House, 1996), 16–35, 203–17; Howard Norton and Bob Slosser, *The Miracle of Jimmy Carter* (Plainfield, NJ: Logos International, 1976); David Kucharsky, *The Man from Plains: The Mind and Spirit of Jimmy Carter* (New York: Harper and Row, 1976); Niels C. Nielsen Jr., *The Religion of President Carter* (Nashville, TN: Thomas Nelson, 1977); James Hefley and Marti Hefley, *The Church That Produced a President* (New York: Wyden, 1977); William Lee Miller, *Yankee from Georgia* (New York: New York Times Books, 1978); James T. Baker, *A Southern Baptist in the White House* (Philadelphia: Westminster, 1977); Kandy Stroud, *How Jimmy Won: The Victory Campaign from Plains to the White House* (New York: William Morrow, 1977), 159–69; Leo P. Ribuffo, "God and Jimmy Carter," in M. L. Bradbury and James B. Gilbert, eds., *Transforming Faith: The Sacred and Secular in Modern American History* (Westport, CT: Greenwood, 1989), 141–59; and Peter G. Bourne, *Jimmy Carter: A Comprehensive Biography from Plains to Post Presidency* (New York: Scribner's, 1997), 31ff., 167–79.

2. E. Brooks Holifield, "The Three Strands of Jimmy Carter's Religion," *NR* (June 5, 1976), 15–17, quotations from 15, 17.

3. Burns Stanfield, "Faith and Politics in the Presidency of Jimmy Carter," M. Div. thesis, Harvard University Divinity School, 1988, 14. Carter later labeled *Reinhold Niebuhr on Politics* (1960) his "political Bible" (Bourne, *Carter*, 171). See also Miller, *Yankee*, 201–25. Before becoming president, Carter read *Justice and Mercy* (1974), a collection of Niebuhr's later sermons and prayers, and June Bingham's *Courage to Change: An Introduction to the Thought of Reinhold Niebuhr* (1972). Carter frequently quoted Niebuhr.

4. Carter, *Living Faith*, 110. See also Kenneth Morris, *Jimmy Carter: American Moralist* (Athens: University of Georgia Press, 1996), 8, 19, 213, 238–39.

5. Ribuffo, "Jimmy Carter," 148. See also Miller, *Yankee*, 193; Wesley Pippert, comp., *The Spiritual Journey of Jimmy Carter in His Own Words* (New York: Macmillan, 1978), 164–65, 186, 192–93, 202–4.

6. E.g., Carter, *Living Faith*, 24–27.

7. Carter had some personal contact with Hatfield and Hughes about matters of politics and faith, but there is no evidence that he read their books. See the Hatfield, Hughes, and Henry files at the Jimmy Carter Library (hereafter CL). See also Robert Eells and Bartell Nyberg, *Lonely Walk: The Life of Senator Mark Hatfield* (Chappaqua, NY: Christian Herald, 1979); Mark Hatfield, *Between a Rock and a Hard Place* (Waco, TX: Word, 1976); Harold Hughes, *The Man from Ida Grove: A Senator's Personal Story*, with Dick Schneider (Lincoln, VA: Chosen, 1979); Carl F. H. Henry, *Aspects of Christian Social Ethics* (Grand Rapids, MI: Eerdmans, 1964); John B. Anderson, *Between Two Worlds: A Congressman's Choice* (Grand Rapids, MI: Zondervan, 1970); and

Steven V. Monsma, *The Unraveling of America* (Downer's Grove, IL: InterVarsity, 1974). Carter also apparently had minimal knowledge of the work of other leading evangelicals who wrote about political life: Paul Henry, Richard Mouw, Richard V. Pierard, James Skillen, Bob Goudzwaard, or John H. Yoder. Carter's presidential library contains only a handful of letters he wrote to evangelicals indicating that their sermons, books, or conversations had been helpful to him.

8. "Religion and the Presidency," National Religious Broadcasters, Oct. 14, 1976, in *The Presidential Campaign, 1976*, 5 vols. (Washington, DC: U.S. Government Printing Office, 1978–79) (hereafter *PC*), Part Two, 965. See also Kucharsky, *Man from Plains*, 67; and Carter, *Living Faith*, 16. The two best discussions of Carter's faith and his presidency are Richard Hutcheson, *God in the White House: How Religion Has Changed the Modern Presidency* (New York: Macmillan, 1988), 114–51; and Richard V. Pierard and Robert D. Linder, *Civil Religion and the Presidency* (Grand Rapids, MI: Zondervan, 1988), 231–56.

9. Interview with Bill Moyers, Public Broadcasting Service, May 6, 1976, in Jimmy Carter, *A Government as Good as Its People* (New York: Simon and Schuster, 1977), 90.

10. E.g., Jimmy Carter, "Remarks and a Question-and-Answer Session at a Town Meeting," Mar. 24, 1979, in *Public Papers of the Presidents of the United States, Jimmy Carter, 1977–1981*, 4 vols. (Millwood, NY: Kraus International, 1983) (hereafter *PP*), 472.

11. The services at Camp David were usually conducted by army or navy chaplains from one of the nearby bases. See Robert L. Maddox, *Preacher at the White House* (Nashville, TN: Broadman, 1984), 21; and Carter, *Living Faith*, 130.

12. Interview with Moyers, 88. Cf. Carter, *Living Faith*, 98.

13. "Religion and the Presidency," 967, 966.

14. Jimmy Carter, "Speech to National Religious Broadcasters," Jan. 21, 1980, *PP*, 181. He added, "I do pray a lot every day, as I move from one event to another" (183). See also Robert Maddox (hereafter RLM) to Anne Wexler (hereafter AW), memorandum for the president, Jan. 18, 1980, CL; Remarks to Religious Broadcasters, President's White House File, Jan. 21, 1980 [1] Box 165, CL. For examples of Carter's commitment to prayer while president, see his *Keeping Faith: Memoirs of a President* (New York: Bantam, 1982), 298, 317, 319, 331.

15. Carter, *Living Faith*, 104–5.

16. Jimmy Carter, "Remarks at the Meeting of the General Council," Nov. 2, 1977, *PP*, 1953; Carter, "Remarks and Question and Answer Session at a Town Meeting," Oct. 21, 1980, *PP*, 2386, quotations in that order.

17. Jimmy Carter, "Remarks and a Question-and-Answer Session at a Town Meeting with New Hampshire High School Students," Feb. 18, 1978, *PP*, 370.

18. Carter, "National Religious Broadcasters," 181.

19. See Nielsen, *Religion of President Carter*, 117–27; George D. Kelsey, *Social Ethics among Southern Baptists, 1917–1969* (Metuchen, NJ: Scarecrow, 1973); and Robert A. Baker, *The Southern Baptist Convention and Its People, 1607–1972* (Nashville, TN: Broadman, 1974).

20. Robert Scheer, "Jimmy, We Hardly Know Y'All," in *PC* I, Part 2, 960–61.

21. Some evangelicals complained that Carter's views of Mormonism and Judaism were too positive, that he rejected the biblical position on female submissiveness, and that he did not believe in biblical inerrancy.

22. Interview with Ralph Blodgett, *Liberty Magazine*, Sept.–Oct. 1976, *PC* II, Part II, 980.

23. Jimmy Carter, "Remarks and Question and Answer Session at Town Hall Meeting," Sept. 2, 1980, *PP*, 1613.

24. Press secretary Jody Powell explained that "sometimes I would put what I thought was an apt [biblical] reference in a speech, and it got taken out" (quoted in Hutcheson, *White House*, 115).

25. Jimmy Carter, "Remarks to the Baptist Brotherhood Commission of the Southern Baptist Convention," May 13, 1977, *PP*, 877. Cf. Interview with Washington Star Group, Aug. 5, 1976, *PC* I, Part II, 452; Interview with Jim Castelli of the Catholic News Service, Aug. 9, 1976, *PC* I, Part I, 453; and JEC to RLM, Oct. 3, 1978, White House Central Files (hereafter WHCF), Religious Matters (hereafter RM), RM-2, RM 3, 10/1/78–5/31/79.

26. Carter, "New Hampshire High School Students," 370.

27. Jimmy Carter, "Remarks . . . at a Townhall Meeting," 1612; Interview with Blodgett, 975, quotations in that order.

28. Interview with Blodgett, 975. Cf. Kucharsky, *Man from Plains*, 52.

29. Jimmy Carter, "World Conference on Religion and Peace," Sept. 6, 1979, *PP*, 1599. Carter, like other presidents, rarely mentioned Jesus. In December 1977, however, he declared "that almost 2,000 years ago, the Son of Peace was born to give us a vision of perfection," humility, unselfishness, and love ("Remarks on the Lighting of the Community Christmas Tree," Dec. 15, 1977, *PP*, 2127).

30. Scheer, "We Hardly Know Y'All," 944.

31. Norton and Slosser, *Miracle*, 87.

32. Interview with Castelli, 459.

33. See Discussant: James S. Wolfe in Herbert D. Rosenbaum and Alexei Ugrinsky, eds., *The Presidency and Domestic Policies of Jimmy Carter* (Westport, CT: Greenwood, 1994), 123.

34. "On Meet the Press," July 11, 1976, *PC* I, Part 1, 296–97. Cf. interview with Blodgett, 975.

35. Carter, "New Hampshire High School Students," 370. Carter later claimed that there were "very few occasions when I felt torn between my own faith and my obligation . . . to 'preserve, protect, and defend the Constitution' " (*Living Faith*, 125).

36. Carter, "National Religious Broadcasters," 182.

37. Bourne, *Carter*, 178–79. Cf. Burton I. Kaufman, *The Presidency of James Earl Carter, Jr.* (Lawrence: University Press of Kansas, 1993), 5: Carter was "not ideological, philosophical, or conceptual."

38. Quoted in Kenneth Briggs, "Carter's Evangelicalism Putting Religion Back into Politics," *NYT*, Apr. 11, 1976, 47.

39. Jimmy Carter, statement to the *World Mission Journal* in Kucharsky, *Man from Plains*, 13.

40. Press Conference, Sept. 9, 1978, *PP*, 1993. See also interview with Castelli. Unlike many other Christian politicians, he claimed that he had never confronted any conflict between his faith and his elected positions. E.g.; "Religion and the Presidency," 967; and Carter, "Remarks to . . . the Southern Baptist Brotherhood Commission," June 16, 1978, *PP*, 1115. Cf. Hatfield, *Rock and a Hard Place*; and Anderson, *Between Two Worlds*, 35–39.

41. Carter, "Baptist Brotherhood Commission," 877.

42. Jimmy Carter, "Remarks to . . . the Southern Baptist Brotherhood Commission," 1115.

43. Jimmy Carter, "Remarks at the Annual Prayer Breakfast," Jan. 18, 1979, *PP*, 59.

44. "The President's News Conference of December 30, 1977," *PP*, 2207.

45. Carter, "Remarks . . . at a Town Meeting," 473. Cf. "Question and Answer Session with New Jersey News Editors," Sept. 9, 1980, *PP*, 1685.

46. Jimmy Carter, "Remarks and Question and Answer Session at a Town Meeting," Oct. 29, 1980, *PP*, 2505–6, quotation from 2505. Cf. Carter, "Remarks . . . at a Townhall Meeting," 1613.

47. See Jerry Falwell, *Listen America* (Garden City, NY: Doubleday, 1980); Ed Dobson and Jerry Falwell, eds., *Fundamentalist Phenomenon: The Resurgence of Conservative Christianity* (Garden City, NY: Doubleday, 1981); and Robert Webber, *The Moral Majority: Right or Wrong?* (Westchester, IL: Cornerstone, 1981).

48. Jimmy Carter, "Remarks and Question and Answer Session at a Town Meeting," Oct. 31, 1980, *PP*, 2590–91; both quotations 2591. Cf. "Remarks at a Rally with Area Residents," Nov. 1, 1980, *PP*, 2628–29.

49. James M. Wall, "Jimmy Carter: Year One," *The United Church Observer*, Nov. 1977, 31–32; first quotation from 31, second and third from 32.

50. Carter, "Southern Baptist Brotherhood Commission," 1117.

51. Carter, "New Hampshire High School Students," 370. See also interview with Blodgett, 976.

52. Carter, "Who Really Cares for the 'Least of These'?" *Seeds*, Apr. 1983, 12. Cf. "Inaugural Address of President Jimmy Carter," Jan. 20, 1977, *PP*, 1.

53. "Religion and the Presidency," 969. Cf. Jimmy Carter, "A Message on Justice," *PC* I, Part 1, 24, 26–27.

54. Carter, "Baptist Brotherhood Commission," 877.

55. Stanfield, "Faith and Politics," 26. See Carter, *Living Faith*, 125, 132.

56. "White House Reception for Black Ministers," Oct. 23, 1980, *PP*, 2428.

57. Carter, "Who Really Cares?" 13.

58. He did say, however, "I believe I was put here on purpose" ("White House Reception for Black Ministers," 2429).

59. See James M. Wall to JEC, Dec. 1, 1978, WHCF, RM 1, RM 1/29/77–12/31/78, Executive. Carter's faith especially helped sustain him after he lost the 1980 presidential election.

60. Norton and Slosser, *Miracle*, 88.

61. Carter, "New Hampshire High School Students," 370.

62. "Jimmy Carter's Code of Ethics," Mar. 1, 1976, *PC* I, Part 1, 92.

63. See Ribuffo, "Jimmy Carter," 151.

64. Carter, "National Religious Broadcasters," 181; Jim White, "Interview with Jimmy Carter," *Deacon*, Oct.–Nov. 1985 (quotation); Carter, *Keeping Faith*, 207.

65. See Gerald Ford, *A Time to Heal: The Autobiography of Gerald R. Ford* (New York: Harper and Row, 1979), 175, 417; *PC* II, Gerald R. Ford, 617, 909, 911, 919, 981; Richard Reeves, *A Ford, Not a Lincoln* (New York: Harcourt Brace Jovanovich, 1975), 110, 113–14. Dallas Baptist pastor W. A. Criswell endorsed Ford. See Charles Mohr, "Pastor of the Largest Baptist Church Hails Ford and Denounces Carter," *NYT*, Oct. 11, 1976.

66. By late May, Carter reported that journalists had written about a hundred articles about his religious life. See *Georgia Baptist Convention News* magazine, May 27, 1976.

67. For a good overview of how Carter spoke differently to various audiences about his faith and religious themes during the campaign, see Betty Glad, *Jimmy Carter: In Search of the Great White House* (New York: W. W. Norton, 1980), 330–40.

68. E.g., Alette Hill, "The Carter Campaign in Retrospect: Decoding the Cartoons," *Semiotica* 23 (1978), 307–32.

69. Glad, *Carter*, 335.

70. Norton and Slosser, *Miracle*, 55–70.

71. Jules Witcover, *Marathon: The Pursuit of the Presidency, 1972–1976* (New York: Viking, 1977), 359–60.

72. *CT* 20 (July 31, 1976).

73. Interview with Castelli, 461.

74. Quoted in Claire Booth Luce, "The Light at the End of the Tunnel of Love," *National Review*, Nov. 12, 1976, 1228.

75. Arthur M. Schleisinger Jr., "The Carter Phenomenon," *WSJ*, April 28, 1976. Cf. Charles Henderson, "The Politics of Love: Religion or Justice?" *Nation*, May 8, 1976, 555; and Roger Rosenblatt, "The Carter Congregation," *NR*, Aug. 7, 1976, 42.

76. James Burnham, "Politics and Morality," *National Review*, Nov. 12, 1976, 1226.

77. Reeves, *New York*, Mar. 22, 1976, 30. Cf. John R. Coyne Jr., " 'Nice-guyin' His Way to the White House?" *National Review*, May 14, 1976, 502; Steven Brill, "Jimmy Carter's Pathetic Lies," *Harper's* 252 (Mar. 1976), 77–80, 82, 84, 88; and James T. Wooten, "The Well-Planned Enigma of Jimmy Carter," *New York Times Magazine*, June 6, 1976, 16, 76–82, 86–89.

78. Eells and Nyberg, *Lonely Walk*, 159.

79. Andrew Greeley, *Catholic Review*, Aug. 27, 1976. Cf. "Carter's Catholic Problem," *Chicago Tribune*, Aug. 9, 1976.

80. Outside conservative Christian circles, the interview helped to reinvigorate the "suspicion that Carter was too strange to be president." See Ribuffo, "Jimmy Carter," 146.

81. See Scheer, "We Hardly Know Y'All," 964.

82. Although Ford publicly refused to comment on Carter's interview, his strategists mailed two million copies of a brochure to rural families that contained a reproduction of the Playboy cover, objections of Baptist ministers to the interview, and Ford's recent interview with religious broadcasters. See Elizabeth Drew, *American Journal: The Events of 1976* (New York: Random House, 1977), 490.

83. Interview with National Religious Broadcasters, Oct. 14, 1976, *PC*, II, Part II, 973. See also *NW*, Oct. 4, 1976, 70; *Time*, Oct. 4, 1976, 34; Andrew Greeley, *WSJ*, Oct. 18, 1976, 24; Martin Marty, *CC* 93 (Oct. 6, 1976), 847; and William Miller, "Candor and Naiveté—Defending Carter's Heresies," *National Review*, Oct. 9, 1976.

84. Gary M. Fink and Hugh Davis Graham, "Introduction," in Fink and Graham, eds., *The Carter Presidency: Policy Choices in the Post–New Deal Era* (Lawrence: University of Kansas Press, 1998), 4.

85. Stroud, *How Jimmy Won*, 419–34, quotations from 419, 424. Carter won 93 percent of the black vote, in part because his Southern Baptist faith enabled him to speak the language of many black evangelicals (170–76).

86. See Albert Menendez, *Religion at the Polls* (Philadelphia: Westminster, 1977), 197–98.

87. Interview with Blodgett, 974, 976.

88. Keith V. Erickson, "Jimmy Carter: The Rhetoric of Private and Civic Piety," *Western Journal of Speech Communication* 44 (Summer 1980), 235.

89. Carter, "Remarks at . . . the General Council," 1953.

90. Interview with Pat Robertson on *700 Club*, 1976, in Pippert, *Spiritual Journey*, 106.

91. Jimmy Carter, "Remarks and Question and Answer Session at a Town Meeting," Oct. 21, 1980, *PP*, 2387.

92. Jimmy Carter, "Address to B'nai B'rith," Sept. 8, 1976, *PC* I, Part 2, 712.

93. Raymond A. Moore, "The Carter Presidency and Foreign Policy," in M. Glenn Abernathy, Dilys Hill, and Phil Williams, eds., *The Carter Years: The Presidency and Policy Making* (New York: St. Martins, 1984), 55.

94. Carter, "Address to B'nai B'rith," 713.

95. "Religion and the Presidency," 971.

96. Carter, "Who Really Cares?" 13.

97. Interview with John Hart, NBC News, March 28, 1976, in Pippert, *Spiritual Journey*, 101.

98. Talking Points for President's Meeting with Jewish Supporters from New York City, Aug. 27, 1980, WHCF, RM 2, RM 3, 5/11/80–1/20/81. See also Carter, *Keeping Faith*, 184.

99. Interview with the National Religious Broadcasters, Oct. 9, 1976, *PC* I, Part 2, 972.

100. Jimmy Carter, "Message to the Congress," May 3, 1977, *PP*, 786–87.

101. Carter, *Why Not the Best?* 175.

102. Jimmy Carter, "To the Ministers of the African Methodist Episcopal Church," June 18, 1976, in Pippert, *Spiritual Journey*, 243.

103. Interview with the National Religious Broadcasters, 967.

104. "My Name is Jimmy Carter and I'm Running for President," in Carter, *Government as Good*, 131; "Remarks on . . . the Community Christmas Tree," 2126, quotations in that order.

105. Interview with Moyers, 93.

106. Carter, "Southern Baptist Brotherhood Commission," first quotation from 1115, second from 1116. See also Carter, *Why Not the Best?* 125; and Carter, "National Conference of Christians and Jews," May 29, 1979, *PP*, 972.

107. Glad, *Carter*, 480.

108. Paul Henry, "Christian Perspectives on Power Politics," in Perry C. Cotham, ed., *Christian Social Ethics* (Grand Rapids, MI: Baker, 1979), 63.

109. Carter, "Remarks on . . . the Community Christmas Tree," 2127.

110. "Religion and the Presidency," 967. Cf. interview with Blodgett, 981.

111. Interview by Castelli, 458.

112. See Jimmy Carter, "Remarks at the Annual Prayer Breakfast," Jan. 27, 1977, *PP*, 24–26. See Reinhold Niebuhr, *Justice and Mercy*, Ursula Niebuhr, ed. (New York: Harper and Row, 1974), 42, 97. See also Carter, "Remarks at the Annual Prayer Breakfast," Jan. 18, 1979, *PP*, 60–61.

113. Carter, National Prayer Breakfast, 1977, 24; Carter, *Government as Good*, 68.

114. Interview with Robertson, 107.

115. Carter, "National Religious Broadcasters," 182.

116. Bourne, *Carter*, 169. Cf. Kaufman, *Presidency*, 10. Since leaving the presidency, Carter has continued to serve God and people through his work with the Carter Center and Habitat for Humanity and his mediation of political disputes. On the other hand, he has produced a spate of books that publicize his achievements in every facet of his life.

117. Carter, "World Conference on Religion and Peace," 1598.

118. Carter, "Remarks at . . . the General Council," 1957.

119. Carter, "My Name is Jimmy Carter," 131.

120. Jimmy Carter, "The U.S.-Soviet Relationship," *State Department Bulletin*, Aug. 15, 1977, 197.

121. Carter, "Remarks at . . . the General Council," 1953.

122. Zbigniew Brzezinski, *Power and Principle: Memoirs of a National Security Advisor, 1977–1981* (New York: Farrar, Straus, Giroux, 1983), 49. See also Gladdis Smith, *Morality, Reason, and Power: American Diplomacy in the Carter Years* (New York: Hill and Wang, 1986), 50.

123. Carter, "Inaugural Address," 2. See also *PC* 1, Part 1,110, 245–46; 3:97.

124. Moore, "Foreign Policy," 57.

125. Smith, *Morality*, 50. Smith contends that U. S. policy was not consistent. Nations were treated differently depending on their strategic importance, military and economic power, and political ideology (52–55). On human rights, see Glenn Mower Jr., *Human Rights and American Foreign Policy: The Reagan and Carter Experiences* (New York: Greenwood, 1987); and Tony Smith, *America's Mission: The United States and the Worldwide Struggle for Democracy in the Twentieth Century* (Princeton, NJ: Princeton University Press, 1994).

126. Mark Hatfield complained that the Carter administration chose to combat human rights violations "only where it coincided with U. S. economic and strategic interests" (Eells and Nyberg, *Lonely Walk*, 159). Wes Michaelson and Jim Wallis, editors of *Sojourners*, questioned Carter's " 'selective morality' " in his human-rights policies and "commitment to military growth and nuclear weaponry" (quoted in Bruce Buursma, "Religion Is a Problem for a Nation Which 'in God Trusts,' " *Louisville Courier-Journal*, Nov. 26, 1978).

127. William Stueck, "Placing Jimmy Carter's Foreign Policy," in Fink and Graham, eds., *Carter Presidency*, 252.

128. Carter, *Living Faith*, 109.

129. Jimmy Carter, "Remarks at a White House Briefing for Religious Leaders," Jan. 10, 1980, *PP*, 49.

130. Jimmy Carter, "Energy and National Goals," July 15, 1979, *PP*, 1237.

131. Carter, "National Conference of Christians and Jews," 971.

132. Interview with Robertson, 99. Cf. Carter, "Who Really Cares?" 13.

133. "At what stage in the development of the fetus it becomes murder, I can't say" (*Face the Nation* Interview, Mar. 14, 1976, *PC* I, Part 1, 107).

134. Interview with Blodgett, 979.

135. Jimmy Carter, "Remarks and Question and Answer Session at a Town Meeting," Feb. 17, 1978, *PP*, 362; Carter, "Remarks and Question and Answer Session at a Public Meeting," July 21, 1977, *PP*, 1325.

136. Jimmy Carter, "Abortion," Sept. 11, 1976, *PC* I, Part 1, 593; "Position on Abortion," *PC*, 92–93; Carter, "Question and Answer Session with Members of the Graduating Class," June 6, 1977, *PP*, 1062; Carter, "Remarks during a Televised Question and Answer Session with Area Residents," May 17, 1977, *PP*, 898; Susan Clough to Mother Theresa, Dec. 20, 1979, Mother Theresa, CL.

137. Jimmy Carter, "Remarks and Question and Answer Session, Clinton Town Meeting," Mar. 16, 1977, *PP*, 392.

138. Carter declared that the abortion issue involved "an inherent conflict" between the right of a woman to control her own body and "the right of the embryonic child to live." He agreed with the Supreme Court position that abortions should be permitted

during the first three months of pregnancy and tightly constrained thereafter ("Remarks...at a Public Meeting," 1325).

139. Telegram from denominational executives to JEC, Sept. 21, 1977, WHCF, RM, Box 1, General. Maddox criticized Carter for not meeting with more people whose views differed from his "on some of the hotter social issues" (*Preacher*, 137).

140. Jimmy Carter, "Remarks...with...College Editors and News Directors," Mar. 3, 1978, *PP*, 464. Carter supported a law restricting Medicaid funding for abortions and demanded that HEW strictly comply. See Eve Rubin, *Abortion, Politics, and the Courts: Roe v. Wade and Its Aftermath* (Westport, CT: Greenwood, 1982), 151–77; and Joseph A. Califano Jr., *Governing America: An Insider's Report from the White House and the Cabinet* (New York: Simon and Schuster, 1981), chap. 2.

141. "President's News Conference," July 12, 1977, *PP*, 1237.

142. Costanza Memorandum to JEC, July 13, 1977, Presidential Handwriting File, 7/15/77 [3], CL.

143. "Interview with the National Black Network," July 18, 1977, *PP*, 1341.

144. Carter, "Remarks...at a Townhall Meeting," 1621. Cf. "The President's News Conference of April 10, 1979," *PP*, 655; and "'Ask the President,'" Oct. 13, 1979, *PP*, 1887.

145. "Interview with the President," Apr. 7, 1979, *PP*, 625.

146. Jimmy Carter, "Catholic Charities," Oct. 4, 1976, *PC* 1, Part 2, 905.

147. Jimmy Carter, "Remarks and a Question-and-Answer Session at a Town Meeting," May 5, 1978, *PP*, 868, 874; "The President's News Conference of April 11, 1978," *PP*, 730; Joseph Califano to JEC, "Alternative to Tuition Tax Credit Proposals," Feb. 4, 1978; Stuart Eizenstat and Frank Moore, Memo to the President, Feb. 6, 1978, Office of Staff Secretary, Handwriting File, Feb. 6, 1978.

148. Carter occasionally met with religious leaders, primarily to defend his policies and solicit their support, either in helping to pass legislation or to explain his policies to their constituents. In July 1978, he hosted twenty-six religious leaders to urge them to work to pass a foreign aid bill. In September 1978, the White House held a briefing with about 250 ministers and lay leaders to build support for the administration's urban policy. See Charles Warren to AW, Sept. 26, 1978; "The White House Briefing on the President's Urban Policy," Sept. 28, 1978, WHCF, RM 1, RM Jan. 20, 1977–Dec. 31, 1978, Executive. In the spring of 1980, Carter met with three different groups of black ministers to discuss administrative initiatives to combat inflation, rising energy costs, unemployment, poverty, and discrimination.

149. Interview with Castelli, 457.

150. "*Los Angeles Times* Interview," Aug. 24, 1976, *PC* I, Part 1, 560.

151. After consulting with other evangelicals, Robertson sent Carter a list of twenty individuals, but none of them received a position. Leaders of the religious right protested that Carter had used them to get elected and now was ignoring them (White House exit interview with Robert Maddox, CL).

152. Maddox reported that as soon as he began his job, he was "swamped with requests for interviews, invited to luncheons, and had many appointments with leaders of religious groups to discuss issues that were important to them: peace, Christian schools, abortion, homosexuality, and legislation that affected non-profit organizations" (*Preacher*, 73). He also handled mail from religious leaders and letters that dealt with moral and spiritual matters (79). In addition to Maddox, Carter's closest religious advisors were Jimmy Allen, who was the pastor of First Baptist Church in San

Antonio, Texas, and president of the Southern Baptist Convention, and James Wall, the editor of *Christian Century*. Carter consulted Allen on many issues, including energy policies, foreign aid, federal health programs, SALT II, the Camp David Accords, and the ratification of the Panama Canal treaty. See JEC to Allen, March 21, 1978; April 28, 1978; June 12, 1979; Aug. 6, 1979; WHCF, Allen, Ji. Wall and Carter talked and exchanged letters frequently, as detailed in various references throughout the footnotes.

153. Maddox, *Preacher*, 135.

154. Quoted in Lovett Weems Jr., "Christian Values and the Carter Presidency," *Mississippi Methodist Advocate*, n. d.

155. RLM, memorandum to AW, Phil Spector, and Ed Sanders, Aug. 3, 1979, Religious Liaison/Religion 7/1/79–3/31/80, Speechwriters File (hereafter SF), Box 26, CL. See also Maddox, *Preacher*, 138–39. Maddox also sought to improve Carter's relationship with Billy Graham. Although Carter's Christian convictions were much more similar to Graham's than any of his three predecessors, Graham had not spent any time privately with Carter and felt estranged from him. Maddox met with Graham in August 1979 to mend fences and solicit his support for SALT II, and the Grahams had dinner with the Carters at the White House in November 1979. See Maddox, *Preacher*, 140–43; AW and RLM, Memorandum to JEC, Oct. 26, 1979, Graham, Billy; Maddox, memorandum to Jimmy and Rosalynn Carter, Sept. 5, 1979, ibid. See also JEC to Ruth and Billy Graham, Nov. 30, 1977; Rosalynn Carter to Ruth and Billy Graham, Jan. 9, 1978; Graham to JEC, May 30, 1978; JEC to Graham, Dec. 20, 1978; Graham to JEC, May 9, 1978; all in ibid.

156. Maddox, memorandum to Jerry Rafshoon and Greg Scheiders, July 27, 1979, religious liaison, Maddox RL.

157. RLM to President and Mrs. Carter, Oct. 5, 1979, WHCF, RM 1, RM 1/20/77–1/20/81, General. See also Maddox, *Preacher*, 80.

158. Maddox, *Preacher*, 157, 162–65, quotation from 157. See also Patricia Y. Bario to John Myers, May 2, 1980, Falwell, Jerry; AW to Tom Lester, July 11, 1980, WHCF, RM1, RM 1/29/77–1/20/81, General.

159. Carter's staff urged him to emphasize the threats posed by the religious and political right and to stress that under his leadership America would continue to champion freedom, compassion, and morality. See AW to Rosalyn Carter, July 30, 1980, RM, Box 111, Jan. 21, 1977–Jan. 20, 1981, F. L. Social Office File.

160. These resolutions were adopted by the SBC in 1978, 1979, and 1980. See SBC, especially, Harold Bennett to JEC, June 23, 1980, CL.

161. Jack Harwell to Jack Carter, June 23, 1977. Harwell was the editor of *Christian Index*, a Baptist paper published in Atlanta. See also JEC to Harwell, Aug. 11, 1977, SBC.

162. "Views Self as 'Populist,'" interview in *USN*, Sept. 13, 1976, *PC* I, Part 2, 736; interview with Hearst Newspapers Task Force, July 22, 1976, *PC I*, Part I, 433.

163. The *Washington Post* referred to Carter's "Catholic problem" (Sept. 9, 1976). Many Catholics denounced Carter's position on abortion and school vouchers. E.g., Edward Walsh, "Bishops Like Ford's Stand on Abortion," *WP*, Sept. 11, 1976; "Catholic Hard Line on Abortion," *Washington Star*, Sept. 19, 1976; "Ford Hopes Linked to Catholic Vote," *NYT*, Sept. 5, 1976; "Courting the Catholics," *NW*, Sept. 20, 1976; and "The Catholic Issues,"*CMW*, Aug. 27, 1976.

164. See Menendez, *Religion*, 188.

165. E.g., Allen to JEC, July 7, 1977, Allen, Jimmy, CL.

166. Jimmy Carter, "Remarks at . . . the National Conference of Catholic Charities," Oct. 15, 1979, *PP*, 1926.

167. See also Presidential Speech Control Sheet, SF, Box 55, Oct. 6, 1979, CL; and Gordon Stewart, Memorandum for the President, Progress Report on Remarks for the Pope's Visit, Oct. 3, 1979, SF, Box 55.

168. "Meeting with Pope John Paul II, Exchange of Remarks," June 21, 1980, *PP*, 1165, 1167, quotation from 1167.

169. See Milton Himmelfarb, "Carter and the Jews," *Commentary*, Aug. 1976, 48; "Carter and the Jews," *CC*, Oct. 26, 1976, 928.

170. See Glad, *Carter*, 529; Himmelfarb, "Carter and the Jews," 45; and Martin Schram, *Running for President: A Journal of the Carter Campaign* (New York: Pocket, 1976), 203–4.

171. Carter repudiated this accusation in a public letter and insisted in a speech that he believed that God listened to the prayers of Jews "just as attentively as he listens to mine" ("Remarks at the Alfred E. Smith Memorial Dinner," Oct. 16, 1980, *PP*, 2311).

172. Mann to JEC, Dec. 22, 1978, WHCF, Box RM-2, RM 3 10/1/78–5/31/79. See also David Indich to JEC, May 5, 1978, ibid., 1/1/78–9/30/78.

173. See Carter, "National Conference of Christians and Jews," 971; Carter, *Keeping Faith*, 287–89.

174. Carter, *Keeping Faith*, 20.

175. Carter, "Catholic Charities," 903–4, quotations in that order.

176. Carter, "Remarks at . . . the National Conference of Catholic Charities," 1927–28; first quotation from 1927, second from 1928.

177. "White House Conference on Families," Oct. 22, 1980, *PP*, 2422–23.

178. Jimmy Carter, "Remarks at the Governor's Annual Prayer Breakfast," May 4, 1978, *PP*, 830–32, quotations from 830.

179. See Jeffrey K. Stine, "Environmental Policy during the Carter Presidency," in Fink and Graham, eds., *Carter Presidency*, 179–201.

180. Interview with Castelli, 458. Carter also sought to increase U.S. foreign aid, ensure that it went to the people who most needed it, alleviate hunger and suffering, and improve the quality of the environment and people's health. See "At Notre Dame University," Oct. 10, 1976, *PC* I, Part 2, 997; Carter, "Address before the General Assembly of the United Nations," Mar. 17, 1977, *PP*, 448.

181. James T. Patterson, "Jimmy Carter and Welfare Reform," in Fink and Graham, eds., *Carter Presidency*, 119. See also Patterson, *America's Struggle against Poverty, 1900–1994* (Cambridge, MA: Harvard University Press, 1994); and Theda Skocpol, *Social Policy in the United States: Future Possibilities in Historical Perspective* (Princeton, NJ: Princeton University Press, 1995).

182. Patterson, "Welfare Reform," 120–35; Laurence Lynn Jr. and David Whitman, *The President as Policymaker: Jimmy Carter and Welfare Reform* (Philadelphia: Temple University Press, 1981).

183. John C. Barrow, "An Age of Limits: Jimmy Carter and the Quest for a National Energy Policy," in Fink and Graham, eds., *Carter Presidency*, 158, 161–62; first quotation from 158, second from 161. For an example of his call for sacrifice, see Carter, "National Religious Broadcasters," 182.

184. Jimmy Carter, "The Energy Problem," Apr. 18, 1977, *PP*, 656. See also Carter, "National Energy Policy," Mar. 2, 1977, *PP*, 274.

185. Carter, "Energy Problem," 657–59, first quotation from 657, second from 658.

186. Jimmy Carter, "National Energy Plan," Apr. 20, 1977, *PP*, 663–72, quotation from 663.

187. Jimmy Carter, "National Energy Plan," Nov. 8, 1977, *PP*, 1981–87; quotations from 1986.

188. Barrow, "Age of Limits," 166.

189. See Carter, "Energy: Address to the Nation," April 5, 1979, *PP*, 609–14. See also Barrow, "Age of Limits," 169; "The Energy Tangle," *NW*, Apr. 16, 1979, 21.

190. See "Camp David Advisors: Who Carter Met," *Congressional Quarterly*, July 14, 1979, 1393.

191. See Christopher Lasch to Jody Powell, June 10, 1979, esp. 3–5, 11–13, Lasc; Jerry Rafshoon, Memo to JEC, July 10, 1979; and Greg Schneiders, Memo to Jerry Rafshoon, July 10, 1979, SF, Box 50, July 15, 1979, Address to the Nation, Energy/Crisis of Confidence [1]; Patrick Caddell, Memo to the President, July 12, 1979; ibid., Energy/Crisis of Confidence [2]; Jerry Rafshoon, Rick Hertzberg, and Gordon Stewart, memo to JEC, July 14, ibid., Energy/Crisis of Confidence [3].

192. Carter, "Energy and National Goals," 1236–37; first quotation from 1236, the remainder from 1237.

193. Ibid, 1236, 1240; first quotation from 1236, second and third from 1240.

194. See Dan F. Hahn's "Flailing the Profligate: Carter's Energy Sermon of 1979," *PSQ* 10 (1980): 583–87; and J. William Holland, "The Great Gamble: Jimmy Carter and the 1979 Energy Crisis," *Prologue: Quarterly of the National Archives* 22 (Spring 1990), 63–79.

195. See "Major Jewish Organizations Hail Carter's Energy Policy," *Jewish Week*, July 19–25, 1979; Office of the White House Press Secretary, July 19, 1979, SF, Box 50, July 15, 1979 [4].

196. RLM, memo to JEC, Aug. 7, 1979; JEC to Adrian Rogers, Aug. 14, 1979, SBC. On January 10, 1980, Carter met with religious leaders to solicit their support for his energy policies. See "Remarks at a White House Briefing for Religious Leaders," 49.

197. Signers included the officers of the National Council of Churches and the National Conference of Catholic Bishops and the heads of numerous denominations. See Office of the White House Press Secretary, July 20, 1979, SF, Box 50, July 15, 1979 [4].

198. Barrow, "Age of Limits," first two quotations from 173, third from 176.

199. "Presidential Commission on World Hunger," Oct. 5, 1978, *PP*, 1712; see also "A Status Report and Brief History of the Presidential Commission on World Hunger," n. d., Records of Presidential on World RG 220, Box 16, General; "Presidential Commission on World Hunger," Sept. 5, 1978, *PP*, 1498; Carter, "State of the Union Address," Jan. 25, 1979, *PP*, 147.

200. "Preliminary Report of the Presidential Commission on World Hunger," Dec. 1979, Presidential Commission on World Hunger, Box 16, Status Report of the Commission [2], I, 1.

201. "Vienna Economic Summit Conference," June 23, 1980, *PP*, 1189–90; quotation from 1189. Also illustrative of Carter's concern about this matter is his administration's Global 2000 Report, completed in 1980, which projected what global conditions in population, agriculture, water and forest resources, energy needs, and environmental quality would be like at the century's end if present patterns continued. See "Global 2000 Study," July 24, 1980, *PP*, 1415–16.

202. Moore, "Foreign Policy," 67.

203. Jimmy Carter, "Address at Commencement Exercises at the University of [Notre Dame]," May 22, 1977, *PP*, 954–59, quotations from 957, 958. See also Carter, "State of the Union Address," Jan. 19, 1978, *PP*, 97; Carter's speech on the 30th anniversary of the Universal Declaration of Human Rights in *PP*, December 6, 1978, 2161–65; Carter, "Before the General Assembly," Mar. 17, 1977, *PP*, 448–51; and Theodore Hesburgh to JEC, Mar. 18, 1977, SF, Box 6; May 22, 1977, Notre Dame Speech [1].

204. Jimmy Carter, "Panama Canal Treaties, Address to the Nation," Feb. 1, 1978, *PP*, 259–61; Carter, "State of the Union Address," (1978), 97.

205. Carter argued in *Keeping Faith* that no Panamanians had helped to negotiate the treaty, its terms were highly favorable to the United States, and Panama's government "had objected bitterly to the terms of the treaty" (152). See also 161, 184; "Panama Canal Treaty," Aug. 30, 1977, *PP*, 1526; and "Conversation with the President," Dec. 28, 1977, *PP*, 2195.

206. Smith, *Morality*, 111. See also Clyde M. DeLoach, "Jimmy Carter: The Effect of Personal Religious Belief on His Presidency and Their Relationship to the Christian Realism of Reinhold Niebuhr," Ph.D. dissertation, Baylor University, 1985, 262–91.

207. Carter, "Panama Canal Treaties," 259, 262, quotation from 262.

208. Carter, *Keeping Faith*, 156.

209. First quotation from Smith, *Morality*, 110; second from Jimmy Carter, "Panama Canal Treaty, Remarks on the Senate Ratification of the Treaty," Apr. 18, 1978, *PP*, 759. See also Carter, "Foreign Policy," *PC* I, Part 1, 372; and "Visit to Panama, Toast at the State Dinner," June 17, 1978, *PP*, 1122.

210. Carter, *Keeping Faith*, 160, 164–66, quotation from 160. On the treaties, see Walter LaFeber, *The Panama Canal: The Crisis in Historical Perspective* (New York: Oxford University Press, 1978); Robert Strong, "Jimmy Carter and the Panama Canal Treaties," *PSQ* 21 (Spring 1991), 269–84; and George D. Moffett III, *The Limits of Victory: The Ratification of the Panama Canal Treaties* (Ithaca, NY: Cornell University Press, 1994).

211. Hamilton Jordan, Briefing on the Panama Canal Treaties for Leaders of Religious Organizations, Jan. 30, 1978, WHCF, RM 1, RM Jan. 20, 1977–Dec. 31, 1978, Executive.

212. Carter, *Keeping Faith*, 273–74, quotations from 274. On how Carter's religious views affected his understanding of the Middle East, also see his *The Blood of Abraham* (Boston: Houghton Mifflin, 1985).

213. Interview with Blodgett, 977; Jimmy Carter, "30th Anniversary of the State of Israel," May 1, 1978, *PP*, 813.

214. Smith, *Morality*, 157. On the larger context, see Steven L. Spiegel, *The Other Arab-Israeli Conflict: Making America's Middle East Policy, from Truman to Reagan* (Chicago: University of Chicago Press, 1985); George Lenczowski, *American Presidents and the Middle East* (Durham, NC: Duke University Press, 1990); and William B. Quandt, *Peace Process: American Diplomacy and the Arab-Israeli Conflict since 1967* (Washington, DC: Brookings Institution, 1993).

215. Carter "familiarized himself with every kilometer of disputed territory, [and] learned the names and populations of scores of villages" (Smith, *Morality*, 165).

216. Sadat praised Carter as a man who held noble ideals, was determined to "pursue what is right," and was committed to the cause of peace. See "Visit of President Sadat of Egypt," Apr. 4, 1977, *PP*, 568.

217. "Visit of Prime Minister Menahem Begin of Israel," July 19, 1977, *PP*, 1281. See also Carter, *Keeping Faith*, 290.

218. Carter, *Keeping Faith*, 282.

219. Smith, *Morality*, 161.

220. "Visit of President Anwar al-Sadat to Israel," *PP*, Nov. 20, 1977, 2043. See also Carter, *Keeping Faith*, 297.

221. Smith, *Morality*, 163.

222. Carter declared, "There is no nobler calling on this earth than the seeking for peace" ("Visit of President Sadat of Egypt," Feb. 8, 1977, *PP*, 290).

223. "Joint Statement Issued by President Carter, President Anwar al-Sadat of Egypt, and Prime Minister Menahem Begin of Israel," Sept. 6, 1978, *PP*, 1501.

224. Bourne, *Carter*, 439.

225. See Maddox, *Preacher*, 157–59; Maddox interview.

226. Hamilton Jordan interview, Miller Center Interviews, Carter Presidency Project, vol. 6, Nov. 6, 1981, 3–16, CL.

227. See *Dallas Morning News*, Aug. 23, 1980, A1, A8–9. See also Rowland Evans and Robert Novak, *The Reagan Revolution* (New York: E. P. Dutton, 1981), 213–14; Jeffrey K. Hadden, "Born Again Politics: The Dallas Briefing," *Presbyterian Outlook*, Oct. 20, 1980, 5–6; Kenneth A Briggs, "Evangelicals Hear Plea: Politics Now," *NYT*, Aug. 24, 1980, 33; and Richard Pierard, "Reagan and Evangelicals: The Making of a Love Affair," *CC* 100 (Dec. 21–28, 1983), 1182–85.

228. See "Conservative Christians Launch Activist Bid," *CC* 97 (Sept. 24, 1980), 872; and James M. Wall, "The New Right Comes of Age," ibid., Oct. 22, 1980, 996.

229. See Doug Wead and Bill Wead, *Reagan in Pursuit of the Presidency* (Plainfield, NJ: Haven Books, 1980); Evans and Novak, *Reagan Revolution*, 205–7; and Ronald Reagan, "God Is Always There for Me!" *Action* (PTL Club), Nov. 1980, 3–4.

230. *LAT*, Mar. 6, 1980, sec. 10.

231. Jerry Falwell, *Strength for the Journey: An Autobiography* (New York: Simon and Schuster, 1987), 365; "Getting God's Kingdom into Politics," *CT* 24 (Sept. 19, 1980), 11; George J. Church, "Politics from the Pulpit," *Time*, Oct. 13, 1980, 28–35.

232. Maddox, *Preacher*, 158.

233. Albert J. Menendez, "Religion at the Polls, 1980," *Church and State* 33 (Dec. 1980), 15–18; Seymour M. Lipset and Earl Raab, "The Election and the Evangelicals," *Commentary* 71 (Mar. 1981), 29; Gerald Pomper, "The Presidential Election," in Pomper, ed., *The Election of 1980: Reports and Interpretations* (Chatham, NJ: Chatham, 1981), 71–73; Center for Political Studies at the University of Michigan data.

234. Ribuffo, "Jimmy Carter," 156.

235. Quoted in Beth Spring, "Republicans, Religion, and Reelection," *CT* 28 (Oct. 5, 1984), 56.

236. Interview with Robertson, 100.

237. Carter, "Inaugural Address," 3.

238. Morris, *Carter*, 241, 245, quotation from 241.

239. See Carter, *Keeping Faith*, 65.

240. Tom Wolfe, "The Me Decade and the Third Great Awakening," in his *The Purple Decades: A Reader* (New York: Berkley, 1983); Nicholas Lemann, "How the Seventies Changed America," *American Heritage* 42 (July–Aug. 1991), 39–49; Jonathan Alter, "All Grown Up and Nowhere to Go," *Esquire*, May 1991, 96–104. See Morris, *Carter*, 9, who called my attention to these sources.

241. Morris, *Carter*, 9–16, quotation from 10.

242. Carter, *Keeping Faith*, 21.

243. Wall, "Jimmy Carter," 30.

244. "Religion without Intellect," *Washington Star*, Feb. 5, 1978.

245. Erling Jorstad, *Evangelicals in the White House: The Cultural Maturation of Born Again Christianity, 1960–1981* (New York: Edwin Mellen, 1981), 133.

246. Quoted in "Pope's Washington Visit Temporarily Blurs 'Tradition,'" *Denver Post*, Oct. 7, 1979, 36.

247. Morris, *Carter*, 160; Bourne, *Carter*, 508; first two quotations from Morris, third from Bourne. See also James Fallows, "The Passionless Presidency: The Trouble with Jimmy Carter's Administration," *AM*, May 1979, 42.

248. On the distinction between Carter's private faith and his public morality, see Erickson, "Jimmy Carter," 221–35; Ronald B. Flowers, "President Jimmy Carter, Evangelicalism, Church-State Relations and Civil Religion," *JCS* 25 (Winter 1983), 113–32; Christopher L. Johnstone, "Electing Ourselves in 1976: Jimmy Carter and the American Faith," *Western Journal of Speech Communications* 42 (1978), 241–49; and James S. Wolfe, "Exclusion, Fusion, or Dialogue: How Should Religion and Politics Relate?" *JCS* 22 (1980), 89–105.

249. Carter, "Inaugural Address," 1.

250. Morris, *Carter*, 213, 239, 246–50; first quotation from 250, second from 247.

251. Anderson, *Two Worlds*, 148.

252. Bob Goudzwaard, *A Christian Political Option* (Toronto: Wedge Pub. Foundation, 1972), 64. See also Mouw, *Political Evangelism*, 41–46. Organizations that might have been helpful to Carter in his attempt to approach politics from a Christian perspective included Sojourner's Fellowship (which relocated in Washington in 1975), Christians for Urban Justice (established in Boston in 1976), the Association for Public Justice (founded in 1977), and Evangelicals for Social Action (founded in 1978). There is no evidence Carter had a relationship with any of these evangelical organizations that sought to apply biblical principles to political life.

253. Alan Otten, *WSJ*, as quoted in Victor Lasky, *Jimmy Carter, the Man and the Myth* (New York: R. Marek, 1979), 21. See also David Lee, "The Politics of Less: The Trials of Herbert Hoover and Jimmy Carter," *PSQ* 14 (Spring 1984), 265–84; and Michael J. Kruskones, "The Campaign Promises of Jimmy Carter: Accomplishments and Failures," *PSQ* 15 (Winter 1985), 136–44.

254. Kaufman, *Presidency*, 210. Also see Fallows, "Passionless Presidency," 35–38; Bourne, *Carter*, 444; and Carter, *Keeping Faith*, 117.

255. Fink and Graham, "Introduction," 2.

256. Kaufman, *Presidency*, 3.

257. Charles O. Jones, *The Trusteeship Presidency: Jimmy Carter and the United States Congress* (Baton Rouge: Louisiana State University Press, 1988), 2–3, 6; first quotation from 2, second from 3. Cf. Carter, *Keeping Faith*, 88. Also see Erwin C. Hargrove, *Jimmy Carter as President: Leadership and the Politics of the Public Good* (Baton Rouge: Louisiana State University Press, 1988).

258. JEC to Allen, Nov. 13, 1980, Allen, Ji. See also Carter, *Keeping Faith*, 110; and Carter, "My Personal Faith in God," *CT* 27 (Mar. 4, 1983), 15–21.

259. Jimmy Carter, White Burkett Miller Center of Public Affairs, University of Virginia, Project on the Carter Presidency, Transcripts, I, 53, VI, 102.

260. Discussant: James S. Wolfe, 127.

261. Ibid.; James A. Speer, "Jimmy Carter Was a Baptist President," in Rosenbaum and Ugrinsky, eds., *Presidency and Domestic Policies*, 92, 94–5, 101–8.

262. Kaufman, *Presidency*, 3.

263. Patterson, "Welfare Reform," 123. See Thomas O'Neill with William Novak, *Man of the House: The Life and Political Memoirs of Speaker Tip O'Neill* (New York: Random House, 1987), 297, 308–11; Kaufman, *Presidency*, 3.

264. Jones, *Trusteeship Presidency*, 217. Cf. Kaufman, *Presidency*, 3.

265. Discussant: James M. Wall in Rosenbaum and Ugrinsky, eds., *Presidency and Domestic Policies*, 117.

266. Miller, *Yankee*, 96.

267. Buursma, "Religion Is a Problem."

268. See Morris, *Carter*, 325; James David Fairbanks, "The Priestly Functions of the Presidency: A Discussion of the Literature on Civil Religion and Its Implications for the Study of Presidential Leadership," *PSQ* 11 (Spring 1981), 214–32; and Martin Marty, "Civil Religion: Two Kinds of Two Kinds," in Marty, *Religion and Republic: The American Circumstance* (Boston: Beacon, 1987).

269. See Pierard and Linder, *Civil Religion*, 255.

270. Fink and Graham, "Introduction," 5.

271. Jerel A. Rosati, *The Carter Administration's Quest for Global Community: Beliefs and Their Impacts on Behavior* (Columbia: University of South Carolina Press, 1987), 7–13, 34–35.

272. Kaufman, *Presidency*, 38. See also "New Approach to Foreign Policy," May 28, 1975, *PC* I, Part 1, 68–70.

273. Stueck, "Carter's Foreign Policy," 261.

274. E.g., Carter, *Keeping Faith*, 143.

275. See Monsma, *Unraveling*, 185.

276. See Carter, *Keeping Faith*, 142–51.

277. Smith, *Morality*, 245, 247, quotations in that order. Smith maintains that Carter thought harder than most political leaders do about human purposes, ultimate values, and the long-term future (4).

278. Monsma, *Unraveling*, 193.

279. See Carter, *Living Faith*, 48.

280. Quoted in Bourne, *Carter*, 385.

281. Discussant: James M. Wall, 121–22; quotations from 121.

282. William Leuchtenburg, "Jimmy Carter and the Post-New Deal Presidency," in Fink and Graham, eds., *Carter Presidency*, 8–9.

283. Smith, *Morality*, 3–4.

284. Moore, "Foreign Policy," 70.

285. Stueck, "Carter's Foreign Policy," 260; Martin Walker, *The Cold War: A History* (New York: Henry Holt, 1994), 45. Cf. Tony Smith, *America's Mission: The United States and the Worldwide Struggle for Democracy in the Twentieth Century* (Princeton, NJ: Princeton University Press, 1994), 239.

CHAPTER 10

1. For bibliographies on Reagan, see Lou Cannon, *President Reagan: The Role of a Lifetime* (New York: Simon and Schuster, 1991), 895–910; and William E. Pemberton,

Exit with Honor: The Life and Presidency of Ronald Reagan (Armonk, NY: M. E. Sharpe, 1998), 259–82.

2. Two anthologies of Reagan's addresses focus on this theme: D. Erik Felten, ed., *Shining City: The Legacy of Ronald Reagan* (New York: Simon and Schuster, 1998); and James C. Roberts, ed., *A City upon a Hill* (Washington, DC: American Studies Center, 1989). See also Amos Kiewe and Davis W. Houck, *A Shining City on a Hill: Ronald Reagan's Economic Rhetoric, 1951–1989* (New York: Praeger, 1991).

3. See Garry Wills, *Reagan's America: Innocents at Home* (Garden City, NY: Doubleday, 1987), 355. John Winthrop applied the words of Jesus to the Puritan mission in America in his sermon, *A Model of Christian Charity.* The theme of a city on the hill was also emphasized by Alexander Campbell, the founder of the Disciples of Christ; Ben Cleaver, Reagan's pastor during his formative years; and Reagan's mother, Nelle. See Wills, *Reagan's America*, 28; and Terry L. Miethe, "The Philosophy and Ethics of Alexander Campbell," Ph.D. dissertation, University of Southern California, 1984.

4. Pemberton, *Exit*, xiv.

5. Founded by Campbell and Barton Stone in 1831, the Christian Church (Disciples of Christ) grew rapidly during the nineteenth century. During the early twentieth century, the Disciples emphasized education, revivalism, and social reform. See Lester G. McAllister and William Tucker, *Journey in Faith: A History of the Christian Church (Disciples of Christ)* (St. Louis: Bethany, 1975); Kenneth L. Teegarden, *We Call Ourselves Disciples* (St. Louis: Bethany, 1975); and David Harrell, *A Social History of the Disciples of Christ* (Tuscaloosa: University of Alabama Press, 2003).

6. On Nelle Reagan's religious commitments, see Wills, *Reagan's America*, 16–17, 22–26; Anne Edwards, *Early Reagan: The Rise to Power* (New York: William Morrow, 1987), 59–60; Stephen Vaughn, "The Moral Inheritances of a President: Reagan and the Dixon Disciples of Christ," *PSQ* 25 (Winter 1995), 109–27; and Paul Kengor, *God and Ronald Reagan: A Spiritual Life* (New York: Regan, 2004), 10–16.

7. Cannon, *Reagan*, 211.

8. Maureen Reagan, *First Father, First Daughter* (Boston: Little, Brown, 1989), 64.

9. Ronald W. Reagan, *An American Life* (Norwalk, CT: Easton, 1990), 20–21. Also see Nancy Reagan with William Novak, *My Turn: The Memoirs of Nancy Reagan* (New York: Random House, 1989), 108.

10. Ronald Reagan, "Remarks . . . [to] Women Leaders of Christian Religious Organizations," *Public Papers of the Presidents of the United States, Ronald Reagan, 1981–1989*, 8 vols. (Lanham, MD: Bernan, 1995) (hereafter *PP*), Oct. 13, 1983, 1450.

11. See Edwards, *Early Reagan*, 58; Vaughn, "Moral Inheritances," 112–13. The Disciples required those being baptized to publicly confess their faith in Christ as their savior.

12. Edwards, *Early Reagan*, 59; Vaughn, "Moral Inheritances," 113.

13. Wills, *Reagan's America*, 18. On Cleaver's life and his close relationship with Reagan, see also Vaughn, "Moral Inheritances," 109–12; and Kengor, *Reagan*, 32–38.

14. Quoted in Jerry Griswold, "I'm a Sucker for Hero Worship," *NYT Book Review*, Aug. 30, 1981, 11. Cf. Edmund Morris, *Dutch: A Memoir of Ronald Reagan* (New York: Random House, 1999), 40.

15. See Morris, *Dutch*, 40–42; and Kengor, *Reagan*, 17–26. Morris and Kengor see clear parallels between the book and Reagan's approach to combating social problems and communism.

16. Morris, *Dutch*, 42. See also Reagan, *American Life*, 32. Reagan told Harold Bell Wright's daughter that his book "set me on a course I've tried to follow even unto this

day" (RR to Jean B. Wright, Mar. 13, 1984, Dixon Public Library, Dixon, Illinois, as cited by Kengor, *Reagan*, 19).

17. Edwards, *Early Reagan*, 84–86, quotation from 85.

18. Vaughn, "Moral Inheritances," 120. Vaughn used Ben Hill Cleaver's papers in the Disciples of Christ Archives in Nashville, the Reagan-Cleaver family correspondence at Culver-Stockton College, Canton, MO, and the Records of the First Christian Church in Dixon, and interviewed a number of people who knew the Cleavers and the Reagans (120).

19. Ronald Reagan, "My Faith," *Modern Screen*, June 1950, 37–39.

20. Moomaw claimed that whenever they were in Los Angeles between 1963 and 1980, the Reagans attended his church regularly (David Shepherd, *Ronald Reagan: In God I Trust* [Wheaton, IL: Tyndale, 1984], 6). He explained that Reagan was "always very attentive in worship" (quoted in Bob Slosser, *Reagan Inside Out* [Waco, TX: Word, 1984], 49). See also Morris, *Dutch*, 351. On Moomaw's life and Bel Air Presbyterian Church, see Laurence Jones, "Reagan's Religion," *Journal of American Culture* 8 (Winter 1985), 62. Patti Davis maintains that her father's participation in worship was enthusiastic and very meaningful (*Angels Don't Die: My Father's Gift of Faith* [New York: HarperCollins, 1995], 78–79).

21. Quoted in Frank van der Linden, *The Real Reagan* (New York: William Morrow, 1981), 90.

22. Slosser, *Reagan Inside Out*, 51.

23. Ibid., 13–20, quotations from 15. See also George Otis, *High Adventure* (Van Nuys, CA: Bible Voice, 1971), 185ff.

24. E.g., Edward Kosner, Karl Fleming, and William Cook, "Ronald Reagan: Rising Star in the West?" *NW*, May 15, 1967, 36; Michael Deaver, "The Elusive Ronald Reagan," *NYT*, Sept. 29, 1999: "he had an unshakable belief that God had a purpose for him"; and Maureen Reagan, "A President and a Daughter," *WT*, June 16, 2000, A23.

25. William Rose, "The Reagans and Their Pastor," *Christian Life* 30 (May 1968), 43–44.

26. A 1976 letter quoted in Rowland Evans and Robert Novak, *The Reagan Revolution* (New York: E. P. Dutton, 1981), 208.

27. Van der Linden, *Real Reagan*, 26. Cf. Helene von Damm, ed., *Sincerely, Ronald Reagan* (New York: Berkley, 1980), 88; von Damm, *At Reagan's Side* (New York: Doubleday, 1989), 61; and Rose, "The Reagans," 43–44.

28. Davis, *Angels*, 48.

29. Ronald Reagan, "Remarks . . . [to] the National Religious Broadcasters Association," *PP*, Feb. 1, 1988, 159. Reagan often emphasized this point in personal letters. E.g., von Damm, ed., *Reagan*, 26, 86, 93, 123–26. See also Morris, *Dutch*, 429–33; and Mary Beth Brown, *Hand of Providence: The Strong and Quiet Faith of Ronald Reagan* (Nashville, TN: WND, 2004).

30. Reagan, *American Life*, 261, 263, quotation from 261. He told his daughter Patti that his own physical healing depended directly on his ability to forgive Hinckley (Davis, *Angels*, 27).

31. Quotation from Morris, *Dutch*, 434. See also Reagan, *American Life*, 262–63; and Michael Deaver, *A Different Drummer: My Thirty Years with Ronald Reagan* (New York: HarperCollins, 2001), 145–47.

32. Tom Freiling, *Reagan's God and Country* (Ann Arbor, MI: Servant, 2000), 9. Reagan had earlier discussed spiritual matters in the hospital with Moomaw. See

Richard Hutcheson, *God in the White House: How Religion Has Changed the Modern Presidency* (New York: Macmillan, 1988), 165. See also Ronald Reagan, "Remarks at the Annual National Prayer Breakfast," *PP*, Feb. 4, 1982, 109.

33. Reagan, *American Life*, 263. See also Reagan, *First Father*, 279.

34. Quoted in Freiling, *Reagan's God*, 10.

35. Slosser, *Reagan Inside Out*, 135–38. The Grahams stayed at the White House twice during Reagan's first term, and the evangelist and president corresponded occasionally. Reagan met several times with Mother Teresa and visited and prayed with Cardinal Cooke in New York in September 1983. See "President Pays Visit to the Bedside of Cardinal Cooke," *WP*, Sept. 26, 1983.

36. See Hutcheson, *White House*, 171; Gary Wills, *Under God: Religion and American Politics* (New York: Simon and Schuster, 1990), 150.

37. Interview with Cardinal O'Connor, Jan. 12, 1989, Religious Matters (hereafter RM) 031 Catholic (600000–end), RM, Box 7, Ronald Reagan Library (hereafter RL).

38. E.g., RR to Stephanie Atkins, May 24, 1982, RM, 020 Prayers, 080001–081200.

39. Davis, *Angels*, 1–2, 5, 46–47, 50; quotation from 5.

40. Ronald Reagan, "Three Grave Threats to Our Way of Life," July 17, 1980, in Alfred A. Balitzer and Gerald M. Bonetto, eds., *A Time for Choosing: The Speeches of Ronald Reagan, 1961–1982* (Chicago: Regnery Gateway, 1983), 235.

41. Ronald Reagan, "Inaugural Address," *PP*, Jan. 20, 1981, 3.

42. E.g., Ronald Reagan, "Remarks at an Ecumenical Prayer Breakfast in Dallas, TX," *PP*, Aug. 23, 1984, 1166. Reagan sometimes used quotations from these individuals that did not reflect the historical context of their remarks.

43. Ronald Reagan, "Remarks at the Annual National Prayer Breakfast," *PP*, Feb. 5, 1987, 110.

44. Ronald Reagan, "Remarks . . . in Observance of a National Day of Prayer," *PP*, May 6, 1982, 574.

45. Reagan, "Prayer Breakfast," 1987, 110. Cf. Reagan, "Women Leaders," 1450.

46. Reagan, "Ecumenical Prayer Breakfast," 1166.

47. Rose, "The Reagans," 23–24; Doug Wead and Bill Wead, *Reagan in Pursuit of the Presidency—1980* (Plainfield, NJ: Logos, 1980), 183–85; Brown, *Hand of Providence*, 14–16, 141–43.

48. Quoted in Freiling, *Reagan's God*, 24.

49. Reagan, "Prayer Breakfast," 1987, 110.

50. Davis, *Angels*, 1, 50, quotation from 1.

51. Cf. RR to Cardinal Bernard Law, Aug. 19, 1985, President's Handwriting File (hereafter PHF), Presidential Records (hereafter PR), Series II, Box 13, 5/29/85–10/31/85, Folder 198, RL; and Reagan, "Remarks at a Candle-Lighting Ceremony for Prayer in Schools," *PP*, Sept. 25, 1982, 1219.

52. E.g., RR to Bill Orozco, Aug. 14, 1985, PHF, PR, Series II, Box 13, 5/29/85–10/31/85, Folder 198; and RR to Phil Regan, Nov. 21, 1988, ibid., Box 21, Folder 341.

53. RR to Mother Teresa, Dec. 18, 1984, PHF, PR, Series II, Box 11, 12/18/84 cont.-2/28/85, Folder 154. The files at the Reagan Library contain hundreds of letters from Reagan to clergy, military personnel, and ordinary citizens, many of which are originally handwritten, that express the same point. E.g., RR to Mrs. Frank Miller, Apr. 14, 1981, RM 000001–030000; RR to Patricia James, Dec. 18, 1984, RM020, Prayers, 280000–304999, Folder 44; RR to Brother Gary Gerke, Dec. 22, 1986, PHR, PR,

Box 17, Folder 271; and RR to Bernard Cardinal Law, Mar. 11, 1987, PHR, PR, Box 18, Folder 282.

54. Dinesh D'Souza, *Ronald Reagan: How an Ordinary Man Became an Extraordinary Leader* (New York: Free Press, 1997), 213.

55. Hutcheson, *White House*, 170. Secretary of the Interior Donald Hodel is the source of this story.

56. Slosser, *Reagan Inside Out*, 172–73.

57. Interview with O'Connor.

58. Reagan, *American Life*, 229, 292, 365. He also thanked God for the release of the hostages from Iran and the success of the military operation in Grenada (ibid., 236, 455). When the dean of the faculty at St. George's School of Medicine thanked him for sending troops, Reagan replied, "We're grateful to God for His help in making our mission a success" (Oct. 29, 1983, PHR, PR, Box 8, Folder 106).

59. Von Damm, ed., *Reagan*, 83; "Ronald Reagan–George Otis Interview," in Wead and Wead, *Reagan in Pursuit*, 181.

60. Freiling, *Reagan's God*, 37. Pastor Harald Bredesen was also impressed by Reagan's knowledge of the Bible (Slosser, *Reagan Inside Out*, 19).

61. Ronald Reagan, "Remarks ... [to] the National Religious Broadcasters," *PP*, Jan. 30, 1984, 118. Cf. Reagan, "Remarks ... [to] the National Religious Broadcasters," *PP*, Jan. 31, 1983, 152.

62. Ronald Reagan, "Proclamation of the Year of the Bible, 1983," *PP*, Feb. 3, 1983, 179.

63. Reagan, "National Religious Broadcasters," 1983, 152. Cf. RR to Rev. Paul T. Butler, May 31, 1985; and Butler to RR, Feb. 22, 1985, both in PHF, PR, Series II, Box 13, 5/29/85–10/31/85, Box 13, Folder 198.

64. Ronald Reagan, "Remarks at the Annual National Prayer Breakfast," *PP*, Feb. 3, 1983, 178.

65. Nelle wrote in her Bible beside this verse, "A most wonderful verse for the healing of the nations" (Reagan, "National Prayer Breakfast," 1983, 179).

66. See Ronald Reagan Facts, Favorites, 1, http://www.reagan.utexas.edu/archives/reference/facts.html. Reagan also gave Psalm 106:2-5 as his favorite passage ("Reagan–Otis Interview," 182).

67. Cannon, *Reagan*, 288; D'Souza, *Reagan*, 214.

68. Ronald Reagan, "Christmas," radio broadcast transcript, 1–2/78, excerpted in Ronnie Dugger, *On Reagan: The Man and His Presidency* (New York: McGraw-Hill), 511.

69. Von Damm, ed., *Reagan*, 90. A letter Reagan wrote to Billy Graham was very similar: Christ "gave us reason to accept literally the miracle of his birth and resurrection. ... Indeed ... either we believe him, or we must assume He was the greatest liar who ever lived" (89).

70. Ronald Reagan, "Radio Address ... on the Observance of Easter and Passover," *PP*, Apr. 2, 1983, 488.

71. Ronald Reagan, "Radio Address ... on Christmas," *PP*, Dec. 24, 1983, 1747. Morris maintains that Reagan's favorite hymns were "Rock of Ages" and "The Old Rugged Cross," both of which focus on Christ's atonement (*Dutch*, 55).

72. Ariel Sergio Malnate to RR, Sept. 13, 1983; RR to Malnate, Nov. 30, 1983, both in RM 180001–204000.

73. Reagan, *American Life*, 319, 321, quotation from 319; Slosser, *Reagan Inside Out*, 130.

74. E.g., Ronald Reagan, "Remarks at the Annual National Prayer Breakfast," *PP*, Feb. 4, 1988, 173; Reagan, "Remarks to Soviet Dissidents at Spaso House in Moscow," *PP*, May 30, 1988, 677.

75. RR to Graham, Nov. 4, 1983, White House Office of Records Management (hereafter WHORM), ME 001–02, 183199.

76. Reagan explained that after he took office, he and Nancy had decided to worship at National Presbyterian Church (which they attended several times before the assassination attempt). See Ronald Reagan, "The Role the Bel Air Presbyterian Church Has Played in Our Lives," Bel Air Presbyterian Church *Images* 12 (Summer 1990), #1. However, the "unholy procedure" of having churchgoers pass through a magnetometer to be checked for weapons, forcing them to wait for the presidential motorcade when coming to and leaving services, and the possibility they could be hurt by a terrorist attack directed at him, compelled the president not to attend church (Reagan, *American Life*, 396).

77. Reagan, *American Life*, 396. Cf. Morris, *Dutch*, 427.

78. "Debate between the President and Former Vice President Walter F. Mondale, Louisville, KY," *PP*, Oct. 7, 1984, 1447. As noted, Reagan had not "regularly gone to church" all his life. Slosser argues that Moomaw urged Reagan to "take the risk" that attending public worship entailed, perhaps by going to different churches and not revealing his plans in advance (*Reagan Inside Out*, 170–71). Moomaw told Hutcheson a couple years later, however, that he agreed with Reagan's decision because his attendance inconvenienced others. The metal detectors, motorcycles, security cars, and countersniper squads up on the roof created "an unnatural atmosphere" (*White House*, 167).

79. *WP*, Apr. 16, 1984, A2.

80. Reagan, *American Life*, 399.

81. Reagan, "Bel Air Presbyterian Church." "Nancy and I have been churchgoers all our lives," Reagan claimed, "and that eight-year absence was hard to take...." *Christianity Today* reported in October 1983 that Reagan had attended the National Presbyterian Church about six times since assuming office (Beth Spring, "Rating Reagan," Oct. 7, 1983, 45).

82. Reitz to Meese, Feb. 26, 1982, RM 030001–750000. See also Meese to Reitz, Mar. 16, 1982, ibid.

83. Shepherd claims Reagan considered this alternative "self-serving, predictable, and religiously safe" (*Ronald Reagan*, 7). For efforts to persuade Reagan to hold private services, see, for example, Thomas L. Munson to Fred A. Ryan Jr., Sept. 20, 1983; Peter Rusthoven to Fred Fielding, Oct, 28, 1983; Frank Hamblen to RR, Mar. 23, 1984, all in RM 161001–180000. Hamblen proposed that Reagan appoint a personal chaplain who could hold services for him and his staff and provide "Biblical counsel on important matters." Ira Lee Eshleman, who initiated pregame chapel services for the NFL, suggested that Reagan hold chapel services or Sunday evening vesper services at the White House or Camp David. See Eshleman to RR, Nov. 14, 1984, RM020, Prayers, 245724–262999. Military chaplains also offered to hold special services for the president in areas where he visited, but he rarely accepted their offers. E.g., David Forden to RR, July 11, 1983; Ryan to Forden, Sept. 8, 1983, both in ibid.

84. See Patti Davis, *The Way I See It: An Autobiography* (New York: Putnam, 1992), 118–19; Ronald Reagan with Richard G. Hubler, *Where's the Rest of Me?* (New York: Duell, Sloan, and Pearce, 1966), 283. An astrologer in Los Angeles, Joyce Jillson,

claimed the Reagans consulted regularly with her and other astrologers while he was governor of California. See OA 17971, Bell, Mariam, Astrology [2 of 4], 9, RL. Carroll Righter alleged that both of the Reagans were his clients during their years in Hollywood. See Linda Goodman, *Linda Goodman's Sun Signs* (New York: Bantam, 1968), 394–403.

85. "Astrology," Nancy explained, "was simply one of the ways I coped with the fear I felt after my husband almost died (Reagan and Novak, *My Turn*, 44). She also prayed continuously and talked with Moomaw and Graham (45). "While I was never certain that Joan's astrological advice was helping to protect Ronnie, . . . nothing like March 30 ever happened again" (47). She was not sorry she had consulted Quigley, but she did regret the embarrassment it caused (47–48). Quigley admits that she never directly gave advice to the president. See Joan Quigley, *What Does Joan Say?* (New York: Carol, 1990), 72–73.

86. Kenneth Franklin Kurz, *The Reagan Years A to Z* (Los Angeles: Lowell, 1996), 18.

87. Donald Regan, *For the Record: From Wall Street to Washington* (New York: St. Martin's Press, 1988), 3–5, 28, 68, 70–71, 72–74, 90, 93, 300–1, 359, 367–70; quotation from 3.

88. Ronald Reagan, "Remarks at . . . the Small Business Person of the Year Awards," *PP*, May 9, 1988, 572; Reagan, "Interview with Foreign Television Journalists," *PP*, May 19, 1988, 611; George Hackett and Eleanor Clift, "Of Planets and the Presidency," *NW*, May 16, 1988, 20; OA 17971, Bell, Mariam, Astrology [2 of 4], 10, 15, 8. See also Reagan, *My Turn*, 49.

89. Edwin Meese, Richard V. Allen, and speechwriter Ben Elliott, all based on interviews with Paul Kengor in 2001 (*Reagan*, 193).

90. Boone to RR, June 4, 1988, OA 17971, Bell, Mariam, Astrology [1 of 4], Box 6.

91. Otis to RR, May 27, 1988, ibid.

92. See Laura Session Stepp, "Astrology Reports Disturb Some Evangelical Leaders," *WP*, n. d., OA 17971, Bell, Mariam, Astrology [4 of 4]. " 'Most of us cherish the notion that Reagan trusts Jesus Christ,' Len Solomon, pastor of the McLean Bible Church, said. 'It has never been confirmed' " that his wife does. See also David Neff, "Suckers for the Zodiac," *CT* 32 (July 15, 1988), 15.

93. Quoted in Hackett and Clift, "Of Planets and the Presidency," 20.

94. Mark Silk, "Reagan's Stargazing Concerns the Christian Right," *Atlanta Constitution*, May 5, 1988.

95. Many petitions are in OA 17971, Bell, Mariam, Astrology [4 of 4]. See also Otis to Mariam Bell, June 27, 1988; News Release of Creative Communications Associates, n. d., both in ibid.; "Petitions from Conservative Christian Urge the Reagans to Reject Astrology," *LAT*, June 21, 1988, Part 1, 21. Otis campaigned vigorously for Reagan in 1980 and 1984.

96. Reagan's sparse contributions to the church and other charitable causes also led some to question the sincerity of his faith. In 1979, he donated only 1 percent of his adjusted gross income to charitable organizations, a pattern that continued while he was president (Hutcheson, *White House*, 165). See also Richard Pierard, "On Praying with the President," *CC* 99 (Mar. 10, 1982), 262. Some argued that Reagan gave considerable sums to needy individuals or groups that did not have tax exempt status. See Slosser, *Reagan Inside Out*, 54; and Edwards, *Early Reagan*, 125–26, 135, 56. See also Kiron K. Skinner, Annelise Anderson, and Martin Anderson, eds., *Reagan: A Life in Letters* (New York: Free Press, 2003), 653–59.

97. Morris, *Dutch*, 11–12.

98. Reagan, *Where's the Rest of Me?* 84.

99. Briefing in Astrology file, 18–9, RL; D'Souza, *Reagan*, 213.

100. For the full description of the incident, see 400–1. See also Fitzwater's statement in OA 17971, Bell, Mariam, Astrology [2 of 4], 19; Davis, *Angels*, 65; and Michael Deaver with Mickey Herskowitz, *Behind the Scenes* (New York: William Morrow, 1987), 106.

101. Jones, "Reagan's Religion," 64–66, provides the most complete description of Reagan's interest in biblical prophecies about the end times. See also Howell Heflin's reported conversation with Reagan in the *NYT*, Oct. 28, 1981; and *Weekly Compilation of Presidential Documents*, 1983, 1708–13.

102. Some critics feared that Reagan might consider nuclear war a divine instrument. E.g., Richard Ostling, "Armageddon and the End Times," *Time* 124 (Nov. 5, 1984), 73; Cannon, *Reagan*, 288–90; Kenneth L. Woodward, "Arguing Armageddon," *NW* 104 (Nov. 5, 1984), 91; "Armageddon and Mr. Reagan," *America* 157 (Nov. 10, 1984), 286; "Critics Fear That Reagan Is Swayed by Those Who Believe in a Nuclear Armageddon," *CT* 28 (Dec. 14, 1984), 48, 51.

103. Ronald Reagan, "Remarks . . . [to] the National Religious Broadcasters," *PP*, Feb. 4, 1985, 118.

104. "President's News Conference," *PP*, Feb. 21, 1985.

105. E.g., Dean Peerman, "Presidential Proof-Texting," *CC* 102 (Feb. 20, 1985), 176; and Allan Fotheringham, "Reagan Recruits the Lord," *Maclean's*, Feb. 18, 1985, 60.

106. Martin Anderson, *Revolution: The Reagan Legacy* (Stanford, CA: Hoover Institutional Press, 1990), 280.

107. Morris, *Dutch*, 427.

108. See Cannon, *Reagan*, 194; and Charles Wick, interview with Paul Kengor, May 17, 2001.

109. D'Souza, *Reagan*, 213.

110. Hutcheson, *White House*, 170; Slosser, *Reagan Inside Out*, 40.

111. Slosser, *Reagan Inside Out*, 117, reporting on interviews he conducted.

112. Quoted in Freiling, *Reagan's God*, 38.

113. Peggy Noonan, *What I Saw at the Revolution: A Political Life in the Reagan Era* (New York: Random House, 1990), 200.

114. Interview with Hutcheson, *White House*, 167–68.

115. Interview with Hutcheson, *White House*, 165. See *NYT*, Jan. 21, 1981; and Graham to RR, Feb. 2, 1981, WHORM, Box FG, Organizations, Box 82. The correspondence between Moomaw and Reagan was limited during Reagan's years in the White House. Moomaw wrote to congratulate him on his reelection, assure him he was praying for him, and inform him about the church's plans. Their only substantial exchange was about claims that American churches were aiding the persecutors rather than the victims in Nicaragua. See RR to Moomaw, July 27, 1987, PHR, PR, Box 18, Folder 297; RR to Moomaw, Oct. 20, 1987, ibid., Box 19, Folder 306; and RR to Moomaw, Dec. 21, 1987, ibid., Box 18, Folder 314. Reagan also regularly received tapes of Moomaw's sermons.

116. Hutcheson, *White House*, 167–68.

117. Sociologist Robert Bellah discusses this type of belief in *Habits of the Heart: Individualism and Commitment in American Life* (Berkeley: University of California Press, 1985). See also Hutcheson, *White House*, 171.

118. Personal conversation with Doug Bandow, Mar. 2002.

119. Martin Marty, "Presidential Piety: Must It Be Private?" *CC* 101 (Feb. 1984), 188. This phrase seems contradictory. D'Souza labels Reagan's religiosity "generic and a little suspect" and argues that Reagan's jokes often lampooned "ostentatious piety" and "the pretensions of the clergy" (*Reagan*, 213). "Yet there is no doubt about the sincerity of his deep faith in God and his acceptance of the fundamental truths of Christianity" (214). While Reagan discusses how his faith sustained him several times in his 726-page *An American Life*, his description of his religious commitments in the work is rather limited.

120. Tom Teepen, "View from the Reagan Pulpit," *Atlanta Constitution*, Feb. 7, 1984.

121. Nicholas Von Hoffman, "Reagan's Piety Is No Match for Carter's," *Arizona Daily Wildcat*, Sept. 18, 1984, 4.

122. Robert Kaiser, *New York Review of Books*, June 28, 1984.

123. Quoted in Kenneth Woodward with Elizabeth Bailey, "Who's a Good Christian?" *NW* 104 (Aug. 6, 1984), 30.

124. "Reagan–Otis Interview" (1976) 173. See also "Reagan on God and Morality," *CT* 20 (July 2, 1976), 39–40.

125. Quoted in David Nyhan, " 'Born-Again' Run the Race for President," *Boston Globe*, May 26, 1980, 10–11.

126. Quoted in Elizabeth Drew, *Portrait of an Election: The 1980 Presidential Campaign* (New York: Simon and Schuster, 1981), 172–73.

127. Quoted in Slosser, *Reagan Inside Out*, 49.

128. Hutcheson, *White House*, 165.

129. "Ronald Reagan's Religious Beliefs," Vertical File, Reagan, Ronald W.— Religion, RL. Later in the statement, however, Reagan asserted that "[p]erhaps there was a dramatic awakening" because he realized anew his need to trust God for direction after being elected governor of California.

130. Ronald Reagan Facts, 6.

131. Robertson's statement is in the *WSJ*, Sept. 18, 1984, 1; Herbert Ellingwood, "Ronald Reagan: 'God, Home, and Country,' " *Christian Life* 42 (Nov. 1980), 50. Ellingwood reported that Reagan told an interviewer that John 3:16 meant "that having accepted Jesus Christ as my Savior, I have God's promise of eternal life in Heaven" (50). See also RR to Charles W. Lowry, Dec. 27, 1985, RM, Box 2, WHORM, RM, 250001–RM010End.

132. Richard V. Pierard and Robert D. Linder, *Civil Religion and the Presidency* (Grand Rapids, MI: Zondervan, 1988), 272.

133. Jim Castelli, "Reagan Religiosity Threatens Separation," *Journal-Constitution*, Sept. 3, 1984.

134. See Paul H. Boase, "Moving the Mercy Seat into the White House: An Exegesis of the Carter/Reagan Religious Rhetoric," *JCR*, Sept. 1989, 3.

135. He addressed the National Prayer Breakfast eight times, the National Religious Broadcasters five times, and the National Association of Evangelicals twice. In these five addresses to the NRB, Reagan quoted the Bible fifty-four times and used some of them to discuss the connection between faith and policy making. He also spoke to many interdenominational, evangelical, mainline Protestant, Catholic, and Jewish groups.

136. His handwritten revisions of his speeches at the Reagan Library provide ample evidence. For an example, see his revision of the speech he gave in September 1982 at

Kansas State University. Reagan contributed much of the religious content of the address, which is restated in many subsequent speeches (PHF, Series 3, Presidential Speeches, Box 6, 8/4/82–10/22/84, Folder 104).

137. Reagan, "Women Leaders," 1450. See also Reagan, "Ecumenical Prayer Breakfast," 1166.

138. Reagan, "Remarks ... [to] the Knights of Columbus in Hartford, CT," *PP*, Aug. 3, 1982, 1110.

139. E.g., Ronald Reagan, "Remarks at the Annual National Prayer Breakfast," *PP*, Feb. 6, 1986, 145.

140. Reagan, "Annual Prayer Breakfast," 1983, 178.

141. Reagan, "Ecumenical Prayer Breakfast," 1168; Reagan, "Remarks at a Question-and-Answer Session with Local High School Honor Students," *PP*, May 23, 1983, 756.

142. Ronald Reagan, "Acceptance Speech," *Vital Speeches of the Day* 46 (Aug. 15, 1980), 642–46.

143. Reagan, "National Religious Broadcasters," 1983, 152.

144. Ronald Reagan, "Remarks following a Meeting with Pope John Paul II in Vatican City," *PP*, June 7, 1982, 737.

145. Ronald Reagan, "Remarks at a Spirit of America Festival in Decatur, AL," *PP*, July 4, 1984, 1001.

146. Ronald Reagan, "Address at the Commencement Exercises at the University of Notre Dame," *PP*, May 17, 1981, 434.

147. Reagan, "National Religious Broadcasters," 1983, 152 (first and second quotations); Reagan, "Prayer in Schools," 1182 (third quotation). Cf. "Responses to *Soir Magazine*," 3; Reagan, "Women Leaders," 1450; Reagan, "Remarks at Kansas State University ... on Public Issues," *PP*, Sept. 9, 1982, 1122. See also Robert D. Linder, "Reagan at Kansas State: Civil Religion in the Service of the New Right," *Reformed Journal*, Dec. 1982, 13–15.

148. Ronald Reagan, "Remarks at the ... American Legion in Salt Lake City, Utah," *PP*, Sept. 4, 1984, 1229.

149. Ronald Reagan, "Remarks at the ... National Association of Evangelicals in Columbus, OH," *PP*, Mar. 6, 1984, 309.

150. Reagan, "Ecumenical Prayer Breakfast," 1167.

151. "Interview with the Knight-Ridder News Service on Foreign and Domestic Issues," *PP*, Feb. 14, 1984, 207.

152. Reagan, "Ecumenical Prayer Breakfast," 1167.

153. Reagan, "American Legion," 1231; Reagan, "Inaugural Address," 1981, 3; Reagan, "Easter and Passover," 488. Cf. "Proclamation [of a] National Day of Prayer, 1984," *PP*, Dec. 14, 1983, 1698; Reagan, "National Day of Prayer," 574; Reagan, "National Association Evangelicals," 1984, 306–7.

154. Reagan, "Women Leaders," 1450; Reagan, "Address at the Commencement Exercises at the U.S. Military Academy," *PP*, May 27, 1981, 462; Reagan, "Remarks at a Meeting with Editors and Publishers of Trade Magazines," *PP*, Sept. 24, 1982, 1214; Reagan, "National Association Evangelicals," 1983, 362; and Slosser, *Reagan Inside Out*, 166. Reagan also often emphasized this point in personal letters. E.g., RR to Blake Steele, Apr. 6, 1983; and RR to Rolf McPherson, May 25, 1983, both in RM 115001–150000.

155. Reagan, "National Association Evangelicals," 1983, 362. Reagan began his calls for spiritual renewal in the 1970s. See von Damm, ed., *Reagan*, 91; "Reagan–Otis Interview," 167–69.

156. Most important were Morton Blackwell, J. Douglas Holladay, Faith Whittlesey, and Carolyn Sundseth. Before joining Reagan's team, Blackwell had worked for the new right leader Richard Viguerie's direct mail operation. An evangelical Episcopalian, Holladay had studied with Francis Schaeffer at L'Abri, directed a Young Life chapter, and worked to establish prayer and fellowship groups among Washington politicians. See "A White House Aide Reaches Out to Reagan's Opponents," *CT* 28 (May 18, 1984), 80–81. Sundseth focused on evangelical, fundamentalist, and conservative women's groups.

157. In May 1984, for example, Reagan aides discussed education, U.S. humanitarian assistance, drug policies, and Reagan's position on the relationship of church and state with a group of mainline Protestant bishops, evangelists, pastors, and lay leaders. See James Johnson to RR, Oct. 4, 1983; and Briefing Agenda for National Coalition of Concerned Citizens, May 7, 1984, both in OA 12271, Holladay, J. D., Nat'l Coalition of Concerned Citizens, May 5, 1984.

158. By Linder and Pierard's count, only four—Watt, Dole, Hodel, and Meese (who later served as attorney general)—of Reagan's thirty-one cabinet appointments were known evangelicals ("Ronald Reagan," 70).

159. Discussing areas where "a God-centered world view" was making a big difference, *Christianity Today* pointed to the work of Koop, Billings, Meese, Douglas Holladay, Dee Jepsen, Reagan's liaison with women's groups, Carl Horn of the Justice Department, and Marjory Mecklenberg and Jerry Regler in the Department of Health and Human Services (Spring, "Rating Reagan," 47–48).

160. See William Martin, *With God on Our Side: The Rise of the Religious Right in America* (New York: Broadway, 1996), 221–22.

161. See *The Christian Embassy Update*, summer 1983; Jones, "Reagan's Religion," 65, 69.

162. See Richard Pierard, "Ronald Reagan and the Evangelicals" in Marla J. Selvidge, ed., *Fundamentalism Today: What Makes It So Attractive* (Elgin, IL: Brethren, 1984), 57–60.

163. Beth Spring to J. Douglas Holladay (hereafter JDH), Apr. 6, 1984; Schedule Proposal, Apr. 19, 1984; Spring to JDH, May 11, 1984, all in OA 12271, Evangelical Press Assoc., 5/8/84, Holladay, J. D.

164. See A. James Reichley, "The Evangelical and Fundamentalist Revolt," in Richard John Neuhaus and Michael Cromartie, eds., *Piety and Politics: Evangelicals and Fundamentalist Confront the World* (Lanham, MD: University Press of America, 1987), 86–87. Also see James David Fairbanks, "Reagan, Religion, and the New Right," *Midwest Quarterly*, Spring 1982, 327–45.

165. E.g., OA 12272, Evangelical Briefing (Virginia), Trible, 4/26/85; OA 12272, Evangelical Press on Freedom Fighters and Budget, 4/19/85; OA 15050, Christian Media, Tax Reform, Aug. 1, 1985, Anderson, Carl, Box 2; and JDH to Chester Crocker, David Miller, and Frank Wisher, Dec. 6, 1985; OA 12266, Holladay, J.D., 9/27/85–1/3/86.

166. Jeffrey K. Hadden and Anson Shupe, *Televangelism: Power and Politics on God's Frontier* (New York: Henry Holt, 1988), 36.

167. E.g., "A White House Aide Reaches Out to Reagan's Opponents," 80; Spurgeon M. Dunnam, III to Elizabeth Dole, July 23, 1981, RM 030 (000001–199999), Box 6.

168. See OA 12271 Mainline Church Briefings, Box 11; ibid. Holladay, J. D., Religion and Politics, Dec. 20, 1984, Box 12. J. Douglas Holladay claimed that most participants appreciated the "openness and informative nature of the meetings" and that many

had "become ardent and active supporters of the Administration's policies" (JDH to Phil Ringdahl, Sept. 19, 1985). See also David Ochoa to RR, Sept. 25, 1985; James M. Dunn to William Keucher, Oct. 4, 1985; Ernestine Galloway to JDH, Oct. 16, 1985. All these are in RL, OA 12272, Mainline Church Briefing in South Africa, 9/23/85, Holladay, J. D., Box 14.

169. E.g., Rev. R. Dennis Macaleer to JDH, July 27, 1984, OA 12271, Holladay, J. D., Briefing—Letters of Response, Box 11.

170. See William P. Thompson to RR, Nov. 4, 1982; Excerpts from Remarks of the President in a Meeting with Hispanic, Labor and Religious Press, and William Clark to RR, n. d, all in RM 115001–150000.

171. E.g., August Wenzel to RR, July 2, 1985, RM 033–08, Lutheran Bodies, RM 031, 340000-RM 039-end; James Andrews to RR, Aug. 28, 1987, RM 033–11, Presbyterian Bodies, RM 031, 340000-RM 039-end.

172. See Steve Askin, "Liaison Works to Align White House, Catholics," *National Catholic Reporter*, Dec. 30, 1983, 6–7.

173. Most of these speeches are referenced in other footnotes in this chapter. See also Ronald Reagan, "Remarks to the Students and Faculty of Archbishop Carroll and All Saints High Schools," PP, Oct. 17, 1988, 1339; Reagan, "Remarks at the St. Ann's Festival in Hoboken, NJ," PP, July 26, 1984, 1097–1100; and "President Reagan's Remarks," *CGA World*, Sept.–Oct. 1984, 29–30.

174. Clark interview with Paul Kengor, Aug. 24, 2001, in *Reagan*, 123. See also William Clark, "President Reagan and the Wall," Address to the Council of National Policy, San Francisco, Mar. 2000, 11. Edmund Morris claims that Clark was the only person in the Reagan administration who enjoyed any type of "spiritual intimacy" with the president (interview with *The American Enterprise*, Nov.–Dec. 1999). See also James G. Lakely, "'God's Plan' Guided Reagan's Life," WT, June 7, 2004.

175. See Reagan, "Pope John Paul II," 736–39; and Reagan, "Remarks at the Welcoming Ceremony for Pope John Paul II in Fairbanks, AK," PP, May 2, 1984. They also talked on the phone and exchanged letters.

176. Ronald Reagan, "Remarks on Presenting the Presidential Medal of Freedom to Mother Teresa," PP, June 20, 1985, 802. See Mother Teresa to RR, June 21, 1985, PHF, PR, Series II, Box 13, File 192.

177. See Rebecca G. Range to Frederick J. Ryan Jr., Oct. 6, 1988, RM031 Catholic, 600000-end, RM, Box 7.

178. All these quotations are from Jeremiah O'Leary, "Vatican Ties Upgraded with Wilson as Envoy," WP, Jan. 11, 1984, 1, 12A. See also Arthur Jones, "Reagan Pushes Full Vatican Ties," *National Catholic Reporter*, Oct. 21, 1983, 1–2; Kenneth Briggs, "Church Groups Denounce Reagan Move," NYT, Jan. 11, 1984; "Recognizing Rome—and Politics," ibid., Jan. 13, 1984: Reagan is "presumably banking on this as a vote-getter among the nation's 52 million Roman Catholics, and [as] not so offensive to...conservative Protestants that they will abandon him." "Appointment of an Ambassador to the Vatican Meets Mild Opposition," CT 28 (Feb. 17, 1984), 40–41, described the Catholic response as "positive but quiet" (41). See also D. Peerman, "The Vatican Connection," CC 101 (Jan. 25, 1984), 67–68; Kenneth Kantzer and V. G. Beers, "That Controversial Appointment," NW 103 (Mar. 16, 1984), 12–13; and "Vatican Tie Challenged," CC 101 (Oct. 10, 1984), 919–20. The Southern Baptist Convention repeatedly urged Reagan to dissolve the post.

179. Henry Hyde et al. to Joseph Louis Bernardin, Dec. 15, 1982, RM 031 Catholic, 000001–124999, RM, Box 6.

180. Sven Kraemer to William P. Clark, Jan. 8, 1983, RM031, Catholic, 125–232368, Box 6.

181. See *NYT*, May 5, 1983. On this pastoral letter, see T. J. Reese, "The Bishops' Challenge of the Peace," *America* 148 (May 21, 1983), 393–95; K. A. Briggs, "Bishops' Consensus," *CC* 100 (May 25, 1983), 519–20; Michael Novak, "The Bishops Speak Out," *National Review* 35 (June 10, 1983), 674–81; and "Catholic Bishops Say No to Nuclear Arms," *CT* 27 (June 17, 1983), 39.

182. Daniel R. Browning, "National Body Opposes Bishop on Nuclear Arms," *Anaheim Hills News-Times*, Mar. 2, 1983, 1.

183. E.g., "The Bishops Take on Conservative Economics," *Business Week*, Dec. 19, 1983, 79–80.

184. See "The American Bishop's [*sic*] Pastoral Letter on the American Economy," RM 204001–211000, Box RM 000001–250000 (quotation); Faith Whittlesey to Frederick Ryan, Nov. 13, 1984, "Lay Commission on Catholic Social Teaching and the U.S. Economy," both in RM 204001–211000, Box RM 000001–250000.

185. Report excerpted in the *NYT*, Nov. 8, 1984.

186. *NYT*, Oct. 29, 1984.

187. Lynch to Archbishop Philip M. Hannan, Dec. 4, 1984. See also Lynch to Edwin Meese, Dec. 5, 1984, both in RM 204001–211000, Box RM 000001–250000.

188. In October 1985, the bishops invited Reagan to comment on the second draft of the pastoral letter. Because the final letter was bound to be unsatisfactory, Patrick Buchanan recommended that the administration take no official stand on it until it was published. See Rembert Weakland to RR, Oct. 7, 1985, RM031, Catholic, 340000–599999, RM, Box 7; Buchanan to Donald Regan, Sept. 30, 1985, RM031, Catholic, 340000–599999, RM, Box 7.

189. E.g., Ronald Reagan, "Proclamation [of] Jewish Heritage Week," May 1, 1981, *PP*, 401–2; Reagan, "Proclamation [of] Jewish Heritage Week," *PP*, Apr. 19, 1985, 462–63; Reagan, "Remarks . . . [to] the National Conference of Christians and Jews," *PP*, Mar. 23, 1982, 357–58; Reagan, "Remarks . . . [to] Jewish Leaders," Feb. 2, 1983, *PP*, 173–75; Reagan, "Remarks . . . [to] the Anti-Defamation League of B'nai B'rith," *PP*, June 10, 1983, 847–48. For Jews' appreciation of his efforts, see Morris Abram to RR, Nov. 5, 1987, RM032, Jewish, 325000-end, Box 7.

190. Reagan's Meeting with Rabbi H. D. Yoseph, Feb. 17, 1983, OA 10854, Breger, Marshall; Moshe Feller, "Rabbis Explain 'Top to Top,' " *American Jewish World*, June 8, 1983.

191. See Al Abrams to Beth Barnes, Feb. 2, 1982, "National Association of Jewish Legislators, OA 10853, Breger, Marshall; UJA Top Leadership White House Briefing, Mar 3, 1983, ibid.; "Talking Points for Meeting with Rabbi Lubinsky," May 17, 1982; and Memorandum for Red Caveney, Feb. 5, 1983, WHORM, RM020, 187310-end; and Jack Stein, Speech to B'nai Zion, June 18, 1981, OA 10852.

192. See "President's Remarks to Jewish Leadership," Nov. 19, 1981; Meeting with the President and Fisher Group, Nov. 11, 1981, OA 10852, Breger, Marshall; Elizabeth Dole, "Meeting with Reagan/Bush Jewish Supporters, Nov. 19, 1981, ibid.; "Meeting with the President and Jewish Leaders," June 7, 1983, OA 10854, Breger, Marshall; National Jewish Coalition, Apr. 4, 1985, OA 10371, and Breger, Marshall, Box 3; President's Meeting with UJA Top Donors, Aug. 6, 1983, ibid.

193. See Cannon, *Reagan*, 391. For his support of Israel, see, for example, Ronald Reagan, "Remarks to . . . Jewish Community Leaders in Valley Stream, NY," *PP*, Oct. 26, 1984, 1652–55.

194. Ronald Reagan, "Remarks at the Jewish Community Center of Greater Washington . . . ," *PP*, Dec. 4, 1983, 1650–51.

195. E.g., "Reagan Fails to Allay Worry at Jewish Parley," *NYT*, Sept. 7, 1984, A14.

196. Marshall Breger to Marshall Wolke, Nov. 2, 1984. See also Wolke to RR, Sept. 10, 1984; Adler to Breger, Oct. 17, 1984; Breger to Samuel Adler, Nov. 5, 1984; and Norman Lent to RR, Sept. 14, 1984, all in RM 235001–250000; and "Conservative Rabbis Urged to Mobilize against Moral Majority," Global News Service of the Jewish People, Apr. 28, 1982, RM032, Jewish, 000001–169999.

197. E.g., Irving Kristol, "The Political Dilemma of American Jews," *Commentary* 74 (July 1984), 23–29; and Lucy Davidowicz, "Politics, the Jews and the '84 Election," *Commentary*, Feb. 1985, 25–30. The quotation is from Richard V. Pierard, "Religion and the 1984 Election Campaign," *Review of Religious Research* 27 (Dec. 1985), 107.

198. See Marshall Breger, "Jews and American Politics, 1984 and After," *This World*, 25–30.

199. Among others, fifty-three senators, his wife, and Elie Wiesel urged him not to go. For Wiesel's concerns, see "Remarks on Presenting the Congressional Gold Medal to Elie Wiesel," *PP*, Apr. 19, 1985, 462.

200. D' Souza, *Reagan*, 233.

201. Ronald Reagan, "Remarks . . . with Regional Editors and Broadcasters," *PP*, Apr. 18, 1985, 457; Reagan, "Remarks at a Joint German-American Military Ceremony at Bitburg . . . ," *PP*, May 5, 1985, 565–68, quotation from 566.

202. Bernard Weintraub, "Reagan Joins Kohl in Brief Memorial at Bitburg Graves," *NYT*, May 6, 1985.

203. Cannon, *Reagan*, 573. Kohl claimed that a presidential snub might topple his administration.

204. D'Souza, *Reagan*, 235.

205. RR to Philip M. Hannan, May 28, 1985, PHF, PR, Series II, Box 12, Folder 186; RR to George Smathers, May 28, 1985, ibid. Reagan told Hannan he had received many letters from World War II veterans, some of whom had been POWs, supporting his decision.

206. Cannon, *Reagan*, 587. Prominent Jewish Republicans met with Reagan staff on April 16, 1985, to try to persuade Reagan not to go to Bitburg (578–79). The fullest descriptions of this episode are Cannon, *Reagan*, 573–89; and Morris, *Dutch*, 521–26.

207. Pierard and Linder, *Civil Religion*, 266.

208. Some evangelicals took a less partisan approach. See Kenneth Kantzer, "Our November Call to Conscience," *CT* 28 (Sept. 21, 1984), 12–13; "Billy Graham: Churches Should Shun Partisan Politics," *USN*, Oct. 8, 1984, 12.

209. Woodward, "Who's a Good Christian?" 30. Woodward noted that Mondale, like Reagan, seldom attended church and was "vague about his doctrinal commitments." Strongly influenced by the Social Gospel, he saw helping others as the "mark of a true Christian and justice as the sign of a Christian society." *Time* offered a different perspective: Mondale was the "pious and principled son of a Methodist pastor" who "apparently feels his faith deeply and knows what he believes" (Kurt

Anderson, "For God and Country," *Time* [Sept. 10, 1984], 10). Also see Steven Tipton, "Religion and the Moral Rhetoric of Presidential Politics," *CC* 101 (Oct. 31, 1984), 1010–13.

210. Anderson, "For God and Country," 8. See also Beth Spring, "Republicans, Religion, and Reelection," *CT* 28 (Oct. 5, 1984), 54–58; and "Partisan Politics: Where Does the Gospel Fit?" *CT* 28 (Nov. 9, 1984), 15–17.

211. Many commentators conclude that Reagan gave only "pro forma support" to the proposals of the New Right for restoring school prayer, tuition tax credits, and a right-to-life amendment. E.g., Leo Ribuffo, "God and Contemporary Politics," *Journal of American History* 79 (Mar. 1993), 1522.

212. Pierard, "1984 Election Campaign," 104. This paragraph depends heavily on Pierard's article.

213. These were Reagan's *Abortion and the Conscience of the Nation*, Bob Slosser's *Reagan Inside Out*, and David Shepherd's edited compilation entitled *Ronald Reagan: In God I Trust*.

214. Pierard, "1984 Election Campaign," 104.

215. Reagan, "Ecumenical Prayer Breakfast," 1167.

216. William Safire, *NYT*, Aug. 27, 1984; Haynes Johnson, *WP*, Aug. 26, 1984; "Church-State Separation Is Still Sacred," *Business Week*, Sept. 24, 1984, 24; "A Christian Country?" *National Review*, Sept. 21, 1984, 18–19.

217. Sidney Blumenthal, "The Religious Right and Republicans" in Neuhaus and Cromartie, eds., *Piety and Politics*, 272–73.

218. "The Theory of Trickle-Down Religion," *Atlanta Constitution*, Sept. 10, 1984. Reagan defended his speech at Dallas in "Informal Exchange with Reporters...," *PP*, Sept. 2, 1984, 1219; and *PP*, Sept. 4, 1984, 1233.

219. Teepen, "Reagan Pulpit."

220. Castelli, "Reagan Religiosity." *Newsweek* called Ferraro's claim that Reagan was not a "good Christian" "an ill-chosen way to dramatize her contention that cutbacks in social programs violated traditional religious notions of charity and compassion." See "Politics and the Pulpit" 104 (Sept. 17, 1984), 25. See also Woodward, "Who's a Good Christian?" 30. For other critiques of Reagan, see Danny Collum, "What's At Stake...and What Isn't," *Sojourners*, Sept, 1984, 12–16; and James Wall, "Looking at Candidates through a Mirror," *CC* 101 (Oct. 10, 1984), 915–16.

221. Stephen Galebach to John A. Svahn and Bruce Chapman, Aug. 28, 1984, RM 220001–235000, Box RM 000001–250000.

222. "Politics and the Pulpit," 26; the quotation is that of the *Newsweek* writers summarizing Mondale's position. See Walter Mondale, "Religion Is a Private Matter," *CS*, Oct. 1984, 12–15; "God and the Ballot Box," *Time* 124 (Sept. 17, 1984), 26; Joseph Carey, "Religion and Politics: Furor Keeps Building," *USN*, Sept. 17, 1984, 29–30; and Charles Krauthammer, "The Church-State Debate," *NR* 191 (Sept. 17 & 24, 1984), 15–18.

223. "Debate between the President and...Mondale," 1447.

224. Quoted in Blumenthal, "Religious Right," 285.

225. "General Plan of Appeal to Catholics," OA 12450 Catholic Strategy, Blackwell, Morton.

226. "A Plan on How to Proceed," OA 12450, Catholic Strategy, Blackwell, Morton, Box 7. See also "Ethnic/Blue Collar Strategy Outline," Dec. 10, 1982; Elizabeth Dole to Edwin Meese, James Baker, and Michael Deaver on Ethnic/Catholic Strategy, n. d.; and Thomas Melady to Michael McManus Jr., Mar. 31, 1983, ibid. These documents

discussed the various Catholic ethnic groups, provided lots of statistical analysis, and proposed specific steps to win Catholic votes.

227. Pierard, "1984 Election Campaign," 109; William Droel and Gregory Pierce, "The Catholic Vote," *CMW* 111 (Sept. 7, 1984), 455–56.

228. Wilson Carey McWilliams, "The Meaning of the Election," in Gerald M. Pomper, ed., *The Election of 1984: Reports and Interpretations* (Chatham, NJ: Chatham, 1985), 172. Numerous Catholic bishops, most notably New York Archbishop John J. O'Connor, Cardinal John Krol of Philadelphia, and Bishop Bernard Law of Boston, supported Reagan, and many Catholic editors sharply criticized Ferraro's position on abortion. See "Politics and the Pulpit," 25; Wilson Carey McWilliams, *Beyond the Politics of Disappointment? American Elections, 1980–1988* (New York: Chatham, 2000), 38–40.

229. See Adam Clymer, "Religion and Politics Mix Poorly for Democrats," *NYT*, Nov. 25, 1984; Albert Menendez, *Christian College News*, Dec. 1984, 1–2; and James Wall, "Both Parties Helped Reagan Win," *CC* 101 (Nov. 14, 1984), 1051–52.

230. Pierard, "1984 Election Campaign," 113.

231. Robert Dugan, "Election '84: Some Surprising Winners and Losers," *CT* 29 (Jan. 11, 1985), 43. Cf. James M. Wall, "Ban Neutrality from Campaign Talk," *CC* 101 (Sept. 12–19, 1984), 819–20.

232. Reagan, "Ecumenical Prayer Breakfast," 1167. Cf. "Responses to *Soir* Magazine," 3.

233. "Reverend Reagan," *NR* 188 (Apr. 4, 1983), 7–9.

234. Wilbur Edel, *Defenders of the Faith: Religion and Politics from the Pilgrim Fathers to Ronald Reagan* (New York: Praeger, 1987), 149.

235. Ronald Reagan, "Address . . . on State of the Union Address," *PP*, Feb. 4, 1986, 128.

236. The bill enabled doctors to perform abortions whenever they concluded that a pregnancy endangered a woman's physical or mental health. See Pemberton, *Exit*, 75–76; D'Souza, *Reagan*, 66–67; Morris, *Dutch*, 351–52; and von Damm, ed., *Reagan*, 100–3.

237. See Meeting with Right to Life Volunteers, Jan. 21, 1988, OA 19222, Abortion, Bauer, Gary, Box 1; See also Meeting with National Leaders of Pro-Life Movement," OA 12448, Blackwell, Morton, 1/23/84.

238. Reagan, "Knights of Columbus," 1012. See also Reagan, "National Association Evangelicals," 1983, 361. "I think it comes down to one simple answer: You cannot interrupt a pregnancy without taking a human life," Reagan told an interviewer. "And the only way we can justify taking a life in our Judeo-Christian tradition is in self-defense" ("Reagan–Otis Interview," 178).

239. Reagan, "National Religious Broadcasters," 1984, 119. Cf. "Responses to *Soir* Magazine," 2; RR to Malcolm Muggeridge, July 9, 1984, PHR, PR, Series II, Box 9, Folder 133; RR to Archbishop John J. O'Connor, Mar. 29, 1985, ibid., Box 12, Folder 176.

240. Reagan, "National Association Evangelicals," 1983, 360–61.

241. Reagan, "National Religious Broadcasters," 1984, 119; "Memorandum Promoting Adoption," *PP*, Nov. 13, 1987, 1329; "Proclamation [of] National Adoption Week, 1987," *PP*, Nov. 19, 1987, 1358; "Proclamation [of] National Adoption Week, 1988," *PP*, Nov. 18, 1988.

242. See Bill Peterson, "New Right Defeated on Abortion," *WP*, Sept. 16, 1982, A1. *Christianity Today* argued that Reagan had been reluctant to "endorse any particular

initiative because prolife groups failed to patch up their intramural differences" (Spring, "Rating Reagan," 50).

243. See Steven Roberts, "Reagan Said to Back Measure to Bar Any Federal Aid for Abortion," *NYT*, Feb. 10, 1987, A20; George Archibald and Amy Bayer, "Anti-Abortion War Resumed by Reagan," *WT*, July 31, 1987, A1; Fred Barnes, "Bringing Up Baby," *NR* 197 (Aug. 24, 1987), 10–12; OA 17976, Prolife Bill Chronology Summary, Bell, Mariam (2), (3), (4) and (5). For background, see Administration Abortion Bill, June 20, 1986, OA 17964, Bell, Mariam, Abortion–General [1] and RR to Henry Hyde, Mar. 19, 1987, OA 17955, Pro-Life (2), Bell, Mariam, Box 1.

244. Pemberton, *Exit*, 124; Blumenthal, "Religious Right," 286; "Reagan Abortion Stand Opposed," *USA Today*, Sept. 4, 1985, 3A.

245. E.g., "Prolifers, Wake Up," *National Catholic Register*, May 4, 1986; Nellie Gray to RR, Jan. 12, 1987, OA 17955, Pro-Life (2), Bell Mariam, Box 1: "It is a puzzlement and great disappointment that actions of your Executive branch do not follow your good words."

246. Jim Wallis, "The President's Pulpit: A Look at Ronald Reagan's Theology," *Sojourners*, Sept. 1984, 21. See also Wallis, "Dissenting from the Right," in "The Roles Religion Plays," *NW*, 104 (Sept. 17, 1984), 32. Cf. Colman McCarthy, "On This Issue, Reagan Is Morally Right," *WP*, May 21, 1983.

247. Collum, "Reagan's Election Crusade," *Sojourners* 13 (Apr. 1984), 4.

248. Julie Johnson, "Reagan Vows to Continue Battle on Abortion," *NYT*, Jan. 14, 1989; "Reagan Says Ending Abortion Will Mean U.S. Is Civilized," *NYT*, Jan. 16, 1989. Cf. William P. Clark, "For Reagan, All Life Was Sacred," *NYT*, June 11, 2004.

249. Interview with O'Connor. "Abortion" is not an item in the index of Reagan's *An American Life*.

250. Reagan, "National Religious Broadcasters," 1984, 120.

251. Reagan, "Message to the Congress . . . on Prayer in the School," *PP*, May 17, 1982, 647–49. See also Reagan, "Message to the Congress . . . on Prayer in the Schools," *PP*, Mar. 8, 1983, 364–65.

252. Reagan, "Candle-Lighting Ceremony," 1218.

253. Reagan, "Prayer," 1182. See also Reagan, "Remarks . . . [to] the National Parent-Teacher Association in Albuquerque, NM," *PP*, June 15, 1983, 871. Reagan made this same point in dozens of letters on school prayer. E.g., RR to Lois Picard, June 13, 1984, RM020, Prayers, 220000–245723.

254. Reagan, "Prayer," 1182.

255. Reagan, "National Day of Prayer," 574.

256. Reagan, "National Religious Broadcasters," 1984, 120. See also Reagan, "National Association Evangelicals," 1984, 309; and Reagan, "Remarks at a National Forum on Excellence in Education, Indianapolis," *PP*, Dec. 8, 1983, 1669.

257. See Elizabeth Dole to Edwin Harper, Apr. 26, 1982, RM020 Prayers, Prayer Periods, 065021–072000; RM020, 207055–334999. Staff assigned to call senators were given key talking points for particular individuals, answers to probable questions, and major public statements by the president on school prayer. Letters from Reagan were sent to all 26,300 individuals who had written to commend him for proclaiming 1983 to be the Year of the Bible. See School Prayer Amendment Letter, Feb. 7, 1984, RM 020, Prayers, Box 4. The file RM020 Prayers, Prayer Periods, 187310–200000 contains letters Reagan sent in 1984 to congressmen on school prayer and letters to religious leaders. See RM020, Prayers, Box 4. See also "Questions and Answers on the President's School Prayer Amendment," Mar. 5, 1984, ibid.

258. See materials in RM 020, Prayers, 150001–180000 for Reagan's talk to pro-school prayer leaders on July 12, 1983.

259. See RM020, Prayers, Box 4; RM020, Prayers, 150001–180000; Robertson to RR, Sept. 9, 1983, ibid. Concerned Women of America, Save Our Schools, the Fellowship of Christian Athletes, and the Southern Baptist Convention all strongly promoted the amendment (RM020, Prayers, 200001–204500, Box 4; RM020, Prayers, Prayer Periods, 072001–072849). See also Tom Wicker, "The Baptist Switch," *NYT*, June 22, 1982. For an example of Jewish support, see Seymour Siegel, "School Prayers—Yes!" *Jewish Spectator*, Fall 1982, 53–55.

260. See Mary Kay Quinlan, "New Push on for School-Prayer Amendment," *USA Today*, July 24, 1985, 4A; Kristen Burroughs, "Coalition Vows Hard Drive for Vocal Prayer in Schools," *WT*, July 24, 1985; and Keith Richburg, "Hill Conservatives, Students Lobby Congress for School Prayer," *WP*, Aug. 3, 1985, B6.

261. Martin, *With God on Our Side*, 233. Beth Spring argued in 1983 that Reagan had "expended very little political capital on the prayer issue" ("Rating Reagan," 50).

262. Morris S. Friedman to RR, Sept. 7, 1984, RM020, Prayers, 245724–262999. See also The Synagogue Council of America to RR, May 4, 1982, RM020, Prayers, Prayer Periods, 075001–080000 (this file also contains letters of protest from other Jewish organizations sent in May 1982). See also Linder, "Reagan at Kansas State," 15; and Charles Krauthammer, "Rectifying the Border," *Time*, Sept. 24, 1984, 79–80.

263. T. R. Reid, "Prayer Bill Foes Attack 'Election-Year Religiosity,'" *WP*, Mar. 7, 1984. More than a dozen Jewish groups and Christian denominations met to reiterate their strong opposition to the amendment. See also, John C. Danforth, "Why Many Religious People Oppose It," *WP*, Mar. 11, 1984.

264. Reagan, "National Religious Broadcasters," 1983, 153. See also Reagan, "Remarks . . . during an Administrative Briefing in Chicago, IL . . . ," *PP*, May 10, 1982, 591. Reagan, "Remarks to . . . Archbishop Carroll and All Saints High Schools," 1341.

265. Reagan, "Women Leaders," 2. See also Thomas P. Melady, "Tuition Tax Relief: Educational Priority," *Catholic Transcript*, Sept. 2, 1983, 2.

266. Reagan, "Knights of Columbus," 1012.

267. RR to Thomas J. Welsh, Apr. 5, 1982, PHF, PR, Series II, Box 3, Folder 34.

268. RR to John F. Meyers, Nov. 29, 1983, RRL, PHF, PR, Series II, Box 8, Folder 107.

269. Paul Kengor explains that Reagan's understanding of communism as an evil empire was influenced by a number of individuals, especially Soviet dissident and author Aleksandr Solzhenitsyn and Whittaker Chambers. See *Reagan*, 77–88. See especially Whittaker Chambers, *Witness* (New York: Random House, 1952) and Solzhenitsyn, *Alexander Solzhenitsyn Speaks to the West* (London: Bodley Head, 1978).

270. Jerel A. Rosati, *The Carter Administration's Quest for Global Community: Beliefs and Their Impacts on Behavior* (Columbia: University of South Carolina Press, 1987), 52–54, quotation from 52.

271. Reagan, "Knights of Columbus," 1013. Kengor, *Reagan*, 329, points out that Reagan referred to God's providential direction of history in most of his milestone speeches, including the 1964 "Time for Choosing," address, both inaugural addresses as California's governor, his 1979 speech announcing his campaign for the presidency, his speech accepting the Republican nomination in 1980, his two presidential inaugural addresses, and his farewell address.

272. E.g., Reagan, "Inaugural Address," 1981, 3; Reagan, "Address . . . on State of the Union Address," *PP*, Feb. 6, 1985, 279; Reagan, "Remarks . . . Marking . . . Captive Nations Week," *PP*, July 19, 1983, 1053.

273. Reagan, "Captive Nations Week," 1053. Cf. Reagan, "State of the Union," 1985, 279; Reagan, "Inaugural Address," 1981, 3.

274. Reagan, "National Association Evangelicals," 1984, 307.

275. Ronald Reagan, "Remarks at the Conservative Political Action Conference Dinner," *PP*, Mar. 20, 1981, 278.

276. Reagan, "Captive Nations Week," 1053.

277. Ronald Reagan, "Address before . . . the Irish National Parliament," *PP*, June 4, 1984, 811.

278. Clark, "President Reagan and the Wall," 2.

279. Reagan, "National Association Evangelicals," 1983, 362–64. Although many pundits accused Reagan of "recklessly and unconsciously provoking the Soviets into war," he claimed he made this speech and others like it "with malice aforethought." Reagan later explained that in his address he wanted to reach Americans "who—like my daughter Patti—were being told the path to peace was via a freeze . . . that if implemented, would leave the Soviets in a position of nuclear superiority" (*American Life*, 568–70). He also insisted that since the Soviet Union clearly was an evil system, "why shouldn't we say so?" (Ronald Reagan, *Speaking My Mind: Selected Speeches* [New York: Simon and Schuster, 1989], 168–69). See also Anthony R. Dolan, "Premeditated Prose: Reagan's Evil Empire," *American Enterprise*, Mar.–Apr. 1993, 24–26. In other addresses, Reagan denounced the idea that the United States and the USSR were "morally equivalent." E.g., Reagan, "Remarks at a Fundraising Dinner for Senator Paula Hawkins in Miami," *PP*, May 27, 1985, 674.

280. E.g., William F. Buckley Jr., "Reagan at Orlando," *National Review* 35 (Apr. 15, 1983), 456; Richard V. Pierard, "Mending the Fence: Reagan and the Evangelicals," *Reformed Journal* 33 (June 1983), 18–21; Beth Spring, "Reagan Courts Evangelical Clout against Nuclear Freeze," *CT* 27 (Apr. 8, 1983), 44–45; James Wall, "Mr. Reagan Speaks Only to Believers," *CC* 100 (Mar. 23–30, 1983), 259; "Presidential Pulpit," *CMW* 110, Mar. 25, 1983), 164–65; and "The Presidential Pulpit," *America* 148 (Mar. 26, 1983), 223.

281. The quotation is from Michael Lienesch, *Redeeming America: Piety and Politics in the New Christian Right* (Chapel Hill: University of North Carolina Press, 1993), 211, who is summarizing the argument of George Marsden, *Fundamentalism and American Culture* (New York: Oxford University Press, 1980), 206–11.

282. Woodrow Wilson, "Statement on Russia," Sept. 1918, in James Richardson, ed., *A Compilation of the Messages and Papers of the Presidents*, 20 vols. (New York: Bureau of National Literature, 1917), 17:8589–92 (see also Wilson, "Address to Congress," Dec. 4, 1917, ibid., 17:8403; and Wilson, "Seventh Annual Message to Congress," Dec. 2, 1919, ibid., 18:8819); Dwight D. Eisenhower, "Farewell Radio and Television Address to the American People," *PP*, Jan. 17, 1961, 1037; the third quotation is from Anderson, *Revolution*, xxxii.

283. Commager as quoted in the *WP*, Mar. 8, 1983. He added, "No other presidential speech has ever so flagrantly allied the government with religion." See also Albert Menendez, " 'The Right Rev. Ronald Reagan'?" *CS*, May 1983, 16; and Morris, *Dutch*, 475.

284. Hugh Sidey, "The Right Reverend Ronald Reagan," *Time* 121 (Mar. 21, 1983), 18. Even Jimmy Carter "never mixed God and government as baldly as Reagan did at

Orlando." See also Arthur Schlesinger Jr., "Pretensions in the Presidential Pulpit," *WSJ*, Mar. 17, 1983, 26.

285. Anthony Lewis, "Onward Christian Soldiers," *NYT*, Mar. 10, 1983.

286. Wallis, "President's Pulpit," 20.

287. Richard Cohen, "Convictions," *WP*, May 26, 1983, C1.

288. Morris, *Dutch*, 473.

289. Robert M. Gates, *From the Shadows: The Ultimate Insider's Story of the Five Presidents and How They Won the Cold War* (New York: Simon and Schuster, 1996), 263. Ironically, a decade later, many Russians acknowledged that their nation had been an evil empire. See also Kengor, *Reagan*, 254–57.

290. E.g., RR to Rabbi Dov Bidnick, June 9, 1981, RM020, Prayers—Prayer Periods, 000001–065019.

291. RR to Stephen Majoros, Mar. 15, 1983, PHF, PR, Box 5, 12/21/82–3/16/83. See also RR to John Kmech, Feb. 1, 1983, ibid.; and to Robert E. Kent, Apr. 18, 1983, ibid., Series II, Box 6, Folder 79.

292. Reagan, *American Life*, 552–53, 550, quotations from 552–53.

293. Reagan, "American Legion," 1230.

294. Reagan, *American Life*, 550, 13, 547, quotations in that order. On Reagan's aversion to nuclear weapons and war, see Edwin Meese III, *With Reagan: The Inside Story* (Washington, DC: Regnery Gateway), 186–87; Anderson, *Revolution*, 72; and George Shultz, *Turmoil and Triumph* (New York: Scribner's, 1993), 189.

295. Ronald Reagan, "Address to the Nation on the Soviet–United States Summit Meeting," *PP*, Dec. 10, 1987, 1502.

296. Reagan, "National Religious Broadcasters," 1983, 154. See also Muggeridge to RR, Mar. 1983: "I am sure that Solzhenitsyn is right, that now...there is a higher percentage of believing Christians in the USSR than in the UK or the USA," despite the concerted effort "to extirpate the Christian faith." See also RR to Muggeridge, Apr. 18, 1983, both in PHF, PR, Series II, Box 6, Folder 78.

297. Ronald Reagan, "Remarks...with Area High School Seniors in Jacksonville, FL," *PP*, Dec. 1, 1987, 1405. On Reagan's fascination with religious revival in the USSR, see also Morris, *Dutch*, 519.

298. Reagan, "National Association Evangelicals," 1984, 307.

299. E.g., Ronald Reagan, "Address to the Nation about Christmas and the Situation in Poland," *PP*, Dec. 23, 1981, 1186–87; Reagan, "Statement in Signing Legislation concerning Human Rights in the Soviet Union," *PP*, Mar. 22, 1982, 350; Reagan, "Remarks on Signing the International Human Rights Day Proclamation," *PP*, Dec. 10, 1984, 1882–83; Memorandum of Conversation, Reagan-Gorbachev Meetings in Geneva, Nov. 1985, Third Private Meeting, OA 92137, Geneva Meetings, Memcons of Plenary Sessions and Tete-a-tete, 11/19/85, Matlock, Jack, Box 6; and Reagan, *American Life*, 675, 698, 706. In meetings with Soviet leaders, Reagan also lobbied for ending religious repression (*An American Life*, 558).

300. Ronald Reagan, "Remarks at a Conference on Religious Liberty," *PP*, Apr. 16, 1985, 437–40.

301. Reagan, "National Religious Broadcasters," 1983, 154.

302. Reagan, "Remarks on Signing...Human Rights Day and Week Proclamation," *PP*, Dec. 9, 1983, 1675.

303. Reagan, "Knights of Columbus," 1014. Among other actions, Reagan allowed Catholic Relief Services to buy unlimited amounts of surplus food at "concessionary

prices" to distribute to the Polish people. See John Cardinal Krol to RR, Aug. 4, 1981, RRL, PHF, PR, Folder 6.

304. Reagan, "Easter and Passover," 488.

305. Ronald Reagan, "Remarks . . . on Religious Freedom in the Soviet Union," *PP*, May 3, 1988, 550.

306. Ronald Reagan, "Remarks to Religious Leaders at the Danilov Monastery in Moscow," *PP*, May 30, 1988, 675. See also, Reagan, "Soviet Dissidents," 676–77. Cf. "New Year's Messages of President Reagan and Soviet Secretary Gorbachev," *PP*, Jan. 1, 1986, 1; and Reagan, "Remarks at Fudan University in Shanghai, China," *PP*, Apr. 30, 1984, 606.

307. See "Man of the Decade, Gorbachev," *Time* 135 (Jan. 1, 1990), 42–45; Strobe Talbott, "Rethinking the Red Menace," ibid., 66–72; and Raymond L. Garthoff, *The Great Transition: American-Soviet Relations and the End of the Cold War* (Washington, DC: Brookings Institution, 1994).

308. George F. Kennan, "The G.O.P. Won the Cold War? Ridiculous," *NYT*, Oct. 28, 1992, A21; Richard J. Barnet, "A Balance Sheet: Lippmann, Kennan, and the Cold War," in Michael J. Hogan, ed., *The End of the Cold War* (New York: Cambridge University Press, 1992), 113–27.

309. E.g., Gates, *From the Shadows.*

310. E.g., Don Oberdorfer, "Reagan's Triumph: Personal or Institutional?" in Kenneth W. Thompson, *Foreign Policy in the Reagan Presidency: Nine Intimate Perspectives* (Lanham, MD: University Press of America, 1993), 159–78.

311. Cannon, *Reagan*, 833.

312. Both Peter Schweizer and Paul Kengor argue that Reagan seemed to believe that God had spared his life to confront communism. See Schweizer, *Reagan's War: The Epic Story of His Forty-Year Struggle and Final Triumph over Communism* (New York: Doubleday, 2002), 3, 134–37, 180; and Kengor, *Reagan*, 198–99.

313. Peter Schweizer, *Victory: The Reagan Administration's Secret Strategy That Hastened the Collapse of the Soviet Union* (New York: Atlantic Monthly Press, 1994), esp. xiii–xx. This strategy also included a "sophisticated and detailed psychological operation to fuel indecision and fear among the Soviet leadership," "a comprehensive global campaign . . . to reduce drastically Soviet access to Western high technology," and "a widespread technological disinformation campaign, designed to disrupt the Soviet economy." See also Schweizer, *Reagan's War*, 152–59, 284, where he provides a breakdown of the financial costs Reagan's strategy imposed on the Soviets. Meese provides an insider perspective on Reagan's strategy in *With Reagan*, 163–73. Samuel F. Wells Jr., "Nuclear Weapons and European Security during the Cold War," in Hogan, ed., *The End of the Cold War*, 63–75, offers a similar perspective. The president and the pope worked to aid Solidarity in Poland to order to puncture the Iron Curtain and foster spiritual renewal. See Carl Bernstein, "The Holy Alliance," *Time*, Feb. 24, 1992, 28, 30; "The Pope and the President: A Key Advisor [William Clark] Reflects on the Reagan Administration," *Catholic World Reporter*, Nov. 1999; and Reagan, *American Life*, 301–3. Beth A. Fischer argues that Reagan did not have a grand design but rather dramatically shifted his approach in late 1983 and early 1984. See Fischer, *The Reagan Reversal: Foreign Policy and the End of the Cold War* (Columbia: University of Missouri Press, 1997), 1–5, 109–43. See also Don Oberdorfer, *The Turn: From the Cold War to a New Era* (New York: Poseidon, 1991), 438.

314. Condoleezza Rice, "U.S.-Soviet Relations," in Larry Berman, ed., *Looking Back on the Reagan Presidency* (Baltimore, Johns Hopkins University Press, 1990), 74. See also Reagan, *American Life*, 551, 660; Schweizer, *Victory*, 107.

315. Schweizer, *Victory*, 281.

316. Pemberton, *Exit*, 155; Gates, *From the Shadows*, 263. Gorbachev claimed that their personal relationship was pivotal to the arms control agreements they reached (Mikhail Gorbachev, "A President Who Listened," *NYT*, June 7, 2004). See also Jack Matlock, *Reagan and Gorbachev: How the Cold War Ended* (New York: Random House, 2004).

317. Statement by Kissinger, video commemoration of Ronald Reagan, Republican National Convention, San Diego, 1996, as quoted by D'Souza, *Reagan*, 134.

318. Reagan, *American Life*, 708.

319. William Clark, "NSDD-75: A New Approach to the Soviet Union," in Peter Schweizer, ed., *Fall of the Berlin Wall* (Stanford, CA: Hoover Institution Press, 2000), 75.

320. D'Souza, *Reagan*, 28–29. Other positive appraisals of Reagan's role in ending the cold war include Andrew E. Busch, "Ronald Reagan and the Defeat of the Soviet Empire," *PSQ* 27 (Summer 1997), 451–66; Douglas J. Hoekstra, "Presidential Beliefs and the Reagan Paradox," ibid., 429–50; and John Lewis Gaddis, *The United States and the End of the Cold War* (New York: Oxford University Press, 1992), 119–32. Gaddis contends that Reagan "had a decisive impact upon the course of events" through his proposal of SDI, endorsement of the "zero option" on intermediate-range nuclear missiles in Europe, real reductions in warheads under START, the quickness with which he engaged in serious negotiations with Gorbachev, and his eagerness to consider alternatives to the nuclear arms race (131).

321. Statement at a Heritage Foundation dinner in 1991, quoted in Meese, *With Reagan*, 173. Taking a very different perspective, some scholars maintain that because the United States paid such a huge economic and social price in waging the cold war that it, like the Soviet Union, lost the war, as Germany and Japan emerged from the "era with healthier economies" than that of the United States. See Michael Kort, "The End of the Cold War," in James D. Torr, ed., *The 1980s* (San Diego, CA: Greenhaven, 2000), 125. See also Richard Ned Lebow and Janice Gross Stein, *We All Lost the Cold War* (Princeton, NJ: Princeton University Press, 1994), esp. 369–76.

322. E.g., Robert Wright, "Legacy: What Legacy?" *NR* 200 (Jan. 9 and 16, 1989), 6; Mark Hertsgaard, *On Bended Knee: The Press and Ronald Reagan* (New York: Farrar, Straus, and Giroux, 1988); Mark Green and Gail MacColl, *Reagan's Reign of Error* (New York: Pantheon, 1987); and Johnson, *Sleepwalking*, 14, 447. For an overview of Reagan's critics, see Anderson, *Revolution*, xxviii–xxxi, xl–xlvi.

323. Joe Dolman, "Carter, Reagan Pose a Religious Mystery," *Atlanta Constitution*, Sept. 18, 1984.

324. "Ronald Reagan's America," *St. Louis Dispatch*, Jan. 13, 1989, in Paul S. Boyer, ed., *Reagan as President: Contemporary Views of the Man, His Politics, and His Policies* (Chicago: Ivan R. Dee, 1990), 270.

325. The first quotation is from James Tobin, "Reaganomics in Retrospect" in B. B. Kymlicka and Jeane Matthews, eds., *The Reagan Revolution?* (Chicago: Dorsey, 1988), 93; the second is from Jeffrey Bell, "Man of the Century: Ronald Reagan," *Human Events* 55 (Dec. 31, 1999), electronic version, 2; the third is from D'Souza, *Reagan*, 11.

326. Pierard and Linder, *Civil Religion*, 259; Robert Lekachman, *Visions and Nightmares: America after Reagan* (New York: Macmillan, 1987).

327. Woodward, "Who's a Good Christian?" 30.

328. Collum, "Reagan's Election Crusade," 5.

329. Cannon, *Reagan*, 794–99, quotation from 798. See also Pemberton, *Exit*, 146; Johnson, *Sleepwalking*, 184–87. On the Iran-contra affair, see Theodore Draper, *A Very Thin Line: The Iran-Contra Affair* (New York: Hill and Wang, 1991); and Lawrence E. Walsh, *Firewall: The Iran-Contra Conspiracy and Cover-Up* (New York: Norton, 1997).

330. Paul H. Weaver, "The Intellectual Debate," in David Boaz, ed., *Assessing the Reagan Years* (Washington, DC: Cato Institute, 1988), 413.

331. "Gone with the Wind," *CMW* 116 (Feb. 10, 1989), in Boyer, ed., *Reagan*, 270–71.

332. Johnson, *Sleepwalking*, 194–96.

333. Alonzo Hamby, *Liberalism and Its Challengers: F.D.R. to Reagan* (New York: Oxford University Press, 1985), 374, 339, quotation from 339.

334. Morris, *Dutch*, 458.

335. D'Souza, *Reagan*, 21, 23, quotation from 21.

336. T. R. Reid, "A Flirtation with Greed, but Bedrock Beliefs Stay Solid," *WP*, Dec. 14, 1989. See also Richard B. MacKenzie, *What Went Right in the 1980s* (San Francisco: Pacific Research Institute for Public Policy, 1994).

337. Spring, "Rating Reagan," 44.

338. E.g., Ed Rubenstein, "The Real Reagan Record," *National Review* 44 (Aug. 31, 1992), 25–26.

339. D'Souza, *Reagan*, 23–24.

340. Pierard and Linder, *Civil Religion*, 281, 283, quotation from 281.

341. Wallis, "The President's Pulpit," 21. Historian George Marsden contended that Reagan expressed a religious nationalism that was not explicitly Christian. His common-denominator appeal favored religion in general instead of Christianity (quoted in Spring, "Rating Reagan," 45). Cf. "Mr. Reagan's Civil Religion," *CMW* 111 (Sept. 21, 1984), 483–85: when Reagan called for a " 'rebirth of faith,' " it was not the "faith of the Talmud" or "of Jesus' death and resurrection" but faith in " 'bedrock values' " he appeared to have in mind (484).

342. Johnson, *Sleepwalking*, 203.

343. Edel, *Defenders*, 208, 152; first two quotations from 208, third from 152.

344. Pierard, "Ronald Reagan and Evangelicals," 60.

345. Pemberton, *Exit*, 137.

346. See Marci McDonald, "Fire on the Religious Right," *Maclean's*, Jan. 18, 1988, 22; Randy Frame, "Were Christians Courted for Their Votes or Beliefs?" *CT* 33 (Feb. 17, 1989), 38.

347. Interview in Martin, *With God on Our Side*, 236.

348. Hadden and Shupe, *Televangelism*, 295, 35.

349. Pierard and Linder, *Civil Religion*, 268. See also Richard V. Pierard, "Reagan and the Evangelicals: The Making of a Love Affair," *CC* 100 (Dec. 21–28, 1983), 1182–85. Most of the blame for the Reagan family problems was placed on Nancy. See Pemberton, *Exit*, 123.

350. Robert D. Linder and Richard V. Pierard, "Ronald Reagan, Civil Religion and the New Religious Right in America," *FH*, 23 (Fall 1991), 58.

351. Wills, *Reagan's America*, 198, 382–86.

352. Garry Wills, "Faith and the Hopefuls: The Race for God and Country," *Sojourners*, Mar. 1988, 15–16.

353. James Combs, *The Reagan Range: The Nostalgic Myth in American Politics* (Bowling Green, OH: Bowling Green State University Popular Press, 1993), 107, 123, 126, 129; first quotation from 107, second from 129.

354. See Pierard, "Ronald Reagan and Evangelicals," 47–53; and William Martin, "How Ronald Reagan Wowed Evangelicals," *CT* 48 (June 22, 2004).

355. Hadden and Shupe, *Televangelism,* 294.

356. Pierard and Linder, *Civil Religion,* 258.

357. Linder and Pierard, "Ronald Reagan, Civil Religion," 66.

358. Reagan, "National Religious Broadcasters," 1984, 119. See also Reagan, "Address . . . on the State of the Union," *PP,* Jan. 25, 1984, 91.

359. Ronald Reagan, "Remarks . . . Honoring Representative Jack F. Kemp of New York," *PP,* Dec. 1, 1988, 1583. Cf. Reagan, "A Farewell Address to the Nation," *PP,* Jan. 11, 1989, 1722; Reagan, "Remarks at the Republican National Convention," *PP,* Aug. 15, 1988, 1081.

360. Reagan, "Farewell Address," first three quotations from 1722, fourth from 1720.

361. Cannon, *Reagan,* 836.

362. "Reagan's World View, *Albuquerque Journal,* Jan. 14, 1989, in Boyer, ed., *Reagan,* 280–81. Cf. Robert J. Samuelson, "The Enigma: Ronald Reagan's Goofy Competence," *NR* 200 (Jan. 9 and 16, 1989), in ibid., 268–69; and David R. Gergen, "Ronald Reagan's Most Important Legacy," *USN,* Jan. 9, 1989, in ibid., 273–74; "America Is Standing Tall Again," *Indianapolis Star,* Jan. 8, 1989, in ibid., 267–68; and "Roosevelt and Reagan," *Denver Post,* Jan. 15, 1989.

CHAPTER 11

1. Howard Fineman et al., "Bush and God: How Faith Changed His Life and Shapes His Presidency," *NW* 141 (Mar. 10, 2003) 25.

2. Elisabeth Bumiller, "Talk of Religion Provokes Amens as Well as Anxiety," *NYT,* Apr. 22, 2002.

3. Weston Kosova, Holly Bailey, and John Kascht, "The Incredible W," *NW* 144 (Sept. 6, 2004).

4. George W. Bush, "Proclamation—National Day of Prayer and Thanksgiving," Jan. 20, 2001, http://www.whitehouse.gov (hereafter WH).

5. Peter Mackler, "Messenger or Demagogue: Bush Parlays Piety into Policy," Agence France Presse, Oct. 6, 2004.

6. Fineman et al., "Bush and God," 30.

7. Derek H. Davis, "Thoughts on the Separation of Church and State under the Administration of President George W. Bush," *JCS,* 45 (Mar. 2003), 229–33, quotation from 233. Cf. Fred Greenstein, "The Leadership Style of George W. Bush," in Greenstein, ed., *The George W. Bush Presidency: An Early Assessment* (Baltimore: Johns Hopkins University Press, 2003), 12.

8. Davis, "Thoughts," 233.

9. David T. Cook, "Interview with Ralph Nader," *CSM,* Apr. 20, 2004.

10. "So Now You Know," *Economist,* 372 (Oct. 9, 2004).

11. Stephen Mansfield, *The Faith of George W. Bush* (New York: Penguin, 2003), 22–24, quotation from 24. See also Barbara Bush, *Barbara Bush: A Memoir* (New York: St. Martin's Paperbacks, 1995), 229, 239.

12. George H. W. Bush, *Heartbeat* (New York: Scribner, 2002), 286. On Bush's faith, see Douglas Wead, *George Bush: Man of Integrity* (Eugene, OR: Harvest House, 1988), passim; George H. W. Bush, *All the Best: My Life in Letters and Other Writings* (New York: Scribner, 1999), 409; and Mansfield, *Faith,* 18–21.

13. George W. Bush, *A Charge to Keep* (New York: William Morrow, 1999), 18–19.

14. David Aikman, *A Man of Faith: The Spiritual Journey of George W. Bush* (Nashville, TN: W Publishing Group, 2004), 42.

15. http://www.blessitt.com/bush.html; Alan Cooperman, "Openly Religious, to a Point; Bush Leaves the Specifics of His Faith to Speculation," *WP*, Sept. 16, 2004; Aikman, *Man of Faith*, 70–71; Mansfield, *Faith*, 63–64. Blessitt's Web site contains a prayer that he claims he prayed with Bush for him to receive Christ as his Savior.

16. Aikman, *Man of Faith*, 71.

17. Bush, *Charge*, 136.

18. Tony Carnes, "A Presidential Hopeful's Progress," *CT* 44 (Oct. 2, 2000).

19. Bush, *Charge*, 136. Bush stated that as a result of his conversations with Graham that weekend, "I searched my heart and recommitted my life to Jesus Christ" (Bush, "Faith Can Change Lives," a sermon preached at Second Baptist Church, Houston, Mar. 6, 1999, in Aikman, *Man of Faith*, 206).

20. Aikman *Man of Faith*, 74–75.

21. Fineman et al., "Bush and God," 26.

22. Bush, *Charge*, 137. See also Richard N. Ostling, "Bush Religious Bio Shows Impact of the Bible Study Movement," AP, Nov. 29, 2003.

23. Carnes, "Presidential Hopeful."

24. Bush, *Charge*, 135.

25. Aikman, *Man of Faith*, 79.

26. Bush, *Charge*, 1. See also "George W. Bush: Running on His Faith," *USN*, Dec. 6, 1999; and Aikman, *Man of Faith*, 75–76.

27. Ibid., 45. See also Bush, "Remarks … at National Prayer Breakfast," Feb. 1, 2001, WH.

28. Cooperman, "Openly Religious." Also see "So Now You Know"; Cindy Crosby and Jeff Zaleski, "'Dubya' Gets Religion," *Publishers Weekly* 250 (Sept. 29, 2003); Kathleen K. Rutledge, "A Methodist in the White House," *Good News*, Mar.–Apr. 2001; Mark Tooley, "George Bush: Just a Methodist," Seattle *Post-Intelligencer*, Mar. 20, 2001; and Michael Paulson, "Bush, Fellow Methodists Don't All See Eye to Eye," *Boston Globe*, Dec. 30, 2000.

29. E.g., Britt Hume, "Interview with President George W. Bush," Fox News Television, Sept. 22, 2003.

30. Bush, "Faith Can Change Lives," 206. Cf. James G. Lakely, "President Outlines Role of His Faith," *WT*, Jan. 12, 2005: Bush declared that he did not "see how you can be president without a relationship with the Lord."

31. Quoted in Elisabeth Bumiller, "Bush Urges Freedom of Worship in China," *NYT*, Feb. 22, 2002.

32. Bush, *Charge*, 6, 138, 139, quotations in that order.

33. Bush, "National Prayer Breakfast," Feb. 1, 2001. Throughout American history, Bush added, "people of faith have often been our nation's voice of conscience," especially as they attacked slavery and promoted civil rights. Cf. Bush interview at http://www.beliefnet.com/story/33/story_3345_1.html; and Bush, *Charge*, 138.

34. Bush, *Charge*, 138; Aikman, *Man of Faith*, 77; Mansfield, *Faith*, 119. Every other year, Bush uses the "one-year" Bible to read from Genesis to Revelation.

35. Mansfield, *Faith*, 120; Cal Thomas, "Interview with the President," Feb. 2, 2005, http://www.townhall.com (hereafter TH).

36. Cooperman, "Openly Religious."

37. Bush, "Faith Can Change Lives," 207.

38. George W. Bush, Acceptance speech at the Republican Convention, Aug. 3, 2000, http://www.cnn.com/ELECTION/2000/conventions/republican.

39. Mansfield, *Faith*, xiv; Bush, *Charge*, 6.

40. George W. Bush, "Radio Address . . . to the Nation," Apr. 14, 2001, WH; George W. Bush, "Remarks at a National Day of Prayer and Remembrance," Sept. 14, 2001, ibid. Cf. George W. Bush, "Remarks . . . at National Prayer Breakfast," Feb. 7, 2002, ibid.

41. George W. Bush, "Remarks . . . at National Prayer Breakfast," Feb. 6, 2003, WH.

42. George W. Bush, "Second Inaugural Address," WH.

43. "Moving Out, Looking Forward," interview with Kenneth T. Walsh, *USN*, Aug. 7, 2000.

44. George W. Bush, "Message on the Observance of Easter," Mar. 27, 2002, WH. Cf. Bush, "Message on the Observance of Easter," Apr. 17, 2003, ibid.

45. Quotation from J. Lee Grady, "PLUS: God and the Governor," *Charisma & Christian Life*, Aug. 29, 2000. See also George W. Bush, "Press Conference," July 30, 2003, WH.

46. Todd Starnes, "George W. Bush Shares Personal Testimony," Baptist Press interview, Aug. 31, 2000, http://www.pastors.com/articles/GWBush.asp; Bush, "First Inaugural Address," Jan. 20, 2001, WH.

47. Cooperman, "Openly Religious."

48. Hume, "Interview with Bush."

49. E.g., John McCaslin, "A President's Prayer," Oct. 19, 2004, TH.

50. "The History of the Presidential Prayer Team," http://www.presidentialprayerteam.org. Each day the site includes prayer requests, specific government leaders to pray for, Bush speeches, statements by presidents about prayer and other religious matters, inspirational messages, features on the nation's "godly heritage," biblical passages, "prayer and faith in the news," troop updates, and other items. Two other groups also enlist hundreds of thousands of Americans and citizens of other nations to pray for those in political leadership positions and for the increase of religious and political freedom throughout the world: the World Prayer Center (http://www.worldprayerteam.org) and Global Harvest Ministries (http://www.globalharvest.org). See John W. Kennedy, "Prayer Warriors: Email Newsletters Are Helping Hundreds of Thousands Pray about the War," *CT* 47 (May 2003), 36–37.

51. Bush, "Faith Can Change Lives," 206.

52. Bush, "National Prayer Breakfast," 2003. Cf. Barbara Walters, "Interview with Governor George W. Bush," NBC *20/20*, July 28, 2000.

53. George W. Bush, "National Day of Prayer," May 1, 2003, WH.

54. Bush, *Charge*, 138.

55. Bush, "National Prayer Breakfast," 2001.

56. Bush, "National Prayer Breakfast," 2003.

57. George W. Bush, "National Day of Prayer, 2003," Apr. 30, 2003, WH.

58. George W. Bush, "Remarks . . . at the National Hispanic Prayer Breakfast," May 16, 2002, WH.

59. Bush, "National Prayer Breakfast," 2001.

60. "Prayer Network Focuses on Bush," *Pittsburgh Post-Gazette*, Dec. 1, 2001.

61. See Carnes, "Presidential Hopeful"; and Aikman, *Man of Faith*, 107.

62. Aikman, *Man of Faith*, 92.

63. Amy Sullivan, "Empty Pew," *NR* 231 (Oct. 11, 2004). See also Sullivan, "The Wafer Watch Continues: Kerry Goes to Church, and Reporters See Controversy. Bush Doesn't, and No One Says Anything," *Gadflyer*, May 12, 2004.

64. Aikman, *Man of Faith*, 198; James L. Guth, "George W. Bush and Religious Politics," in Steven E. Schier, ed., *High Risk and Big Ambition: The Presidency of George W. Bush* (Pittsburgh: University of Pittsburgh Press, 2004), 129: Wes Allison, "Man of Faith," Jan. 16, 2005, http://www.stpetersburgtimes.com/2005/01/16/news. Mansfield claims Bush hates to miss church (*Faith*, 119). Howard Fineman and Martha Brant report in "This Is Our Life Now," *NW*, Dec. 3, 2003, 29, that Bush also sometimes attends a small church near Camp David, which has become his "spiritual home."

65. Bill Minutaglio, *First Son: George W. Bush and the Bush Family Dynasty* (New York: Times, 1999), 170.

66. Quoted in Aikman, *Man of Faith*, 62, 130.

67. See Bob Woodward, *Plan of Attack* (New York: Simon & Schuster, 2004), 186; and Peter Schweizer and Rochelle Schweizer, *The Bushes: Portrait of a Dynasty* (New York: Doubleday, 2004), 303, 331, 333, 342, 438, 473.

68. Quoted in Fineman et al., "Bush and God," 24.

69. Aikman, *Man of Faith*, 152–53, 156; Bob Woodward, *Bush at War* (New York: Simon & Schuster, 2002), 119–20; Bill Keller, "God and George W. Bush," *NYT*, May 17, 2003. Bush said he told Jiang "that faith had an incredibly important part in my life..." ("President Bush and President Kim Dae-Jung Meet in Seoul," Feb. 20, 2002, WH). See also Elisabeth Bumiller, "Bush Urges Freedom of Worship in China," *NYT*, Feb. 22, 2002.

70. Bush, 2000 acceptance speech.

71. George W. Bush, speech to B'nai B'rith, Aug. 28, 2000, http://www.beliefnet.com/story/40/story_4049_1.html.

72. George W. Bush, "Remarks...at Houston Power Center," Aug. 2003, WH.

73. Bush, "National Prayer Breakfast," 2001.

74. Guth, "Religious Politics," 128.

75. Bauer was president of the Family Research Council and a respected member of the Christian right. Keyes's adamant pro-life stand appealed to many religious conservatives. Senator Hatch of Utah was a devout Mormon. See Kenneth L. Woodward and Martha Brant, "Finding God," *NW* 135 (Feb. 7, 2000); and "In God We Trust," *Economist* 353 (Dec. 31, 1999).

76. See Minutaglio, *First Son*, 210–24; and J. Lee Grady, "The Faith of George W. Bush," *Charisma & Christian Life*, Nov. 2000, 48.

77. Fineman et al., "Bush and God," 28.

78. Aikman, *Man of Faith*, 114; Mansfield, *Faith*, 108–11.

79. E.g., "Graham Planted 'a Seed in My Soul,' Bush Says," *PL*, Jan.–Feb. 2001, 1, 11.

80. Kevin Phillips, "Crusader," *CC* 121 (July 13, 2004).

81. Karen Hughes asserts that Bush had not anticipated this kind of question and thus had not prepared a specific answer (Aikman, *Man of Faith*, 11–12); Carnes, "Presidential Hopeful."

82. Maureen Dowd, "Playing the Jesus Card," *NYT*, Dec. 15, 1999.

83. Michael Gove, "Thank God for Politicians Who Take Their Cue from Above," *London Times*, May 6, 2003.

84. Quoted in "In God We Trust."

85. Quoted in Fineman et al., "Bush and God," 28. See also Franklin Foer, "Running on Their Faith," *USN* 127 (Dec. 6, 1999).

86. Woodward and Brant, "Finding God."

87. Foer, "Running." Cf. Woodward and Brant, "Finding God."

88. Cathy Young, "Beyond Belief," *Reason* 36 (Oct. 2004). See also Ellen Willis, "Freedom from Religion," *Nation* 272 (Feb. 19, 2001).

89. "Values Shaping the Elections," *CC* 117 (Aug. 30, 2000).

90. Foer, "Running."

91. "In God We Trust."

92. J. Lee Grady, "The Spiritual Side of Al Gore," *Charisma & Christian Life*, Nov. 2000, 49; Gore, speech to the Salvation Army's Adult Rehabilitation Center, Atlanta, May 25, 1999 (quotation); Ceci Connolly, "Gore Urges Role for 'Faith-Based' Groups," *WP*, May 25, 1999; Karen Tumulty, "Taking a Leap of Faith," *Time* 153 (June 7, 1999).

93. Woodward and Brant, "Finding God." See also Laurie Goldstein, "White House Seekers Wear Faith on Sleeve and Stump," *NYT*, Aug. 31, 2000, A1, A16; and Kenneth T. Walsh, "The Lost Years of Al and Dubya," *USN* 127 (Nov. 1, 1999).

94. "Values Shaping the Elections."

95. Quoted in Dave Boyer, "Bush Campaign Says It's in the Bag," *WT*, Nov. 6, 2000.

96. Quoted in Foer, "Running."

97. John M. Swomley, "Another Theocracy: The Ties That Bind," *Humanist* 61 (Nov.–Dec. 2001).

98. Guth, "Religious Politics," 121.

99. Patricia Miller, "Conservative Catholics and the GOP," *USA Today Magazine* 131 (Nov. 2002).

100. The two basic explanations of religious alignment in American politics are the ethnocultural theory and the culture war theory. The first posits that ethnic identity and denominational affiliation strongly influence how Americans vote. The second theory maintains that the fundamental divide in contemporary politics is between orthodox and progressive elements within the nation's religious communities. Arguing that the "culture war" hypothesis is too simplistic because the moral battle lines shift from issue to issue and because large numbers of citizens remain noncombatants, most scholars combine these two perspectives in explaining the outcome of the 2000 and 2004 elections (Guth, "Religious Politics," 118–19). See also James Davison Hunter, *Culture Wars: The Struggle to Define America* (New York: Basic Books, 1991).

101. Kevin Phillips, *American Dynasty: Aristocracy, Fortune and the Politics of Deceit in the House of Bush* (New York: Viking, 2004), 215 (quotation); James Guth and John Green, *The Bible and the Ballot Box* (Boulder, CO: Westview, 1991), 16–19.

102. John Green, Mark Rozell, and Clyde Wilcox, *Prayers in the Precincts* (Washington, DC: Georgetown University Press, 2000), 42.

103. Phillips, "Crusader."

104. Tony Carnes, "The Bush Agenda," *CT* 45 (Jan. 8, 2001).

105. David Frum, *The Right Man: The Surprise Presidency of George W. Bush* (New York: Random House, 2003), 9.

106. Guth, "Religious Politics," 122–24. The Third National Study of Religion and Politics devised these categories.

107. See John C. Green and John DiIulio, "How the Faithful Voted," Ethics and Public Policy Center, http://www.eppc.org/publications/pubID.1542/pub_detail.asp,

Jan. 2001, 3. See also Mary C. Seegers, ed., *Piety, Politics, and Pluralism: Religion, the Courts, and the 2000 Election* (Lanham, MD: Rowman and Littlefield, 2002); and John K. White, *The Values Divide: American Politics and Culture in Transition* (New York: Chatham, 2002).

108. Guth, "Religious Politics," 126.

109. Ryan Lizza, "Salvation," *NR* 224 (Apr. 23, 2001). Also see Gertrude Himmelfarb, "Religion in the 2000 Election," *Public Interest*, Spring 2001.

110. Quoted in Mark O'Keefe, "Will Democrats Get Whacked on Religion?" *CC* 121 (Jan. 27, 2004). See also Walter Shapiro, "Religion on the Stump Could Add a New Dimension to Election," *USA Today*, June 11, 2004.

111. Jim Wallis, "Putting God Back in Politics," *NYT*, Dec. 28, 2003, Section 4, p. 9.

112. All the quotations are from Carnes, "Swing Evangelicals." See also "Democrats Try to Regain Ground on Moral Issues," Dec. 8, 2003, Crossmap News.

113. E.g., Jodi Wilgoren, "Kerry Invoking 'Values' Theme to Frame Issues," *NYT*, July 3, 2004; David Brooks, "Values, Values Everywhere," *NYT*, July 17, 2004; and Jodi Wilgoren and Bill Keller, "Kerry and Religion: Pressure Builds for Public Discussion," *NYT*, Oct. 7, 2004.

114. Quoted in Frank Rich, "On 'Moral Values,' It's Blue in a Landslide," *NYT*, Nov. 14, 2004.

115. "Conventional Wisdom," *NW*, Jan. 3, 2005, 37.

116. "Religion and Politics: Contention and Consensus," Pew Forum on Religion & Public Life, July 2003, http://pewforum.org/docs/index.php?DocID=26.

117. "*George W. Bush: Faith in the White House* Documentary Releases an Alternative to Fahrenheit 9/11," PR Newswire, Aug. 13, 2004. It is based primarily on Aikman's *A Man of Faith* and Tom Freiling's *George W. Bush on God and Country*. Bush supporters who were interviewed included Reagan's Secretary of Energy Don Hodel, James Robison, Rabbi Daniel Lapin, Catholic publisher Deal Hudson, and author Stephen Mansfield. Bush critics included Susan Jacoby and Robert Sheer of the *Los Angeles Times*, Jim Wallis, actor Richard Gere, Ralph Nader, and Barry Lynn, executive director of Americans United for the Separation of Church and State (Mark Moring, "George W. Bush: Faith in the White House," *CT* online, Aug. 24, 2004).

118. Frank Rich, "Now on DVD: The Passion of the Bush," *NYT*, Sept. 30, 2004. Going beyond "the civic piety practiced by previous presidents," Bush claimed "godlike infallibility."

119. Both quotes from Gloria Borger, "Closing the God Gap," *USN* 137 (Oct. 25, 2004). See also Kenneth T. Walsh and Jeff Kass, "Separate Worlds," ibid.

120. "Religion Plays Major Role in Bush Campaign," Oct. 23, 2004, Cox News Service.

121. Phillips, "Crusader."

122. E.g., Dan Gilgoff, "The Morals and Values Crowd," Nov. 15, 2004, *USN*; "Down to the Wire," *NW*, Nov. 15, 2004.

123. David D. Kirkpatrick, "Bush Campaign Seeks Help from Thousands of Congregations," *NYT*, June 3, 2004; "Bush Campaign Plan Draws Fire," AP, June 12, 2004; Kirkpatrick, "Bush Allies Till Fertile Soil, among Baptists, for Votes," *NYT*, June 18, 2004; "Bush Woos the Faithful with Religious Fervor," AP, June 26, 2004; Kirkpatrick, "Churches See an Election Role and Spread the Word on Bush," *NYT*, Aug. 9, 2004.

124. Tony Carnes and Mark Stricherz, "Wooing the Faithful," *CT* 48 (Oct. 2004).

125. An April 2004 survey reported in *Religion & Ethics Newsweekly* found that evangelicals gave higher priority to these issues than the general population.

126. Carnes and Stricherz, "Wooing."

127. Steven Waldman, "On a Word and a Prayer," *NYT*, Nov. 6, 2004.

128. Steven Waldman, "Evangelicals for Bush," Sept. 2, 2004, *National Review* online.

129. Mark A. Noll, "None of the Above," *CC* 121 (Sept. 21, 2004), 8–9.

130. Walter Shapiro, "Bush's Certainty Rallies the Faithful," *USA Today*, Sept. 9, 2004.

131. Viveca Novak, "Translating Faith into Spanish," *Time* 164 (Oct. 25, 2004); Carol Curiel, "How Hispanics Voted Republican," *NYT*, Nov. 8, 2004.

132. See Borger, "Closing the God Gap."

133. William Sloane Coffin, "Despair Is Not an Option," *Nation* 278 (Jan. 12, 2004); Lynette Clemetson, "Clergy Group to Counter Conservatives," *NYT*, Nov. 17, 2003.

134. "Democrats Try to Rethink the Value of Religion," AP, Nov. 13, 2004.

135. Some argue that the major political development of the past decade is the growth and cohesion of the secular left and its increasing impact on the Democratic Party. See Louis Bolce and Gerald De Maio, "The Politics of Partisan Neutrality," *First Things* 143 (May 2004), 9–12; Geoffrey Layman, *The Great Divide: Religious and Cultural Conflict in American Party Politics* (New York: Columbia University Press, 2001); Daniel Henninger, "The Nonreligious Left," *WSJ*, Oct. 17, 2003; and Richard N. Ostling, "Dems Increasingly Rely on Secular Voters," AP, Aug. 28, 2004.

136. Quoted in Eyal Press, "Closing the 'Religion Gap,'" *Nation* 279 (Aug. 30, 2004).

137. Wilgoren and Keller, "Kerry and Religion."

138. "Kerry's Acceptance: 'We Have It in Our Power to Change the World Again,'" *NYT*, July 29, 2004.

139. Barack Obama, "The Audacity of Hope," July 27, 2004, http://www.ameri canrhetoric.com.

140. Wilgoren and Keller, "Kerry and Religion."

141. Press, "Religion Gap."

142. Katharine Q. Seelye, "Kerry Ignores Reproaches of Some Bishops," *NYT*, Apr. 11, 2003; and Seelye, "Kerry Attends Easter Services and Receives Holy Communion," *NYT*, Apr. 12, 2003.

143. Wilgoren and Keller, "Kerry and Religion."

144. Quoted in "Kerry Latest Test over Policy, Faith," AP Apr. 24, 2004.

145. Quoted in O'Keefe, "Bush, Kerry Take Vastly Different Approaches to Religion in Public Life," Newhouse News Service, Sept. 13, 2004.

146. "Bush Faith Has Dems Talking God," AP, Jan. 31, 2004.

147. Diane Salvatore, "Supportive Partners," an interview with John and Theresa Heinz Kerry, *Ladies Home Journal*, Aug. 2004.

148. See Ted Olsen, "Kerry's Religion Is Today's Big Politics Story," *CT* online, Mar. 29, 2004; Nedra Pickler, "Bush Campaign Blasts Kerry's Bible Quote," AP, Mar. 28, 2004; and Karen Tumulty and Perry Bacon Jr., "A Test of Kerry's Faith," *Time*, Apr. 5, 2004.

149. O'Keefe, "Bush, Kerry."

150. Laurie Goodstein, "Kerry, Candidate and Catholic, Creates Uneasiness for Church," *NYT*, Apr. 2, 2004; Katharine Q. Seelye, "Kerry Attends Easter Services and Receives Holy Communion," *NYT*, Apr. 12, 2004; Young, "Beyond Belief."

151. See Robert Novak, "Kerry and Communion," May 3, 2004, TH; John Leo, "The Bishops and the Pols," TH, May 10, 2004; "Democrats Criticize Denial of Communion by Bishops," NYT, May 20, 2004; Kenneth L. Woodward, "A Political Sacrament," NYT, May 28, 2004; and Daniel J. Wakin, "A Divisive Issue for Catholics: Bishops, Politicians and Communion," NYT, May 31, 2004.

152. Laurie Goodstein, "Politicians Face Censure from Bishops on Abortion Rights," NYT, June 19, 2004.

153. Deal Hudson, "Did John Kerry Lie about Abortion?" Catholic Exchange, Feb. 23, 2004. See also Laurie Goodstein, "Vatican Cardinal Signals Backing for Sanctions on Kerry," NYT, Apr. 24, 2004.

154. George Neumayr, "The New Saintliness," American Spectator, Apr. 21, 2004.

155. David D. Kirkpatrick and Laurie Goodstein, "Group of Bishops Using Influence to Oppose Kerry," NYT, Oct. 12, 2004. See also Charles J. Chaput, "Faith and Patriotism," NYT, Oct. 22, 2004; Robert Novak, "Catholic Wars," Oct. 20, 2004, TH; Mark W. Roche, "Voting Our Conscience, Not Our Religion," NYT, Oct. 11, 2004; and "Making a Political Play: Presidential Race Prompts Clergy to Action," AP, Oct. 16, 2004.

156. Wilgoren and Keller, "Kerry and Religion." A Time survey in the late spring of 2004 showed that only 7 percent of Americans considered Kerry to be a man of strong religious faith (cited in David Brooks, "A Matter of Faith," NYT, June 22, 2004).

157. Joe Klein, "The Values Gap," Time 164 (Nov. 22, 2004).

158. George Neumayr, "Kerry's Conceptions," American Spectator, July 7, 2004; Marvin Olasky, "Is Kerry a CINO—Catholic in Name Only?" Oct. 7, 2004, TH.

159. E.g., Todd S. Purdum, "Electoral Affirmation of Shared Values Provided Bush a Majority," NYT, Nov. 4, 2004.

160. "The Triumph of the Religious Right," Economist 373 (Nov. 13, 2004). A subsequent Pew Research survey found that 27 percent of voters had considered moral values decisive.

161. "Catholics Go for Bush," America 191 (Nov. 15, 2004). Cf. Klein, "Values Gap."

162. DeWayne Wickham, "Bush Faces Keen Pressure to Reward Faithful," USA Today, Nov. 8, 2004.

163. http://www.cnn.com/ELECTION/2004. Evangelicals accounted for 23 percent of the electorate and Catholics for 27 percent. People who were concerned about terrorism, moral values, and taxes voted for Bush; those who worried most about the economy and jobs, health care, education, and war in Iraq cast their ballots for Kerry. See Paul Kengor, "Kerry Loses His Faith," American Spectator online, Nov. 5, 2004; and "Catholics Go for Bush."

164. Maureen Dowd, "The Red Zone," NYT, Nov. 4, 2004; Thomas L. Friedman, "Two Nations under God," ibid; Garry Wills, "The Day the Enlightenment Went Out," ibid. See also Alan Cooperman and Thomas B. Edall, "Evangelicals Say They Led the Charge for GOP," MSNBC, Nov. 7, 2004; "The Evangelicals and the Election," NPR, Nov. 6, 2004; David Klinghoffer, "What Bush Voters Share: In God We Trust," LAT, Nov. 8, 2004; and Richard N. Ostling, "Election Reinforced Religious, Moral Divide," AP, Nov. 6, 2004.

165. "Triumph of the Religious Right."

166. David Brooks, "The Values-Vote Myth," NYT, Nov. 6, 2004.

167. Morris Fiorina, Samuel J. Abrams, and Jeremy G. Pope, Culture War? The Myth of a Polarized America (New York: Pearson Longman, 2005), as analyzed in Alan

Wolfe, "The Referendum of 2004," *Wilson Quarterly* 28 (Autumn 2004). They contend that there is more competition within the red and blue states "than the polarization thesis allows." They argued that "if the views of all Americans . . . are evaluated, Americans are more centrist than they've been for some time."

168. Leon Wieseltier, "The Elect," *NR* 231 (Nov. 22, 2004).

169. William Bole, "Democrats' 'Religion Gap' Not Full Story," *CC* 121 (Feb. 24, 2004). See also David Kirkpatrick, "Some Democrats Believe the Party Should Get Religion," *NYT*, Nov. 17, 2004; and "Democrats Try to Rethink the Value of Religion."

170. Dana Milbank, "Religious Right Finds Its Center in Oval Office: Bush Emerges as Movement's Leader after Robertson Leaves Christian Coalition," *WP*, Dec. 24, 2001.

171. Phillips, "Crusader."

172. Quoted in Paul Kengor, *God and George W. Bush: A Spiritual Life* (New York: Regan, 2004), 164.

173. Transcript of *The Jesus Factor*, May 10, 2004, 18–9.

174. Elisabeth Bumiller, "Evangelicals Sway White House on Human Rights Issues Abroad," *NYT*, Oct. 26, 2003.

175. Guth, "Religious Politics," 131, Thomas B. Edsall, "GOP Eyes Jewish Vote with Bush Tack on Israel," *WP*, Apr. 30, 2002; Frum, *Right Man*, 246–60.

176. Goegelein belongs to a Lutheran Church, Missouri Synod congregation. See David D. Kirkpatrick, "Aide Is Bush's Eyes and Ears on the Right," *NYT*, June 28, 2004; Melinda Henneberger, "Tending to the Flock. Soul Man: A White House Aide Keeps Faith with the Faithful," *NW*, Sept. 13, 2004; Bill Berkowitz, "Tim Goeglein: Selling Brand Bush to the Christian Right," Mar. 23, 2005, http://www.media transparency.org/story.

177. Tim Goegelein, speech at Grove City College, Feb. 19, 2004.

178. Aikman, *Man of Faith*, 139.

179. Justin Webb, as cited in Aikman, *A Man of Faith*, 158.

180. See Tom Raum, "Bush Acting to Block Last-Minute Clinton Rules," AP, Jan. 20, 2001.

181. Frum, *Right Man*, 19, 16–18; first quotation from 17, second from 18.

182. Quoted in Mansfield, *Faith*, 118.

183. Frum, *Right Man*, 3–4. See also Jack Beatty, "In the Name of God," *Atlantic* online, Mar. 5, 2003; and Garry Wills, "With God on His Side," *NYT*, Mar. 30, 2003.

184. Fineman et al., "Bush and God," 29.

185. See Corrie Cutrer, "No Place Like Home," *Today's Christian Woman* 26 (Nov.–Dec. 2004), 56–58; and Karen Hughes, *Ten Minutes from Normal* (New York: Viking, 2004).

186. On Ashcroft, see Marvin Olasky, "A Higher Authority: Why Democrats Should Love John Ashcroft," *World*, Feb. 3, 2001; Laurie Goodstein, "Ashcroft's Life and Judgments Are Steeped in Faith," *NYT*, Jan. 14, 2001, 22; and James Bovard, *The Bush Betrayal* (New York: Palgrave Macmillan, 2004), 185–97. On Rice, see Sheryl Henderson Blunt, "The Unflappable Condi Rice," *CT* 47 (Sept. 2003), 43–48.

187. On the role of Christians in Bush's White House, also see Jim Whittle, "All in the Family: Top Bush Administration Leaders, Religious Right Lieutenants Plot Strategy in Culture 'War,'" *CS*, May 2002; Robin Toner, "Conservatives Savor Their Role as Insiders at the White House," *NYT*, Mar. 19, 2001; Jim Vandehei and Elizabeth Cowley, "Bush Keeps the Faith with Religious Right," *WSJ*, June 13, 2001; and Esther Kaplan, *With God on Their Side: How Christian Fundamentalists Trampled Science,*

Policy, and Democracy in George W. Bush's White House (New York: New Press, 2004), 68–90.

188. Aikman, *Man of Faith*, 115–19. Bush delivered addresses at several major events at Evans's church, and in 2003, he spoke at Caldwell's church.

189. Bumiller, "Evangelicals Sway White House"; Rich Lowry, "The Moral Force of Bush's Foreign Policy," Sept. 30, 2003, TH; Chuck Colson, "An Evil We Can't Ignore," Aug. 2, 2004, TH; George W. Bush, "Remarks . . . at the National Training Conference on Human Trafficking," July 16, 2004; "Putting the Sex Trade on Notice," *NYT*, Jan. 9, 2004; "President Bush Addresses United Nations General Assembly," Sept. 23, 2003, WH.

190. "A Resolution to Honor President George W. Bush," National Religious Broadcasters, Feb. 8, 2003, http://www.nrb.org/partner/Article_Display_Page/0,,PTID 308562%7CCHID567536%7CCIID1532458,00.html.

191. Carnes and Mark Stricherz, "Wooing."

192. Quoted in Wickham, "Bush Faces Keen Pressure."

193. Quoted in Ostling, "Religious, Moral Divide."

194. "Of Prayer and Payback," *NW* 144 (Nov. 22, 2004), 46. Cf. Wickham, "Bush Faces Keen Pressure."

195. Chuck Colson, "It's Not Payback Time," Nov. 8, 2004, TH. See also "Same Song, Second Term," *CT* 49 (Jan. 2005), 26; Karen Tumulty and Matthew Cooper, "What Does Bush Owe the Religious Right?" *Time*, Feb. 7, 2005, 29–32. For evangelicals' policy goals for Bush's second term, see David Neff, "Post-Election Faith at Work," *CT* 48 (Dec. 2004), 5; and "For the Health of the Nation," National Association of Evangelicals, http://www.nae.net/images/civic_responsibility2.pdf.

196. John C. Green, "Bush's Religious-Right Challenge," *CSM* 93 (Jan. 23, 2001).

197. Molly Ivins and Lou Dubose, *Shrub: The Short but Happy Political Life of George W. Bush* (New York: Vintage, 2000), 76.

198. Keller, "George W. Bush."

199. Lizza, "Salvation." Cf. See Adam Clymer, "Bush Aggressively Courts Catholic Voters for 2004," *NYT*, June 1, 2001, A14.

200. Miller, "Conservative Catholics."

201. George W. Bush, "Remarks to Catholic Leaders," Mar. 23, 2001; George W. Bush, "Interview with Foreign Journalists," July 17, 2001; Bush, "Remarks at the Dedication of the Pope John Paul II Cultural Center," Mar. 23, 2001, all at WH; quotations in that order. See also Kathryn Jean Lopez, "On the Same Page? Assessing Bush's Outreach to Catholics," *National Catholic Register*, July 22–8, 2001.

202. Kenneth T. Walsh, "Coveting the 'Catholic Vote,'" *USN* 130 (May 28, 2001).

203. John M. Swomley, "Another Theocracy: The Ties that Bind," *Humanist* 61 (Nov.–Dec. 2001). See also the journal of Catholics for a Free Choice, *Conscience*, Summer 2001; and "God and Man in Washington," 32.

204. E.g., Anna Quindlen, "In the Name of the Father," *NW* 138 (July 16, 2001).

205. Frum, *Right Man*, 247–49; quotation from 248.

206. Malcolm Foster, "Jews Get Evangelical Christian Backing," AP, Feb. 1, 2003.

207. Mansfield, *Faith*, 160. For a negative assessment of Bush's position on Israel, see Kaplan, *With God*, 23–29.

208. Robert G. Kaiser, "Bush and Sharon Nearly Identical on Mideast Policy," *WP*, Feb. 9, 2003, A-1. Cf. Donald Lambro, "Jewish Voters Approve of Administration's Policy in the Middle East," *WT* National Weekly Edition, Apr. 29–May 5, 2002, 19;

Donald E. Wagner, "Marching to Zion: The Evangelical-Jewish Alliance," *CC* 120 (June 28, 2003), 20–24; Rabbi Daniel Lapin, "Why Many American Jews Will Vote for President Bush This November," http://www.elijahscry.org/index.php?name= News&file=article&sid=4; Caroline Glick, deputy managing editor of the *Jerusalem Post*, "What Bush Understands," Oct. 30, 2004, TH; and William Safire, "Arab and Jewish Votes," *NYT*, Oct. 25, 2004.

209. The samples are not large enough to be reliable, but they suggest substantial support for Bush. See Phillips, *American Dynasty*, 223, 362.

210. George W. Bush, "Remarks . . . at Islamic Center of Washington, D.C.," Sept. 17, 2001, WH.

211. Bill Salmon, *Fighting Back: The War on Terrorism—From Inside the Bush White House* (Washington, DC: Regnery, 2002), 160.

212. Bush, "Islamic Center."

213. E.g., Diane West, "Bush and Muslims," *WT*, Oct. 31, 2003.

214. Frum, *Right Man*, 154–55.

215. Jerry Falwell, *60 Minutes* interview, Oct. 6, 2002.

216. Franklin Graham, interview in Wilkesboro, NC, Oct. 2001; interview with NBC, Nov. 16, 2001, quotations in that order. See also Franklin Graham, "My View of Islam," *WSJ*, Dec. 9, 2001; and interview with Graham at *Newsweek* online, Jan. 3, 2005. Other conservative Christians applauded Graham's remarks. E.g., "Hurrah for Franklin Graham," *World*, Dec. 1, 2001. Other evangelicals protested Bush's frequent assertion that Christians and Muslims prayed to the same God. E.g., "Bush's Remark Draws Criticism," Religious News Service (hereafter RNS), Nov. 29, 2003.

217. "Remarks by . . . Bush in a Statement to Reporters . . . ," Nov. 13, 2002, WH.

218. See George W. Bush, "Remarks . . . at Iftaar," Nov. 19, 2001; Bush, "Message for Ramadan," Nov. 15, 2001; and Bush, "Roundtable with Arab and Muslim-American Leaders," Sept. 10, 2002, all at WH.

219. George W. Bush, "Remarks . . . on Eid al-Fitr," Dec. 5, 2002, WH.

220. Nicholas D. Kristof, "Giving God a Break," *NYT*, June 10, 2003.

221. On Bush's relationship with Muslims, see Kengor, *Bush*, 135–45. For a critical appraisal, see Kaplan, *With God*, 12–20; and "Defaming Islam," *WP*, Oct. 6, 2002.

222. Lisette Poole and Tahir Ali, "2004 Election Sees Second American-Muslim Bloc Vote," http://www.washington-report.org/archives/Jan_Feb_2005/0501025.html.

223. Fineman et al., "Bush and God," 25.

224. Bush fund-raising letter, May 23, 2003.

225. Bush, "First Inaugural Address."

226. Quoted in Kathleen Parker, "Bush the Un-Zealot," Dec. 8, 2004, TH.

227. Bush was especially influenced by Olasky's *The Tragedy of American Compassion* (Washington, DC: Regnery, 1992) and Myron Magnet's *The Dream and the Nightmare: The Sixties Legacy to the Underclass* (New York: William Morrow, 1993).

228. Bush, *Charge*, 229–35; first quotation from 230.

229. "A Blueprint for New Beginnings—7. Champion Compassionate Conservatism," WH.

230. Bush, "First Inaugural Address"; Bush, "Remarks . . . to the Southern Baptist Convention 2002 Annual Meeting," June 11, 2002, WH; Bush, "Compassionate Conservatism," Apr. 30, 2002, WH, quotations in that order.

231. E.g., George W. Bush, "Remarks at Religious Broadcasters' Convention," Feb. 10, 2003, WH.

232. John DiIulio Jr., "The Future of Compassion: President Bush's Social Program Hasn't Gotten a Chance," *Philadelphia Inquirer*, Dec. 3, 2002.

233. Frum, *Right Man*, 274.

234. Elisabeth Bumiller, "Bush's 'Compassion' Agenda: A Liability in 2004?" *NYT*, Aug. 26, 2003.

235. Robin Weinstein, "The George W. Bush Presidency: A Review of Compassionate Conservatism and Its Effect on the American Poor," presented at Symposium on Religion and Politics, Calvin College, Apr. 29–May 1, 2004. See also Bob Herbert, "Suffer the Children," *NYT*, July 11, 2002.

236. Nicholas Kristof, "The God Gulf," *NYT*, Jan. 7, 2004.

237. Press, "Religion Gap." Other Christians voiced similar views at "Pentecost 2004," a conference "designed to rally a broad coalition of religious leaders against poverty."

238. See Joe Loconte, "Leap of Faith," *National Review* 51 (July 12, 1999). Bush's office published "Faith in Action: A New Vision for Church-State Cooperation in Texas."

239. Bush, "Faith Can Change Lives," first quotation from 209, second from 211.

240. Mary Segers, "President Bush's Faith-Based Initiative," 1, in Jo Renee Formicola, Mary C. Segers, and Paul Weber, *Faith-Based Initiatives and the Bush Administration: The Good, the Bad, and the Ugly* (Lanham MD: Rowman and Littlefield, 2003). Also see Jim R. Vanderwoerd, "Is the Newer Deal a Better Deal? Government Funding of Faith-Based Social Services," *Christian Scholar's Review* 31 (Spring 2002), 301–18; Mary Jo Bane, Brent Coffin, and Ronald Thiemann, eds., *Who Will Provide? The Changing Role of Religion in American Social Welfare* (Boulder, CO: Westview, 2000); Charles Glenn, *The Ambiguous Embrace: Government and Faith-Based Schools and Social Agencies* (Princeton, NJ: Princeton University Press, 2000); Lewis D. Solomon and Matthew J. Vlissides Jr., *In God We Trust? Assessing the Potential of Faith-Based Social Services* (Washington, DC: Progressive Policy Institute, 2001); George W. Bush, "Rallying the Armies of Compassion," Jan. 30, 2001, WH; Jo Renee Formicola and Hubert Morken, eds., *Religious Leaders and Faith-Based Politics* (Lanham, MD: Rowman and Littlefield, 2001); and Amy E. Black, Douglas L. Koopman, and David K. Ryden, *Of Little Faith: The Politics of George W. Bush's Faith-Based Initiatives* (Washington, DC: Georgetown University Press, 2004).

241. See U.S. Department of Heath and Human Services, The Center for Faith-Based and Community Initiatives, "What Is Charitable Choice?" Dec. 12, 2002, http://www.hhs.gov/fbci/choice.html. See also Center for Public Justice, *A Guide to Charitable Choice* (Washington, DC: Author, 1997); and Stanley Carlson-Thies, "Charitable Choice: Bringing Religion Back into American Welfare," *Journal of Policy History* 13 (2001), 109–32.

242. Segers, "Faith-Based Initiative," 19.

243. E.g., George W. Bush "Remarks . . . at Habitat for Humanity Event," Aug. 8, 2001, WH; and Richard W. Stevenson, "Bush Invokes Faith's Power to Cure Society's Ills," *NYT*, Jan. 21, 2003. See also Bush, "Remarks to the White House National Conference on Faith-Based and Community Initiatives," June 1, 2004, WH.

244. George W. Bush, "Commencement Address University of Notre Dame," WH.

245. Amy Sullivan, "Faith without Works," *Washington Monthly* 36 (Oct. 2004).

246. "Bush Pushes Program to Help Those in Need," Feb. 10, 2003, Fox News online. Cf. George W. Bush, "Remarks . . . to the National Leadership of the Hispanic Faith-Based Organizations," May 22, 2001, WH.

247. Mansfield, *Faith*, 121–22; Bush, "Remarks . . . to the American Jewish Committee," May 3, 2001, WH. See also Joe Loconte, *God, Government, and the Good Samaritan: The Promise and Peril of the President's Faith-Based Initiative* (Washington, DC: Heritage Foundation, 2001).

248. George W. Bush, "Faith-Based Initiative," Apr. 11, 2002, WH. Cf. Bush, "Remarks . . . in Announcement of the Faith-Based Initiative," Jan. 29, 2001; and Bush, "Hispanic Faith-Based Organizations."

249. George W. Bush, "Establishment of White House Office of Faith-Based and Community Initiatives," Jan. 29, 2001, WH.

250. Sullivan, "Faith without Works."

251. See Elizabeth Bumiller, "Preaching to the Choir, Bush Encourages Religious Gathering," *NYT*, June 2, 2004; and "New Rules, More Money," *CT* 47 (Nov. 2003), 32.

252. Tony Carnes, "The Twelfth of Never," *CT* 48 (Jan. 2004), 28.

253. On Catholics, see Jo Formicola and Mary Segers, "The Bush Faith-Based Initiative: The Catholic Response," *JCS* 44 (Autumn 2002), 693–715.

254. Dave Donaldson and Stanley Carlson-Thies, *A Revolution of Compassion: Faith-Based Groups as Full Partners in Fighting America's Social Problems* (Grand Rapids, MI: Baker, 2003), as quoted in Arthur E. Farnsley II, "Faith-Based Politics," *CC* 121 (Aug. 24, 2004).

255. Formicola, Segers, and Weber, *Faith-Based Initiatives*, 169.

256. Michelle Cottle, "Save It," *NR* 224 (Feb. 26, 2001). Cf. Black, Koopman, and Ryden, *Of Little Faith*, 283–86; and Kaplan, *With God*, 53–55.

257. "Jewish Leaders Criticize Faith-Based Initiative," *WP*, Feb. 27, 2001, A4; "Church, State, and Money," *CMW* 28 (Feb. 23, 2001), 5–6.

258. First quotation from Jeffrey H Birnbaum, "Blacks Find Religion in the GOP," *Fortune* 144 (July 9, 2001); second from Pat Robertson, "Mr. Bush's Faith-Based Initiative Is Flawed," *WSJ*, Mar. 12, 2001, A15.

259. "God and Man in Washington: George Bush Is Redefining the Religious Right," *Economist*, May 19, 2001, 32. Deborah Caldwell, "Falwell: 'Deep Concerns,'" Beliefnet, Mar. 6, 2001, http://www.belief.net/story/70/story_7040_1.html. Carnes and Stricherz found that many evangelicals across the country were worried about "government-church entanglement" ("Wooing").

260. Quoted in Laura Meckler, "Bush Moves to Aid Faith-Based Groups," *WP*, Jan. 30, 2001, A1. See also Laurie Goodstein, "Bush's Charity Plan Is Raising Concern for Religious Right," *NYT*, Mar. 3, 2001, A1; Matt Porio, "Keeping the Faith Has Its Cost," *Newsday*, Mar. 23, 2003; and Kaplan, *With God*, 59–63.

261. "Using Tax Dollars for Churches," *NYT*, Dec. 30, 2002. See also Paul Krugman, "Gotta Have Faith," *NYT*, Dec. 17, 2002.

262. Quotation from the bipartisan Roundtable on Religion and Social Welfare Policy report, released on August 16, 2004. The full report is available at http://www.religionandsocialpolicy.org. See also Laurie Goodstein, "Church-Based Projects Lack Data on Results," *NYT*, Apr. 24, 2001, A12; and Robert Marus, "An 'Aggressive' Faith-Based Initiative," *CC* 121 (Sept. 7, 2004).

263. Formicola, Segers, and Weber, *Faith-Based Initiatives*, 15, 167–69, 172–77, quotation from 15. See also E. J. Dionne, "Not Conservative, Not Compassionate," *Courier Journal*, Feb. 8, 2003, A7; and Melissa Rogers, "The Wrong Way to Do Right: A Challenge to Charitable Choice," in E. J. Dionne and John DiIulio, *What's God Got*

to Do with the American Experiment? (Washington, DC: Brookings Institution, 2000), 138–45.

264. In July 2004, the Freedom from Religion Foundation filed suit against the administrators of Bush's faith-based initiative, arguing their actions unconstitutionally favored religious organizations. Jim Towey told Religion News Service that "President Bush has made very clear that we're to level the playing field, not to favor faith-based groups" (*CC* 121 [July 13, 2004], 15).

265. E.g., Bob Wineburg, "The Underbelly of the Faith-Based Initiative," *Sightings,* July 31, 2003, http://marty-center.uchicago.edu/sightings/archive_2003/0731.shtml.

266. Sullivan, "Faith without Works." Cf. Eric Alterman and Mark Green, *The Book on Bush: How George W. Bush (Mis)leads America* (New York: Viking, 2004), 165–67.

267. David Kuo, "Please, Keep Faith," Feb. 15, 2005, http://www.beliefnet.com/story/160/story_16092_1.html. See also Stanley Carlson-Thies, "Faith and Action in the Faith-Based Initiative," Public Justice Report, second quarter 2005, http://www.cpjustice.org/stories/storyReader$1286. John DiIulio has also strongly criticized the faith-based initiative in numerous speeches and essays.

268. Kate O'Beirne, "Uncharitable Choice," *National Review* 53 (July 9, 2001).

269. Formicola, Segers, and Weber, *Faith-Based Initiatives,* 169. Cf. Sullivan, "Faith without Works."

270. Bush, *Charge,* 240.

271. George W. Bush, "State of the Union Address," Jan. 28, 2003, WH; Bush, "Second Inaugural Address."

272. Bush, "Southern Baptist Convention."

273. George W. Bush, "Securing Freedom's Triumph," *NYT,* Sept. 11, 2002.

274. Bush, "Compassionate Conservatism."

275. Bush, "State of the Union," 2003; George W. Bush, "Remarks . . . to . . . the German Bundestag," May 23, 2002, WH; first two quotations from first speech, third from second speech.

276. E.g., Charles Colson, "Africa's AIDS Crisis," May 2, 2003, TH.

277. Bush, "State of the Union."

278. See "A Serious Response to AIDS," *NYT,* Feb. 1, 2003; Sheryl Gay Stolberg, "$15 Billion AIDS Plan Wins Final Approval in Congress," *NYT,* May 22, 2003.

279. George W. Bush, "Remarks . . . on Global HIV/AIDFS Initiative," Apr. 29, 2003, WH. See also Charles Colson "Bringing Down the Numbers: The Global AIDS Bill," May 15, 2003, TH; "Bush Signs AIDS Plan: Tells Europe to Follow Suit," Reuters, May 27, 2003; and "Bush to Sign Global AIDS Bill," AP, May 27, 2003.

280. Peggy Noonan, "Be Proud of What We Stand for," *Ladies Home Journal* 120 (Oct. 2003), 118–20. See also Elisabeth Bumiller, "Bush Proposes Doubling U.S. Support for Education in Africa," *NYT,* June 21, 2002.

281. E.g., "America's Promises," *NYT,* Jan. 28, 2005.

282. Bush, "Securing Freedom's Triumph."

283. Bush, "State of the Union," 2003. Cf. George W. Bush, "Remarks . . . in Roundtable Interview with Print Journalists," May 29, 2003, WH.

284. George W. Bush, "Remarks . . . at . . . the National Endowment for Democracy," Nov. 6, 2003. Bush emphasized that predominantly Muslim countries were making democratic progress and that more than half of the world's Muslims live under democratically constituted governments. Cf. Bush, "Remarks . . . at the Royal Banqueting House," London, Nov. 19, 2003, WH.

285. David E. Sanger, "In Bush's Vision, a Mission to Spread Power of Liberty," *NYT*, Oct. 21, 2004.

286. "Remarks by President Bush and Senator Kerry in the Third 2004 Presidential Debate," Oct. 14, 2004, WH. Cf. George W. Bush, "State of the Union Address," Jan. 20, 2004, WH.

287. George W. Bush, "Proclamation—Religious Freedom Day, 2002," Jan. 21, 2002, WH.

288. The National Security Strategy of the United States of America, II: "Champion Aspirations for Human Dignity." http://www.whitehouse.gov/nsc/nss.html.

289. George W. Bush, "Remarks and an Exchange with Reporters...in St. Petersburg," *Weekly Compilation of Presidential Documents* 38 (June 3, 2002).

290. "President Bush Speaks at Tsinghua University," Feb. 22, 2002, WH. See also Charles Hutzler, "Bush's Focus on Religion May Strain China Ties," *WSJ*, Feb. 25, 2002, A14.

291. Tony Carnes, "The Bush Doctrine," *CT* 47 (May 2003).

292. Fred Barnes, "Stop Dean," *Weekly Standard*, Dec. 22, 2003; Fineman et al., "Bush and God," 25.

293. Carnes, "Bush Doctrine."

294. Richard Lacayo et al., "Spiritual Influence," *Time* 164 (Nov. 15, 2004).

295. Carnes, "Bush Doctrine."

296. Woodward, *Bush at War*, 341.

297. Carnes, "Bush Doctrine"; David Domke, "Bush Weds Religion, Politics to Form World View," *Seattle Post-Intelligencer*, Aug. 22, 2004; Domke, "A Matter of Faith: The White House and the Press," *Nieman Reports*, Summer 2004, 68–70.

298. Quoted in Jay Tolson, "Looking behind the Bush Doctrine," *USN* 136 (Feb. 16, 2004). See also Ivo Daalder and James Lindsey, *America Unbound: The Bush Revolution in Foreign Policy* (Washington, DC: Brookings Institution, 2003); and Richard K. Herrmann and Michael J. Reese, "George W. Bush's Foreign Policy," in Colin Campbell and Bert A. Rockman, eds., *The George W. Bush Presidency: Appraisals and Prospects* (Washington, DC: CQ, 2004), 191–225.

299. John Lewis Gaddis, "A Grand Strategy of Transformation," *Foreign Policy*, Nov.–Dec. 2002, 50–57. Cf. Lloyd Ambrosius, *Wilsonianism: Woodrow Wilson and His Legacy in American Foreign Relations* (New York: Palgrave Macmillan, 2002), 10–18.

300. John Lewis Gaddis, *Surprise, Security, and the American Experience* (Cambridge, MA: Harvard University Press, 2004).

301. Tolson, "Bush Doctrine." See also James M. McCormick, "The Foreign Policy of the George W. Bush Administration," in Schier, ed., *High Risk*, 205–23; and Fred Barnes, *Rebel-in-Chief: Inside the Bold and Controversial Presidency of George W. Bush* (New York: Crown Forum, 2006), chap. 6.

302. Phillip Berryman, "The Bush Doctrine: A Catholic Critique," *America* 190 (Feb. 23, 2004).

303. George W. Bush, "Address to the Nation," Sept. 11, 2001, WH.

304. Salmon, *Fighting Back*, 158.

305. Bush, "National Day of Prayer and Remembrance."

306. Tony Carnes, "Bush's Defining Moment," *CT* 45 (Nov. 11, 2001), 40. See also T. Trent Gegax, "Bush's Battle Cry: Drawing on Prayer and a Sense of Personal Mission, W Becomes a War President," *NW*, Oct. 1, 2001, 24.

307. George W. Bush, "Address to a Joint Session of Congress and the American People," Sept. 20, 2001, WH.

308. Gary L. Gregg II, "Dignified Authenticity: George W. Bush and the Symbolic Presidency," in Gary Gregg II and Mark J. Rozell, eds., *Considering the Bush Presidency* (New York: Oxford University Pres, 2004), 100.

309. Frum, *Right Man*, 137.

310. Bush, "Faith-Based Initiative."

311. Woodward, *Bush at War*, 131.

312. "Afghanistan, Then and Now," Nov. 11, 2002, WH; "Rebuilding Afghanistan," May 19, 2003, ibid.

313. Carnes, "Defining Moment," 386. The last quotation is of Timothy Goeglein.

314. Mansfield, *Faith*, 137; Frum, *Right Man*, 136.

315. "Stated Clerk Sends Letter to President Bush Outlining PC(USA) Concerns," *News of the PC(USA)*, Oct. 26, 2001, 6–8.

316. Anthony Lewis, "Right and Wrong," *NYT*, Nov. 24, 2001; Alan Wolfe, "The God of a Diverse People," *NYT*, Oct. 14, 2001; Berger, as quoted in Carnes, "Defining Moment," 41. See also Richard Miniter, *Shadow War: The Untold Story of How Bush Is Winning the War on Terror* (Washington, DC: Regnery, 2004), and Richard S. Conley, ed., *Transforming the American Polity: The Presidency of George W. Bush and the War on Terrorism* (Upper Saddle River, NJ: Pearson/Prentice Hall, 2005).

317. Quoted in Mackler, "Messenger or Demagogue." See also Kenneth Walsh et al., "Sticking to His Guns," *USN*, Mar. 10, 2003; Jeffrey Sheler, "Drawing on the Divine," ibid; Stan Crock, "Bush, the Bible and Iraq," *Business Week* online, Mar. 7, 2003; John Dart, "Bush's Use of Religious Imagery Divides Faithful," *CC*, Mar. 8, 2003; "Bush's Worldview," ibid.; and Spencer Ackerman and John B. Judis, "The Selling of the Iraq War," *NR* 228 (June 30, 2003), 14–18, 23–25.

318. Phillips, "Crusader"; Arnon Regular, "'Road Map Is a Life Saver for US,' PM Abbas Tells Ha'aretz," *Ha'aretz*, June 26, 2003.

319. Kaplan, *With God*, 10.

320. Norman Podhoretz, "How to Win World War IV," *Commentary* 113 (Feb. 2002).

321. E.g., Ari Fleischer, July 1, 2003, briefing, WH.

322. See "Religion Plays Major Role."

323. Woodward, *Plan of Attack*, 379.

324. Jim Wallis, "Is Bush Deaf to Church Doubts on Iraq War?" *Catholic New Times*, Jan. 5, 2003. See also "Black Evangelicals Vote Moral Values," AP, Nov. 20, 2004.

325. Jim Wallis, "Disarm Iraq . . . Without War," *Sojourners*, Nov.–Dec. 2002.

326. Mar. 24, 2003, press release entitled "Nobel Peace Laureate Maguire, US Bishop to Lead Action Wednesday in DC."

327. Gary G. Kohls, "US President Professes Too Much," *Catholic New Times*, Mar. 16, 2003.

328. Mark Tooley, "Religious Coalition Opposes War on Iraq," *PL* 35 (Oct. 2002), 15.

329. NCC 2002 General Assembly Resolution "After September 11, 2001: Public Policy Considerations for the United States of America," Nov. 16, 2002. See also Bill Broadway, "Religious Leaders' Voices Rise on Iraq," *WP*, Sept. 28, 2002, B11.

330. See "Ad to Bush: Let Jesus Change Your Mind," RNS, Dec. 7, 2002.

331. Quoted in David Earle Anderson, "Not a Just or Moral War," *Sojourners*, Jan.–Feb. 2003.

332. "Remarks of Jim Winkler, General Secretary of the United Methodist General Board of Church & Society," Feb. 26, 2003. See also Daniel J. Wakin, "Some Doubt Fellow United Methodist (the President)," *NYT*, Apr. 7, 2003.

333. Frank Bruni, "Pope Calls the Potential War in Iraq 'a Defeat for Humanity,'" *International Herald Tribune*, Jan. 14, 2003. See also Johanna Neuman, "Pope's Emissary Meets with Bush, Calls War 'Unjust,'" *LAT*, Mar. 6, 2003.

334. "Is Bush Too Christian?" http://www.catholiceducation.org/articles/politics/pg0080.html, Mar. 15, 2003, 2.

335. Jimmy Carter, "Just War—or a Just War?" *NYT*, Mar. 9, 2003; Susan Thistlethwaite, "President Bush's War against Iraq Is Not a 'Just War,'" *Chicago Tribune*, Oct. 15, 2002; "Make the Case—War and Peace," *CC* 120 (Jan. 11, 2003); Methodist Federation for Social Action, Sept. 3, 2002, http://www.mfsaweb.org. See also "GAC Calls for U.S. Restraint on Iraq," *News of the PC(USA)*, Oct. 11, 2002, 7–8; and "Churches Speak Out," RNS, Oct. 12, 2002.

336. "'Just War' Questions Ignored by Bush," RNS, Oct. 19, 2002. See also "Ethicists, Divinity School Oppose War with Iraq," RNS, Sept. 28, 2002; and "Religious Groups Join in on Anti-war Coalition," RNS, Dec. 14, 2002.

337. CWS Board of Directors on War in Iraq, Mar. 19, 2003, http://www.churchworldservice.org/news/Iraq/board-statement.html.

338. Henry Kissinger, "Our Intervention in Iraq," *WP*, Aug. 12, 2002, A15; Eric Schmitt, "House G.O.P. Leader Warns against Iraq Attack," *NYT*, Aug. 9, 2002, A6; Brent Scowcroft, "Don't Attack Saddam," *WSJ*, Aug. 15, 2002, A12.

339. James P. Pfiffner, "Introduction: Assessing the Bush Presidency," in Gregg and Rozell, eds., *Bush Presidency*, 11; Thomas J. Friedman, "Iraq Upside Down," *NYT*, Sept. 18, 2002, A31; Graham T. Allison, "The View from Baghdad," *WP*, July 31, 2002, A19.

340. Woodward, *Bush at War*, 351.

341. Amos Oz, "The Protestors: Right for the Wrong Reasons," *NYT*, Feb. 19, 2003.

342. "Power and Leadership: The Real Meaning of Iraq," *NYT*, Feb. 23, 2003. Cf. "Saying No to War," *NYT*, Mar. 9, 2003; and "War in the Ruins of Diplomacy," *NYT*, Mar. 18, 2003.

343. Maureen Dowd, "Casualties of Faith," *NYT*, Oct. 21, 2004.

344. "Chicago Faith Leaders: 'Give Peace a Chance,'" *CC* 119 (Dec. 18, 2002).

345. "Ethicist Argues Bush Has Moral Case for War," RNS, Feb. 22, 2003. See also "Preachers on All Sides of the Issue of Likely Iraq War," RNS, Feb. 22, 2003; and Laurie Goodstein, "Catholics Debating: Back President or Pope on Iraq?" *NYT*, Mar. 6, 2003.

346. "U.S. Church Leaders Press against War in Talks with Blair," RNS, Feb. 22, 2003; "American Church Leaders Take Their Message of Peace to Downing Street," *News of the PC(USA)*, Mar. 7, 2003, 12–13.

347. "Church Leaders Propose No-War Iraq Peace Plan," RNS, Mar. 15, 2003.

348. "New 'Just War' Rules Advocated," RNS, Feb. 8, 2003.

349. Michael Novak, "'Asymmetrical Warfare' & Just War: A Moral Obligation," *National Review* online, Feb. 10, 2003; John L. Allen, "In Rome, Novak Makes the Case for War," *National Catholic Reporter*, Feb. 21, 2003.

350. "Ethicist Argues Bush Has Moral Case for War." See also Jean Bethke Elshtain's *Just War against Terror: The Burden of America Power in a Violent World* (New York: Basic Books, 2003). See especially the appendix "What We're Fighting For," 182–98, a letter signed by sixty leading scholars and ministers.

351. E.g., Charles Colson, "The Safety of a Great Nation," Jan. 21, 2004, TH.

352. Laurie Goodstein, "Evangelical Figures Oppose Religious Leaders' Broad Antiwar Sentiment," *NYT*, Oct. 5, 2002; "Faith Conservatives Back Bush on Iraq," RNS, Oct. 19, 2002.

353. "Church Leaders Propose No-War Iraq Peace Plan." Howard Fineman contends that Bush satisfied himself that an attack on Iraq would be a just war in Christian terms, not by studying Augustine, Aquinas, and Luther or by discussing the issue with Christian theologians and ethicists. He simply "decided that Saddam was evil, and everything [else] flowed from that" ("Bush and God," 30).

354. John McCain, "The Right War for the Right Reasons," *NYT*, Mar. 12, 2003. Cf. Donald H. Rumsfeld, "The Price of Freedom," *NYT*, Mar. 19, 2004. For a very different perspective, see "One Year After," *NYT*, Mar. 19, 2004.

355. Pew Center, "Different Faiths, Different Messages," *Pew Forum on Religion and Public Life*, Mar. 19, 2003. "Poll: Sermons on Iraq Influence Few in Pews," AP, Mar. 22, 2003; Mark O'Keefe, "Church Leaders' Anti-War Message Fails in the Pews," RNS, May 2, 2003; "Anti-War Pronouncements Ignore People in the Pews," *PL*, Apr. 2003, 6–7; "Few Churchgoers Say Religious Beliefs Shape View of War," *America* 188 (Apr. 14, 2003).

356. Gumbleton is quoted in "2003 Saw Conflicts Abroad and at Home," RNS, Dec. 27, 2003; Paula R. Kincaid, "Iraq War Declared 'Unwise, Immoral and Illegal,'" *PL* 37 (July 2004), 16. See also Jerry L. Van Marter, "Presbyterians Opposing U.S-Iraq War," *News of the PC(USA)*, Feb. 21, 2003.

357. "The Party of God." The quotation is from the White House Advisory Group on Public Diplomacy's study of the Middle East.

358. Gore Vidal, *Dreaming War: Blood for Oil and the Cheney-Bush Junta* (New York: Thunder's Mouth, 2002), 195.

359. Robert Bellah, "Righteous Empire," *CC* 120 (Apr. 4, 2003). Cf. Bob Edgar, "The Role of the Church in U.S. Foreign Policy Today," Apr. 15, 2003, http://www.voxpax.org/BobEdgar2003.html.

360. Emmanuel Todd, *After the Empire: The Breakdown of the American Order*, C. Jon Delogu, trans. (New York: Columbia University Press, 2002), xvi–xix; David Haney, *The New Imperialism* (New York: Oxford University Press, 2003), 2–6 and passim; Daalder and Lindsay, *America Unbound*; Chalmers Johnston, *The Sorrows of Empire: Militarism, Secrecy, and the End of the Republic* (New York: Metropolitan, 2004); George Soros, *The Bubble of American Supremacy: Correcting the Misuses of American Power* (New York: Public Affairs, 2004); Tariq Ali, *Bush in Babylon: The Recolonisation of Iraq* (New York: Verso, 2003); and James Mann, *Rise of the Vulcans: The History of Bush's War Cabinet* (New York: Viking, 2004), 362–63.

361. Haney, *Imperialism*, 19, 203, quotations in that order.

362. Jim Wallis, "Dangerous Religion: George W. Bush's Theology of Empire," *Sojourners*, Oct.–Nov. 2003.

363. Robert Jay Lifton, "American Apocalypse," *Nation* 277 (Dec. 22, 2003). Cf. Lifton, *Superpower Syndrome: America's Apocalyptic Confrontation with the World* (New York: Thunder's Mouth, 2003); and Coffin, "Despair Is Not an Option."

364. James Carroll, "The Bush Crusade," *Nation* 279 (Sept. 20, 2004). See also Carroll's *Crusade: Chronicles of an Unjust War* (2004); and Alterman and Green, *Book on Bush*, 252–301.

365. Kengor, *Bush*, 211.

366. E.g., Mona Charen, "A Matter of Integrity," Jan. 30, 2004, TH. Kerry, Tom Daschle, Nancy Pelosi, and Ted Kennedy all took this position.

367. Kaplan and Kristol, *The War over Iraq: Saddam's Tyranny and America's Mission* (San Francisco, CA: Encounter, 2003); Ronald Kessler, *A Matter of Character: Inside the White House of George W. Bush* (New York: Sentinel, 2004), 280–81.

368. For an early glowing assessment of the invasion, see Joe Loconte, "Anti-Liberation Theology: The Clerics Got It Wrong on Iraq," *Weekly Standard*, May 5, 2003.

369. George W. Bush, interview with Tom Brokaw of NBC News, Apr. 24, 2003.

370. E.g., Kaplan, *With God*, 68–90, 271–76.

371. Frank Rich, "Religion for Dummies," *NYT*, Apr. 27, 2002. Cf. "Bush Brings Religion to the Bully Pulpit," AP, Feb. 10, 2001; and Judy Klein, "President's Faith Is a 'Great Comfort' to Him, but Some Worry Frequent Prayers Mix with Policy," *USA Today*, May 18, 2001, 6A.

372. "Bush's 'God-Talk' Puts Off Some in Religious Community," RNS, Feb. 15, 2003.

373. See Bruce Lincoln, *Holy Terrors: Thinking about Religion after September 11* (Chicago: University of Chicago Press, 2003), 30–32. Bush allegedly uses biblical references, allusions to hymns, and specialized vocabulary to convey his underlying religious themes. See Lincoln, "Words Matter: How Bush Speaks in Religious Code," *Boston Globe*, Sept. 12, 2004. Key Bush speechwriter Michael Gerson repudiated the allegation that Bush's speeches contain code words only evangelicals understand (Alan Cooperman, "Bush's References to God Defended by Speechwriter," *WP*, Dec. 12, 2004).

374. Wallis, "Dangerous Religion."

375. Paul Bedard et al., "Washington Whispers," *USN* 134 (Feb. 24, 2003).

376. Delia M. Rios, "Critics Call President a Zealot," RNS, Jan. 22, 2005.

377. "Running on His Faith."

378. Quoted in Bumiller, "Talk of Religion." Cf. Ruth Conniff, "Public Piety," *Progressive* 67 (Mar. 2003).

379. Durbin is quoted in Robert Marus, "Amended Faith-Based Bill Approved by U.S. Senate," http://www.bjcpa.org/news/docs/rftc_030416.pdf; Lynn is quoted in "Bush Launches Unprecedented Assault on Church-State Separation," Jan. 29, 2001, http://www.au.org; Nadler is quoted in "Faith-Based Plan Does Not Meet the Constitutional Test," Jan. 28, 2003. http://www.house.gov/nadler/archive108/SOTU2_012803.htm.

380. Press, "Religion Gap."

381. Carnes, "Presidential Hopeful." Similarly, Bush confided to Ed Young, a leading Southern Baptist pastor in Houston, "I believe I am called to run for the presidency" (Aikman, *Man of Faith*, 120).

382. Land, "Bush and Religion," Oct. 17, 2004, *NYT*, 6.

383. Steven Waldman, "Faith-Based, Heaven Sent: Does God Endorse George Bush?" Sept. 13, 2004, http://slate.msn.com/id/2106590/.

384. Bill Keller, "The Soul of George W. Bush," *NYT*, Mar. 23, 2002.

385. Woodward, *Bush at War*, 67.

386. Quoted in "Bush's 'God-Talk.'" See also "Religious Leaders Uneasy with Bush Rhetoric," *Pittsburgh Post-Gazette*, Feb. 12, 2003; and David Gergen: Bush clearly feels that "he is somehow an instrument of Providence" (quoted in Laurie Goodstein, "A President Puts His Faith in Providence," *NYT*, Feb. 9, 2003).

387. Duffy is quoted in Wallis, "Dangerous Religion"; Ron Suskind, "Without a Doubt," *NYT Magazine*, Oct. 17, 2004. Cf. Mark Dowd, "A Bush That Burns: Who Does Dubbya Think He is? Moses? St. John? Or Jesus Himself?" *New Statesman*, Nov. 2004, 22–23.

388. "The President Rides Out," *London Observer*, Jan. 26, 2003. Cf. the statement of Tim Goeglein: "I think President Bush is God's man at this hour" (quoted in Joel Rosenberg, "Political Buzz from Washington," *World*, Oct. 6, 2001).

389. Quoted in "Without a Doubt," *Hamilton Spectator* (Ontario), Oct. 23, 2004, F04.

390. Dowd, "Casualties of Faith." Cf. Maureen Dowd, "Vote and Be Damned," *NYT*, Oct. 17, 2004: "The president's certitude—the idea that . . . God tells him what is right . . .—is disturbing. It equates disagreeing with him to disagreeing with Him." See also Robert Wright, "Faith, Hope and Clarity," *NYT*, Oct. 28, 2004.

391. Suskind, "Without a Doubt." Cf. Ron Suskind, *The Price of Loyalty: George W. Bush, the White House, and the Education of Paul O'Neill* (New York: Simon & Schuster, 2004), 292; and Alterman and Green, *Book on Bush*, 188–89.

392. E.g., Richard Reeves, "The Chosen People" *New York Magazine* 37 (Oct. 25, 2004), 26–27.

393. Wallis is quoted in *The Jesus Factor*, May 10, 2004, 17, http://www.pbs.org/wghb/pages/frontline/shows/jesus/. The second quotation is from Keller, "George W. Bush."

394. George F. Will, "Paradoxes of Public Piety," *NW* 143 (Mar. 15, 2004).

395. Land is quoted in *The Jesus Factor*.

396. George W. Bush, "Remarks . . . during the National Day of Prayer Reception," May 3, 2001, WH. Cf. Bush, "National Hispanic Prayer Breakfast": "We have never asserted a special claim on His favor." At the National Prayer Breakfast" in 2003, Bush declared: "We don't own the ideals of freedom and human dignity, and sometimes we haven't always lived up to them."

397. Bush, "Second Inaugural Address."

398. Davis, "Thoughts," 231–32. To conclude that any society cannot become a democracy, Bush avers, is "cultural condescension." In making this argument, George Will maintains, Bush is severing the strong connection many of his fellow evangelicals see between Christianity and democracy ("Paradoxes of Public Piety"). See also Wilfred M. McClay," The Soul of a Nation," *Public Interest*, Spring 2004; and Clifford Orwin, "The Unraveling of Christianity in America," ibid.

399. Wills, "With God."

400. Jackson Lears, "How a War Became a Crusade," *NYT*, Mar. 11, 2003.

401. Martin E. Marty, "The Sin of Pride," *NW* 141 (Mar. 10, 2003), 33. Cf. Wieseltier, "The Elect."

402. Cooperman, "Bush's References."

403. Quoted in *George W. Bush: Faith in the White House*, Grizzly Adams Productions documentary.

404. Neuhaus and Frum are both quoted in Cooperman, "Openly Religious." Also see "Friends: Bush a Believer, Nothing More," Jan. 22, 2005, AP. Neuhaus declared that Bush "in no way believes his decisions necessarily reflect God's will or that God acts through him."

405. Keller, "George W. Bush." Cf. O'Keefe, "Bush, Kerry." Others echo these assessments. Journalist Bob Woodward, who examined the role Bush's faith played in

decisions about the Iraq war, concludes that his approach is not unusual (see Carnes and Mark Stricherz, "Wooing"). Cf. Joe Klein "The Blinding Glare of His Certainty," *Time*, Feb. 18, 2003.

406. On Roosevelt, see chapter 6. Churchill described the war as a fight between "idolatrous paganism" and "the Christian nations." See Stephen Mansfield, *Never Give In: The Extraordinary Character of Winston Churchill* (Nashville, TN: Cumberland, 1996), 32.

407. George W. Bush, "Remarks Following a Meeting with the National Security Team," Sept, 12, 2001, WH. Cf. Bush, "Address to . . . Congress and the American People."

408. George W. Bush, "Remarks . . . at 2002 Graduation Exercise of the United States Military Academy," June 1, 2002, WH; Bush, "German Bundestag."

409. Carnes, "Bush Doctrine."

410. "Yes They Are Evil," *WP*, Feb. 3, 2002. Cf. Brad Knickerbocker, "As 'Evil Axis' Turns, Bush Sees No Blur of Right, Wrong," *CSM*, Feb. 6, 2002.

411. Alessandra Stanley, "Understanding the President and His God," *NYT*, Apr. 29, 2004.

412. Dunn is quoted in Brad Knickerbocker, "As 'Evil Axis' Turns"; Stanley Fish, "Condemnation without Absolutes," *NYT*, Oct. 15, 2001.

413. Steve DeVane, "Campolo: War on Terrorism Hurts Missions," *Baptist Standard*, Apr. 8, 2002.

414. Juan Stam, "Bush's Religious Language," *Nation* 277 (Dec. 22, 2003). Cf. Lincoln, *Holy Terrors*, 20.

415. Bush, "State of the Union," 2003.

416. "Bush's Messiah Complex," *Progressive* 67 (Feb. 2003). Berlet is quoted in this article. See Chalmers Johnson, *Blowback: The Costs and Consequences of American Empire* (New York: Henry Holt, 2004).

417. See Phillips, *American Dynasty*, 232–33. Cf. Molly Ivins and Lou Dubose, *Bushwhacked: Life in George W. Bush's America* (New York: Random House, 2003), 222–24.

418. See Debora Caldwell, "George W. Bush, Presidential Preacher," *Beliefnet*, Feb. 17, 2003, 1.

419. First quote is from Paul Boyer in "Bully Pulpit: George W. Bush's Religious Rhetoric," *CC* 120 (Mar. 8, 2003); the second and third are from Phillips, "Crusader."

420. Quoted in Cooperman, "Openly Religious."

421. Ron Csillag, "Burning Bush of Faith," *Toronto Star*, Oct. 23, 2004.

422. Wallis, "Dangerous Religion."

423. Tony Karon, "W Goes to Finishing School," *Time*, June 13, 2001.

424. Jonathan Chait, "The Case for Bush Hatred," *NR* 229 (Sept. 29, 2003); Robert Novak, "The Anti-Bush," Aug. 7, 2003, TH. Cf. Robert C. Byrd, *Losing America: Confronting a Reckless and Arrogant Presidency* (New York: W. W. Norton, 2004), 18–20; and William Buckley, "Bush Is Evil," Sept. 10, 2003, TH.

425. Chait, "Bush Hatred."

426. David Brooks, "The Presidency Wars," *NYT*, Sept. 30, 2003.

427. James Traub, "Learning to Love to Hate," http://www.furnitureforthepeople.com/traub.htm.

428. Maureen Dowd, "A Plague of Toadies," *NYT*, Nov. 18, 2004.

429. Bruce Bartlett, "My Misgivings," Apr. 21, 2004, TH.

430. E.g., David Gergen, "The Power of One," *NYT*, Nov. 19, 2004.

431. Paul Krugman, "Just Trust Us," *NYT*, May 11, 2004. Cf. Krugman, "To Tell the Truth," *NYT*, May 28, 2004. Krugman and others especially point to Bush's efforts to prevent an independent inquiry of 9/11 and to hinder oversight of Iraq spending ("Where's the Apology?" *NYT*, Jan. 30, 2004).

432. Paul Krugman, "This Isn't America," *NYT*, Mar. 20, 2004. Cf. John Dean, *Worse Than Watergate: The Secret Presidency of George W. Bush* (New York: Little, Brown, 2004).

433. E.g., Maureen Dowd, "Nuclear Fiction," *NYT*, Oct. 10, 2004; and Deborah Tannen, "Being President Means Never Having to Say He's Sorry," *NYT*, Oct. 12, 2004.

434. Jonathan Chait, "Blinded by Bush-Hatred," *WP*, May 8, 2003, A31.

435. Nicholas D. Kristof, "Calling Bush a Liar," *NYT*, June 30, 2004.

436. http://bushwatch.org/bushlies.htm. See also http://www.lies.com.

437. Byron York, "The Truth about Bush's 'Lies,'" *National Review*, June 16, 2003. See also Alterman and Green, *Book on Bush*, 6–9; Harold Meyerson and Eric Alterman, "Bush Lies, Media Swallows," *Nation*, Nov. 7, 2002; and "The Most Dangerous President Ever," *American Spectator*, May 2003.

438. Nicholas D. Kristof, "Missing in Action: Truth," *NYT*, May 6, 2003; "Was the Intelligence Cooked?" *NYT*, June 8, 2003; Paul Krugman, "Denial and Deception," *NYT*, June 24, 2003; Krugman, "Checking the Facts, in Advance," *NYT*, Oct. 12, 2004.

439. Nicholas Kristof, "Pants on Fire?" *NYT*, Oct. 27, 2004.

440. Dana Milbank, "For Bush, Facts Are Malleable," *WP*, Oct. 22, 2002, A1.

441. Quoted in Bob Herbert, "Masters of Deception," *NYT*, Jan. 16, 2004.

442. E.g., David Limbaugh, "The Left's Real Issue," Oct. 29, 2004, TH.

443. Kathleen Parker, "Sex, Lies and Yellowcake," July 13, 2004, TH. Cf. William Safire, "Sixteen Truthful Words," *NYT*, July 19, 2004; Michael Barone, "The 'Bush Lied' Folks Can't Be Taken Seriously," July 19, 2004, TH.

444. Woodward, *Plan of Attack*, 250.

445. Bob Herbert, "Bush's Echo Chamber," *NYT*, Nov. 19, 2004. Cf. Paul Krugman, "Looting the Future," *NYT*, Dec. 5, 2003.

446. "State of the Union Abroad," *NYT*, Jan. 21, 2004.

447. Byrd, *Losing America*, 212–13. Cf. Bovard, *Bush Betrayal*, 1–7, 273–77; Jack Huberman, *The Bush-Hater's Handbook* (New York: Nation, 2003), vi–xi; and Douglas Kellner, *From 9/11 to Terror War: The Dangers of the Bush Legacy* (Lanham, MD: Rowman & Littlefield, 2003), 62–63, 72–75, 136–37, 223, 225–28, 242–43, 252–59.

448. Bob Herbert, "Bait and Switch," *NYT*, Jan. 30, 2003; Herbert, "Bush's Duty, and Privilege," *NYT*, Feb. 13, 2004, quotations in that order.

449. Alterman and Green, *Book on Bush*, 331–32.

450. E.g., George Will, "A Summer of Conservative Discontent," July 24, 2000, TH; Jonah Goldberg, "Bush Becomes 'Big Government Conservative,'" July 18, 2003, TH; Jeff Jacoby, "The Party of Big Spenders," Dec. 12, 2003, ibid.; David Brooks, "Running on Reform," *NYT*, Jan. 3, 2004; and Gary Mucciaroni and Paul J. Quirk, "Deliberations of a 'Compassionate Conservative': George W. Bush's Domestic Policy," in Campbell and Rockman, eds., *Bush Presidency*, 158–90.

451. Doug Bandow, "Righteous Anger: The Conservative Case against George W. Bush," Dec. 11, 2003, http://www.cato.org/research/articles/bandow-031211.html.

452. Nicholas D. Kristof, "Mr. Bush Talks the Talk," *NYT*, June 28, 2002.

453. Frum, *Right Man*, 272.

454. Ibid., 275, 278, 282; first and second quotation from 275, third from 278.

455. Kessler, *Character*, 290.

456. See also Jonah Goldberg, "Bush's Strong Foreign Policy Successful," Dec. 24, 2003, TH. He pointed to Saddam's capture, Iran's openness to nuclear inspections, Syria's seizing of millions of Al Qaeda funds, and the more cooperative approach of Saudi Arabia. Cf. David Brooks, "Make No Mistake," *NYT*, Dec. 21, 2004; Daniel Pipes, "The Bush Doctrine," http://hnn.us/roundup/comments/17739.html; and Bill Steigerwald, "Pipes Calls War a Successs," *Pittsburgh Tribune Review*, Apr. 1, 2006. Pipes praises Bush for his goals but is critical of how he is implementing many of them.

457. David Limbaugh, "The 'Dangerous' Faith of President Bush," Oct. 19, 2004, TH.

458. Wallis, "Dangerous Religion."

459. E.g., John McCloskey, director of the Catholic Information Office in Washington, DC, labels the president "a totally uninformed Christian" because he has not read Thomas Aquinas or studied major events in church history (quoted in Aikman, *Man of Faith*, 199).

460. Maureen Dowd, "Stations of the Crass," *NYT*, Feb. 26, 2004.

461. Arthur Schlesinger Jr., "The White House Wasn't Always God's House," *LA Times* online, Oct. 26, 2004; Oct. 22–23, as quoted in Marvin Olasky, "Belief without Advocacy Is Dead," Oct. 28, 2004, TH.

462. Young, "Beyond Belief."

463. Glasgow *Herald*, Sept. 1, 2004, 13.

464. "The God Gulf," Jan. 7, 2004.

465. Glasgow *Herald*, Sept. 1, 2004, 13.

466. Davis, "Thoughts," 233.

467. Kengor, interview with Olasky, Feb. 5, 2003, *Bush*, 163.

468. Aikman, *Man of Faith*, 201; Mansfield, *Faith*, xviii–xix.

CONCLUSION

1. Numerous others shared many of the same convictions, most notably John Adams, James Madison, John Quincy Adams, Andrew Jackson, Rutherford Hayes, James Garfield, Grover Cleveland, Benjamin Harrison, William McKinley, Herbert Hoover, Harry Truman, Gerald Ford, George H. W. Bush, and Bill Clinton.

2. William Miller, "Candor and Naiveté—Defending Carter's Heresies," *National Review*, Oct. 9, 1976, 17–19.

3. Christopher Levenick and Michael Novak, "Religion and the Founders," National Review online, Mar. 7, 2005.

4. George Washington Papers, Library of Congress, 1741–99.

5. John Adams, "To the Officers of the First Brigade of Third Division of the Militia of Massachusetts" in Charles Francis Adams, ed., *The Works of John Adams, Second President of the United States*, 10 vols. (Boston: Little, Brown, 1851–65), 9:229.

6. James David Fairbanks, "Reagan, Religion, and the New Right," *Midwest Quarterly*, Spring 1982, 336–37, 342.

7. *NYT*, Jan. 17, 1953.

8. Carter, however, displayed much less personal piety than many other presidents whose faith was not nearly as strong. Ribuffo suggests that "because he was so pious, Carter felt little need for official declarations of piety." See Leo P. Ribuffo, "God and

Jimmy Carter," in M. L. Bradbury and James B. Gilbert, eds., *Transforming Faith: The Sacred and Secular in Modern American History* (Westport, CT: Greenwood, 1989), 151.

9. David M. Abshire, "The Wartime Faith of Washington, Lincoln, and Roosevelt," General Theological Seminary 2003 Alumni/ae Address, 6.

10. E.g., Fred Barnes, "God and Man in the Oval Office," *Weekly Standard* 8 (Mar. 17, 2003); and Terry Mattingly, "Bush Isn't Speaking in Unknown Tongue," AP, Jan. 22, 2005.

11. Hugh Sidey, "Taking Cues from on High," *Time*, Mar. 19, 1984, 27.

12. Ed Dobson and Cal Thomas, *Blinded by Might* (1999), as quoted in Thomas, "Using and Abusing God: Part Deux," Jan. 19, 2005, TH.

13. Franklin D. Roosevelt, Undelivered address for Jefferson Day, Apr. 13, 1945, *PPAFDR* 13: 616.

14. Foxman is quoted in Carter M. Yang, "Religion Plays Big Role in Bush Presidency," May 21, 2001, http://www.hvk.org/articles/0501/75.html; Martin Marty, "Presidential Piety: Must It Be Private?" *CC* 101 (Feb. 1984), 187–88, quotation from 188.

15. Charles Krauthammer, "Alabama, Faith, and the Senate," Aug. 29, 2003, TH.

16. Armstrong Williams, "Bush's Faith Reflects Society's Beliefs," Feb. 1, 2005, TH.

17. Charles Colson, "The Lures and Limits of Political Power," in Richard John Neuhaus and Michael Cromartie, eds., *Piety and Politics: Evangelicals and Fundamentalist Confront the World* (Lanham, MD: University Press of America, 1987), 176.

18. Stephen Monsma, "Concluding Observations," in Monsma, ed., *Church-State Relations in Crisis: Debating Neutrality* (Lanham, MD: Rowman and Littlefield, 2002), quotations from 261, 262, 263, in that order.

19. Richard G. Hutcheson Jr., *God in the White House: How Religion Has Changed the Modern Presidency* (New York: Macmillan, 1988), 236.

20. Ibid., first two quotations from 265, third from 266, fourth from 267.

21. Ibid., 268–69.

22. TJ to Samuel Miller, Jan 23, 1808, *WTJ* 11:428–30.

23. Few Americans, except outspoken secularists, want a naked public square. Mainline, evangelical, and fundamentalist Protestants, Catholics, Jews, and Muslims all insist that public life should rest on basic religious values. Although Americans disagree about whether public buildings should be allowed to display the Ten Commandments, most of them concur that their principles—reverence for God, honesty, fidelity, integrity, and respect for life and property—should direct corporate as well as individual life. Two Christian intellectuals have especially promoted this argument: Richard John Neuhaus, editor of the journal *First Things* and author of *The Naked Public Square* (Grand Rapids, MI: Eerdmans, 1984), and Yale Law School professor Stephen Carter, who wrote *The Culture of Disbelief: How American Law and Politics Trivialize Religious Devotion* (New York: Basic Books, 1993) and *God's Name in Vain: The Wrongs and Rights of Religion in Politics* (New York: Basic Books, 2000). They contend that the effort to broaden the concept of the separation of church and state in order to eliminate religious perspectives, values, and symbols from public life and to inhibit the participation of religious groups in discussions of public policy is at odds with the First Amendment as it has been understood throughout American history. In *Divided by God: America's Church-State Problem and What We Should Do About It*, New York University law professor Noah Feldman argues that the current debate over religion in the public arena is largely between two camps he labels

"legal secularists" and "values evangelicals." He insists that almost all Americans want to ensure that the nation's religious division and diversity does not pull us apart. "Values evangelicals think that the solution lies in finding and embracing traditional values we can share"; "legal secularists think that we can maintain our national unity only if we treat religion as a personal, private matter." He proposes a bargain: greater tolerance for the public expression of religion "in exchange for tighter restrictions on government funding" of religious institutions and activities. He urges values evangelicals to "reconsider their position in favor of state support for religious institutions and re-embrace the American tradition of institutionally separated church and state" because "state funding actually undercuts, rather than promotes, the cohesive national identity that evangelicals" want to restore. See also Michelle Goldberg, *Salon*, July 23, 2005.

24. Ibid., 232.

25. Charles P. Henderson Jr., "Civil Religion and the American Presidency," *Religious Education* 70 (Sept.–Oct. 1975), 474.

26. Mary E. Stuckey, *The President as Interpreter-in-Chief* (Chatham, NJ: Chatham, 1991), 1.

27. Hutcheson, *White House*, 238.

28. Ibid., 237.

29. *Inaugural Addresses of the Presidents of the United States from George Washington 1789 to Richard Milhous Nixon 1973* (Washington, DC: Government Printing Office, 1974), 2.

30. Abshire, "Wartime Faith," 4–5.

31. Martin Marty, "Two Kinds of Two Kinds of Civil Religion," in Russell Ritchey and Donald Jones, eds., *American Civil Religion* (New York: Harper, 1974), 144–47. See also Robert Linder, "Universal Pastor: President Bill Clinton's Civil Religion," *JCS* 38 (Autumn 1996), 733–49.

32. Robert D. Linder and Richard V. Pierard, "Ronald Reagan, Civil Religion and the New Religious Right in America," *FH*, 23 (Fall 1991), 66.

33. Ronald Isetti, "The Moneychangers of the Temple: FDR, American Civil Religion, and the New Deal," *PSQ* 26 (Summer 1996), 692. He is only discussing Roosevelt's use of civil religion. Carter's version of civil religion "was more infused with Christian principles" than that of most presidents (Discussant: James S. Wolfe in Herbert D. Rosenbaum and Alexei Ugrinsky, eds., *The Presidency and Domestic Policies of Jimmy Carter* [Westport, CT: Greenwood, 1994], 125).

34. Marty, "Two Kinds of Two Kinds of Civil Religion," in Ritchey and Jones, eds., *Civil Religion*, 146–47; Richard V. Pierard and Robert D. Linder, *Civil Religion and the Presidency* (Grand Rapids, MI: Zondervan, 1988), 295. See also James Fairbanks, "The Priestly Functions of the Presidency," *PSQ* 11 (Spring 1981), 214–32; and Paul Carter, "The Pastoral Office of the President," *Theology Today* 25 (Apr. 1968), 52–63. Scholars debate whether civil religion has a positive or negative impact on American society. While some applaud civil religion for stressing a set of "external, transcendent truths which provide a standard of morality and justice for [evaluating] all national endeavors," others denounce it for using religious-national symbols to mobilize political support (Fairbanks, "Priestly Functions," 220). Some insist that this common religion supplies a cosmic frame of reference to help validate the nation's goals and values, promote solidarity, and reduce its conflicts and cleavages (e.g., Peter Berger, *The Sacred Canopy: Elements of a Sociological Theory of Religion* [Garden City, NY: Doubleday,

1967], 22–28, 51). Others emphasize that civil religion furnishes ultimate standards for judging a nation's ideals and practices (Robert Bellah, "Civil Religion in America," in Ritchey and Jones, eds., *Civil Religion*, 24–25, 33–35). By providing a common language, civil religion enables Americans who espouse different worldviews to discuss their deepest convictions in the public arena. Others counter that the effects of civil religion are largely negative. They denounce it as "a shallow celebration of the American Way of Life." Civil religion prompts Americans to consider themselves superior to others because of their military might or wealth and promotes complacency ("Mr. Reagan's Civil Religion," 483; cf. Sydney Ahlstrom, *A Religious History of the American People* [New Haven, CT: Yale University Press, 1972], 8, 954). Numerous Protestants, Catholics, and Jews castigate civil religion as banal, theologically naive, detrimental, and even idolatrous. See, e.g., Conrad Cherry, "American Sacred Ceremonies," in Phillip Hammond and Benton Johnson, eds., *American Mosaic: Social Patterns of Religion in the United States* (New York: Random House, 1970), 304; and Will Herberg, *Protestant-Catholic-Jew* (Garden City, NY: Doubleday, 1960), 263. It has typically been used to justify the nation's actions and celebrate its virtues and righteousness, others complain, rather than to provide a transcendent standard to censure its transgressions and vices. Critics also deprecate American civil religion for promoting the nation's interests and goals and ignoring the ideals, needs, and aims of the world. Moreover, it has tended to exclude African Americans, Native Americans, and the poor (Cherry, "Introduction," 17–18; Bellah, "Civil Religion," 41, 36; Michael Novak, *Choosing Our King: Powerful Symbols in Presidential Politics* [New York: Macmillan, 1974], 303ff.; and Robert Jewett, *The Captain America Complex: The Dilemma of Zealous Nationalism* [Philadelphia: Westminster, 1973]). Many theologians condemn American civil religion as an "idolatrous competitor to 'true' religion" (Pierard and Linder, *Civil Religion*, 294).

35. Henry A. Kissinger, "Morality and Power," in Ernest W. LeFever, *Morality and Foreign Policy: A Symposium on President Carter's Stance* (Washington, DC: Ethics and Public Policy Center, Georgetown University, 1977), 59.

36. Alan Dawley, *Changing the World: American Progressives in War and Revolution* (Princeton, NJ: Princeton University Press, 2003), 369, fn. 29. See Wilson, speeches to the Grand Army of the Republic, Sept. 28, 1915, *PWW* 34:146; Feb. 10, 1916, 36:361.

37. Dawley, *Changing the World*, 128.

38. Dwight D. Eisenhower, "Second Inaugural Address," Jan. 21, 1957, *Public Papers of the Presidents of the United States: Dwight D. Eisenhower*, 8 vols. (Washington, DC: Government Printing Office, 1960–61), 5:64.

39. Kennedy quoted these words in his "Annual Message to the Congress on the State of the Union," *Public Papers of the Presidents of the United States, John F. Kennedy*, 3 vols. (Washington, DC: Government Printing Office, 1962–64), Jan. 30, 1961, 1:28; Franklin D. Roosevelt, "Radio Address Summarizing State of the Union Message," Jan. 6, 1945, *PPAFDR* 13: 517.

40. William Weeks, *John Quincy Adams and the American Global Empire* (Lexington: University Press of Kentucky, 1992); first three quotations from 184, fourth from 186.

41. William Lee Miller, *Lincoln's Virtues: An Ethical Biography* (New York: Alfred A. Knopf, 2002), 89.

42. Martin Marty, "The Sin of Pride," *NW*, Mar. 10, 2003, 33; Maureen Dowd, "Casualties of Faith," *NYT*, Oct. 21, 2004; Ron Suskind, "Without a Doubt," *NYT*

Magazine, Oct. 17, 2004; Mark Dowd, "A Bush That Burns: Who Does Dubbya Think He Is? Moses? St. John? Or Jesus Himself?" *New Statesman*, Nov. 2004, 22–23.

43. Derek Davis, "Thoughts on the Separation of Church and State," *JCS* (Mar. 2003), 234.

44. Paul Johnson, "A God-Fearing White House Is Safer," *Forbes* 168 (Aug. 20, 2001).

45. Thomas C. Reeves, *A Question of Character: A Life of John F. Kennedy* (New York: Free Press, 1991), 14–15, quotation from 14.

46. Ibid., 14.

47. James David Barber, *The Presidential Character: Predicting Performance in the White House* (Englewood Cliffs, NJ: Prentice Hall, 1972).

48. Hutcheson, *White House*, 230–31, quotation from 231.

49. Jefferson was a bachelor during his first alleged indiscretion and a widower during his second.

50. Reeves, *Character*, 419.

51. John W. Chambers II, "The Agenda Continued: Jimmy Carter's Post-presidency," in Gary M. Fink and Hugh Davis Graham, eds., *The Carter Presidency: Policy Choices in the Post-New Deal Era* (Lawrence: University of Kansas Press, 1998), 267–85.

52. Glenn A. Phelps, "The President as Moral Leader: George Washington in Contemporary Perspective," in Ethan Fishamen, William D. Pederson, and Mark J. Rozell, eds., *George Washington: Foundation of Presidential Leadership and Character* (Westport, CT: Praeger, 2001), 11 (including the quotation). See also James P. Pfiffner, "Presidential Character: Multidimensional or Seamless?" in Mark J. Rozell and Clyde Wilcox, eds., *The Clinton Scandal and the Future of American Government* (Washington: Georgetown University Press, 2000), 225–55.

53. Quoted in Robert S. Alley, *So Help Me God* (Richmond, VA: John Knox, 1972), 120.

54. Susan Jacoby, *Freethinkers: A History of American Secularism* (New York: Henry Holt, 2004), back cover.

55. Pierard and Linder, *Civil Religion*, 297.

56. Reeves, *Character*, 419.

57. Francis J. Lally, "Religion and Public Life," *CMW* 69 (Dec. 19, 1958), 314.

58. Ibid.

59. Reeves, *Character*, 418.

60. Wilfred M. McClay, "Two Concepts of Secularism," in Hugo Heclo and McClay, eds., *Religion Returns to the Public Square: Faith and Policy in America* (Washington, DC: Woodrow Wilson Center Press, 2003), 51–52, first two quotations from 51, third from 52. See also Robert P. George, "What Can We Reasonably Hope For?" *First Things*, Jan. 2000, 22–24.

INDEX

Abbott, Lawrence, 498n48

Abbott, Lyman, 134, 142, 156, 519n188

Abercrombie, James, 27

abortion, 4, 5, 14, 303, 318, 344, 345, 346, 347, 348, 373, 374, 375, 379, 380, 384–85 (*see also* Bush, George; Carter, Jimmy; Kerry, John; and Reagan, Ronald)

Abrams, Elliot, 343, 386

Abrams, Morris, 343

Absalom, 74

Acheson, Dean, 429

Acton, Lord, 290

Adair, Douglas, 84–85

Adams, Abigail, 53, 64

Adams, John, 53, 406; and the afterlife, 32; attack on by James Callender, 83; on the Constitution, 416, correspondence of with Jefferson, 54, 58, 64; death of, 89–90; and the election of 1800, 69, 70, 72; faith of, 436n29, 630n1; as an intellectual giant, 34; and national days of prayer, 77; on religion as essential to morality, 62; religious views of, 436n29; resentment of Washington's exalted reputation, 50; as a theistic rationalist, 26; view of the trinity, 462n65

Adams, John Quincy, and the Bible, 366; criticism of Jefferson of, 53–54; 458n5; on the death of John Adams and Jefferson, 89; emphasis of on God's providence, 134; faith of, 436n29, 630n1; foreign policy of, 395; inability to accept the Christian conception of salvation, 102; integrity of, 428; reticence of to discuss religious views, 92; as a Unitarian, 141, 501n109; on the U.S. as God's instrument, 107; on the U.S. as a model of democracy, 114

Adams, Samuel, 45

Adams, Sherman, 239

Addams, Jane, 138, 208

Addison, Joseph, 35

Adger, John, 491n300

affirmative action, 345

Afghanistan, 318, 321, 352, 356, 397, 412, 424

Africa, 87, 136, 209, 214, 249, 280, 290, 315, 324, 356, 393, 548n150 (*see also* South Africa)

African Methodist Episcopal Church, 344

Age of Reason, 71, 73

Aikman, David, 369, 413

Airport, 319

Albanese, Catherine, 42

Alien Act of 1917, 521n225

Allen, Jimmy, 318, 578n152

Allen, Richard, 40, 340, 591n89

Alley, Robert, 6, 9, 278

Alliance for Progress, 274, 290

All in the Family, 320

Al Qaeda, 397, 404

Alterman, Eric, 411

ambassador to the Vatican, 266, 267, 270 (*see also* Carter, Jimmy; Kennedy, John F.; Roosevelt, Franklin; and Reagan, Ronald)

Ambrose, Stephen, 226

Ambrosius, Lloyd, 189, 525n300, 525n301

America, 239, 267, 273, 275, 302

America as a chosen nation, vii, 5, 15, 16–17, 44, 93, 107–8, 114, 124, 180, 337–38, 361–63, 372, 374, 403, 405–7, 409, 416, 425–27, 440n55; criticism of the concept of, 425–27 (*see also* individual presidents)

America's Fund for Afghan Children, 397

American Bar Association, 185

American Bible Society, 132, 229

American Catholic Conference, 342

American Civil Liberties Union, 14, 208

American Coalition for Traditional Values, 345

American Committee for Hebron Yeshivah, 210

American Council of Christian Churches, 203, 232, 242–43, 550n181

American Council for Judaism, 275

American Federation of Labor, 185

American Freedom and Catholic Power, 266

American Jewish Congress, 209

635